THE *New* EXECUTIVE PROTECTION BIBLE

By

M. J. Braunig

ESI Education Development Corporation, Aspen, Colorado

The *New* Executive Protection Bible
by M.J. Braunig
Copyright © 2000 by Martha J. Braunig

Printed in the United States of America

ISBN: 0-9640627-3-9

Published by ESI Education Development Corporation
225 Teal Court
Aspen, CO 81611
(970) 925-3630

ACKNOWLEDGEMENTS

In the original edition of The Executive Protection Bible, much credit for the evolution of modern executive protection was given to the United States Secret Service, for providing a model for the professional executive protection agent. That is still true. We also acknowledged an equal debt owed to those professional educators and practitioners in the field who have continually refined the body of knowledge, and who have unstintingly contributed to the growth of professionalism in the industry. That is also still true.

My personal acknowledgement goes to Bob Duggan, President of Executive Security International, Ltd. (ESI), and to the many ESI instructors and graduates who have cumulatively added knowledge, skills, and experience to make this book possible. Bob Duggan has, over the past twenty years, carried the banner for professional education of the executive protection agent. The material about corporate executive protection owes much to Kirk Marshall, a skilled practitioner and instructor of executive protection. Material on domestic violence stalkers is courtesy of Victim Protection Services of Denver, Colorado. Judith Robinson, Shanti Khalsa, and Sharon Frink contributed the material on female agents. Material on audio surveillance and countermeasures came from Martin Kaiser. Guiding me through the pitfalls and dangers of bombs were David Richmond and Jack McGeorge. Dick Barber contributed his knowledge of defensive shooting and driving. Last, and far from least, I would like to acknowledge the contributions of Jack McGeorge of the Public Safety Group in Woodbridge, Virginia. Jack McGeorge is the embodiment of the executive protection agent. His knowledge, professionalism, and energy are remarkable. Jack McGeorge contributed to the material contained in this book, both in written and lecture form. I have tried faithfully to translate his spoken word into writ. All errors are mine.

M. J. Braunig

INTRODUCTION

When we published The Executive Protection Bible in 1993, it was our intention to produce the most detailed, most complete book on executive protection to be found on the open market. While a number of worthwhile books, articles, and monographs had been written, there was no complete, "how-to" manual for the protection agent, security director, and corporate risk manager. The available books, we believed, fell short in that they tended to give more of an overview of the job, as opposed to the nitty-gritty of *doing* the job. Apparently, we met our goal. The Executive Protection Bible has been extremely well received, having been sold to corporations, government agencies, non-profit entities, and numerous individuals. Now, in the year 2000, we sat down to analyze the changes which have taken place in the field in the last seven years. We found a number of changes and have incorporated them in The *New* Executive Protection Bible.

Since the 1993 publication of The Executive Protection Bible, much has happened to expand the role of the professional protection agent. Increasingly, he (and she) is being asked to perform much as an executive assistant, providing support in a number of areas: intelligence collection and analysis, counterintelligence, contingency planning, special event security, estate management and security, management of violent employees in the workplace, stalker problems, and asset protection. In this updated edition of the "Bible," we have addressed these areas.

Today's executive protection agent must be able to blend in with any business and social situation. Often, the most successful agents combine executive protection with other skills, such as business management, or computer technology, or paralegal, to expand their job possibilities. You see, reality is that a good executive protection agent is expensive, so he and she may find that there are not enough employers who will pay someone simply to stand around and protect them. Being able to take on other (related) chores may cinch a job. Cross-training is definitely in. Nannies are learning executive protection, as are personal chefs, secretaries, corporate drivers, executive assistants, and private pilots.

These changes and enhancements to the executive protection profession are all to the good. Finally, we're "getting some respect." No longer viewed as knuckle-draggers, the executive protection agents are acquiring the dignity of a recognized profession. And as such, the agent can view the profession with pride and integrity. It is a multi-faceted profession.

Just as the image of the executive protection agent has changed, so has the scope of the job. As has already been pointed out, executive protection agents function very efficiently in other sectors of the private security field, often working as estate managers, corporate security personnel, and personal or administrative assistants. Many private investigators find that, by acquiring executive protection skills, they double their marketable skills (and vice versa).

With The *New* Executive Protection Bible, we have undergone a more or less complete revision of the original book. There have been changes and additions made to each chapter, resulting in the addition of 180 pages. New chapters were added for Terrorism, Stalkers, and Threat Interventions & Management. The Terrorism chapter examines the emerging right-wing groups, including militias, "lone wolves," and hate groups. The Stalker chapter is extensive and includes information on celebrity, dignitary, domestic, and cyberstalking. The Threat Interventions and Management chapter takes a close look at available intervention options and the need to interface with the law enforcement and mental health communities.

New material was added on Violent Employees in the Workplace, Threat Assessment, Predictions of Dangerousness, Intelligence Collection, and Biochemical Threats and Responses. Information has been included regarding executives traveling in "hot" areas overseas. Emphasis is given to the need for the agent to actively participate in the protection of proprietary information, now that the Cold War has given way to Information Warfare and corporate spying.

All information has been thoroughly updated to reflect our rapidly changing world. The material is timely and detailed, written to fulfill the needs of the new executive protection agent.

A word about job titles. As with the 1993 Executive Protection Bible, we have used, interchangeably, the terms, "executive protection agent," "protection agent," "protection specialist," "personal protection agent," "agent," and "bodyguard." You will find that these titles are used in the industry, with "bodyguard" being the most limiting.

A word about the author, who is the Vice President for Executive Security International, Ltd. (ESI). ESI is certainly the largest, and arguably the best, school for private security in the United States. A unique feature of ESI's Executive Protection Program is the home study component of 450 hours. The author, whose responsibilities include the design of the home study materials, continually researches and reviews the available off-the-shelf material and textbooks.

Having come full-circle, we have arrived at the reason for this book. As the executive protection agents' image and scope have changed, there is a need for an in-depth, greatly expanded body of knowledge for the training of these agents. Incidentally, we hope that the employers of the agents will review this book, to understand the complexity of the job which, when coupled with the absolute willingness to protect a client at cost of limb and life, constitutes the modern executive protection agent.

A few comments about the make-up of this book. Some of the material may seem overly basic, even boring, but so be it. In the section on THE THREAT, for example, those of you new to the profession will find that your client is not very likely to be threatened by terrorists, but instead, he is more likely to fall down the stairs and hurt himself or to have a heart attack. The section on overseas travel assumes that the reader has no experience in this area and, therefore, many very basic details are included for the first-time traveler.

Some material, such as corporate crisis management, may seem at first glance not to be applicable. But, read it! Learning about corporations, how corporations function, and how they react to a crisis, can prepare you for work in corporate security--steady work, with many benefits!

Finally, the author greatly values suggestions and additions to the body of knowledge which, over the years, has been codified here and invites any and all such applicable information. If you feel that we have overlooked or slighted some area of executive protection, please write to me. The mailing address is M.J. Braunig, ESI Education Development Corporation, 225 Teal Court, Aspen, CO 81611. Telephone (970) 925-3630. e-mail <braunig@sopris.net>

CONTENTS

CONTENTS

The players in the very serious game of executive protection are the *agents*, the *clients*, and the *intruders*. Their roles are fairly obvious. The client wishes to be protected from harm to his person, his reputation, or his sense of well being; and security from intrusion. The agent's role is to provide that protection to his client. The intruder wishes to kill, kidnap, hurt, annoy, or merely embarrass the client, and, in doing so, must remove or evade the agent. It is almost like a chess game and just as complicated.

AGENTS

Who are these executive protection agents and what motivates them to enter the profession? To begin, there are no longer any typical profiles of agents. At one time, it was thought that only large men, preferably ex-football players, special forces veterans, or martial artists could handle the job of protecting a client. And, to be honest, in some circumstances, this is still true. One tends to see very large bodyguards working with certain rock stars and performers. At one joint performance given before a huge, screaming audience, Kenny Rogers and Dolly Parton entered from the back of the auditorium, walked down the aisle, and onto the stage. It was a study in styles. Four extremely large, muscled men flanked Dolly Parton, brushing aside hands and keeping her safe from her adoring fans, all of whom seemed bent on touching her. By contrast, Kenny Rogers walked in front of two regular-sized guys, accepting the reaching-out and touching of his fans. I certainly do not criticize Dolly Parton. She is actually a woman of small physical stature who probably hates being jostled and touched and needs a visible deterrent to avoid these unwanted tokens of esteem. The point being, the client is an individual whose need for protection varies greatly.

Some clients, who have possibly read too many paperback thrillers, like to have their protection team armed to the teeth, and take a vicarious thrill from seeing their guys strong-arm their way through crowds. This style of behavior, however, is rapidly becoming a thing of the past. Too many lawsuits have stripped the glamour away. Let it be stated at the outset that executive protection agents do not have any police powers (unless they are, indeed, police officers, working an official assignment). It is unlawful to lay hands on, manhandle, or otherwise assault another individual, unless it can be *proven* that the individual being manhandled was intent on doing physical harm to the agent, the client, or the client's family. Aside from the legal and liability issues, strong-arm tactics are unnecessary and unattractive, and a true professional agent does not want to work with a client who expects this kind of behavior. There are tales of clients who expect their bodyguards to whip their servants, procure drugs for them, and share ribald adventures of drinking and wenching. While these may seem like pretty exciting activities, they are terrible for business and are destined to provide short-lived protection careers. Clients are notorious for jettisoning any employees who embarrass them by getting caught doing something illegal or reprehensible. Fortunately, the freebooting, out-of-control client is becoming extinct, except possibly in the drug trade.

Perhaps this is a good point to discuss "low profile" versus "high profile" protection. The Dolly Parton example is one of high profile. It is intended to be a visible deterrent. It says, "I'm here and I'm going to protect my client against any intrusion." It is visibly preventive and proactive. It is also becoming increasingly rare. More often, low profile is the role of choice. Low profile blends into the client's environment and is often not detected as a protection measure. Many clients do not want protection but realize that, for one reason or another, they must have it. In these cases, a low profile protection individual or team is more palatable to the client. Remember, when the client is an executive, he or she is generally older, having risen to top management over the years. He has established a life and business style and enjoys the esteem of friends and associates. He is used to being in control, and the last thing he wants is to lose that control or appear powerless. Low profile protection provided by someone who looks and acts like one of his business colleagues is much, much more acceptable to him, thereby making the job of protecting him easier. If you are not an annoyance, you will be able to get closer to him, and that is where you want to be, not exiled to the outer door.

Low profile means dressing like, acting like, and speaking like the client. Sometimes this requires homework, boning up on the subjects, hobbies, and sports which pertain to the client. If the client likes to jog, clearly his bodyguard will be jogging one pace to the right rear. If the client takes ski vacations, his agent had better like cold, crisp days spent doing suicidal things on the mountain. It has been said that President Eisenhower's secret service agents were right there on the fairways and greens with him. It should be obvious that in low profile situations a weapon is never visible. Generally, this is fairly easy to accomplish, unless one happens to be on the beach!

Blending in is made easier if the agent has a basic knowledge of literature, art, music, and film, much of which can be acquired simply by reading the newspapers. This is a perfect time to make a pitch for reading at least one major newspaper, plus the local paper, *every day.* This is the minimum if you wish to be informed. Major national and metropolitan newspapers pay goodly sums of money to their reporters to investigate and report on national and international political, economic, religious, and cultural events. Reading a newspaper means more than skimming. It is a cover-to-cover endeavor. Want to find out which terrorist groups are operating in Mozambique? Read the *New York Times, Washington Post, Chicago Tribune, Los Angeles*

Times, or one of the other notable newspapers. The *Christian Science Monitor* and the *Wall Street Journal* are also excellent. How about books? The *New York Times Book Review* will tell you everything you need to know at a basic level. Art, movies, theater? All are covered by critics who know what they are talking about. And, if you can manage it, the *Jim Lehrer News Hour* (television) is one of the best, because it discusses important issues in depth as opposed to the three-minute coverage afforded by the regular television news stories. The smaller local newspaper may depend on the wire services for much of its international coverage of news but, at the local environment within which you will be functioning, the local news coverage is unique. And, to round out the resources, *National Public Radio,* heard in the morning on its *Morning Edition* and late afternoons on *All Things Considered,* is the best of the best.

All this information is not intended to make you a chatterbox; nor does it give you license to foist your opinions on the client or his friends. You may, on occasion, find yourself sitting down with the client at a social occasion and, rather than looking like a bump on a log, you will be able to hold your own with the table conversation.

Low profile clothes--you will need a good, basic wardrobe, something that fits you well, is comfortable, durable, and costs more than you will want to spend, but will pay back over and over again. It is an investment. You want to make top dollar? You have to look like top dollar. A cautionary note, since we are talking about blending and low profile; the look is conservative and timeless, not trendy or flashy. You want to look like you belong with the client, and that you are a competent and trustworthy person. A rule of thumb is that you never out-dress the boss and you never stand out.

Clearly, there are many advantages to working low profile, not the least of which is that you may remain anonymous to anyone who aims to harm your client, and thereby avoid the danger of being eliminated at the outset of an incident. In almost every kidnap or assassination incident, the bodyguard is the first to be shot. He is considered a nuisance to have around and is, therefore, expendable. Count on it. Would-be kidnappers and hostage-takers want only the client. Low profile may save your life as well as your client's. If your low profile "cover" is good enough, the client's associates will not be tempted to gossip about you. Low profile means that the fewer people who know your real role the better.

If low profile is a process of blending in and remaining anonymous, what is high profile? High profile is high visibility with no attempt to remain anonymous. On the contrary, high profile is intended to deter a possible incident. It generally includes large individuals with dark glasses, non-smiling faces, and visible weapons, who make no attempt to seem sociable or approachable. High profile protection may be seen in strike situations or in estate protection, which makes use of patrolling guards and dogs. In strike situations, protection agents functioning as video photographers poised to capture any events on video tape are extremely useful in preventing violent incidents. Estate protection may include roving patrols, guard dogs, firepower, and high-tech electronics. High profile is the way to go when your purpose is *deterrence*, giving the appearance of being too tough to tackle. While certain individuals and groups determined to harm your client will take on suicidal missions, most terrorist groups and sensible criminals want only to attack those individuals and institutions that appear to be easy. No terrorist worth his salt wants to die or appear ineffectual. Individuals and groups bent on personal gain want an easy target. Therefore, visible and effective protection has an important role to play. It is a responsibility of the professional executive protection agent to assist the client in determining the level and breadth of protection required.

There are those situations which require both high and low profile protection, with low profile being the back-up, close-in deterrent. Each protection situation requires its own analysis to determine what kind of protection will be provided. At some point, the executive protection agent will need to deal with budgets, and no matter the advantages or

disadvantages, a certain course of action will be dictated. The executive protection agent will find himself/herself working high profile at times, but more often low profile. The important point is that the client may often feel that high profile is what is needed, whereas in reality, low profile is more desirable. In this situation, the agent's diplomatic skills will be in high demand to convince the client of the proper level of protection.

If the trend is toward low profile, who are the individuals filling the role of protection agent? They are not all cut from the same cloth. A high percentage have some background in the military, law enforcement, and/or the martial arts. Many have worked in other aspects of private security. It is not unusual for a bodyguard to have worked as a night club bouncer or a security guard. Law enforcement is a very useful experience, as it often provides the individual with a network that can be helpful. The military experience teaches discipline and provides good physical training. The martial arts teach excellent defensive tactics and good reflexes and, even more importantly, teach a philosophy of integrity that is parallel to executive protection. The samurai of history was a master of the martial arts, and his job was to defend his "master" even unto death. But, it should be emphasized that, while useful, it is not necessary to have any of these profiled backgrounds to be successful as an agent. The modern executive protection agent may have been an accountant, a computer programmer, a university professor, a cowboy, or simply a person who has never before had a real purpose in life. Agents have emerged from backgrounds of poverty and tough times, including inner city ghettos. One very successful agent was a male nurse before moving into the protection environment. His was probably the most useful background of all. This agent has saved three lives, none of which were saved by a gun or a fast getaway. All were medical emergencies.

Women have made great inroads in the profession. One of the best female agents took up the profession after having raised five children while working at a humdrum support job. Another woman was a graphics artist for a very successful, if somewhat racy, magazine before entering the executive protection profession. Yet another female graduated from the most prestigious military establishment in the country and then decided to change careers.

Of more importance than background experience is motivation, the force that drives an individual to enter the profession. At one point, the author surveyed 200 agents on this issue. A high majority responded that the most important reason for taking up the profession was the desire *to protect and support others*. The second most important reason was the desire *to change their profession and their lives*. Third, not surprisingly, was *the desire to make decent money in an interesting and challenging profession*. Clearly, the ones who make it in the profession are dedicated individuals who often make great personal sacrifices to achieve their goals. It speaks well for the profession.

Does this mean that all bodyguards and agents are splendid individuals of equal skills? No, it does not. It is a tough, demanding profession, and a lot of motivated individuals have more heart than ability. The profession is tough in several ways. It can be dangerous, and, conversely, it can be boring beyond belief. Think about it. If the agent does the job properly, nothing happens, and yet the agent is never able to fully relax. Constant vigilance is the name of the game, and that usually goes hand-in-hand with stress. It's a tough profession in that it may not be constant; that is, a good agent may work intensively and profitably for a few days or weeks, and then not work at all for an equal time. Unless one works in a steady position as protection agent for a family or within a corporation, it is a matter of living with erratic income. Yet, in spite of these factors, executive protection is a rapidly expanding profession with a projected growth rate that is very attractive.

In addition to the monetary rewards, there is the sense of doing a job well, of making a difference, of maintaining an integrity in a world that sometimes seems filled with shoddy values, violence, and craziness. There is the increased self-confidence that comes with the turf, the certain knowledge that one has acquired life skills of importance. The agent's job, or trade, is actually a way of life, since it requires constant vigilance and attention to detail. If you like the idea of demanding, challenging work that demands your best at all times, it is probably the profession for you.

Newcomers to the profession are often surprised to find that they use their brains far more than their weapons, cars, or defensive tactics. About 100:1 times more often. Planning and attention to details, with unceasing concentration, are the bedrock elements of the agent's job. There are numerous U.S. Secret Service agents who have never drawn their guns except to practice-fire on the shooting range, and to unholster at night. When was the last time you read about a shootout that involved Secret Service agents? Never, is the answer. Meticulous planning and attention to detail could be the official slogan of the executive protection agent's profession. Conversely, flexibility and good reflexes, with an ability to take decisive action instantly, is an absolute necessity. Good planning will take care of 95%, maybe 98%, of the potential problems which could occur, but decisiveness, vigilance, and excellent reflexes are needed for the other 5% to 3% of possible contingencies. If you have ever seen the tapes of the John Hinckley assassination attempt on President Reagan, look for two important things. The police are looking at the President, not at the bystanders, which included Hinckley. More importantly, notice the *instant* reaction of the Secret Service agent closest to Reagan. Within probably one second he had Reagan in the car; no hesitation--bang, into the car, and away! This is very difficult, to go from ho-hum business as usual to instant action. It is all part of the agent's job.

Agents work either as a team or single-handed. A general rule of thumb is that the single agent works in low risk situations, and teams are required for high risk assignments or for work with families and children (multiple clients). This is not 100% true, and the single agent will often find himself improvising to provide additional protection. However, whether it is a one-man operation or a team, the principles of protection are the same. Teams take more organizational and management skills. One-man operations require improvisation and a lot of self-confidence. If it's a one-man operation, that one man has to have the confidence to know that he can take care of his client. He can make decisions. He has good judgement. And, as an in-between stopgap measure, a lone protection agent may find that he occasionally needs to call in additional agents to assist in taking care of the client for a short-term situation. Some agents work better on their own and prefer the one-man assignments. Others like being members of a team.

The best agents are the ones who have the self-confidence to realize when they have done the job and to take pleasure from that knowledge without breaking their arms patting themselves on the back. This is not to say that it doesn't pay to advertise, and the best advertising in the protection business is word-of-mouth. You should realize that the world of private protection is essentially a very small one. Practically everyone knows practically everyone else, referrals are the name of the game, and networking is very important. Do a good job and your reputation helps you into the next job. Do a bad job and you are, very quickly, dead in the profession. For anyone getting into the executive protection business and who intends to make it a lifetime career, it is of primary importance to develop a professional code of ethics and behavior and to stick to it through thick and thin. Sometimes this means selecting your client, even turning down an assignment.

The accepted philosophy which is at the heart of modern executive protection rests on a few fundamentals: conflict avoidance; the use of proactive measures whenever possible rather than reactive measures; cover and evacuate; and, when avoidance and evacuation are not possible, decisive use of reactive measures.

Conflict avoidance in this context means avoiding hazards (including accidents), dangerous situations, confrontations, and embarrassments. This is such an important issue that good executive protection agents will spend 90% of their time practicing conflict/hazard avoidance. The most desirable problem is the one you never have.

Proactive measures include all of the activities which the executive protection agent will take to avoid problems. Advance surveys, threat assessments, intelligence gathering, armored cars, bomb detection, electronic detection and countersurveillance--these are but some of the proactive measures taken by agents to protect their clients.

If avoidance and proactive measures fail to deter the problem, the agent must cover and evacuate his client whenever possible, as opposed to standing fast and either slugging it out or shooting it out with the bad guy. Agents are not law enforcement officers; they have no duty (nor right) to confront, pursue, or arrest offenders. Therefore, unless it would be unsafe to do so, the preferred measure of conflict avoidance is simply to get the client away, safely, from the problem.

The reactive measures of muscle intervention, gunplay, evasive driving, martial arts, and other unarmed defensive tactics should be undertaken only when all proactive measures have failed. There is a caveat to this--when reactive measures are needed, the agent must be fully prepared to use them and should be capable of doing so instantly and decisively!

The old-style bodyguards relied heavily on reactive skills, which often led to disasters involving the client and themselves. Studies of terrorist incidents reveal that, where proactive measures were not taken to protect a client, reactive measures taken by the bodyguards failed almost every time. The terrorists, having the elements of surprise and heavier firepower, won the incident. Case histories prove over and over again that the overwhelming majority of organized attacks are successful--the bodyguards usually all die, and the bodyguards' gunfire almost never affects the outcome of the incident (the bodyguards rarely fire their guns effectively and sometimes never get off a shot).

In non-lethal situations, such as dealing with a belligerent drunk, using strong-arm methods will result either in a lawsuit aimed at the client or grave embarrassment to him. At this point, the agent becomes a liability, not an asset.

The level of protection provided a client is dependent upon budget and resources. The first level of protection consists of the agent, or agents, in closest proximity to the protectee. Their job is to anticipate and identify problems, to avoid or deter those problems, and to react to close-in hazards, whether those hazards are armed assailants, pushy drunks, stalkers, overeager autograph seekers, or troublemakers of any variety. The second level of protection consists of the technical support provided the agents. This support may include intrusion detection systems, armored vehicles, bomb detectors, and other aids. The third level of protection is achieved through the gathering of intelligence (information) which allows the agent(s) to predict problems and plan avoidance solutions. This intelligence gathering can include known or suspected threats, adversary profiles, safety hazards, and general crime potential. These are the levels, or assets, which can be provided a client under normal conditions. The depth, or extent of the protection level is dependent on the amount of money allocated. Will the client expend the dollars for a full protection team or only one person? Will an armored vehicle be within the budget? If the dollars are not there, the agent(s) must do without some of the protective features.

If the client is a government dignitary or national leader, two additional levels of protection may be available: law enforcement and military. Law enforcement support typically available for a state governor, senator, or the President of the United States could include uniformed and plain-clothes police, sniper/countersniper teams, F.B.I. investigative resources, and others. A national leader's protection might include military aircraft, communications, and troops.

CLIENTS

Which brings us to the clients--the individuals, groups, or corporations who find themselves in need of protection. Each situation is different, but the techniques of protection are much the same, differing only in degree. The world has changed sharply in the past few decades. President Harry Truman loved to walk daily through the streets of Washington, DC with only minimal Secret Service protection. When President Clinton jogs, be assured he has a full team with him and that he chafes at the loss of his personal privacy. Many believe that it was the assassination of President Kennedy and the turmoil of the 1960's that so greatly changed and increased the need for protection. The past 35 years spawned international terrorist networks with assassinations-for-hire and deliberate attacks on military, government, and corporate entities. Within the United States, drugs, street gangs, and an escalating increase in violent crime have jumped the more-or-less traditional barriers of gangland and now threaten individuals at all levels. Home-grown fanatic groups, ranging from the Aryan Nations to animal rights activists, target individuals who never before felt at risk. Disaffected employees, brooding over job terminations, have killed dozens of former supervisors and fellow workers. Stalkers are so numerous and constitute such a problem that every state plus the federal government has passed legislation to make stalking a crime. Clients, therefore, include a wide range of individuals and entities.

Political figures are still targets of choice around the world. In this category you should include individuals such as Malcolm X and Dr. Martin Luther King. They were in the thick of political activities and were reliant on their bodyguards to protect them. Unfortunately, their bodyguards failed. Political figures are hard to protect. The nature of their profession means that they are up front working the crowds, shaking hands, and trying their best to seem approachable. They can't be sealed off completely, and unless the client is the President or Vice President of the United States, there are limits to the affordability of protection. It is not uncommon during a presidential campaign for candidates to solicit volunteers from the private security sector to augment their protection. Politicians, when they can, utilize local law enforcement to beef up their security. State Governors most often have their security provided by the State Police. Ex-politicians, on the other hand, especially the controversial ones or those running for their next office, are usually dependent on private protection (except for ex-Presidents of the United States).

Foreign political figures, sometimes on unhappy terms with their governments, engage protection agents. Some leaders of Middle East countries find themselves threatened by dissident groups from within their own country. Others, such as Salman Rushdie, author of the *Satanic Tales*, are victims of political regimes and live under constant threat, in hiding, with protection. In this country, members of the royal family of one Arab country employ many, many bodyguards. This client group, alone, accounts for a high percentage of the executive protection agents working today.

Many corporate executives, especially those at the highest management levels, have added executive protection to their corporate security. Corporate executives are in some real peril. Many represent companies which some view as "harmful." Exxon is a case in point. The Alaskan oil spill left this corporation looking less than perfect to some environmentalists. Corporations using animal research to develop products (cosmetics, chemicals, pharmaceuticals, genetically altered food products) have suffered a great deal of damage to buildings and threats to executives. Corporate executives, as well as bankers, have often been viewed as kidnap targets, with ransom as the goal. The 1992 kidnapping and subsequent death of an Exxon executive rattled corporate board rooms across the country. Overseas, corporations seem perfect targets, representing as they do oppressively rich American interests in third-world countries. Rising nationalism has focused on these corporations, and executive kidnappings have not been unusual. Providing protection for a corporate executive is serious business and, even within the

richest corporations, there is rarely enough budget to provide the number of bodies needed. On the other hand, a corporate executive generally does not have the same need as the politician to get out and shake the public hand. On the contrary, most executives today maintain a high level of anonymity. Lee Iacocco was a rarity, using his personal image and charisma to guide Chrysler Corporation as its CEO through difficult years.

Corporate protection is strictly suit, tie, shirt, and polished shoes--all up scale. It can be steady work and fairly low-risk, provided the agent can avoid becoming embroiled in corporate politics. A distinct advantage to corporate work is the support infra-structure provided by the corporate secretaries, chauffeurs, pilots, and security department. Yet another advantage for some is the fact that corporate work is not necessarily all close-order work. The executive is one of the hardest-working individuals you will encounter, and he works surrounded by others. It would be very difficult to kidnap or kill a Fortune 500 CEO sitting at his desk on the 19th floor of the company headquarters. His vulnerable points are, primarily, getting from home to office and back home again plus any travel or personal appearances. Unless, of course, that executive has received a direct threat, which ups the pressure.

Rock stars and other high-visibility celebrities almost all have some kind of protection. Often, it is a friend, member of the family, or other novice. But, increasingly, these celebrities are hiring professional agents to protect them. Crowds can be very scary even when they love you. When they stop loving you, it's even scarier. The murder of John Lennon made an indelible impression. Entertainers are somewhat like politicians in that they work hard, close-in to the public. Their fans are wild about them, and that means lots of money. Entertainers must look like they, in turn, love their fans, tossing hugs and kisses to the crowd. The protection is the thin barrier that separates entertainer from fan. Never forget that the star works like a dog. A singing tour can last a year, constantly on the move, constantly on edge. As much as anything, that star wants privacy away from fans, hangers-on, and entourage. Frankly, some agents love this work and others hate it. It is tough, tough work, sometimes done in spite of managers and sycophants who do not appreciate having a body between them and the star. Never forget, the agent can't manhandle the fans or the entourage, and he should never get involved with any kind of funny business on the side, such as drugs or teen-age girls. It's a different, very special kind of life, calling for different clothes and attitudes but no less professionalism. There seems to be a trend toward less craziness in the rock star world, and this is helpful.

There have been stalkers around for a very long time, but never before have there been so many. Stalkers have fastened their attention on movie stars, television figures, and other high-visibility figures, as well as on many non-celebrities. No one has true statistics on how many ex-wives and ex-girlfriends have been attacked and murdered by stalkers. It is a very dangerous situation, since stalkers seem so obsessed in reaching their victims that they are unmindful of any deterrents. One young Colorado woman was pursued by her ex-boyfriend stalker up the steps to the door of the police station, where he shot and seriously wounded her. The zeal of the stalker is similar to the fanaticism of the religious terrorist in Lebanon. The problem for many intended victims is that these (almost always) women cannot often afford to hire bodyguards. One very intelligent executive protection agent put together a non-profit corporation to provide this kind of protection and tried funding it with corporate and foundation grants. This is very innovative and is a win-win situation for everyone except the stalker. The women gain badly needed protection, the agents get work, and the giftgivers are contributing to a highly visible and worthwhile cause.

Families of means, sadly, often find themselves in need of protection. The greed factor surfaces in family feuds and violence is sometimes the result. Custody battles all too often end with one parent kidnapping a child or children. Protection for a family is often steady work, with an agent or team

of agents working for a year or longer. Some agents prefer this work. It's relatively low risk and, if you like being around children, it can be pleasant. The distaff side is that it can be boring, something like being an armed nanny, and living that closely with a family can be stressful. There are agents who have lived and worked with the same family for five years. And there are families who wear out agents like shoes, changing them every three to 12 months. A family has its own habits, manners, culture, and preferences, and that family is not going to change anything for the convenience of the agent.

Many agents exist primarily on short-term assignments which they acquire through referrals and networking. Agent A, who lives in New York, has contacts in all parts of the country plus a few in Europe and other countries. His client, headquartered in New York, is planning to make a fast visit to Los Angeles. Agent A is a one-man protection team. Agent A calls Agent B in Los Angeles. They know each other well and have worked together before. Agent A gives Agent B his client's itinerary and asks him to do an "advance" (more on this later) for him, since Agent A cannot do the advance and stick with his client at the same time. Or, Agent A, who is usually a one-man team, discovers that his client is going to be involved for ten days in a high-risk endeavor. Agent A calls three other agents in the area whom he trusts and brings them in for short-term, beefed-up protection. Many jobs are referred through the network but only to trusted professionals of integrity who can work together as a team. Team leader on one assignment may find himself a team member taking orders from another team leader in another assignment. There is no room for prima donnas in these situations. A true professional does his or her job--period. Having a network of agents whom one respects makes this easy.

There are other clients, but the ones we have covered fit most situations.

INTRUDERS

There is as much variety with intruders as

there is with clients, and they have been discussed to some degree. But, for our purposes we are going to divide them into simple categories.

There are those intruders who mean to do physical harm to the client and who are mentally unbalanced or obsessed with their goal or gripped with a fanatic fever. This intruder frequently knows no fear, doesn't care if he or she is killed, and, in fact, may visualize being killed or committing suicide after the event. This is extremely dangerous and makes the protection job a tough one. This intruder may be crazed but can still function very cleverly, often improvising to gain access to the client. It is a high risk situation and requires intense vigilance. Fortunately, many of these unbalanced intruders are not so clever, being more impulsive than organized and, in fact, some are more nuisance than threat. An obsessed fan invaded talk show host David Letterman's home so many times, claiming to be his wife, that it should be recorded in the *Guinness Book of Records*. Of course, one never knows when obsession and longing will turn into resentment and anger. Some intruders long for notoriety and "telegraph" their movements, hoping to appear on the evening news. In any case, cranks, obsessed fans, disaffected employees, stalkers, and religious fanatics must be taken very, very seriously. Obsessions have a history of being long-lived. Some stalkers carry their obsessions for years. One television anchorwoman has moved several times to illude an obsessed fan, only to find that the fan has moved with her.

A second category of intruders is the cool, calm, organized intruder with a purpose, perhaps a kidnap and ransom, perhaps a hijacking, perhaps extortion. Well-organized terrorist groups with funding are the best examples of this kind of intruder. Again, this is very dangerous. If a terrorist group in Argentina, or Chile, or other country decides that the CEO of the Yankee oil company in their country represents a chance for kidnap and ransom, plus the enormous public relations value of showing their strength, this group will plan for weeks or months and spend whatever it takes, involving perhaps dozens of people, just to complete the mission. There are some definite moves which can be taken to evade these people and this will be covered in depth in the material which follows in this book. One major advantage in this situation is that the group or individual wishes to be successful; i.e., wishes to accomplish its purpose and remain alive and unharmed. If the target appears to be too well protected, another more accessible target may be selected as a substitute. This is a distinct advantage. If there are two major corporations using animal research in their operations, and one is tightly protected while one has no visible protection, it is not difficult to determine which corporation will be selected for attack.

Then there are the amateurs who want to be cool, calm, and organized but generally lack the professional skills. Parents planning to kidnap their children often fall into this category. The fact that they often succeed is not so much a testimonial to their skill as it is evidence of the naivete of the target. Very often, the intruder's job is made easy by simply appearing at a school and driving off with a child. Clients who recognize a threat and bring in protection generally find that this situation can be controlled with a low-to-medium risk.

There are short-term threats that cool down. This is similar to the second category above, with individuals and groups who wish to accomplish a "hit" but also wish to be successful. A determined individual bent on revenge, given time, may decide that life is sweet and the client is too well protected. Threats of this nature must be taken quite seriously, because the visible protection which results may deter the attack.

Probably the most difficult threat of all is the accidental or indiscriminate threat. This is the violence that occurs purely because the client happens to be in the wrong place at the right time. This includes the bombing of the Belfast train station, or the armed hold-up of the 7-Eleven just as the client decides he needs a pack of cigarettes. It can be and usually is unplanned, violent, and somewhat unpredictable, but not altogether so. The protection agent has, as a responsibility, the very real duty of preventing his client(s) from being placed in unpredictable circumstances. Sometimes, when all else fails, the agent simply has to do his job by covering and evacuating his client, and actively protecting him.

There are threats that are not necessarily of the life-and-death variety but which hold equal importance in the mind of a client, and they may be totally accidental. Clients do not like to be embarrassed, not from a drunk, not from a fan, not from anyone. Totally unforgivable in the mind of a client is the following scenario. A presumably devoted follower/employee/fan comes forward with a

bouquet of flowers, and, just as he reaches the client, he throws a bottle of blood or a cream pie on the client. (A similar incident happened to Bill Gates of Microsoft.) This is a preferred method for certain groups who wish to make a point. If the media are present and snapping live pictures the catastrophe is complete. These intruders are just as dangerous in their own way as the guys with the guns.

There are low risk, medium risk, and high risk situations. All must be addressed, much in the same way but to different degrees. The principles are the same. The differences are usually dictated by *budgets*, a subject which will be discussed continually, along with the trade-offs which must be made to accommodate budgets.

The stereotypical approach to executive protection is to focus all attention on preventing bad-guy intruders (usually terrorists) from intentionally harming the client. In reality, there are three security objectives: preventing *unintentional injuries, embarrassing situations, and intentional injuries.*

Note that *intentional injuries* is listed last. This is because the likelihood of a bad guy attack (particularly a terrorist attack) on a client is less than the likelihood of the client's suffering an unintentional injury or an embarrassing situation. Statistics show that international terrorist attacks against non-military American targets have declined in the past few years. Hijackings have declined as well. The flip side of this is that life within the United States for corporate executives and high profile figures has become increasingly dangerous, in spite of a decline in violent street crime. None of this should be construed as unconcern for the problem because, even though the client may not statistically be faced with a high likelihood of intentional injury, the results of an intentional attack can be catastrophic. The threat of intentional attack is difficult to counteract and, therefore, much of the material in this book is directed toward protection against intentional attack.

The probability of unintentional injuries and embarrassing injuries occurring with a client are high and are an everyday opportunity. If the agent focuses all of his attention on preventing terrorist attacks and overlooks the possibility of unintentional injuries and embarrassing situations, he is not doing his job. What good is it if the client doesn't get killed by bullets today but instead falls down the stairs and breaks a leg just as he was going on stage to receive an award. Is it the agent's job to make certain that the stairs are well lighted or marked with reflective tape? Yes, it is, as well as the many other preventive measures which the agent must take to smooth the way for the client. These are the day-to-day activities which the client can see and have confidence that, when the agent is on the job, there is no problem. The agent has his client's safety and welfare in mind.

The executive protection agent must carefully balance his job activities to deal with the low probability/high penalty intentional attack, and the high probability/low penalty unintentional injury or embarrassing situation. If the agent does his job properly, he can provide protection against each of these contingencies for his client. This makes the agent a very valuable employee. It also marks him or her as a true professional, totally different from the old-style bodyguard with arms crossed guarding a door.

UNINTENTIONAL INJURIES

Vehicular accidents are great examples of unintentional injuries. There are hundreds of thousands of vehicular accidents which occur every year, probably every month. This is a high probability event. Because of this, the executive protection driving schools have changed much of the content of their driving programs. There is less attention focused on the escape and evasion maneuvers, with more time and practice devoted to comfortable, safe driving. There remains a balance of attention on these activities, as it is still true that the majority of intentional attacks on a client occur in and around the vehicle. Escape and evasion driving techniques are important, without question, and are invaluable when needed. However, on a day-to-day basis, the client wants to have a smooth ride with no accidents and no hassles. For years, defensive driving (or driving defensively) has placed emphasis on the avoidance of accidents.

Random accidents are another high probability event for clients. Random accidents can include falling down the stairs, being hit by a golf ball, hitting someone else with a golf ball, slipping in the bathtub, and a myriad of other innocent but damaging incidents. Random accidents can include many other less innocent activities. Some clients get drunk and fall down in public. Others injure themselves by smashing their hands through windows. Teenage children of clients are often prone to indulge in these sorts of fun affairs. Some bodyguards are hired primarily to keep the clients from doing bodily harm to themselves or others.

Medical emergencies are right at the top of the list of bad things that will probably happen to a client. The probability of this is so high that the professional executive protection agent who hopes to make a long-time career *will*, absolutely, deal with numerous medical emergencies. These will not be inconsequential band-aid incidents. They will include heart attacks, blood, and other life-threatening events. The serious executive protection agent should invest the time needed to acquire Emergency Medical Technician (EMT) training. If it is important to learn to shoot straight, it is ten times more important to learn how to deal effectively and decisively with medical emergencies. Relying on calling 911 to save a client is simply not good enough; the client could die. EMT training will generally enable an agent to keep the client alive until competent medical help can be reached. This is particularly true if the client is in a remote area, overseas, or in third-world countries. Example: The client likes to vacation at his back country Montana ranch, reached by dirt roads some 30 miles from the nearest town and 80 miles from the nearest decent emergency hospital. The client likes to hunt elk, and prides himself on being able to hike far back in the mountains. The client accidentally shoots himself, and, in doing so, bleeds copiously. Try calling 911. This is a life-and-death situation, and the agent had better be able to deal with it.

Special medical problems often occur with clients. If the client, particularly a non-celebrity client, can afford to hire executive protection, he or she is probably no youngster, having worked a number of years to become Chairman of the Board or CEO of a major corporation. He is probably in his 50's, 60's, or 70's. He is very likely not in top physical health, having worked intensively for years at a sedentary occupation. He probably has one or more special medical problems, and may be reluctant to be forthcoming about them. It could be diabetes. It could be epilepsy. It could be cancer. The client may very well be embarrassed at having his medical problem. He likes being CEO and does not wish to exhibit any weakness to the Board of Directors or associates who might interpret a medical problem to be grounds for retirement. Unless the client has total confidence in his agent, he may try to hide the medical problem. It's a delicate situation. The client does not have to divulge his medical problem. Time, trust, and diplomacy can sometimes provide the solution. If this doesn't work, the agent may have to play detective. If the client leaves medicine or pill bottles lying around, it may be necessary to quietly take a sample to a pharmacist to see if it can be identified, and the medical condition for which it has been prescribed. Sometimes the client's wife can be helpful, since her concern lies more in keeping her husband alive than exposing a vulnerability.

There are some medical problems which present serious problems for the agent. AIDS is the best example. AIDS is a special problem for the client and is a potential problem for the agent. What happens if the client is shot, with blood pouring out? What about CPR? It has happened that a team of agents worked a short-term assignment with an AIDS-stricken client. The client was up-front about his medical condition, which made it easier for the agents to determine if they could provide an acceptable level of protection to the client without risking infection to themselves. After some investigation and consultations with the client's doctor, it was agreed that the assignment could be undertaken with certain restrictions. Special equipment could be used in the event CPR was needed. If the client were to sustain a bleeding injury, the agents would not be able to expose themselves to the blood. Both parties agreed to the contract. There is, after all, some potential risk in any assignment. If an agent is willing to take the risk of being shot, he or she should be willing to take some medical risks.

There is another special problem which an agent may, at some time, have to deal with--what to do if the client takes illegal drugs. The decision as to whether the assignment should be taken is up to each individual agent. Technically, what the client does in the sanctity of his or her bedroom is his business. However, the agent needs to have a clear understanding with the client that he, the agent, will not collect the drugs, and he does not want to be in the same room with the client when the client is indulging this illegal habit. The agent must never be in a position of appearing to condone the use of illegal drugs or of having to testify as to what he saw happening. Agents are not priests, and they are not cops, but it can be discouraging to spend time and energy protecting a client only to have that client kill himself. Again, for every agent, it is an individual choice.

EMBARRASSING SITUATIONS

The media can present some special problems for high-visibility, newsmaker clients, particularly political and corporate clients, although they can also give some bad moments to celebrity clients. All too often, individuals who are in the news and the individuals who write about and photograph the news end up as antagonists. When this happens, it is often the fault of the security people and the client's organization. Do some clients have foot-in-mouth disease, and are some media people real sharks out for blood? Sure, but even these folks can be managed with proper care.

Some of the most visible aspects of bad press relations and the most awful management of those bad press relations could be seen in the presidency of Richard Nixon. President Nixon made no bones of the fact that he did not like the press, and the press, in turn, delighted in showing Nixon in the worst light, sometimes literally. Those dark, glowering photographs were sometimes deliberately shot from down low with dark lighting. Media relations with the White House became a problem of mammoth proportions (for the White House).

Richard Nixon wasn't the first person who went to war with the press. It is astonishing how many otherwise intelligent individuals will try either to ignore the press or to prevent them from doing their job. Corporate executives often have this failing. Let an unpleasant event befall the company, and more often than not, the people in charge will either stonewall, lie, or naively make it impossible for the media to do their job. It always, always comes back to haunt them.

Let's dispel a myth here. The media has been maligned for years, having been represented as bloodthirsty scavengers who will do anything to get a story, preferably a story that makes somebody look bad. Well, folks, it simply is not true. The media are like anybody else with a job to do. They are paid to investigate and report on stories. They are tightly managed by editors who know that, if the story is not scrupulously reported, the newspaper, magazine, or television station can be sued for a lot of money. The majority of the media reporters and interviewers adhere to a code of ethics and try to do a fair job. The best ones go through a lot of self-examination, worrying about the power of the press. They are also just as human as anyone else. They like certain people and they dislike others. Now, if you treat the media like dogs, lie to them, refuse to give them facts, and openly show your lack of respect, it is easy to see how the media will respond. Do you have something to hide, something that will embarrass you? Watch out, *the media will inevitably find out and be ever so delighted to report every nuance of the embarrassment.* On the other hand, if you are open, honest, courteous in your treatment, and try to facilitate the media's job, you are generally going to receive fair treatment.

Let's take a simple example. Your client is hell on the media and loses no opportunity to make this clear. As he is leaving the stage after a speech, he trips and falls on his rear. The media at that event are going to show him sprawled on the ground in living color, over and over, on the evening news and in every newspaper with a wire service. Did it happen? Yes. Is it fair reporting? Sure, it's a piece of news that your client is a klutz, and it's fair to let the rest of the world in on this secret.

An opposite example. One of the most popular First Ladies was Barbara Bush and the press loved her. She was honest, forthright, and courteous. If Barbara Bush had tripped over her dog, Milly, and sprawled on the White House lawn, would this have made the news? Probably not. After all, it was a minor non-event, and the press are not obligated to show all of the warts and pimples on good people. Do you see the difference?

It often becomes the job of the executive protection agent to deal with the press. Later, in the material dealing with special events, there is a discussion of arrangements for media attending the event. Suffice it for now to state that the agent can make very big points with the media by helping them to do their job, making it possible for them to be situated where they can get photographs and where they can hear the speeches. It is also much safer. The last thing any agent wants is to have a pack of frustrated reporters and cameramen swarming toward the client because they had been stuck in some far-off corner and failed to get their story. Keep in mind that the media has been invited, and, if they have taken the time to respond, they want a story. Making it easy for the media to get their stories makes for *better* stories, with a nice opportunity to score some points for the client. Sometimes, when the media build a good feeling of trust, they will go out of their way to check out a potentially embarrassing story before printing it, giving the client an opportunity to recover some ground. Even if a not-so-nice media shark prints a lurid story, the good guys in the press will often actually defend an individual. Hilary Clinton, President Clinton's wife, is a case in point. Some press harpies were unable to resist sniping at Mrs. Clinton's career, clothes, and presence in the power circles. Gratifyingly, many of the top press people in the country counteracted by taking Mrs. Clinton's part and defending her. Hilary Clinton is a professional, and she is too smart to lash out at the media. She conducted herself with dignity and was treated very fairly in the highest-stakes game in the world.

The very last thing any agent ever should do is push, hit, verbally abuse a media person, or snatch a camera for its film. It is unforgivable, and, if the media person doesn't sue the agent, his client should fire him on the spot. You can't just shoo the media away, either. If it is a public event they have a perfect right to be there, and an agent has no authority to ask them to leave. If it is a private event, this is another matter. At a private event certain media are invited and credentialed. If someone from the media who is not invited or credentialed shows up the agent has the right to deny them entrance. An agent cannot deny them the right to stand on the street and take photographs of the client. This being the case, sometimes it is a good idea to set up a decent place for them so that there is a chance to keep them in a small, confined area rather than chasing the client down the street.

Even if the client hates the media, the agent should never compound the problem by reflecting his client's attitude. The agent is a professional. So is the media person. Professionals need to be able to communicate with each other in a civilized fashion. There are other advantages to getting along with the media. Top media people, both television and press, like to interview experts for their stories. Some top executive protection agents have received excellent news coverage and credibility by virtue of the fact that they earned the trust of the media. And last, on occasion it is very useful to be able to ask a television reporter for a copy of her video tape of a particular story. If relations are cordial, this is often possible.

Very often, clients are in the public spotlight as speakers, recipients of awards, givers of awards, or participants in some ceremony. It is important that the client not be allowed to fall down on his way to the stage or suffer any other accidental injuries or embarrassments. This means that the agent must anticipate potential problems. Temporary stages which are hastily assembled for a special event can have poorly constructed steps, bad lighting, and no handrails. These will present a problem to the client, particularly if he is elderly or clumsy. The agent's job is to conduct a survey of the stage and seating arrangements and request any *reasonable* changes as far in advance as possible. It is unrealistic to demand elaborate, costly changes and additions for the sheer sake of showing off. And, not very much can be accomplished thirty minutes in advance of the client's arrival. If done early, a reasonable request for some safety feature(s) will usually be accommodated. It also helps to request the changes in a courteous, but firm manner. If all else fails, strips of silver reflective tape can be a big help in marking the steps.

Some potentially embarrassing situations occur as a result of the client's private life. More than one U.S. President has had a family member who was a source of embarrassment, and who was protected by the U.S. Secret Service as much to prevent harm to himself as to avoid being a problem for the President. Children can be big problems and sometimes have their own bodyguards as a restraint mechanism. Celebrities tend to attract friends and family who are less than desirable. Clients who find themselves unable to control unruly family members may wish to pass this responsibility to the agent. While it is the agent's job to prevent embarrassment to the client, it is not a good idea to become so strung out that the agent cannot do his primary job of protecting the client. At that point, the agent may need to have a discussion with the client to clarify the situation, and establish priorities.

This is as good a time as any to state that, in view of the interpersonal relationships inherent in any protection work, the executive protection agent must know exactly what his job is. His job is *to protect the client and perhaps the client's family*. It is not his job to become the client's friend or confessor. Unless the agent is careful, private life problems can become too attractive. Once the agent becomes enmeshed in family relationships, it becomes very difficult to perform the real job of protecting the client.

Entertainers and others who acquire and use illegal drugs can present an uncomfortable private life problem for the agent. Clients have been known to ask the (armed) agent to pick up the drugs. Answer-- never! In some areas of the country the police like to hassle entertainers because of their reputation with drugs. This is very uncomfortable for the agent, who may live in that particular area and does not want to be on the wrong side of the local law enforcement people. This is definitely the time for a heart-to-heart discussion with the client, at which time it should be made crystal clear that no one should buy or use illegal drugs in the presence of the agent. An agent may suspect that his client is taking drugs, but he has no obligation to report or testify about what he suspects. As long as the agent does not see the client or anyone else using drugs in his presence, he cannot testify to that fact. This is an advantage to the client, and generally the client will agree to these limits.

Rarely, there are other private illegal activities which the client indulges in. There have to be some clear limits, and the agent has a duty to protect himself. For example, if the client drags home a drunk, underage teenager and then attempts to rape her, the agent has a moral and legal duty to protect the teenager. Clearly, there must be an understanding between client and agent. The other solution, of course, is for the agent to decline or terminate the assignment. When this happens, the decision to terminate an assignment should be done in an unemotional and professional manner. Recriminations and moral invective are not helpful. What is at issue is primarily a legal one.

It should also be pointed out that clients are human beings, and a great many will not share their agent's moral code. So long as it is legal and doesn't hurt anyone, that's their privilege. The line needs to be drawn when the client's activities are a threat to the agent and the agent's ability to perform his job, or something clearly illegal and compromising is happening, or someone is being hurt.

INTENTIONAL INJURIES

Intentional injuries are any criminal attacks against person or property, random or indiscriminate threat, and organized terrorist attacks. It should be noted that criminal attacks are not always carried out by hardened criminals. Assault is a crime, whether it is committed by an ex-convict, an ex-employee, or an ex-husband. A terrorist attack may be a real threat by the Abu Nidal gang or by an extremist sector of the anti-abortionist group. Firebombing an abortion clinic and menacing an abortion doctor are acts of terror. It's important to deal with modern reality, which is that violent attacks and crimes are now committed by a very wide number of people.

Criminal threat is a problem. Clients are, for the most part, people of property; otherwise, they would not be able to afford executive protection. They have lovely homes, lots of possessions, nice cars, and a potential for being snatched in return for a reward. A great many individuals, having been enriched by the rambunctious stock market, have an enormous amount of money which can make them targets of choice for kidnapping or, more often, burglary. The problem with burglary is that it has been transformed in recent years from a fairly benign, non-violent crime into a violent crime. Some street gangs have, as a requirement for acceptance, a rule that the novice member steal a particular car or shoot someone. More often than not, this results in a random attack, but it can be targeted.

Individual clients are targeted for death or injury by members of their family more often than is generally imagined or reported. Family-owned businesses add the element of power to money, and, if a son, daughter, or nephew feels slighted in the division of power or money, revenge can be a powerful motivator.

Intentional attacks and injuries are the dangers which prompt clients to hire executive protection agents. Learning to prevent these attacks, therefore, forms the bulk of the material contained in this book.

Random threats are another security problem. Drugs, street gangs, and street criminals are not only expanding in numbers, they are leapfrogging over some traditional barriers. The use of so-called recreational drugs by "nice people" has opened the door. A stunning development is the growth of "yuppie gangs," teenage children of affluent families who have formed their own gangs and who pursue many of the same violent initiation rites as the ghetto gangs. Carjackings, most of which are randomly done, have declined but are still a problem. 7-Eleven stores are routinely held up, as are all-night gas stations. The chances of being victimized in a random attack are excellent. The Justice Department published an alarming report. As a baseline it focused on 12-year-old children in the United States. It stated that 83% of all 12-year-old children in this country will be victims or intended victims of violent crimes at least once in their lifetime. One out of every 133 Americans will become a murder victim and one out of every 12 women will be the victim of a rape or attempted rape. The National Crime Prevention Council stated that violent crime is 100 times more likely to strike than pneumonia death or death in an auto accident, eight times more likely than death from heart disease, and 16 times more likely than death from cancer.

Organized terrorist attacks are the problem which certain clients have to deal with, and against which they need protection. Terrorist attacks should be divided into international terrorism and domestic terrorism. This division makes it a little easier to understand, although protection against these groups is roughly similar. Modern international terrorism has a longer history than domestic terrorism. It has thus far been more deadly; it is better funded; it has learned to network; and it has developed some very elaborate scenarios. International terrorism has benefitted from client governments who often find terrorism to be a very cost-effective form of warfare to subvert governments. If a client is an executive in an international company which has divisions located in third-world countries, and if the client travels on business to these branch locations, the client has now greatly increased the possibility of a targeted threat to himself. While international terrorism directed toward non-military Americans has been somewhat on the wane, it is still a very real threat, and a high percentage of executive protection agents are employed to protect clients against this threat. In fact, one of several reasons for the lessening of international terrorism threats is that American companies have recognized that they have a responsibility to protect their employees, and, therefore, have developed defensive strategies which make them less attractive targets.

During the 1960's and 1970's, Americans felt that they enjoyed high international prestige as good guys, and there was a general feeling that, if you didn't do anything offensive or foolish, you were perfectly safe. The author traveled many times to Europe, the Orient, and the Middle East during the period between 1965 and 1975, while working for an international hotel chain, and felt absolutely safe, foolishly so. By 1975, Beirut was a gunpowder keg with armed gangs roving the highway between the airport and my hotel, the Phoenicia, in Beirut. Yet, I spent several hours walking the streets of Beirut, taking in the sights, alone, with the utter confidence that no harm would ever come to an American citizen. This phoney feeling of security permeated American corporations as well. American companies were felt to be inviolate. That's why they became such good targets. Since the mid-1980's, corporations and executives have toughened their protective defenses and developed strategies to protect themselves and their assets. This coincides with a general lessening of international terrorism, fewer client governments hiring hit men, and the collapse of many communist regimes. These events are cyclical,

and it will be interesting to view what happens, for example, in Germany with the rise of Neo-Naziism, or in Russia with the uncertainty of power, and the constant division of once-powerful countries into many small states. These events could engender feelings of hopelessness and anger, providing an impetus for terrorism.

A new threat on the international scene is that of crime. Crime in Russia is a new phenomenon. Perhaps it existed before the collapse of the central government, but it was never before considered a threat to Americans. With the emergence of international economies and the disappearance of some former national boundaries, crime is apt to become a major problem.

At the same time, domestic terrorism has been on the rise. While some of the fizz has gone out of the Aryan Nations and their fundamentalist comrades, there are now a number of quite virulent extremist groups. Environmentalist, anti-abortion, and many other legitimate groups have their violent spin-offs. A very real threat to American executives emanates from these violent spin-offs.

The challenge to the executive protection agent is to protect his or her client against any and all intentional, unintentional, and random threats. This is a real challenge.

3

THE THREAT

In executive protection, the term "threat" is generally intended to mean threat of intended, or targeted, attacks. These attacks are perceived to come from an assortment of dangerous individuals and groups. The majority of adversaries could be identified as:

- Cranks & crowds.
- Terrorists.
- Hate groups.
- "Good cause" extremists.
- Displaced and disaffected persons, primarily refugees from other countries.
- Violent employees and violent members of employees' families.
- Criminals.
- Cults.
- Gang members.
- Stalkers.
- Assassins.
- Serial killers.

All of these people represent some degree of threat to a client, although the probability of the client becoming involved with each grouping varies, depending upon several factors. If the client is the CEO of an international corporation with branch offices in Lebanon and South America, his exposure to a terrorist incident is significantly higher than the female country music star. Her exposure to a stalking incident, however, will be much higher.

Since the professional protective agent will, in his and her career, undoubtedly work with a number of different clients, it is well to understand the difference in the psychological make-up of each of the potential adversary groupings.

Some of the groups show a high similarity to each other and, in fact, sometimes fit within two or more categories. Terrorists certainly perform criminal

acts, often for the same reasons--to acquire money. Some serial killers choose their victims indiscriminately, pouncing on the first likely (easy) victim to appear, while others methodically identify and stalk specific victims. Violent employees may kill indiscriminately or may target their victims and may stalk victims before killing them. The Charles Manson cult spawned the Sharon Tate murders and the assassination attempt against U.S. President Gerald Ford by cult member Lynette (Squeaky) Fromme. Assassins and assassinations are most closely linked to public figures such as heads of state (U.S. President John Kennedy, Egyptian President Anwar Sadat) and other highly public and often controversial figures (Robert Kennedy, George Wallace.)

While some assassinations are purely politically inspired and carried out, others are the victims of non-political stalkers who, for various reasons, follow their victims until an opportunity presents itself (John Hinckley's attempt on the life of U.S. President Ronald Reagan).

ADVERSARIES

Thus far, we have looked at the social, cultural, and environmental influences which affect every strata of society. Now it is timely that we look at some of the influences that are specific to certain adversaries. While a stalker, violent employee, activist, or terrorist may be generally conditioned by the social influences which affect us all, what is it that specifically triggers him/her to "cross over the line" and become dangerous.

Crowds, Cranks and Stalkers

Inevitably, the client will find himself involved with friendly and unfriendly segments of the public. There are stockholder meetings, political rallies, concerts for rock and country music stars, speeches, employee meetings, striking labor mobs, and numerous other opportunities for the client to be placed in either a potentially dangerous or compromising situation.

Crowds are different from mobs, but both can be dangerous. A friendly crowd can hide the presence of a killer. Crowds can stampede if something triggers their panic button. Agitators can whip a docile crowd into a raucous crowd or a mob. Crowds tend to lose some of their normal inhibitions, and individuals lose their identities within the crowd. On the one hand, a friendly cohesive crowd will tend to remain friendly; on the other hand, leaders can adversely influence crowds, particularly when the issues are emotional. Hopefully, a client will never have to face an angry mob, but if there is a possibility that the crowd will become a mob, provisions should be made for crowd control with police, guards or both. Uniformed officers have a strong deterrent effect on rowdy crowds. Most people are either law-abiding or afraid to break the law openly; therefore, the presence of the law tends to put a damper on unruly behavior, though not always. Sometimes, the presence of armed, baton-wielding police officers can actually inflame emotions within the crowd. Uniformed officers are a visible deterrent so long as they do not appear as a bunch of armed thugs. Bashing heads is not a choice option.

Cranks tend to focus upon individuals in power. This means that Members of Congress, the President of the United States, State lawmakers, CEO's of corporations, heads of regulatory agencies, and the like are clear targets. If the client belongs to one of these groups and is high profile or highly visible, he/she is almost certain at some point to attract one or more cranks. Cranks tend to fixate upon real or imaginary problems. These can include delusionary problems such as little green men from outer space beaming deadly rays into their tooth fillings or the CIA opening their mail. It can also include complaints about an imaginary love affair between the target and the crank which must be consummated.

Cranks generally operate from a negative posture; that is, inherently, they are labeled cranks because of their crankiness, always complaining about something. They can be woefully persistent, sending multiple letters and telephone calls or calling on the press to register a complaint.

Cranks sometimes have legitimate causes and reasons for their crankiness. Often, they merely want to be heard, to register their complaints with someone in authority. It is when their behavior becomes more of an obsessive nuisance or dangerous that they must be regarded as a real security risk.

Cranks should be taken seriously. Ignoring them does little good as they seldom go away on their own. If the crank does not find an audience, he may simply escalate the level of his behavior, as he now feels justified in pursuing his goals.

At some point the client is almost certain to attract the attention of one or more cranks, and if he/she is high profile, this likelihood will increase proportionately.

What is the difference between a crank and a stalker? For the purposes of this book, we shall define the crank as generally more nuisance than physically harmful, and as someone who may be persistent but does not actively stalk his target. A crank may send multiple letters or may wait for hours outside the client's office but does not follow the client from home to out-of-state functions and back again. Cranks come in all sizes and shapes. Some are merely nuisances and some are potentially dangerous. Some are mentally disturbed, and others are merely angry or determined to accomplish some objective.

Cranks can be dangerous and, for that reason, can never be dismissed out-of-hand. A determination should *always* be made as to whether the crank represents a physical threat to the client or to himself. Cranks, if they stick with their crank obsessions long enough, can gravitate into the role of stalker, presenting yet another reason for intervening as early as possible to rid oneself of the crank.

Stalkers, a category of threat that will be dealt

with in a subsequent chapter, are a relatively new, rapidly emerging threat. Stalkers can be dedicated beyond belief and can be lethal. True stalkers will obsessively follow their target almost as a full-time occupation, often traveling long distances and demonstrating great skill in positioning themselves close to their target. Stalkers often lose all regard for their own safety and will follow a target into any situation. Truly obsessed stalkers apparently lose all feeling for the normal inhibitors which restrain most of us as they pursue their prey.

Cranks and stalkers often show similar characteristics. One distinction is that we normally think of cranks as those individuals who are negative or hostile, or who may have some fixated notion which they wish to relay to a public figure or other client. Stalkers, on the other hand, may be either hostile or benign. Benign (non-dangerous) stalkers may be genuinely "in love" with the object of their stalking and wish nothing more than to express that love to the stalkee.

Violent Employees and Violent Members of Employees' Families

This is a rapidly increasing category of potentially violent adversaries, or threats, to our clients. It is a relatively new phenomenon. Because of the importance of this category of individuals and the skills required to correctly identify, assess, and manage them, there is lengthy material in a later chapter devoted to them.

Terrorists

In the fall of 1999, a Federal advisory commission report warned that the United States faces increasing threats from terrorism in the next 25 years. The report warned that the U.S. will be vulnerable to an increasing range of threats against American forces and citizens overseas, as well as at home, from terrorists or rogue states. It stated that threats could involve unannounced attacks on American cities by terrorist groups using germ warfare, as well as cyber-attacks on the air traffic control system.

Terrorism has been a serious concern for the past three decades. There was a brief period at the end of the Cold War when many believed that terrorism would no longer be a problem, that without prominent state sponsors, the terrorists would lay down their guns and disappear. It soon became evident that this was not to be the reality; in truth, terrorism never went away--it simply mutated.

The very definition of terrorism has changed, along with the scope, profile, tactics, and targets of terrorists. During the late 1980's and throughout the 1990's, the right-wing side of terrorism surfaced with a vengeance. Hate groups expanded their activities via the Internet. And America, which heretofore had experienced little domestic terrorism, was shocked by the bombings of the World Trade Center and the Oklahoma Federal building.

As the level of violent rhetoric has escalated, the threat emanating from domestic extremist groups-- among them the anti-abortion, ecoterrorists, animal rights groups, the growing number of extremist militia and white supremacist groups, as well as refugee militants--must be taken into consideration.

Internationally, the danger lies as much from the insurgent movements of a number of countries as it does from individual terrorist groups. Compounding the problem is the new globalization of business, requiring our executives to put themselves in harm's way by traveling to some very dicey, oil-rich regions.

And, last, the bombings of two of our American embassies in Africa are reminders of the dangers posed by fundamentalist extremists.

Because of the seriousness and scope of the terrorism issue, a separate chapter has been devoted to this subject.

Criminals

Why does an individual become a criminal? If you can answer that question you will win a prize. There are numerous explanations of criminal behavior, and probably all are correct if not complete.

One theory states that crime is situational, meaning that criminality relates to the opportunities present for a criminal act. For example, a thief may steal from a vegetable stand if the owner is not looking, but will not do so if the owner is vigilant.

A second theory is that crime is related to the earlier history of the criminal and is dependent upon birth circumstances, home, community environment, and socioeconomic conditions.

Yet another theory poses that criminal behavior is learned behavior and is learned in association with others.

A theory that has strong acceptance for the crime in today's society places the blame upon social disorganization, meaning that the social pressures for conformity on the part of the person are not uniform and harmonious. In this condition, the society does not possess consensus with respect to societal goals or else does not possess consensus regarding means of achieving agreed-upon societal goals. Thus, the individual is confronted with alternative goals or means. He finds that behavior which is "right" or "correct" in one group is "wrong" from the point of view of other groups.

Controversies have raged surrounding theories of genetic and/or racial predispositions to criminal behavior versus environmental pressures, but at the current time the prevalent theories tend to center around the environment, social pressures, dysfunctional families, the self-reinforcing gratifications of crime and violence, and the easy availability of the weapons of crime.

What is the future of crime? Surprisingly, the futurists, while not necessarily a cohesive group themselves, do not support this doomsday theory. They have made some rather surprising forecasts of crime trends which are sketched in the following paragraphs.

The primary criminals of current times--the young, male, poor, and undereducated--will be replaced by older, more upscale offenders. Crimes committed by women will increase in non-traditional areas such as white collar crime and violent crimes. Senior citizens will enter the crime arena, and teenagers will commit more violent crimes. The good news is that the chances of becoming a street victim will diminish, and the bad news is that crimes will be more sophisticated and more profitable. The trend to migration back to rural communities, more active Neighborhood Watch programs, and increasing numbers of individuals who work from their home offices will help to decrease the number of burglaries.

Demographic trends show that the size of the teenage population will shrink in coming years. Because a high proportion of crimes are committed by teenagers, this means a decrease overall in the amount of crime. However, increased domestic violence and illegitimate births by underaged single mothers will continue to produce the conditions that lead young men into violence; hence, a decreasing number of teenagers will create a high proportion of the violence in crime. The same demographic trends show an enormous increase in the numbers of retired workers and a subsequent increase in the numbers of crimes committed by older persons.

Any retrenchments in the workplace and corporate downsizing, with the subsequent loss of jobs, should this occur, could create a class of middle class unemployed workers. Demoralizing circumstances and diminished living conditions would then lead the way to more middle class crime, involving primarily older males. Violence in the workplace would also increase, as a corollary to lay-offs with the resulting stressful home life.

Crime will not be contained within geographic areas--it is already showing strong tendencies to travel outside specified neighborhoods. It has, in fact, become mobile. Crime has already traveled from the industrial cities to the suburbs and rural areas. Drug gangs in coastal cities, seeking new clients, have traveled to cities located in the central areas of the United States to set up shop.

White collar crimes, primarily vested in

technology and a cashless community, will increase. Computer crime will greatly increase.

There are faint stirrings now and these stirrings will become a strong movement to curb the violence seen in motion pictures and on television. There will be strong pressures, if not regulation, to remove much of the violence now seen. This same trend will move more strongly on pornography. The futurists believe that the curbing of violence and pornography will have a beneficial effect in reducing violent crimes.

At the same time, not without a grimace, some consensual crimes (drug abuse, prostitution, gambling) will be legalized. And, yes, there will be increasing pressures to impose some measure of gun control, making it more difficult for criminals and potential criminals (teenagers, young people) to obtain guns.

Traditional crime-fighting strategies will be increasingly replaced by non-personalized, high-tech strategies. As it is, databanks now exist which make it possible to obtain an extensive background record on an individual within hours and to locate elusive individuals without ever leaving one's desk. In ways there were not possible until very recently, computers can and will talk to each other, sharing information. Individual privacy will go out the window.

To solve the crime problem, some of the civil liberties won with such hard effort in the 1960's and 1970's will disappear. The price for maintaining these civil liberties will be deemed too high to pay. The continued rise of the fundamentalist, conservative, ultra-right will increasingly view the civil liberties surrounding crime as impediments.

An increase in the use of private security will continue. There will be a growing emphasis on privatizing public space, denying access to intruders. All architecture, public as well as private, will be designed to make buildings more defensible and less accessible.

It remains to be seen if the futurists are right

in their predictions. The last three years have actually shown a downturn in violent crimes. Some attribute this to more effective policing while others claim that we are locking up more criminals and keeping them in prison for longer terms. Perhaps a booming economy and a shortage of workers has something to do with it.

For our clients, the dangers of becoming victims of violent crime remain as either indiscriminate crime--being in the wrong place at the wrong time--or the targeted crimes perpetrated for money and other reasons. Of equal or greater concern are the white and blue collar crimes, so-called "victimless" crimes. There is no question that corporate espionage is a rapidly growing problem, involving millions, perhaps billions, of dollars. If the futurists are correct and violent crime decreases, protective agents will find that they need to add to their existing protective skills the ability to investigate and identify the crimes of fraud and business espionage. The protection provided a client will expand from purely personal protection to the additional areas of asset and corporate protection.

Teenagers and Gangs

No one knows how many gangs and gang members there are in the United States. One figure puts 90,000 youth gang members in Los Angeles County alone. Gangs which were traditionally located on the west and east coasts of this country have spread into the interior or have served as models for newer gangs in Denver, Omaha, Kansas City, Albuquerque, Little Rock, and other cities. Suddenly, there are gangs in just about every major city in the United States, and their numbers are growing.

This growth factor is attributed to a number of factors, not the least of which is illegal drugs, in particular crack cocaine and, more recently, heroin. Not all gangs deal in drugs, but some gangs have become heavily involved in the trafficking of these illegal drugs, often sending advance "soldiers" into new urban areas to open new markets. Once in the new areas, they have helped to form the gangs needed for the distribution network.

If the reasons for gang behavior and gang violence are complex, the solutions are equally complex. Simply banning guns and drugs and building more prisons will not solve the problems. It is going to be much harder. The root causes of poverty and alienation must be tackled. Education and jobs must be provided. And, somehow, we must find ways to provide positive role models and cultural alternatives to the violence which has become so attractive and acceptable to young people.

These solutions will be painfully long in coming, which means that the problems will be around for a long time, as will the dangers.

Cults

Not all cults, as we regard them today, are violent, but in increasing numbers many are very destructive. With all due respect to those cults, or sects, or "churches," which are composed of passive, loving, nonviolent individuals, the focus of our work here is to evaluate those cults viewed as destructive (physically and/or emotionally).

Most cults are founded by a charismatic leader whose objectives are usually control, money, and/or ego fulfillment. The word "cult" is derived from the Latin "cultus" which means to worship. The word "cult" is often used interchangeably with "sect." An inherent characteristic of cults is the blind, slavish devotion of the members of the cult to a central figure.

It is estimated that there may be as many as 5,000 groups in the United States. The majority of these groups are small but others have tens of thousands of members. The Falun Gong, the group which has received international attention for its Beijung, China protests and arrests, claims a worldwide membership in the millions.

Contrary to popular misconceptions that cult members are wild-eyed or drugged-out crazies, research shows that most cult members are relatively normal. They include the young, middle-aged, elderly, poor, wealthy, educated, and non-educated

from a background spectrum that includes almost every well-known ethnic and religious background.

The 1950's

Cults began to emerge during the 1950's, when two of the biggest and most controversial religions or cults--the Church of Scientology and the Unification Church--entered the scene.

Church of Scientology. Science fiction writer L. Ron Hubbard founded the group as a church in 1954, based on a form of self-help psychotherapy he called "Dianetics." Scientology's spiritual counseling, for which people pay money, involves an "audit" in which people confess painful or embarrassing moments while using a lie detector-type device. Scientologists follow Hubbard's belief that a person is neither mind nor body, but a spiritual being - a soul.

FBI raids on Scientology offices in the 1970's uncovered evidence that adherents had infiltrated government agencies and harassed people, but Scientology officials said they purged offenders from their ranks. The church won a hard-fought battle for tax-exempt status as a religion in the U.S. in 1993.

So much controversy has been generated by pro- and anti-Scientology individuals and groups that the truth is impossible to separate from the propaganda. Like many other new emerging faith groups, Scientology has been accused of ethics violations, brainwashing techniques, swindling people, etc. Their opponents have been accused of violating copyright laws, violating the civil rights of Church members by kidnapping, confining and brainwashing them, etc.

Unification Church. It was in 1935 that the Reverend Sun Myung Moon claims to have received his first major revelation from God, reporting that he had a vision in which Jesus appeared to him, telling him of the important role he was to play in bringing the Kingdom of Heaven to the Earth.

Moon formally founded the Holy Spirit

Association for the Unification of World Christianity on May 1, 1954. Unification Church goals are to provide resources for objective understanding; encourage appreciation of religious diversity; and promote religious tolerance.

A U.S. congressional probe in 1976 demonstrated ties between the Unification Church and the South Korean government. The church has promoted an ideological war against communism and used its substantial financial resources to build political alliances with conservative leaders. In 1982, Moon was convicted of income tax fraud and sentenced to 18 months in prison.

The Unification Church has been controversial in the United States since the early 1970's. Controversies usually revolve around the following points:

. The group may be best known for its mass weddings. Some involved in the ceremonies are married but re-commit to their wedding vows. Others marry spouses picked by Reverend and Mrs. Moon.

. Charges have been made by those who oppose the Unification Church that it engages in brainwashing and deception. No evidence has been brought to substantiate these charges.

. The Unification Church has huge financial resources. It has been viewed as a cult in both Korea and the U.S., and it has spent considerable effort and money in pursuing legitimacy. The Church owns *The Washington Times* which, apparently, consistently loses money. Since the *Times* is a conservative newspaper, it is thought that this provides Moon and the Church with a vehicle to reach influential backers. Money spent to back right-wing politics has had good results, albeit strange ones. Some organizations sponsored by conservative evangelicals which have received money from Moon feel compelled to reject his doctrines as heretical and label his group as a dangerous and destructive cult. The sources of Unification Church wealth has long been a source of much speculation.

. The Unification Church announced in 1992 that Reverend Moon is the Messiah, or the second coming of Jesus Christ as prophesied in the Bible. Counter-cultists regard this as heresy.

. Reverend Moon's eldest son by his current wife, Hyo Jin, was once thought to be his successor; however, in 1995, his wife left him with their five children, reporting physical and emotional abuse as well as Hyo Jin's addictions to cocaine and pornography. The problem comes in that, in theory, the Reverend Moon as the Messiah is believed to be sinless, that his wife is the perfect woman and, hence, they would produce sinless children.

The 1960's

Cults really took hold in this country during the 1960's. This was the time of "self awareness," "consciousness raising," and "encounter groups." As society began to reel from the shock of new ideas, new freedoms, and new drugs, many young people began to search for new social structures or communities within which they could find an anchor-- a form of security and an answer to troubling questions and problems. A great many young people, caught up in the frenzy of new ideas, found that their belief systems had been shattered, and they needed desperately to find a "new way."

College programs began to expand to include new studies on religion and politics. International travel was cheap, easy, and safe. Inevitably, many young people found themselves backpacking not only in the known areas of Europe, but in India, Nepal, Kashmir, Japan, and other exotic regions. Thus were discovered the Far Eastern concepts such as mantras, I Ching, and Karma, as well as brown rice and vegetarianism. These concepts and religions formed a foundation for the acceptance of cults in the United States. It is paradoxical that many young people, who fought for individual freedoms in the 60's voluntarily relinquished their freedoms by joining groups, cults, and communes which were founded on the principle of total obedience.

Hare Krishna. The International Society for Krishna Consciousness is a spiritual sect developed from Hinduism. In 1965, a number of centers were opened in New York and California. The group's membership eventually grew to more than a million. Hare Krishna members became a familiar, and often unwelcome sight in public, usually with shaved heads, chanting and aggressively asking for alms.

The key belief of the Krishnas is that Krishna is the supreme or "all-attractive." When the Krishna chant (or mantra) is recited, it is a way of putting oneself in harmony with Krishna or in the natural state. A core belief of Hare Krishnas is reincarnation. Another core belief is the rejection of meat-eating, intoxication, illicit sex, and gambling. A strict vegetarian lifestyle is followed.

In its own official journal, the Hare Krishna movement has published a candid expose of widespread physical, emotional and sexual abuse of children who were sent to live in the group's boarding schools in the U.S. and India in the 1970's and 1980's. Parents were often unaware of the abuse because they were traveling, soliciting donations in airports and on the streets, leaving their children in the care of Hare Krishna monks and young devotees who had no training in educating children and often resented the task. In May 1996, ten former Krishna pupils testified that they had been regularly beaten and caned at school, denied medical care, and sexually molested and raped homosexually at knife point.

Charles Manson. On the night of August 9, 1969, Sharon Tate, who was 8-1/2 months pregnant, was stabbed to death, then hung from a rafter in her living room. Also killed were Abigail Folger (Folger's Coffee heiress), Voityck Frykowski (a Polish filmmaker), Jay Sebring (hairdresser), and Steven Prent (friend). Written in blood on the walls were messages such as "Death to Pigs." The next night, Rosemary and Leno LaBianca were stabbed to death in their home located in an upper-middle-class neighborhood. Again, bloody messages were scrawled across the walls. The killings were dubbed the "Helter Skelter

Murders" by the press.

Three months after these events, police arrested a scraggly band of cult members devoted to ex-convict Charles Manson. Manson was their father figure and they called themselves the Manson family. The "family" indulged in drugs and sex.

Manson has newly become something of a cult hero and his popularity has been boosted by the Internet. Manson receives as many as four fan letters a day, addressed to him in jail. Manson and three of his cult members are serving life sentences.

The 1970's

In the 1970's, the make-up of cults changed in certain ways. Whereas in the 1960's cults, for the most part, were small home-grown groups, peaceful in nature and informally organized, during the 1970's hard-core, strictly organized mega-cults were formed. Many of the cults became actively evangelistic, recruiting members from college campuses, conferences, marches, and meetings. For good reasons! Cult members often worked extremely long hours for little or no recompense other than food and housing to build "retreats" and to solicit donations. Cult leaders, meanwhile, often lived lives of luxury.

Peoples Temple (Jim Jones). This was a destructive doomsday cult founded and led by James Jones. The Peoples Temple was originally founded as an interracial mission for the sick, homeless, and jobless and grew to include over 900 members. When questions arose as to some of his practices, Jones moved the group to California. Jones preached the imminent end of the world in a nuclear war. Jones also urged his elderly members to turn over to the Temple their social security checks, promising them lifetime care. After a magazine expose during the mid-1970's raised suspicions of illegal activities within the Temple, Jones moved most of the members to Jonestown, Guyana. On 4,000 leased acres, the Temple members raised animals for food and tropical fruits and vegetables for food and sale. During the late 1970's, it is alleged that Jones abused prescription drugs and appears to have become increasingly paranoid. Rumors of human abuse motivated U.S. Congressman Leo Ryan to visit Jonestown in 1978 on a fact-finding mission. As Ryan was leaving, some 16 Temple members decided to leave with him and his entourage. While Ryan and the others waited at the local airstrip, armed members of the Temple's security guards arrived and started shooting. Ryan and four others were killed and 11 others wounded. Feeling that their situation was hopeless, Jones and his advisers decided the only way out was to commit group suicide. Of the roughly 900 members, some voluntarily drank the cyanide-laced kool-aid; others were "helped" by poison injection or gunshots. A few fled into the jungle and survived.

In the late 1970's, U.S. Senator Bob Dole chaired a special inquiry into "the cult phenomenon" that focused chiefly on the Unification Church.

The 1980's

In the 1980's, many Christian fundamentalist groups adopted lower profiles but continued recruiting worldwide. Political extremism, meanwhile, spread quietly in the United States. Groups espousing anti-authority and anti-government philosophies took hold in rural areas.

The 1990's

The 1990's initiated some dramatic and significant changes in the tenor and focus of cults, sects, and unorthodox religions. The "flower children" of the 1960's and the mildness of the 1980's were obscured by more violent overtones. The encroaching millennium was an irresistible force, and the emergence of the survivalist/militia/anti-government groups sometimes met in ways not previously known. Several small groups made sensational, and tragic, news in the 1990's.

Branch Davidians. The group known as the Branch Davidians actually trace their roots back to a splinter sect that broke away from the Seventh Day Adventist Church (SDA) in 1942. Basic beliefs of the Branch Davidians (BD) follow those of the SDA; namely, emphasis on the imminent arrival of Jesus Christ, dietary rules, the infallibility of the Bible, etc.

Koresh was able to persuade married women within the group to join him as "spiritual wives," which, of course, included sexual access. Husbands and wives were separated and only Koresh was allowed to have sex with the wives while the husbands remained celibate. Koresh fathered children with females whom he alleged to be as young as 12 or 13, although this has not been proven. There were rumors that Koresh sexually and/or physically assaulted children, but this was never established and is now in doubt.

The BD assembled large supplies of arms in their Waco, Texas compound, prompting the Alcohol, Tobacco and Firearms (ATF) to try to arrest David Koresh. A group of 76 armed ATF agents entered the compound on February 28, 1993 and attempted to serve a search warrant. A shot was heard--it is unclear as to who or which side fired--in the ensuing firefight, 6 Davidians and 4 ATF agents died, and an additional 24 agents and one BD were wounded. (Given their doomsday beliefs, the BD saw this as the predicted Apocalypse and Battle of Armageddon.) A 51-day siege which followed ended with a fire that killed Koresh and 81 followers.

The Waco events have rallied many splinter groups and dissident "lone wolves." Waco is said to have been the trigger that sent Timothy McVeigh to bomb the federal building in Oklahoma City.

Order of the Solar Temple. This group of several hundred people was virtually unknown until 1994 when more than 50 members, including founder Luc Jouret, killed themselves in Canada and Switzerland. More Solar Temple suicides occurred in 1995 and 1996.

Jouret persuaded members to give up jobs and turn over assets to the group. He convinced his followers that he was a member of the 14th century Christian Order of the Knights Templar during a previous life and that he would lead them after death to a planet which revolves around the star Sirius. They regard death as an illusion and that life continues on other planets. They follow a form of Christianity mixed with New Age philosophy, homeopathic medicine, and high finance. Solar Temple groups were organized in several countries.

For many months prior to the suicides, rumors of financial mismanagement had circulated within the Solar Temple. An infant, aged three months and thought to be the Anti-Christ, was killed in 1994 at their Canadian site by driving a wooden stake through his heart.

The Solar Temple group continues to exist; it is believed to have over 30 surviving members in Quebec and from 140 to 500 worldwide. No doubt the Millennium will provoke more doomsday activities.

Aum Shinri Kyo (Supreme Truth). Shoko Asahara and members of his Buddhist sect were accused of releasing a lethal nerve gas, sarin, on crowded subway cars beneath Tokyo in March, 1995. A study revealed that the cult had also mounted several biological attacks on different targets in Japan, including the Legislature, the Imperial Palace, and the U.S. base at Yokosuka. These prior attacks failed as they lacked either sufficient lethal virulence or the delivery method failed.

In 1989, a counter-cult lawyer, Tsutsumi Sakamoto, his wife and child were kidnapped and murdered by Aum members. Sakamoto had been engaged by families of some of the cult's members to investigate and reveal details of the cult's illegal activities.

Aum Shinri Kyo began operating as a religious organization in July 1987. The head of the cult, Shoko Asahara, claims to be the "one and only person who has acquired supreme truth" and has attributed to himself supernatural powers. In August 1989, the cult formed its own political organization, the Shinri Party, which contested the 1990 general

election. None of the 25 candidates won seats, a failure which fostered a feeling of frustration among members. A revised doctrinal basis was "the plan to save mankind facing the ultimate chaos of Armageddon." The cult arranged for the mass production of a thousand Russian K-74 rifles. It also purchased a helicopter (for air delivery of chemical weapons) and made repeated attempts to enter the plant facilities of major private sector enterprises in an effort to spy and steal advanced military technology.

Aum Shinrikyo planned to produce and use 70 tons of sarin. They built a large scale chemical plant to manufacture sarin and other nerve gases.

By the time of the Tokyo attack, the cult had grown into an organization of some 10,000 Japanese members with branches in Russia, Germany, the United States, and Sri Lanka. Aum's assets have been estimated at between 300 million and one billion dollars. The money came from the savings that new members turned over to the cult, from tax-exempt businesses staffed by cult members, and from fraud and extortion.

The cult has been very successful in recruiting trained scientists and graduate students in physics, chemistry, biology, medicine, and electrical engineering.

World Church of the Creator (W.C.O.T.C.) This is a non-Christian religious organization. Members regard themselves as being motivated by a love for the White race and an antipathy toward Blacks and Jews. The group was organized by Reverend Matt Hall, who styles himself *Pontifex Maximus*, in 1996. Hale was formerly the head of the National Socialist White American's Party. The group's beliefs mirror those of many other right-wing extremist groups. Some of the most flagrant are:

.   Persons who are not white are of a "mud race."

.   Envisioned is a racial holy war (RAHOWA) in the future between the white and non-white races.

. Love and hate are the most powerful emotions; having both is healthy and essential to life. Enemies should be hated.

. American culture is becoming more decadent, as evidenced by black crimes, growing acceptance of homosexuality, interracial marriage, increasing drug use, and lack of racial identity among white people.

. Jews were responsible for World War II, and the Nazi holocaust never happened.

. Jews are in control of the United Nations.

There are many more W.C.O.T.C. beliefs and tenets which echo the above.

In July 1999, a senior W.C.O.T.C. member, Benjamin Nathaniel Smith, went on a shooting rampage through the mid-west, killing one Afro-American and one Korean-American. Six orthodox Jews and three Afro-Americans were wounded.

Heaven's Gate. In March 1997, 39 men and women, all dressed alike, were found dead in a mass suicide at an estate in Rancho Santa Fe, California. Fifteen died one day, 15 the next and the remaining nine the third day. The suicides were choreographed, with every person dressed alike and laid out neatly underneath a purple shroud. The house was clean, and the garbage had been emptied. The dead were members of a little-known computer-related cult called Heaven's Gate.

Heaven's Gate denounced sexuality and many members were castrated. The group believed a UFO following comet Hale-Bopp would take them to a higher level existence. The philosophy which evolved combined elements of Christianity with unusual beliefs about the nature of UFOs.

The cult talked of philosophical bonds with other millennial groups and self-appointed messiahs, including the Branch Davidians, the Unabomber, the Freemen, and the Solar Temple. They believed that the world had become corrupted and that its institutions and religions had been seized by Lucifer.

Like every other group in society, religous cults have embraced the global Internet, using it as a means to communicate among themselves and distribute their millennial messages. The Internet has proven a powerful recruitment tool for cults. It allows them to cheaply disseminate information and to reach upper middle class loners who may be more likely to own computers. Heaven's Gate is only one of a growing number of small, computer-connected cults that have flourished in the last decade, and particularly in the last five years.

Many of the cult adherents are extremely negative about the state of the world, warning that the government, the wealthy, and moral leaders are controlled by evil space aliens, who have also used all religions to deceive humans about God. They warn, too, of a coming Apocalypse that will destroy civilization (gang wars and ethnic cleansing are offered as proof the process has begun); later, there will be a "restoration period" in which another civilization will be born. (With some changes and terminology, the same philosophy applies to a number of extremist right-wing groups.)

The cult still exists; not everyone lived and died in the compound.

The Millennium and Apocalypse

Toward the end of 1999, the Federal Bureau of Investigation (FBI) published a special report entitled "Project Meggido." Some of its key points have been reproduced here.

. Many extremist individuals and groups place some significance on the next millennium. The significance is based primarily upon either religious beliefs relative to the Apocalypse or political beliefs relating to the New World Order (NWO) conspiracy theory. Several religiously motivated groups envision a quick, fiery ending in an apocalyptic battle.

. Religiously based domestic terrorists use the

New Testament's Book of Revelations--the prophesy of the endtime--for the foundation of their belief in the Apocalypse.

.   Under the most common extremist ideologies, many extremists view themselves as religious martyrs who have a duty to initiate or take part in the coming battles against Satan. For apocalyptic cults, especially biblically based ones, the millennium is viewed as the time that will signal a major transformation for the world, and that the federal government is an arm of Satan. Therefore, the millennium will bring about a battle between cult members/religious martyrs and the government.

While predicting violence is extremely difficult and imprecise, there are certain characteristics that make some cults more prone to violence.

.   Sequestered groups - members of sequestered groups lose access to the outside world and information preventing critical evaluation of the ideas espoused by the leader.

.   Leader's history - the fantasies, dreams, plans, and ideas of the leader are most likely to become the beliefs of the followers because of the totalitarian and authoritarian nature of cults.

.   Psychopaths - control of a group by psychopaths or those with narcissistic character disorder.

.   Changes in the leader - changes in a leader's personality caused by traumatic events such as death of a spouse or sickness.

.   Language of the ideology - groups that are violent use language that contain the seeds of violence.

.   Implied directive for violence - most frequently, a leader's speeches, rhetoric, and language does not explicitly call for violence; rather, it is most often only implied.

.   Length of time - the longer the leader's

behavior has gone unchecked against outside authority, the less vulnerable the leader feels.

.   Who is in the Inner Circle - cults with violent tendencies often recruit people who are either familiar with weapons or who have military backgrounds to serve as enforcers.

Apocalyptic cults see their mission in two general ways. They either want to accelerate the end of time or take action to ensure they survive the millennium. An analysis of millennium cults by the FBI's Behavioral Science Unit describes how rhetoric changes depending on whether the leader's ideology envisions the group as playing an active role in the coming Apocalypse or a passive survivalist role.

A cult that predicts that "God will punish" or "evil will be punished" indicates a more passive and less threatening posture than the cult that predicts that "God's chosen people will punish." As another example, the members of a passive group might predict that God or another being will one day liberate their souls from their bodies or come to carry them away. The followers of a more action-oriented group would predict that they themselves will one day shed their mortal bodies or transport themselves to another place.

A cult that displays these characteristics may then produce three social-psychological components: isolation, projection, and anger.

The city of Jerusalem is cherished by Jews, Christians, and Muslims alike. There were, and are, many concerns that Jerusalem will be inundated with apocalyptic-oriented cults throughout the millenium year of 2000. It is felt that the most likely targets would include the Al-Aqsa Mosque or the Dome of the Rock or the Temple Mount. Some millennium cults hold that these structures must be destroyed so that the Jewish Temple can be rebuilt which they see as a prerequisite for the return of the Messiah.

One group decided to get in place well in advance of the Millennium. In January 1999, Israel ordered 11 members of the Denver-based Concerned

Christians doomsday cult deported and brought two others before a magistrate on suspicion they plotted a Jerusalem shoot-out in hopes it would bring Jesus Christ's return. Members of the cult began selling their Denver homes in the fall of 1998. Their leader, Monte Kim Miller, believed he would die on the streets of Jerusalem in December and be resurrected. Since this did not happen in 1999, he may try again in 2000.

Cult critics, in particular parents, perceive cults as irresponsible and damaging. Many cults discourage members' contact with parents, loved ones, and friends, describing them as "agents of Satan" and "negative influences." In some cults, mail is censored, and new members are assigned cult companions who accompany them everywhere, depriving them of privacy and any opportunity to cultivate doubts. Time spent not working or fundraising is devoted to the reading of cult literature, chanting, singing, and group activities. Some cults promote the concept of "free love," thus eliminating another area of privacy. Many cults are quasi-religious, preaching spiritual fulfillment through total devotion. Some cult leaders have even claimed to be messengers of God.

Cult critics have accused cult leaders of "brainwashing" their members, which is not entirely correct, although their methods of mental persuasion are often quite effective. Simply to set the record straight, brainwashing as it was portrayed in the film, *The Manchurian Candidate*, is not realistic. Brainwashing was regarded during the years of the Korean War in the 1950's to be a process whereby the victim's ideological beliefs and morals could be irreversibly reconstructed; i.e., that prisoners could be brainwashed and then sent back as programmed killers or devout Communists. It began when a number of Korean War prisoners "confessed" to crimes which they did not commit and was popularized in books and movies. Later research proved that brainwashing, as then perceived, was not a realistic process. The Chinese techniques, long regarded as the most insidious and successful, were a form of conditioning referred to as "coercive persuasion," and were intended to create behavioral

conformity rather than ideological conversions among prisoners. Researchers found that ideological conversions were rare and were almost always found in those prisoners who appeared to be most sympathetic initially to the Communist philosophy (and who also spoke fluent Chinese).

Other cult critics claim that young people are kidnapped and held captive within cults. This is almost completely untrue. It would be counter-productive and it is certainly unnecessary. No--cult members join not out of coercion or brainwashing. They are persuaded to join and to remain, giving up home and hearth, and working for the greater good of the cult.

The persuasive techniques employed owe a debt to some of the Chinese techniques, which have been described as a three-step process. In the first phase, beliefs and attitudes held by the individual are quickly and severely disrupted. The individual may already be undergoing belief changes or may merely be receptive to them. Changes in environment, physical location, name, (many cults assign new names to recruits), companions, and exposure to radical ideas can create mental dislocation. Students going off to college alone, for example, can experience the effects of sudden and severe dislocation.

In phase two, once the individual has lost his/her sense of stability, he/she seeks for a new set of beliefs and attitudes, which can then be provided by mentors who suggest new directions. Group uniformity is a compelling force, and within a cult there is complete conformity. The cult's ideology becomes the only "real" ideology. Recruits are helped through the process by other members of like background who have "seen the light" and can testify to the satisfaction of acceptance of the cult's beliefs.

In the third phase, acceptance of the new ideology is reinforced and strengthened within the recruit. As the recruit lengthens and intensifies his/her membership in the cult, he/she may be encouraged to recruit others to the cult and to serve as the mentor/role model.

Throughout the process, every effort is made to persuade the new recruit to give up or suspend his critical faculties. Information is closely controlled. Reinforcement techniques are constantly applied--to believe without question is to elicit praise from the group--to ask critical questions is to receive negative feedback. Often, the cult divides the world sharply between cult members (the good people) and the outside world (ruled by Satan). Those members who show signs of wanting to leave the cult may be told that this will lead to eternal damnation, because now the recruit has been shown the "truth," and to backslide is to invite retribution.

This kind of environment can be hypnotic and beguiling. No questions--no doubts--no problems. Suspending one's critical faculties does not mean that they are lost forever, but they can be so successfully blocked that it becomes frightening to consider having to use them.

Cult members "rescued" (kidnapped/forcibly removed) from cults often show signs of total fright and panic, convinced at a visceral level that they have been dragged into a nest of Satin-worshippers and are unwilling to communicate with family and friends at any level. Some, who have been taught to chant within the cult, may chant incessantly to retain their moral strength and to resist the "forces of evil." If the recruit has a history of alienation from normal society, he may be so wedded to the cult that he cannot be "deprogrammed." It should be made clear, however, that a majority of individuals who join cults do not suffer from mental or psychological disturbances. They may simply be vulnerable in terms of emotional nuances. They may, for example, so fear having to compete with others that being able to live in a noncompetitive environment seems wonderful.

Many of the more radical cults use sex both as a recruiting device and as a persuader for remaining with the cult. Ego-stroking is another recruiting technique. Cult members may zero in on a potential recruit and flatter him/her with their total attention. Never has he/she felt more loved, totally accepted, and important than with his/her new friends.

Once recruited, the new member may undergo a period wherein his attitudes and behavior are systematically recast into new ones. The cult ideology is likely to be intense and emotional. Concepts are seen in black and white terms. Language will be absolute, dramatic, and emotional. If, for example, the economy is troubled and the world is going through troubled times, the cult leaders have a perfect opportunity to exploit these difficulties by preaching the philosophy which states that the world is getting its just fate, having subscribed to Satan's temptations of material wealth, and salvation is only possible through the cult. Guilt manipulation is a favored cult strategy.

Now, comes the question--while cults may be damaging to their members, what is their potential for outside violence? *Potential* should not be confused with *ability*. A strong cult, led by a charismatic leader preaching extreme radical philosophies, certainly has the ability to veer into violent activities. Those small cults which are based in radical politics or (more likely) radical religious beliefs, and whose "hidden persuaders" rely heavily upon drugs and/or sex, have the potential for violence. The larger cults, whose leader(s) have as a hidden agenda the accumulation of wealth and power, may have no interest in violence. Why should they? Violence would only attract the media and the law, and would likely terminate the ability to attract donations. The exception to this is when the cult feels threatened by exposure. If the cult leaders believe that an ex-cult member or anyone else has the ability to, and intends to, disclose information harmful to the cult, violence is a distinct possibility.

It is the psychological make-up of the typical cult, and the thought control practiced by many cults which have the potential for aberrant behavior and possible violence.

Assassins

"Assassin" is the word which, within this book, we will use to describe only those individuals who kill or have attempted to kill prominent political figures. It should be noted that assassins are also, somewhat necessarily, stalkers in that they must stalk their victims in order to kill them. However, we will assign a distinction to the assassin in that his/her primary goal is the killing of the victim, as opposed to the stalking process itself. (While many stalkers kill their victims, often the stalking process is in itself sufficient for stalkers who merely wish to be near the person whom they are stalking.) The dictionary specifically uses the word "assassin" in the context of the killing of a political figure. Because of the involvement of religious figures in politics, the term "assassin" is also assigned to the murdering of politically active religious figures. Also, in recent years, abortion doctors have been assassinated.

Between 1835 and the current time, 16 documented assassination attempts have been directed toward nationally prominent political figures in the United States. This does not include the reported planned assassination attempt against President George Bush outside this country, which was attributed to the government of Iraq. A number of other world political figures have been assassinated outside the United States, including Indian Prime Ministers Indira and Rajiv Gandhi and Egyptian President Anwar Sadat. An assassination attempt was made against the Roman Catholic Pope, John Paul II, an attempt which severely injured him.

On the one hand, 16 attempts in 158 years does not seem an overly high figure. It is undoubtedly not a correct figure either. Certainly, other political figures have been either threatened or killed, but they may not have qualified as sufficiently "prominent" to have their plight documented. Also, there have, without question, been numbers of foiled attempts which never came close to the target. That is, there are surely numerous threats to prominent figures which are thwarted by the U.S. Secret Service or the FBI, but the would-be assassin is prevented from coming close to the target. The U.S. Secret Service is to be commended on its ability to keep most Presidents alive and well in spite of the numbers of people who would like to assassinate them.

Are all assassins mentally disturbed (i.e. crazy) individuals? For many years, this was the prevalent opinion, that in order to commit this heinous act the assassin must suffer from some mental disorder. It became a stereotype. And, it is not correct. To view all assassins as crazies is to believe that only crazies assassinate, which is a dangerous conclusion. It is sufficiently difficult to protect a target without looking for the wrong profile of assassins.

In the excellent U.S. Department of Justice booklet, *Protective Intelligence and Threat Assessment Investigations*, by Robert A. Fein, Ph.D and Bryan Vossekuil, the following is stated:

"Mental health histories of ECSP (Exceptional Case Study Project) attackers and near-lethal approachers include the following:

. Many had contact with mental health professionals or care systems at some point in their lives, but few indicated to mental health staff that they were considering an attack on a public official or figure.

. Almost half had histories of delusional ideas, but few of these ideas led directly to a near-lethal approach or attack.

. Few had histories of command hallucinations (imagined voices ordering the individual to take action).

. Relatively few had histories of substance abuse, including alcohol abuse."

The report further states:

"Person who *pose* an actual threat often do not *make* threats, especially direct threats. Although some threateners may pose a real threat, usually they do not. However, most importantly, those who *pose* threats frequently *do not make* threats."

Recent studies have shown that there are several profiles, or types, of assassins. These conclusions were reached after research into the background, prior history, and subsequent interviews with the assassins and others who knew them. The profiles drawn undoubtedly have value, in that they may help to identify other violent individuals--for example, violent employees. Assassins are not notably different from other violent individuals other than the fact that they kill or attempt to kill prominent political figures, and the results of the assassinations are very wide-reaching.

The first category of assassins may be the "purest" of all. These are the individuals who kill for political, ideological or religious principle, and do so fully knowing and accepting that they may be caught. They do not seek recognition or attention. These are not the media freaks. They kill because they believe that they are justified in doing so--must, in fact, do so--not for revenge, but for the higher good. These are rational people who have committed to a principle and a deed. Their reasons are not personal, nor do they stem necessarily from unhappy childhoods or dysfunctional families. They are difficult to defend in court because of their rationality and because they refuse to back away from the act or recant their beliefs. Sirhan Sirhan, typical of this type of assassin, to this day refuses to show remorse for the killing of Robert Kennedy and will, as a consequence, undoubtedly spend the rest of his life in prison.

Sirhan Sirhan is a true assassin who killed for political principles (and undoubtedly to expiate his rage). His victim, Robert Kennedy, a candidate for the presidency of the United States, was perceived by Sirhan to hold strongly biased views on the Arab-Israeli issue, favoring Israel. When, in 1968, President Johnson declared his intentions not to run again, with no formidable competition for the office, Robert Kennedy appeared to be destined for the presidency. Senator Kennedy had strongly supported the sale of 50 supersonic jet aircraft to Israel and had met privately with Israeli Premier Eshkol. Sirhan began to fear that if Kennedy were elected President the Arab homeland would be forever lost, with no hope of his returning to his birthplace in Jerusalem. He then determined to kill Kennedy and began to stalk him. Incredibly, he was able to enter the back corridors of the Ambassador Hotel, where Kennedy had just finished delivering a speech, wait there, and

then step forward and fatally shoot Kennedy. He is reported to have said, "I did it for my country."

A second type of assassin typifies the individual who kills for personal motives but who rationalizes these motives as being political and of a higher nature; i.e. for the greater good. This type of assassin typically has suffered from a deprivation of, or withdrawal of, love and/or affection from family (mother/father), wife, lover, friend, or peers. The assassination may be a "pay-back," either directly to the target who has presumably caused or contributed to the assassin's woes, or to the "significant other(s)" who have deprived the assassin of the love and attention he/she needs. This type of assassin is likely to be beset with personal anxieties and/or very real problems (loss of homeland, loss of job, loss of spouse). This type of assassin also shows little remorse for the act, and thus defies all attempts for rehabilitation. Lynette Fromme, who attempted to assassinate President Ford, did so with extremely convoluted reasoning. Her commitment to Charles Manson (as a member of that cult) was personal, not political, and her assassination attempt was an attempt to create enough disharmony that Manson would be released from prison or would be presented with an opportunity to escape. President Ford was, therefore, not a personal target so much as a generally effective target. Lynette Fromme had suffered badly from dysfunctional relations with her father and viewed Charles Manson as her "father." She was found sane, free of drugs, and competent to stand trial.

Yet another category of assassin is typified by rage. This is the individual who is unloved and unloving, who cares not one whit about politics or moral values, and who seeks an outlet for his/her rage and need for revenge against the society which has denied him/her true acceptance and love. A political target may embody the elements of the society which has "rejected" the assassin, and thus can serve very nicely as a sacrificial lamb. (This is another parallel to the violent employee, as well as to the stalker.) This type of assassin is, again, not crazy in the usual sense. He/she does not necessarily suffer from delusions, black-outs, schizophrenia, or other symptoms of mental disturbance. However, these individuals tend to suffer from severe emotional disturbances. They are often "loners," isolated by their rage and anti-social behavior. These are frightening people, as they sit on the borderline of rational vs. irrational thought processes. Revenge is a strong motivator, either personal revenge for a reality-based wrong, or revenge against a society which has rejected them in a single act of contempt and deprivation.

Arthur Bremer shot Presidential candidate George Wallace and injured him so severely that Wallace was paralyzed from the waist down. Wallace was not Bremer's first intended victim. Bremer had previously stalked Richard Nixon but found him too well protected, then had settled upon George Wallace as being more accessible. Bremer apparently had no loving relations and found most of his sexual education through cartoons and pornography. His single attempt to relate to another person, a younger girl, ended disastrously as he behaved absurdly and outrageously in an attempt to impress her. She refused to see him, and that denial seems to have completed his contempt for others and his rage at having been rejected by society. At his trial, with the psychiatrists deadlocked on the issue of whether Bremer was insane, he was found guilty.

Yet another type of assassin is the more typical stereotype--the individual with severe emotional and mental disturbances. The individuals in this group may suffer from one or more psychological deficiencies. These are the true "crazies." They may suffer from delusions. They may hear "voices." They may believe that God has directed them to a single, world-shaking, violent act.

A strong influence in the area of assassinations is the power of the media. The modern phenomenon of performing a violent act before the television cameras has become, unwittingly and unpremeditated on the part of the media, a possible contributor to public violence. For those individuals who have a craving for recognition, who feel they have failed at everything in life, and who are desperate for self-esteem, killing a prominent figure (preferably on camera) becomes irresistibly attractive.

Even if the assassination does not take place on camera, subsequent interviews, selling one's life story, and publicly documented trials provide the attention that life has denied them. Media attention is not a cause for assassination, but it may be a compelling supportive element in the decision to assassinate. The appeal of appearing on the evening news may tilt the balance for all but the "pure" first category of assassins.

A disturbing circumstance is that Lynette Fromme and Sara Moore (both of whom separately attempted to assassinate President Gerald Ford) had made threats before their attacks, and these threats were ignored. It is imperative that the stereotypical attitudes be discarded, and that there be a recognition that *rational, seemingly "normal" people* be considered as threat imperatives.

Assassins, much more than kidnappers, are very focused people who target an individual for killing. They may also be terrorists, criminals, or lone wolves. There are various reasons for assassination, political and religious motivations being the most common. Assassins motivated by religious reasons are often prepared to carry out their mission even in the face of great danger and death to themselves. Within the most extreme sector of the Shiite fundamentalist movement, religiously inspired assassins have been given funerals in advance of their suicidal mission, thus assuring the assassins places in the heavenly garden. Assassinations are highly focused attacks.

Serial Killers

At the very top of the list of horrific, twisted crimes are the serial killers, also called motiveless killers, recreational killers and lust murderers. The problem may be more widespread than previously thought. According to the FBI, in 1983 alone, approximately 5,000 Americans of both sexes were killed by murderers who did not know them and who killed them for "fun," or sexual gratification, or simply for an emotional "high." In 1987, it is estimated that 25 percent of all homicides were perpetrated by serial killers.

These are clever, cunning killers who are very difficult to catch, since they do not fit the investigative "norm." Once the serial killer murders his first one or two victims, he (and it is almost exclusively a male killer) becomes practiced at his game. The serial killer is a different kind of killer. He rarely, if ever, kills in a fit of passion, nor does he usually know his victim. He is clear-headed, calm, completely unbothered by compassion, and is therefore able to methodically stalk and acquire a victim. Victims often fit a profile. The killer may choose to prey upon prostitutes, or young men, or women in their early 20's with long, blond hair, or homosexuals, or elderly women. This, too, makes it easy for the killer, who is able to haunt certain areas until the next victim comes along, and he or she is instantly recognizable as fitting the victim profile. Serial killers almost never kill their friends and acquaintances; they prey on strangers.

The serial killer may confine his activities to a certain geographic area, such as the "Green River Killer" in Seattle, or may be mobile, as was Ted Bundy who killed and moved, then again killed and moved. Many serial killers are so fascinated with the game of killing that they remain close to the area, sometimes taunting the police. This is, of course, opposite to the behavior of more traditional killers who flee, hide, or melt into backgrounds within which they can hide. The traditional killer does not wish to be caught--the serial killer does not think he *can* be caught. Success makes him feel god-like. He may, after all, have murdered 10, 12, 20, 40 times over a period of years, and the police have not come close to identifying him. When it seems that the police are getting too close, or the level of fear is so high that attractive victims are becoming scarce, the killer may move on to untouched areas. Thus, Ted Bundy (who preferred young, attractive women) moved across the country, finally settling in Florida in a college town, where he murdered and was caught, again.

Ted Bundy, who murdered a number of young women, had been caught and jailed twice, and escaped. Bundy was probably one of the most attractive and most clever of known serial killers.

Adding to the difficulties of finding these killers is that the victims are often chosen for the fact that they, too, are mobile, or at least not likely to be missed for some time. If the victims are runaway teenagers or prostitutes, for example, missing person reports may not be filed at all, or may have been filed in another state. The number of missing person reports nationwide is staggering. No one police department can possible investigate even a small percentage of these reports. The FBI believes that the numbers of serial killers are growing, as are the numbers of victims killed by each serial murderer. It is estimated that as many as 500 serial killers may be "working." Thus, the numbers of murders attributed to serial killers is very high. Even professional contract killers may account for less than five victims. A serial killer may kill as many as 100!

Until recently, serial killers were almost an exclusive American phenomenon. One report shows that the United States has produced 75 percent of the documented serial killers. This statistic will undoubtedly change, as evidenced by media coverage of serial killers operating in the old U.S.S.R. and other areas. It is certain that repressive governments tend to restrict the opportunities for serial killers to operate. As repressive governments are replaced by more democratically oriented governments, affording greater civil liberties and mobility to their citizens, all crimes are increasing.

Serial killers are particularly gruesome in that they often torture their victims, record their sufferings, and sometimes keep body parts as souvenirs. One pair of serial killers was stopped by the state police on a traffic violation, only to have the lower part of a female torso discovered in the back seat of their vehicle. There is a high quality of control and dominance which marks many of the murders. Victims may be kept alive for 24 hours or longer.

It is not just the act of killing. The serial killer has made his killings a way of life. He maintains a double life, often living in a neighborhood and working in a normal job. But, always, there is the fantasy world which lures him to the next victim and his next "fix." This may be triggered by playing tapes, or viewing pictures or, fondling the souvenirs of his victims.

While some serial victims experience feelings of guilt immediately following a murder, this is soon sublimated or entirely forgotten. There are no reformed serial killers; these are lifetime pursuits and are as deeply ingrained as terminal drug habits. Serial killers such as Ted Bundy may maintain a cold, compassionless, unrepentant psyche all the way to the grave, while others seemingly show relief when caught. Serial killers, once caught, often cooperate closely with police in identifying and locating the remains of victims. They rarely appeal their cases, and they seek the death penalty.

Serial killers are almost exclusively male, white, and most are, or at least when they begin their killing careers, in their early 20's. Working either alone or with one partner, they may appear on the surface to be normal, sometimes attractive people. Most have developed an "MO" (modus operandi, or method of operating) which aids them in acquiring victims. Ted Bundy often used a fake arm or leg cast to appear harmless and to elicit sympathy. Serial killers do appear to prey on relatively defenseless victims, those who are unsophisticated, vulnerable, or are seeking help. It is no accident that serial killers do not prey on football linebackers, karate experts, or soccer players.

What is it that drives these men to kill? Studies show that there are some common factors or events in their backgrounds. The majority of serial killers were themselves the victims of abandonment, molestation, or humiliation, most during their very early formative years. They were (and are) intelligent and may have been quite sensitive. Being victims without recourse, they may have been so inculcated with rage that they became walking volcanos waiting for a triggering event to explode.

One interesting theory is that the killer never receives the satisfaction which he had hoped for in the killing and, thus, must do it over and over again to get it right. A second theory is that he succeeds through practice in getting it right, but that, after the first few times, the thrill diminishes and he must escalate the numbers of victims and degrees of violence to receive satisfaction.

Not surprisingly, many serial killers like to read about other serial killers and may even copy some of their exploits. There are some experts who believe that these killers view themselves and other serial killers as "stars" and are entranced by their press reports. No one as yet has been able to give definitive reasons for the rapid growth of the numbers of serial killers.

Serial killers are particularly dangerous in that they strike without warning and it is often difficult to tie the killer to the victim. This is not a terrorist targeting a government official or corporate CEO or an extremist shooting an abortion doctor. This is a nameless, faceless adversary.

Some Conclusions

So much attention has been given over the past twenty years to the terrorism threat that other threats have been largely overlooked. Two areas of threat--stalkers and violent employees--are relatively new and are rapidly growing. These two groups will be examined in some detail within this book both because they are each a relatively new phenomenon and because they represent a very real threat to clients.

ADVANTAGES OF THE ADVERSARY

The adversary has a number of advantages, not the least of which is that he, the bad guy, knows a great deal about his target, while the target almost never knows who his adversary is. It is true that defensive measures call for the collection of intelligence, and your files may be bulging with information about every known terrorist group, but how do you know which group has targeted your client for a violent act? The threat may be coming from a new, not yet identified terrorist group or from a determined individual. This is a big advantage for the adversary, having the ability to remain anonymous and invisible while making plans and surveilling the target. The adversary will have more information on the target than the target will have, specifically, on him. If the threat is coming from an area in which other terrorist attacks have been mounted, there may be information available to the agent on how these attacks were carried out. This will give the agent some knowledge of the techniques employed to help him plan his defenses. In this regard, the terrorists often make life a little easier for the defenders by announcing their responsibility for terrorist acts, thus establishing a "signature."

The adversary almost always has the advantages of numbers and equipment. Terrorist groups are notoriously well funded, as are criminal groups. They can bring more bodies and more guns and equipment to the attack than can the protection people. Agents and bodyguards, even when working for very wealthy individuals and corporations, have to live within a budget, and those budgets never provide for enough agents or equipment. If a target perceives a threat and looks for additional protection, he may put the job out for bids. The proposal which wins may not be the proposal which outlines the best protection; it will be the proposal which offers a reasonable protection plan for the least amount of money. The executive protection team will never have as much money as they feel they need to provide complete protection. Terrorist groups tend not to have these problems. Not only are they given large sums of money by governments unfriendly to America, they extort money from friendly governments, they steal money, and if they run short, they can always kidnap a Yankee executive for ransom.

The adversary has access to weapons which an agent will never legally be able to possess. A horde of weapons--hand-held rockets, sophisticated tracking devices, and the like--are now afloat in the international market, looking for buyers. Some will end up with unfriendly governments but a certain amount will undoubtedly go to dissident groups and criminals.

The adversary has a chance to develop

plausible scenarios and rehearse the action. The best that the target can do is to develop and rehearse several generic scenarios. There is a lot of "what if" that takes place in executive protection. There are also precedents, case studies of terrorist attacks, which provide food for thought. There are certain "givens," such as, most terrorist attacks occur in and around the vehicle. Therefore, some scenarios can be projected for defense against an attack on the client's vehicle. However, the adversary is the party which can rehearse specific maneuvers. The adversaries know each other, and from the beginning have worked together on a particular assignment. The defense team, if hastily assembled to meet a perceived threat, may not know anything about the other team members. If they are lucky, they will have a day or more to get used to each other, to fit their movements together, and to agree on a common security language. It is not uncommon for an agent, or agents, to be brought into a corporate situation to meet a short-term need for beefed-up security, only to find that time is wasted by having the full-time corporate protection people fighting to defend their jobs and positions against the newcomers. The adversary, however, is very clear as to who does what and who is in charge.

Motivation is on the side of the adversary. Assassins, terrorists, kidnappers, and like adversaries spend a lot time talking about what they are going to do and why. They are pumped up, on the edge, ready to move. The agent or protection team may be motivated to protect the client, but it is a general motivation, not a cause. It is professional, not emotional. And no agent can stay pumped up all the time. Alert, yes, but not pumped up to the maximum.

The adversary has the advantage of surprise. He launches his attack from a defensive position, never a frontal assault. If the adversary knows where the target is going, what time he intends to get there, and what route he will follow, there is an excellent chance that an attack can be launched from the adversary's most advantageous position. Adversaries launch attacks against the target's soft spots. To have surprise as an advantage, the adversary must have information about those soft spots and predictable knowledge about the movements of the target. Denying that information to the adversary removes at least some of the element of surprise.

One advantage to the protection team lies in the fact that criminal and terrorist groups around the world tend to develop and use their own specific attack scenarios, using the same types of weapons, and they will use those same techniques over and over again. They are not particularly open to new and innovative ideas. They have, after all, been successful in the past and feel safe using the same techniques again and again. Knowing how a particular group operates, say, in Chile, when the threat to the client is also in Chile, gives the agent some knowledge as to how to counteract the threat.

TARGET SELECTION

There are some motivations for target selection, and the order of their importance varies from group to group, and individual to individual. However, money is right up there, either as #1 or very close. Money may be the end goal, or it may be merely the lubricant that keeps the group operative in pursuing its real goals. If an individual or corporation is rich, he, she, or it is a potential target.

If the target has a position that makes him, or it, a subject of media focus, this may guide target selection. Will kidnapping a particular individual or blowing up a certain research laboratory bring the media into the picture? Will this result in wide media coverage to relate the adversaries' demands and highlight their cause? This is a powerful motivator and one that was at the heart of many airplane hijackings in the mid-1980's. The media covered the hijacking stories for weeks, providing an intoxicating showcase for the terrorists. Media stories are not merely ego-building. They give heightened credibility and an odd sort of semi-respectability to a group, particularly if hostages are later released unharmed.

Revenge and its cousin, hate, provide great motivations. In the United States, a booming economy has allowed chief executives to make enormous salaries and bonuses while, at the same time, closing plants and forming mega-mergers. Let us take the example of Corporation X, which announces that it is closing five plants and laying off 15,000 workers. One of those workers may now be in desperate straits with no money, no future, no health insurance, and one child who is going to need long-term, continuing medical care. If something happens to that child, the father worker may, in his anguish, be motivated to seek revenge on the corporate CEO who announced the lay-offs. Another example: Corporation A wishes to get rid of Company B, a small nuisance competitor, and through some super-tough, semi-shady marketing manages to drive Company B into bankruptcy. The owner, distraught at the loss of his family-owned company, plans to revenge himself by attacking the CEO of Corporation A. Revenge is a targeted motivation which is tough to discourage.

Political viewpoints provide endless motivations for attacking a target. American corporations in third-world countries often are perceived as the wealthy oppressors who exploit the natives and prop up corrupt governments. This makes the corporation the target of a political viewpoint. The corporation can also be a target for money. American corporations are attractive targets for several reasons. Some corporate executives are targeted for attack by activist groups motivated from a political viewpoint. An example may be the corporation which manufactures surgical equipment and which uses animals in its research. At least one animal rights group has tried to kill the CEO who is the visible symbol of the corporation. Politicians and heads of state are targets motivated by a political viewpoint. Indira Gandhi, assassinated several years ago, was the victim of a political attack. While politically motivated attacks can be targeted, such as in the case of Indira Gandhi, many are uncaring about a specific target so long as the target justifies the motivation and accomplishes the purpose.

TARGET SELECTION CRITERIA

Any good attacker who wishes to succeed

needs to consider a list of criteria which will help him select the best target. If the attacker is obsessed with a particular target, he may not care about the criteria, but he then has a higher risk of failure.

What is the *accessibility* of the target? Can it be gotten to and how easily? The President of the United States today is considerably less accessible than was Harry Truman, who took strolls through the streets of Washington, DC. To be able to successfully attack a target, one must be able to penetrate its defenses to reach the target, or the target must come to the attacker.

Vulnerability is a consideration. Even if the target is accessible, how vulnerable is it? If an armored car carrying the target comes down the street predictably at the right time, it may be accessible but is it vulnerable? Not if it is armored to a degree to withstand the firepower of the attacker. It is the issue of vulnerability which has made armored cars very useful in high-risk situations. Physical security is usually an element of vulnerability. If the perimeter barriers are sufficiently strong, the target may be neither accessible nor vulnerable. The Catholic Pope, John Paul, II, was gravely injured several years ago in an assassination attempt. The attack was launched while he was riding in an open jeep in the courtyard of the Vatican. He was highly accessible AND vulnerable. The Pope survived and still tries to remain somewhat accessible, or at least visible, but he is no longer so vulnerable. His defence has been strengthened with bullet-resistant glass and other measures.

Criticality is sometimes part of the criteria. Is the target critical to gaining some purpose? If the corporation is one that manufactures nuclear materials and is the only corporation in the country doing so, and the attacker is the anti-nuclear group, that corporation is pretty critical. It does no good to blow up the corporation that manufactures surgical equipment if the objective is to get out the anti-nuclear message and deter the production of any more nuclear materials.

Recuperability is another consideration. Using the example above, if the corporation manufacturing nuclear materials is able to quickly recuperate from an attack, part of the motivation is lost. True, the corporation was forced to shut down for 30 days, and a fire bombing was good for some media attention for the anti-nuclear group, but if the corporation is back in business 30 days later, with the President of the country present for a ribbon-cutting celebration, not much damage has been done. Killing Martin Luther King was a devastating blow, but his movement survived and recuperated. That attack did not stop the Black movement; if anything, it gave it greater meaning.

What will be the *effect* of the attack? Will it achieve such great results that it may topple a government? If so, it will probably be worth any risk. Will it have the opposite effect; that is, will the attack so enrage the people that they will turn against the attacking group, which may have, until then, enjoyed good will among the populace? This is the criteria which is probably most often misjudged by the attacker. Attackers have egos just like other people, and they like to think that their attack will drag down governments while promoting their cause. Sometimes it works, and other times the attack is ill-advised.

Risk is the criteria which must be carefully weighed. Generally, the higher the perceived risk, the less enthusiasm there is for the attack. The element of risk is very carefully evaluated, and if the target appears too tough to take or potential casualties too high, the attack may shift to a different target.

IS THERE ANY HOPE?

With, seemingly, most of the advantages on the side of the adversary, can a client be protected? Indeed, he can, by "hardening the target." As we have seen, success is important to the adversary, and easy targets are the first choices. Therefore, subsequent chapters are devoted to examining the most effective countermeasures which can be developed to deter the adversaries.

Before you can discourage or deter an attack, you must understand the threat. You need to know as much as possible about the people who are threatening the client, how vulnerable the client is to the threat, and what countermeasures can be taken to cure the vulnerabilities. In business terms, you must evaluate the problem and come up with solutions. It is not possible to plan for the correct type and amount of protection for a client unless the type and strength of the threat is established. Since budgets are a consideration, money for defense may be a problem. It is important that money not be wasted on what is not needed but, instead, is used for essentials. The client cannot be protected from any and all contingencies, but he can be protected from the most *likely* dangers.

THREAT MODEL

The primary purpose of designing a threat model is to identify probable attackers and to define their important characteristics. If you have specific information about your adversaries, the threat model can be more exact but this is not usual. Instead, threat models define the characteristics typical of all probable attackers.

Putting together a threat model has to start with some basic facts. Is there a *known* threat, a *perceived* threat, or simply *a desire for protection* over and above that which the client already has?

If there is a known threat, there may be indicators of who is posing the threat. If we know who is behind the threat, there is a good chance that we can also determine numbers, methods, equipment, skill, and dedication of the threat. All possible information about the suspected threat must be analyzed. How was the threat received? Was it identified as to who sent it? Does the message contained in the threat indicate the motivation of the

sender? Does it contain any details as to how the threat will be carried out? Was the threat sent to a specific individual or to a corporation in general? Let us set up an example. The client owns an abortion clinic located in a major city where two other abortion clinics have been damaged by bombs. No one has been injured in the blasts, as they were set during the early morning hours. The client has received a telephone threat. An unidentified man has called twice, did not ask for anyone in particular, but said, "You saw what happened to those other abortion clinics, and you know we mean business, so if you're smart, you'll shut down that baby-killing clinic." On the second call, the caller also said, "This is your second warning--you won't get another one." The caller then added a couple of details known only to the police, who determined that the threat is real. The clinic is determined to remain open and hires an executive protection team to protect the clinic, its employees, and patients.

The protection team begins with a threat analysis. Yes, it appears to be a real threat. It is logical to think that the attacker is the same adversary as the one(s) who bombed the other two clinics. On the other hand, this could be a "copy-cat" threat, possibly from someone who is more disposed to violence than the person or group who bombed the other two clinics. It is probably fair to assume that the threat is primarily a bomb. The second call indicates that time is running out. It seems to be a threat in general, not aimed at any specific individual. In analyzing the threat, the team must collect all information available about the other two clinic bombings. What type of explosives were used? Were the bombs set inside or outside the building? Information can be obtained from the police, personnel from the two clinics, and from newspaper clippings and television coverage. A profile must be drawn of the possible attackers, their strength, and their expertise. With this information, the protection team can begin to assess the vulnerabilities of the client and devise countermeasures.

A perceived threat is one that is not direct. No written or telephoned threats have been received, but the environment and circumstances are such that a reasonable person could expect an attack. Let's look at a second scenario. John Jones is the Regional Vice President for an American oil company located in Venezuela. The country is unsettled, with rumblings of discontent from the populace. The district manager of the Coca Cola plant in Venezuela was kidnapped two weeks ago, and it is feared that he is dead, since negotiations have broken down with the kidnappers. The kidnappers have not identified themselves or their affiliation to any group. John Jones's company has been vandalized twice with messages of "Yankees, go home" sprayed on the walls. John Jones has good reason to fear that there is a threat either to himself, to another company executive, or to the company itself. He asks for a threat assessment and additional protection. The threat modeling will include gathering all information possible on the abduction of the Coca Cola district manager and about any dissident groups or terrorists known to be operating in that part of Latin America, specifically Venezuela. What is known about the dissident groups in terms of numbers, weapons, equipment, techniques, expertise, and dedication? Was the Coca Cola executive kidnapped at gun point? under what circumstances? What kind of guns were used? Was he kidnapped at home, en route to the office, or at work? How does this compare to the known information about terrorist groups in the area? Since John Jones has not received a specific threat, an attack could be of any nature, including kidnapping, bombing, or assassination. In collecting information about known terrorist activities in the area, what is the likelihood of a kidnapping as opposed to a bombing or assassination?

Many prudent individuals, who have never received a direct threat, nor been given reason to think there might be a threat, hire executive protection agents because they believe that circumstances are such that they could be regarded as

an attractive target for an attack. For our third scenario, let us take the case of Dr. Tom Brown. Dr. Brown has an international reputation for his work in genetic engineering. Dr. Brown believes that, by using genetic engineering techniques with monkeys, he can develop strategies for producing stronger, more disease-resistant human beings. Dr. Brown is married with two children aged seven and ten. Dr. Brown is high profile, as he is often asked to give speeches, and he travels internationally. Dr. Brown is aware that many deeply religious people feel that "tampering with God's work is prompted by the devil." On a recent nationally televised talk show, the pros and cons of genetic engineering were discussed, with call-in questions, many of which were virulent and hostile in nature. Dr. Brown believes that, even though he has never received a threat, he cannot overlook the fact that he and his family might be the focus of a threat for some time, at least until the field of genetic engineering has passed the point of controversy. He quietly hires an executive protection agent, who will live with the family and provide some visible protection.

This scenario calls for a different threat assessment. Since there is no direct or perceived threat, the assessment must be more general, with a goal of correcting the more obvious vulnerabilities surrounding Dr. Brown and his family. While anything can happen to anyone at any time, the likelihood of someone actually attacking Dr. Brown is relatively low. The agent will certainly want to do a search of the major newspapers, perhaps the *New York Times*, to see if there are any reported incidents concerning individuals or entities in the genetic engineering field. He might interview other people in the field. But, he is going to concentrate his activities on shielding Dr. Brown and his family from any intrusion or attack.

The results of the threat assessment and threat modeling should give the agent a fairly good idea of what he must guard against, and how to do so within the confines of budgets and cost constraints. Obviously, the abortion clinic has a bigger problem than Brown, and it's going to take different measures to fix the problem. John Jones has a bigger problem than Brown, and it will take more money to fix.

Threat modeling is somewhat like a doctor trying to put together a first aid kit for a client who is going into Honduras on a bird-watching vacation, and who has diabetes plus a bad back. What is the "threat" to this patient's health? We know he has diabetes and a bad back, so certain medicines can be prescribed, plus a back brace. There may be some exotic tropic diseases which can drop our patient like a stone, thus incapacitating him. Not every disease lurks in the jungles of Honduras, but there are at least two known problem diseases. And, of course, there is a slight chance that all of the old guerrillas have not laid down their arms in the general amnesty, so a gunshot wound is not out of the picture. However, it is not likely that the patient will encounter bombs. This patient will only lug around so much luggage, so whatever he takes has to have applicable and realistic value to the potential problems.

In order to put together a threat model, there must be as much information gathered as is practicable. There are several sources for acquiring information about terrorist and criminal groups, and other security problems, in a particular area. People who live in and do business in the area can be queried. If the client works for a corporation, there are undoubtedly some very knowledgeable people working for the corporation in the target area. This includes citizens of that country, plus the American expatriates. These are the "old hands" who know what's going on. Local law enforcement officials can, if willing to do so, provide information on any terrorist or criminal activities.

The U.S. State Department has, in recent years, produced a great deal of valuable information about every area in the world, and the Department continually updates its data banks. The State Department Overseas Security Advisory Council (OSAC) is particularly helpful to U.S. businesses overseas. OSAC maintains an Internet website at <www.ds.state.gov/osac>. Information may also be obtained from the Department of State's websites at

<http://travel.state.gov/travel_warnings.html> and <http://travel.state.gov/>. Travel warnings are reasonably up to date, but not necessarily complete. The State Department is reluctant at times to post negative information about countries which are U.S. allies or countries with which the U.S. is involved in delicate negotiations.

American embassies and consulates are obligated to advise American citizens or business representatives on possible terrorist threats in foreign countries. The security officer at a diplomatic or consular post can provide information about general terrorist activities in a country, local laws and regulations regarding weapons possession, agencies available for security and background checks on employees, and may be able to smooth the way to networking with the local law enforcement officials.

One of the best sources of information is the media, both national and local. If the threat is outside the United States, the local newspapers and television news broadcasts can be monitored. If language is a problem, translations can be provided. Bear in mind that in those countries with repressive governments all events may not be reported, or reported accurately. In countries unfriendly to the United States, the reports may be biased against American businesses located there. A quick overview can be obtained in this country by using a news clipping service. Any good library will carry, on microfiche, entire copies of the *New York Times*, which are indexed by subject matter. This can produce a lot of information in a very short time. Outside the United States, short wave broadcasts from the *Voice of America* and the *BBC* can be informative. Increasingly, *CNN* is the top producer of information. During the Gulf War, many U.S. officials were getting their best and most available information from *CNN*. Altogether, the media is an extremely valuable source.

There are private firms which are in the business of collecting and providing, for a fee or subscription, in-depth and up-to-date information about terrorist groups and security problems anywhere in the world. The information is excellent, and it is expensive. If time is short and the budget will allow it, this is a viable source. If the budget will not allow for this, remember that these private firms collect their information from the same sources listed in this book.

After all of the information is collected, it must be analyzed and evaluated. Simply having bulging files of information is of no use. What is needed is good information that has been pared down to the necessary facts which suggest how a threat can be defeated. These facts should, ideally, give some idea of the numbers of people involved in the threat. This indicates how many protection people will be needed to deal with the threat. It also indicates the seriousness of the threat; the more people committed to the operation, the higher the interest level of the group.

The methods of the threat group, if known, can be projected into practice scenarios. The protection team can, and should, devise various scenarios which might be used by the adversary, and then construct defensive strategies for use against the scenario attacks. What equipment will be used by the attackers? Do they have hand-held rockets, or are they more apt to use handguns? The answer to this question may dictate the use of an armored car.

The skill level of the adversary is important to know. If the suspected threat is one with a big record of successful attacks carried out with ruthless efficiency, they are going to be very tough to defeat and will require a higher (and more expensive) level of protection. If, however, the adversary is perceived to be fumbling and amateurish, spending mega-dollars on defense is not called for.

The dedication of the adversary is one to be considered. If the adversary is absolutely willing to be hurt, killed, or captured, he is going to be a very tough adversary. He may be an amateur, but he may simply not quit. If the dedication level is marginal, the attacker may be discouraged by a visible level of protection which he believes poses too much risk for the operation.

DATA COLLECTION

It is important to find out what the adversary knows about or is able to learn about the protectee, the protectee's protection, and the vulnerabilities in that protection. This means collecting information (data) about the protectee from the viewpoint of the adversary. We know (or should know) what our weaknesses are but this is irrelevant. It is what the adversary knows about the target's weaknesses that matters, because it is the adversary who will do the attacking, not us. In the field of product design, there is a process known as "reverse engineering" where an engineer takes a product apart in order to find out how that product was engineered, along with its strengths and weaknesses. The data collection process is much the same. As agents, we need to step into the shoes of the adversary and "take the client apart" to discover his strengths and weaknesses.

What data can an adversary collect about the client? An intelligent and creative adversary will be successful in obtaining and analyzing an enormous amount of detailed information. In actual cases where terrorists and/or determined criminals have been picked up, the authorities were astonished to find the amount and accuracy of information which had been accumulated on specific targets.

The most important information for an adversary is a description of the client's daily activities. The adversary needs to know where the victim is likely to be at any given time and by what route he will arrive at that location. Because of the criticality of this information, the adversary will invest as much surveillance time as it takes to study the habits and characteristics of the target. Surveillance will include following the target, taking photographs, establishing primary routes, making detailed maps and sketches of the target's residence and office, and noting all security measures used for the target's protection. The same information will be assembled about the client's family, if such exists. This is crucial information to the attacker. The more predictable the client's movements, the higher probability there is for a successful attack. Predictable movements on the part of the client give the adversary the advantages of rehearsal and surprise.

Information about the client's work, family, and social activities will be carefully assembled by the adversary. This is easily obtainable by the adversary if he surveils the client and his family and does his homework in the local library. Libraries contain a lot of information that you might not know about, kept for the most part in the reference section. "Who's Who" books (and there are several) and listings of major corporations with their executives are readily available. Many states and major cities publish magazines which, once a year, list the 100, or 300, or 500 largest corporations, with ancillary information. Local newspapers are kept on file for years. These newspapers can be scanned as to local news, business news, and social events. For example, let us say that the client and his wife were shown in a photograph in the social column of the local newspaper, with a small paragraph identifying the client as the Chairman of the Beaux Art Association. It can now be surmised that the client and his wife will attend the next Beaux Art shindig. The more high profile the client, the more information about him which is available.

Corporations publish annual reports which contain information about the net worth of the company plus listings of major executives and other useful facts. Many corporations publish in-house newsletters which (if you can obtain copies) are a wealth of inside information. Most have "News of Our Employees" columns and might include something like this. "Mr. Client, CEO of our company, has been designated to receive the Widget Award on December 16, at the Hilton Hotel. This annual banquet honors those . . . " We now know where the client will be on the night of December 16.

A quick look around the corporation's parking lot may indicate to an adversary where the designated parking spots are for top executives.

Children's routines are generally very predictable in that they go to school at the same time every weekday. It usually does not occur to a parent,

delivering the children to school, to vary the route; therefore, an adversary may well be able to predict where the children will be at a certain time. If the school is close to the family residence, the children may walk back and forth to school. Because of the high number of child kidnappings by one parent, kindergarten and pre-school teachers are more aware of the need to provide some protection for young children. However, this is still a potentially weak point, open to a clever adversary. If young children are involved, a visit should be made to the school to assess the security procedures. Are the children watched at all times, or are they allowed to play unsupervised in a yard with only a small fence? What are the procedures for allowing anyone other than the parent-in-charge to pick up a child? What would happen if someone arrived with a note stating that the child's parent had been injured in an automobile accident, and this person had been sent to pick up the child?

Physical and electronic security are the next most important elements to be analyzed. If the perceived threat seems to be against a plant, clinic, or other building(s), the physical deterrents must be looked at with a critical eye. How accessible is the building to the attacker? How easily can an unauthorized person gain entry? If the threat is directed toward a person or family, the client's home must be similarly assessed. Is there any electronic security? Should there be? How careful is the family about locking doors and windows, drawing curtains, and refusing to give out information over the telephone to strangers? Does the client have a dog? Where is the dog kept, particularly at night and will the dog bark? It is amazing how many people all but invite in the attacker by opening doors to strangers, moving about in a lighted house without drawing the curtains, and opening windows at night. One reads again and again, in a news story about a burglary, rape, or murder . . . "The intruder apparently entered through an unlocked window in the victim's bedroom."

Some attention should be given to key employees and servants. These are the people who can provide access to the client. Have background checks been made at any time? If so, how long ago? Do the servants have keys to the house? If regular deliveries are made to the residence, can the deliverymen be identified? Who, besides the family, has access to the house?

Is there any discernable information about the client which will reveal a vulnerability to attack, and is this information available to the adversary? This is the goal of the data collection. Depending upon the severity of the threat or perceived threat, the data collection may need to done very quickly, if not perfectly. If there is no perceived or actual threat, and an agent or team has been brought in to provide a prudent level of protection, a more detailed analysis can be made, including a Personal Profile of the client. The Personal Profile will contain many more details including medical data, passport numbers, driver's license numbers, club memberships, and social security numbers.

The Personal Profile goes by several names: Protectee Biographical Profile, Emergency Data File, Family Fact Sheet, and others. The names are unimportant. The purpose is to gather the pertinent information which an agent should have to prepare a threat assessment, to protect the client, and to react to an emergency. Clients are not always happy about having the really intimate and confidential details of their lives recorded. Some will balk at giving medical data. Others are reluctant to give out the number of their safety deposit box or other confidential details.

There are two or three ways to address the problem. The client must be convinced that there is a need for the information to be recorded. He must know absolutely that his agent can be trusted to keep the information confidential. And, if it gives him a better feeling of comfort, the Personal Profile can be sealed in an envelope and given to his lawyer or lodged in the corporate safe. The agent may not need to know all of the details contained in the Personal Profile until an emergency occurs, and then that information may be vital. If the client is kidnapped, confidential information disappears with him. A

Personal Profile is somewhat like a will; it gives vital information in the absence of the person who made the will. A typical Personal Profile may be found in the Appendix of this book.

ANALYSIS, VULNERABILITIES, AND SCENARIOS

Once you have completed the threat model and collected that data on the client which an adversary would collect, you are ready to begin analyzing vulnerabilities and creating scenarios. These scenarios should be reality-based. Given the information the adversary now possesses, where and how would he attack, and is the existing protection sufficient to deter the attack? Can the existing vulnerabilities be reduced? Should additional countermeasures be considered?

A word about scenarios. It is well to be creative but any scenarios which are devised should be based in reality. The new agent who hires on with a family living in a low-risk, no-known-threat situation is apt to see danger lurking in every corner when, in truth, the potential threat may be quite small. The author has read Threat Assessment and Countermeasure reports submitted by fledgling agents that would make you blush, as they call for the need for concertina wire and a $1,000,000 electronic security system to defeat the many imagined threats. Clients are not impressed by this unless they are hopelessly paranoid about their safety. One should never fall victim to the disease of believing that the mere creation of a threat assessment requires that it show a long list of vulnerabilities.

On the other hand, a thoughtful assembly of practical scenarios, based on the threat level, is very useful. If the threat would appear to be a fire bombing of an abortion clinic, and that threat seems fairly imminent, who will attack, how and when will they attack, how determined are they to attack a specific clinic, and what are the vulnerabilities of that specific clinic? Is it locked up, with lights out, by 9:00 p.m. each night? Can we not put together a scenario that makes it an easy, no-sweat hit on the clinic? Is there an alternate scenario that makes it possible for someone to gain entrance to the clinic under peaceful guise during the daylight office hours and plant a bomb that either has a timer or can be remotely detonated? And so on. If the agent has done his job well in putting together a threat profile and a vulnerability study, he should be able to stand on the corner opposite the clinic and, looking through the eyes of the adversary, figure out exactly how to fire bomb the building.

COUNTERMEASURES

If countermeasures are called for, they may include changes in physical security; i.e., technical security devices such as intrusion detection systems, lights, locks, barriers, safe rooms, bullet-resistant materials, access control within buildings, patrolled parking lots, and additional security guards.

It will also include briefing the client on some basic security measures to take for his own protection and the protection of his family.

The threat may be of such a nature that the client and his family can only be adequately protected with an executive protection agent or a protective team. Much has been written in this book about protective details and protective teams; however, the inherent principles of the protective detail apply almost equally to the individual agent. Teams are more complicated, because there are more bodies involved. Lone agents learn to be creative in supplementing their protection. There are circumstances and budgets which dictate the use of a protective team, and there are many more which make do very nicely with one agent. Protective details do not stop bullets. Protective details are only one element of countermeasures. Working within the confines of a budget, the bottom line is, what is the best use of the dollars available to you? It may mean bodies (a protective detail) or it may be technology.

In the Appendix you will find a real-life Threat Assessment which was prepared for an overseas client (photos deleted for confidentiality.)

PROTECTIVE INTELLIGENCE & THREAT ASSESSMENT INVESTIGATIONS

Mention was made previously of the excellent U.S. Department of Justice research study, the Exceptional Case Study Project (ECSP) by Robert A. Fein, Ph.D and Bryan Vossekuil. This study was conducted by the U.S. Secret Service in an effort to provide useful information to State and local law enforcement officials who have responsibilities in the areas of physical protection or protective intelligence. However, the information provided is almost equally adaptable to threat assessments in the private sector. Key passages from the ECSP report are reproduced here, with permission from the U.S. Department of Justice.

Elements of a Threat Assessment Program

Designing and implementing a protective intelligence program in a law enforcement or security organization involves two steps. The first step is to define the problem, conceptualize the program and its functions, and establish objectives. The next step is to assess what capabilities are needed to implement the program and to plan so that essential functions can continue over time.

In completing the first step, certain questions must be answered:

. How does the organization define its protective responsibilities? What protective responsibilities does the organization now have? What responsibilities is it likely to have?

. What approaches to protection are currently being used? What kinds of protective services and programs are most likely to fulfill the organization's responsibilities?

. What is the legal basis for protection?

. How often is the organization faced with the task of responding to a threat or a concern about possible violence directed against a public official or figure?

. What currently happens when a threat is received by a protected person's office?

. What should occur when an individual who might be interested in harming a public official or figure comes to attention? For instance, who should be notified?

. Is the organization faced with other targeted violence investigative concerns such as stalking or workplace violence?

Protective services encompass a range of functions, including protective intelligence and physical protection, designed to shield potential targets of violent attacks or assassinations. Visible protectors, such as uniformed officers and security agents, are deployed to defend against any attempted attack on a protected person. Other physical protection measures, such as metal detectors, may keep persons with weapons away from a protected person and deter would-be attackers from trying to approach with a weapon.

Protective intelligence--a less visible aspect of protection--consists of programs and systems aimed at identifying and preventing persons with the means and interest to attack a protected person, from getting close enough to mount an attack and, when possible, reducing the likelihood that they would decide to mount an attack. Protective intelligence programs are based on the idea that the risk of violence is minimized if persons with the interest, capacity, and willingness to mount an attack can be identified and rendered harmless before they approach a protected person. This involves three key functions:

. *Identification* of persons who might pose a threat.

. *Assessment* of persons who are identified as a potential threat.

. *Case management* of persons and groups deemed a threat to a protected person.

The second step in developing a threat assessment program involves determining what is needed to complete protective intelligence tasks, examining what is needed to conduct threat assessments, and deciding how to maintain the threat assessment program. Again, several questions must be answered:

. Who will carry out protective intelligence responsibilities? What kind of staffing is needed?

. How will the knowledge and expertise developed by protective intelligence investigators be maintained and shared over time?

. How will new investigators learn, and how will experienced investigators teach?

. What balance of specialized threat assessment expertise and general investigative experience is desirable?

. Can the protective intelligence program build ways to learn from its experiences?

. How will case information be sorted and retrieved for individual and aggregated case analysis?

The needs of agencies responsible for protective intelligence mainly depend on their activities. For instance, an organization like the U.S. Secret Service, with responsibility for protecting the President and other national leaders, needs to have the ability to respond immediately to information that a person or group may pose a threat to a protected person. Likewise, a police department in a major city may have a substantial need to fulfill ongoing protective responsibilities as well as intermittent needs to support other targeted violence investigations. A security organization responsible for protecting celebrities may require extensive protective intelligence abilities. Smaller security organizations or those with limited or episodic protective responsibilities may have less extensive needs.

Key Functions of a Protective Intelligence Program

A protective intelligence program involves three key functions; identifying those who might pose a threat, investigating and assessing those individuals, and engaging in case management of those who have been deemed a threat to a protected person.

Identification

Identification is the process by which persons who might present a risk to a public official or figure come to the attention of agencies responsible for protective intelligence.

Some persons self-identify--they call, write, e-mail, or approach a public official or figure or indicate an unusual or inappropriate interest in a person. These individuals often give their names or provide other information that leads to easy identification.

The threatener--someone who communicates a direct, indirect, or conditional threat--is the classic example of a self-identifier. Such a person may threaten for various reasons: to warn of a possible attack, to ask to be stopped, to demand help or attention, to express frustration or anger, or to communicate distress. Threats should always be investigated; even if a threat is not an early warning of attack, making a threat is usually a violation of law, which is a valid reason for opening an investigation.

Other persons self-identify by expressing an inappropriate interest in a public official or figure. They may feel that they have (or should have) a special relationship with the potential target, a unique assignment or role to play, or extraordinary information or expertise that must be shared directly with the public official or figure.

In addition to self-identifying, people also come to the attention of law enforcement by being noticed by others who:

. Recognize that the behavior of the individual is of concern.

. Believe that the individual should be brought to the attention of authorities.

. Understand that authorities want to know about persons who might pose a risk to public officials or figures.

. Know how to contact the proper law enforcement or security organization (or know someone who knows how to contact authorities).

Individuals can be brought to the attention of the authorities by various second parties, including other law enforcement agencies, State agencies, security professionals, family members, neighbors, co-workers, mental health practitioners, and correctional staff. But before this can happen, protective intelligence program staff must decide on identification criteria--which kinds of persons the unit wants to be informed about: Those who made threats against a protected person? Those who indicate to others that they are considering an attack on a protected person? Those who demonstrate inappropriate interest in a protected person?

Once identification criteria are determined, decisions must be made about education: Who should be informed about how to report cases of potential concern? What should family members, associates, and staff of a public official or figure know? What should be said to the public about reporting cases of potential concern?

Liaison between protective intelligence agencies and the public is a key function of the identification process. Law enforcement and security agencies will receive information only if the public is aware that they have protective intelligence capacities and know how to contact protective intelligence personnel.

In addition, liaison is important within a given organization and with other organizations. Access to information is increased when the protective intelligence unit previously has engaged in liaison efforts designed to educate organizations and individuals who may have information on potential threats about the mission and functions of the protective intelligence unit. People and organizations with information may be more willing to share information if they are aware of the responsibilities of the protective intelligence unit and if they previously have met or become acquainted with protective intelligence staff. For instance, information from other city agencies about possible threats to the mayor's safety is more likely to come to the police department if staff know that the police department has a protective intelligence capacity. In a corporate environment, reports about persons of possible concern will come more readily to those responsible for an executive protection unit if employees know that the unit exists and how to contact unit staff.

Assessment

After an individual who poses a possible threat to protected persons comes to the attention of agencies responsible for protective intelligence, an initial evaluation is conducted and a decision is made about whether to conduct an investigation. If an investigation is opened, investigators gather information about the individual and then evaluate the information collected to determine whether the individual poses a threat to a protected person. The quality of an assessment is related to both the relevance and the range of information gathered. Key facts of a case should be authenticated and corroborated, with appropriate investigative skepticism about the credibility, accuracy, and veracity of witnesses and informants.

Sources of information. Protective intelligence investigators should make use of all the information available about an individual that will help them answer the fundamental question of threat assessment investigations: Does this subject pose a threat to protected persons? Investigators should emphasize factual data that can be corroborated, rather than the opinions of those who know (or purport to know) the individual.

Sources of information include interviews with the individual and those who have had contact with or appear to have information about the individual (employers, co-workers, neighbors, relatives, associates, caregivers, arresting police officers), records from agencies and institutions that have had contact with the individual, writings by or about the individual, and receipts from the individual's purchases and travels.

A variety of strategies and tools are used in protective intelligence investigations, including interviews; searches of people, residences, automobiles, etc.; background checks; reviews of weapons purchases, credit card purchases, phone records, and travel verifications; and consultations with threat assessment professionals.

The processes of information gathering and evaluation occur simultaneously; they are distinct, but influence each other. Newly developed information affects the ongoing evaluation of the risks an individual poses to protectees. At the same time, the evaluation process may suggest new investigative leads or directions of inquiry.

Case Management

When sufficient information is gathered to permit a full evaluation, a decision is made about whether the individual being investigated poses a threat to a protected person. If investigators believe that the individual does not pose a risk, the investigation ends and the case is closed. However, information about closed cases should generally be retained for a period of at least several years. An individual may come to an agency's attention as a potential threat again, in which case information from the previous investigation may be invaluable.

If the individual is deemed a threat, a plan to manage the individual and possible risks is developed and implemented. Such a plan may be as simple as periodically confirming the whereabouts, for example, of an individual confined to a correctional or mental health facility for an extended period of time. A case management plan also may involve a pattern of specified contacts with the individual and others around the individual--such as family members, police officers, co-workers, and caregivers--designed to prevent the individual from approaching a protected person and to decrease the risk of violence posed by the individual. In developing and implementing a case management plan, consultation with threat assessment and other professionals is useful. In all cases, the plan should include informing targets or their designated protectors.

Once developed, a case management plan is implemented until the protective intelligence agency decides that an individual no longer poses a threat of violence. At that point, the investigation is concluded and the case is closed.

Building a Database and Sharing Information

Information about the persons who are subjects of threat assessment investigations should be organized and maintained in a manner that permits search capabilities, efficient retrieval and analysis. Some individuals come to the attention of the authorities more than once, sometimes months and even years after the initial investigation was completed and the case closed. In these cases, prompt retrieval of case materials fosters an informed decision of what additional investigation, if any, is needed.

Developing a database also permits later analysis of behavior patterns that come to the attention of threat assessment investigators. A database containing both anecdotal and statistical information about individuals who have been investigated could promote future development of training materials and teaching programs for agencies with protective intelligence and physical protection

responsibilities.

Creating a database of threat assessment cases is also useful for interagency cooperation. Attackers and would-be attackers often consider multiple targets who may live in different jurisdictions with various law enforcement agencies and security organizations responsible for physical protection and protective intelligence. To facilitate the detection of patterns of behavior in known would-be attackers, law enforcement agencies should implement information-sharing programs with other such organizations. Under most circumstances, law enforcement organizations are permitted to share such information. In many cases, law enforcement organizations can receive information, even though they may not provide information to other agencies. Other organizations and individuals often understand these restrictions and may be willing to give information that may help prevent attacks.

Opening a Case

An individual may come to the attention of protective intelligence professionals after exhibiting inappropriate or unusual interest in a protected person or by threatening a protected person. The information may be general ("I'm going to the State capital to even the score") or specific ("John Smith wrote the mayor's name on a .45 caliber bullet last night"). The person may be acting alone or as part of a group. Sometimes, an individual is a person acting alone who becomes a fringe member of an extremist group, using the rhetoric and rationale of "the cause" for personal reasons.

Inappropriate or unusual interest

Much of the information that initially comes to the attention of protective intelligence professionals appears on the surface to be relatively innocuous. When initial information (provided by either a suspected individual or another person) suggests that the suspected individual has an inappropriate or unusual interest in a protected person, it is reasonable to presume that the individual eventually will be deemed to not pose a threat. The investigator's task is to search for information that rebuts this presumption and suggests that the individual does pose a real threat. Often, a relatively brief investigation will confirm that the individual has neither the interest, motive nor means to mount an attack against a protected person, thus supporting the presumption that the individual is not a threat.

However, initial information sometimes suggests that the individual already has *taken action* on his or her inappropriate or unusual interest, such as going to the target's home or office or approaching the target in a public place. The combination of *inappropriate or unusual interest* coupled with *actions* based on that interest makes the case more serious.

In even more serious cases, the individual's actions involve weapons-seeking or weapons use. It is then reasonable to presume that the individual poses a real threat. Investigators of these persons should gather information refuting the assumption that the individual poses a threat, if such information is available or exists.

Threats

An individual may come to the attention of authorities after making a threat against a protected person or after being accused of making such a threat. Threats should always be taken seriously and investigated. Although many people who make threats against protected persons do not pose a real threat, some make threats in order to convey a warning that they are prepared to act. These individuals may interpret a lack of investigative interest in their threats as permission or encouragement to mount an attack.

Also, some people make threats against protected persons to signal that they are in danger of losing control and hurting someone. Making a threat is a way for them to get attention from authorities who they believe can prevent them from acting violently. Ignoring these threats might make the individual more desperate, possibly increasing the risk

of violence to others, such as family members of the individual.

Occasionally, anonymous threats by phone, letter, or electronic mail come to the attention of law enforcement authorities. Individuals have various motives for communicating anonymous threats. ECSP information suggests that a few attackers and near-lethal approachers of prominent persons who made anonymous threats were trying to warn authorities that they were considering attacks. These individuals were ambivalent about attacking and were communicating with the hope that they might be stopped. Yet they did not want to identify themselves and make it more likely that the attack would be prevented.

Anonymous threats, though rarely acted upon, should be taken seriously and investigated to the fullest extent possible. Specific threats indicating that the threatener has plans to attack or that the threatener may have been in proximity to a protected person should be regarded with special concern.

Investigating a Case

Once a case has been opened, the protective intelligence investigator develops an investigation plan with the primary goal of collecting information and evidence that will help determine whether an individual has the interest, motive and capacity to mount an attack on a target.

A protective intelligence investigation differs from other kinds of assessments of danger because the goal is to prevent a particular kind of violence: attacks directed against public officials or figures. For example, a parole board may try to assess the likelihood that an inmate, if released, will commit another crime. A mental health professional may attempt to predict whether a mentally ill person is likely to act violently if he or she is not hospitalized. These are different kinds of evaluations than the assessment required in a protective intelligence investigation.

Interviewing the subject

Traditionally, protective intelligence investigators have relied on their interview of the individual who is the focus of a protective intelligence investigation as a key (if not the key) source of information. But this rule is not ironclad--for example, if the subject is known to be a member of a radical or militant group, any interview should be considered only within the context of the overall strategy for investigating the group.

The timing of the interview is often a major question. It usually makes sense to first gather preliminary information about a subject's background and interests before conducting an interview, as background information can guide an investigator during the interview. Such background information may lead the interviewer to areas relevant to whether the person poses a threat to particular targets.

Interviews can provide investigators with valuable information about subjects' thinking, motives for engaging in the behavior that initially brought them to the attention of the authorities, behavior that might be of concern, and leads for further investigation. Interviews may corroborate subjects' statements and be the basis for judging their veracity. Interviews also give subjects the opportunity to tell their personal stories, to be heard, and to reassess and redirect their behavior away from activities that concern investigators.

If at all possible, an interview should be conducted in a subject's "natural environment"--for example, at home--permitting the investigator to observe and gather nonverbal information and evidence that is relevant to the investigation, such as writings, pictures, and weapons that are within sight. Also, the investigator will learn about the subject's overall lifestyle and personality traits.

Investigators must sometimes interview persons who appear to be mentally ill. Such interviews often require special patience. Investigators should remember several basic principles

regarding interviews with mentally ill subjects:

. Any subject, including a mentally ill subject, will behave in accord with how he or she perceives reality. Thus, to understand how a mentally ill subject has behaved or may behave in the future, investigators must learn how the person perceives reality. For example, a subject who believes that aliens are controlling his mind and telling him to attack the Governor may feel that he is being forced to stalk the Governor, even though he sees himself as generally law-abiding and knows that attacking the Governor is illegal. An investigator who dismisses this thinking as crazy, concluding that the subject is unlikely to act, and who stops the interview may not explore whether the subject has made efforts to get a weapon or travel to sites where the Governor is likely to be.

. People, including those who are mentally ill, are more likely to reveal their thoughts and actions when treated with respect. Mentally ill subjects who perceive their interviewers as interested in hearing what they have to say are more likely to tell their stories than those who feel humiliated or scorned.

. Someone who is acutely or chronically mentally ill may still be able to think clearly in some areas and to determine whether an investigator is speaking truthfully. Interviewers who use a style that is clear, direct and nonjudgmental are more likely to solicit useful information than those using an approach in which they pretend to agree with a subject's delusions. An interviewer needs to be an active listener and to communicate a genuine interest in hearing and understanding the subject's story, no matter how outlandish it may seem. However, listening and understanding do not mean agreeing; an investigator should take care not to inadvertently reinforce the views of a delusional subject. Respectful skepticism will elicit more useful information: "I haven't had that experience, but I'm very interested in what you believe."

Although interviews can provide valuable information, relying too heavily on interviews does present problems. The information provided by the subject may be incomplete, misleading, or inaccurate. The interviewer may fail to solicit the information that is most relevant to the protective intelligence strategy called for in the investigation. The interviewee may present different information at different points in time, depending on his or her current circumstances, degree of desperation, mental health treatment, or other factors. In some cases, a subject's mental condition may be worsened by the interview.

Content of a protective intelligence investigation

Protective intelligence investigations differ from many other kinds of investigations in that the ultimate goal of these investigations is to prevent an attack, not to secure an arrest or conviction or to verify facts. Thus, any errors should be made on the side of safety and violence prevention.

Corroborated information and evidence. A primary task of a protective intelligence investigator is to seek and collect information and evidence to corroborate the statements of the subject of the investigation. Corroborated information about the individual's thinking and behavior facilitates assessment of the subject's interest, motives, and capacity to attempt to attack a protected person.

Corroborated evidence is more useful to investigators than subjective information and opinions. For instance, in a more traditional investigation, a detective would not ask a subject's wife, "Do you think he would ever pass a bogus check?" Likewise, asking the relative of a subject or a mental health professional questions such as "Do you think he is the type of person who would try to attack the mayor?" are rarely useful.

Areas of inquiry. A protective intelligence investigation of a subject should seek information in five areas:

The facts of the situation that initially brought the subject to the attention of the authorities. The first area of inquiry concerns how the subject came to

the attention of the protective intelligence unit. In cases where the subject went to the mayor's office with "special information only for the mayor that will keep the city safe," the answer is obvious. But other situations may be less clear. For example, a threatening letter from the county jail to a judge signed John Doe, Inmate 502, may have been written by inmate Jones to get Doe into trouble. An anonymous call to the local police by a "concerned citizen" about Mary Smith's disparaging comments about the mayor and her recent purchase of a gun may be from a disgruntled employee who hopes to embarrass her by a visit from law enforcement agents. Providers of information may have multiple motives, and eyewitness accounts of people's behavior are notoriously inaccurate. Protective intelligence investigators should carefully establish the facts of a case to determine if the subject being reported is a victim and if the "informant" is the true threat.

General information about the subject. Three kinds of general information about a subject are gathered in a protective intelligence investigation: identifiers, background information, and information about the subject's current life situation and circumstances.

.   **Identifiers.** Identifying information (identifiers) includes the following:

    .   Name and aliases.

    .   Date of birth.

    .   Social security and military identification numbers.

    .   Current address.

    .   Names and addresses of close relatives.

    .   Physical description and current photograph.

    .   Handwriting samples.

. **Background information.** Background information includes the following.

. Education and training.

. Criminal history.

. History of violent behavior.

. Military history.

. History of expertise with and use of weapons.

. Marital and relationship history.

. Employment history.

. Mental health history (with special attention to involuntary psychiatric commitments, episodes of depression or despair, including suicidal thinking and behavior, and violent behavior while mentally ill).

. History of grievance.

. History of harassing others.

. Interest in extremist ideas of radical groups.

. Travel history, especially in the previous year.

There are four purposes for gathering background information: to learn about past behaviors, interests, and lifestyles of subjects that may influence their current interests, motives, or capacity to attempt an attack; to develop sources of information, if further inquiry into a subject's life (past and present) is needed; to develop information that could help investigators locate the subjects in the future; and to assist in managing cases that are deemed serious.

. **Current life situation and circumstances.** A third area of general information sought in protective intelligence investigations concerns the current living arrangements and environment of the subject being investigated. Inquiry about a person's current situation is based upon the knowledge that some persons engage in extreme behavior or reach out to law enforcement authorities when they are in transition, in crisis, or in an unstable living situation.

Protective intelligence investigators should consider a number of issues related to a subject's current situation. Is the subject in a stable living situation, with basic needs for food, clothing, shelter, and human contact being met? Is the subject currently employed, and how stable is the subject's employment situation? Is the subject currently or soon likely to be in transition or crisis? For example, has the subject recently left a marriage, job, or community? Will the subject soon be discharged from a correctional or mental health institution? How does the stability of the subject's current living situation compare with past living situation and with the subject's likely living situation in the near future? Does the subject appear to be on a downward course? For example, has the subject recently appeared to be giving up hope, becoming more desperate, losing important contacts and supports, or becoming suicidal? Who is the best source to identify and convey this information?

Information about attack-related behaviors. ECSP examinations of the thinking and behaviors of persons who have attacked or approached to attack prominent persons in the United States suggest that many attacks and near-lethal approaches are preceded by discernible attack-related behavior. This behavior is often observed by people in the subject's life; the protective intelligence investigator who discovers such behavior in a subject will recognize it as a warning sign.

The idea that most assassins and near-lethal approachers engage in similar attack-related behaviors is consistent with an understanding of what is involved in mounting an attack on a protected person. An individual must select a target, locate the target, secure a weapon, travel to the vicinity of the target, and try to thwart whatever security measures are in place. These efforts may provide clues, indicating that the subject being investigated has been planning an attack. Protective intelligence investigators should look for evidence of attack-related behaviors, which can be categorized by whether or not weapons are involved.

Behaviors of concern in a threat assessment include:

- **An interest in assassination.** Manifestations of such an interest include gathering information about murder or assassination, writing to or about assassins, following news accounts of violence directed at public figures, visiting sites connected with assassinations, and emulating assassins.

- **Ideas and plans about attacking a public figure or official.** Evidence that a person has been thinking about or planning an attack may be revealed in comments to others, notes in a diary or journal, recent attention to the activities or travel of a public person, inquiries about law enforcement protective measures, travel patterns, attempts to breach security, or recent efforts to secure a weapon.

- **Communicating an inappropriate interest in a public official or figure, especially comments that express or imply an interest in attacking the person.** ECSP information suggests that attackers and near-lethal approachers rarely communicate direct threats to their targets or to law enforcement agencies, but many communicate information that indicates their intention to harm a target to relatives, coworkers, neighbors, or others.

- **Visiting a site linked to a protectee.** Appearance at an event or site where a public official or figure is, is believed to be, or will be in the future, is significant. Visits to these sites, when there is no obvious reason for the subject's appearance there, may be evidence of attack-related behavior.

- **Approaching a protectee.** To attack a protected person, an individual usually must travel to an event or site where the public official or figure is scheduled to be. Information that an individual has approached a target by visiting a site under these circumstances may be cause for concern.

Evidence of attack-related behavior involving a weapon should be taken very seriously by protective intelligence investigators. Of special interest is information about subjects purchasing or otherwise acquiring a weapon around the same time as they develop or hold an inappropriate or unusual interest in a public official or figure. In these circumstances, investigators must determine the intended use of the weapon.

Investigators should presume that an individual who has engaged in attack-related behavior involving a weapon or who has breached security is interested in attacking if given the opportunity. Investigative efforts in such a case should focus on ruling out the possibility of an attack. For example, investigators might establish that the individual had valid reasons, unrelated to a possible attack on a protected person, to carry a weapon or to travel to a certain site.

Motives. A thorough protective intelligence investigation involves careful attention to a subject's motives, because motives may determine whether a public official or figure is being targeted for attack and, if so, which persons are at greatest risk.

As noted previously, the 83 American assassins and near-lethal approachers studied by ECSP researchers had some combinations of eight motives. However, U.S. Secret Service case experience suggests that the motives of protective intelligence subjects who did not engage in near-lethal behavior have included the following:

. Bringing themselves to the attention of persons they perceived to be authorities.

. Instigating their involuntary commitment to a mental health or correctional institution.

. Effecting change in a current living situation viewed as intolerable (for example, to be moved from one prison to another).

. Obtaining help; e.g., being stopped from acting violently.

. Getting someone else in trouble.

. Obtaining attention or notoriety or bringing a concern to public attention.

. Achieving a special relationship with a public official or figure.

. Correcting a perceived wrong.

. Being injured or killed.

An investigator's opinion about the rationality of the subject's motives has no bearing on whether the subject will take action. Because subjects' acts are based on their perceptions of reality, the investigator's views will not determine a subject's future course of conduct. It may not matter whether the motives are illogical or rational, foolish or realistic, self-destructive or in the individual's best interests.

For example, a subject who believes that she is a relative of a public figure and that she has been invited to move into the public figure's residence is unlikely to be dissuaded by an investigator's rational analysis. Such a person is likely to continue to believe that she is related to the public figure despite facts to the contrary. The interviewer's tasks in such

a case are to understand how the subject views her situation, not to reinforce any delusional ideas, and to try to gauge what action the subject might take based on her perceptions and beliefs.

The motive of suicide can also be a factor in near-lethal approaches or attacks on public figures and officials. This phenomenon--"suicide by cop"--has received considerable attention in the past ten years. An individual who wants to die, but is not willing or able to take his or her own life, may believe that instigating gunfire by approaching a protected person with a weapon is a way to get killed.

When coupled with an individual's wish for fame or notoriety, suicide becomes an even more ominous motive. An individual whose motives are notoriety and suicide may consider attacking a political leader, even though he or she has no political interest and no negative feelings about the protected person. The only issue that matters is that the public official is protected by armed law enforcement officers and will be accompanied by news media that will record the assailant's death.

Target selection. Many attackers and near-lethal approachers may consider several potential targets and change their primary target several times.

For example, the published diary of Arthur Bremer (who shot Alabama Governor George Wallace in 1972) suggests that his first target was President Richard Nixon. After unsuccessfully attempting to position himself to shoot the President during a trip to Ottawa, Canada, Bremer shifted his interest to Wallace, by then a Presidential candidate. Other near-lethal attackers have shifted from one target to another based on their perception of the importance of a given target. One subject shifted between attacking a Governor, a Senator, and a Presidential candidate, settling on the candidate because he thought a "Presidential candidate is much more powerful."

When gathering information, therefore, investigators should be alert to the possibility that a subject has considered, is simultaneously considering, or might consider in the future a number of public officials or figures as possible targets. Selection of a primary target may depend on many factors, such as the subject's motives, ability to travel, financial situation, and opportunities to approach a target, as well as the perceived importance of, the media attention given to, and the perceived security afforded a target.

Evaluating A Threat Assessment Case

A protective intelligence investigation, at least in part, is an effort to predict specific future violence. Two points about violence prediction are worth consideration. First, violence prediction is conditional--not a yes-no, "this person will be violent or will never be violent" proposition. A prediction of violence is a statement that, given certain circumstances or conditions, a specified risk exists that a particular subject will act violently toward a particular target.

Second, targeted violence is different than other kinds of violence, and attacks on public officials or figures appear to be a specific kind of targeted violence. An attack on a Mayor, Governor, or President is a different kind of behavior than an armed robbery, rape, or attack on a roommate. A murder of a celebrity or a business leader is a different kind of violence than a murder of a parent or neighbor. ECSP information about attackers and would-be attackers of prominent persons suggests that some factors that have been seen as general predictors of violence, such as a history of violence, may not specifically predict violence toward a public official or figure.

Principles to Guide a Protective Intelligence Evaluation

After information about a subject has been gathered, this material must be organized and evaluated. A two-stage process is suggested. First, information should be examined for evidence of behavior and conditions that would be consistent with

the likelihood of a violent attack on a public person. In the second stage of evaluation, the protective intelligence investigator will determine whether a subject appears to be moving toward an attack and, if so, how rapidly.

Protective intelligence investigators should conduct threat assessments using two principles as guides:

- Assassination is the result of an understandable and often discernible process of thinking and behavior.

- Assassination stems from an interaction of the potential attacker, event, situation and target.

Questions to Ask in a Threat Assessment

Investigators should ask a number of questions of both the subject and collateral sources throughout the investigation. The answers to these questions will guide the evaluation:

- What motivated the subject to make the statement or take the action that caused him or her to come to attention?

- What, if anything, has the subject communicated to someone else (target, law enforcement, family, friends, colleagues, associates) or written in a diary or journal concerning his or her intentions?

- Has the subject shown an interest in any of the following?

    - Assassins or assassination.

    - Weapons (including recent acquisition of a weapon).

    - Militant or radical ideas/groups.

    - Murders, murderers, mass murderers, and workplace violence and stalking incidents.

. Is there evidence that the subject has engaged in menacing, harassing, and/or stalking-type behaviors? Has the subject engaged in attack-related behaviors? These behaviors combine an inappropriate interest with any of the following:

  . Developing an attack idea or plan.

  . Approaching, visiting, and/or following the target.

  . Approaching, visiting, and/or following the target with a weapon.

  . Attempting to circumvent security.

  . Assaulting or attempting to assault a target.

. Does the subject have a history of mental illness involving command hallucinations, delusional ideas, feelings of persecution, etc., with indications that the subject has acted on those beliefs?

. How organized is the subject? Does the subject have the ability to plan and execute a violent action against a target?

. Is there evidence that the subject is experiencing desperation and/or despair? Has the subject experienced a recent personal loss and/or loss of status? Is the subject now, or has the subject ever been, suicidal?

. Is the subject's "story" consistent with his or her actions?

. Are those who know the subject concerned that he or she might take action based on inappropriate ideas?

. What factors in the subject's life and/or environment might increase or decrease the likelihood that the subject will attempt to attack a target (or targets)?

In addition, an investigator should address troubling or unresolved issues about a particular case, which could include missing information or new information that might clarify the subject's motives and interest.

Attacks on public officials and figures are rare; all cases that are serious enough to be opened deserve a thorough investigation. Usually, information gathered during the investigation will lead to the conclusion that the subject does not pose a threat. However, sometimes the facts cause the investigator to become concerned about the risk a subject poses. These cases require particularly painstaking investigative efforts and consideration.

In most cases, an investigator should consult with other professionals before drawing a conclusion about whether a subject poses a threat to a public official or figure. Another investigator with protective intelligence experience is often the most effective consultant. However, people with special expertise that might pertain to the facts of a given case can sometimes offer a useful perspective. For example, a mental health professional who has experience assessing mentally ill persons who act violently and who is familiar with the operations of law enforcement agencies could help assess information about a mentally ill subject.

Documenting and keeping a record of the information gathered and evaluated in a protective intelligence investigation is vital. A well-documented record permits others to review the case and offer assistance, and shows that the investigation was performed with care and attention. Also, a carefully documented case file provides baseline information about a subject's thinking and actions at a certain point in time, which can be invaluable if the subject is investigated again or if future investigators need to determine whether the subject has changed thought or behavior patterns.

Protection

Those charged with protection of the targeted public official or figure must be notified about cases of concern, and the information should be incorporated into protection activities. The structure and operations of an organization should determine how threat assessment data are connected to protection activities. For instance, if an organization has one unit responsible for protection and one for threat assessment functions, this often can be accomplished through intramural briefings. Briefing of protectors usually includes a description of a subject's identifiers, behavior, interests, and current location and situation. However, such briefings should be two-way exchanges of information, because protectors often have information that can be important in a protective intelligence investigation as well as in follow-up investigations used in monitoring the subject.

Managing A Protective Intelligence Case

In most protective intelligence cases, based on the information gathered, investigators determine that an individual does not pose a risk to a public person. The majority of these cases are closed following the investigation, unless a criminal violation occurred (for example, the subject threatened a public official) or protectors feel that the subject may harm a person other than the original target. If a criminal violation has occurred, the case may be presented to the prosecutor's office for possible charges. If investigators believe that a subject is a threat to an unprotected person, they can attempt to direct the subject to the appropriate resources or otherwise intervene to prevent violence.

When a thorough investigation suggests that the subject has the interest, motive, and ability to attempt an attack on a public official or figure, the investigator's task is to manage the case so that violence does not occur. Successful case management involves considerable time and effort and is composed of two functions: efforts directed at protection, so that a target is shielded from the potential assailant, and efforts directed at monitoring, controlling, and redirecting the subject.

Monitoring, Controlling, and Redirecting the Subject

The central premise of case management efforts is that violence directed against a protected person is in no one's best interest, including that of the potential assailant. Coordinated, consistent efforts to tell the potential attacker that an attack will not be permitted and that it is not in anyone's best interest to attack can increase the chance that a subject will abandon the idea of assassination.

Unless there is reason to do otherwise, the subject should be made aware of the investigation and told that unacceptable interest in a protected person and unacceptable behavior must change. This message should be communicated to the subject clearly and professionally. However, in certain investigations--for example, those involving a member of a radical or militant group--it may not be appropriate to alert the subject.

Many people who are considered a threat want attention and will accept ongoing contact with the law enforcement or security organization responsible for protective intelligence. Therefore, the subject should be asked to cooperate with being monitored by the investigator and the law enforcement or security agency. For example, the agency might ask the subject to report all planned travel and to check in with the investigator on a regular basis.

Many subjects see law enforcement officers as important authority figures in their lives. Regular, respectful interviews, in which investigators listen while delivering a consistent, clear message about unacceptable behavior, are key to supporting these subjects as they attempt to change. For a mentally ill subject, simply reinforcing the idea that he or she must remain connected to and cooperative with mental health treatment professionals may be sufficient. Other cases, such as those involving terrorists, call for different strategies.

Effective case management is aided by a systems perspective. That is, investigators should identify existing social systems that might help them manage persons who are potential threats. Social systems that might work cooperatively with the investigator to engage, neutralize, and redirect the potential attacker include the following:

. Criminal justice system (prosecutors, courts, probation officers, correctional officials).

. Health and mental health care organizations (managed care organizations, public mental health agencies, local hospitals).

. Social services organizations.

. Religious organizations to which the subject belongs or in which the subject is interested.

. Community organizations.

. Family and friends.

Ending Monitoring

The purpose of connecting the subject to services and systems that will aid and encourage change is ultimately to enable the investigator to discontinue monitoring. After monitoring is ended and a case is closed, the subject may continue to be involved with service systems that aid successful functioning.

The investigator will be able to end monitoring after performing the following tasks:

. Assessing whether (and to what extent) the subject has changed unacceptable thinking

and behavior over time.

. Developing and supporting intervention strategies that encourage and help the subject to change.

Sources of postassessment information

To evaluate changes in behavior, an investigator should develop a baseline of the subject's behaviors of concern and then collect information over time about the subject from multiple and consistent sources. Such a strategy takes into account the likelihood that the living conditions may change, as may the law enforcement or security staff with responsibility for ongoing investigation of the subject.

To permit later comparisons to baseline behavior, the investigator should write detailed descriptions of the subject's initial attack-related behavior and worrisome thinking and actions when he or she was first deemed a threat.

A list also should be compiled of persons and organizations who can be contacted at regular intervals for information about the subject's behavior. Collateral-source information can corroborate or clarify information gained directly from interviews with a subject during the case management process. An interview with such a subject might be followed by interviews with others who are in regular contact with the subject to determine whether he or she behaves in a manner consistent with his or her statements to the investigator.

For example, a prison inmate who tells an investigator that he is no longer interested in the Governor but who is described by the shift commander on the cell block as being intensely interested each time the Governor appears on the news might be suspect in other comments about his interests and behaviors.

Similarly, seeking an opinion from a doctor in a mental health unit who has little contact with a subject about the likelihood that the patient will try to kill the Governor may prove less useful than interviewing a mental health worker who frequently interacts with the patient.

Closing a Case

A protective intelligence investigator can close a case when he or she is able to:

. Articulate why a subject was originally considered to pose a threat.

. Document changes in the subject's thinking and behavior that negate the original concerns.

. Describe why the subject is unlikely to pose a future threat to protected persons.

If postassessment contacts have been made, closing the case involves ensuring that the subject understands that the protective intelligence investigator will initiate no further contact. For some subjects, cessation of contact with the investigator may be a desired goal and a relief; for others, the thought of ending contact with officials who they viewed as helping them may be difficult. In most cases, therefore, it makes sense that discontinuance of contact be gradual, rather than abrupt. Ongoing contact with other organizations, such as mental health or social services agencies, can help these subjects function after their contact with the law enforcement or security organization has ended.

In order to know whether an attack is being planned against your protectee and how to avoid or defeat it, you need good, reliable *intelligence*. One definition of *intelligence* is *organized information*. In order to produce intelligence, one must select, evaluate, analyze, and, of course, act upon the intelligence results. To be effective and to avoid "spinning your wheels," you need to know what information to collect and where to collect it. The "what intelligence to collect" should emanate from your threat assessment. Who is likely to target your client for an attack? You should avoid spending excessive time researching and cross-indexing the names of all adversary groups or particular individuals. This information rarely proves useful, since it is over-kill; you are interested only in that information which is specific to your client. Then, that information must be evaluated, validated, and analyzed.

Intelligence is collected from several information sources: police, commercial sources, print media, television, the Internet, computerized databases, and human collection.

POLICE AND LAW ENFORCEMENT SOURCES

As you might surmise, law enforcement personnel usually have the clearest picture of what is happening in their jurisdiction. Does this mean that an executive protection agent can simply walk in and ask for intelligence about terrorists, gangs, and criminals operating in their area? No, and in fact, they will probably make that agent feel very foolish before they show him the door. Public law enforcement personnel usually harbor some suspicions against the private security community in general--in many cases for good reason. Private security personnel have not always distinguished themselves for their ability to protect anyone, or worse, have caused a good deal of grief for the police. It should be noted that this attitude is changing. As police budgets continue to be cut, and crime continues to rise, it is apparent even to the most regressive law enforcement personnel that the private sector is now providing, and will continue to provide, the majority of the protective services. There is also a greatly heightened understanding of, and respect for, the role of the professional, trained executive protection agent.

There are other reasons why the police do not greet all requests for local intelligence with enthusiasm. They are very busy people and truly do not have the time or inclination to sit down and thoroughly brief the agent. They may be apprehensive about giving out too much information if they feel it compromises their own intelligence sources; i.e., their snitches. And, as with any hierarchy, it helps to come through the door with an introduction. So, how does one deal with this situation? Do your homework first and, if at all possible, arrange for an introduction to the Chief, the top decision maker in that department.

There has been prior discussion in this book about the need to collect information. Before an agent visits with the local police he or she should already have gathered as much local intelligence as possible, either from private firms or from one's own files. The agent's files constitute his most valuable intelligence asset, containing as they do ongoing collections of clippings from the print media. Before the agent walks through the door of the local police department, he should already have put together a summary of information about local conditions, focusing on *who are the threat, what are their numbers, weapons and skills, and level of dedication*. If there is more than one group who might pose a threat, this information needs to be included. If there are no clearly identifiable groups who might pose a threat, a summary of crime problems in the area might be the answer. Once this is done, with the proper introduction an agent can usually visit with the police, asking them to look over his summary and verify his findings or add information. This is far more professional and is a lot easier for the police to deal with since the agent has done the major part of the work.

If ever there was a tight network, it is the law enforcement network; therefore, it behooves the executive protection agent to join that network when possible. It is generally possible in any locale in the country to join some sort of law enforcement reserve program. Reserve deputy sheriff is one of the most accessible roles; reserve police officer is another. Sometimes this requires additional training for which several weeks or even months may be required to complete. In other circumstances, it may be possible to acquire reserve deputy sheriff status by contributing time and services. For example, if the agent has any aptitude for giving instruction and is an accomplished shooter, he or she may volunteer to instruct the department in defensive shooting techniques. Several agents have achieved their goals in this way. Yet another agent instructs personnel in the sheriff's department in certain specialized subjects, such as financial fraud investigation. There are many advantages to gaining legitimacy in the law enforcement arena. It opens doors and effects introductions; it may provide a license to carry a concealed weapon; and it provides a support system.

Now, when the agent/reserve deputy sheriff wants to acquire intelligence in another community, he first puts together his summary of local conditions, and then he asks his law enforcement Chief to call the law enforcement Chief in the target area, arranging an introduction. This is using the law enforcement network to its best advantage. Incidentally, one should always try to reach the Chief, the top decision maker in any department, since any personnel in his department will first want the Chief's approval before any information is given out, or any support services provided. This is true in any organization, whether it be law enforcement or business.

If, for some reason, the agent is not able to join the local law enforcement agency on reserve status, the next best opportunity is to join a network organization such as the National Sheriffs Association or the International Association of Chiefs of Police (IACP). Often, if one does not meet the membership requirements (such as actually being a Chief of Police), it is possible to join as an "Associate Member" (non-voting). All organizations like to increase their memberships; they are, after all, dependent on dues and attendance at conferences to provide funding for the organization's staff and activities. After joining, one should attend at least a minimum number of meetings, seminars, and conferences, should volunteer for committee work, and campaign for elective office within the association. Using this route, the agent can ask his local chapter of IACP or National Sheriffs Association to call or write to the local Chief or Sheriff in the target area, recommending the agent as a brother member for the Chief's help.

It is important for the agent to conduct himself as a true professional when he pays his call on the local police Chief or Sheriff. This means dressing for the part, looking as much like the Secret Service or FBI image as possible, with business suit, shirt, tie, polished shoes, briefcase, and business card. It means shaking hands, introducing oneself and stating one's business up front, "Good morning, Chief, my name is John B. Agent. I'm handling the security for J. B. Client, who will be visiting in your city. I appreciate your taking the time to let me meet with you," and then extending one's credentials. This is not only the first impression which the Chief will receive of the agent, it is the lasting impression, and the one which will determine the amount of support the agent will receive. It is well to keep in mind that the local police do not *have* to give any cooperation whatsoever. While they may have a certain vested interest in seeing that clients and notables are safe in their city, they may decide that they can handle it without the agent. Now, in order to earn his salary, the agent must merit the cooperation of the law enforcement community, and he achieves this as one professional to another. The worst thing an agent can do is wear his concealed weapon into the police station, the next worst is to demand that the local

Chief give aid and assistance, and the third worst is to walk in wearing black leather, shaved head, goatee, and mirror glasses.

Once the agent has established his credentials with the local Chief, the Chief will probably ask, "What can I do for you?" At this point, the agent can pull out his intelligence summary and itinerary. "Chief, here is a copy of the schedule for my client, subject to change. We would appreciate your keeping it confidential. And, I would also appreciate your looking over my intelligence estimate and telling me if I have the correct picture of what goes on in your city." The agent has now asked the Chief to review his analysis, not write it for him. At that point, the Chief will generally cooperate and extend the courtesies of his department. There is a caveat here which is, one should never abuse the departmental courtesy by asking for anything that one does not actually need.

PRIVATE FIRMS

There are private firms that collect useful information and, in turn, offer it for purchase in the form of newsletters or special reports. The reports and newsletters are broad-based and somewhat generic; that is, these reports rarely focus on a specific issue. They tend to cover a wide range of groups, incidents, and issues gathered on a worldwide basis. These firms generally charge a hefty price for their services and may offer only a small quantity of information actually relevant to any particular security program. For the most part, private firms collect their information from public sources--newspapers, magazines, and television reports, sources available to any enterprising agent. They do a good job of this and have numerous subscribers. They are, however, expensive, and this must be balanced within the budget as to whether it is the best use of available dollars.

IN-HOUSE FILES

In-house files remain one of the most cost-effective ways to collect and organize relevant

information as the information is gathered from media stories printed in newspapers and magazines. To be effective, a variety of publications should be used. *Time, Newsweek, U.S. News and World Report, Washington Post, New York Times*, and the *Christian Science Monitor* would be good examples. The information being collected covers anything that is, or might be, relevant. Typically, the clippings might be about terrorists, emerging activist groups, crimes, street gangs, bombings, killings, assassinations, kidnappings, etc. For example, the 1992 kidnapping and subsequent death of the Exxon executive is a subject for a file. Who kidnapped him, why, how was it done, and what went wrong?

The print media is an excellent source for intelligence gathering. Journalists are trained gatherers of information. They know how to get information (often through informants and other sources of their own), how to analyze and organize information, and how to produce that information as a coherent, complete story. Often, the best print stories contain pictures, graphics, maps, and other very useful information that would be unavailable to the agent working on his own. Governments and agencies often "leak" information to reporters. Reporters are in the business of collecting the best information available. Newspapers are extremely competitive and hire reporters who can produce information that is the best available, or even better, exclusive to that newspaper. Now, not every newspaper is a great source of national and international intelligence. The major newspapers such as the *New York Times, Los Angeles Times, Chicago Tribune*, and *Washington Post*, have Pulitzer Prize reporters on staff and in regional offices around the world; therefore, their information is first-hand, factual, and complete. Smaller local newspapers are not particularly good sources of national and international news, as they depend upon syndicated stories for much of their news coverage. They do not have the budgets to maintain large staffs of on-site reporters. Local newspapers are, however, excellent sources of local news. If a major event occurs, say, in Denver, the national newspapers will pick up on the story. If, however, it is a relatively minor event on the national scene, it will not be covered by the major newspapers other than as a small paragraph in the back section of the newspaper. However, if the agent and protectee live in Denver and the story is significant to them, the in-depth coverage of that local event in the local newspaper will be well worth collecting.

News magazines can be an excellent source of information, often giving the most complete, in-depth coverage of a story. During the time of the many airplane hijackings, some of the best stories were being provided by *Time* and *Newsweek*, with maps, photographs, interviews, and priceless information.

Files should be opened with a purpose in mind. The file could cover the situation in Kosovo, or Lebanon, or could cover a specific event such as the kidnapping of the Exxon executive, or be about the recent elections of Islamic reformists in Iran, or bombings of abortion clinics and the torching of the Vail ski area mountain resort. Files are often cross-indexed; for example, a file on executive kidnappings in the United States could generate another file with some of the same information about a specific kidnapping.

Some tips are: xerox newspaper articles for the files (original newsprint turns yellow and fades with age); keep files in chronological order; keep files in logical order; don't be a glutton (keep only pertinent information); keep it simple; don't let the clippings pile up (it is easier to stay current with clipping and filing); and read at least one newspaper per day and two news magazines per week. If a story is significant, it is helpful to collect different versions of that story from several newspapers and magazines. This is not a chore for one's secretary; this is a must-do activity for the agent. Only by *reading*, clipping, filing, and committing to memory is the intelligence gathered of value.

A new news phenomenon is the cable television newscast, *CNN* being a prime example. *CNN* newscasts of significant events are now monitored avidly by government agencies. A case in point is the coverage of the Gulf War. *CNN* not only

had widespread coverage, it had a reporter in Baghdad who was allowed to regularly broadcast stories from the Iraq capital while the battle was going on. Were his broadcasts censored? Yes, but nonetheless, news was being sent out which was real and reasonably accurate. There are some excellent *PBS* newscasts and stories. To stay fully informed, an agent should try to watch one or more of these programs every day. There are numbers of documentary stories produced for television, some of which are excellent. For example, there was a story about the rise of modern terrorism in Lebanon produced several years ago. It is one of the best sources of the history of this movement that one could hope to find. It is sometimes possible to buy copies of newscasts and documentaries which are good intelligence sources for an agent's files.

In-house files should be considered an adjunct to a personal library. The most successful agents maintain both, because the files, video tapes, and library complement each other. It is useful to get on the mailing list of catalogs from major suppliers of books of particular interest to the executive protection field. There are publishing houses that specialize in books for private security and law enforcement. There are so many facets to the agent's job that it requires the accumulation of books and files dealing not only with terrorism and crime, but also with pertinent legal aspects, electronic security technology, computer security, celebrity protection, white collar crime, cyber crime, and the list goes on and on.

PUBLIC INFORMATION

A startlingly uncomfortable amount of information can be obtained about individuals. Much of it is now computerized, while a certain percentage is still sitting in paper form in state and local government offices.

One of the best sources of information lies within the public library. Good libraries have subscriptions to various newspapers and magazines, free for the reading. Libraries store back copies of newspapers and magazines on microfiche, and information thus stored can be conveniently printed out. This is very helpful for researching data on a particular story or subject.

Good libraries maintain a reference section which contains marvelous information: lists of associations, *Who's Who in America*, telephone books from every major city in the United States, criss-cross directories (cross-referencing street addresses with telephone numbers), and much more. Libraries also contain numerous annual reports of major U.S. corporations. And, best of all, librarians are generally very helpful. Sometimes, one little piece of information can be obtained simply by calling the library and asking the librarian for it. It has been said that the library is the spy's best friend. Surely, this can be applied as well to the executive protection agent.

Many of the public records compiled on a person can be found with the Clerk-Recorder at the county courthouse. These can include traffic records, birth/death records, marriage records, civil records, criminal records, real property sales records, auto tag registration, hunting and fishing licenses, probate records, real property tax records and voter registration. State records include auto tag, driver licenses, vehicle title, corporate business names, and state highway patrol records.

Birth and death records. To obtain information, particularly if you are making your request in writing, include, if possible, the following: full name of person; sex and race; parents' names, including maiden name of mother; month, day and year of birth or death; place of death (city, town, county, state); reason for requesting the information; and your relationship to the person.

Marriage records. Marriage records reside with the vital statistics office either at the state level or locally in a city, county, or other office. To obtain information by written request include when possible: full names of bride and groom; month, day and year of marriage; place of marriage (city, county, state); purpose of request; and relationship to person(s).

Divorce records. These records are also kept with the vital statistics office at state, county, or city level. Information to include with the request is similar to requests for marriage records and includes: full name of husband and wife; date of divorce or annulment; type of final decree; purpose of request; and relationship to subject.

Voter registration records. Information to be learned from these records includes: subject's full name and current address; telephone number; sometimes a social security number; party affiliation; registration date; and whether the registration is a new or changed address.

Court records. Court cases, either criminal or civil, are within the public domain, meaning the records are available to the public. Records can be accessed in the court clerk's office where the case was tried. Do not overlook the following:

. Bankruptcy.
. Civil proceedings.
. Credit judgements.
. Divorce actions and child support hearings.
. Estate filings and probate actions.
. Small claims.
. Trust formations.

If these do not appear to be good sources, think again. Divorce proceedings between hostile parties can reveal a great deal. In more than one case, the divorce proceedings uncovered devious business dealings, secret assets, kickbacks, and more. Probate actions when conducted with warring and/or disinherited heirs can pinpoint assets and reveal names of trustees, partners, executors, associates, and the like. For example, the probate of Howard Hughes' estate, together with the libel suit filed against him by a former associate, produced hundreds of boxes of material, sufficient to enable writers to write a biography of Hughes.

In some states, persons attempting to establish property settlements in divorce cases may be required to submit tax returns. In some criminal cases, tax returns are subpoenaed.

Tax liens filed at the county, state or federal level are civil claims seeking to attach money and/or property to pay taxes due.

U.S. Tax Court. This court is located in Washington, D.C. and is the scene of battles between the Internal Revenue Service and a taxpayer (taxpayers). Trust the IRS to discover all there is to know about the subject(s). The IRS has a vested interest in uncovering hidden assets and placing all business dealings under a microscope.

DATABASES

Databases are the true mother lode of information! There are hundreds of databases, some better than others, and many that are almost useless because the information contained in the database is badly organized, incomplete, and out-of-date. The really good databases are worth their cost, but be aware that the cost can be quite high. Before progressing any further into the world of computer information collection, it would be remiss not to state that a *huge* amount of information can be researched from the Internet, using a PC and modem, with costs at a minimum depending upon the amount of time spent online. Almost all government agencies at the federal level and some at the state level offer information on the Internet. The decision as to whether to pay the cost for securing information from a proprietary (commercial) database may well be founded on these considerations: how much time you have to devote to the project; how quickly you need the most up-to-date information; budget; and whether the information is available anywhere else. For example, credit information on a person is not available by merely browsing the Internet--it must be bought in the form of a credit report issued by a database company whose business is the credit information business.

Computer databases offer a wealth of information and are used (for our purposes) to investigate backgrounds of individuals and businesses

and to corroborate that information. Information provided often leads to other connections and links which can be explored. For example, if one is researching a corporation or an individual, a database may provide news articles which would refer to names of people involved with the company, claims against the company, and so on.

Before going any further, it must be stated that *not all information which stems either from the Internet or from computer databases is necessarily correct or even current.* Much of the information obtained from databases is provided by the subject him/herself and, as we all know, sometimes the subjects lie, or perhaps exaggerate, or even provide false information in a deliberate attempt to deceive. In other cases, there are simply mistakes, either mistakes made by the subject or by the person in front of the computer inputting information. What keeps the information from being overly contaminated is that it is an *aggregate* of data supplied from different records. If a subject fills in several forms (credit application, drivers license, real estate license, etc.) it is likely that the record will begin to resemble the truth. Clerical errors are another matter and numerous well documented cases have occurred because upstanding, credit-worthy individuals have had their lives turned upside down with credit denied for mortgages, automobiles, and credit cards--all because of clerical inputting error. This also means that in trying to locate an individual, clerical error can send an investigator to the wrong address or wrong employer or both.

How is the information in these databases acquired? From a plethora of sources, including credit applications, all those public records described earlier in this chapter, and the numerous forms which we all fill out (warranty cards, trial subscriptions, etc.)

Databases exist in several areas, primarily: government (including law enforcement); proprietary (commercial databases, industry analysts, professional associations, special interest groups); media (newspapers, magazines, industry); and libraries/colleges/universities/science and research agencies networking together.

Government Databases

Government Law Enforcement Databases

Some of the largest, most valuable databases belong to the federal government and not all are available to non-government, non-law enforcement, non-classified individuals.

. **Federal Bureau of Investigation's National Crime Information Center (NCIC)**. This database, available *ONLY* to law enforcement agencies (specifically a government agency meeting the definition of a criminal justice agency or an agency under the management control of a criminal justice agency) contains records on millions of Americans, indexed by such things as fingerprint classification, name, date of birth, and social security number. Over a million requests for information per 24-hour period are processed every day from federal, state, and local systems that interface with the NCIC system. The FBI includes the following files kept in the NCIC.

    Wanted person file--this includes information about individuals for whom federal warrants are outstanding or who have been named in warrants for a felony or serious misdemeanor, and for which the offenses are extraditable. As can be imagined, the information is as complete as can be obtained re name, description (height, weight, scars and other marks), birth date, type of offense, date of warrant, and identity of the agency holding the warrant.

    Foreign fugitive file--persons wanted in Canada for an extraditable offense.

    Missing persons file--entries concern those persons who may have a physical or mental disability; who are thought to be endangered (feared to be in some form of physical safety endangerment); involuntary disappearances (abduction); juveniles; and catastrophe victims. These files contain as much information as possible both about the individual and about the circumstances surrounding the disappearance.

. **Unidentified person file**--entries for unidentified deceased individuals and living persons unable to identify themselves (amnesias, infants, senile persons). Data entered is similar to that in the missing persons file.

. **U.S. Secret Service protective file**--contains information about individuals who may pose a threat to the president and other protectees. Information includes name, description, identifying factors, and known whereabouts of the subject.

. **Vehicle file**--unrecovered stolen vehicles, vehicles wanted in conjunction with a crime, etc. Information includes VIN number, license plate, description, date stolen, and reporting agency.

. **License plate file**--stolen/missing license plates.

. **Gun file**--serially numbered stolen guns. Information includes, when available, serial number, type, make, calibre, and date of theft (approximate), plus reporting agency. Note that the serial number of the gun is the most important piece of information.

. **Article file**--stolen property. Must have serial number to qualify for entry and desirable is a description of type, brand name and distinguishing characteristics.

. **Boat file**--stolen boats. Must have registration and document data, hull serial number or owner-applied number, name of boat manufacturer, and year of manufacture.

. **Securities file**--stolen stocks and bonds, travelers checks, money orders, and currency that are serially numbered, along with security date and issuer.

Canadian Border Anti-Smuggling Intelligence Center. Maintains information on narcotic, currency, weapon, and alien smuggling, international and domestic terrorists, Asian crime and culture gangs, and motorcycle gangs. Communications flow between the Royal Canadian Mounted Police, U.S. Customs, Drug Enforcement Administration, U.S. Marshal's Service, FBI, and northern border ports of entry. Records are maintained on wanted persons, stolen guns, wanted vehicles, fraudulent passports and stolen immigrant visas, smuggling activities, and much more.

Canadian Police Information Center (CPIC). This database, an NCIC counterpart, is operated in Canada by the Royal Canadian Mounted Police. Information contained is limited to accredited police agencies and agencies complementary to law enforcement who function in a support capacity and data may be used only for law enforcement purposes. There are four principal databases--investigative, identification, ancillary, and intelligence. Included in the four databases are: vehicle files; marine files; persons files (wanted, charged, parolees, missing); property files; major crimes files; criminal records files; motor vehicle registrations; drivers license records; and intelligence files (surveillance, criminal intelligence).

El Paso Intelligence Center. Managed by the Drug Enforcement Administration, EPIC monitors narcotics activities worldwide in participation with the Bureau of Alcohol, Tobacco and Firearms, Border Patrol, Coast Guard, Customs Service, Federal Bureau of Investigation, Federal Aviation Administration Immigration, Internal Revenue Service, and the U.S. Secret Service. Inquiries for information are received from federal, state, country, and city agencies. Data is maintained on weapons and narcotics activities and on individual offenders.

Federal Court System. There are several courts which are online and which contain up-to-date information on cases in their jurisdiction. This information will probably include names of all individuals involved, as well as ancillary information. BRB Publications, located in Denver, Colorado, publishes the *Public Record Research Library*, a set of reference books on where and how to find public records, including U.S. court locations, Federal Records Centers, state public records, and listings of local court and county record retrievers who do retrieval of criminal, civil, and probate case files, plus U.S. District and bankruptcy courts. The *Library* also publishes other information useful in searching public records and in asset/lien searching.

Regional Information Sharing Systems. Intelligence and investigative support is provided to member agencies. Participating members must have arrest powers. Participating are:

.	**Mid-States Organized Crime Information Center.**

.	**Middle Atlantic Great Lakes Organized Crime Law Enforcement Network.**

.	**New England State Police Information Network.**

.	**Regional Organized Crime Information Center.**

.	**Rocky Mountain Information Network.**

.	**Western States Information Network.**

.	**White Collar Crime Project.**

There are many other government databases which are not particularly appropriate to our needs; however, several are worthy of note.

.	**Central Intelligence Agency.** One of the, if not the, premier U.S. intelligence collection and analysis entities. The CIA ostensibly does not have law enforcement powers, nor are they empowered to engage in internal security functions within the United States. The CIA mandate is national security.

. **Department of Agriculture.** Inspects, investigates, monitors, promotes, and protects agricultural products and some aspects of land resources. Keep an eye on this Department, which is sure to heat up with the current genetically altered agricultural products controversy.

. **U.S. Forest Service.** Maintains records on forest, mining, and pasture leases. This department is often targeted by ecologically motivated extremists.

. **Department of Commerce.** Primarily concerned with promoting U.S. commerce, both within the U.S. and internationally. It heads a number of agencies. Watch this one, as the controversy over the World Trade Union continues at fever pitch.

. **Department of the Interior.** A "hotspot" agency, Interior has the responsibility for overseeing and administering several hundred million acres of federal land, including Indian reservations, and is responsible for conservation and development of such natural resources as minerals (oil, mining, timber-cutting, etc.), water (dams, hydroelectric power systems), fish, and wildlife. Interior seems almost constantly under attack by conservationists, developers, ranchers, etc., alike. Watch the current news for stories about this department, gambling casinos, and highly placed officials. There is major opportunity for corruption since the undeveloped mineral and oil resources, alone, are worth fortunes.

. **Bureau of Indian Affairs.** This agency oversees many activities on indian reservations, including gambling casinos. Reservation gambling, once a relatively small business, has mushroomed into enough business to attract corruption.

. **Bureau of Land Management.** This agency has endured, despite attempts to get rid of it by those who resent its management of federal lands with minerals, timber, oil, gas, wildlife, recreation areas, public range lands, and endangered plants and animals.

. **National Park Service.** This agency has, until recently, been considered a fairly benign one, with responsibilities for the management of our national parks and the concessionaires who provide food, lodging, and entertainment services. The National Park Service is now overwhelmed with the task of maintaining the parks in the face of a flood tide of tourists. Crime, heretofore almost unknown in the parks (except for petty theft), is now of such concern that many park rangers are provided firearms and training in their use.

. **United States Fish and Wildlife Service.** This agency has a number of responsibilities, including: endangered and threatened species; hunting; preservation of wetlands as natural habitats; and the protection, rearing and stocking of wildlife resources.

. **Drug Enforcement Administration (DEA).** This agency and the Federal Bureau of Investigation are undoubtedly the two best known federal enforcement agencies. DEA has its hands full investigating and enforcing the narcotics and controlled substances laws and regulations. DEA has wide enforcement powers. It maintains its own drug intelligence system, keeping records of users, pushers, and suppliers of narcotics, as well as licensed narcotics dealers.

. **Federal Bureau of Investigation (FBI).** The FBI has the responsibility for enforcing federal laws and the jurisdiction over federal criminal, civil, and domestic security (terrorist) violations. The FBI also provides support services such as fingerprint identification, laboratory services, and training for other law enforcement agencies. The FBI maintains the National Crime Information Center (NCIC). The FBI has enjoyed wide powers, but its reputation has suffered over the last few years with the confrontations at Ruby Ridge and Waco and the accusations that its vaunted laboratory has been less than perfect. Getting information from the FBI, even for bonafide law enforcement officers, is often difficult.

. **Immigration and Naturalization Service.** This agency administers and enforces laws relating to admission, deportation, and naturalization of aliens. INS maintains records on naturalization--names of witnesses to naturalization proceedings, accounts of deportation proceedings, financial statements of aliens, and details on persons sponsoring their entry. INS also maintains lists of passengers and crews on ships from foreign ports, passenger manifests, and declarations such as information pertaining to ship, date, and point of entry into the U.S. Within its framework is the U.S. Border Patrol--another agency all but overwhelmed by the numbers of attempted illegal entries along the borders of the United States.

. **Interpol--U.S. National Central Bureau.** The USNCB is the conduit to Interpol--it coordinates, collects, and transmits information regarding international investigations between U.S. federal, state and local law enforcement agencies and, through Interpol, with other countries. Information is of much the same variety as that in the NCIC; that is, information about missing persons, weapons traces, etc. USNCB is staffed by members of the federal law enforcement agencies, with representation from the DEA, U.S. Marshals Service, U.S. Secret Service, Internal Revenue Service, Customs Service, Bureau of Alcohol, Tobacco and Firearms, and others. As globalization spreads, Interpol becomes ever more important.

. **National Institute for Justice/National Criminal Justice Research Service.** This criminal justice information network funds some research projects and provides reams of information and statistics on a wide variety of crime-related and law enforcement subjects. It is "user-friendly" and can be reached by telephone, fax, e-mail, electronic bulletin board, and mail. Recommended is the free bimonthly publication listing books and publications on criminal justice. Accessibility through the Internet provides an opportunity to search the agency's archives. Custom searches are available for a fee.

. **U.S. Marshals Service.** This agency has the primary responsibility for providing security for federal courtrooms, federal judges, attorneys, and jurors. It also has the responsibility for guarding and transporting federal prisoners from their arrest to incarceration. There is a Special Operations Group which cooperates with other law enforcement agencies in cases of civil disturbance and terrorist incidents. This agency has become better known through two motion pictures, "The Fugitive" and "U.S. Marshals."

. **Department of State.** This very important department has the huge responsibility of advising, coordinating, supervising, and implementing U.S. foreign relations and for the protection of U.S. citizens and U.S. State Department workers outside the United States.

. **Bureau of Consular Affairs.** Issues passports and visas and maintains offices to advise and evaluate various matters.

. **Bureau of Diplomatic Security.** This office provides security and protective services for diplomatic personnel. It is heavily involved with counterterrorism planning and threat analysis programs. The Bureau publishes reports and statistics of terrorist incidents; it also issues State Department communiques to business people and tourists with information about security and safety conditions in foreign countries.

. **Department of the Treasury.** This department recommends economic, tax, financial, and fiscal policies and serves as the financial agent for the United States government. A mundane function is the manufacturing of coins and currency. A far more exciting aspect of the department is enforcing the law in certain areas.

. **Bureau of Alcohol, Tobacco and Firearms.** This agency keeps its personnel busy enforcing firearms and explosives laws. They have been in the news in recent years as part of the response teams investigating the World Trade Center and Oklahoma City bombings, and firearms caches hidden by some segments of the Freemen. BATF is also responsible for enforcing those laws relating to the production, use, and distribution of alcohol and tobacco. The criminal enforcement activities of the bureau are aimed at eliminating illegal possession and use of these products. Other important activities include overseeing compliance in the payment of taxes and revenues due from the alcohol and tobacco industries and the correct issuance of licensing and permits. BATF can trace any firearm (manufactured or imported after 1968) from manufacturer or importer to retailer. BATF keeps records of distillers, brewers, and persons or firms who manufacture or handle alcohol, as well as inventories of retail liquor dealers, names of suppliers, and names and records of bootleggers. It maintains complete lists of all federal firearms license holders and federal explosive license holders.

.   **Financial Crimes Enforcement Network.** This organization collects, analyzes and disseminates intelligence on financial crimes. As with several other federal organizations and agencies, FinCEN is staffed with personnel from a number of federal agencies including the Internal Revenue Service, U.S. Customs Service, U.S. Secret Service, Office of the Comptroller of the Currency, and several federal bank regulatory agencies. It is not an enforcement agency; its functions are focused on intelligence collection and analysis. It maintains a number of databases, including commercial databases, law enforcement and government databases. Future databases, now being developed, will add to the value of this important organization. At least one or more databases will focus on undercover money laundering investigations.

.   **U.S. Secret Service.** While the Secret Service is best known for its protective responsibilities for the President, Vice President, candidates for those offices, and family members, as well as other designated individuals, it also has the responsibility for counterfeiting and forgery investigations, computer access fraud, electronic funds transfer frauds, and like incidents.

.   **Environmental Protection Agency.** Regulates air, water, and noise pollution; responsible for cleanup of hazardous dumps; regulates disposal of waste in particular hazardous chemicals; regulates use of pesticides. This is a well-hated agency by those groups and individuals who wish to get rid of ALL government regulation.

All of these regulatory agencies maintain Internet websites. Depending upon your needs, you might find it useful to dial up these websites.

State Government

All state governments maintain records which contain very good information. In fact, these state government offices are often the first place that an experienced investigator looks for open information. Computerizing state government records has been a long process and, while much of the information is available to the public, it may not be *readily* available. Service varies from state to state and department to department. Also, the precise names of each state government department may be slightly different from state to state. State government databases include those maintained by:

.   Any regulatory agencies.
.   Law enforcement agencies.
.   Tax bodies.
.   Departments of highway safety.
.   The state court system.
.   Offices of vital statistics, etc.

Several states permit direct on-line access to their Department of Highway Safety database or the equivalent. Others may be accessed through vendors who have "batch" access, or by phone call or walk-in. Drivers' tracking systems may include the subjects' address, driver's license number, social security number, date of birth, physical description, and other data. Name and date of birth are usually a minimum requirement for querying the database. Some states, in particular the most populous ones, maintain excellent computerized files. Information contained in their databases will, at a minimum, usually contain fingerprint files, name files, summary case history files (rap sheets), and wanted and missing persons files.

Local Government Sources

City and county records, more so than state records, vary from locality to locality. In very small communities some government functions are combined. However, one will generally find the following:

.   **Assessor.** This person (usually County Assessor) appraises and sets a value on all real and personal property subject to taxation. Records, arranged either alphabetically or geographically or both, include the names of the legal owners, addresses, improvements made to the property, and date of last assessment.

.   **Auditor or Controller.** The chief local financial officer who authorizes government expenditures and maintains records of expenditures.

.   **Clerk-Recorder.** This is a key department within local government, with the highest (and usually most productive) records. These include: birth and death certificates, marriage licenses, passport applications, property deeds and titles, voter registration roles, and much more.

.   **Courts.** Documents on suits and judgments are open to the public and include information on bankruptcy, civil proceedings, divorce actions and child support hearings, estate filings and probate actions, credit judgements, and small claims.

.   **Fire.** Maintains records of fire inspections

and investigations of fires, and issues permits for use of explosives.

.   **Planning.** Responsible for development and implementation of master and other plans.

.   **Public Administrator.** Responsible for the administration of the estate of person who dies without apparent heirs. May be appointed by the court to serve as guardian for minors or elderly who are incompetent to manage their own affairs.

.   **Police.** Perhaps the preponderance of police work is done at a local level and, thus, perhaps the greatest concentration of records is initiated at local and municipal police and sheriff's departments. In general, information is "keyed" by the subject's name and includes date of birth; physical description; offense, circumstance or reason for contact; case number; and booking number if subject is arrested. Entries may include: wanted persons; missing persons; individuals having felony and/or misdemeanor records; operator license suspensions; persons on probation and parolees; arrest reports; and juvenile records.

Other files probably include accident and incident report files; identification and criminal history files; arrest files; and stolen and recovered vehicle files. In smaller communities, one might even find bicycle theft files and fraudulent check offenses files.

In larger metropolitan areas, intelligence files are maintained on organized crime operations, youth gangs, and subversive organizations

Almost all police agencies restrict the release of information to those persons, agencies, and organizations with a need for, and authorized to receive, the information.

.   **Public Works.** Issues building permits and enforces building codes.

.   **Redevelopment.** Urban renewal and housing programs.

.   **Social Services and Welfare.** Administers federal, state, and local welfare programs as well as funding for service agencies--drug and alcohol abuse treatment facilities, counseling centers, rape crisis centers, etc.

.   **Tax Collector.** Collects taxes and maintains records of payments made by companies and individuals.

Private and Public Databases

There are a number of public and private databases filled to overflowing with information. For the most part, the best public databases are found in libraries. Library databases offer access for searching periodicals, newspapers, and other media both by key word and by name (author or title). The InfoTrac system used by many libraries offers access to hundreds of journals and periodicals, to business indexes, to newswire releases, to major law reviews, and to full text reports by major investment research firms and covering thousands of companies.

Private libraries and their databases are to be found in corporations, many of whom employ full-time staff to maintain their collection; in colleges and universities; and within professional associations. These libraries, of course, may not be accessible to "outsiders."

Data collected and maintained by consumer groups, environmental groups, special financial interests, commercial database providers, and any other group who gathers, uses, or stores large amounts of data is usually available through one or more online vendors. There are hundreds of databases and to list all of them is beyond the scope of this manual; however, do not be intimidated, there is help. In some cases, several or many databases are offered as a packaged service by some vendors. **DIRECTORY OF ONLINE DATABASES**, publisher Gale Research, Inc., Detroit, MI, is accessed through **DIALOG**, an information retrieval service with several hundred databases in such areas as biographic, scientific, medical, and technical reports, business,

newspaper files, and professional journals. The **DIRECTORY OF ONLINE DATABASES** is also available in hardcopy form.

To work your way through the world of databases, be aware that there are various breakdowns. There are specialized networks and specialized services catering to a specific group of people. There are major online vendors, such as **DIALOG, NEXIS/LEXIS** and **COMPUSERVE** offering a "one-stop shopping" array of dozens or hundreds of databases. In addition, there are gateway vendors and information brokers. Gateway vendors can access online sources which might be prohibitively expensive if you were to pay the normal set-up and subscription fees and communications surcharges. Information brokers will do the entire search for you. If you are limited on time, expertise, and money, gateway vendors and information brokers are often the most cost-effective way to go. A good information broker has usually developed his and her network of sources and can extract the information much faster than the average computer-literate person.

Be aware that there are hundreds of proprietary databases, many of which are focused on specific areas of information. For example, **ENERGY DATA BASE** covers technical literature and patent information in the energy field. **FINDEX** locates market studies and research reports published by market research houses and Wall Street analysts. **MEDLINE** covers medical literature throughout the world.

Media Databases

The media has always been a valuable source of information. Reporters live and die (professionally) by their investigative and reporting skills. It was the media and those dogged reporters who were instrumental in effecting the Freedom of Information Act. Major newspapers and magazines are very well funded, wildly competitive, and ruthlessly flog their reporters to get the facts. There are several ways to piggyback on the information gathering skills of the media.

Excellent information is available either through the Internet or by subscription with one of the several media databases. The *New York Times* provides articles from its archives (only for the prior 365 days) of articles for a fee, as does the *Christian Science Monitor*, and can be accessed in minutes via the Internet. This service is also available from a number of prominent newspapers and magazines. A good subscriber database, the **NATIONAL NEWSPAPER INDEX** provides a complete index of the *Wall Street Journal, The New York Times,* and the *Christian Science Monitor.* **NEXIS**, one of the top database services, can provide full-text copies of articles from dozens of newspapers, magazines, newsletters, and wire services. Most newspaper libraries (formerly called "morgues") are now computerized and searches can be conducted by name, subject, or key word for articles about individuals, corporations, agencies, etc. These searches can be conducted by the newspaper or magazine librarian and, often, by the reference librarian of a good public library. Any fees charged are usually quite modest.

NEWSGRID is an on-line service specializing in key word searchable business-oriented news. The **BUSINESS WIRE** offers continuously updated information and press releases from hundreds of different companies. **JOURNAL GRAPHICS** is the largest producer of printed transcripts for television broadcasts, including such shows as: *Nightline, CBS 60 Minutes, Larry King Live, Frontline* etc. **BUSINESS DATELINE** provides articles from more than one hundred regional business publications in the U.S. and Canada.

As with all commercial databases, accessing any of those mentioned can become very pricey unless you define the information required, avoid information gluttony, and carefully interpret the search results.

Personal Records Proprietary Databases

Marquis Who's Who. A database of North American professionals. Information includes, as usual, name, date of birth, family, education, career history, civic/political activities, corporate and foundation board memberships, professional associations, and military history. If the individual being researched is of noteworthy position, this is a good source. There is a caveat, however -- almost all of the information provided is submitted by the subject him/herself and, thus, without verification, open to question.

Metronet (and others). These providers compile generic, inexpensive, superdatabases from telephone books, directories, mailing lists, voters' registration records, magazine subscriptions, Department of Motor Vehicles, etc. Their value is dependent upon their accuracy and *timeliness.* Searches by surname, if they do not find the subject, may lead to relatives. Searches can also be done by telephone number (to determine the name of the telephone owner) and by address. There are some limitations which include:

.   The subject must have a listed telephone number (unlisted numbers won't work).

.   Searches for common surnames (Jones, Smith, Davis, etc.) must be narrowed down, usually by the addition of a first name or initial and a considerable narrowing of the geographic area to be searched.

.   Females may not list a full name, preferring to list only a first initial.

National Change of Address (NCOA) database. This database is available to and marketed by vendors and so can be classified as a commercial database. The database can be accessed directly and instantly for a very small sum. One can also request from a vendor a magazine subscription forwarding address check. If the subject has failed to register a change of address with the post office for his mail (knowing that this information is readily available to the public), he may believe that changing the address on his magazine subscriptions will not be similarly available. However, magazines and mail order houses are notorious for selling their subscription and mail order lists to other vendors.

Credit Bureau Databases.

When a person applies for credit or a loan, he and she is asked to fill out an application. Depending upon the amount of money involved (such as a mortgage loan), very detailed information may be required. The credit grantor (bank, store, etc.) will then exchange information with the credit bureau. The credit grantor also updates the credit bureau as to outstanding loan balances, non-payments and late payments, and any collection problems with the borrower. Credit bureaus also collect public record information such as foreclosures, bankruptcy, press clippings of criminal convictions, change of name, and more. Credit bureau members are encouraged to report any negative information about their loan/credit grantees. At the same time, positive information is introduced to the credit bureau's files on a request basis. Information may also be updated and/or corrected upon request by the person whose information is on file. Credit bureaus are by no means infallible and a fairly alarming amount of false information is entered, usually by accident.

Credit bureau files contain only factual material of a non-discriminatory nature. No reference is made to race, religion, etc. These files usually include:

. name(s)
. marital status
. age
. current and previous places of residence
. current and previous places of employment
. estimated income
. paying habits
. outstanding credit obligations
. recommended credit limitations
. member experience with the account

While there are others out there, the most prominent providers of credit reports are: TRW, CBI Equifax, and Trans Union. Between them, just about every person in the United States has a record on file. Credit bureau searches are among the most common searches, because they reveal a plethora of information, much of which is *current*, an attribute not found in many other records.

TRW Credit Data Services is probably the largest in-file credit reporting agency. TRW handles, on a daily basis, hundreds of thousands of inquiries from banks, retailers, credit card companies, banks and financial institutions, and more. TRW **ACCU-SEARCH** allows expanded address searching as well as searching based on nicknames and aliases.

CBI/Equifax is the in-file credit-reporting arm of the Equifax Corp. of Atlanta. Equifax Canada is one of the four principal sectors of the company. Equifax Marketing Services supplies information about customer preferences, gleaned from mall-intercept research, focus groups, and telephone interviews.

Trans Union Credit Information Co. executives have boasted that their company has information on every adult in the U.S., including credit histories of 200 million Americans. Trans Union's **TRACE** program conducts searches based on social security number. Its **ATLAS** system locates people nationwide by address, telephone number, and inquiries to neighbors. **ATLAS** makes use of NYNEX **FASTRACK**, digital telephone directories, the U.S. Postal Service's Notification of Change of Address (NCOA) file, and the files of the circulation departments of magazines and direct mail marketing firms. Trans Union's **WATCH** service analyzes good credit accounts for indications that they may go bad.

INTELLIGENCE COLLECTION-- AN ONGOING ACTIVITY

Clearly, good intelligence collection cannot be done overnite, nor as a last-minute frenzied response to a threat. From Day One on the job, a protective agent must begin the task of collecting pertinent information, analyzing it, and maintaining and updating in-house files. It is an integral, important, often overlooked part of the agent's job.

The group responsible for ensuring the safety of a particular person (the protectee, also called the principal) is called the protective detail. The total number of protective detail members available for protectee duty is divided into groups based on their working hours. Each group (working shift) is headed by a senior person commonly known as the shift leader, who is responsible for the deployment of the detail members and ensuring that they are present as required, properly clothed and equipped. The shift leader reports to the detail leader, who has the overall responsibility for the safety of the protectee.

A protection team (the protective detail) has three primary day-to-day responsibilities: the duties of the security agents accompanying the protectee; operation of one or more command posts; and security advances.

The day-to-day responsibility of the working shift is to guard the protectee. These detail members are the ones who are seen by both the public and potential attackers. The sharper and more professional the detail looks, the less likelihood there is of an attack. When the attacker has a choice, history has shown he will usually select the easier (softer) target.

The protective detail operates under the protective philosophy of doing whatever needs to be done to avoid problems, using meticulous planning, and, whenever possible, taking *proactive/preventive* measures. If the proactive measures fail, the *reactive* measure of choice is to *cover and evacuate* the client. The last thing the agent wants is to find himself engaged in a blazing gun battle. Chasing bad guys and shooting them is the job of the police. Much of police work is reactive, quite different from the job of the executive protection agent. If enough preventive measures are taken, the threat will almost always diminish or go away. If the threat (adversary) persists

and, against all odds, creates a life-threatening situation, and the client cannot be safely evacuated, then the extreme reactive measures of defensive shooting, evasive driving, or whatever is needed must be taken.

PERSONNEL

The protective detail working shift, whether it is a one, two, or four-man team, is composed of those individuals whom you think of as the visible manifestations of protection; they are the people (perhaps) carrying guns, wearing sunglasses, and keeping a watchful eye on everyone.

What kind of individuals make good protective agents? In the past, bodyguards were often viewed as "muscle" and "bullet-blockers," and included gunslingers, karate experts, muscle-bound knuckle draggers, ex-prize fighters, and ex-football players. These individuals provided an intimidation quality and may have deterred the more timid adversaries, but they did not have a significant impact on the outcome of an armed attack by a dedicated adversary. In the majority of instances the bodyguards were all killed. The professional agent of today is proactive, placing his primary emphasis on preventing the attack from taking place, while continuing preparations to react in the event of an attack. It is this proactive strategy that separates the professional security agent from the muscle-bound "bullet-blockers" of the past.

What qualities, then, does a good protective agent possess?

Not surprisingly, intelligence and mature judgment are at the top of the list of desirable agent qualities. Every day on the job an agent must make judgmental decisions as to whether an apparently hazardous or dangerous situation is a coincidence or an ambush about to be sprung. The car which stops suddenly in the street in front of you and the strange car parked on the street two days in a row near the protectee's driveway are examples of the need for quick, enlightened decisions. The agent cannot see attackers hiding around every corner; nor can he or she fail to see the one person who represents a potential threat.

Mature judgement does not necessarily mean an older person; valuable life experience and common sense can be gained at a relatively young age.

The agent must have a high degree of initiative, self-confidence, and creativity. The successful protective agent has to be a take-charge problem solver who can "get it done," no matter what the circumstances are. There is always a considerable amount of work to do and rarely enough time in which to get it all done. Agents must necessarily be self-starters.

The ability to organize is another primary requirement for agents. Advance surveys are purely organizational exercises and are constructed out of a multitude of details. Certainly, the lone agent on a one-man team must be a super organizer in order to cover all of his (or her) bases.

The agent must be in good, sound physical condition. Long hours are routine in the executive protection business. Often the protective agent is the first person the protectee will see in the morning and the last person he or she sees at night. It is not necessary to be a world class athlete, but an agent should be generally fit and possess a healthy share of stamina. It simply doesn't work to call in sick, so the agent must maintain good eating, sleeping, and exercise habits to stay in top condition.

An agent is most successful when his or her appearance and demeanor blend with that of the person being protected. Whether the protectee wears casual clothing or business suits, the agent should conform to the protectee's attire at any given time.

This will necessarily require that the agent invest in a suitable wardrobe, and that he is meticulous in his personal grooming. The agent's demeanor, the way in which he conducts himself, will have a lot to do with success on the job. He or she must fit in with the protectee's work and social environments. This sometimes places an unusual demand on the agent, particularly one whose background is very different from the protectee's environment. Good manners and a knowledge of social behavior are necessary attributes; if these are lacking in the agent, he must make an effort to acquire them.

It is helpful if the agent has a good basic educational background, and agents should possess good communication skills. Communication skills are needed in interacting with the protectee and the protectee's family and associates and in dealing with other team members. An advance agent (one who conducts an advance) will need to procure information, set up arrangements, and often ask for special things to be done, all requiring good communication skills. Whether by education or experience, the agent should possess at least minimally good language skills in grammar, punctuation, and expression.

The agent should be a disciplined worker, attentive to detail. Coming to work with a clear head is a must and requires monitoring one's personal life. The protective agent is a far cry from James Bond and necessarily must put personal considerations aside while on duty. Patience is a required virtue, since nothing may happen for long periods of time. Clients are not always perfect ladies and gentlemen, and children can be taxing. Diplomacy and sensitivity are qualities which should be added to this list. They will be needed in large measure in dealing with clients, adoring fans, the media, and family members.

The agent must be a team player, ready and willing to take on post assignments and back up the other team members. He must be able to work well with different people in widely varied settings. Teams which are brought together for brief periods may never have worked together before. It is not always possible for all team members to like each other, but it is certainly possible to respect each other and to work together as professionals. Learning to work together in all kinds of situations is part of the "can do" philosophy. Sometimes it is necessary to work with other protective details, and this must be done smoothly and cooperatively. If two dignitaries, each with his own protective detail, are scheduled to appear at the same event, there must be willing coordination. Sharing information, and sometimes sharing posts, can make best use of manpower and avoid duplication of effort.

What is appropriate background experience for a protective agent? The ideal combination of experience would probably include one tour in the military to learn discipline and self-reliance, and a period of time spent in the federal law enforcement field in one of the major agencies to acquaint the individual with law enforcement procedures and to establish some of the contacts that he or she is going to need over the years as sources of information and assistance. Experience gained working in the uniformed division of the U.S. Secret Service is very valuable.

It should be emphasized, however, that these backgrounds are not necessary. Many very successful agents have no military or law enforcement background--indeed, many have come full-blown from other careers which added greatly to their usefulness. Experience with business, law, accounting, computer technology, construction, and electronics all give the agent useful skills which can be put to use on the job.

TRAINING

If in-house training is provided for members of the protective detail, it should include a number of subjects, and sufficient time should be devoted to the training for true acquisition of skills. Protective agents are made, not born. While a certain amount of on-the-job training can take place, classroom and simulation training are preferable. Just as one does not want one's surgeon learning on the job, one does not want his protection agent learning through his

mistakes. This could be fatal.

Identification of Adversaries and Threat Assessment. The trainee should be thoroughly briefed on any known, probable, and possible adversaries with profiles on their numbers, past actions, methodology, known capabilities, and specific techniques used. To sharpen the agent's powers of observation, he/she should be given surveillance training and exercises. Time should be spent learning how to gather intelligence data and how to put together a threat assessment.

Detail Organization and Operations. The organization and daily functions of the detail should be thoroughly explained. Each member of the team should be completely familiar with his or her responsibilities as well as those of all other personnel. Cross-training of agents is very important so that agents can function in a number of jobs. Rotating agents through the command post is an excellent idea. Intensive training should be given in positioning of agents in relation to the protectee (working the client), protective formations, and the immediate action to be taken in the event of any incident or emergency. Sufficient hours of practice should be devoted to this particular facet of training to assure that the appropriate responses are virtually automatic and need no thought or discussion.

First Respondent Medicine. Emergency medical care instruction should focus on those medical emergencies which are most likely to occur with a protectee. In particular, training should stress an understanding of the functioning of the body's respiratory and circulatory systems, heart attacks, bleeding, and shock. Agents should be able to diagnose the cause and effect of a problem and provide the most effective treatment. The goal should be that each agent is capable of keeping a mortally wounded protectee alive for at least ten to fifteen minutes.

It is highly recommended that serious executive protection agents take EMT (Emergency Medical Technician) training, currently about 80 to

100 hours. This area of expertise is so important that some companies pay a bonus to their agents who are EMT's. The probability of the agent becoming involved in a firefight is remote, but the potential for an agent's protectee hurting himself or having a heart attack is excellent.

Legal Aspects. Every agent should become familiar with and understand the civil and criminal laws and regulations which pertain to his job. He must know the extent of his authority and the liability he and/or his employer would incur if he acts negligently. He must certainly know the law regarding the carrying of a concealed weapon.

Physical Security. Agents should have a basic working knowledge of intrusion detection systems, bullet resistant materials, locks, barriers, and lights. The agent should have a sufficient knowledge of physical security to perform a basic survey, detect any weaknesses in the physical security, and contract for changes or upgrades to the system.

Communications and Electronic Security. All agents should be generally familiar with audio surveillance and countersurveillance techniques. Training should prepare the agent to be aware of how to prevent the implanting of surveillance devices, to be able to look for and detect them, and to nullify their effectiveness.

Defensive Driving Skills. Agents should be drilled in basic driving skills as well as defensive, evasive, and offensive driving techniques. Emphasis should be given to safe, careful, comfortable driving skills. Because of the high number of terrorist and criminal incidents which occur in an around the vehicle, sufficient time should be devoted to this area of training to insure that the agent is proficient.

Firearms and Defensive Shooting Skills. The duty of a protective detail is to cover and evacuate-- not to engage in gunfights. This has been, and will be, repeated many times in this book. It is not the job of the agent to chase and apprehend bad guys. And, if the detail is forced to stop in a well-planned ambush, they probably will not live long enough to return fire.

However, we live in an imperfect world, and the time may come when the agent(s) will need to use his or her weapon in a defensive posture. Therefore, sufficient time should be devoted to firearms training to ensure that each agent, if required, will be able to employ his or her weapon with maximum efficiency and without shooting himself, other detail members, or innocent bystanders.

Unarmed Control Techniques. This does not mean martial arts, although many techniques have been borrowed from the martial arts. Control techniques are simple, useful techniques which can be used in lieu of punching, kicking, or shooting an adversary. These techniques are humane, effective, and are not likely to put the agent into a liability posture.

Interpersonal and Social Skills. Good manners are important and, sadly, many people have never bothered to learn them. Even Fortune 500 corporate executives are going back to school to learn proper table manners, how to order a meal, how to introduce people properly, and a myriad of manners which constitute acceptable social behavior. Some otherwise highly qualified agents have not succeeded in executive protection because they were simply unattractive to be around.

It is very important that all phases of training be practiced on a regular basis and evaluated through realistic practical exercises. As with many professions, training and education is an ongoing process. There are a number of community colleges which offer courses in security or law enforcement. Several publishers specialize in books and manuals for private security.

EQUIPMENT

Equipment requirements for a protective detail include the equipment used by, and shared by, the entire team, and the equipment needed by each detail agent. Usually, though not always, the team equipment is provided by the protectee. For example, on a short-term assignment, all equipment might be provided by the protective team and its use charged to the client. A professional agent will usually accumulate high quality equipment for his own use (weapon, holster, belt, etc.)

Each agent on a detail should, whenever possible, be issued individually a two-way radio with microphone, earpiece, belt holster, weapons, and flashlights--unless, of course, the agent already possesses these items. The agent's personal equipment includes credentials, passport, immunization records, and credit cards, although a detail leader and advance man might be issued a credit card by the client to cover business expenses.

Radio. An agent's most valuable piece of equipment is the radio. Without it, his or her flexibility and general usefulness is greatly reduced. Effective communications means good radios operating unobtrusively at peak efficiency and clarity. This means that team personnel can talk to each other, between the client's vehicle and the advance man, between cars in motorcades, inside and outside buildings, and to and from the command post.

Good radios are expensive and are worth every penny. Reliability is the number one requirement, and the ability to get it fixed quickly anywhere when necessary is number two. It should have multi-channel capability; four channels are usually sufficient. Output power should be about five watts. Operating frequency band will depend on local regulations, but higher is usually better. Frequency allocations change from one country to another; check before going abroad to make certain you'll be able to use your standard frequencies.

The radio should be equipped with a detachable hand microphone and molded earpiece to accommodate indoor assignments. There are unobtrusive little mikes that fit in the hand and transceivers which plug into the ear. The wire can be worn under the shirt, strung down the arm, and taped

at the wrist to allow just enough slack for the mike to be cupped in the palm of the hand. If you see a good, professional team working, you will undoubtedly see an agent talking into his hand. The transceivers look like hearing aids, and the good ones are custom molded to the ear for a comfortable fit. Each agent should have a leather, metal, or plastic belt holster that will effectively secure the radio when he or she needs to run or be highly active.

Having an extra radio or radios is great. If it is a one-man operation, one radio can be given to the client and another loaned on a temporary basis to, say, a security guard or anyone reliable who can be brought into the operation, as needed.

Batteries are important. Detachable rechargeable batteries are the most cost effective over the long run; however, because of the logistics involved, the most convenient are the replaceable batteries. Because of the heavy use of the radio, spares should be carried. The built-in rechargeable batteries are not a good idea at all, since the radio is out of commission while the battery is being recharged. A problem with any rechargeable battery is determining whether the battery has been sufficiently recharged. Detachable rechargeable batteries are heavy. The most efficient, easiest to use battery is the replaceable battery.

Cellular Telephone. Another piece of communication equipment that is very useful is the cellular telephone, particularly for one-man operations. The lone agent, equipped with a cellular telephone, can use it to call ahead to double-check arrangements from the car. Inside the house, if something should go wrong with the regular telephone system (lines cut or knocked out by a power outage), the cellular phone is still operative. A cellular telephone is a must-have piece of equipment for a client safe room.

Flashlights. A homely but essential piece of agent equipment is a small flashlight. Agents working the late shift, particularly outdoors, need a flashlight that is small, light, easily carried, and powerful. The availability of very rugged miniature flashlights (sometimes referred to generically as "maglites") which can be carried in belt holders is a boon to the protective agent. These powerful little flashlights are affordable and easily available.

Weapons. Is there a best choice of handgun for executive protection? The answer is no--and yes. Experienced agents usually find, through trial and error, the handgun which best fits their purpose. There are excellent guns--revolvers and semiautomatics--produced by various manufacturers. However, in the final analysis, the issues of brand, magazine capacity, stocks, sights, and numerous fancy add-ons take a back seat to some basic considerations.

The first issue is reliability. If the gun does not perform, if it jams at the worst possible moment, every other feature is insignificant. If the weapon is overly sensitive to environmental conditions, it may be more trouble than it is worth--ditto for weapons which require constant maintenance.

It must be able to stop an assailant, which means that it must shoot ammunition that is sufficiently powerful to do the job, preferably with one or two shots. Your first shot is the one that counts. If your weapon is a little peashooter that only slows the assailant but does not put him down, you have a problem.

It must be accurate. Generally, if the weapon fulfills the other conditions, it can be engineered for accuracy.

It must be concealable and comfortable, which generally dictates carrying a small gun. Smaller guns are easier to conceal and are more comfortable since they produce less drag on a belt holster and have less tendency to poke and nudge the wearer.

Concealability is highly important since the agent wants to keep a low profile. The protectee (unless he is mafia or a drug dealer) does not want his friends and associates to think he is accompanied by

a gunslinger. If the agent is working within a corporation, the people with whom he will come in contact will not feel comfortable being around someone who is carrying a gun. And, of course, if the gun brings the agent to the attention of the police, even with a permit to carry concealed, the resulting hassles can be time-consuming and potentially embarrassing.

The best holsters are those that hold the weapon securely in a position where it can be readily grasped when needed and safely returned with one hand when danger has passed. High-ride, pancake style hip holsters are usually the best choice. Shoulder holsters are a poor choice and should not be used except by women, who may have few other suitable ways to carry a weapon concealed. Jackets have a way of opening and showing the weapon, and it is almost impossible to safely reholster a weapon in a shoulder holster with one hand.

Except for high risk situations, it is not usual that a protection team would need or carry a shoulder weapon. It is not likely that any police jurisdiction is going to allow a protection team to openly carry shoulder weapons on the streets. Shotgun barrels must be at least 18 inches long according to federal law. That, coupled with the federal mandate of minimum 26-inch overall length, makes a shotgun inconvenient to conceal for law abiding persons. Non-law abiding persons simply cut down the length of the barrel making it less inconvenient to carry on a sling beneath a coat.

Circumstances which might suggest enhanced firepower could include estate protection (patrolling the perimeter), and within the residence; i.e., on and within private property. Some teams carry shoulder weapons in the trunk of the vehicle, and some even insist on including 9mm submachine guns, theoretically because shoulder weapons are favored by terrorists. The reasoning is faulty in at least two ways. First, almost all 9mm ammunition will penetrate through bodies and walls, presenting a real danger to innocent bystanders. Second, if one has to hop out of the car and open the trunk to secure a shoulder weapon, the battle will be over and the bodyguards dead long before the weapons can be brought into play. There are exceptions to this and every rule, but the call for shoulder weapons should occur rarely, if ever.

However, if a shoulder weapon is required, a twelve-gauge pump action shotgun is an excellent weapon. Loaded with buckshot, it is intimidating and yet offers the minimum danger to innocent bystanders, particularly indoors. In reality, the shotgun is best utilized in a stationary position of cover, since the length of the weapon makes it difficult to use in confined places.

Credentials. There are several types of credentials which are useful to the executive protection agent. The first credential which every agent should procure and carry is a picture identification card. This is the equivalent to the badge which police officers carry and the identification carried by FBI and Secret Service. It gives the agent an aura of legitimacy and authority. Identification cards are valuable because they are expected by those with whom the agent is likely to come in contact. Not having some form of legitimate identification diminishes the agent's authority and authenticity and will limit his or her effectiveness. The card should contain:

.   a head and shoulder photograph, preferably in color.

.   the name of the issuing agency--either the employer company, government agency, or the agent's own self-owned company.

.   the agent's name and title.

.   descriptive information such as race, weight, height, and hair color.

.   the agent's social security number or other identifying number.

.   a sample of the agent's signature.

Often included on the identification card, either at the bottom or on the back, is a brief description of the agent's protective responsibilities together with a request for cooperation with his or her mission.

Identification cards can be made up by a printer, to order. Stores which cater to law enforcement sometimes have identification cards which are useful.

A second useful form of credential is a distinctive lapel pin. It is an unobtrusive form of identification for the wearer and may, additionally, permit the wearer access to restricted areas. It may also serve as an indicator that the wearer is armed. Obviously, for the lapel pin to serve its purpose, all law enforcement, security, and other individuals in positions of authority must be aware of the significance of the pin.

Lapel pins can either be designed and created in quantity for use by protective agents working for the same company, or they can be hastily assembled for a one-time assignment. On one assignment, impromptu pins were created by using fingernail polish to paint different colored stripes on upholstery tacks. One color indicated that the bearer was armed; another permitted free access to all areas; and other colors restricted the wearer to specific areas.

Every agent should obtain and maintain a current tourist passport and an up-to-date record of vaccinations. Government agencies typically issue their agents either official or diplomatic passports for international travel on official business. For overseas travel, some countries require visas for entry and exit into the country. Because of the time required to procure a passport, working agents should obtain it, even if they have no immediate use for it. It has happened on more than one occasion that agents were contacted to work on an overseas assignment NOW, and unfortunately, some of the best agents did not possess a passport and were not able to take the assignment.

There are a minimum number of vaccinations, such as yellow fever, which are required for entry into some countries. Other vaccinations, such as for cholera, diphtheria/tetanus, polio, and hepatitis, while not officially required, should be made a condition of employment. These diseases are extremely debilitating and are easily avoided with vaccinations. Regular booster shots will often maintain the agent's vaccinations.

There is extensive information about passports, visas, shot records, and travel documents in the chapter on Foreign Advances.

Credit Cards. Credit cards are essential to the protective agent because they provide immediate, extreme financial flexibility. Almost anything can be charged to a credit card including charter aircraft, boat rentals, limousines, entertainment, and guides, in addition to the more common billings for meals and lodging. It behooves the agent to use his cards frequently and pay in full promptly to build a good, high-maximum-limit credit availability. The best credit cards (those accepted just about everywhere in the world) are American Express, VISA, and Mastercard. American Express generally allows the most flexibility in charges and is considered somewhat more prestigious, while VISA and MasterCard are more widely accepted. U.S. petroleum company cards are usually not accepted abroad. Major automobile rental cards are accepted at almost all of the issuing companies' outlets worldwide.

On assignment with a permanent protective detail, one or more agents may be issued a company credit card for official use; however, agents should also carry their own personal credit cards. There might come a time when an agent would need every scrap of credit he or she could obtain to extract his client and his team from an emergency situation. The agent's "can do" persona and his ability to solve all problems includes the ability to pay for whatever is needed, immediately.

Other Equipment. Other useful equipment an agent may wish to bring along includes a multipurpose knife (such as a Swiss Army type) and a set of lock picks, if these can be obtained legally. Frequently, it becomes necessary to gain access to locked doors, cabinets, desks, and luggage that must be searched when time does not allow for locating the right maintenance person or secretary.

Detail Equipment

Detail equipment includes those items which are used by and shared by the detail agents. Depending upon the size of the team and the criticality of the assignment, detail equipment could be minimal or extensive. Any team, even a one-man team, should include at a minimum: medical equipment; fire extinguisher(s); communications equipment; command post equipment; and alarm system(s). For a full team working a high-profile, high-risk assignment, shoulder weapons and X-ray/metal detector equipment might well be included.

Medical Kit. An appropriate medical kit is essential for any detail. Some medical kits appear to be capable of sustaining a miniature hospital emergency center, but anything this elaborate is not generally needed or even particularly desirable. Attention should focus on equipment which could be used for those injuries most likely to occur with a protectee or agent.

Fire Extinguishers. Stationary fire extinguishers should be located within the protectee's residence and offices. Portable fire extinguishers should be available for each vehicle and the command post.

Communications Equipment. The most often required communications equipment includes: radios sufficient for all team members, plus one or two spares; command post radio base station; portable repeater; spare radio antenna; spare radio microphone and earpieces; cellular telephones; fax machine; spare batteries or battery charger(s); computer equipped with a fast modem; printer; and answering machine.

X-Ray and Metal Detectors. With a small,

low-risk, low-budget detail, there may be no dollars available for X-ray and/or metal detector equipment. However, if there is sufficient budget and sufficient risk to warrant the expenditure, this equipment is extremely effective in screening personnel, parcels, and baggage for possible explosives and/or firearms. The cabinet model fluoroscopes and walk-through metal detectors are particularly useful at access control points in office buildings or for use at special events where a high number of people must be screened quickly and efficiently. Portable fluoroscopes and handheld metal detectors, available from a number of suppliers, are best for a traveling detail.

Alarm Systems. Alarm systems of some kind will be required by a protective detail. Intrusion detection, smoke, and panic alarms are the sensors most likely to be of use. Alarm systems are usually permanently installed in the protectee's residence or office and are usually monitored either by the command post or by an outside service. Portable alarms are available which can be used in hotels and temporary residences.

A pocket panic alarm, usually a small radio transmitter, is small, unobtrusive, and very useful. The protectee can carry it in a pocket and place it by the bed at night. The alarm can be activated to summon help in an physical or medical emergency.

Fire and smoke alarms sensors can be linked with the command post either by wire in the case of a residence or office, or by radio frequency transmission from the protectee's hotel suite to the command post room. Portable smoke detectors are available and can be easily mounted by using foam tape.

Intrusion detection systems provide electronic protection at the residence or office. These systems vary widely in complexity and cost. The portable alarm systems are necessarily simple and basic, but are reasonably effective.

Audio Countermeasures Equipment. Audio countermeasures equipment has increasingly become an important addition to the protective detail's equipment list. This equipment varies considerably and can range from a basic kit assembled primarily with off-the-shelf components from Radio Shack to highly sophisticated and very expensive detection equipment.

Protectee Equipment. Armored vehicles are a consideration, depending upon the level of threat. Increasingly popular are armored four-wheel drive vehicles such as a Bronco or Cherokee, as opposed to the limousine. The smaller cars are easier to armor and cost less to do so. Their straight windshields save many, many dollars over the limousines with their curved windshields.

If the client will agree to wear it, a bullet-resistant vest can be obtained for use in high exposure conditions. Bullet-resistant briefcases are an option, but have limited applicability. There are other bullet-resistant garments (coat, cape, woman's slip) but the vest remains the most used of these protective garments. Some high visibility dignitaries have a bullet-resistant coat or cape which can be wrapped completely around the body and provide protection from some handguns. They are heavy and generally require someone to carry the garment.

Giving the protectee a radio to use is often a very good move. This, together with a panic alarm, a smoke alarm, and a door alarm are fairly standard for use when the protectee is staying in hotels. It gives him instant contact with the command post.

DETAIL OPERATIONS

A protective detail has several primary responsibilities on a day-to-day basis:

. Communication, administration, and organization of logistics.

. Command post operations.

. Protectee security ("working the protectee").

. Advances.

With a full protective detail, these responsibilities are shared by team members; however, with a one-man detail, the lone agent must accomplish all responsibilities single-handedly.

On the other hand, if the risk and budget are sufficient, a protective detail may be formed for each of several protectees. When multiple protectees travel together or base themselves from a common residence or office, their security should be coordinated from a single point. This is not only more economical, but provides less opportunity for dangerous confusion as to who is doing what.

The detail leader is the individual responsible for communicating with the client and team, for assigning responsibilities, and for organizing the logistics of the team. Typical logistical requirements include handling arrangements for food, lodging, and transportation for the detail and the protectee's party while on a trip, as well as transportation arrangements to and from meetings and events. The handling of these logistical responsibilities will have a direct effect on the ability of a detail to accomplish its mission.

Some protectees extend these basic responsibilities by asking the detail (or detail leader) to assist in purchasing and shipping goods, accompany family members and guests on shopping trips, accompany children and teenagers to and from school and on dates, procure amusements, and arrange for parties and special events. In unusual circumstances, agents have been asked to perform some fairly exotic chores. One agent assisted his protectee in purchasing large ranches and stocking them with cattle and horses. Another agent (a former chef), was required to stage elaborate dinner parties for his protectee and family.

The extent to which these responsibilities should be accommodated is an individual choice. Firms offering protective details for hire and individual, self-employed agents should carefully consider the advantages inherent in being viewed as accomplished logistical technicians. The reality is, very few agents or teams will ever save a protectee's life! If the team does its job efficiently and creatively, it will discourage the potential attacker. Therefore, a client who is not knowledgeable about executive protection may not see that his protective detail is accomplishing anything that is real and tangible. On the other hand, if the protectee views his agent as the person he can rely on to get things done, that agent's worth is proven every day.

As with so many other jobs, good administration and smooth organization may seem dull chores, but they are at the heart of the protective function. Shooting and evasive driving skills, while essential in an emergency, may never be needed during the life of a protective assignment, but handling of logistics will be needed every single day.

Financial Considerations

Whatever the size and configuration of the protection team, it cannot function without a significant flow of money. Money is needed to pay personnel, hotels, and restaurants, and for airline tickets, rental cars, limousines, gasoline, taxis, tips, and incidentals.

In the case of a government or large corporate detail, this money is paid out directly as salary checks, payments to the travel agents, car rental companies, etc. Only a relatively small portion is made available in cash to the detail.

A company providing executive protection will arrange for payment for personnel and expense funds through a written contract with the client. The contract should clearly state what charges will be allowed for reimbursement, expense estimates, per diems for agents, agent salaries or fees, and regular, timely payments of salaries and expense reimbursements. Whenever possible, a reasonable cash advance should be obtained from the client to cover at least one week's salaries for personnel, employee benefits, use of equipment, projected expenses for the client and team, and any significant logistical expenses (charter aircraft, etc.) If the protection company (or agent) does not secure a cash advance, it will find its cash flow requirements increasing enormously during the operation of the detail. Few executive protection companies can afford to "front" all salaries and expenses, then wait 30 to 60 days for reimbursement. Meticulous recordkeeping and careful invoice preparation are necessities.

Payroll represents a considerable expenditure. Salaries for agents are substantial, and, if agents accrue unscheduled overtime, this can contribute significantly to salary expense. With long-term, permanent details, some companies and agencies pay their detail agents an additional fixed percentage of their salary for unscheduled overtime. This saves a great deal of paperwork and recordkeeping.

Transportation can represent a considerable expense. If the protectee's itinerary is fixed and unchanging, the charges for airfares and rental cars can be easily handled by the protectee's organization. Often, however, the protectee's schedule becomes fluid. When that happens, the agent or detail leader may find himself charging considerable sums on his credit card for airline tickets, charter aircraft, and rental vehicles. This is one reason for maintaining credit cards with sufficiently high charge limits.

As noted earlier, the protectee can provide a card number to which all significant expenses are billed, or each detail member may be encouraged to apply for his own card with the understanding that any business-related charges will be promptly reimbursed. If it is a permanent or long-term detail, the employer usually picks up the annual card member fees. If the agent, detail leader, or executive protection company is routinely paying for expenses, it is extremely important that there is a clear agreement with the protectee for prompt reimbursement.

If the protectee provides a company credit card for use in paying expenses, careful records must be maintained and receipts furnished to provide an accounting of all charges to the card. All charges to the card should be authorized and business-related; at no time should any personal charges be made on the company card.

Detail Organization

In a large organization with full protection, a detail is comprised of a headquarters section and two or more squads of agents. The detail leader who has overall responsibility and authority, his deputy, and administrative and technical support personnel (if any) constitute the headquarters section. The teams of agents are called working shifts. The shift leader for each shift is the man or woman in charge and is responsible for the actions of the agents on his shift.

Every detail has certain administrative duties which it must fulfill. These can include: coordinating with the protectee, the protectee's family, and his working staff; planning and overseeing the daily protective functions; coordinating all logistical requirements; handling paperwork, such as expense reports, work schedules, etc.; and taking care of any other administrative requirements.

The protection activities, or jobs, which the agents perform can be categorized as "posts." Post assignments include surveillance posts, command post, checkpoints, drivers, and as visible close-in protection for the client. When the team is composed of one agent, that agent must, of course, attend to all responsibilities. Since one agent can only be in one place at one time, he or she must assign some duties to others. When needed, security guards and others can be used at checkpoints or for other duties.

With a low-risk situation, the protective detail may consist of anything from a one-man team to two, three, or four individuals. The detail leader is the person, overall, in charge, and the others are team members. If it is a four-person detail, it may be split into shifts, in which case there is a shift leader. The same administrative and daily working jobs must be performed--they are simply performed with fewer people.

A close working relationship with the protectee, with good interactive communication, is very important to the ongoing success of the protective detail. This is why it is essential that, from the very beginning of an assignment, the functions of the protective detail are fully understood by the protectee, his family, and working associates. Establishing this good working relationship requires diplomacy and patience.

The protective detail must interact with the protectee's staff on a positive basis. For example, the detail must be quickly informed of changes to the protectee's itinerary to avoid logistical disasters and potentially serious lapses in security. This is information generally known by secretaries and administrative assistants, if not by the protectee himself.

The detail leader should be the principal point of contact between the protectee and the detail. Problems are created when the protectee feels that any one member of the team can be used as a conduit and he will casually mention his plans to whichever agent is close at hand. This should (diplomatically) be discouraged. By serving as the principal point of contact, the detail leader can be certain that his detail speaks with one voice and that he is aware of the protectee's intentions at all times. This can not, of course, be an inflexible point of contention. The protectee must not be made to feel that he must always "go through channels" to communicate with his protective detail. Nurturing a good relationship and communications should be the responsibility of the detail leader, not the client. Therefore, clear communication must be established within the detail to make certain that all information flows up and down.

While it is desirable to establish a close working relationship with the client, the detail leader and all members of the team must take care to ensure that the relationship remains strictly professional. When the relationship becomes that of good buddy, best friend, lover, or conversely, servant, the effectiveness of the detail goes out the window. The

relationship should be, at all times, totally reliable and trustworthy, but non-emotional. A good visual description of this relationship can be seen in the film "The Bodyguard" which starred Kevin Costner. It is easy to see how personal emotions can derail the protection function.

Next to knowing of any threats to the client, the most important information to the protective detail is the client's itinerary. Once the protectee's anticipated daily schedule is known, the detail can make plans to meet the perceived security challenges and logistical requirements. Any changes to the client's daily routine must be factored into the detail's schedule of preparations.

Post assignments in and around the protectee's residence and office remain relatively unchanged on a day-to-day basis unless new information is received which causes changes to the normal routine.

Command Post

Command posts are either fixed and stationary (on an estate, or in the protectee's house, or office), or they are mobile. The protective detail's command post is the center of all information. The command post monitors all communications; keeps track of the whereabouts of the protectee and the protective detail; provides back-up for the working shift; and coordinates all logistics for the detail and supporting services.

An important part of communications is between the command post and the detail, noting when the protectee leaves and keeping track of when the detail should be calling in to advise of their arrival at some destination. If the command post personnel should fail to receive that call, they would have cause for concern. They would initiate an inquiry and, failing to receive a satisfactory answer, would immediately summon assistance.

The command post is used as the monitoring point for any intrusion detection or fire alarms installed in the protectee's residence, suite, or offices. The command post is also used to house various equipment needed by, and shared by, the detail. A command post log book is utilized primarily to keep a record of telephone calls, messengers, visitors and guests, and any unusual events.

Command posts vary in size and appointments, but generally are not elaborate. An office, spare room, studio, basement, or existing guard shack is often adequate. Hotel rooms are used as command posts when the protectee travels. The command post should be close to the protectee's residence or hotel suite, but not so close as to be an intrusion or annoyance to the protectee. Command posts should be completely secured.

Command posts are 24-hour business operations. Wherever it is located, the command post should be organized, efficient, and attentive to duty. These are not agent "lounges" where off-duty agents can congregate and gossip. The post should be kept clean and look good, so that the protectee and any visitor can stop by without embarrassment. If at all possible, the command post should have a bathroom for the protective personnel.

Since command post personnel cannot usually physically see what is happening, it is important to assign only seasoned staff to this post. Their experience will help them to visualize what is being described to them and anticipate its effect. It is a good idea, however, to rotate protective detail members through the command post, when possible, as cross training and a way of relieving job boredom.

To function efficiently a command post should have adequate equipment. The following suggested items should be considered.

.   A radio or some form of communication with the detail and the protectee. Spare batteries and/or battery recharger.

.   A telephone to communicate with police, fire, emergency, protectee's office, key contacts, and others. Also, one or more cellular telephones which can be used in the event of a power failure and which can be issued to team members for use in mobile assignments.

.   Typewriter (handy for typing envelopes and short notes).

.   Computer w/modem and printer, with Internet connections. (Actually, two different printers may be desirable, one for heavy print production and one that is portable and is used for limited copies.)

.   Fax machine and answering machine (some machines serve both functions).

.   Copy machine. (Note: most fax machines now have copy functions, but these are only useful for small copy jobs. A separate copy machine is needed; it is more cost-effective, for the production of numerous copies.)

.   Telephone numbers--emergency numbers, names of contacts.

.   Daily/weekly schedules for detail members.

.   Copies of primary and secondary routes to be used by the protectee and detail.

.   Intelligence reports.

.   Agent schedules and post assignments.

.   A log book.

.   Bulletin board and chalk board to post assignments, current information, schedules, routes, etc.

.   Office supplies.

.   Table or desk, and straight-back chairs.

. Extra keys (vehicles, house).

. Long cords for use between the telephone handset and the telephone body and between the telephone body and the wall.

. Medical kit.

. Extra weapons and ammunition.

. Fire extinguisher(s).

. Flashlights.

. Camera, preferably a Polaroid, that can take instant pictures. (Very useful for photographing suspicious looking individuals.)

. Smoke mask(s).

. Small tool kit with set of screwdrivers.

. Heavy duty grounded extension cords.

. Portable alarms and monitoring equipment (when traveling).

. Key block lock to secure hotel key-in-door lock from outside (when traveling).

Protective Formations

The standard formation used for close-in protectee security in protective details is composed of four people, and is called the "diamond formation." There will not always be the luxury of four people, but because in many ways it is the ideal number, it is the formation which is used when possible. When there are less than four people, some obvious formation adjustments must be made.

A few executive protection practitioners recommend the use of several different formations, including the "wedge," "box," and "circle," all of which require six to seven agents. They also use six

agents in the diamond formation. In reality, unless the threat is extremely high, one almost never sees these formations. There is no need for six or seven bodies and the danger of agents shooting each other or tripping over each other is fairly high. The cost would be prohibitive, and the logistics required to transport six or seven agents from Point A to Point B would be complicated. If the threat were sufficiently high to permit the use of numerous bodyguards, the extra agents could be put to better use in surveillance or at checkpoints.

Diamond Formation. The basic placement of agents around the protectee is the diamond formation. The diamond is formed by four agents and usually includes the detail leader and the shift leader. The detail leader almost always positions himself slightly to the rear on either the right or left flank of the protectee. The shift leader takes the opposite flank position. These two people work within an arm's length of the protectee--not so close as to crowd him, but able to reach him in one step. These two flanking positions are joined by a point man and a tail man who remain a few paces in front and to the rear, respectively, of the protectee.

Contrary to what you may have heretofore been told, the principal duty of agents accompanying the protectee is not to function as "bullet blockers." Their principal duty is *observation*. Each agent has his and her own sector of visual surveillance responsibility.

In a diamond formation, this sector is approximately 90 degrees. The point man is responsible for observing all that occurs directly in front of the protectee. The shift leader and the detail leader observe what is happening with the left and right sides while the tail person is concerned with what is happening to the rear. It should be emphasized that each agent should concern himself almost exclusively with his/her own sector of surveillance. In doing so, each agent must trust his team members to concern themselves with their sectors; otherwise, the system breaks down. If shift leader to the left rear of the protectee begins surveilling in front of him, he will lose track of what is occurring in his sector, and no one else on the team will be observing his sector.

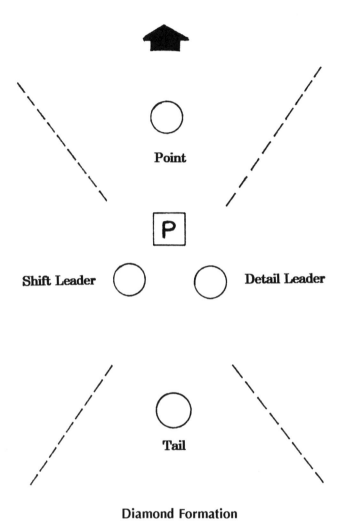

Diamond Formation

How far in advance should the point man be? That depends upon the perceived threat level and the density of the crowd. If there appears to be an immediate or imminent threat the detail closes around the protectee; if the crowd is dense, the same occurs so as to keep the crowd from getting between the detail members and the protectee. If the threat level is low, and/or the crowd is loose or nonexistent, the detail opens up and the point man may be as little as six feet or as much as 15 or 20 feet in front, surveilling the area. Historically, most of the ambushes occur in front, waiting for the protectee.

The point man's job is to identify any threat and signal (radio) this to the detail. If an actual problem develops, the point man is in a position to confront and, if necessary, engage the threat while the detail covers and evacuates the protectee. It should be noted that the Secret Service style is to keep the point man closer to the protectee; this is because they have the luxury of numerous bodies, some of which are in front, thereby leaving the point man back only six feet from the protectee.

Cover and Evacuate

In the event that a suspicious, unfriendly, or hostile act occurs, the agent observing the act alerts the others in clear plain language as to the nature and general location of the threat. For example, if the detail leader observed someone to the right pulling a gun from his coat, he would call out "gun right" or something similar. The agents closest to the protectee, usually but not always the shift and detail leaders, would immediately close in on the protectee, bend him over at the waist to reduce him as a target, cover the protectee with their own bodies (see illustration), and rapidly evacuate him away from the hazard. While these two agents are evacuating the protectee the remaining two agents must decide whether to assist in evacuating the protectee or engaging the threat. An agent within a pace or two of the adversary might attempt to block or disarm him. A worst-case scenario would be in facing an assailant who has a gun and is firing or attempting to fire it. If he presents an ongoing danger, one agent might be forced to engage him while permitting the other agents to evacuate the protectee. However, whenever possible, the primary responsibility should always be to get the protectee away from the threat, rather than getting involved in gunplay, fistfight, or confrontation.

Single Agent and Other Formations. If the team is composed of only one agent, he or she is usually best positioned slightly to one side and slightly to the rear of the protectee in the usual shift or detail leader position. This sole agent then has the responsibility for observation of all sectors. If a second agent is added to the team, he should take the point position. In the great majority of cases, attacks emanate from the front rather than the rear; therefore, it is critical to cover the front, then the sides, and last, the rear areas relating to the protectee. If a third agent is added to the team, he or she should take the unoccupied flank or tail position. And, of course, if a fourth agent is added, the formation is then completed.

Special Situations. The special situations in which the protectee may be involved are most likely to include banquet seating, receiving lines, and, with politicians, working the crowd along "fencelines." The diamond formation will not be useful in these situations; however, life is not perfect and these special situations call for creative accommodation of existing protective needs. There is no magic to the shape of a formation; its purpose is to prevent harm from coming to the protectee through surveillance (observation) and in covering and evacuating the protectee.

Banquet seating will usually physically separate the protectee from his team. The team will probably split up, with one person covering the area in back of the head table where the protectee is seated (if possible). Options for the other team members are: two agents covering both sides of the room and one agent seated in the banquet area maintaining eye contact with the protectee and the other agents; agents covering all doors into the banquet area, including the door from the kitchen and no one seated in the banquet area; any combination of the above which fits the situation. Placement of agents will depend upon the size of the detail, the layout and configuration of the room, access control, screening of employees, and inclusion of non-team members at doors (uniformed personnel, event sponsors, etc.)

If the protectee is a politician, or perhaps a celebrity, he or she will seek out handshake opportunities in order to "reach out and touch" his or her constituents and fans. These opportunities are most likely to involve a receiving line or fence line crowd. It will almost never be possible to position an agent directly between the protectee and the crowd or guests.

On the contrary, the protectee wishes to be perceived as approachable. Therefore, the team must concentrate on ensuring that all individuals approaching, leaving, or already in the immediate vicinity of the protectee are under careful observation. Why only the immediate vicinity? Almost all attacks in public places take place close to the target. The sheer number of bodies will usually prevent an attacker standing far back in the crowd from getting a clear shot at the protectee, much less a knife attack. A sniper attack is possible, but not likely.

In addition to the possible danger of an attack is the much higher probability of a determined or overenthusiastic person who wishes to hang onto the protectee and refuses to turn loose his hand.

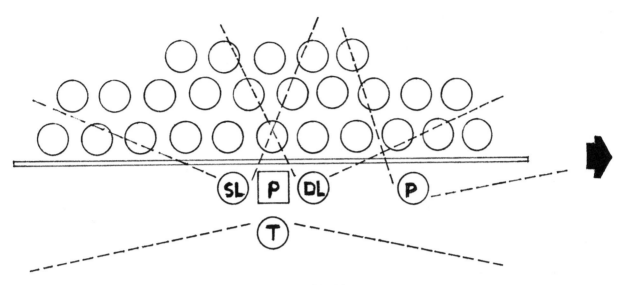

Fenceline and Agent Positions

Often, these individuals hope to have their picture taken with the protectee. The agent closest to the protectee should be alert for this and be prepared to disengage the protectee from the handshake when the protectee indicates that he wishes to move on. A polite "Excuse me," accompanied by quick, minimal pressure to the individual's hand will usually work.

In a receiving line the conditions are more easily controlled, as guests approach in single fashion, making it possible to carefully watch hand movements. The receiving line occasion is such that guests are usually screened and, additionally, an event sponsor or staffer will almost always be at hand to identify guests to the protectee.

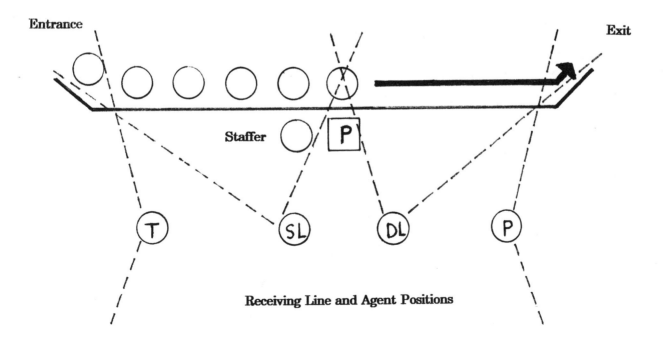

Receiving Line and Agent Positions

Stairs. With a detail and the protectee going up stairs, the point man should quickly go up the stairs, look around, and signal the detail to proceed up. As soon as the point moves out and up, the shift leader moves up and in front of the protectee, and the detail then proceeds up the stairs. Once at the top of the stairs, the detail can re-form.

Elevators. The drill for the detail and the protectee to take an elevator is for the point man to move up front and ring for the elevator. When the elevator doors open, he looks inside, and if it looks secure he enters, and the detail and protectee follow with two members of the detail standing in front. If, however, when the elevator door first opens, it does not look secure, the detail does not enter, but rings for another elevator.

ADVANCE WORK

When a trip to any location is planned, an advance survey (called an advance) should be made of the location site. The agent who performs the survey is referred to as the advance agent. The advance survey is one of the most important functions of the protective detail. A meticulously executed advance will reveal potential problems and will plan solutions. Because of the importance of this element of protective work, two chapters have been devoted to advances.

POST ASSIGNMENTS

Preparation of post assignment schedules is usually the responsibility of the detail leader. In very large details, this might be handled by a security operations person who coordinates with other (non-security) personnel for inclusion in the overall schedule. Schedules include, and are often based upon, information received in the survey received from the advance agent.

A fixed post assignment schedule should include specific information about the following:

Location and/or description of the post.

. Name of the post stander (for each post) and his post hours (when he is to report and when he is relieved).

. Agent's attire and identification to be used, who is permitted access and to which specific areas, reporting procedures, and emergency measures to be taken.

Scheduling is one of the administrative chores which enable the protective detail to operate smoothly, without hitches. Every member of the team should be aware of the entire schedule, as well as his/her own scheduled responsibility. At the same time, it should be recognized that schedules can change, often abruptly. Therefore, each detail member should regularly check in with the command post and/or the detail or shift leader to become aware of changes. Each team member must be reachable by telephone or beeper within a short period of time in the event that the detail leader or anyone else needs to locate him.

Examples of two types of schedules can be found at the end of this chapter.

CONTRACTUAL PERSONNEL

Outside the federal governments of various countries, the mafia, and highly successful drug dealers, there is never enough money to employ and maintain a sufficiently large protective staff to meet every circumstance. Reality is that the protective detail--one to several agents--must, on occasion, be supplemented by bringing in outside protection staff. There are some choices.

A known, or well-recommended outside protection agent (or agents) can be brought in for short-term assistance. This is an expensive option but can be worth its weight in gold if solid, tested expertise is required for a short period.

Off-duty police officers may be a good option. These individuals know the territory, have a "license to carry" should this be necessary, are networked into the law enforcement community, and are familiar with the local and state legal issues. They have received at least some, often extensive, training. They generally make excellent drivers and are equally useful for perimeter assignments. The disadvantage is in their conflict of interest. In an emergency, will they cover and evacuate the protectee, or will they engage in a pursuit and shoot-out of the bad guys? What are their sworn responsibilities?

Another choice is a well-recommended and reliable security guard service. These are the people who can maintain remote guard posts, perimeter control, and airport security, and who can assist with access control. This is usually one of the more cost-effective ways of maintaining low-risk security.

Yet another option is an executive protection firm. If this option is exercised, the firm should be chosen carefully--not simply from the Yellow Pages, unless, of course, this is a last-ditch emergency effort. This is one of the best examples of why protective agents should maintain an active network of fellow practitioners. But, let us assume for the moment all else has failed. You dial the executive protection firm. What are you looking for? What are your requirements? How do you qualify them?

Do not be fooled by glossy brochures and advertisements. The firm may be headed by a qualified individual, but what about the worker bees? Are they qualified? If time permits, ask for a client list and call these people. Were they satisfied? Were there problems?

Ask for evidence of the firm's license, liability insurance, license to carry firearms, etc.

Ask for specific information as to what services will be provided, who will provide them, a background of the individual (or individuals) who will provide them, and details on this (these) individual(s). Check the information with the local law enforcement authorities. Has the individual a clean record? Is the firm in good "odor" with the local law enforcement?

Examine the contract with a minute eye--look for hidden charges--make certain who is responsible for providing security equipment.

Try, whenever possible, to have the outside security personnel responsible to, and under the command of, the in-house security team.

COUNTERSURVEILLANCE

It has been proven many times that even the most efficient protection team cannot always deter a determined, well organized opponent. In a high risk situation it is safe to assume that the protectee and his team may be under surveillance by adversaries. One strategy is to assign a member of the protection team to perform in an undercover role; that is, outside the team formation. This agent's job would be to follow the protectee and team, observing them and, more importantly, observing any suspicious activity around them. His job, then, would be countersurveillance. By staying on the outer fringes and mingling with the crowd, he would have at least a chance to spot any suspicious persons and/or activities. This agent would also have the responsibility of focusing on the vehicles and individuals normally in the vicinity.

A number of protection teams are employing this strategy.

-POST-

Montclair Resort Hotel, Kansas City, MO

Post #   Area and Responsibilities

1   Checkpoint post in hallway immediately outside door of command post located in room #515. Protectee is housed in suite #505, two doors down and west of the command post. Members of the protectee's party occupy rooms #504 and #506. The command post checkpoint is between the protectee's suite and the bank of elevators. The responsibilities of this post are: to deny entry to unauthorized personnel to the protectee's suite, as well as rooms #504 and #506; and, if needed, to evacuate protectee (and members of his party if possible) to safety.

                 Other hotel guests are located on the same floor as the protectee and have free access to their rooms. Hotel personnel on duty are also free to access hotel rooms not occupied by the protectee's party. Only hotel personnel wearing a red identification badge are allowed to access the protectee's suite and rooms #504 and #506. Anyone attempting to access the protectee's suite, and who is not previously identified or expected, should be asked to wait in the command post until the protectee can be contacted for permission. Should an evacuation become necessary, the post stander will quickly escort the protectee (and members of his party if possible) to the west stairwell, and from there evacuation will be continued to the lobby. If the west stairwell is blocked, evacuation will take place via the east stairwell.

2   Command post located in room #515. The primary responsibility of the command post is to maintain constant contact with the protectee, the protectee's party and the protective detail. The command post will be staffed around the clock, for the two days/nights of the visit.

3   Close-in protective assignment with protectee, performing advance surveys and accompanying protectee to and from visitation sites, primarily Board of Directors meeting at XYZ Co.

                 Agents on post duty are to wear business attire at all times. All shifts will be twelve hours. Post stander on post #1 will check in with command post every thirty minutes. Post stander on post #3 will check in with command post upon departure and arrival. Meals for command post will be taken in the command post. Meals for hallway post stander will be taken just inside the command post. Benson will handle the combined command post and hallway check post between 2000 and 0800. All post standers will report to their post ten minutes early to receive information and briefings.

DAILY ASSIGNMENT SCHEDULE

#1--Hallway

Jones   0800-2000
Benson 2000-0800

#2--Command Post

Dawson   0800-2000
Benson   2000-0800

#3--Protectee

Perry   Variable, dependent on protectee

A schedule made for a traveling detail will be more fluid and narrative in style. The following schedule reflects a visit by the protectee to Denver, where he will attend the Annual Meeting of the Shareholders for the Nuclear Corporation of America. This corporation has received a number of threats, because of its nuclear activities, and because of its involvement with the much-maligned Rocky Mountain Nuclear Arms Plant.

VISIT OF MR. BRONSTEIN TO DENVER
ANNUAL MEETING OF THE SHAREHOLDERS
NUCLEAR CORPORATION OF AMERICA

Feb.2

2200   Advance agent Sinclair proceeds to Stapleton Airport in grey Ford rental vehicle to meet arriving flight UA-2035 and picks up arriving agents Barber and Denton. Agents collect two rental vehicles (black Lincoln Continental for protectee and blue Plymouth station wagon for lead car) from Avis (303-629-1515). Agents will proceed to Red Lion Inn at Quebec and Martin Luther King Boulevard (303-629-8890) where they will spend the night.

Feb.3

0715   Advance agent Sinclair will proceed to Nuclear Corporation of America, at Rocky Flats (303-889-1868). Sinclair will double check the security arrangements, placement of security guards at the gates, and will conduct a sweep within the meeting area for surveillance detection and bombs.

0830   Agents Barber and Denton arrive at Stapleton Airport and prepare for arrival of Mr. Bronstein and detail leader Duggan, scheduled to arrive at 0915 on UA-380. Airport contact is United Airline Service Representative Mary Browning (303-629-3366).

0910   Duggan, Barber and Denton depart airport with Mr. Bronstein and proceed to Nuclear Corporation of America, using Route A. Route B is alternate. Hospital closest to airport is Swedish Medical on South Colorado Boulevard (see map), and hospital closest to Nuclear Corporation (28 miles west) is Denver General Hospital on Speer Boulevard.

1400   Duggan, Sinclair, Barber, and Denton depart Nuclear Corporation with Mr. Bronstein and proceed to Stapleton Airport, in three rental cars. Duggan accompanies Mr. Bronstein inside the airport to United Red Carpet Club. Sinclair, Barber, and Denton return rental vehicles, then join Duggan and Mr. Bronstein for return flight UA 992.

Vehicles:

Advances and follow-up	Gray Ford, Driver Sinclair
Lead car	Blue Plymouth station wagon, Driver Barber
Client car	Black Lincoln Continental, Driver Denton

ADVANCES

When a protectee makes a trip of any duration, either to another city, overseas, a restaurant, or a meeting, it is highly desirable for an agent to travel to the site in advance of the protectee. Advance security survey, or simply "advance," is the term used to describe the procedures and actions undertaken by the agent(s) in making the necessary logistical and security arrangements for the client's trip. Note that the advance serves two purposes: it makes certain that all of the logistical details are prepared and checked to ensure a smooth, hassle-free trip; and it makes certain that all security arrangements are made for the protection of the protectee and his party.

Since the primary goal of an advance is to minimize risk, a well executed, meticulously detailed advance will have a direct bearing on the probability of avoiding or surviving an attack. Conversely, trips taken without the benefit of an advance or with a sloppy advance are invitations to disaster. Many experienced executive protection agents, those who have been most successful in the business, consider advances to be the most important aspect of executive protection.

An advance will cover arrangements for travel, lodging, meals, vehicles, meetings, and special events. It includes liaison with local law enforcement and security, emergency services, and will decide on routes of travel. The advance must also include security and logistical arrangements for the other protective detail agents.

Because every advance is unique, not every imaginable situation has been covered in this book. However, the principles are the same regardless of where the advance takes place and the nature of the event being advanced.

The thoroughness of the advance is dependent on several factors, among them: the perceived threat level, the number of bodies available to do the advance, and the time allotted for the advance. If it is a one-man operation, the advance may be accomplished by that one agent, or it may be contracted out to someone in the business who performs the advance for him. Let us say that Client A wants to go from his home base in Long Island, New York for a one-day visit to Los Angeles. Client A has one agent for protection. The agent can do several things. He can make a number of telephone calls and collect as much information as possible in advance. He can jump on a plane and make a fast 24-hour advance to Los Angeles, and perhaps in his absence bring in a networking professional to take his place with the client while he is gone. Or, he can call a professional agent in the Los Angeles area, give him or her the client's itinerary, and contract with that agent to perform the advance. It helps if the two agents have worked together in the past, and perform advances in a similar manner.

If the protectee has a protective detail of two or more individuals working for him, one of the agents can be sent ahead to do the advance. Good advance men and women are detail-oriented and meticulous in their planning. Some agents specialize in doing advance work, smoothing the way, working out the details in advance, and planning against any and all foreseeable contingencies. A well-done advance reduces the risk of attack, intentional or unintentional, to an acceptably low level. Obviously, in a high-threat situation, the manpower and time allocated to the advance should be increased.

Sometimes, advances must be done almost in a matter of minutes. For example, the protectee's wife convinces him at 5:00 p.m. that she would really like to get out of the house and have dinner at the newly opened Vietnamese restaurant in the Asian quarter of the city. They agree that they will change clothes, have a drink, and leave for the restaurant at 7:00 p.m. If there is only one agent, and he has the time, he may have to drive quickly to the restaurant, do a quick advance of the seating arrangements, exits, and parking, and be back by 7:00 p.m. to drive Mr. and Mrs. Protectee to the site. The agent may not even have that luxury; he may have to drive Mr. and Mrs. Protectee to the restaurant, go first into the restaurant for a quick look-around, seat Mr. and Mrs. Protectee in a protected area in the bar, and do a five-minute advance to locate restrooms, exits, and the best available seating from a protection standpoint. Is this good enough? In all probability, yes. The client decided only two hours in advance that he was going to that particular restaurant, making it almost impossible for an adversary to plan in advance for an attack.

On the other hand, advances can be highly complex and can require a day or several days to complete. If the client is a controversial figure who is going to the Philippines to speak at a convention of 2,000 people, and who then intends to travel on to meet with some business associates in Russia to investigate new market areas, the advance work will be lengthy, complicated by language and cultural difficulties, and fraught with some risk potential. It is to be hoped in such a case, that the client has a protective detail working with him, and that one member of the team can be sent ahead to make all of the advance arrangements.

Advances can be expensive even under the best of circumstances; thus, every effort must be made to hold costs down. From the get-go, a budget should be put together and reviewed to make certain that, while important items are covered, there are no unnecessary or simply "nice-to-have" expenditures included.

PRE-DEPARTURE PREPARATIONS

The advance work begins before the advance agent leaves his base of operation. The agent needs to collect information and make certain preliminary arrangements.

The first step is to put together a preliminary threat assessment based on the locales to be visited, the conditions in those locales, and the purpose of the visit. If the client is this country's most prominent and controversial advocate of women's rights to abortion on demand, and the trip is being planned for the city of Boston with its high population of Irish Catholics, the threat assessment may be very different from one done for a trip to San Francisco, where abortion is not the hot issue. On the other hand, if the trip is low level, say a ski vacation to Vail, Colorado, and there have been no threats to the client, the threat assessment can be done very quickly.

The agent's second step is to gather and review documentation: reports, floor diagrams, maps, etc. from any prior advance done at the location to be visited. Advances should be meticulously recorded and important data kept for future use. Keeping a log is an excellent idea. Maps, floor plans, names of contacts, telephone numbers, special problems, and client preferences--the wealth of information that is accumulated during an advance and subsequent visit--can be of enormous help in planning other advances or in returning to the same site. For example, if the client's party stays at the InterContinental Hotel in the site city, and the Resident Manager was unusually helpful, a call to him (or her) might smooth the way for a visit to another InterContinental Hotel in a different city.

This is a good time to state that, after the visit is completed, thank-you letters and letters of commendation (for services provided) should be promptly sent to all the individuals who have helped the protection team. A letter to the General Manager of the hotel, praising his facilities and the helpfulness of his staff, in particular the Resident Manager, Mr. ....., is worth gold to the recipients, is helpful toward gaining a promotion for them, wins everlasting appreciation, and assures future help.

When this background information has been assembled, the advance agent should concentrate on ensuring that he has correct and complete information concerning the upcoming event. If it is a short-term protective assignment, the agent or protective detail leader must obtain the information one way or another, either from the client or a knowledgeable associate of the client.

Pre-Departure Information.

This should include as much of the following information as possible.

. Location(s) and site(s) to be visited, the dates of the visit, and an itinerary. The itinerary will indicate the local sites to be visited, the people visited, and any special events.

. Names, titles, and description of the protectee(s) and other members of the party. (If this is a one-time assignment, the advance agent may never have met the protectee.) In large delegations, there is always the problem of protocol which dictates where to room the various members of the group, in order of rank. This must be clearly indicated to the advance agent before he/she leaves.

. Transportation arrangements for getting the protectee and party to the locale/site. Have transportation reservations been made? How is the billing being handled?

. Name and address of the residence or hotel the protectee and party will use. Have reservations and billing arrangements been made? What are the arrangements?

. Type of local transportation to be used at the site; i.e., rental cars, limousines, etc. Have reservations and billing arrangements been made?

. Amount of baggage which will accompany the party. Will this require special handling? Will all bags be coded to indicate owners? Once at the arrival site, baggage must be correctly delivered to rooms, and coding and identification will be crucial.

. Any special requirements of the protectee and party; i.e., special diets, room with a view, king-size beds, separate room for spouse, special diets, etc.

. Protectee's known medical problems and medical requirements, including prescription drugs. Are extra quantities of prescription drugs being brought, or will these need to be procured at the visitation locale?

. Transportation and billing arrangements for the advance agent and the protective detail.

. Housing arrangements for the advance agent and the protective detail. Have reservations and billing arrangements been made? How many protective detail agents are authorized per hotel room?

. Budget authorization. Although this is not normally a function of the advance agent, the advance agent may also be the man-in-charge. If so, he needs to know whether he can hire extra people on site or rent radios, and how to deal with other types of miscellaneous expenses authorized for the protective detail, such as tips, meals away from the hotel, etc.

. Special dress requirements which will involve the protective detail (black tie, beach, ski attire, etc.)

. Billing arrangements for any other significant expenses.

. If going out of the country, will an interpreter be necessary? Will a local driver be needed to facilitate getting around the city/country?

. Transportation and customs requirements for any special protective equipment (alarm kit, radios, weapons) required by the protective detail.

. Will local part-time security personnel be needed? Are there other anticipated protective detail requirements?

. List of key contacts, with telephone numbers. This could include business associates, company employees, law enforcement contacts, U.S. State Department, friends, professional contacts.

Preliminary Telephone Contacts

The advance agent needs to make some important telephone calls before he leaves. Contact should be made with the following sufficiently in advance to be effective:

. The protectee's local contact at the site to be visited, either a company contact or the host, to advise them of the advance agent's arrival time, itinerary, and any assistance required.

. The hotel, to insure reservations for the advance agent, plus reconfirming the reservations for the client and his party.

. The auto and/or limousine rental agencies, if rental vehicles are required, for the advance agent and the client's party.

. Any local law enforcement or intelligence agencies as suggested by the detail leader, and any federal or state authorities if this is appropriate. In lieu of direct contact, a call should be made to the agent's local law enforcement contact, asking for an introduction to law enforcement officials in the host city.

. The travel agency being used to arrange transportation for the protectee and party. All travel arrangements should be reviewed and confirmed. If the protectee is to travel by private, charter, or corporate aircraft, the captain and crew must be contacted to determine certain information. The advance agent will need to know the following details in order to check on the arrival of the protectee and party.

. Departure and arrival times.

. Type of aircraft, owner, call signs and tail number.

. The FBO (Fixed Base Operator) at the departure and arrival sites, with their telephone numbers.

. Any logistical details such as, will ramp steps be required for the aircraft? Are they available at departure and arrival sites? Will additional cabin crew be required?

. Storage location for the aircraft at the visit FBO. Is security adequate?

. Alternate arrival site in case weather conditions make it impossible to land the aircraft.

. Any special requirements by client for meals, beverages, etc.

ARRIVAL AT THE SITE/CITY OF THE VISIT

Upon arrival at the visit site/city, the advance agent should go to work immediately, beginning with the airport. He/she needs to observe the general layout of the airport. How good is the security? Are there problems? Are there adequate emergency services within the airport complex? Will it require unloading and processing the client in a special place? How is the baggage handled? Who is the Airline Service Representative? This is the person who will be of invaluable help in making special arrangements for seating the protectee, loading baggage, and maintaining good security.

The advance agent will need to obtain a good map of the area and orient himself in terms of important reference points such as the airport, residence or hotel, downtown area, hospitals, police station, and touristic points of interest. The advance agent will be the key person in orienting the protective detail as to the physical layout of the visit site. Since the best-laid plans can go astray, the advance agent must be fully aware of the physical characteristics and major routes of the visit site/locale.

The agent should proceed to pick up the rental car which he will use during his advance. At the same time, he should reconfirm reservations for additional rental vehicle(s) for the protectee and party and the protective detail. Any special requirements should be discussed and made sure they are clearly understood and will be available. Billing arrangements should be reconfirmed.

Using his city map, the agent should drive to the hotel, observing traffic and road conditions and making notes regarding the general topography and prominent landmarks. A bit later in the advance, the agent will need to map out primary and secondary routes to and from sites. The route from the airport to the hotel offers the opportunity for a general reconnoitering of the area.

The agent will continue to the hotel and check in. He/she should make notes regarding the parking areas, lobby configuration, elevator locations, areas of congestion, restaurant locations, emergency exits, visible security, and other items of interest. Somewhat later, after meeting with the hotel Director of Security, the agent will have an opportunity to do a walk-through of the hotel.

Immediately after checking in, the agent should telephone the home office to notify the detail leader of his arrival, telephone number, and room number. If there are any last-minute changes in the site, itinerary, or arrangements, they can be relayed to the agent at this time. Any items of particular interest noted by the agent can, in turn, be related to the detail leader. For example, if the advance agent has noted any significant security problems, this may require a re-deployment of agents scheduled to travel with the protectee.

If there is a host, sponsor, or other specific contact, the agent should call those individuals to notify them that he/she has arrived, and to make any appointments to meet with them.

Whenever possible, it is desirable to bring local law enforcement into advance preparations. This is somewhat dependent upon such factors as the identity of the protectee(s), the protectee's need for anonymity, and the need for local intelligence information. Local law enforcement officials can be very useful to the advance agent in providing (or reviewing) intelligence, assistance in selecting routes, and as a source of part-time help. The advance agent

should remember that he is asking for, and is not in a position to demand, assistance. He should not expect the local sheriff or police chief to do his job for him. Best results are obtained when he arrives at the Chief's office with most of his questions already answered, seeking only the Chief's review and comments on his plan.

The advance agent must always consider the advantages and the disadvantages of revealing a protectee's identify and/or plans. Unless a protectee is very recognizable or his visit has been made public, it is usually advisable to do as complete an advance as possible while not jeopardizing protectee anonymity and itinerary plans.

HOTELS

At the host hotel, the initial contact should be made, if possible, with the General Manager or Resident Manager. Every effort should be made to get to the highest authority, because there are certain things which need to be done and which can only be done with the cooperation of the hotel hierarchy. As with all organizations, and perhaps in hotel hierarchies even more so, there is a status quo. Employees in hotels know what they are expected to do in terms of providing service to their customers, and they can even handle a few minor special requests, but they have no authority either at the worker or mid-supervisory level to handle major special requests. This authority is reserved to the General Manager or, in his absence, the Resident Manager. The Resident Manager is the number two person in the chain of command. This is the person that the agent wants on his side, and it is usually fairly easy to accomplish this.

Hotels are operated on the premise that they provide a safe, comfortable environment for the traveler. The last thing that a hotel wants is an incident, and if the agent's requests are presented from a security viewpoint, there is every likelihood that the hotel will wish to cooperate. Hotel operators have become far more security-conscious in the past few years, having learned the hard way. In the 1980's, there were devastating fires (Las Vegas MGM

Grand and Hilton Hotels, Stouffers, etc.), and there was a marked increase in violent crime within many hotels, including assaults, rapes, and murders. The resulting litigation and lawsuits brought a higher awareness of the hotel's responsibility for the safety of its clientele. With the increase in business and international travel, the better hotels are now used to providing special arrangements for their customers, and to safeguarding the anonymity of those customers who wish to remain low profile. Indeed, part of the hotel service is protecting, discreetly, the identity of its guests.

The advance agent, properly dressed, business card in hand, should ask for the General Manager's office. This office will be staffed with a (usually) very efficient secretary, someone who has been in that particular hotel for a long time and who shares some of the same power as the Resident Manager. The agent can quickly make an ally of this invaluable person by introducing himself, extending his business card, telling her that he has a special client coming into the hotel who will require some special security arrangements, adding that he would like to speak directly with the General Manager or Resident Manager, and will appreciate her help in arranging this. This will, in almost every case, guarantee a meeting, and usually quickly. Once having obtained an introduction to the General Manager or Resident Manager, the agent should come straight to the point. They should, in almost every case, be told the identity of the client. Major hotels have entertained Presidents, Arab royalty, major entertainers, gangsters, and CEO's of Fortune 500 companies without batting an eye and without calling in the media. They should be told the reasons for any special security arrangements and given a brief rundown on what is included in those arrangements. Last, the agent should request a meeting with the Reservations Manager (sometimes called the Front Desk or Rooms Manager), Security Director, Night Manager, Food and Beverage Manager, Chief Hotel Telephone Operator, Head Bellman, Concierge, and Head Housekeeper. If possible, he should arrange a meeting with all of these individuals at one time. While it is difficult to get key personnel together at one time, the hotel management will realize that this

is a time-saver for all involved and will usually try to make it happen. If all cannot be present at one time, the Resident Manager should arrange for separate meetings with those personnel not present at the general meeting.

Once the meeting is set up, it is most important to be organized and to move quickly through the list of requests, as this may be the only opportunity for such a meeting. It is very helpful to have a list of requirements (actually, requests) made up in advance, which can be handed out, first to the General or Resident Manager, and subsequent copies to department heads. There is a cardinal rule which applies to this meeting; *do not ask for anything that is not necessary*. While there is a temptation when standing in front of the key department managers of a major hotel to ask for a lot of "nice to have," don't do it. At best, special requests are a burden to a regular routine, and the hotel personnel will appreciate having to perform only those special requests which seem reasonable and necessary. At this meeting, the agent should obtain the name, hotel phone extensions and, if possible, home phone numbers of the General Manager and Resident Manager, and the key personnel at the meeting. Very often, the General Manager's secretary will supply these numbers and will serve, along with the Resident Manager, as a logistical focal point. At this meeting, a request should be made for the names of hotel personnel who will be regularly assigned to service the protectee's suite and members of his party; i.e., valet, waiters, housekeepers, room service. If the security detail is armed, this fact should be made known to the people at the meeting. It should be emphasized, however, that all arms will be kept out of sight at all times, even in the guest rooms.

Let us look at the key personnel represented at this meeting and the reasons for their inclusion. The General Manager is the most powerful person in the hotel. Unlike many other organizations, the hotel General Manager's "word is law." He can, if he wishes, authorize just about anything that isn't illegal. If he gives his blessing to the advance agent, everyone will fall into line. How the agent conducts himself will determine how gracefully and happily the staff cooperates. The Resident Manager speaks for the General Manager in the General Manager's absence, and carries (not quite but almost) the same authority as the General Manager.

The Reservations Manager is sometimes called the Front Desk Manager or Rooms Manager, or these may be separate functions. In some hotels, the Reservations Manager reports to his superior, the Front Desk Manager. It is important to contact the correct person in authority, the decision-maker in the department. From this person, the agent will request special room arrangements. This Manager will know who is in certain rooms and for how long, which rooms are connecting, and which rooms and suites are under long-term contract. Corporations sometimes lease hotel suites for their executives. If the client requires a block of rooms located all together, the Reservations Manager may be able to shift reservations to provide this block. If the client requires only one room, but good security means finding out who is on either side, above, and below the client, the Reservations Manager can reveal this. He may be helpful in locating the client in a room or suite that is sandwiched between reliable, long-term guests or corporate suites, none of which constitute a danger to the client. Most importantly, the front desk personnel will have to be informed that no information regarding the protectee is to be given out to anyone stopping at the front desk. Anyone asking for the protectee can be connected by house telephone to the command post, for handling.

The Security Director has, perhaps second only to the General and Resident Managers, the highest vested interest in making certain that the protectee is safe and secure in his hotel. That is his specific job. Many major hotel Security Directors in the United States are ex-law enforcement--police officers, FBI, etc. As when meeting with any law enforcement person, the agent will make points by looking like, and conducting himself like, the Secret Service and FBI. It helps to use some diplomacy, since this is the Security Director's turf. He can be helpful in using his security personnel to aid in protecting the client. The Security Director has people on staff who patrol the hotel at all times; they can provide extra eyes and ears to note anything unusual which might affect the protectee. If he is a good Security Director, he has established a rapport with the local police and fire departments. He will be able to advise on the local crime scene and can point out any shady characters who might hang out in the bar, restaurant, or lobby. He knows who belongs, and who does not belong, to the hotel.

The Security Director can conduct the agent on a walk-through of the hotel, checking entrances, exits, parking, emergency equipment, banquet and conference rooms, and the non-public areas: kitchens, maintenance, engineering, employee locker rooms, employee entrances, and storage areas. It is a good idea to ask to visit the Security Office. The Security Director is usually proud of his office and is only too happy to show diagrams and floor plans of the hotel, all of which are kept in his office. The Security Director and the Maintenance Engineer are the ones in charge of emergency procedures and equipment. Modern hotels have complex command posts of their own, which control heat, light, elevators, emergency generators, fire suppression systems, and smoke detectors.

The good Security Directors are very good. They keep up with modern security technology and, within their mini-world of the hotel, they deal with every crime in the book, including theft, robbery, assault, rape, murder, drugs, purchasing kickbacks, prostitutes, and carjackings. The Security Director can be a great help. The Security Director may, in the larger hotels, control the parking and can secure the invaluable advantage of reserving the two or three closely guarded parking spaces right in front of the hotel which are usually allotted to the hotel limousine or vans.

The Night Manager generally does not have much authority, unless this function is served by the Resident Manager. The Night Manager is there to maintain a presence and to solve minor problems. It is important, however, that he be aware of the client's presence and security requirements.

The Food and Beverage (F&B) Manager

generally supervises the Banquet Manager (but not in every case) and is in charge of the hotel's restaurants and room service. This is the individual who can handle special food requests. The agent should determine room service hours and request that they be extended if necessary. A schedule of room service hours, together with a menu, should be posted in the command post. Arrangements should be made to place room service orders through one or two designated (and trusted) hotel staff persons. This will generally expedite delivery, and preserve security.

Arrangements should be made with the Food and Beverage Manager so that, when placing food orders for the protectee(s), his identity will not be indicated to the kitchen; instead, the protectee's room service orders will be delivered to the command post. Arrangements should be made for coffee, soft drinks, etc. for command post personnel, and for coffee and sandwiches for the late night shift if there is no 24-hour room service. These special requests can easily be handled by the F&B Director's Room Service Manager. The F&B Manager should be able to vouch for the reliability of any food and beverage employees who will come in contact with the client. If meals are to be taken in the hotel restaurant(s), the F&B Manager can introduce the agent to the Restaurant Manager and/or Maitre d'Hotel, who can arrange for special tables.

The Chief Telephone Operator will be invaluable in screening calls to the client. She will need to be informed of the identity of the client. If special telephones need to be installed, she will make the arrangements. As a matter of practicality, it is not realistic for all calls to the protectee to be routed through the command post; this requires too much logistical handling. Calls can be routed, if desired, through someone in the protectee's party, or simply to the protectee's suite.

The Head Bellman and the Concierge can be regarded together for our purposes. Sometimes the Head Bellman reports to the Concierge, but not always. Not every American hotel has a Concierge, but instead gives these duties to the Head Bellman. Almost without fail, every decent European hotel, and the better third-world hotels, will have a Concierge.

In the United States, the Concierge or Head Bellman can be very useful, and in Europe the Concierge is invaluable in dispensing information and making arrangements. They change American dollars into foreign currency, arrange for transportation, and can procure anything: taxis, guides, excursions, shopping, theater tickets, extra security guards, babysitters, ski tickets, and the list goes on and on. The Concierge can usually arrange for a typewriter and/or computer, xerox and fax machine(s) for the command post, secretarial help, and can arrange for access to the hotel copying (xerox) machine. Are these services available after hours, and if not, can special arrangements be made? Tip: if there is no Concierge, the General Manager's secretary can be very helpful in arranging for access to the hotel's telex and copy machine, and can usually produce a typewriter.

First-class and luxury American hotels almost all now maintain suites which come equipped with copy, fax, and answering machines, and can arrange for computers.

The following frequently desired services are usually, but not always, available within the hotel: barber, drug store, beautician, masseuse, clothing store, shoeshine, health club. If these services are not available within the hotel, the Concierge can provide assistance in locating them nearby. A good Concierge is worth gold in saving time, effort, and frustration. Often, the parking attendants are supervised by the Head Bellman; if not, determine to whom they report. One of the considerations will be secured parking. Note that in Europe, parking is often controlled by the hotel doorman, who plays a much more important role there than does his counterpart in the United States.

The Head Housekeeper is generally in charge of the maids (who clean guest rooms) and housemen (who clean the public areas), and works closely with the maintenance people. The Head Housekeeper is the person who will arrange to move furniture out, or in, the command post, procure extras (sheets, blankets, TV sets, telephones), and arrange that only the most reliable housekeeping staff is scheduled to work in and around the protectee's rooms.

As a reminder, all names, telephone numbers, and special notes should be recorded for future use. After the trip is over, with the assignment finished and the protectee leaving, the agent should personally thank each individual, and hand over the tips to be distributed. The protocol in hotels is that the management staff (all Managers) are not tipped, although they may be given thoughtful gifts. Tips for the restaurant and room service personnel are usually signed on the guest tickets. Tips for the maids and housemen may be handed over in an envelope to the Head Housekeeper. Telephone operators are usually not tipped, although this is not a firm rule, and if the operators have been particularly helpful, an envelope with tips may be given to the Head Telephone Operator. The Concierge and Head Bellman are tipped according to how much use has been made of them, services provided, and the degree of their helpfulness. If anyone has been particularly helpful, including restaurant, room service, and kitchen personnel, a tip or gift is greatly appreciated.

If there is any confusion as to how much to tip, the Manager of that department or the Resident Manager will usually be helpful. Ask them what is appropriate and for whom it is appropriate. In countries outside the United States, tipping customs vary. Information about overseas tipping is usually available in guidebooks. In Japan, for example, tipping is frowned upon for any employees; it causes the employee to "lose face." In Europe, a 15% service charge is usually automatically added to the check, but a small additional tip for especially good service is in order.

The Security Director will appreciate a "gift of the trade;" for example, a special knife and, if you can manage it, a set of lock picks will make him very happy.

Everyone, including the General Manager, will appreciate receiving letters thanking them and commending them for their good service. These letters are highly prized, often going in the employee's file for promotion, or posted on bulletin boards, or useful in gaining points for Employee of the Year.

ROOMS

The first priority after the meeting is arranging for the rooms and suites which will be needed for the client, the client's party, the protective detail, and the command post.

Protectee's Suite

Unless the protectee insists or there is some overriding reason for doing so, the protectee's suite, or room, should not be located higher than the sixth floor. That is the maximum distance that many fire departments' ladders can reach. If the fire trucks cannot be brought directly next to the hotel (fire lanes blocked, etc.) the stretching of the ladders may make only those floors up to the fifth floor accessible.

The second consideration is the location of the suite on the floor. It should not be next to or opposite stairwells, elevators, closets, or storerooms. What is above, below, opposite, and on either side of the protectee's suite? Whenever possible, these rooms should be filled with protective detail members, the official party, or regular guests known to the hotel. The Reservations Manager will be aware of those people who are regular guests and where the corporate suites are located.

Rooms and suites that have an exposure to adjacent buildings should be avoided. In some downtown areas, older hotels occasionally have rooms with windows that are only a few feet from the windows of adjacent buildings. The suite should not be accessible from common balconies or fire escapes. Some very large suites may have rooms located on two floors connected by internal stairways, or may have a number of access doors leading into multiple hallways or service areas. This presents some security problems. When possible, the suite selected should have a minimum number of entry doors, all of which open to a common hallway on one floor. Any other arrangement will require an increase in manpower to provide visual surveillance and security for all areas.

A thorough examination should be made of the protectee's suite with particular emphasis on safety, security, and comfort concerns. Rooms with false ceilings offer considerable opportunity to conceal explosives or audio surveillance devices, and should be avoided if possible. All lights, switches, gauges, and electrical connections should be checked to be certain they are in good working condition. Frayed cords, torn places in the carpet, or anything that could cause unintentional harm to the client should be corrected. If there are small children in the protectee's party, the agent should make certain that their room(s) are safely furnished, and that anything that could present a hazard to a small child is temporarily removed or moved to a higher location. Any special needs or desires of the protectee such as twin/queen/king-sized bed, bar, extra TV, VCR, radio, refrigerator, video machine, etc., should be attended to, if available.

The location of emergency exits, fire extinguishers, fire hoses, and smoke alarms should be noted. This includes establishing an exit route to the nearest stairwell, plus a secondary route to an exit stairwell at the opposite end of the hallway, and walking up and down the stairwells to make certain they are not blocked. Establishing an escape route means counting the number of doors to the stairwell because, in the event of a fire, the smoke may be so dark that one cannot see the stairwell. Hotel fires can be devastating, not only because of the fire, but because of the smoke and toxic fumes. Many of the furnishings in hotel rooms are plastic or chemically produced and can emit deadly fumes. One should always establish a fire escape plan.

If a fire should occur, and the hotel guests are alerted either by alarm bells or a call from the hotel Operator, you will have to make some decisions. Let us say that the alarm is sounding, or you hear shouts of "Fire, Fire!" First, grab the door key, your wallet or purse, and if handy, some clothes or a coat. Touch the door. If it feels cool, open it carefully; if it feels

hot, don't open it. The fire may be in the hallway, and opening the door could blow the fire straight in. If the door is cool, you should walk or, if there is smoke in the hallway, *crawl* along your pre-selected route to the nearest stairwell (if the path is not blocked or heavy with smoke) or to the alternate exit. As you leave, close and lock the door behind you, making certain first that you have your room key. Do *not* attempt to use the elevator. The controls on some elevators are heat-responsive and could automatically open on the fire floor and refuse to budge. In modern hotels, the elevators will be brought to the ground floor and impounded for the use of the firefighters. Once in the stairwell, try to walk (not run) down to the lobby. Smoke rises, as do flames, and the last thing you want is to be trapped on upper floors that are not accessible to the fire ladders. Be very careful not to get involved with panicking guests all hurtling and pushing down the stairs. There are some commercially available smoke masks which are lightweight and which will filter out smoke for five to ten minutes, long enough to crawl down a hallway and reach the stairwell.

A second scenario is, after you have been alerted to the fire, you touch the door and it is red-hot. Don't open it! Call the hotel Operator; tell her that you believe the fire is outside your door and you are staying in your room, and then call 911 and the Fire Department and give them the same information. Hotel rooms, to meet code, should be rated for at least one hour of resistance to the fire. Shut off the air conditioning and air handling units. Run some water in the bath tub, soak the towels, and place them along the cracks around the door to keep out the smoke. Open the window, if possible. If smoke is infiltrating the room, you may have to smash the window to bring in clear air; if so, try to make only a small hole. If smoke begins to rise outside the building, you may have to stuff a towel in the hole. Hang a bedspread or colorful garment outside the window to flag the firefighters as to which room you are in and stay in touch with the hotel Operator.

Another safety precaution, when making hotel reservations, is to inquire about the hotel's fire safety system. Do all rooms have sprinklers? Be aware that many hotels are not sprinklered, except in the public areas. The fire experts all agree that nothing is as safe as sprinklers, and some hotels have committed the considerable funds needed to retrofit all of their hotel rooms with sprinklers. Generally speaking, the newest hotels have sprinkler systems because of the stringent fire codes enacted after the dreadful MGM and Hilton Hotel fires in Las Vegas. The older hotels in many cities, however, have been allowed under "grandfather" loopholes to install alarm systems only.

If your client is scheduled to participate in a public event within the hotel, part of your survey should be to inquire about evacuation plans from the public areas. Some of the most tragic fires have occurred in public areas, with a high number of deaths due to trampling, panicky crowds and locked security doors. You should have a back-up plan as to where you and client will go if you are separated in an emergency.

Room Selection for Balance of Party

Whenever possible it is desirable to create a security buffer zone around the protectee's suite, utilizing the rooms to either side, across the hall, and above and below. Every effort should be made to make certain that these rooms are assigned to persons accompanying the protectee, his or her staff, and/or security agents.

When planning room assignments for a large group, it is always desirable to reserve the whole floor or wing for the protectee's exclusive use, if possible. If this can't be done initially when the protectee's party is moved in, a list of the rooms not under the protective detail's control should be kept and members of the party moved as adjacent rooms become available. The logistics of a large client group are sufficiently difficult as it is; therefore, it is easier if the entire party is kept together.

Room assignments for the protectee's party can be a touchy subject, and it is wise not to make too many assumptions. The protectee will certainly occupy the largest, most desirable room or suite, and his wife will usually stay with him. If it is a suite, the protectee's small children may stay in the same suite, but possibly not. While the agent can make a tentative plan, he must get information from someone in charge who can guide him in the room assignments, particularly in assigning the rooms on either side of the protectee.

All rooms should be checked to make certain that they have the required number of beds and that adjoining doors are locked. A quick check should be made to ensure that lights, air conditioning, heat, electrical connections, etc. are in good working order. A list should be made of who in the protectee's party is occupying the rooms, room numbers, and telephone extension numbers.

Command Post

The command post is responsible for keeping track of the protectee and coordinating the activities of any supporting groups such as the ambulance crew, fire department, and local police. As the distribution center for all information, the command post must be in radio or telephone communication with all parties. Once the protectee and the main protective detail arrive, the command post takes over many of the duties set up by the advance agent.

The command post should be close to the protectee's suite; however, it is better if it is not located next to, or across from, the protectee's suite. It should be situated between the protectee's suite and any general traffic areas for other hotel guests, such as the elevator bank. The command post, if there is a full team working, can be a noisy operation, and it is better that it not be on the other side of the wall from the protectee. In addition, if the protectee's party is large enough to warrant a command post, the rooms on either side of the protectee, as well as the room across the hall, will be allotted to the official party. If the protectee is alone or accompanied only by one or two persons, and there is a single agent, the command post will double as the agent's sleeping room and may well be the adjoining room to the protectee.

Since the command post is a 24-hour

operations control center for security and support activities, it is essential to provide a businesslike atmosphere. If only one agent is on duty in the command post, and he needs to monitor the traffic coming and going down the hall, the door to the command post may be open or partially open. It is important that the room be tidy and professional. It is not a flophouse for the protective detail. If an agent is off-duty he should not "hang out" in the command post; he has his own room for relaxing. Off-duty personnel in the command post only create confusion and babble, and if the protectee looks into the room, he does not want to surmise whether he is paying personnel simply to stand around or sleep!

If possible, and with the help of the Head Housekeeper, some of the regular furniture should be moved out. This includes the beds, the dresser, and all of the overstuffed, comfortable chairs--anything that is unnecessary or will tempt an agent to go to sleep. The regular tables and desks are fairly useless and should be replaced, if possible, with the six-foot tables used in the conference and banquet rooms and with straight-back chairs, arranged so as to allow for agent briefings and meetings. One table and chair should be designated as the command post desk. Arrangements should be made with Housekeeping for extra hand towels and wastebaskets and to have the command post cleaned daily during "off peak" hours; i.e., when the protectee(s) and his party are out or sleeping.

Arrangements should be made to install a very large chalk (or white) board; this is easily done in a hotel, since all hotels now have conference materials. The chalk board is used as the information center. Telephone numbers, including emergency numbers for fire, police, hospitals, ambulance, key contacts, and hotel staff, etc., are listed on the board. Any information applicable to everyone can be written and changed on the board. If a bulletin board can be obtained as well, this is also helpful. A copy of the itinerary should be conspicuously posted on the board, available to all. Also posted should be much of the same information which would be found in a permanent command post, plus information specific to the trip.

. Room assignments for the protectee's party and the security detail, with telephone numbers.

. Written instructions and a diagram showing where the cars will be parked. Driver assignments and motorcade instructions should be listed.

. Itineraries, with any special instructions.

. Schedules and assignments for agents.

. Diagrams and/or floor plans of sites to be visited showing access points, parking, and security posts.

. Threat models, intelligence information, and any publicity surrounding the visit.

. Maps showing the primary and secondary routes in and out of each site, and the fastest routes to the hospital.

. Diagrams of hotel emergency evacuation routes and reassembly points (fire, natural disaster).

. Location of pre-determined safe place for protectee(s) in event of emergency not occurring in the hotel.

Some sort of arrangements should be made for the exchange of information and communications between agents and the detail leader and for messages. This can be handled by using large envelopes or folders, one for each agent with his or her name on it. All messages, expense vouchers, and notes can be placed in the envelope where they are accessible to all agents at all times without a lot of chitter-chatter.

Other items, information, and supplies which should be kept in the command post include local telephone books, extra pens, paper, legal pads, paper clips, stapler, expense vouchers, time sheets, tags for labeling keys, etc. Keys to the vehicles are kept in the command post, and extra keys should be provided. Arrangements can usually be made to obtain a typewriter or computer and printer, often through a rental company.

Better yet is a laptop computer (also called a notebook computer) with built-in modem and a small portable printer assigned to and carried by the protection team. This contains necessary files, has e-mail and Internet search capability, and can perform any number of chores. Lists, maps, itineraries, memorandum, etc. can be altered, revised, and produced in a matter of minutes. Just as the cellular telephone has become an essential tool for the protection agent, the computer has attained this status. Prices on the laptops have decreased, although the powerful ones are not cheap. To be totally efficient, a laptop should have CD-ROM capability, as well as a port for a scanner. It also calls for a knowledgeable user/agent. Any protection agent who is not computer-literate is WAY behind the times and needs to correct this deficiency immediately.

Typewritten and printed schedules and communications look much more professional and are more easily read than handwritten ones. (Tip: schedules, directions, and memos are more easily read if they are double-spaced with wide margins for penciled-in notations, on white paper.)

If possible, a master hotel room key ("E" key) should be obtained, so that only one key is needed to open the doors to the protectee's suites, as well as all other rooms occupied by the official party. This is, however, quite difficult, as the master key also opens all other rooms on the floor, and the hotel is reluctant to part with its master keys. Therefore, duplicate keys to the protectee's group rooms should be kept in the command post.

To handle the telephone communications, a long cord should be obtained for the hotel phone. This makes it possible to move around the room and out to the hall with the telephone. A long cord on the handset gives moveable freedom. If the detail has a cellular phone, this is very helpful as well.

If appropriate, a hallway checkpoint, using a chair and small table, should be set up in front of the command post, so that it does not obstruct the hallway. The agent manning this checkpoint does not have any authority of his own to deny access to anyone; he is not acting in the name of the hotel, but rather in the private capacity of security for a hotel guest. However, to be realistic, this checkpoint serves the purpose very nicely. The hotel people will be aware of the checkpoint and will have received instructions from their supervisors; further, they will be wearing identification. All mail, packages, and room service should be routed to the command post, before being delivered to the protectee. Hotel guests on the floor not belonging to the protectee's party have every right to proceed past the checkpoint to their rooms. Guests of the protectee should be identified by the Front Desk and a call made to the command post before directing them to the protectee's suite.

Total strangers who might slip through the screening process represent the only potential problem. They should be asked to identify themselves and politely requested to wait while a call is made to the protectee or someone in his party, who can then escort the guest to the protectee if this is desired. All hotel staff should be instructed to check in with the command post before attempting to enter the protectee's suite. All persons should be escorted into the suite, and an agent should remain with them until excused by the protectee or until they depart. Exceptions for family, friends, or business associates should be discussed with the protectee in advance to avoid misunderstandings. While the agent does not have the authority to deny access to anyone, the protectee has every right to deny access to his suite to anyone.

A temporary command post should contain much the same security equipment which is kept in a fixed command post. Again, it must be emphasized that, in a one-man operation, much of this equipment will not be made available, nor will it be necessary. But, in a full-on operation, the temporary command post should include: any extra weapons or shoulder weapons with ammunition; heavy duty flashlight with batteries; key block locks; smoke masks; set of lock picks; portable fire extinguisher; portable alarms; and two-way radio(s), charger(s), and spare batteries.

A fully stocked portable medical kit should be kept in the command post.

The protectee and members of his party will often leave money, jewelry, briefcases, and other items of value in the command post for safekeeping. The correct handling for this is to ask the protectee or guest to place the items in an envelope and seal it before custody is taken. The agent in charge of the command post should list the contents on the outside of the envelope, then obtain a signature from the owner of the item(s). Briefcases should be locked and the key retained by the owner.

A location in the command post should be selected where the shoulder weapon, medical kit, and security equipment will be kept at all times when the protectee is in residence. It may be necessary to move quickly with the protectee, and there will no time to look for gear. Professionalism requires that the agent be prepared and be prompt. The storage location should be readily accessible to the command post agent in the event of emergency but should not compromise the confidentiality of the equipment, particularly the shoulder weapon.

The command post should, at all times, look professional, organized, and sharp. It will be a focal point for many people. The protectee will look in from time to time, as will members of his party, the hotel Security Director, guests of the protectee, and perhaps the local police. The client does not want to be embarrassed by a room with equipment scattered all over the floor, messages tacked on the wall, dirty plates of leftover food, etc. He wants to see a replica of a Secret Service command post. Every effort should be made to avoid damage to the hotel property. Papers taped to the wall not only look unprofessional, they tend to peel off the paint when removed. Feet should be kept off the chairs. And, nothing should be broken; this is simple carelessness. If room service is ordered for the agent on duty, dirty dishes should be cleared by calling the room service number and asking for removal. Ask the housekeeper for a tray to hold dirty glasses and a large waste basket for the bathroom to hold dirty towels. It may be desirable to ask for a stack of paper towels, the

kind that are used in public restrooms. These can be used to mop up spills, wipe hands, and serve a multitude of other uses. A certain level of tidiness, as opposed to a real mess, wins many points with the housekeeping staff.

Post Assignments

Post assignments on a trip will closely resemble post assignments at home and will include checkpoint posts, surveillance posts, and special assignment posts. Checkpoint posts on a trip are important as they limit access to a restricted area. Access can mean access of people and screening of mail, packages, etc.

In order to limit access, you must have two things; the authority to deny access to a person, and the means to recognize those people who do have access. In order to recognize those people who have access, there must be a list of those people, and they must either be able to show their own credentials and identification, or there must be some sort of visible and recognizable identification, such as a pin.

There can be confusion, as well as danger, in relying on the regular identification supplied to individuals such as hotel workers. For example, let us say that the hotel provides its employees with a clip-on badge showing their picture, name, and physical description. Fine, but that only tells us that this particular individual works for the hotel. It does not tell us whether this individual has been cleared as "the" maid or room service waiter assigned to the protectee's suite. A special form of identification can easily be provided by using a pin, perhaps a different color for each day, something that is given out each day and returned each day. This system can be even further refined. Different pins or different colors may be assigned to different areas of the hotel (or other sites), so that red bordered pins might identify housekeeping personnel, and blue bordered pins restaurant personnel, and so on. This limits internal access to employees.

There are now available some very sophisticated, easy to produce identification cards.

Polaroid and other manufacturers have equipment which will take a picture and imprint identification information in a matter of moments. This represents an expense, but if the protectee and detail travel a great deal, it may be an identification solution.

The job of the surveillance post agent is to keep an eye on things, to report any suspicious activities to an authority, and either to take action or wait for someone else to come and take action. Examples of surveillance posts might be a lobby assignment, or someone watching the cars.

Examples of special assignment posts are: advance man, luggage handling, driving the principal, driving the follow-up car, and manning the command post, although the command post also qualifies as a checkpoint post.

General Considerations

How well known is the protectee and has his visit been publicized? If the answer is, the protectee is high profile and his visit has been touted in the media, additional arrangements must be made. It may be desirable for someone to officially greet the protectee. The greeter might be the hotel general manager, or a city, state, or political official. There can, in fact, be a group or committee assembled to greet the protectee. Will this be done outside at the entrance to the hotel or inside? If possible, it should be done inside, since this will be a more secure setting.

Will there be a photo session, perhaps accompanying the official greeting? This should be handled inside the hotel, not on the street, and preferably in the protectee's suite or a room other than the lobby. This keeps a low profile and provides protection from crowds. If the protectee is a celebrity, he/she may prefer to have a more public audience, making it more difficult to exercise strict security and crowd control. In all cases, the protectee will dictate the answer to these questions.

The agent should make certain that there are sufficient baggage handlers with carts for all arrivals

and departures of the protectee's party. If the baggage has been coded, it makes for fast, competent delivery. The agent should arrange for tipping the baggage handlers.

Whenever possible, the protectee and his party should be pre-registered to avoid standing in lines at the Registration Desk. At the same time, room keys should be obtained. This clears the way for the protectee to arrive at the hotel and move immediately to his room or suite.

If circumstances seem to warrant the expense, the protectee's room or suite may need to be secured a day in advance. This insures that it WILL be available at the appointed time, that the protectee is pre-registered, that sufficient time has been allocated to thoroughly inspect the room/suite for hidden devices (bomb, surveillance), and opportunity has been provided to stock the in-room refrigerator with snack and bar items favored by the client. When this expense can be included, it is highly desirable--it is the only way to guarantee "no surprises." If the expense is not acceptable, the advance agent should arrange for pre-registration and room inspection at least an hour before the protectee's arrival.

Double check with the protectee's staff and hotel personnel the arrangements for billing rooms, meals, and expenses. Hotels are able to set up master ledgers which effectively combine all room, telephone, valet, and restaurant charges on one bill, which can be paid with a credit card or by billing to the client if advance arrangements have been made for this. Be sure you know the policy on tipping. Except for the hotel restaurants, tips are almost never charged to the rooms account. Will the protectee's staff handle them or do detail personnel handle the tipping and bill the protectee? How often will the protective detail members be reimbursed for expenses--weekly, semi-weekly, end-of-assignment?

Many successful trips have been quickly ruined by a last-minute dispute over expenses. To avoid this, the detail leader must insist on detailed expense reports with back-up receipts from his/her team members, presented either daily or not later than immediately upon the end of the trip. A billing for expenses should be presented to the protectee immediately upon the conclusion of the trip, and any items that have been "forgotten" may simply have to be canceled as uncollectible.

RESIDENCES

An advance survey for a residence is somewhat defined in scope by whether the residence is to be used temporarily (short-term) or for a longer duration, such as an overseas assignment. However, for either situation, an examination of the interior and exterior of the buildings and property must be completed. Depending upon risk factors, locale, and other considerations, the advance may require background checks for the residence staff and occupants.

As with any advance, it is a good idea for the advance agent to contact the local police and fire departments, advising them of the protectee's presence and the address. The protocol of this contact has been described earlier. The police and fire officials should be advised of any weapons which will be stored at the house. Emergency response time for the police, ambulance, and fire department should be determined. Primary and secondary routes to the nearest fully equipped emergency/trauma hospital must be mapped out.

The residence interior survey will include examination of the exterior and interior doors, door frames, hinges, and locks, as well as window fittings and locks. The residence should be inspected for utility access ways, main circuit breakers, plumbing shut-off valves, and heating and air-conditioning controls. A diagram or blueprint showing these locations, as well as the layout of each floor showing all windows, doors, closets, hallways, and stairways, should be provided for the command post. Intrusion and fire alarm sensor locations should be included in the diagram.

Recommendations should be made for improvements in the physical security. However, if the visit is to be a short one, say for a week's vacation, and/or the residence being occupied belongs to a friend, it is not realistic to think that any structural improvements will be made. Security will be largely dependent upon the protective team.

The exterior survey will include a study of the terrain surrounding the residence. A diagram should be prepared which includes the location of any high ground, drainage ditches, bodies of water, embankments, fencing, lighting, vegetation and trees, roads and pathways, and other homes.

A diagram of the exterior terrain and features with their relative positions to the residence should be prepared for the command post. The diagram should also show the locations of all exterior power outlets and any alarm sensors or cameras. A description of the intrusion system, if it exists, should be prepared as a companion piece to the diagram. Is the system monitored? By whom? If an alarm is triggered, what is the anticipated response? What type of system is it? Does it have a history of false alarms?

If alarms have not previously been installed, and the residence will be occupied for a sufficient period of time to warrant the expense, recommendations should be made to install at least a basic intrusion and fire detection system. This could include both perimeter and interior detectors. For a trip of short duration, portable alarms, including a panic alarm, are convenient solutions.

Either fixed or portable fire extinguishers should be placed in key areas and, if not already installed, portable smoke detectors should be considered. If the residence has two or more levels, any bedrooms above the first story should have a collapsible ladder available for emergency exit. An emergency and fire evacuation plan should be prepared.

A "safe room" should be set up in an easily accessible area of the residence. A "safe room" is an enclosed area which ideally has been strengthened and can provide protection for a limited time from attack or intrusion, though not fire, unless escape from the fire to the outside were impossible. In case of fire, the protectee and his family should make every effort to exit the residence to a designated assembly area.

In a permanent or long-term situation, the safe room should have a reinforced door and walls, have an independent air supply, and be equipped with a cellular telephone and a battery-operated CB radio. Safe rooms are typically equipped with a first aid kit, protectee medications, a weapon, and water.

For a temporary residence, a bedroom or other area close to where the protectee will sleep might be designated as a safe room. It is not practical in a short-term situation to consider strengthening the room to a greater degree than installing a deadbolt lock and making certain that the door is safely anchored on its hinges. A cellular telephone and a weapon should be kept there.

If the temporary residence is a condominium, the advance will combine some of the elements of a residence and a hotel survey. The advance agent will need to contact the building management staff and any on-site security personnel. A survey should include the grounds, lobby, elevators, and garage or parking area, much as one would perform a walk-through inspection of a hotel.

A command post, if located in the residence, is best kept away from the center of the protectee's daily activities. The command post can be tucked away in the basement, an office, or a studio. If possible, a private telephone line should be installed. Diagrams, floor plans, duplicate keys to the residence and vehicles, itineraries, and the same items a traveling detail staying in a hotel would need should be contained in the command post. Photos and information on all domestic help should be collected in a file, kept in the command post.

As with any command post, it is a professional, working center. It should be off-limits to any staff other than the security staff. In a long-term situation it will house the CCTV monitors (if any) and may serve as the alarm station. It should have its own security system. Security personnel may, or may not,

be housed in close proximity to the command post.

If the protective operation is a one-man team, the command post may be a simple office in the protectee's house, but even so, it will be a miniature version of a full-scale command post.

If it is agreeable to all of the occupants of the residence and the protectee, all mail, gifts, and packages delivered to the residence should be checked first by the security agents. If it is a high-risk situation, a portable metal detector or X-ray machine might be installed in the command post.

All household staff should be instructed as to the proper procedures for handling telephone inquiries and deliveries. They should be cautioned to be alert for any suspicious circumstances. A list should be made of all temporary help (gardeners, plumbers, garbage men, pool service, laundry service, newspaper carrier) showing the approximate times when they are due to be at the residence. This list should be used to brief the agents and then kept in the command post. As with all command post procedures, a daily log of activities involving the residence should be kept.

Prior to the protectee's arrival, the advance agent should make a sweep of the residence to detect any surveillance devices or bombs. A word of caution: none of these procedures should be of such proportions that they are intrusive or upsetting to the owners and residents of the house.

There is extensive material about residential security in various chapters in this book, and checklists can be found in the Appendix which deal both with security and with advances.

SPORTS, FITNESS & ENTERTAINMENT

If the protectee is a fitness buff, he may also be a jogger. If he regularly runs for a specified period each day, even when on a trip, the advance agent must scout out the most accessible and safest jogging route. If the protectee is a golfer and the trip is planned to include one or more golfing excursions, the agent must check out the chosen facilities. Undoubtedly, the protectee belongs to a private club at home, and managers of that club can recommend a club or golf course in the target city which can be contacted in advance to make arrangements. Good exercise spas can be found in all major first-class hotels.

If the client intends to visit a museum, art gallery, or theatre, the advance agent must include these in his advance survey. Tickets should be procured in advance whenever possible and an on-site inspection made to locate telephones, restrooms and exhibits. Major museums, such as the Metropolitan Museum of New York are gigantic and often confusing. However, there are Information Desks staffed by helpful individuals who can supply floor plans and maps, lists of exhibits, location of elevators and escalators, restaurants, tearooms, and gift shops. These maps should be carefully scrutinized and committed (in a general sense) to memory.

If the protectee is high profile and well known, the agent should contact the museum/gallery officials, introduce himself, and make arrangements for a member of the staff to be available at the time the protectee intends to visit the facility. Almost certainly, these officials are happy to oblige and are quite discreet, considering that a major portion of the facility acquisitions and upkeep are dependent upon donor contributions. Following the visit, a modest donation will be greatly appreciated.

For a theatre visit, discretion is the name of the game. The protectee will, of course, want the most desirable seats in the house, but these may not be the safest seats. The agent should call upon the theatre manager and ask to be given a quick inspection of the theatre prior to seat selection.

Routes to all of the above should be scrutinized, selected and captured as a separate section of the city map showing travel routes. Parking accommodations should be pre-determined.

RESTAURANTS

Advances in restaurants are fairly simple. The advance agent should arrive at the restaurant prior to the protectee's arrival, allowing himself about 30 to 45 minutes to complete his advance if the restaurant is new to him. If the restaurant is familiar to the agent and has been used before, the advance will take no more than a few minutes. As soon as the advance agent reaches the restaurant he should contact the command post personnel, advising them of the time and distance from the protectee's location, best travel route, and how he can be reached, either by telephone or by radio. At that time, the command post personnel can advise him if there has been any change of plans since his departure. The command post should be reminded to contact him as soon as there is a departure, so that the advance agent can be on hand in front of the restaurant in time for the protectee's arrival.

If the advance is done a day or several days beforehand, the agent should produce a simple sketch of the restaurant showing the arrangement of the rooms, the tables, the entrances, exits, emergency exits, kitchen, and restrooms. Sometimes, in hotels for example, there may be more than one entrance into the restaurant; this should be verified and their locations marked.

In hotels, it is generally easy to work with the Restaurant Manager, Maitre d'Hotel, or Hostess, in protecting the identity of the client, and in arranging in advance for the best (most secure) seating. In free-standing restaurants (not associated with a hotel), it is not always so easy. Provided that the advance is done sufficiently in time, however, most Restaurant Managers will, with a little help, agree to the seating. The agent will need to know if the protectee has any preferences as to his seating.

If it is a small party with only one or two agents, it may be possible to accomplish one's mission without revealing the protectee's identity, by simply approaching the Manager to say, "I would like to make some special arrangements for dinner (lunch) tonight (next week), and will appreciate your help. I particularly like *that* table, and would like to have it held in my name for 8:30 tonight. Is that possible? I will really appreciate it, as this is a special occasion." In all likelihood, the Manager will agree. At that point, it is perfectly appropriate to give him a $20.00 gratuity, again expressing appreciation and thanks.

If the Manager is not so cooperative, or if the protectee is arriving with a large party, or there are several agents, or this is being done only 45 minutes in advance, a different approach is called for. The Manager or Maitre d'Hotel should be advised that a V.I.P. will be visiting his/her establishment and that you desire his/her assistance in making the stay safe and enjoyable for all. The agent should not, if possible, divulge the name or position of the client. The agent might say, "I would really appreciate your doing your best to help me out. Your restaurant has been highly recommended to my client, and he would like to come here more often if he feels comfortable. Please do your best for us," and hand over the tip. That will usually do the trick. If all else fails, the agent may have to confess to the identity of the protectee and try to twist the Manager's arm, figuratively speaking, by letting him in on the secret, and getting his cooperation.

Much depends upon the reputation and nature of the restaurant. If it is a small, hole-in-the-wall restaurant which has been chosen precisely because of its low profile nature, it will be somewhat more difficult to arrange for special seating. In a first-class restaurant, the Managers are used to their customers requesting special tables. It is always appropriate and is desirable to tip the Maitre d'Hotel in advance, and if you think you are going to be back, tip him again as you leave, expressing once again your appreciation. If all this fails to produce the most desirable table from a security standpoint, there is usually a second, almost-as-good choice. What the agent wishes to avoid is having his client stuck in an indefensible spot, or conspicuously in the open.

Restaurants which do not take reservations but seat people as first-come-first-serve are the worst choice, as there is no control over where or when the client will be seated. In addition to being given the worst table in the restaurant, the client may be forced to wait in an exposed lobby or waiting area for his table.

If the protectee is a recognizable person, the restaurant people may identify him. At that point, the agent should ask their cooperation in keeping his presence confidential. Besides providing additional security coverage, an agent posted by the main entrance will discourage the Maitre d' from leaking this information to other patrons.

If the advance agent has the final responsibility for making the arrangements for the visit, he should choose a convenient, private entrance into the dining area which is as close as possible to the protectee's parked vehicle. The more private the entrance the better, particularly if it avoids main hallways or foyers. The most desirable seating for the protectee is away from the entrance, in a fairly private area, away from the majority of the other diners. It is not a good idea to locate the protectee where everyone who comes into the restaurant must pass by his table. Tables next to windows are terrible, as anyone on the street can see the protectee. A table close to the emergency exit is the best, particularly if it is possible to park close by. If there is only one door into and out of the restaurant, there is a problem, since seating the protectee away from the door makes it impossible to get him out of the restaurant by that door quickly. However, there is always a service entrance into the kitchen, and sometimes another access door by a storage area or the restrooms. Extra exit doors are mandated by fire codes. The agent needs to be aware of these extra doors, both from a security standpoint and for use as a possible emergency exit. Therefore, the agent should walk around the building, locating all doors and parking areas. He should know the location of restrooms and telephones and, if possible, arrange for the protectee's use of a private area for both (perhaps the manager's office). This is another good opportunity for the use of a cellular telephone.

The agent should determine where the

protectee's vehicle(s) will be parked. If the vehicles are to be moved to another area he should make sure he has a way of contacting their drivers quickly. One vehicle should be parked by an alternate exit from the dining room (if possible) for use in the event of an emergency. The driver of this vehicle must be informed when and if it is determined that the departure will be via the primary route. It is highly desirable to leave an agent with the cars to keep them under secure surveillance and to make sure the vehicles are lined up properly and ready for departure

After the agent has completed his restaurant advance he should contact the command post again to give the detail leader a situation report and to find out if the protectee has departed for the restaurant. If this has not yet occurred, the advance agent should stand by for a telephone or radio confirmation of the protectee's departure. As the protectee's vehicle approaches, the advance agent should be in contact with the driver by radio or telephone, directing the vehicle to his location. He should stand curbside by the entrance to be used into the restaurant, ready to open the protectee's door and lead the party to their table. At departure, the advance agent should lead the party to their vehicles. If the vehicles have been parked at some distance from the restaurant door, the drivers will need to be alerted in advance to proceed to the entrance.

Circumstances vary as to whether the agent(s) will sit at the protectee's table. In large details this does not normally happen. With a low profile, long-term, single agent assignment, the agent may be invited to join the protectee if the protectee is dining alone or only with family. If there are outside guests, the agent is rarely invited to join the table.

The advance agent should arrange for a separate table for the agents, if they are expected to eat. This table should be located so that it is in close proximity to the protectee and, at the same time, allows the agents an unobstructed view of the restaurant, kitchen, doors, and halls. If possible, the agents' table should be located in the same waiter "station" as the protectee's table. This makes it easier to coordinate the service to the protectee and the

agents. (Restaurant dining areas are divided into "stations" and waiters are assigned to a specific "station.")

If the agents are served a meal, they must continue to be vigilant and pay attention to business. They should not linger over their food. It is a good idea to ask the waiter what menu items can be served quickly and to ask him to rush their order. The waiter should be asked to inform the agents periodically on the progress of the protectee's meal and to warn the agents when the protectee shows indications of leaving. For example, if after-dinner coffee or drinks are served, this is usually the closing activity of the meal.

If there is more than one driver and they wish to eat at this time, there are several options. They may be allowed to eat (quickly) at another nearby location in shifts, or one driver can obtain food for all at a carry-out restaurant. If possible, the drivers should avoid eating in the car, but if they do so, the vehicle *must* be cleaned and aired out prior to the arrival of the protectee. If there is only one vehicle, it must not be allowed to leave. In this event, sometimes the restaurant will agree to have food delivered to the car via the kitchen entrance.

Arrangements should be made in advance to have all meals and drinks put on one ticket which, together with the tip, can be paid with one credit card or in cash. It should be very clear as to who is going to pay the check--either the protectee, someone in his party, or the agent in charge. This should never be left up in the air, as it will create confusion at the end. It is sometimes a good idea, when making these arrangements, at the beginning of the meal, to hand over a credit card to the Maitre d'Hotel with instructions to include all of the meals for everyone, saying, "Please take care of this for us, and add a 20% tip, which I leave up to you to distribute. I would appreciate it if you would bring me the bill and credit card voucher immediately after we have (the protectee has) finished coffee." This is the cleanest, fastest way to handle the bill.

Restaurants chosen on the spur of the

moment are usually not advanced, nor is it particularly necessary. If no one knows the protectee is going to be in that restaurant, it is hard to plot against him. A quick walk-through, with a tip to the Maitre d'Hotel to gain the best table(s) available, will usually be sufficient.

BALLROOMS, BANQUETS AND AUDITORIUMS

In advancing special events held in ballrooms, banquet rooms, and auditoriums, the agent should meet with the people in charge and identify the appropriate liaison person(s) for the banquet management, caterers, facility management, program manager, media/public relations, sponsor, and host committee. It is important to get the correct spelling of their names, their titles, and their telephone numbers. The agent should make certain that these people know how to contact him.

The agent must determine the answers to several questions. What is the purpose of the function--fundraiser, awards banquet, etc.--and how many people are expected to attend? The nature of the function gives an indication of the type of people who will be attending, and the level of security which should be provided. Is the event or its sponsor of a controversial nature? Are there likely to be demonstrators? If this event has been held before, were there any incidents? (If it is a recurring event, the advance agent should obtain any available intelligence on the event from newspaper and publicity files.) Is the location of the event a concern? What are the crime statistics on the area? Will there be entertainment and is the entertainment or star performer controversial? Will there be other V.I.P.'s attending the event, and will they or the entertainers bring their own security? If so, you should try to coordinate with them.

If any gifts or awards are to given to the protectee, arrangements should be made with the host to have these mailed after the presentation. It is very awkward to find yourself carrying a bulky object, knowing that you have compromised your ability to react quickly to an emergency. If the protectee later decides to keep the gift with him, it should be passed along to a staff member as soon as possible.

What is the program? Not the printed program which is given to the guests, but the minute-by-minute schedule, which tells when the guests will be seated, when the speeches will be given, and all logistical arrangements. During the program, will there be a time when the lights go off, perhaps for a slide presentation, a film, or simply for special effects? If this is known in advance, there will be no cause for alarm. However, if suddenly, without warning, all of the lights go out, all agents should go on red alert. This could be embarrassing if it is a legitimate, but unrevealed, part of the program.

Will there be a reception or cocktail party held before the main event, and is the protectee expected to attend? Where will it be held? Who and how many will be invited to this event?

Is it a black-tie affair? Will dark business suits be acceptable for the agents, or will they also be expected to be in formal attire? Should the ladies wear cocktail dress, formal gown, or business dress? Agents should dress as any other guest, whenever possible, to protect their anonymity. Information on proper attire should be obtained sufficiently in advance to allow time to reserve tuxedos and to allow for fittings if required. In some locales, there is a heavy call for rental tuxedos. If not enough time is allowed, agents may find themselves unable to obtain their proper sizes and wearing ill-fitted, awkward-appearing tuxedos.

The agent should obtain a floor plan showing the room(s) to be used. Using the floor plan, the agent should perform a thorough walk-through of the site, parking, and indoor facilities--including an inspection of catering facilities, storage rooms, catwalks, back stage area, projection booths, elevators, stairwells, electrical outlets, power input, exits, and seating. The floor plan should be diagramed by the agent to show the entrance and exit routes under normal and emergency conditions, location of a holding room, vehicle parking, fire extinguishers, protectee's location, agent posts, and other pertinent information. Copies will be made and provided to each agent.

The agent should determine if there will be an engineer on duty during the event to oversee the controls for heat, air, light, and sound. If possible, an agent or other trustworthy person should be assigned to this area since the function could be severely disrupted by any tampering of the engineering controls.

The agent should identify the arrival point for the protectee's vehicle. Ideally, it should be arranged so that it is separate from the regular arrival point used by the general public and other guests. The protectee's entrance, when feasible, should be the shortest, quietest, and most easily controlled. There will, however, be times when this is not possible, and at fundraisers the protectee may wish to walk through the crowd.

Where will the protectee's vehicle be kept during the function and can that location be made secure?

What is the departure point for the protectee from the event area? There must be some sort of plan for getting the protectee out of the room, either for an early departure before the crowd breaks up, or after the room has been cleared, or simply through an exit different from that used by the crowd. Otherwise, the event will break up, and the protectee will be lost in the sea of people, all leaving at one time, using the same exits.

The agent should arrange for a holding room where the protectee can rest, review a speech, or conduct business in private. If possible, it should have a telephone and a private restroom. The holding room ideally should be located near the entrance/exit point into the event area.

The table set-up (arrangement of tables) is usually controlled by the Headwaiter, or instructions will be given by the Banquet Manager. Usually, there are standard set-ups for each room which vary dependent upon the number of guests, whether there is a head table and/or podium for a speaker, and

guest preference. These are known in advance and are usually designated or diagrammed on a Function Sheet provided by the Banquet Manager or the Banquet Sales Manager. A typical Function Sheet lists date, time, number of guests, menu, cocktails, drinks, wine, table set-up, sometimes number of waiters and busboys, and the name and telephone number of the guest contact person.

If the protectee will be seated at the head table, the agent should determine where it will be located. He should survey what is above, below, and behind it. In many ballrooms and auditorium arrangements there is a wall, back stage, storage space, orchestra pit, and other rooms located directly adjacent to the head table site. If so, how can access be controlled and the area made secure? Are there lighting booms, movie screens, or heavy curtains above? Will they be adequately secured?

There are several types of head table set-ups or configurations, each of which has security considerations which the agent must review.

One of the most commonly used, and more informal, head table set-ups is the simplest. The table is only slightly separated from the other tables, and is not raised. There may be a table-top podium from which speeches are given and awards presented, or a standing podium may be located to the side of the table. This table arrangement is usually used with a smaller audience, most of whom know each other. While some security is compromised by having little physical separation from the other tables, it is assumed that the audience is better screened and identified.

The raised head table is another commonly found set-up. The head table will be located on a platform raised to any height from one foot to several feet, mandating steps to ascend to the platform.

A less commonly found head table configuration is the tiered arrangement, consisting of two or three tiered platforms. It is a very good arrangement from a security standpoint, since it establishes elevated barriers between the protectee and the audience.

A stage is commonly used for events which are high visibility, since the height and separation of the stage from the audience allows everyone to see the people seated on the stage. The security advantage to this arrangement is that it provides a barrier of four to five feet minimum. The disadvantage is that the stage will almost always have behind it and to the side numerous doors, curtains, catwalks, equipment, and people. Access control is a strong security consideration.

Unless there is a strong physical separation between head table and audience (such as with a stage), it may be desirable to have a buffer in front of the head table. This is particularly desirable if there are to be reporters and cameramen present. A buffer prevents anyone from approaching the protectee too closely. A simple but effective buffer can be accomplished by placing plants or potted shrubs in front. Or, it is perfectly acceptable to rope off the area in front of the head table with velvet rope like that used in theaters and concert halls.

The agent should personally inspect the podium, raised platform, stage, and steps for general stability, lighting, and any hidden hazards such as loose carpet, wires, or obstructions that could trip the protectee. He should inspect the chair in which the protectee will sit and the table at which he or she will be seated--topside and underneath. Be aware that these tables and chairs may be the folding or collapsible type, and it is important to make certain that chair legs are fully extended and locked. The agent should make certain that the table is not seated too close to the back of the platform where a chair could inadvertently be pushed back over the edge, dumping the occupant on the ground.

After the agent has completed his survey, he must select or make recommendations for agents' posts for the event. One difficulty is in making certain that the agents' posts and seats are not compromised. If the agents are to be seated, their seats should be clearly marked for use by security personnel. Event sponsors and guests at the table should be asked not to rearrange the seating of the agents. Latecomers should not be invited to take over the agents' seats, even though they may be unoccupied at that moment. One way to handle this is to seat one agent early, so that he can make certain that other agents' seats are not changed or occupied.

This is often a non-problem, as the agents may be stationed at the exits, far right, far left, and backstage, where they must have a clear observation of the protectee, the doors, and the room at large. The agent may be seated in a chair, or could be required to stand throughout the evening. Depending upon the situation, an agent may be placed on the stage, back against the curtain, although this is not common. The agent should not be seated at the head table.

If a meal is to be served, meal tickets may be required of the guests. This is a common procedure at large meal events, making it easy for the catering company to know how many meals have been served and can be billed to the sponsors. Whenever meal tickets will be required, and agents will be seated among the guests, the advance agent should obtain a sufficient number of meal tickets for the seated agents. If the event is a fundraiser, there will be a high price tag on seats at the table, and it will be most difficult for an agent to obtain a "free" seat.

When agents are seated at table, it is permissible for them to eat, and, indeed, they should do so in order not to draw attention to themselves. They should keep in mind, however, at all times that they are working, by maintaining eye contact with other agents in the room, observing the protectee, and surveilling the room and general area. They should be polite and professional with the guests at the table but should not become distracted by engaging in lengthy conversations. If wine is served, it should be refused politely by the agent. An agent should never drink alcoholic beverages while on duty; instead, he should request a plain soda or sparkling water. Since, in today's health-conscious world, many people do not drink alcoholic beverages, this is very acceptable and does not call attention to the person.

When possible, an agent should select at random the meal to be placed before the protectee. This should be done as the meals are served. This is not always possible, unless the protectee is a notable V.I.P. If the agent foresees that it will be a problem, some prior arrangement may be made with the Head Waiter. It should be handled discreetly, not by charging through the ranks of the waiters and snatching dishes away. Wait staff at banquet functions are highly orchestrated and work under severe time constraints. Stumbling through their ranks can create unacceptable confusion.

Who are the waiters and waitresses? Meet them, if possible, and let them know who you are. Provide a distinctive pin or button for easy identification. Prevail upon the Banquet Manager, Captain, or Maitre d'Hotel for his oldest and most trusted employees for head table service. If the situation warrants it, the agent may attempt to obtain names, date of birth, and social security numbers for the wait staff, and request local law enforcement to verify their status.

Access Control

Access control for a special event is very important. If one is able to control who comes into the room, it is much easier to protect the protectee. Access control is also a potential problem. Invited guests are not necessarily happy about being stopped at the door; therefore, good procedures must be set in place, and this requires prior information.

Is entry free and open to the general public? Were tickets sold? If so, what was the price range? The price of tickets is a good (but not absolutely reliable) indicator of the type of crowd to expect. Is this event by invitation only? What were the qualifications for receiving an invitation? Are the invitations numbered and cross-referenced by name on a master list? May a guest who chooses not to attend give his invitation to another without notifying the host/sponsor?

Find out from the sponsoring or host organization how many people are expected. It is not unusual in the case of fundraisers for a sponsoring group to oversell a function anticipating that there will be some no-shows. A problem arises when there is a capacity crowd with no seats for latecomers who are holding tickets. While this may not seem a security matter, it is quite possible that blame will attach itself to the protectee if he or she is the featured speaker or guest.

Where is the main access control point? Who will be there to check tickets or verify invitations? Will guests who claim to have lost or forgotten their tickets be admitted and issued new invitations or turned away? By whom? And, most difficult of all, will guests' handbags be searched? Ideally, there should be at least two people at each door, with one in uniform who can politely ask for the ladies' handbags to be searched, and the second a representative of the sponsoring organization to check the guest list. Guests are generally more willing to relinquish a handbag or other objects to a uniformed person. On the other hand, if there are any discrepancies in the tickets, one of the sponsor's knowledgeable people may recognize each guest, making the job much easier.

There should be another checkpoint slightly removed from the main access door to take care of problems. If a guest arrives without his or her ticket ("I lost it; I forgot it"), or there is another problem, this person can be politely escorted to the secondary checkpoint where the sponsoring representative can work it out without holding up the main line. It is more efficient and less embarrassing to the person with the problem.

How will access via service or stage entrances be limited to authorized personnel? How will authorized personnel be identified as such? Who will enforce these procedures?

How will exit to the guest restrooms and re-entry be controlled? Guest restrooms are almost always located outside the dining and auditorium areas. If they are outside the secure area of the function some procedures must be devised to handle this, perhaps by issuing passes or a small rubber stamp mark on the hand.

Media Coverage

Media coverage is always potentially troublesome for a protectee, particularly if the protectee is high profile and/or controversial. The advance agent should determine if both the print and broadcast media have been invited. Will the media be accredited and, if so, who will check their credentials? From a security standpoint it is highly desirable to have only accredited media personnel at an event. If there is to be a press conference or press interviews, arrangements should be made to identify and set aside a room for this purpose so that it can be done under controlled conditions. Will the press attend the main function, or will they be limited to an interview/press conference?

Depending upon the answers to these questions, the agent may find it advantageous to make certain that the logistical needs of the media are well attended to. Generally, for any major event, the sponsoring organization will have one person assigned to liaison with the media; however, this does not mean that the liaison person knows precisely how to take care of logistical needs. If the media are crammed into an unworkable area, can't see or hear, and do not have enough electrical connections, there is sure to be a problem. The media, having been invited to the event, have a job to do and every right to expect that they will be able to do that job. A knowledgeable agent can often be a problem solver, thereby avoiding embarrassment or damaging fallout to his client.

The media need to have a workable space prepared and dedicated for their use. A television crew needs approximately five feet by five feet, or 25 square feet of space, to set up camera, lights, and equipment. Electrical outlets are needed, one for each television crew. They need to have a "feed," one for each crew, from the amplifiers so that they can get clear, decent sound. They need to be located in a spot that is at eye level with the speakers on the stage. And, they can't be bunched behind each other. Each crew must be "up front" to get a clear picture.

Wires and cables need to be taped down. By making it possible for the media to get their stories without a great deal of commotion, there is a good opportunity to keep them from crowding the stage or rushing the aisles.

If there are to be any special interviews or a press conference, these should be set up away from the stage and the crowd. A special room or area should be set aside and the media informed in advance so that they can set up their cameras and lights. If any media person requests a private interview with your client, you should pass along the request to him. This is a decision which should be made by the client or his public relations consultant.

Protective personnel should endeavor to stay out of the limelight and to avoid, if possible, having their pictures taken or appearing on television. They should not reveal any security measures which are in place and politely refuse to comment on the security system. This is merely common (security) sense.

Having stated this, there are protective specialists who have actively sought out the media to gain exposure and--business. It's tempting. It can also be a career-wrecker. A good interviewer can expose all the warts, glowers, foolish utterances, and stupid comments that an interviewee possesses, and there it is in living color on the six o'clock news. It also "blows the cover" of the agent. Yet another trap lies in the fact that the interviewer wants confidential information and will try to pry that out of the interviewee; if successful, the hapless interviewee agent expert will be out of work by the time the program ends. Seeking media attention is a very, very tricky business.

Demonstrations/Diversions

If your protectee is high profile, there is certain to be someone or some group that disagrees with his opinions, actions, or just his notoriety. Therefore, if there is any publicity about the event, it is fairly likely that hecklers or demonstrators may choose this event to voice their displeasure and capture media attention. This is one of the hazards of public events. Many groups, such as the anti-abortion groups, have become both sophisticated and effective in their harassment campaigns. Their actions may include picketing, heckling, harassing, shouting, and blocking vehicles. A dedicated heckler who has heard too many slogans and impassioned rhetoric from one of the extremist groups may decide to attempt deadly violence.

Diversionary tactics--the creation of a disruption or an incident at some distance away from the target--provide an opportunity for other members of the group closer to the protectee to launch an assault or create an embarrassing incident. An agent's first obligation is to the protectee. If all the agents look and respond to the diversion, none are left to protect the client. Instead, any disruption should immediately be viewed by the agents as a possible diversionary move. Rather than responding to a problem area, the agents should close the distance between themselves and the protectee.

If the event is such, as indicated by advance intelligence, that the advance agent believes there could be problems which would require more protection than the team could provide, he may wish to engage local law enforcement or outside security to assist in crowd control and site protection.

OUTSIDE EVENTS

Approximately the same advance must be made for outside events as for indoor events held in ballrooms and banquet rooms. Most of the same kind of information must be acquired. This means establishing a liaison with the organizers of the special event and getting all of the appropriate information as to the purpose of the event, who will be there, timing, and itinerary. A diagram or sketch of the area should be made, marking the spots where the protectee will arrive and depart, the stage or grandstand (if there is one), and where the protectee's vehicle will be parked. It is very important that the vehicle be parked so that it can, if necessary, get away quickly. Is the dress attire strictly business-like with suit and tie? If it is a nighttime event, who is handling the lights? Is there a back-up generator?

The stage must be checked for loose wires, handrails, and lighting (if at night). A survey should be made of the area, paying particular attention to high ground, anything that will overlook the spot where the protectee will be standing or seated. Local police and/or security guards are best utilized to cover any sensitive spots.

The security arrangements must be checked. Who is handling security? Are there enough bodies for crowd control? Should the security be augmented with local police? Have the local police been contacted? Who will be directing the parking? Has someone arranged for emergency services, ambulance, and paramedic? Crowds, especially in the summer, are notorious for producing accidents. People faint, fall down, and otherwise hurt themselves. While some of these responsibilities are not directly related to the agent's job, if anything goes wrong, it can kick back to the protectee. In the entertainment field, outdoor events are common, and some have produced violent incidents, even death, none of which helped the star entertainer's career. Having one's name associated with a violent or embarrassing incident can be very damaging.

Access control can be a real problem at these events. Open areas are harder to control than closed buildings. Spectators, especially large numbers of spectators, may be present, without the benefit of having been specifically invited; as for example, at a political or religious rally. How do you control the spectators and provide protection for the protectee? Some method has to be devised that will confine the spectators to certain areas. It may be a seated affair with folding chairs lined in front of and to the sides of the stage. If so, this provides some orderliness, and it is also possible to control who sits in the front seats. If it is a stand-up affair, containment can be accomplished by using barrels half-filled with water, and rope, two strands if possible. (Wooden barricades are not very useful, as they are too light-weight and can be easily knocked over.) Two sections can be set up with a smaller area roped off up front. It is not possible to control the movements of, or observe, each and every person in the crowd; there may be hundreds, or thousands. What is necessary is to control the movements of the people in the front section. How?

One way is to fill the front section with trusted friends. These can be members of the protectee's political, religious, or business organizations in the area such as Knights of Columbus, Boy Scouts, and the like, and they can be invited to occupy the front section. Any organized group of people who know and recognize each other, are friendly to the protectee, who will be dressed appropriately, and look good on camera are desirable. They will undoubtedly be delighted to have an invitation to occupy the choice spots. They can organize themselves, and they can identify and vouch for each other. They are not apt to have someone with them who wants to shoot, attack, or embarrass the protectee. And, they are not likely to allow a stranger to take over one of their choice spots. These people should be asked to arrive early, as early as possible, so that there are no problems getting them situated in the front rows. If the threat is kept out and away from the front rows of spectators, there is little chance that anyone standing in the back rows can create a security problem.

If the media are in attendance, an area must be dedicated for their use, just as is done for indoor events. Some sort of platform, trailer truck, or other elevated area should be provided for the television crews and electrical outlets provided for them, if at all possible. It is very useful to designate another area which can be set up and roped off for photo opportunities, interviews, and press conference. A time should be set up before or after the main event to allow the protectee to meet with the media people.

Weather will be a factor in these events, so there needs to be a foul weather plan, as well as several large umbrellas on hand. Golf umbrellas are great for this purpose; they are super-large and very sturdy. Frequently, outside events are held in a tent and, if so, a representative of the company who is familiar with rigging should be on hand to handle any problems.

What do you do if the event is canceled? Let

us say that the protectee arrives in the city and checks into the hotel just hours ahead of a downpour or a snowstorm, which effectively shuts down the event. He may choose to sit in his hotel room and catch up on some work. If his family is with him, they may wish to entertain themselves. An alert agent will already have captured some of those brochures found in the racks in the hotel lobby or will have talked with the Concierge or Head Bellman and investigated any special entertainment attractions in the area. The agent may find himself taking the wife and kids to the world's biggest shopping mall, or a museum, or art gallery, or the IMAX theater. Does this present an opportunity for danger? Hardly, since the excursion is spontaneous and unplanned, and the husband may be safely tucked away in his hotel suite. A foul weather contingency plan is very helpful.

GROUND TRANSPORTATION

A very important component to any trip is the ground transportation. It also presents some potentially vexing problems which could alter the successful performance of the detail. When establishing contact with the transportation agency, it is best to deal whenever possible with the owner or manager. He should be told specifically what will be needed and the quality of performance expected. It is almost always better to deal with the top two or three national rental car agencies, regardless of expense. They are #1, 2 and 3 because they have more extensive, comfortable, and reliable services, and they charge accordingly. The difference in expense is negligible. Another advantage to these agencies is that they have offices all over the world. It is advantageous to acquire the "executive" or "club" credit cards issued by these agencies, as this brings enhanced services, including express check-in and check-out, a real time-saver. Major credit cards are also a must, since most rental agencies *will not* accept cash. In addition, major credit cards now provide automatic daily auto insurance which will take care of large and small accidental damage.

Limousines are not always the best idea; they send a "rich" high profile signal, and they almost always come with a driver. It is almost impossible to rent a limousine without the driver. The driver may be an advantage or a hindrance. Traditionally, limo drivers have been comfort and service oriented, unskilled in any protection skills. Limo drivers like to spring out and open doors for the client and provide other services which are more likely to produce tips. As with other service providers (waiters, waitresses), these drivers are dependent upon tips as a significant part of their livelihood. Limo drivers are very careful about avoiding any damage to their vehicles and are not likely, therefore, to ram a block car if necessary to escape from a threat situation. On the other hand, an increasing number of limousine companies are advertising "executive protection trained drivers," and sometimes (though not always) these drivers are security-conscious and competent. Other limo companies advertising "executive protection" may employ off-duty policemen. If a limousine is to be rented, some advance investigation should be made to determine if the driver is security competent. If so, this can be an advantage, adding an extra body to the team. Dealing with the larger limousine companies rather than the one-car operations is generally the best course. The larger companies are more likely to have well-maintained vehicles with all the necessary parts (spare tire, jumper cables, etc.), and they can produce more than one car for an operation.

If a limousine is not required by the protectee, one of the larger, heavier rental cars such as a Lincoln Town Car or Ford LTD is most desirable. These cars are more comfortable and can most easily retain their balance and operating capabilities if emergency driving maneuvers become necessary. Under certain circumstances, other vehicles may be a better choice. If there are winter snow and ice driving conditions, a four-wheel drive vehicle such as a Jeep Cherokee is a fine choice. Jeep Cherokees have great traction, off-road capability, good balance and comfort, and are reasonably low profile since they are now extremely popular. Their disadvantage is in the small size and diminished luggage space. If there is to be much luggage and equipment, a Jeep Wagoneer or a four-wheel drive SUV is another good choice.

It is the advance agent's responsibility to check any vehicles prior to the arrival of the protectee. Not all rental vehicles, including limousines, are equally furnished and maintained, so the agent must pay attention to the overall condition of the vehicle, as well as checking for specific items. The vehicle should be clean inside and out, and kept clean at all times, certainly on the interior. There should be a full set of tires plus a spare, in good condition, properly inflated. If using a rental car, before leaving the rental agency, a check should be made of the fluid levels--oil, water, automatic transmission, power steering, and windshield cleaner-- and a general examination made of the condition of the under-the-hood mechanisms. All controls should be tested: air conditioning, heat, power windows, power locks (you definitely want power locks!) automatic seat belts, and radio. The vehicle should be equipped with jumper cables, jack, small tool kit, and an extra ignition key. Any extra junk should be removed from the trunk. If reservations were made in advance for the vehicle, and there is any danger that the identity of the protectee is known, a visual inspection for explosive devices and/or audio surveillance devices must be made.

Driver Briefing

If someone other than a regular team member will be driving the vehicle, he or she will need to be briefed, and made to understand that the briefing is very important. The first priority is to make the driver understand that the *agent* is in charge, and will be issuing the orders, not the client. There must not be any confusion on this issue. Beyond that, the following are some specific do's and dont's, which can be typed in advance and handed to the driver.

.   Report with a clean car and a full gas tank. Car should be refilled at end of day when no longer required by the protectee.

.   Speak only when spoken to. Unnecessary chatter can not only be unwanted, but can pose a problem if the agent is concentrating on traffic, route, etc.

. Do not leap out to open the door for the client will open and close the client's door.

. Once the client and agents are inside the vehicle, lock all windows and doors.

. Do not leave the limo unattended. Stay with the limo at all times unless you are relieved. Provisions will be made for meals, restroom breaks, etc. If you must leave, you are to notify the agent, the command post, or other drivers as to where you can be reached and how long you will be gone. Keys to the vehicle should be left in the vehicle (unless it is unattended), at the command post, or with the agent until you return. The advance agent should make certain that all drivers know how to contact the agent and the command post. A second set of vehicle keys should be maintained by security agent(s).

. When the vehicle stops at its destination, the vehicle doors should be unlocked, the engine is kept running, and the driver remains behind the wheel of the vehicle. Do not open and close the car doors for the protectee or the agents. The agent riding in the limo will open and close the passenger's side rear door, and the follow-up agent (if any) will control the driver's side rear door.

. Do not remove keys from the ignition unless absolutely necessary in the event it should become necessary to leave immediately. If the trunk needs to be opened, use the inside release.

. Alcoholic beverages must not be drunk within twelve hours prior to reporting for work or during work. Do not drink any beverage while driving.

. Food should not be eaten in the car, nor should the vehicle be used to drive to an eating place. The agent will arrange for meals. If it should become necessary to eat in the car, the vehicle must be completely cleaned out and aired before the protectee returns.

. Do not smoke in the vehicle.

. Drive smoothly, safely, and conservatively,

obeying all traffic laws. Stop, start, and turn gradually and smoothly, signaling turns well in advance. Pace your driving so that you do not run yellow lights. This is especially important if there is a follow-up vehicle. Do not sound the horn except in an emergency.

. Do not turn the radio on unless requested to do so by the protectee or agent. Pre-program the radio to stations with either classical or "easy listening" music in addition to a good news station, preferably one which has National Public Radio broadcasts.

. In a high profile motorcade, keep the headlights on.

. In a motorcade or convoy, drivers must be instructed to stay approximately one car length from the vehicle ahead of them. The distance should be such that the vehicles do not run into each other and, at the same time, do not allow other vehicles to get in-between. If a problem develops with a vehicle, the driver should drop out of line rather than hold up the motorcade. Once lined up, the vehicles should keep their assigned positions unless a problem develops or a blocking maneuver is executed.

The driver(s) must be furnished with route maps and queried as to whether they understand the routes to be followed.

Other Vehicles Needed

A "stash car" is an extra car used for emergency evacuation or when the normal departure by the protectee's limousine is not desirable. The stash car, because of its primary use as an emergency getaway vehicle, remains at the hotel or residence, and is not normally used for other purposes. It must be available on a 24-hour basis. If it is felt that a stash car will be needed, the advance agent is responsible for making the arrangements to rent one.

The stash car should be parked in a secure, but readily accessible place. As a part of his briefing, the advance agent should describe the vehicle and its parking location to the other agents. The keys to the stash car should be kept in the command post along with duplicate keys to all vehicles. No one else should be given a description or location of this vehicle.

If a stash car has been obtained, the limo driver should take the protectee's vehicle home or to the limousine garage at the end of the day; i.e., when the protectee has no further use for the limousine. The agent should already have ascertained, as a part of his driver briefing, the phone number where the driver will be, how long it will take him to get back if needed, and what time he is to report back to duty. The driver should be given telephone numbers for the command post and/or the agent.

If agents are staying at a location different than their protectee, it will probably be necessary to provide a shift change vehicle for use in transporting agents to and from work. This sometimes is the situation with extended trips. For example, the protectee's party may occupy a high-rise condominium, keeping only one or two agents with them, and the rest of the team may be housed in a nearby hotel or apartment.

The stash car should not be used as a shift change vehicle.

Additional Considerations

What happens if the limousine breaks down? The lead vehicle can be used as a back-up client car, at least until such time as a replacement vehicle can be obtained. This is yet another reason for dealing with a top nationally known agency. Their vehicles are generally in newer and better condition, and the agency has sufficient vehicles to produce a replacement quickly.

All vehicles used by the protectee must either be kept in a secure place under constant surveillance or, as is more often the case, if they are left unsecured, these vehicles must be visually checked before they are used.

If portable radios are being used, they should be assigned to the protectee's vehicle, follow-up vehicle, and lead vehicle. The medical kit, which should be taken on each movement, should be placed in the protectee's vehicle.

It is standard procedure with a team for the agent or driver assigned to the protectee, prior to a departure, to contact the agent at the next stop by radio or telephone. Both parties should understand the route which will be taken by the protectee's vehicle and the estimated travel time.

Public Transportation

Protective details almost never use public transportation, particularly buses and subways. There is no reason to do so, and subways can be terrible traps, often besieged by crime. Taxi cabs are another matter. In those cities which have horrendous traffic problems and there is little use for a rental car, taxis are not all bad. Taxi drivers generally know the city, they are low profile, and it is unlikely that an attacker (unless he has you under surveillance) will know that the client or the agent is in the taxi. Overseas, taxis are often a very good way to move about the city. Many countries and cities require that their taxi drivers take special training, and these drivers are licensed and carefully regulated by the local police. A hotel Concierge can obtain the services of such a driver. These licensed taxi drivers often have big, fairly comfortable vehicles, and they are accustomed to being hired not only for one ride, but often for several hours or days, doubling as tourist guides. The rates for a car and driver can be surprisingly inexpensive. Many licensed taxi drivers speak English fairly fluently, as it may be a requirement of their training. Some cities, London being one, are famous for their good taxi service. And, London taxicabs are among the most comfortable in the world.

There is one cautionary note. In some cities, for example in Tokyo, cab fares are incredibly, unbelievably expensive, sometimes costing over $100 for a ride in from the airport to downtown. If the plan calls for a taxi ride in from the airport, one should first look for a dispatcher and inquire as to taxicab fares. Very often, the dispatcher will quote a straight price and may even write out a ticket. This is always preferable simply to jumping into the first cab, whose driver may have no compunction about adding in a few fees for baggage, tolls, etc. Transportation overseas often seems better organized than in the United States. More people in other countries utilize public transportation. In this country, another form of "public" transportation is the limousine hired only for the pick-up or delivery from one point to another. This is usually a hassle-free, though somewhat more expensive, way of obtaining transportation from or to the airport, with a driver standing by and ready to assist.

Travel Routes

In picking a travel route, there are several considerations. You will always plan a primary and a secondary route to each destination, especially if the protectee is involved in a publicized event. What is needed is the safest, yet shortest point from start to finish. Utilizing limited access (freeway) routes is highly desirable. Freeways (except during rush hour) move traffic quickly, and there are very limited opportunities for anyone to ambush the protectee's car. A drive-by shooting is a remote possibility, but the danger of being attacked on a freeway is infinitely smaller than being ambushed on a side street. The quickest way to pick a route is to ask advice from the police officer who is in charge of traffic for that city. No one knows more about the movement of traffic within the city, nor the proximity to emergency services than that person. And, in addition, that officer may have been asked to chart the same route for other dignitaries in the past. If a route has already been pre-selected, it is a good idea to visit with the same police officer and seek his opinion on the route chosen. This officer can furnish the agent with the telephone number of the city department that handles road construction and repair. A telephone call to this department can reveal whether any construction is currently underway or is being planned along the chosen routes.

All routes should be driven in advance, preferably more than once. The agent must map out the distance between locations, plus the time required to travel the route under normal traffic conditions and with heavy traffic conditions. He must note the proximity to hospitals and safe areas (police station, military facilities, etc.), traffic problems, and potential delaying conditions such as construction, railroad crossings, and toll booths. Any security or travel problems should be noted.

Routes should be driven at approximately the same time as will be driven with the protectee. That is, if the actual travel will be done during rush hour traffic, then the primary and secondary routes must be advanced at those same hours. If the travel is to be done at night, the routes must be advanced at night. How difficult will it be to see at night? Can some kind of landmarks be identified to help with turns? Freeway access entries and exits must be noted by number. Everything must be done to ensure that the drivers will have clear directions and no problem in identifying turns. Nothing is more embarrassing than getting lost, particularly at night.

The secondary route should closely parallel the primary route so that, if it must be utilized, it can be reached quickly and without problems.

Once the primary and secondary routes have been established, they must be recorded in such a way that they are crystal clear to all drivers. This is done by marking a map and by giving typed street directions.

An excellent route map can be put together by first obtaining a large scale map of the city or area. These maps can usually be purchased in a 7-Eleven or other convenience store, or from a bookstore, and sometimes from a service station. These maps are in color and, while they look very nice, they are not going to be very useful in color for marking a route. A useful trick is to photocopy (xerox) the map, if possible enlarging it to show more detail of your route. A clean photocopy in black and white will show all of the important detail, and is ideal for marking the route with a highliter (not a magic marker). Use one color for the main route and a different color for subsidiary routes. Use a third color for emergency hospitals and safe havens. Each route should be shown completely from destination A to destination B on one map. If the route is too long, the photocopy can be reduced in size; this makes it harder to read, but it gets everything on one page.

About copy machines--these wonderful machines can do many useful things. They can produce different sizes: 8-1/2 x 11 (regular size); 8-1/2 x 14 (legal size); and 11 x 17 (large size). The material being copied, in this case a map, can therefore be reproduced in larger type on a larger piece of paper, etc. The route maps should be of a size that is not awkward to handle, and if there are several maps, they can be fitted in a 3-ring binder, in the order in which they are to be used, primary route first, followed by secondary route. Copiers can also make double-sided copies, in which case you might show the primary route on the front, and the secondary route on the back.

The typewritten route directions should be clearly indicated and double-spaced. These directions can also, if desired, be photocopied in enlarged form. Most computer printers have large type, which is useful for this purpose. It is best to describe turns as left (west), or right (east). "Left" and "right" are always easier to figure out than east and west; however, sometimes the street signs are indicated as east and west. It is always a good idea to write directions as follows: "From the WOODBRIDGE Exit, #274, turn left (west) on the first cross street BELLEVIEW--proceed to the 2nd stoplight and turn right (north) on SPRING--proceed 4 blocks to a stop sign, with a 7-Eleven on the corner--turn . . . . ." The driver now has, in addition to his map, very clear directions which tell him numbers of blocks, directional turns, and street names. At night it is very difficult to read street signs, and if the directions do not indicate approximate distances and landmarks (the 7-Eleven store, a Texaco station, etc.) it is easy to miss the turn. In some cases, the streets do not have street signs. The directions must make it foolproof to navigate without them. If the lack of street signs or anything else makes a fairly substantial problem, a Polaroid camera shot of the corner where the turn is to be made can make life easier.

When the route maps and directions are given to the drivers, the agent should review them with the driver(s) to make sure everyone clearly understands them, with any problems discussed in advance. Freeway exits can sometimes be quite confusing, and a wrong turn can place the vehicles in a very bad situation, with many twists and turns to get back on the right route. Any problems of this nature should be pointed out.

AIR TRANSPORTATION

Since the protectee will almost always travel longer distances by air, airport advances are an intrinsic part of the advance survey.

Airports are divided into areas which cater to commercial aviation, private aircraft, and cargo handling. Agents rarely are involved with the cargo handling areas, except possibly in small towns when they might be expecting delivery of large air cargo items. The commercial aviation areas are strictly controlled, provide their own security, and regulate all flights of commercial airlines. The private aircraft area is known as the General Aviation, or more often, the Fixed Base Operation (FBO). The FBO will administer services to private aircraft, corporate aircraft, and charter aircraft. The FBO is generally more relaxed and caters more to the individual needs of the customers. FBO's provide landing and storage space for aircraft, gasoline and oil, sometimes repairs, and often quasi-concierge services; i.e., will recommend hotels, restaurants, secure taxicabs, etc. Corporate aircraft make extensive use of the FBO's. Sometimes, in a metropolitan area, one FBO may be at the main airport, and yet another FBO will be located at a smaller airport in a different location. In Denver, for example, there is an FBO at Denver International Airport, the major commercial airport, and another FBO many miles south at Centennial Airport, a smaller, but many feel more secure, airport.

The building housing the FBO will usually be marked with big letters, GENERAL AVIATION, or sometimes with the name of the FBO, such as COMBS GATES, or BUTLER AVIATION. Generally, the FBO will not be on the same street as, nor even very close to, the main streets into the commercial aviation area of the airport.

Charter and Private Aircraft

Aircraft (planes) can be chartered in almost any area in the country. Charter companies are listed in the telephone yellow pages under "Aircraft, Charter, Rental & Leasing." If arrangements and payment are to be made by the agent, he will need a credit card with a high charge limit, as charter fees are quite high. The charter companies operate from the General Aviation (FBO) facilities.

In leasing a plane, the agent must make certain that the aircraft can fly in and land at the destination site, and that it has the correct safety equipment. For example, if the flight is destined for Aspen, Colorado in the middle of winter, does the aircraft have proper de-icing equipment and oxygen to fly at the 16,000-foot level required to get over the mountains? It doesn't hurt to ask to see the maintenance record for the aircraft.

What will be the capacity of the aircraft for people and baggage? Will the aircraft have internal ramp steps for entry and exit from the plane?

The advance agent is responsible for making arrangements for food and beverages, if these are required. Services and prices vary widely among charter companies, with some companies catering to upscale executives while others offer more or less "bare bones" transportation. The more expensive charter companies may be able to provide an aircraft with the interior equipped as an office, with full communications and flight attendant(s).

The crew should be instructed not to accept any baggage, equipment, or items unless it has been vetted by the protection agent or the protectee or protectee's family. Only passengers or crew should load items onto the aircraft. A list or manifest of the aircraft's cargo should be drawn up, particularly when flying to a foreign country where undoubtedly such a list will be required by customs.

If the flight is destined to another country, the agent must make certain that the charter company, or corporate aircraft, has the proper licensing, insurance, and immigrations and customs documentation.

The advance agent will need to contact the operations supervisor at the FBO arrival site. This is the individual who can keep the agent posted on the pending arrival of the protectee's aircraft and accommodate special requests. For example, he can arrange permission for limousines and baggage vehicles to drive directly to the aircraft.

Some general aviation facilities have more than one Fixed Base Operator. The agent must make certain he knows which FBO is being used and has identified the exact location where the craft will arrive, be serviced, and depart.

In advancing the FBO facility, the agent will need to obtain a diagram or map of the airport and ramp areas. The FBO operations supervisor can provide the agent with a general overview of the airport topography and relationship to access roads. The advance agent must map out the primary and alternate routes into and out of the airport complex, and to and from the closest full facility emergency hospital. The agent will need to provide route maps to each of the protective detail drivers and brief them on any specific facts.

Does the FBO provide ramp steps for aircraft, and do the ramp steps "fit" the aircraft which the advance agent has chartered?

Within the FBO facility, restrooms and telephones must be located. Is there any private or semi-private area which can be used for a V.I.P. holding area? If the media is expected, will this area be large enough to accommodate the media? If not, is there an appropriate outside area that can be used for greeting guests, fans, and/or other audiences, and have working space for the media?

The agent should ascertain and note the hours of airport operation, and he must obtain the names and telephone numbers (including home numbers, if possible) of airport supervisors.

Private aircraft pilots communicate with the FBO personnel, just as commercial pilots are in communication with the control tower at the commercial airport. Therefore, the communications people at the FBO can provide incoming arrival times to the protective agent if they have certain information. They must know the following: type of aircraft the protectee is traveling in, call signs, tail number, and owner of the aircraft. Knowing when the protectee is expected to arrive is, of course, important to waiting guests, dignitaries, security personnel, limousine drivers, and the media if they are to be present. All these people need time to prepare for the impending arrival, and will be relying on the advance agent for status reports on its progress.

Once the protectee's aircraft is on the ground, the advance agent should connect with the pilot, noting his and the crew's phone numbers and hotel or local residence numbers where they will be staying. The advance agent should make certain that the pilot has the most up-to-date itinerary, and he should ascertain the time that the plane will be available for loading luggage and passengers for departure. The agent should coordinate with the pilot as to arrangements for any food, beverages, or other servicing arrangements.

The agent should determine if the plane will be guarded while it is on the ground; in all likelihood, it probably will not be if it is simply left up to the FBO for security. Typically, there may be one guard who might, or might not, patrol the area. Security of the aircraft is usually an air crew responsibility, although this does not mean that a crew member is going to sit at the airport watching the plane.

There are some things which can be done to upgrade security. The agent can request that the plane be parked on a ramp close to the FBO building, in a well lighted area. *Any maintenance that might be required, as well as servicing, should be done with a crew member present.* Aircraft doors should be locked whenever the crew is not on hand and

alarm systems activated. If it is determined that additional security is warranted, the operations supervisor at the FBO can recommend a guard service acceptable to him. If the situation warrants it, the advance agent may recommend that one or more agents be assigned to security posts at the FBO. These posts might include any high ground which could be infiltrated by a sniper, the area around the plane, and the FBO building facility.

Before boarding the aircraft, the crew, who understand the aircraft, should inspect it carefully, inside and outside, for any signs of tampering.

Well in advance of leaving for the airport which will be handling the protectee's departure, the agent should check with the operations supervisor at the airport for a weather report that covers the entire flight, and the expected length of flight time to the next destination.

If agents are included as passengers on the aircraft, one agent should remain outside the aircraft while another stands just inside the door until the plane is ready to taxi. This provides continued surveillance until immediately before the plane begins to move. Agents' weapons should not be exposed nor left unattended either on the aircraft or within the FBO facility.

If there are agents or other individuals at the next destination preparing for the arrival of the protectee, these people should be contacted with information about arrival time.

Helicopters

If a helicopter is deemed necessary or desirable, the agent must coordinate with the helicopter leasing service to determine what conditions will be necessary for landing the craft. Will a landing pad be necessary? What are the conditions (overhead wires, lights for a night landing, etc.)? Helicopters are limited by size and weight as to how many passengers and how much baggage can be carried. **It is absolutely essential to learn the safety**

rules for boarding and disembarking. No one wants to lose a client to a spinning rotor.

Corporate Aircraft

Many corporations own their own jet aircraft; large corporations, in fact, may own a fleet of planes. Where there is a corporate aircraft, there will be a crew to fly the plane, and the crew will have the primary responsibility for overseeing the maintenance, servicing, safety, and security of the aircraft. By and large, corporate pilots and crew are competent and conscientious. Some, in fact, have acquired executive protection training. However, they often do not have as detailed an understanding of security measures as one might wish.

It is, of course, important that the agents work closely with the corporate flight crew. As with other aspects of corporate protection, tact and diplomacy will help to accomplish a close working relationship. Flight crews often tend to exhibit some proprietary or slightly arrogant attitudes about their abilities to perform all tasks in and around the aircraft, but these attitudes can be overcome with a friendly exchange of information and an establishment of mutual respect.

Strong consideration should be given to acquisition of an alarm security system. In general, there are two general alarm systems--on-board systems and portable systems. On-board systems are expensive, very expensive, but well worth cost if one considers the cost of the aircraft (in the millions of dollars) and the worth of the passengers.

If a security system is deemed necessary for the protection of the aircraft, the crew will be essential in designing the system since they, more than anyone else save the designer, will understand the vulnerabilities of the plane. Once a security system is installed, it should be used, always, even if the aircraft is to be parked for as little as an hour. Portable systems are much less expensive and are quite handy if the aircraft is not owned by the client. For example, if charter aircraft is used, a portable system, while not as complete as an on-board system, is quite effective.

Corporate travel is generally handled through one of the many corporate departments, and this means that itineraries and schedules can become garbled, restrictive, or withheld from the agents. However, this information always is given to the flight crew(s)--another reason to establish a close working relationship between agents and crew.

Tip: offer to give the flight crew instruction in shooting and driving. It wins their hearts, and it may provide a back-up contingent.

Baggage

The control of baggage--getting it intact from Point A to Points B and C--is a homely but essential element in the success of a traveling detail. This is one of the many executive protection chores which are non-exciting but highly important.

All bags should be *counted* and *identified* before departing a residence or aircraft terminal. For rapid identification, all bags and particularly those belonging to the protectee, the protectee's party (by name), agents, and the ones going to the command post should be distinctively coded. The markings should be different for each category. The name of the protectee and/or his corporation should not appear on his bags. If the protective team is sufficiently large, whenever possible an agent should be assigned to the baggage. This is not to consign the agent as a baggage handler, but he/she can verify that all of, and the correct number of, the bags coming off one mode of transport are the same ones being loaded onto the next, whether it is vehicle to plane or vice versa.

The agent assigned to baggage duty should count and verify the movement of bags. It is most efficient to have the same agent repeat this process at every stop. The agent should plan on having the baggage loaded into one vehicle, thus making it easier to control the movement of the baggage. This vehicle should be scheduled to leave at least 30 minutes before the departure of the protectee. The agent assigned to the baggage should check with the protectee's staff to make certain that no bags have been left behind.

With baggage (in hotels and airports) comes baggage handlers, and this means tips. If tips are to be distributed to the baggage handlers it is always better to determine, prior to the transfer of bags, how this will be handled. Will a member of the protectee's staff handle this, or will an agent be expected to tip and then voucher tips with other expenses? This is another one of those small details that can cause endless confusion at the end of a trip unless it is anticipated and handled in advance.

Commercial Airlines

The Airline Service Representative is a valuable contact as a fixer of problems with anything concerned with the commercial airlines. This is not the person behind the counter in the "Customer Service" area. The Airline Service Representative is usually a very experienced staff employee with an office somewhere behind either the ticket counters or in the vicinity. This person can often arrange for a holding room for arrival and departure with phone and restrooms; special seating aboard the aircraft; permission for protectee to board last; baggage stored top-side or loaded last into the baggage compartment so that they can be off-loaded first; off-load luggage into vehicle or baggage truck on ramp; and perhaps arrange to board the party from the ramp instead of walking through the terminal.

Understand that the Airline Service Representative does not *have to do* any of these things, but usually can do so if he or she understands the urgency of the situation. As always, one should only ask for those things that are really necessary. Get the name of the Representative, keep the name for future reference, and write a thank-you note.

It is very useful to belong to one or more airline clubs. The larger airlines, including United, Continental, Delta, and American, have private club memberships. Being a member entitles you to admittance into the private club room located conveniently in the airport. There is at least some form of security (anyone entering must show identification). Beverages and snacks are available, as well as telephones and, sometimes, fax machines. Club personnel are very helpful in arranging changes in flight plans. It is a much better environment than sitting exposed in the public waiting areas.

Airlines are at the mercy of the weather and mechanical problems, either of which can mean canceling a flight. When that happens, the agent should have a contingency plan with alternate flight times or some way of dealing with the problem. For example, the agent and his protectee arrive in Denver on United Airlines, only to be informed that, due to weather conditions, all United Express flights into Aspen have been canceled. Other than staying overnight in Denver, what are the options? There are, from time to time, other, smaller airlines which operate in and out of Aspen, using different type aircraft than United. Are any of their flights still operative, and is there space on the next flight? Is there a flight to Grand Junction, 140 miles west of Aspen and at a lower altitude? If so, how soon is the next flight, and can a vehicle be reserved there for the 2-1/2-hour drive to Aspen? Better yet, there is an airport at Eagle, Colorado, 70 miles from Aspen -- are there available flights? Is there a limo service to Aspen from Denver, a five-hour drive in bad weather? There should always be a fall-back plan when flying.

Agents meeting a commercial airline should consider going unarmed so as not to create problems with local and federal authorities.

Agents traveling aboard commercial aircraft should turn radios off during the flight. Don't carry mace, tear gas, knives, etc. Put all individual weapons (unloaded) in one bag and declare that bag as containing firearms. Make sure weapons in the command post kit are unloaded, and declare the command post kit as containing firearms.

One agent or staff member should have all tickets and boarding passes. If there is an attempted hijacking of the aircraft, no action should be taken unless absolutely necessary.

International Travel by Air

If the protectee has been traveling overseas an agent will usually be detailed to meet him and his party upon arrival back in the United States. By contacting the Airline Service Representative, the agent may be able to secure that person's assistance in processing the client through Customs and Immigration (C/I). Whenever possible, the protectee should be met at the C/I area rather than the public portions of the airport. If the protectee has diplomatic status, the agent should notify the C/I personnel, and they will often be able to expedite the procedures through their facilities.

EMERGENCY SERVICES

The three emergency services which must be advanced are hospitals, fire and ambulance, and police. Whenever possible, these services should be physically checked, not merely identified by location. There is a variation in services, particularly with hospitals, and all hospitals do not have emergency services.

Hospitals

The advance agent must identify and locate the major full service hospitals at the visit site area and must physically visit them to make certain that they will be suitable. The first requirement, of course, is that the hospital must be able to accept patients; that is, it is not a military or government hospital with restricted admittance. Second, the hospital should have a 24-hour emergency room or shock/trauma unit, with a doctor on duty 24 hours a day. Other desirable attributes would include a burn care center, ample whole blood supply, well equipped operating room, good high-tech equipment, and rapid access to specialists such as neurosurgeons, cardiologists, and orthopedic surgeons.

The advance survey will include a brief walk-through of the facility to locate the emergency entrance and the route leading to this entrance. Some hospitals inexplicably "hide" these entrances or make

it necessary for a driver to be quite familiar with the streets surrounding the hospital to reach the emergency entrance quickly and unerringly. Is there either a designated helicopter landing area or a clear area which could be used for this purpose if needed? The agent also needs to know if there is a V.I.P. hospital room and space for security.

The primary and alternate routes to the hospital(s), with descriptions as to how to reach the emergency entrances, should be mapped out and given to the driver(s) of the vehicles to be used by the protectee and his party.

It is very important that the advance agent know before departure the general medical condition and any particular health problems of the protectee. This information will aid him in his advance survey of site hospitals. Ideally, the detail leader should have obtained a medical history on the protectee which would include any special problems, blood type, allergies, etc. If the client is reluctant to provide this information, it can usually be handled by asking him to fill in one of those typical Medical History Questionnaires which the doctors and hospitals use. The protectee can fill it in, place it in an envelope, seal it, and keep it with him until just before departure, at which time he should turn over the sealed envelope to the agent. The agent will only open the envelope in an emergency and will return it to the client at the end of the trip. If the protectee is traveling with his family, a medical history should be available for each member of the family.

In major metropolitan cities there are pharmacies which are open 24 hours a day. As a part of the advance, the agent should locate one or more of these pharmacies. This is particularly useful if the protectee takes prescription drugs.

Fire and Ambulance

The agent should find out the response time of the Fire Department to the various locations where the protectee will be. Response time to residences in small town locations may be a real problem, particularly if the residence is located up a winding road, ten miles outside of town, in the winter, with snow on the ground. Effective response time could be 30 minutes or longer. Beyond that, there is not much involved with the Fire Department in the advance. If it is a small town, the agent might wish to check on the amount and quality of the equipment.

Ambulance services may be provided either through a hospital, a volunteer service, or a private service, and there can be a significant difference in the level of care provided. The agent should determine the response time of each ambulance service, and try to obtain recommendations from some knowledgeable source as to which ambulance service provides the best trained personnel. This is a good place to put in a recommendation that every professional executive protection agent should not only be well schooled in First Respondent Medicine, but also be a certified Emergency Medical Technician (EMT). During his or her career, an agent may never have reason to pull his or her gun, but *will*, guaranteed, be called upon to deal with some medical problem that will range from serious to life-threatening. This includes keeping a careful eye on the ambulance personnel called to administer to a protectee, to be certain that *they* do not cause further damage. This bears repeating. Ambulance personnel range from barely trained in first aid to highly skilled, extremely competent individuals. If there is an accident or incident, the agent's responsibility to his client does not end when the ambulance arrives. This is not to say that the agent should be a nuisance or take it upon himself to tell the ambulance personnel what to do. He should only intervene if he feels that the handling and treatment of the client is actually causing further damage.

Police and Sheriff

The advance agent, as has already been discussed, should make contact professionally with the local police. The agent needs to know response time and distance from the police station. He will certainly want to check with the police as to local conditions, presenting his intelligence analysis for the Chief's review. If the agent perceives a need for

additional security, he may wish to inquire about hiring off-duty police. It is not at all uncommon for off-duty police to fill in as security personnel. There are some distinct advantages to this. Police officers can carry concealed weapons legally, know the area, can make arrests, may agree to run background checks on employees, and won't get lost going to various locations. Typically, they make good security drivers. It will undoubtedly cost more than hiring a contract guard but may be well worth the money if a higher level of security is needed.

If the situation is such that the protectee is a high ranking political figure or foreign dignitary, the police may be called upon to provide escort services, and liaison should be established for this.

The Sheriff's department may be a source of obtaining permission to carry a weapon concealed--perhaps. If the agent is a Reserve Deputy Sheriff in his home area, he may be able to convince the Sheriff to extend the same privileges to him in the guest city.

Disaster Planning

Disasters are normally of the fire, earthquake, flood, hurricane, and tornado category. The probability of a disaster is not very high, but the consequences of one can be enormous. Almost all communities have disaster plans. For the agent, the most important issue is finding a relocation site. The most likely disaster is a fire in the hotel where the protectee is staying. If there is a fire or a hostage situation which requires evacuating the hotel, there should be a relocation site identified in advance and transportation arrangements made to get there. While police stations offer safety, they make poor emergency relocation sites, unless they are in small towns. They tend to be filled with noise, confusion, holding cells with unattractive people, and hard benches which may have to be shared with people you would not wish to spend time with.

Hotels have greatly improved their own disaster planning, often providing for relocation of their guests. In hurricane or earthquake-prone areas, many hotels have safe areas in which to take refuge, and have organized evacuation procedures. This issue should be discussed with the hotel Security Director.

DETAIL BRIEFING

A detailed briefing of all team members must be given by the detail leader or advance agent. The briefing should consist of more than merely handing out pieces of paper. Advance information should be organized as itineraries, route maps, intelligence assessments, diagrams, names of contacts, telephone numbers, description of special problems, everything that the detail must know.

The detail leader or advance agent will give a description of the protectee(s), including any special (health) problems, plus a description of the members of the official party, if any.

The destination(s) and itineraries should be reviewed in detail and integrated with agent assignments. Transportation, routes, hotel, special events, hospital, police and emergency--all information needs to be discussed. Responsibilities for the protective equipment, baggage, tickets, etc. must be assigned.

Intelligence reports and threat assessments should be discussed and any special instructions given. If identification pins are to be used, they should be described or passed around. Names, telephone numbers, and contacts should be made available for everyone.

If the trip is to be made overseas, any information regarding the customs and cultures of that country should be given. It may be useful to give each member of the detail a small guidebook to the area (obtainable in bookstores), and make it required reading.

Detail members should be kept up to date on changes in itinerary, post assignments, and intelligence information. Copies of this information should be posted in the command post. With a traveling detail, this is the kind of information that should be posted on the bulletin board or chalkboard and reinforced with periodic briefings by the detail leader.

CAVEAT

This is one of the longer chapters in the book, which should indicate the importance of advance surveys. Good, thorough advances can be, and are, complex and time consuming. Is it worth the time, effort, and expense? Absolutely. If the protectee is at risk, and there are adversaries trying to get to him, a thorough advance will either deprive them of the opportunity to attack, or convince them that their target is too well protected to proceed.

But, what if time, manpower, and budgets do not permit the luxury of a full scale advance? What if the agent is working alone and has only the time for a brief two-minute advance survey--is this still a worthwhile effort? Of course it is. The agent should never permit his protectee to enter the unknown. A quick look around to detect any obvious problems will eliminate 90% of the potential for problems. Hopefully, that will be enough.

Foreign advances and those done within the United States are conducted similarly. A foreign advance will cover transportation, hotels and residences, restaurants, travel routes, emergency services, and special events and functions--the same areas which must be included in a U.S. advance survey. There are, of course, some differences, and these differences are rooted in the different cultures, customs, attitudes, politics, and economic conditions which the agent will encounter. This is why it is so important to do some quick advance reading about the country or area to which the protectee will be traveling. Equally important is the need for a good sense of awareness and sensitivity to others' reactions. If you feel that you are making someone uncomfortable, you probably are correct. You may have to modify or soften your approach in seeking information.

In many countries, dignity and respect are extremely important. Any requests for information should be couched in such a way that the other person does not feel that he or his country is being criticized or demeaned. Be generous with courteous expressions such as "Please," "Thank you," "I will greatly appreciate your help in arranging. . .," and "Would it be convenient for you if I . . . ?" As with any culture, good manners will carry the day.

PRE-DEPARTURE PREPARATIONS

In addition to the information which an advance agent will need and which has been covered in detail heretofore, he will need a *passport*. He may need one or more *visas*; some countries require them, others do not. He should have a *shot record*, showing immunizations and dates they were administered. An *international driver's license* is not always necessary, but, if it is only needed once, it pays to obtain one, easily done through the AAA automobile clubs located throughout the U.S. First,

however, is intelligence acquisition.

Intelligence Acquisition

The U.S. State Department can provide useful information with a call to the "desk officer" for the country to which you are traveling. The handy booklet published by the Superintendent of Documents, U.S. Government Printing Office in Washington, DC, *Key Officers of Foreign Posts/Guide for U.S. Business Representatives*, will list names of embassy and consulate officers with addresses and telephone numbers for each country. A call in advance can obtain answers to some questions.

A separate division, or department, of the State Department is the Overseas Security Advisory Council (OSAC). OSAC consists of 21 organizations from the private sector and four U.S. government departments and agencies. There are 1,400-plus private sector organizations that participate in the Council's activities and are recipients of the information and guidance it provides.

As part of its security program, OSAC has prepared publications containing suggested security and emergency planning guidelines for American private sector personnel and organizations abroad. OSAC has also published a number of booklets dealing with terrorism threats, catastrophes, crime, and theft of information. The OSAC Internet website is at < http://ds.state.gov/osac/ >

The State Department maintains a website < http://travel.state.gov/travel_warnings.html >which is quite helpful, if not totally current. It issues travel warnings as well as a wealth of information on visa and immunization requirements, crime, known terrorism, etc.

The Department of State publishes

Background Notes on countries worldwide. These are brief, factual pamphlets with information on each country's culture, history, geography, economy, government, and current political situation. The *Background Notes* are available for approximately 170 countries. They often include a reading list, travel notes, and maps. To purchase copies, you can contact the Superintendent of Documents, U.S. Government Printing Office, Washington, DC 20402, or call (202) 512-1800.

Yet another State Department Internet website < http://www.state.gov/www/global/terrorism/index. html> is the home page for the Office of the Coordinator for Counterterrorism. It is physically located at: Office of the Coordinator for Counterterrorism, Office of Public Affairs, Room 2507, Dept. of State, 2201 C Street NW, Washington, DC 20520.

All of these resources should be tapped as part of a pre-departure advance plan and added to the in-house files.

Passports

By definition, a passport is an official warrant certifying the citizenship of the bearer and affording protection to him when traveling abroad. While on the one hand, a passport is an absolute necessity when traveling in most countries outside the United States, and while it still carries an important image, it is not a guarantee of U.S. rights or special treatment. Break the law in another country, and you will pay the penalty; however, a U.S. passport still signifies the interest of the United States government and has bailed many a hapless traveler out of sticky situations. Canada and Mexico do not require passports of U.S. citizens, but because of the significance of, and importance of, the U.S. passport, it is an excellent idea to carry one even in those countries. A passport is a record of unchallenged identity (unless the passport, itself, can be proved to be fraudulent), and for that reason will be required by almost all hotels and rental car agencies abroad.

Passports can be obtained through a U.S.

Passport Office located in various locations throughout the United States, at many Federal and state courts, probate courts, at some county/municipal offices, or at most U.S. post offices. The post office does not, itself, issue the passport but will collect the necessary documents from the applicant and then forward them to the proper authorities. The entire process will usually take six to eight weeks (25 working days from receipt of the application at the passport agency) and so should be applied for well in advance. If you wish or need to receive your passport sooner, you may request expedited service for processing of the passport within three business days from receipt of the application by a passport agency. Currently, the fee for expedited service is $35.00 in addition to the regular passport fee. If you request expedited service, your departure date should be clearly shown on the application. (Sending in your application data by overnite service also saves time.)

Any professional agent should automatically obtain a passport so that he or she has it at all times for immediate use. The process takes much less time if you request it in person at a U.S. Passport Office, perhaps as little as one or two weeks. In an emergency, it is possible to obtain a passport from a U.S. State Department office within a matter of hours if you appear in person, and if you are holding a valid plane ticket for departure within, say, 48 hours, and have with you your birth certificate and passport photos.

In order to obtain a passport you will need the following:

. A certified copy of your birth certificate, or previously issued U.S. passport (if you have one).

. If born abroad, a naturalization certificate.

. Two identical 2" x 2" front-view passport photos.

. Completed passport application, signed in front of an officer of the U.S. Passport Office, a clerk of a court, or the post office employee who accepts the application.

. Additional documentation (proof) of identity, such as a driver's license, with your photo attached.

. A check in the correct amount.

If you cannot obtain a birth certificate, submit a notice from a state registrar stating that no birth record exists, accompanied by the best secondary evidence possible. This may include a baptismal certificate, a hospital birth record, affidavits of persons having personal knowledge of the facts of your birth, or other documentary evidence such as early census, school, family Bible records, and insurance papers.

The name which you use to sign the passport application form is the name which will appear on the passport. What does this mean? Let us say that, for reasons of anonymity, you sign your application as "M. Browning," rather than your full name of "Martin J. Browning." "M. Browning" will appear on your passport, thus partially disguising the name. You are required, of course, to use your legal surname.

Passports are valid for ten years from date of issue. One should never leave the country with a passport that is close to expiration. Better to go through the process of having a new passport renewed six months prior to expiration than to take a chance on suddenly needing to go overseas with a passport due to run out in two weeks. If it appears that you will be traveling a great deal, request a passport with extra sheets (as many as 48) for visas.

You can obtain a renewal of your passport if the expiration date is less than eight years away (within two years of expiration). It is obtained in the same way as obtaining the original passport, through a Passport Office or the post office. You will need the old passport, two passport photos, completed renewal passport application form, and a check in the proper amount.

There is one other way to expedite getting your passport if you live in an area where there is no U.S. Passport Office. There are firms that specialize in handling passport and visa applications and can

obtain these in record time--two days in an emergency and two weeks for regular processing. For a first-time passport, you must still go to the post office, fill in and sign the application, and send with photos, birth certificate, and check. For a renewal, you must send a signed application, old passport, two photos, and check. Either TRAVISA in Washington, DC (1-800-222-2589) or PASSPORT PLUS in New York (1-800-367-1818) will do the legwork, standing in line, following through and overnight expressing the passport to you. Be prepared to pay for the service, but, in a real pinch, it's worth the price.

For complete information on obtaining and renewing passports, check the State Department's website< http://travel.state.gov/yourtripabroad.html >

Passports are extremely valuable and should be carefully safeguarded. If you lose your passport, there are some real difficulties in obtaining a new one, the suspicion being that the original passport was sold to an alien. If your passport is lost or stolen in the United States, report the loss or theft immediately to Passport Services, 1425 K Street, NW, Department of State, Washington, DC 20524. Should your passport be lost or stolen abroad, report the loss immediately to the nearest U.S. embassy or consulate and to the local police authorities.

There are diplomatic, military, and civilian passports and, in the modern era of hijackings, a civilian passport is probably the safest one to carry. If you already have a military or diplomatic passport, it is possible to also obtain a regular tourist passport. While a diplomatic passport brings undoubted privileges, particularly in customs and dealing with foreign police, it can be a hazard when dealing with terrorists in a hijacking or hostage incident. Terrorists always collect passports, and have often shown more brutal treatment of military and U.S. officials. It is a matter of individual decision for you and your client. Hijackings seem to have abated for the time being, but this could, of course, change at any time.

Passport agencies are located as follows:

Boston Passport Agency
Room 247, Thomas P. O'Neill Federal Building
10 Causeway Street
Boston, MA 02222

Chicago Passport Agency
Suite 3808, Kluczynski Federal Building
230 South Dearborn Street
Chicago, IL 60604
(312) 341-6020

Honolulu Passport Agency
First Hawaiian Tower
1132 Bishop Street, #500
Honolulu, HI 9685
(808) 541-1919

Houston Passport Agency
Mickey Leland Federal Building
1919 Smith Street
Houston, TX 77002-8049
(713) 751-0294

Los Angeles Passport Agency
Room 13100, 1100 Wilshire Boulevard
Los Angeles, CA 90024-3615
(310) 575-5700

Miami Passport Agency
3rd Floor, Federal Office Building
51 Southwest First Avenue
Miami, FL 33130-1680
(305) 539-3600

New Orleans Passport Agency
One Canal Place
Corner of Canal & North Peters Streets
New Orleans, LA 70113
(504) 589-6728 and (504) 589-6161

New York Passport Agency
376 Hudson Street
New York, NY 10114
(212) 206-3500

Philadelphia Passport Agency

U.S. Custom House
220 Chestnut Street, Room 103
Philadelphia, PA 19106-2970
(215) 418-5937

San Francisco Passport Agency
Suite 200, 525 Market Avenue
San Francisco, CO 94105
(415) 974-7972 and (415) 974-9941

Seattle Passport Agency
Room 992, Federal Office Building
915 Second Avenue
Seattle, WA 98174-1091
(206) 442-7941 and (206) 442-7945

Stamford Passport Agency
One Landmark Square
Broad & Atlantic Streets
Stamford, CT 06901
(203) 969-9000

Washington Passport Agency
1119 19th Street, NW
Washington, DC 20524
(202) 647-0518

Visas

Whereas passports identify individuals as being citizens of certain countries, visas are the diplomatic permission which a country extends to a citizen of another country to visit its country. Some countries require visas; others do not. Department of State Publication M-264, *Foreign Entry Requirements*, is available from the Consumer Information Center, Dept. 438T, Pueblo, CO, 81009, telephone (719) 948-4000, Internet <www.pueblo.gsa.gov> -- and from the State Department's Internet website at <http://travel.state.gov/foreignentryreqs.html>. In this era of the European Common Market, and with other trade coalitions forming daily, an increasing number of countries do not require visas. If there is any question, contact the consular office of the country to be visited. The publication, *Foreign Consular Offices in the United States*, contains the

U.S. addresses of all foreign diplomatic offices; it is available from the Superintendent of Documents, U.S. Government Printing Office, Washington, DC 20402.

Visa requirements should be checked with the consular officials of the embassies for the countries to be visited well in advance of departure date. Some visa approvals require only a few days for processing while others may take two weeks or longer, even if you apply in person. Information which you will need is as follows:

.   Immunization documents.

.   Currency restrictions--there may be a limit to the amount or kind of currency which you can bring into the country.

.   Exit requirements.

.   Number of visa photos (usually two).

.   Travel restrictions within the country and from country to country.

.   Licensing, insurance and any needed permits for a vehicle.

.   Items that may not be carried into the country, in particular weapons, radios, tape recorders, cameras, and other security equipment.

The visas will be issued, usually in duplicate form, stapled in your passport. One copy of the visa will be handed over to customs upon entering the guest country and one copy must be surrendered upon departure. Take care of *all* copies and do not throw any away. The duplicate copy is not for you. Not having the exit visa can present a real problem, as the first suspicion is that you have sold your exit visa to someone else.

In some cases, the visa permit will be stamped directly on a page in your passport, which may require leaving your passport with the consulate authorities for a day or so. Note that a visa will not

be granted to anyone whose passport is due to expire prior to the expiration of the visa. If your passport is due to expire in six weeks, and the standard visa into a particular country is for a minimum of six months, they will not issue the visa, since your passport would expire before the expiration date of the visa. This is one of the reasons one should renew one's passport six months before it is due to expire. If you plan to make several trips to one country over, say, a six-month period, you should inquire as to whether you can obtain an extended visa. Some visas are available for different lengths of time: six weeks, three months, six months, or a year. However, you should be careful with this, as the longest visas may be "business" visas, and may require more explanations than you care to give.

Some Middle Eastern or African countries will not issue visas or allow entry if your passport indicates travel to Israel. There may be a similar problem with visas from Nationalist China and Peoples Republic of China. These countries are usually willing to stamp their visa on a separate piece of paper rather than (indelibly) in your passport. Be watchful, however; even when the visas from these three countries are only stapled into the passport, you must watch when you actually enter the country to make certain the Customs and Immigration official there does not stamp your passport. Consulates are used to being asked for a stapled form (which can later, after you leave, be removed from the passport). If, in spite of everything, you find that an offending visa has been stamped in your passport, you can, when it is feasible and you have the time, return your old passport and request a new one. This is also desirable if you travel a great deal to many countries, or to many troubled countries, and you do not wish to appear suspiciously like a secret agent to immigration officials.

It is wise to carry several extra passport-size photographs, as it is easier to obtain additional visas or a replacement passport if you have extra photos with you. Sometimes, during the trip, plans change and this may call for visiting a country for which you do not have a visa. It is usually possible to arrange, upon entry through the Customs and Immigration for that country, to obtain a temporary visa without too much trouble; however, it will require usually two pictures. It is very handy to have six or eight extra pictures in your passport folder at all times.

Because passports and visas are so important, many airlines ask to see them before allowing you on the plane. Were you to arrive at your destination without your passport, the airline may be fined by the entry country, and you will find yourself restricted to the plane. For this and other reasons, you should plan to arrive at the departure airport two hours in advance for an international flight to destinations that require passports and visas. Rushing into the airport 20 minutes before an international departure is almost guaranteed to lose your seat on the plane.

You should always make two photocopies of your passport and visas, one copy to be carried with you in case you lose your documents and one to leave behind in the office where a telephone call might help in replacement.

Immunizations, Shots and Health

The purpose of the International Health Regulations adopted by the World Health Organization (WHO) is to ensure maximum security against the international spread of diseases with minimum interference with world traffic. While most countries require no immunizations, some do. This represents a real change from years back, when immunization against smallpox, cholera, and yellow fever was almost standard. The booklet, *Health Information for International Travel*, stock number 017-023-00202-3 can be ordered from the Superintendent of Documents, U.S. Government Printing Office, P.O. Box 371954, Pittsburgh, PA 15250-7954. It provides relevant up-to-date information and is updated yearly. Cost for the 1999-2000 edition is $22.00 and can be ordered by telephone (202/512-1800), using a credit card. Information is also available from the Centers for Disease Control and Prevention's 24-hour hotline at 1-888-232-3228, from their automated faxback service

at 1-888-232-3299, or check the Internet page at <http://www.cdc.gov>. Another useful website is <wysiwyg://108/http://www.cdc.gov/travel/>.

If vaccinations are required, they must be recorded on approved forms, such as those in the booklet PHS-731, *International Certificates of Vaccination as Approved by the World Health Organization*. If your doctor or public health office does not have this booklet, it can be purchased for $1.00 from the Superintendent of Documents at the above Pittsburgh address.

Under the International Health Regulations adopted by WHO, a country under certain conditions may require an International Certificate of Vaccination against Yellow Fever. Smallpox was deleted from the diseases subject to Regulations in 1982. A cholera vaccination is no longer required for travelers coming into any country direct from the United States. However, between various countries, a cholera vaccination may be required. Depending upon where one travels, it is recommended to receive both cholera and yellow fever vaccinations so as to avoid any problems which might arise during a trip if you were routed through a country with these health problems.

Beyond what is required in vaccinations, there are a number of preventive health strategies which should be considered. Traveling outside the United States, and particularly in third-world countries, can present some health challenges. Hepatitis, for example, is fairly common around the world but can usually be avoided by taking certain measures. For an agent traveling overseas to fall ill is a minor disaster even if it is simple diarrhea, the most common ailment; he or she cannot work.

Local health departments, physicians, and agencies that advise international travelers are helpful in recommending additional shots and in taking along medicines which can be taken if one falls ill. A diphtheria/tetanus shot should be routine. If you are planning to travel to *hot, humid, possibly jungle areas*, such as parts of Central and South America, and Africa, you should check with a physician who specializes in tropical diseases, for his or her advice on preventive shots and medicine. All shots should be recorded in a *Shot Record*, which shows dates and types of shots. Just as you must renew your passport at intervals, you should seriously consider keeping your shots renewed. There are two advantages. Booster shots are often of lesser intensity and therefore less debilitating, and an up-to-date shot record gives the ability to travel anywhere at any notice. There can be some adverse reactions to shots, and for that reason they should be taken well in advance of a trip. Warning: try to avoid having to take any shots at the point of entry into another country. The sanitary conditions may be suspect, and with the spread of AIDS, the last thing anyone should do is voluntarily "exchange fluids" or come in contact with another's blood or bodily secretions encountered on an improperly sanitized needle.

With no disrespect to the continent of Africa, it should be pointed out that most of the really exotic and often fatal diseases, as well as more common diseases, can be found on this continent. Only a physician can recommend preventive shots. One must exercise excessive care in eating and drinking in any African country, with the exception perhaps of South Africa. Do not be fooled by the appearance of high-rise office buildings in a capital city; the sanitation may leave much to be desired.

In other countries, there are some common diseases which have long been conquered in the United States, but which may be found in poor, rural areas.

Cholera. Cholera is an acute intestinal infection. Infection is acquired primarily by ingesting contaminated water or food. Currently, no country or territory requires vaccination as a condition for entry. Local authorities, however, may continue to require documentation of vaccination. Currently available vaccines have been shown to provide only about 50% effectiveness in reducing clinical illness for three to six months after vaccination, with the greatest protection for the first two months. Travelers to cholera-infected areas are advised to avoid eating uncooked food, especially fish and shellfish, and to peel fruits themselves. Carbonated bottled water and soft drinks are usually safe. Ice is usually not and, therefore, drinks containing ice should be avoided.

Diphtheria and Tetanus. These remain as worldwide health problems. Immunization is recommended.

Giardiasis. This occurs worldwide, including in the United States. Transmission occurs from consumption of contaminated water.

Hepatitis, Viral, Type A. Transmission may occur by direct person-to-person contact, or from contaminated water, ice, or shellfish harvested from sewage-contaminated water, or from fruits, vegetables, or other foods which are eaten uncooked but which may have become contaminated during handling. Immune globulin (IG) prophylaxis is recommended for travelers to developing countries, especially those who will be living in or visiting rural areas, eating or drinking in settings of poor or uncertain sanitation, or who will have close contact with local persons. A single dose of IG of 0.02 ml/kg is recommended if travel is for less than three months. For prolonged travel or residence, 0.06 ml/kg should be given every five months.

Malaria. Malaria transmission occurs in large areas of Central and South America, Hispaniola, Africa, the Indian subcontinent, Southeast Asia, the Middle East, and Oceania. The risk varies markedly from area to area. Malaria is transmitted by mosquitos or possibly contaminated blood transfusions. Travelers should take protective measures to reduce contact with mosquitoes, remaining in screened areas, using mosquito netting, wearing clothes that cover most of the body, and using an insect repellent. Quinine tablets have been used in the past to ward off malaria, but it is best to seek preventive medication from a physician.

Poliomyelitis. Travelers to countries where poliomyelitis is epidemic or endemic are considered to be at increased risk and should be fully immunized.

Typhoid Fever. Typhoid vaccination is not required for international travel, but it is recommended for travelers to areas where there is a recognized risk of exposure to the fever. It is transmitted by contaminated food and water and is prevalent in many countries of Africa, Asia, and Central and South America.

Yellow Fever. Urban and jungle yellow fever occur only in parts of Africa and South America. For purposes of international travel, yellow fever vaccines produced by different manufacturers worldwide must be approved by WHO and administered at an approved Yellow Fever Vaccination Center. A number of countries require a certificate from travelers arriving from infected areas or from countries with infected areas. Some countries in Africa require evidence of vaccination from all entering travelers.

There are some general rules which, if followed, will limit the exposure to disease, infection, and diarrhea. As a general rule, *don't drink the water,* including iced drinks (ice in drinks), and don't brush your teeth with tap water. There are several ways to have safe liquids. You can drink bottled water, wine, beer, and carbonated drinks. If the bottled or canned drinks have been sitting in water, that water may be contaminated and the containers should be wiped clean. You can brush your teeth with alcoholic drinks or with bottled water. You can boil water. You can carry a water purifier, the kind that campers use. And, you can obtain pills which can be dropped in the tap water and left to stand for a number of hours, for purification. Cloudy water should be strained through a clean cloth into a container to remove any sediment or floating matter, and then the water treated with double the recommended number of tablets, and/or an extended amount of treatment time. While the water may be perfectly safe in a good hotel in Europe, water is still the chief culprit in causing problems worldwide. U.S. embassy officials can advise as to the safety of the local water.

Food should be selected with care. All raw food is subject to contamination. Particularly in areas where hygiene and sanitation are inadequate, travelers should avoid salads, uncooked vegetables, unpasteurized milk, and milk products such as cheese. They should eat only food that has been cooked and is still hot, or fruit that has been peeled by the traveler. Undercooked and raw meat, fish, and shellfish may carry various intestinal pathogens. Cooked food that has been allowed to stand for several hours at ambient temperature may provide a fertile medium for bacterial growth and should be thoroughly reheated before eating. Some species of fish and shellfish can contain poisonous biotoxins. These fish include barracuda (the worst), red snapper, grouper, amberjack, sea bass, and a wide range of tropical reef fish. Crab and shrimp can be poisonous. These are fish that may swim in contaminated areas.

Diarrhea is acquired through ingestion of fecally contaminated food, both cooked and uncooked, and/or water. Especially risky foods include raw meat, raw seafood, and raw fruits and vegetables. Tap water, ice, and unpasteurized milk and dairy products may be the culprits. The place food is prepared appears to be an important variable. No one should risk buying food from street vendors or from quaint little hidden restaurants. No available vaccines are available against diarrhea.

Diarrhea can be extremely debilitating. If you are not bedridden, at the very least you will be severely hampered in your inability to be further than a few steps from a toilet. Therefore, if, in spite of all your efforts, you are struck down, you must be prepared with some effective medication. Before departing, you should check with your doctor and obtain a good medication for diarrhea. Lomotil is very effective. It is a prescription drug in the United States but is available in many other countries over-the-counter. (*Warning–it can be addictive.*) Pepto Bismol is slow but effective for controlling simple diarrhea and stomach pains caused by diarrhea. Imodium pills, now available without prescription, are very effective in curing the diarrhea symptoms, though they do not cure the infection. Drugs, or a prescription for drugs, to cure the infection need to be obtained from a physician. Bactrim and Septra have been recommended by some physicians, but, before taking any drugs, you should *consult a physician*, who can advise you as to any side effects and test you for allergies. You may also wish to take with you a good, strong medicine for pain, something to provide comfort if you or your client is injured. For the best advice, try to find a physician who is familiar with the health conditions of the countries you will be traveling in.

If you are incapacitated, you are of no use to the protectee. Carry with you several weeks' extra supply of any prescription medications you may be taking. It will be difficult to renew prescriptions out of the country. Warning--leave all medicine in the prescription bottles; don't toss them into an empty container. Customs officials may mistake them for illegal drugs.

Swimming in contaminated water may result in skin, eye, ear, and certain intestinal infections. Generally, only pools that contain chlorinated water can be considered safe places to swim. In real tropical areas, even bathing may present a problem with contamination; certainly, washing one's hands with tap water may transmit infection. It helps to carry something of a disinfectant nature to wipe the hands and lightly wipe the body.

If medical care is needed abroad, travel agents or the American Embassy or Consulate can usually provide names of hospitals, physicians, or emergency medical service agencies. The International Association for Medical Assistance to Travelers (IAMAT) is a worldwide association that offers a list of approved physicians and clinics whose training meets American standards. IAMAT is located at 417 Center Street, Lewiston, NY 14092, (716) 754-4883; in Europe at 57 Voirets, 1212 Grand-Lancy, Geneva, Switzerland. More medical information may be found in the Department of State Bureau of Consular Affairs' brochure, *Medical Information for Americans Traveling Abroad*, available by autofax service at (202) 647-3000

There are some companies which can provide overseas medical coverage and can also provide emergency services overseas, including evacuation from areas without adequate medical care, or blood screened for AIDS. These include: Carefree Travel Insurance at 1-800-323-3149; Travel Guard International at 1-800-782-5151; Health Care Abroad, International Group at 1-800-394-2500; and International SOS Assistance at 1-800-523-8930. A subsidiary of International SOS Assistance (Security Overseas Services) provides crisis emergency services in case of civil unrest and other volatile situations.

There are, in addition, a HUGE number of air ambulance/med-evac companies. The author does not endorse them; the agent should gain information from <http://travel.state.gov/medical.html>, a website provided by the State Department.

You should contact your own insurance company as well, to make certain that your coverage extends outside the United States.

"Jet lag" is the debilitating but mostly harmless condition which affects many overseas travelers for 24 to 48 hours after arrival. It can totally destroy an advance agent's schedule if he is a victim of jet lag, and can't properly function for the first day or two. There are anti-jet-lag diets and formulas which your physician can advise about. There are some helpful hints as well. Most people agree that you should rest as much as possible for 24 hours preceding your overseas flight, and try to sleep on the plane, perhaps with the help of a mild sleeping pill. Avoid alcoholic beverages and stimulants while on the plane and for the next 24 hours. Try to program yourself for several days in advance to get on the local schedule of the area to which you are traveling, by gradually adjusting your hours. Change your watch as soon as you get on the plane and gradually adjust it to the local time. Your mental attitude has a lot to do with the severity of jet lag. Stop thinking (and saying) "If I were home, it would be midnight," when the local time is 5:00 p.m.. You will talk yourself into a mental attitude of midnight and want only to go to sleep. Forget the time back home.

International Driver's License

Many countries do not require an International Driver's Permit in order to rent and drive a vehicle, but a few do. It is easy to obtain this license through a local AAA automobile club. There are some advantages to belonging to AAA and holding a license. The AAA agency can provide you with maps, routing, and local information about the area you will be in. The license often facilitates getting the rented vehicle through entry/exit points leaving one country and entering another. Last, it may allow you to contact the offices of the AAA club located in the country where you are going, and that local club can be very helpful in giving information about local driving regulations, laws, availability of gasoline, and roadside lodging.

If you rent a car, always purchase the liability insurance. If you do not, this could lead to financial disaster.

Some countries have both a minimum and maximum driving age. Check all driving laws before you drive in any country. As an example, many countries require you to honk your horn before going around a sharp corner or to flash your lights before passing.

If the drivers in the country you are visiting drive on the opposite side of the road than in the U.S., practice driving in a less populated area before attempting to drive during the heavy traffic part of the day.

Credit Cards and Currency

The most widely accepted credit cards, worldwide, are American Express, Visa, and Mastercard. Visa and Mastercard are almost universally accepted; American Express is still the more prestigious card and carries a higher potential charge limit. American Express also has travelers checks which, if you lose them, are rather easily and quickly replaced. Be sure to photocopy your credit cards or make a list of them with their numbers, carry a copy with you, and leave a copy in the office. Get the call-in telephone numbers for lost credit cards so that, if you lose your cards, you can contact the credit card company immediately. You should check with the company before departure to determine what are your spending limits for each credit card you are carrying. Separate the traveler's checks and currency so that they are not carried all in one place; if part is stolen, you may still have access to some funds.

You need to become knowledgeable *in advance* about the foreign currency you will be using and the exchange rates (available at any major bank), so that you can easily translate the amounts needed for taxis, meals, rentals, hotels, and purchases.

You need to calculate continually how much you have charged on your credit cards, so that these are not overloaded. One very good tip is to prepay a certain amount on your credit cards before you leave, to prevent running out of charge money. If you think you are going to spend, say, $2,000, and you prepay $2,000, and your charge limit is $2,000, you now have the potential for spending $4,000 before your card is shut down. Carrying two or three cards also elevates your spending potential, since each card will have a spending limit.

It is always useful to carry $50 or $100 in U.S. one-dollar bills, and a few U.S. five-dollar bills. These come in handy for tips, taxis, and small purchases. Handing a $50.00 bill to a taxi driver on a $3.00 ride and expecting change will not work.

Travelers checks can be replaced if lost and are widely accepted. Make certain that you purchase at least half in small denominations. Be sure that the travelers checks you buy are accepted in the country where you are traveling; not all travelers checks are accepted everywhere. Almost certainly, your personal check will *not* be accepted, even with impeccable identification.

Computers

Before leaving, check to make certain that

you and your client will be able to carry a notebook computer into a foreign country and that it will not be subject to being held and checked. Some countries insist upon checking the contents of the computer and may even make copies of files. The same applies to diskettes.

Travel Arrangements

If your client has corporate contacts, either in the United States or overseas in the target country, this support should be utilized to make flight arrangements and hotel reservations. If you are on your own, you should find a good travel agent, one who specializes in, or is very familiar with, overseas travel and can guide you in your selection of airline carrier, hotel, etc.

The U.S. State Department can provide information; contact the "desk officer" for the country to which you are traveling. The handy booklet published by the Superintendent of Documents, U.S. Government Printing Office in Washington, DC, *Key Officers of Foreign Posts/Guide for U.S. Business Representatives*, will list names of embassy and consulate officers with addresses and telephone numbers for each country. A call in advance can obtain answers to some questions.

In choosing an air carrier, you may be limited in your choices if you are flying to some remote area or off-beat destination. However, for major world capitals, many airlines fly to them. Some airlines, including U.S. airlines, have been targeted for incidents. Many people believe that the air carriers most likely not to be targeted for a terrorist incident are the air carriers of such neutral countries as Switzerland or Scandinavia. Try to get a direct flight, one that is not routed through other cities. Some airports have been, either fairly or unfairly, viewed as unsafe airports, having been accessed by terrorist travelers in the past. Every time a plane lands and new passengers come on board, the risk of a terrorist incident is increased. If you have a choice, it is well to avoid traveling on any of the dates which signify key events for terrorists, as for example September 5,

the date of the attack at the Munich Olympic Games by Palestinians, or October 6, commemorating the Yom Kippur War. In the past, commemoration dates have triggered terrorist attacks.

You should book a return flight whenever possible at the same time you buy your ticket, especially in those countries which do not have many flights, thus avoiding being stuck in some area waiting for the twice-a-week flight which is filled for the next two weeks. On overseas flights, you are obliged to confirm your return flight either upon arrival in the foreign country or within a specified period prior to departure.

It is generally conceded that the rear of the plane is somewhat safer than the front end. Whether to sit by the window or on the aisle is a judgement call. An aisle seat may be the best choice in a crash, having greater flexibility for getting out. In the case of a terrorist incident, the window seat is probably the better choice. In the past, terrorists have established a pattern of taking over the cockpit and first class sections, and picking on aisle passengers for abuse. Seats close to an exit are generally always desirable for quick emergency exiting. While first-class is undoubtedly more comfortable, many international travelers avoid it, simply because of its history of abuse in terrorist hijackings.

A few tips on what you should and should not take with you in your luggage. Do take anything that you absolutely will need; don't depend upon being able to find items such as spare batteries, note pads, and pens. Sure, they are *there*, but it takes some getting-used-to to know where to buy various items. On the other hand, be sensible; don't take anything just because it is new, or fancy, or "nice-to-have." You will rapidly grow tired of the millstone of luggage, which grows heavier with each step. If you need a pocket calculator, fine, take it along; if not, leave it at home. A Swiss Army Knife is indispensable. Maps and small guidebooks which describe the customs of the country are very useful. Good little guidebooks will list hotels, restaurants, touristic attractions, local currencies, customs, maps of the major cities, a map of the country, emergency telephone numbers, electric current, climate and temperatures, tips on what to bring in the way of clothing and accessories, and some basic phrases in the local language which you can rehearse while on the overseas flight.

You should buy one or two security devices for keeping your passport, travelers checks, and currency. Available are money belts with inner zipper compartments, leg wallets which strap to the leg inside the trousers, half slips for women with compartments built into the hems, and an underarm wallet which fits inside a jacket. As a security item, you should include photos of family, wife, and children. If you are not married, borrow some; in the event of a terrorist incident, having family pictures may save your life.

Do not carry with you the *Communist Manifesto, MiniManual of the Urban Guerilla,* the latest guide to military tactics, or anything that might be construed as offensive such as girlie magazines, or that might leave the impression you are someone other than you claim to be.

Luggage

The best luggage is the luggage which can take the most abuse without spilling open. Recommended is the soft, reinforced ballistic type. Luggage should be inconspicuous, not obviously expensive, and carry no labels other than a sturdy tag (inside and out) so that, if your luggage is lost, it can be identified and delivered to you. ID luggage tags should show only an office address, not a home address, and a curtailed name. It is not a good idea to use a phoney name, as your luggage will never find its way to you in your hotel. Luggage should always be locked.

With you, not packed in the checked luggage, should be your airline ticket, passport, visas, international driver's license, medical shot record, health insurance card, list of telephone numbers and contacts, travelers checks, money, local currency, and credit cards (most of them thoughtfully hidden in one of the personal security devices). Any items of value need to be on your person. In your hand luggage should be anything you might need if your checked luggage were lost.

A lot of luggage is misrouted, misplaced, and just plain lost. To increase your chances of reaching your destination together with your luggage, you may want to take a proactive stance. When checking your luggage, watch to make certain that each piece has a baggage tag correctly stamped with your destination. (The author once watched as the harried airline clerk put a ROME baggage tag on her two bags, while her ticket read PARIS.) Then, wait a few moments to make sure the bags get onto the conveyor belt or the streetside baggage cart. If you check your bags streetside, do tip the porter well. There are no guarantees that tipping the baggage handler will get your bags to their destination; however, if you do not tip him, he may be tempted to be careless. Put a piece of tape or something that is easily identified on your bags. Many experienced travelers put a line of strapping tape (the strong, translucent tape) around their bag, passing it underneath the luggage handle, to discourage thieves and to keep the bag together if it is accidentally dropped thirty feet. (Strapping tape is a godsend, useful in many, many situations; always carry a roll.) Get to the airport in plenty of time. Rushing in at the last minute will almost certainly land your luggage on a different flight. And, last, if you have very little time between stops, your luggage may not make the connection; you may want to consider picking it up yourself and carrying it to the connection.

Be certain that you receive duplicate baggage check tags, so that you can claim your luggage. Copy down the numbers, in the event that you lose your tags. Sometimes the luggage claim tags will be stapled to the envelope enclosing your plane tickets. When you check in at another stop, be sure that the tags are not thrown away when the clerk helpfully puts your plane ticket in a clean envelope. It is always a sound idea to watch the airline counter clerk to make certain that only the requisite ticket coupons are removed. Count them. If too many coupons are inadvertently removed, they will be lost to you.

En Route

Once on the plane, take some precautionary emergency measures. Just as you would walk the route to the emergency exits of a hotel, you should do the same in the airplane. Find the exits and count the numbers of aisle seats from you to all exits, front and back. In the event of a crash, there will be a lot of smoke and terrible confusion. A smoke mask should be in your carry-on bag. This can provide you with a few precious moments of safe breathing in the event of a fire on board.

If you are in the habit of not listening to the emergency and evacuation instructions given by the flight attendant, break that habit and pay attention. It's like a fire drill; you need to have the instructions down pat. Look under the seat or wherever the life preserver cushion is kept and make certain that you have one. If you take your shoes off, keep them handy to put on in a hurry. Look for an unobtrusive place where you could, in the event of an incident, hide any identification or objects which might target you as someone the terrorists would want to interrogate.

Get comfortable and try to get some sleep. It helps to find, or ask for, a pillow and blanket. If you want to work on the plane, going over your notes or reading your guidebook, this is also a good idea, but getting sleep is very helpful.

ARRIVAL AT DESTINATION

While you are on the plane, or as you enter a country through their control Customs and Immigration area, you will be asked to fill in a Landing Card, also called a Disembarkation Card. There are several questions, among them, "Where are you staying? How long will you be in the country? *Why* are you entering the country?" In answer to this last question, be careful that your answer is consistent with the reason given for your visa. If one question

asks, "What is your occupation?" answer with something that is non-specific. If you answer "security," or "protection," it will undoubtedly cause a great many problems. You are apt to be mistaken as CIA or a hit man, and definitely a potential problem. You are inviting surveillance, among other things. "Security" and "protection" in other countries often have different meanings. Otherwise, answer all questions as honestly as possible. If a visa is required, all answers must match; whatever was stated on the visa should be stated on the Landing Card. Keep the Landing/Disembarkation Card, as it will have to be surrendered, along with your passport (and visa, if needed) in Customs.

Whenever you are traveling with the protectee or a team to a foreign country, it usually saves time and is more efficient if one staff member carries the passports and the declaration cards for all members of the party. Otherwise, some one individual in the party is certain to misplace his passport and cause the entire party to be delayed.

You may also be asked to fill out a Customs Declaration of some sort, stating how much money you are bringing into the country and/or other questions about what goods you are bringing with you. In some countries, you must account for your U.S. dollars and other currencies, both going into and exiting from the country. This means that you must change your dollars at approved government outlets-- banks, hotels, etc.--where you will be issued receipts for money changed. Those receipts, plus the remaining dollars must be accounted for when you leave the country. *Save those vouchers.* Resist changing your dollars on the black market, even though the rate is much better. Many black market people are informants. It is also not wise to change too many dollars. If you should end your trip with a large wad of the local currency, it may be harder to exchange back to dollars. Monitor your expenses and try to predict how much local currency you will need, saving enough at the end to handle tips. In many countries, U.S. dollars will be accepted to pay for goods and services, though the exchange rate is almost always lower than the bank rate. It is a good idea to change enough dollars at the airport currency exchange booth to pay for the taxi and/or other small expenses until you reach the hotel or a bank. Tip: it is possible to change U.S. dollars for one of the better-regarded currencies (English pound, French franc, Italian lire, etc.) in some U.S. banks before leaving the States.

In declaring goods, one should always declare anything with serial numbers--guns (if allowed into the country, and unloaded), radios, tape recorders, cameras, etc.--with a full description and the serial numbers. If you do not do this, there will be a problem at exit time, as well as at arrival back in the States. There must be no doubt that the items are personal, were bought in the States, and not purchased overseas. The consequences may be confiscation or a hefty charge for import duties.

Guns. One should always check in advance to determine if a gun may be brought into the country. You may find that you are allowed to bring in a shotgun, but not a handgun. If the country allows firearms, these should be placed, unloaded, in a bag, and a separate Declaration filled in for them. This is done at the ticket counter (not curbside) in the U.S. before leaving. An airline red tag will be filled out and placed INSIDE the bag; the bag is then locked and sent to the baggage area, to be reclaimed at the other end, where it must be declared in Customs. The gun must be in a container within the suitcase. There must be no ammunition of any kind or caliber within that same suitcase. Ammunition must be in separate, locked luggage, no more than eleven pounds of it, and it must be in appropriate containers; i.e., not loose or in speedloaders or magazines. The suitcase should be a hard-shell style, not soft shell.

It will save time to make a list, in advance, of the serial numbers and descriptions of all guns and security equipment and make several copies for use in Customs and Immigration. Incidentally, one should never buy guns overseas and attempt to bring them back to the U.S. Guns must be legally imported into the States, which requires a dealer's permit.

If it is possible to make advance preparations for someone to meet you upon arrival, this person may be able to expedite clearance through Customs and Immigration and to arrange transportation from the airport to the hotel. Unless you know the person, you will need to set up some means of identifying each other and arranging a place to meet. If you are not being met, you will need to either hire a car or take a taxi into town, remembering that, in some parts of the world, taxis are extremely expensive.

If no one is meeting you and local transportation has been prearranged, make sure it is waiting outside the C/I area.

Hotels

On an advance, hotel reservations should already have been made, either by the client's corporation or through a good travel agent. There are some differences of opinion as to where one should stay, but for the agent and his client the best choice is probably a major American hotel, such as InterContinental, Hilton, Sheraton, and the like. These hotels almost always operate more efficiently than the locally operated hotels, and provide the services which the client will expect. Some exceptions to this can be found in London, Paris, Rome, Madrid, and other world capitals, where luxury hotels with a century's experience of providing excellent, discreet service makes them outstanding. One caveat is to make certain that the hotel is reasonably fire safe, has smoke detectors, and preferably sprinklers. Old hotels often are firetraps, being constructed with a great deal of wood and no real fire protection.

Location of the hotel is a consideration. Ideally, it should not be located next to any structure which might be considered a target, such as the Israeli Embassy or the Turkish Tourist Office.

A foreign advance covers the same procedures as an advance in the States, with some differences. It is likely that setting up a meeting with hotel personnel will not be quite as easy. In Europe, particularly, the long history of providing guest service to kings, queens and other notables may leave a foreign staff less receptive to requests for extra security measures. On the other hand, European hotels have an equally long history for discretion and protecting identities of distinguished guests.

If the hotel is a first class one, known for its well-heeled business clientele, there is a good chance that the suites and rooms are routinely bugged. Industrial espionage is now increasingly encountered, as businesses and entire countries try to get an economic edge on their competitors. One published report stated that the first class passenger seats on Air France airlines were routinely bugged. A thorough sweep should be made of the protectee's rooms, including agents' rooms and command post, daily. One should assume that the telephones are bugged and, therefore, no confidential information should be discussed over the phone.

Arrangements should be made to pre-register the protectee and his party, and to obtain room keys in advance. This makes it easier to whisk the protectee and party to their rooms with minimum public exposure. Room keys for the protection team may be given to them upon arrival at the airport.

One should always carefully safeguard passports, visas, travelers checks, and any sensitive papers. This does not include leaving them in the hotel room. In many countries, the hotel rooms are routinely searched. Passports are very valuable and are the object of theft, as are money and jewelry. The hotel safe deposit box is a good place to leave articles of value.

If the hotel is located in Muslim countries, the room search should include looking for any contraband items, which may have been deliberately planted. One diplomat's wife, having just arrived on a visit to Libya, idly looked through the hotel's desk drawer and, in the back of the drawer, discovered a bottle of half-empty wine. She wasn't sure whether a previous guest had left it or if it had been deliberately placed there to embarrass her. Thinking quickly, she

telephoned the Reception Desk and shrieked, "How dare you place me, a religious woman, in a room that has ALCOHOLIC SPIRITS in it? This is an insult. I shall complain to my embassy immediately!" She was hastily moved to another room, amid profuse apologies.

U.S. Embassy or Consulate

The advance agent should plan to visit with the Regional Security Officer at the American Embassy at his earliest opportunity. The RSO can supply information to add to the intelligence acquisition obtained in the pre-departure phase--information such as:

.   updates on new or emerging political issues which could pose a problem, and any activist groups associated with them.

.   standard emergency evacuation plans.

.   recommended hotels, restaurants, as well as areas to avoid.

The RSO can be very helpful in providing local police contacts and suggestions for reliable vehicles for hire, drivers, and interpreters. To the extent possible, the agent should share some general facts about the protectee's itinerary, as the RSO may have suggestions or warnings. For example, if the protectee plans to drive into the hill country outside the capital city, or is the guest speaker at a rally, the RSO may have some thoughtful ideas about the safety of doing so.

The RSO can advise as to the general health and sanitary conditions of the country, and will know whether the water is safe to drink. The agent should ascertain from him whether the emergency hospital(s) are adequate and where they are located.

The American Embassy is able to arrange, for status individuals, something called "courtesy of the port." "Courtesy of the port" provides for expeditious clearance through Customs and Immigration. If it is deemed desirable, the agent may try to secure this privilege for the protectee, the traveling party, and the baggage.

The Political/Consular Officer at the U.S. Embassy is a very valuable contact. This is the person who worries about Americans within the country. If problems develop and someone ends up in jail, he is the person who will try to solve the problem. It is a very good idea to check in with this person upon arrival, and when leaving. The Political/Consular Officer is responsible only for American citizens. If the protectee is a foreign national, U.S. Embassy interest will end abruptly.

U.S. consular officers will do their best to assist U.S. citizens abroad. However, they must devote priority time and energies to those Americans who find themselves in the most serious legal, medical, or financial difficulties. Because of limited resources, consuls cannot provide routine or commercial-type services.

Do you need an interpreter? Probably not. Since the majority of the agent's travels will be to Europe, Asia, and the Middle East, these areas have a high proportion of local people who speak at least a rudimentary English. All major international hotels such as InterContinental, Hilton, and Sheraton, have English-speaking employees. Many licensed taxi drivers and tourist guides speak English. The Concierge at the hotel can be especially helpful in writing out directions in the local language for use with taxi drivers who do not speak or understand English. Often, the Concierge will call the cab and personally give directions to the cab driver. One should always have the Concierge write down in the local language the name, address, and telephone number where the agents and protectee are staying, so that they can always find their way back to the hotel. Another handy name is the U.S. Embassy.

Everyone should have some of the local coins, and be able to operate the local telephone. If all else fails, a call to the hotel or the Embassy can send help. If business transactions mean a more complicated need for language, the Concierge or the American Embassy can arrange for an interpreter.

A guidebook to the local customs and culture, as noted earlier, can be very helpful. There are pitfalls in every country in terms of affronting someone without intending to do so. In many countries, it is considered rude to photograph other people. It may be against the law to photograph military installations. In many Arab countries, women are veiled, and it is considered rude even to inquire in the most superficial way about someone's wife or female family members. There are different rules of business and different hours. These and many other details are important to know.

One custom, a delicate one, is that of bribes, called baksheesh in many countries. In some countries, bribes are a way of life and constitute a part of an official's "salary." However, it is not necessarily an *open* custom. It is most often encountered in Customs and Immigration, and in getting permission to do something in third-world countries. These are not the million-dollar bribes passed illegally between corporations and governments to secure contracts. These are petty $20 bribes to get the visa stamped *now*. If it appears that a small bribe is expected, it should be done quietly and without fuss, perhaps by way of a folded bill inside the passport folder or left casually on the counter. One should never openly offer it or speak of it. In this way, if the official accuses you of offering a bribe, it can be plausibly denied.

There is a separate chapter in this book dealing with protecting executives traveling and living abroad.

Physical security has been discussed in various chapters of this book; however, because of the importance of this first line of defense, this chapter contains additional information.

It should be pointed out that physical security is only as good as it is current. An initial site survey, with blueprints of the building(s) and grounds in hand, should be performed and should be repeated on a regular basis, depending on the level of perceived threat. These regular surveys should coincide with maintenance of the physical security system, whether performed by the protection agent or by outside contractors. Repairs should be made as quickly as possible. Recommendations for improvement to the system should be presented in a businesslike manner, with costs detailed, for review and approval by the client.

Perimeter Security

Perimeter barriers are generally designed to keep the fainthearted out, to delay the intruder, to warn the residents of the intrusion, and, in some cases, (as with CCTV) to identify the intruder. All local ordinances regarding perimeter barriers should be checked for compliance. Environmental conditions will also affect the design of your perimeter system.

Obviously, the stronger the perimeter barriers, the more successfully your system can meet its objectives. In a maximum security setting, walls should be used in place of fences, but clients often object to being walled in. If a masonry wall is used, it should be at least eight feet high including a topguard similar to that required on a chain link fence, or set with broken glass.

An excellent, albeit unsightly, fencing is either number 9 or number 11 American wire gauge, with 2-inch mesh openings, topped by three strands of barbed wire, angled outward and upward at a 30 to 45 degree angle. The bottom of the fence should be within two inches of solid ground. Natural topography, such as lakes, can be used as natural obstacles, but can also provide intrusion opportunities which call for additional security devices. Fencing can be electrically alarmed, and, in a maximum security setting, two parallel sets of fencing may be used, thus forming a double barrier.

Openings such as culverts, tunnels, and utility access should be properly secured. As a general rule, perimeter gates and other entrances should not exceed the number required for safe and efficient operation and should be locked when not in use. It should be obvious that perimeter gates should be constructed of material and in a manner which provides protection equivalent to the fence or wall. Clear zones on both sides of the fence/wall are an excellent help to security. Cars, boxes, or other materials alongside the fence can be quickly spotted if they are found in the clear zone. Debris should never be allowed to accumulate, as it can provide hiding places for intruders or suspect material. An interior all-weather perimeter road may be provided for guards and allows for quick car patrol. If guards are used to patrol the perimeter areas, they should do so on an irregular (unscheduled) basis with frequent changes both in schedule and routine.

Shrubbery should be cut back from windows and entrances. Many residences, in particular, have shrubbery which is planted to shield the windows from the casual outsider. The problem, of course, is that the intruder can take refuge in the shrubbery. There should be a clear zone immediately around the circumference of the residence or office which can be lighted to readily show an intruder. Flower beds are a very sensible addition; in addition to their sightly qualities, they can clearly show footprints. There are some plants and bushes which contain sharp spikes or thorns such as thorny roses, holly, barberry, locust, and which are not hospitable to intruders.

Guard dogs are extremely effective, and, if properly trained, will resist falling into the trap of accepting tainted or poisoned food. There are a number of excellent guard dog training organizations. These dogs can be placed in three categories: the alarm dog, the harassing dog, and the attack dog. Be aware that the potential for lawsuits is very high with dogs, as tradespeople and other innocents can inadvertently stumble into your guard dog's turf. At the very least, you should provide for clearly designated "BEWARE OF DOG" signs. (An ancient form of guard animal are certain breeds of geese, who are sensitive to strangers and disturbances and provide a distinctive, loud noise.)

Protective Lighting

Security lighting serves a number of purposes. At the top of the list is deterrence, followed by observation and identification. Good lighting serves to deter the intruder. It permits observation by the security agent of the perimeter, and it can aid in the identification of intruders or suspicious people lurking in the vicinity. Designing a lighting system for maximum security requires professional help from a contractor or lighting engineer. Attention must be given to light level and the power requirements to produce it. Certainly, the light level must be coordinated with the alarm system, particularly if CCTV is used at the perimeter. As with any segment of the intrusion system, the power source must be adequately protected, with back-up power for emergencies. Periodic testing of the back-up system should be scheduled.

Gates, entrances, and penetration points may require extra lighting. The angle and placement of lighting is important in that you may wish to leave the interior area in comparative darkness to avoid backlighting the guards or producing glare in their eyes. The angle should be such that the glare is directed toward the intrusion zone.

Maintenance of the lighting system should include immediate replacement of burned-out light bulbs and a check of the wiring and housing elements. Underground wiring is generally less vulnerable to tampering. There should be a system for replacing all light bulbs before they burn out, perhaps by tabulating time averages. All lights, lamps, switches, and controls should be housed in weather-resistant tamper and damage proof casing.

When high intensity light is not used, lighting can be improved by bouncing it off white or very light colored walls. The same principle can be applied to paved areas, such as parking lots, by painting them white or applying a reflective surface. If a white gravel or stone is used, an added advantage is in the sound produced by anyone crossing the surface.

The contractor or lighting engineer will advise as to methods of emplacement to overcome any environmental problems, such as poor drainage, shifting soil, high winds, etc.

In very sensitive, high-security areas, consideration might be given to the installation of back-up lighting, on a separate circuit, which would remain solely under the control of the security personnel. It would be activated only in emergencies or to provide additional lighting during an incident.

Controls can be programmed to switch the lights on and off at preset times. In addition, there are alarm systems which include a feature that turns on the lights if an intruder is spotted. A handy little device is on the market which can be carried in the purse or pocket and allows the owner to turn on his lights from outside the house, just as he can use his garage clicker to open the garage doors.

Lighting can be used as a weapon of sorts, as in the case of glare lighting directed against intruders, temporarily blinding them. Stroboscopic (rapidly flickering) illumination can cause disorientation. There are hand-held super flashlights on the market which emit immense blinding candlepower that can temporarily incapacitate intruders.

If the interior lighting of a residence is on a timer with the purpose of deceiving potential intruders into thinking you are home, make certain that you can program the timer to activate the lights at different times. If the residence is under surveillance, it is certain to be suspicious if your lights come on in certain rooms precisely at the same time every night.

Doors

According to the FBI, the majority of all burglaries involve entry through the front or back door. Doors may be vulnerable in several ways. In any maximum security situation, exterior doors and/or doors to interior safe rooms should be of solid material rather than hollow core, with a metal sheet facing (which can, in turn, have a decorative wood covering, if desired). The thickness of the sheet metal should be no thinner than 18 gauge. There are four major types of doors: flush wood, stile and rail (panel) wood, metal, and sliding glass. Flush doors come in two types: hollow core and solid core. A hollow core door is two sheets of a thin veneer overlaying a soft filler. Solid core doors are wood all the way through. They add sound insulation and fire resistance as well as increased security.

Frames for maximum security doors should be as carefully designed and as strong as the door itself. Doors should be fitted so that as little "give" as possible exists between the door and the frame. A favorite method of illegal entry is simply to pry the door away from the frame, using a crow bar or hydraulic jack. Most wooden door frames constructed today have solid wood for about 3/4-inch to an inch. Beyond this, there is usually a 4- to 6-inch gap for air between the frame and the first stud. Construction of this type provides very little resistance to forced entry. The door frame can be strengthened by securing 2-by-4-inch studs directly behind the facing. Another method is to attach the frame to the first stud in the wall using long wood screws.

Door glass should be as far as possible from the door lock to avoid someone breaking the glass and reaching inside to unlock the door, and the glass

should be unbreakable glass. You can also install a double cylinder deadbolt lock, one that requires a key to open it from both sides. Remember, though, that in an emergency, you may not be able to find the key quickly enough to open the door; at the very least, the key should *always* hang next to the door, just far enough away that it cannot be reached from the glass opening.

Double doors are generally quite vulnerable unless the locking system is strengthened. If there are double doors, it must be possible to make one door inactive by a sturdy deep-seated lock and mount, top and bottom, and the active door should be joined with a deadbolt lock. Dutch doors should be fitted with deadbolts top and bottom.

Steel security storm doors (the ones with bars and glass) provide good additional security, and can be decorative. The steel should be heavy duty and the glass tempered safety glass.

It is an excellent idea to replace the (probably) hollow core door into the master bedroom with a solid core door, using the same security measures as with the front entry door, and install a deadbolt lock. This presupposes that an adversary breaches the outer front door and gains access to the house. Having a strong bedroom door with a deadbolt lock provides an additional barrier between the occupants and the intruder.

The security value of the door hinge is often overlooked. A well-secured hinge protects a home, apartment, or office against two types of forced entry: forcing the door out of the frame by applying pressure to its hinged side, and lifting the door out of its frame after removing the hinge pins. From a security standpoint, the most important consideration of a hinge is whether it is located on the inside or outside of the door and, if the hinge is on the outside, whether or not the pins are removable. If the hinge pins are on the outside, they can be removed and the door removed from the frame. There are several ways to deter this. One is to weld the pins to the hinges. Although this method is effective, it is also permanent. Another technique is to drill a small hole through the hinge and into the pin and insert a second pin or small nail flush with the hinge surface. A third method is to insert a large pin or screw into the door (or the door jamb), leaving the head exposed about 1/2 inch. A matching hole is drilled on the opposite side, so that the screw head fits into it when the door is shut.

Vehicle doors and garage doors are often extremely vulnerable to attack. Not only should they be strengthened, but the door leading from the garage into the residence or installation should meet maximum security standards. Garage doors should always come equipped with an electric door opener, making it unnecessary to get out of the car to open the door.

Sliding glass doors, of the sort usually found leading to patios, are particularly vulnerable to intrusion. If the occupants insist on their use, the glass should be as strong as possible and bullet resistant. The moveable door panel should always be located on the inside of the stationary panel, with a fair overlap, to make it more difficult for an intruder simply to lift the door out of its track. It is not sufficient to prevent the doors from being moved laterally. They must also be secured vertically since the channel in which they ride may provide wide, sloppy tolerances. Most locks designed for this type of door take into consideration both the lateral and vertical movement, preventing the door from being lifted out of the channel. There are locks designed specifically for sliding glass doors, as well as "charlie bars." These are available at any good hardware store.

Some of the same devices used to secure windows can also be used with sliding glass doors. Drill a hole through the channel and the frame. Insert a pin or nail to prevent the door from being opened. Sheet metal screws can also be inserted into the upper channel, allowing screws to protrude far enough to prevent the door from being lifted out of the channel.

There should be peepholes and intercoms to identify visitors before opening the door. All doors and vulnerable windows should be incorporated into the alarm system. There are heavy-duty chains which can be installed on doors, and, while chains are not entirely reliable (the small, thin ones can be breached by a good shoulder hit or boot thrust), the heavy-duty ones add another security dimension.

Windows

Windows pose more complex security problems than doors. They come in a much greater variety of styles and sizes, with emphasis on ventilation, lighting, and aesthetics rather than security. Windows are particularly vulnerable to intrusion and, unfortunately, the methods used to strengthen them are often unattractive or inconvenient to the occupants.

Louvre windows are a high security risk because the individual panes can be removed easily. Louvre windows should be replaced with solid windows of tempered, shatter-resistant glass.

Several techniques can be used to upgrade the security of windows with movable sashes. The simplest measure, which works equally well with single- or double-hung windows and horizontally sliding windows of all types, is to drill one or more holes through the sash and frame and insert a pin or nail to prevent the window from being opened. Key operated locks for windows are also available, but they pose a safety hazard in the event the window is needed for escape in a fire or other emergency.

If bars are used, they should be fitted internally and set back from the outer wall, grouted at both ends into solid masonry to a depth of three inches. When bars are longer than, say, two or two and a half feet, cross bars should be either welded at the intersections or fitted into the masonry as well. Bars should be solid rather than hollow. With wooden window frames, bars should be secured with substantial bolts and reinforcing. Ornamental grilles should be fitted, if possible, internally or anchored adequately to resist prying apart or removal. A cautionary note is that solidly anchored bars or grillwork can be hazardous in case of a fire.

Provision must be made for the occupants to exit quickly in case of fire. This can be achieved by inserting an exit opening in the bars, which can be locked. Local fire code provisions should be checked for compliance.

If bars are not acceptable, a grille made from expanded metal or welded mesh affixed to a metal frame can be fitted to the window on the inside and secured with permanently fixed coach-bolts or with a heavy-duty padlock. This method of window security is frequently used with basement and cellar windows.

Toughened glass, laminated glass, bullet resistant glass, and barrier glass offer options for security where bars or grills are not permissible.

Roofs

The most secure roofs, such as poured concrete with steel reinforcing, are to be found in plants and other commercial installations and are generally not an option for a residence; however, there are some security measures which can be taken to upgrade existing roofs. In a high security situation, the roof should be factored into the intrusion alarm system.

A flat roof presents special problems. It can be scaled by use of a grappling hook. A helicopter can hover close enough to drop intruders. To prevent scaling, shielding should be installed to prevent the hook from finding an anchor point. The installation of poles (such as a flag pole) or other barriers can deter an attack by helicopter. All openings in the roof, such as skylights, air-conditioning, and ducts, should be secured so as to deny access to an intruder. Metal grilles welded into the opening are a good option.

Locking Devices

The most commonly used and least secure lock is the key-in-the-knob lock. These locks are adequate for interior doors to aid in privacy, but should never be considered in a high-security situation. These locks are easily picked and can be

opened by slipping a celluloid card between the frame and the door. From a security point of view, these locks are the least desirable of all lock types.

Single-cylinder deadbolt locks are popular auxiliary security locks. They are usually installed above the primary lock. The best designs have steel bolts and cylinder guards so that they cannot be twisted, pried, or broken. Double-cylinder locks could be dangerous in an emergency since a key is required to get out. Some municipal codes prohibit use of this type of lock.

Cylindrical lock sets with deadbolts combine all the best features of a good security lock--a deadbolt function with a deadbolt lock. The better designs incorporate a 1-inch throw deadbolt, a recessed cylinder to discourage forcible removal, a concealed armor plate to resist drilling, and a cylinder guard that spins freely when the deadbolt is in a locked position. This last feature makes it virtually impossible for an intruder to wrench the cylinder or cylinder guard off the door. Finally, these sets include a panic feature that assures that the knob will turn freely from the inside to permit rapid exit in case of emergency.

Mortise locks are a step up in security, as they have both the privacy latching feature and a deadbolt. The knob is not a part of the deadbolt and cannot be opened with a credit card. If the bolt is an inch to an inch and a half in length, it is almost impossible to pry the door open. Additional security can be obtained by attaching a cover plate to the lock to prevent prying at the screws. Since the introduction of the cylindrical lock, mortise locks have declined considerably in popularity. Mortise locks are far more expensive to install than cylindrical locks because large sections of the door and jamb have to be specially mortised to fit the lock.

A rim lock with interlocking bolt is a very good security lock, particularly when it is added as a second lock. It is not "jimmy-proof," but it is very difficult to defeat.

The striker plate is an integral part of a lock's

total security value. The striker plate must be affixed securely to a sturdy door frame or it will be forced easily. Also important is a close fit between the lock and the striker plate so that there is little room for movement when the door is closed.

Much has been done to improve cylinder design, and as much consideration should be given to choice of cylinders as to locks. Twisting pin-tumbler key cylinders and dimpled keys are but two examples of the newer high-security key cylinder designs. The dimpled key requires a special machine for duplication, and each key has a serial number which requires an authorized signature to obtain a duplicate key.

Pushbutton locks have achieved some popularity, since they are "pick-proof" and convenient, with no key required and a simple combination to memorize. The obvious disadvantages are: the combination can be forgotten (particularly in moments of stress), and the combination can be observed by an unfriendly outsider. Some experts claim that, with heavy use, the code buttons will eventually show more wear than the non-coded buttons.

Card reader systems have found increased acceptance. All good hotels use them, many offices and high-security installations use them, and they can be found in some residential environments. There are a number of advantages to the good card reader systems. The card is difficult to duplicate. It "logs" the holder in and out and provides a record of that individual's comings and goings. There is instant access change, so that whenever a coded card is lost or stolen the controller can be reprogrammed to void the continued use of the card. These systems are particularly useful in access control situations, where the card holder may be granted access to certain areas only, at restricted times.

In far too many situations, the weakest link in the locking system is in the issuance and control of the keys. Keys are often given out to people for convenience, or as symbols of authority, or as "perks" to trusted employees. Many homeowners who build

in sophisticated access systems to their residences hand out keys to employees, servants, and repairmen. The lock is only as good as the key control. It is axiomatic that, whenever moving into a new residence, the locks and/or cylinders and keys should be changed, no matter what assurances have been given that "no one else has a key." At the office or plant, key control is a major issue and should be carefully supervised to prevent keys ending up in the wrong hands.

There are good portable locks on the market. One of the more popular is the box lock used by real estate brokers. For security in traveling, one or several top quality portable locks should be included in the protection agent's travel kit for use in hotel rooms and/or temporary residences. Another simple security device is the rubber door stop, which can be used within the hotel room to jam under the door.

Safe Rooms

A "safe room" is a designated, strengthened, enclosed area either in a residence or office which can provide protection for a limited period if an intrusion or attack is imminent. *It should not be used in case of fire unless all hope of evacuation is denied, and a call to the fire department alerts firefighters to the fact that people are in the safe room and its location.* Safe rooms offer temporary sanctuary against an adversary and should be equipped not only to repel the intruder, but to call out for help. Safe rooms do not necessarily have to be additional rooms. They can double as a bedroom, bathroom, office, or conference room. They should have only one door, and preferably contain no windows accessible to intrusion. If there are windows, bullet-resistant glass should be installed. In a residence, a safe room is usually located upstairs where, at the first hint of danger, children can be gathered together with the parents into the safe room. In an office, the safe room is usually placed close to the chief executives, since they are generally singled out as targets for attack. The safe room should be rated as fire-safe for at least one hour, in the event that the intruders set fire to the building.

Safe rooms should contain, at a minimum, a cellular phone or a telephone that is on a separate line and not vulnerable to tampering. It is essential that the occupants be able to call for help. A two-way radio is also very useful. A secured source of light and air must be provided. A battery-operated light can be used, and at least one or two maglites should be kept there, along with extra batteries. A first aid kit may be useful. Any weapons should be brought into the safe room. A fire extinguisher should be available. Food and water are not usually needed, because of the temporary need for the safe room; however, water is reassuring, and, when under stress, people become thirsty, so a gallon jug of water is a useful addition.

Ideally, a safe room should have steel sheeting, sufficient to repel bullets, attached to the walls and door. Doors, in addition to steel reinforcing, should be hung so that the hinges are on the inside with heavy duty hinges and bolts. The door frame, itself, should be reinforced with steel. The door lock must be state-of-the-art, lockpick-proof, and, in addition, there should be a heavy-duty steel bolt which secures the inside of the door. On the outside of the door, a steel plate covering the lock should be installed.

Electronic Security Systems

A threat analysis and thorough site survey is needed before an adequate security system can be designed. Many security systems are installed that do not protect the assets they were intended to protect, either because the purchaser did not understand what was needed and what was tolerable in a living situation; or because the alarm installer did not understand the requirements and/or sold the equipment in stock as opposed to the equipment needed. Expert advice should be sought in the design and installation of an electronic security system, as it needs to be integrated with the existing physical security plan. In large facilities, and, in particular in high-rise buildings, electronic detection systems are complex and highly sophisticated. In residences, the system can be simplified but very effective.

A number of questions must be answered. What is the value of the "asset" being protected versus the cost of the system needed to protect it? Do the existing physical security measures provide strong deterrence? What is the perceived threat? Are there guards patrolling the area? dogs? How far out should the detection system stretch? Will the system be monitored? on the premises? linked to a central station? Is the system going to be user-friendly, or will it become such a nuisance or create so many false alarms that it will not be used properly? Who will maintain the system, and how much maintenance will be required? These and a great many other questions must be considered.

For our purposes, suffice it to say that electronic detection systems are very effective and should be integrated into the protection plan.

Fire and Safety Considerations

Both in permanent and temporary situations, consideration should be given to fire and other safety conditions. Fire and smoke alarms should be installed and a response/evacuation plan devised and practiced at regular intervals. Smoke detectors are generally used for early fire warning because smoke generally precedes the intense heat of a fire. Two types of smoke detectors are in widespread use: photoelectric and ionization. The photoelectric type uses a bam-break or light-scattering principle to detect the presence of smoke. The ionization type, considered by some to be more efficient, detects the electrically charged ion particles associated with smoke in the early stages of fire. Smoke detectors incorporating both types of detection in a single unit are called combination smoke detectors.

A good portable smoke alarm, with spare batteries, should be in the security agent's travel kit.

At home, particularly where children are involved, frequent practice of fire evacuation plans should be utilized. You should practice evacuating in the dark against the possibility that the electricity could fail. Each bedroom should have a flashlight in a handy spot, as well as a folding ladder for upstairs bedrooms to allow escape from the second floor. There should be portable fire extinguishers, regularly checked and refilled when necessary, kept at strategic locations in the garage and house.

Without question, sprinkler systems can save lives. Tragic hotel fires have now mandated the installation of fire sprinklers in all new hotels in this country. If sprinklers were installed in homes, death by fire in the home could almost be eliminated. Unfortunately, sprinkler systems, especially if they have to be retrofitted into an existing home or office, are very expensive. However, with any new construction, this should be a recommendation to a client.

Other safety considerations involve surveying the residence (and hotel room) for safety hazards. It is a fact that a majority of accidents occur in and around the home. Scalding bath water, torn carpeting, slippery bath surfaces, inadequate interior lighting--these are but a few of the many, many potential hazards which can cause accidents or death. It is as important to maintain the homely repairs as it is to keep the intrusion system in top working condition. Falls, cuts, and burns are at the top of the accident list, and a physical survey should make note of any hazards that could contribute to these incidents. Where children are concerned, any poisonous substances, drugs, and medicines must be kept out of reach, or under lock and key.

STAYING WITH FRIENDS AND TEMPORARY RESIDENCES

Your client and family may visit with friends, staying overnight or longer in their home. Or the client may be offered the use of a house, or rent one, for vacation use. You must first determine if you are going to be allowed to stay in the house with your client. Count on the fact that you are going to be regarded as something of a nuisance to the host/hostess and their household staff. Therefore, you should immediately introduce yourself to the appropriate people, courteously inquire as to the house rules, and determine how and where you will

take your meals. If you are carrying a gun, you will probably be regarded with alarm, so keep it out of sight. Unless you are in a high-risk situation, you may be advised to leave your gun locked in your suitcase, particularly if there are children in the household. Flowers and candy are thoughtful gifts to make your presence more acceptable. A friendly and understanding staff will make your job much easier. Any problems should be handled diplomatically. Under no circumstances will your client allow you to take a tough line with his friends or their employees.

You will need to quietly and discreetly survey the house and grounds to determine any vulnerabilities. You will probably not be able to change anything, but at least you will be aware of any problem areas. Make inquiries as to availability of emergency services in the area and pay a friendly visit to the local law enforcement authorities to present your credentials. In essence, you will be conducting an advance to obtain information, although you may not be able to implement all of the security procedures which you would normally include.

If your client wishes to rent a vacation house or condominium, try to persuade him to allow you to visit the area and do an advance prior to committing to a particular property. Professional rental agents, particularly in major resort areas, are generally very knowledgeable and helpful, and can make your job much easier. They can provide you with descriptions, floor plans, and pictures of various properties, put you in touch with services such as security companies, recommend restaurants, and supply tourist maps. They are accustomed to providing these services (for different reasons) to their clients. If your client's choice is to stay in a condominium, the rental agent can usually identify who is staying in adjacent units.

In order to maintain a low profile, you should equip yourself with appropriate clothing to fit into the vacation environment. If your client's choice is the beach, carrying a weapon concealed in skimpy beach clothing can be a problem. As always, when traveling, check the local regulations regarding the carrying of a weapon.

COMMUNICATIONS SECURITY

If a switchboard is utilized it should be located away from the mainstream in a protected area, with restricted access. Open wires and terminal boxes should be inspected frequently for damage and wire-tapping. Telex, fax, and other communication machines should be located in a secure area. Copy machines should have restricted access to discourage the copying of sensitive documents, and a shredder should be provided. A system that is cost-effective and helps to maintain control of the copying process is the issuance of coded keys to authorized personnel.

Computers should be in secure areas and accessed by password. Sensitive and confidential papers should be kept under lock and key unless the computer operator is actually working with them.

Some general guidelines should be established for telephone security. You should always either know with whom you are talking or be prepared to verify by calling the party back. Try to obtain verbal identification to include name, company or affiliation; then, look up the telephone number yourself. This procedure is particularly necessary when the caller is seeking information about the client or the routines and systems of the residence. There are many, many seemingly legitimate, but suspicious, calls and an infinite number of clever scams to elicit information. Any calls which you consider suspicious should be documented and checked out. An unusually high number of wrong number calls should be noted and documented.

At the same time, your client will not be happy if his or her calls are handled rudely or too tersely. Each call should be answered promptly and courteously. Take all information down in writing and make certain that messages are delivered promptly to the client. Do not use sloppy language or refer to your client in overly familiar terms. Legitimate callers should not be made to feel they are unwanted, or held in suspicion.

Radio transmission security can be improved by observing some basic guidelines. Two-way radios should always be regarded as professional equipment for business use only, by keeping transmissions to a minimum. Develop your own codes and make certain that your authorized staff (only) are trained in the use of the codes and use them. Your code system should have a back-up to verify any emergency situations. You should be aware that it is possible for intruders to violate your radio transmissions. Avoid using excessive power or transmitters that exceed your range. Keep your transmission clear, particularly in emergencies or in stressful circumstances. Have a fully developed plan for responding to emergency calls or failure to check in by a station. If an employee leaves, and certainly if an employee is fired, the codes should be changed.

GUARDS AND PROTECTIVE SERVICES

There will be times when you will work in circumstances where guards and guard services are employed. If you are a one-person protection team you may, on occasion, need to bring in one or more extra protection people. It is well to know some facts about guards and security companies.

Guards or security officers compose the largest percentage of all persons employed in private security. For a number of years, there has been a phenomenal growth in the industry, with some larger companies (such as Wackenhut, Pinkerton's, and Wells Fargo) maintaining offices in most major metropolitan cities, offering a variety of security services. In the past, there were numerous problems with contract guards, due largely to poor pay, lax hiring procedures, and lack of training. There have been definite improvements, and now a number of guard companies maintain their own training programs. The trend is toward greater and greater use of guard services and the industry is rushing to keep pace.

It pays to check out the company you choose to provide guard services. To a degree, you get what you pay for, and, if you insist on the least expensive service, you may run the risk of obtaining poorly trained or unreliable personnel. Obtain references if possible. A local chapter of the American Society for Industrial Security (ASIS) can be helpful in recommending services to fit your needs.

Insist on meeting with the guard company official(s) at their offices and be prepared to ask the right questions. What equipment will the company provide their guards and what equipment will you be expected to provide? What kind of supervision will be given? Will the guards be armed? What kind of liability insurance does the company provide for its guards? If the contract guard shoots someone on your premises, who will be held responsible, you or the guard company?

If your need is for a more highly trained protection specialist, you have, in some areas, three sources: bodyguard companies, security companies offering executive protection services, or an executive protection training school. In some states there are companies listed in the telephone yellow pages as providing executive protection or bodyguard services. Security companies and contract guard companies will sometimes provide these services. If you strike out in your own area, you can contact one of the schools (such as Executive Security International in Aspen, Colorado) who train executive protection specialists and who can recommend graduates on either a temporary or permanent basis. Insist on seeing a full resume which includes job skills and references.

Your new member of the protection team should be fully briefed on his job. Make it clear how you will work together.

OFFICE SECURITY

For the executive protection agent, reality is that the client's business probably comes equipped with a Security Director who is usually quite capable of providing the physical security needed by the client's business. Security Directors, particularly of Fortune 500 companies, are generally well experienced and capable of implementing the security

measures which protect the client's business, though not necessarily the client's personal protection needs. A good working partnership, nurtured with a high degree of diplomacy, can usually be established between the protection agent and the corporate Security Director. Generally, unless the client has a small business, his office security is well attended to, and the executive protection agent should coordinate personal security with the Security Director. However, in the event that this does not happen, the following provides some guidelines to the agent.

All of the security principles which apply to doors, windows, locks, etc. are equally suitable for residences or offices with one exception; office buildings and plants often do not reflect quite as much concern about appearances as residences. Whereas the client may object to a cyclone fence encircling his residence, he may not have the same qualms about his manufacturing plant. And, where all-night lighting may not be suitable for a home, it may be quite acceptable for an office building.

As always, office security begins with a security survey, starting with the perimeter environment: landscaping, fencing, gates, lighting, guards, dogs, and alarm system. Next, and very important for an office environment, is the area of access control. Who is allowed on the premises? What controls are in place to direct the movement of employees and their access to various portions of the office? How are visitors controlled in their movements and their access to company property? To reduce the problem to its most basic elements, the issues are: how vulnerable is the property to access (invasion) by strangers, and what can be done to reduce this vulnerability? Corporate Security Directors are generally knowledgeable in these procedures. They are concerned about internal and external theft and, therefore, have implemented good access control procedures. The weak link is sometimes in the area of visitors. A visitor is still viewed as a guest, and security procedures are often sacrificed for comfort and hospitality.

There are at least three potential problems not normally dealt with in the corporate security environment. In a great many offices, a slick visitor may arrive, business card and briefcase in hand, with a plausible story. While waiting in the reception area, that same visitor may conveniently leave the briefcase in a corner, behind the couch, or in the restroom, and quietly slip away. That briefcase may contain a bomb.

A second potential problem is with the same slick visitor who, with a good cover story, is able to penetrate the inner sanctuaries of the executive offices carrying a briefcase that contains either a bomb or a gun.

A third problem which is a fairly recent phenomenon, involves the disaffected or terminated employee who has had some sort of access in the past, who is now very angry, and who wishes to invade the inner areas of management to kill or injure a supervisor or co-worker.

Personnel & Visitor Identification

While access control procedures are important, of equal importance is awareness training of personnel, particularly those employees who control access areas. Secretaries, receptionists, and guards can do a great deal to limit access by strangers, and to notice anything out of the ordinary. The premises should routinely be checked for objects that are out of place and do not belong there.

If an employee identification card or badge is used, there must be a system to control the issuance of the badges and the safekeeping of any extra badges. Lost or damaged badges must be accounted for, and, if this compromises the system, the identification should be changed. It should be evident that all tradespeople must show identification which can, and should, be checked. Employees should be encouraged through their security awareness training to question any non-badged strangers wandering about a facility, courteously inquiring, "May I help you?," and then escorting the strangers to the reception area.

Reception areas should never be left unattended, and scheduled relief periods for the receptionist must be arranged. The reception area should be kept clean and clear of extraneous objects, so that any "foreign" object immediately stands out. In high security situations, the guard station is usually located either in or near the reception area, and access is very strictly regulated.

Empty offices, restrooms, and storage closets should be kept locked, particularly those located in or near public areas, with potential access by strangers. Executive offices should not be marked with names or titles, nor should routes to executive offices be marked. Doors used as barriers between the receptionist or administrative assistant and the executive office should be locked. A silent duress system from the receptionist to guards and administrative assistants, and from the executive's office to administrative assistants and guards, should be installed.

Cleaning people should be supervised and their access to sensitive material restricted. It is a favorite ploy of spies to use cleaning people to implant listening devices in offices and conference rooms.

If the situation warrants it, a visitor procedure should be established. Either a visitor escort program or a visitor identification process can be used to track visitors.

If badges are utilized, they should be clearly distinguishable from employee badges, so that visitors who are in unauthorized areas can be spotted quickly. Visitor badges should be turned in as the visitors leave, to avoid re-entry by them or others. A visitor's log should contain full information as to the visitor's name, company, purpose of visit, person visited, and time in and out. If at all possible, an advance list of expected visitors and guests should be given to the reception desk, and, in high security situations, identification should be requested of these visitors when they arrive. Since identification can be forged, this should be scrutinized with care. Consideration should be given to the inspection of briefcases and/or packages carried by visitors.

Escort procedures insure that all guests are accompanied from the reception area to their destination.

Package Control and Search

Letters and packages should never be given directly to the client without first being inspected. If a visual search is conducted, and, if the package is accompanied, the visitor should be asked to open it. Briefcase and pocketbook compartments should be examined. Personnel should be trained in search techniques, as it has become increasingly difficult to recognize some very clever surveillance devices and innocent-appearing weapons. Many people will take umbrage at having their briefcases and pocketbooks searched, and the entire procedure must be handled with diplomacy. Great care should be taken with personal possessions. A courteous "thank you" will help to assuage miffed feelings.

Packages delivered by courier or mail should be carefully checked and opened by trained personnel before delivering to the client. If you have any reason to suspect that a package or letter contains an explosive, don't touch it. Call the police bomb squad and ask for their help. Unidentified packages or parcels which appear "out of the blue" should always be regarded with suspicion.

Some material incorporated within this chapter is taken from the U.S. General Services Administration publication, "Security Guidelines for Government Executives." We are deeply grateful for the opportunity to work with the U.S. General Services Administration on this project, and for their permission to use this material.

Electronic security, as it applies to the protection agent, encompasses two protection applications: intrusion detection (electronic alarm systems); and electronic surveillance and countermeasures (prevention, detection, and nullification of "bugs").

INTRUSION DETECTION SYSTEMS

Intrusion detection (alarm) systems are an enhancement of physical security, though not a replacement of sound physical security. The most effective security system combines well-designed physical security with an alarm system that fits the requirements, threat level, and lifestyle of the client. Note the word "lifestyle." Unless the threat level to the client is very high, he will rarely submit to an alarm system that forces him to do more than slightly alter his comfort level. If the system is not user-friendly, convenient, or makes allowances for his dogs and children, he won't use it. Also, he will probably not open his pocketbook for unlimited expenditures that turn his home into Fort Knox.

It is not necessary that the protection agent have the same in-depth knowledge of an alarm system that a dealer/installer must have. The protection agent will not install the system, nor fix it if it breaks down. What is important is that the agent be able to specify the kind of system which best fits the site, and identify and work with a reliable dealer/installer.

Without an electronics background, how does an agent pick up enough knowledge to be able to specify a security system? There are some magazines which cover the subject on a regular basis: *Security* (magazine), *Security Distributing and Marketing*, as well as some issues of *Security Management*. There are trade shows sponsored by American Society for Industrial Security (ASIS), and Cahner's (publisher of *Security*) which are crammed with dealers who are

eager to hand out copious amounts of literature on alarm systems, and who will tirelessly explain their products. There are books, one of which is *Intrusion Detection Systems*, 2nd Edition, author Robert L. Barnard, publisher Butterworths, that explain in more detail than you may require how each system component works.

The material in this chapter relating to intrusion detection systems is basic and over-simplified, but it will serve to reduce a daunting subject to manageable terms. Further exploration of the subject is up to the agent.

The non-recommended substitute to acquiring the right security system is simply to pick out a dealer from the yellow pages, then ask him to design the system. The dealer is, remember, in the business of selling products, and the more unscrupulous ones may sell more than is needed. In addition, if a dealer does not have or understand the products you may need, he is not likely to send you to another dealer. He is more apt to sell what he has, not necessarily what the client needs.

In very general terms, an intrusion detection system is a combination of some form of sensor which has the capacity to detect movement, sound, or heat, and a device which relays the information to someone. That "someone" can be a central monitoring station which has contracted to provide an alarm monitoring system, or it can be someone(s) on the premises, including the client himself. Once the alarm signal has been transmitted, the next steps are to establish the validity of the signal (false alarm or bad guy) and to respond in some way.

Intrusion sensors are found in two modes--passive and active. Passive systems can be mechanical, requiring that someone or something pull, move, or break a connection. This category includes the microswitches which are installed at doors and windows. Someone opens the door, thereby breaking the connection, and the intrusion is reported in some form. Passive systems also include heat sensors that are designed to react to patterns of radiated heat, such as are produced by the human body. A third type of passive sensor is the acoustic sensor which, like a microphone, picks up noises.

Active systems use light beams, usually infrared or radio frequency energy. Radio frequency systems take the form of sonic, ultrasonic, and microwave motion detectors. Light beams, as you might expect, produce a beam which, if broken, triggers an alarm signal.

Each of these sensors has its own characteristics, advantages, and disadvantages. A complete security system may use a combination of different categories of sensors. The system must work compatibly not only with the client's lifestyle, but with the environment, since some sensors cannot "see" efficiently around corners, or through fog or snow. Additionally, a system designed for a residence and one designed for an office building or plant, and using essentially the same equipment, will be very different.

Establishing the Parameters

Joe Agent has only recently been hired by Bob Client to provide executive protection for himself and his family. Bob Client believes that, because he is the CEO of a group of three abortion clinics, he needs to upgrade his residential security. Until now, he has preferred to live without an electronic intrusion detection system, but believes that now one must be designed and installed both for his home and his three clinics. He wants Joe Agent to rough-design the systems, make recommendations, identify a reliable dealer, oversee the installations, and make arrangements for the systems maintenance.

Joe will not rush out and spend as much money as possible to make certain that Bob and his clinics are safe. Before making recommendations, Joe

will take several steps, which is the progression to be followed by agents in any similar situation.

The first step is to sit down with the client and discuss with him some important points. It is highly recommended that the client's spouse be included in the discussion, since all matters concerning the residence are mutual to husband and wife. What are the client's expectations--what does he expect the system to do for him and his family? What are his priorities? What does the client perceive as the risk? The client's expectations may not be realistic, since no system is foolproof; and his priorities may be expensive in light of the perceived risk.

Getting to know the client's lifestyle is important. How much security is the client willing to live with? Are there small children and pets who will be difficult to "housebreak" in terms of living with the security system? Are the pets free to come and go, particularly at night? Is the residence empty much of the time, due to the client's travels or the fact that it may only be a vacation home? Are there frequent house guests, or renters, who will be expected to live with the security system? If the security system does not fit the lifestyle and habits of the client, it will not be used or will be a source of constant irritation.

What is the value of the assets being protected? Aside from the perceived personal risk of (in this case) the client's role in owning abortion clinics, is there an impressive million-dollar art collection which must also be protected? If so, this will add other components to the security system. If it is a manufacturing plant, what are the assets of the corporation in terms of equipment, computers, inventory, and other considerations? If the plant were destroyed, would an irreplaceable something worth $20,000,000 be lost? On the other hand, is the plant fully insured, with excellent physical security in terms of fences, gates, locks, and access control? The two situations require a very different system in terms of budget.

The next step is to conduct a threat

assessment, to include a site survey and intelligence gathering. How good is the physical security--fences, doors, locks, landscaping? The intrusion detection system must interface with the physical security. A visit to the police will provide an insight into the crime statistics and general nature of the neighborhood. Are other houses in the surrounding neighborhood equipped with alarm systems, and how extensive are these systems? The agent will check the corporation's files, as well as the newspaper files. Have there been any threats or incidents? Are there any criminal or violent groups operating in the area?

With some idea of the client's expectations and preferences, the value of the assets to be protected, and the results of the threat assessment, the agent now has a fairly good idea of what a security system designed to meet those needs will cost. The agent must meet with the client to discuss the budget. Is the client willing to spend the money required, or must the system be scaled back? If the system is to be scaled back, the client must know what is being given up, and how it affects the agent's ability to provide the required protection.

System Design Approach

A generally accepted approach is to design a security system that will delay, detect, alert, and respond. That is, to delay and then detect an intruder, to alert someone to the intruder's presence, and to respond in some manner.

Delay tactics comprise the physical barriers which are erected to delay the intruder. These include fences, walls, gates, landscaping (water, hedges, thorn bushes, etc.), doors, windows, and locks. A determined adversary may defeat all of these, but he will be delayed while doing so.

Detection includes the electronic security devices and sensors that detect violations of protected areas or zones. For planning purposes, there are five zones of detection: perimeter penetration detection; exterior area between perimeter fence or boundary and the facility being protected; building penetration;

motion detection; and proximity detection.

In the alert phase, a signal is transmitted to someone, either to an outside monitoring station or to someone in or around the facility. If the alert phase includes an audible alarm, it also alerts the adversary as to his detection. An alert includes audible and silent alarms and may trigger the turning on of indoor and/or outdoor lights.

The response to an alarm can include evacuating the client to a safe room and notifying the police, and/or sending a guard force to intercept the intruder(s).

Zone One--Perimeter Penetration Detection

The objective of the sensors in Zone One is to detect climbing, cutting, lifting, or penetration of a perimeter fence.

One method includes fence disturbance sensors, used primarily on chain link fences and mounted directly on the fence. The sensors react to mechanical vibrations that are larger in amplitude and usually higher in frequency than natural intruders such as wind, birds, and small animals. A disadvantage to these systems is their visibility. The sensors and the connecting cable are simply strung along the fence and attached to the fence posts.

Yet another method includes taut wire switches. Line sensors provide a linear detection zone. An alarm is activated when an intruder moves across the line established by the sensor. Taut wire switching is a simple switch assembly and is triggered by a trip wire or a cord. The wire is either stretched along the top of the fence or along the line where detection is desired.

Fence disturbance sensors and taut wire switches require that the intruder come in contact with the fence in order to trigger the alarm. If the intruder is able to vault over the fence, nothing will happen.

Zone Two--Exterior Zone Protection

The purpose of this zone is to detect anyone running, walking, crawling, or driving between the perimeter fence or boundary and the facility walls. There are several choices of systems.

Electrostatic Field Sensors (E-Field Fence or EFF).

A crystal-controlled field generator imposes an electrostatic field on a combination of field wires and sense wires running parallel to each other. An alarm is triggered dependent upon the mass or size of the intruder, how close the mass is to the EFF, how long the mass is near the EFF, and the rate of speed with which the mass moves. The sensors should ignore the frequencies generated by the wind, flying debris, birds, and small animals.

When mounted on a perimeter fence, the EFF is considered a Zone One system. When it is free-standing and located inside the fence, it is Zone Two protection.

Some advantages of EFF are that it can "see" through (function in) bad weather--rain, snow, fog. It is easy to install, in that it requires no ditching or trenching. It is a single-end feed. Also, line of sight is not necessary--you can follow nature contours of land with it. Last, it is inexpensive.

Buried Sensors.

Because they are buried, these sensors involve more expense; however, they are considerably more sightly, and, while this might not be a consideration when used around a plant, it is usually important for a residence. Another advantage to these sensors is that, being buried, they are not apparent to an intruder, making it very difficult for him to evade the system. These include geophones, piezoelectric transducers, strain, ferrous metal detectors, and seismic energy detectors. These buried sensors are described below.

.   **Geophones.** Geophones buried in a trench with densely compacted dirt, sand, and gravel detect the seismic energy reflected by anyone crossing the line of geophones. Geophones are very sensitive and false alarms are sometimes a problem unless the sensitivity level is adjusted to eliminate the low seismic energy generated by the wind or small animals.

.   **Piezoelectric Transducers.** When an intruder stresses the transducer, a quartz crystal generates an electrical signal based on the applied pressure and causes an imbalance which becomes an alarm via a signal processor.   As with geophones, these transducers should be buried with densely compacted sand and soil.

.   **Strain/Magnetic Line Sensors.** Combined strain and magnetic line sensors detect both the pressure or strain produced in the ground by someone crossing the sensor line. They can also detect ferrous metals. False alarms can be a problem with these sensors if they are located close to utility lines, and they can be affected by electrical interference such as switching substations and radar. Alarm signal, power, and any other electrical cables should not be buried in the same trench as the strain/magnetic line sensors, as the electrical signals on the additional cables could cause false alarms.

.   **Ferrous Metal Detectors.** These buried detectors are used for vehicle detectors.   An advantage is that they detect only metal and are not, therefore, a problem for animals (except for horses with iron shoes). They are best used in locales where there is little chance of lightning, heavy snow, and no strong source of electromagnetic energy close to the sensor line.

.   **Seismic Energy Detectors.** Intruders emit seismic energy when walking or running. Seismic detectors pick up mini-shock waves going through the ground. These are also affected by deep snow.

Outdoor Motion Detectors.

These include outdoor infrared beams and outdoor microwaves. Both systems are line-of-sight systems. If there are obstructions or hills, the area behind the obstruction will not be protected.

Outdoor Infrared Beams. Outdoor beams project an infrared beam along the path between source and receiver. When the path is broken by an intruder, the amount of energy picked up by the receiver is reduced and alarms are activated. When fog rolls in and slowly interrupts the beams, they are turned off automatically. The housings also contain heaters to keep condensation from building up, keeping the lenses fog-free. The operative protective range for infrared is approximately one thousand feet on level ground.

Newer outdoor systems using beam generating lasers have overcome the drawbacks caused by bad weather. Lasers generate a beam several times more intense than any LED and a stronger, narrower beam can be directed with precision over distances of one thousand feet.

A simple set-up of the infrared intrusion detection system is from post to post. The transmitters and receivers can be hidden in bird houses, hollowed-out tree trunks, or hidden behind shrubbery as long as the beam is not broken. A "fence" can be created by a series of "posts," each with several separate stacked transmitters and receivers. A disadvantage to outdoor infrared beams is that if the intruder spots the housings he can crawl underneath. An advantage, however, is that if they are set high enough, dogs can be allowed to run free and add to the protection without triggering false alarms. Infrared energy is very much affected by rain, fog, and snow and, for that reason, may not be a good choice for very damp, snowy climates.

Outdoor Microwaves. Most outdoor microwave systems have a transmitter and a receiver set up at opposite ends of a straight line which defines the protected area. Microwave systems also provide a fence pattern similar to that of the infrared in which a microwave energy field is created between the transmitter and receiver. The fence pattern can be a tight pattern, approximately two hundred feet long and several feet wide or up to one thousand feet long with a thirty-foot-wide center.

Microwaves are much less affected than infrared systems by rain, snow, and fog. Microwave detectors are less affected by air turbulence than is true with ultrasonic detectors.

Zone Three--Building Penetration Detection

These are the systems used to detect an intruder who has breeched the perimeters of the facility through a wall, window, door, or ceiling.

Contacts. Contacts detect openings and closings of doors, windows, skylights, etc. Interruption of the circuit creates a signal. These switches contain two basic components, a magnetic reed switch and a permanent magnet, each with separate housing. The reed switch is sensitive to the local magnetic field. It will open or close depending upon its proximity to the magnet. The most common arrangement calls for the reed switch to be attached to a door or window frame and the magnet attached to the door or window. With door or window closed, the switch assembly has a closed circuit. Opening the door or window breaks the circuit and signals are triggered. This is considered a normally closed circuit. A normally open circuit works in the reverse way. When the magnet and the reed switch are close together, the reed switch is held open. When a door or window is opened, the magnet is removed from the proximity and the reed switch closes, sending the signal.

Foil. This is thin metallic tape that can be bonded to windows or walls. When it is broken, the current passing through the foil is interrupted and an alarm is activated. The detection area is defined by the pattern of the foil over the protective surface to which it is bonded. On windows, the usual pattern runs around the edge of the pane, three inches from the frame. Depending upon the surface covered, foil may be easily bypassed; however, it is inexpensive and may be a visible deterrent.

Window Bugs. Window bugs are about the size of a fifty-cent piece and are installed in the corners of sheets of glass up to four by eight feet.

When the glass is broken, the bug picks up the sound of breaking or cutting glass.

Glass Sentry. This is similar to a window bug but is monitored.

Vibration Detectors. These detectors sense vibrations of sufficient magnitude to signal an alarm. They are small, adjustable leaf switches.

Magna-Vib. This is a combination of a magnetic contact and a vibration detector.

Shock Sensors. Shock sensors respond to the shock waves of breaking materials, a condition that generally occurs when an intruder is trying to gain access to the perimeter of the building through a wall, window, or door. They are mechanically filtered, solid-state electric sensors designed to respond only to shock waves with intensities associated with break-ins. The sensor will remain open from three to five seconds and then reset itself.

Sound Discriminators or Audio Sensors. Audio detection, also called passive acoustic, is a system of microphones in the protected area which detect the sound produced by an intruder. An alarm is initiated when the system detects sounds that match the sensitivity and logic of the system. The pattern is normally omni-directional; the range depends on the sensitivity setting within the protected area and the amount of background noise. For situations that have varying background noise, audio detection systems are not very useful. Filters, however, can cut out extreme high and low frequency noises, but audio systems work best where the noise level is low and continuous. Some systems combine a pick-up microphone with a loudspeaker. These are used mostly in empty buildings during the nighttime hours. If the central station receives an alarm, the operator can tune in the microphones and actually hear what is going on in the protected areas.

Alarm Screens. An alarm screen is a frame of wood or aluminum with wire or fiberglass wire cloth. It is much like standard screen installed in homes; however, it is interwoven at intervals with wires which make a protective circuit. Entry through the screen requires breaking one or more of the wires, which interrupts the circuit and triggers the alarm. The frames are fitted with magnetic switches and mercury switches so that, if the frame is removed from the window casing, it will trigger the alarm.

Heat Sensors (Ionization). These sensors are used in areas where the intruder might use a cutting torch, such as a vault or safe.

Mercury Switches. These have closed contact points with floating mercury between. As long as the mercury is in place, it connects the two contact points at the closed circuit. When a switch is tilted, the mercury will drop from one of the contact points, thus opening the circuit and causing an alarm.

Panic Buttons. Panic buttons are operated in an emergency situation and work even if the premise alarm is turned off. Emergency buttons should be located in some of the bathrooms, kitchen, entrance ways, bedrooms, and the garage. The emergency panel operates twenty-four hours a day. When the panic button is hit it can either send a silent alarm or activate your audible and visual alarms.

Hardwire vs. Radio. For reliability and maintenance, hardwire is used to connect the different sensors in any one premise. Sometimes, an occasion occurs when it is impractical to run a wire from a sensor back to the control panel. A transmitter works without use of wires and sends a radio signal. Each transmitter is monitored continuously for both alarm and maintenance conditions. The transmitter transmits periodically, anywhere from twenty seconds to forty seconds, telling the master control that there is no intrusion, and that the system is working correctly.

Zone Four--Interior

This is the zone within the facility, and detects anyone who has entered the building and is moving within the protection zone.

Pressure Mats or Flex Switches. Mats can be placed under rugs where an intruder may walk. When placing mat switching under carpets, it is not necessary to alarm the entire surface, only the strategic areas.

Light Sensors. These are light-sensitive diodes that activate an alarm when they receive a light source. They are installed inside safes, walls, etc., where they are turned on while in total darkness. They are so sensitive they can pick up a cigarette glow in an enclosed, darkened room.

Infrared Beams. The zone of protection for these devices is defined by the optical path of the beam from the source to the receiver. The use of mirrors produces geometric paths other than a straight line so you can get several beams for the price of one. They are low in false alarms and are disguised as wall outlets. If they are installed high enough off the floor and away from furniture, you can have pets inside the house with the interior system on.

Ultrasonics. Ultrasonic sensors consist of transmitting and receiving transducers. The transmitting transducer converts electronic oscillations into sound waves which flood the immediate area, reflecting off any hard surface and are picked up by the receiving transducer. The receiver converts sound waves to electrical signals which are sent to the control panel for processing. The outgoing and returning signals are processed for frequency shifts-- either more cycles per second or less. A certain difference generates an alarm. The detection pattern in an unobstructed volume is generally tear-drop shaped with a range of 15 to 30 feet. Detection patterns may be shaped to fit any volume configuration by placing transmitting and receiving transducers in appropriate locations.

The advantage of ultrasonic is that its coverage saturates the volume being protected. The units can be triggered by air turbulence (air conditioning units and forced air heaters), loud sounds of certain frequencies (hissing noises from escaping steam and ringing bells), and moving objects. The better ultrasonic systems have built-in air turbulence compensation/filtering, clutter rejection, and other compensating devices.

Microwaves. Similar principle to ultrasonics, but higher frequency. A variety of patterns are possible, and microwave energy has the advantage of being able to penetrate glass, wood, and cinder block to some extent. The units can be mounted to go through several walls, thus protecting several rooms and/or floors. The disadvantage to this is that the microwave may detect someone moving beyond a partition in an unprotected area or outside a wall, thereby causing false alarms. Metal objects (file cabinets, metallic wallpaper, etc.) can reflect microwave energy; therefore, metal objects detected within the microwave energy pattern can trigger false alarms. Microwave detectors should never be pointed toward any moving metal objects.

Sonic. Similar to ultrasonic but less sensitive to small insects, cats, and rodents than ultrasonic. This is due to the fact that the wavelength of sonic energy is much longer than that of ultrasonic. The high-intensity sound of sonic detectors can be heard outside the protected area and can be annoying; hence, sonic detectors might best be used in warehouses and schools where this will not be a noticeable disadvantage.

Passive Audio. Passive audio listens to sounds on open microphones placed in protected areas. These sensors work best in protected areas with background noises low and continuous. These systems can have a listening monitor and two-way communication capabilities.

Stress Systems. Sensors are attached to support beams underneath large expanses of floor and are set up to read a similar resistance. If one or more of the stress sensors are triggered it creates an imbalance with the other sensors and activates an alarm.

Passive Infrared. Every object transmits a certain amount of infrared energy. The intensity of the energy depends on the surface temperature of the object. Passive infrared detectors receive this energy directly through a system of lenses. A person who walks through the protected area will cause a change in the intensity of the infrared energy that is registered by the detector. The design of the system is such that a moving object cannot be seen by both the active elements simultaneously. A moving object will therefore cause an unbalanced signal which triggers an alarm. Conversely, changes in background temperature are received by both elements simultaneously, resulting in a balanced signal which is not registered as an alarm. False alarms are further reduced by the fact that the circuitry requires both sides of an individual detection zone to be crossed before an alarm is registered. This circuitry rejects insignificant background motion without any reduction in sensor range. Passive infrared systems are extremely stable and have ranges similar to ultrasonics and microwaves. They do have blind areas since they cannot see through building materials.

Television-Imagery or Video Alarm Systems.
Basically, these systems are combinations of closed circuit television with motion detection. Video cameras examine a video field and an image is pre-logged. Any change within this field is fed into comparison logic circuits for evaluation; significant deviations are programmed to initiate an alarm signal.

Zone Five--Proximity Detection

The purpose of this zone is to detect approaching, removing, attempting to remove, or penetration of a protected container.

Wafer Switches--Weight and Unweight.
These provide the same function as pressure mats but are much more sensitive and much smaller. They can be placed under valuable objects.

Light Sensors.
Placed in safes or vaults (see above).

Heat Sensors.
Detects cutting of the protected area or protected container with a torch.

Sound.
(see above.)

Capacitance Discharge System.
This is the main type of system recognized by insurance companies for protection of safes and vaults. Proximity detectors or capacitance discharge detectors protect ungrounded metal storage containers and objects. These devices operate by making the protected object part of the electronic capacitance system. The object is set off the floor by insulating blocks connected with conducting straps or wires to the capacitance system. An intruder coming too close or touching the protected object will alter the circuit and initiate the alarm. The range extends a small distance from a protected object. The pattern conforms to the object protected. The system is vulnerable to false alarms caused by humidity, poor ground insulation, and static charge build-up and discharge.

Cargo Nets.
The net is placed over the object or vehicle to be protected. Any attempt to lift or cut the net immediately triggers an alarm.

Portable Detection Systems.
These are self-contained systems which include detection, arming components, and their own power supplies. A variety of types of detectors are available, including sonic, ultrasonic, microwave, and infrared. A time-delay feature allows the keyholder time to exit the area before the unit goes into an alarm condition. The system also allows approximately ten to thirty seconds for the protected area to be re-entered and the unit deactivated by key before going into an alarm condition. These units can emit audible alarms or transmit wireless signals to a remote location. Some systems can be used in hotel rooms, left in automobiles, or used in temporary offices. The larger systems can be used in vacation homes and can be kept available for supplemental protection on an irregular basis.

Closed Circuit Television--CCTV.
This requires a basic system consisting of a video camera,

cabling, and video monitoring. An assortment of lenses increase or magnify a protection area. Cameras can be connected to detection sensors and activate simultaneously with an alarm signal.

Fire and Smoke Systems

In designing a system, the agent should be aware of basic safety requirements, including fire and smoke detection systems.

Heat Detectors. Heat or thermal detectors are sensitized to go off at a fixed temperature. These are inexpensive units and are very stable; however, fire must be present before they react.

Rate of Rise Detectors. These react like a heat detector when the temperature reaches a certain reading. They are more sensitive because they sound an alarm when the temperature rises ten degrees within a ten-minute period.

Smoke Detectors. These operate on a photoelectric principle. Detectors activate an alarm after smoke particles entering the chamber are illuminated and the scattered light from the particles cross the beam. There are also radioactive smoke detectors.

Ionization Detectors. These respond to the first traces of fire in the form of invisible products of combustion and/or visible smoke. Detectors usually contain two ionization chambers and a sensitive semi-conductor amplifier switching circuit. One chamber detects products of combustion; the other serves as a reference to stabilize the detector's sensitivity to environmental changes.

Infrared Detectors. These detectors respond directly to the presence of flame. Detectors sense infrared radiation which must occur for several seconds.

Utilities

So, as long as you are designing a system,

why not make it all-encompassing, and include utilities and other safety factors.

Pressure Detectors. These detectors are installed in utility areas where pressure has to remain constant. If the pressure in a pipe or container changes, an alarm would be activated.

Flow Switches. These are paddle-type units installed in a pipe carrying water or other liquid. As long as the liquid in the pipe is standing still, the switch remains in a stable condition. When the water flows, it moves the paddle switch. These are used in fire systems so that water flow is checked before too much damage is done.

Water Switches or Moisture Switches. These are basically installed to guard against water leakage, burst pipes, rusted-out water heaters, etc.

Gas Detectors. These detectors are usually set up for propane.

Swimming Pool Detectors. These were originally developed so that parents could hear a child falling into a pool. When a small buoy is bounced by rippling water it transmits an alarm via radio frequency to the home.

Heat Loss Detectors. This is basically a heat thermostat with a high and low setting. If the heat in a house drops below the pre-set temperature the alarm will activate. Very useful in vacant houses where pipes could freeze.

Access to the Alarm System

How do you turn your alarm system on and off? What makes it work?

Keys. One key type actuates a momentary switch. The second key type is a shunt lock, which is a bypass switch.

Digital. These look similar to key pads on the telephone. They can be instantaneous or have entry/exit time-delays. They have several characteristics.

.   They turn the alarm system on and off.

.   They have shunting capabilities. From the key pad you can enter a code and turn on the perimeter or the interior system, or you can enter another code and turn the entire system on.

.   You can change the code for security reasons.

.   You have ambush capability. If someone is behind you with a gun and they tell you to turn the alarm system off, you enter the ambush code and the system appears to be off, while sending a silent signal.

.   They have a tamper code. If someone starts playing with the key pad it will even reject the correct code. You can enter a tamper code added to your correct code and that will clear it, or there will be a time delay once a wrong code is entered. There is approximately a five-minute time delay before the correct code can be entered and the system will activate or deactivate.

.   They have the capability of identifying who turned the system on or off.

.   They have the capability of recording times of entry and exit or activation and deactivation.

Other applications include the following:

Voice Actuation. Voice-actuated access controls are available in two types: actuation by a word or by voice print. Actuation by a word is less expensive.

Time Locks. The alarm system access is automatically turned off for certain periods of time and automatically turned back on, so that it is only accessible for certain periods of time.

Card-Key Access or Card/Card-Key. These electronic access readers employ various coding elements including lettering, mechanical hole position, optical or magnetic tape.

Cards and Codes. These are combinations of card readers and coded units. Both the card and a memorized code are needed to gain access to the alarm system. The card is inserted in the reader, and a code is entered on a digital. Since two elements are involved, a greater degree of security is provided.

Hand Geometry Card Readers. Verification is provided by using an individual's hand geometry characteristics, which are measured and compared by a machine. Tolerances can be established so that the possibility of cross-identifying fingerprints can be reduced to one out of thousands.

Signature Verification. This system measures (with respect to time) the pressure applied to a writing instrument when one signs his own name. Statistics show that each person's pressure pattern is unique to the individual and remarkably constant from one signature to the next.

Control Panels

The control unit of an intrusion detection system contains the signal processing logic. The signals from various sensors are processed and alarm signals are initiated. The control unit contains the system's on/off switch, the re-set line, the alarm and circuit test, a power source, and various switches for bypassing or hook-up. It also contains power filters and power supplies. Power supplies and filters help during black-out and brown-out periods to keep the voltage to the control panel consistent. The control unit also contains automatic cut-offs which will automatically shut down the alarm after a given period so that the neighbors are not annoyed by a continuously ringing bell or flashing lights.

Control panels also contain automatic re-set features. If the intruder damages some piece of equipment (foil on the window, etc.) the system will not re-set itself. However, if the system has been violated through an open door and the door is closed within a given period of time, the system will automatically re-set itself.

Zones and zone switching are located in the control panel. It is very useful to separate the first floor perimeter, second floor perimeter, and other levels of perimeter. Control panels have the zones of the outside alarm system and their back-up zones. For example, if Zone One were violated, it could automatically eliminate Zone One from the system. It can also trace the intrusion and signal the intruder's location to the monitoring station.

Computers

There are several types of computers associated with security systems: analog, band pass, pac-adapts, and general. These different computers are the intelligence system to the control panel through which is programmed the intruder profile (size, pressure, etc.). Intrusion detection sensors, line supervision, control, monitoring, and display functions, as well as access control system, can all be tied into a computer. Notification functions are handled by the computer communicating with either the security control center or the police. Computerized systems are designed primarily for facilities such as a plant or an office building or a high-level residential compound. The obvious disadvantage of any computer system is that when it goes down, everything is shut down.

Alert (local)

Audible Alerting. This includes bells, sirens, lighting with strobes, and floodlights. Activating the system should set off a local alarm light, usually a strobe located on the roof of the house, possibly even in the house. The lights should be of high intensity and floodlight instantly. The alarm should alert the security center and the local police or response force.

Alert (Independent Location)

Central Station. The central station is an independent location and privately owned, or a police

station where the alarms are monitored.

Guard Station or Proprietary Alarm Stations. This is the same as the central station except that it is on the premises of the area being protected.

Transmission of Alarm from Location to Receiving Station

Direct Lines. These are direct lines or wires from the alarm location to the receiving station. There are several different types.

.   **Private.** With a private line, the owner of the alarm system provides his own facilities to get the line from one place to another. In a new building, the wires can be built in. Adding them later means stringing visible cables or burying them.

.   **Leased line.** A dedicated pair of lines, used only for alarm transmission, can be leased from the telephone company. There is no other traffic on the lines. There is an installation charge for hook-up and a monthly charge.

.   **Supervised.** These leased lines are supervised by a variety of methods, but basically they carry the voltage charge in a continuous flow to and from the central station. When they are interrupted or cut, the central station knows that it is no longer receiving a signal from the premise, and an alarm is triggered. It is indicated as a line interruption. The police or patrol may not be dispatched to the home immediately, but a central station should check with the telephone company to see what has caused the interruption and if the telephone company was responsible for it. If the telephone company did not cause it, a response force should be dispatched to further check whether the line has been deliberately cut.

.   **Polarity Reversal.** With these lines, one wire going out carries a positive charge, the wire returning carries a negative charge. When there is an alarm at the premise, the control panel reverses the voltage. This is indicated as a total switch from the normal condition to the alarm condition at the central station. When the line is cut no voltage is received, so it drops to a relaxed position which is read as a break in the line.

. **Resistance Readings.** As opposed to the reverse polarity, there are resistance readings. This is a newer method of providing security for private and leased line security transmissions. The resistance is read from the central station to the premise and back again. The resistance is so carefully monitored that, if someone attempts to interrupt the circuit, an alarm will be received.

. **Encode and Decode.** You can encode several alarm signals into one signal, transmit across the private line to the other side of town and decode at the central station. You then have several premises using one pair of wires.

. **Multiplex.** With multiplex, transmissions from a number of protected facilities can be made over a signal communication channel.

. **McCulloch Loops.** This refers to a single pair of wires being split from the central station running from premise to premise in one large loop. Costs of one large line are shared among several premises. The disadvantage to this system is that if there is a break in the line all of the premises located on the line after the break lose their transmission ability.

Dialers. These are unsupervised, less expensive, and much less secure methods of transmitting an alarm message.

. **Tape Dialers.** Dialers automatically make a telephone call for you. When an intrusion occurs on the security system, a pre-recorded message is dialed through your telephone to as many as four pre-designated telephone numbers. The major disadvantage is that it is not supervised. If no one is at home to receive the message, no one is aware of the alarm. Also, if the telephone line is not working, the central station does not receive an alarm signal.

. **Digital dialers.** These require a receiving unit at the central station, and they are more efficient, taking just seconds to make the call with a series of beeps.

Alternate Methods of Alarm Transmission. These include radio transmission, microwave transmission, and laser communication transmission.

Additional Points

Any security system must satisfy two additional points. It must conform to and satisfy any local ordinances. It must also be a system that is low-maintenance and does not require constant fine-tuning to make it work. The system, however, must be regularly inspected, checked, and provided any needed maintenance.

The agent has the responsibility of working with the dealers in designing and bidding out the system, and has an equal responsibility at the installation phase. He or she should be on hand during installation to make certain that the installers deliver the right system, and that any glitches are corrected on the spot.

It is one thing to design a system on paper and quite another when it comes to life on-site. Unforseen circumstances or environmental impediments may necessitate changes. The agent must be totally familiar with and able to operate the system, as he will be the individual who must "train" the client and the client's family and employees.

Confidentiality and protective control of the security system is important. Any security system can be invaded if the adversary knows certain details. Blueprints of the system should be kept under lock and key. Employees and strangers should not be given confidential information. And, the client should be dissuaded from discussing his system with anyone.

This also argues for the need for great care in selecting an electronic system provider. The provider must have impeccable credentials and reputation.

ELECTRONIC SURVEILLANCE AND COUNTERMEASURES

Electronic surveillance is a way of life in today's world. Whereas it once was relegated to "cold war" issues, James Bond, and national governments spying on each other, it is now commonplace, particularly in the business environment. It has been estimated that American businesses lose many billions of dollars each year to business espionage. Much of the espionage is conducted by foreign governments and foreign companies. In fact, however, some American companies have resorted to this form of "research" to gain a competitive edge. A major story of February 24, 2000 discussed a report by a special European Parliament commission which stated that an electronic intelligence gathering network had the potential to violate the privacy of millions of European citizens and suggested that it has been used to benefit U.S. corporations in economic and industrial espionage.

In truth, information is fairly easy to access, and, while most corporations use perfectly legal intelligence gathering methods to produce "competitor intelligence," no one can accurately estimate how many are breaking the law by using illegal electronic measures to acquire valuable data from their competitors.

Remember, there are a lot of out-of-work spies roaming the universe, looking for meaningful employment. Hiring a spy to steal information is infinitely cheaper than spending millions of dollars in the development of new products.

Many clients are more concerned about loss of privacy or loss of sensitive company information than of being kidnapped. Perhaps so, but electronic surveillance, as well as physical surveillance, has been used extensively by terrorists in planning kidnappings and hostile attacks.

It is probably fair to say that, if your client is not currently being bugged, he has been bugged in the past or will be bugged in the future. It behooves the professional agent, therefore, to understand the basic principles of electronic surveillance and the countermeasures needed to defeat the surveillance. Increasingly, knowledgeable clients expect a professional bodyguard to protect them from electronic intrusion as well as from physical harm.

Anyone with an electronic background will simply love electronic surveillance countermeasures. Agents without an electronic background may wish to enroll in a basic course offered either by a community college, correspondence school, or trade school. However, take heart. The material, while not simple, can be mastered.

As not all eavesdropping is electronic, many people prefer the term "audio surveillance," and the U.S. government has used the term "technical surveillance." In his reading, the agent may expect to encounter these designations.

For years, the United States, the U.S.S.R., Israel, and all major national governments spent hundreds of millions of dollars in experimenting and developing the most exotic, sophisticated, and difficult to detect methods of technical attack. The agents trained in these technical methods were and are extremely good at their trade. The best electronic devices and countermeasures equipment are extremely expensive and are probably unaffordable or not cost-effective for use in low risk situations. Some devices may not, in fact, be available to the general public. Foreign espionage agents, however, are supported by the full resources of their governments and money, therefore, may not be a barrier.

Reality for the executive protection agent is that he and she will be working with fairly unsophisticated equipment and will use physical search as the primary method to detect implanted electronic devices. In almost every instance, this will be sufficient, since the usual technical attack will be equally unsophisticated. Outside the government, there are few adversaries able to finance a very exotic attack. Criminals and terrorists are apprehensive about running afoul of the law and tend to build their own electronic spy gadgets.

In order to know how to defeat a technical attack you must understand the various ways in which attacks are made. How do clever spies access information?

Non-Electronic or Mechanical Attack

One of the most important devices used to gain information is the human ear. Sometimes it is not necessary to invest in sophisticated audio countermeasures equipment to discover how information is being leaked. The problem may lie with the secretary sitting immediately outside the conference room or private office. A clever spy who knows how to listen can learn a great deal.

A crude but effective hearing enhancer is a water glass with a moistened rim. Yes, it works, although it works better against some walls than others. Used against a wall with little insulation, it can be very useful. A stethoscope placed against the wall is another simple, but effective, hearing enhancer.

It is a matter of acoustic attenuation, which translates as the ability to block the transmission of sound. For example, soundproofing represents total attenuation of audible sounds. Acoustic attenuation depends upon the type of material and construction, the thickness of the wall, the rigidity of the wall, and other variables.

Another type of mechanical attack is the use of a tape recorder which is smuggled into the target space. Excellent miniature tape recorders which are voice actuated and which can easily be carried in a pocket are available, as are briefcases with built-in recorders. It is easy, then, for a person to attend a meeting or conference with the tape recorder hidden on his person.

A favorite spying method is to hide a recorder in a conference (or other) room before a meeting. If the device is equipped with a voice actuated switch (VOX switch) the recorder is active only when there are conversations. There are any number of small recorders which can tape for several hours under these circumstances. The recorder can be brought into the room by anyone, including a cleaning person. Spies make good use of cleaning and maintenance people to smuggle tape recorders in and out of critical areas. Using a tape recorder (as opposed to a permanent, wired-in microphone) is particularly useful for gaining information from one-time events, such as conferences. It is simple and clean. Retrieving the tape recorder quickly lessens the possibility of discovery in a routine countermeasures sweep.

Visual Or Optical Attack

Included under optical attacks is simple observation using telescopes, binoculars, photography with telephoto lenses, and video cameras. These devices are often used together with lip reading. This has become a favorite method of criminals, who use binoculars and knowledge of lip reading to spy on people using public telephones equipped with credit card reception. The telephone companies have been bilked out of hundreds of millions of dollars.

Accomplished lip-readers, especially with a language capability, and using binoculars, have been used by spies very successfully. Private discussions held in the park or visible through a window have been invaded. Of course, the agent himself need not be a lip-reader if he merely films the action for analysis at a later date.

Video Attacks

Video cameras provide a threat in those areas where the attacker has a chance to gain access to the target space and hide a camera, or where he occupies an adjoining room or space. Video technology continues to improve, as does video surveillance. Retail stores have provided the impetus for the development of very sophisticated video cameras which can be hidden almost anywhere; for example, in the head of a ceiling-mounted sprinkler. You have undoubtedly heard of "pinhole cameras," which are cameras that can be aimed through a hole the size of a pinhole, and can take pictures of quite acceptable quality. Light levels are not terribly critical, as the state-of-the-art of low light level television systems has improved markedly over recent years. The use of light amplification tubes such as those used in the military with even standard vidicons (television tubes) produces satisfactory results. Even if the light is insufficient to produce an acceptable picture, the sound recording will be extremely helpful. It goes without saying that the more sophisticated video equipment is expensive, but this may not be a consideration for a dedicated spy.

It is now possible to use fiber optics with the lens of a video camera. These fiber optic units enable a television camera to be mounted back some distance, and the image can even be transmitted around corners. Depending upon the conditions, however, the results may not be wholly acceptable. This is due to the less than ideal light transmission characteristics of the fiber optics as well as a very pronounced loss of resolution.

Information recorded by a video camera can be retrieved in three ways: video tape, which can be retrieved depending upon access to the camera; hard wire, whereby it is routed from the camera to the monitor via cable; and video transmitter, where the signal is transmitted to a distant location like a miniature television station.

Light Attacks

Light devices are somewhat exotic and represent the wonderful stuff seen in spy movies. In the real world, it is unlikely that the agent would encounter these devices. However, they are a real threat and some understanding of them is needed.

For our purposes there are three types of light sources used for surveillance attacks: infrared (IR), light-emitting diodes (LED), and the laser.

Infrared light is that light which is found just below visible light in the electromagnetic spectrum. It has been used for some time for night vision devices as it normally is invisible to the human eye. Light-emitting diodes are solid state devices which have come about by way of the transistor. When an external electrical power is applied to a light-emitting diode, it produces a narrow beam of light.

Both the light-emitting diode and the infrared source are used in a similar manner. A microphone is attached to electrical components which convert the room audio picked up by the microphone to the electrical energy needed to modulate the light beam.

It is necessary for the light transmitter to be placed in a position so that it can transmit an uninterrupted beam of light to the listening post where a receiver reverses the procedure. A disadvantage is the need for an optical path to the listening post, which makes it a bit complicated. There are advantages, one being that, although the light from a light-emitting diode is usually somewhat visible, it has a much narrower beam than does the infrared transmitter, and can be noted only if one is on axis with the light beam. Another real plus is that the device is very hard to detect as its transmission cannot be monitored by audio countermeasures search receivers.

In some ways, the laser resembles the light-emitting diode in that it produces a very narrow beam of light when stimulated by large voltages. Unlike the light-emitting diode, however, light emitted by a laser is coherent; i.e., it is at a specific wave length and is in phase. Because of this, the beam remains very narrow for extreme distances. This, combined with the high voltage applied to it, allows the beam to transmit considerable power. Larger lasers can drill through steel or glass, and the laser has been applied in certain types of eye surgery.

When a conversation takes place in a room, all objects in the room vibrate or resonate due to the acoustic energy produced by the room audio. Rigid objects vibrate more so than soft ones. This, of course, is how a microphone works; the diaphragm moves back and forth as it is vibrated by room audio, and this mechanical energy is changed to electrical energy.

If we train a laser beam on one of these objects, the vibration of this object will modulate the reflected return beam. Room audio can be recovered from this beam, and there is no need to plant a microphone in the target space. Any flat, reflective surface will do--a mirror on the wall, a picture, a polished ashtray, etc. The beam can be used on the window panes or even on one of the venetian blind slats if they are drawn, as these objects, too, are resonated by room audio.

Under ideal circumstances, the laser can be highly effective and very difficult to detect and is one of the few ways to "bug" a room without the need of physical access.

There are, however, certain disadvantages to the laser beam audio interception. There are the size and power limitations of the laser itself, which are closely related to its great expense. It is also necessary to have an optical path from the target to the listening post, although it does not have to be in the line of sight. A judicious placement of mirrors or similar reflective surfaces would allow the beam to be bounced from point to point on its way to the target.

A major problem is noise. For example, if a window pane is used as a target, it is being modulated by room audio. Outside street noises, wind, and even passing airplanes will affect it even more and, in many cases, entirely mask the room audio. Fixed objects in the target area will also resonate to other ambient sounds--people working, plumbing noises, and so forth, further decreasing the clarity of the received signal. In summation, the laser is exotic but not cost-effective. It is fairly easy to defeat.

Microphone and Wire

This is probably the oldest of the technical attacks dating back to the days of carbon microphones and huge, tube-type amplifiers. Today, the technology has advanced to the point where there are highly sensitive microphones one-quarter inch in length which can transmit information over super-thin copper wire or even, in some cases, electrically conductive paint. There are a multitude of small, inexpensive microphones openly available to the general public which are suitable for audio surveillance.

While microphones differ in design or specific operating principle, they all do the same thing; they convert acoustic (mechanical) energy to electrical energy. As a group, microphones fit into that general class of electrical components known as transducers. A transducer is simply a device which changes mechanical energy to electrical energy or vice versa. Thus, a radio loudspeaker is a transducer as is the window pane which modulates a laser beam. This interrelationship is of interest because of the fact that a loudspeaker, especially an efficient one with a stiff speaker cone, can be used as a highly effective microphone.

It is perhaps a sign of the times that so many of the areas which must be protected have speakers mounted in the walls or ceilings to accommodate a piped-in music system or the public address system. Any time one of these speakers is not actually being used for its designed purpose, it can be used as a microphone by an adversary. All that is necessary is to intercept the pair of speaker wires at any point and attach an amplifier. It is not even necessary to enter the target room as the audio in the room will cause the speaker cone to resonate in exactly the same manner as would the diaphragm of a microphone.

Perhaps the most familiar example of a transducer functioning both as a microphone and a speaker is the hand-held transceiver such as those used by various police agencies, or many of the Citizens-Band walkie-talkies. Most of these use the loudspeaker as the microphone and as a speaker.

There are a variety of types of microphones

on the market such as the moving coil, carbon, crystal, ribbon, condenser, etc. Each has its particular advantages and disadvantages. The potential attacker would carefully consider which one to use in view of his needs for certain characteristics such as sensitivity, current drain, frequency response, impedance, and signal output. It is not necessary to go into the differences between the varieties of microphones. Suffice it to say that the technical spy would choose the proper microphone with the same care as would an assassin in choosing his weapon. Microphones may be placed into three groups; the carbon microphone, other microphones, and contact microphones.

Carbon Microphones. The carbon microphone is characterized by its very high output compared to most other types. The mouthpiece of a telephone handset is a carbon microphone. Carbon microphones require that voltage be applied to the microphone to make it work. This requirement, plus a progressive loss of sensitivity over a period of time, has caused the carbon microphone to become unpopular for clandestine uses.

Other Microphones. The other microphones generally do not need an external power applied to make them work. It is sufficient simply to attach two wires from the amplifier to the microphone, similar to the technique used with the loudspeaker. Not only are these microphones very small, but they contain such refinements as preamplifiers (to boost the output signal) and automatic gain control (AGC), circuitry which increases the sensitivity when there is little ambient noise, and decreases it to prevent overloading when there is quite a bit of noise. (Automatic gain control is the feature that keeps a car radio at a constant volume even though the signal varies due to buildings, bridges, or similar obstacles).

A modern microphone equipped with automatic gain control can pick up conversations in an average room regardless of where it is placed, especially if the room is acoustically dead. These microphones are very difficult to detect due to their small size. Additionally, they are commonly "fed" via acoustic tubing, a narrow plastic tube from 12 to 16 inches long. Thus, the microphone itself does not have to be in the target area as the tubing provides an excellent acoustic channel while, at the same time, protecting the microphone from magnetic microphone detectors.

Although very thin electrical wire or electrically conductive paint is quite satisfactory, it is easier for an attacker to use existing electrical conductors such as power lines, phone lines, or wires which have been abandoned but remain in place inside the walls. A "wire run" of this nature is very difficult to detect and is one of the most commonly employed methods of microphone use.

Contact Microphones. The contact microphone is usually a form of crystal microphone. It is employed by placing it against a common wall or by inserting it into the wall (spike mike). The crystal element of the microphone, when placed against the wall, uses the entire wall as a diaphragm. Audio from the target area causes the wall to resonate and these vibrations are converted directly into electrical energy by the crystal.

Under ideal circumstances, a contact microphone is very effective when coupled to a high gain amplifier. There are, however, definite disadvantages. The wall does not transmit frequencies equally; thus, there often is a significant loss of intelligibility. Most important, however, is the fact that all other sounds in the building are also transmitted through the wall to the extent that they often mask the audio from the target area. Many a technical man can recount stories of attempting to listen to a conversation which was all but obliterated by toilets flushing and doors slamming throughout the building. For practical intents and purposes, the contact microphone is the ear and water glass technique supplemented by electronics, and limited to a great extent by the same inherent drawbacks.

"Shotgun" Or Parabolic Microphones. Although the shotgun or parabolic microphones differ in design from one another, they both have the same purpose, the detection of audio at relatively great distances. Both are highly directional in that they focus sound waves upon the diaphragm of the microphone somewhat like a telephoto lens focuses light. The most common example of the use of the parabolic microphone is found in televised broadcasts of professional football, where sound technicians along the sidelines train them on the quarterback in order to pick up signal calling. They are also used in wildlife photography to record bird calls and similar sounds.

Both the shotgun and the parabolic microphone have another characteristic in common; their effectiveness has been grossly exaggerated. They work well at distances of less than 100 feet, provided that the ambient noise level does not block out the targeted conversation. As the distance increases, so does the problem of what engineers call signal-to-noise level. In other words, it is harder to distinguish target audio from background or unwanted audio. Under ideal circumstances, the best directional microphones might have a range of three hundred feet, but 100 feet or less is much more realistic for voice reception.

These devices actually work quite well for bird calls, for two reasons. The sounds are quite loud, certainly much louder than a normal conversation. The sounds are higher in frequency. High frequency sound is generally more directional. Additionally, the human ear tends to perceive these higher than normal voice frequencies much more easily under marginal conditions.

In short, unless the attacker has an unusual interest in wildlife, it is unlikely that he would select one of these directional microphones to further his technical efforts.

In summary, the microphone and wire attack is still very much with us and quite a few of the devices found by technical surveillance countermeasures agents in overseas areas have been microphone and wire attacks. Indeed, Department of State technical surveillance countermeasures personnel found and removed 52 microphones from the U.S. Embassy in Moscow in 1964, the same year in which 55 microphones were removed from the U.S. Embassy in Warsaw, Poland. The availability of the devices, their low cost, and the relative lack of technical expertise required by the user makes it highly likely that audio countermeasures efforts will continue to reveal such devices.

Free Space Transmitters.

For purposes of clarity and convenience, radio frequency transmitters can be broken into two broad categories; the free space transmitter, and the carrier current transmitter. This distinction is necessary, as they differ markedly in the way that information is transmitted from the target area to the listening post. The countermeasures employed against each category must also differ.

Earlier, it was pointed out that a transducer is a device which changes mechanical energy such as human speech to electrical energy. The proper term for this electrical energy is electro-magnetic energy (EM energy). Electro-magnetic energy travels in waves which vibrate a given number of times per second. Various forms of electro-magnetic energy vibrate at different rates; this rate of vibration is called the frequency of an electro-magnetic wave and is measured in cycles per second. Relatively recently, the scientific community decided to honor one of its own, a certain Dr. Hertz, by using his last name as a unit of measurement. Thus the term, cycles per second, abbreviated cps, became simply, hertz (Hz). One hertz equals one cycle per second. Old ways die hard, and many people still use cycles per second instead of hertz, but hertz is the preferred term.

Scientists often refer to the electro-magnetic spectrum, which is a group of electro-magnetic energy in order of frequency. At one end of the spectrum is energy that does not vibrate at all. This is direct current (DC) such as that produced by a battery. At the upper end we have visible light, x-rays, and cosmic rays. The energy of concern at the moment is radio frequency (RF) energy, and is generally considered to be the electro-magnetic energy in the spectrum band from 10,000 Hz to infrared light. As these are very large numbers, it is a good time to look at some abbreviations. Another way to say 10,000 Hz is 10 kilohertz, which is abbreviated 10 Khz. The letter "K" (for kilo), is the common abbreviation for "thousand" in the scientific community. One million Hz is one megahertz, abbreviated 1 Mhz. The last term is one which is used for 1,000 Mhz, one gigahertz, which is expressed as 1 Ghz. The abbreviations "M" and "G" are frequently used in science as abbreviations for "million" and "billion" respectively.

Back then to the transducer. The electro-magnetic energy that it produces is in what is referred to as the audio range; i.e., from 20 Hz to 20 Khz, the same range as the sounds in the room. All the transducer has done is to convert the mechanical energy (sound) to this low frequency electro-magnetic energy. Because it is low frequency, the energy will flow along the wires attached to it and into an amplifier. Consequently, the only way that the low frequency information can be retrieved from the target area is along this hard wire path.

If, however, the intercepted information could be shifted to a much higher frequency, a whole new picture would develop. A certain amount of energy would still flow down the wire, but some of it would radiate outward from the wire along its entire length. If the frequency were to be increased further, greater amounts would be radiated into free space and could be intercepted by a radio receiver tuned to the same frequency.

Of course, there is a device which can convert audio range electro-magnetic energy to radio frequency energy; it is called a transmitter. The transmitter takes the audio range information fed to it and converts it to a specific frequency in the radio frequency range. The transmitter includes an amplifier used to magnify the converted signal. The amount of electric power used in amplifying the radio frequency signal is expressed in watts. As was noted, the radio frequency energy will radiate from the wire

leading to the listening post. If the wire is cut, the radio frequency energy will continue to radiate from the section still attached to the transmitter, especially if it is of a certain length in relation to the transmitter frequency. This piece of wire is called an antenna, and the ideal size is referred to as its resonant length.

Add to the above a power supply, and you have a simple broadcast station. However, similar though the operating principles may be, there is a great deal of difference between a full-fledged commercial broadcast transmitter and a clandestine or "bug" transmitter.

The first difference is gross physical size, as the bug must be very small for ease of concealment. The famous "martini olive" transmitter is a good illustration of this.

The requirement for electrical power needed to operate the transmitter and broadcast the signal varies widely. The need to use either small batteries or to "parasite" electrical power from the target area's telephone or power lines sharply limits the output power of the clandestine transmitter. Another limiting factor of output power is fear of detection. Normally, there is no need to broadcast great distances as most listening posts are located within a few hundred yards or less of their target. While commercial broadcast stations use thousands of watts of radiated power during transmission, and hand-held walkie-talkies use two to four watts of power, the modern clandestine bug transmitter can effectively employ as little as 20 milliwatts (a milliwatt is 1/1,000 of a watt), making their detection exceedingly difficult.

Another factor affecting detection of bug transmitters is the type of modulation used. A look back at the simple transmitter may be in order at this point. If the transmitter operates at a frequency of 100 Mhz (as an arbitrary example), it emits a radio signal at that frequency. Somehow the electrical information from the transducer must be impressed onto this signal so that the information can be transmitted. The way in which this intelligence is superimposed upon the 100 Mhz signal (which is referred to as the carrier wave or signal, or quite often, just "carrier") is referred to as modulation. The carrier wave is changed or modulated by the audio intelligence which is impressed upon it during transmission.

There are a number of ways in which this carrier wave can be modulated. The most common are amplitude modulation (AM) and frequency modulation (FM). These, of course, are the two types used in commercial broadcasting. It is not necessary to understand the technical differences between them. What is important is that the search devices detect as many types of modulation as possible. If a choice must be made, an AM detector should be used. This type of detector can readily slope detect FM and other special modulations.

Clandestine transmitters come in a variety of configurations and degrees of sophistication. The martini olive transmitter exists but in reality is not overly practical. There is seldom a need to build a transmitter as small as a martini olive. One of the basic considerations in transmitter construction is operating time which is determined by battery life. Generally, the larger the battery, the longer the transmitter will last. Size is not normally critical if the transmitter is to be secreted in a wall or in a location adjacent to the target area, or if a microphone and wire run are to be employed.

There have been transmitters found in recent times which have been remotely switchable; i.e., the transmitter could be turned on and off by a broadcast tone or other signal. The advantages of this are obvious. Not only does it greatly conserve battery life by allowing the device to be turned off when nothing interesting is being said or when the building is empty, but it can be switched off at the first sign of an audio countermeasures survey, which would eliminate any chance of its detection by means of a search receiver.

There has been an increasing use of these so-called "drop" transmitters, in part due to the increased physical security of target installations. The drop

transmitter is a relatively small, disguised device which can be quickly slapped into place during a pretext visit.

One of the more bizarre types of free-space transmitters, a type which has no batteries and no electronic components, but in spite of this lack was used successfully against the United States for a number of years, is the so-called resonant cavity transmitter.

This device was concealed in the Great Seal of the United States in the U.S. embassy in Moscow. As has been reported extensively in the media, a wooden wall plaque was presented as a gift with the suggestion that it be mounted on the wall behind the ambassador's desk which, in turn, conveniently faced a window. Many may recall the photograph of Ambassador Lodge pointing to a bug concealed in the back of the plaque. The bug was a resonant cavity transmitter and, although the principle of operation was well known, this incident marked the first time that technical surveillance countermeasures experts had detected such a device in use.

The resonant cavity transmitter is a disarmingly simple device technically known as a passive radiator; i.e., one which lacks an internal source of energy. In constructing the device, a diaphragm is stretched across a closed tube, which is of a specific size, and a wire "tail" which functions as an antenna is attached to the base of the cavity. The cavity is then flooded with a beam of radio frequency energy from an external source (usually in the microwave region, 1 Ghz and up). The size of the cavity and the length of its antenna are carefully calculated so that the radio frequency energy which bathes the cavity is re-broadcast back via the antenna. The diaphragm acts as a transducer, and the audio range electro-magnetic energy modulates the returned radio frequency signal which, in turn, is picked up by a receiver in the nearby listening post.

The free-space transmitter remains one of the most prevalent forms of technical attack. As with the other forms of electronic eavesdropping, the most sophisticated of these are used only by government agencies. It is unlikely that resonant cavities or transmitters with very tricky modulation will be encountered on the non-government level. The most likely threat comes from one of the plentiful miniature transmitters, many of Japanese origin, which use FM broadcast band or are returned to operate just above or below it. In some instances, standard size Citizens Band walkie-talkies have been used as listening devices. Nonetheless, regardless of sophistication, all free-space transmitters pose a threat which must be given serious consideration during the course of an audio countermeasures survey.

Carrier Current Transmitters

Technically, carrier current transmitters are the same as the free-space transmitters. They differ, however, in how the intercepted room audio is transmitted from the target area to the listening post.

In the case of the carrier current device, the radio frequency energy is impressed upon either a power line or other conductor, and is retrieved by a receiver located outside the area. A common example of this is the so-called wireless intercom.

The basic concept is that radio frequency energy at lower frequencies and power levels, when placed on a conductor such as a power line, will flow along the line as if the conductor were a pipe. The conductor does not act as a radiating antenna as it would if the radio frequency energy were at a higher frequency. There are some obvious advantages to such a system. One is that the electrical energy needed for the transmitter can be taken from the power line, thus eliminating the need for a battery in the transmitter. Consequently, a carrier current device can be left in place for years without the need for replacement of exhausted batteries.

Such carrier current devices are easily concealed and cannot be found by a "sweep" of the radio frequency spectrum with a search receiver because the radio frequency signal leaves the target area via hard wire. Some carrier current transmitters

are remotely switchable and can be turned on by a broadcast radio frequency signal. Their presence on an electrical line also enables them to be switched on or off easily by either pulses of high voltage or a tone signal, both of which may be impressed on the electrical line to which they are attached.

Carrier current devices are commonly built into such innocuous looking objects as wall plugs, light switches, lamp sockets, and even telephone instruments. Sophisticated types are exceedingly difficult to detect.

There are also disadvantages to carrier current devices. The major disadvantage is that it is necessary to gain physical access to the target area in order to plant the bug.

Another drawback is distance. The attacker's listening post, if the device is placed on a power line, must be on the same side of the utility company power transformer as is the device because the radio frequency signal cannot pass through the transformer.

There is some problem also with noise. The normal electrical power 60 cycle AC hum must be filtered out and the lower frequencies tend to be inherently noisy due to both natural and electrical machine interference.

In summation, the carrier current transmitter is a serious threat confronting the audio counter-measures expert, particularly if it has been installed by an adversary skilled in the concealment and effective use of one of these devices.

Telephones

The Watergate affair served to focus public attention once again upon the vulnerability of a telephone system to technical attack. Such concern is warranted because any telephone located in a sensitive discussion area presents a serious hazard to the audio security of the entire room, regardless of whether or not the telephone is on or off the hook.

There are two different types of technical attacks which may be made upon the telephone; the "tap," and the "compromise."

The telephone tap is an interception of telephone communications. The interception may be of conversation or of non-oral telephone communication such as teletype, facsimile, or computer data. The tap is characterized by the fact that it entails the interception of intelligence information only when the phone is in use. A tap does not require physical access to the target space because the telephone lines may be attacked anywhere between the target phone and central telephone office.

There are a multitude of ways to tap a telephone, ranging from direct connection with the line to what is called inductive coupling which does not require a physical connection to the line. The latter uses a so-called induction microphone which is not truly a microphone as it does not convert acoustic energy to electro-magnetic energy as do all transducers. The inductive microphone or coil works on the following principle; electro-magnetic energy flowing down a telephone conductor wire creates an electro-magnetic field around the conductor. The information flowing down the telephone wire is, of course, electro-magnetic energy which has been modulated by the information impressed upon it. This modulation causes the electro-magnetic field to vary at the same rate as does the energy on the line. If an induction coil is placed on or near the line so that it is within this electro-magnetic field, it causes a similar electro-magnetic energy flow to be induced into the coil. This induced signal is then fed into an amplifier and the information is recovered. The inductive tap is then fed into an amplifier and the information is recovered. The inductive tap is effective but lacks the fidelity of a direct tap, and suffers from noises created by other nearby sources of electro-magnetic fields such as power lines or electric motors.

A "compromise" is an attack upon a telephone which transforms it into a listening device capable of intercepting audio in the targeted area at all times, regardless of whether or not the telephone is on the hook. A telephone can be compromised in a number of different ways, all of which require physical access to the telephone.

A transmitter, either carrier current or free space, can be easily concealed inside a telephone and can be very difficult to find even when the phone is opened up for inspection, especially if it resembles a legitimate telephone part. One of the most common of these transmitters is made to resemble and replace either the telephone earpiece or mouthpiece transducer. (Technically, the mouthpiece transducer is called the transmitter and the earpiece is called the receiver). This drop-in transmitter device draws power from the telephone. Transmitters can also be hidden within internal parts of the phone such as the network or ringer coil, thus masking them from visual inspection.

Every telephone contains at least three transducers. One of these is the telephone mouthpiece transmitter, a carbon microphone. The telephone mouthpiece is not the ideal transducer to attack because, like all other carbon microphones, it requires that voltage be applied to it to make it work, thus limiting its use to that time when the telephone is off the hook.

The second transducer is the earpiece receiver which is a highly sensitive dynamic microphone. This is the natural point of attack because it works very effectively as a transducer for either radio frequency transmitter or a wiring modification.

The third and usually the most unreliable transducer is the telephone ringer unit. The ringer units of most telephones are resonant and a large number of them are modulated by room audio in their vicinity. If a telephone ringer is sufficiently resonant, a high-gain amplifier can retrieve conversations emanating nearby it. The range of its sensitivity is quite limited; generally some three to five feet from the instrument is the maximum range that it can pick up conversations. The conversations can, however, be picked up regardless of whether the phone is on the hook or not. Incidentally, it is not the bell portion of the ringer which resonates. Rather it is the "clapper" whose oscillations produce the audio intelligence.

An explanation of what a telephone hookswitch does will help to understand how easily phones can be compromised. The hookswitch is the device which ostensibly disconnects the telephone from central office (the telephone exchange) when the handset is placed on the cradle. A telephone in this position usually has about 48 to 50 volts of DC line voltage. When the handset is lifted off the cradle (off-hook position), the telephone handset receiver and transmitter are connected to central office and the on-line telephone voltage drops to 7 to 9 volts DC.

In the standard, single line instrument, all that separates the telephone handset transducer from the outside world is the hookswitch. From time to time, one of these hookswitches will become accidentally bent, or some conductive deposit will build up on one of the electrical contact points. Under these circumstances the handset is "hot" all the time. A high-gain amplifier placed across the pair of telephone wires under such circumstances will retrieve room audio with astonishing fidelity.

By the same token, there are numerous ways that a hookswitch can be bypassed to allow room information to be retrieved in the listening post. A simple rearrangement of wires takes only minutes and is very effective. It has the added advantage of being a deniable compromise; i.e., it may never be possible for the audio countermeasures expert to determine whether or not the rewiring was an attack or merely human error. Additionally, it is possible to insert into a telephone any number of devices such as four-layer diodes or neon bulbs which can be turned on remotely by sending a pulse of high voltage towards the phone. These devices have the added advantage of automatically shutting off when the handset is picked up due to the resultant voltage drop (from 48 volts DC to 7 to 9 volts DC).

Probably the most famous telephone attack is the so-called "infinity transmitter" or "harmonica bug." This is just a variation of the remotely switched radio frequency transmitter described earlier, and, as with those devices, the attacker must gain access to the target area or at least arrange for a gimmicked phone to be placed in the area. (The device can also be placed elsewhere along the telephone line). The transmitter is turned on by dialing the number of the targeted phone and blowing a whistle or harmonica. The device is tone activated and the whistle or harmonica acts as the tone source turning on the device. Once on, the infinity transmitter usually stays on until the handset of the target telephone is lifted from the cradle. The resultant voltage drop from 48 volts DC to 7 to 9 volts DC switches it off, thus preventing its detection by the user of the telephone.

In summation, the telephone is extremely susceptible to a variety of technical attacks which vary in sophistication and are very effective and quite difficult to detect. The telephone is particularly appealing to anyone planning a technical attack as it provides its own source of power which can be "parasited." The telephone is large enough to facilitate concealment of a variety of bugging devices. The telephone provides a hard wire path out of the target area. The telephone does not require any additional microphones because the normal transducers in the telephone instrument may be employed if desired.

Because of its attractiveness for and susceptibility to technical attack, the telephone remains as one of the most dangerous and commonly employed electronic surveillance devices in the world.

Audio Countermeasures

An effective audio security program should encompass two basic considerations:

.   Isolation and nullification--the measures to be taken which will complicate or prevent a technical attack.

.   Audio countermeasures survey--the measures to be taken which will detect the presence of a technical attack.

However, prior to undertaking either plan, an initial step is the assessment of the threat. First it must be determined:

.   Who is the target?

.   What is the potential value of the information?

.   Who would be the most likely person (or persons) to mount a technical attack?

.   What are the potential attackers' resources?

Intelligence sources should be used to the maximum extent so that the agent can gain a reasonable feeling as to what to expect in order to allow him to establish his defensive priorities. Obviously the nature of the threat will be affected by the type of facility which is involved.

Isolation and Nullification

Generally the areas to be protected will fall into one of the three basic categories:

.   Permanent facilities such as offices used on a daily basis, residences, conference and meeting rooms, etc.

.   Facilities used temporarily or infrequently such as hotel rooms, conferences in hotels and meeting halls, or public buildings.

.   Automobiles.

Each category of facility presents a different challenge, primarily as the result of variations in the amount of control the agent has over the audio environment of the facility.

As was previously noted, isolation and

nullification relate to actions to be taken before the fact which will sharply limit the opportunity for a successful audio surveillance attack. The actions which can be taken along this line become more apparent if we consider the possible techniques which can be used against the area to be protected. Notwithstanding the variety of techniques which were previously described for technical attacks, there are only four ways that audio can be taken from a target area:

.   It can be carried out. All of the techniques discussed under the heading of mechanical attacks apply.

.   It can be transmitted out--the free space technique applies.

.   It can be retrieved optically--the visual/optical techniques apply.

.   It can be retrieved via hard wire--the carrier current, microphone and wire, and telephone techniques apply.

There is no technique which does not utilize one of the above methods. Therefore, these four methods must always be considered during the development of an effective isolation and nullification program. For purposes of this material, isolation pertains to those actions which tend to prevent the mounting of a technical attack, whereas nullification relates to those techniques which would tend to hinder or even prevent the attack from producing useful intelligence.

The basic component of isolation is physical security. A highly effective physical security system would deny an attacker access to the target space, which would in turn sharply limit his selection of techniques. However, the security must be round-the-clock and cannot consist solely of physical protective devices such as locks or vaults. All such physical security systems must be buttressed with either an effective alarm system or a twenty-four hour per day guard. There is no lock available today which can withstand the determined attack of an expert adversary. Obviously, the amount of protection that can be given a facility will depend upon which of the three categories into which it falls as well as limitations on time and resources available to the security officer or agent.

The easiest facility to protect is, of course, the permanent facility. An agent attempting to create an ideal audio security environment in this instance should first identify those areas wherein sensitive discussions may take place. These areas normally are private offices and/or conference rooms and an attempt should be made to confine sensitive discussions to these specific areas, which then permits concentration of security resources on just one or two rooms rather than an entire building.

Acoustic Barriers. Consideration should be given to the type of construction of the room with a view towards the acoustic attenuation characteristics of its perimeter; that is, the ability of the walls, ceiling, and floor to act as a barrier to sound. Acoustic attenuation is greatest when there is a barrier consisting of two different types of insulating materials. This creates what engineers call an acoustic impedance mismatch. This use of dissimilar materials, particularly when there is air space between them, is much more effective than mere thickness. For instance, a double wall consisting of 1/4-inch plywood nailed to 2 x 4-inch studs will attenuate more sound than four inches of cinder block. Double pane, 1/4-inch glass with a 1/4-inch airspace is even more of a barrier.

One common insulating material which should not be used is acoustical tile. This tile was not developed to function as an insulator. Rather, it was designed to minimize reverberation or reflexed sounds with radio broadcast studios. Its use in a room will facilitate a technical attack by making the target area as acoustically "dead" as a recording studio, an ideal situation for a clandestine microphone. Additionally, the presence of thousands of dampening holes in the tile gives an opponent just that many more places to conceal a microphone, as

the diameter of any of these holes is ample for such a purpose.

The sound-absorbent nature of acoustical tile actually facilitates the passage of sound through the wall. It is far better to use a dense sound-reflective material such as plywood, plaster, or masonite. If the reverberations in the room become annoying to its occupants, heavy draperies will soften the sounds considerably without an adverse effect upon audio security.

Room Doors. One security aspect often overlooked is the door. Although a heavy, solid core door is often quite adequate, there is considerable sound transmission around the edges and underneath the door. This can be eliminated or reduced by the installation of an inexpensive rubber gasket around the edges of the door.

Room Duct Work. Air conditioning or heating vents provide audio paths which can be exploited. There are various acoustic baffles which can be installed, but the most inexpensive approach is usually the application of nullification techniques. One example of nullification which is applicable in this situation is masking.

Audio Masking. Masking is the generation of sufficient noise at the perimeter of the secure area to cover or mask any conversations within the room.

There are a number of commercially available tape systems designed for this purpose. A tape deck capable of playing as long as 24 hours at a time is connected to a series of speakers. These speakers are mounted facing towards the exterior of the room, so they may be played at a loud volume without disturbing the occupants. The transducers are mounted in the air vents and in any other possible avenue of technical attack. As long as there is music playing through them, the speakers virtually eliminate the chances of a successful attack using a contact microphone or any other transducer mounted on the perimeter. The wiring of the music system should be installed so that it cannot be tampered with (ideally, it should not leave the secure area), and so that it can be easily inspected.

Although the tape system is best, an FM radio is also generally adequate. However, the radio should be kept as far from the vicinity of any sensitive conversations as possible, as some FM radios can act as transmitters under certain conditions. This is an inherent trait of FM radios due to the radiation of what is called the "local oscillator," which can be modulated by room audio. For practical purposes, the hazard presented by an FM radio is far outweighed by its ability to provide audio masking under circumstances where an AM radio may not even play due to the shielding effects of various buildings.

Room Windows. Ideally, there should be no windows in the secure room. If there are windows, they should be equipped with venetian blinds and heavy draperies. If both the drapes and blinds are drawn during any discussions, it virtually precludes the possibility of any visual or optical attack. If there are no windows, the visual/optical attack possibility is reduced to almost zero.

Room Wiring. All wiring leaving the secure area should be accounted for, and any that is not being used should either be removed or have the ends tied together to prevent its technical exploitation.

Room Telephones. Telephones should not be allowed in discussion areas--they are that much of a hazard. A persuasive agent can present a good argument for their removal from conference rooms, but there is no way a public figure can be talked out of having a telephone in his office. Thus, although the ideal situation is to have no phone, it will be necessary to take steps to minimize the hazard it presents.

The telephone instrument should be equipped with a positive means of secondary disconnect; i.e., it should be disconnected from central office by devices other than the standard hookswitch. The cheapest and simplest means is the plug and jack arrangement

similar to that used in home extension telephones. The phone is then left unplugged at all times that it is not in use. With this arrangement, it is necessary to install a separate ringer to annunciate incoming calls, as the ringer in the telephone is, of course, also disconnected when the phone is not plugged in. Ideally, the ringer should be a special, non-resonant ringer. This would preclude an attacker using the ringer as a transducer.

Realistically, an acceptable degree of security could be gained by the use of a standard Western Electric Ringer, particularly if it were mounted as far from the immediate discussion area as possible (a distance of ten feet would probably suffice). Notwithstanding apocryphal stories to the contrary, there is no way that an unplugged telephone can be technically attached. At best, it could be used to conceal a transmitter needing its own power supply. Thus, a relatively inexpensive modification as described above nets a tremendous increase in audio security.

However, practical experience has shown that the inherent weakness in this system is human nature. It is extremely difficult to motivate the executive to plug and unplug the telephone, especially if he uses the phone heavily.

Telephone Disconnects--Switches. There are disconnects available, including plug and jack arrangements, which sound an audible alarm if the handset is placed on-hook with the telephone still plugged in. It is suggested that contact be made with the local telephone company security office to ascertain what similar varieties of disconnects are available locally. It should be noted, however, that standard "push to talk" buttons do not provide any particular increase in security as they only disconnect the carbon microphone in the mouthpiece. As was pointed out earlier, it is the dynamic microphone in the earpiece which presents the greatest threat.

If there are no funds available for purchase of the above equipment, the implementation of some of the following procedures will still provide a significant increase in security.

Telephone Disconnects--Key Telephones. Most large offices use key telephones; i.e., those telephones equipped with several buttons for selection of various lines. Usually these buttons are located on what is called the key strip along the bottom of the telephone instrument. The buttons often control such functions as "hold," choice of outside lines, and intercom. Two inherent characteristics of the key telephone can be used to benefit audio security. The first is the fact that if all of the buttons are in the "up" position, and no line is engaged, the key strip then provides an additional disconnect feature to supplement the hookswitch. The easiest way to get the buttons in this configuration is to hang up the phone at the conclusion of the conversation, and then depress the "hold" button. Although the protection afforded by this countermeasure is not nearly as effective as that provided by a positive means of secondary disconnect, it does complicate any technical attack and increases the amount of access time needed to effect such an attack.

The other characteristic is that key telephones require the support of auxiliary equipment known as key telephone systems which provide for such functions as "hold," "lamp flash," and "intercom." If these units are located within the secure area (in order to prevent interception of the line pairs between the telephone and the auxiliary unit) there is a large increase in security. There are some audio countermeasures experts who argue that the presence of the equipment within the secure area coupled with the use of the "buttons up" countermeasure affords an adequate amount of security against all but the most sophisticated attacks.

Security of Telephone Instrument. Again, physical security is paramount. The simple countermeasures will work only if the potential adversary is denied an opportunity to gain access to the telephone instrument. As one attack technique consists of replacing the entire telephone with one that has been re-wired, it is a good idea to discreetly mark the telephones so they can be quickly, visually inspected. A control number can be engraved on the bottom of the instrument, for instance. Yet a better method is to mark the phone in some manner with a material that fluoresces under ultraviolet light.

Telephone Taps. The adaption of all, or at least a substantial portion of, the above procedures will prevent any but the most highly sophisticated attacks. However, a word of explanation is in order. The attacks prevented are compromises, not taps. Short of the use of encrypted or "scrambler" telephone systems, there is no way to guarantee that a telephone is either not now or soon will be tapped.

There are some private technical security services which claim that their audio countermeasures surveys include an inspection of all telephone lines to ascertain whether or not they are tapped. Realistically, however, all that they can say with any certainty is that there are no obvious or gross technical interceptions.

There has been an investment of considerable time and effort on the part of many investigators to perfect a system that can detect all tapes, but, to date, no system has been developed which can reliably find all possible attacks.

The problem is created by the fact that the line pair can be intercepted at any point between the telephone instrument and central office, which can mean miles of unprotected wiring. A direct tap can be made with careful attention to impedance matching, which would be very difficult to detect. Certainly, the telephone subscriber would be unaware of it, as there would be no telltale clicks or noises on the line. A carefully installed induction tap would also be very difficult to uncover.

On the other hand, chances of a successful tap are complicated by good physical security practices. The simplest tap is made at the nearest terminal or connecting block where the target line pair is tied to either a large "house" cable or to an "outside" cable. The line pair at this point is spread out on the connecting block and is easy to both identify and attack. The terminal board or connecting block is usually found within the same building as the telephone, although it may be on an adjacent telephone pole, especially if the telephone is located in a residence. Consequently, if there is good physical security, it would possibly deny an adversary this easier point of attack. He would then be forced to spend some time and effort to identify the line pair even closer to central office where it would be just one of hundreds or even thousands of line pairs. Although the target lines could be located by means of a telephone company cable chart, it would be necessary to obtain the chart from the telephone company. As its acquisition would have to be via illegal means, such as purchase from a corrupt telephone company employee or outright theft, it probably would eliminate attacks by inexperienced or unorganized eavesdroppers.

Although the isolation and nullification procedures described so far are primarily applicable to permanent facilities, it should be obvious that many of them can be effectively applied to occasional-use facilities and, in some cases, to automobiles. Audio security like any other form of security is a percentage proposition in that every positive preventive action taken will yield a certain percentage increase in security. Therefore, it is incumbent upon the agent to implement as many countermeasures as possible, consistent with resources and common sense.

A careful analysis of the isolation and nullification techniques discussed above will reveal two basic points common to all the recommended countermeasures:

.   threat analysis

.   physical security

The agent must decide the most likely means of attack and plan his defenses accordingly. The material thus far presented should clearly indicate the overwhelming importance of good physical security, security which would have to be present in any event

to safeguard the personal safety of the client.

If all applicable isolation and nullification techniques have been applied, then a potential technical penetrator has been denied several means of attack. His most viable option would be the planting of a remotely-controlled transmitter, either free space or carrier current, and even then it would require him to breach physical security, either before or after the security perimeter was established. In short, if the security perimeter is perfect and all the isolation and nullification recommendations implemented, a successful technical attack would be virtually impossible to carry out. However, security is never perfect or foolproof. Therefore, the agent cannot consider his audio security program complete until he has arranged for and conducted the second major program component, the audio countermeasures survey.

The Audio Countermeasures Survey

The audio countermeasures survey is an essential component of an effective audio security program even when isolation and nullification techniques have been assiduously applied. It becomes necessary for two reasons.

.   A technical attack may have been perpetrated prior to the initiation of the audio countermeasures program.

.   An attack may have been successfully launched as a result of overlooked weaknesses or human error in the maintenance of adequate physical security.

As with the approach used with isolation and nullification, the survey may be conducted on a sliding scale of sophistication ranging from a simple physical examination of the area to the application of the most complex and detailed audio counter-measures equipment. As might be expected, the effectiveness of audio security tends to increase, as does the expense, proportionately. However, the application of audio countermeasures techniques described in this section will certainly add to the overall audio security already present as a result of previously applied isolation and nullification techniques.

Timing of the Audio Countermeasures Survey. Perhaps the first question to be considered is when an audio countermeasures survey should be conducted. This is dependent upon several factors, the first of which is whether the facility is permanent or only used once or occasionally.

With a permanent facility, the most important question is the overall effectiveness of the isolation and nullification program and the degree of physical security. If all isolation and nullification techniques have been implemented, one audio countermeasures survey every one or two years is sufficient. Any time there is extensive modification of the area, new construction, new electrical wiring, or any other activity which gives outsiders relatively unsupervised access to the sensitive area, a survey should be conducted upon the completion of the disrupting activity.

The survey should always be conducted during normal working hours to facilitate the discovery of remotely switchable devices. With occasional-use facilities, the survey may be conducted at any time prior to its scheduled use. Upon completion of the survey, physical security procedures must be implemented. Additionally, if the activity to be protected is a conference or discussion, the agent should arrange for some additional monitoring of the radio frequency spectrum during the initial stages of the conference in order to detect any radio frequency devices missed during the survey, but remotely turned on to intercept the sensitive discussion. A survey will be required for the occasional facility each time there is a break in the physical security provided it. The same applies to automobiles.

The chances of an audio countermeasures survey detecting a clandestine device are greatly enhanced if the survey can be conducted in as non-alerting a manner as possible. If the opponent learns

in advance of an audio countermeasures survey, he may have an opportunity to remove any clandestine equipment before the survey can be conducted. And, if the adversary has advance notice, hears the audio countermeasures specialist in the conduct of the survey, or overhears someone in the target area mention that such a survey is in progress, he may switch off his remotely switchable transmitter, preventing its detection by means of a search receiver. At the very least, he would have an opportunity to abandon his listening post, negating any chances of arresting him. It also precludes any chances of exploiting any devices found by using them to transmit false information.

This concept of strict secrecy in the conduct of audio countermeasures surveys cannot be overemphasized. Technical surveillance counter-measures specialists on the federal level take these restrictions so seriously that a high security classification is attached to all information regarding scheduled technical surveillance countermeasures surveys. This secrecy is, in fact, regarded as one of the technical surveillance countermeasures specialist's most important tools.

Searching for Radio Frequency Transmitters. Generally, the most important and most sensitive part of the audio countermeasures survey is the search for radio frequency transmitters, both free space and carrier current. This is done by the use of electronic devices and through physical search.

The most effective electronic equipment available to assist the agent in the detection of clandestine transmitters is a high quality search receiver or spectrum analyzer, preferably one capable of tuning from at least 100 Khz to 1 Ghz. Such devices are available in a price range of several to many thousands of dollars.

This cost factor may be prohibitive and is budget-dependent. However, there are some relatively inexpensive feedback detectors which can also be very effective. Some secrecy is lost, however, by their use.

The first step, then, in the conduct of an audio countermeasures survey is the search of the radio frequency spectrum. Upon the completion of the "sweep" of the spectrum, the power lines should be checked for the presence of a carrier current device. A similar check is made of the telephone lines at the same time that the telephone system is checked for any compromises.

Inspection of Telephone System. The next step in the audio countermeasures survey is an inspection of the telephone system. The easiest and most efficient way to accomplish this is to check the outgoing area. Generally, buildings have a telephone locker where the various line pairs are spread out on terminal boards. This is where they are patched into the cable which eventually goes to central office. There are at least two wires on the terminal board for each outside line. The telephone company calls the two lines "tip and ring." Some specialized telephones use a four-wire system. In this case, there will be a tip and ring for the talk pair (the pair connected to the transmitter), and a tip and ring for the pair connected to the receiver.

In telephone systems using key telephones, many of the wires on the board are not tip and ring; rather they are auxiliary conductors for such functions as the "hold" circuit and "lamp flash." Although it is possible to tell which is which by the use of a voltmeter (tip and ring will show 48 volts DC between them if the line is not being used), it is really necessary to know which is which for the purpose of a survey since, under certain circumstances, an adversary may have decided to use one of the auxiliary wires in a technical attack.

One of the audio countermeasures expert's most useful tools is a high gain transistorized amplifier. There are any number commercially available that offer the user a choice of input impedance and which are rather inexpensive. The higher-priced models will include a 60 Hz filter, a tone generator, and a means of producing voltage in order to turn on a carbon microphone. Along with the amplifier there should be a set of earphones (the

stethoscope type which cover both ears are best) and a twin wire lead terminating in alligator clips.

To check a telephone line, one clipped wire is to "tip," the other to "ring." If the amplifier allows a selection to input impedance, 500 K Ohms is a good choice, as it allows for very high gain. All that is necessary is to turn up the volume control and listen. If the telephone is in use, the conversation will be heard as this is essentially a tap. If the telephone is not in use and room audio is heard, the telephone hookswitch has been bypassed in some fashion, either by accident or on purpose. Of course, it is important to have some sort of sound source in the secure area, such as a radio playing or people conducting routine business. Under these circumstances, the sound of room audio will be unmistakable.

The above procedure should be followed with all line pairs leading to the central office. If a technical attack has been initiated on a telephone in the secure area which does not utilize a radio frequency transmitter, this procedure will detect it in almost all instances, provided that the inspection procedure is carried out in a non-alerting manner.

Upon completion of this audio check, the procedure should be repeated using a search receiver. If both the radio frequency check and the audio check are negative, there is reasonable assurance that the telephone system has not been attacked, unless by a particularly sophisticated means, which would be negated if the recommended isolation and nullification techniques are implemented. A disassembly of the individual telephone instruments will be covered later in the survey.

There is a device available for counter-measures use called a telephone analyzer or telephone test set. This equipment, costing in the range of low thousands of dollars, performs certain audio countermeasures functions and has achieved some acceptance by technical surveillance countermeasures experts on the federal level. Although these units are generally effective, there are drawbacks to them. There are devices which they cannot detect for a variety of technical reasons. Also, they require a lot of time to use. Typically, one of the best models takes close to 20 minutes to test a five-line key telephone. If the space to be surveyed includes several telephones the time can be excessive, especially when time spent at the terminal board will detect the majority of the unsophisticated attacks employed on the non-government level.

One of the major determinations which the security must make is the value per audio security dollar. The cost of a telephone analyzer may be better used in the purchase of secondary disconnect equipment to establish an effective isolation and nullification program. In short, the telephone analyzer may not be the most cost-effective equipment for general audio countermeasures use.

Total Area Inspection. Prior to initiating the audio countermeasures survey, a cursory, non-alerting inspection should have been made in order to decide the possible location of listening posts and to decide the best location from which to conduct the radio frequency "sweep." Now that the most critical portions of the survey have been completed (the search for remotely switchable devices), it is not as important to remain completely non-alerting, although it would be best to remain so, consistent with effectively completing the survey. The next step is a more detailed inspection, starting from outside the facility.

Stand back a distance from the building. Are there any strange wires running from it that may be used as a microphone and wire run? Is there any evidence of an attempt to hide a wire run such as freshly turned earth at the base of the outside wall or fresh mortar surrounding the bricks of a brick building? Check the roof. Is there any sign of a penetration or spurious wiring or antennas? Where are the nearest buildings which could serve as a listening post or an observation post? It may be that there is no logical site for an observation post. If so, the chances of an optical or visual attack on the space is remote. If the nearest place for a listening post appears to be too far for a surreptitious wire run, then

either the listening post is within your building or the attack will be other than microphone and wire. Thus, under certain circumstances, it is possible to eliminate two out of four possible attacks on your area merely by a "common sense" threat analysis.

The inspection should continue on the inside of the building. Are there any places in the building that might function as listening posts such as a microphone and wire run terminating in a closet where all interceptions are recorded on tape and the tape retrieved on a daily basis? Are the telephone closets locked to hinder access by unauthorized personnel? Is physical security good? Does it seem adequate to prevent a "carry-out" attack utilizing a tape recorder? Does the perimeter of the secure area provide an adequate acoustic barrier? What conductors leave the secure perimeter? Every wire must be accounted for in the event it is being exploited for clandestine purposes.

Room Searching. Following generalized exterior and interior building examination, the potential target area itself should be considered. By this point in the audio countermeasures survey, the agent will have a good idea of what any possible technical attack must involve. At this juncture, it is obvious that the greatest threat comes from a transmitter or a microphone and wire feeding a nearby transmitter. Consequently, he should have a fairly good idea what to look for as he starts a detailed, physical search of the area.

The procedures used to search the facility are quite similar to those used to search for explosive devices, and the equipment used is the same. Thus, a good tool kit containing a set of screwdrivers, various pliers, wrenches, inspection mirrors, and a flashlight is the basic minimum needed to do the job correctly.

Priority should be given to those areas closest to where discussions normally take place such as desks, chairs, sofas, and telephones. Items such as pictures and wall plaques should be removed from the wall and closely inspected for microphone parts.

Remember that the acoustic passage can be little bigger than a pin hole. There have been instances where transmitters have been secreted in picture frames.

An examination should be made of the underside of all furniture. Wooden furniture should be inspected for the presence of tack holes in such a pattern as to suggest that a drop transmitter such as the Soviet "stick" transmitter may have been recently removed. Furniture should be picked up and moved to ensure that it does not conceal microphone wires.

Any and all grates or grills for air conditioning or heating ducts should be removed and the interiors inspected. Be alert for any signs of recent entry such as tool marks or disturbed dust patterns. Use of an ultraviolet light is helpful in detecting recent alterations.

Examine baseboards carefully for signs of recent modification. These are popular places to hide microphones and/or wire runs. Roll back any carpeting to make sure that it does not hide a device. Again, an ultraviolet light is useful.

If the room has a false ceiling, the space between it and the true ceiling must be inspected. Be particularly alert to the wires which often abound in these spaces. Remember that all conductors must be accounted for.

Pay particular attention to the backs of file cabinets or bookcases as these are good hiding places. It would be worthwhile to examine all hard-bound books as these have been successfully used in the past to hide transmitters.

The walls should be carefully inspected for any signs of microphone holes. Be alert for any portions of the wall where there is a mismatch of paint or where there are signs of recent modifications such as new plaster. The ultraviolet light can be of assistance as it tends to highlight paint or plaster differences better than does standard light.

As light switches and electrical outlets are favorite places to plant carrier current devices, these must be carefully examined. The protective plates must be removed and, especially in the case of light switches, the back of the component inspected to determine whether or not there are any extraneous electrical parts which might be a "bug." There are quite a few "off the shelf" carrier current devices commercially available which are packaged within wall plugs, electrical outlets, and light switches. These must receive careful attention during the audio countermeasures survey. _**A word of caution--it is always best to conduct this kind of inspection with the power turned off, if possible.**_ If this is not possible, then take care to use insulated tools and not to touch two conductors at the same time. Most experienced technical surveillance countermeasures experts can ruefully attest to the shocking power of 117 volts AC (or, in some cases, 220 volts AC), and most technical surveillance countermeasures tool kits contain at least one partially welded and badly scarred screwdriver. Always bear in mind that 117 volts AC is more than sufficient to kill under the right conditions.

Physical Inspection of Telephones. A physical inspection of the telephone system takes some advance preparation. If one is to gain anything useful by disassembling a telephone instrument, he must first know what a normal telephone looks like. For this reason, the agent should examine a representative number of telephones prior to conducting an audio countermeasures survey in order to give him a general understanding of normal telephone circuitry. This will enable him to better recognize a gross attack on the instrument, such as where a device has been dropped into the telephone. More sophisticated attacks will not be detected in this manner as the devices may be hidden in other telephone components such as the network. Alternatively, a careful audio and radio frequency check at the terminal board should detect this type of an attack.

The handset is easily examined in the following manner. Unscrew the earpiece and examine the transducer. It will have only two wires (usually white) attached to it which run into the center of the handset. There is a small device (usually green) called a varister which is attached between the two terminals. There should be nothing else. The presence of any other components such as resistors, capacitors, or excess wiring may represent a device.

When the mouthpiece is unscrewed, the transducer will drop out into your hand as it is not wired in. Examine it carefully for any abnormal signs, as a common attack is the replacement of the standard transducer with a drop-in device which will function as the normal transducer. Hold the transmitter near your ear and shake it. You will hear the carbon granules inside if it is unmodified. (This, of course, is not a positive test as a cleverly modified microphone may still have the number of granules needed to make this noise).

There is a plastic cup with two contacts located under the carbon microphone. This can be lifted out and an inspection will reveal two wires are attached to it (normally red and black). Any additional wiring, or the presence of any other electrical components is indicative of a technical attack.

The wire leading from the telephone should be followed to the junction box. The cover of this box (or wall jack with single line instruments) should be removed and an examination made to ensure that it does not contain a device. Key telephones are usually interconnected by means of a 50 pin plug called an amphenol plug. These should be taken apart to ensure that they do not conceal a small transmitter. Any suspicious bulges in the telephone cabling should also be carefully examined as many devices are designed to fit within an ordinary telephone cable.

Audio Countermeasures--Automobiles

Automobiles present a somewhat different problem. The basic difficulty with automobiles is that they are not afforded sufficient physical security to warrant the investment of concerted audio countermeasures efforts upon them. Consequently, a physical search is probably the most cost-effective countermeasure, and much of it could be done at the same time as any search for explosive devices. There are only two viable surveillance attacks against an automobile; a transmitter, or a tape recorder. A cursory physical search should quickly uncover a tape recorder, especially if the obvious places are covered such as under the dashboard (especially the top of the glove box), under the seats, the trunk, and the underside of the car.

Transmitters can be easily hidden but usually cannot be as small as a device used to attack a building. The main reason for this is the need for greater power to compensate for the variable distances from the listening post as well as shielding effects created by the metal car body and by adjacent buildings and other automobiles. This need for transmitter power is illustrated by the fact that in one technical attack a standard five watt walkie-talkie was concealed in the fender well of the target vehicle.

Remember that an attacker's choice of microphone placement must always be influenced by an inherent characteristic of the automobile noise. For this reason, it follows that the microphones must be placed as close to the potential discussion area as possible. Thus, one would presume that in a chauffeur-driven VIP car, the target area would be the back seat area rather than the front. Consequently, physical search efforts should be concentrated in that area.

In short, experience and common sense will eventually formulate the audio countermeasures search procedures most effective for any given situation.

The importance of the physical search cannot be overemphasized, particularly if the audio countermeasures survey was conducted without the benefit of a radio frequency "sweep." By the same token, its effectiveness should not be underrated. It is a fact that more electronic eavesdropping devices have been found by physical search and examination than by any other means. Even if a good search receiver is utilized during the audio countermeasures survey, at least 60% of the total man-hours expended should be devoted to the physical search.

The audio countermeasures survey is only part of an effective audio security program. True audio security can be gained by the adoption of isolation and nullification techniques as well. Although, ideally, all of the recommendations should

be incorporated into an overall audio security program, implementation of even a few will significantly decrease vulnerability to a technical attack.

In the final analysis, the decision as to what techniques to adopt must be made by the agent or security director in consonance with his conception of the threat and the fiscal and operational constraints with which he is confronted.

Good executive protection driving skills rank at the very top of the skills needed and prized by professional agents. It is, in fact, essential that the agent possess a wide range of information and skills related to vehicle and driving security. There are several reasons for this.

Reason # 1. Automobile accident statistics vary from year to year, but your chances (and your protectee's chances) of being involved in a serious auto accident are very good. During the Viet Nam War years the death toll was heartbreaking, but in the same years we killed many, many more people on the highways--approximately ten times as many. Good, basic, safe driving skills with an emphasis on accident avoidance can significantly decrease the potential for a vehicular accident involving the client.

Reason # 2. An astonishingly high percentage of kidnappings and assassinations and a considerable number of bombings take place in or around the vehicle. You do not read many stories about killing attacks against dignitaries and executives in their offices or their homes, but the files are full of attacks which were launched against the protectee in and around his vehicle.

Reason # 3. At a more mundane level, the protectee wants an efficient, comfortable, reliable ride, with no problems. He does not wish to be involved in a fender-bender. He wants to be able to drink a cup of coffee without a quiver, read a newspaper, or carry on a conversation as easily as if he were in his living room. The client needs to have a feeling of complete trust in his driver's ability to perform safely and smoothly, avoid accidents, react correctly to emergencies, and to get away from danger.

SAFE DRIVING VS. ACCIDENTS

Figures from the National Safety Council on the cold hard facts of dollar loss attributed to auto accidents pegs the cost to the nation at about $43,000,000,000 per year. That figure may be about 75% of the dollar cost of the "War in the Gulf". Yet, much of this cost is avoidable, as motor vehicle "accidents" are seldom truly accidents. These "accidents" are usually driver-induced collisions. Collision avoidance is learned, directly or indirectly, through life experiences, common sense, training, and a desire to survive.

Driving tends to promote a dangerous feeling of power and un-touchability which may lead to a great many problems. High speeds, stress, excitement, danger--all can produce adrenalin rushes that cause the driver to take unwarranted risks, often with disastrous results. The best antidote is skill, knowledge, and confidence in one's ability to perform calmly and precisely in any situation. As a driver, you should always remember that you are in control of a tool with the potential of deadly force. Your actions, if performed in an unprofessional manner, are not only unpleasant to your client but could result in injury to yourself or others.

Concentration is a must--not the rigid concentration seen on the faces of other drivers who stare fixedly straight ahead, white knuckles on the wheel--rather, it is a state of total awareness. Awareness is the driver's ability to notice, forecast, and react to his changing and moving environment. Like a computer being fed new data, his mind must process the changes which it perceives.

How fast am I going? Who or what is behind me and how far away? Is anything close to me on either side? Is there enough space between the car in front and my car to brake or evade if he suddenly jams on his brakes for some reason? Does it appear that something might be getting ready to exit the driveway ahead?

You should be aware of who and what is behind you and how close they are, checking every ten seconds or so. You should know whether someone is approaching too rapidly from the rear and ask yourself if it could be a bad guy threat. Or, could it be a threat just because they are going too fast for the road conditions? (It is more than a little uncomfortable to have the driver of the car passing you suddenly start to hydroplane on wet roads or slide on snowy roads.)

You should be mentally prepared to take evasive action if you notice in your rear view mirrors that the car closing on you from behind:

.   is weaving around on a dry road. Is he drunk or ill? Will he drive right into the back of you? Could he side swipe you in passing?

.   seems to have some object slightly protruding from a window on the right side of the car.

.   has been closing on you at a high rate of speed and suddenly slows down and paces you at a distance of five or six car lengths. There is plenty of room for him to pass, but he doesn't do so.

The good driver allows his vision to fluctuate from near to far, from instruments to close-proximity road, to horizon, to rear view mirrors. You should *not* be staring at the end of your hood. You *should* be looking as far ahead as you can see. Your peripheral and secondary vision will alert you to hazards that are near and you can look at those hazards, if you need to, at that time. When you are going around a curve, do you look at the inside curb line and the inside edge of the roadway? You shouldn't. You should look as far around the outside of the curve as possible. Since you have already seen the point where you are now, you need to be looking far forward around the curve. You need to know what you will be approaching. By looking far forward, your hands and eyes help guide the steering wheel to that point rather than to the road right in front of the car. Of course, you will be glancing at your instruments and mirrors too. You need to know what is behind you, where you are, and what is ahead, as

well as what your car is doing. No one in the protection industry said that driving was as easy as most people seem to think it is. Awareness is one of the things which sets you apart from the common everyday driver.

Physical condition is of great importance. Racing drivers know this very well, and the best of them work hard to keep their bodies in shape. Sports and competitive activities provide good training and keep reflexes finely tuned. There are many sports which, in addition to providing fun and relaxation, help to develop coordination and quick reflexive reaction. Exercise, sleep, a healthy diet, and good physical conditioning are an unbeatable combination for top driving form.

Conversely, fatigue, alcohol, and drugs (including prescription drugs) are driving killers. Top-level racing drivers will not take an alcoholic drink within 24 hours before a race. Alcohol reduces the mind's ability to recognize, diagnose, and react to visual, physical, and audio stimuli. Prescription drugs that have an effect on your driving include tranquilizers, antihistamines, anti-depressants, and analgesics.

Most collisions could be avoided or minimized if the driver would take the correct action, even if the correct action were taken at the last moment. There are things that a good driver can do when faced with a seemingly impossible situation. If action is taken at the last moment, you may no longer be able to totally avoid colliding with something, but most experts will agree that you should make every effort to lessen the severity of a collision. Never give up control of your vehicle--for that matter, never give up, period.

Above all, *make every effort not to hit anything head on.* The impact of two heavy objects hurtling toward each other is devastating, almost always killing or maiming the automobile occupants. If a collision of some sort is unavoidable, try to control the damage by: hitting something soft rather than something hard; hitting something going your way rather than a stationary object; and hitting something stationary rather than something coming toward you. These are tough options, to be taken only when a collision is inevitable.

Race car drivers insist that the best way to avoid a collision is to drive away from it. What they mean is that you should not jam on the brakes and skid into it. Make every effort to steer away from the collision while reducing speed. Improper use of the brakes is the leading cause of drivers losing control of their vehicles. Understand--brakes do not stop the car--they only stop (and can lock) the wheels. Brakes and wheels, when locked, create a skid.

To repeat, automobile collisions are the direct result of driver ignorance, negligence, error, lack of awareness, and slow reflexes. The executive protection driver who can consistently drive efficiently and safely is the one who maintains employment. The driver who is too relaxed, too comfortable, and too unaware of his surroundings is unsafe. He is the driver who usually scrapes the tires against the curb when he parks because he doesn't really know where the car is. The next step is scraping another car.

THE VEHICLE AND ITS PARTS

As with everything, the budget and client preferences will determine the type and number of vehicles included in the protectee's protection plan. It would be ideal to have at least three vehicles: a lead vehicle, the protectee's vehicle, and a follow-up car.

The lead car serves the same purpose as the point man in a diamond formation; the lead car's purpose is *surveillance* and functions as something of a lightning rod, being the first into any potential trap. The protectee's vehicle should be in the center of the circle of protection but able to navigate independently and to evade problems. It sounds heartless but, in the event of an ambush, the protectee must be evacuated, if necessary leaving the lead car to find its own way out of the predicament. The follow-up car in a three-car formation provides the back-up muscle, is the repository of extra equipment, and can be used as a

"hospital unit." The follow-up vehicle is, ideally, a station wagon, one of the old-fashioned cars with BIG back ends, or a van, or one of the big SUV's (sports utility vehicles) such as a Suburban. In an emergency, it can be used to place the protectee for emergency care. There should be ample room to lay the victim down and perform CPR.

When there are only two vehicles, the second vehicle functions as the lead vehicle. Okay, tradition has designated the follow-up vehicle. But, there is little reason for the second vehicle to be in the rear, while it makes more sense for it to be in the forefront, surveilling, looking for possible problems, checking out the situation and, yes, being the first into the danger zone. Remember the iron-clad principle--one *never* allows one's protectee to proceed into an unknown situation.

Having said this, there is one circumstance which might dictate that the second car be placed in the rear. In the past, overseas in other countries, there were a number of killing attacks carried out by terrorists in cars or on motorcycles. The technique was to overtake the target's vehicle from behind, almost always on the left, and, when alongside, to use concentrated gunfire to kill driver and client. This type of terrorist incident has been on the wane in recent years. Still, if it were perceived that the threat would most likely be a killing attack from the rear, it would make sense to position the second vehicle in the rear to keep strict surveillance toward the rear.

The client's car and the back-up car(s) should be of sufficient size, power, and weight to provide maximum safety and to be able to function reliably in escape and evasion maneuvers. Lincoln Town Cars, Ford LTD's, Chrysler New Yorkers, and big Cadillacs are good choices. It is best to choose a four-door car that blends in, rather than standing out, and that has the best chance of withstanding a crash with minimal damage. Reliability is important. Does it start in all weather and have a low repair need record? Vanity plates should be completely avoided, as they are easy to spot.

Many options which can add to the safety

and security of the vehicle are now easily available from the car dealers. In rapid succession, some car manufacturers are adding, or have in the planning stages, high-tech computerized options which are very helpful to the protection agent and his client. As a cautionary note, however, be aware that some of these high-tech (primarily comfort) options take away some of the control which the driver can exercise over the vehicle.

Transmission. An automatic transmission is usually much preferred over a manual shift transmission for executive protection driving. It provides more freedom for the hands and feet as well as providing smoother shift points than most drivers using manual shift can perform. You also appreciate it when stuck in bumper-to-bumper, stop-and-go traffic. Always choose the heaviest duty option available for that car. It should also be minimally a four-speed automatic (four forward gears). Most American manufactures have a built-in automatic override which eliminates the possibility of accidentally changing down to a low gear at speeds which would damage the engine. It is important to determine if this override is included. Ask the dealer and check the owner's manual.

Coming on the market are "intelligent" automatic transmissions. These transmissions use computer logic to better simulate the gear selection a driver would make with a manual transmission. The simplest will put the transmission in a lower gear when you are going downhill, rather than up-shift and make you brake harder. They also downshift earlier at stoplights.

Engine. When cost is not an overriding factor, choose an optional higher powered engine if one is available. You won't be sorry, as you will discover the first time you have to drive a high mountain road or safely pass a slower-moving vehicle on a two-lane road.

Commercially available engines are usually either diesel fueled or gasoline fueled. The advantages of diesel are more miles per gallon and

much cooler engine operating temperatures. Diesels have commonly run several hundred thousand miles. Other parts wear out, but the engine seems to keep going. However, the disadvantages are many. You will spend possibly thousands of dollars more to get the diesel instead of the gas fueled engine. You will get possibly thousands of dollars less at trade-in time. The diesel is noisy, smelly, and needs expensive turbo charger(s) if you intend to operate at altitudes higher than sea level. If you operate the diesel in cold weather country, de-gel additives are a must for each tank of fuel.

Gasoline fueled engines may have a carburetor which mixes fuel and air before putting them into combustion chambers, or they may have fuel injection. Carburetion, spoken of as "normally aspirated," is generally recognized as more horsepower-efficient at sea level than fuel injection but less gasoline-economy-efficient. Government mandates for more fuel economy have given rise to the increased use of fuel injection and decreased use of carburetors.

Fuel injection allows the engine to work harder with less fuel and is easier to control with internal computers. The usable horsepower delivered to the drive wheels is less affected by higher elevation than normally aspirated engines. A diesel, for example, loses three percent of its usable horsepower for each 1,000-foot increase in elevation. That is a serious consideration for persons who will be driving over mountain passes of ten or twelve thousand feet of elevation. (Ever wonder why airplanes don't use diesel engines? Now you know!) Some companies use "throttle body" injection which puts the fuel/air mix into the engine in a manner similar to the carburetor. Some companies use "port" injection which places the fuel/air mix directly into each chamber through small nozzles. Most American luxury cars come equipped with some form of fuel injection system.

A turbo-charger may be added to either a diesel, normally aspirated, or fuel injected engine. Turbos have been used in racing circles for years. They started gaining prominence in this country as a necessary item for boosting the horsepower on under-powered diesels as well as on the small engines dictated by the fuel economy mandates. Turbo chargers dramatically increase horsepower output by recycling escaping fuel and hot air in the exhaust. Turbos typically spin at about 170,000 rpm. The high rotations per minute allow the escaping fuel to be forced back into the combustion system, under high pressure, for more complete burning. The client desiring extra horsepower, whether due to vehicle weight, or simply as a toy, might be encouraged to seek such an add-on. Some factories will perform this service. If, however, the client goes outside the factory for his turbo, you should advise him that this add-on may void his engine warranty.

Whether it is factory or non-factory installed, insist on a turbo oil pressure booster; it is available at most speed shops. It may take a minute or more for the turbo to wind down after the engine is shut off. The booster will hold oil pressure in the turbo during this wind-down. Without the booster, normal turbo life may be decreased to about 50,000 miles.

The turbo will increase horsepower by 50% or more in gasoline-fueled engines and, although expensive, is a very desirable option. Another "charger" option is called a super charger. It provides nearly as much power increase as a turbo charger but at a lower cost. A person willing to spend the extra money can take a car to a reputable performance shop. Thanks to racing technology, the expertise to double the manufactured horsepower of a given car exists in these shops. If warranty and trade-in are not overriding factors, the person willing to pay for the benefits of substantial power will be pleased with the performance results.

Radiator. Always order the heaviest duty radiator available. If it is not listed with the usual options, ask about availability. You will need all the cooling capacity you can get when stuck downtown in the heat of summer in slow moving traffic. Determine from the cooling system charts the amount of anti-freeze needed for either summer or winter driving. Depending on your geographic locale, the amount may vary. Short trips, slow driving, and high temperatures mean that you should faithfully change the anti-freeze and have the system back-flushed annually. Don't go over two years at most before having your service shop back-flush the cooling system. The dividends it pays in good cooling operation are worth every penny.

Heating/Air Conditioning. These creature comforts are virtually standard items on most cars today. Quite often the "Climate Control" variety is a very desirable option because you don't have to fiddle with the controls. You set the desired interior temperature and the computers do the rest. A rear window defogger is a must, whether you drive in snow country or the regions in warm country which are subject to high humidity. Have you ever been confronted with a car full of people on a frosty morning and had their breath cause the windows to fog over? You want the visibility it allows you to have through the rear window. If the rear window wiper/washer option is available for the car you are buying, get it. You will come to appreciate the increased rear visibility on slushy or rainy roads. An option that is more uncommon is de-icing for outside mounted rear view mirrors. If you spend much time in snow country, you might want to consider this option.

Alternator. Insist on the heavy duty alternator option when available. The alternator output should be a minimum of 80 amp and at least 45 amp at idle speed of 700 rpm. If you have add-on equipment such as telephones, televisions, cb radios, fax machines, cold bars, and additional internal and external lighting, they will create a heavy drain on the battery. The heavy duty alternator should be able to provide the battery with sufficient power to accommodate these needs. Drainage problems are not noticed at highway speeds. The usage drains show up when stuck in slow-moving traffic and waiting in the bank drive-through line. The engine does not have enough rpm to turn the alternator fast enough to keep the battery at peak performance.

The older dual belt drive systems were better

in some ways but newer cars are going to a very reliable, single wide belt drive system. The belt drives the radiator fan, water pump, power steering, brakes, air conditioner, and alternator. While belt failure is uncommon under 30,000 miles, it is important that the belt be checked for cracks and slippage. Have this done at least at one-half of the interval the manufacturer recommends. A slipping belt reduces the efficiency of the components it drives.

Battery. Never get less than the biggest and highest capacity battery available for the car. American cars have 12-volt systems. The battery should be the maintenance-free variety and have at least 465 cold cranking amps with a 70 amp/hour rating. If you have a big electrical system with many demands, you need a big battery. You may also have an additional battery installed to be used for powering many of the add-on accessories.

Brakes. Power disc brakes help with emergency stops, and anti-lock brakes may be desirable (see the material following on tires for additional comments.) Anti-lock brake (called ABS) systems use sensors on each wheel to detect rotation speed. When a central computer interprets a significantly higher deceleration rate at one wheel than the others, it momentarily reduces brake pressure on that wheel to allow it to start rolling again, then clamps the brakes back on. The system provides maximum braking force short of allowing a skid.

Traction Control. Traction control uses the same hardware--sensors, computer, and brake controls--to slow down spinning wheels. When the car starts on ice, for instance, the traction control computer brakes the spinning wheel until its speed matches the other drive wheel's. So, both wheels get traction.

Some expensive traction control systems go further. They actually reduce the engine's power in addition to applying the brakes. This means that the driver's foot no longer directly controls the throttle; electronics systems do. When the driver floors the gas, the pedal sends a signal along a wire, telling a computer how much the driver wants to accelerate. The computer then decides whether to open the throttle wide or--if it receives a signal that a wheel is spinning--to throttle back. No matter that the driver is still standing on the gas pedal.

Stability Control. Another ABS add-on, stability control, works to prevent spins and understeering--plowing ahead in a corner. The system uses a sensor to measure steering-wheel angle and a yaw sensor, which measures the rate the car's body is actually turning at. Some systems also monitor speed, throttle, and wheel and rotation. If the computer finds a difference between steering angle (where the driver wants to go) and yaw angle (where the car is actually going), it brakes one or two wheels to correct course.

For example, if a car is spinning to the right, stability control will slow only the left front and right rear wheels to rotate the car back into line.

Headlights. Quartz-halogen high beam lights are standard on many of the more expensive cars. However, even if your car is very expensive, don't assume you have them. The added power of these lights make them a wonderful item, especially when driving at night in rural areas. The addition of grille or bumper mounted fog lights and spotlights or driving lights may also be a consideration, depending upon the security profile of the vehicle, the geographic locale, and weather conditions of the area. If not illegal in your area, an alternating flashing headlight system is an attractive option which can be used as a warning device in the event of emergency driving.

High-intensity back-up lights are another option, for use in fast-speed backing under poor light conditions.

High intensity spotlights are available, some with incredible, blinding intensity, and, if legal in your state, can satisfactorily discourage pursuers. One such light can be installed on a swivel so that it can be directed up front or in back. ***Warning: using such a light could cause an accident--it should never be used except in an emergency.***

Tail Lights. Again, if not illegal in your area, a cut-off switch which allows you to turn off the brake and tail lights while allowing the headlights to remain on is an attractive add-on. This could be a comfort if you are pursued by bad guys at night. However, if the pursuer has flashing red or blue lights, you should not even consider using the tail light cut-off switch. If used, remember to deactivate it when returning to traffic so the tail lights work again.

Interior Lighting. The installation of a cut-off switch is a good security measure. It allows you the option of having the interior lights on or off when opening a door. Directional reading lights are more desirable than lights which simply flood the interior with illumination.

Alarms. Some cars now come equipped with built-in alarm systems. If not, consider investing in a good vehicle alarm system. Something that will both sound an alarm and disable the engine until deactivated is much preferred over the alarm-only variety. On the market are also remote control devices for locking and unlocking the doors, starting the ignition, warming the car, and checking for ignition-connected bombs. The desirability of these devices is a matter of practicality and the security profile of your choosing.

Gauges. Warning lights are designed for the ignorant, normal, everyday driver. They tend to flash red when the oil is all gone and the damage is done. You want to watch the dial that indicates your oil pressure. If it isn't in the proper range, you need to have the vehicle checked. The temperature gauge will show you if the engine heat is too high. The amp/batt gauge (indicating (amperes/battery/charge) will show you instantly whether your battery is charging.

A tachometer is a must for performance driving. It shows the engine rpm and allows you to

determine if your mph speed is too great to drop down one gear to get braking through use of engine compression.

Locking Systems. These should be of the type that are tamperproof and include locks for the hood, trunk, and gas tank. Newer locking systems have a clicker for locking and unlocking the doors from the outside. It is an excellent idea to have the trunk lock equipped with an inside catch so that the trunk can be unlocked and opened from the inside.

Window Glass. All windows should be the heat-absorbing tinted type. This is standard on most American cars. There are some darker factory installed options you may or may not find desirable. Lowered interior visibility when viewed from outside the car is probably a desirable option on a limo for the side windows. Dark windows should not be a deliberately purchased item for the front door windows on a limo. The driver must have adequate visibility for both day and night driving. Very dark front door windows severely limit the driver's vision at night. Normal tint for windshield, left front, and right front windows is desired. Darker tint, if desired for client privacy, may be installed behind the driver for all side windows. Most states allow factory installed tint of 35% gray, 35% gray-2 ply, or 35% bronze. Other than a limo type vehicle, standard factory tint windows should be used to maintain a low security profile.

Suspension. Do you want a soft, mushy, comfortable ride or do you want a ride which will give you the optimum in handling control for performance driving? To the best of our knowledge, there is no vehicle made which will provide both features. Computer controlled, flick-the-switch, automatically adjustable controls are a compromise at best. If your desire is for a good executive protection vehicle, you still must determine how it is to be used. Will it be a street limousine? Will it be used on rural gravel roads that are subject to washouts and potholes? Will it be driven much on rural mountain dirt roads? Will it be subjected to deep snow or soft sand at the beach? Will it be driven much in tightly spaced parking lots? Will it be parked in a low-roof underground parking facility? A car with stiff suspension on bumpy roads is a teeth-jarring experience. A van or other tall vehicle will not fit under the clearance limits of many underground garages. A car that is too long may be difficult to turn in narrow parking lots. All wheel or four wheel drive might be a consideration in some areas of the country.

Whether the need is for a more maneuverable short-wheel-base car, or a more comfortable long-wheel-base car, the suspension should be heavy duty with heavy duty shock absorbers front and rear. Additionally, heavy duty front and rear stabilizer bars are essential. They will reduce body roll and assist with flat cornering. If you anticipate carrying 100 pounds or more of gear in the trunk, get the load leveler option. The rule of thumb is that, if there is a heavier duty something available for the car, get it. The heavy duty items quite often mean less maintenance. If the "police package" is an available option, get it, because it will normally have many of the heavy duty options included in the price.

And now--for the good news. There are now available active suspension systems which measure wheel movement over bumps and adjust suspension firmness accordingly. With these systems you are no longer faced with the trade-off between a smooth ride, which requires a soft suspension, and good handling, which requires a firm one. Active handling makes the same car do both. Suspension sensors measure the frequency, abruptness, and height of bumps and pass the information on to a computer.

The computer interprets sharp, high-frequency movements as bumps and opens valves in the shock absorbers to soften the ride. When the car heels over in corners, the tall, low-frequency suspension movements trigger the computer to add resistance to the shock absorbers.

Some active suspension systems can also raise and lower the car to help passengers get in and out or to improve aerodynamics on the highway.

Steering. Power steering is a must with all heavy cars. Some of the newer systems provide alternating power steering with easy steering at low speeds and tighter steering at higher speeds. The addition of a power steering cooler to the power steering unit is desirable for city driving on hot days. Tilt steering wheels are a nice driving comfort item for the driver and available on most cars. They also provide the driver with a little more room for easier entrance and exit. The thicker, padded steering wheels are a better option than the older, skinny, slick plastic style wheel.

Tires. Why save tires for the last item? Sometimes you save the best for the last. Tires are one of the most overlooked items when purchasing a car. They are certainly overlooked when it comes time to replace them. Tires should match and they should be radial. Snow tires will provide traction needed in winter months in snow conditions. They will not provide the best traction for all around driving on streets and highways when there is no snow. Studded snow tires will provide even more traction on snow and ice impacted roads. (If studded snow tires are used, don't just put them on the two driving wheels; put them on all four wheels.) They provide the least traction on dry streets and highways.

Tire speed ratings are European specifications. "S" indicates the tire is safe for sustained driving at 112 mph. "H" indicates 130 mph and "V" indicates somewhere beyond 130 mph. There are even higher speed ratings than "V" that we will not concern ourselves with since they are track and competition high speed ratings.

Every tire sold in the U.S. must carry an American rating which the Department of Transportation (DOT) calls a temperature-resistant grade. The scale goes from C to A. The C grade represents the minimum heat/speed capability for all tires sold here. The A rating falls roughly between the European H and V ratings. B rated tires are in the vicinity of the European S rating. DOT ratings do not cover higher speed tires. You can usually determine from your dealer the top speed your car is capable of achieving. That will be your guide as to which heat or speed rating your tires should be. When in doubt, go with the next higher rating. If the car is to be armored, ask for the armorer's recommendation. The car is only as good as the tires. A top line all-season radial with a DOT rating of A is usually a good choice for most American luxury cars.

Inflation--don't permit the typical, under-inflated tire installation. Tire installers often typically inflate tires as much as five or ten pounds below the recommended tire pressure inflation. The tire is softer and gives a nicer ride while going in a straight line at city speeds. The tires on the typical American luxury sedan will usually have pressure ratings of 32 to 36 pounds. The tires with V speed rating, found on some of the faster sport type cars, will sometimes have pressure ratings of 44 pounds or more. Conventional tires and under-inflated tires will distort badly at high speeds. They also have a nasty tendency to roll right off the rim during hard cornering activity. For good performance, a recommendation is that tires, rather than being under-inflated, be slightly over-inflated by, say, two pounds. Some performance driving schools insist that five pounds is the amount to over-inflate tires. Either way, make certain that all tires are inflated to exactly the same pressure. Under-inflation may provide a softer ride, but it also causes more wear and lowered fuel economy.

Whenever tires are changed or rotated, they should be checked for balancing. If you feel the slightest sustained shimmy in the steering wheel or the seat of your pants, the tires may be out of balance. The vibration means the tire is not rolling smoothly and needs a small amount of weight added or deleted from the wheel rim. The more technical "spin balancing" is usually recognized as a better form of balancing than "bubble balancing" for high speed use. Balancing for a minimum of 80 mph will usually be sufficient for speeds up to 100 mph. Tires which are out of balance will provide less than optimum performance, not only for high speed driving, but for turning and braking as well.

There are "run-flat" tires on the market which

can be driven for a fair distance even when punctured. They are reasonably effective if the damage is not concentrated. One or two bullet holes will not damage the tires sufficiently to cause them to go flat immediately, but a shotgun blast causes too much damage; the hole is too big, and the tire will flatten instantly.

Be certain that the spare tire is of the same make and quality as the four tires on the car. Many new cars are now delivered with miniature tires good only for very mild driving and distances not exceeding 35 to 50 miles. When leasing a car, keep that in mind!

A comment about ABS systems is in order when talking about tires. The Anti-Lock Braking Systems seem to be a hot selling option. They are marketed as a life saving device. If you have an ABS option, you must make absolutely sure that all tires are inflated to exactly the same pressure. Also make sure that the wheel alignment is correct on all four wheels and that the tires are properly balanced. If anything is out of proper adjustment, you can have anything from insufficient braking to the uncomfortable experience of one wheel locking up and possibly putting the car into a sudden spin.

Rear View Mirrors. These should be mounted on the outside of both front doors. They should be non-glare glass, and each mirror should have at least 14 square inches of usable viewing area. That is slightly smaller than a 3" X 5" card. The outside mirror on each side of the car should be electronically adjustable from the driver's position. The driver is the one who needs to use them.

Power Door Locks. Some power door locks automatically activate when the transmission is put in drive and are a convenient safety feature. Unless you override the feature, they do not deactivate until the transmission is put in park or neutral.

Power Windows. These are a must and are included on many cars. Try to avoid the "push the button once and it automatically goes all the way down" option. The driver should be able to control how far down he wants the window at any given time. There are occasions when you may wish to open the window only an inch or so to speak with someone, while avoiding the danger of that person reaching inside the car or throwing something inside.

Cruise Control. While this is a desirable option, it should not be used in city driving. Nor should you attempt to use it while driving on crowded highways. You should use it for normal driving on non-congested highways. It can be used to relieve some of the physical tension associated with keeping your foot on the throttle during long drives. Just be sure to deactivate it when you start closing on another car. Simply lifting your foot from the throttle will not cause the car to decelerate in preparation for possible evasion when the cruise control is in operation.

Mercedes-Benz plans with its top-of-the-line to use a cruise control which uses a laser to measure the distance to the car in front. If you get too close, the cruise control automatically slows down. When traffic opens up again, it automatically resumes the speed you set.

Mercedes-Benz uses the same laser plus one in the back to function much as "curb feelers"--when you are parallel parking, the lasers measure the distance to the cars in front and behind. Get close, and a beep sounds inside. The beeping gets faster the closer you get.

Fire Extinguisher. Ideally, you should equip the vehicle with two fire extinguishers, one for the trunk and one for the floor of the front seat area. The latter should be mounted close to a door for easy access by either the driver inside or someone outside.

Cellular Telephone. A hands-free cellular telephone is a wonderful addition to a car's safety equipment. It can be used to summon help and to call ahead to alert advance personnel of the protectee's arrival. It should be equipped with the capacity for programmable telephone numbers. In an

emergency, you will not have time to look up numbers; you will need to call immediately without losing time. The integrated cellular phone includes speakers and a microphone hidden in the car, so drivers can keep their hands on the wheel and their eyes on the road. The phones automatically mute the stereo during calls and allow the driver to dial by speaking the phone numbers.

GPS Navigation Systems. Many automakers offer global positioning satellite (GPS) navigation systems in their luxury cars. The systems combine a touch screen in the dashboard, a flat satellite antenna, and a gyroscopic sensor to track which way the car is pointing. The system satellites triangulate the car's position to within ten yards and plot it on a map on the dashboard screen. The system can locate businesses, bank machines, attractions, and street addresses through an on-board CD-ROM database. The driver can enter a destination, and the system will sound out turn-by-turn directions as the car arrives at each intersection.

On-Star. General Motors combines satellite navigation and a hands-free cellular phone with this security system. The cellular phone is also linked with some car controls. On-Star has no navigation screen or in-car CD-ROM database. Instead, it has its own in-house support base. Lost? Press the On-Star button on the built-in phone. Call-center employees can see your location on a screen and give you directions by phone. Lock your keys in the car? The center can unlock it. Car stolen? The center always knows where it is. Broken down? Service people can find you. In an accident? Any time the air bags go off, the car automatically calls the center and help is dispatched. (Ford offers a similar, but less comprehensive, system called Rescue.)

VEHICLE MAINTENANCE

All drivers should know something about the maintenance requirements for their vehicle. The periodic maintenance schedule is described in the owner's manual. This includes things like rotation of tires, changing or adding engine oil, changing or adding transmission oil, lubrication, changing air and oil filters, checking the anti-freeze, and the myriad of other things necessary to validate your warranty and keep your car running well. There are other items the executive protection driver should concern himself with on a frequent basis. The following areas should be checked weekly.

Tires. Tires should be checked weekly or even more frequently. The first and easiest check is for proper inflation. Whether you decide to use standard maximum recommended pressure, the two pounds over pressure, or the five pounds over pressure, you should maintain the pressure *exactly*. Pressure gauges may vary in accuracy so a good quality gauge should be purchased from the local auto parts store. All four tires, as well as the spare tire, should be the same pressure. Even one tire with two pounds less pressure than the other three tires can drastically alter the performance potential of your car. It will make a difference in the steering, pulling you slightly to one side rather than keeping you in a straight line. You can feel this in the steering wheel. The under-inflated tire creates more drag and less traction.

Tire inflation will also play a part in the wear and life span of the tires. Under-inflated tires wear appreciably faster. The tread depth wears away, and the tires are unable to grip pavement in the rain and achieve traction in snow and mud. Do not under-inflate tires for better traction in mud and snow. The lowered pressure has the reverse effect. The treads are prone to close in on themselves when under-inflated, thus negating traction.

It is a handy idea to keep a can of tire inflator/sealer in the trunk for each of the four tires. If it has to be used as an emergency inflator, the culprit tire should be repaired or replaced at the earliest opportunity. Also, since most pressurized cans of this sort utilize a flammable gas as the pressure propellant, the tire changer should be made aware of this before he changes and repairs the tires. Visibly check the rubber valve stems for cracks next to the wheel. If there are any, have them replaced.

Front Wheel Alignment. Another wear factor on tires is misalignment of the front wheels. If one side of the tire tread shows more wear than the other side (less tread depth), the front wheels need to be aligned. Depending on the amount of wear, the tires may also need to be replaced. Many factors can cause this but usually it is caused by hitting a curb, a chuck hole in the road, or other obstacle. It literally knocks the wheel slightly out of alignment. The tire rolls at a slight angle to the road surface and wears faster on one side than the other side. The rear wheels on most American cars are mounted straight because they are not required to lean for turns. They have no adjustable wheel alignment. When uneven wear is noticed the problem should be addressed promptly. Get the car to a good alignment facility. Either your factory dealer or a good frame and axle shop should be able to correct the alignment.

Lug Nuts. If the vehicle is driven frequently, check the lug nuts at least monthly to determine they are all secure. If the lug nut wrench is all screwed together with the jack and spare tire, you might consider the purchase of a standard jack handle or star wrench that fits your lugs. It can be wrapped in cloth and laid in the trunk for easy access. If you suddenly find yourself in the middle of an evasion procedure, loose lug nuts can cause serious problems. The loose mounting may actually allow the wheel to snap off during hard turns. Be sure to properly seat the wheel covers back in place after checking the lug nuts. It is not necessary to jack the wheel off the ground to perform this check.

Wheel Rims. These should be visibly checked monthly, especially if other people drive the car. Someone could have hit a deep hole in the road or a curb and not mentioned it. If you notice a bend in the wheel rim, the wheel should be replaced. It can allow some air to escape through the bead seal. The tire could roll off the rim during hard cornering. If hit severely enough, the wheel could even have a crack in it which could lead to wheel failure at a bad time.

Windshield Wipers and Washers. Double

and triple edge wiper blades are now available which can greatly enhance the overall performance of your wipers. They should be replaced annually, but check them weekly. Have any small metal clips become bent or broken? Does the wiper make a clear path on the wet windshield on each cycle, or does it appear to skip over areas of the glass, then make contact again? Are there any nicks in the rubber edges? Wipers that don't work properly must be replaced. Occasionally, even a new car will have a wiper blade that is less than the best. If they don't work, your vision is hindered in inclement weather. Replace them.

Check the level of the windshield washer fluid even though you may not have used the washers. Make sure the washers do, in fact, squirt onto the glass. Fluid can leak out of the container and foreign material can get into the line or the nozzle. Resist the temptation to simply add water if the container level is low. Usually a 50-50 mix of washer fluid and water is recommended. Never use only water except in case of an emergency. The water will freeze in winter and evaporate in summer. It also does not have the cleaning properties necessary to remove impacted bugs from the windshield. Be sure to use windshield washer fluid-antifreeze, not engine antifreeze.

Products such as Rain-x or Protect-all may be applied, according to instructions on the container, to all glass, both outside and inside. These products assist in preventing the formation of steam, smoke film, fogging, and other vision hazards on the glass. Annual or biannual application of these types of products will greatly aid in the ease of removal of accumulated film, dirt, and bugs. Keep the windshield and windows sparkling clean. Sunlight, headlights, and street lights are all diffused by the dust and smoke film on the glass. This glare contributes to dim vision through the windshield and affects your peripheral vision as well. Clean the glass.

Windshields, especially, may become pitted and contribute to glare. Sand, salt, and dirt particles blasting against the windshield make tiny pits. The resulting glare is as bad as dust film on the windows.

The damaged windshield may be repaired in some cases, but replacement is usually a better option.

Electrically Controlled Side Mirrors. Check the adjustment of the mirrors before you drive the car. Others may have adjusted them. Don't wait until just before the client gets into the car prepared to leave. You will have no time to make adjustments then. Remember that changing the seat position will probably require some mirror adjustment.

Hoses and Belts. With the engine off, use a flashlight to check all hoses under the hood for any signs of moisture or leakage. Moist or oily spots should not be noticeable. Look at and feel the fan belt. Look for any cracks on the underside of the belt. Try to find any "strings" that seem to be working loose. Have any of these items replaced at the first sign of anything being out of the ordinary.

Additional Items to Check. Check the pressure on your interior mount fire extinguisher as well as the one in the trunk. Be sure they have not been used and that the pressure dial still indicates normal charge.

The inventory list of tools in the trunk should also be checked weekly. Make sure the shovel, kitty litter or sand (for traction in mud and on ice), flares, fire extinguisher, flashlight, tire sealers, tool kit, medical kit, spare tire, (two are preferred), nylon tow chain (minimum 20,000 pounds test), jack, lug wrench, jumper cables, extra motor oil, and engine coolant are all intact. If the car is radio or telephone equipped, perform your test check.

Visibly inspect the battery posts and cables for cleanliness; if the battery doesn't work, nothing else will either. Check the hazard warning lights to be sure they work at all four corners of the car. See if the tail pipe has a sooty appearance. You may need a timing adjustment so the engine runs more efficiently. The car should be washed and kept clean outside and underneath; this makes it easier to spot signs of tampering or extraneous objects (bombs, surveillance devices).

ARMORING

Does your client need an armored vehicle? Perhaps. If the threat is high enough to warrant, an armored vehicle offers vastly improved protection. However, there are some fairly significant trade-offs for the added protection.

Armoring a car adds weight, which cuts down on its speed and maneuverability. To hold up the weight of the armored vehicle requires a custom-built chassis, usually made of truck components. The engine must be extensively reworked or replaced to provide the additional horsepower and torque needed to pull the vehicle. The steering system must be able to guide the vehicle, and the brakes capable of stopping it within a reasonable distance. Power must be sufficient for the vehicle to cruise without laboring up a hill. Bullet resistant glass must be free of optical distortion.

All of this adds up to money, a great deal of money. An armored vehicle will cost upwards of $200,000, and a heavily armored vehicle can reach $750,000. Think carefully, therefore, about the comfort, maneuverability, and financial trade-offs before recommending this as a ready solution to the client, making certain that the threat warrants it.

If the conclusion, or client preference, is to purchase an armored vehicle, the agent (you) will undoubtedly be given some, if not all, of the responsibility for overseeing the project.

The first decision will be the careful selection of the armored car manufacturer. There are, literally, only a small handful of competent, trustworthy armored car producers in the United States, and it is imperative to identify a highly recommended vendor who will work with you, and who will provide you with names of individuals or companies who have purchased armored vehicles from him.

You will need to interview these vendors and get specifications. You must ask the right questions and get the best advice you can find. There are unscrupulous salesmen, some of whom make false promises and some who merely leave out part of the facts. They may claim that their armor will stop bullets when what they really mean is that their armor will stop bullets at 100 yards, or at an angle, but not at point blank range.

Be prepared to request interviews with the armoring manufacturers' clients and to ask the right questions having to do with vehicle performance.

Different levels of protection have to do with these factors: *the resistance to various calibers of bullets, at specific ranges, for single and multi-shots.* As a condition of your vendor selection, you should insist on the right to conduct test firing at the armor plate selected, at close range, at various intervals during the construction.

You should know that "armor" can be constructed of glass, acrylics, polycarbonates, ceramics, glass-reinforced plastics, fabrics, steel, and aluminum.

Glass. Bullet-resistant glass, which is generally constituted of soda lime float glass, is used primarily for windshields and side windows in an armored vehicle. Protection against small caliber handguns can usually be accomplished with a single layer of 3/8 inch glass. Protection from larger caliber handguns, shotguns, and rifles may require two to four layers of glass which are laminated together with a bonding agent and joined with a backing material. This can result in two or three inches of very heavy glass. It is not only very expensive to produce but is prone to distortion.

Distortion is, in fact, a major problem. You should insist upon glass that is virtually free of distortion, particularly in geographic areas where extremes of temperature can create or enhance distortion.

Acrylics and Polycarbonates. Acrylics, like glass, are transparent. They are stronger and lighter than glass, but are prone to scratching.

Polycarbonates are also transparent, are highly resistant to breakage, are much stronger than either acrylics or glass, but are also prone to scratching. Both acrylics and polycarbonates are flammable.

Fabrics. Kevlar, the most well known name in bullet-resistant fabrics, is used primarily in the production of protective garments--vests, capes, and women's undergarments. It is an aramid fiber which was first introduced in 1972 as a fiber to strengthen radial tires. As with other bullet-resistant materials, Kevlar derives various levels of protection by the use of multiple layers (in this case, fabric). Simply purchasing a Kevlar vest does not guarantee that it will stop all bullets. Multiple, multiple layers of Kevlar are required to protect against a 9mm or .44 magnum attack. There is a use for Kevlar in the interior of the vehicle to provide added protection; however, because of its bulk, it is not easy to "work" the fabric into any other than very simple applications. Allied Signal has more recently come on the scene with its soft body armor vest called Spectra-shield. It is a tough modified polyethylene plastic.

Ceramics and Glass-Reinforced Plastics. Ceramics are the "Cadillac" of bullet-resistant materials. They are extremely hard and efficient, and, because of their light weight, they are sometimes found in aircraft, primarily helicopter seats for pilot protection. They are, of course, (there is always a catch) very expensive. Glass-reinforced plastics also possess excellent bullet-resistant properties and are sometimes combined with ceramics.

Steel and Aluminum. These are the bullet-resistant materials most commonly found in armoring vehicles. Steel is used when the threat is more likely to include attacks with machine guns and rifles. To armor against the threat of sub-machine guns requires the equivalent of 1/8th inch specially hardened steel. To armor against the threat of rifle caliber machine guns requires the equivalent of 3/8 inch specially prepared steel. These special steels will probably not stop armor-piercing machine gun bullets; they will not stop .50 caliber machine gun bullets; and they will

not stop most remote controlled bombs.

Aluminum armor, certainly one of the most popularly used vehicle armoring materials, is used when the threat is perceived to include nothing more powerful than 9mm bullets. It is, in many ways, a compromise of protection, comfort, practicality, and money.

The additional modifications and options which must be considered when designing an armored vehicle include the following.

. **Tires.** Tires are a priority. At least one manufacturer makes self-sealing, inner liner (second tire inside the outer tire), bullet-resistant tires. If the outer tire is shredded by dense fire power, the inner tire will still hold the car off the rim for better maneuverability. You can run the gamut from self-sealing to liquid filled with baffles or to virtually solid tires. A set of four bullet-resistant tires may cost $2,000.

. **Radiator Shield.** Either reinforced metal baffles or ceramic panels to shield the radiator will deflect, if not stop, bullets. The car will still run for several minutes with a pierced radiator until the engine finally gets too hot and seizes up. Metal, Kevlar, Spectra-shield or ceramic panels installed to deflect bullets away from key components in the engine compartment will go a long way toward helping insure the continued running of the engine. The shielding needs to protect not only the front and top of the radiator but also radiator hoses, hydraulic lines, gas line, electrical modules, and wiring. This additional installation also requires the ducting of additional air to the radiator and the installation of an 8-or-more-bladed radiator fan. These panels may be attached to the hood and side walls and behind the grille. They may also be placed, in modular form, over the protected components.

. **Windows.** Factory-installed windows are made of safety glass. Sheets of glass are laminated together so that, if broken, the glass has less tendency to burst into tiny fragments which shower the occupants. Additional sheets of lamination and/or tinted sheets of plastic are available and, when applied to the inside of the window, will have a higher safety potential and not interfere with the operation of the windows. The thinness allows the windows to work in the existing window slots in the door. Again, this option is not bullet-proof but will aid in the deflection of bullets and will further contain glass showers inside the car. Bullet-resistant glass can be as much as three inches thick and requires re-working of the doors. Another option is the installation of Kevlar or Spectra-shield curtains. These are easily affixed to the doors and back window. The trade-off is severely limited visibility.

. **Roof, Floor, Door, and Back Panels.** Kevlar or Spectra-shield panels may also be installed inside the roof liner and door panels. Panels must overlap each other at least 1-1/2 inches because, just as with personal soft body armor, the seams are the weak link. Additional panels may be installed behind the back seat. Panels may be placed under the floor carpet and seats. Unless radio equipment or something explosive is located in the trunk there is not much advantage to panels inside the trunk lid, unless you just want the additional security from rear assaults.

. **Transmission.** The addition of all this extra weight puts a heavier burden on the transmission. For that reason, a transmission oil cooler, usually available in the "Trailering Package," is a must. All the horsepower in the world will not save you if the transmission overheats and burns up. You most certainly will want the addition of the skid plate mounted under the housing. It will not only deflect bullets but rocks and curbs as well. If escape situations arise and you need to jump a curb, the skid plate will take the blow instead of the transmission housing.

. Additionally, some companies will install a solid plate across the entire underside of the vehicle. The idea is more for hindering the placement of an under-the-car bomb than it is for protection from tossed bombs or bullets. There are some minor problems associated with routine servicing and oil changes with this installation.

. **Gas Tank.** The rubberized, heavy duty, self-sealing gas tank is an expensive but nice addition, especially if you chose to disregard panel or plate protection. You should not be too concerned about someone shooting holes in the tank, as you have seen in the movies, and stopping the car because it runs out of gas. Be more concerned about the fire hazard. It is possible that fragments of bullets can get to the tank. It is also possible for high speed backing over a curb to burst the tank or tear it. A high-impact collision to the rear of the car could also damage it. A burst gas tank is a sudden fire hazard.

You should insist on your vehicle (whether armored or not) being equipped with Safoam, a plastic sponge-like material, which can be installed inside the gas tank. Safoam goes a long way to reducing fire and explosion in the gas tank.

. **Bumpers.** The addition of reinforced bumpers, especially the front bumper, is a consideration sometimes overlooked. If the necessity for armoring exists, the necessity for reinforced bumpers to allow for ramming also exists.

. **Gas Line.** One item which is often overlooked is the gas line, the cheap plastic line from the gas tank to the engine. It often is loosely placed along the rails of the chassis. Be sure that it is placed out of view and above the chassis. It is quite possible for bullet fragments, pieces of rocks or concrete or other debris, driven with sufficient force, to penetrate the gas line. If the engine does not get the required amount of fuel, the internal computers quickly shut down, along with the engine. The fuel line should be protected with soft or hard armor wherever it is exposed.

. **Gun Ports.** Resist the addition of gun ports in the sides of the car. Whether gun ports are invisible from the outside of the car is not relevant. What is relevant is that you can not deliver aimed and accurate fire from a small opening on the inside of the car. Each bullet that misses the intended target is a piece of potential liability. Shooting from inside the car in such a manner that the muzzle of the gun is placed into a gun port opening or between the seams of the armor, then fired so the bullets will pierce the outer skin of the car, is an exercise in futility. The outer skin of the car will virtually guarantee the first shots to be inaccurate due to deflection and distortion of the bullet as it passes through the metal. And, certainly, no one who has been inside a closed car when a .357 magnum revolver discharged would ever recommend such a procedure.

.   **Bomb Blanket.** A readily accessible bomb blanket for the use of the client may also be used to provide additional protection. It can be used to immediately throw over the client in a gunfire attack. The client should be instructed in its use and know how to cover himself on the floor in an emergency. Of course, the client should always be instructed to get on the floor if attacked, whether he has a bomb blanket or not.

Of great importance is balancing the weight of the armor on the vehicle to maintain safety and maneuverability. An overloaded vehicle will accelerate and brake slowly, be hard to handle on steep grades, and sluggish in any situations except straightforward driving. If too much weight is added too high on the body of the vehicle, it could cause the car to become destabilized, thereby causing it to roll, pitch, and even overturn. Too much weight up front, or in back, could also destabilize the vehicle, causing the car to squat on its rear axles or skid. It takes a skilled, knowledgeable armorer to know how much armor any one vehicle can carry, and where it should be placed.

Driver training will be needed, as driving a heavily armored vehicle is a challenge. It simply is not going to accelerate or stop as easily and quickly as one is accustomed to experiencing. Stopping power is extremely important and simply adding heavier brakes is not enough. The entire rear axle may need modifying. Even so, one should be prepared to take a longer stretch of road to stop the

vehicle. Turning corners must be done more carefully to avoid either sliding off the road or flipping the car over.

It is impossible to armor a vehicle that will protect it against all bombs. Armored vehicles have survived grenade attacks but little else in the way of direct or immediately adjacent bomb attacks. One vehicle was blown sky-high, landing on top of a five-story building. The best defense against a vehicular bomb attack is still prevention--not being there when the bomb goes off.

One tends to think only of armored limousines, but consideration should be given to other mid-sized automobiles, as they have a somewhat lower profile. Four-wheel drive vehicles like the Jeep Cherokee can be an excellent choice, providing off-road flexibility. If the car is being used primarily in another country, a car more typical of that country might be used; for example, a Mercedes in Germany.

Finally, do not be lulled into a feeling of false security by relying on an armored vehicle to provide full protection. Armoring is only as efficient as its strength. A mortar round will easily dispel that good feeling. All of the protective measures employed with an unarmored vehicle should be used with an armored vehicle.

VEHICLE SECURITY

Basic security for the executive protection driver means insuring the security of the client's car. Government agencies may be able to provide 24-hour security for specific cars but most clients in the private sector do not find that degree of security cost-effective. Even though the vehicle may be secured in a locked garage overnight, there probably is not someone in visual contact with it at all times. When the client goes to the office and the car is parked in a municipal garage, or even in the garage in his own building, there usually is not someone in visual contact with it all the time. Even if there is, the executive protection driver/agent leaves nothing to chance. If the driver is not with the car at all times, he inspects it before the client gets into it.

A basic means of keeping any vehicle secure is to equip it in such a way that a break-in is difficult. Obviously, the vehicle should be kept locked at all times, preferably inside a locked garage.

There are various kinds of automobile alarm systems and all of the really effective ones should be installed by a knowledgeable dealer or mechanic.

.   A switch alarm is a basic system with switches placed on the doors, trunk, and hood of the car. The system is activated when one of these is opened. This is very similar to the basic house, or office, alarm which is audible.

.   A motion detector alarm utilizes a mercury switch activated when someone tries to break into a door or window. Unfortunately, strong wind can sometimes rock the car enough to activate this alarm.

.   A pager-type alarm offers an added feature. In addition to an alarm going off, a pocket-pager device signals the owner or driver. The range is generally fairly short and may be compromised by the steel and concrete construction of the typical underground parking facility.

.   Coded start systems generally utilize an electrical switch that requires a coded input to release it. It may also sound an alarm and/or ground out the ignition.

.   Disabling devices represent another dimension of security. A fuel shutoff will allow the car to start, but it will run for only a short distance before shutting down. A battery disconnect operates with a switch which shuts down all electrical power to the car. A brake lock will lock up the master brake cylinder which locks up all four brakes. There are steering wheel bars and locks which make the steering inoperative. All of these devices work to one degree or another. They are also very inconvenient and a hindrance if one needs to get the car moving NOW! Most of these disabling devices are designed

to prevent theft of the car. In executive protection, auto theft is generally not at the top of the worry list. What is important is to deny an intruder the opportunity of placing a bomb in, on, or around the car.

The term "car bomb" can be used to describe various kinds of bombs. Bombs can be placed within the car or engine area. Virtually no one other than an amateur attempts to wire the bomb to the ignition. The danger of missing the intended target is too great unless the client is the only one who drives the car. Bombs are usually placed under the car near the gas tank. The taped-together sticks of dynamite, used in the past, are rarely seen today. Modern explosives can be molded into virtually any desired shape. If you have reason to suspect that a bomb has, indeed, been attached to the car, it is a job for experts. They may literally have to dismantle the car to disclose the bomb.

Bombs are very tricky and very, very dangerous. They are almost impossible to prevent in all circumstances. However, there are some steps which can be taken to guard against car bombs. These steps may be extended and accelerated depending upon the level of risk.

To repeat, no unauthorized person should have access to your vehicle. Access control will go a long way toward thwarting a potential bomber's plan. If the bomb can't be hand-carried to the car, you have little to fear from planted car bombs. At home, the car should be locked within a garage even if it is left unattended for only a few minutes. The garage should be protected at night with an alarm system. A shaft-driven automatic garage door opener should be installed, as it securely locks the door. Chain driven automatic doors are easily forced. Any windows in the garage should be included in the alarm system and they should be coated so that vision is denied from the outside. At work, the vehicle should be in a well-lit, controlled area, preferably in a patrolled or guarded area. If the car is left in a public area, it should be highly visible.

One should get in the habit of walking

around the car before entering, if the car has been out of sight, unguarded. Take note of any footprints, marks of a jack, debris, smudges, oily stains, tool marks, wires protruding, strange objects in the tire wells or tailpipe, or anything that looks suspicious. Is there dirt under the car which wasn't there when you left?

Look underneath the car to see if anything is obviously out of place or newly placed. The underneath area of the vehicle should be kept as clean as possible so that any foreign objects become more obvious. A handy instrument to use for looking under cars is a mirror mounted on an angled pole; however, a thorough check can only be made by lying underneath the vehicle and examining every possible place of concealment. A flashlight will be needed to look into dark spots. In particular, you should look up into the motor compartment and under the area of the driver and passenger seats. Search thoroughly around the exhaust pipe, gasoline tank, and chassis. Be on the alert for any fine, almost invisible, fishing line which can be attached between a bomb device and moving parts as a trigger mechanism. Make a thorough check under the wheel arches for any unusual items under or on top of the wheels. Check for signs that the tires may have been slashed or cut to cause a blowout at high speed. Check and remove the hubcaps.

Look through the windows before touching or entering the car to see if anything looks suspicious. (This is an excellent reason for keeping the vehicle clear of all loose items, packages, letters, etc. at all times.) *If there is any reason to suspect that a bomb has been placed, the search should halt at this point and an expert team brought in to complete a detailed search.*

Often, car bombs are placed so that they go off when the doors, hood, or trunk are opened, or when the motor is activated. Unlock and gently disengage the car doors, but leave on the safety latch. Before completely unlatching and entering, use a piece of plastic (a credit card will do) to move slowly along the edges of the door. This should detect any wires or devices placed to detonate as the door is opened. The same technique can be used along the hood and trunk edges.

When you enter the car, look carefully around the car, inside the glove compartment (open carefully), tape deck, under the seats and dashboard, and behind the visor and headrests. Any dangling or unidentified wires could indicate wiring leading to a bomb in the engine. Check under floor mats, but first run your hand gently over the mats to see if you can feel a bump indicating something under the mat. Check ashtrays, door pockets and panels, rear window ledge, and the ceiling.

A quick inspection of the engine area and the trunk should be made. First, unlock the hood but do not completely unlatch it until you have checked carefully along the edges. Use a flashlight to peer through the slight opening to spot anything that looks suspicious. Disconnect the battery, then check clutch, brake, accelerator, and steering linkage for actuating devices. Are there any suspicious wires attached to the battery?

Use the same careful two-stage maneuver when opening the car trunk, leaving it on half-latch while you check the edges and look inside. Check the floor mat, spare tire, tool kit compartment, brake lights and other rear lighting.

A cursory search for bombs will generally be sufficient (and consume all the time you can afford) unless you have reason to believe that a bomb threat is a high probability. Complete, seam-to-seam bomb searches of a car can take many hours and require expert assistance. If you have reason to believe that you have spotted a bomb in or around your car, *call for professional help!*

If the threat seems sufficiently high, a remote control device can be acquired that starts the car from a distance (it will also start the heater in the winter!)

If you have reason to believe that your client is under surveillance, your car check should include surveying for hidden "bugs" and location finders.

DRIVING SECURITY

One of the most vulnerable "soft spots" for the protectee is in his vehicle traveling to and from Point A to Point B. This can be driving from home to office and back, or every Sunday morning at 9:00 a.m. from home to church, or driving to the highly touted testimonial dinner at the Waldorf, news of which has appeared in all of the local newspapers. Aldo Moro, Texaco executive Kenneth Bishop, and Hans Schleyer were all ambushed in their cars. More recently, an Exxon executive was taken from his car at the end of his own driveway. Since these are classic examples of how easily the adversaries accomplished these crimes, let us briefly examine two of these incidents.

Hans Martin Schleyer

Dr. Hans Martin Schleyer was president of the Federation of German Employers' Association. Dr. Schleyer had a high visibility and for over two years was a matter of concern to the German Ministry of Interior, who believed him to be a likely target of a kidnap attempt or assault by one of the terrorist groups operating in West Germany. Matters began to come to a head in August, 1977, as intelligence indicated that Dr. Schleyer might be in imminent danger of attack. The Ministry ordered 24-hour maximum protection for him, and Dr. Schleyer was accompanied by a team of police officers both at home and at work.

On September 5, 1977, the attack took place. The adversaries, having conducted a successful surveillance, knew that Schleyer would be on a particular street in a general time frame. Schleyer traveled in a limousine with a driver and was followed by one car containing three police guards.

As Schleyer's chauffeur turned a corner on a one-way street only two blocks from the residence, a yellow Mercedes in the opposite lane and driving in the wrong direction suddenly veered in front of his limousine. It appeared that the Mercedes swerved to avoid a woman pushing a blue baby carriage across

the street. The Mercedes stopped at an angle across the street, blocking the sidewalk and half the street. The driver of the limo braked sharply. The escort car, which had been following closely, was unable to stop and collided with the rear of the limousine. Five assailants, armed with two .223 caliber semi-automatic rifles, two shotguns, and a submachine gun opened fire on the follow-up car. One police officer was able to fire a burst from his submachine gun and another fired a couple of shots from his pistol. The police bullets had no effect, and all three officers and the chauffeur were killed in less than 30 seconds. Schleyer was dragged from his car and forced into a Volkswagen bus, which escaped from the scene. Schleyer was later killed and his body stuffed into the trunk of a car.

Reviewing this incident, it is clear that intensive surveillance was carried out against Schleyer and his protective personnel. The assault was well planned and executed. Lessons to be learned include: Why was Schleyer's escort car in the rear instead of the front, where it could have been the first to spot the trap? The Mercedes was driving in the wrong direction and swerved; why was this not seen immediately as suspicious, particularly since the threat level was perceived as imminent? Why were the drivers not trained to avoid crashing into each other, and to practice evasive driving? Why didn't the chauffeur drive around or ram past the Mercedes? Was there no radio communication between the two vehicles? Why was Schleyer's vehicle not armored?

Aldo Moro

Aldo Moro was a very high visibility Italian political figure. A leading member of the Christian Democratic Party and a former prime minister, Moro was viewed as a candidate for the presidency of the Italian government. Italian politics rely heavily upon compromise and coalitions, and Moro was seen as able to unit various political factions, thus providing an alternative to the growing strength of the Italian Communist Party.

Aldo Moro was either uncaring about his safety or ignorant of ways to protect himself. He always took the same route to the Parliament and rode in an unarmored vehicle. His driver was chosen because he had proven to be a safe driver, not because of any specific executive protection or counterterrorist training. Moro's bodyguard, who traveled with him inside his vehicle, was 52 years old, had worked with Moro for 13 years, and was more an aide than a bodyguard. He had no special training nor real qualifications for the job; Moro simply liked him. Moro was provided with an escort car, containing three police officers.

On March 16, 1978, Mr. Moro left his Rome residence in a vehicle containing himself, his driver, and his bodyguard, with the police escort in the follow-up position. Moro planned to attend a crucial Chamber of Deputies meeting for a vote of confidence to the newly named government. In Italy, these votes can determine whether a government stands or falls.

At 9:02 a.m., as the two-car motorcade, proceeded along a residential street, a small station wagon braked suddenly in front of the principal's car. The driver of Aldo Moro's car ran into the rear of the station wagon, causing the follow-up car to run into the rear of Moro's vehicle. Two terrorists leaped out of the station wagon and shot Moro's driver and bodyguard, killing both. At the same time, additional terrorists attacked from a position along the side of the road, firing on the officers in the follow-up car. Only one of the three policemen was able to exit the vehicle and return fire, and all three police officers died in the attack. The officers' car had an automatic weapon, but it was locked in the trunk of the car for safekeeping. Moro's bodyguard's gun was so badly rusted that it was inoperable. After holding Moro for a well publicized period of time, his attackers later killed him.

The attack was well planned and executed. It is believed that 11 men and one woman took part in the attack, using at least five vehicles and one motorcycle.

Moro was not the terrorists' first choice as a target. They originally planned to attack Enrico Berlinguer, the First Secretary of the Italian Communist Party. They are believed to have changed their plans to take Berlinguer because their intelligence revealed he always traveled in an armored sedan accompanied by a two-car escort of police and bodyguards. His bodyguards were former partisans and trained extensively in anti-terrorist assaults. Since the attackers hated the Communist Party and the Christian Democrats equally, they opted for a "soft" target (Moro) instead of Berlinguer.

Aldo Moro and his escorts made so many mistakes one wonders why the terrorists thought they needed 12 people for such an easy target.

Why was Moro's car not armored? Why did he travel the same predictable route? Why was the escort vehicle in the rear rather than in front? Why were the drivers not better trained to avoid a rear-end collision? And why was the automatic weapon locked up, uselessly, in the trunk of the car?

In addition to the lessons learned from the foregoing incidents, there are some specific aspects to good driving security, starting with alertness and awareness.

Getting to and from the car is often the most critical part of vehicle travel. It is a time for top alertness during which you are looking for anything that might be suspicious. The agent should always precede the client to the car, checking the area and looking for anything that might be suspicious. Don't linger around the car. Get the client inside the vehicle, lock the doors, and leave. Once having arrived at a destination, the car should be stopped as close to the door into the building as possible so that the protectee is not exposed for any longer than necessary.

Once inside the car, the safety rules include fastening seat belts, adjusting all equipment for maximum efficiency, and making certain that the car is in top condition. The gas tank should always be at least half full.

You have read several times that the most

important element of good security driving is to alter your schedule and route, but it is worth stating again. Do not be predictable! Stay alert, and pay attention to any details along your route which might be suspicious or different from the norm.

A state of constant alertness should be maintained as to driving conditions and signs of trouble. If you think you are being followed and are under surveillance, check it out. Take some evasive action by turning several times quickly, varying your speed and stopping at a safe place. Well planned surveillance can and usually will involve at least two teams in different cars or on motorcycles--even on bicycles. Women drivers and children are often used. Surveillance can mean that an incident is being plotted. Keep a good distance between your cars and those ahead of you. When you stop at lights, it is a good idea not to pull up exactly opposite other cars; this makes you too vulnerable. Better to stop opposite an adjacent car's rear fender.

If an attack is made on the vehicle, it can emanate from an ambush, road block, barricade, fake accident, cut-off, gunfire, or bomb.

The most realistic prevention against an implanted bomb is to vary routes and routines so that the client's movements are unpredictable. Driving with the car doors locked and the windows rolled up to within an inch of the top will prevent the entry of hand-thrown bombs. It also prevents having other things tossed in the car or a car door being opened by intruders at a stoplight. This means that the vehicle should be air conditioned for comfort.

Whenever possible, choose a route that requires the fewest possible stops and is wide enough to prevent blocking the vehicle. Well traveled routes are better than shortcuts, and detours should be regarded with suspicion. Routes traveled past police or fire stations are usually a good choice, since a number of official vehicles will travel the same area. When traveling on a multi-lane road, drive in the left lane to minimize the likelihood of someone trying to force you off the road. In the great majority of vehicle attacks the attack has been launched at the driver's side.

The noise level within the car should be kept as low as possible to avoid distractions. Alertness can be maintained by constantly checking the car mirrors. Notice the make and color of cars. If you suspect you are being followed, take evasive maneuvers and get to a safe haven. You should know where the nearest police and fire stations are located along your route.

Extreme caution should be exercised when anything--repeat, anything--causes an abnormal stop. Women and children have been used as decoys, often in connection with a faked accident. If an accident appears to be real, drive on and report it to the authorities. Another problem situation can be one that involves your car in a created accident; for example, a car that stops abruptly in front of you and causes a rear-end collision. Keep a safe distance between your car and others to avoid being boxed in. If there is a fender-bender, stay in the car with the doors locked and the windows up, motor running, and prepared to drive off instantly if anything suspicious happens.

Never pick up hitchhikers, even children with small pets. If the situation calls for it, report what you see to the authorities and let them handle it.

Bear in mind that a terrorist scenario can involve a large number of people playing different and seemingly unrelated roles. Phoney "police" checkpoints, bicyclists, and women with baby carriages have all been used as parts of terrorist scenarios. The difficulty comes in sorting out the legitimate from the fake. If possible, back up, drive away, avoid the incident, and refuse to become boxed in.

Cars stalled or pulled across narrow streets should be viewed as danger signals. The cardinal rule is to *keep moving*. Drive around, and even through, barriers or be prepared to execute quick evasive turnarounds. (An excellent exercise is to practice backing the car at higher than normal speeds--carefully and safely, of course.) Case studies of attacks on vehicles reveal that in the successful attacks the terrorists were able to *stop the vehicle*. Once stopped, the occupants were sitting ducks. Far better to damage the car breaking out of the trap than to lose the client and your own life.

A heavy car can be a fortress of sorts and can sustain an incredible amount of damage and continue to move. If your client's life (and yours) is at stake, you must move quickly. Your car can run with flat tires and a radiator belching steam, climb curbs, and perform heroically for a short period of time and distance, which may be just enough to break out of a trap. Never willingly get out of the car and run if there is a chance of driving out of the trap.

There is a caveat to this, of course. In today's litigious society, one must be aware that the consequences of ramming can involve civil or criminal litigation. A driver may be called on to convince a reasonable jury that his ramming was performed because he feared for the life of his client and his own, and why he felt that fear. He may also be called upon to explain why he felt he had no other option. Any time you use your vehicle as a weapon, you will have to justify that use just as if you had used a gun. You must be able to do so.

Obviously, it is better to avoid the trap rather than having to escape from it.

A tactic seen more in overseas countries than in the United States is the mobile attack, also called the travelling ambush. Sometimes the attack takes place at an intersection, when the target car stops for a red light. More often, a motorbike will simply maneuver alongside the target car while both are in traffic. When the attackers are close enough to the window they want, one rider starts shooting at that window. The maneuverability of the motorbike makes it a good choice for an attack and escape vehicle. It can go down alleys and sidewalks, move between cars stopped in traffic, and go through narrow openings between buildings.

The mobile attack is often difficult for a single car to defend against if the driver is untrained. However, the motorbike attacker is also vulnerable to the actions of the trained driver. What are the driver's defensive options, once he or she is convinced that an attack is about to take place? Options include brake and evade maneuvers, takeouts, and sudden acceleration when stopped, to name a few. It is *not* an option to stay put and shoot it out with the bad guys unless the car will not move.

SURVEILLANCE DETECTION

Potential adversaries are very good at surveillance because they need information--where the target lives and works, his schedule, route(s) of travel, and life style. To get this information, surveillants are in the vicinity for long hours, watching and recording movements, and following the target's vehicle. Does the target leave the house at the same time, sit in the same seat in the car, travel the same streets, park in the same place, and use the same entrance? Wonderful, this makes the attacker's job easier.

How do you recognize and counter auto surveillance? It is helpful to know some of "the tricks of the trade." In most situations, simplicity is a key aspect of appearance both for the surveillants and their vehicles. If the surveillance is being conducted by automobile, the surveillants will generally select the most common, garden-variety car used in the area. Colors of choice are blue, green, gray or other subdued colors, with no distinguishing features--no bumper stickers, fancy wheel covers, hood ornaments, or anything that would draw attention to the vehicle. Surveillance cars are usually neither brand-new or very old, nor are they shiny clean or very dirty. Mid-size cars are usually most easily driven in traffic rather than the very small compacts, and no surveillant worth his reputation would use a big Cadillac or stand-out Jaguar.

Many surveillants use rental cars; however, not for more than a one-time gig, since the license plate may be a giveaway. Rental cars which boldly show the rental agency's name are avoided--they are too easy to spot.

Some surveillance cars are equipped with cut-out switches. A single headlight or taillight can be turned off, then switched back on at will, to easily disguise the car at night.

Rear-vision views have blind spots. This means there are areas behind any car which make it difficult for the driver to observe who may be following him. Cars with both right and left side mirrors have better rear-vision coverage than those with only a driver-side mirror.

Some surveillants carry simple change disguises in the car with them and don them while the subject is turning the corner or momentarily out of view. These simple disguises may be a cap, hat, wig, sunglasses, or jacket which are quickly donned and discarded.

Most serious surveillance is conducted by at least two people to a car, a woman and child being the most innocent appearing team. Two or more teams may be deployed to observe the subject, and they are often in radio contact with each other. In that way, one car can "pick up" the subject, follow him for a distance, then drop off and "hand him over" to the next team. The most usual driving position is for the lead surveillance car to follow the subject car in the lane to the right, keeping one or two cars between itself and the subject car. The backup surveillance car follows approximately the same distance behind the lead car in the left lane. These cars can change positions easily. If a third surveillance car is being used, it may lead the subject car, or it may be stationed at a position along the known route to pick up after the subject car passes by, or it may travel in a parallel direction one street to the left or right. The third car and even a fourth may also follow at a distance of a block or so and switch off periodically with cars one and two.

Sophisticated surveillance may make use of electronic tracking devices. Some beeper devices have a range of up to five miles. Part of your regular survey of your automobile is to look for a possible bug. Most of the bumper beepers need an antenna, which can be a piece of wire. Many are attached by a magnet. Surveillants generally carry binoculars so

that they can track the subject car from a greater distance.

In highway driving along semi-deserted areas, a surveillance car may pass the subject car, then pull into a crossroad when out of view of the subject car. While he waits for the subject car to appear, he may disguise himself and his car. When the subject car passes he can then pick up the chase.

For nighttime surveillance, in addition to cut-out switches, sophisticated teams use night vision equipment. Either the driver or the passenger may use night vision goggles. These do not give the user good depth perception but will allow him to follow at nearly normal speeds without lights, undetected.

Surveillance is often conducted by motorcycle or van. A motorcycle is particularly mobile but may be more easily spotted by the subject. In some areas where speeds are low, such as a residential neighborhood, a bicycle may be used by at least part of the surveillance team.

Detecting surveillance can be difficult, particularly when sophisticated electronic equipment is used and several rotating teams are employed. However, this is fairly unusual unless you are in a very high-risk situation and have been targeted by a top funded group. Even these teams will make mistakes, particularly if your movements are both cautious and unpredictable.

Surveillance generally begins at the target's residence and continues to his destination. If you think you have spotted surveillance, do not rush to elude the surveillants. First, make notes as to time, place, type of vehicle, description of occupants, and all other details, including license plate numbers. If the surveillance continues, notify the authorities, and increase your own security.

As you enter the client's vehicle, look at everyone--pedestrians, bicyclists, dog-walkers, and people in parked vehicles. Make a mental note of their presence. If they suddenly fall in behind you and follow you, you may have a problem. Be a mirror watcher as you drive and look for anyone who seems to pull in and stick to your tail, even if they are several cars back. Watch carefully as you turn corners to see if your suspected tail follows you.

If, after a day or two of observation, you think that you are under surveillance and want to check it further, ask an associate or friends to follow you at a distance of several car lengths or even a block or more behind. When they observe the suspected tails, they can then follow the tails.

Unless you feel you are in eminent danger, be careful about making overly dramatic movements to elude your tail. It will surely tip them off to your knowledge of their presence. That can have two results. The surveillance team may simply change, or it may precipitate some action for which you are not yet prepared. First, you need to report your findings to the authorities who can help you. You have just made the first step in articulating a possible later defense of your actions.

If you suspect that you are being tailed, there are several tactics you may employ. There are low-level tactics which, when performed casually, will not necessarily tip your hand to the surveillants.

You can vary your speed while you watch to see if anyone ahead or behind matches your changes. You can turn a corner and park. Be sure to leave yourself escape room when parking, just in case your surveillant also stops. This is particularly effective at night. If you park and cut your lights (foot off the brake pedal), you will probably spot your tail and you may even fool him. If he is intent on catching you, he may speed past you. When he is gone, you can then reverse direction and leave. Be careful, however, for if the tail is intent on doing you immediate harm and finds you parked, you are vulnerable. You should usually leave the motor running for hasty escape purposes.

You can time your entry into a traffic light by dawdling until just before the yellow light turns red, then driving through, thus stranding your tail. If someone follows through the red light and continues after you, it is possible that you are being followed.

If you can find a freeway off-ramp with an on-ramp directly opposite, you could drive down the off-ramp, cross the boulevard, then slowly drive up the on-ramp while watching for tail activity.

In a residential neighborhood with side streets and alleys, you may quickly turn off the street and into an alley. Rapidly drive to the opposite end of the alley and stop where you can see the corners of the street in front of you. If the tail is using parallel streets he will have duplicated your turns or he will have lost you because you unexpectedly turned into the alley.

There are some more dramatic moves which will undoubtedly tell your tail that you are aware of him. You may wish to employ these only if you think you are in danger, or if your destination is highly secret and you need to get rid of your tail. Making a sudden U-turn or turning the wrong way into a one-way street will generally lose a tail. You must, however, be careful that you do not box yourself into a dangerous situation or endanger anyone else by your maneuvers.

If you are on a freeway, stay in the left, or middle, lane. Wait until you can see an exit ahead, pick your spot and, without using your turn signal, move swiftly into the exit lane at the last moment. With luck, your tail will be trapped in traffic. If he is following closely enough, and if you wait for the last possible moment to make your turn, he may not have enough time to react to be able to exit. You may also try changing lanes in an attempt to get behind the tail, then slow down and exit as he passes the turn-off.

ESCAPE AND EVASION DRIVING

If you anticipate that you may be involved with high speed and/or evasive driving, your high speed radial tires should have 35 pounds of air pressure to prevent rolling the tire off the rim during a J-turn. (Low air pressure also increases the hazard of hydroplaning.) Conventional, off-the-shelf tires will not sustain the heat buildup in high speed driving, and you will need to consult with your tire dealer to procure the best quality available. Police special tires and European specification radials of S, H or V ratings are recommended for speeds over 100 miles per hour. American tires must be marked for heat rating C to A; C is not suitable for high speed driving or escape and evasion maneuvers. Tire and other vehicle related tests are reported in magazines such as *Road and Track*, and *Car and Driver*.

Seat belts and shoulder harness should be used *at all times*, and are an absolute necessity for evasive driving techniques.

There is an inherent risk in escape and evasion driving. While the maneuvers described in this book can be life-saving they are included with a cautionary note.

They should be utilized in emergencies only. Vehicles must be in top condition and equipped with safety devices. Speeds must be kept at a safe minimum, and any practice and execution should be monitored by a professional driver. Do not attempt to perform these maneuvers alone!

Before you can become proficient in performing the tricky escape and evasion maneuvers, you should practice until you have perfected some rather mundane procedures: left-foot braking; trail braking; and, using a vehicle equipped with automatic transmission, changing gears without looking at the gear shift panel. By perfecting these procedures, you will save enough time to perhaps buy that extra margin of time in an emergency, and you will have better control of your vehicle.

Please note that all maneuvers are described for performance with automatic drive equipped vehicles. All vehicles should be of mid-to-large size and sufficiently heavy in weight with good balance.

Left-Foot Braking

Left-foot braking can save vital seconds in an emergency, when instant responsive action is needed. While it seems awkward at first, with practice you can become proficient in using this technique. However, do not let your left foot hover over or upon the brake.

With left-foot braking, you keep your left foot on the floor until it is time to brake. Bring your left foot from the floor to the center of the brake pedal, utilizing the ball of the foot rather than the toes for maximum application of foot pressure. As soon as you have completed the braking maneuver you should remove your foot entirely from the brake pedal and put it back on the floor. The exception is when you have stopped and need the brake pedal to remain stopped until you move the car again. Be certain not to "ride" the brake pedal as it will cause the brakes to overheat and wear out sooner than is normal.

Trail Braking

To put it simply, with trail braking you gradually increase brake pedal pressure to maximum braking, hold that pressure, then gradually decrease pressure. Let us use the example of approaching a blind curve at speed. As you approach the curve start to apply brake pedal pressure and gradually increase the pressure until you have achieved desired brake adhesion (do not jam the brakes to the floor). Continue to hold that pressure as the car slows, and as it slows continue to gently increase some brake pressure. As you reach the entry point, you must gradually decrease the brake pedal pressure because you will need more of the adhesion for turning than stopping. Continue to release more brake pressure, gradually, attempting to keep the forward/backward weight balanced, until you have completely released the brake pressure. Then gradually start to accelerate as you reach the apex of the curve.

Gear Selection Without Looking

While most drivers of automatic transmission equipped cars look at the gear marks each time they move the gear selector lever, it is not necessary. With practice, you can do this blindfolded.

Generally, on almost all cars, the lever does not have to be lifted first, nor the thumb button release punched, when moving from REVERSE to

NEUTRAL or DRIVE, or from DRIVE to NEUTRAL. Moving from REVERSE to DRIVE requires only a gentle downward pull until the lever stops by itself. The only time you should have to pull the lever or push the button first is when taking it out of PARK. All other times the lever should be moved until it stops, then the button pushed or the lever gently pulled.

To Change from PARK to DRIVE. If the shift is a steering column mount, you must lift the lever gently toward your face, then pull down gently toward the floor. When you have passed the first felt or heard click, you can continue pulling toward the floor but let the spring action pull it back toward the dashboard. It will stop in DRIVE. You will bypass DRIVE if you fail to let the spring pull the lever back toward the dashboard.

If the shift is a console mount, you must push the release button with your thumb and gently pull the handle toward the rear. When you have passed the first felt or heard click, you may continue pulling toward the rear, but you must release the thumb button. It will stop in DRIVE. You will bypass DRIVE if you fail to release the thumb button.

To Change from REVERSE to DRIVE. Do not lift lever and do not depress thumb button. Gently slap the handle down. It will stop in DRIVE.

To Change from DRIVE to REVERSE. Push the lever up until it stops. Depress the thumb button or gently lift the lever. Gently move the lever up one felt or heard click. You are now in REVERSE.

K-Turns

There are two basic types of K-turns. Both may be done from either the right or left lane. The first one is called the same-side backing K-turn and is done while you are still moving forward.

Same-Side Backing K-Turn. Usually, when stopped on a street, a car will be on one side of the street or the other. If it is stopped in the center of the

road, the driver can make a backing K-turn to either side of the road. In this example, the car has stopped on the right side of the road. Traffic is blocked ahead, and the driver does not have enough road width to enable him to make a full U-turn. The driver has the left foot on the brake and the selector lever in DRIVE. Seeing that the traffic is blocked and that there are cars coming up behind him, the driver decides to quickly perform a backing K-turn.

While keeping an eye on cars in front and behind, and without wasting time to look at the gear selector indicator, immediately shift to REVERSE and start backing slowly. At the same time, gradually start turning the steering wheel to the left. As the right front tire gets farther from the right edge of the road, increase steering input by palming the wheel around with the left hand until the wheel has reached full lock; that is, 100% left. It is important to remember when the front tire is close to the curb or edge of the road to gradually increase steering input as the car moves backward.

If there is too much turn too soon, the arc of the front of the car turning will carry the tire off the roadway or into the curb. When backing, turn the steering wheel in the direction you want the rear of the car to go. If you want the car to back to the left, turn the steering wheel left. If you are on the other side of the road and want the back of the car to move toward the right, turn the steering wheel to the right.

Regardless of which side of the road you start on, back as far as possible to the other side of the road while turning the wheel 100% as soon as possible. Stop the car just before the rear wheels reach the edge of the road or curb. Without wasting time looking at the gear selector lever, drop it down to DRIVE. Remove the left foot from the brake. As the car starts to creep forward, immediately palm the wheel 100% in the direction you will be going and begin to accelerate. As the car starts toward the desired lane, let the wheel start coming out (rather than steering it out) as you move forward.

SAME SIDE BACKING K-TURN

Blockage

Start input of gradual turning arc.

Start increasing turning arc toward 100%.

100% turn.

When stopped, turn right to 100%

Start letting wheel come out.

Straighten wheel as you angle toward the new lane.

CROSSOVER K-TURN

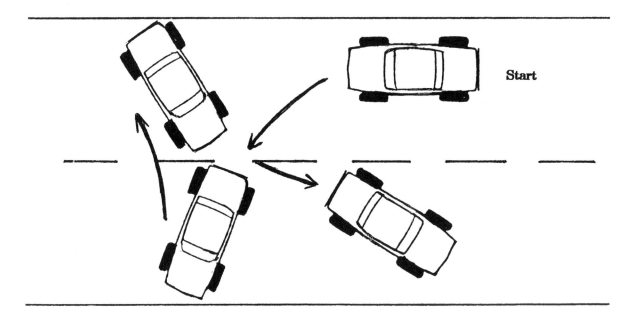

Crossover K-Turn. In this example we shall assume the car is in the right lane and driving forward at 30 mph. The driver sees that traffic is blocked in front and that there are cars coming up behind him.

Trail brake to under 10 mph while driving in a straight line. Continue trail braking while starting to turn the steering wheel to the left. About halfway across the road the speed will have been reduced to under 5 mph. Start trail braking off while palming the steering wheel 100% left. Complete the stop just before the front wheels reach the edge of the road. Without wasting time looking at the gear selector lever, immediately go from DRIVE to REVERSE with the left foot on the brake pedal. Release the brake. When the car starts moving back, palm the wheel 100% right and continue backing until the rear wheels reach the edge of the road without going off, and stop. Again, without wasting time looking at the selector lever, drop down to DRIVE, then remove the left foot from the brake. As the car starts to move forward, palm the wheel back to the left 100% and continue to accelerate. Start letting the steering wheel come out and continue on down the street.

The driver was in the right lane going

forward. He trail braked and turned across the road into the left lane and, immediately upon stopping, backed up into the right lane. As soon as he stopped, he immediately pulled forward to the new direction of travel. There was no wasted motion; he utilized the full road without hitting a curb or dropping his tires off the pavement. Properly executed, this K-turn is clean, quick, and causes no discomfort to the occupants of the car.

K-turns are illegal on many city streets. If you wish to practice these turns, you should check with your local police authority for a legal place to do so.

FORWARD AND REVERSE 180'S

The fastest way to reverse direction of travel in an attack situation is to perform a "180." When performed on hard, dry surfaces, this type of turn can be very damaging to the automobile transmission, suspension, and tires. If performed incorrectly, the transmission can be damaged to the point that the car is no longer driveable. This, of course, severely limits escape potential. It is dangerous. There always exists the possibility of rolling the car. These facts mean that *the maneuver should be attempted only in an extreme emergency, when under imminent life-*

threatening attack. This maneuver should never be practiced alone--there should be a certified, qualified instructor present to supervise the practice session.

It is important to remember that the maneuver should always be performed at slow speed. The objective is to swap ends on the car and immediately escape. Not only is it very dangerous to perform this maneuver at speeds higher than 30 mph, it is unworkable. Consider this example. The driver moving forward at 60 mph performs a Forward 180 without rolling the car; however, his forward momentum is too great and, although he has swapped ends, the car is still travelling in the original direction, backward. When he attempts to accelerate and escape, the wheels try to spin in the opposite direction from the momentum, creating too much stress on the transmission and the engine. As a result, the engine stalls, or the transmission breaks from the strain. Either way, the driver has swapped ends but has not escaped. Even at speeds in excess of 30 mph, the forward momentum may be too great for the car to completely stop and immediately reverse the direction of travel. When doing a Forward 180, the objective is to synchronize everything so that when the back of the car has completely turned to the 180 degrees, the forward momentum has also ceased, and the car can accelerate immediately in the other direction. If the momentum is too great in the original direction, you cannot change direction until the momentum has been depleted.

The maneuver can be performed when driving forward or when driving in reverse. When driving in reverse, the direction of the original momentum does not have to be reversed; therefore, there is less strain on the transmission if the procedure is properly performed. If the procedure is done incorrectly, the strain on the engine and transmission is the same as with the Forward 180. The Forward 180 is performed by locking only the rear wheels and turning the steering wheel quickly. The Reverse 180 is accomplished by turning the steering wheel sharply and shifting. Depending upon the speed you are going in reverse, you may or may not want to use some braking. The best performance is achieved at low speed with no use of the brakes.

A 180 is used to escape from the direction of an attack without taking the time to make a U-turn or K-turn and without driving off the road. The emergency brakes must be in good working order for the Forward 180 because they are required to independently lock the rear wheels. The driver should be in a good seating position and properly belted in with both the lap belt and shoulder harness. Without them, the driver will find himself sliding across the front seat unable to reach the controls. Finally, the driver must allow himself a brief moment for a thought process--which way he will be turning the car. If he is on the right side of an alley and attempts a Reverse 180 to the right, the rear of the car will end up in the building wall on the right, thus stopping the car. He is now a "sitting duck," pinned broadside in the alley.

J Turn or Reverse 180 (to the Left)

.   If the car is moving forward, come to a stop, and put the car in reverse. The left hand is on the steering wheel at 1:00. Slide it down to the right so that the back of the hand is facing you, and the grip is at about 5:00.

.   Floor the throttle and accelerate only three or four car lengths.

.   Brace the left foot on the floor--keep it there.

.   Push gear selector lever down to NEUTRAL.

.   Yank the steering wheel hard around, all the way from 5:00 back to the top and continue around and down to 6:00 (more, if you can do it). This nearly full circle motion should be done in one constant movement and as hard and fast as possible. The movement is extremely aggressive, nearly equal to the force needed to throw a baseball.

.   When the car has reached about a three-quarter rotation, push the gear selector down the final notch to DRIVE and start gradually depressing the throttle. Let the wheel start coming out. Accelerate and drive away.

REVERSE 180 TO THE LEFT

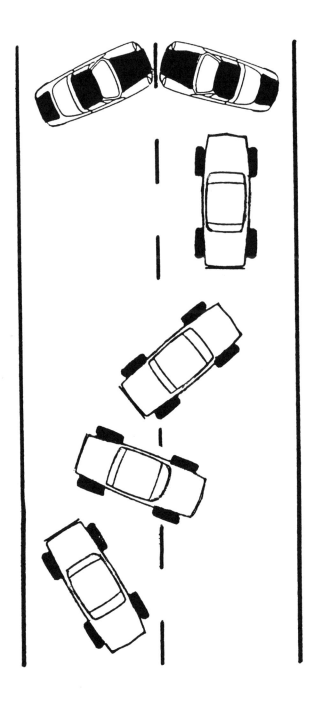

A.   When car is at full stop, put in reverse. Full throttle backward for three car lengths and drop it into neutral.

B.   Take foot off throttle, yank steering wheel to the left 360 degrees. From 5:00, around to 6:00. Yank as hard and fast as possible.

C.   Hold the steering wheel in place while the front slides around. Do not touch the brake.

D.   As the car begins to reach 180 degree rotation let the wheel start coming out, shift into drive. Start accelerating away from the blockade.

Reverse 180 (to the Right)

The procedures are the same as with the Reverse 180 to the left except:

. The car starts on the left side of the road.

. The left hand is placed at 7:00 rather than at the 5:00 position.

. The left hand turns from 7:00 to the top and continues around and down to 6:00.

180's performed on wet or slippery surfaces cause less strain on the car as there is less friction to overcome. Nonetheless, it induces stress that the car is not designed to accept. It follows, therefore, that this is not a maneuver you should perform "for fun" with your best vehicle.

When performing a Reverse 180 you should remember that it is usually better to perform it as soon after starting backward as possible. As long as the car is going backward in a straight line, you are still a good target for incoming fire through the windshield. The sooner the car starts spinning around and spoiling the attackers' aim, the better. You must be sure that the car will not slide backward into a wall or off the road while reversing, so do a quick thought process as to which way you want to turn the wheel. If there is not enough width to perform the maneuver, you have little choice other than to continue backing in a slalom manner until there is enough space to perform the reverse.

Bootleg Turn or Forward 180 (to the Left)

Car Equipped with Foot Pedal Emergency Brake.

. Drive forward at 20 mph on the right side of the road. The left hand holds out the brake release knob. The left foot is poised to jam down the emergency brake pedal (using the strength of the ball of the foot). The right hand is palm down on the wheel at 12:00.

. Jam down and hold the emergency brake pedal to lock the rear wheels (you should hear and feel them sliding).

. Jog the steering wheel slightly to the right, to upset the balance; then, immediately hard left to 6:00. The steering wheel must be turned quickly and aggressively.

. As the car approaches 180-degree rotation, remove the left foot from the emergency brake pedal, release the left hand from the brake handle, and start acceleration. Don't floor the throttle; just start pressing it.

. As the car starts accelerating, let the steering wheel start coming out, and proceed in the new direction.

Car Equipped with Hand Emergency Brake Lever. These are essentially the same procedures as with the foot operated emergency brake pedal except:

. Grip the handle with the right hand; depress and hold the release button with the right thumb.

. Left hand on the steering wheel at 12:00.

. Yank up and hold the lever rather than jamming the foot pedal.

. As the car approaches 180-degree rotation, quickly lower the right hand lever and start acceleration.

Forward 180 (to the Right)

The procedures are the same as for the Forward 180 to the left except:

. Drive on the left side of the road.

. The steering wheel will now be jogged slightly to the left and quickly turned hard right to 6:00.

FORWARD 180 TO THE LEFT

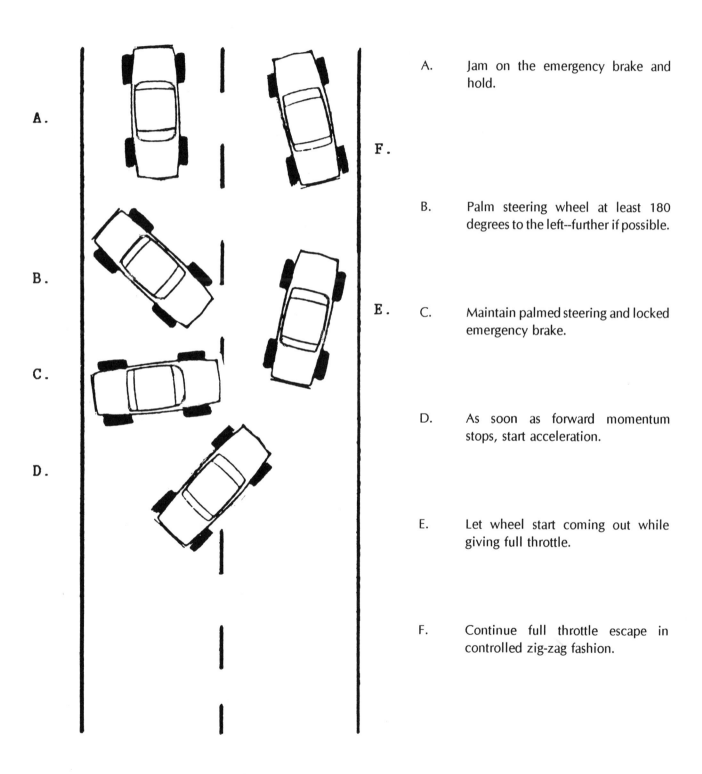

A.   Jam on the emergency brake and hold.

B.   Palm steering wheel at least 180 degrees to the left--further if possible.

C.   Maintain palmed steering and locked emergency brake.

D.   As soon as forward momentum stops, start acceleration.

E.   Let wheel start coming out while giving full throttle.

F.   Continue full throttle escape in controlled zig-zag fashion.

Brake and Evade

Brake and evade is the procedure a trained driver will use to avoid a sudden hazard, rather than the untrained and typical driver's reaction of locking all wheels in panic and skidding right into the hazard. Usually, evasion braking is aggressive and firm but with a great deal of finesse, and is often referred to as "threshold braking." This can be used in conjunction with trail braking to allow aggressive steering wheel movement without losing turning adhesion. When confronted with a sudden hazard or obstacle, the driver must be able to brake and slow down, then steer around the hazard or stop before hitting it.

Threshold braking means rapidly escalating brake pedal pressure to the point just before wheel lock-up occurs. It is similar to trail braking except that the pressure is applied quickly. Since it is very easy to lock the wheels when this procedure is used, it is important to remember to release a pound or two of pressure when you hear the tires start to slide. This allows the tires to start barely rolling again.

Threshold braking, when used in conjunction with turning movements, will require release of several pounds of brake pedal pressure while turning.

Threshold braking is basically the application of faster, heavier trail braking. You still hinge the pressure on. The difference is that you hinge it faster and harder. The objective is to reduce all the speed you can prior to reaching the hazard, so that you can input the aggressive turning necessary to steer around the hazard. When aggressively turning, some of the brake pedal pressure must be relieved. When most of the tire's capacity for traction is used for braking, there is not enough left over for turning. If most of the tire's traction is being used for turning, there is not much left over for braking.

Improper threshold braking leaves the wheels locked too long, and the melting rubber causes you to skid into the hazard. Proper threshold braking started at the same speed and distance will allow you to stop in time. Proper threshold braking coupled with improper turning will likely put you sideways in the road or worse, off the road.

These are the basic rules for brake and evade:

1.   ON THE BRAKES! Rapidly input brake pressure until tires make noise but are not locked (just before lockup). This noise will sound more like a low pitched moan than a loud screech. (This is the 15% skidding and 85% rolling.)

2.   OFF THE BRAKES! You are removing some of the tires' braking traction so they have sufficient capacity for turning. Rather than taking the foot completely off the brake, take off two or three pounds of pressure. If the wheels do lock, release enough pressure within one second to allow them to start turning. Keep the *reduced* pressure applied to the brakes through the turning movement.

3.   TURN! If you are not able to stop in time, you must steer around the hazard while lightly braking. You must turn the steering wheel very hard and fast. The turn will be more like a severe yank on the steering wheel rather than simply guiding the wheel. Movement of the wheel should not be overly exaggerated. Movement will usually only be about 12 to 16 inches one direction (depending on the steering on your car); then it should immediately be brought back to center position.

4.   TURN! Turn the wheel very hard and fast in the other direction. You have already turned one direction sharply and then centered the steering wheel to the straight-ahead driving position. Immediately return the wheel to the center position.

The amount of the braking and steering input will depend on proximity to the hazard, the speed you are travelling, how wide the opening on either side of the hazard is, etc. The idea is to brake before trying to turn rather than turning hard first and then attempting to brake, and to turn the steering wheel no more than is absolutely necessary to steer around the hazard.

One last word on wheel lockup. You might hear a squeal from the inside rear wheel during the turning movement. Since there has been so much weight transfer away from it during the turn the noise and minimal lockup of that wheel is, by itself, of little consequence.

Takeouts

A take-out of another car is a maneuver used to escape from a moving attacker without losing control or driveability of your car. Make no mistake, the procedure is not intended to be used indiscriminately against any driver whom you think *might* be an attacker; you must be certain that you are being attacked. As with many of the other maneuvers described in this book, *the laws governing use of deadly force apply to take-outs.*

If an attacker has pulled up next to you and is attempting to force you off the road or fire at you or your client, you must quickly evaluate your escape options. Can you out-horsepower the attacker and escape through traffic? Will you shoot it out while driving? Will you smash into him, side by side, just like in the movies and force him off the road into the guard rail? None of the above are very viable alternatives. If necessary, you can perform a take-out on a much heavier car than the one you are driving and still escape in your original direction of travel. You must use good technique to spin the attack car off the road without losing control of your own vehicle. *Remember that you are using potential deadly force.* If the maneuver is performed at speeds of 35 to 40 mph or more, you run the risk of flipping the attack car and killing its occupants. If you panic and hit your own brakes in the middle of a higher speed maneuver you run the risk of t-boning the attack car with a second impact and possibly disabling your car. If you try a take-out against a professional at a speed of 35 or 40 mph he may have enough momentum to simply go with the flow, perform a 360-degree turn, and be right back on your tail. If he is good enough, he can also recover from speeds as slow as 25 or 30 mph. Many police officers are routinely taught this recovery maneuver.

The take-out maneuver should be performed at relatively slow speed. It maximizes your potential

to spin the attack car off the road and sideways, so that he will have to use several precious seconds trying to get his car going straight again. In the meantime, you will be able to escape. If an attack takes place while you are driving 55 mph, and your decision is to perform a take-out, you must brake and slow down. Usually, the best speed to perform the take-out is about 20 mph, at which speed you can take out the attacker without damaging your car extensively. If hits are performed while going too fast, you run the risk of caving your fender into the tire, restricting both your forward motion and your steering.

An attack car approaching from the rear is not an attack car until you can articulate how he is attacking. If he is simply approaching at a high rate of speed and there appear to be several occupants in the car, you may have trouble explaining why you took him off the road when he attempted to pass you. If you see guns pointing at you, a defense is possible. If he makes contact with you, a defense might be possible. If you had previously received information from the authorities that a certain group was trying to kidnap or kill your client and that they had been seen driving a late model gray Toyota sedan, and such a car appeared, you will *not* have enough legitimate reason to take it off the road. You do have reason to watch it closely, play the "what if" game, and be prepared.

One approach to performing the take-out maneuver is to do it as he overtakes you in the other lane. The other approach is to do it as you overtake him. The better technique is to take him out as he overtakes you. To do so, you must reduce speed, quickly, to 20 to 25 mph, to minimize disabling damage to your car. You must brake hard, (he soon will, too) time your contact, and drive him off the road. You must drive the extreme front corner of your car into his "sweet spot" for maximum results. This spot is toward the back and on the side of his car closest to your car. It is defined as the area on the side toward you, measured forward from his back bumper no more than 18 inches. It is undesirable to hit near his rear wheel or any point forward, especially if he is heavier than you. The only reason for deliberately hitting farther forward is to attempt to spoil the attackers' aim if they are shooting back toward you. The weight of the car you are trying to take out is relatively unimportant unless you miss the sweet spot and hit too far forward, around the wheel or forward of it. If that happens, you must slow down and time your second hit for the correct spot.

The procedures for the take-out are as follows:

. Allow the attack car to slightly pass you, not more than two feet to the side. One foot apart is better. If you are too far apart, you telegraph your movement to the attack car and allow him time to maneuver. Also, you may just slam into him at contact, rather than driving through him.

. Aim the front corner of your car at his sweet spot. If you turn into him just when his rear wheel reaches your front bumper, you will miss the sweet spot unless he is moving much faster than you are. You must wait until his rear wheel is past your front bumper.

. Turn your wheels into the attack car, contact the sweet spot, and accelerate full throttle. Maintain acceleration and steering while the front of your car pushes him on around. You must accelerate all the way through impact and not lift up on the throttle. The other car will actually roll around in front of yours, off the side of the road, leaving you free to accelerate and speed away. You must resist the normal urge to apply brake pressure. Either lifting up on the throttle or applying brakes will reduce your momentum and ability to push him around.

The basic principles of leverage are what allow you to push a heavier car off the road. If you hit forward of the sweet spot you will be attempting leverage against his two axles which carry the full weight of his car. If you push as far behind his rear axle as practical, you leverage behind one light axle (the rear of the car) and force his car to pivot on the other (the front axle with the weight of the engine and transmission).

If an attacker is attempting to take you out and you are unable to avoid him, there are some steps you can take to recover.

. Do not attempt to overcorrect your steering; that is, do not turn in the direction of the skid.

. Do turn away from the skid. If your back end is being pushed to the left, turn sharply to the right. If being pushed to the right, turn hard left. Allow your car to spin.

. You are now faced with two options. You may continue the spin for a full 360 degrees and come back up on his tail. Your second option is to reverse your direction of travel and escape in the opposite direction. Your choice will probably depend upon the density of traffic and the distance to an exit.

Because of the inherent danger of this maneuver it should never be practiced without safety equipment (helmet), a reliably equipped and powered vehicle, and the supervision of a trained, competent instructor, nor should it be practiced at speeds higher than 20 to 25 mph.

Ramming

Without question, the most extreme of all the evasion maneuvers performed with a vehicle is ramming. The technique is designed to allow the driver to successfully ram and escape from a vehicle roadblock without losing his driveability. As with the other evasion maneuvers, ramming is best done at slow speeds. The technique is not designed to be used on heavy busses, dump trucks, or bulldozers. It is designed for the usual cars or vans. The sweet spot of the attack car referred to in takeouts is also utilized in ramming maneuvers. The objective is to push steadily through the barricade rather than colliding with it and disabling your own car.

Under what circumstances would you ram through a barricade? Let us take the following situation. You and the client are in the client's car and are being pursued by a car whose occupants have already fired at you. The police have been

TAKE-OUT. Drive to within one foot of the side of car. Keep speed at 20 mph or less!

A. Line up the sweet spot.

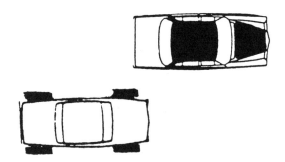

B. Turn into sweet spot. Do not lift on the throttle.

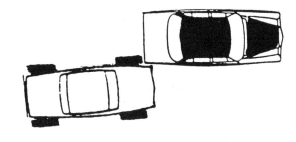

C. Maintain gentle steering arc and constant throttle pressure.

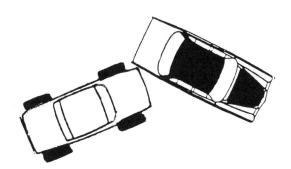

D. Do not brake and do not lift on the throttle.

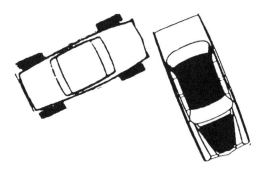

E. The momentum of his back end throws him out of the way.

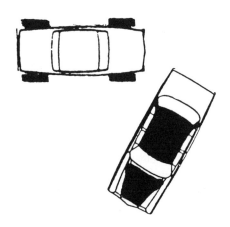

F. Accelerate!

notified by car phone, and your line is open to them. They are en route but not yet there. As you crest a hill, you see directly in front of you a car parked broadside, blocking the road. Flames are coming from the interior of the car, and at least two people pointing guns at you are crouched on either side of the road. There is no avenue of escape to either side, and the other attackers are close behind you. You certainly do not want to stop and shoot it out with them. Your decision is to ram the road block, escape, and hope the police will arrive soon.

Once the decision to ram is made, you must drive into the sweet spot on the block car, push it out of the road and escape. If you are going too fast when you hit the blocker, you may push him out of the way; however, you may not be able to drive your car away.

A reminder is in order: *this is an extreme and dangerous option. The driver must weigh whether the apparent life-threatening circumstance is worth accepting the inherent risks to life and limb by ramming.*

Once the decision is made, the driver must slow the vehicle. His ram speed should not exceed 10 mph. (Yes, most cars can be pushed away at 10 mph.) Do not entertain the thought of completely stopping the car, just prior to the ram, in an attempt to "fool" the attackers. When you stop, even momentarily, you have done what they wanted to make you do. Stopping the car makes you a better target. They will not wait for you to stop the car and get out to negotiate before using all their available firepower.

Your goal should be to brake hard, timing it so that you have slowed to 10 mph no more than one car length before impact. Then, begin to accelerate. Hit the sweet spot, and drive right through the block car.

These are the correct ramming procedures:

.   Approach the block car. Brake hard to slow the car to 10 mph and time your braking so that you

reach that speed about one car length prior to impact.

.   Aim for the lightest end, as it is the easiest to push. The lightest end, of course, is usually the trunk end. The heavy end with the engine will not push around as easily as the end without the engine.

.   Determine the sweet spot on the block car and use only that same amount of the corner of your front bumper. Again, the sweet spot will be the last 15 to 18 inches of the block car.

.   When you are about one-half car length from the block car and lined up with the sweet spot, accelerate hard and continue. RAM THE BLOCK CAR. You must make contact with the sweet spot to insure maximum momentum and leverage. DO NOT LIFT OFF THE THROTTLE AND DO NOT BRAKE!

.   At contact, continue to accelerate and push the rear end of the car away from you. Your intent is not to hit him hard and knock him around. Your intent is to make contact with enough momentum that you can continue to push him out of your way.

.   If you hit the block car at 25 mph, you run the risk of caving your front fender in against your tire and stopping your own car. If you hit his wheel with the center of your car, you run the risk of driving his axle into your engine. If you hit the block car at speeds higher than 25 mph, you will run the risk of injuring or killing yourself.

.   If you hit him broadside in a t-bone fashion, you will probably stop your car in the side of the block car.

.   Follow through and escape. As the impact happens, continue acceleration and drive through the collision. There is a normal tendency to hit the brakes at some point before or during the collision. Resist this urge. You will stop in the middle of the place you don't want to be.

.   As soon as you feel your car break loose from the impact, continue acceleration and commence to zig-zag in a shallow S-curve manner. This will assist

RAMMING

Slow to 10 mph and line up on the sweet spot. At 1/2 car length from stopper. Floor the throttle and make contact with the side.

Continue acceleration and push stopper car around. Maintain acceleration and straight steering.

Escape while continuing to accelerate and drive in a controlled zig-zag manner.

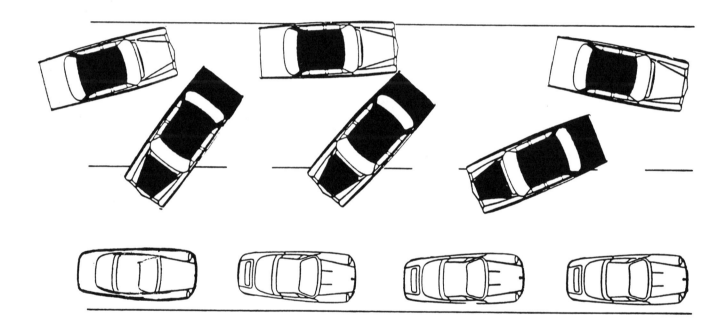

in spoiling the attackers' aim until you are out of effective range.

If, for any reason, you have to ram the engine end of the block car, cut the sweet spot area down to 12 inches, ram, and accelerate through.

Ramming maneuvers should never be practiced on your own. It is imperative to have proper equipment, safety helmet, and the guidance of a trained and competent instructor.

MOTORCADES AND CONVOYS

Motorcades are troublesome and are particularly so if the agent has no logistical control over them. Your client may never need to be a part of a motorcade, but, if he is, you must be prepared to deal with several contingencies. Some problems are: your client may be asked to ride in an open car; your client will probably be asked to ride in a car without you; and/or there may be confusion as to exactly where he is to ride and with whom.

Try to position yourself so that you are not separated from your client. One ploy is to ask if the protectee can provide his own car and driver, which provides you with an excuse to remain with your client and to keep control of your own situation. If there is a problem, get your client away! This means that you must be familiar with the route, the emergency services located nearby, and the best means of reaching them.

If you can do so, eliminate motorcycle escorts. Motorcycles are noisy, can be unstable, and attract attention. Because of the slow speeds of most motorcades, the motorcycle riders have a difficult time simply keeping their machines steady. It has happened more than once that a motorcycle rider has slipped under a motorcade vehicle. If you must have motorcycles, try to restrict their use to intersections for traffic control. Marked cars are preferable for lead cars and can be very useful.

If yours is the responsibility for selecting the motorcade route, you should select both a main and subsidiary route. Get a good map and drive the route yourself, preferably at the same time as the scheduled parade, with the same traffic conditions. Then, check it out with the police. Don't expect the police to select your route for you, but ask them to review your plan. Keep in mind that your route should be one that allows you to control some of the safety factors. Identify the closest hospitals with emergency rooms and be aware of the best emergency routes to reach them. Get recommendations on the available ambulance services. Some are volunteer services, and unregulated. Many times an ambulance service will

take you only to specific hospitals, not necessarily to the hospital of your choice or the nearest one.

Put together a scenario, taking a close look at any potential trouble spots along the route where you may wish to increase speed. Decide how many cars you will need, the order of procession, need for escorts, and the number of security agents who will be needed to protect your client and other dignitaries. Arrange for radio communication between your car and the lead and follow-up cars. Find out the size of the expected crowd, whether any demonstrators are expected, and any known threat factors.

Be certain that your driver(s) know the route. Provide them with a map that is marked with color pencil or highliter, together with typed instructions that can be clearly read.

Intersections and turns can be physically marked by placing reflective silver duct tape on the telephone poles or street signs. This stands out even at night. Small motorcades have lost their way in the past. It is extremely embarrassing to have your motorcade meandering aimlessly through the city.

Liaison must be established between the private security and the law enforcement contingent. All motorcycle and marked car escort drivers must be briefed as to route and the intersections which need to be blocked. Contingency plans must be set up for handling of, and response to, any incidents or accidents. Who will be in charge? Someone must have an overall responsibility and authority for the operation. Will this person be on site during the motorcade? Where? How will radio communication be handled? Very high level security motorcades require the use of advance cars and possibly a helicopter to over-fly and scout the area.

The first advance car should drive the route about 15 to 20 minutes before the departure of the motorcade, visually checking for stalled vehicles, possible threats, unplanned construction, etc. The second advance vehicle should run the same route five minutes before motorcade departure. Any problems encountered by either advance car can be reported back, and departure delayed.

Extremely high level security motorcades, such as the visit of the Pope, require extraordinary planning measures. Entire streets may be blocked off with rope barriers, mail boxes and trash containers along the entire parade route examined and sealed, manhole covers sealed, and culverts and storm drains examined. Businesses along the parade route will be interviewed and employees background-checked, upper floors of buildings checked out, and a request made to keep windows closed. Empty buildings and overpasses may be manned with security, parked cars removed, and SWAT countersnipers posted on roofs of buildings along the route.

Convoys

Under most conditions, you will find yourself at best with a two-car convoy, with the second car used to provide back-up security. However, depending upon the extent of the protective coverage given your client, you may find yourself in a convoy of three to five cars. The goals are simple: to provide protection and a smooth ride, to avoid creating an accident, and to not lose each other! It may sound simple, but it can be difficult to execute on a crowded freeway. Convoy driving is difficult and demanding. The convoy driver needs all the skills of the single car driver and, additionally, must be alert to radio communications and anticipate convoy movements. Convoy driving requires training and practice.

In convoy driving, the distance between the cars must be kept to a minimum to avoid letting other cars get in between, and yet not rear-end each other. A constant in any convoy situation is that the cars should be no closer than one car length apart and not more than 1-1/2 car lengths apart. Left-foot braking is useful for the instant response and added control it provides.

Radio communication is important to signal lane changes, passing maneuvers, exits, and any problems. There are two schools of thought on radio commands and acknowledgement. One school recommends that drivers respond with an acknowledgement to the detail leader's commands. The second, and recommended, school of thought maintains that communications be kept to an absolute minimum. The detail leader does the communicating and the other driver(s) usually does not respond verbally; his acknowledgement is to respond immediately! The exceptions to this are radio check procedures and the need to communicate suspicious activity or potential threat to the leader.

The radio check should be simple. The leader is usually in the lead car. The cars are numbered by their position in the convoy at that particular time with the lead car being Car 1 and the tail car being Car 5. The client car is usually Car 3 and is not identified on the radio as "client car." The leader asks, "Car 2 ready?" The reply is, "2 ready." The leader will ask, "Car 3 ready?" The reply is simply, "3 ready." The same procedure is used to check all the other cars. It is not necessary to reply, "Car 2 is ready--over." The simple acknowledgment, "2 ready," is sufficient. The driver of the car has just acknowledged to the leader that he has the specified people in his car, the radio is working, the engine is running, and he is ready to go. If, for example, the engine on Car 4 has not started, the driver says, "4 not ready". The leader does not ask him for a specific reason; he simply waits a moment and re-checks. On the second check, if the driver of Car 4 is still not ready, he then advises the leader of the problem so a decision can be made. If he is now ready, he just responds, "4 ready." There is no additional reply necessary at that time.

The next communication from the leader is, "Convoy--forward." This signals all drivers to start moving in unison. The driver behind has the responsibility of maintaining space with the car in front of him. Drivers maintain their spacing while accelerating, driving steady, slowing, or turning. If each driver waits to start moving until after the car in front of him has started to move, the lead car may be doing 20 mph while the tail car is still standing still. That violates the spacing principle.

Since convoy vehicles do not have flashing red or blue lights, you have no authority to drive faster than the speed limit. You have no authority to stop people or block roads. You have no authority to cut in front of other traffic. Nonetheless, you may be ordered to do something of this nature by the team leader. You can only perform his orders when it is safe to do so. Any driving violations are your responsibility, not his, and not the client's. If you have a collision with another car while performing any maneuver, the local traffic laws apply, and you will probably be cited by the authorities. If you hit another car while performing a maneuver and continue on with your convoy, you will be guilty of felony hit-and-run in most states.

You must remember that even though you are driving in a convoy in a high risk threat situation, you are still responsible for your own driving actions. If you perform a lane change or attempt to block another car from coming around or run him off the road, you must be able to articulate why that car was an imminent and dangerous threat to you or the client. If you make an attempt to block a car, hit him in the process, and fail to stay there until the authorities arrive, you have problems when it is determined later that the car was not a threat to the convoy, merely an aggressive driver who had the legal right to be in that lane. *Extreme caution must be used when performing any convoy maneuver.*

Maneuvers

It is understood that when the leader commands a maneuver other than "Convoy--forward," Car 2 pulls out for it first. He automatically does it unless the detail leader specifies another car. If the leader calls for two maneuvers, Car 2 pulls out and automatically performs the first maneuver called. Car 4 pulls out immediately after Car 2, and performs the second order. They do it automatically and without being designated. The first car called out is the first car to come back into the convoy automatically. It is the responsibility of the detail leader to call the cars out in the proper order for performing and returning to the convoy.

"Lane change left -- now!"

(A)   Car 2 immediately pulls into the left lane and slows to at least one-half speed.

(B)   The instant Car 3 clears the front of Car 2, Car 2 responds, "clear." Cars 1 and 3 immediately pull into the left lane in front of Car 2 and continue at regular speed. The only car slowing is Car 2. You now have old #'s 1, 3, and 2 in the left lane.

(C)   As Cars 1 and 3 are moving into the left lane, Car 4 accelerates to the old Car 2 slot. Car 5 clears Car 2.

(D)   When Car 5 clears the front of Car 2, both 4 and 5 merge into the left lane. You now have the old numbers 1,4,3,5,2 in order. Without any additional communication, cars are renumbered in order 1,2,3,4,5. The only cars maintaining their old numbers are 1 and 3. There is no further communication after 2 responds "clear" as a signal for 1 and 3 to move in front of him. It is the detail leader's responsibility to make certain that all lane changes are called far enough in advance to allow completion of the maneuver before coming to the proximity of slower traffic in the right lane. When done properly, 1 and 3 merge into the left lane in unison, then 4 and 5 merge into the left lane in unison. When in doubt, think Car 1 is always 1. There is almost always a car between 1 and 3. Car 3 is the client car unless it becomes disabled. Cars now take on the number and responsibility of the new space they are in.

A lane change to the right is a mirror image of a lane change to the left. When travelling on a street that has two lanes in the direction of travel, lane changes may be utilized at will to aid in getting the cars through traffic. The driver of Car 2 acts as a rolling block for traffic in the lane he went into. In effect, he will slow down any traffic in the lane behind him. By severely reducing his speed, he allows the rest of the convoy to come around him in the shortest possible space and time. Car 2 must time his acceleration as Car 5 merges in front of him so that the spacing interval is maintained. When the lane change is completed, the cars take on the new position number in the convoy according to their new

LANE CHANGE LEFT

A.

B.

C.

D.

position. Rather than each car having a specific name or number, they are simply numbered according to position, which changes with each maneuver.

"I need a block left--now!"

The convoy is approaching a certain intersection and the leader wants to block off the traffic coming from the left. The reason for the block left could be a suspicious car lingering at the intersection. For the purpose of this exercise, we will assume there is a stop sign for that traffic. At the command, "now," Car 2 changes lanes when safe to do so and passes Car 1.

Car 2 proceeds to the intersection and stops perpendicular to it. As soon as Car 2 vacates his position in the convoy, the other cars close the gap to maintain the proper spacing. The convoy continues on as four cars until they have passed the intersection Car 2 is blocking.

Car 2 must anticipate the arrival of Car 5 and time his acceleration so that he is able to jump right in behind as soon as Car 5 passes him. He is to maintain the convoy spacing.

When Car 2 catches up with Car 5, the old #'s in order would be 2-5-4-3-1 from back to front. As soon as practical, 4 will then automatically pass 3 and merge between 3 and 1. The old #'s in order will then be 2-5-3-4-1.

When in doubt, think "1 is almost always 1, and the client is usually 3." In the previous example, 3 is in the 2 position so one of the last two tail cars must come around and merge between 1 and 3. Car 4, having the shortest distance to go should be the one to pass and merge. As soon as practical, 4 will then automatically pass 3 and merge between 3 and 1. The drivers of 1 and 3 will start to open the space to accommodate him as soon as they see him coming in their mirrors. When 4 vacates his position to come up and merge, 5 immediately closes the gap to maintain the spacing interval.

"I need a block left and block right, -- now!"

This calls for Car 2 to pull out as described before. At the same time, Car 4 pulls out to block the intersection to the right. The first command is for Car 2 and the second command is for Car 4. They do it without being designated by number over the radio. It is understood, without being said, that they will both block the first intersection they come to. When the remaining three cars in the convoy pass the intersection, Car 2, being the first called out, is the first car to come back to the convoy. Car 4 is the second. This leaves the configuration of the convoy as illustrated below.

As in previous examples, when in doubt, think Leader is 1 and Client is 3. There should be a car between them. In this case, 5 has the shortest distance to travel so he should pull around and merge between 1 and 3 as soon as it is safe and practical to do so as illustrated below. When Car 5 vacates his position to come up and merge, 2 immediately closes the gap to maintain spacing interval.

The maneuver is now completed so they take on new #'s, 5,4,3,2,1.

While the convoy is travelling, the leader sees a traffic light ahead that will probably turn red before the convoy can get through. His first communication to the convoy is in the form of decreasing speed. (He verbally tells the lead car driver to slow down if the convoy can't all make it through the light.)

The drivers in the convoy are using left foot braking with the foot poised over the brake. They are looking through the windows of the cars in front of them so they can better gauge increasing and decreasing speeds. When they realize they are decreasing speed, they anticipate the possibility of some maneuver even though the reason for the decrease may be nothing more than just slower traffic. The second communication from the leader is radioed, "Convoy--halt!" The other cars, having seen the reducing speed, are prepared for some possible maneuver. When the leader said "convoy" they were

I NEED A BLOCK LEFT -- NOW!

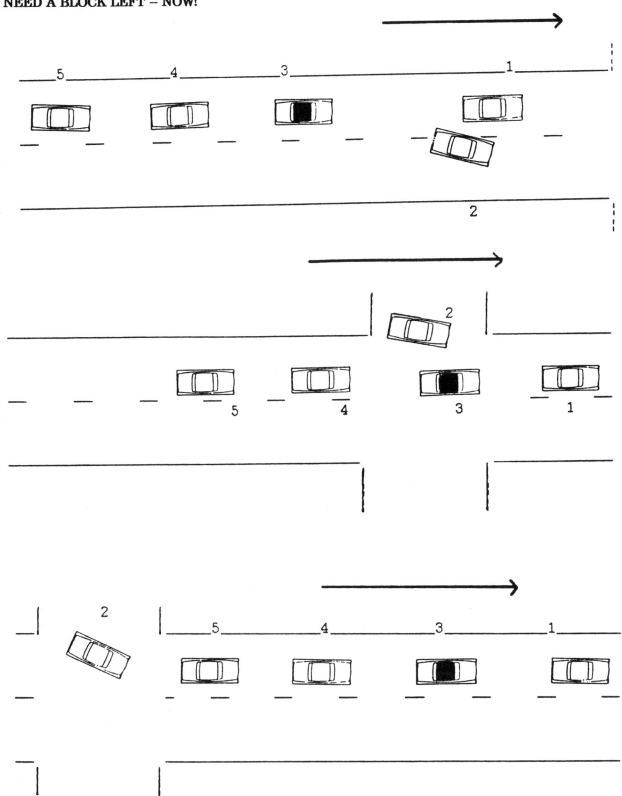

poised for braking. When he said "halt!," they came to a smooth stop. They anticipated a maneuver and were ready to perform it. They were able to maintain the convoy spacing even when stopping.

When the light turns green the leader commands, "Convoy--forward." At the command "convoy" they are prepared to do something. At the command "forward" they immediately begin accelerating in unison while maintaining the convoy spacing. There is a natural tendency to leave more room than necessary during the starting-up phase. Don't do it. All convoy cars must anticipate the movement of 1 so they can move in unison. Maintain the interval. If the spacing is not maintained, a car too close to the rear of another does not have enough room to maneuver around him in an emergency. A car too far from the rear of the car in front is inviting other traffic to interject themselves into the convoy.

"I need a U-turn left -- now!"

This one is pretty straightforward. Everybody simply follows the leader as he makes a U-turn to the left. However, if he decides that he needs the oncoming traffic lane blocked while the U-turns are completed, his command is, **"U-turn left with a block right, behind me--now!"**

Car 2 peels off to block to the right as he approaches the oncoming lane. When Car 2 peels off, there is a big hole and someone should immediately plug it up. Car 4 should start for it as soon as 2 pulls out of line. He does so by making a tighter turn than the rest of the convoy and then making a beeline for the slot 2 was in. Car 4 should be merging into the slot about the time 2 is coming back to the last position following his block.

"K-turn -- now."

If the leader in Car 1 saw suspicious activity on the road or a barricade indicating potential ambush, he could call for a K-turn when the road is too narrow for a U-turn. If the convoy were still

moving forward he could opt for either a crossover K-turn or a same-side K-turn. If the convoy is stopped, it is understood that the K-turn will be a backing K-turn and not a crossover. In this example, the convoy has been given the order, "Convoy--halt!" This gives the leader a moment to study the situation and make a decision. Normally, it is preferable for him to have made his decision and ordered the K-turn while still moving. When he orders, "K-turn--now!," all five cars back to the opposite side of the road in unison. After they have stopped, they will pull forward in unison.

Since 1 is now the tail position, he will, when safe and practical to do so, pull out and pass all four cars to resume his position as the lead car. When he passes Car 3, immediately 3 will pull around the car in front of him and resume the 3 position.

Old 2 must start to close the gap between himself and 4 as soon as 3 pulls out to go around the car in front of him.

"Rolling block -- now!"

Another maneuver the detail leader has at his disposal is the rolling block. When the leader commands, "Rolling block--now!," Car 5 pulls up next to Car 4 so both lanes are blocked. The cars will maintain convoy speed unless the leader orders them to slow down to further hinder the progress of traffic from behind. For example, Car 5 may have radioed to the leader, "Car coming from the rear, high speed, straight line, right lane, 100 yards." The team leader may have decided that the car poses a potential threat and orders a rolling block.

It is understood that Car 5 will pull out of line and fall in beside Car 4. They will maintain that position until ordered back in by the leader. When ordered back in, Car 5 can either pull in front of Car 4 or he can drop back to the old 5 position. It will depend on which lane the blocked car is in or how close he is. If there is reason to believe the car might really be an attack car, the leader will have the rolling block slow down, allowing the rest of the convoy to

U-TURN LEFT WITH BLOCK RIGHT--
BEHIND ME

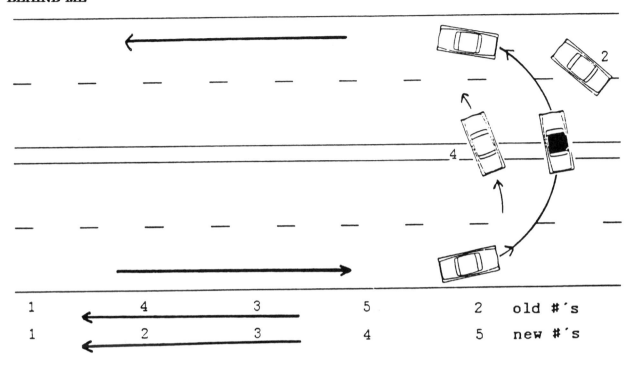

| 1 | 4 | 3 | 5 | 2 | old #'s |
| 1 | 2 | 3 | 4 | 5 | new #'s |

BACKING K-TURN

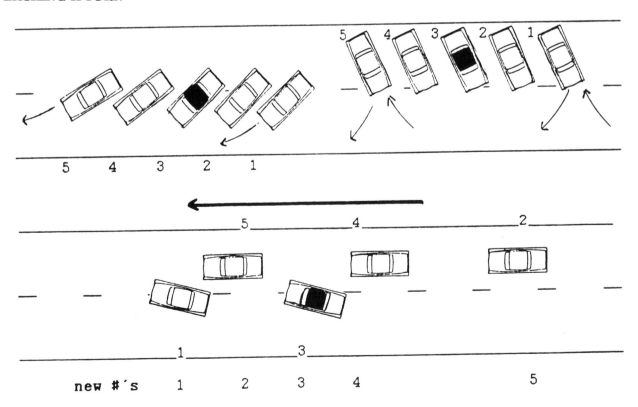

new #'s   1   2   3   4   5

ROLLING BLOCK

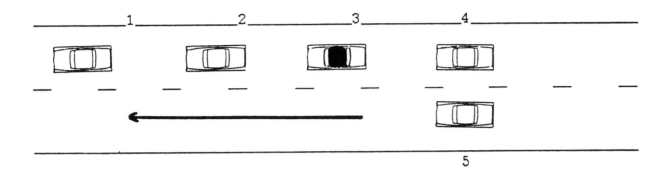

move some distance ahead as a three-car convoy. The attackers, not wishing to tip their hand, and realizing the target is getting some distance past their planned killing zone, may simply pull off and try again another day when the situation might be more favorable. If they actually do start the attack, the drivers in Cars 4 and 5 have several options: takeouts, backward rams, or even stopping for a gunfight. The important thing is that the three-car convoy is still protecting the client and moving farther away from the attackers.

Moving the Client Between Cars

A situation could arise during a convoy operation which would require moving the client from his car to another one. Perhaps his car had a flat tire. Car 3 would communicate, "3 has a flat tire." The leader would then command, "Convoy-- halt!" It is understood that the client would be moved to the vehicle in front of his in such an event. Also,

Car 3 would stop very close to the rear of Car 2 to shorten the distance that the client is exposed while outside the car. Drivers of Cars 1,2,4, and 5 remain with their cars. The protective detail personnel in Car 2 would come back to Car 3, form a protective detail, and escort the client to Car 2. Those same persons wait with the driver of Car 3 and assist with the tire change and protection while the rest of the convoy leaves the scene as a four-car convoy.

COMMON SENSE

Having learned some aggressive escape and evasion driving techniques, it is only common sense to practice them ONLY in emergencies. Aggressive driving techniques are not for everyday use and should never be used to gain petty little advantages. The protection agent should NEVER be involved in displays of "road rage," nor any maneuvers calculated to inflame another driver. There should be no game-playing or p-----g contests.

Bombs are extremely effective. They maim, destroy, and kill with tremendous success. Like arson, they have a visceral attraction for those individuals who are emotionally unstable or who have a specific need to vent their hate and disaffection. Bombs make very satisfactory noise and flames for people who need this kind of Armageddon expiation. Also, it can be tough to catch bombers unless they do something really stupid, or unless the authorities are willing to commit the massive dollars and people to fully investigate a bomb incident. This is particularly true if the bomber is "faceless"--he is not a known terrorist, nor has he ever made a threat. He simply does not like your client, carries a grudge, and has fanned the inner flames of his discontent until he finally constructs and plants a bomb in your client's office building or under his vehicle.

Without question, bombs are the favorite terrorist tools. Which accounts for the fact that terrorist bombings were top news in the decade of the 1990's and continue into the year 2000. Among the more famous, of course, were the bombings of the World Trade Center in New York City, the Oklahoma City federal building, the exploits of the Unabomber, and the destruction of the two U.S. embassies in Africa, which made the name of Osama Bin Laden a household word. Bombs have long been the signature weapon of the Provisional Irish Republican Army (PIRA), the Greek 17 November, and other groups. The U.S. Department of State found that from 1990 to 1997 over 60% of all terrorist attacks worldwide were attributed to bomb attacks.

While it is probably impossible to deter a totally committed, clever bomber, there are measures which can be taken to minimize the potential, and subsequent damage of, a bomb incident. The best ammunition which can be used is, as always, prevention. Not letting the bomber have access to your premises or vehicle is the single, best deterrent

against a bomb incident. Physical security and access control are the deterrent weapons. However, if and when your deterrent system breaks down, you must be prepared to recognize, react to, and manage the incident.

It is highly likely that, in the course of his professional work life, the executive protection agent *will* be a participant in a bomb incident. Even though the incident may be a bomb threat hoax, it will involve search procedures and management of the threat incident. In order to determine if a suspect item is actually found in the search, the searcher (in this case the agent) should have some knowledge of the appearance and workings of a bomb. Having found the suspect item, it is also helpful if he is able to make some sort of determination as to the nature of the bomb. How dangerous is it? Most importantly, how is this bomb and the people adjacent to it going to be managed? Must an evacuation be ordered? *Note: nowhere within this chapter will you find information on physically handling or disarming a bomb. This is NOT the agent's job, nor should the bomb be handled by anyone other than a trained bomb removal expert and/or team.*

BOMBS

Bombs can be composed of two, three, or all four of these elements: explosive, initiator, power source, and delay device. Many bombs contain only explosives and initiators. Power sources are relevant only in electrically initiated systems.

Explosives

Explosives are generally classified as either High Explosives (HE) or Low Explosives (LE). The differences between them is that low explosives are said to deflagrate at speeds ranging from a few centimeters to around 400 meters per second, while high explosives detonate at speeds in excess of 1,000 meters per second. The term for detonation velocity is "brisant," which means shattering effect. For example, a very large boulder has dropped onto the steep road leading up to your client's mountain cabin, effectively blocking the road. The county engineer wishes to remove it. He can use a low brisant explosive and heave the boulder up (more or less intact) and down the mountain into a neighbor's yard, or he can use a high brisant explosive and shatter it like gravel.

The more tightly packed (higher density of) the explosive, the more powerful, as detonation velocity will be increased. A small bomb with higher detonation velocity may create the same or greater damage as a larger bomb composed of a low explosive.

Low explosives are said to "deflagrate," not "detonate." Low explosives burn very fast, but they do not detonate as do high explosives. From a practical standpoint, this may make no difference. Either is capable of causing intense damage. With low explosives, although the blast effects may not be as great as those of high explosives, there are significant shrapnel effects.

Low explosives include black powder, which is readily available and, hence, a favorite among bombers. Other examples are smokeless powder, firecracker powder, photoflash powder, matchheads, and sugar/chlorate mixture. Smokeless powder is commonly used as a propellant. Both black powder and smokeless powder are used in pipe bombs.

Solid-type low explosives such as black powder or propellant powder tend to be hygroscopic; that is, they absorb moisture. This means that, depending upon the environment and circumstances, their performance may be degraded to the point where there will be no explosion. This is not likely to be the case with a bomb planted inside a building and a threat called in. It may be the case when a device is stumbled upon accidentally in some out-of-the-way place.

Even though some low explosives are hygroscopic they should *not* be immersed in water, as this may set off an electrical firing system. All bombs are sensitive to heat, shock, and friction. Therefore, while immersing a bomb in water solves the heat problem, it does not solve its sensitivity to shock and friction. Bombs do go off underwater.

Low explosives, as a class, are more sensitive to heat, shock, and friction than high explosives. What does this mean? It means that you do not need a blasting cap to set off a low explosive; usually a flame is all that is required to set them off. The practical effect of this is that they are not as susceptible to discovery by metal detector as are high explosives.

Low explosives are also more commonly available, in that a low explosive can be created using available materials purchased in the hardware, grocery, and/or feed store. These two reasons make low explosives attractive to some terrorists; they can make a bomb from materials which will not identify them later. Try buying blasting caps or any constituted explosive, and you will find yourself signing your name as to why you are purchasing these materials.

High explosives are classified as primary high explosives and secondary high explosives. For the most part, primary high explosives are used for blasting caps, detonating cord (det cord), and military detonators. They are extremely sensitive, and, for that reason, they are used in small quantities. In and of themselves, they produce violent, shattering shock.

Secondary high explosives are used for explosive boosters and for the main explosive charge. They include ammonium nitrate, TNT, dynamite, blasting gelatins and slurrys, nitroglycerin, and plastic explosives.

Typical explosive boosters include PETN, pentolite, tetryl, and RDX. PETN is the explosive used in detonating cord. It is extremely powerful (extremely high detonation velocity) and is relatively insensitive to friction and shock. RDX is the key component in industrially made plastic explosives. It is highly sensitive. Pentolite is a combination of PETN and TNT.

Dynamite is one of the better known secondary high explosives; however, you probably did not know that it comes in different types: straight dynamite, ammonia dynamite, gelatin dynamite, ammonia-gelatin dynamite, and military dynamite. With the exception of military dynamite (which contains no nitroglycerine), all other dynamites are extremely sensitive to shock and friction. Dynamite can be exploded when primed with a blasting cap or det cord. The sensitivity of dynamite decreases at diminishing temperatures until the dynamite freezes, after which it becomes extremely sensitive. Old dynamite may be recognized by the oily substance collected on the casing or by stains appearing on the wooden packing case. Droplets and crystals of nitroglycerin form on the surface. Dynamite in this state is extremely sensitive and dangerous to handle.

While military dynamite is yellowish-white to tan in color, commercial dynamites tend to be tan to brown in color. Dynamite appears in the form of sticks wrapped in brown paper.

Dynamite has, to some extent, been replaced by water gel high explosives. Water gels can be used, pound for pound, as a replacement for dynamite, though they are more stable than the nitroglycerin-loaded dynamite. They are packaged so that they look like a sausage or a long tube. The material packed inside can look smooth and creamy, or chunky; or it can be beige in color or bright silver.

TNT (trinitrotoluene) at one time was the most popularly used military explosive, though it has now been replaced with Explosive D (or Composition D) and other explosives to a great extent. TNT blocks (bricks) are pressed powder, weighing one pound, half-pound, or quarter-pound. When new, it is light green in color, but rapidly turns yellow and, if left in the sun, becomes more brown than yellow. Overseas, TNT is packaged in blocks weighed in grams, and usually marked with a yellow dot or stripe--yellow being a color internationally associated with TNT.

C-4, called a plastic explosive, is the latest of the Composition C series, and is probably the best high explosive made in the world. It is largely composed of RDX and some form of non-explosive plasticizer. C-4 is considered a military explosive, although it is not illegal for civilian use. It is simply too expensive and too powerful for civilian application. The most frequently encountered of the C series are C-2, C-3, and C-4. C-2 and C-3 are yellow and oily, sometimes scaly, in texture. C-4 is very light in color, has an acrid taste, and is formed into rectangular blocks. When warm, it has the consistency of putty and can be molded into any shape; when cold, it becomes hard and brittle. It should be noted that plastic explosives are also molded into slabs, flat sheets, tubes and rolls.

Semtex, the Czech-produced explosive, has been highly reported to be the most awesome of explosives. This, however, is not true, although it certainly is powerful and will do the job nicely. An enormous amount of Semtex has been sold to countries throughout the Middle East.

One of the newer types of explosive is the liquid binary explosive. This comes as two bottles of liquid, each on its own being relatively harmless, but when mixed together become quite explosive.

Incendiary devices are sometimes used, often for arson. The arsonist will use anything that comes to hand, but is more apt to use white phosphorus, metallic sodium, sodium peroxide, etc. because of their ease of ignition or resistance to suppression.

Incendiaries can be liquids, powders, or solvents. One example of an incendiary device is the "Molotov cocktail." This very simple device is nothing more than a glass bottle filled with gasoline and a cloth stuck in the open end. It is effective under some circumstances, and relatively ineffective under others. If, for example, a molotov cocktail is thrown against a moving car, (as has happened in some strikes) it will be largely ineffective as the movement of the car will generate a breeze/wind which will quickly burn out or put out the flame. However, if the car windows are down and the device is thrown inside the car, it is very effective. A molotov cocktail, unless it finds something to ignite, will fairly rapidly burn out.

Firing Trains

A firing train is a preplanned sequence of events which results in an explosion. From the point of view of the person who desires the explosion, the result should be dictated by: the happening of a specific event (activation of a trip wire, or by a clock delay, or by command); which initiates a further sequence of events (the lighting of a fuse to fire a blasting cap, or the electrical ignition of an electric blasting cap); causing the main charge of the explosive to detonate.

The elements of a firing train, then, are: an initiator, a booster charge (more typical of munitions than of improvised or civilian explosives) and a main charge.

Blasting caps are commonly used as initiators (detonators) for detonating high explosives. Blasting caps are very sensitive and must be protected from shock and extreme heat. Blasting caps should never be stored or carried together with other explosives. Commercial blasting caps vary in size and power. Thus, a more powerful blasting cap is used to set off a less sensitive explosive and vice versa. These devices are about the thickness of a pencil, are slim copper or aluminum tubes, and contain small amounts of relatively unstable explosives. There are two kinds of blasting caps--electric and non-electric.

Non-electric blasting caps are crimped on to either a piece of time fuse or detonating cord (det cord). The difference between time fuse and det cord is that time fuse burns very slowly, usually not more

than several feet a minute, while det cord detonates as fast as several thousand meters per second. In both instances, some initiating event is required to ignite the fuse or det cord. Improvised initiators frequently make use of handgun or rifle cartridges with the bullet and the propellant charge removed.

Det cord, while it comes in various sizes, is typically less than 1/4-inch in diameter, and comes in a variety of colors and stripes. Orange-colored det cord can easily be confused with orange-colored time fuse. The way to distinguish between them is to slice the end off a piece--if the interior is black, you have time fuse--if the interior is white, you have det cord. Usually, det cord is composed of PETN, one of the most powerful explosives. When used in det cord, PETN has a very high (fast) detonation velocity. It is relatively insensitive to friction and shock. Det cord is used to prime charges and to simultaneously explode a number of separate charges. One could, for example, have branching det cord, tied together, leaving Point A and carrying the initiating explosion along three lines of det cord to set off bombs located at Points B, C, and D--and use only one blasting cap to do so. Partially water-soaked det cord will detonate if initiated from a dry end.

Electric blasting caps are used when a source of electricity is available. They have embedded in them a small electric circuit which requires .9 volts to initiate the explosion.

The question is often asked, can a radio set off an explosion. The answer is, yes and no. A radio receiver cannot do so, and a radio transmitter that is not transmitting cannot do so--but, a radio transmitter that is transmitting might set off an electric blasting cap, which would initiate an explosion. Electric blasting caps can also be set off by an induced electrical charge resulting from a strong enough radar emitter or strong enough microwave emitter.

Blasting caps are inserted into the next element of the firing train. In munitions this might well be a booster charge, an explosive which is slightly more stable than the initiator and is, therefore, found in greater quantity than the initiator, but is less stable than the main charge and is found in smaller quantity than the main charge. However, the agent is more likely to run into situations where the blasting cap is plugged directly into the main charge.

The main charge is the bulk of the explosive. In munitions, it is usually a fairly stable compound, manufactured to be relatively immune to shock, heat, and the normal effects of being moved around. Improvised munitions and explosives are frequently very unstable and must be approached with extreme caution.

Time blasting fuse transmits a flame from a match or igniter to a non-electric blasting cap or other explosive charge, providing a time delay wherein blasters may retire to a safe distance prior to the explosion. There are two types: safety fuse and time fuse.

Safety fuse is limited standard and is used in general demolitions. It consists of black powder tightly wrapped with several layers of fiber and waterproofing material and may be any color, orange being the most common.

Time fuse is similar to safety fuse and may be used interchangeably with it. The fuse is a dark green cord with a plastic cover, or it may be any color externally. On the inside it should be black or gray in color. Externally, time fuse closely resembles det cord, and care must be taken never to confuse the two. Time fuse burns slowly (det cord does *not*), and at a uniform rate, thus allowing the person firing a charge to reach a place of safety before the charge explodes. It has a distinctive odor of sulphur.

Methods of Initiation

A firing system can be initiated by a number of methods. A remote initiation can be as simple as a man sitting with something that generates a small amount of voltage (battery) connected to a few hundred feet of wire hooked to an explosive device. Or, it can be as complicated as a radio-controlled

explosive device with the same man sitting a couple of miles from the scene. Timing can be precisely controlled.

Other initiating sources include pull/trip, time delay, pressure, vibration, magnetic, intrusion sensors, chemical, mechanical, and others. Devices can be simple and seemingly innocent: a letter bomb, a "mouse trap," a bomb rigged to a car battery, a bomb which explodes when a drawer or door is opened, a briefcase with a timer, and many, many others. They are, as the old expression goes, limited only by the imagination of the bomber. These include some fairly exotic initiators.

Chemical delay devices usually involve the process of an acid eating its way through some delaying material, such as a metal wire or membrane, to either release a cocked, spring-driven striker or to interact with a flame-producing chemical. Another type of delayed-action device involves metal fatigue. In this device, a spring-driven striker is held back from impacting a fuse by a piece of lead alloy which has been inserted in a wire frame. The wire frame (attached to the striker) is prevented from allowing the striker to fall until it cuts through the soft lead alloy.

Any device, be it a microphone, a photo-electric cell, a vibration switch, or a reed switch which acts as a switch in a circuit with an electric source, can be used to set off a bomb.

Sources of Explosives

A potential bomber generally obtains explosives: through purchase of civilian manufactured explosives; through theft; through "home" manufacture; and through supply by various terrorist organizations and their backers. The relevance of this information is that knowledge of the source of the explosive will tell the specialist something about its stability. For example, military explosives manufactured in the United States are extremely stable, whereas "home" manufactured explosives tend to be extremely unstable, often blowing up the unlucky manufacturers.

Throughout the world, the open purchase of explosives usually involves the filling out of forms, the provision of documents of identity, and the obtaining of permission from local security authorities. For these reasons, terrorists and criminals seldom seek to openly purchase their explosives. They usually resort to stealing them, or stripping the explosives out of war souvenirs or stolen munitions, or referring to one of the many "how to make a bomb" books on the market. Not surprisingly, the Internet has sprouted a number of websites with bomb-making information. *Caution: many (if not most) of these "how to" sources are dangerous, since they give formulas but often fail to disclose that the formulas generate an exothermic reaction, which tends to produce an explosion.*

Explosives Screening and Detection

Equipment is available which aids in the identification of bombs within suspect items. At the current time, x-ray and fluoroscope equipment provide probably the most cost-effective, yet reliable, mechanical means to detect explosives. These allow the viewer to scan the contents of a letter or package without opening it. Static x-ray with lead-glass shielding is considered to be safer than unscreened x-ray. With any of this equipment, the user must exercise tight precautions to avoid being hit by and absorbing dangerous x-ray levels.

Metal detectors are also cost-effective and are reasonably reliable at detecting explosive devices containing metal. However, without the presence of metal to detect, they are limited in their application. For practical purposes, metal detectors are not of much value in detecting C-4.

Sniffers (vapor detectors) are sensitive to a degree but are vulnerable to environmental conditions and the type of explosive used. In warm conditions they can be very good; in cold conditions, their effectiveness is affected adversely. They cannot detect some explosives at all.

A fairly new device, called a neutron backscatter, is quite effective. It can also be dangerous when the operator is careless, and little neutrons get a chance to dissolve human body cells.

Dogs are effective sniffers for those explosives that emit an odor, specifically an odor which the dog has been trained to detect. The dog does not inherently know it is detecting "a bomb." It knows that it is being asked to detect an object which emits one of several odors which it knows from training. Dogs are incredible sniffers and have been used very effectively in searching large areas such as auditoriums and buildings which are difficult to search by humans. It is considerably more difficult to employ a trained dog in a mail room or residence. There are additional drawbacks. Dogs can work only for limited periods, at most four hours in a 24-hour period which include regular breaks. To remain effective, dog sniffers must receive regular booster training and work closely with a specific handler. There is also the question of cost, which can be surprisingly expensive when one factors in the original cost, training cost, medical attention, and maintenance.

A visual search, tedious as it may be, and sometimes dangerous, is probably the most effective search method. A visual search, combined with the greatest tool of all, common sense, has detected more bombs than all of the mechanical detectors. However, having mechanical detectors, sniffers, and dogs to aid in the search is definitely helpful. As with all protection issues, the budget and level of threat will dictate search resources.

MAIL AND PACKAGE BOMBS

Letter and package bombs are not new. While most letter bomb incidents have involved political terrorism, such bombs are made for a wide variety of motives. Hate crimes are increasing and will undoubtedly find letter bombs to be an easy way to reach a target. Letter bombs appear to be more common than package bombs, which is fortunate, since a typical letter bomb weighs less than 12 ounces. Letter bombs, while they do not usually have wide destructive power, are devastating to anyone in the immediate vicinity. The explosive force, which causes explosive shock and blast pressure, is generally contained within a relatively small area. However, letter bombs containing C-4 or another plastic explosive could pose a more severe problem.

Package bombs, often containing larger amounts of an explosive, could be very damaging. Several years ago, the king of all package bombs--a giant of a bomb--was delivered to a Nevada casino gambling hotel as part of an extortion attempt. The large, heavy package eventually detonated, causing millions of dollars in damages.

Usually, the purpose of the letter/package bomb is not to cause property damage so much as damage to one or more individuals. While the letter is generally addressed to a specific individual or title (President, General Manager, etc.), it is often opened by innocent, non-targeted individuals such as secretaries.

The particular form of these bombs varies in size, shape, and components. They may be very basic in shape, form, and construction, or they may have sophisticated firing systems utilizing electric and non-electric detonating caps. Package bombs can be and are sometimes rigged with more than one triggering device, in an attempt to trap anyone trying to defuse the bomb.

Letter bombs are almost always designed to detonate upon opening. This is an important point, since in most cases they are safe until someone opens the letter. They have, after all, usually travelled through the U.S. Postal Service without exploding. The trick lies in recognizing those letters and packages which should not be opened.

The sophistication level of terrorist letter bombs has improved, making it somewhat more difficult to identify suspect letters and packages. Amateurs, trying to kill the company CEO because of his involvement with animal research, are more likely to construct cruder, more easily identified devices.

Without the use of screening equipment, it is impossible to visually identify all letter bombs. However, there are some clues.

.   All unrequested packages delivered either to the office or residence should be viewed as suspect.

.   The experts advise that foreign mail, particularly foreign mail received from someone not known to the recipient, should be viewed with suspicion. This is probably the case because of the prevalence of foreign terrorist groups. However, in our increasingly global economy, large corporations and many individuals receive a high proportion of foreign mail, so that this may no longer be a major clue. Foreign mail from countries such as Lebanon or Iraq might continue to receive more than casual attention. If the letter is from a foreign source and matches some of the following clues, it should be treated as suspect.

.   Air mail, express mail, and special delivery mail are somewhat more likely to be chosen as the conveyance for a bomb than ordinary mail. Again, this is not, of itself, enough to warrant attention since an enormous amount of mail is sent this way. The reasons for choosing these non-ordinary mailing systems might be speed of delivery and the belief that it will attract the attention of the intended target. Many people use express mail because they feel it looks important and has a sense of urgency that will entice the person to whom it is addressed to open it him/herself. Also, as mail systems now function with somewhat less efficiency than in the past, there is a feeling that more expensive (express, priority) mailings are better guaranteed to reach their destination correctly and quickly.

.   Special markings such as "Personal" or "Confidential" are also a strategy intended to get the envelope delivered to the target for opening. Many executives have a policy of forbidding anyone else to open mail addressed to them in this fashion.

.   Imprecise, excessive postage is a very good clue, particularly from a foreign source. Letters containing bombs tend to weigh more than ordinary mail. If the sender wishes to preserve his anonymity, he may shy away from taking his letter to the post office to have it weighed for the correct postage. To make certain that the letter is not returned for additional postage, the sender will often place noticeably excessive postage on the letter.

. Hand-written and clumsily typed addresses are also good clues. If a hand-written, smudgy letter with excessive postage, addressed to the CEO arrives, it will stand out from the rest of the mail.

. If the targeted person's name is incorrectly spelled, and/or his title is omitted or is incorrect, or the letter is being sent to "President" or "General Manager" (or other title), this is a clue, but a low-level one. The same holds true for letters with obvious misspellings of any kind, such as misspelling the company name.

. Odors, oily or greasy stains, fine powder leakage, and discolorations represent strong clues. Many explosives emit odors (sulphur, marzipan) and leave a residue of oil, grease, or powder. If this soaks through or escapes from the envelope, it is hard to imagine what, other than an explosive, might be enclosed.

. If there is no return address, or if the return address does not match the postmark, this should sound an alarm, because it is very unusual for business correspondence. The sender, you see, is in a quandary. If he places a return address, and for some reason the letter bomb does not blow up and destroy the envelope, the return address will send the authorities straight to the source. Of course, if he places a bogus address on the envelope, using a city located two hundred miles from home, and then drives to that city to post the envelope, the trail starts to grow cold.

. If the letter seems to be heavier than normal and contains one or more other clues, it should be viewed as suspect. Bombs, other than the more sophisticated variety, tend to be heavy--certainly

heavier than paper.

. Any unusual shapes that are lopsided, overly stiff, or bulge unevenly should be viewed as highly suspect. Almost no legitimate business correspondence fits this description.

. It is hard to imagine that an adversary with any brains would send a letter bomb with protruding wires or tinfoil, but if he should do so, or they manage to work their way through the envelope, call for the demolition squad immediately.

. Excessive securing material used to wrap and tie a package provides another clue. While many legitimate people (the author being one) are obsessed with the need to wind excessive amounts of tape around a package, this is a real necessity for the package bomber. He does not want his bomb to be crushed or fall out of the package.

. Booby-trapped packages have arrived under the guise of gifts and curiosities, all of which should be treated as suspect. Candy boxes, hollowed-out books, and other devices have been used. Remember the old expression from the days of Troy and the wooden horse--"Beware of Greeks bearing gifts."

These clues have been recapped in a list at the end of this chapter. The list should be reproduced as a poster and placed in the mailroom, and should be incorporated in a training program for all personnel assigned to open the mail.

What other measures should be taken to detect and eliminate mail and package bombs?

Training is the first step, whether at work or at home. On the home front, family members, servants, and employees should be alerted not to accept unexpected packages, and all packages should be routed to the command center if this exists. Personnel should be provided with a list of the clues used to identify suspect letters and packages. If the threat level is high and the budget will allow, some form of screening device (probably a fluoroscope or x-ray) could be installed and all letters scanned before opening. If this is not affordable or practical, very strict visual inspection should be made of all envelopes and packages before opening. One person, probably the agent, could be assigned the task of screening all mail and packages before handing them over to the recipients. Whenever possible, this should be done in the command center.

If the office is a small one and an incoming mail room has not been set up, one should be recommended. This need not be elaborate. If space is limited, the designated mail area should be as far removed from other people as possible, and not accessible to strangers. In a large organization, the mail room should be somewhat isolated, away from other workers, and removed from any areas vital to the organization. Should a mail bomb detonate, you don't want to lose your telephone equipment, computers, or research data; nor do you want it blowing up next to hazardous materials.

All mail, including hand-delivered and express mail, and all packages should be routed to the mail room before delivery to recipients. Mail room employees should be fully trained to visually scan mail and in the safe use of any mechanical scanning equipment. Is it practical, in a very large organization, to screen all mail? Probably not. In a huge organization, there may be too much mail to make this realistic. However, it is practical to screen all mail addressed to executives and key individuals. This does not eliminate the possibility that a crazed individual, or someone nursing a grudge against the entire company, might send a "blind" letter or package to the company with no specific individual targeted. Therefore, mail room employees should be regularly reminded to check the clues for visual scanning. Since almost all mail is innocent, it forms a pattern--it looks just like all other mail. Suspect mail, hopefully, will look different.

Procedures should be developed for use in the event that a suspect item is found, and all mail room employees should be trained in these procedures. Safety first should be the underlying

theme of all training.

Once a suspect item is found, a supervisor should be notified. The supervisor, in turn, should notify the appropriate company safety person--security director, safety officer, etc.

The next step is to isolate the suspect item. There are special containers which have been constructed to hold suspect mail/package items. An improvised blast suppression isolation chamber can be constructed, using a couple of old automobile tires, filled with sand, and stacked upon one another. Whether your company has a container or not, the suspect item can *probably* safely, but carefully, be carried to a spot where it will not be disturbed and can remain until a trained demolition person can handle it. It has already travelled through the mail without exploding. On the other hand, if the item was hand-delivered, maximum care should be exercised and the item should be left undisturbed. In extreme circumstances, such as overseas hot spots or locations which receive a high number of bomb threats, a special blast-suppressing isolation chamber might be considered. The isolation area should be away from people, preferably outside, and the route to reach it from the mail room should not traverse any areas where personnel are located; otherwise, the route must be evacuated prior to transporting the item.

All mail room personnel and employees in adjacent areas should be evacuated to a safe distance. If the suspect item is a letter, the evacuation is fairly shallow (involves fewer people and smaller adjacent areas); if it is a package, the evacuation must be deeper. Windows and doors in the isolation area should, if possible, be opened to vent any explosion. This is difficult in the majority of modern buildings with sealed windows.

The safety officer should check with the intended recipient to determine if that individual is familiar with the return address, is expecting such a letter or package, and can shed any light on the incident. If the recipient cannot provide any clues to the letter or package, the police should be notified and asked to send a bomb scene officer to take control of the incident. In communicating with the police, all information should be given as to: what is the item, why it is regarded as suspect, and what action has been taken to isolate it. *It is not the responsibility of any untrained civilian or employee to make a positive identification of an item as being a bomb--his/her responsibility is only to determine that the item is suspect and to be able to articulate the reasons for regarding it as suspect.* The bomb scene officer will determine what action needs to be taken, such as calling in the bomb squad, etc.

Employees should be instructed not to re-enter the mail room or isolation area until the item is cleared or removed.

There are several actions that should *NOT* be taken. The suspect item should not be directly covered with a bomb blanket, although a bomb blanket might be rigged in such a manner as to help suppress explosive results. For example, it might be suspended in some way to cover a door, or provide cover for nearby equipment. But, to repeat, one should never place a bomb blanket so that it touches the suspect item, or will be difficult to remove without disturbing the object. Pity the bomb squad who must attempt to drag the bomb blanket away from an item that could be pressure-sensitive. Do not handle the item more than is necessary and do not move it other than to an isolation area. Do not shake, rattle, or immerse the item in water. Do not open it.

HAND DELIVERED BOMBS

Mail bombs constitute only a fraction of the bombs used and are generally not as destructive as those bombs which are delivered by a person, either on foot or by car. In recent years, the car/truck bomb has been increasingly utilized, with massive destruction. This was true for the World Trade Center, the Oklahoma City federal building, and the U.S. embassies in Africa, as well as the bombings of American personnel in Lebanon and Saudi Arabia. In addition to the car bomb's destructive capability, it is

often easy to conceal the delivery vehicle, then detonate it either with a timing device or from a distance. When concealment is not an issue, as with suicide bombers, the certainty of reaching the target and succeeding with an explosion is the chief factor.

Courier-delivered bombs have reached their destination both by innocent individuals and by those designated within the group to undertake the task. Innocent individuals have been given briefcases and suitcases by kindly strangers and boyfriends and asked, as a favor, to transport them. In one of the more cynical incidents, a young, pregnant girl engaged to a Middle Eastern person, was sent by him on a trip innocently carrying a suitcase bomb. Fortunately, she was intercepted by officials before she or her suitcase could board the plane.

During the hot-and-heavy terror days of the IRA and Northern Ireland, briefcase bombs were used, being casually left in bars and other public places, timed to explode.

The best defense against the courier-delivered bomb is awareness, vigilance and preventive measures--measures that deny the bomber access to the premises. In public areas, such as bars and hotel reception areas, unfortunately, these measures are--well--largely ineffective. Bars are apt to be crowded, with people constantly coming and going, and little attention paid to a briefcase lying on its side by the wall. Worse is a hotel reception area, which is rife with potted plants, stuffed and cushioned furniture, hordes of people with suitcases, etc.

It is a good deal easier to screen unwanted persons and bombs from a client's office facility. As otherwise noted in this book, good physical security is essential, which includes access control. The intruder must be kept out whenever possible. If the intruder enters, he/she must be monitored, kept under observation, and not allowed to indiscriminately wander the premises. Screening procedures are dependent upon the perception of risk and threat level. In a small facility with no perceptible threat, screening procedures can be kept to a minimum. In a higher risk environment, stricter measures must be employed.

With visitors, access control starts by identifying him/her and the purpose of the visit. Good, tightly run companies issue ID badges and assign someone to accompany the visitor to his destination. Packages and briefcases may be checked and a notation made in the visitor log book. If the visitor entered with a briefcase/package, he must have that same briefcase/package when he leaves, or a credible reason must be given.

If the visitor is asked to wait in the reception area, he/she must be under clear observation. Surveillance cameras in the reception area are very helpful, provided, of course, they are monitored. Bombs have been left in potted plants, waste cans, smoking urns, or stuffed under sofa cushions. The visitor should never be left unattended. ANY abandoned objects left in reception areas, lobbies, hallways, and offices should be viewed with suspicion. If the visitor were to disappear (perhaps having slipped unnoticed out the door), an instant "red alert" should be sounded.

If the visitor asks to use the restroom, a company employee should check the restroom after the visitor exits. Did the visitor carry anything with him when he entered the restroom? Depending upon how long he was in the restroom, a quick check should be made of trash containers, napkin dispensers, commodes (lift the top), and anything that could contain even a small packet. CAUTION: this must be done carefully--if there is any indication of a suspicious object, the search should halt and trained security alerted.

Covert delivery of a bomb is more often accomplished during those hours when the facility is closed down. If physical security is good, the bomber may not be able to penetrate the building itself, but may leave the bomb along the perimeter or adjacent to the building. Security patrols must be particularly alert to any abandoned or unidentified objects. In a high-risk situation, a daily check should be made of

the areas outside the facility most likely to conceal a bomb--trash cans, air ducts, utility boxes, service inlets, drain pipes, shrubs, and plants. When possible, these areas should be locked. Those interior areas most accessible to an intruder--restrooms, storage closets, utility rooms, stairwells, etc.--should be routinely checked.

One of the more vulnerable pipelines for a courier-delivered bomb is via an employee. For the most part, violent and disaffected employees have resorted to the use of firearms to accomplish their purpose, but the use of bombs should not be ruled out. This potential threat can be best controlled by access control, to include searches of packages brought in and taken out of the facility. If a particular employee has exhibited evidence of hostility and/or been involved in on-premise incidents, a fairly close observation should be made of the individual and the individual's access to areas outside his particular workplace. CAUTION: management must never find itself in the position of being accused of harassing an employee.

Much of the above information also pertains to residence security. Physical security is essential. Visitor identification is also essential, as is true for service and delivery people.

When all is said and done, security *awareness* is undoubtedly the most important element. Everyone--the client, employees, and security personnel--must be constantly aware of the potential for intrusion and harm. No one wants to be surrounded by a number of paranoid individuals who see bogeymen behind every bush, but a healthy dose of security awareness is extremely useful. Security should be viewed much as we perceive good health. It is simply a fact of life that can, and should, be managed--not agonized over.

It is one of the most effective and cost-efficient ways of expanding the security factor--adding the eyes and ears of each employee. Many companies accomplish this by including regular articles in the company newsletter, by establishing hotlines, and by maintaining open lines of communication between employees and management. One more point. It is much easier to enlist employee support of good security if the employee is made to feel important, to understand that he/she is *really* part of the team, is appreciated and cherished, and is given a feeling of "ownership."

BOMB THREATS

Some organizations never receive a bomb threat, while others are regularly pestered with hoax calls. Depending upon whose statistics you believe, between 90% and 99% of all bomb threats are pure hoaxes. Threats are made (the vast majority by telephone) by pranksters, by employees or students who want the day off, by disaffected employees who want to scare the pants off the boss, by angry customers or someone with a grudge, by individuals with a cause who hope to frighten the company/clinic into closing, and by anyone who is bored and sees the company name. It is a pity that anyone with a quarter and an adjacent telephone booth can make a call that will disrupt business and demoralize employees. It is also very effective, since every call must be considered as to whether it is the "real thing."

Yes, some threats are real. The bomber may wish to cause property damage rather than people damage and will call in a warning to get the people out of the building. A friend or relation of the bomber may know that the event is going to happen and secretly calls in a warning. The really insidious warning is intended to get the people who are thinly scattered throughout a building out of the building to an area (more accessible to his placement of a bomb) where they are more densely packed, for a devastating explosion.

Bomb threats, real or bogus, can be costly. If the business must be shut down for an evacuation, productivity and dollars are lost. People can be injured if they panic in an evacuation. Bomb threats are very demoralizing, which can lower efficiency and cause good people to leave the company. It is

important, therefore, to handle and manage bomb threats as efficiently as possible.

The great majority of bomb threats are called in, and they are generally called in "blind"; that is, the caller talks to whoever answers the telephone. This is convenient to the bomber and is harder to trace than a written threat. The first step, therefore, is to make certain that all individuals who regularly answer the telephone for incoming calls should be trained in how to handle a bomb threat call so as to elicit the most vital information quickly. The caller wants to make the call quickly and hang up. He or she may be highly excited and babble. The telephone operator cannot afford to panic but must, instead, get the basic information needed to determine whether the call is "for real" and, if it is, obtain certain facts.

There are no guarantees that the caller will divulge the following information, but the telephone operator must try to get answers. The most important facts are:

.		When is the bomb scheduled to go off? If the answer is, "in five minutes," this will be a very brief conversation.

.		Where is the bomb? If the caller is very specific about its location, and that location is a real one, the call must be treated with higher credibility. Knowing the location of the bomb will greatly aid in evacuating that area.

.		What does the bomb look like? This would be a big help in identifying it, and, if the caller is specific, again the call becomes more believable. The caller may be proud of his accomplishment and wish to brag about it.

.		What kind of bomb is it? If an answer can be obtained, it will be of help to the bomb squad.

.		Who are you (caller)? He/she will almost certainly not reveal a specific name or identity, but may leave a clue, by saying something like, "You bastards killed my wife" (to a hospital), or "baby killers" to an abortion clinic. If the caller refuses to answer this question, he/she might answer to this one--"Why did you plant the bomb?" The answer may aid in determining whether this is to be an ongoing threat.

When a bomb threat is called in, the Operator should remain calm and courteous, and, without interrupting more than is necessary, should keep the caller on the line as long as possible. Writing down exactly what is said or taping it is important. The caller should be asked to repeat the message. If the caller does not indicate the location of the bomb or the time of possible detonation, he should be asked for this information. The caller should be informed that the building is occupied and the detonation of a bomb could result in death or serious injury to many innocent persons; this may elicit more information. These are the most important facts and relate directly to the problem which now exists--making a determination if the threat is real and, if so, how to minimize danger to people and damage to property.

A few words on taping bomb threats. In some states, it is illegal to tape telephone calls unless both parties agree to the taping. The author does not advise anyone to break the law. However, a taped bomb threat can be of crucial importance in investigating a threat or consequent explosion. The agent is advised to talk with the local authorities in his/her area to find guidance in making the decision to tape.

The following can be noted, probably later: any peculiar or distinctive background noises (music, motors running); voice quality (calm, excited); male or female; accents; and speech mannerisms and impediments. This is information which could be useful in the follow-up investigation, but is not vital at the moment. Vital is getting the basic facts.

Since called-in bomb threats do not occur every day, and when it happens an instant anxiety attack will occur, it is strongly recommended that a Bomb Threat Check List be provided the Telephone Operator(s). It should be readily available.

There is a Check List at the end of this chapter which is suggested for use. However, something short and less formal could also be provided, perhaps a card kept underneath the telephone with the following words printed in big letters on it:

WHEN

WHERE

WHAT

WHO

WHY

Once the operator has taken down all of the information she/he can elicit from the caller, she must notify her supervisor and the safety officer, who will then notify the crisis management team. Subsequent action and response procedures should be carefully articulated in the company's crisis management plan. (Subsequent chapters cover information on crisis management and crisis management plans.)

Using Caller ID may, or may not, give the telephone number for the caller. In a small facility, such as an abortion clinic, this is a good procedure and should be employed immediately. In a very large facility using a multi-line PBX system, this procedure may be useless.

Although comprising a smaller percentage of bomb threats, the written threat must be evaluated as carefully as one received over the telephone. Once a written threat is recognized, further handling should be avoided in order to preserve fingerprints, handwriting, typewriting, postmarks, and other markings. Placing the letter and envelope in separate protective see-through covers can handle this nicely.

Threat response requires deciding whether or not to take a communicated threat seriously.

Although the majority of attackers with serious lethal intent (suicidal drivers of car bombs) do not provide warnings, a sufficient percentage of threats are given which turn out to be real. Thus, threats cannot be ignored. Since there is no clear, accurate means of assessing whether or not the threat is real, the determination of its validity becomes a matter of subjective judgement. Generally speaking, a specific threat with detailed information is more likely to involve an actual explosive device than the one wherein the caller simply says, "There's a bomb in your building and it's about to go off--get everybody out of the building," then hangs up. The more common threat is relatively non-specific, but it cannot be ignored.

The company's crisis management plan must include provisions for dealing with a bomb threat that is received after hours when the establishment is closed, and it should specify who will be notified and the subsequent response. For example, evacuation becomes much less of an issue, but additional help may need to be called in to assist in searches.

Evacuations

Having evaluated the credibility of the threat, it is necessary to decide whether to: take no action; search without evacuation; initiate a partial evacuation; or conduct a complete evacuation and search.

The company is caught between a rock and a hard place on evacuation decisions. It has a duty to protect its employees, but it is also subject to proximate cause. What if, by evacuating, an employee is injured--did the company decision to evacuate contribute to the injury of the employee?

Evacuation is not always a good policy since the vast majority of threats are hoaxes. When it becomes known that the company always evacuates when a bomb threat is received, then the number of these bomb threats may dramatically increase, particularly on sunny days.

It should be noted that unnecessary evacuations of large numbers of people can create panic and/or injuries, clogging stairwells and running the risk of someone falling or being pushed. Evacuating a one or two story building is very different from evacuating a huge 30 or 50 story building. In the World Trade Center, for example, hundreds of different companies occupy the approximately 200 office floors. Are there employees who will find it difficult to evacuate, such as pregnant women, handicapped individuals, and employees with health problems who will suffer from panic and severe exertion? Can a total evacuation even be effected, or will some employees necessarily have to remain behind to monitor critical equipment?

A blanket policy to evacuate can be a costly decision in terms of production and man hours. While the company can endure one such event, if frequent threats are received, or it becomes known that the company policy is to always evacuate, this can become an unendurable expense. In the current times of industrial espionage, bogus bomb threats that cause evacuation of critical areas leave these areas open to covert espionage by unscrupulous employees.

A factor to be considered in arriving at a decision to evacuate or stay put is whether the area can be effectively searched without at least a partial evacuation. If a search is to be conducted while employees are in the immediate area, it will undoubtedly affect both morale and efficiency. Every time the searcher opens a drawer, the bystanders will listen for the boom.

In deciding whether to evacuate, management should consider whether their intelligence indicates that the threat could be real. Have threats been received in the past, and were they similar to the one just received? Have other companies in the area or industry received threats?

Do not look to the police or the public safety officials to make the decision for you. They will be extremely reluctant to become involved at this point. The crisis management team, together with the safety officer, security director, and agent must make the evacuation decision and should do so as close to immediately as possible. This is not the time for indecision and lengthy discussions of pros and cons. The longer the decision is postponed, the greater the chance that a bomb might go off and injure people. Management indecision will be perceived by employees as weakness, and an unauthorized employee decision to evacuate might ensue. Should this happen, panic could be the result.

The crisis management plan should include clear guidelines as to the criteria to be used in a decision to evacuate either a portion of or the entire building. The CMP should also develop detailed evacuation procedures and designate those individuals who will be in authority. Specifically, the CMP should designate who will make the decision to order an evacuation and who is that person's deputy, available when the decision-maker is absent.

Evacuation teams should be selected and trained in advance. Properly trained teams familiar with evacuation procedures, possible hazards, and primary and alternate routes can help to reassure employees and visitors. If the evacuation teams are working in very large buildings, where the occupants of a floor or section may not even know each other, the teams should have some sort of identifying badges which establish their authority. This could be an arm band, cap, vest, or jacket. It is important that the evacuation team members establish their authority immediately and get the evacuation underway without argument.

Primary and alternate evacuation routes should be pre-selected, with people routed for evacuation so that they do not have to pass by the suspect area. The crisis team and safety officer should decide upon the route and instantly communicate this information to the evacuation team members. When possible, the evacuation routes should be searched, even quickly, before people are routed through them.

The size, type, and location of the bomb, as well as other factors (specificity of the threat,

intelligence) will determine the area of evacuation. If the building is a small one, everyone should be evacuated. In large buildings, the entire floor plus the floors above and below might have to be evacuated.

Before evacuating an area, the windows and doors should be opened to help in venting the blast should the bomb go off--unless it has been established that the device is an incendiary. Incendiary devices which are intended to produce hot fires should be contained. Open doors simply spread the flames and open windows provide oxygen to fan the flames. Employees should take with them purses, wallets, and eyeglasses, as well as coats in cold weather, if these can be quickly collected. In addition, computers, radios, and electrical equipment which have been under someone's observation (not accessible to the bomber) should be turned off. This will help to minimize damage, will lessen the chance of an electrically-inspired explosion, and will make the job of searching easier since it will eliminate extraneous noises. Drawers and file cabinets should be unlocked and, if in an open position, left open. This will also be of help to the searchers.

For a total evacuation, some sort of evacuation signal may be required to notify all employees, who will be scattered throughout the building in work areas, bathrooms, cafeteria, closets, supply rooms, and dark corners. All employees, in their indoctrination training, should receive information about fire drills and evacuations. Route maps should be posted in each area, with instructions as to routes, methods of egress (can they use the elevators or must they use the stairs?), and safe assembly areas.

For the total evacuation of a very large building, occupants may have to be evacuated one floor or section at a time. To have hundreds or thousands of people trying to leave at one time could create a worse problem than a bomb.

There should be a designated safe destination for evacuated occupants, and this safe area must be searched prior to its use. The bomb threat could be a decoy, designed to lure the occupants away from the building to an exposed area where the "real" bomb can kill numerous people. Safe areas should offer some comfort and protection against the weather and should be located away from any potential hazards and flying debris in the event of an explosion.

As evacuation is underway, floor wardens should verify that all occupants are out of the area. The evacuation teams must include specific individuals responsible for checking restrooms, closets, and all maintenance and public areas. After evacuation, there should be some way of verifying that all occupants from the danger area have, indeed, been evacuated. Floor wardens and supervisors should be prepared to take a head count. A quick search of the building may be necessary to make certain of this, if all people cannot be accounted for.

If the bomb threat is viewed as a serious one, the crisis team will need to make a decision as to cutting off gas and electricity to the building, to minimize damage in the event of an explosion. Also, preliminary notification should be given to police, fire, and medical services that an evacuation has been ordered and that a search will be instigated. In evacuating large numbers of people, even without verification that a bomb exists, emergency medical services should dispatch an ambulance to stand by in the event that someone is injured or suffers a heart attack as a result of the evacuation.

Communication and security must be maintained during an evacuation. The crisis team must be able to communicate with each other, with management, with security, with employees, with public safety officials, and possibly with the media. Of help will be a command center, even if it is only a temporary one designated for use during a partial evacuation. If an entire evacuation has been ordered, the command center must be located in a pre-designated area outside the building, and must be capable of maintaining communications and security. The command center, whether permanent or improvised, should be searched. If the command center is permanent and is tightly secured, the search

can be a very quick one.

Security must be posted to prevent employees and occupants from prematurely re-entering the building, and to prevent unauthorized individuals from sneaking into the building.

The evacuation team is a logical group of individuals to leave in charge of the safe area, to reassure the employees that events are under control, and to regularly communicate progress. Nothing is more demoralizing than the opposite; that is, evacuating people to a common area and then leaving them "in the dark" as to what is transpiring. If a building search is to be a lengthy one, a decision should be reached by the crisis team as to whether to release the employees, either for the shift or for an hour or two, with instructions to reassemble in the safe area at a specific time. Trying to corral and hold a number of people comfortably for a period longer than 30 minutes or so is very difficult.

BOMB SEARCHES

A bomb search may be conducted prior to, simultaneous with, and following an evacuation. For example, a non-specified bomb threat is received. There is no history of violence against the individual or company and no reason to suspect that this is anything but a hoax. Depending upon company policy and (in the case of a private client) personal preference, the search may be instituted without evacuation. Another example might be a called-in threat which states that a bomb has been placed in the public restroom on the first floor of the building. The only employee within any likely distance of the public restroom might be asked to temporarily vacate her desk while a search is made of the restroom. One Denver hotel reported an average of four bomb threat hoaxes every month for over a year. Their decision, after the first month, was not to evacuate but to conduct a limited search. These are examples of searches conducted prior to evacuation. Obviously, if a suspect device were to be found, a full or partial evacuation would have to be ordered.

Several factors--time, urgency, numbers and location of people--might make it desirable to initiate a search while an evacuation is being conducted, provided it could be done safely without endangering any of the building's occupants or interfering with the evacuation itself.

Search techniques and procedures should be clearly covered in the crisis management plan (CMP). Any search teams designated in the CMP should be given training in search techniques and provided with equipment to aid in searching.

Covert vs. Overt Searches

The first decision to be made is whether the search will be a covert or overt search. In theory, if it is considered a low-level threat, a covert search conducted by supervisors, security, or a search team can quickly and efficiently search the area without having to order an evacuation, and without disturbing other employees and occupants or causing a panic. In actuality, covert searches can almost never go unnoticed unless they are conducted in an area not occupied by other employees, such as a basement maintenance area. Employees tend to notice everything that a supervisor does, and if they see a supervisor covertly examining their file cabinet or poking in their trash basket, they are very likely going to distrust the whole process. Employees, like most people, like to think that management is treating them as adults, and that they deserve to be well informed. Additionally, if a bomb were to be found in a covert search, it could cause a real panic with no time for an orderly evacuation. "Oh, my God" yells the supervisor, "It really *is* a bomb." Every employee in the room is going to make a concerted rush for the door.

There are other disadvantages to the covert search. Because the searchers may not be familiar with the area and/or do not want to make their search obvious, the search will not be thorough or efficient. Will the covert searchers, for example, examine handbags, look through trash baskets, and pull up the carpet?

For all these reasons, overt searches are considered to be much more effective.

Who Searches?

Overt searches can be conducted by supervisors, security personnel, trained search teams, employees and occupants, or a combination of the above. By having individual employees search their own work areas, an overt search may be completed more quickly and thoroughly. Each individual knows his and her area, and can easily identify an object (handbag, briefcase, radio, box) as belonging there or not. Supervisors might be able to do so, but not as effectively as the employees and occupants. Trained search teams and security personnel will not be able to distinguish between objects that belong and foreign objects. It is, therefore, very desirable to ask employees to assist in searching their own areas. It should be pointed out that agreement to participate in a search is purely voluntary. If an employee were to be ordered to aid in a search and a bomb were found and detonated, thereby injuring said employee, there would be hell (not to mention massive dollars) to pay in the ensuing litigation.

There are some weaknesses to the theory of having employees search their own areas. If they have not been properly trained, they may fail to search as thoroughly as is required. Will they search all corners and crawl spaces or only their individual desks and file cabinets? They cannot be asked to actually search; that is, to probe, open drawers, roll up carpet, etc. They cannot do much more than merely point out familiar and unfamiliar objects, unless they have been adequately trained. Without training, they will fail to search thoroughly and the potential danger would be too great.

Trained search teams are the most thorough searchers and should be used at the very least in the public and outside areas, which are the most vulnerable areas in any case. These teams need not be outside professionals. They might be composed of security, supervisory, and maintenance people. These are the people who will have the greatest familiarity with the building and grounds, will have access to building plans, will understand how the machinery works, and will have less hesitancy about pulling up carpet and taking down ceiling panels.

The training of a search team should include efficient and safe search techniques as well as identification of suspect items (bombs). Bombs can be cleverly disguised as almost anything. Training is needed to be able to identify an innocent-appearing object as being suspect, for reasons which can be articulated. Training should also include a thorough orientation to the layout of the building and its equipment. Floor plans--which include the electrical system--should be provided during the training. This will be very important should a serious threat need to be dealt with and searched. Training should cover the procedures articulated in the crisis management plan, policies regarding notification and response. Additionally, first respondent medical and fire suppression training would equip the search team to give valuable aid in the event of an explosion.

A good combination search might involve employees/occupants conducting a preliminary surface search of their own area and, after identifying all suspicious or unfamiliar objects to the search team, turning over the search to the professionals. While the employees and occupants search their own areas, the trained search team(s) could search the outside and public areas. If the threat is received after regular office/plant hours, your only alternative may be a combination of trained team(s) and supervisors, who can be called in from home to conduct the search.

Search Techniques

Searches should be thorough, systematic, and time-conscious. Unless the building is shut down and the teams have many hours, even days, to search for a suspect item, the search will necessarily have to be completed as quickly as possible. If the threat is received during working hours, there will be pressure on the search team(s) to finish the job. To expedite the search, several teams will be needed. Three teams will be required to simultaneously search the

outside areas, the public areas, and the work areas and offices. Intense concentration is required for thorough searching; hence, the teams will tire and will need to be replaced for rest periods. This requires either a relief team or the search must be extended to allow for rest periods. All teams should be provided with floor plans and diagrams.

Normally, two people are needed to search most areas. Two people tend to watch out for each other and will often do a more thorough job because each is aware that he is also responsible for his partner's safety and is accountable to his partner. Reckless behavior, such as an overwhelming curiosity to open the suspect item, will more likely be curbed by a partner. Two people always make a tedious job more acceptable and less boring. The exception to the two-man team occurs when very large or very open areas, such as garages, parking lots, and auditoriums, must be searched. In that event, the area must be divided and delineated, and a larger team or several teams put to work simultaneously.

There is an accepted theory that building searches should start simultaneously with the exterior, the public areas, and the individual areas, and that it should start at the lowest level of the building and work up. This is because of the more ready access to the bomber to the outside, the public areas, and the lower floors. This is the way a majority of searches are conducted. However, to a certain degree, searches should be prioritized. If a bomb has been identified by the caller as having been placed on the top floor of the building, this becomes an obvious first choice for a search. Evacuation routes, safe areas, and the command center are high priority, as are any areas where critical equipment or hazardous materials might be stored. Any areas with high density of people or critical personnel should be searched early. Critical personnel would include any individuals who have been threatened specifically or who are thought to be the intended target.

A search plan and room search cards should be made available to the searchers. The search plan should identify the team members and their assignments, the areas to be searched, the priority order of search, location of the command center, any information about the search gained from the caller or from security's intelligence files, notification procedures, and actions to be taken should a suspect object be found.

The room cards should be posted in the rooms that they pertain to. As the searching of the rooms is completed, the cards are turned in to a supervisor or coordinator. If area occupants are assisting in the search, the card could allow space to accommodate their comments. This would eliminate the need for the trained search teams to hunt down the occupants to debrief them. The card serves two purposes. It contains instructions to the search personnel, telling them what and how to search, and it provides this information in the form of a checklist which the searchers can initial when completed. This is a good help for non-professional searchers. The weakness of the card system is that searchers may search only the items and areas listed on the card, leaving out all other objects. A thorough search means that *everything* must be searched, leaving nothing out.

The search plan and the room cards should be carefully safeguarded, since they (hopefully) provide legal evidence that the company fulfilled its responsibilities. In the event that an explosive device detonates, there is bound to be litigation and the insurance company will be involved. All documentation showing the company's concern about safe procedures and defensive measures will be helpful.

A systematic search means that each area and room must be searched in exactly the same manner. While the method of the search is not carved in stone and may be varied for each situation, the search being conducted must be done systematically--meaning, the same way. You can't have one team searching a room one way and another team searching a different room another way. What happens if you must provide a rest break for a team while they are in the middle of a search? Anyone walking into the room

should be able to determine immediately how the room is being searched, and how much of it has been searched.

With an outside search, the team should pick an initiation point to begin the search and identify sectors for the search. These should be clearly understood by the team members, and use should be made of an easily visible line delineator. This translates as a cord or rope. Each member of the team has a length of cord which he moves as he searches. Everything within the cord has been searched--everything outside the cord has not been searched.

Outside searches are very tough. If the adversary has had access to the area, the bomb can be hidden very effectively. The job is made somewhat easier if the area is kept spotlessly clean so that foreign objects stand out. If trash has been allowed to accumulate, every little scrap must be examined.

The outside search should start with the walls of the building and move outward. There is little advantage for the adversary to blow up a section of lawn or pavement 200 yards from the building. If the bomb is outside, he wants to get it as close to the building or to a vulnerable area as possible. There are a great many closed containers outdoors including incinerators, fuse boxes, manholes, culverts, dumpsters, and mail boxes. More or less open containers include flower boxes, window ledges, and building ornaments. Obvious spots such as shrubbery, signs, fire escape ladders, and trash should not be overlooked. While the entire outside area may have to be searched, priority should be given to searching anything next to, on, or attached to the building, or located within one hundred feet from it. Automobiles and bicycles parked next to or close to the building will need to be searched.

Inside searches are generally a little tidier than outside searches. When the two-man team enters the room, they should first visually scan the area, looking for any suspicious objects or obvious disarrangement of furniture, and noting any scuffs or scratches along the walls or floor. They should then stand absolutely still and listen so as to familiarize themselves with the background noises of the room and the building. Unusual noises can be unnerving unless they are identified. If the lights are off in the room, it may be advisable to leave them off, since it is very easy to booby-trap a light switch or light fixture. With a serious threat, it may be deemed expedient to cut off all external power so that bombs utilizing the internal power system are disabled. Search teams should have access to flashlights, battery-operated lanterns, and other auxiliary lighting.

The next action is to decide how the room will be divided for the search and to what height the first searching sweep should extend. The first searching sweep will cover all items resting on the floor up to the selected height.

The room should be divided into two equal parts or as nearly equal as possible. This equal division should be based on the number and type of objects in the room to be searched, not the size of the room. An imaginary line is then drawn between two objects in the room; for example, from the window on the south wall to the doorway on the north wall.

The first searching height is usually designated as hip high or waist high, but this is dependent to a degree upon the average height of items in the room. It could also be a designated height of, let us say, three feet and a mark placed on the wall. That mark could then be matched to each person's body, tall and short.

After the room has been divided and a searching height has been selected, both men go to one end of the room division line and start from a back-to-back position. This is the starting point, and the same point will be used on each successive searching sweep. Each man now starts searching his way round the room, working toward the other man, checking all items resting on the floor around the wall area of the room. When the two men meet, they will have completed a wall sweep and should then work

together and check all items in the middle of the room up to the selected height. This first searching sweep should include the floor under the carpet, rugs, and items mounted on or in the walls such as air-conditioning ducts, baseboard heaters, built-in wall cupboards, etc., if these fixtures are within the designated height. This first sweep is usually the most time-consuming.

A determination should next be made of the height of the second sweep. This height is usually from the hip or waist to the chest or top of the head. Again, a specific height can be marked and compared to each person's body. The two team members return to the starting point and repeat the searching techniques. This sweep usually includes pictures, built-in bookcases, tall lamps, plants, etc.

When the second searching sweep is completed, the third searching height is selected, usually from the chest or top of the head to the ceiling. The third sweep is then made. It will often include high-mounted air-conditioning ducts and hanging light fixtures.

If the room has a false or suspended ceiling, the fourth sweep involves investigation of this area.

It is recommended that, during the room searches, the same kind of line delineator be used as was used outside. It is a great help and leaves no one wondering precisely what has been searched.

Once the room has been swept, the room card should be filled in, initialed, and turned in to the supervisor or other appropriate person. Some identification should be placed on the door to indicate that the room has been searched. This can be a card or sign, but better is a colorful tape stretched across the door to prevent re-entry by anyone. If anyone breaks the tape and the reasons for doing so are unknown, the room may need to be searched again.

Searches must necessarily include some hard-to-access areas. These include storage areas, employee lockers, restrooms, cafeteria kitchens, and maintenance rooms--all of which may be locked. Someone must be available to provide keys for unlocking these areas.

Elevators, shafts, and wells must (ugh!) be checked. Elevator wells (the bottom of the shaft) are usually one or more feet deep with grease, dirt, and trash, and must be probed by hand. To check elevator shafts, the searcher must get on top of the car, then ride the car slowly, moving one floor at a time, searching with a powerful lantern or flashlight for any suspicious object. There are a surprising number of nooks, crannies, closets, false panels, and walkways located within elevator shafts. The counterweights, which move down as the elevator goes up, must also be checked.

Auditoriums, convention halls, and amphitheaters provide problems simply because of their sheer size. Dogs, x-ray and fluoroscope equipment, sniffers, and metal detectors are useful for these searches. Thousands of seats must be checked on hands and knees. The searcher is looking for cut or unfastened seats with a device inserted into the cushion or back. The stage area, storage areas, dressing rooms, and numerous other rooms and offices must be searched. The stage area with its trap doors, tunnels, and crawl spaces is a real challenge, as is the electrical and air conditioning system. Lights and hanging fixtures must be searched. Because of the enormity of the search required for an such a building, it should be tightly secured after the search is completed so that it does not have to be repeated.

Once a search is initiated, it should be completed. This can mean continuing the search even after a suspect device has been found. The device found may be an easily found low-level bomb. A second, more sophisticated and more powerful device may have been hidden within the building.

Tools of the Trade

.   **Stethoscope(s)**. These may range from the extremely expensive electronic types to simple rubber

acoustic types. Since sophistication is generally not that great an issue, and since loss of equipment is an important factor to consider, purchase of the less expensive models is recommended.

.   **Flashlights**. You will need more than one kind of flashlight. You will obviously need a flashlight with a lot of power, in the event that external power is cut off. The second kind of flashlight is the small flashlight with fiber optic attachments used by doctors and car mechanics, the kind which allows you to illuminate hard-to-reach areas.

.   **Batteries**. Spares for the flashlights.

.   **Wrench kits or a universal wrench**. You will frequently need to get into areas or dismantle machinery for which wrenches are handy tools. A universal wrench will fit both metric and English bolts.

.   **Screwdrivers**. You may need a hex, phillips, flat, torx, offset phillips, halfmoon, or other head. You can either go all out and purchase an entire set, or buy one screwdriver with a set of detachable points.

.   **Pliers**. Useful for many purposes.

.   **Colored tape**. Useful for several purposes.

.   **Plastic cards**. These can be old credit cards, playing cards, or any other kind of card which is non-conducting. They are used for detecting trip wires and the like.

.   **Mirrors**. Two kinds of mirrors are needed. One is a small mirror attached to the end of a three-foot (or more) stick. These are commercially available in auto parts stores and are used by mechanics and security agents for detecting things in hard-to-reach places. The other kind of mirror is large (around two by three feet) and is used for sliding under a car to search the underside.

. **Plastic knitting needles.** These are very useful for probing soil and for slipping easily through the weave of the fabric in furniture and automobile seats. Buy several of different diameters.

. **Coveralls.** There will be times, usually when you are dressed in your most expensive suit, when you will be required to search underneath a car or crawl through an air conditioning system.

. **Canteen, jacket, hat, and any survival or comfort equipment.** The job may require you to work in uncomfortable, cold, wet, dark circumstances. If you do not have the equipment to make the job tolerable, your attention span will degrade.

. **Bomb blanket and sand bags.** Bomb blankets are placed strategically to deflect the bomb blast away from people and critical equipment. Sand bags serve the same purpose and you can afford to use more of them.

. **Geiger counter.** With increasingly sophisticated terrorists, we will surely see the use of radioactive material in devices.

. **First aid equipment.** If a bomb explodes, you probably won't be able to do much for anybody in the immediate vicinity; however, you might be able to take care of other minor injuries.

. **Communications equipment.** If you have to direct the operations of a large search team, you will need some kind of radio equipment.

. **Ladders.** Extendable, light-weight aluminum ladders will be of significant help if you are to search ceilings, roofs, catwalks, etc.

. **Remote starters for cars, airplanes, and boats.** These can be very handy as a safety device.

. **X-ray and fluoroscope equipment, metal detectors, vapor sniffers, and dogs.** These vary wildly in price and may be simply unaffordable. They are useful, particularly in high-risk situations and for searching large areas.

. **Bomb-sniffing dogs.** Useful, but almost impossibly complicated and expensive for use in non-government situations.

Locating Suspicious Objects

So, now you have located a suspicious object, one that you cannot identify, but it doesn't belong there. What do you do now?

The location and an accurate description of the object must be reported to the appropriate person and/or the crisis management control center. The control center, safety officer, or security director should immediately notify the police, fire department, and emergency medical services. When the officers arrive, they should be met and escorted to the scene.

If an evacuation has not already taken place, either a partial or complete evacuation must be ordered, and evacuation routes and safe areas searched.

If it can be safely done, the search should be continued to determine if another device has been planted.

The danger area should be blocked off and identified with brightly colored tape. Access to the area must be secured so that no unauthorized people can gain entry.

Doors and windows should be opened to minimize damage. If power and utilities to the building have not been previously turned off, consideration should be given to doing this now.

Bomb blankets, sand bags, and even mattresses should be placed strategically to help suppress the bomb blast. However, none of these items should ever be placed directly on or over the bomb. (Note as follows--with a liquid incendiary device, a bomb blanket may usefully be placed or thrown over the device.)

How effective are bomb blankets and what are they? Think of a bomb blanket as a protective shield--though not a foolproof one. Bomb blankets are constructed, for the most part, of ballistic nylon cloth or some similar material, which is then covered with a water and fire resistant outer layer of material. They are heavy and may need two men to carry the larger ones. Some bomb blankets have small holes or vents to aid in allowing the explosive gases to escape.

The effectiveness of bomb blankets in general, regardless of type or expense, is limited by the type and size of the bomb against which they are being used for protection. They are, for example, fairly effective with an incendiary device. If placed over an incendiary they will retard the spread of flames and deny oxygen to the device. With a thermite incendiary, however, a bomb blanket has very limited use, as the thermite will generate such high temperatures that the blanket will melt. Also, thermite devices generate their own oxygen, making it much more difficult to smother the flames.

Bomb blankets are, in spite of limitations, fairly effective in reducing the damage caused by fragmentation in small, low explosive bombs such as a pipe bomb. If it can be rigged in some way so that it does not touch the bomb (which might set it off), but forms a barrier over and/or around it, this can be a useful way to minimize damage caused by fragmentation. It will also serve to lessen the blast pressure, particularly if it has inner vents. A bomb blanket provides some safety against the fragmentation and blast pressure of a small high explosives bomb. With a large bomb composed of high explosives, it is the least effective. The sheer power and velocity of the bomb renders it virtually powerless to provide any measurable security.

Once a suspect device has been identified and the police arrive, they will advise as to further actions to be taken to preserve human life and minimize damage. They will, in fact, take control of the incident. They may or may not be able to immediately disarm the device and so must plan a removal route to get the device out of the building.

Tight security and crowd control will be needed as there are no guarantees that the bomb will not explode before it can be removed from the building.

If there really is a bomb and it detonates, the aftermath of the incident will be complex and potentially devastating. There will be many, many steps which must be taken. These actions are better reviewed in the chapters devoted to crisis management.

All of the procedures described in this chapter are equally applicable to the sole agent working with a private client within a private residence. The procedures must, of course, be scaled down to fit that situation.

VEHICULAR BOMB ATTACKS

Vehicular bomb attacks generally fall into two categories--bombs inserted in or attached to a vehicle, and bombs launched against or exploded from the outside while the vehicle is moving. Bombers have exercised creativity in both categories of attacks.

Bombs have been attached to gas tanks, engines, tailpipes, wheel wells, radiators, ignition systems, and any number of spots underneath the vehicle. For this reason (as noted in the chapter on Vehicle and Driving Security), the vehicle should be washed and kept clean outside and underneath, thus making it easier to spot signs of tampering or extraneous objects. Bombs have also been introduced into the vehicle's interior disguised as a briefcase or package. Pressure bombs have been inserted under carpets. Plastic bombs can be molded into any shape.

The protective measures against this type of bomb attack fall primarily into the area of prevention, with a healthy dollop of vigilance and awareness. Because of its importance, a small segment of the information given in the chapter on Vehicle and Driving Security is repeated here.

Bombs are very tricky, and very, very dangerous. They are almost impossible to prevent in all circumstances. However, there are some steps which can be taken to guard against car bombs. These steps may be extended and accelerated depending upon the level of risk.

No unauthorized person should have access to your vehicle. Access control will go a long way toward thwarting a potential bomber's plan. If the bomb can't be hand-carried to the car, you have little to fear from planted car bombs. At home the car should be locked within a garage even if it is left unattended for only a few minutes. The garage should be protected at night with an alarm system. A shaft-driven automatic garage door opener should be installed as it securely locks the door. Chain driven automatic doors are easily forced. Any windows in the garage should be included in the alarm system and they should be coated so that vision is denied from the outside. At work, the vehicle should be in a well-lit, controlled area, preferably in a patrolled or guarded area. If the car is left in a public area, it should be highly visible.

A basic means of keeping any vehicle secure is to equip it in such a way that a break-in is difficult. Obviously, the vehicle should be kept locked at all times, preferably inside a locked garage.

There are various kinds of automobile alarm systems and all of the really effective ones should be installed by a knowledgeable dealer or mechanic.

. A switch alarm is a basic system with switches placed on the doors, trunk, and hood of the car. The system is activated when one of these is opened. This is very similar to the basic house, or office, alarm which is audible.

. A motion detector alarm utilizes a mercury switch activated when someone tries to break into a door or window. Unfortunately, strong wind can sometimes rock the car enough to activate this alarm.

. A pager-type alarm offers an added feature. In addition to an alarm going off, a pocket-pager device signals the owner or driver. The range is

generally fairly short and may be compromised by the steel and concrete construction of the typical underground parking facility.

Government agencies may be able to provide 24-hour security for specific cars, but most clients in the private sector do not find that degree of security cost-effective. Even though the vehicle may be secured in a locked garage overnight, there probably is not someone in visual contact with it at all times. When the client goes to the office and the car is parked in a municipal garage, or even in the garage in his own building, there usually is not someone in visual contact with it all the time. Even if there is, the executive protection driver/agent leaves nothing to chance. If the driver is not with the car at all times, he inspects it before the client gets into it.

One should get in the habit of walking around the car before entering, if the car has been out of sight, unguarded. Take note of any footprints, marks of a jack, debris, smudges, oily stains, tool marks, wires protruding, strange objects in the tire wells or tailpipe, or anything that looks suspicious. Is there dirt under the car which wasn't there when you left?

Look underneath the car to see if anything is obviously out of place or newly placed. The underneath area of the vehicle should be kept as clean as possible so that any foreign objects become more obvious. A handy instrument to use for looking under cars is a mirror mounted on an angled pole; however, a thorough check can only be made by lying underneath the vehicle and examining every possible place of concealment. A flashlight will be needed to look into dark spots. In particular, you should look up into the motor compartment and under the area of the driver and passenger seats. Search thoroughly around the exhaust pipe, gasoline tank, and chassis. Be on the alert for any fine, almost invisible, fishing line which can be attached between a bomb device and moving parts as a trigger mechanism. Make a thorough check under the wheel arches for any unusual items under or on top of the wheels. Check for signs that the tires may have been slashed or cut to cause a blowout at high speed. Check and remove the hubcaps.

Look through the windows before touching or entering the car to see if anything looks suspicious. (This is an excellent reason for keeping the vehicle clear of all loose items, packages, letters, etc. at all times.) *If there is any reason to suspect that a bomb has been placed, the search should halt at this point, and an expert team brought in to complete a detailed search.*

Often, car bombs are placed so that they go off when the doors, hood, or trunk are opened, or when the motor is activated. Unlock and gently disengage the car doors, but leave on the safety latch. Before completely unlatching and entering, use a piece of plastic (a credit card will do) to move slowly along the edges of the door. This should detect any wires or devices placed to detonate as the door is opened. The same technique can be used along the hood and trunk edges.

When you enter the car, look carefully around the car, inside the glove compartment (open carefully), tape deck, under the seats and dashboard, and behind the visor and headrests. Any dangling or unidentified wires could indicate wiring leading to a bomb in the engine. Check under floor mats, but first run your hand gently over the mats to see if you can feel a bump indicating something under the mat. Check ashtrays, door pockets and panels, rear window ledge, and the ceiling.

A quick inspection of the engine area and the trunk should be made. First, unlock the hood but do not completely unlatch it until you have checked carefully along the edges. Use a flashlight to peer through the slight opening to spot anything that looks suspicious. Disconnect the battery, then check clutch, brake, accelerator, and steering linkage for actuating devices. Are there any suspicious wires attached to the battery?

Use the same careful two-stage maneuver when opening the car trunk, leaving it on half-latch

while you check the edges and look inside. Check the floor mat, spare tire, tool kit compartment, brake lights and other rear lighting.

A cursory search for bombs will generally be sufficient (and consume all the time you can afford) unless you have reason to believe that a bomb threat is a high probability. Complete, seam-to-seam bomb searches of a car can take many hours, and require expert assistance. If you have reason to believe that you have spotted a bomb in or around your car, *call for professional help!*

If you have reason to believe that your client is under surveillance, your car check should include surveying for hidden "bugs" and location finders.

In-Transit Bomb Attacks

In-transit bomb attacks have been a long-standing favorite of terrorists, some with spectacular results. Bombs have been triggered when the target vehicle passed a certain point; others have been launched against the vehicle.

Countermeasures place heavy emphasis on prevention--denying the attacker an opportunity to attack the client.

As with all threats, intelligence collection and threat assessment are key tools. Because of the prevalence of this kind of attack and the inherent vulnerability of the vehicle and its passengers, intelligence collection and threat assessment should be a continuing activity--simply a fact of life for the protection agent.

Prevention also includes unpredictability--changing travel routes, varying routines, safeguarding travel plans, and generally making it difficult for the attacker to get close to the protectee. Not enough can be said on this subject. It is incredibly frustrating to note the case studies which show that the target was *predictable*, adhering to the same routines, schedules, habits, and travel routes.

Prevention is bolstered by awareness. To successfully launch a bomb attack, the attacker must surveil the target. The protection agent must, then, practice countersurveillance; indeed, all employees must do so. Employees generally know if there is any unusual activity in the neighborhood. If they are made a member of the team, given some awareness training, and encouraged to report anything unusual, they can be very helpful. Building security personnel can be enlisted to provide "eyes and ears." Video cameras are useful for surveillance. Tapes should be routinely reviewed to determine if anything out of the norm has been caught by the cameras.

Unusual activity could include any and all of the following, plus more.

. Construction and/or utility and/or service vehicles and personnel in the neighborhood for an unusually long time, and with little productive activity observed.

. An unknown vehicle, either occupied or unoccupied, parked in the neighborhood, especially if parked for a lengthy time.

. An identifiable vehicle (or vehicles) slowly cruising the neighborhood or slowing when passing the protectee's home/office.

. Persons who seem "out of place" either in dress or demeanor, or who seem to display an inordinate interest in the home/office.

. Bogus salespeople and survey-takers, who attempt to either gain entry or who ask questions.

. Telephone calls seeking information, often disguised as marketeers selling free airline tickets, etc.

. The same vehicle(s) which appear to follow the protectee's vehicle.

. Unusual or suspicious construction activity

along the travel route.

It is interesting in reviewing cases of bomb attacks and plane hijackings to note that, in almost every case, someone said, "You know, I noticed that. . . but then I forgot it and didn't do anything about it."

Armoring

In a high-risk situation, and if the budget can afford it, armoring the vehicle may be a good option. For more information on armoring, review the chapter on Vehicle and Driving Security.

BIOLOGICAL WEAPONS

Do you remember this story? In 1998, three men were arrested for allegedly planning to assassinate President Clinton and other government officials, using a cactus thorn coated with a deadly toxin. The three men allegedly told informants that they were members of the Republic of Texas, an antigovernment group that believes Texas is an independent nation. The men planned to modify a cigarette lighter so it would expel air instead of propane in order to fire a cactus needle tipped with anthrax, botulism, or the AIDS virus.

Much has been written in the past ten years about "germ warfare" and "weapons of mass destruction" and "bioterrorism." It is a real and vital concern--one, for example, that has occupied any number of investigators searching for Iraq's biochemical weapons. At a time when the U.S. is enjoying global military supremacy, rival nations and terrorists, unable to match convention U.S. military capabilities, are looking to harness the massive killing potential of chemical and biological weapon, the recipes and components of which are widely available.

U.S. officials say much remains of a Soviet program that, until 1992, employed thousands of people and stockpiled tons of lethal material. European and U.S. intelligence reports say that not only some smallpox but also anthrax strains and other agents were taken over by the Russian military and shrouded in secrecy. Although details are classified, U.S. officials believe that freelance Russians are helping Third World countries solve specific problems in weaponizing pathogens.

The relatively low-tech requirements of biological weapons are surprising simple for governments to obtain, especially since most elements also have legitimate uses in medicine or science. This was evident in Iraq's case, at least until that country invaded Kuwait in 1990. Before Saddam Hussein came to be seen as a threat, it is believed that Iraq obtained anthrax from an American lab. European companies supplied equipment and expertise. Iraqi scientists studied in Western universities. By 1995, 17 countries had been named as biological weapons suspects, including: Iran, Iraq, Libya, Syria, North Korea, Taiwan, Israel, Egypt, Vietnam, Laos, Cuba, Bulgaria, India, South Korea, South Africa, China, and Russia.

Biological weapons have an extraordinary destructive power and are considered the world's most lethal substances. Because biological agents are so lethal, terrorists/activists do not have to stockpile large quantities--a little bit goes a long way.

Governments are not the only entities interested in biological experiments. On March 20, 1995, the nerve agent sarin was set loose in the Tokyo subway system, killing 12 people and injuring 5,500. That thousands did not die from the Tokyo attack was attributed to an impure mixture of the agent. The cult responsible for the sarin attack, Aum Shinrikyo, was developing biological agents as well.

On May 5, 1995, Larry Harris, a laboratory technician in Ohio, ordered the bacterium that causes bubonic plague from a Maryland biomedical supply firm. The company mailed him three vials. Suspicions were, however, aroused, so company contacted federal authorities. He was later found to be a member of a white supremacist organization. To get the plague bacteria, Harris needed no more than

a credit card and a false letterhead.

Fortunately, biological terrorism in the United States has thus far been limited to very few cases. One incident occurred in September 1984, when about 750 people became sick after eating in restaurants in an Oregon town called The Dalles. In 1986, Ma Anand Sheela confessed at a federal trial that she and other members of a nearby cult that had clashed with local Oregonians had spread salmonella bacteria on salad bars in four restaurants.

But, wait, isn't the danger of bioterrorism largely unfocused, intent on killing masses of people and not individual targets? Not necessarily true. Remember the story of the intended attack on President Clinton? And, what about white supremacist Harris--what was his intent?

A news report dated December 29, 1998 from California stated that a telephoned anthrax threat forced about 800 people to be quarantined for several hours inside a dance club Sunday--at least the fifth such hoax in Southern California in December. Other threats involved two courthouses, a U.S. Bankruptcy Court, and an office building.

In January, 2000, in Birmingham, Alabama, an abortion clinic where a bomb killed a security guard in 1998 was evacuated after employees were told an anthrax-laced letter was delivered with the day's mail. Other clinics and offices around the country received similar threats. Among the other locations involved were the Planned Parenthood clinics in Providence, Rhode Island, Manchester, Connecticut, and Naples, Florida. Sporadic threats of contamination with the potentially lethal anthrax bacterium date back several years. They often arrive in bunches, at 10 or 15 similar targets in a city. The targets have included: abortion clinics, Catholic schools, nightclubs, department stores, hospitals, post offices, courthouses, news media offices, FBI offices and even the Old Executive Office Building beside the White House. Anthrax scares rapidly became the equivalent of bomb scares in the 1990's.

Oh, yes, targeted bioterrorism is possible. Lethal biological agents can be produced easily and cheaply. One highly placed U.S. official said that quite decent biological weapons can be made for less than $10,000.

On the plus side, the U.S. government is very concerned and has, for the past few years, begun implementing defensive and reactive measures to deal with bioterrorism. Mock scenarios have been held which involve all emergency response units. And, the United States has pushed to enact an international treaty forbidding the use of biochemical weapons.

At the more private level, the protection agent needs to be ever aware of this new danger. As with other issues, protection lies in prevention and awareness--and, in this case, education. Most of us were only vaguely aware of anthrax, ebola, and botulism a few years ago, and we were quite certain that smallpox had been eradicated (samples reside in laboratories around the world). It behooves the protection agent to learn as much as possible about these biological agents: their makeup and properties; symptoms; lethal qualities; vaccines and treatments when available; and potential threat. This is all part and parcel of the intelligence gathering process. A great deal of information is available via: the Internet; microbiology periodicals; biology and microbiology college textbooks; and research papers published by the U.S. and the U.S.S.R. dealing with microbiology.

.   What are they?
.   Who has, or might have, them?
.   Where are they likely to be used? When?
.   Why?

All incident management plans must now include a response to a biological threat or incident. This will require liaison with the health community as well as with law enforcement. Most authorities now believe that it is not a question of whether biological threats will be forthcoming--only when.

Biological agents are disease-carrying substances and organisms. Possible agents include:

.   bacteria, for instance plague.
.   viruses, such as yellow fever.
.   rickettsiae, for example typhus.
.   fungi, for instance coccidioidomycosis.

Suitable lethal agents include:

.   smallpox.
.   various forms of encephalitis. and haemorrhagic fevers
.   Ebola fever.
.   Rift Valley fever.
.   yellow fever.
.   anthrax.

Many view anthrax, smallpox, botulin toxin, and plague as the more likely to be used agents.

Anthrax. Upon exposure to air, anthrax forms a spore, which can become airborne and can cause disease by coming in contact with abraded skin or wounds; inhalation; or ingestion. Antibiotics have long been used to treat skin anthrax and have been shown to be effective in the laboratory. However, while effective against the bacillus, antibiotics do not reduce the amount of virulence factor in victims.

With skin exposure, one to five days will pass before the presentation of symptoms. The disease starts as a small lesion, which grows into a puss-filled blister which then turns into a coal black scab. Symptoms include fever, malaise, and headache. Mortality ranges from 20-25% without treatment, less than one percent with treatment.

Pulmonary anthrax starts with inhalation of anthrax spores. after an incubation period of one to seven days, an exposed individual develops flu-like symptoms that persist for two to three days. After a leveling of symptoms or improvement, severe respiratory distress with symptoms of difficulty in breathing, upper respiratory obstruction, cyanosis (bluish skin color), increased chest pain, rapid heart rate, and excessive sweating develop. Within 24 to 36 hours, the victim dies. Mortality rate is 95-100% despite antibiotic treatment.

Ingestion anthrax has an incubation period of 2-5 days. Symptoms include nausea, vomiting, fever, and severe abdominal pain. Mortality rate is 95-100% despite antibiotic treatment.

Anthrax is readily susceptible to a number of antibiotics. Penicillin G has long been the drug of choice used for the treatment of anthrax.

An anthrax vaccine has been developed and has been adopted, though not without controversy, by the military. There are drawbacks to the vaccine. Immunized personnel must maintain a regular schedule of booster shots. And, the vaccine is effective only after an 18-month course of injections.

Smallpox. Smallpox has not been a problem for a number of years and, in fact, smallpox vaccinations have not been administered for some time. (Stored smallpox vaccine is now considered to be almost unusable due to age and instability.) Over the years, immunizations built up to an extent that experts now believe the body's natural protections are all but gone, leaving us more vulnerable to the disease.

Smallpox has been around for thousands of years and has accounted for catastrophic wipe-outs of entire populations. It is estimated that 3.5 million Aztecs died as a result of smallpox infection introduced by Hernan Cortes's invasion of Mexico. In Europe, smallpox regularly took the lives of hundreds of thousands of people.

After a person is exposed, the virus spreads rapidly through the body for about two weeks. Then, the symptoms appear. The head, back, and muscles ache, accompanied by very high fever. In about two days, fever and aches give way to pockmarks. At first, they appear on the tongue and roof of the mouth and then break out over the face and spread to the arms and legs. Flat and red at first, the pox turns into small blisters and fill with pus, after which scabs form. About one-third of the victims die.

Smallpox spreads easily once the rash appears

in the throat or skin, with each infected person typically passing on the virus to others.

In 1972, the U.S. stopped routine vaccinations of smallpox. Thus, those Americans born after that date are vulnerable. No one is certain of the life span of vaccinations and cannot, therefore, predict whether those vaccinated well before 1972 are still protected.

There are caches of vaccine stored in the United States, in several other countries, and with the World Health Organization. Unfortunately, there are serious quality control problems. The U.S. is now embarked on a program to produce new quantities of the vaccine, but it is estimated that the new vaccine will not be available before 2005. There is also research being conducted to find an anti-viral drug which might be administered long after exposure to save infected victims.

Botulin Toxin. This is a protein which is created as a by-product of the life of the bacteria clostridia Botulinum. It is an anaerobic bacteria, meaning that it will only grow in the absence of air. The fact that the toxin is a protein means that it will become useless if exposed to heat (useless in exploding munitions). It is best used in an aerosol form. A very small amount--ingested, inhaled, or introduced through a cut or sore--can kill you, even a DROP.

Plague. In humans, plague occurs in three forms: bubonic plague, pneumonic plague, and septicemic plague. Bubonic plague is the best-known form and is identified by the appearance of enlarged, inflamed lymph nodes, in the groin or armpit or on the neck. Pneumonic plague is most often transmitted by sprayed droplets, either from an infected person or by more insidious means. The infection may spread from the lungs to other parts of the body, resulting in septicemic plague (infection of the blood). Septicemic plague may also be initiated by direct contact of contaminated hands and objects.

Untreated bubonic plague is fatal in 30 to 75

percent of all cases, pneumonic plague 95% of the time, and septicemic plague almost invariably. Mortality in treated cases is 5 to 10%.

In bubonic plague, the first symptoms are headache, nausea, vomiting, aching joints, and a general feeling of ill health. The lymph nodes of the groin or, less commonly, of the armpit or neck, suddenly become painful and swollen. The temperature, accompanied by shivering, rises to as much as 105 degrees. The pulse rate and respiration rate are increased, and the victim becomes exhausted and apathetic. In nonfatal cases the temperature begins to fall in about five days and approaches normal in about two weeks. In fatal cases, death results in about four days.

Plague is treatable with antibiotics and care. It is no longer considered the scourge it once was; however, it can be debilitating.

Some Generalizations

While some biological agents can be ingested through food or water contamination or even through the skin, it is generally believed that inhalation of chemical or biological agents is the most effective method. Thus, protection of breathing airways is of paramount importance. In an airborne attack, many biological agents are heavier than air and would tend to hover close to the ground. This would recommend a strategy of seeking upper levels of safety.

The experts recommend that decontamination procedures include thorough scrubbing with large amounts of warm soapy water or a mixture of 10 parts water to 1 part bleach--applied, of course, as soon as possible.

If water is not available, talcum powder or flour can be used to decontaminate liquid agents. The procedure is to sprinkle the flour or powder liberally over the skin area, wait 30 seconds, and brush off with a rag or gauze pad. If at all possible, rubber gloves should be used.

Generally, chemical agents tend to produce an immediate noticeable effect, but many biological agents will take days before symptoms appear. *In any case, if exposure is suspected, medical attention should be sought as quickly as possible.*

Most chemical and biological agents which are airborne break down fairly rapidly when exposed to the sun, diluted with water, or simply blown away.

Since many agents are odorless and colorless and may cause no immediately noticeable effects or symptoms, one should be alert to the following indicators of a possible attack.

. Droplets of oily film on surfaces.

. Unusual number of dead or dying animals.

. Unusual odors--smell of bitter almonds, peach kernels, or newly mown hay or green grass.

. Unusual or unauthorized spraying the area.

. Low-lying clouds of fog unrelated to weather; clouds of dust; or suspended, possibly colored, particles.

. People dressed unusually (long-sleeved shirts or overcoats in the summertime) or wearing breathing protection, particularly in areas where large numbers of people tend to congregate.

If an attack is strongly suspected, here are some steps which should be taken:

. Get away from the area quickly and, at the same time, cover the mouth and nose with a piece of cloth. Move upwind.

. If unable to leave the immediate area, one should move indoors and upward to an interior room on a higher floor. Close all windows and exterior doors and shut down the air conditioning or heating systems.

.   Cover the mouth and nose. Cover bare arms and legs.

.   Wash or powder/clean all exposed areas.

.   If the suspected agent is contained in an envelope, or the envelope contains a threat of biological poisoning, the face and hands should be washed with warm soapy water immediately.

.   If in a vehicle, shut off outside air intake vents and roll up windows.

Additions to a safe room should include:

.   Plastic sheets and sealing tape to cover all windows and openings (if attacked, a water-soaked cloth should be used to seal gaps under doors.

.   Biological/chemical rated gas masks.

.   Waterproof clothing.

.   Rubber gloves.

.   A 3-day supply of food, water, prescription medicines, television set, and items to help pass the time (games, toys, books, etc.)

CHECK LIST WHEN YOU RECEIVE A BOMB THREAT

EXACT WORDS OF CALLER:_____
_____
_____
_____

QUESTIONS TO ASK:

1.   When is the bomb going to explode?_____

2.   Where is the bomb right now?_____

3.   What kind of bomb is it?_____

4.   What does it look like?_____

5.   Why did you place the bomb?_____

6.   Who are you?_____

7.   (Optional) Do you know that there are innocent people, women and children, in this building who might

      be injured? Would you want that to happen?_____

_____

DESCRIPTION OF CALLER'S VOICE:

Male_____ Female_____ Young_____ Middle_____ Old_____ Accent_____

Tone of voice_____ Is voice familiar?_____

If so, who did it sound like?_____

Other voice characteristics_____

Background noises_____

Time caller hung up_____ Remarks_____
_____
_____
_____

Name of Operator_____ Telephone #_____

Address_____
_____

Time and Date reported_____ How Reported_____

LETTER AND PARCEL BOMB RECOGNITION POINTS

- Foreign Mail, Air Mail, Express Mail, and Special Delivery
- Restrictive Markings such as "Confidential," "Personal," etc.
- Excessive Postage
- Hand Written or Poorly Typed Addresses
- Incorrect Titles
- Titles but No Names
- Misspellings of Common Words
- Odors, Oily Stains or Discolorations
- No Return Address
- Excessive Weight
- Rigid Envelope
- Lopsided or Uneven Envelope
- Protruding Wires or Tinfoil
- Excessive Securing Material such as Masking Tape, String, etc.
- Visual Distractions (Candy Boxes, etc.)

The last thing that a good professional executive protection agent wants is a shoot-out. There is an adage in the protection business which goes something like this: If you have to use your gun you have already failed in your mission. However, this may be a trifle harsh, since the best and most vigilant advance planning may, in the final extremity, leave protectee and agent in an unplanned, unwanted, indiscriminate, violent situation. If this happens, the agent must be totally prepared and equipped to shoot--yes, to kill if necessary. Most agents go through their professional careers without having to draw a gun in defense. However, should the day arrive when this is necessary, this chapter provides some insights into the ramifications of a shooting incident. The legal aspects of the use of deadly force are covered in a separate chapter.

Handguns are easy and convenient to handle, carry, and use. However, there is a significant responsibility to handgun ownership.

In the hands of a properly trained person, the handgun is a powerful defensive tool. In the hands of the untrained person, more harm than good can be the tragic result. Improper operation encourages dangerous results. Proper operation encourages effective protection if and when it becomes necessary.

A defensive firearm is not used as a conversation piece, as a show-and-tell item, or as a toy. It is a deadly serious tool to be used to defend your life. Firearms should not be lying around in the open and visible to the casual observer. Advertising the presence of firearms is an invitation to unwarranted handling and unintentional discharge. When carrying a gun, you have constant direct control over it. A gun left in the home is usually unattended with no direct control over it. As such it is liable to theft and unauthorized use. Defensive handguns have been great allies and have saved many

lives. Careless storage and use have resulted in unending grief. When you live with guns, you find there are many opportunities for careless behavior. As with so many other elements of protection, constant vigilance is needed to safekeep your firearm(s). The responsibilities of handgun ownership are great and are not to be taken lightly.

HANDGUN SELECTION

When considering what make and model you want in a defensive handgun, the first priority must be reliability. The gun must be well designed and made, mechanically sound, and able to function with the brand of ammunition you choose. While it is preferable that it function flawlessly with any commercial brand of your specific caliber choice, this isn't always possible. Some of the 9mm 147 grain Federal Hydrashock brand do not consistently and smoothly eject live rounds in some 9mm autoloaders due to the extra length of the bullet. Some Silvertip HP in short case autoloader loadings do not feed reliably in many older style 9mm and .380 autoloaders due to the angle of the feed ramp and the short, wide configuration of the bullet nose.

The gun must also function reliably under wide-ranging, adverse environmental conditions. Suppose it is 120 degrees in the shade or 20 degrees below zero, with a 30-mph wind. Suppose you are caught in a rain storm or in the desert with blowing sand.

Will it work despite rough treatment? If you drop it, will it still work? If you are shoved against a wall or knocked to the ground, will the gun be affected?

All defensive firearms should be conscientiously maintained. However, under actual field conditions, when gunk and stuff get into the works of the gun, it must function reliably nonetheless. Start with good equipment and take care of it. Firearms that have exceptionally tight tolerances, such as a fine competition handgun, are more prone to failure in tactical field conditions than others. Your personal guns must be tough and wear-resistant to hold up to heavy use for many years. Stick with name brand, high quality guns rather than off-brand bargains. That lesser brand that is "just like" the name brand usually ends up out of adjustment and with broken parts far sooner than the name brand.

The second priority is carryability. The preferred method of carry is the "strong side directional draw" method. However, this is not always feasible for several reasons. For the present, simply concern yourself with whether you feel comfortable carrying your choice of defensive handgun for eight to sixteen hours a day. A handgun carried next to the body all day should be light rather than heavy, short rather than long, slim rather than bulky, and smooth (without burrs and snags). A big .44 magnum with an 8-3/8 inch barrel is usually not a good choice for a carry gun. It is neither light, short, nor slim. If you shoot it enough, you will be using rubber wraps around your elbows because of the long-term effects of the heavy recoil. A .380 Walther PPK/S is light, short, and slim but you may need to carry three or four of them to accomplish your mission. The defensive handgun that is slim and smooth is less likely to snag on clothing when drawn. Whether you carry it in a belt holster, a shoulder rig, or an ankle holster, you must consider the comfort and bulk of the gun when carrying it. If it is too fat, too long, too cumbersome, or too heavy, you will probably not carry it.

The third priority is maintainability. A few defensive type handguns are difficult to field strip for maintenance. Some have tiny parts to keep track of when doing this maintenance. Some require special tools for field disassembly. The major parts of your gun should break down into readily identifiable components which are easy to handle and reassemble. You should not need a barrel wrench to remove a barrel bushing or a pry bar to remove a

slide lock lever. The gun should not need frequent trips to the gunsmith to keep it operational. If, after instruction, you can't field strip it with your bare hands and reassemble the components, don't buy it!. There is probably a similar one in the display cabinet that works better. If the gun is difficult to field strip, you will be less likely to properly maintain it. That leads to accelerated wear and malfunctions. Some production model guns have burrs that make field stripping difficult. If you want that particular gun, demand that the store gunsmith remove the burrs at no charge before you pay for the gun.

Even the best guns on the market will sometimes need new parts. If you stick with name brands, the local gunsmith is more likely to have the part you need in stock.

Also under the category of maintainability is the caliber of choice. Calibers of .38 Spl, 9mm, and .45 ACP are easily available in gun shops and hardware stores. Less popular ammunition like 10mm, .44 magnum and .41 magnum may be difficult to locate in some remote locations. Some ammunition like .357 Maxi-Mag may be almost impossible to find, even in non-remote locations.

The fourth priority in your selection process is capacity. Assuming your hands are large enough and fingers long enough to accommodate the "double-stack" configuration of many of today's defensive firearms, you have many choices to consider. Double-stack means that the rounds are not directly on top of each other in the magazine. They are lying somewhat offset from side to side to allow more rounds in the same vertical space. In the single stack, the rounds are layered directly on top of each other. If your hands are smaller, you are limited to the "single-stack" configuration or the revolver.

Magazine capacity is the number of rounds the magazine is designed to hold. The revolver holds six rounds. Most single-stack autoloaders hold eight to ten rounds. Double-stack autoloaders usually range from 13 to 18 rounds. Some manufacturers also offer very long 30-round extended magazines for SWAT type work. Great for SWAT, but poor for concealed carry. If you truly feel the need for a substantial number of rounds, opt for the double-stack configuration. There are advantages and disadvantages to each configuration and capacity. Be aware, there is no best gun or ammunition combination for every need.

The Revolver

For many years, the revolver was the handgun of choice, and, with older law enforcement officers, it is still their favorite. Though its use is on the wane, it continues to offer some strong advantages.

The revolver is a simple handgun which uses a revolving cylinder to chamber rounds (bullets) one at a time into the gun barrel. Revolvers are often referred to as "wheel guns" because the cylinder revolves on a central axis much like a wheel revolves on an axle. Individual cartridges are loaded into the individual chambers of the cylinder. The cylinder must be rotated and lined up with the barrel for each successive shot. When the rounds have been fired, the spent cartridge cases are removed and six fresh (live) ones loaded into the chambers.

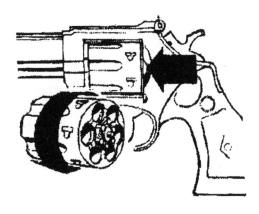

Revolver Cylinder

The cartridges are loaded into the open chambers and the cylinder closed. The hammer must then be cocked and a chamber of the cylinder lined up with the barrel. The trigger is pulled, releasing the

hammer to fall forward. The firing pin (either in the frame or on the hammer) hits the primer and causes it to detonate (fire).

There are two basic types of revolvers. The single-action revolver functions manually. It is fired by first cocking the hammer, then pulling the trigger. The double-action revolver can be fired two ways. It can operate in the single-action mode. It may also be fired by simply pulling the trigger without first cocking the hammer. When fired in the double-action mode, the hammer is self-cocked by the action of drawing the trigger to the rear. In both types the cylinder rotates and lines up the next chamber with the barrel as the hammer rises to the rear. If your choice of a defensive weapon is a revolver, only the double-action revolver should be considered. The time required to manually cock the hammer in single-action guns is unacceptable.

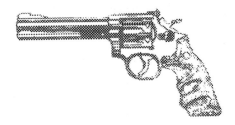

Double Action Revolver

Reloading the double action revolver is accomplished by activating the cylinder release located on the left side of the frame. The cylinder then swings out. The ejector rod is pushed and the extractor lifts the empty cases from the chambers. The chambers can be loaded individually or the preferred method is to use a speed loader which holds six rounds in readiness. After the cartridges are released into the chambers, the cylinder is manually closed and locked. When the trigger is pulled, the cycle starts.

Good double action revolvers are manufactured by Smith & Wesson and by Ruger. Double action revolvers are probably the easiest of the handguns to learn how to use and carry safely. They are the least likely to fire unintentionally. They are also more forgiving of negligent handling than the autoloaders. Even though they hold fewer rounds than the autoloaders, the double action revolver is still an excellent choice for many persons as their defensive handgun.

Autoloaders

Autoloading handguns (autoloaders) use a spring-loaded magazine to store reserve cartridges and reload the chamber with a bullet every time the weapon is fired. Autoloaders enjoy great popularity, and there are many excellent choices.

The cartridges are loaded into (charge) a magazine. The charged magazine is inserted into the base of the grip (handle) and pushed into place. The slide of the gun is pulled completely to the rear and suddenly released. This action cocks the hammer and chambers one cartridge. As the slide is moved to the rear, it pushes the hammer or striker back and cocks it in place. As the slide moves forward, it strips one cartridge off the top of the magazine, pushing it forward and up into the chamber.

The gun is fired by pressing the trigger all the way to the rear and holding it there. The trigger releases the cocked hammer which falls forward and strikes the firing pin. The firing pin strikes the primer of the chambered cartridge. The primer ignites, then, in turn, ignites the powder in the cartridge. The burning powder releases gasses which push the bullet from the cartridge and out the end of the barrel (the muzzle). While the bullet is leaving the barrel, the remaining gasses continue to burn and expand and push the slide to the rear. As the slide is moving to the rear, it ejects the fired cartridge case and cocks the hammer again. The slide returns forward, chambering another round. The trigger is then released a little bit. When the trigger is pressed all the way to the rear, the whole cycle is repeated. This is a very simplified version of the actual mechanics and does not address model variations and levers and buttons, but it serves to illustrate the basic function of an autoloader.

There are three basic types of semi-automatic handguns. These types are defined by the method used to cock the hammer. The hammer is a spring-loaded lever or linear striker that is first drawn back or "cocked." The action of the trigger releases the hammer or striker from the cocked position and allows it to fall forward to hit the firing pin.

One type of autoloader is "squeeze-cocking." A spring-loaded panel is integrated into the front of the grip. Squeezing the panel as you grip the gun causes the internal striker (hammer) to cock in the full back position. Releasing the pressure on the grip panel decocks the hammer, rendering the gun "safe." H&K popularized this style with their P-7's.

Another type of autoloader is "slide-cocking," so-called because the trigger will not cock the hammer for firing if the hammer is in the down position for any reason. The hammer must be manually cocked prior to firing the shot. This is usually accomplished by pulling the slide to the rear and suddenly releasing it. It is also accomplished when the gun fires and the slide functions normally. This type of gun is normally carried in the "cocked and locked" mode. The hammer is in the cocked position, and the external safety lever is pushed and locked in the up position. This version is predominantly found on Colt and Browning styles.

Another version is found on Glock. The striker is in the cocked position, and simply removing the finger from the trigger releases an external safety bar and locks the mechanism in place. To fire the Colt/Browning, the "safety" is swept down with the shooting hand thumb, and the trigger will release the hammer. To fire the Glock, application of the finger to the face of the trigger depresses the external safety. Increasing the pressure activates the trigger allowing striker to drop and the gun to fire.

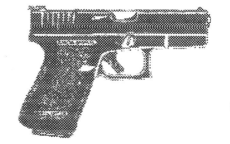

Glock

The third type of semi-automatic is "trigger-cocking." This refers to the ability of the gun to be fired by pulling the trigger and firing the gun with the hammer in the uncocked (forward) position. The action of the trigger cocks and releases the hammer, firing the first shot. It is not necessary to manually cock back the hammer by thumbing it back or manually cycling the slide prior to firing. (This assumes there is a round already chambered.) After the first shot, the hammer is cocked again by the action of the slide, (slide-cocking mode). After the first shot the gun is in the slide-cocking mode rather than the trigger-cocking mode. Trigger-cocking autoloaders are further classified by the method of decocking a cocked hammer without firing the gun again. Double-action revolvers utilize the trigger-cocking method.

Once the autoloader has been fired, leaving the hammer in the cocked position, there must be some reliable means of getting the hammer back down to the uncocked (forward) position without firing, so that the gun can be safely returned to the holster. These guns are designed so that the decocking can be done quickly and safely by the operator without touching either the trigger or the hammer. The manufacturers of these guns use various levers and decocking mechanisms to accomplish this.

Autoloader Slide

The slide is the distinguishing feature of autoloaders, as opposed to the cylinder found on revolvers. The slide is the heavy part on the upper portion of the autoloader. It moves back and forth (slides) on the frame. The slide is held under tension by a recoil spring, and its normal position is fully forward--referred to as being "in battery." When the slide is pulled back, you can feel the spring tension. When you release your grip on the slide, it suddenly springs forward. Most autoloaders have some sort of slide lock lever, usually located on the left side. This lever allows you to lock the slide in place after having pulled it to the rear. This function allows the shooter to visually inspect the chamber area at the back of the barrel and the magazine well inside the grip. Autoloaders are designed so that when the last round is fired from the magazine, the slide locks itself to the rear. This signals the shooter that the magazine is empty.

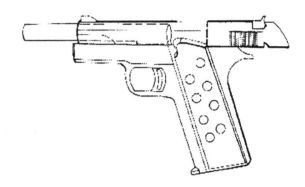

Slide Locked Back

After loading a fresh magazine of cartridges, the slide can be grasped, pulled to the rear, and suddenly released. The slide moving forward strips the top round off the magazine and chambers it. The gun is then ready for firing.

You should consider the safety features and cocking mechanisms on any handgun which you choose. You will undoubtedly feel more comfortable with one cocking mechanism than another, depending upon your facility and hand size. One reason for the popularity of the revolver is its trigger-cocking mode--it is simple and straightforward. Squeeze-cocking for those who do not have facile hand control will probably be a dangerous nuisance. Whichever weapon you choose, give equal consideration to what is needed to *de-cock* the weapon, and which you consider to be the safest for carry.

Revolvers Versus Autoloaders

In making your handgun choice, you may

wish to consider the following features of the revolver and the autoloader.

Revolvers are simple, are easy to learn to use, are dependable, are relatively inexpensive, and are forgiving of rough handling. They are extremely easy to clean and maintain; in fact, they require no disassembly at the user level. However, if the revolver does malfunction, or is seriously mishandled, it requires an armorer's attention to remedy. It has limited ammunition capacity and is slower by far to reload than an autoloader. If you are confident that any gunfight you are likely to be involved in can be won with the first two or three shots, a small-frame, snub-nosed revolver may be the gun for you. It might also be a good back-up gun choice. Revolvers are often chosen as guns to be issued to security guards when training is fairly minimal.

Autoloaders tend to have opposite characteristics of revolvers. Autoloaders are generally more expensive and more complicated, requiring more training to become expert in their use and handling. They can shoot larger, more high-powered ammunition and have greater ammo capacities. For all their larger ammo capacities, autoloaders are available in sleek, small size. They are engineering marvels in this respect. Autoloaders are not very forgiving of careless, rough handling and can fairly easily malfunction; however, malfunctions are almost equally easily remedied. Autoloaders are sturdy and do not often require other than user maintenance, but they must be disassembled for cleaning.

There are many excellent and reliable autoloaders, each with slightly different features, too numerous to cover within this book. Suffice it to recommend that, before purchasing any weapon, you carefully consider the options offered. Go to a firing range and, if possible, rent different weapons. There is no perfect gun which suits everyone. Choosing a weapon, for a professional protection agent, is even more serious than choosing an automobile. Since it represents your livelihood and your life, it should be the weapon that you will carry, use, trust, and rely upon in all circumstances.

Carrying A Concealed Weapon

In order to carry a concealed weapon, you must apply for a permit to do so (unless you are a member of law enforcement). Be prepared for a long drawn-out process with no guarantee of success. The laws regarding the right to carry a concealed weapon are diverse, with different requirements in each state. Because of the confusion, you should seriously consider asking an attorney to help you with the process, particularly in those jurisdictions which take pride in denying any and all civilian requests for a permit. Also be aware that, even if you are successful in obtaining a permit in your local jurisdiction, other jurisdictions may not recognize or uphold your permit. There is NO nationwide permit for civilians not involved in government or law enforcement work. Although, in some more liberal jurisdictions, it may be possible to show your local concealed carry permit and have it honored for a specific time period (such as when traveling with your protectee) within the "host" jurisdiction.

For this reason, it becomes very important to obtain a local permit. You may have some success with this endeavor if you can show that you are well trained in the use of firearms, have a definite need for a weapon in protecting your client, and have a demonstrated record of working positively with the law enforcement community. You may wish to consider taking training with the local police academy or sheriff's department to acquire "Reserve" status.

If you carry concealed, even just from time to time, the gun is carried only to protect yourself or others in your charge. You should not be tempted to intervene in a crime in progress that does not affect you directly. I know--this is a judgement call. If, by jumping in with your gun, you could save some innocent person's life, you may have a moral responsibility to do so. But, short of that possibility, resist the impulse to be a hero. You could be shot. Police responding to the scene have every right to mistake you for the perpetrator and will undoubtedly be less than polite until identities have been established. At best, you will probably find yourself involved in a tiresome and time-consuming hassle before the details are sorted out.

If you carry a concealed handgun, then do so consistently. It is impossible to predict when you might need your weapon, since armed attacks happen when they are least expected. If you have a permit to carry a concealed weapon, then do it. Also, if you carry, be consistent with position of carry; that is, where you keep the gun on your body. When reflexes cause you to reach for it at the belt, it is difficult to remember that you put it in an ankle holster this morning rather than your belt holster. Be consistent in what you carry. Carrying a government model .45 ACP in a shoulder rig while working today, but wearing a five-shot revolver in an ankle rig for the party tonight, is not an example of consistency. Due to different clothing styles and seasons of the year, consistency of gun and position of carry are not always compatible. However, any changes should be kept to a minimum and certainly not become a habit.

The handgun and its gear should be thoroughly checked each time you put it on. Check for proper function and cleanliness and make certain it is loaded to capacity. Be sure that you have additional loaded magazines or speedloaders available, if needed.

If you carry concealed, the strong-side, directional draw position is generally considered the best method of carry. The holster may be either an inside-the-pants or outside-the-pants version. It is the fastest and most reliable position to draw from. It is comfortable (if it is the right gun for you). And, it represents the most defensible position. (Try defending your weapon when it is in a shoulder holster!) Inside-the-pants holsters offer greater concealment than outside-the-pants holsters, but to be effective must have some rigidity so that the weapon can be reholstered with one hand. They must also be firmly attached to the belt to avoid pulling the holster out, along with the gun. Outside-the-pants holsters are somewhat easier to deal with since there is less material to snag the gun on its way from holster to firing position.

Most men can wear a gun in this manner and

maintain it in a vertical position. However, belt lines on most women's fashions are closer to the navel. For a woman wearing slacks, the gun may tend to be in less than a vertical position. The top of the gun leans in toward the waist while the bottom of the holster tends to flair out toward the hipline. This makes it very difficult to draw straight out of the top of the holster. Sturdy belts are not high-fashion items, either. Most women choose alternate modes of carry. Some alternatives are leg or ankle holsters, shoulder holsters, and handbag holsters. For more casual dress, the simulated fanny pack holsters are an option for both men and women. All these methods are less than good when compared with the best method and should be considered only as alternatives.

COMPONENTS, FINISHES AND ACCESSORIES

As with any combination of handgun and ammunition, there is no best group of accessories. Individual needs and wants differ. Situations are different. There are different requirements for a carry gun than for a gun which will only be used as a home defense gun. The focus for the agent is the carry gun for self protection and protection of the client.

Your defensive weapon is a working tool, and it represents an investment on your part. It behooves you, therefore, to protect your investment by choosing a weapon that will be sufficiently durable to last a long, long time. That shiny, deadly-looking gun which glitters in the dealer's showcase is just like the shiny red convertible sitting in the automobile dealer's showroom. It has a sexy appeal. Be strong! Resist the impulse to buy the biggest, shiniest gun you can find. It probably will not perform at maximum efficiency; it will tear up your clothing; it will be a giant pain-in-the-rear to carry every day; it will be hard to maintain; and it will undoubtedly wear out long before you are ready to invest several hundred additional dollars to replace it. To avoid making a costly mistake, you need to know some of the more mundane facts about handguns.

Modern-day handguns are constructed

primarily from steel, aluminum, polymers, or any combination of the three in the same gun. For example, Glock frames are made of a tough and durable polymer, while the slide and barrel assembly are of steel. Regardless of the manufacturer, virtually all handgun barrels and chambers are constructed of various steels.

More and more frames are constructed of aluminum. Aluminum is popular due to the fact that it is lighter than steel. As ammunition capacity increased in autoloaders, attempts to reduce the weight of autoloaders increased. While less popular in revolvers than autoloaders, aluminum alloys do substantially reduce the overall weight of handguns. For example, compare the empty weights of a small frame, five-shot, .38 Spl. revolver made by Smith and Wesson. The model 36, blued steel, weighs 19-1/2 ounces. The same configuration, model 37, but with aluminum alloy rather than blued steel, weighs 13-1/2 ounces. The model 37 still has a blued carbon steel barrel and cylinder. Most of the internal parts are also steel. The weight reduction is almost entirely attributed to the basic frame.

While it is true that six ounces is an appreciable weight difference, there is also a trade-off. By using aluminum, rather than steel, the sacrifice is that the basic frame will not last as long under repeated firing. Higher pressure rounds will accelerate the wear. Basically, you trade weight for strength in this situation. Some owners have a perceived need for reduced weight and are willing to sacrifice strength for that gain. Again, there is no "best" gun, finish, construction, ammunition combination for all handgun owners and shooters. Each person needs to make his or her own determination as to what meets the needs and situation best.

Finally, stainless steel should also be considered. While it is really not a finish but a material of construction, more and more handguns are appearing in stainless steel. The stainless guns are less affected by rust than the carbon steel counterpart.

Stainless steel, in its more traditional forms

like dishware, is extremely hard. It is therefore less suitable to the manufacturing processes associated with firearms production. To make this material less difficult and costly to work with, the amount of chromium in the alloy is reduced. This reduces the corrosion resistance inherent in more traditional stainless steel configurations.

Yes, stainless steel handguns do rust. Not as easily as carbon steel materials, but they will rust. An advantage to stainless steel parts is that they do not wear as rapidly as conventional carbon steel parts. Another is that holster wear does not take the "finish" off as with blued guns because there is no finish to wear.

A carry gun is infinitely more fragile than it appears. It is subjected to more environmental stress than the typical home defense weapon. A carry gun is carried next to the body and therefore subjected to warmth and moisture. Perspiration, essentially little more than warm salt water, is very destructive. Body acids, plus the grit and grime accumulated in normal use and the acids in the leather holster, can and do seriously damage the weapon unless it is assiduously cleaned and maintained. Because the carry gun in its naked state is vulnerable to rust and corrosion, surface finishes are extremely important. Finishes have evolved from being simple, basic, and marginally efficient to high-tech, expensive, very efficient add-ons to the defensive weapon. Your choice should be a balance of personal choice, budget, environment, and intended use.

Numerous surface finishes have been marketed which are basically one of three textures: matte, satin, and gloss.

A matte surface provides a rough surface with "pores." Because of the pores, it retains oil, which must always be kept (a light film) on the surface since the pores also attract moisture (sweat). Rusting can be a problem for this reason. Its dull finish is desirably low profile since it does not reflect light nor attract undue attention.

A satin surface does not reflect light and,

therefore, is also suitably low profile. While it also has "pores" it is not as porous as the matte finish and is more resistant to rusting.

For the protection agent, the glossy surfaces are not desirable, since they reflect light and are unsuitably flashy.

Once the surface textures are created, special finishes can be applied.

Finishes

What color is it? For most of the middle 1900's, a handgun was either blue steel or nickel plated. The most desirable blues were created using a cyanide chemical process. This process produced a deep, rich, lustrous blue color. Since bluing uses cyanide, the cyanide fumes were vented from the factories by using big fans and chimneys which put the fumes directly into the air above us. Eventually, someone figured out that the process was not the safest idea for people outside the factory and the technique has pretty much been abandoned.

Now a similar process, but without the cyanide, is used. The result is a slightly darker but very similar color. However, it is not as deep and rich looking as the old cyanide process. Essentially, bluing is accomplished by dropping the part in a hot tank of chemicals and salts. Temperature and elapsed time are critical. If the fluid is too hot, if the part is left in too long, or the mixture is not quite correct, the finish comes out with a slightly cherry tint in the blue. The alloy composition of the metal also affects the final result. It is not uncommon for the basement bluer to turn out a shotgun barrel of one color and a magazine tube of a different shade of that color. Bluing is an exacting process which takes place on the surface of the metal only. When the blue wears away, the bare steel beneath will easily rust and pit. In short, bluing is done to protect the steel beneath it.

Nickel plating is done for the same reason. A very thin layer of nickel alloy is applied to the surface of the steel. The plating is very hard and wear-resistant. The advantage is that, since it is harder to wear off than blue, the gun lasts longer and is less likely to rust. Both bluing and nickel plating are common in handgun manufacturing today.

Among the older versions of the newer finishes is Parkerizing. Parkerizing is zinc or manganese phosphate coating and can only be applied to a matte surface. It will not adhere to aluminum, stainless steel, or chrome. (Chrome steel alloy is a soft metal favored around the turn of the century as being easy to work with during the manufacturing process.) While it provides some protection from rust, it is considered only slightly better than bluing. It remains popular because it is relatively inexpensive. Parkerizing is available as light gray, dark gray, or black.

Anodizing is used on aluminum. It provides a very hard, but thin, layer of aluminum oxide. It can be dyed virtually any color and wears relatively well under normal conditions. It tends to scratch and chip easily because it is so thin.

Electrolytic nickel, as the name implies, is an electrical process. The surface is electroplated first with copper, then with nickel. Electroplating processes tend to go on somewhat unevenly and may even leave tiny pinholes where the material is thin. It is soft and will wear through to the copper when the gun is carried in a holster. It is subject to body acids and some cleaning solvents.

Hard chrome was once a hot item in gun finishes but is now not considered as desirable as some of the newer ones It is very hard, almost brittle, and for that reason will sometimes peel. Because it is an electrical process, the application is uneven in thickness. It does not adhere well to aluminum but can be used on steel. It offers excellent protection against surface wear, but only fair protection against rust (those uneven surfaces!). Normal hard chrome is whitish or silvery in appearance. Black chrome is hard chrome with an additional process causing the chrome to blacken. Neither the chromes nor electrolytic nickels are highly recommended for today's defensive handguns.

Electroless nickel is newer and nearly as hard as hard chrome. It is not an electroplating process--it is a chemical process, which eliminates the problem of uneven plating. Thus, it provides better protection against rusting, body acids, and various cleaning solvents. Like hard chrome, it adheres more satisfactorily to steel than to aluminum.

Teflon--in this case, Teflon-S--is a step up in finishes. Rather than plating, it is sprayed on and can be applied to almost any metal surfaces. While it offers excellent protection against rust and body acids, it is soft and will wear quickly. It is self-lubricating and requires no further lubrication until it wears, of course. One hitch is that it is applied as a much thicker surface than other treatments, and because of this, refitting may be needed after treatment to make certain that the weapon will function as smoothly as intended.

One of the most highly recommended finishes is NP3, which is a wonderful hybrid of teflon and electroless nickel in a single surface finish. It is very hard, is corrosion resistant, does not peel or chip, and is self-lubricating. The NP3 process is owned by Robar Inc. of Phoenix, Arizona.

Less expensive than NP3 is an epoxy coating. Robar's version of this finish is called Polymax. It is self-lubricating and moderately wear-resistant, though it is not as hard as the metallic finishes. While similar to teflon, it is applied in a much thinner treatment and requires no refitting of the weapon after treatment.

Tennifer is a finish which is available only on Glock guns and is applied at the factory. It is a very good hard metallic treatment and is recommended for Glock owners.

Sights

Sights are an integral and necessary part of any firearm. Yes, you can hit a target without the use of sights. Yes, you can hit a target using one hand. But, can you hit a target reliably (every time) in a defensive encounter (shooting at a live person who is trying to kill you), within ranges of fifteen yards? The target, in this case, is about a nine-inch circle; it is the area which you must hit in order to incapacitate your adversary.

Sights need to be large, sturdy, and easy to see without hanging up or snagging on clothing or holsters during the draw. If the sights are not sturdy, they can come off the gun. If too flimsy, they can break. Some front sights are just peened in. Some have a small screw securing them to the gun. Eventually, either process will allow the sight to come loose. It is preferable that sights be dovetailed or welded if possible. While many people actually prefer adjustable rear sights for the flexibility of point of aim/point of impact adjustment for different ammunition, few if any of them will hold up to abuse. Most will not survive a drop test of three feet if the gun lands on them. If the gun you will be working with has adjustable sights, it is strongly suggested that you consider having them replaced with sturdy fixed sights.

In addition to being strong, good sights should be low profile and free of sharp corners and snags. Those sharp edges will attach themselves to your clothing, slowing down your draw and tearing up your good suit. If the sight becomes truly embedded in your clothing, you won't be able to draw and fire. With autoloaders, a bristly rear sight will scrape your hand as it grips the slide.

Learning to use a defensive handgun involves learning to use the sights quickly and effectively. Many front sights are too difficult to see and use. For best lateral accuracy, the light bars (space seen between outside edges of front sight and inside edges of rear sight notch) on either side of the front sight, when viewed properly through the notch of the rear sight, are equal. For defensive handguns, holding the gun in front of you with two hands and looking through the notch of the rear sight, each light bar should be about one-half the width of the front sight. There must be sufficient light bars to quickly find the front sight. If the light bars are too narrow, the time taken to find the front sight increases. If the front sight is narrowed to increase the light bar, it becomes too flimsy. This narrow front sight is also more difficult to pick out quickly. Since you will be aligning the target, front sight, rear sight, and your eye all in one line, the quicker you can find and align the front sight, the better. If light bars need to be increased, replacement or opening of the rear sight is the necessary remedy.

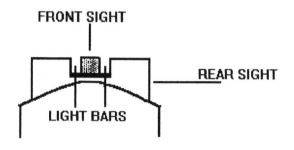

**Looking Through the Rear Sight
at the Front Sight**

The correct sight picture on a defensive handgun may not be the same as on a target or competition handgun. Some forms of competition target shooting allow enough time for a very precise sight picture, a luxury not found in defensive shooting.

In defensive shooting and some forms of competition shooting, the need for speed and accuracy must be balanced against each other. Once shooting skill is developed and practiced so that all the fundamentals are exercised smoothly and reliably, the defensive shooter knows that as soon as he sees light bars he is close enough to start applying trigger pressure. In slower forms of competition that require a great deal of accuracy and precision, shooters don't start their trigger pressure until the sights are in perfect alignment. Defensive shooters are only as accurate as they need to be. This is usually not as accurate as the precision shooter. It does not mean the defensive shooter is inaccurate--just slightly less accurate. It means that he is a hair less precise than the precision shooter and a *lot* quicker.

Self-luminescent sight systems have progressed a long way from their inception. Usually

called night sights, the newer and better systems use a tritium gas capsule which has a service life of five to ten years. The original night sight systems were little more than luminescent paint which lost its luster in a very short time. Newer versions of night sights are great for very dim light encounters in that they can be aligned quickly when it is too dark to see your normal colored sights. They do not illuminate or locate the target, but they do show you where your sights are. It goes without saying that, if it is too dark to identify your target, you have no business shooting at it anyway.

For those situations like dusk on a cloudy day where there is enough light to identify the target but not enough to see your sights for the first shot, night sights allow you to align the sights. A drawback of night sights is the luminescent material. It is bright enough to cause the target to fade when your eye attempts to focus on the front sight. The way to properly use night sights is to align them without focusing on them, look through the sights at the target, then start the trigger press.

Sight inserts, small pieces of colored plastic or resin, are found on several types of handguns. Experience has shown that they tend to fall out at the most inopportune times. Inserts, busy white lines, and little shiny dots and bars all tend to be nice marketing gadgets that make the sights look different. The human eye sometimes has difficulty sorting out all the clutter in front of the gun. Younger shooters usually are distracted by them. Older shooters sometimes feel they need them to more readily identify the front sight. The preponderance of shooters find that non-glare black sights serve their needs quite nicely.

Stocks

The stocks of a handgun are the panels on either side of the handle. They are referred to as the stocks, the grips, the handle, or numerous other names. Newer Smith & Wesson autoloaders utilize a composition one-piece plastic stock which comes in different sizes according to the frame size. With a Glock, the stock is molded as part of the frame during manufacturing. In revolvers, stocks can be a very personal and individual thing. Wooden stocks may be carved or machined to fit nearly any hand, whether large or small, thick or thin, long or stubby. There are fewer actual stock choices available to the autoloader shooter but there are more models and sizes of handguns available in autoloaders. This is to accommodate different hand sizes and situational needs.

When a handgun is carried concealed, it is positioned under an article of clothing. As the owner goes through his workday activities he sits, stands, stoops, walks, runs, etc. The clothing should slide back and forth across the gun. If the gun is positioned incorrectly or if the clothing binds, the outline of part of the gun or holster is revealed. This immediately notifies other observant people that you are carrying a gun. Large bulky stocks outline under clothing more easily than flatter stocks. Longer stocks or extended length magazines are also harder to conceal. Fabric slides across smooth wood and composition or plastic stocks more easily than soft rubber stocks. Rubber stocks usually facilitate a better grip of the weapon when wet, as from sweating palms, rain, snow, or blood. It seems the world is full of trade-offs, and grips are no different.

Moderate checkering is okay. Sharp checkering or stippling should be avoided as it will snag on clothing and is hard on the hands when performing malfunction clearance drills.

Any replacement stock, whether rubber or otherwise, should not interfere in any way with any external lever, plunger, or button. The stock on an autoloader is too fat or too big from front to back if you are unable to reach and easily manipulate the trigger, magazine release button, safety, and/or decocking lever with the fingers of your shooting hand while the gun is held in that hand in a firing position. The grips on a revolver should be scooped out on the left side so that you can line up a loaded speedloader with the six chambers in the fully opened cylinder. This alignment usually means that the side of the loaded speedloader makes contact with the side of the gun frame.

Handgun Modifications

There are numerous modifications which can be made to a handgun, most of which are not only unnecessary but are simply a bad idea. Unnecessary modifications can mean further modifications to accommodate the first modification! Some alterations are actually dangerous. Most are cosmetic rather than intrinsic.

Rather than substantially altering a gun, it is a better idea to shop until you find a handgun which suits your purposes.

Acceptable modifications include exclusion of night sights, bumper pads on the base of the magazines, minor stock modifications for hand fit, anchoring of and possible adjustment of fixed sights, and filing off any sharp corners which will snag clothing and hands.

Leather

This includes the belt, the holster and the speed loader or magazine carrier. Previously, all three items were manufactured of good leather. Increasingly, of late, good leather is becoming more and more scarce. As cowhide becomes less and less easy to obtain, more manufacturers are turning to composition plastics and resins for production of holsters, carriers, and even belts.

Regarding belts, you should choose a belt of at least 1-1/4 inch width. It not only holds up your trousers but several pounds of gear as well. Thin flimsy dress belts do not hold gear in place comfortably. Numerous sturdy belts are available that are moderately priced and will serve your needs quite nicely. Belts which are lined and double-stitched are more durable and won't break down as easily from the weight of all the gear suspended from them.

Carriers come in many styles and prices and vary greatly in their efficiency. Right-handed shooters wear the carrier on the left side of the body to facilitate weak hand loading. Left-handed shooters wear the carrier on the right side of the body. This holds true for both revolver and autoloader shooters. If you wear a uniform while carrying the gun, the carrier should have a snap strap which covers and retains the magazine or loader. Velcro straps are a last resort. They have an irritating habit of hooking shut again as soon as you release them from the opening motion. If you are not in uniform when carrying a gun, the retaining strap is less necessary. In uniform, the magazine or loader in the carrier is open to the elements. When concealed, there is less probability of foreign material invading the carrier. There should, however, be an internal retaining spring, or the carrier should be constructed in such a way that the magazine or loader will not fall out when you are running.

Loose, open-top canvas, nylon, or soft leather carriers are an invitation to unnoticed loss of equipment. Whether the carrier has a strap or is open top, the devise should attach to the belt by sliding the belt through slits or loops. While there are some brands that attach to the belt by spring metal clips, few of them hold the carrier securely. When confronted with a reload under stress, it is very likely to come away from the belt with the loader or magazine still inside it. Suddenly, there is simply too much extraneous stuff in your hand to fit into the gun.

Leather which is somewhat stiff will hold its shape better in the long run than lightweight, flimsy material. The funny-looking magazine carriers made by Glock for their magazines offer good retention, are relatively inexpensive, extremely durable, very thin, and light. While they look and feel flimsy, they are an excellent choice for concealed carry if you have a Glock.

Another exception to the light and flimsy is the "auto-clip holder" made by Safariland. It is all metal and clips onto the belt. This spring clip is substantial, will stay on the belt, and is light and easy to use. This offers another low-cost option for the economy-minded. It is flat and a good choice for concealed carry for both revolver and autoloader.

Holsters, holsters, holsters. There are a great many sizes, shapes, colors, and smells to choose from. Not all manufacturers make holsters which will fit all the makes and models of handguns on the market. Some models are manufactured by more than one company but under different names with nearly undetectable differences. Of necessity, catalogs change with each edition, as models that do not sell well are dropped and new styles are added. There are so many changes annually that no one can keep up with the hundreds of models.

Regardless of make or model, your holster should retain the gun during a backward roll. If it accomplishes that, the gun will stay secured when you run or lean over. If the holster is long enough to completely cover the rear sight, so much the better. This means less interference from clothing and other snags when drawing the gun. Leather holsters should be double stitched at all stress points.

The top of the holster must remain fully open after the gun is withdrawn. When you find yourself holding a two-way radio in your weak hand, you can't gracefully use that hand to open the top of the holster to holster the handgun. If your weak hand is full of a determined but unarmed attacker, again, you cannot quickly put the gun in the holster one-handed. One-handed holstering eliminates all but a few of the ballistic nylon holsters.

The strong-side belt holster is generally considered the best choice for concealed carry. Inside-the-waistband holsters on the strong side may be a good choice. If that is your option, make sure it has the following features. The holster must be secured to the belt by snap straps or loops. Don't trust the metal clip-on-the-belt variety. You may find yourself drawing the gun and pointing a loaded holster at an adversary. The holster must have a steel, plastic, or other kind of liner around the top. This is absolutely necessary to preserve the shape of the mouth of the holster after the gun has been drawn. If the mouth collapses, rapid holstering is difficult, to say the least. In most situations you are far more likely to holster quickly and do something with your hands than you are to shoot. When you holster the gun, you must do it quickly and that cannot be done with a holster that has closed at the top. A drawback to these holsters is body moisture in the area of the holster. It can soak the holster and increase moisture on the gun. Also, thin people sometimes have difficulty with body chafing where the holster rubs.

A shoulder holster is a comfortable method of carry for many people who have to spend a lot of time sitting. It is accessible to either hand while sitting. Unfortunately, it is also very vulnerable to frontal attack due to the cross draw method of operation. When the user reaches across the chest to draw the gun, a close adversary will find it relatively easy to capture the gun hand and arm, break the elbow, and put the user face first in the ground.

However, the most dangerous aspect to the shoulder holster is not during the draw. Rather, it is during the act of holstering. Since the gun must be pointed at some part of the body when holstering, most manufacturers now state that the only safe way to holster is to remove the rig, holster the gun, then put the rig back on. It is still a favorite carry option with many chauffeurs who are less likely to use a defensive handgun.

The cross draw belt holster is not recommended. It is vulnerable to a gun grab by an adversary.

Leg or ankle holsters are a favorite of people who routinely do not wear a jacket or similar outer garment and are used by many for a back-up weapon. There are some trade-offs. It is a slower and more awkward draw. Pants cannot be very stiff or snug at the bottom. And, special care should be taken not to cross the legs while sitting; if the pants are not long enough, the bottom of the holster may show while simply sitting.

Better leg holsters have a wide garter strap, lined with sheep skin, below the knee and above the calf. The garter should be about four inches wide for comfort and to avoid restricting circulation. The holster then hangs from an adjustable strap while a narrower strap at the base of the holster holds it against the leg.

Ankle holsters actually rest on the ankle bone. They should be heavily padded and fit snugly. The ankle holster is more accessible but is also more difficult to conceal. Both holsters are usually used only for small-frame handguns like a five-shot revolver or single stack .380 or very small 9mm. Preferred wear is on the inside of either leg, butt forward or backward, depending on the method of draw.

A number of "fanny pack" designs on the market hold any of the popular defensive handguns. These are available through larger police supply stores. Some styles use velcro closures which are ripped open with the weak hand; then the strong hand pulls the gun from the holster secreted inside. Some have ambidextrous zipper closures. The weak hand unzips and the strong hand plunges into the opening to remove the gun from the holster inside. Again, the obvious drawback is that quick holstering is nearly impossible. As with any alternative to the strong-side belt holster, they are slower to draw and not intended for constant concealed carry. However, they work if you need to be in shorts and tee-shirt. The police versions are preferable to a standard fanny pack which does not have an internal holster. If using this method for temporary carry, the pack may be worn over the strong hip or toward the front, but never in the back or fanny position. That position leaves the gun accessible to everyone but you.

Handbags have long been used by women to carry any number and variety of weapons, from fingernail files and scissors to bombs and handguns. However, there are distinct drawbacks to using this device to carry a gun. A handgun carried in a regular purse is going to be in contact with lint and other debris typically found in handbags. Further, any time the purse is opened, the gun may be visible to others close by. If the bag must be unzipped to access the gun, it will be a very, very slow draw. It is, however, the only feasible option open to many female protection agents. The best handbag for use in carrying a handgun is especially made for this purpose. Essentially, the handbag is separated into two pouches (a common design for women's purses), with a hidden compartment located between the two pouches. The gun is carried in the hidden compartment which has a velcro closure. While it is somewhat bulky, it offers a near-perfect hiding place and cleaner environment for the gun. If the user senses danger, one hand can actually slip into the compartment and grip the gun.

Carrying a gun in a pocket is not the best method for any handgun. However, some people routinely carry a small backup weapon in their pocket. Firing from inside a trouser or jacket pocket is possible and may be advisable but there are some considerations. Sights are not usable, so shooting should only be done at virtual contact range and as a last resort. The hammer may be restricted from falling to the firing pin by the proximity of fabric. The travel of the slide of an autoloader may be restricted and fail to produce subsequent rounds for firing. Simply removing a hammer spur will not ensure unrestricted hammer travel. Smith & Wesson makes at least two versions of the J-frame five-shot revolver with either a shrouded or enclosed hammer. Either of these bodyguard styles afford the best opportunity for firing from inside your clothing.

Magazines and Speed Loaders

The magazine is the "food tube" all defensive autoloaders rely on. Regardless of the cost or quality of the gun, it is only as good as the magazines which supply the ammunition to the chamber. Magazines will be a high replacement item if you do much shooting. The primary wear happens at the lips at the top of the magazine. They get bent and cracked from normal and repeated insertion into the magazine well. They are also damaged from normal and repeated dropping from the gun when reloading. Either situation will eventually cause malfunctions. Defective magazines will not always lock the slide to the rear when empty. It may be that a round will not feed freely and bind the slide before closing all the way. It may also mean that more than one round will try to feed. This happens when the slide moves to the rear and allows a round to pop up from the magazine. As the slide moves forward it strips another round as it should and you are left with two rounds cluttering the ejection port area. Repeatedly dropping magazines on a hard surface is not advised.

The stress can cause cracking or other weakening of the floor plate area. This can lead to the floor plate falling off during firing. This allows the plate, spring, follower, and all unexpended ammunition to fly out the bottom of the gun.

Older magazine springs had the reputation of becoming fatigued when stored fully loaded for long periods of time. Today, different magazine springs are used than the types of forty years ago. Smith & Wesson, as well as other manufacturers, routinely fill and store magazines for five years and longer, then test fire them. It is no longer considered necessary to relieve magazine spring tension periodically to avoid spring fatigue.

Ammunition carried in your magazines or speedloaders should be replaced with fresh ammunition every six months. It can become contaminated by gun lubrication, body moisture, and other circumstances. It is probably unnecessary to purchase all new ammunition; properly stored ammunition is suitable for replacement.

Any time a magazine or speed loader fails to work properly, relegate it to the practice box and never carry it again except to the practice range. Mark it in a distinguishing manner so there is no chance you will get it mixed up with good ones.

Do not waste time and money on imitation magazines. If your gun is made by Sig, for example, purchase Sig-made replacement magazines. If you want to use non-factory supplied magazines, use them in pistol matches or for practice. There is no harm done other than a bruised ego if a magazine malfunctions there. When utilizing them in a defensive situation, a malfunction could cost your life. The few dollars saved with an imitation product is not worth that cost. Good factory magazines for the most popular autoloaders might range from $25 to $60 each.

As a minimum you should have at least three magazines--one in the gun, one for primary reload, and one for spare. All three will be carried at the same time and rotated. The first magazine that causes a problem is notice to you that you should immediately purchase three new ones. The same holds true for revolver speedloaders, except they are not supplied by the factory. Safariland and HKS make good speedloaders for most revolver configurations of five-shot and six-shot cylinders. Be sure to check that the speedloader is for your particular revolver model.

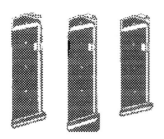

Glock 9mm Magazines
Standard, Left--Extended, Center--Compact, Right

Magazine carriers normally come as a single or double. The double holds two magazines side-by-side in individual pockets. If doubles are used, make sure the magazines are separated by at least the width of one finger. When the magazines are too close together, some people have difficulty grasping only the front one. Magazines should be inserted with the bullet nose facing the front and should not fall out during a backward roll.

Whether you have a speedloader or magazine, it should be function-tested several times with your carry ammunition before you allow yourself to carry it in conjunction with your defensive handgun. You must make sure everything functions and fits. The middle of a shooting encounter is no time to discover that the magazine or loader does not work "as advertised." Speedloaders should be visually inspected as often as magazines. That translates to every time you put the gun on. Speedloaders are relatively inexpensive when compared to magazines and retail in the $6 to $16 range for most models.

Speedloader carriers are available in single, double, triple, and stack pack. The stack pack contains four loaded loaders with one pair side-by-side stacked on top of another pair. As with autoloader magazines, the loaders should not fall out during a backward roll. A revolver shooter should carry at least two loaded speedloaders for his gun.

Body Armor

Body armor, as sold commercially, is not bullet-proof. When you read or hear that someone was "wearing a bullet proof vest," it is not true. If soft body armor were truly bullet-proof it would be too bulky and heavy for most people to move while wearing it. If you could find a bullet-proof vest that would stop .50 cal AP bullets or 20mm cannon bullets, and could be worn consistently every day, you would make a great deal of money.

In 1972, Dupont introduced "Kevlar." This material was designed as a fiber to strengthen radial tires. It did not take long for someone to come up with the idea of sewing layers of this material together in different thicknesses and marketing these panels for use in a vest of soft body armor. Numerous companies market soft body armor for law enforcement and the military. The basic differences are in the weave of the fabric and the envelope, or carrier, for the panels.

The strength of any particular vest was designated by its "threat level." The common levels of threat protection are I (one), Ia, II (two), IIa, and III (three), with I being the lowest and III being the highest level of protection. Designed primarily to defeat handgun bullets, a level I or Ia should stop .25 auto, .32 cal., .380 auto, and some slow, heavy .38 cal. Level II should defeat many .38 spl and some .45 acp. Level IIa should stop most .38 spl, 9mm, and .45 bullets. Level III is advertised to handle most handgun cartridges.

Many of the vests have an optional removable insert of hardened steel or ceramic for stopping some rifle cartridges. When worn with the insert in place, the vest is too heavy and bulky for everyday use and is used primarily in tactical situations. The idea behind the soft body armor vest is to spread the impact of the bullet over a large area, thereby reducing injury and prohibiting the bullet from penetrating the torso.

The bullet actually penetrates several layers of Kevlar material but hopefully is contained within the material. Even if the handgun bullet penetrates the vest, much of the energy is dissipated while going through the vest, leaving little energy for getting deep enough in the torso to damage organs. Even though the trauma is spread over a large area, there will be severe bruising and possibly cracked or broken bones. While these are extremely painful in their own right, it is considered preferable to the alternative. While any soft body armor is hot, bulky, inconvenient to wear, and reduces the wearer's mobility, it does save lives!

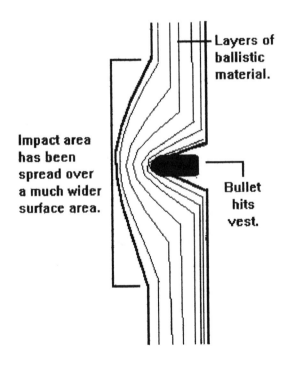

Bullet Hitting Vest

In 1989, Allied-Signal of Richmond, Virginia, began marketing a material, Spectra Shield, to compete with Dupont's Kevlar. It is a tough, modified polyethylene plastic. Allied-Signal advertises that their level II vests consistently stop "everything from 9mm to 44 Magnums." They claim, "in test after test, Spectra Shield has proven itself against high velocity threats, angle-shots, and multiple hits." Field and laboratory tests and experiences have largely validated their claims. More and more authorities in ballistic materials rank Spectra Shield as the superior product.

Whether your choice is Kevlar or Spectra Shield, it will do you no good if you are not wearing it at the time it is needed. High profile situations call for it. A major drawback is that good vests retail in the neighborhood of $600 or more. Most wearers look at it in the same way as they consider a good defensive handgun. They cost about the same and both can save your life if you have them when you need them.

If you buy body armor, make certain that it can be washed, since in wearing it will become stained and redolent of perspiration. Resist, however, buying a "waterproof" garment, since it will be very uncomfortable and lack the softness you will need for comfort.

Other Devices

It is hard to imagine a situation which would deem it necessary or even desirable for the protection agent to use a silencer on his defensive weapon. As you remember from the movies, the bad guys use silencers to kill their victims. Much of this is hokum, incidentally, particularly the devices which are pictured as silencers. Real silencers are sound suppressors which reduce and alter the sound of a gunshot so that it is not recognizable as a gunshot. The gunshot is, however, audible. Silencers are normally used in covert assault operations.

Silencers are considered by the U.S. Treasury Department to be Class III items and, as such, must be registered with the federal government. They are, therefore, as legal or illegal as a fully automatic firearm.

Light/optical attachments include gun mounted flashlights and red dot or laser optical systems. While the attachment of a small flashlight might be a good thing to have in a tactical building search during low light encounters, it is considered an extreme inconvenience on a defensive carry gun. Basically, a mount is secured to the gun in which a small flashlight can be secured, usually in line with and below the barrel. A wire connects the light, the battery pack, and a pressure pad switch. This switch is secured to the gun in a position where it can be pressed by the palm of the hand, a thumb, or other finger while the gun is held in the firing position. The theory is to allow the user to keep both hands on the gun while performing building and area searches in reduced light. The light can be activated, when the shooter desires, in short light bursts while searching for targets.

The laser optics and red dot optics are wonderful for fast, accurate target acquisition. A sighting optical tube like a small scope is mounted to the top of the gun. The user activates the on/off switch and brings the gun to eye level. A small red dot appears in the scope and shows where bullet impact will be if the gun is fired at that instant. The other optical system, the laser, is usually mounted to the side or under the gun. When activated, a narrow beam of red light, visible to the naked eye, is projected on the target where the barrel is pointing. The gun can be held at eye level, waist level, or any level you choose. The red light shows where the gun is pointing. However, any of the light and optical systems add considerably to the bulk of a defensive carry gun and render them too bulky to carry daily. Their place is for use in tactical situations. For example, a protective agent, assigned at a gate house, could have an auxiliary weapon so equipped and available in the gate house should the need arise. It would be supplemental weaponry, stored in the gate house, and available to him for special situations.

RECOMMENDED HANDGUNS

As by now you recognize, the selection of a handgun is not a simple matter. There is no perfect gun for everyone. Listed below, however, are handguns which have proven their durability,

efficiency, and usefulness. It is a short list and may not include your favorite handgun. No matter--as they say, "that's what makes horse racing."

What is important is that you choose a pistol that you feel comfortable with, one that allows you to operate the trigger, buttons, and levers with only your shooting hand.

45 ACP

Colt/Browning system autoloaders include Springfield Armory or Springfield, Inc. Government Models and Colt Government Model, Officers Model, Commander, or Commander Lightweight. Better quality and durability for the Colt is found in the Series 70 or older models. The newer production Colt in Series 80 might be a distant third choice. There are many copies of the Colt pistols available. Many have manufacturer stamping indicating a Colt look-alike was assembled outside this country. The only .45 ACP Colt/Browning systems recommended are those previously mentioned.

Trigger cocking (D/A) models from Smith & Wesson or Sig-Sauer with slide-mounted or frame-mounted decock levers are also recommended. Glock is highly recommended.

40 S&W

Currently, the only recommended styles are those made by Smith & Wesson and Glock.

9MM

Glock is a modern phenomenon. Glock guns sell so fast that many dealers must place your name on a waiting list to purchase either the Glock M19 or M17. These guns are very well engineered and durable, as well as light, safe, and easy to use. They are highly recommended. Persons with "basketball player-sized hands" will probably choose the longer grip of the M17. The M17-L is a light trigger competition version with a long slide and is not conducive to concealed carry.

H & K P-7 series is one of the most desirable systems on the market. However, the cost is in excess of $1,000, taking it out of the realm of most persons.

Beretta 92 series offers both a full size and a compact size. The full size is larger than many hands will accommodate but both are very reliable. They also offer single stack versions in the 92 series. Beretta has the longest trigger pull of the recommended guns, which adds slightly to the firing time. The lack of forward magazine base extension makes it more difficult to remove a sticking magazine.

Smith & Wesson offers full size and compact versions in double or single stack configurations. Choices of finish, size, and capacity are numerous. Anything except the old style 2 digit model or 2 digit dash numbers are recommended.

Sig has a shorter trigger pull than some of the Smiths and offers both full size and compact versions.

Ruger makes a big, strong, reliable pistol. Persons with small hands would be better advised to chose another pistol. Except for size it's a very good gun.

Browning Hi-Power is an "oldie but a goodie." There are numerous versions of this pistol on the market and the only one recommended is stamped "Made in Belgium." It is the MK-II. The only acceptable alternate is Browning Hi-Power assembled in Portugal.

Walther P5 and P88 are other high dollar recommendations like the H&K P-7. The P5 is small and the P88 is full sized. The P5 has the ejection port on the left side which makes it a favorite of high roller left-handers.

38 SPL or 357

Small frame. It is not uncommon for defensive shooters to carry a "backup" gun in a trouser or jacket pocket. The smallest revolver suitable for this purpose is a five-shot S&W J-frame with fully concealed or shrouded hammer in the "Bodyguard" or "Centennial" series. Other types should be avoided due to possible hammer snag when fired from inside the pocket or when drawing the pistol. Additionally, this pistol has a barrel length of only two inches. The Ruger five-shot is slightly larger that the J-frame.

Medium frame. Another short barrel (three inches or less) backup is available from S&W in the round butt, six-shot, K-frame series. The Ruger version is the SP101.

Approved large frame revolvers are the S&W L-frames and the Ruger GP100. Both are available in short barrel versions for primary carry and should be carried with .357 Magnum rounds rather than .38 spl loads. Primary carry of revolvers with barrel lengths exceeding four inches should be avoided.

.380 AUTO

This small frame autoloader should be considered only as a backup carry gun in the same vein as a five-shot revolver. Reasonably priced Walther PP down to PPK/S versions are good choices when loaded with ball ammunition. Browning BDA could be considered as an alternate; however, the thickness of the handle makes this somewhat bulky for concealed carry. If you can hide the wide BDA, you would be better served to hide a 9mm.

RECOMMENDED HANDGUN AMMUNITION

The "Big-3" ammunition manufacturers in this country are still Federal, Winchester, and Remington. Their products are recommended due to their consistency and proven track records. Offerings from CCI in Idaho are also excellent and widely available. Imports worth considering include offerings by PMC (Pan Metal Corporation) and IMI (Israeli Military Industries). It should be remembered that good marketing techniques call for refinements in old products and introduction of new products. Ammunition manufacturers are no different. The better ones constantly strive to satisfy the demands for the "newest and best" thing on the market. When in doubt as to what is currently the "best," call your local police department and talk with someone in their firearms training unit. They are usually aware of the newest or most popular law enforcement loadings and manufacturer.

For 45 ACP

Recommended is Federal 230 grain "Hydra-Shok." It combines good feeding characteristics with good penetration and expansion. 230 grain ball by any of the major manufacturers is also a good choice for defensive work. The admirable track record going back many decades makes it a favorite of soldiers and lawmen alike. If your preference is for "fast," Remington 185 grain +P is a good choice.

For 9mm

Either 147 grain "Hydra-Shok" by Federal or 147 grain "OSM" by Winchester is a good choice. The Federal round is very long and does not live-eject well from some Glocks. Make sure it functions reliably in your gun before purchasing large quantities. Another excellent choice is 124 grain Nyclad by Federal. It has good penetration and expansion and feeds well in most 9mm handguns.

Do not use IMI "Carbine" ammunition in your handgun. It will chamber in most 9mm handguns but is designed for use in shoulder weapons like the UZI and H&K. It is loaded to higher pressures than handgun ammunition and can create excessive wear and breakage when used in handguns.

It should also be noted that some manufacturers of 9mm pistols specify in their literature, "Do not shoot non-jacketed ammunition in this pistol." Lead bullets, fired at standard 9mm velocities, tend to lead the barrel excessively. Some manufacturer's concerns are that this leading will build up in a barrel to the point that additional bullets will actually swage (press) the barrel out of shape as they are forced down the barrel. In actual practice, the problem is often negligible if the barrel is frequently inspected and cleaned. If any lead bullets

are fired through your gun, you should thoroughly clean the barrel after each magazine has been fired. Also be aware that firing lead bullets may cause the accuracy of your barrel to deteriorate as it is swaged out of shape. Even though lead bullets do not cause any particular problem in many guns, if it happens in yours, it is a problem.

For 10mm or .40 S&W

Any Federal Hydra-Shok offering available is a good choice. None have a sufficient track record to legitimately offer a valid recommendation. Popularity currently tends to lean toward the .40 S&W.

For 38 spl

Small frame revolvers. Federal 125 grain Nyclad "Chiefs Special" is a good choice. The 158 grain RNL is usually considered a better performer but due to somewhat severe recoil, many people find it very unpleasant to shoot.

Medium frame revolvers. Federal 129 grain Hydra-Shok +P or a 158 grain LHP +P by any of the "Big-3" is probably the best choice. Winchester seems to have less muzzle flash than the others in this caliber and weight.

For 357 Mag

Winchester 145 grain Silvertip is a good choice for those who can handle the recoil. Federal 125 grain HP is also a preferred round.

For 380 Auto (9 mm Kurz)

As a minimum caliber for defensive work, RN ball ammunition of any major manufacturer should be the only choice. Numerous hollow points are readily available but none offer sufficient velocity or weight for adequate penetration.

MAINTENANCE

Like automobiles, guns must be regularly

cleaned, checked, and maintained. In addition to (possibly) saving your life, a good handgun represents a sizeable investment of dollars. Taking care of it assiduously will help to prolong its life. Good maintenance will certainly go a long way toward preventing untimely breakdowns. (Remember the story of Aldo Moro's bodyguard's rusted gun?)

Maintenance begins with the arrival of your newly purchased handgun. Having spent a good deal of money for it, you would surely expect it to be in perfect condition. That expectation is erroneous. Your new gun (unless it has been serviced) will have been packed with heavy grease, and will likely contain minute metal chips and grinding grit left over from the factory. To be on the safe side you should instantly take your newly purchased gun to an armorer who can disassemble it, thoroughly clean it, and check all moving parts to make certain they function properly and have not been damaged in shipping. He will then apply a light coating of oil, and you are now ready to test-fire your new weapon. The shop where you purchased your gun can recommend a reliable armorer. Do not allow anyone who has not been properly trained to disassemble your gun. Also, be aware that simple dunk tank ultra sound type cleaners are not considered a viable alternative to detail strip cleaning. This process tends to leave sludge in hard-to-reach places around springs and plungers.

Make certain that you have been given instructional material which (like an automobile manual) will give you excellent information about the care and keeping of your gun. Read it carefully and follow all maintenance instructions. The people who wrote the material manufactured your weapon. They know more about it than anyone else. If you do not follow their maintenance requirements, you may violate your warranty.

When the pistol is returned from deep cleaning, take it to the range and fire two or three hundred rounds. Usually, if something is going to break, it will do so with that amount of shooting. It will also enable you to determine that your sights are adjusted for POA/POI at twenty-five yards with the

ammunition you will be carrying. POA is point of aim or the specific place on the target you are holding your sights. POI is point of impact or the specific place the bullets are actually hitting on the target. POA and POI should be the same. Handguns are routinely rough-zeroed at the factory at distances of seven to fifteen yards.

After this test firing, the unloaded pistol can then be field stripped, cleaned, and inspected. The factory literature that comes with your pistol gives detailed information on the proper manner of field stripping that gun. It also advises you not to disassemble the gun any farther than indicated in the literature. Pay heed to those words. When you take it apart farther than your training qualifies you to do, you may cause damage that the factory is not responsible for repairing.

You should clean the pistol after every firing. Whether it is just a few rounds or many is not the issue. Any rounds fired will leave some residue inside and outside the pistol. All of it is harmful when left on for long periods of time. Fresh residue of grit, lead, and dirt can be wiped away easily; however, if it hardens, you have a much tougher cleaning job. The gun won't rust away if you don't clean it immediately. However, that kind of treatment does accelerate the wear of the finish as well as internal parts. Firing even one round creates heat which starts eroding the internal lubricants. When fired again, those parts with less lubrication than necessary will wear more quickly. It's best to form the good habit of cleaning within a day after firing any rounds. Immediately after completing your range session is even better.

Cleaning your gun provides you with the opportunity to check it for hairline cracks, loose attachments (sights, etc.) and any other oddities.

You should clean your gun at regular intervals even if you do not use it, particularly if you carry it consistently, since body perspiration and oils will damage the gun. You should test-fire the gun (and your shooting accuracy) every month or so, which means more than shooting a few rounds.

This may sound unnecessary but, nonetheless, **before cleaning your gun be certain to unload it completely!**

To clean the pistol you need some basic tools and supplies. The items that come in the box with the gun are minimal and marginal. These supplied tools will allow you to clean the bore and little else. Merely cleaning the bore and perhaps wiping off the outside does not constitute cleaning the pistol.

Your list of actual supplies should include:

1.   Cleaning patches or clean, soft fabric, disposable rags, or cloth.

Something like part of an old tee-shirt is good. Don't use the whole tee-shirt as you should dispose of the rag when finished. Don't keep the rag to wash because you will leave lead contaminate in your clothes washer which in turn will be deposited into any clothing washed later.

2.   00 Steel wool.

Steel wool is available in numerous textures. Double 0 is readily available at hardware stores and is fine enough not to mar a finish but strong enough not to disintegrate while using.

3.   Cleaning rod.

Most pistols come with some sort of factory furnished rod. Virtually all will accept threaded universal cleaning brushes except those made by Glock. You don't need a 16-inch long rod to clean a four-inch barrel. A standard handgun cleaning rod of six to eight inches in length is recommended. Aluminum rods are softer than steel and less likely to mar the bore.

4.   Chamber brush.

This is a round brush with copper or stainless steel bristles in rows which screw onto the threaded end of a cleaning rod. The chamber brush is used *only* for the chamber. It is not intended to go into the bore and it is not intended to be used to scrub any other part of the pistol. It must be of the appropriate caliber. Don't mash a .45 cal brush into the chamber of a .38 spl.

5.   Bore brush.

This is a round brush like the cylinder brush but with slightly smaller diameter. It is not quite big enough to adequately clean the chamber. Like the chamber brush, the bore brush has one use. It goes down the bore, period. Don't bend and kink the bristles by using it to scrub other parts of the gun and never wrap a cleaning patch around it to final-finish the bore. The brush alone goes in the bore on the end of the rod.

6.   Stiff bristle toothbrush.

For light to medium work the military brush works best. It has standard toothbrush-looking nylon bristles on one end. The other end is very narrow and usually has a single row of short, stiff bristles. This narrow end is for use under the point of the extractor. Stainless steel bristle toothbrushes are also available for areas of heavy buildup.

7.   Pressure spray de-greaser.

Pressurized cans of lubricants such as WD-40 won't get all the greasy residue out of the gun. WD-40 should not be used anywhere near chamber areas. Products similar to Gun Scrubber or Gunk-out work very well but should not be sprayed on tritium night sights.

8.   Synthetic grease lubricant.

A one-ounce tube of synthetic grease will work better than gun oil for slides and rails on autoloaders. A single tube should last a long time unless you use it to grease a howitzer. PGL, manufactured for Pachmayr, is very good and there are other excellent choices on the market. The synthetic grease lubes are non-penetrating and, unlike some gun oils, do not tend to work into the primers of ammunition and kill them. Further, it is not as runny and messy as others. It tends to stay where you put it. It does not gum up or become too stiff to work at 20 degrees below zero or run out the bottom of the gun when it's 120 degrees. Finally, it does not tend to attract lint and other airborne debris as easily as gun oils.

9.   Inexpensive safety glasses.

Clear plastic eye protection is good to have in the unlikely event that a part flies out during the disassembly. Glasses also protect your eyes from the tiny particles flying about during the cleaning process.

10.   Disposable rubber surgical gloves.

These will protect your hands from the lead contaminate and residue. They are thin enough to allow "feel" of small parts.

To actually perform the entire cleaning process, you will go through ten individual steps. It is best to complete your cleaning without interruption in a private, quiet area where you can concentrate on the task at hand--the "gun cleaning mental mode."

CHECKLIST FOR HANDGUN CLEANING

1.   Enter the gun cleaning mental mode.

2.   Take your cleaning supplies to your cleaning area.

3.   Lay down a protective covering.

4.   Unload the pistol and separate the ammunition.

5.   Perform the cleaning process.

6.   Thoroughly check all cleaned parts.

7.   Reassemble the pistol and test functions.

8.   Secure the pistol and refrain from handling until after step 10.

9.   Clean up work mess, yourself, and dispose of the debris.

10.   Exit the gun cleaning mental mode.

SUPPLEMENTAL DEFENSIVE WEAPONS

Supplemental firearms include firearms not normally carried on the person. They are used in special circumstances when the primary or backup handgun is not sufficient for a particular task at hand. Such firearms include the shotgun, sub-machine gun, and rifle. These three kinds of firearms are used as shoulder weapons. That is, they are normally held to the shoulder when fired. As with handguns, shoulder weapons have sights and a trigger. They differ in the types of sights, method of trigger operation, grip, and manner of loading. They all have longer barrels than standard defensive handguns.

Backup Guns

In addition to his primary handgun, the prudent agent carries an additional gun concealed on his person. This gun needs to be accessible but not necessarily as readily accessible as the primary one. Favorite methods of carry are:

.   Inside the shirt. This can be an inside-the-pants holster carried on the side or in the small of the back. Under-the-arm shoulder rigs are also popular.

.   A small pocket pistol carried in the support-side pocket.

.   Leg holster or ankle holster.

The objective is to have another gun concealed on the person, one that is not visible to anyone who might capture you. A backup gun is usually smaller and therefore more easily concealed. Numerous lives have been saved by a backup when the primary handgun has been lost during an encounter. At the first opportunity, the backup gun is drawn from the place of concealment and used. Numerous lives have been lost when the backup gun failed to operate. The usual cause of failure to fire in such cases is accumulated lint, grime, and grit in the mechanism. Since most people who carry a backup gun rarely fire it, they do not perceive the need to clean it. In actuality, the need for armorer-level detail maintenance is usually higher than for the primary gun. Because the backup is very close to the body, it is subject to more body moisture and compacted particles of lint and dirt.

In the two examples shown, the Bodyguard model on top has a shrouded hammer (outer shroud conceals the hammer from the sides). The Centennial model below it has an internal hammer that does not snag on clothing, even from the back. Both are five-shot two-inch .38 spl revolvers.

SHROUDED HAMMER

CONCEALED HAMMER

Backup Guns

Most shooters prefer to carry a backup with the same caliber and frame configuration as the primary gun. While this is desirable, it is not necessary. If you carry a backup with the idea that it is a last ditch, final resort, up close, and personal method of defense, a very small .22 or .25 cal. handgun fired into an eye socket, is a very good

defense. The point is, the gun should be small enough that you can carry and hide it along with your primary gun. Carrying only a very small backup is not considered sufficient for defense. Laws governing the carrying of concealed firearms do not differentiate between primary carry and backup carry. Concealed is concealed. A backup handgun should be fired and cleaned whenever you fire and clean your primary handgun.

Shotgun

Few commonly carried weapons possess the destructive power of the shotgun. It has been a mainstay of military and law enforcement since the trench warfare days of World War I. Pointing a 12-gauge shotgun at someone nearly always gets their attention. This firearm is intimidating and versatile due to the variety of basic configurations and availability of specialty ammunition. While they are not usually as heavily restricted by law as handguns, they are big, heavy, and inconvenient to use. Shotgun barrels must be at least 18 inches long according to federal law. That, coupled with the federal mandate of minimum 26-inch overall length, makes it inconvenient to conceal for law-abiding persons. Non-law abiding persons simply cut down the length of the barrel making it less inconvenient to carry on a sling beneath a coat. It is easier to carry a shotgun in the trunk of a car or to keep it handy for home defense from a stationary position of cover. From a tactical perspective, the length otherwise makes it difficult to use in confined places.

Shotguns are available in three basic configurations and numerous models.

1.   Single barrel/single shot.

2.   Single barrel/repeater.

These include the manually operated pump action and lever action, as well as the semi-automatic. The pump is cycled by pulling the forend stock to the rear, then pushing it back to the front. The lever action is cycled by pulling down a long, hinged lever by the trigger guard, then pulling it back up into place. These actions release a round from the tube or box magazine on the back (down) action, then chamber that round on the forward (up) action. The semi-auto is cycled by pulling back the bolt handle releasing a round from the magazine and the forward motion of the bolt chambers that round.

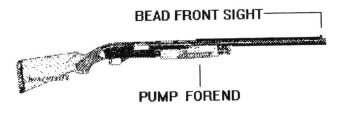

BEAD FRONT SIGHT

PUMP FOREND

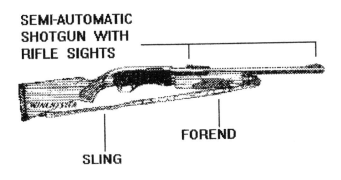

SEMI-AUTOMATIC SHOTGUN WITH RIFLE SIGHTS

FOREND

SLING

Shotguns

3.   Double barrel.

Double barrel shotguns are available in either side-by-side or over-and-under models. The side-by-side model is usually referred to as a "double barrel." Identically chambered tubes are joined parallel to each other and centered on one common frame and stock. They usually have two triggers in the same trigger guard (one trigger for each hammer and barrel). The over-and-under shotguns are also double barreled. One barrel is mounted directly on top of the other. The barrels are usually the same caliber but it is not uncommon for the top barrel to be a small caliber rifle barrel with the bottom barrel a shotgun barrel.

The bore of a shotgun barrel is smooth and without rifling. Rifling is used to create laterally rotating bullet spin for stability in flight. Since the bore of the shotgun is smooth, a slang term for shotguns is "smooth-bore." The caliber (diameter) of a shotgun bore is called "gauge." The smaller the number of the gauge, the larger the diameter. A very heavy recoil 8-gauge is best fired by someone other than yourself while a light recoil 20-gauge is easily controlled by almost anyone.

A rifle shoots a bullet while the shotgun is designed to shoot multiple projectiles from each cartridge. These projectiles are called "shot." Buckshot contains large pellets and birdshot contains very small pellets. The individual pellets are sometimes referred to as BB's. Shotgun rounds loaded with shot are available in various sizes. Shot size called number nine (#9) shot is very small and used for hunting small birds, snakes, etc., and was used in riot control in the past. It is also a favorite of some trap and skeet shooters because there are several hundred pellets per shot and the recoil is manageable. The small shot is not very penetrative and usually travels less than 300 yards. Number five (#5) shot is a larger birdshot favored by many when hunting larger birds such as pheasant. While it is more penetrative, it rarely carries to 300 yards either. The larger the shot number, the smaller the pellet size.

Buckshot consists of much larger pellets than birdshot. As with birdshot, the lower the number, the larger the size and the fewer that fit into a cartridge. They range in size from #'s 4, 3, 2, 1, 0, 00, and 000. For 12-gauge loading, #4 buckshot contains 27 pellets. The 00 (double-aught) is the recommended choice for defensive 12-gauge loads. Each of the nine pellets are approximately the size of a .32 caliber bullet. A 00 magnum cartridge containing 12 pellets is also available. Buckshot was originally designed for deer hunting. From a defensive cartridge perspective, the 12-gauge loaded with 00 is very effective to 25 yards. Some combinations of gun and ammunition consistently keep all nine pellets from one shot on a man-sized silhouette target up to a range of 45 yards. Penetration using buckshot is substantially deeper than that of birdshot. Penetration is similar to that of handguns but with many more projectiles in the same area.

There are other commonly available cartridges known as rifled slugs. These are a single solid projectile. Shot and buckshot are round balls while the slug is somewhat elongated like a normal bullet and has rifling around its outside diameter. The rifling creates a stabilizing spin similar to that which a barrel with rifling creates on a smooth-sided bullet. A 12-gauge rifled slug weighing 437 grains can be fired accurately in excess of 100 yards. A very skilled shooter with the right combination of gun, sights, and ammunition can fire with devastating accuracy up to 200 yards. The large diameter (about the size of a dime) coupled with great penetration makes this choice a very destructive round. When fired at a car door, it will often penetrate to the interior with enough energy to produce lethal wounding of an occupant.

If you have a choice in stocks, synthetic materials are recommended over wood. The plastics available today are tougher than wood and do not warp. Since the plastic is unattractive right from the beginning, the small scratches and blemishes that occur do not detract from the overall appearance. Plastic is much less likely to break during a defensive butt stroke than wood. Bottom line is--you get wood for "pretty" and plastic for work.

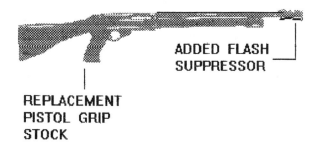

ADDED FLASH SUPPRESSOR

REPLACEMENT PISTOL GRIP STOCK

Shotgun with Pistol Grip

A solid stock is usually more comfortable for shooting than folding or collapsible stocks. However, if you need to carry the shotgun in a suitcase or conceal it beneath a coat, the reduced length available by folding or collapsing the stock makes the task easier. Under most circumstances, to achieve accurate firing, the folding stock should be extended before use. Solid stocks are often available with an integral pistol grip. This makes sense in a defensive shotgun as it makes the shotgun more controllable.

Shotguns are commonly carried in estate protection and strike (asset) protection.

Rifle

In most urban situations, the shotgun is the only feasible shoulder weapon which should be used. Rifles are simply too penetrative and long-range for consideration. A bullet from a high-powered rifle can reach a distance of one mile, and still have enough energy to injure or kill someone or something. However, should you be trapped with your client on his ranch 50 miles from effective help, a good scoped rifle is useful. If the attacker is armed with a rifle, firing from cover at a distance of 100 or more yards, a shotgun will not do much good. You will need a rifle to successfully thwart the attack and protect yourselves.

A lightweight, short-barrel version of a rifle is a carbine. There are a number of compact carbines available with a wide assortment of stocks, sights, finishes, and chambers. Some are even chambered to accept pistol cartridges. The most popular of these is 9mm but you will also find .357 magnum, .44 magnum, and a few .45 ACP. Carbines are classified as rifles in this country; therefore, they must have a barrel of at least 16 inches in length. Depending on the propellant used, bullets travelling at pistol velocities tend to stop accelerating in a barrel at about seven to seven and one-half inches. You actually gain little increased accuracy from the longer barrel on a carbine. You do gain a little increased bullet spin stability and a longer sight radius (distance from the front sight to the rear sight). The longer sight radius creates the illusion of more precise sight picture. For this reason, a pistol bullet seems more accurate at seventy-five yards to 100 yards when fired from a carbine rather than a pistol.

Most military and some civilian rifles are configured as semi-automatics. Other popular actions are the bolt action and lever action. Pump actions are popular on low-powered rifles such as .22 caliber plinking rifles. As with shotguns, the advantage to semi-auto rifles is that much of the recoil is absorbed by the gas-operated action. The disadvantage is increased weight.

Browning Semi-Auto Rifle

With the bolt action rifle, the bolt is operated by means of the attached lever which usually extends from the bolt and down the right side. The advantage of the bolt action is that it is lighter. It provides equal accuracy to that of the semi-automatic. A disadvantage is the extended time it takes to operate the bolt for each shot. The lever is rotated upwards with the strong hand, pulled all the way back to eject a case, pushed all the way forward to strip a round off the magazine and chamber it, then locked in place by rotating it back down. Tight bolt lockup (at least equal to that of the semi-automatic) is necessary for long-range accuracy.

Winchester Bolt Action Rifle

The third type of action, the lever action, has evolved from the "saddle" carbine of the Old West days. The lever is usually pulled down with the strong hand. As the lever goes down, the bolt comes back ejecting the case. A round is also released from the tube magazine located parallel to and under the barrel. As the lever is pulled back up, the round is chambered and the action locked.

The short barrel and quick operating action have made it an old favorite of hunters in brush and mountain country. It is usually chambered for lighter cartridges such as the .30-.30 cal. or .35 Remington. Chambered in this fashion, it does not possess the extreme long-range accuracy potential of the other two rifle actions. However, it is often credited with getting more deer over the years than any other type of rifle.

Winchester Lever Action Rifle

There are dozens of excellent rifle calibers in common use. While each has special advantages, at the current time two are recommended. Both are universally available and both are widely used in military applications. The first is .223 Remington, also named 5.56mm. The second is .308 Winchester, also named 7.62mm X 59. A shorter version of this cartridge, 7.62mm X 39, is used in the AK-47 and is common in former Eastern Bloc and Asian countries.

The AK style gun is considered by many to be the best military battle rifle ever designed. Whether that is true or not is subject to debate. Which ammunition is best and which gun is best? Any of these listed cartridges allows a good, practiced rifle shooter to consistently hit human targets at ranges of two hundred or more yards. All possess nearly identical accuracy qualities at those ranges. The lighter weight .223 is more likely to be blown slightly off-course by wind deflection than the heavier .308. The .308 creates greater penetration at extreme ranges and is regularly fired by counter-snipers at ranges of 1,000 yards. Even though the .308 travels at more than 25 percent less velocity than the .223, the recoil is substantially heavier, because the bullet weighs three times as much. Unless extreme ranges are anticipated, most riflemen equip themselves with something like a Ruger Mini-14 chambered for .223 cal. cartridges. This or similar configurations are lighter than full-size military battle rifles. Recoil is more manageable, accuracy to the recommended sight-in distance of 100 yards is excellent, and ammunition is inexpensive enough that extensive practice is feasible.

As with shotguns, replacement stocks of composition plastic and an integral pistol grip are desired. The gun will probably be subjected to more abuse than a recreational rifle. Collapsible stocks for rifles should be avoided unless there is a specific need for concealment or transport. A good flash suppressor is necessary to avoid night vision wash-out or revealing your position from any direction other than directly to the front. A military peep sight at the rear with a generous sized sighting hole is also desirable. The larger sighting hole allows for quicker target acquisition. The front sight should be protected as it is vulnerable to the rough use given many rifles.

As any hunter knows, scopes provide an added measure of accuracy; however, the scope has some disadvantages. It is bulky, and it often requires more time for sighting the target than using the basic rifle sights. Reality is that the attacker is more apt to use a high-powered scope than the person being attacked.

As a compromise, a scope with slight magnification is usually better than extreme magnification, as it will provide increased accuracy (and identification) at short ranges and you will probably not be using your rifle to fire long distances. Extreme magnification causes the target to dance and waver in the scope unless solid support is used, much like using an extremely long lens on your camera.

Cheaper utility scopes work as well as good ones in bright daylight. The quality scopes have superior light-gathering capabilities under cloudy or dim light conditions. For clarity, light-gathering ability, and resolution, the best scopes in the world are the German Zeiss and the Austrian Kahles and Swarovski brands. They are also extremely expensive.

Since the scope is no better than the mounts that attach it to the rifle, get good quality mounts and have the scope and mounts installed by a reputable gunsmith. This is not something to be trusted to the neighborhood armorer. Because a scope is fragile and subject to damage through mishandling, the iron sights should not be removed when the scope and mounts are attached. The iron sights beneath the scope must be usable in case the scope becomes unusable.

As with all defensive weapons, the rifle and shotgun should be as smooth and sleek as possible, and free of sharp corners and burrs to catch on clothing and other extraneous objects. The weapon must be comfortable to carry, reliable, durable, and accurate; otherwise, it has limited, if any, value to your defense. You must, of course, practice with your rifle and shotgun to maintain your accuracy and comfort level; then, clean, check, and provide any repairs to keep it in tip-top condition.

Regardless of your choice of shotgun or rifle, be certain that you have the availability of dealer service and spare parts. Often, people are surprised to find they have purchased a neat gun that they cannot get serviced. Name manufacturers with nationwide dealer networks are often a better choice for shopping than the local gun show. Go to gun shows for fun and bargains rather than for defensive firearms.

SUB-MACHINE GUNS

A machine gun fires rifle or larger-sized caliber cartridges. A sub-machine gun (sub-gun), fires pistol caliber rounds. Both guns have the capability of firing more than one round every time the trigger is pressed. A short gun that looks like a sub-machine gun but only fires one round each time the trigger is pressed is not a sub-machine gun.

The old-style weapon favored by gangsters and law enforcement alike during the prohibition era was the Thompson sub-machine gun. A slang name for it is "Tommy Gun." Its popularity extended through World War II. It holds a whole box of ammunition in a single round "drum" magazine, but the compression of the spring makes it somewhat difficult to load. A disadvantage is the long magazine spring which sometimes kinks or jams and fails to feed all the rounds. Additionally, the weight makes it difficult to carry after longer periods of time.

Modern sub-machine guns are much more light, compact, user friendly, and dependable. One of the most popular and efficient styles is the UZI. Modern sub-guns are normally equipped with collapsible shoulder stocks which make them relatively easy to carry and conceal. Sub-guns usually are equipped with a selector switch which allows firing modes to be switched from safe to full auto mode or single shot mode. Some guns have an additional position for firing a three-shot burst. A sub-gun can be fired like a rifle, using the sights and firing one shot at a time. However, the sub-gun is best used in close environments where targets are moving rapidly.

The ideal cyclic rate of fire for a sub-gun is about 850 rounds per minute. This means the bolt cycles and fires at a rate that would expend 850 rounds in one minute if you had a magazine capable of feeding it. If you hold the trigger back for one second, you fire about 14 rounds. A trigger technique known as "trigger bump" actually lets you fire as few as two to four rounds per bump. Best accuracy is obtained by moving the selector switch to the single shot mode. Best tactical accuracy is obtained by firing three rounds per burst. Absolutely the most fun is to hold the trigger back until the 30-round magazine is emptied.

H&K MP5 is another excellent choice and is the most accurate sub-gun when fired in the single shot mode. The UZI has the smoothest feel when fired in full auto mode. The advantage to sub-guns is that they are superior to other firearms at close range against fast moving targets. They are not superior in other aspects. Unless used in the single shot mode, the danger of all those bullets careening around is simply unacceptable. Every single bullet will find a target; that is, it will hit *something*. That something might be a child or other innocent bystander. Again, it is the bad guy who is more apt to carry a sub-

machine gun, since the probability of an innocent casualty is fairly acceptable to him.

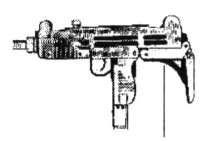

UZI Sub-Machine Gun with Collapsible Stock

Because all true automatic firearms are severely regulated by the federal government, most people will never be able to possess one. In this country, sub-guns remain a curiosity for the vast majority of shooters. However, after first mastering their other personal firearms, serious shooters should have some experience with them. There are numerous indoor ranges around the country that legally rent sub-guns for use on their premises. Unless you are involved in an extremely high-risk, sanctioned assignment or work for the government, using a rental sub-gun at a range may be your only opportunity to handle one.

THE SHOOTING INCIDENT

Hopefully, as with the U.S. Secret Service, you will never have to use your defensive weapon for any purpose other than target shooting on the range. On the other hand, you will spend a fair amount of your time mentally and mechanically preparing for that dread moment when all threat assessments and proactive measures fail, and the incident "comes down." If and when that happens, you must be fully knowledgeable of the actualities and repercussions of a shooting incident. Even if you and your client survive without a scratch, a lot of unpleasant side effects await you.

Stopping Power

What happens when a person--someone else

or you--is shot? If you glean all of your information from the movies you undoubtedly believe that all bullets hit their intended target and that most gunshot wounds are dramatic and fatal. You rarely see, in the movies or on television, shots that miss their target, and when they hit, they immediately incapacitate the target(s).

Fortunately, or unfortunately as the case may be, this is not the norm. Shooting accuracy, even among the bad guys, is fairly poor, particularly at longer distances, and performed under conditions of total surprise, fear, nervousness, and stress. After all, it is not an everyday occurrence. Imagining a shooting incident is a far cry from actually experiencing one. This is why your training and practice must be regular and consistent, not erratic. You must become so proficient with your defensive weapon(s) that your reactions are instant, effective, and visceral--no time to think, merely to assess and react.

If the incident is well planned and the adversary is in sufficient numbers, well-entrenched, and outguns you in firepower, you are in severe trouble. This, however, is the situation that your intelligence-gathering, threat assessments, and advance planning should eliminate, and, if they don't, your escape and evasion driving skills should take hold.

No, your problem may well be a complete surprise, something that should never have happened, when a total stranger with a gun appears out of the shadows and starts shooting. What are the chances that he/she will hit you? It depends, of course, upon distance, light, his shooting skill, your immediate reactions, and other factors. The fact is, you may not be hit (although someone else may be struck). The mere fact that someone else has a gun does not guarantee that you are helpless and almost dead.

Can you draw your gun and hit him first, and *will that stop him*? Let us assume that, because of your assiduous practice, you can hit him. Whether or not that stops him is another question.

In truth, a great many people who are hit, even with powerful bullets, not only do not die, they are not incapacitated sufficiently to make them helpless. There are numerous instances of individuals being hit with multiple bullets who did not die and who created a lot of damage before they succumbed to their wounds. Strong, enraged individuals who were shot in the heart have demonstrated that it may take agonizingly long seconds to die, meanwhile using a gun or knife effectively enough to damage or kill others. This is one of the reasons why you should not merely try to "wound" a real adversary. Therefore, merely hitting him is not enough--you must incapacitate (stop) him. Okay, what must you do to incapacitate him?

Loss of blood pressure. This is probably the most effective "stopper." Bullet wounds which cause massive and sudden bleeding and resulting loss of blood pressure will stop an adversary--although he/she may still take more time than you would like to cease causing damage to you and your client. It is a fact that loss of blood pressure to the brain will incapacitate an individual. Note that mere loss of blood is not the stopper. It is loss of blood pressure. The body's circulatory system depends upon the heart, liver, kidneys, spleen, major arteries, and aorta to supply blood. Massive traumatic damage to one or more of these organs will cause instant loss of blood pressure and, unless reversed, death. Though not instantaneous, this is a reliable and fast stopper. Bullets aimed at upper body mass (mid-chest) will have better results than bullets aimed at knee caps, shooting hand, shoulder, or even, perhaps, the head. If necessary to preserve your life and your client's, you must be prepared to fire more than once, since you must cause enough damage to stop him, not merely hit him.

Damage to the Neurological (Nervous) System. This is an equally effective, but much more difficult, stopper since to cause incapacitating damage the shot must be to the brain or spinal column. A head shot, unless performed at extremely close range, is difficult and not guaranteed to either penetrate the brain or cause sufficient damage. Because the brain is of such major importance to the well-being of the body, it is well protected by nature and the skull. Trying to shoot someone in the spinal column is extremely difficult unless you are within close range. However, if the person is hit in the spine, he will reliably collapse.

Psychological or Emotional Reaction. Since we know that bullets do not always incapacitate an individual, we can only hope that our adversaries do not share that knowledge, because there is a good possibility that merely being hit may shock them into stopping. There are recorded cases of individuals who thought they were shot and immediately collapsed, when in reality they were merely frightened. A determined adversary will probably not succumb to this, but an amateur might do so. If the adversary is pumped full of alcohol or drugs, he may not even know he has been hit.

To summarize, immediate incapacitation of the adversary can only be guaranteed through sufficient damage to the central nervous system (CNS). A bullet striking the basal ganglia, (the base of each quadrant of the brain), the brain stem, or the cervical spinal cord will nearly always cause immediate incapacitation. While this immediate incapacitation will cause the person to cease motor function, there can still be an involuntary muscle spasm of the hand and fingers--a twitch or flinch. If the person were pointing a gun, it could be fired by a sudden trigger finger spasm.

For example, a terrorist is holding a gun to the head of your client. You decide that you can make a frontal brain shot in the hopes of immediately incapacitating the terrorist and neutralizing the situation. If you elect to take that shot, you must weigh the possibility that the finger muscles of the terrorist holding the gun might immediately spasm. You might decide, under those circumstances, to keep your sights aligned and wait for him to move the gun from the client's head.

The cerebellum, a small area at the rear base of the brain, controls muscle functions. Severe damage to this area is virtually guaranteed to cease all muscle activity, including involuntary muscle spasms. Therefore, law enforcement countersnipers are taught to consider that area as a target if confronted with a hostage-taker pointing a gun at the head of a hostage. They are also taught that such a shot is very difficult in the best of circumstances and that they must usually be to the rear or side of the target.

Merely beheading the hostage-taker with a shotgun blast still allows the possibility of trigger finger spasm. A bullet entering the brain from the front can allow a spasm to start before the bullet can reach the cerebellum. This area at the base of the brain is quite small and very difficult to intentionally hit. Since the skull is relatively thick, handgun bullets do not reliably penetrate the skull. Unlike high-powered rifle bullets, handgun bullets fired at angles of deflection over 20 degrees are more likely to ricochet off the skull unless fired from close range. It is therefore not recommended that a person armed with only a handgun attempt to take a cerebellum shot to save a hostage unless there is no other recourse available. In a defensive encounter rather than a hostage situation, a CNS shot is still desirable, if practical. A bullet in the brain is very effective. The person will immediately become immobilized and unable to function in a coordinated manner. A bullet that severely damages the spinal cord will usually result in the person losing control of his body below that wound. This, of course, causes the person's legs to buckle and he falls to the ground.

Handgun bullets, more so than high-powered rifle bullets, do not tend to follow a straight line after impacting in the body. Density of tissue, bone, cartilage, and deformation of the bullet are among the reasons for this. A bullet fired directly at the spinal cord from the front of the body is unlikely to penetrate deep enough to cause sufficient damage to the spinal cord and unlikely to travel in a straight line even if it does have enough penetration. So you see, while it may be more desirable to attempt a CNS shot, it is not very practical during shooting encounters to intentionally attempt it. If you do happen to hit the spinal cord, by accident or by luck, great. However, it is not something you can count on.

The more practical approach to a shooting encounter is to fire into the chest where the heart and lungs are located. The brain requires oxygenated blood to maintain consciousness. Blood pressure loss is the desired result of shooting someone. It makes little difference how drugged-up, crazy, or dangerous, the assailant may be. Like more ordinary individuals, he needs blood pressure to remain functional. Handgun bullets are limited as to what they can do but they are capable of causing massive damage to major components of the blood supply system. This damage causes sudden loss of blood pressure leading to lessened motor abilities and probably unconsciousness, though it may take several seconds for these events to take place. Until the attacker has totally collapsed into unconsciousness there is danger. Be prepared to shoot until the attacker no longer poses a threat.

Even after the threat has ceased, you must continue readiness for a possible re-encounter or for new entrants to the incident. Do not immediately holster your gun unless the police are on the scene or until you are certain there is no danger.

If an attacker is shot by you and immediately drops to the ground due to his own psychological reaction, so much the better. If he does so, drops his gun, and poses no danger to you or your client, you may NOT shoot him.

You must strive to be more accurate than you think you need to be. Take the time to get proper hits. One proper hit coupled with five or six marginal hits is less likely to stop an attacker's aggressive actions in a timely manner than two or three proper hits. It sounds simplistic, but you do not have time to miss your shot.

What should you do if you are hit? Take courage; the odds are that you will not die unless you choose to do so. You can sustain dreadful wounds and continue to function in a defensive posture--and live a long life. Some of the useless things you should not do are to: instantly fall to the ground, dropping your gun; scream "I'm hit" (no one can help you at the moment and it will only encourage your

attacker); frighten yourself into immobility; or beg for mercy. Your best hope is to forget your wounds (there will be little or no immediate pain), react positively and aggressively, and determine that you *will* survive. The sooner you can end the confrontation and incapacitate your attacker, the sooner you can seek help for your wounds.

Stress Factors

Not surprisingly, scientists know a great deal about stress, its causes and effects. They know, for example, that severe and sudden stress can produce changes in the body and brain which are unavoidable and involuntary. These changes have been analyzed and labeled as the "tachy-psyche effect." While these stress-induced changes are unavoidable in their totality, they can be recognized while they are happening and reduced to some extent if the individual is aware of what is happening to him or her.

Hand-eye coordination, tunnel vision, and mental coordination are three important components of the tachy-psyche effect. Fine, controlled movements of the hands and fingers are greatly diminished. Fine, precise movements of fingers used to locate and operate small buttons and levers will begin to break down under stress (fear, anger, anxiety). Physical coordination is much less than normal when under this kind of stress. Adrenaline and other hormones which surge into the blood stream during severe stress cause muscles to tighten. Tightened muscles cause shooters to miscalculate the amount of pressure the finger is applying to the trigger. Under stress, trigger control is dangerously impaired and unintentional firing is highly probable.

Since the degree of precision necessary to finesse a light trigger breaks down under stress, you should avoid these hair-triggers on your defensive weapon.

Tunnel vision is a phenomenon that takes place under stress. Your total attention becomes fixed only on the imminent source of danger to the total exclusion of everything else. Danger factors to the sides and rear, and even immediately adjacent to your focal point may not be seen or assessed. The only way to break tunnel vision is to physically turn the head (when it is safe to do so). Simply rotating your eyes from left to right is not adequate to completely break the tunnel vision. A similar accompanying effect is that peripheral sounds can be blocked out under severe stress. You may fail to hear shouted instructions or warning cries. For this reason, you should not change position until you have broken tunnel vision and viewed your next position. Physically turning your head from side to side helps break auditory tunnel vision as surely as it does visual tunnel vision.

There are other effects and symptoms of the tachy-psyche effect. Time and space distortion often occurs during the course of the incident. Stress distorts your perceptions of elapsed time and distances. The incident may appear to be happening more slowly than in "real time." Objects may appear closer than they actually are. The space-distance distortion, in particular, will affect your shooting.

Recollection of times and distances differ greatly with witnesses suffering the tachy-effect. Witnesses may vary greatly in their recollections depending on their level of stress resulting from the incident. That is why you hear of descriptions that read something like: The killer was 5'2" or 6'1", with sandy hair or black hair, wearing brown shoes or gray boots. Time-space distortion is particularly severe during and immediately following a stressful incident. With time, a more factual recollection may occur. This is one reason why you should refrain from making either verbal or written statements about a lethal confrontation until you have had an opportunity to calm down and to talk with your attorney.

Just as physical coordination (fine finger movements) is affected by stress, so is mental coordination. This is why it is almost impossible in a firefight to remember how many bullets you have fired. When combined with tunnel vision, you may have difficulty remembering how many team members are with you and where they are located.

There is no guaranteed antidote to the tache-psyche stress factors, although realistic training exercises help. Some shooting courses try to re-create violent shooting incidents, using multiple "shoot-don't shoot" targets and house-clearing exercises. Even in these simulated circumstances, stress will take over and govern, to some extent, the participants' behavior. If it is any comfort, the bad guys are equally vulnerable to stress effects. Understanding the changes which will take place within you gives you some advantage.

The Aftermath

The experts tell us that everyone who is the survivor of a violent incident is affected emotionally to some degree. During World War II it was called "battle fatigue", and any Viet Nam veteran can enumerate the personal damage created by exposure to the violence of a conflict. Police officers are familiar with the term "post shooting trauma." As if the physical, legal, and financial repercussions were not enough, surviving the emotional consequences of a fatal shooting is close to devastating. As the survivor of a fatal shooting incident, you may, like a rape victim, be forced to justify your actions. If you survive a fatal shooting incident, you should then look to surviving the post-violence feelings that many survivors encounter.

If your shooting incident involved killing the most notorious terrorist of the decade or a loathsome and reprehensible serial killer, you may be only moderately affected by the aftermath emotions of the incident. On the other hand, if the dead victim was a wildly confused, emotionally distraught fan from a broken home who decided to take your client with him to a better world in the sky, you may be trapped by extended post-shooting trauma.

You may experience an immediate euphoria, an adrenaline rush brought on by the knowledge that you and your client are alive and well, and that good triumphed over evil. Do not expect that particular feeling to last long. Very quickly, your euphoria will be replaced by numbness, detachment, perhaps denial, lethargy, and depression.

You will undoubtedly dream. Even daytime events may trigger "flashbacks." If the nightmares are severe, you may find that you are afraid to sleep and insomnia will result. Loss of sleep may make you tense and irritable, which can lead to anti-social behavior. You may feel that your friends and loved ones do not understand you, and your irritability and mood swings can drive them further away.

You may lose interest in food and sex. You may, in fact, experience nausea. Sexual dysfunction will only add to your feelings of helplessness and guilt.

This gloomy picture, while true, is not complete. For most individuals, this aftermath of emotional repercussions will eventually diminish and fade away to a very manageable level. The survival instinct which brought you through the shooting incident will kick in to help you through the post-incident coping and get-well stages. Friends and loved ones will help you if you will allow them to do so. Professional counseling is something which should be considered.

There are some don'ts. Don't wallow in self-pity. If you were prepared and did your job, you did the right thing. Be strong enough to accept the unpleasant facts. Don't, above all, turn to alcohol or drugs to "help you through" the crisis. They are guaranteed to deepen and widen the problems. Don't shut out your friends, even when their efforts to help seem clumsy. Of course they do not understand exactly how you feel, but that does not diminish their love and regard for you. Don't be so dramatic--this has happened to many, many others who lost more than you and went on to become happy, useful members of society.

Do get on with your life, and leave the emotional and psychological refuse behind.

This is a good point at which to repeat--you will almost assuredly never be involved in a fatal shooting incident. The better prepared you are, the less likely an incident will occur.

Shooting, Safety and Other Issues

There are issues and information which cannot be covered in this chapter because they are too lengthy, and this book is sufficiently long as it is!

This chapter, for example, does not teach you how to shoot your weapon, nor does it describe the various shooting stances, or concealed cover shooting, or how to clean your gun. For answers to these issues you must look elsewhere. Highly recommended is to attend one of the excellent defensive shooting schools in the United States. If this is not feasible, you should find a good, professional shooting range, either indoor or outdoor, and a shooting instructor. There are a number of books and magazines about guns and shooting. Membership in the National Rifle Association (NRA) will access NRA sanctioned shooting ranges and a ream of pamphlets and other literature. There are gun shows, replete with manufacturers' booths and free literature, as well as demonstrations.

The purpose of this chapter is to provide you with information relating to the protection agent's particular needs and applications. It is assumed that the reader will, like any good professional, learn the basics of shooting (and driving) on his/her own. This book should provide you with the specialized information about executive protection applications which you will not receive from other sources.

Having stated this, it would be remiss to leave this chapter without a few words on the all-important topic of gun safety.

Gun Safety

There is more to safety than a device or rule; safety is an attitude and commitment which must be consistently practiced. If you carry a firearm or keep one in your home, you probably handle it often. You must take the responsibility in learning how to handle it properly.

There are several facts which you must accept at the outset.

.   Guns do not accidentally discharge--something or someone causes them to discharge.

.   All bullets discharged from a gun hit something or someone--fortunately, most hit benign substances, but some "accidental" bullets hit innocent bystanders, family members, and animals.

.   Firearms injuries and fatalities are almost 100% avoidable, in that they are caused by intent, negligence, carelessness, laziness, or ignorance. The gun fired because someone caused it to fire, or allowed it to fire.

.   Owning and carrying a gun is similar to being pregnant--there are no half-way measures. You can't be almost safe--100 percent is the only way.

.   Being safe includes being fully knowledgeable about the firearms and ammunition which you possess and shoot. This includes the cleaning and maintenance of the firearms.

.   All firearms should be considered to be loaded, even when the weapon is and has been under your control. This means that, if you empty and clean the gun, then leave it on table for an hour while you are in the front yard, before handling it again you check it to make certain it is empty. If you checked it last night when you went to bed, you check it again in the morning. (Could someone have sneaked into your room? Are you a sleepwalker?)

.   When checking your firearm or when handing it over to someone else, open the action to determine whether a round is chambered. The gun is handed over with the action open for his/her inspection. The same precaution should be taken whenever you accept a gun from someone else.

.   Unloaded firearms should be handled exactly as you would handle loaded firearms. Even when you have verified that the weapon is unloaded, you should observe all safety rules. Even when your weapon is unloaded and the action is open, keep your finger away from the trigger and point it in a safe direction.

.   The muzzle of the firearm must always be pointed in a safe direction. Often, a safe direction is hard to find, particularly if your ammunition has a high penetrative ability over long distances.

.   If you are outdoors and you are loading or unloading, the gun muzzle can be pointed three or four feet in front of you and into soft earth or sand. Indoors, you should never point the muzzle at the floor or an interior wall. There could be someone in the next room or downstairs and bullets *will* penetrate these flimsy barriers. One option is to point the gun exactly in the corner of two walls and toward the bottom of the corner. There are usually joist and frame members which come together at that joint. Another option is a dresser full of folded clothing or a paper-loaded file cabinet.

.   Your fingers should contact the trigger of the gun *only* when you are going to fire. This means your fingers are off the trigger when drawing the gun, when moving from point to point, when holstering, and when covering someone. Remember how difficult it is under stress circumstances to control those fine finger movements.

.   Be sure of your target and everything adjacent to, behind, and generally in line with it. Be aware of the danger of ricochets and penetration.

.   There are no "free" shots; every shot counts. This means no "warning" shots or guesswork shots. You are not justified in shooting at shadows, unidentified movement, or through doors or walls. You must be able to testify (if necessary) that you knew exactly what you were shooting and where your bullets were going.

Not surprisingly, many executive protection agents have a history of martial arts training. The samurai of old was a superb warrior and defender of his master. Through the years, the art and philosophy of defensive fighting skills have been preserved in a relatively pure form, and are practiced in a number of disciplines in dojos around the world, in exhibitions, and now in the Olympics.

In recent years, an interesting evolution has taken place. A handful of martial art practitioners in the United States recognized that, while mastering the precise nuances of a martial art form and the progression through various degrees (belts) could take years to complete, it was possible to extract a few of the more practical martial art techniques and teach them to law enforcement and security personnel in a short time period. These techniques are now universally accepted within this country and are referred to as "control techniques."

There are several reasons for the acceptance given to these techniques. They are effective; that is, when used properly, they enable the police officer or security agent to restrain or control an adversary. The techniques are humane; again, when used properly, the adversary can be controlled without injury, although they are based upon pain compliance. There is a caveat--if used improperly, these techniques can cause severe injuries. They must be learned from a professional instructor and practiced under controlled, safe conditions.

The techniques presented in this book were developed by Bob Duggan, President of Executive Security International (ESI) of Aspen, Colorado. Duggan is a fourth degree black belt in the art of Hwa Rang Do, a very old and very complex martial art form, and he is a pioneer in the adaptation of martial arts techniques for practical (street) use. These techniques are taught to executive protection students during their resident training at ESI.

While it is very helpful for the agent to have some form of martial arts training, it is not necessary. So long as you are in good physical condition, the techniques presented in this chapter can be learned in a very short period of time. Once learned, of course, it is mandatory that regular practice be scheduled to stay on top of your acquired skills, just as you must regularly practice your defensive shooting skills. A side benefit of engaging in this practice is the increase in physical well being--it is very good exercise.

The Cants

The first section in this chapter examines a single series of joint locks referred to as "the Cants." While the entire spectrum of joint locks form a complex, comprehensive system, recommended for use by the protection agent are the Vertical Cant, the Parallel Cant, and the Horizontal Cant. One advantage of the Vertical Cant, in particular, is its relatively low profile. There are no kicks and fancy throws--it is a fast, simple "Come-Along."

The name "Cant" is rooted in the fact that the technique operates off of a spiral and it is "Canted" or tilted off the center axis. The Cants are particularly simple, effective, and very easy to learn.

These are potentially injury-inducing exercises and you should practice them with great care, using a padded flooring, and with knowledgeable, professional instruction. It is not intended that the material in this chapter be used as a self-sufficient training course. It is offered as an introduction to unarmed defensive techniques and/or a refresher for those individuals who have received training.

The Vertical Cant

Capturing the fingers is the key to an unsuspecting joint lock. As the fingers are gripped with the right hand, drop the weight of your body into your opponent's fingers, and begin twisting clockwise and upwards. The left hand circles around from behind and grips the knife edge of the opponent's hand. Thinking of the joints as a chain link, each joint will reach its limit of rotation very quickly. As the point of resistance is attained, it will put pressure on the next higher joint until you are able to control the opponent.

Key Points: Regard the forearm as the center axis of a vertical line directly under the elbow, and Cant the knife edge of the opponent's hand towards the center of his body. The rotation will continue until the opponent is under control and ceases to resist the technique. If you maintain the tension inwards and upwards, the opponent will be under control and capable of movement in whatever direction you desire. This technique is an excellent "Come-Along."

The Parallel Cant

The approach and lock are identical to the Vertical Cant. Gripping the fingers and dropping into a point just below the knuckles, you rotate the opponent's hand clockwise and upwards through the center axis line. This results in a firm control of the opponent. But the Parallel Cant is aimed at the resolution of a higher level threat than the Vertical Cant.

Following through with the line of the Parallel Cant, one is capable of breaking all three joints of the wrist, elbow, and shoulder. It is appropriate only under the immediate threat of grave bodily harm to you or your client. Abuse this technique and it is very likely that you will be the one who ends up in court.

WHEN PRACTICING, THE RULE IS: NO FAST JERKY MOVEMENTS!

Key Points: To execute the Parallel Cant correctly, bring the opponent's hand in towards the body until the knife edge is parallel with the opponent's bicep. This is not a control technique! It is set for a break, sometimes multiple breaks. The line of the break cuts the opponent's upper and lower parts of his body in half. The motion is not a pull under the arms as much as a full circle.

Exercise extreme caution when practicing all joint locks, but especially this one!

The Horizontal Cant

The Horizontal Cant is most appropriate as an arrest technique. Follow the same approach as the Vertical Cant technique until you have locked the opponent up and have him effectively under control. Raise the knife edge straight up until the forearm and the bicep are on a "horizontal" plane. Keep the knife edge straight in line with the forearm; do not bend the hand towards the body. Pivot your body outwards until you confront the opponent face to face without disturbing the plane.

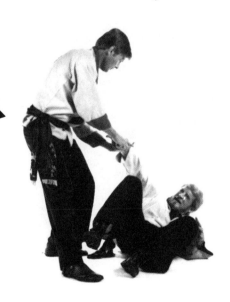

Key Points: Looking down the line of the knife edge and forearm, begin twisting the fingers in a spiral around the center axis of the forearm and pressing downwards. The whole plane will drop as if it were a plate. Once on the ground, maintain your grip on the fingers. By slightly increasing the pressure on the spiral, the opponent will have to roll over on his face. By shifting your position so that you can plant your knee in the center of his back, you can release the fingers and handcuff his free hand.

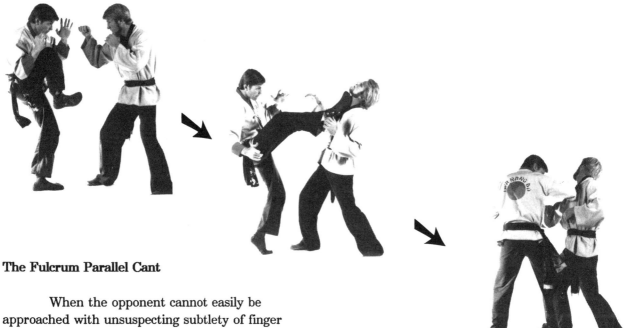

The Fulcrum Parallel Cant

When the opponent cannot easily be approached with unsuspecting subtlety of finger joint locks, the Fulcrums may become the next line of defense. Close the distance quickly and form a wedge high on the inside of the trigger point of the forearm and from below on the ulnar side of the wrist. Quickly shock the arm with a short, sudden drop, followed by a cut of the elbow upwards in a small circle as you pass under the opponent's arm and pivot. As you pivot, lock your hand over your gripping hand. You will notice that you recreate a fulcrum without shifting the hands on the grip.

Key Points: Drop the weight of your body with a shudder, much in the manner of a thrust punch, except that the line of direction is downwards. Execute this drop explosively, simultaneous with an upwards motion of the wrist which acts as the lever on the fulcrum. Break the balance of the opponent and the strength of the arm with a short circle.

BE CAREFUL! This lock is capable of breaking all three joints of the arm as in the Parallel Cant.

The Fulcrum

In physics, a fulcrum is the point of axis about which a bar or a lever will rotate when force is applied at any distance from the axis. The muscle system of vertebrate animals operates on a leverage principle and thus involves a biological analogue of the fulcrum.

The human forearm, when bent at a right angle, provides an excellent example of a relatively simple lever system; the elbow joint is the biological analogue of the fulcrum and the forearm is the lever. The purpose of the fulcrum and lever is to multiply power and motion. Given leverage over a fulcrum, we can move much more weight with least force. If we invert the fulcrum and place it at the muscle trigger of the forearm and the grip on either the ulnar or radian side of the wrist, we have a lever, except that gravity now pulls on the fulcrum.

The fulcrum offers two advantages. First, it is based on simple, gross hand traps; and second, it allows the thrower to maintain his guard under a flurry of punches until he feels the wedge of a trap. Of course, it is still necessary to use the feet, hands, elbows, shins, and knees to set up the trap.

Once the wedge of the trap is set, the force of fulcrum breaks the opponent's balance and the strength of his arm simultaneously. Despite the fact that you only have control of a small portion of the opponent's body, you are capable of moving a much larger weight because that is the function of a fulcrum.

Fulcrums allow one to apply grappling techniques offensively without the liability of precise finger grips on the opponent in order to execute an effective throw or place the joints in locking position.

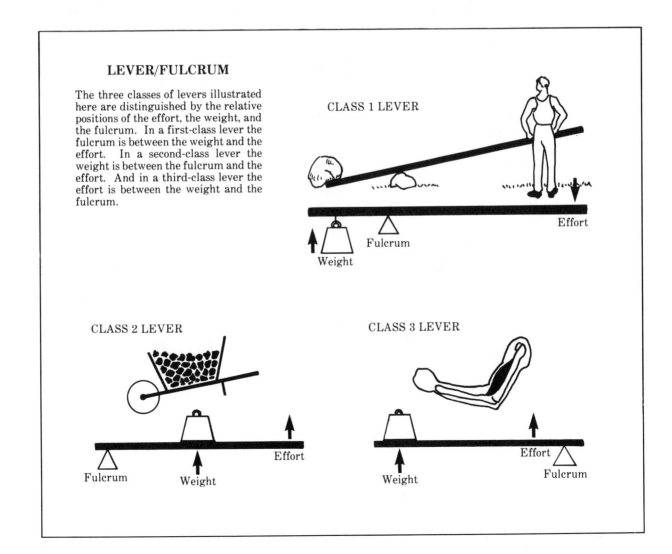

LEVER/FULCRUM

The three classes of levers illustrated here are distinguished by the relative positions of the effort, the weight, and the fulcrum. In a first-class lever the fulcrum is between the weight and the effort. In a second-class lever the weight is between the fulcrum and the effort. And in a third-class lever the effort is between the weight and the fulcrum.

CLASS 1 LEVER

Effort

Fulcrum

Weight

CLASS 2 LEVER

Effort

Fulcrum   Weight

CLASS 3 LEVER

Effort

Weight   Fulcrum

Outside Dropping Fulcrum

A typical set-up may begin with jabs to the head, followed by a low shin kick to the thigh and elbow attacks to the head again. Set up the trap with your forearm over the opponent's trigger point high on his radial forearm, and the low grip on the underside of the wrist. Explosively drop the body into the opponents' forearm as you pull upward on the low grip of the wrist. As you hit the ground, strike the face with elbow and set the arm in an arm bar.

Key Points: Drop the weight of the body with a shudder, much in the manner of thrust punch, except that the line of direction is downward. The sudden and explosive drop to the ground is aided by snapping the foot upward in order to allow gravity to play its inevitable role.

Follow-up with arm bar. Grip thumb and rotate outwards!

Set the wedge with forearm over the opponent's trigger point and grip on ulnar side of wrist.

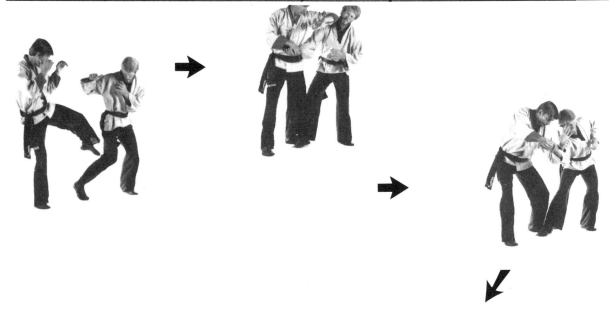

The Pivoting Fulcrum

The set-up might include the illustrated shin kick to the thigh and elbow strike to the face. When the trap is caught, shock the arm with a sudden drop and quickly cut your elbow upward in a small circle as you pass in front of the opponent and pivot. As the hands pass around the crown of the head, lock your hand over your own wrist. When the opponent hits the ground, lock him up with a Torqued Gooseneck.

Key Points: Break the balance of the opponent and the strength of the arm with the short circle. Notice that, as you lock the hand on the wrist, you recreate a fulcrum without shifting the grip.

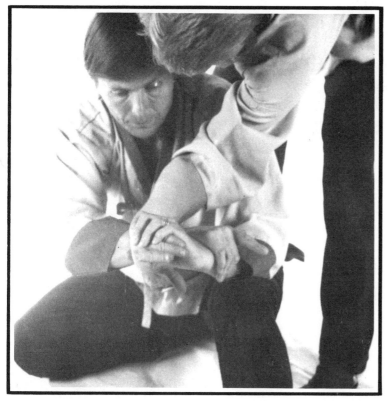

Recreate a fulcrum after the pivot the instant before he is thrown.

Reverse Pivoting Fulcrum

This technique could be set up with a leg sweep and the trap. The arm is caught and shocked in the same way as the Pivoting Fulcrum except that the follow-through is executed with a reverse pivot. Once you have the trap, step backward and pivot. Swing the trapped hand around the crown of the head as you drop low to the ground; this keeps the lock close to the center of gravity, and consequently more difficult to escape with a counterspin.

Key Points: The success of the Pivot depends upon the combination of the initial dropping shock and the speed of the small upward circle

Ground position for a reverse pivot.

Reverse Shoulder Drop

Stomp the instep and set up exactly as in the Reverse Pivoting Fulcrum. The only difference between the two techniques is the depth of the reverse step. The result of the deep reverse step is that you are planted behind and below the opponent.

Key Points: The lock can be set outward at a 45-degree angle for a dislocate or vertically for a back drop.

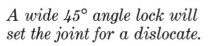

A wide 45° angle lock will set the joint for a dislocate.

Rear Straight Arm Fulcrum

The set-up could begin with a side kick to the knee, and entering on the outside for the trap. The trap is caught high on the arm and low on the radial side of the wrist. Weight is dropped through the elbow initiated from the legs and hip. This is done explosively, simultaneous with a lifting motion of the wrist. Follow through with a drop to the floor, pressing on the muscle trigger in the tricep which allows for a high arm lock or chicken wing.

Key Points: The fall of the body, like the Outside Dropping Fulcrum, is committed in a sudden shudder as you raise the lower lever (wrist).

Capture the wedge high on the tricep and low on the wrist.

Weapon Disarms

The material on weapon disarms included in this book is somewhat specialized. That is, the opportunity for and success of an effective weapon disarm depends on the distance, the intent of the assailant, reflexes, training of both parties, and other variables. If the right set of opportunities are presented, there is a fairly good chance to disarm a loaded weapon from an assailant.

There are no guarantees that these techniques will work. There are too many imponderables. If not executed properly, or if the assailant is well trained, the results could be grievous. On the other hand, there may be no other good options.

You cannot know precisely what you will do under any particular circumstance until it happens, but having the training and the knowledge of what to do can make the difference should the opportunity arise.

You must be within range of the weapon. If the weapon is out of reach, do not attempt to take it. If you have to take a step to reach the weapon, you do not have time to reach it before the adversary can react.

Assuming that the assailant does not fire at the first opportunity, what is his intent? There is no way of knowing this, but, if the assailant is at close range and the weapon is within reach without your having to take a step, you have a distinct advantage.

The one who decides to act first will determine the outcome of the event. If the gun is within reach and you act first, you have two-tenths of a second of reflex action on your side. It is not possible for him to react any faster to an action that you have initiated; if he decides to act at the same instant, the margin is reduced to zero, but then you have nothing to lose anyway.

There is an aspect of reflex that must be considered. When you slap the gun hand from the outside moving inward towards the center, the reflex of the hand muscles clench. This means that the gun is likely to go off in your direction. If, however, you slap the gun from the inside moving outward, the reflex of the hand opens. It is a natural tendency. The gun, therefore, must be moved to the outside. There are exceptions to this rule. For example, if an innocent person or your client is standing in the outside position, this will change the approach.

The Technique

The initial impact against the weapon should come from wherever the hands are at the instant you make the decision to go for the weapon. You do not have time to raise your hand and then strike. The slap must come up or down in a sudden explosive motion. It will tend to wrap around the weapon rather than bounce away.

The striking target is simply the largest center mass. It matters little whether the slap strikes mainly the gun or mainly the hand. What is important is that you deflect the barrel and wrap your fingers around the gun hand. Do not, however, strike the forearm, because that will bend the wrist toward you.

At the same instant as you slap, pivot on the right foot (assuming the assailant is holding the gun in his right hand). The body will swing open like a door a full 90 degrees, aiming a simultaneous firing of the gun past the body. It is important to allow the left arm to pivot out of the line of fire until the weapon is captured with the right hand before making a second grab. The pivot is always done with the weight of your body over the ball of the foot, while the left foot remains stationary.

The grip on the weapon is crucial. The slapping hand must wrap over the gun hand. The second hand needs to grip the gun in an opposing position, because the hands are the strongest when holding the weapon in this way. The second hand strikes the gun at the trigger guard. Strike the trigger guard as if it were a punch, and close the fingers around the assailant's trigger finger.

The barrel of the weapon must follow a line of least resistance. That is, a line in which there is little or no possibility of stopping the disarm technique because of muscular strength or shifting of position. That line is above and parallel to the forearm.

The completion of the disarm is a complete circle. If the grip on the gun hand is held tight, the assailant will probably lose a finger since the trigger guard will cut it to the bone.

Great care must be exercised in practicing these techniques.

THE GRIP

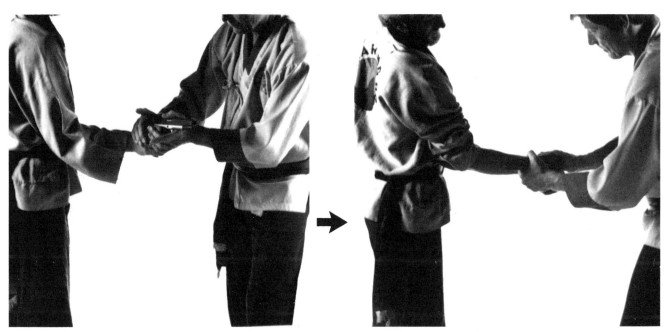

The Grip in opposing hands.

Punch the Barrel Parallel to the forearm.

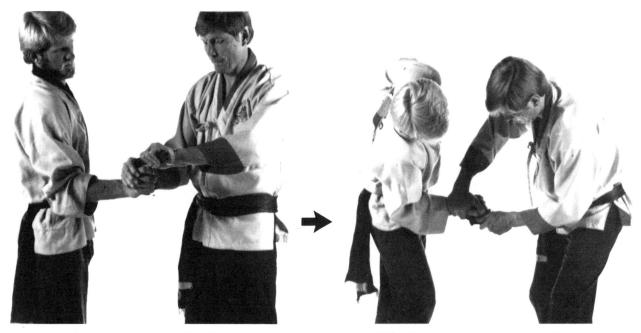

A Lethal Mistake. The Grip is not in Opposition.

The Result. It is Impossible to Prevent a Rotation of the Barrel.

Another Common Mistake. The Grip is Opposed to the Bicep.

The Result. A Natural Reflex to Withdraw the Weapon.

Different Method, Same Result. Very easy for the Assailant to Block the Disarm.

The Weapon is within Reach. Relax!

Pivot and Slap with Thumb-Up. Note Left Arm Swings Out.

THE FRONT STANDING DISARM

The Tiger Mouth Punch.

Same Position, Hands Up.

Same Pivot.

Back out.

The Line Parallel to the Forearm.

Breaking his Grip and Completing the Circle over the Forearm.

Key Points: Be aware! All upper body movements telegraph the intent. The initial explosive motion in the Pivot and the Slap begin from the ground up! This makes the movement both more powerful and concealable. It will happen before the assailant can see it coming.

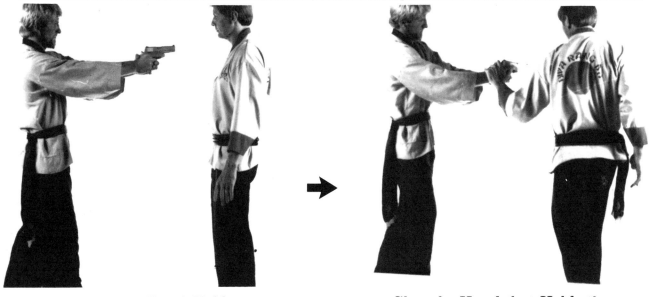

A Double Hand Hold.

Slap the Hand that Holds the Weapon.

DOUBLE HAND HOLD

Key Points: You must now slap to the inside. Since the assailant is holding the weapon with two hands, you cannot disarm it parallel to the inside forearm. It must inscribe an elliptical circle between the forearms.

Up, over, and circle through!

Remember to point the barrel at the nipple, and the weapon will break through the thumbs, the weakest point of the grip.

Tiger Mouth Punch and Push Up and Over.

Protect the Weapon and Back Out.

Press Down Between the Forearms.

Point the Barrel at the Nipple.

REAR BODY DISARM

Key Points: Maintain contact with the weapon until you have a firm grip on it. The free hand passes over the top because this provides you with a wedge to trap the hand in the event that he withdraws the gun.

Pivot and Block the Weapon.

*The Weapon is Within Reach.
(You feel it or you look.)*

Trap the Weapon.

*Pivot and Turn the Weapon
Inwards Parallel to the Forearm.*

Pivot and Block.

Trap the Weapon.

REAR HEAD DISARM

The Weapon is Within Reach.
(You feel it or you look.)

Key Points: When you pivot, swing as deep to the rear of the assailant as possible. Do not pivot in place, because he may back out and still have you in front of the weapon. Maintain contact with the gun hand until you have a firm grip.

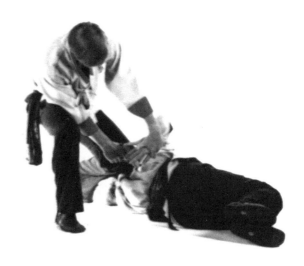

Pressure on the Wrist at this Angle will Automatically Roll the Assailant Over.

Grip the Weapon with Opposing Hand.

Turn the Weapon Inwards Parallel to the Forearm.

Press Downwards on the Wrist and the Assailant will Drop to the Ground.

Disarm him. Retain the Wrist Hold and Press the Hand Towards the Armpit.

BODY GRABS AND WEAPON CONTACT FROM THE REAR

Key Points: Keep the technique simple. The principles are identical to the Front Standing Disarm. As long as you have space to move within his grip, you can pivot and he cannot keep the weapon pressed against your body. It is, in fact, a great advantage to have the pressure of the weapon pushed into the body, because as you pivot, the weapon will slip by you.

Wait Until you Feel the Space to Move.

This is Where Accidents Occur.

*Pivot and Block the Weapon into
the Assailant's Arm.*

*Trap the Weapon and Turn it
Parallel to the Forearm.*

BODY GRABS FROM THE FRONT

The Weapon is Pressed Against the Body.   *Pivot and Trap the Weapon.*

Turn the Weapon Parallel to the Forearm.

Punch the Trigger Guard with the Tiger Mouth of the Open Hand.

Complete the Circle, Holding his Finger in the Trigger Guard.

Of all the skills which an executive protection agent must possess, perhaps none are more important than the skills needed to deal with medical crisis situations. An agent may go through his or her entire career without confronting a single assault on a client, but it is extremely likely that he and she will be involved in some type of medical crisis situation once or more in their careers.

In a protective operation, the need for medical intervention can be complicated by several facts. The client may not reveal some of his medical problems to the agent, making it difficult for the agent to foresee possible medical problems. The client is very likely to be someone who travels often and to many areas that are either far removed from competent medical professionals and a fully equipped hospital, or to areas where the level of medical care is substandard. And, finally, if the client is at risk, there is an increased likelihood of traumatic injuries.

The more sophisticated client will expect his team to be qualified to plan for various medical contingencies and to be able to provide emergency medical assistance. The client expects his team to save his life, irrespective of the nature of the threat.

The entire subject of First Respondent Medicine is too lengthy to be included in this chapter. Therefore, the material must be narrowed down to those issues which the protective agent is most apt to encounter, including heart attacks, massive bleeding, shock, and traumatic injuries. It is presented in a streamlined, simplistic style. The author strongly recommends (as do all thoughtful professionals) that the agent invest the time to acquire in-depth knowledge and training.

THE MEDICAL THREAT

Heart and blood vessel (cardiovascular)
disease. The combined group of cardiovascular diseases accounts for nearly one million deaths in the United States annually.

Heart attacks are but one manifestation of cardiovascular disease; however, deaths due to heart attacks outnumber all other causes of death combined. The number of deaths from heart attacks is followed closely by those from strokes and high blood pressure, all of which are consequences of cardiovascular disease.

Cardiovascular diseases claimed almost one million lives in the United States in 1997. This is 41.2 percent of all deaths. It is also generally true that more than half of those who die from heart disease die before reaching the hospital, and they die within the first two hours of the onset of symptoms. As a result, sudden death due to heart disease is the most prominent medical emergency in the United States today.

As a result of so many cardiac deaths occurring outside the hospital, the community itself is being recognized as the "ultimate coronary care unit." This is because life-saving care is most effective when begun immediately in the field. Without this immediate intervention, many victims will not survive a heart attack.

This has obvious application for the protection agent. If the protectee suffers a heart attack, and the team is prepared for the threat, they may save the protectee's life. They may also save the life of someone dear to the protectee, which can be even more meaningful to the protectee than having his or her own life saved. Conversely, without emergency caregiving capabilities, the team provides only a substandard level of service on borrowed time.

Cancer. Trailing the number of deaths

caused by cardiovascular diseases are those caused by cancer (539,577 deaths in 1997). Here, the protection agent also has an opportunity to effectively intervene. A cancer-afflicted client can benefit from an informed agent's ability to provide emotional support and understanding of physical limitations in this difficult situation.

In addition, actual medical assistance may be needed when a worsening of cancer symptoms results in an acute illness or even a life-threatening event. Besides the direct threat of cancer, its treatment alone can cause severe illnesses. For example, nausea or other gastrointestinal disturbances can occur due to chemotherapy or radiation-therapy, as can bleeding and generalized weakness. Cancer can produce such life-threatening events as heart attacks, strokes, and other acute illnesses.

Trauma (Wounds and Injuries). Trauma follows cardiovascular disease and cancer as the third leading cause of death in the United States. In 1997, accidents accounted for 95,644 deaths. To place this in perspective, 43,000 American soldiers were lost during the Vietnam War. During those same 11 years, 25 times that number of people died from trauma, with over 40% of these dying from traffic accidents alone.

Trauma is the leading cause of death for all groups of people up to age 38, and it kills more people between the ages of 15 and 24 than all other causes combined. The most frequent major cause of trauma death is from motor vehicle accidents. The next most common cause of trauma death is from firearms, followed by jumps and falls, then drownings, poisonings, burns, etc. A primary function of the protective team is moving the client from one location to another using automobiles. These statistics demonstrate the high level of personal vulnerability for the protectee and agents that is associated with being transported by automobiles.

MEDICAL CREDENTIALING

For the executive protection agent seeking to obtain education and credentialing in the emergency health care field, it is useful to know what resources are available. Also, knowing the kind of credentials to pursue is critical in terms of time and money constraints. Basic medical credentials should first be pursued by the agent, as these skills are most likely to be the ones needed first. As they progress with their professional careers, agents tend to distinguish themselves by areas of expertise, and medicine might be a choice.

The American Heart Association

The development of modern cardio-pulmonary resuscitation (CPR) began in 1960, but it was not until 1973 that CPR was extended to the general public. During this time, the use of CPR by emergency health care providers was defined, and solutions to medical-legal problems relating to CPR began to be explored. In 1979, CPR was expanded to include resuscitation of infants and children and was renamed basic life support (BLS). In 1973, the American Heart Association also developed the advanced cardiac life support (ACLS) educational program.

Since 1973, over 40,000,000 people have been trained to perform CPR and tens of thousands of health care providers have been trained in ACLS. The development of modern emergency medical services (EMS's) has also greatly contributed to the success of CPR. It helps, of course, that the public has become more aware of the causes of cardiovascular disease such as hypertension (high blood pressure), cigarette smoking, fatty diets (the evil cholesterol), and improvements in medical and surgical care for cardiovascular disease.

Presently, CPR training and practice is ultimately administered by the American Heart Association, which continually evolves CPR practice standards using reviews of scientific data and clinical experience. As a result, CPR practice is constantly changing and requires continual updating and recertification to be current.

Basic life support (BLS) is the "first-line" of care required by a victim of a heart attack who is breathless and pulseless. BLS (also known as cardiopulmonary resuscitation or CPR) presently saves about 150,000 lives each year.

BLS involves recognizing the early warning signs of a heart attack, attempting to prevent complications if a heart attack is in progress, reassuring the victim, and providing emergency breathing and cardiac compressions via CPR if the heart and/or lungs stop. Regardless of the level of training or skill possessed by the responder, these basic functions must be provided in order for other treatment to be successful for the heart attack victim.

Initial certification for American Heart Association BLS usually requires a six-hour class and test time. Recertification, including a review of recent updates, takes about a half-day. Recertification is required every two years.

The advanced cardiac life support (ACLS) program is also administered by the American Heart Association and is designed to provide additional treatment for the heart attack victim over that provided by BLS. Even though the prompt administration of BLS is the key to survival, other therapies are usually required. If CPR is initiated within the first four minutes of a cardiac arrest and ACLS is administered within the first eight minutes, the victim has the highest possible opportunity (statistically) of surviving the attack.

ACLS is only available to licensed health care professionals authorized to administer medications (other advanced knowledge and skills are required to complete an ASLC course). These professionals include some paramedics and emergency medical technicians, pharmacists, nurses, and doctors. This is generally a two- to three-day initial course and a half-day every two years for recertification.

American Red Cross

The American Red Cross teaches CPR, basic first aid, and advanced first aid courses.

First Respondent Medicine

First responder certifications are offered and recognized in many communities and were designed to provide members of law enforcement, fire departments, and other community servants with limited, but skilled, care. The knowledge and skill level is designed to be far greater than that offered by the Advanced First Aid provider and, for many reasons, is an excellent basis of knowledge for personal protection specialists. These courses typically require about 24 hours of education.

Emergency Medical Technicians (EMT's) and Paramedics

These are generally classified as either A (Basic), I (Intermediate) or P (Paramedic). These certifications require completion of an approved Department of Transportation National Standard Training Program or its equivalent and must be additionally certified by a state emergency medical services board or other authorizing agency.

EMT's classified as either A or I are well prepared to assess patients, using advanced knowledge of disease processes. They can provide basic life support, render special splinting procedures, stabilize suspected spinal injuries, administer oxygen, and provide greater field treatment of shock. These courses typically require about 180 hours of education.

EMT-P can also initiate advanced life support and is certified to perform advanced medical procedures consistent with ACLS protocols. These courses typically require about 800 hours of education and 500 hours of clinical work.

EMT's and paramedics are also employed in various areas of hospitals, including emergency rooms and intensive care units, although it is generally nurses and doctors who are the primary care providers in emergency rooms.

LEGAL ISSUES

In spite of what you might think to the contrary, the legal system is not designed to convict caregivers who are performing within their level of education and experience. It is designed to protect these caregivers from frivolous lawsuits and to protect care receivers from care providers who are not performing safely.

Standards of Care

"Standards of care" is a legal concept which tests the quality of service delivered by one individual against that delivered by his or her peers. For example, if allegations of negligent or improper care are directed toward a medical care giver, "standards of care" criteria will be applied to the occurrence so that a reasonable comparison can be made between the care that was given and that which would have hypothetically been given by peers in that same situation. In making a comparison in this manner a decision can be made as to whether the care in question was delivered in conformance with standards. Specifically, comparisons are made between the individual caregiver's training, experience, and the conditions under which the care was delivered.

An important point, therefore, is that medical care providers must always perform only those procedures which they know they can perform safely and have been trained and certified to perform. If the care provided is not up to these standards, the caregiver (and his employer) may be sued and held liable for his actions.

Good Samaritan Laws

Good Samaritan laws were developed to protect good-intentioned individuals from being sued for providing medical care, in good faith, at the provider's level of training, and at the provider's best ability. However, if these laws exist in the state in which you practice, they only apply if care is provided on a volunteer basis.

Negligence

The basis for most lawsuits involving pre-hospital care is negligence. For the kind of care most protective professionals will probably be giving, negligence is defined as a failure to provide the expected standard of care, which results in additional injury to the patient. More specifically, negligence is:

. not doing what is expected; that is, not performing to standards of care, or

. doing something carelessly; that is, not performing to the best of one's ability and according to training received, and

. the patient is injured as a result of this improper care.

Negligence is also construed as abandoning the patient after care has begun, but before care has been properly transferred to someone of superior training, such as EMT's or paramedics who arrive on the scene.

ORGAN SYSTEMS AND SHOCK

Before jumping into the first respondent care which the agent should be able to provide, it will be useful to learn a little about how the human body functions, and what happens when the system does not function properly.

Organ Systems

There are three organ systems that are essential for the maintenance of life: the heart, also known as the cardiac system; the lungs, also known as the respiratory or pulmonary system; and the blood and blood vessels, also known as the circulatory system.

These organ systems are essential for life because they provide other organ systems with the substances they need to maintain their respective functions. For example, the nervous system, which consists of the brain, spinal cord, and nerves, maintains consciousness, reasoning abilities, and muscular coordination in a normal individual. The nervous system is composed of billions of specialized, individual units called cells which work together to perform the complex functions of this particular system. Therefore, to maintain the life of these cells means the function of the individual's nervous system must be maintained. And, for these cells to be maintained, they must be continually supplied with life-giving substances by the cardiac, respiratory, and circulatory systems. If these essential systems become ineffective due to disease or injury, the organ systems they support, such as the nervous system, become ineffective and start to die. This is how the organ system works.

. **Oxygenated blood leaves the heart.**

One of the primary substances required to maintain life is oxygen, which is carried to the cells by the essential body systems. This blood-carrying oxygen is known as oxygenated blood. The heart is responsible for circulating blood to the rest of the body using blood vessels.

. **Blood is transported via arteries.**

These blood vessels, which carry oxygenated blood to the body cells, are collectively known as arteries. When severed, arteries bleed bright red blood, as opposed to the blue blood carried by veins. Arteries often bleed with a pulsation and surging of blood, sometimes called spurting.

. **Arteries branch into arterioles.**

As oxygenated blood is carried farther from the heart, the arteries that carry it branch, and they become smaller and smaller as they approach the size of individual cells. It is the circulatory level of the arterioles where blood pressure is controlled.

. **Arterioles branch into capillaries.**

At the individual cells, arterioles branch into

vessels which are microscopic in size.

. **Capillaries give up oxygen and nutrients to individual cells.**

It is at this level where oxygen is given over to the various cells of the body.

. **Carbon dioxide and wastes are absorbed.**

Waste substances generated by the cell's metabolism are also given up to the circulating blood which carries them to other organs to be eliminated. For example, carbon dioxide is major waste substance carried to the lungs for elimination, which is accomplished through the process of breathing.

. **Capillaries converge into veinules, then veins.**

The circulatory system from this level becomes increasingly larger, progressing from the size of the single cell and converging into slightly larger veinules, then into the largest vessels, veins. The primary difference between arterioles, veinules, arteries, and veins is whether they carry oxygen: arteries and arterioles do, and veins and veinules do not. Another way of looking at this is that arteries and arterioles carry blood away from the heart, and veins and veinules carry blood to the heart.

. **These return blood to the heart.**

As blood is pushed into increasingly larger veins it eventually is pushed into the right side of the heart.

. **Where it is then pumped into the lungs.**

The heart is completely divided into two separate sides called the right and left sides. Each side has pumping functions; however, the location where these sides pump blood is different for each side. For example, blood returning from the body (which is very low in oxygen but is high in carbon dioxide) is pumped from the right side of the heart directly to the lungs. Here, the blood gives up carbon dioxide and accepts oxygen.

.   **Blood circulates through lung alveoli where gases are exchanged.**

It is at a location called the alveoli where the movement of gasses, specifically carbon dioxide and oxygen, occurs. At this location, blood most closely comes into contact with actual air as it moves in and out of the lungs. It is the movement of gasses into and out of the lungs that complements the movement of gasses in blood.

Specifically, a high concentration of oxygen and low concentration of carbon dioxide is inhaled with each breath. This oxygen is then pulled into the blood and is pumped to body cells which require it to live. As blood returns from these cells, it has negligible quantities of oxygen but high quantities of carbon dioxide. As this blood flows into the alveoli, it gives up this carbon dioxide, which is then transported out of the lungs during breathing, and oxygen is again picked up, and the cycle begins again.

.   **Back to the left side of the heart.**

After the blood in the lungs rids itself of carbon dioxide and accepts oxygen it returns to the left side of the heart, where it is pumped again to the body's cells.

Shock

Shock, in medical terms, means the failure of the cardiovascular system to adequately supply blood to all parts of the body. Left untreated, shock is always fatal. It is a normal consequence of any major traumatic injury that results in blood loss, either internal or external. Shock is also a consequence of many illnesses. As the illness progresses and the patient weakens, early signs of shock can be diagnosed. Recognition and treatment of shock is critical, since the victim may die as a result of shock rather than precisely as a result of the causative

wound or illness.

Often, signs of shock emerge due to a lack of oxygen getting to the body's cells such as those in the nervous system, cardiac or other muscles, kidneys, and other body systems. It also shows the body's inability to rid itself of by-products of cellular activity.

When cells are deprived of oxygen or have an over-accumulation of carbon dioxide, they show problems that are specific to the kind of cells which are being deprived. For example, cells that comprise heart muscle show signs of this stress differently than cells of the nervous system. The protective agent can learn how to identify signs of shock by knowing how certain organs show the stresses of lack of oxygen or an abundance of carbon dioxide.

.   **Lack of Oxygen to the Lungs.**

One consequence of a lack of oxygen to generalized body tissues, including the lungs, is a sign of shortness of breath or air-hunger. This can be seen in a patient who complains of being short of breath, saying "I can't catch may breath," and having a panicked or anxious facial expression, or by recognizing an increase in respiratory rate and depth of breathing. Of course, these observations must be carefully weighed against the usual breathing characteristics of the individual and the appearance of other signs of shock before this sign should be considered a signal of developing or worsening shock.

As shock progresses to near irreversible levels, the respiratory rate will decrease, and the depth of respirations will be shallow. However, in recognizing this, the observer will see other signs of impending death such as deteriorations in skin color, texture, and moisture, and other findings.

The normal adult respiratory rate is 12 to 20 breaths per minute, with most people in the 12 to 16 range. Older adults tend to breathe more slowly than young adults, and infants breathe much faster. One breath is defined as one inspiration (breath in) and one expiration (breath out). The respiratory rate is taken by watching the patient's chest as it moves up and down while appearing to monitor the pulse, as the patient will tend to vary his respiratory if he knows someone is watching his breathing.

. Lack of Oxygen to the Heart.

One consequence of a lack of oxygen to the heart is weaker heart contractions. Whenever a muscle goes without oxygen it is temporarily weakened. The body cells sense this and report it back to the heart. The heart then tries to compensate for weaker contractions by pumping faster. The faster pumping can be recognized by taking the pulse of the patient. Of course, an increased pulse is not always a sign of shock. Other factors, such as anxiety, fear, and fever, can cause an increased pulse rate.

Another consequence of a lack of oxygen to the heart is increased irritability of the heart muscle. This can result in an irregular rhythm. An irregular rhythm would be detected by taking the victim's pulse. The agent would feel a rhythm which seemed not to have the consistent rhythm normally found in that specific victim. The agent should recognize if the rhythm change is new or old. If it is new and is associated with other signs of shock, it is an ominous sign and would require the immediate attention of the EMS system. On the other hand, if it is old, it is probably something the patient has experienced for some time and it is not significant. If possible, the protectee's normal heart rate and rhythm should be determined by the agent as soon as possible upon taking a new protectee assignment, especially if the protectee is known to be in ill health. This information can be obtained from the protectee's doctor with permission from the protectee, or from the protectee himself or herself.

The normal heart rate is 60 to 80 beats per minute. Below 60 beats per minute is usually considered to be slower than normal but this can be normal for some people. Greater than 80 beats per minute can be caused by many other factors besides shock, such as anxiety and fear.

. Lack of Oxygen to the Brain.

A consequence of a lack of oxygen to the brain is first recognized by a change in the victim's level of consciousness. A normal person is someone who is alert and talkative in an appropriate way, and is oriented to where and who he is, as well as having an awareness of the time and environment. If a change in the level of consciousness occurs, the individual will first become agitated, restless, or confused. If lack of oxygen continues uncorrected and is allowed to worsen, the changes will become more severe, resulting in loss of consciousness and inability to arouse the victim (which is known as coma).

. Lack of Oxygen to the Skin.

Recognizing this consequence of lack of oxygen is extremely important for the protective agent because it is a very sensitive indicator to the body's ability to compensate. Whenever oxygen becomes less and less available to the body's cells, it attempts to compensate by shunting blood to vital organs, thus maintaining their efficiency but allowing other organs such as the skin to go relatively uncompensated. As a result, changes in conditions of the skin are among the first changes to be seen, as deterioration in overall body processes occur. An obvious advantage of using the skin to observe deteriorations is that it is easily seen in anyone simply by observing the hands, face, and other exposed areas, and it does not require special equipment or skills to monitor.

If deterioration in overall body processes is due to lack of oxygen, the skin will change from its normal characteristics of pink, warm, and dry. Instead, it will first become cool, pale, and dry. If progression continues, the skin will become more moist, sweaty, or clammy. This sweatiness is often most easily observed on the forehead, arms, and chest. If progression is allowed to continue, the pale color will deteriorate to a bluish hue. This is most easily observed in skin areas around the mouth, lips, and generalized face, as well as finger tips and under the fingernails (called nail beds). If oxygen deficit worsens, skin in these areas will become purplish until the entire body is purple, probably indicating near-death.

As with other symptoms of shock, changes in skin color and temperature should be considered in context with other symptoms and outside temperatures. The normal effects of cold temperatures causes paling of skin and can progress to a bluish hue if cold exposure is allowed to continue. Warm weather, on the other hand, could disguise skin symptoms of shock as heat makes the skin pinker than it would be normally.

People with dark skin pigmentation, such as those who are Black, Hispanic, or Asian, can be more difficult to assess due to this natural skin coloring. In these individuals, nail beds often will continue to be a reliable location to assess skin color. For assessing color in anyone, the mucous membranes are infallible and should be considered in those with dark skin pigmentation as well. The most easily found mucous membranes are the inner eyelids. Other areas are the inner lips and cheeks or the tongue. These areas are usually bright pink; however, if they become pale or purplish, the effects of shock may be occurring.

.   **Lack of Oxygen to the Gastrointestinal (GI) System.**

The GI system is comprised essentially of the mouth, throat, tube leading from the throat to the stomach (called the esophagus), stomach, small and large intestines, rectum, and anus. Like the skin, the organs of the GI system are selectively given less oxygen for the benefit of maintaining other essential body systems. As a result of lack of oxygen to the GI system, the patient often exhibits symptoms of thirst, nausea, and vomiting. Thirst is an extremely important symptom of shock as it is often the very first symptom to alert the agent that shock is impending.

.   **Lack of oxygen to the kidneys.**

Much of the fluid that is drunk by a person is absorbed through the small and large intestines into the blood. After entering the blood, it bathes body cells and carries out other byproducts of cellular metabolism in the form of urine. The primary function of the kidneys, therefore, is to regulate the quantity of water in the body and serve in the removal of metabolic byproducts.

The kidneys are an organ system that must have a certain amount of blood flowing through it to sustain its ability to remain healthy. If the amount of circulating volume falls too low, as in the case of blood loss, the kidneys may fail entirely. The kidneys, therefore, are one of the last body organs to be without oxygen if the body can prevent it. However, if the entire body becomes compromised due to inadequate oxygen supply to the cells or due to overabundance of cellular byproducts, the kidneys will decrease urine output. This is an attempt by the kidneys to maintain as much circulating fluid volume as possible.

It should be noted that assessing kidney function is probably not possible at the scene of an injury. However, if the situation allows itself, it may be possible to determine whether urination is decreasing.

A decrease in urination does not necessarily mean shock; it can result from many causes. For example, in someone who has been vomiting or has had diarrhea or has had a prolonged fever with sweating, the body may be relatively dehydrated and the kidneys may try to retain the water that is available and thus decrease urine output.

<u>Kinds of Shock</u>

For the protective agent to better identify other factors which may be present if symptoms of shock are noticed, an overview of the kinds of diseases which most commonly can cause shock should be considered. It should also be noted that many actual illnesses and shock conditions result from more than one kind of shock occurring in the same person at the same time. Also, shock can develop in varying degrees and may be observed in only slight symptoms or may be profound with the potential of rapidly threatening life.

. **Respiratory (lung) shock.**

The primary cause of respiratory shock is an inability of the lungs to adequately move oxygen in and/or carbon dioxide out. This inability can be caused by any disease or injury which affects the lungs. For example, asthma, emphysema, allergic reactions, drowning or near drowning, and high altitude sickness are all possible causes of respiratory shock. In addition, injuries to the neck, such as those sustained during an automobile accident, are also possible sources of respiratory compromise resulting in respiratory shock.

. **Cardiogenic (heart) shock.**

Cardiogenic shock refers to "shock originating from the heart." This kind of shock is caused by the heart's failure to pump an adequate amount of blood to the body cells. Cardiac shock, heart shock, or cardiogenic shock is the leading cause of shock death. This kind of shock usually results from heart disease such as a heart attack. However, it can also result from direct injury to the heart muscle or the delicate sack which covers the heart. Such an injury can be caused by an automobile accident in which the driver is thrown forward and strikes the steering wheel with his chest.

. **Hemorrhagic (bleeding) shock.**

This kind of shock is what laymen think about when they think of shock. It is caused by an actual loss of circulating blood. When part of the volume of circulating blood is lost, it prevents the body from transporting oxygen efficiently to cells. Hemorrhagic shock, therefore, can be caused by an open, visible wound such as a cut to a major blood vessel (especially an artery), or can be caused by internal bleeding.

Internal bleeding can occur due to a fracture of a large, long bone such as the thigh bone (called

the femur). A broken (or fractured) femur can result in as much as a half gallon of lost blood without any sign of visible bleeding. A fractured pelvis can also result in a huge blood loss. Obviously, the tearing or rupturing of a major internal organ such as the liver or spleen will cause the kind of hemorrhage that can result in hemorrhagic shock.

. **Septic (dirty blood) shock.**

Septic shock is caused by overwhelming infection due either from bacteria, viruses, or fungus in the blood. Such an infection places such demands on the body that many different kinds of organ systems can be compromised to the point that they are unable to function. For example, the normal tone of the arterioles is what keeps blood pressure under control in the healthy individual. If the arterioles suddenly relax for any reason, they suddenly are able to hold much more blood than they usually hold. As a result, they act as a reservoir for blood which should normally be moving quickly to the heart and to body organs. This causes the body's organs to react as if they are not getting the oxygen supply they require and exhibit signs of real shock. In the hospital, septic shock is the second leading cause of shock death.

. **Neurogenic (nerve) shock.**

Normally the nervous system controls the "tone" of arterioles (see septic shock section). Neurogenic shock, therefore, is caused by the nervous system's inability to control the arterioles' regulation of blood pressure. This kind of shock can result from injury to the spinal cord, as in a fall from a height causing a broken back or neck.

. **Anaphylactic (allergic) shock.**

Allergic shock results from the body's overreaction to some kind of substance that it normally has a mild allergic reaction to. It is always caused by the body responding to something it has previously encountered. This kind of shock often results in swelling in the face and neck and can result in airway closure which immediately leads to respiratory shock. Loss of blood vessel tone, as in septic and neurogenic shock, can also result. The most common cause of allergic shock is a reaction to penicillin. Also, reactions to fish and iodine can cause this kind of shock.

. **Psychogenic (fainting) shock.**

This is a form of mild shock resulting from loss of tone to the blood vessels, caused by the kind of things that normally cause fainting. It is usually caused by some kind of psychological shock to the "mind."

. **Metabolic (body fluid imbalances) shock.**

Metabolic shock is caused by some kind of alteration in body fluids due to a mineral, acid/base, or cellular by-product imbalance. A common cause of this shock is diabetes, which causes an abnormally high blood sugar.

General Signs and Symptoms of Shock

To bring this information into perspective, it may be helpful to briefly review the most common signs and symptoms of shock. Symptoms may develop gradually, causing restlessness, confusion, combativeness, weakness, sleepiness, nausea, thirst, fear, and anxiety. They can also proceed rapidly, and quickly progress into unconsciousness. Statements of being thirsty, can't catch his or her breath, and complaints of nausea are all possible and are common to shock.

Breathing is often rapid and may be either shallow or deep. Heart rate will often be rapid and may be either weak or strong. Skin may be initially warm and flushed and then, as shock progresses, may become cool and clammy. There may be either slight dampness to the skin or profuse sweating. Vomiting is also a possibility.

A late sign may be pale skin which, if it progresses, may result in bluish discoloration around lips or mucous membranes. Loss of consciousness, slow pulse and respirations, and loss of control of bladder or bowels are signs of possibly irreversible shock and probable death.

Treatment of Shock

Treatment of shock must be quick and precise.

. **Lay the patient down and provide reassurance.**

This minimizes the demand for more oxygen. Someone at rest requires much less oxygen and also produces much less metabolic byproducts than someone engaged in even minimal activity. If the individual collapses, he/she is demonstrating his/her need to do this anyway. Rest also results in a degree of psychological relaxation. This relaxation places less physical stress on the body and decreases demand on the essential systems. To further enhance rest, the agent should also attempt to calm and reassure the patient.

. **Check for pulse and monitor vital signs.**

If there is no pulse, you must initiate CPR. Watch for changes in pulse rate and quality, respiratory rate and quality, level of consciousness, and skin condition.

. **Keep airway open.**

The airway must be kept open regardless of the level of consciousness. If vomiting occurs and the person is partially conscious or unconscious, he is at risk for inhaling his vomitus, which would likely result in respiratory arrest. As a result, the person should be observed closely for this possibility. If it occurs, the patient should be carefully turned to the side (see below) so that contents of the mouth can fall out and allow the airway to remain clear. If proper instruction and liability issues have been adequately addressed, oxygen can also be administered.

.   **Control external bleeding and splint major fractures.**

.   **Properly position patient, and be alert to spinal injuries.**

The head should be turned to the side if vomiting is a concern. *Caution: If spinal injuries are suspected, this turning must be accomplished by turning the body as a unit, keeping the head in precise alignment with the chest and shoulders, and without applying any pulling force away from the chest.* If spinal, pelvic, or leg injuries are not present, the patient can be laid on his/her back with the feet and legs elevated. This prevents available blood from pooling in the legs and keeps it circulating around the vicinity of the internal organs and brain where it will do the most good. The head and shoulders of the patient can also be slightly raised so that if vomiting does occur it will clear more easily than if the head is flat; however, it will still have to be turned to the side.

.   **Keep patient warm but do not overheat.**

Changes in skin condition result in skin cooling. This process should be kept to a minimum by insulating the victim from a cool ground or air temperature.

.   **Give nothing by mouth.**

Regardless of the amount of thirst, if shock is definitely suspected or nausea is present, do not give anything by mouth as this will undoubtedly encourage vomiting. In addition, never give anything by mouth to someone who is either unconscious or barely conscious--he must always be fully conscious to avoid inhaling the fluid given.

ASSESSING INJURIES AND ILLNESSES

In performing a patient assessment, the agent should proceed in a specific and deliberate manner. To go about the process haphazardly increases the possibility of overlooking problems, particularly when enduring the stress of treating someone known to the agent, and with a severe injury.

The first step in a medical emergency is to establish a safe scene for yourself and other responders. If there is an automobile accident which has knocked down "hot" electrical wires, or there are toxic gases or flames present, or other life-threatening conditions, you will do the client no good by becoming a victim yourself.

You must gain access to the victim. For example, if he is trapped in a car, and you see that he is massively bleeding, you must get to him immediately. Conversely, the victim should be moved only under certain conditions. If the scene is safe, moving an injured victim has resulted in even more, and more severe, injuries to the victim. This is especially true of fall or car accident victims who sustain neck or other spine injuries that are not visible. When carelessly moved, many of these victims sustain extended damage to the spinal cord and become paralyzed. For injuries at the level of the neck, the cord damage can result in instant death. *Moving an injured person requires trained knowledge, care, and precision.*

There are only four reasons to move an injured victim:

1.   If leaving him or her there would increase the threat of his or her injuries or injury to other responders.

2.   A patient's chin can be moved if the airway is obstructed and a chinlift must be performed to open the airway.

3.   The patient can be log-rolled if it is necessary to assess or treat life-threatening injuries to the back, or to turn the patient to remove vomitus from the mouth in an unconscious patient to open the airway.

4.   To transport the patient to a medical care facility.

The next step is the patient assessment (which will be discussed later in this chapter). Once the assessment is completed, you must provide basic emergency care. Remember, this is the care which the provider has been trained and certified to provide. For the lone protective agent, it is important to think through, in advance, how others at the scene, such as bystanders, can be asked to help in providing care. They can be asked to call for an ambulance, notify the police authorities, meet and escort the ambulance crew to the victim, and perhaps help in holding back onlookers and securing the scene.

As soon as the need for additional medical care is recognized, the Emergency Medical System (EMS) must be accessed, which can be done by dialing 911 in many U.S. urban locations. This must be done as soon as possible due to many unavoidable delays in their response. This is a very important reason for having at least one cellular telephone in the vehicle and another on a member of the protective team.

The EMS system can either be called by the agent at the scene, or the agent can direct someone else to make the call while he/she administers first responder care. If someone else is directed to make the call, that person should be instructed to return to the scene, if possible, after making the call. By returning, confirmation is assured that the call was made, and the agent will have another person at the scene if additional assistance is needed.

Before the call is made, the caller must know where to direct the ambulance crew so that a minimum amount of time is lost in getting to the victim. These directions must then be clearly communicated to the operator or dispatcher at the time of the call.

The time required for better trained and equipped responders to arrive may be prolonged, depending upon the location of the victim. However, until they arrive and accept care, the agent must continue any care-in-progress. The only reasons for discontinuing care, other than handing over to a

better trained responder, are that the caregiver becomes so exhausted that no further care can physically be given, or the victim is pronounced dead by a qualified medical doctor.

When care is transferred to more qualified providers, pertinent information regarding the patient should also be transferred. If it cannot be communicated by the victim, this must be provided by the agent. This information includes the victim's allergies, significant past medical history, and list of current medications. If the agent is not injured, he/she must find some way to accompany the protectee to the hospital.

When to Call EMS

A crunch point comes in determining when to notify the EMS system. Clearly, if the client is lying in the road unconscious, and blood is pouring from the chest, this is the appropriate time to call 911. But, what about those times when it is not so clear? The client falls down in his residence, or there is a minor automobile accident. Do you call 911? A great deal of liability can result if the agent makes the wrong decision; i.e., does not call for EMS when he/she should do so. Here are some of the reasons to access the EMS system.

.   Any unexplained worsening of breathing.

.   Any unexplained change in mental status.

.   Any visible bleeding of a quantity more than two tablespoons.

.   Any signs of shock.

.   Any injuries, such as falls, which could result in fractures of the head, spine, pelvis, or upper legs.

.   Any open fractures.

.   Any crushing injuries.

.   Any injuries to the head, eyes, face, neck,

chest, abdomen, pelvis.

.   Any sudden onset of chest, jaw, back, or arm pain unrelieved by rest, and lasting more than five minutes.

The Primary Survey

The primary survey is always the first step in dealing with medical crisis situations. It takes precedence over all other procedures. The primary survey is a process of rapidly identifying any immediately life-threatening conditions and taking necessary action to correct those life-threatening conditions that are present. It provides a brief, but vital, overview of the situation.

Is the scene safe? Does the patient need to be moved due to environmental dangers?

If dealing with trauma, what caused the injury? Based on the cause of injury, what would you expect for injuries? For example, in a fall from a height, such as from a second-floor balcony, more severe internal injuries are likely than from a fall off the curb. The internal organs most often affected by a fall from a height are the liver and spleen, which tear with the impact and therefore begin to bleed. Such an injury could, either slowly or almost immediately, result in hemorrhagic shock. Another organ vulnerable to this kind of injury is the delicate brain, spinal column, and spinal cord. If any signs of head injury are apparent, the neck and spine should be presumed to also be injured until cleared by x-rays and medical doctors. As a result, the head, neck, and back should be correctly immobilized if movement is required before better qualified responders assume care.

How many patients need to be treated? Have the client and two members of his family been injured, or only the client himself? Who needs attention first, second, etc.? How many ambulances are needed?

Is the victim conscious or unconscious? A conscious patient indicates there is breathing and circulation. It does not necessarily mean that the breathing and circulation are adequate, only present. An unconscious patient may or may not have breathing and circulation present. You must carefully check the status of the airway, breathing, and circulation in every unconscious patient. Unconsciousness makes finding injuries more difficult because the patient cannot tell you where it hurts.

Does the patient have an open airway? A person needs a clear, unobstructed conduit from the mouth to the lungs to breathe normally and easily. A clear, open airway is absolutely mandatory to patient survival. Without an adequate airway none of the other procedures that you can perform will prevent death. At this time, check the chest for holes in the chest wall that will interfere with oxygen exchange. If present, seal immediately before continuing with the primary survey.

Is the patient breathing adequately? Look, listen, and feel for adequate air exchange. Is the patient breathing spontaneously? Are the depth and rate of the respirations adequate? Based on these questions, does the patient need assistance with respirations?

There are two aspects to consider in evaluating circulatory status--does the patient have a pulse, and is there massive bleeding present? In determining whether there is a pulse, use the carotid artery in the neck, as this pulse is the most reliable in an emergency situation. If no pulse is present, you must initiate CPR. If a pulse is present, check for presence of life-threatening bleeding. You are concerned primarily with bleeding from major arteries, veins, and traumatic amputations. You must control all major bleeding points and anticipate shock.

Secondary Survey

While the main purpose of the primary survey is to identify and correct any immediately life-threatening conditions, the purpose of the secondary survey is to identify injuries or medical problems that could present a threat to life or limb if left untreated. It is critically important that you not jump to the secondary survey before you have performed the primary survey. This is a very common error, even for seasoned EMT's and paramedics.

The secondary survey is a brief head-to-toe examination to determine the presence of any associated injuries such as minor bleeding sites, fractures, burns, sprains, etc. The following is a basic format for a secondary survey, starting at the head, because you are already in this position from evaluating the ABC's, and proceeding downward in an organized fashion.

. **Head.** Check for lacerations, contusions, deformities, depressions.

. **Face.** Check skin color. Look for blood or clear fluid draining from the nose or ears, indicating skull fracture. Check for blood coming from the mouth (airway), and check for obvious facial fractures.

. **Neck.** Check the neck for pain, deformity, tenderness to touch. Check the front for evidence of injury to the windpipe and for any medic alert necklace.

. **Chest and Upper Back.** Look for signs of injury--lacerations, bruises, deformities. Look to see if chest is expanding when the patient breathes. Feel front and back for holes in chest wall or obvious bleeding sites. Feel chest for signs of rib fracture.

. **Abdomen and Lower Back.** Look for obvious signs of injury--lacerations, bruises, bowel protruding. Feel for bleeding sites front and back and for pain, tenderness, or deformity.

. **Pelvis.** Use "compression" test to check pelvis for fractures. Check genital area for signs of injury, if applicable.

. **Legs and Feet.** Check lower extremities for signs of injury--lacerations, bruises, deformities, or obvious signs of fractures. Run hands along legs to check for bleeding sites. Check pulse, movement, and sensation in each foot.

. **Hands.** Check upper extremities for signs of injury--lacerations, bruises, deformities, or obvious signs of fractures. Run hands along arms to check for bleeding sites. Check pulse, movement, sensation in each hand.

. **Back.** If you can do so safely (for the patient), check the back for signs of injury--bleeding, bruises, lacerations, deformities.

A common error, particularly when dealing with gunshot and stab wounds, is failure to check the entire body, including the back.

Estimating the Severity of Injury or Illness

Having completed the primary and secondary surveys, the next step is to determine just how severely the patient is injured or ill. There are certain parameters within which you must work with a minimum of equipment. Unlike an EMT or paramedic, you may not have a stethoscope or blood pressure cuff. You must use your senses to observe the vital signs.

. **Level of consciousness.**

Changes in a patient's level of consciousness frequently are early indications as to the severity of his condition. An anxious, restless, or agitated patient may indicate lack of oxygen or an injury involving possible blood loss or damage to the breathing process.

. **Skin color, temperature, and texture.**

Changes in skin color, temperature, and texture are excellent early indicators of blood loss. Normal skin is dry to the touch, warm, and usually pink. Patients with significant blood loss, internally or externally, tend to have pale, cool, moist skin. Some patients with heart conditions and respiratory conditions may have bluish skin color (cyanosis).

This sign signals danger as the patient is severely compromised.

.   **Capillary refill and eyelid test.**

While you probably will not have a blood pressure cuff to gauge the patient's cardiovascular status, you do have two very reliable indicators that require no equipment. The first is called the capillary refill test. Pinch the patient's fingernails. If normal, the nail will be pink to start and then blanch white with pressure. When you release the pressure the nail bed should promptly return to its pink color. If it takes longer than three seconds to return to color, or if the color does not return at all, this indicates a decrease in blood pressure, hence a blood loss somewhere.

Another simple test is to peel the lower eyelid downward to expose the inner eyelid. In normal, healthy people, the eyelid will be moist and pink. In patients with blood loss and low blood pressure, the eyelid will be pale.

These two tests are valuable in determining shock.

.   **Pulse.**

A normal pulse is easily felt at the wrist or the neck. It is full and beats at a rate of approximately 60 to 80 beats per minute. When patients are in shock, the pulse becomes difficult to feel, is weak, and the rate increases to 100 to 140 beats per minute. While pulses are excellent indicators of blood loss, they do require some skill and a certain feel for normal versus abnormal qualities.

Based upon the findings of the primary and secondary surveys and your estimation of severity of the patient's condition, you must now set your priorities in treating the patient(s).

Immediate patients need prompt attention and transport to survive. They include: airway problems, breathing problems, massive internal or external bleeding, open chest wound or massive injuries to chest, and wounds to head and chest areas.

Urgent patients may initially be stabilized at the scene but soon require transport to a hospital. These include: most stab wounds; less severe head, neck, chest, or abdominal trauma that does not threaten the ABC's (airway, breathing, and circulation); most fractures; and most medical conditions.

Delayed patients are those whose condition is not a threat to loss of life or limb, but who do require medical attention. These include: sprains, strains, some minor medical conditions, and minor lacerations and fractures.

Minor patients are those whose injuries do not have to be evaluated at a medical facility; for example, a bruise or laceration that does not require sutures.

Setting Priorities in Assessing and Treating Injuries and Illnesses

Despite the enormous distractions at any injury scene, you must prioritize your treatment to ensure patient survival. It is necessary to put the patient's injuries in the order of their severity, and to treat them in that specific order.

A.   Airway.

After securing the scene, your first priority is always the airway, as the brain cannot survive more than a few minutes without oxygen. Airway blockages may include blood, teeth, vomitus, food, or tongue. Snoring sounds indicate obstruction by the tongue. Noisy respirations mean an obstruction. (Also, any large opening of the chest must be sealed at this time.)

Once you have opened the airway with the head tilt or jaw thrust methods, you must clear the airway of debris and determine if the patient needs to be positioned on his side to maintain an open airway.

B. Breathing.

After the airway is secured, all injuries and illnesses that threaten the ability to breathe normally must be corrected. You must assess the breathing status and, if necessary, begin artificial respirations. Gunshot wounds, stab wounds, and chest injuries from vehicular accidents, as well as heart failure, respiratory conditions, and strokes, may all affect the respiratory efforts.

C. Circulation.

Now turn your attention to the circulatory status. If there is no pulse, you must begin CPR. In addition to pulse, you must assess internal and external bleeding and attempt to estimate the severity of blood loss. Internal blood loss, usually caused by blunt trauma associated with punches, kicks, falls, and automobile accidents, is difficult to assess. A patient may literally be bleeding to death with little external evidence, all the time slipping deeper and deeper into shock. The vital signs must, therefore, be constantly evaluated. All external bleeding must be controlled, and the patient treated for shock.

D. Delicate nervous system.

The delicate nervous system includes the spine, spinal cord, and the brain. Spinal cord injuries can be the most tragic of all traumatic injuries, causing paralysis that may be permanent. The most common causes of spinal injuries include vehicular accidents, sports injuries, diving injuries, falls from heights, and gunshot and stab wounds. It is extremely important to remember that if the injury circumstances suggest the possibility of spinal cord injury, you must treat the patient as if you were certain he had a spinal injury. All unconscious trauma patients are presumed to have a spinal injury as well.

Part of the function of the brain is to control the respiratory system and the cardiovascular system. An injury to the brain can adversely affect the breathing process as well as affecting the heart's ability to function as a pump. Any injury to the head or spine must alert you to the possibility of ABC impairment, which is always life-threatening. All head-injured patients are assumed to have a spinal injury until proven otherwise.

E. External Wounds.

After securing the ABC's and attending to head and spinal injuries, you may now turn your attention to external wounds. These include lacerations, cuts, abrasions, impaled objects, eviscerated tissue, burns, and amputations. If any of these wounds involve major blood vessels or cause massive bleeding, they would be categorized under priority C. If burns occurred involving the respiratory tract or if massive burns cover a large surface area of the body, they would be placed under category A, B, or C.

Treatment includes controlling bleeding, preventing contamination, keeping the injury immobile, and possibly treating for shock.

F. Fractures.

While fractures tend to be gruesome in appearance, causing enormous anxiety in the patient and the rescuer, they are normally less of a priority for care than life-threatening injuries. However, certain fractures can result in a threat to the ABC's. These would include fractures of the thigh and fractures of the pelvis, which can result in massive bleeding. Also, fractures of the skull may cause an injury to the brain which would result in possible ABC problems.

When treating fractures, do not waste time with fancy splints. Learn to use what is at hand. The goals of fracture care are to keep the extremity immobilized (splinted) and prevent further injury. Splinting reduces pain, and helps to prevent further damage to tissues, further bleeding, and permanent injury to nerves, arteries, and veins. When possible, you should immobilize the injured body part in the position it was found in.

G. General Other.

Under this category will fall most of the medical emergencies that you are likely to encounter: seizures, diabetic emergencies, strokes, minor heart attacks, and minor respiratory ailments. Most medical conditions need general support care, calm reassurance, and monitoring of vital signs until help arrives. If the patient has both traumatic injuries as well as a medical emergency, you should proceed in the normal order of treatment--A through H. An example of this might be a patient who has a heart attack while driving and causes an automobile accident.

H. History.

Obtaining an accurate history is an important part of assessing and treating a patient, if time permits. History refers to the events surrounding the current injury plus a brief statement of the patient's past medical history. For example, it would be helpful to know if a traumatized patient has a history of several major medical conditions. This would alert the rescuer to the fact that this patient could not tolerate the injuries as well as a healthy young patient might. As a protection specialist, it would be in the client's best interests that you have knowledge of his medical history so that you can relay that information to those caring for him or her later.

This system of prioritizing injuries and illnesses will greatly help in treating the most serious, life-threatening injuries first.

For example, your client is a 70-year-old man. While driving to a benefit concert, you are struck by another vehicle. Your client sustains numerous injuries. You examine him and find the following: he has pain in his neck area; a fracture of the forearm; an obvious open fracture of the thigh; numerous small lacerations; and a large hole in his chest wall. In what order do you treat him?

A. Airway. The hole in his chest threatens the airway, as well as--

B. his breathing.

C. Circulation. The fracture of the thigh may cause massive blood loss and shock.

D. Delicate nervous system. The pain in the neck may indicate a fracture of the neck and damage to the spinal cord.

E. External wounds. The numerous superficial lacerations need to be attended to in order to prevent further bleeding.

F. The fracture of the forearm needs to be splinted.

EMERGENCY INJURY AND ILLNESS MANAGEMENT

The following covers some of the most basic guidelines to procedures of emergency injury and illness management, covering those traumatic situations which the agent is most likely to encounter. The professional agent is strongly recommended to acquire in-depth training for first responder procedures.

Heart Attack

In assessing what he believes may be a heart attack, the agent should regard that any middle-aged or older patient with chest discomfort is assumed to be having a heart attack. Heart attack patients frequently deny that anything is wrong; take this as a positive sign that something is, indeed, wrong, and make note of the following questions.

Is the patient breathing? Is there a pulse? Does patient have a history of heart trouble? Is the patient complaining of chest pain? Is the patient short of breath? Is the patient sweaty? Nauseated? Weak? Is the patient anxious? Scared? Restless?

Basic management of the heart attack for the agent includes the following:

.   Maintain the ABC's and monitor vital signs.

.   Make certain that an ambulance has been called, if possible.

.   Keep patient resting, quiet, and calm. Any agitation can lead to worsening of the condition. Be reassuring.

.   Loosen all restrictive clothing, and make the patient as comfortable as possible.

.   If known heart patients take medications, you may assist a conscious patient in locating and taking his/her medication.

Spinal Injuries

In assessing spinal injuries, ask these questions. What caused the injury and does this suggest spinal injury? Is the patient paralyzed? Can the patient move hands and feet? Can he feel you touching him? Is there numbness or tingling in his arms, legs, or both? Is there pain and/or tenderness in the neck? Is there deformity along the spine? If the patient is unconscious, pinch his arms and legs to see if he moves them in response.

You must assume all unconscious patients have a spinal injury for treatment purposes.

.   If spinal injuries are suspected, the patient must not be moved before the ambulance arrives *unless* you or your patient are in immediate danger, *or* you must initiate CPR or correct other immediately life-threatening circumstances associated with the ABC's.

.   The ABC's should be maintained with a minimum of movement.

.   Any external bleeding must be controlled, and the patient treated for shock.

.   The patient's head, neck, and body should be immobilized as a single, straight unit.

Chest Injuries

With chest injuries, you should consider the following questions. Is the wound open or closed? Is the breathing process affected? Is there evidence of internal or external blood loss? Are there multiple rib fractures? Are there entrance wounds? Exit wounds? Impaled objects? Is there evidence of shock?

Be aware that blunt injury to the chest can cause catastrophic internal injury to lungs, heart, and blood vessels with very little external evidence of injury. Any injury to the chest can result in airway, breathing, or circulatory problems.

.   Establish an open airway.

.   Pay close attention to breathing and watch for respiratory distress.

.   Check circulatory status; especially check for massive bleeding. Control external bleeding.

.   Anticipate shock and treat it aggressively.

.   Check for entrance and exit wounds.

.   Cover "sucking" chest wounds. Try to seal the wound with an air-tight dressing such as saran wrap, aluminum foil, sandwich bag, etc.

.   Monitor vital signs.

Abdominal Injuries

With abdominal injuries these are the points to check. Is there pain or obvious injury? Is the injury blunt, or penetrating? Is there external blood loss? Is the bowel protruding? Is the abdomen tender? Rigid? Is there evidence of shock?

Blunt or penetrating abdominal trauma can cause massive bleeding; be prepared to treat for shock. Check for injuries front and back, particularly if dealing with gunshot or stab wounds.

. Assess the ABC's.

. Control external bleeding.

. Stabilize impaled objects--do not remove!

. Immobilize if spinal injury is present.

. Treat for shock.

. Do not attempt to push protruding organs back into the abdomen. If bowel protrudes, cover with moist dressing, then cover with dry dressing to maintain warmth.

. If practical, elevate the knees for comfort.

. Monitor vital signs.

Shock

Shock has been covered in some depth in this chapter; however, it is so important that a short review may be valuable. Every significant injury and illness carries with it the possibility of shock, and shock which is untended may be fatal. You should suspect and treat for shock in cases of gunshot and stab wounds, explosions, high speed vehicular accidents, falls from heights, and severe beatings. The agent must look for the following indicators.

Is there any injury that threatens the airway, breathing, or circulation? Is there major bleeding? Are there major, multiple fractures or other traumatic injuries? Is there a severe crushing type injury to chest, abdomen, or pelvis?

You should take note of these shock indicators: rapid, weak pulse; shallow respirations; pale, cool, moist skin; pale eyelids; patient restless, anxious, thirsty, weak, and/or trembling.

. Maintain an open airway and adequate breathing.

. Check for pulse; if none, initiate CPR.

. Identify and control all major bleeding sites.

. Treat for spinal injury if this is apparent.

. Control less severe bleeding sites from all external wounds.

. Splint all fractures.

. Keep patient warm.

. Do not give anything by mouth to the patient.

. Monitor vital signs.

Fractures, Dislocations, and Sprains

Without x-ray equipment, it is difficult to distinguish between a non-visible fracture and a sprain. If this is the case, the injury should initially be treated as a fracture.

Is pain or tenderness present in the injury? Is there an obvious deformity? Are there bone ends protruding from the skin? Is there swelling present? Is the patient unable to use the extremity?

Treatment is fairly straightforward, unless there is massive bleeding, accompanied by shock. If necessary, cut away clothing to see what you are doing. Try to not move or walk the patient unless the scene places you and your patient in danger.

. Assess the ABC's.

. Control bleeding and open fracture sites by normal means--direct pressure, elevation (where appropriate), pressure points.

. Check circulation, movement, sensation.

. Fractures near the joint or dislocations need to be immobilized in the position they are found to prevent permanent nerve and muscle damage.

. Apply appropriate splint(s).

.   With upper body fractures, you should use the patient's body as a splint, immobilizing the fractured limb to the torso. With lower extremity fractures, the same principle applies; use the uninjured leg as a splint for the fractured limb.

.   Reassure patient, as the sight of fractures can be quite unnerving.

.   Monitor vital signs.

External Wounds

In cases of blunt trauma to chest or abdomen, you should suspect internal bleeding and anticipate shock.

Is the bleeding bright red and spurting (arterial) or dark maroon with a steady flow (veinous)? Is the tissue exposed? Are there puncture wounds near vital structures? Is there an impaled object? What is the estimated blood loss? Does the skin, nailbed, and eyelid color suggest major blood loss? Are there any associated injuries?

In treating external wounds, do not waste time looking for fancy materials; use whatever is available at the scene (shirt, hand, towel, etc.). If necessary, cut away the clothing to examine the wound.

.   Assess the ABC's.

.   Control all external bleeding with direct pressure, elevation, pressure point or, as a last resort, tourniquet application.

.   Treat for shock.

.   Treat spinal injuries present.

.   Check entire body front to back and head to toe for bleeding sites.

.   Stabilize impaled objects in place--do not remove!

.   Splint all fractures. Avoid elevation if the limb is fractured.

.   Do not try to push protruding organs back into the body; cover with a warm, moist dressing if possible.

.   Move only if necessary to avoid hazards at the scene.

.   Keep patient still and calm.

.   Monitor all vital signs.

Burns

Before burn injuries can be assessed and treated, it is necessary to understand the differences between first, second, and third degree burns. All second and third degree burns should be treated as serious emergencies.

First degree burns involve burns of partial thickness of skin layers. The skin is red, may be swollen, and is usually painful. Sunburn is an example of a first degree burn.

Second degree burns still affect a partial thickness of skin layers, but the burn is deeper. The skin is red, blotching, blistered, "wet," and moderate to severe swelling may be present. These burns are extremely painful.

Third degree burns are those in which all layers of the skin are damaged. These burns usually appear charred, gray, leathery, and dry to the touch. They are usually painless due to destruction of the nerve endings.

Burns may cause much anxiety in the rescuer; however, treatment must proceed with the priorities in the normal fashion. Treatment must not be withheld in an emergency for fear of damaging burned skin.

.   Assess the ABC's. Burns frequently result in

airway and respiratory damage.

.   Control external bleeding and treat for shock.

.   Treat spinal injuries if present.

.   Splint all fractures.

.   Monitor vital signs.

.   First degree burns--soak in cool water or run cool water over the burned area for several minutes; then, cover with a dry (sterile if possible) dressing.

.   Second degree burns--if covering a small area, soak in cool water. If covering a larger area, dress with dry dressing to prevent heat loss, separating fingers and toes if they are involved.

.   Third degree burns--cover with dry dressing, maintain body warmth and treat for shock.

Stroke

Stroke occurs when there is damage to the brain by either a blocked blood vessel or a blood vessel that ruptures. Depending on the location of the vessel in the brain, a wide variety of signs and symptoms can manifest themselves. Frequently, patients with chronic high blood pressure are at risk of experiencing a stroke, particularly if they do not take their prescribed medication regularly.

Be aware that stroke patients may act in an irrational manner. Do not overlook this fact and assume that the patient is just drunk. These patients have no control over what they are doing.

Is the patient conscious? Is the patient complaining of headache or blurred vision? Is the patient paralyzed on one side of the body? Is the patient having a hard time speaking or swallowing? Is the patient confused? Is he/she able to stand or walk? Is there a noticeable change in facial features?

Stroke patients need gentle reassurance as

they may be frightened by their condition. Even unconscious stroke patients may still be alert enough to understand what is going on around them even though they seem totally unresponsive.

.   Assess the ABC's. Stroke patients frequently have trouble maintaining their airway.

.   Keep the patient reassured and still, if possible.

.   Place the patient in a head-elevated position or on his/her side to protect the airway.

.   Protect paralyzed limbs from injury.

.   Monitor vital signs and keep a keen eye on the airway.

Diabetic Emergencies

Diabetes is a disease which is characterized by the patient's inability to produce the hormone "insulin." Insulin is necessary to allow the body to use glucose as a primary energy source. While all cells of the body need glucose to survive, the brain and nervous system are the most sensitive to a lack of glucose for fuel. The brain needs a constant, uninterrupted source of glucose to function normally. If glucose is withheld for a considerable period of time, brain damage and eventually death result. There are two major diabetic emergencies: diabetic coma and insulin shock.

Diabetic Coma. This occurs when the blood sugar becomes too high, either because the insulin dose was too low or was forgotten altogether. It may also occur when too much food is eaten for the dose of insulin taken. In assessing diabetic coma, several points must be addresses.

Is there a history of diabetes? Did the patient take insulin today? Has patient eaten today? Does the patient know if the blood sugar is too high? Too low? Is the patient thirsty? Hungry? Need to urinate excessively? Is the patient's breathing unusually deep or rapid? Is the skin warm, dry, flushed? Is there a fruity odor on the breath?

.   Assess the ABC's, especially if the patient is unconscious.

.   If conscious, lay patient on his/her side to protect the airway.

.   If conscious enough, administer sugar (mixed in orange juice, a candy bar, or sweetened drinks).

.   Keep patient relaxed, calm, and at rest.

.   Monitor vital signs.

Insulin shock. This is a condition of too little sugar in the blood stream. It is usually brought on by taking too much insulin, eating too little, or a combination of both. Unlike diabetic coma which develops slowly over several days, insulin shock develops very rapidly. Brain damage can quickly result from lack of glucose. Patients often act in a bizarre manner, even combative. They may (mistakenly) appear to be drunk. If a patient has a history of diabetes and is acting in an abnormal, bizarre fashion, you should assume patient is experiencing diabetic problems.

Many symptoms are common to both diabetic coma and insulin shock. It is not always possible for the non-medical person to distinguish between diabetic coma and insulin shock. When in doubt, you should treat for insulin shock by administering sugar in some form; it may be life-saving.

Is there a history of diabetes? Has patient taken insulin today? Has patient eaten today? Is the patient acting bizarre? drunk? combative? Is speech slurred and uncoordinated? Is headache present? dizziness? Is skin pale, moist, cool? Is pulse rapid and weak?

For the first responder, the treatment is the same for both diabetic coma and insulin shock.

Seizures

Seizures are the result of a massive discharge of neuron activity in the brain. This discharge causes collapse and then generalized, purposeless motor activity throughout the entire body. The patient is unable to control this activity and may also lose bladder and bowel control. Many conditions may cause seizure activity; however, by far the most common cause of seizures is a condition known as epilepsy. In epileptics, the seizure condition is usually well controlled with medication. If the patient stops taking his medicine for a period of time, seizures may result.

The protection agent should always question a patient or relatives about an epileptic history and whether the patient takes medications for seizures. This information will be of help in making an assessment of a seizure.

Does the patient have a history of seizures? Does patient take medication for seizures? Has patient been taking medications regularly? Is the patient incontinent? Did anyone witness the seizure? Did patient bite his or her tongue? After the seizure is the patient tired? confused? disoriented?

The chief concern in caring for seizure patients is to protect against accidental damage to head and limbs during a seizure activity.

.   During seizure activity, roll patient on his/her side. Protect patient from striking his head on the floor, or his limbs from striking an object.

.   NEVER insert anything into the mouth of a seizure patient as this may cause a fatal airway obstruction.

.   When seizure activity ceases, roll patient on his/her side to protect airway and allow for drainage of blood and mucous.

.   Gently reassure patient as his or her level of consciousness gradually returns to normal.

. After seizure activity, keep the patient at rest.

. Be alert for an onset of multiple seizures.

Coma (Unknown Cause)

You may encounter a situation where a patient is unconscious, and no one is available to give you information as to the reasons for the unconsciousness. However, the treatment includes many of the same elements. In assessing the situation, these points should be addressed.

Unconsciousness may result from a number of causes, including alcohol, epilepsy, diabetic coma, insulin shock, underdose of essential medication, traumatic injuries, massive infection, stroke, or psychiatric reasons.

Does the patient respond to your voice or to shaking or painful stimulus? Is the airway open? pulse present? patient breathing? Is there evidence of head trauma? spinal trauma? Is there a previous medical history to indicate diabetes, cardiac problems, or stroke? Is there a smell of alcohol present? Does the patient have a history of drug abuse?

Remember, any unconscious trauma patient is assumed to have a spinal injury; therefore, treat accordingly.

. Carefully assess the ABC's.

. Identify if a spinal injury is present and treat accordingly.

. Lay the patient on his/her side to maintain airway *unless* there is suspicion of spinal injuries.

. Control external bleeding and treat for shock, if necessary.

. Splint fractures.

. Keep patient as still as possible to avoid aggravating a spine injury.

. Try to obtain a medical history.

. Monitor vital signs and monitor level of consciousness.

PROTECTIVE DETAIL MEDICAL KIT

One of the essential pieces of equipment which any agent or protective team should have is a medical kit. There are some kits available, commercially, but all too often they are either understocked or overstocked. Beware of medical kits that are so loaded with equipment that they become too heavy and cumbersome to conveniently carry. The protective agent will not be performing field surgery. His role is to administer first responder care and to keep his client alive for the time needed to either access an ambulance or transport him to a hospital.

The following is recommended for a basic, appropriate medical kit for a protective detail.

. Refillable oxygen cylinder, regulator and mask capable of supplying at least six liters oxygen per minute for at least fifteen minutes.

. Bulky trauma dressings big enough to stop copious bleeding, such as military battle dressings or Security Co. multi-trauma dressing.

. Universal poison antidote.

. Oropharyngeal airway set.

. Wire ladder splints.

. Roller gauze bandage material.

. Triangular bandages.

. Surgical tape.

. Ace bandage.

. Non-mentholated shaving cream (good for

covering/coating burns.

. Band aids.

. Imodium, or Pepto-Bismol.

. Seat belt cutter.

. Antihistamine and decongestant.

. Tylenol or equivalent.

. Di-Gel or something equivalent to settle upset stomachs.

. *Small folded pocket mask (to protect the user from infection from contagious disease while performing mouth-to-mouth resuscitation.

. *Pair (or several pairs) of disposable medical examination gloves.

. Sunscreen and sunburn medication (aloe vera products are helpful).

. Insect repellant.

. Medical history of protectee(s).

. Extra supply of protectee(s) prescription medication.

AIDS and hepatitis represent real and present threats to your life and they must be recognized, and appropriate self-protection measures taken.

The experienced protection agent usually has an additional "field" medical kit which is small, streamlined, contains only the rock-bottom essentials to deal with the life-threatening ABC's, and can be carried on his or her person. If the client is hiking on his ranch in Montana, or skiing the back side of Aspen Mountain (somewhat removed from the ski patrols), and he has an accident, it is not helpful to know that the fully equipped medical kit is in the trunk of the car. A bulky trauma dressing, airway set, splints, bandages, tape, and a pain-killer may be all that is needed, under these conditions.

If you and your client are planning to spend considerable time in a really backward area, one in which there are no doctors or medical facilities within easy accessibility, you should consider buying a book entitled *Where There is No Doctor, a village health care handbook,* (Revised) by David Werner, published by The Hesperian Foundation, P.O. Box 1692, Palo Alto, CA 94302. This one really covers the basics, but is of limited use for dealing with life-threatening emergencies.

Warning--the material contained within this chapter does not constitute a complete training course in First Respondent Medicine. The agent is advised to seek further training in order to perform any of the procedures listed, as attempting to render emergency procedures without proper knowledge could result in further injuries.

Far fewer corporations hire executive protection agents than you might think, and the corporations who do hire them generally do so because of reaction to a specific incident, or because of specific threats, or in some cases simply as a prudent security measure. Having absorbed this fact, it should also be stated that, while only a few years ago very few corporations were even aware of executive protection as a profession, there is growing respect now for the professional protection agents and awareness as to the need for them.

The need for heightened protection overseas has been recognized since the 1960's, when terrorists began to target Americans and American corporations. Until fairly recently, however, domestic terrorism tended to target the government (anti-Viet Nam, anti-tax) or specific individuals (Ku Klux Klan, Aryan Nations) as opposed to corporate America. No longer. Corporations and the executives who run them are increasingly being singled out with anger, frustration, and violence on the part of people with causes. These include the animal rights activists, anti-abortion extremists, anti-nuclear protesters, and environmental extremists.

The banking industry has traditionally been a target for kidnapping, hold-ups, and bombs, and they are even more targeted in hard times. Bank foreclosures, a reluctance (or inability) to extend loans, and the smelly business of the S & L scandals have contributed to a generally bad feeling about the banking industry.

Corporations are also under attack internally. Disaffected employees, those who have been fired or chastised, are a frightening new problem, having created numerous violent incidents including killing fellow employees and supervisors. With the downsizing of corporations, plant closings and subsequent employee lay-offs, the internal anger will continue to grow and present a new threat to the security of the corporation and its chief executives.

Additionally, chief executives, the CEO's themselves, are being held accountable as never before for the actions of the corporations. If Corporation X uses animal research to perfect its line of cosmetics, the CEO of Corporation X is held personally responsible by the animal rights activists for this practice. Good cause extremists are not just looking at the corporation; they hold the CEO to be directly responsible.

Shareholders, too, have "come out of the closet." There was a time when corporate shareholders were, except for the holders of large blocks of shares, generally a fairly quiescent group. This is no longer true; shareholder meetings have become unruly shouting matches, often with the shareholders locked in verbal combat with the chief executives. Stockholders in some corporations have demonstrated such strong feelings about the management of their corporations that some stockholder meetings are held with the chief executives speaking from behind bullet-resistant podiums.

Along with the threats of violence against corporations and corporate executives comes a new, non-violent, but extremely damaging threat--industrial espionage perpetrated, for the most part, by foreign governments. According to one well regarded survey, of 165 corporations responding to a survey, 35% stated they were aware of technology having been stolen. They reported that 75% of known thefts of technology occurred domestically and 25% occurred in international locations. Of those corporations targeted for information, 55% were targeted for product data, 31% for manufacturing data, 10% research, and 4% for sales data. As international competition heats up, the race is, increasingly, being won by the swiftest possessor of saleable information. Stolen company secrets have cost the victimized corporation millions of dollars in business. The battle has shifted for the major powers from nuclear war to industrial and economic war. There are a huge number of unemployed government spies worldwide, many of whom are going to work for corporations.

One other factor contributing to the corporate awareness of its need for specialized protection stems from the Board of Directors. The Board of Directors has a responsibility to provide a reasonable level of safety for its employees. If there is a known threat, or a reasonable, prudent person might believe in the strong potential of a threat, the corporation has a moral and legal responsibility to provide protection for the person or persons being threatened. There is a profit motive as well. If a strong, decisive CEO of a major corporation were kidnapped and either held for an extended length of time or killed, the corporation could suffer semi-paralysis at the decision-making level, costing perhaps millions of dollars. That CEO is one of the corporation's most valuable, perhaps irreplaceable, assets. Increasingly, therefore, Fortune 500 Boards of Directors are dictating the acquisition of specialized executive protection for key executives.

The bottom line to these facts is that corporations are becoming increasingly aware of the threats against them and the need for specialized protection, protection not traditionally provided within the corporate structure. To supply the specialized protection needed by corporations, a protection agent must be multi-faceted and multi-trained. Corporations, even very large corporations, may not be able to justify the employment of an agent who is too narrow in focus, even if that agent is very adept at executive protection. To succeed within a corporation, a protection agent must be conversant with:

. Corporate structure--it is impossible for the executive protection agent to function effectively within a corporation unless he, or she, understands how the corporation works, the departmental lines, and the politics involved. The corporate environment is highly competitive, and an agent is apt to be perceived as a detriment by corporate staff unless the agent is able to demonstrate an understanding of the various jobs and people.

. Business management--at least at a minimal level, to understand that the sole motivation of the corporation is *profit*, and the means whereby corporations achieve profits.

. Physical and electronic security--an increasingly complex, high technology subject, especially as it relates to securing executive suites, critical information, and facilities.

. Information and computer security--to prevent the selling, or taking, of company secrets that can, literally, bankrupt a company.

. Guard force utilization and management--using guards in the most effective manner to provide the protection needed for company assets.

. Executive protection--the specialized protection of key individuals and their families within the corporate structure, domestically and overseas.

. Special event security--for corporate-sponsored national and international sporting events, stockholders' meetings, and social events.

. Internal threat management--relating to workplace violence issues.

. Crisis management policies and procedures--as they relate to the protectee (kidnapping, hostage taking, bomb threats).

Are not some of these security areas the responsibility of the corporate Security Director, rather than the executive protection agent? Perhaps, but as is the case in other arenas, if the job needs to be done and is not being done satisfactorily, the agent may need to pitch in. The agent and the Security Director must work together as a team, harmoniously, with an understanding of each other's job. Make no mistake, the Security Director is very likely to view the newly hired executive protection agent as a rival. A top priority for the agent is to change this impression, and to establish a professional working relationship with the Security Director.

Ideally, for the protection specialist to do his job, the corporate Security Director should advocate the use of personal protection when it is truly needed. The Director should realize that specialized corporate needs require specialized skills, and that the employment of a protection specialist will complement skills which already exist within the security organization.

It helps if the Director honestly believes that the person hired for the agent position possesses the necessary training and intelligence to fulfill the requirements and has personality traits which are complementary to the protectee. A trusting relationship must be established which will reassure the Director that his or her career will not be threatened by the close relationship which will surely develop between the agent and the protectee.

There will be so many occasions when the Security Director and the protection agent must work together that, unless a good relationship is established, the agent simply will not be effective.

Corporate Structure

A corporation can be any size from one person to the mega-corporations such as General Motors and IBM. For the purposes of this book, we will be referring to those large, multi-national corporations which are apt to have the kinds of problems that would call for the services of an executive protection agent or a team of agents.

At the very top of any corporation are the stockholders (also called shareholders), the individuals who own shares in the corporation. The shareholders are the ultimate "boss." They meet on at least an annual basis (called the Annual Meeting of the Shareholders) and at that meeting, among other issues, they elect a Board of Directors for the corporation and select auditors to check and report on the finances of the corporation. Generally, the shareholders elect Directors and auditors according to a slate of candidates presented to them.

The Board of Directors, also called Board members, have certain guidelines as to which decisions they can make for the corporation, and those guidelines are quite broad. The Board meets on both a regular and an as-needed basis. The Board, at its Annual Meeting (usually immediately following the Annual Meeting of the Shareholders), elects the Officers of the Corporation. In addition, the Board makes decisions on major issues affecting the corporation, and the Board has a legal responsibility for these decisions. Sometimes, the CEO of the corporation will also serve as a Board member. Boards are extremely powerful, and the most powerful Board member is the Chairman of the Board. The Chairman of the Board may, or may not, hold an active management role in the corporation. Depending upon his active involvement with the corporation, the Chairman of the Board is a likely candidate for executive protection. The Board may designate an Executive Committee, usually three to seven Board members who will meet frequently and play an active role in the management of the company.

It should be explained that, usually, the top executives of the corporation are very influential in proposing the names of Board members, and those individuals are usually a shoo-in for election at the Annual Meeting of the Shareholders. Therefore, a prominent Chief Executive Officer (CEO) has enormous influence over the corporation.

The Chief Executive Officer (often but not always President) is the top salaried officer in the corporation. He usually has great influence with the Board of Directors and the Executive Committee. Therefore, he makes many crucial corporate decisions and is often the most visible person, from a public relations standpoint, in the corporation. He or she is probably the strongest candidate for executive protection.

The Chief Operating Officer (COO), who may

also hold the title of President or Executive Vice President, is the number two salaried Officer and executive in the organization. Whereas the CEO looks at the "big picture" of corporate policy and strategic goals, the COO concentrates on the organizational issues of "making it happen." Depending upon his responsibilities, he may be a candidate for executive protection. Generally, this person's risk level is lower than the CEO and/or Chairman of the Board due to lesser identification with the corporation as viewed by the public.

Many corporations have subsidiaries located either within the United States or overseas. At the head of the subsidiary is generally a President, since most subsidiaries are separately incorporated. If the corporation does not have a separately incorporated subsidiary, it may operate one or more branches of the company in different locations, in which case the head of the branch may have a title of Vice President, or Manager. The President or Manager of the subsidiary/branch may be a candidate for executive protection, particularly if his subsidiary corporation is either controversial or is located overseas. The public frequently identifies the title of President with the top position in a corporation, even if this President is only in charge of a relatively small corporate subsidiary.

There are many, many, divisions and executives heading these divisions within a major corporation and, for the most part, the executives within these divisions do not require executive protection. There is one exception--when a supervisor has been threatened or feels he could be threatened by an unhappy employee. It is useful to have some understanding of the divisions within a corporation, since an executive protection agent working within a corporation will have to interface with at least some of them.

The technical division contains the research, development, and engineering personnel. In many corporations (computer, pharmaceuticals, etc.) this is a huge division, and the work performed by this division is highly protected, since it is particularly attractive to industrial espionage. Theft of a newly developed product could be very costly if a competitor could bring the product to market more quickly than the original company.

The legal department provides legal counsel. The federal and state relations department conducts the lobbying efforts for the corporation. The planning department contains, usually, the finance people and the strategic planning and economic development personnel. The financial controllers are powerful people within the corporation and may be supportive of executive protection if they perceive a financial threat to the corporation through the loss of a key executive. By the same token, the legal advisors may support executive protection services if legal counsel believes a legal responsibility exists to the shareholders to protect its executive "asset." The financial and legal staff are apt to take a risk management approach to the issue of executive protection (more about this in the chapter on Crisis Management).

The operations department may contain the sales, marketing, advertising, purchasing, and distribution functions. Again, there may be little interface with these departments.

The personnel department is very active as it handles hiring, background checks, training, benefits, promotions, and a multitude of services, almost all of which will interface with the agent's job.

Security, engineering, and maintenance are important departments that interact with each other and will be of real importance to the agent. These departments are responsible for many of the safety and security functions of the corporation.

Other departments contain public relations, community relations, and shareholder relations. This department is important to the agent in several ways. Public and community relations people like to publish information about corporate executives, information which may unknowingly violate security. The public and community relations people will be intrinsically involved in the special events sponsored or held by the corporation--the bicycle races, charity events, sporting events, employee picnics, and shareholder meetings--all of which must have strong security measures.

The executive support staff which surrounds the protectee executive is of vital importance to the agent. The support staff can include the following: one or more administrative assistants who interface with the various departments; a secretary who may control the executive's itinerary; speech writer(s); consultants; travel agents; flight operations personnel; drivers and vehicle maintenance; and security personnel. At a personal level, the support personnel may include physicians, wardrobe buyers and tailors, barber or hairdresser, family and friends.

There are two situations which the agent may face with his new position within the corporation. If he is the first professional executive protection agent to be introduced into the company, the protectee and his staff may hold unrealistic, even unflattering, preconceptions of him and his role. They may feel that he is going to come in with guns blazing and swift ninja-like movements, or that he will look and act like the bodyguard stereotype, muscular and arms crossed but not much between the ears. It is possible that bodyguards have been brought in on occasion and that the results were not harmonious. It is the agent's job to change those wrongful expectations.

Because of the closeness of the support staff, both to the protectee and to each other, they may view the agent as an intrusion rather than an asset. The agent will not be able to perform his or her job effectively if he cannot gain acceptance by the staff. This acceptance is greatly facilitated if the protectee "makes it happen" by giving his full support, and if the agent is able to convince the staff that he is non-political; i.e., not a threat to the staffperson's position. The agent is most effective when he or she functions as a facilitator, someone who can help the staff function more efficiently, and who can maintain communications, particularly when the protectee is away from the office. The agent must, through diplomacy and patience, convince the staff that he is not a threat to their positions; rather, he is performing a job just as they are, a job so specialized that only the agent can do it.

To gain acceptance and respect, the agent must project a profile that is acceptable. He has to look like the corporate image, properly dressed, clean, mannerly, and able to use proper language and communication skills. The agent must have respect for the other staff people. He must make a real effort to understand what everyone else does and how their jobs contribute to the success of the corporation. If, for example, an executive assistant fumes at some delay caused by a security measure, it helps to say, "I'm sorry that this has caused a problem, and I know the time constraints you are under because of your special project. I'll try to make it as easy for you as I can."

The agent must also project an image of reliability and integrity, actually to a higher degree than is expected of others. It seems trite, but if the agent is late or careless about an assignment, can it not be assumed that he will be equally inept at protecting his executive? The agent is the problem-fixer; if things start to go wrong, he can help to set them right. Integrity comes with being non-political and being thought of as trustworthy. The agent has one job--to protect his client. That does not include pointing out to the protectee that his executive assistant likes to smoke a joint in the men's room, or that the secretary was late twice last week. If there is a security problem, such as a couple of employees who are careless about leaving important documents on their desks when they go to lunch, there are ways to handle the problem without running to the client.

The agent will inevitably be privy to confidential information about the corporation, the protectee, and other staff personnel. Within a corporation, information, especially secret information, is power. The agent must guard that information zealously, and resist *any* temptation to relate that information to anyone. If he is perceived as trustworthy and not one of the corporate "power players" (hence, the enemy), he is not regarded as a threat; indeed, he can be everyone's ally and confidant.

Conversely, nothing will damage an agent's ability to work with the staff more than to ask for special privileges, brusquely order people about, gossip about other personnel, brag about his personal relationship to the boss, dress like a slob, make inappropriate sexual and ethnic remarks, and run to the client with every real or imagined infraction of the corporate rules. This kind of behavior guarantees a short career.

Ultimately, acceptance of the agent will depend upon the staff's and protectee's perception that the agent knows his job, is good at his job, and brings a positive addition to the organization. If possible, key staff personnel should be allowed to understand why the agent is there. Was it a Board decision? A reaction to a threat? It would be extremely helpful if the protectee, himself, were to meet with key staff personnel to explain these issues, introducing the agent and asking for support from the staff. This sets the right tone.

If the decision to provide executive protection has been made by the Board, with the reluctant concurrence of the protectee, the agent is going to have a tough time unless he can persuade the protectee that he (the agent) is there as a facilitator, and not a nuisance. He will have to sell himself into the job.

Corporate Power, Politics & Influence

There are power and influence levels in every corporation; there are also politics. **Power** is the ability to influence decisions and control resources. Managers and professionals often have power because of the authority granted by their positions. **Influence** is close in meaning to power, though influence is more subtle than power. Power and influence do not necessarily reside in title. In a real sense, the CEO's personal assistant may not have the same power as the Vice President of Finance, but might wield more influence with the CEO. Power and/or influence can also be conferred on an individual based on his or her inherent abilities, expertise, personality, trustworthiness, and loyalty. **Politics** are the avenues and strategies employed by individuals hoping to gain power and influence.

Of the three--power, influence, and politics-- politics is the wiliest and least trustworthy. However, not all politics are necessarily bad, especially when political tactics are used to produce good results.

It is essential for the protection agent to understand the following issues within the corporation:

. **Corporate culture.** Is the corporation set in its ways? Is change of any kind resisted? Does one often hear, "Oh, we've always done it that way," and "Oh, we would never do that--it would be too (undignified), (disruptive), (etc.)." Is there an atmosphere of fear, which leads the key individuals to simply entrench themselves? Do they regard all newcomers as rivals for their job?

Conversely, is the corporation in the "fast lane," changing almost every day? Does it embrace new ideas? Will security and protection be viewed as necessary elements for the health of the corporation?

Is the CEO "lean and mean" with a tendency to scoff at the thought of personal risk? After all, he spends his (business) life dealing with the risk of competition and changing markets.

The protection agent should have a good perception about the corporate culture of an organization before he or she accepts the job, and, once having accepted the job, he/she must be prepared to function within that culture.

. **Power and Influence.** Understanding how the power/influence forces work within a corporation is essential to accomplishing the protection agent's goals. There will be-- guaranteed--one or more powerful decision makers who will resist the notion of spending money on security, and/or who see the protection agent as an unnecessary appendage and nuisance. Also guaranteed is the fact that at least one powerful executive will declare that he knows better than the protection agent how to provide protection. In fact, that individual may be the protectee himself.

So, now, what is the hapless agent to do? Enter the mentor.

. **The mentor.** A mentor is one who can perform at least two functions: guide the (in this case) protection agent through the complicated paths of that particular organization's corporate culture, power, and influence; and who can quietly intervene to support and assist the agent in accomplishing his/her goals.

Logically, the mentor should be recruited from the ranks of senior management. While lower level supervisors may be of great help, they have no power, for example, to influence the budget or gain access to the CEO's office. The mentor must have **access** to the decision makers, must be able to communicate with them at "eye level." Mentors can be found in several areas, but a good bet is someone from the following departments: operations, finance, legal, personnel and human relations, and from the CEO's administrative staff.

A mentor must not only have access; he or she must have **respect**--must be viewed as trustworthy, level-headed, objective, and less motivated by political shenanigans than others. There is one in every corporation, an individual who has weathered the internal corporate storms, who maintains an open-door policy, who really *listens* and evaluates new ideas, who has the courage to swim against the tide, who has a good track record of success, and who is likeable.

Once the mentor is identified, the protection agent must present his ideas in a clear, succinct way. If the mentor has the above qualities, he will listen carefully. If he understands that the measures being presented will benefit and protect the corporation, he

can be persuaded to help. If, however, he senses that either the agent doesn't know what he is talking about and is presenting some sort of fuzzy, indeterminate, overly ambitious set of ideas, his mentoring support will be nonexistent. He did not achieve his access and respect by supporting bumblers. One way to avoid this is for the agent to ask the potential mentor what *his* ideas are--how he views the security and potential threats--and his advice on how to tackle the situation, beginning with an overall threat assessment.

Conducting A Threat Assessment

Executives are high-powered people, used to making decisions and acting with a great deal of independence. They are not, then, apt to submit to a great many restrictions. They will certainly not wish to change their lifestyles or agree to any measures that will alter the corporation's ability to prosper. For example, if the CEO likes to personally wade into labor disputes and treasures his ability to personally get problems resolved, he is not going to agree to turn over this function to his assistant because you, the agent, think it's too risky. The last thing the protectee wants is to have his Board of Directors or his ambitious, would-be successor think he has lost power or guts.

It is important, as early as possible, to determine what the protectee's expectations are of his agent or protective team. After that, it is up to the agent to gain the protectee's confidence, so that when changes are necessary to preserve security, those changes can be presented as options to which the protectee will listen with respect. In establishing this rapport, the agent will find a mentor's help to be most useful.

However, before any changes are suggested, a first step is to conduct a risk assessment, beginning with the protectee. What does the protectee perceive as the threat? What does he see as the agent's primary role? What does he see as his, and the corporation's, vulnerabilities? If appropriate at this time, the agent should query the protectee on certain aspects of his life, such as his involvement with community activities, political activities, participation in other corporations (does he sit on other Boards?), and any activities which might put him at risk.

It is extremely important that the protectee understand the critical relationship between having a professional threat assessment conducted and the actual quality of the protection offered. In other words, there cannot be a professional level of protection in the absence of a professional threat assessment. Therefore, it is the agent's task to convince the protectee of its importance and gain his/her support, as the agent must be able to speak with those individuals and access those resources which the agent believes are necessary to obtaining good, reliable information. A mentor can facilitate this process, opening doors that might otherwise be closed.

On the other hand, if the agent were to conduct the assessment, even in good faith, *without* the executive's approval (or at least knowledge) this action would likely be seen as an invasion of the executive's privacy and an overstep of the agent's responsibilities. Such an overstep would obviously be a grave mistake at a time when it is critical to build trust in the protector/protectee relationships. If there is a problem with gaining access to a key resource, the agent must inform the executive that the data is required for a thorough assessment and that without it, an incomplete assessment will result.

If the agent has the backing of his protectee he can use that backing to obtain the additional information he needs for his risk assessment. He should interview the executive assistants, especially those personnel who screen calls, open mail, make social and travel arrangements, and control itineraries--all with an eye to reviewing the procedures for protecting proprietary information about the protectee and his family. Part of the agent's job will be to heighten the security awareness of all personnel who control sensitive information. He should request calendar and itinerary information for upcoming events, so as to review security for these events as far in advance as possible, or he should request that he be informed of such events based on previously agreed-upon criteria.

He should meet with the corporate Security Director and establish his credentials. From the Security Director he should determine whether there are procedures for dealing with suspicious mail and handling negative or threatening telephone calls; how visitor access is controlled; telephone, computer, and document security procedures; and overall physical and electronic security of the office building.

He should request that the Security Director do a walk-through of the property with him to inspect the overall security, and perform an introduction to the building maintenance and engineering staff.

He should request permission to review any incident files, threats either from outside or from employees, union disputes, or other perceived or real risks. He should determine if there is a corporate crisis management plan for handling bomb threats, worker violence, kidnappings, natural disasters, etc.

The agent should determine whether there are procedures which are regularly employed to detect outside electronic surveillance in offices, conference rooms, and boardrooms. Has evidence of surveillance been detected? How effective are the countersurveillance methods being used?

The agent must establish cordial working relationships with the Security Director and staff. These people will be vital in the overall protection of the executive.

A meeting with the Risk Manager will determine how the corporation balances its risks and what measures are taken, such as the purchase of insurance, to ameliorate risk.

A meeting with the Legal Affairs department will help to establish certain guidelines to aid in avoidance of liabilities.

A meeting with the Personnel (or Human Resources) Director should explore hiring practices. Are references checked? Does the corporation use background checks? on all employees, or just on management personnel? How are employee terminations handled? With the growing number of employee violence incidents, a prudent suggestion would be to establish a practice of reviewing personnel records prior to termination for indications of dangerousness, substance abuse, fighting, or disciplinary actions. The agent should inquire about any recent firings or currently employed disgruntled employees and any union problems. The agent, if possible, should review the files of close-quarter personnel, those staff people working closely with the protectee. The agent should set the pattern for an ongoing close relationship with the Personnel Department to ensure that current information is related to him in a timely manner.

The agent should access data available from the Public Relations (PR) Department as this department is responsible for distributing to the media any officially released information about the corporation or its employees. The PR Department also interprets media coverage and the public's response to releases. The agent should request, and review, the file of press clippings about the corporation. He should also determine if a complaint file is kept and review it. All this data can provide the protective agent with valuable historical, up-to-date, and ongoing information about controversial issues.

Almost all corporations maintain very good proprietary libraries, managed by a capable manager and researcher. Much useful information can be obtained here.

If the corporation maintains its own corporate aircraft, the agent should meet with the Director of Flight Operations and review security procedures. Flight departments almost always believe they already have adequate security measures in place. The role of the protection agent, then, is to offer subject matter expertise regarding vulnerabilities that specifically relate to the security of key executives while at that facility, or during ingress and egress from the aircraft, or while aboard company aircraft. If there is no flight security plan, he will need the cooperation of the flight personnel in developing one.

The agent should meet with all corporate drivers to do the same. He needs to determine if the drivers have adequate training and experience to function as protection drivers; if not, a recommendation should be make to provide that training. The agent should consider putting together a security manual for the drivers, utilizing executive protection procedures. A security seminar for the drivers is even more useful, as it allows for an exchange of ideas and provides an opportunity for the agent to demonstrate his knowledge.

The agent should introduce himself, his credentials, and his responsibilities to the top local law enforcement personnel, and obtain information on general crime statistics and specific crime patterns in the neighborhood of the corporation property and the protectee's residence. The law enforcement authorities keep incident records and should be able to relate any problems connected to the corporation from their standpoint.

In determining risks, by now the agent should know if there are any specific threats against the corporation or the protectee himself. In the absence of specific threats, the risks to a corporation and, hence, an executive are several. Random street crime is a threat to the corporate protectee, just as it is to any individual.

At the corporate level, the disgruntled employee probably poses the most worrisome threat either of violence, theft, or of sabotage. Employees, angry with the corporation, have been known to kidnap and kill executives, plant bombs, commit arson, shoot fellow workers and supervisors randomly, destroy computer information and softwear, steal items of great value, and sabotage valuable property. Large corporations employ many, many employees who probably represent a realistic cross section of the general American public. This means that a certain percentage take drugs, beat their wives, own guns, gamble, drink to excess, are in debt and beset by creditors, are deeply resentful of authority, or are committed to violent behavior simply out of frustration. For one or all of these reasons, the angry employee who has been reprimanded or terminated may feel driven to violent behavior one more time. Because corporations and the people who run them are often perceived as authoritarian and uncaring, they are easily blamed for personal problems and failures; hence, revenge! The trend is rapidly approaching epidemic proportions.

A rising risk for some corporations comes from the extremist proponents of "causes." This is not to be taken lightly. These groups often employ classic terrorist tactics, albeit at a level of relatively low intensity. A number of violent incidents have been perpetrated against corporations using animals for research, abortion clinics, nuclear plants, and environmentally insensitive companies. More than one corporate CEO has a protection team with him night and day, precisely because his company falls in one of these categories.

Disgruntled customers and dissatisfied shareholders are both risks of varying degrees. They fit more into the area of embarrassing or nuisance incidents, of which there are many. The protectee is not happy when confronted either by a drunk or a tomato-throwing shareholder. Anyone can become a shareholder simply by purchasing shares in the corporation, which entitles him or her to attend the shareholders' meeting. This means that shareholders represent a cross section of society, subject to the same worries, frustrations, and violence.

The risk of kidnapping for economic or political gain is slight in the United States as compared to the higher risks overseas. In third world countries with political disruptions, this risk becomes significant. In fact, the risk assessment becomes a different and highly focused ongoing undertaking. Overseas, the problem of corporate politics becomes significantly lower, whereas actual security threats take a higher priority. Americans overseas are too far removed from the corporate seat of power to have the overriding concerns of ambition which preoccupy their colleagues in the States. From a security viewpoint, expatriates (foreign workers in a country) are more concerned about the issues of terrorism, religious restrictions, clan disputes among workers, theft, sanitation and health, and mechanical breakdowns. Thus, the risk assessment becomes a very different matter.

Once the threat assessment (risks, vulnerabilities, and recommendations for improvement in security) is completed, the agent should meet with the client to discuss the results. A corporate risk assessment may not necessarily be done in writing. The decision whether to do it in writing or verbally depends on the protectee's level of interest in the subject and the writing abilities of the agent. An interactive discussion with the protectee in a private, relaxed atmosphere may suffice. In addition, the threat assessment will probably change so frequently that any written document will quickly become obsolete and will soon serve only as a baseline for comparison. However, it is recommended that separate security surveys be written on each facility that has been included in the threat assessment, such as aircraft hangars, executive residences, and offices. (These documents, when combined with an overall threat assessment, can become quite time-consuming in the writing.)

If the threat assessment is written, it should be written in a clear, not overly long, form and should contain up front an executive summary, a one-page summation of risks, vulnerabilities, and recommendations (see Target Study in Appendix). The client is a busy man and he does not wish to read overly detailed, insignificant reams of detail about non-existent problems. He wants to know, in the shortest time possible, what is the problem, why is the problem, what will it take to fix the problem, and the costs of doing so. He will also want to have options for fixing the problem, and those options will *not* involve reinventing his corporation. The client may agree to the purchase of a cellular telephone, or a medical kit, or the safeguarding of his itinerary, but he will be noticeably cool to the suggestion of replacing his Security Director, or the hiring of a team of eight additional protection agents, etc., etc.

If possible at this time, the protectee and the agent should come to some sort of agreement as to what security measures will be set up as routine for the protectee, and the basis upon which the protectee and agent will relate to each other. This is setting up the guidelines, and should be done with tact and understanding. Vulnerabilities should be discussed and solutions agreed upon.

The agent may offer to conduct personal security awareness training for family members, and for staff members. Rather than brusquely dictating changes, department by department, it is generally more efficient to bring key personnel into the security procedures. Making key personnel aware of security needs is one way of extending this knowledge into the front line of employees and making them part of the security team. All recommendations must be made in a cooperative light. Simply telling people what they must do brings resistance, the kind of resistance that will sink the good intentions of the agent and result in no further opportunities for consultation. On the other hand, having successful partnerships with key facility managers can enhance the agent's reputation for good client management.

The agent may offer to conduct a more thorough security survey of the corporate operations which directly affect the protectee, and to request that the protectee ensure his involvement in the security arrangements for executive travel, special events, and board meetings. The agent should request permission to sit in on the meetings of the Crisis Management Team. He should try to persuade the protectee that he (the agent) should be informed as early as possible about any events or incidents which might affect the protectee, such as upcoming social and special events, media conferences, problems, labor disputes, and travel. He should emphasize his role as a facilitator, and a proactive preventer of problems.

The agent should describe the advantages of the advance surveys which should be conducted for the protectee's activities and travels. The executive protectee understands the efficiency of advance preparation. He understands the need for proactive measures. He is used to this in his corporate mode of doing business.

Suggestions might be made for improvement in security within the corporation, but the agent should expect to meet with some resistance. This is not an immediate problem; after all this situation has existed for some time, and it will require time to effect change. Unless there is an immediate and imminent threat, all changes can be, and probably will be, made with time so long as the recommendations for change are worthy.

This may, or may not, be the time when the agent requests that the protectee fill in his or her Personal Profile (see Appendix). It depends upon the level of trust which will exist at that time between the protectee and the agent. Sometimes, these things take time.

This is definitely the time when the agent should offer to conduct a security survey of the protectee's residence, and to recommend any changes or security upgrades. If the protectee agrees, he will probably wish to have his wife involved in the process. Any security upgrades should be made only if necessary, and should be realistic in terms of the family's lifestyle. If changes are made, the agent's role is to interview the contractors (for know-how and dependability), to put the job out for bids, and to obtain the best prices for the product. The agent should be on site during installation and during the hand-over, the time at which the installer walks the client through the system and explains it. The agent should be the on-site expert in terms of how the system works and how to maintain it.

Working the Client

The threat level against the executive will almost always determine the size of the protection team assigned to the protectee. If there have been actual threats or incidents, the protection team may consist of two, three, or four people, four being considered the ideal size. In maximum threat situations, there may be two teams of four, or even more. A four-man team means that three eight-hour shifts can be worked around the clock, with the fourth person providing days off, relief time, and/or available for advance work. Or, two people will work twelve-hour shifts, leaving one person to provide for relief time and the Detail Leader free to handle administrative matters and liaison with the protectee. Sometimes, two agents will work the daylight shift, thus allowing one to function as driver and the second agent to ride "shotgun," and one working the night shift. For special, very public events, all four may work twelve-hour shifts to afford maximum protection manning access control, surveillance, and command posts.

The team Detail Leader will provide leadership to the team and will be the primary contact between the team and the protectee. The Detail Leader will write the threat assessment, make recommendations, brief the protectee, establish the law enforcement liaison, and establish interface relationships with the protectee's support staff and corporate management. The Shift Leader is the man or woman in charge of the team while on shift and, in the absence of the Detail Leader, assumes the Detail Leader's responsibilities.

Large details are more complex and are often better equipped because they are designed to counter a known, or higher level, threat. The threat will be perceived as sophisticated, dedicated, and organized. In turn, the protection team must be sophisticated, dedicated, and well organized.

If the threat level is perceived as being low, or protection has been brought in primarily to satisfy the Board of Directors, the team may be one person only. That one person, the sole protection agent, must necessarily be multi-faceted, since he or she must provide all of the services needed for protection of the client. There are several problems. How can the agent be with the client and do advances at the same time? If the agent is with the protectee, who is watching the car? What happens when there is only one agent and the protectee wants protection for himself and his family? Can the client and agent tolerate being with each other *all the time*? How does the agent maintain any kind of life of his own if he is working with the client alone?

The agent in the one-man team is an organizer, a diplomat, a communicator, a facilitator, and a creative solver of problems. He is heavily reliant on other people to help him achieve his protection goals, and must sell himself and his mission to the protectee's staff. For example, if the agent needs to do an advance for an upcoming special event, leaving the protectee at the office with a security-aware secretary, good visitor access control, a locked office door, and a panic button will do nicely.

The agent can't watch the car all the time, but then, does he have to? The car may be parked in a secure zone at the office, or in an unmarked slot in the garage, or, simply, the perceived threat level may be sufficiently low that constant surveillance of the vehicle is unnecessary.

Solving the problem of too much togetherness is relatively simple. If the residence has been surveyed, security improvements made, and a good intrusion detection installed, the agent may not be needed every night; may not, in fact, live on the premises in a low-threat situation. This provides both the protectee and the agent with some relief from each other. In terms of protecting the client and his family, the client has to make the decision on this one, since it should be readily apparent that one agent cannot be in more than one place at a time. It helps greatly if the client understands what needs to happen, thus allowing the agent and the protectee to function more as a team. Perhaps the client would enjoy learning more about defensive driving, and, if he is willing to vary his times and routes of travel, he may be reasonably safe driving himself on occasion, leaving the agent to the managing of other security matters.

The difficulty comes when there is a high risk situation and a low-ball budget; that is, the client has been threatened, it is real, and there is no money for more than one agent. Unless this is a situation of short duration, it will rapidly become intolerable. As the level of threat escalates, the security must be enhanced. At the very least, two agents become necessary, one to work in close proximity with the protectee and the other to do advances, stay with the car, and provide some relief for the other agent.

Advances are essential, and particularly so for the single agent. Knowing where to go, how to get there, where to park, who will be there, and the names and telephone numbers of key people is required for a successful operation. For example, you note on the client's itinerary, or you are informed by the protectee's administrative assistant, that he is scheduled to meet with the CEO and Board of another, highly controversial company, called the ABC Nuclear Energy Company. An advance would start by contacting the other CEO's administrative assistant, telling him (or her) that you will be accompanying the executive as his personal assistant (never as his protection agent) to the meeting, and that you are calling to see if you might get together with him for a few minutes. You have been asked to drive the executive (protectee) to the meeting and wish to find out about parking and other arrangements.

There is some corporate protocol which must be followed in this situation. Always inform the protectee's administrative assistant that you are contacting the other executive's administrative assistant(s), thus keeping her/him "in the loop." When telephoning the other administrative assistant(s) never mention the word "security" or imply that the advance is for a security purpose. If you describe yourself as security you could place your client in an embarrassing situation, requiring him to explain to the other executive why he needs security. Such a situation could significantly detract from the purpose of the meeting, which would define you as more of a problem than a solution. In addition, to divulge your true purpose is to advertise your protectee as someone who warrants personal protection to those who might be looking for an available target and advertises yourself as the person who needs to be removed in order to gain access to him. Instead, describe yourself as your boss's personal assistant, whose purpose is to facilitate transportation to and from appointments, and who increases his time efficiency in general. Any administrative assistant will understand this, as her purpose is also to increase the efficiency of her boss.

You should then plan the best primary and secondary routes to the site of the meeting, noting proximity to emergency room hospitals, possible construction hazards, and any problems along the route. It is useful to arrive early and to walk around the building, noting parking, entrances and exits, and security within. When meeting with the ABC administrative assistant you should inquire about securing a parking place to be reserved for the executive (protectee) close to an entry/exit for the building. Go over the itinerary. Will lunch be served, and where? Establish the fact that you will not be a part of the meeting but that you will wait in the outer office or lobby. Ask the administrative assistant to call you if there are any changes in the schedule. Give her your pager or cell phone number.

Conclude the meeting with thanks but, before leaving, drive through the parking garage if one is used. Parking garages can be the darkest, most confusing places in the world, poorly signed, and easy to get lost in. Sketch out a little map, noting the entrances and exits, emergency phones, and elevators. How well secured is the garage? Would it be a good idea to ask the protectee if a fellow employee could drive with you and the protectee to the meeting, and wait with the car while you accompany the protectee inside.

There are some helpful aids for the single agent. A cellular telephone with speed dialing and memory can become his best friend. The phone is used for advances, for staying in touch, and for emergencies. A pager is also necessary. There are other helpful gadgets on the electronic market. One such gadget can be programmed to contain hundreds of names and telephone numbers, and will dial the telephone for you. Other electronic gadgets and electronic organizers are almost as good as having a traveling secretary, since they can be programmed to contain itineraries and schedules, and can be re-programmed for changes. Notes and reminders can be included. And all of this comes in one handy gadget. This can be immensely helpful to the agent who is accompanying the protectee, his family, and guests on a trip, and who has the responsibility for baggage; vehicles; wake-up calls; advance checklists; contact names and telephone numbers; passport, visa, and credit card numbers; expenses; currency exchange rates; hotel addresses; room numbers; and the multiple details which must be kept available for instant use.

Warning--gadgets can break down, so all information should be kept in written form, located in a secure area (but readily accessible) as well. It takes longer to access written information and it is cumbersome, but it doesn't need batteries.

The greatest help, however, will be found in other people: the Security Director, security personnel of other facilities, administrative assistants, receptionists, and the liaison people for other executives. The protectee spends much of his time with other executives, many of whom will have their own protection. Teaming up with other protection agents can double the protection (and keep one from stumbling over the other).

As difficult as it may seem, the single agent protection job is one which many agents prefer, since it gives them an opportunity to excel at their work. They like being in charge, knowing that they have full responsibility for all of the protection chores. They are adept at getting other people to help. They are creative in solving logistical snags. The single agent job can be deeply satisfying, and while it lacks the bells and whistles of teams and command posts, it is rarely boring. It is the essence of executive protection work.

Armed or Unarmed Protection

The delicate question of whether the protection agent should carry a weapon must be decided up front, and the decision must rest with senior management (who will undoubtedly ask for Board ratification). The liability potential--not to mention the embarrassment potential--is too severe for the agent, himself, to make the decision. If the decision is affirmative; that is, the agent will be armed, some working guidelines must be agreed upon to determine when and where the agent will be armed. There must be management concurrence on this point, and the appropriate staff must be informed.

The decision can not be made lightly. Management must fully understand the risks involved. Input from the Legal department will be helpful, as will advice from the Risk Management department. The Risk Manager must weigh the risk against the company's liability insurance.

There may already exist a corporate policy on the carry and use of firearms if the company employs either contract or in-house guards. If such a policy exists, or is to be placed in existence, strict criteria must be defined. Some aspects to be considered include:

. Careful screening of all individuals permitted to carry a weapon, irregardless of whether these individuals are employed by the corporation or are employees of a contract company. Screening should include drug testing, appropriate psychological tests, and complete background checks. NO ONE with a felony record should ever be allowed to carry or use a firearm.

. Training and re-training requirements, to include recognized certification (National Rifle Association, etc.).

. Weapon ownership--individual or company-issue.

. Establishment of clearly stated guidelines as to the appropriate use of firearms--when, where, and under what circumstances.

. Clear and ongoing supervision for adherence to company policy.

It goes without saying that the *agent* must fully understand the legal parameters and implications of the use of deadly force. If the agent is to be armed on any occasion, he must have a license to carry a concealed weapon, and he must understand the state, regional, and local laws governing the use of concealed firearms. For example, if the agent has a license to carry in Virginia, will he be allowed to carry a concealed firearm in the District of Columbia?

Issues such as these can be a source of intense embarrassment to the client if they are misused.

Commercial Contractors

The growth of commercial security firms has paralleled the overall growth of the security market. There are now several huge security firms with branch offices throughout the United States and in some countries overseas; and there are also numerous small companies which you will find listed in the yellow pages of the telephone directory. Some of these firms provide good to excellent services, and some are hopelessly ineffective. There are times when the single agent will need to bring in supplemental people to help provide needed protection. How, then is the agent to separate the good from the bad? As with so many aspects of executive protection, the answer can usually be found with intelligence collection. Here are some guidelines.

.   Start with a face-to-face meeting with the owner(s). Spend a little time "feeling them out."

.   Ask for their resumes--you can check on these after you leave their offices.

.   Ask to see a copy of their contract(s) and ask for clarification on the services which they provide.

.   Ask for a list, or at least four or five names, of their clients and request their permission to contact these people--which, of course, you will do in order to determine if these clients were satisfied with the service.

.   Ask about screening, hiring, training, re-training, and certification practices.

.   Ask about their licensing at the state and local level.

.   Ask about their insurance coverage-- types and amounts. Do they have Comprehensive General Liability Insurance, with adequate limits per occurrence?

Generally, a limit of $1,000,000 per occurrence is considered adequate, although there may be a cap on total (multiple occurrence) coverage.

.   Ask for a face-to-face interview with the person(s) who will be serving in an executive protection supplemental role.

.   Be very clear about the type and quality of the equipment which the security firm will provide, including an inspection of any vehicle(s).

.   Make certain that you understand precisely what costs are involved.

.   In the initial meeting, sketch out the services which you will require. In a subsequent meeting, after you have checked references, etc., you will want to provide a more precisely detailed listing of your requirements, which will then be incorporated within a contract.

.   If the initial meeting has been favorable, the agent should do a background check on the company. The (state) Secretary of State's office will reveal incorporation status and a listing of owners and officers.

.   A credit check is a must, to determine the company's financial standing. A separate check should be made of the firm's owners and the person(s) they are recommending for protection.

.   The client list must be checked and questions asked as to client satisfaction.

.   A telephone call to the local law enforcement agency may elicit additional information.

.   The security firm's contract should be reviewed by the agent's Legal department.

.   All arrangements must be approved by the protectee and the Security Director.

The need for protection of executives overseas stems from such threats as terrorism, crime, consequences of political instability, health, and substandard medical care. The likelihood of terrorist incidents occurring varies from country to country, depending upon the politics of the region at any given time. American businesses and their employees abroad often have been singled out as targets of terrorists. While there is no absolute protection against terrorism, there are a number of reasonable precautions that can provide some degree of individual protection and can serve as psychological and practical deterrents to would-be terrorists. While to some degree terrorist incidents have been on the wane, there are no guarantees that this slackening will continue. There are many post-cold war frustrations which could feed and nourish terrorist groups.

More frightening than old-style terrorists are the ethnic and tribal wars and insurgencies which are being fought in a number of countries. Many of these bloody affairs are being fought in countries which are rich in those resources coveted by the industrial world. Oil, for example, can be found in a number of third-world countries ruled by warlords, cutthroats, and insurrectionists. (One of the author's agent friends was hired to accompany a client to Sierra Leone--the country where the rebels delight in cutting off the hands of just about everyone. It was an extremely dangerous, extremely tricky assignment.)

In addition to outright terrorist incidents is crime, which is greatly on the increase in Europe, Russia, Africa, Eastern Europe, and the Orient. Crime, particularly street crime and drugs, is on the rise throughout the former hard-line communist countries, as local opportunists take advantage of the political upheavals to feather their own nests. In many countries, the insurrectionists are also criminals looting the oil, diamonds, and other resources. The term "mafia" is now being applied to Russia and other former communist-bloc countries.

As in the United States, security abroad, therefore, continues to be a priority for corporations and individuals. This chapter deals with some security issues of visiting, living, and/or doing business abroad, as these issues involve the executive protection agent.

Although it has been pointed out in prior chapters, it bears repetition to state that outside the United States there are different laws, different customs, and different ways of doing business. While 25 years ago, a U.S. passport was almost a guarantee of safety no matter what, this is no longer the case. The notion of U.S. supremacy and untouchability ended with the taking of the U.S. embassy hostages in Iran, the taking of hostages and holding them for years in Lebanon, and the terrible death toll of the bombing of the Marine barracks in Beirut with the subsequent withdrawal of U.S. Marines from Lebanon.

Having stated these facts, it must also be pointed out that, with some exceptions, it is still safer to live abroad than to walk the streets of New York or Los Angeles. While crime, particularly violent crime, is on the increase abroad, it must be placed in context. Up from where? The United States is still one of the most violent countries in the entire world. Therefore, while one must be cautious, proactive, and security-conscious abroad, security measures must be kept in perspective. As always, the objective is deterrence. The adversary tends not to attack what he perceives to be a tough, protected target.

The executive protection agent not only has a duty to protect his client and the client's family, but also a duty to familiarize them as to the everyday security procedures which will keep them safe from harm. Some of the material in this chapter will be directed toward the everyday life activities of the protectee and his or her family.

While the deterrent power of the United States may have been somewhat diminished in the past few years, it still wields a mighty stick. The U.S. embassies and consulates around the world are an American citizen's and business's best friends. Just what will an embassy do for you, an American citizen and businessman, in a foreign country?

Embassy personnel and the U.S. Department of State can furnish information on terrorist incidents and crime statistics in an area. Embassy personnel can also furnish some details on bombings, kidnappings, muggings, and street crimes which may be helpful in developing protective strategies. They can identify local government and police officials and can help in establishing liaison with these individuals. They can recommend guard services and professional security help. The embassy provides an ongoing connection; in the event of an uprising or civil disorder, the U.S. embassy will assist in medical and security evacuation.

The embassy can advise as to local laws and is the best source of assistance if a local law is broken. It can help in obtaining local legal counsel to represent an individual or corporation accused of breaking the law. You should, of course, plan to access competent legal help. One source is International Recovery, at (215) 977-9982, e-mail address <dickatkins@aol.com>, an organization which provides legal assistance abroad in arrest, divorce, child custody, and other legal areas.

The embassy can advise as to local medical resources, the purity of the water, prevalence of local diseases, and whether the local supply of blood is safe. (You are advised to avail yourself of other sources as noted in the chapter on Foreign Advances.)

The embassy issues new passports to replace lost or stolen ones. The embassy may provide notary services for Americans.

In the case of a terrorist action against an American citizen or company, the embassy or consulate can facilitate communication with the home office and the family of the victim if normal channels are not adequate; it can help establish useful liaison with local authorities; and it can provide information and suggest possible alternatives open to the family or company of the victim. The U.S. government cannot, however, decide whether or not to accede to terrorist demands and will discourage any resolution that is not consistent with U.S. policy. Such a decision can only be made by the family or company of the victim, but it should be in consonance with local law.

The official U.S. Counterterrorism Policy is to not make any concessions of any kind to terrorists, which includes not paying ransom. It is important to understand this as a clear goal held by U.S. government officials, and it may be divergent from the wishes of the victim's family and corporation.

It should also be noted that the actual incident management will always be left to others, including local police agencies. Rarely will the U.S. government assist in hostage release negotiations on behalf of private U.S. citizens. As a result, corporations which have verifiable concerns regarding kidnappings should seek, in advance of need, the assistance of qualified private security agencies which specialize in preempting and managing these problems.

There are a number of things embassy personnel will not do. They will not cash or guarantee checks, provide legal services, settle disputed bills or transactions with local hotels, shops and businesses, or provide bail.

Unlike some U.S. government employees who enjoy diplomatic immunity while living and working in the host country, U.S. private sector employees and their families are subject to all laws of the host country. The constitutional safeguards enjoyed by all Americans in the U.S. do not apply to the actions of foreign governments.

There are limitations to what any U.S. embassy will do for you (usually dependent upon your clout with U.S. senators, representatives, and government officials). Embassy personnel are a resource, not a panacea for all problems. When used in a local advisory role, they are usually very helpful. Beyond that, individuals and businesses must be prepared to institute their own security strategies as they are ultimately responsible for their own security. As always, proactive measures are the most successful, with a provision for reactive measures as needed.

The places where U.S. citizens most often come into difficulties for illegal possession of firearms are nearby--Mexico, Canada, and the Caribbean. Sentences for possession of firearms in Mexico can be up to 30 years. In general, firearms, even those legally registered in the U.S., cannot be brought into a country unless a permit is first obtained from the embassy or a consulate of that country, and the firearm is registered with foreign authorities on arrival. If you take firearms or ammunition to another country, you cannot bring them back into the U.S. unless you register them with U.S. Customs before you leave the United States.

In many countries you can be harassed or detained for photographing such things as police and military installations, government buildings, border areas, and transportation facilities. This could become a problem if the agent takes photographs as part of an advance survey (or attempts to play spy). If you are in doubt, ask permission before taking photographs.

What To Do If Arrested

A hostile or even friendly intelligence organization is always on the lookout for sources who are vulnerable to coercion, addictions, greed, or emotional manipulation. It then behooves the protection agent and his client to avoid any behavior which might bring them to the notice of these agencies.

Foreign police and intelligence agencies detain persons for a myriad of reasons or for no other reason than suspicion or curiosity. (This is the reason you do not want to list "Security" or "Protection" under Occupation on your Visa or Landing Card.)

The best advice is to exercise good judgement, be professional in your demeanor, and maintain a low profile. If you are detained, here are some points to remember:

. Do ask to contact the nearest embassy or consulate representing your country. As a citizen of another country, you have this right; but that does not mean that your hosts will allow you to exercise that right. If you are refused or just ignored, continue to make the request periodically until they agree.

. Stay calm, maintain your dignity, and do not do anything to provoke the arresting officer(s).

. Do not admit anything or volunteer any information.

. Do not sign anything. Often, part of the detention procedure is to ask or tell the detainee to sign a written report. Decline politely until such time as the document is examined by an attorney or an embassy/consulate representative.

. Do not accept anyone on face value. When the embassy representative arrives, request some identification before discussing your situation.

. Do not fall for the ruse of helping the ones who are detaining you in return for your release. They can be very imaginative in their proposals on how you can be of assistance to them. Do not sell yourself out by agreeing to anything. If they will not take no for an answer, do not make a firm commitment or sign anything. Tell them that you will think it over and let them know. Once out of their hands, contact the embassy and your company for assistance in getting out of the country.

In preparation for an overseas trip, a threat assessment should be made of the local conditions. If the protectee is a corporate executive, the threat assessment should include: any prior incidents against the company or company officials; hostile references to, or attacks against, the company in the local press; and incidents against any other American companies, executives, government, or other entities which could appear to represent U.S. interests in the area. Corporate executives should be given a security briefing. Even if the executive has been provided with one or more executive protection agents, the protectee and his family must undertake some personal responsibility for their own safety. If the protectee is a private individual, a briefing is still called for. This becomes even more important if the agent is a one-man team. The agent cannot be everywhere nor provide complete protection for several people at one time. Each member of the party must be aware of local conditions and security self-protection strategies. A briefing is important to all members of the protection team.

When a corporate executive and his family are transferred overseas for extended residence in a foreign company, a much more detailed briefing should be given.

Corporate Briefing

A typical corporate briefing may be put together by the Security Director, but it is more likely to be organized by the executive protection agent, the advance agent, or the detail leader.

An excellent source of information is the U.S. Department of State's Overseas Security Advisory Council (OSAC). OSAC is a cooperative effort between the U.S. government and corporate security officials. OSAC resources are available to corporations which become members. OSAC also publishes via the Internet information about trends in crime, terrorism, political stability, and health. This data is reasonably accurate and is continually updated and available via electronic mail. To apply, a security representative of a U.S. corporation doing business and having personnel overseas must submit an application.

An OSAC Advisory might include:

. Up-to-date information about political unrest, ethnic unrest, and internal conflicts.

. Crime and personal security, types and

methods of crimes, police response to crime, avoidance of crime, and personal response to a crime.

. Health precautions.

. Emergency numbers.

. U.S. embassy numbers, and hours of business.

. National holidays.

Other sources of overseas security information and conditions can be obtained by calling the U.S. Department of State's touch-tone interactive pre-recorded Citizen's Emergency Center at (202) 647-5225, or the Desk Manager of the country (or countries) which you are interested in. The Center publishes several helpful pamphlets.

The Regional Security Officer (RSO) assigned to the U.S. Embassy within the target country is continually advised of all security issues which concern U.S. citizens in that country, and can provide very good information.

In addition to information garnered from U.S. State Department sources, a briefing should also include information about local currency, temperatures, passports, vaccinations required and/or recommended, languages spoken, important contact telephone numbers, and any special requirements. If the agent is writing and conducting a briefing for a protectee and family leaving for extended residence in another country, he should include information about the customs of the country, foreign officials, police and militia, schools, and past history of terrorist incidents. The briefing should include information on travel and pre-departure activities. Maps are helpful additions.

At the end of this chapter is a model for an executive briefing. This is a security briefing for executives and their families to be used prior to a short trip rather than an extended residence overseas and is not to be confused with the briefing given by the detail leader or advance agent to the protection team. The detail leader's briefing to the team is more concerned with the actual logistics of the trip, hotel, motorcades, routes, and special events. An executive briefing concentrates on everyday security problems which are likely to be encountered by the executive and his family, usually overseas. A briefing should be carefully tailored to the needs and circumstances of the client.

While executive briefings require some research and effort to put together, this is largely a one-time effort, which is then updated with current political information. Information for the briefing can be acquired from a variety of sources: company employees familiar with the host country; the U.S. Department of State; the embassy or consulate in the host country; a knowledgeable travel agent; a good guide book; and the agent's own intelligence files. Booklets, called *Tips for Travelers*, are available from the Superintendent of Documents, U.S. Government Printing Office, Washington, DC 20402, at a cost of $1.00 each, for any country in the world. These booklets contain information about passport and visa requirements, customs and currency regulations, recommended inoculations and vaccinations, crime and personal security, and other matters of interest.

In addition, there is an excellent little paperback book entitled *Travel Can Be Murder*, by Terry Riley, published by Applied Psychology Press in Santa Cruz, California. It contains over 500 safety and security tips all designed to make the traveler more aware and more responsible for his own safety. We recommend that you include this book in the briefing packet.

Executive briefings can be longer and more detailed and should include pertinent health risks and data for accessing local quality health care, but it is sometimes difficult to get the executives to read them, so they should be kept concise and factual. Any information specific to the country should be included. Written briefings are often followed by verbal briefings which can expand upon the information or review highlights.

If you are accompanying the protectee overseas and his family does not accompany him, there are some areas of activity which may appeal to him, and for which you, the agent, must make some choices. Prostitution is regarded somewhat differently in other countries than in the United States. In some hotels, the Concierge can arrange a discreet liaison with a prostitute acceptable to the hotel. Cruising in grungy areas for a prostitute is as dangerous, if not more so, in other countries as in the United States. If there is a dispute about prostitute fees or drink prices in a seedy bar, an American cannot depend upon much help from the local police and may even find that the police will side with the locals. These clip joints are an accepted tourist attraction in many countries, and any unwary tourist who cries "foul" will probably find himself severely damaged or in jail. The tourist, especially the naive and stupid tourist, is fair game.

Illegal drugs are certainly available, and drugs in other countries are particularly tempting, often existing in much more pure form than can typically be found in the States, but the logistics and consequences of purchasing them are horrendous. There are several problems: language difficulties which make the deal complicated; dealers who double as informants (they know they will likely not have you as a regular customer); and draconian penalties. While one might be able to bail out of drug-related problems with reasonable ease in some parts of Europe, in other countries such as Turkey, the authorities are apt to lock up the offender and throw away the key--20 years to life imprisonment with no appeals. A growing number of countries--Saudi Arabia, Malaysia, Pakistan, Thailand--have implemented the *death penalty*! The United States has put considerable pressure on countries which have acted as drug conduits in the past. The result is that penalties in these countries are relentlessly stringent. If someone is caught with either soft or hard drugs overseas, he is subject to local and not U.S. laws. Penalties for possession or trafficking are often the same, and prisons are extremely unpleasant.

Illegal drugs are often smuggled with the unwitting help of tourist travelers. Drugs have been stowed away on corporate aircraft and insinuated into innocent travelers' baggage. One must be vigilant to avoid being a victim to drug smuggling. Never leave luggage unattended unless it is checked in with an airline prior to a flight. It is important that these facts be emphasized to all family members, especially to teenage children and young adults. Never offer to carry a wrapped "gift" to a relative or friend unless you are absolutely sure of the people involved, to know it does not contain drugs.

Prescription medications should be left in their original labeled containers if the medicines contain habit-forming drugs or narcotics. A copy of the doctor's prescription should be carried as verification. A number of Americans have been arrested for possessing prescription drugs, particularly tranquilizers and amphetamines, that they purchased legally in certain Asian countries and then brought to some countries in the Middle East where they are illegal. Others have been arrested for purchasing prescription drugs abroad in quantities that local authorities suspected were for commercial use.

RESIDENTIAL SECURITY

If you, the protectee, and his family, are to live for a period in another country, a residence must be selected. In some countries, particularly third-world countries, expatriates (non-citizens) live in compounds with fencing, guards, and other security measures. These are usually good choices, since everyone in the compound can serve as a kind of neighborhood watch, being similarly aware of security problems. If there are no sequestered residential areas, a suitable residence must be chosen.

Given a choice between apartment or single dwelling living, a high-security apartment with secure parking access generally offers greater protection against criminal intrusion. An apartment above the second floor presents a more difficult target, provides the tenant some degree of anonymity, provides the benefit of close neighbors, and is almost always easier to secure and less expensive to modify with security hardware. In the event of an emergency and loss of communications, neighbors can often be relied upon to come to another tenant's assistance. At the very least, they can notify the authorities.

Apartments on the first or second floors should be avoided because of their immediate and easy accessibility from the street level or from trees, tops of large vehicles, or porch roofs. Foreign objects can easily be introduced to first and second floor apartments from the outside area accessible to the public. Apartments above the firefighting capabilities and access of the local fire department should be avoided.

Apartments are only as secure as their access. Access to the lobby should be tightly controlled by a doorman or an electronic system. All residences should be equipped with several battery-operated smoke detectors.

The private or single dwelling allows the occupant greater opportunity to establish more rigid, more specific access control to the property. Also, the protectee may have such a high profile that he feels he must have a private residence. If this is the case, selection of the residence and its locale is important. The local police, the Regional Security Officer at the U.S. Embassy, company personnel, and other American residents can provide information and advice.

As important as the location of the residence is the route which the protectee will have to travel from residence to office and other frequent locations. A preponderance of kidnappings have taken place in and around the vehicle, often within a few blocks of the residence. Will the protectee be forced to travel through narrow, congested streets which can easily be blocked? Is parking allowed on the streets, thus permitting the placing of a bomb in a parked vehicle? Is there high-density foot and car traffic? If so, this could provide a perfect shield for surveillance. One-way and dead-end streets should also be avoided.

The type of residences in the area will give some idea of the income level of the neighborhood. You should examine the quality of lighting at night time, pedestrian and vehicular traffic patterns, parks, playgrounds, recreation areas, the existence of public or commercial enterprises intermingled with residential dwellings, fire hydrants, and police call boxes. Note the overall security precautions that are taken in the neighborhood, such as barred windows, security fences, extensive lighting, large dogs, and security guards. Such visible precautions may indicate a high level of security awareness and/or a high crime area.

Once the residence has been selected, the building and grounds should be surveyed. The survey should be based on the threat assessment drawn up for the area and the protectee. It should include the perimeter security, fencing, lighting, alarm system, locks, doors, windows, roof, interior, and safe room. As a result of the survey, the physical survey components should be reviewed and, as needed, changed and/or upgraded. In areas abroad where forced entry of a residence is commonplace, or where an active terrorist threat is present, the use of a good residential alarm system is highly recommended. Minimum desired alarm system features should be capable of operating on the local electrical current and have a rechargeable battery backup. It should be relatively easy to install and trouble-shoot, as local electricians may not be capable of installing or repairing a complex alarm system. All additions to physical security should be in compliance with local codes.

After you and the protectee and his family have moved in and registered with the U.S. Embassy, it is time to get acquainted with the neighborhood. You should walk around the neighborhood and drive around the area to get a good idea of where you are located, noting the layout of the streets, particularly one-way streets. Drive around at night. Get acquainted with the neighbors. They can help in identifying any surveillance and may provide a safe haven in the event of an incident. Know beforehand where you will turn for help. Familiarize yourself with the identities of nearby neighbors, their servants, and their vehicles. This will facilitate the identification of a stranger or an unauthorized individual in the area.

Learn the location of the nearest hospital and police station. Drive the route to the hospital emergency room in daylight and at night. Check on traffic conditions during rush hours and at other times, noting the time required to get to the hospital and police station.

Obtain emergency fire and safety equipment as soon as possible, including but not limited to fire extinguishers, first-aid kits, blankets, matches and candles, flashlights and battery operated radios with spare batteries. Store a seven-day supply of food, juices, water, and staples. Family members and domestic employees should be trained and tested on the use of each item of emergency equipment. Be aware of host country fire regulations and telephone numbers. Determine if the emergency number has someone on the other end who can understand you in English. Obtain one or more cellular phones.

You should assess the police protection available to your residential area. Are there enough police with communication and means of transportation to respond in a timely manner? You should determine the attitude of the government, police, and the populace towards other nationals, particularly Americans. A strong anti-American attitude may be cause for diminished police responsiveness.

Where police capability is in doubt, the use of a private guard service should be considered. All guards should be subjected to a security check, and recommendations should be obtained from the U.S. Embassy's Regional Security Officer (RSO). Guards may be poorly trained, and there are certain to be some cultural differences which require clarification. This will require additional training and very specific instructions, both in the local language and in English. All instructions regarding job performance should be in adherence with local law, in particular as regards the use of deadly force. Guards should be provided a uniform to demonstrate a visible deterrence and also provided with at least a minimal amount of equipment: two-way radio, flashlight, alarm panic switch, etc.

Domestic Employees

Domestic employees can either be a valuable asset to residential security or a decided liability. The chances of obtaining the services of a reliable servant can be improved by hiring one recommended and/or employed by a friend or neighbor.

Prospective applicants should be required to produce references and should be interviewed thoroughly. All references should be checked for integrity and qualifications. In some countries, the U.S. embassy, local private security companies, or other authorities will conduct background investigations upon request. In some foreign countries, it is an accepted practice to request full personal data from applicants for employment. You should not accept the applicant's word as to name and date of birth without an authentic government document to back up the claim. When a servant has been hired, a record should be made of his/her complete name, date and place of birth, identity card number, telephone number and address, as well as the names of spouse, parent, or close relative.

Domestic help should be briefed on security practices--visitor access, telephone handling, mail and package delivery, emergency telephone numbers--and on how to be alert to possible surveillance. Whenever possible, the servants should answer the door rather than the protectee or his family. They should be trained to query all deliverymen and repairmen by requesting identification and by asking the residents whether something is expected. If either of these conditions is not satisfactory, the item should be refused.

Domestic employees should not be allowed to overhear family plans and official business. Sensitive and confidential papers, including travel itineraries, income or other financial matters, and competitive business information, should be safeguarded as closely at home as at the office. Domestic employees should not have access to information that would benefit a terrorist, a criminal, or a business competitor.

As a word of caution, do not, in front of domestic employees, make comments which could be construed as being disrespectful of local customs or people. Even when they make critical remarks about themselves or their government, do not join in.

There is a temptation in foreign countries to regard a good domestic employee as trustworthy simply because they often seem to be sympathetic caregivers. One must, however, face harsh reality. Life can be difficult for these people. They may be subject to police or political pressure to act as informants, and/or they may be vulnerable to hefty bribes.

Children and the Family

The focus of terrorist activities in the past has been against the male head of the house--the male executive or individual in the family. Spouses have not been the focus of kidnapping or assassination, probably because of concerns about bad publicity. Terrorists rarely commit criminal acts without trying to mask these activities under banners of "freedom" or "doing good for the populace." Kidnapping women and children is a crime that does not fit into this mold and is hard to camouflage as a good deed. Terrorists, however, have practiced surveillance on spouses and children to learn more about the vulnerabilities of the protectee. If spouses and children are not sufficiently aware of the need for security and confidentiality, vital information can be passed that is potentially damaging. A child can say, in all innocence, "My daddy is going to Paris next week," or, "My daddy plays golf every Saturday. I wish he would stay home with me." Spouses, unaware of the need for tight security, can reveal social itineraries and travel plans.

As crime, pure crime as opposed to terrorist crime, increases around the world, the unspoken ban against preying on women and children may lift. Children are frequently abducted in South America and Asia by criminals. Women tourists have been attacked and raped in Moscow and other cities. As crime increases, it is somewhat predictable that women (spouses and female executives) and children will increasingly be targeted for attack.

It is vitally important, therefore, for several reasons, that the family act together as a self-protective unit. It is one of the protection agent's jobs to make certain that the family is made aware of the need for security and is instructed in the ways in which good personal security can be practiced.

Children can learn some simple rules. It should not be complicated. Nor should it instill fear. It should be a positive "can do" process. Practicing "let's pretend" or "what if" with children can ingrain good security habits. (This is also helpful for adults and domestic staff.) These security rules should include:

.   Do not answer the telephone by stating the person's name or the name of the family.

.   The spouse or child should not give the residence telephone number or the names of the residents.

.   Wrong number calls should be reported to the parents, and a repetitive number of wrong number calls should be regarded as suspicious.

.   Children should not converse with strangers on the telephone for any reason.

.   Children should never reveal that they are home alone.

.   Children should be taught at the earliest age possible to dial the public telephone, and given coins to use in the telephone.

.   Children should be taught to memorize a few vital telephone numbers: home, police, U.S. embassy.

.   Children should travel in pairs or groups and walk only in well travelled streets.

.   Children should never leave school with a stranger unless a school official says it is alright. In addition, an emergency code name should be given to the children so that, if any stranger attempts to collect the children, they (the children) can ask for the code.

.   Children should always tell their parents where they are going and how long they will be gone.

.   Children should never accept packages, mail, or deliveries, either made at home or on the street.

.   Children should be given a safe retreat, some place to go in an emergency.

As in the United States, arrangements should be made with the school to make certain that no unauthorized persons are allowed to pick up the children. A real danger could be an emergency call to the school reporting a supposed accident and stating that a certain individual will pick up the children. A code for callback is essential to check the information.

Leaving children with domestic employees is a risky business at best and should only be done when the employee's credentials have been thoroughly checked and verified. The easy babysitter solution of the United States is not a viable solution overseas. The family members must become aware that they are a self-reliant unit with added responsibilities.

OFFICE SECURITY

Executive protection agents are not often asked to design the security system for an overseas corporate installation; the corporation undoubtedly has a Security Director whose job it is to do this. However, it does happen that the protectee will ask his agent for advice. Too, some top agents gravitate into consulting roles, one of which is to conduct threat assessments and vulnerability studies of existing installations (see Appendix for an actual survey done by a top protection consultant). Therefore, it behooves the agent to have an understanding of office security standards.

In the initial stages of a corporation's

presence in a foreign country the corporate office will probably be located in an existing office building or other structure where security upgrades must be retrofitted and designed with existing structures and tenants in mind. This approach to office security will likely continue the entire time a corporation has a presence in a foreign country, due to cost and convenience factors. In fact, major proprietary structures built by corporations in a foreign, hostile environment are extremely rare because of their prohibitive costs. When undertaken, they require complex design and installation cooperation between corporate business and financial executives, architects, various construction engineers and managers, interior decorators, corporate security managers, local security consultants, and local fire and safety engineers. The assistance desired from the protection specialist will likely be to address issues relating to the personal security of the executive and support staff.

To some extent, physical security is the same for office and residence. That is, perimeter, fences, lighting, alarm systems, doors, windows, roofs, and locks must be designed to prevent and detect intrusion. However, office security is frequently more complex and less concerned with sightliness than is true for residences.

The U.S. Department of State has published some guidelines for overseas corporate installations. Ideally, and if indicated by threat assessment, office buildings should be situated at the high point, if any, of a land tract and located away from main thoroughfares. When possible, there should be a 100-foot minimum setback between perimeter and building exterior with space for employee and visitor parking outside the compound in a secure area. In addition, there should be sufficient space for construction of a vehicular security control checkpoint, a pedestrian security control checkpoint, and an outer perimeter barrier or wall.

Floor load capacity must be able to maintain the weight of public access control equipment (ballistic doors, walls, windows), security containers, disintegrators, and shredders. Exterior walls should be smooth shell, sturdy, protected to a height of 16

feet to prevent forced entry, and conducive to grilling or eliminating all windows below the 16-foot level. Windows should be shatter-proof glass.

For manufacturing plant and laboratory facilities, security equipment such as closed-circuit television cameras and monitors, intercoms, card readers, and special glass protection should be considered.

Physical and psychological boundaries (signs, closed doors, etc.) should establish four areas with increasing security controls beginning at the property boundaries. The areas are defined as: perimeter and property boundaries; exterior, lobbies and docks; interior and employee space; and restricted--executive offices, laboratory and computer rooms.

Vehicular traffic signs should clearly designate the separate entrances for trucks and deliveries, visitors, and employee vehicles. Control points should be provided near the site boundaries, and sidewalks should channel pedestrians toward controlled lobbies and entrances.

If the threat is considered to be high, there should be a smooth faced perimeter wall or combination wall or fence, a minimum of nine feet tall and extending three feet below grade, constructed of stone, masonry, concrete, chain link, or steel grillwork. If needed, any newly constructed wall should be designed to prevent vehicle penetration, and should use a reinforced concrete foundation wall, 18 inches thick with an additional 1-1/2-inch concrete covering on each side of the steel reinforcement, and extend 36 inches above the grade. This type of wall is designed to support three wall toppings: masonry, concrete, or steel picket fencing.

At facilities with less than optimum barriers, or at locations where the terrorist threat or building location increases the vulnerability to vehicular attack, bollards (a device constructed to protect against a ramming vehicle attack) or cement planters can be used to strengthen the perimeter boundary. At walled or fenced facilities with insufficient setback from the perimeter fence, bollards or planters can be installed outside the perimeter to increase the setback of the buildings.

Vehicular entry-exit points should be kept to a minimum; ideally, only one regularly used vehicular entry-exit point is necessary. Where two entry-exit points are used, the use of one would be limited to employees' cars, while the other would be used by visitors and delivery vehicles. Depending upon the size and nature of the facility, a gate for emergency vehicular and pedestrian egress should be installed at a location that is easily and safely accessible by employees. Emergency gates should be securely locked and periodically checked. The primary gate should be positioned to avoid a long straight approach, to force approaching vehicles to slow down before reaching the gate.

Primary entrances to a facility should have a booth for security personnel during business hours and automated systems for remote operations during other periods. Options are: electrically-operated gates to be activated by security personnel at either the booth or security control center or by a badge reader; CCTV with the capability of displaying full-facial features of a driver and vehicle characteristics on the monitor at control center; an intercom system located where drivers can communicate with control center; sensors to activate a CCTV monitor and the gate. Lighting should illuminate the gate area and approaches, and signs should instruct visitors where to park and enter the building.

At facilities not having perimeter walls, the security officer booth should be installed immediately inside or just outside the facility foyer. If justified by the threat, the security officer booth should be completely protected with reinforced concrete, walls, ballistic doors, and windows; and equipped with a duress alarm and intercom system.

The only parking permitted inside the perimeter walls should be, whenever possible, only for employees and predesignated VIPs. Security should be considered in the parking areas, and all parking facilities should have an emergency communication system installed at strategic locations.

Exterior lighting should illuminate all facility entrances, exits, parking areas, perimeter walls, gates, courtyards, garden areas, and shrubbery rows.

Doors, door frames, windows, grillwork, roofs, hinges, and locks should meet the standards described in the chapter on Physical Security. Exterior fire escapes should be retractable and secured in the up position. Local fire codes must be considered. It may be desirable to install a local alarmed panic bar on one or more doors which have no outside hardware, to allow quick emergency exiting for employees.

Landscaping and other outside architectural and aesthetic features should minimize creating any area that could conceal a person in close proximity to walkways, connecting links, buildings, and recreational spaces. Landscape plantings around building perimeters need to be located at a minimum of four feet from the building wall to prevent concealment of intruders.

The number of building entrances should be minimized. A single off-hours entrance near the security control center is desirable. The main entrance to the building should have space for a receptionist during the day and a security officer at night, with the security control center located adjacent to the main entrance lobby. The design of public areas should prevent concealment of unauthorized personnel and/or objects. Ceilings in public areas should be made inaccessible with securely fastened or locked access panels installed where necessary to service equipment. Doors to restricted access areas should be designed to resist intrusion and accommodate controlled-access hardware and alarms.

Building vaults or metal safes may be required to protect cash and valuables. Vault construction should be made of reinforced concrete or masonry and be resistant to fire damage. Steel vault doors are available with various fire-related and security penetration classifications.

All elevators should have emergency communications and emergency lighting. All cable termination points, terminal blocks, and junction boxes should be within controlled space.

Stairwell doors in high rise facilities, particularly in a multi-tenant building, present a potential security problem. These doors must be continuously operable from the office side into the stairwells. Re-entry should be controlled to permit only authorized access and prevent entrapment in the stairwell. Re-entry problems can be fixed if you provide locks on all stairwell doors except the doors leading to the lobby level and approximately every fourth or fifth floor, or as required by local fire codes. Doors without locks can be fitted with sensors to transmit alarms to the control center. Doors to the roof should be secured to the extent permitted by local fire codes.

Every facility should be equipped with a secure area (safe room) for immediate use in an emergency, as described in the chapter on Physical Security.

Ideally, if you have a security control center, it should provide a fully integrated console designed to optimize the operator's ability to receive and evaluate security information and initiate appropriate response actions for access control, CCTV, life safety, intrusion and panic alarm, communications, and fully zoned public address system control. The control center should have emergency power and convenient toilet facilities. It should be protected to the same degree as the most secure area it monitors.

Alarm system sensors should be resistant to surreptitious bypass. Door contact monitor switches should be recessed wherever possible. Surface-mounted contact switches should have protective covers. Intrusion and fire alarms for restricted areas should incorporate a backup battery power supply and be on circuits energized by normal and emergency generator power. Control boxes, external bells, and junction boxes for all alarm systems should be secured with high-quality locks and electrically wired to cause an alarm if opened. Alarm systems should be fully multiplexed in large installations, and should interface with the computer-based security

system and CCTV system.

Security sensors should individually register an audio-visual alarm located at the central monitoring location and alert the security officer. A single-CRT display should have a redundant printer or indicator light. A hard-wired audible alarm that meets common fire code standards should be activated with distinguishing characteristics for fire, intrusion, emergency exit, etc. All alarms ought to be locked in until reset manually.

CCTV systems should permit the observation of multiple camera transmission images from one or more remote locations. Switching equipment should be installed to permit the display of any camera on any designated monitor.

Satellite ground stations, microwave parabolic reflectors, and communications towers and supports should be located on rooftops, with limited access to the public. Where this is not possible, the equipment should be installed with fences and alarms. CCTV with video recording capability should be considered and included where justified.

Telephone systems should incorporate an external direct line telephone link for security and life safety independent of the internal telephone network dedicated to the location. This line should feed into the secure area. Communications should provide radio transmission equipment for communications between security personnel. Intercom systems should have the capacity to accommodate all remote access control points.

Security systems in new buildings or buildings undergoing renovation should be installed with distributed wiring schemes that use local telecommunication closets as distribution points. This will provide expansion capability, future networking capability, ease of maintenance, and full function implementation of the security system. At a minimum, the communications link and interface between the sensor, output devices, and computers should include conduit, multiconductor twisted shielded cable and terminal cabinets. Fiber-optic cables should be considered in planning the wiring distribution scheme. Data distribution and gathering closets used for security wiring must be secure. Where possible, the security wiring should be integrated with other systems such as telephone, paging, energy management, etc. In every case, the design of the communications link should permit ready installation and interconnection of cameras, sensors, and other input-output devices. All life safety equipment and accessories should be Underwriters Laboratory (UL) approved.

Outlying facilities should link security systems to the nearest security control center. All new systems should be compatible with existing systems or the existing system should be replaced. Such offices should also have secure communication rooms where telephone and fax transmissions, as well as critical conversations and meetings, cannot be eavesdropped upon. Other considerations would include secure telecommunication systems with encryption algorithms, caller and recipient authentication, key management, tamper resistant design, simultaneous voice and data transmission capability, cellular capability, flexible power options and convenient operation.

The executive offices should have a physical barrier such as electromagnetically operated doors, and a silent trouble alarm button with a signal terminating in the security department or at the secretary's desk. Secretaries should not admit visitors unless they are positively screened in advance or known from previous visits. Visitors should be escorted, wherever possible, to their destination.

Unusual telephone calls, particularly those in which the caller does not identify himself or those in which it appears that the caller is misrepresenting himself, should not be put through to the executive. Notes should be made of these calls for investigation by the security department or local police. Under no circumstances should the executive's secretary reveal to unknown callers the whereabouts of the executive, his home address, or telephone number. All workmen and cleaning people should be identified and escorted and supervised. The secretary, and/or the receptionist, should be alert to strangers in or around the office, and should be alert to strange or suspicious objects in the public areas.

All personnel should be briefed periodically on security measures and about any incidents which might be suspicious. Alert, informed company personnel provide an extension of security to the installation. Security awareness training should be provided all personnel, as part of an indoctrination, and as an ongoing measure. Confidentiality should be stressed in all training.

BUSINESS INFORMATION SECURITY

Economic espionage, serious today, will certainly continue to increase as international relations become more and more a matter of economic, rather than military, competition.

This threat is exacerbated by the increased use of extremely vulnerable electronic communications. We simply must assume that all overseas telecommunications are intercepted, recorded, organized into reports, and reviewed for economic intelligence by everyone interested in the information. To stay with our foreign competitors, we must "button up" all competitive and proprietary communications.

Increasingly, executive protection agents are being asked (even required) to assist or take a leading role in the protection of proprietary corporate information. An enormous amount of corporate spying and espionage takes place on a regular basis. The following material should be of some help to the agent charged with overseas protection.

The majority of competitive information theft cases which occur in the United States involve a company's own employee(s). We know of no reason why this should be any different overseas.

Behind many of these cases are the same motivations and human frailties which we experience in other types of thefts: illegal or excessive use of drugs or alcohol, money problems, personal stress, and just plain greed.

A difficult problem is presented when a foreign intelligence agency is involved in attempting to coerce or persuade its nationals to provide competitive information. A local or foreign employee who is otherwise a good corporate citizen may feel the pressure of patriotism or intimidation by an all-powerful government agency to provide competitive information belonging to his/her American employer.

An employee's rank in the company is not necessarily commensurate with the interest of a foreign intelligence agency. Researchers, key business managers, and corporate executives can all be targets, but so can support employees such as secretaries, computer operators, technicians, and maintenance people. The latter frequently have good, if not the best, access to competitive information. Additionally, their lower pay and rank may provide fertile ground for manipulation by an intelligence agency.

Because they are so easily accessed and intercepted, corporate telecommunications present a highly vulnerable and lucrative target for anyone interested in obtaining trade secrets and competitive information. Increased usage by businesses of these links for bulk computer data transmission and electronic mail makes telecommunications intercept efforts cost-effective for intelligence collectors worldwide. As an example, approximately half of all overseas telecommunications are facsimile transmissions which, because they are emanations, may be intercepted by foreign intelligence services since many of the foreign telephone companies are foreign owned. In addition, many American companies have begun using what is called electronic data interchange, a system of transferring corporate bidding, invoice and pricing data electronically overseas. This type of information is invaluable to many foreign intelligence services which support their national businesses.

A typical economic espionage operation scenario might be as follows:

1.   A foreign intelligence service rents an office near the targeted U.S. firm or in another location strategically selected to provide easy access to telecommunications facilities or transmissions used by the U.S. firm.

2.   Sophisticated electronic listening posts are set up in the office and manned around the clock.

3.   The listening posts eavesdrop on telephone, fax, telex, and computer communications.

4.   All intercepted communications are fed into computers, which sift through the material for valuable data.

5.   Reports and briefs are prepared and passed to the foreign rival of the U.S. firm.

Electronic Transmissions Routine Procedure

Most foreign common carriers are government-controlled or owned. Trade secrets, data, marketing strategies, and personnel information which are discussed or sent over host country telephone lines are easily obtained for foreign interests.

Electronic Media Path

Electronic data is recovered easiest when a signal is not multiplexed or mixed with other data signals; i.e., data transmitted from a telephone instrument to a telephone switch. Only a minimal investment is required to retrieve data not masked with other voice or data. For this reason, it is better to use standard dial-up versus dedicated lines. Data/voice that is routed on major transmission paths (such as microwave, satellite transmission) have less likelihood of being monitored by hackers or low cost monitoring operations, because the cost of sifting through such a volume of information to access one target is often cost-prohibitive. However, a well-financed intelligence gathering operation may find satellite or microwave transmissions the best intercept opportunity, since they can be monitored at great distances with little or no threat of detection.

Electronic Transmission Threats & Vulnerabilities

Threats

1. Many foreign phone systems are either owned or controlled by the host government. This allows the government to easily monitor transmissions of selected U.S. corporations.

2. Intelligence agencies of third party nations, terrorists, and criminals also monitor electronic transmissions. While monitoring is more difficult for them than for the host country, the equipment required for such surveillance can be easily obtained by almost anyone.

3. Business and technical data obtained from U.S. corporations may be, and often is, provided to foreign competitors and potential customers.

4. Personal information obtained may be used to kidnap executives for financial gain or political purposes.

5. Electronic equipment such as facsimile machines, telephones, and desktop computers, may be altered to make electronic monitoring easier. These alterations may be made either to the transmitting/receiving device itself or to the lines leading to and from the devices.

Vulnerabilities

1. Telecommunications monitoring may be done at a phone company's switching facilities; phone lines may be tapped or bugged; or microwave transmissions may be intercepted anywhere between the two microwave transmitters. In any event, tele-communications monitoring may be virtually undetectable.

2. Telephones do not necessarily cease transmitting once they are hung up. Conversations taking place near a phone may be transmitted to the foreign state's phone system switching facility and can be monitored anywhere between the phone and that facility.

3. Employees of U.S. corporations are often not aware of the threat to their transmissions.

4. Most international U.S. corporate telecommunications are not encrypted. Some countries do not allow encryption of telecommunications traffic within their borders, but it should be considered where feasible for any transmission of competitive information.

5. Many telecommunications transmissions will contain "key words," used to identify information of interest to a third party. A key word can be the name of a technology, product, project, or anything else which may identify the subject of the transmission.

6. Encryption should be the first line of defense since it is easier for foreign intelligence services to monitor lines than to place "bugs;" however, encryption will provide little if any security if a careful examination for audio "bugs" elsewhere in the room is not conducted.

Suggested Countermeasures

Below is a list of suggested actions which may be taken in order to improve the security of the telecommunications transmissions.

1. The reader should note that computer links, facsimile transmissions, e-mail, and voice transmissions can all be encrypted. Encrypt electronic transmissions whenever possible. The National Institute of Standards and Technology (NIST) conducts validations of products for conformance to cryptographic standards for encryption and publishes the results quarterly in the *Validated Products*

List. Subscriptions are available from:

National Technical Information Service
U.S. Department of Commerce
5285 Port Royal Road
Springfield, VA 22161

2. Neutralize the vulnerability of telephones. A small, company-controlled switch installed within the facility can help ensure that conversations are not transmitted through handsets which are hung up, and can also serve to decrease the threat of covert line access.

3. Avoid key words or phrases which may be used by intelligence agencies and others to search recorded conversations for subjects of interest. Examples would be project names, product names, the names of persons of interest such as heads of state, CEOs, etc., and classification labels such as "sensitive" and "confidential."

4. Positively identify all parties participating in phone conversations or receiving the facsimile transmissions.

5. Whenever possible, utilize your corporate transmission facilities instead of those of the host government.

6. Corporate offices should be located whenever possible in facilities totally controlled by the corporation.

7. Always keep at least one telephone and facsimile machine secured in a container equipped with a combination lock, and restrict access to the combination. This will help maintain the integrity of that equipment.

8. Check connecting lines to telecommunication devices (telephones, computers, fax machines, etc.) monthly to ensure that the line has not been replaced or modified by unauthorized personnel.

9. Placing stickers on phones warning of hostile monitoring will be helpful to maintain awareness.

Effects of Telecommunications on Computer Security

Hacking into computers is now a standard tool for those involved in espionage and computer crime. Once an intruder has gained entry, he/she may be able to view, change, or destroy valuable company data and information. Electronic terrorism, placing a corporation's information assets at risk, is also possible.

Consider the following tips to reduce the possibility of unauthorized access through networks:

1. Apply access control software and procedures to the corporation's networks; keep the intruder off the "highway." Also, ensure that the corporation's computer systems are protected.

2. Mandate that all users change passwords at least once every 60 days, allow no more than three consecutive invalid passwords before suspending a user identification, and ensure that all passwords are at least six characters in length. Also, encourage employees to use passwords which do not relate to their lives (names of family, pets, sports teams, etc.). Hackers often gain entry by simply guessing passwords. These precautions will make their job harder.

3. Control the phone numbers to the corporation's networks and computer systems as competitive information. Minimize their distribution and notify corporate employees that the numbers should be guarded.

4. Test corporate networks for the existence of unauthorized modems which could provide access to eavesdroppers.

5. Encrypt computer to computer sensitive transmissions to include electronic mail.

6. Require all personnel to agree in writing before they are granted access to corporate networks and computer systems that they will keep competitive information confidential and will abide by the corporation's information protection standards.

Video Conferencing

The threat to video conferencing is essentially the same as that to other types of telecommunications, in that adversaries can purchase or replicate specific equipment used by an American company and then either tap into the line or use other means to monitor both audio and video. Although encryption is available for some video conferencing installations, many countries do not allow any type of encryption and others allow only that type which they can break.

The International Business Traveler

Business travelers who carry and use personal or laptop computers are at risk--particularly if they are unaware of common sense security measures which should be adopted to protect computers and their contents from theft and unauthorized data access.

Computer Theft

It is obvious to a knowledgeable observer by the distinctive shape of the carrying case and the special care taken by the owner when a person is carrying a computer. Because of this, the PC is a clear target for its intrinsic value. A ready market for stolen equipment and the computer's compact size make the theft a very lucrative, low risk venture for the criminal.

A personal computer should never be checked with other luggage, but should always be part of your carry-on baggage that will stay with you at all times.

Likewise, it should never be checked in a temporary airport or train station storage locker, even for a short time.

Greater risk is associated with the information stored on the hard disk of the personal computer. There has always been a degree of risk associated with carrying competitive information in a briefcase, although the bulk and weight of documents limit the number. However, it is possible to store thousands of notes, memos, and full documents on a personal computer hard disk drive. Therefore, the loss or theft of a PC poses a significantly greater risk of valuable information loss than ever experienced in the past.

Unauthorized Access

Unauthorized access occurs when someone accidentally or deliberately reads, modifies, or deletes computer files without your specific permission. Because personal computers do not typically impose data access controls, it is your responsibility to protect your data. While using your computer, protect the information from casual, over-the-shoulder viewing by others. Log-on and data encryption software can provide additional protection.

Obviously, as the size and clarity of portable computer screens continue to increase, so too does the vulnerability to unauthorized observation by people in airport waiting rooms, cafeterias or snack bars, as well as in your plane seat. Positioning oneself so that it is impossible for others to observe the screen can be achieved in a restaurant or snack bar, but is very difficult if not impossible in one's plane seat. One possible strategy is to work on more mundane, non-confidential, non-sensitive work on the plane, and make the presumption that the screen will indeed be observed. Sometimes the aircraft crew will prohibit use of a portable computer on the aircraft.

Foreign Customs

A portable computer is a valuable asset, and national requirements for bringing in such a device vary from country to country--some countries forbid bringing in a personal computer except one made in that particular country. Before even starting on the trip, it is important to check with your legal and security offices concerning customs requirements and necessary documentation. Otherwise, long delays, risk of confiscation, and possible frustrating experiences in attempting to communicate in another language may await the traveler at the airport.

Working From Hotels

Persons traveling in the U.S. expect high quality telephone service. It would not be appropriate to assume that the same will be the case when traveling overseas. In many countries, the telephone service is owned and operated by the national post, telephone, and telegraph company. The quality of service, as well as the technical standards and conventions used, will vary dramatically from country to country. For example, in many countries, it is impossible to simply pull the removable jack from the telephone handset in the room, and plug it into the modem in the PC. Types of jacks and connections differ from country to country, and sometimes within the same country. (A modifier may be the solution.)

Your company may be targeted by a foreign intelligence service which is able to monitor your communications. In most foreign countries only a few central switching points serve to control all international telephone calls whether voice, fax or data stream. Intelligence agencies can tap into these sources without indicating to you that such activity is underway.

Special Risks When Using Cellular PCs

The cellular portable computer is relatively new technology, having unique security considerations which one might easily overlook. The system is essentially a personal computer with an integrated modem, which is a device used to change signals understood by telephone technology into signals understood by computers, and vice versa. There is also a built-in cellular telephone which allows a person with a single action to place a call to a computer system, connect the personal computer to it, and interact with a host computer. Sometimes overlooked with this technology is the fact that cellular telephone communications use radio signals and are, therefore, vulnerable to unauthorized

interception, recording, and subsequent analysis. The necessary monitoring equipment is readily available to foreign intelligence services and to the more sophisticated business espionage agent. Therefore, one should consider carefully whether such interception is acceptable.

Virus Contamination And Detection

Special care must always be taken when receiving a PC program from someone else because the program being given to you may have been contaminated by a computer virus without the knowledge of the person giving it to you. Unfortunately, many viruses are intended to destroy files on a person's hard and/or floppy disks, which could have a catastrophic effect on the user of the PC. Whenever someone copies a program from a bulletin board, or receives a floppy disk from someone else, that program or floppy disk should be scanned to identify any known viruses present within the programs in question. Many such virus scanning programs are available at reasonable cost, and their use is highly recommended.

COUPS D'ETAT AND EMERGENCY EVACUATIONS

If a political event results in a sudden forced change in government (called a coup d'etat or, simply, coup), certain instant decisions must be made. It may, or may not, call for evacuation of Americans from the country. At times like this, nothing is more important than staying in touch with the U.S. Embassy or Consulate. Information of a reliable nature will be hard to come by. It will be almost impossible to distinguish the good guys from the bad guys. Coups d'etat are rarely achieved without violence, which can spill out into the community and permit old quarrels to erupt--violently. It is a time to draw in the protective shell and stay in touch. Short wave radios prove their usefulness at these times. Should one leave? Is it safe to leave? What is the safest method and route to leave? Is it safe to stay? It is vital to monitor the local news. Time spent in the past cultivating local contacts may pay off dramatically at this point. If your emergency supplies are adequate, you may well be able to weather the emergency without too much problem. Staying in touch with local events, contacts, and the State Department should dictate the actions to be taken.

Conversely, it is essential to be prepared to evacuate instantly. If a coup brings in a government that is virulently anti-American and its henchmen are roaming the streets with guns, it may be necessary to get out. This is the time when it is vital to have cash both in the local currency and (because the local currency may become worthless overnight) in U.S. dollars. You should already have mapped out alternate routes of evacuation from the residence to safe havens (the U.S. Embassy being the primary safe haven in a coup or uprising). Passports are essential. An evacuation plan, prepared well in advance, will take care of the essential details. This is where the agent's ongoing intelligence gathering and liaison-building with the local authorities pays off. There should not be any surprises. If the agent has done his job, his contacts should already have provided some warning.

Corporations have a more difficult, and logistically far more complex, job of dealing with coups. Irrespective of its legal obligations, a U.S. corporation has a moral obligation to extend protection to its personnel, at the very least by providing employees with information regarding security and health threats involving their business assignments. This is, of course, particularly true in terms of U.S. citizens. Unfortunately, "nationals" (citizens of that country) are far more vulnerable. While it is unlikely, the agent's protectee may have the unhappy job of staying behind as other U.S. personnel are evacuated. This is the time to retreat into the "bunker" of the corporation, staying calm and stoic in the face of insult and imminent danger. It is well to remember that, with few exceptions (the U.S. Embassy in Iran being one), American expatriates are finally delivered to safe havens. They may be harassed and insulted along the way, but there is still a tacit deterrent that prevents rebels from gunning down American civilians.

If evacuation becomes inevitable, some hard decisions will have to be made.

In a real evacuation, this is the scenario. For starters, the pets, maids, and friends will be left behind. If time allows, personal belongings, luggage, and portable household items will probably be boxed, sealed, and (according to instructions issued by the corporate manager) delivered to a warehouse or some designated place where (hopefully) at some point, someone will ship them to the owners in America. Or, the owners may be allowed to return, collect their belongings, and resume residency. Instructions should be given in advance for labeling, customs declarations, and any additional paperwork. Additional instructions should be given in regard to airplane and/or bus tickets, travelers checks and money, and exit visas. It is important that all paperwork be filled out correctly; the slightest mistake can delay departure.

In all probability, a bus will be assembled to carry American expatriates and luggage (probably one case per person) to the point of departure. If you are not living in a city with a viable airport, you may be bussed dozens, or hundreds, of miles to the nearest international airport. You will be stopped often, and swaggering officials carrying heavy arms will board the bus to check papers and look for contraband. Dogs and cats, heretofore concealed, will be discovered, removed, and killed. Guns will be rammed indiscriminately into stomachs and insults given, with pauses to see if anyone is suicidal enough to invite resistance. After a requisite time, the bus will be allowed to continue to the next checkpoint and series of insults. Waving the American flag will not do zip. The agent's job becomes twofold: keeping an eye on the ball (getting out), and restraining the protectee from informing everyone within hearing that he is an "important person to the United States." The last thing any protection agent wants is to have a client who is important to the United States during a coup or uprising. The agent's job may be to keep the client quiet and smart. The coup-winners will have some sense of not wanting to harm expatriates. It is the agent's job to make certain that they do not have a reason. Eventually, the evacuees will reach safe shelter somewhere. Even in Iran, after the U.S. Embassy had been taken and the occupants made hostage, American expatriates working in Iran were safely evacuated.

(There is a copy of a corporate evacuation plan in the Appendix.)

FAR AWAY PLACES

Since *The Executive Protection Bible* was first published in 1993, there has been a marked increase in the travels by highly placed executives to some exotic, resource-rich, dangerous places. Great quantities of oil and other desirable resources such as gold and diamonds seem to be perversely located in relatively undeveloped areas peopled with some incredibly dangerous people. Angola and Sierra Leone are good examples--lots of diamonds and numerous rebels rampaging and fighting for control. The Congo, rich with natural resources and now, having sustained one coup, is now being fought over not only by rebels but by rebels backed by at least five outside governments. In both cases, the combatants do NOT quibble at hacking off limbs, kidnapping for profit, shooting down helicopters and planes, and just plain shooting anything that moves.

Resource-rich Colombia is riddled with insurgents and heavy-duty drug producers. In the last decade alone, some 100,000 people have been killed. Colombia has the honor of being named "the kidnap capital of the world," due to the huge number of kidnappings which take place there, now estimated at four per day.

Azerbaijan is afloat with huge oil reserves and is being courted by all of the Western nations--and, of course, as luck would have it, it is located on the borders of Russia and Iran and not all that far from Chechnya. Azerbaijan has been engaged in a bloody struggle with Armenia and it has its own share of tough guys, tribesmen living in remote areas, and infiltration from neighboring countries bent on Muslim control. The United States does not want to see oil from this country being routed through Iran, preferring

instead to see it flowing by way of Turkey. Iran is a theocratic state--Turkey a secular state.

South Africa, one of the more enlightened African countries, is riddled with crime. Indonesia, viewed during the 1990's as the Asian jewel, has almost collapsed under the weight of corruption and factionalism.

And, these are only a few of the countries and regions where American (and other) executives are flying to in hopes of doing business.

Naturally, the oil, gold, and diamonds are located way, way back in almost unreachable areas-- areas which may be mined and will most certainly contain a number of avaricious, unpleasant people.

(Before going further, the author does not wish to leave the impression that everyone in the countries named (and unnamed) are lawless butchers. Pity the poor inhabitants who simply want to have a safe and peaceful life; these are the decent people who have been routinely killed and uprooted by the rebels or by neighbors engaged in ethnic cleansing. In Rwanda alone, it is estimated that 500,000 Tutsis were slaughtered by their Hutu neighbors.)

Protecting a client in these areas presents an incredible challenge. The protection agents who are doing this are no doubt rewriting the "rules of engagement." At the same time, the basic principles of protection are applicable. Essentially, the agent is going to be doing the same things, perhaps more intensely, and is definitely going to realize that he/she must be flexible and inventive. Traditional advances may not be possible or may have to be altered on the spot. Overall, the agent should be prepared to be more reactive than he or she would like to be.

Intelligence

Good intelligence will be imperative, and it must be current. It is essential not only to identify the potential dangers but also to have a way of distinguishing the good guys from the bad guys. NOTE: It is entirely possible that the client will be doing business with some unsavory people who just happen to be in charge--what is important is to determine if these people can and will guarantee safety for the client. What arrangements will they make? Do these arrangements seem credible? If one is dealing with the head of the country or top government officials, they will generally arrange for military escort. This may or may not suffice to protect the client. In Colombia, for example, the rebels are as strong as the government military.

Does the client have company representatives on the spot? Have company personnel recently returned from the proposed travel site? These people should be routinely debriefed; they will provide much more reliable information, in some respects, than the local government (which may downplay any problems). The essential information you want is:

.   Who's in charge and can make decisions? Are they (relatively) trustworthy?

.   Who are the combatants and where are they?

.   Is there active fighting going on?

.   Why are they fighting?

.   Does either side actively prey on foreigners-- kidnappings? murders?

.   Is there an active anti-American or anti- Western sentiment with any group?

.   Where are the safe zones? Is the capital city relatively safe?

.   Anything you can learn about back country areas to which the client may want (or need) to travel--particularly safety issues. Are there land mines?

.   Is the military considered competent? (In the event a military escort is provided the client.)

The agent must coordinate with the client and other company officials to determine whether any upcoming business trips are sanctioned with the U.S. State Department. Does the State Department oppose it? This could add to the potential problems. Conversely, does the State Department view it with favor as being good for the national interest, and, if so, can help and support be provided by our own government?

One should never forget to do a quick read on the culture, religion(s), and customs of the target country. Most of these third-world countries have long-standing cultural mores which are intensely felt. Many the deal has fallen flat because an insensitive American trod on the cultural toes of the local people. The history of U.S. intervention in other countries has not endeared us. Many feel that they have been cheated and treated with contempt, and that we Americans have tried to impose our religious and civil rights issues on them. It helps to see and understand their point of view, though not necessarily agree with it.

A necessary pre-departure chore is to determine the kind and prevalence of exotic diseases to be found in the target country--particularly when that country is one that the client would otherwise never visit except for its oil reserves. For example, there is:

.   African Sleeping Sickness - found in tropical Africa.

.   Dengue Fever - found in Central and South America, Africa, South Pacific, Asia, Mexico, and the Caribbean.

.   Ebola River Fever - Congo.

.   Leprosy - Africa, India and elsewhere.

.   Rift Valley Fever - Egypt and East Africa.

as well as a few dozen other really terrible afflictions. The prudent agent will see a physician familiar with exotic diseases to undertake any vaccinations or preventive measures, and to acquire available medications.

Advances

Advances will not be as neat and tidy as advances to, say, Los Angeles or Rome or Berlin. There may only be one or two first-class hotels, if that, and the General Manager will be much less likely to accede to any special requests. If the client plans to travel from the capital to the back country diamond mine, an advance may not be possible or even practical, since the situation is fluid. If Rebel Group A is in control today, he might be dead tomorrow. However, the agent needs to do his absolute best to assess the situation and to put together the best plan available. It is then up to the client as to whether he wants to go through with the trip.

As previously emphasized, the agent should check in first, or as early as possible, with the U.S. embassy or consulate. This is extremely important in high risk areas.

A word on travel. Whenever possible, fly on the bigger, better known world airlines and avoid the third-world national airlines or local charters. Many of these small regional airlines are badly maintained, pilot skills may be marginal, and safety standards virtually unknown. You may not have a choice, but you should know in advance that the incidence of small plane crashes is MUCH greater than the big birds. If the local government is providing a military flight, the safety factor is higher but not guaranteed. All internal travel must be sanctioned by *someone*, either the government or the controlling rebel group, warlord, or religious leader. In an active fighting zone, a flak jacket or armored vest is an excellent idea.

In dealing with local individuals, it is essential to remain neutral and "above the fray." One should never comment on, respond to, or become involved with local politics, intrigues, religious or ethnic conflicts, or power plays. Remember, the politics are volatile and ever-changing.

The agent must avoid any behavior which might label him a spy, a CIA agent, or provocateur.

Taking pictures, drawing maps, and writing copious notes will undoubtedly be viewed with suspicion.

Special Dangers

Drugs. Many third-world countries rich in oil, gold, and diamond reserves are also rich in the poppies and coca bushes used to produce heroin and cocaine. Other countries which are not producers are transhippers of drugs. Some of the countries involved with production or shipment of drugs are: Tajikistan, Kazakhstan, Krgystan, Turkmenistan, Uzbekistan, Afghanistan, and Turkey, as well as Colombia and Mexico. Colombia, Peru, Mexico, Panama, Bolivia, and Nigeria are involved with the cocaine traffic. Thailand and Myanmar are noted for their busy opium and heroin trade. Where there is drug traffic, there is danger.

Terrorists, Insurrectionists & Criminals. Where there are internal conflicts and insurrections, bombings are a constant threat. It is sometimes difficult to separate the bad guys from the good guys-- some play both ends. Insurrections, coups, and governments have often financed their activities either by getting involved with the drug trade or by kidnapping foreigners.

Rebels. THEY want the diamonds, gold, and oil as much as we do. These people may be backed by one or more foreign governments who either want to create mischief or who ALSO want control of the resources.

Kidnappings. Kidnapping is a cottage industry in some countries. Unfortunately, some of these kidnappings have resulted in executions or in deaths related to failed rescue attempts. From the kidnapper's point of view, the business traveler is the ideal victim, since he is probably connected to a well-heeled corporation, and the company may carry kidnap insurance. If the kidnapping has been done for political reasons, Americans are a definite plus, since the U.S. government may apply covert pressure on the local government to gain the release of its citizen(s). Latin America wins the prize for the highest number of kidnappings. In some countries, the kidnappers are in cahoots with the police.

Land Mines. One figure places the number of land mines at as many as 110 million, buried in more than 60 countries. They are, for the most part, uncharted or poorly charted, and are unmarked. Over a dozen African countries have several million mines between them, with Angola being the most heavily mined. Among the most heavily mined countries in the world are: Egypt, Iran, Afghanistan, Cambodia, Iraq, and Croatia. Less heavily mined but nonetheless extremely dangerous are: Mexico, Guatemala, El Salvador, Honduras, Costa Rica, Zimbabwe, Tunisia, Laos, Tajikistan, and Myanmar.

Some sound advice in mine avoidance is to:

. Find out in advance as much as possible about the land mine situation in the area. Those who lay the mines often follow a pattern or set modus operandi in the way they operate (much as other bombers do).

. Stay on well-traveled roads--do not take shortcuts or isolated foot paths--follow others' tracks.

. Avoid being the first person or vehicle-- whenever possible, follow others, preferably a heavy truck. Stay well back; if there is an explosion, shrapnel will be deadly.

. Do not stray off the road onto the shoulder-- these were often mined. Do not park on the shoulder. Execute turns on the pavement.

. If a mine explodes, stand still, then carefully retreat backwards, staying in your own tracks.

. Never pick up or handle a suspicious object.

Handy Resources

There are some very good books and publications available which focus on international and third-world situations.

. *Fielding's The World's Most Dangerous Places*, by Robert Young Pelton with Coskun Aral and Wink Dulles, published by Fielding Worldwide, Inc.

. *Third World Guide*, published by New Internationalist, 55 Rectory Road, Oxford, England OX4 1BW.

. *The Economist*, 111 West 57th Street, New York, NY 10019.

Some material included in this chapter was excerpted from the U.S. Dept. of State Overseas Security Advisory Council (OSAC) publications, "Security Guidelines for American Families Living Abroad," "Security Guidelines for American Enterprises Abroad, and "Protecting Business Information Overseas." We are grateful to OSAC for their permission to use this material."

CONFIDENTIAL
PRE-DEPARTURE SECURITY BRIEFING
XYZ CORPORATION EMPLOYEES

January 2000

The material contained within this briefing is confidential. It is to be read and used only by employees of XYZ Corporation on a need-to-know basis.

GERMANY

Passport, Tourist:	Required
Passport, Business:	Required
Visa, Business and Tourist:	Not required for visits up to three months; longer stays generally require a visa
German Tourist Offices:	747 Third Avenue, New York, NY 10017, 212/308-3300 444 So. Flower St., Los Angeles, CA 90071, 213/688-7332
Vaccinations Required:	None
Currency:	Deutschemark (DM), divided into 100 pfennings (pf). Bills are DM 1,000, 500, 200, 100, 50, 20, and 10. Coins are DM 5, 2, and 1, and 50, 10, 5, 2, and 1 pf.
Rate as of 12/15/99:	DM 1.76 to the U.S. dollar. (Currency rates found daily in Wall Street Journal.)
Import of Currency:	No restriction
Language:	German/regional dialects. English is commonly spoken.
Sanitation and Health Standards:	Excellent
Climate:	Temperate; cold in the winter in the Alps and higher regions. As of week of 12/15/99, highs Berlin 30's, lows 20's, with rain and sleet, which is typical for December.
Time:	6 hours later than New York (EST).
Banks:	Times vary; generally open weekdays from 8:30/9:00 a.m. to 3:00/4:00 p.m.
National Holidays:	January 1; April 19; April 20; May 1; May 28; June 8; October 3; November 18; December 25 & 26.

CONFIDENTIAL PRE-DEPARTURE BRIEFING
XYZ CORPORATION EMPLOYEES

POLITICAL BACKGROUND

The reunion of East and West Germany, while heralded with much fanfare, has been a slow, complex, painful process. Many believe that it will require a generation to complete the reunification of Germany. The cost of shoring up the East German economy has been much higher than anticipated and, as a result, taxes have been raised.

After a euphoric beginning, reality has tested the mettle of the West Germans, who are appalled at the work ethics and lack of environmental concerns of the East Germans. The East Germans, on the other hand, resent losing their former guaranteed employment, even when it meant a lower standard or quality of life than that enjoyed by the West Germans. Many East Germans are now unemployed or are working only part-time.

There remains a great deal of confusion. Traveling between East and West Germany means encountering problems with currency and business relations. The basic infrastructure of East Germany is dilapidated, services are erratic, and the environment has suffered badly from Communist unconcerns.

In mid-1990, the government voted to move the seat of government from Bonn to Berlin, allowing a period of twelve years to make the transition. This makes for a certain amount of confusion.

The Germans are eager to open their borders to free trade, and have not resisted being absorbed into the European Union.

The most alarming and troublesome political development is the rise of Neo-Naziism and the "skinheads," who have resorted to violence against Turkish expatriates in their country in particular.

GENERAL CRIME INFORMATION

Germany, while undergoing internal strife, egged on by the Neo-Nazis, is still relatively safe from the violent crime encountered in some other countries. Pickpockets and purse snatchers are a problem in Germany, and due care must be taken to avoid losing one's valuables. However, if one exercises reasonable care and prudent behavior, crime is not a big concern.

Remember to obtain your passport, visa, and travelers checks well in advance of departure. You should make two photocopies of these instruments, one to carry with you and one to leave with the office. You should make certain that you have a safe place to carry these items.

It is always wise to keep any details about your trip confidential, shared only with family and close associates. Be particularly alert to faxed itineraries sitting unattended at fax machines. However, a copy of your itinerary and list of contacts should be provided to the office, so that the company is aware of your whereabouts at all times.

CONFIDENTIAL PRE-DEPARTURE BRIEFING
XYZ CORPORATION EMPLOYEES

PRE-DEPARTURE SECURITY PREPARATIONS

While it may be company policy to provide first class flight accommodations for company executives flying on company business, you may wish to consider flying coach, males on the window seats and females on the aisle. It is unlikely that there would be a terrorist incident but, if there were one, historically the first class and aisle passengers have been subjected to abuse. Those male passengers sitting on the aisle have often been singled out for interrogation and ill treatment. It is also well to leave valuable jewelry at home and to dress inconspicuously. Expensive suits and a show of wealth are magnets to criminals. Dressing casually for the flight will be more comfortable and more prudent. If you have a choice, ask corporate travel or your own travel agent to book you on a direct flight or one that makes as few stops as possible, as some stopovers are known to be riskier than others.

You should carry with you a generous supply of any prescription medicine in its original container which you may need, an extra pair of eyeglasses, extra hearing aid and batteries, your eyeglass prescription, and a medical card with your blood type and any allergies. All business cards, stationery, or papers which identify you with the corporation should be locked in your checked baggage. It is best not to carry any cards which identify you with a religious or political group; nor is it wise to carry political, sexy, or religious literature. These items, if you wish to have them, should be locked inside your checked baggage. Do carry pictures of your children in your wallet.

It is recommended that you update your will. While the likelihood of something happening to you is remote, it is only prudent to bring one's affairs up to date. You may wish to consider giving a power of attorney, including authorization powers for children's medical emergencies, to your attorney or a trusted friend to be exercised in your absence, and, because a power of attorney is not valid when you are dead, you may wish to establish a joint checking account with your wife if she is not accompanying you on your trip, or to a trusted signer. A key to your safety deposit box and a list of securities, assets, mortgages, bills to be paid, insurance, and any other vital information should be left.

Please plan to arrive at the airport well in advance of your flight to go through customs and passport check. Your tickets should include a boarding pass which will eliminate your having to stand in line. The less time spent in public areas the safer. You should go through the security check and wait for your flight in the airline private club lounge. Airline club lounges have solid walls and are not accessible to terrorists except by forced entry (or if they hold a membership). In the terminal and at the departure gates, try to avoid standing near windows or glass doors and, if you must stand by a window, place your back to the window in the event the glass is shattered.

STREET CRIME

While pickpocketing and purse snatching have always been the most common overseas crimes and should not be minimized, violent crimes are on the increase. In areas that once were relatively crime-free, primarily because of totalitarian control, crime in general increases every year and in some areas is blatant.

-3-

CONFIDENTIAL PRE-DEPARTURE BRIEFING
XYZ CORPORATION EMPLOYEES

Muggings, rapes, as well as assaults, have become increasingly common. For example, in Russia, Moscow in particular), violent crimes against tourists and business people are alarmingly high. As in the United States, security awareness is the best defense. Victims are usually targeted because of their preoccupation with business, sightseeing, shopping, or simply the rigors of coping with a foreign environment. Other victims are chosen because of their obvious show of wealth (jewelry, gold, expensive wristwatches, fur coats), or simple carelessness. You should get in the habit of looking at people in the hotel and in the street. Trust your sixth sense. It is often correct. If something looks suspicious, avoid it.

Some simple strategies are recommended to avoid becoming a victim. It is best to wear inconspicuous clothing that fits into the local environment and to leave all jewelry, but particularly dangling jewelry, at home. A cheap wristwatch to wear in public at all but social occasions is a good idea. You should not carry your passport at all times (normally recommended while in a foreign environment), or more than one credit card, unless you need them, and if you must carry them, place them in a secure inner pocket, preferably one that closes with a zipper. Carrying a photocopy of your passport will generally suffice to establish identification. For many years, the advice to those who lived or visited New York City was to carry no more money than was needed for one day; this advice is excellent for overseas trips as well.

A brisk, confident walk will deter some assailants. Knowing where you are going in advance and having memorized a map will indicate that you are not lost, nor an easy mark. Knowing a few phrases of the local language helps, and you should always have pocket change in the local currency to use for the public telephones.

Be watchful of street vendors and groups of children who may be pickpockets or purse snatchers. They may also work in pairs. If you are jostled in a crowd, or something is spilled on you, be careful--someone may be trying to steal your belongings. A venerable purse snatching technique is for the perpetrator to ride his motorcycle by the victim, snatch her purse, and quickly ride off. This sometimes results not only in acquiring the victim's purse, but in knocking down and injuring the victim. Other techniques involve using a knife or razor to slice a strap or the bottom of the purse. Groups of children begging for coins are often shills for pickpockets, or are themselves skilled in lifting wallets. Accidents and distractions are often staged to cause confusion, making it easier to steal wallets and purses.

Don't invite danger by going to quaint and colorful, but high-risk, tourist places. If you are walking, whenever possible you should try to walk with a companion or a group. Make sure that someone knows where you are going and when you are expected to return. Using a taxi procured for you by a doorman or concierge is generally safer than wandering about on foot.

Taxicabs abroad fall into two categories: licensed and gypsy. In some countries there are two kinds of licensed taxis, a private cab transporting only one person or party, and a jitney taxi that picks up several fares and delivers them along certain routes. There has been an increase in taxicab robberies directed toward the passengers; therefore, it is safer to avoid the gypsy and the jitney taxis, taking only those taxicabs which are licensed and which are procured by the concierge of the hotel or a doorman. If you must call for a taxi at your residence, be sure to use a trusted taxicab company, and, when calling for the cab, ask for the driver's name; then check his identification when he arrives.

-4-

CONFIDENTIAL PRE-DEPARTURE BRIEFING
XYZ EMPLOYEES

If you should be confronted with an assailant, do not take chances. It is better to give up your wallet than your life. Remain calm, do not make any sudden movements, and follow your adversary's instructions. If you have to reach inside a pocket or coat, you should say aloud, "I am reaching for my wallet, using two fingers." Once you have handed over your valuables, stay still. You should never attempt to overpower, chase, or capture the assailant; that is not your job, and it is very dangerous. Any crime should be reported to the police, to the corporate security staff, and to the American Embassy.

If you feel that an assault is inevitable and that you must either suffer grave physical harm or fight back, do so with all your strength. Yell, kick, scratch, pummel, and run like the wind. The choice of submitting or fighting back is a personal one, a judgement call that must be made on the spot. You should be prepared to make that decision.

Women alone, without escorts, are apt to be annoyed by unwelcome male attention in certain countries. It is best to clearly indicate, in no uncertain terms, that these attentions are unwelcome. Learning the local words for "no" and, "Please leave me alone, or I will call the police," may be helpful.

DRIVING SECURITY

If you are not familiar with the city, local traffic regulations, legal system, and language, and if you do not have proper driving credentials and insurance, hire a driver or a car with driver. A driver should also be hired if there is any potential for your being personally targeted by terrorists. Rent a car or hire a driver with a car, equipped with a cellular telephone if it is available.

Good security driving techniques are the same overseas as in the States. If you rent a car, select one that is inconspicuous but has sufficient power to get away in a hurry if there is danger. You should always lock all car doors and roll up the windows whether you are inside or outside the car. Whenever possible, the vehicle should be parked in a secure location. Try to drive always on well traveled streets and avoid any barricades or construction work. Bogus accidents are sometimes contrived to entrap a victim. If you see an accident, drive away and report it. If someone drives into you from behind you, do not get out of the car. Keep the motor running and be prepared to drive away if anything looks suspicious, noting the license number of the car involved. Never allow yourself to become boxed in. A much-used terrorist technique is to block the target car front and back. If necessary, drive through the blockade, slowly but steadily ramming through the back end of the blocking car.

TERRORISM AND HOSTILE SURVEILLANCE

U.S. businesses and businessmen have long been targets of terrorist interest. Often perceived as oppressors or friends of oppressive governments, U.S. corporate executives have been targeted for kidnap and hostage taking. While there have been a number of incidents, the percentage of U.S. businessmen kidnapped as opposed to the total number traveling and living abroad is very, very small. On the other hand, it is only wise to take all precautions to avoid becoming a kidnap target.

CONFIDENTIAL PRE-DEPARTURE BRIEFING
XYZ CORPORATION EMPLOYEES

Terrorists and kidnappers are rarely impulsive. Sometimes they target a specific individual, but more often they will select several targets, and then put a team or teams to work watching every move their target selections make. The target who appears to be the most vulnerable and least careful is then chosen. Even after the target is chosen, there will be intensive surveillance to determine where and when the target travels, and if the target is predictable in his habits. A time and place is then chosen for the incident.

It therefore behooves you to appear too difficult as a target (in comparison to other potential targets) to an adversary. The single most useful defensive measure you can take is to vary your travel routes and times, and the next most important step is to be vigilant and alert to possible surveillance. Terrorist surveillance is so intensive that an alert person will notice something that is out of the ordinary, something that is not quite right. This could be a van that is parked for no apparent reason, or a woman walking a baby carriage or a dog every day past your residence, strangers calling or inquiring about you, a car, bicycle or motorcycle that always seem to follow you. To notice anything unusual you must first know what is normal. Look around, introduce yourself to the neighbors, notice the regular shopkeepers. If you believe you are being followed, stop abruptly (in a safe place) and look your follower in the eye. If you suspect that you are under surveillance, report it to the police and to the American Embassy. Remember the security rules. Do not be predictable. Be alert for surveillance. Avoid areas where you could be trapped. Drive only on well traveled streets. Be alert to blockades or contrived accidents. Keep your private life and itineraries confidential.

Due to the specialized knowledge held by protection agents, they are often asked to assist in both the planning and implementation of crisis management plans.

First, to deal with some terminology. In corporations, one hears the terms, *risk management, crisis management,* and *contingency planning. Risk management* is a term used primarily to describe any measure taken to protect an insurable item. This is greatly oversimplified, but true. Insurance can be bought to cover almost any conceivable situation--at a price. The price may be expensive, staggering, or simply unaffordable, depending upon the value of the assets to be protected. Let us take some examples. Very few museums (if any) can afford to purchase insurance that will cover the costs of the loss of even one virtually priceless painting. Imagine, therefore, trying to insure the collection of paintings at the Metropolitan Museum of Art in New York City, paintings worth untold millions, even billions, of dollars. Therefore, risk management steps in. How great is the risk? What security and safety measures can be implanted to lessen the risk? To what degree can the risk be reduced? How much insurance needs to be purchased to cover the risk that cannot be reduced by security and safety measures?

A plant manufacturing highly inflammable products will undoubtedly install a sophisticated fire prevention and suppression system, have rigorous safety training sessions and, in addition, will purchase insurance. However, because of the highly sensitive nature of the products, full insurance will cost so much money that the company cannot afford full coverage. Risk management in this case will weigh the value of the products and plant against the likelihood of a fire, considering the fire safety measures practiced in the plant, and then purchase the insurance which can be afforded to cover the exposed risk.

In short, this is managing, not eliminating, the risk. It is similar to executive protection where a threat assessment is made and evaluated, and as much protection as is affordable and necessary is applied to the threat. Risk management enters the arena of executive protection when the corporation looks at its CEO and key employees and decides whether the risk (threat) is sufficiently high and the asset (the CEO) sufficiently valuable to warrant bringing in a protection agent or team to protect the CEO, and possibly to purchase kidnap and ransom insurance. If the CEO is virtually indispensable to the ongoing operations and good health of the corporation, and there is a perceived threat to the CEO or the corporation, good risk management will look at its security options, and these could include the provision of, or upgrading of, an executive protection component. If corporate decision-makers believe the loss of the CEO, through any cause, would result in a drastic devaluation of stock prices due to loss of confidence in the company's management, and recognize that security threats exist, they will likely consider personal protection. Decision-makers may also recommend the use of personal protection to help manage any risks of losing the executive through preventable circumstances, such as being shot in a random street mugging or dying of a heart attack, when merely initiating CPR and calling for emergency medical services would have saved his life. In such cases, the corporation does not want to be seen by the shareholders as ignoring such basic responsibilities of asset protection. It is a decision over which the protection agent will have some possible input but no direct control. It will often be decided at the Board level.

Crisis management is more or less what you would expect; it is the planned and reasoned management of, and response to, corporate crises, whether these are natural crises (earthquakes, hurricanes), environmental crises (oil leaks, nuclear plant breakdowns), corporate crises (strikes and civil unrest), or political/terrorist/criminal inspired acts (kidnappings, bombings, skyjackings, product tampering, and evacuations from overseas countries).

Just as a good protection agent does his advance work, so should a corporation. The corporation's advance work consists of forming a Crisis Management Team, which formulates policies and procedures for preventing and responding to crises. In other words, the CMT (Crisis Management Team) manages crises. When a corporate crisis develops, there is no time to think about it; scenarios must already have been developed that dictate action. The analogy of crisis management to executive protection is an apt one. Just as the agent is proactive in attempting to prevent incidents, so the CMT is proactive in setting up policies and procedures to prevent crises. And, as the protection agent must respond to an incident, so must the CMT respond, swiftly and surely, to a crisis. It is the area of Crisis Management that can, and should, involve the protection agent. Whether the crisis is an act of God or a terrorist kidnapping, the corporate protectee will be at the center of the crisis.

Many kinds of plans may be developed which are specific to providing protective services. These may include (but are not limited to) responding to medical or security emergencies at the protectee's home, office, or special events; responding to a situation of a missing protectee such as when he/she does not report to work, does not check into a hotel where reservations are made, or does not pick up a reserved rental car; responding to a corporate aircraft hijacking; responding to downed corporate aircraft; kidnapping; extortion; and conducting a medical or security evacuation from a foreign country.

Contingency planning is a term sometimes confused with, or used interchangeably with, crisis management. It is also a term that is heard in executive protection jargon when the protectee is a private (not corporate) individual. What are the contingencies (possible incidents), and how does one plan to prevent or deal with them? Contingency planning is also a phrase used within corporate

marketing departments. What will happen if our competitors get their product to market before we do?

In this chapter, we will look at an overview of Crisis Management within the context of how it involves the executive protection agent. The subject is too broad to examine in depth, and it would be rare for a corporate protection agent to develop and implement an entire corporate Crisis Management Plan. However, because elements of the plan parallel the agent's job in protecting the corporate client, it behooves the agent to understand the principles of Crisis Management. Also, it will become readily apparent that the way in which Crisis Management functions is very similar to the agent's functions of threat assessment, vulnerability studies, intelligence gathering, and scenarios. In addition, the training received by the agent is directly applicable to the process of planning and managing for crises. As a result, the protective agent can be very helpful and is a likely candidate to participate in developing and implementing crisis management plans.

Crisis management has been a hot topic with American corporations since the 1960's because it makes perfect sense, the stakes are extremely high, and there have been some staggeringly expensive crises in terms of people and money. Take one disaster, the malfunctioning of the nuclear plant at Three Mile Island. Repairs and cleanup have cost almost a billion dollars, and this was a *good* disaster-- if the meltdown had continued, the result could have been destruction of, literally, millions of lives. Any American company which does not have a crisis management plan that is active and constantly updated is flirting with the undertaker.

There are some pitfalls associated with crisis management plans. Some plans are so minutely and complexly developed that they become static instruments which no one understands or could possibly comply with. Or, the plans are considered too "confidential" to share with employees who might be expected to lend aid and support during a crisis. At the opposite end of the scale, some plans are too narrow, being heavily weighted toward natural disasters, with too little attention paid to crises brought about by crime, terrorism, or product tampering. Sometimes the plans lack imagination. Who, for example, would have developed a scenario for an oil tanker which had an "indisposed" captain and an inexperienced hand at the helm that drove the tanker on the reef, spilling millions of gallons of oil on a pristine Alaskan coastline? Quite possibly, the problem may be that a corporation develops an effective crisis management plan, but fails to manage its own resources and employees. The best crisis management plan in the world will fail every time if the company can't manage the day-to-day operations of its own business.

The organization of a Crisis Management Team and production of a Crisis Management Plan in its entirety requires a huge amount of time, work, and commitment, and the effort must be headed up by someone with authority within the corporation. The plan will cut across departmental lines and require the commitment of top management. In all likelihood, the coordination of this effort will not become the responsibility of the executive protection agent, although certain portions of the plan may become the agent's job to develop. The agent may be expected to write, or contribute greatly to, the plan for a terrorist incident, a violent crime, a bomb threat, or a harassment incident.

Although it is not always possible, ideally the protection agent or Detail Leader should have a voice in the CMT, since the crisis may involve his (or her) client. If the agent is not a member of or advisor to the CMT, he should at least be privy to the plan, to know what will happen if the protectee or corporation is attacked. Crisis management is a very complex operation involving almost every department of the corporation. If a protection agent is ambitious and zestful to acquire knowledge, this is an area of real interest. An agent who adds crisis management to his or her portfolio, adds great value to his or her future employment capabilities.

The Crisis Management Team

The first step in Crisis Management is to put together the Crisis Management Team (CMT), who

will then develop the Crisis Management Plan (CMP). The CMT must necessarily be part of top management, as the members will need to access company resources and make decisions which cannot be questioned. In an emergency, let us say for a kidnapping, a decision may be whether to provide ransom money. This is not up for a thoughtful request for departmental discussion; a decision will need to be made and carried through NOW, no questions asked. So, CMT members must be from the ranks of senior management, with authority. They should be capable of cool behavior under fire and able to act in a level-headed manner (in fact, a CMT member may be called upon to negotiate with an adversary during an incident). Every member should be an authority in an area of expertise; legal, financial, communications, etc. The most efficient CMT's are small in number, since too many members will provoke endless comments, discussions, and eventual logjam. Ideally, a CMT may be composed of, say, five to ten individuals, with a sub-strata of subject matter experts who give advice and input. These experts can include psychiatrists, professional negotiators, insurance personnel, law enforcement, overseas personnel, terrorist experts, etc. This secondary level to the team does not hold team credentials but is, nonetheless, very important. The secondary level has expert input, but no authority.

CMT members must be available, able to be contacted at any time. There should be an alert call list and procedures in place so that all members can be contacted in the shortest possible time. All team members and advisors should also practice the process of convening and responding to mock scenarios under the direction of someone who has extensive experience in managing corporate crises, often someone hired to consult on this subject from outside the corporation. This is not a purely honorary appointment. Therefore, CMT members should, logically, reside in the same area or in close proximity. The members must be, frankly, a tough bunch, capable of making unemotional decisions and able to take creative actions instantly. It is a difficult role to fill. The CMT must devise a thoughtful plan for prevention of crisis incidents and also plan against the most bizarre events. Fortunately, corporations are used to filling these diverse roles.

A core CMT might be devised as follows:

. **Chairman (or Coordinator) of the CMT.** This individual has to be, in many ways, "superman" or "superwoman." The Chairman/Coordinator must have responsibility and authority, possess cool, level-headed skills, and be capable of sustaining the emotional trauma of making decisions under fire. This is the individual who may have to tell the terrorists, finally, that the corporation will not negotiate, thus condemning the hostage to a long incarceration or death. This must be an individual who can withstand pressure (sometimes from his or her own people) and can keep his team members together as a cohesive action group. He, or she, must be seen as wise, capable, and trustworthy.

. An alternate must be designated for the Chairman (or Coordinator) of the CMT. If a crisis should develop while the Chairman is out of the country or ill, events must still be dealt with.

. **Security Director.** This individual is responsible for overall security and incident prevention strategies. He, or she, will probably have a major responsibility for implementing the CMP strategies. The Security Director may be required to develop the threat assessments, develop a security training program, conduct bomb searches, make recommendations for security equipment and electronic intrusion detection systems, and maintain liaison with law enforcement agencies. Depending upon the nature of the crisis (explosion, etc.), the Security Director will have the responsibility of providing security to control and prevent further damage. He or she will also organize personal protection for family members of victims or others in the corporation who may need it during the crisis.

. **Legal.** This individual is highly necessary. This is the person who will advise as to the legalities of the incident, the litigious potential, the local laws of the overseas country, the liaison and communications with law enforcement, the legal

responsibilities of the corporation during a hostage or hijacking incident, and the myriad additional details of crises.

The legal implications of any incident are enormous. A Pan Am airplane is blown up in mid-flight. Families of the victims sue Pan Am. Was Pan Am to blame? Were prudent and sufficient security measures employed? Were warnings received and passed on to passengers?

Or, Company ABC's overseas manager is kidnapped. The overseas host country has a "no-negotiation policy" with terrorists. ABC quietly arranges for the payment of ransom and release of the company manager through a third country. Is ABC breaking the laws of the host country?

Or, an employee has been terminated from his job. He makes threats, then goes home, loads up an automatic weapon, and returns to his old job, where he shoots and kills ten people. Is the company liable?

. **Financial.** A corporate financial officer at the highest level must be included on the team. The time may come when a decision is needed for ransom or an opinion on payouts to victims of food poisoning or child-killer toys. A financial officer capable of projecting financial outputs and aware of financial alternatives is essential to the team. The financial officer must deal with the insurance companies.

. **Communications.** This is a very important but often overlooked function. There are several aspects to the communications function which may be handled by one or more members of the CMT.

. **Corporate communications.** If the crisis occurs at a subsidiary location, this is the communication that takes place between the crisis site and the corporate headquarters. Senior management at headquarters must be kept informed, factually and fully. This function will probably be handled by the CMT Chairman.

.   **Adversary communications.** Some one person must handle all communications with the adversary if there is one (barring a natural disaster such as an earthquake). Ideally, this person should have some understanding of the adversary, his goals, motivations, and tactics, although this information can be supplied by an advisor from the CMT support group. The important point is that all communications between the corporation and the adversary must be channeled through one person. This person may also be a skilled negotiator, although it is not always the case. Someone on the CMT should either have received training in hostage negotiations or should agree to do so, since all dealings with the adversary will involve negotiations. The person fulfilling this role might be the person within the corporation who handles union negotiations, although it is usual for a trained law enforcement negotiator to be in charge of negotiating with kidnappers and extortionists, whether the incident is in the U.S. or overseas.

.   **Public relations.** This role is crucial, as the potential for a public relations disaster is enormous. As is true with the person handling adversary communications, all information flowing back and forth between the corporation and the media must be handled by one spokesperson. Depending upon the extent and location of the crisis, the media may be a constant presence, complete with television cameras. Daily, even hourly, briefings may be a necessity. This individual must be in constant touch with the CMT, skilled at communicating under pressure, and able to answer questions without being provoked into intemperate answers. Press releases are a big help. Press (or information) releases should be factual but not compromising. They should not be emotional. If the news story involves legal considerations, legal counsel should review

the releases. Two cardinal rules are: *never lie to the media*, and *never get into an argument with the media*. If a question cannot be answered, either because the spokesperson does not have an answer or because the answer may be compromising, he should simply say, "I can't answer that question, sorry." He should never say, "This is off the record." If you say it, it's on the record. One should not patronize the media, nor underestimate their intelligence.

.   **Internal communications.** This function involves communications with the corporate employees and the family or families affected by the crisis. It also includes controlling rumors which are apt to fly, all of which will be negative and could cause panic. One person should handle this function and do so continually, with a calm and orderly manner. This person will work closely with the personnel/human relations department, or may even be the Human Relations/Personnel Director.

.   **Government liaison.** Depending upon the nature and location of the crisis, a certain level of liaison with government agencies will have to be maintained. If it is a kidnapping or hostage taking, the FBI will be involved in addition to the local police. If it is an evacuation overseas, the U.S. embassy, as well as the host country government officials, must be kept in constant contact. The person handling this function may be the CMT Chairman, or the Security Director, or the individual handling adversary communications. These are all interactive roles.

.   **Personnel/Human Relations.** The CMT person representing this department will have the chief responsibility in dealing with families affected by the crisis. In the case of a natural disaster, this becomes a huge task, as hundreds may be affected. If the crisis is a kidnapping, it is still an important role but less involved. If it is an overseas evacuation, the personnel person may be dealing, again, with hundreds of individuals, whole families who must be relocated to safe havens or brought home.

. **Medical & Relief Operations.** If the crisis is a natural disaster of major proportions, a liaison must be established with the Red Cross and other relief agencies. The subject of disaster operations is highly specialized, with its own rules and procedures. Will the National Guard be called out? What will the Red Cross provide? How can this be coordinated with the corporation's resources? The complexity of providing lifesaving services in a timely manner was never more apparent than with Hurricane Andrew, the Florida mega-disaster, when the sheer size of the disaster overwhelmed private and public sources.

A Crisis Management Plan has several major components: identification of possible crises, establishing measures to prevent those crises, and preparing for responses to crises. The prevention part of the Crisis Management Plan includes many, if not all, of the strategies which have been discussed in this book. Threat assessment, intelligence gathering, physical security, technical support, advances, detail operations, and executive briefings are all preventive strategies. However, the primary and overriding reason for a CMP is to establish procedures for responding to an emergency, so that is the function to which this chapter is devoted.

Establishing Policies

Once the CMT is chosen, it should meet on a regular basis with all members present, or if a member cannot be present, he or she should send a delegate to take his or her place. The first step is to establish corporate policies. This could, and should, include the corporation's policy toward, and assumption of responsibility for, any employee who is kidnapped. Will the corporation purchase kidnap insurance? If an employee is kidnapped overseas, in a country whose policy is not to negotiate with terrorists, what will the company do to effect the release of its employee? Will the company continue

to pay the kidnapped employee's salary to his family?

If an overseas evacuation of employees becomes necessary, will the corporation pay transportation costs for the evacuating employees? Will the company pay relocation costs? shipment of household goods? compensate employees for loss of household goods?

If there is an explosion which closes the plant, will there be any ongoing compensation to those employees who are now out of work? Will the company make money available for re-training of employees if a disaster closes the plant, forcing employees out of work? If there is a bomb threat, what are the guidelines and policies regarding evacuation of employees from the building?

These and many other questions must be examined and a corporate policy written that will cover these details. The CMP and its policies should be considered confidential, known to senior management, and shared with individuals outside the CMT and management on an as-needed basis only.

Team Participation

Each member of the CMT should be given areas of responsibility for writing procedures which use his, or her, expertise. Each member will be expected to amend and update his segment of the CMP. All members of the CMT, however, should be involved in the review and discussion of all CMP policies and procedures, so that they are thoroughly familiar with all components of the CMP. Once the simulation stage is reached (the point at which practice exercises are performed), each CMT member will be expected to participate. If a crisis should occur, the team will need to work well and smoothly together as a team, not as individuals.

Any reports generated by the CMT or by the secondary strata of support experts should be reviewed by all CMT members. One person should take on the responsibility of converting all reports, policies, and procedures into written form. This person will have his hands full and therefore should not have other CMT responsibilities. This can be an administrative assistant or secretary.

Crisis Management Center

A Crisis Management Center must be selected (similar to the command post employed by the protection agent). The Center should be staffed and supplied with necessary communications and work equipment. If a crisis occurs, this will be an operations center and must have adequate, protected, sophisticated communications equipment with back-up power. Computers, printers, copiers, fax machines, all of the equipment for the support of communications, must be included, as well as trusted support staff. Written briefings, public releases, internal communications, and reams of printed memorandums will be produced. It is a good idea to include at least one television set to monitor the media newscasts. (It is reported that during the Gulf War, most government agencies stayed tuned to CNN.) If it is a terrorist incident, there will be interviews granted to the media which would never be given to the corporation. Television may provide the best intelligence which will be received during the crisis. Recording equipment should be on hand and hooked into the telephone system to record calls to and from an adversary. Adequate and assured power for the Center is essential. Without power, the crisis will run wild, with no coordinated response.

Many of the same supplies used to stock a command post should be included in the Crisis Management Center, including a first aid kit, long telephone cords, extension cords, office supplies, and trash baskets. The Center must provide for bathroom facilities and should have water or beverages available.

The Center must be large enough to accommodate Center support staff and CMT members. Pressures will be great, tempers will be stretched, and cramped quarters will only add to the problems. Emergency equipment must be supplied, and security for the Center provided to ensure that it can operate without interruption or interference.

One person must be designated as having Crisis Management Center authority. This is the person who will run the Center and keep it running through thick and thin, and who will coordinate the logistics for everyone. Personnel to work the Center, shift schedules, and practical exercises must be selected. The Personnel/Human Relations designate on the CMT can be of great help in this regard, helping to select staff and providing telephone numbers and emergency codes. A routine must be established which could be used in an emergency to reach Center staff during off-hours, to call them in.

A second area, designated as a briefing room, should be chosen. In a crisis, the media will need a place to set up shop, probably with television cameras and lighting. They may also need desks and telephones in order to communicate to their newspapers, magazines, and television stations. A copy machine and fax machine would be helpful. The media need to get their job done, and it is best to facilitate this effort rather than trying to keep them out. The briefing room should not be located close to the Crisis Management Center, as it may interfere with the Center's operations.

During a crisis, a log should be kept, and it must be as detailed as possible. In the aftermath of the crisis, there is sure to be the possibility of litigation, and a log which details the actions of the corporation will be invaluable in demonstrating that the corporation fulfilled its obligations to the best of its ability. It will also be very useful in determining whether the CMP worked and where it should be modified. Were the CMP procedures adequate? Did communications function properly? Is additional Center staff recommended? Is additional training needed for staff, CMT members, or other employees? The log should be maintained in the Center during the crisis, where it can be added to on the spot and safeguarded.

CMT Activities

The functions of the CMT include:

Conducting an assessment of the nature and

degree of the threat to corporate interests (personnel, facilities, information and other assets).

.   Determining, based on this assessment, the vulnerability of company personnel, facilities, or assets to these threats.

.   Developing specific plans to safeguard personnel and property.

.   Developing job descriptions and specific procedures to be followed for several possible crisis situations.

.   Developing organizational structures within the company's functional areas to implement the CMP and support CMT member functions if they are indisposed and/or dealing with a crisis.

.   Communicating the contents of the CMP to employees.

.   Testing the plan on a regular basis to insure that it is feasible and realistic.

.   Maintaining key names, phone numbers, and whereabouts of employees, government agency contacts, and private organizations or individuals that the CMT should consider briefing or consulting with prior to, during, or directly after, an emergency situation.

Threat assessments and vulnerability surveys are a familiar topic, and need not be further addressed. Developing specific plans to safeguard personnel and property and developing job descriptions and specific procedures to be followed for several possible crisis situations entail a great deal of work. The CMT members must develop and write, or delegate to be developed, precise procedures to be followed in the event of the most probable crises. Once written, the procedures must be communicated to the employees and other individuals who will be involved. Then, simulation exercises should be conducted. A familiar simulation exercise is the bomb threat evacuation plan which every corporation conducts at regular intervals. In many communities,

the emergency response teams in the area conduct simulation exercises for, say, a plane crash at the airport with multiple victims.

Simulation exercises should be as serious and as realistic as possible. The CMT members are an integral part of the exercises, and it helps if senior management will agree to participate. The time and place of the exercise should be clearly understood and publicized. The exercise should be conducted as if it were real. In corporations that take their Crisis Management seriously, simulation exercises can involve almost the entire company, or a series of exercises can be held to involve only certain departments and staff. If it is not physically possible (or is too costly) to move people through the simulation, good results can be achieved by involving the CMT and the Crisis Center. Some work is being done with softwear computer programs that allow for simulation reproductions.

Whatever form the exercises take, it is important to review the results of the simulation exercises. They must be analyzed, and additions and revisions made to the plan. Any weaknesses revealed by the exercises should be dealt with, and new or amended procedures written.

Another very important component to the CMP is the "getting back to normal" plan. It is not useful to handle a crisis magnificently only to fail to take positive action to get the company and its personnel back to normal. Many plans fall apart at this stage. Let us take the example of a very successful corporation whose oil tanker goes aground and creates a major oil spill that pollutes a coastline. Obviously, the preventive sections of the CMP failed. Let us say that the corporation's CMP does provide adequate immediate response to the crisis; teams are set to work to clean up the spill and stabilize the environment. Now what? The corporation and its employees must also be stabilized. The employees must be made to feel that the corporation feels a moral responsibility and is fulfilling that duty. The public must be persuaded that the corporation is behaving with compassion and care. In other words, after the hurricane, or explosion, or meltdown, or strike, there is a clean-up and public relations process which is of equal importance.

Dealing with the Media

Earlier in this book, we discussed the media and the need to work with them, as opposed to working against them. This has never been more true than during a crisis. Whether it is a terrorist incident, fire, explosion, labor strike, poisoned products, or a kidnapping, the media will get the story. That's their job and their right. Therefore, the corporation has a responsibility to make sure the media gets the right story. Simply saying "no comment" won't prevent the press from talking to spectators and employees. The communications member of the CMT should and must be the official spokesperson for the corporation. Providing the media with a briefing room, a place to work, communications, and regular briefings will go a long way to getting the right story in print and on millions of television screens. The spokesperson should have an official alternate who remains in close and constant touch with him. The alternate may be needed if the spokesperson is unable to meet with the press or if there are two or more locations contained in the crisis. Because the spokesperson will undoubtedly end up on the television screen, it helps if that person is calm and cool under pressure, and presentable looking. The spokesperson should give the impression that he, or she, and the corporation have the situation under control, and are behaving responsibly and compassionately towards crisis victims.

Depending upon the extent and length of the crisis, the media will need a continuing flow of information and stories, which means lots of briefings. Briefings should be held at times that are useful to the media meeting their deadlines, deadlines which will differ for newspapers and for the television "6:00 news," or "10:00 news." All briefings should be carefully prepared, factual, and as complete as possible without giving out crucial information. Anything said by the spokesperson and subsequently printed or televised will reach the adversary. On the other hand, it must always be perceived that the corporation, through its spokesperson, is

communicating honestly and responsibly.

Some helpful hints for the spokesperson are: never say "no comment"; if you don't have an answer or some facts, say so and offer to get the information; if certain information must be withheld (as in hostage negotiations) say something like "I'm sorry, I can't comment on that at this time"; and don't count on being able to say "this is off the record" unless you absolutely trust the media person. Be courteous and responsive. Dodging telephone calls from the media is as bad as saying "no comment."

And what do these concerns about company spokespersons dealing with the media have to do with the protection agent? The "company" may be a family, and the protection agent may end up, willy-nilly, as the spokesperson. And/or, in a small company, the executive protection agent may be the person most familiar with the process. The agent knows the threat--the incident--the response--and understands what needs to be done to bring a successful conclusion to the crisis.

RESOURCES

For the individual who inherits the responsibility of heading up, or participating in, a Crisis Management Team, there is help available.

There are a number of books on the subject. Several are listed with the American Society for Industry Security (ASIS) catalog and can be ordered by telephone (703) 519-6200. A handy, easy-to-read little book is *The Handbook for Effective Emergency and Crisis Management*, by Mayer Nudell and Norman Antokol, published by Lexington Books.

There are federal agencies, chief among them the Federal Emergency Management Agency (FEMA) in Washington, DC, (202) 646-2500, and the State Department, (202) 647-4000. There are private sources, almost all of which will be listed with the American Society for Industrial Security (ASIS), (703) 518-1471, and American Red Cross, (202) 737-8300. There are also a number of organizations and consultants who specialize in crisis management.

It is often difficult to visualize an actual plan. No matter how much information one has, the actual plan remains a mystery. In the Appendix can be found a model corporate Crisis Management Plan dealing with an overseas evacuation plan. This model plan is a sample security evacuation plan which could be developed by the agent to be used for evacuating a large group of personnel from a politically unstable country. While not complete, it covers many of the planning priorities that the protection specialist should be prepared to help manage.

While all crises have some effect on a protectee, the crisis situations more commonly dealt with by the executive protection agent are: abduction (kidnapping); hostage taking (either on the ground or in the air); bomb threats and explosions; and overseas evacuation either for security or medical reasons. It is less common for an American executive to be assassinated or to become embattled in a direct attack either on his home or office. While these less common contingencies should be dealt with in the Crisis Management Plan, they are not addressed in this chapter.

Victims of a hostage-taking, kidnapping, or hijacking are probably not greatly concerned about the terminology which defines their situation. For our purposes, however, there should be a distinction made between these three situations, because there are some differences in how to avoid them, in the probable length of detainment, and in the negotiations related to each of the three types of incidents.

A hostage-taking can be planned or accidental; for example, a bank robber who hears the police sirens approaching and decides to barricade himself inside the bank with the employees and customers, or the gunmen inside a 7-Eleven holding customers and cashier at gun point. These hostages were not targeted; they simply were in the right place at the wrong time. Avoiding these incidents is not a matter of planned prevention. What is important is correctly reacting to them. An incident of this nature is usually short-term and is often (but not always) successfully concluded without harm to the hostages.

We are all familiar with another form of hostage-taking, the taking of the American Embassy in Teheran and the kidnapping of the various westerners in Beirut. These hostage incidents are quite different, primarily because of the very long incarceration of the hostages. The motivation behind these incidents differs from the short-term, spur-of-the-moment hostage-taking, and the negotiations for the release of the hostages operate at a completely different level, often becoming extremely complex with governments acting as intermediaries.

While the airline targeted for a hijacking is a deliberate decision, hijackings are planned incidents of generally indiscriminate nature. This means that a specific airplane is hijacked without regard to who is aboard; it is the hijacking incident, itself, which is of importance to the hijackers. It is conceivable that a plane could be hijacked specifically because of the presence aboard of someone(s) highly desirable to the hostage-takers. There are always exceptions, as with the famous (targeted) hijacking of the primarily Israeli passengers which ended in Entebbe Airport. Hijackings are generally short-term, lasting no more than a few days, although in at least one publicized incident passengers were removed from the hijacked plane and incarcerated in secret places. While a specific hijacking is not preventable, there are measures which can be taken to minimize, overall, one's chances of being hijacked.

A kidnapping is usually specific to a particular person. The kidnap target may be rich, famous, influential, conspicuous, or of media value. A kidnap incident can be of long or short-term duration, depending upon the reasons for having kidnapped the victim. Much of the material contained within this book is directed toward preventing such a kidnapping.

There are, of course, numerous incidents of the kidnapping of innocent people, usually women, who are often never heard from again or whose bodies sometimes are found in ditches and fields. These gruesome incidents are not specifically dealt with in this section of the book. Nor have we addressed the family-related hostage incidents, where an emotionally charged husband holds wife and children hostage at gun point.

HIJACKING

The probability of a client becoming involved in a hijacking is, currently, very low. At one time, hijackings were a favorite terrorist tool. As long as there were countries friendly to terrorists, a hijacking could be carried out with relatively low risk, and the access to media exposure for highlighting terrorist causes was intoxicating. Hijacking has, in the past few years, declined. The PLO has tried to clean up its image and has ousted some of its more radical splinter groups. The PLO and other Palestinian groups are making a determined effort to reach some kind of peace accord with Israel. Most traditional state sponsors of terrorism, including the U.S.S.R., Libya, Syria, and Iran, no longer see the advantages of supporting the PLO and other Islamic fundamentalist groups, but instead are seeking to normalize relations with the United States. As a result, sponsors and former sponsors tend to exert their influence by keeping violent incidents in check. Terrorist incidents which affect large numbers of innocent people are now largely out of favor, with the exception of the insurgency areas--Bosnia, Kosovo, East Timor, Congo, etc. Upgraded airline security has just about put the casual domestic hijacker out of business--no more trips to Cuba.

There is, of course, no guarantee that hijacking will become a permanent thing of the past, any more than thinking terrorism is going to decline. There is too much volatility in the world. Preventive measures against hijacking are still a prudent measure and should be part of a Crisis Management Plan.

Pre-Departure Preparation

If the protection agent has done his and her job well, the client may never have to face a hostage or kidnap situation. But, it is only wise to be prepared for all contingencies. Evasion and avoidance are the first line of defense, and the second line of defense is the ability to survive a hostage

incident. A hostage-taking could involve the client, the client's family, or a single member of the family, and could include the protection agent. Knowing what to do and how to react could well save a life, perhaps your own.

These preventive measures have been touched on in an earlier chapter, but it is sufficiently important to bear repeating. One does not have to be scheduled to spend six months on assignment in Beirut to be motivated to take the steps necessary to protect families and businesses. Because the hostage incident can be purely accidental and happen to anyone at any time, there are some prudent preparations which should be made in advance, by your client.

The basics of preparation should include a current will, lodged in a place that will be accessible to family and attorney, not hidden away in a secret deposit box. Hopefully, the client has established a joint checking account with his spouse, with enough money to pay expenses for the family over a certain period. If the client does not have a business manager or accountant who pays his bills, then a schedule of payments for regular expenses should be available.

Other arrangements should include a power of attorney for a spouse or trusted associate to deal with business matters. All important papers--deeds, insurance, will, mortgages, list of stocks and bonds, tax records, etc.--should be kept in a safety deposit box with copies given to an executor and spouse. A guardian should be named for the children, in the event of both spouses being captured or killed.

The client and each member of the client's family should have medical and dental records, with a list of prescribed medications, stored in a safe place. A personal file should contain photographs, updated often (every six months for children), fingerprints, biographies, distinguishing marks, medical and dental records. (See Appendix for model Protectee Profile.)

If the client believes there is a genuine risk of kidnap or hostage-taking, a frank discussion should be held with the members of the family and a plan developed to deal with this contingency. Certainly, the family should be provided with information as to avoidance procedures and children briefed on self-protection measures. Survival techniques should be discussed in a positive manner. The family is a team and, in an emergency, must be mutually supportive while also maintaining a degree of self-sufficiency. If the client is kidnapped or taken hostage, his chances for survival will be greatly enhanced if he has a certain peace of mind about his family.

Similar plans should be in place within the client's business. If the client is a key executive in a major corporation, his loss could immobilize the company and cause the stock to be drastically devalued. Every company should have a crisis management plan in its files, updated regularly. Key man insurance is an excellent hedge against loss of a key executive due to accident, health, or a terrorist/criminal incident. The protectee should be given a security briefing prior to departure, using information on the host country being visited.

Hijack Avoidance

The rash of airplane hijackings in the mid-1980's represented something of a benchmark. There were more of them; they were widely publicized; and they became more violent, with an American serviceman deliberately killed in one incident. Simultaneously, there were bloody incidents which took place inside airports. These incidents produced a body of information to help travelers avoid and survive similar incidents.

Every country has its national and religious holidays, and some areas of the world have a tremendous amount of emotional energy attached to their special, or significant, days. The Middle East, which has spawned much of the terrorist violence, celebrates Ramadan, a 30-day religious holiday, during which time food may not be taken during the daylight hours. It is a highly charged, emotional, stressful period and should be avoided whenever possible. The various Palestinian groups have days of commemoration, such as the PLO's Black September.

A call to the State Department will give valuable advice on these times-to-be-avoided. The State Department can also provide up-to-date information on trouble spots around the world and their current status. At the time of publication of this book, there is a Traveler's Hotline at the State Department (202) 647-5225.

There is some disagreement among the experts as to which airlines are safest. There was a time when U.S. airline carriers were considered safer than many others. This is no longer necessarily the case, as since 1986, Americans have been targeted for hostage-taking incidents. Many experts advise flying the more neutral carriers of European airlines (Swissair, Scandinavian Airlines). However, there is still a case to be made for flying on U.S. airlines, as their security is consistently more thorough. Also, in an international incident, with a hijacking that crosses many national boundaries, and where there is no clear authority for intervention, the United States may feel a clearer authority to extricate its nationals from a hijacked U.S. airplane. If a TWA airliner departs from Rome airport, is taken over by terrorists in the air over Greece, and lands at Beirut, which country has the international authority to negotiate or, in a final extremity, storm the airplane and release the passengers?

It is widely reported that El Al, the Israeli carrier, employs the most stringent (and successful) security procedures of any airline. The trade-off is the amount of time it takes to go through the security procedures and the fact that El Al must surely be the most desirable airline target for a hijacking.

A fair modus operandi has emerged which shows that most hijackings take place aboard smaller airliners (easier to control the smaller number of passengers in the limited space), during daylight hours, and involve schedules which contain two or more stops. Therefore, whenever possible, travel should be non-stop, on a large, wide-bodied plane.

First-class, while more comfortable, should be avoided. The terrorists like to operate from first-class, since it accesses both the cockpit and the main exits.

It is also more comfortable for them. First-class passengers may, therefore, attract too much attention to themselves and will almost certainly be uprooted and sent back to tourist class, without seats of their own.

In high-risk areas, or for that matter in traveling to all overseas locations, it may be advisable for government and military personnel to travel with a plain blue tourist passport. In most hijackings, the passports are collected and the official passport holders are singled out. A copy should be made of the passport number, date of issue, place where it was issued, and the copy placed somewhere other than a wallet or handbag (as these will undoubtedly be taken away.) There are now some products on the market which offer inconspicuous hiding places on your body, such as an underarm, or inner thigh, pouch. These items are hard to detect unless the wearer is stripped.

Liquor, girlie magazines, religious tracts, anti-Communist literature, and books on the Arab-Israeli controversy should be left at home. Also to be left at home or stowed in the checked baggage are identification cards for organizations which might be considered politically or morally controversial or threatening, including record of military or law enforcement service. Class rings and jewelry can also identify a military or religious background. Included as "dead giveaways" are business cards, company letterhead stationery, and business papers, all of which should be in the checked luggage. Briefcases will probably be appropriated along with money and valuables. Any individual identified as an executive of a widely known international corporation may be considered a valuable hostage prize.

Hijackers may be religiously motivated, but they also consider it perfectly appropriate to rob the passengers of money, jewelry, and valuables. It has been reported that the loot from one widely publicized airplane hijacking was $ 250,000 from the passengers. Flashy jewelry will also mark the passenger as someone who might have kidnap value. Anything that calls attention to an individual can be dangerous in a hostage-taking incident. A minimum

of cash should be carried, with the balance in travelers checks. Credit cards should also be kept to a minimum, with one copy of the card numbers left at home and another checked in the cargo baggage.

The traveler should carry with him, preferably in a coat pocket, a minimum ten-day supply of any prescription and/or medicines necessary to his health. Clothes should be comfortable, loose fitting, and conservative, with nothing that draws attention. If traveling with children, any necessary supplies for several days survival should be hand-carried aboard.

There are pros and cons as to the safest airplane seat location. One theory reasons that, since terrorists are more apt to mistreat those passengers on the aisle, it is best to request a seat next to a window. On the other hand, if there is a fire, or a chance to escape, one may be better off sitting on the aisle and as close to an exit as possible. One solution is for the men to take the window seats and leave women and children in the aisle seats, theorizing that the terrorists will not be as likely to mistreat them.

Airports are no longer safe, benign havens. A number of bloody terrorist incidents have taken place there. They have also become crime-centered, particularly in the fringe areas, which include parking garages and lots, and airport hotels. Rapes, muggings, assaults, and thefts have been reported in broad daylight.

Airports worldwide have beefed up their security, but extreme caution should be exercised. Many airports now limit access by denying entrance to all but ticket holders. Certainly, outside the United States, it is prudent to bid farewell to family and friends at home or in the car rather than in the airport.

It is desirable to spend as little time as possible in the airport, particularly within the public access areas. One should always call ahead to determine if there will be flight delays. Tickets should be purchased in advance to cut down on the time spent in the check-in lines. Many travel services can now provide seat selection and boarding passes in advance, along with the tickets. If several members of a family are checking in at the same time, one person should stand in line to handle all the tickets. Baggage for international travel will probably not be accepted for curbside check-in, but will be required to accompany the traveler to check-in.

One should proceed as rapidly as possibly through the security checks and wait in as private an area as is available. The airline private clubs are excellent for this purpose and are very comfortable. Many airline clubs will handle the check-in procedures for members.

In any event, it is prudent to avoid crowds. If you must wait in a public area, stay on the fringes and determine in advance a safe retreat. Look around and spot the emergency exits, as well as any convenient hiding places. It is also wise to avoid those large expanses of glass found in terminals. A bomb blast would create shrapnel of the glass. Any unattended luggage should be viewed with suspicion and, if it remains for long, should be reported to the airport security people. Trash containers seem to be attractive bomb receptacles as well.

If there is an alert, one should get away quickly; have a plan. And remember that, particularly with bombing incidents, there is always the likelihood of a second bomb in a different location or in the same spot, programmed to go off at a later time.

Once inside the airplane, look around at your fellow passengers. Prior to almost every hijacking incident, someone(s) noticed the hijackers (because of their agitation), but either thought that these people were simply nervous travelers or they were too embarrassed to report the suspects to the authorities. One's intuition, and certainly one's trained observational talents, can usually be trusted. Check underneath your seat and in the overhead compartment, as well as the seat pocket in front of you. Any suspicious items should be reported. Hopefully, the airline crew will check the toilets, but since a number of terrorist takeovers have been helped along with a gun hidden in the toilet, it might give you a feeling of comfort to take a quiet look

inside the toilets. Lift the lids, check underneath, look to see if anything looks as if it doesn't belong there.

Dealing with the Crisis

In all likelihood, if a hijacking involving a corporate executive were to occur, the executive's corporation will have no direct role in negotiating with the hijackers. It is extremely unlikely that a terrorist or criminal would hijack a full load of passengers merely to acquire one individual; it would be easier to kidnap him. Therefore, the hijack negotiations will probably be handled at an international level, involving the air carrier's home country, the country within whose air space the hijacking occurred, and the country which provides (willingly or unwillingly) a landing spot for the hijacked air craft. The officials of the air carrier will have an involvement as well.

For the hijacked protectee, it will be a matter of survival (more on this later). For the protectee's corporation, there will be operational problems caused by the taking of the executive. The Crisis Management Plan (CMP) should outline procedures to be followed as a result of a hijacking.

The Crisis Management Center (Center) should be activated and staffed. The Crisis Management Team (CMT) will assemble and begin to implement CMP strategies. Legal counsel will advise on the international laws. The financial advisor and human relations advisor must contact the hijacked executive's family and provide advice and support. As the drama plays out, the executive's wife may wish to fly to the overseas area to be on hand for a possible release. Public relations must prepare to deal with the media, making certain that the hijacked executive is portrayed as a compassionate and responsible person with a family. The internal affairs advisor will prepare briefings and bulletins for internal consumption to demonstrate to all employees management's concern and care. Liaison must be established with government authorities at the highest level, to obtain current situational information and to offer support at a private level. The hijacked executive's job responsibilities must be delegated to other management officials.

There must be a provision in the CMP for eventual release of the hijacked individual and the subsequent support effort. Has the executive been injured? Does he have a medical problem? Must arrangements be made to fly him back to the United States? Will the corporate jet, a charter, or a regularly scheduled airline be used? Some legalities will need to be dealt with; he will probably not simply be allowed to walk off the hijacked plane and immediately fly back to the States. Will financial assistance be needed? Will his family wish to fly to his release point and accompany him either to the hospital or a debriefing center, and return home with him? A company spokesperson may need to be on the spot to control any public appearances of the executive or his family. Emotional counseling should be provided for the executive and his family as quickly as possible, to deal with post-incident trauma. The sooner the executive can be brought back to normal, the sooner the company can effect its own recovery.

There may be residual legal and financial matters to be dealt with. If the executive was posted overseas without proper security briefing, he may feel that the corporation was partially at fault and, hence, that the corporation carries some liability. On the other hand, if the CMP has worked properly, and both preventive and reactive procedures were followed, the company's liability exposure will be greatly reduced.

KIDNAPPING

Kidnappings are carried out by criminals and by terrorists. There are some differences between the two. The criminal kidnapping is almost entirely driven by a demand for ransom money, and the entire incident is apt to be short in duration. Notification of the kidnapping and demands are made, usually, very quickly; in fact, demands for ransom may require that the money be delivered within 48 hours. Whether ransom is paid or not, the kidnap victim may not survive.

Terrorist kidnappings, on the other hand, may be driven by political motives or a combination of political and monetary motives. Demands may include ransom money or/and other stipulations such as release of political prisoners or some form of media notoriety. Terrorist kidnappings for monetary reasons are usually successfully negotiated and the prisoner is released after payment of ransom, although the duration of the incident may be considerably longer than the criminal kidnapping incident. Terrorist kidnappings for political reasons may end with the victim dead or held for a very long duration, thus becoming a hostage situation.

Legal Issues

There are some complicated potential legal liabilities involved with kidnapping and hostage taking. Although the legal code is not entirely specific, some aspects exist within the common law general definitions. The corporation has a duty to warn employees of dangers in the workplace and to take reasonable steps to protect its employees, even if the employees have willingly agreed to work in potentially dangerous circumstances. The duty to protect employees kidnapped in a foreign country may extend to a responsibility to make reasonable efforts to recover the victim. The next part is tricky. The corporation may fall under the "good samaritan" proviso if it undertakes to recover the victim, but in doing so behaves negligently and thereby contributes to death, injury, or extended incarceration of the victim. As an example, if the corporation were to enter into negotiations with the kidnappers, agree to pay ransom money, and then renege on the payment, with the result of the victim being killed, there might be a liability involved for wrongful death.

The employee, on the other hand, must take reasonable measures to protect himself, and if he contributes to the negligence, it may free the corporation from liability. For example, during negotiations the victim attempts to escape, is caught, and killed; this action on the part of the victim might be viewed as contributory negligence.

If the kidnapping happens in a foreign

country, the laws of that country must also be considered. Some countries prohibit negotiations with terrorists and may forbid the payment of ransom money. If these laws are contravened, the corporation may be fined or subject to seizure.

Crisis Management Plan Considerations

The Crisis Management Plan must take into account all of the legal aspects, just as it must include all preventive measures. The preventive measures include all of the material in this book! The CMP should include the elements of threat assessment, vulnerability surveys, intelligence gathering, executive protection, enhanced and upgraded security measures, and executive briefings. These preventive measures may succeed in averting a kidnapping and will go a long way to limiting the liability of the corporation should an incident occur.

Other CMP considerations should include the subject of ransom money. Is there a written corporate policy, sanctioned by at least the Board of Directors, which will permit negotiations with the kidnappers and the payment of ransom money? Is there a limit to the amount of ransom money which the corporation will pay? How will the ransom money be assembled in cash, quickly? Is there a written policy regarding the purchase of kidnap insurance? Were there any people (bodyguards, drivers) injured or killed in the incident, and what are the corporation's liabilities regarding these people? Have procedures been set in place to provide immediate notification of the police or host government and of family members? Should professional negotiators be brought in at corporate expense to deal with the kidnappers, or will this be handled internally? Has a spokesperson been assigned to the family to handle communications? All of these questions, and many more, must be answered in advance and incorporated within the CMP.

Response

Most extortion messages are received by telephone. The message may be given to the kidnapped individual's family or to the office. All such messages should be treated as legitimate and there should be a procedure for taking such a message. These procedures should be included in the CMP. Simulation exercises should be regularly practiced, not only among the CMT members but should also include telephone personnel, since the caller may wish to speak to the first person who answers the phone.

Whoever takes the call should remain calm, make notes of the entire conversation, and try to obtain as many details as possible. The caller should be dealt with courteously and patiently, all the time explaining that while she/he does not have the authority to meet the caller's demands, these demands will be given the most serious consideration. The caller may demand immediate compliance to demands, and the caller must patiently and calmly explain why this is not possible, but assure the caller that every effort will be made to comply. All instructions given by the caller should be repeated for accuracy, and to assure the caller that his demands are being taken seriously.

An attempt should be made to verify that an abduction has actually taken place by asking to speak with the victim. If the abductor refuses, a request should be made for details about the victim which would establish that the kidnapping is real. Every effort must be made to make certain that ongoing communication will take place. A code word should be suggested that will be used by the kidnapper in all communications to prevent complications by copycat callers.

Since it is difficult to remember everything under stress, an Extortion Demand Telephone Checklist should be developed and made available to telephone personnel and any others (including family members) who might receive an extortion call.

An Extortion Call Checklist is included at the end of this chapter.

Although it is an old trick, the caller on an extortion call should be kept on the line as long as possible. If there is a recording device available, it should be used to record the call (if legal), since all details will be important. There is now technology available that will show the caller's telephone number; it is recommended for standard operating use.

The Crisis Management Team must be immediately notified. First priority must be given to verifying that the individual in question has actually been kidnapped and that the call is not a hoax. Once the kidnapping has been verified, the Crisis Management Plan must be put into effect. The police authorities must be notified, although the kidnappers may state that the victim will be killed if the authorities are notified. There really are no good choices. Without the involvement of the authorities, the chances of recovering the victim are slight, and any ransom insurance may be invalidated. If the incident has occurred overseas, the U.S. embassy must be contacted immediately; the embassy will assist in contacting the host country government authorities.

The family must be notified and given support. A spokesperson should be assigned to the family to handle communications with the media, although every effort must be made to keep the kidnap incident confidential and under cover. The involvement of the media will greatly complicate recovery efforts. A company representative should be assigned to the family to handle any communications from the kidnappers; the police will probably also have someone stationed with the family to provide security and liaison with the kidnappers. Medical assistance may be required, as well as counseling. Financial support will be needed, and good communications between the family and the corporation must be established. The family must be made to feel that the corporation shares their concerns and is making every effort to gain the release of the victim. If the incident has occurred overseas, the family will feel particularly isolated and helpless, since the local government and police may seem ineffective to deal with the crisis.

A negotiating team must be designated. If the incident has occurred overseas or in a subsidiary location, the negotiating team may be required to leave immediately for the site, along with a company representative of senior authority capable of making decisions at the highest level. Communications must be set up between the negotiating team, field representative, and corporate headquarters. If a terrorist group is involved, someone must collect intelligence. What is the history and modus operandi of the group? Have they kidnapped before? What were the results? Can they be bargained with? What have they demanded in the past? A ransom policy should already have been established which outlines the limits of ransom participation. How much ransom is the company prepared to pay? Trying to "wing it" with a negotiation stance will be costly, either in terms of money or lives. Kidnappers almost invariably ask for more money than they are willing to settle for.

If the incident is in an overseas country, the negotiations may be long and protracted. Terrorist groups tend to expect agonizingly long negotiations and, if an agreement is reached too quickly, they may feel that they demanded too little, whereupon the demands are increased. Pressure from the victim's family to gain an early release will complicate matters.

If the kidnapping is in the United States, the negotiations will probably be of shorter duration and will become increasingly tense. Whereas the terrorist has a safe haven and is often protected by others in his environment, domestic kidnappers rarely have these advantages. They are likely to become increasingly nervous about having a live victim on their hands. Negotiations must, therefore, insist upon verification of the fact that the victim is alive.

Security is an issue for everyone. The negotiators, the family, company representatives, and employees must all be given additional protection. If the kidnappers become frustrated, feel they have been mislead, or simply wish to up the ante, they may decide to abduct additional hostages.

Considerable thought must be given as to the selection of the person or persons who will deliver the ransom money. If the kidnappers have specified small bills, the entire amount could be extremely heavy and bulky. Simply counting and packaging the money may require a team of people. The police may wish to either mark some of the bills or record them. If time permits, photocopying some of the bills may be very useful. There will be stress, anxiety, and always the potential of danger in delivering the money. Delivery may be attempted and fail, only to have the kidnappers re-contact with new delivery instructions. If acceptable to the kidnappers, it is generally safer to have two people involved in the ransom delivery process.

Many CMPs include the option of mounting a rescue effort to retrieve the victim. It may be an option, but it is generally an unrealistic and dangerous one. In the case of a domestic kidnapping, if all hope is lost and it appears that the victim will, indeed, be killed, the police may themselves use this last resort of attempting a rescue operation. Rescues have been "successfully" carried out against hijackers, meaning that the rescue ended the incident. But, hostages have died along with the hijackers. Attempting to rescue hostages from a foreign country is well nigh impossible, although there are companies which specialize in extraction operations.

The Crisis Management Plan should provide for post-incident operations. If the negotiations are successful and the victim is retrieved, he and his family must be provided with much the same support provided to hijack victims, as outlined earlier in this chapter. The CMP should be reviewed in detail to determine if it worked, and what changes and improvements should be made. Post-incident communications internally with employees should be maintained until normalcy is regained.

Ransom and Kidnap Insurance

The decision as to whether the corporation will pay ransom must be reached by top management, the Board of Directors, and possibly a representative of the shareholders. When push comes to shove, there are few corporations with a no-ransom policy. When Mr. CEO of Corporation ABC is kidnapped, anywhere in the world, it is difficult to imagine that ABC Corporation is going to say "no" to the kidnappers. Humanitarian and economic reasons will prevail. Mr. CEO may be worth three to ten times the amount of his ransom money to the corporation, and the shareholders would have a reason to question why the corporation failed to rescue the man. In addition, the black image it would create with family, employees, and the public would probably deal the corporation a killer blow.

The reasoning behind a no-ransom policy, of course, is that paying ransom rewards the deed and encourages more kidnappings. This is true, and it is the reason why the most in-depth preventive measures must be taken to deter kidnappings and to make the effort of kidnapping someone too costly to the kidnappers.

The hostage taking may have nothing to do with money. Many hostages have been taken for political reasons, and conditions for release have been predicated upon political considerations such as release of political prisoners or distributions of food to the poor. On the other hand, hostage taking borders closely upon kidnapping for money. Many terrorist organizations have financed their operations by robbing banks and kidnappings for ransom. In the final analysis, it doesn't matter; the company must decide if it is going to provide ransom money, and purchase kidnap insurance. Considerations include the cost of insurance premiums which can be quite high, the degree of potential risk, and the ability of the corporation to self finance the ransom. This is another aspect of risk management. If the potential risk seems low, if prudent preventive measures are employed, and if the corporation believes that it could survive the financial burden of paying ransom, a decision may be made not to purchase kidnap insurance. There is one more consideration. If the corporation chooses to self finance the ransom, can the ransom money be acquired in cash, within 48 hours, as is within the norm of kidnapper demands?

The Crisis Management Plan must examine the issue of kidnap and ransom insurance. Will the corporation provide kidnap insurance for its key executives, and for how many executives? It is a complicated issue. Many countries, including the United States, have a policy of not providing ransom money for hostages. Some countries even forbid the payment of ransom from companies or individuals for hostages. The insurance, itself, comes with disclaimers and provisions which must be met before ransom is paid.

There are conditions attached to kidnap insurance, just as there are with any insurance, which are sometimes referred to as limiting. Those conditions may define what responsibilities the insured corporation has in a kidnap situation and what actions the corporation must undertake in order to validate the payment of kidnap (ransom) money by the insurance company. The insured corporation may have to agree to certain stipulations: a valid Crisis Management Plan; agreement to work with authorities; agreement to keep confidential the issue of kidnap insurance; agreement for the insurance company to participate in the negotiations for ransom; independent investigation on the part of the insurance company to determine whether fraud was involved; and assistance in the recovery of the ransom money and prosecution of the wrongdoers.

Legal and financial counsel are needed by the corporation to make certain that all stipulations and conditions can, and are, being met.

The purchase of kidnap insurance should always be kept confidential. Adversaries who look at possible kidnap victims may consider those who have kidnap insurance to be prime assets.

HOSTAGE TAKING

Hostage takers can be professional criminals, terrorists, mentally disturbed or emotionally charged individuals. Law enforcement officials generally regard the criminal as easier to deal with than either the terrorist or the emotionally disturbed hostage taker. The criminal does not wish to die, has nothing to gain by harming the hostages, and can genuinely be negotiated with, as he will be bargaining either for his own safety or a less stringent charge. In short, he knows the rules and how the game is played. The emotionally disturbed are very difficult to negotiate

with, since logic may play no part in the incident.

Terrorists are generally well organized, well funded, may hold their hostages in areas friendly to their cause, and can be extremely difficult to negotiate with, because often there is no immediate danger to, or pressure on, the terrorist group. They can afford to hold out indefinitely and negotiate on their terms. If their demands include the release of political prisoners or fellow terrorists, the negotiators may not be able to meet their demands, thus creating an impasse.

To simplify the issue, hostage taking in the context of executive protection can be generally divided into three situations: an accidental hostage taking, generally a criminal incident; a holding of employees hostage within the corporation by a disgruntled employee or former employee; and a planned hostage taking, primarily for political purposes, by terrorists. There have been other hostage taking incidents, with diplomats kept hostage in an embassy and much subsequent public negotiating; but these incidents are few in nature.

The unplanned, accidental hostage incident can happen to anyone, and there are few direct preventive measures other than to avoid suspicious neighborhoods at any time and to practice all of the sound general preventive measures. These are the events where a would-be bank robber is trapped inside the bank and takes hostages. Or, you stop one night for cigarettes at a 7-Eleven store and find a robbery in progress which aborts with hostage taking. Generally, these incidents are of short duration and are non-deadly to the hostages. Negotiations for the release of the hostages will usually be carried out by the law enforcement authorities.

The taking of hostages by an employee or ex-employee within the corporation is an increasing problem. Unfortunately, when an employee turns on his fellow workers and supervisors, he usually attacks and kills them. There have been increasing numbers of these incidents. Preventive measures include: more background checks on new employees; recognition of potential violence and dangerousness in employees; tight control of employee job terminations and termination interviews; better visitor access control; and good physical security measures. Negotiations for the release of the hostages may be a joint effort of the law enforcement authorities and the corporation.

The kidnapping and holding of political hostages, primarily overseas, has been until recently the most feared hostage incident. There have many such incidents and they have been devastating. Many hostages were killed, and almost all were held for long periods of time, even years. With the release of the Lebanese hostages, the era of hostage taking seems to have abated for the moment. However, it is always a real and imminent danger. If the incident occurs in a country which refuses to negotiate with terrorists, the negotiations may be the responsibility of the corporation. Although the U.S. government may provide advice and support, it will not negotiate with terrorists (at least openly). Negotiations often involve consultants who are experts in negotiations and could include the involvement of neutral governments.

Hostage Negotiations

The primary goal of hostage negotiations is the safe release of the hostages, and the secondary goal is the safe capture of the hostage taker(s). Negotiations are tedious, stressful, and require great skill. A hostage situation is not the time or place for amateurs. There are police negotiating teams and private firms which specialize in negotiating. In a protracted hostage situation, two or more negotiators will be needed to spell each other. If one negotiator fails to make progress with the hostage taker(s), a fresh negotiator may be able to achieve results.

The negotiator must have a calm, reassuring, trustworthy personality and be willing to listen patiently, without making judgmental comments. A negotiator must establish a rapport with the hostage taker, and do so as rapidly as possible so that they can reach a mutual conclusion to end the stalemate. Once the rapport is established, the negotiators must be the official communicators with the hostage takers.

There is general agreement that hostage takers fall into three groups: terrorist, criminal, and unstable personality. Going a bit further, the personalities of the hostage takers, regardless of which grouping they fall into, will differ; therefore, their responses to negotiations will differ. A skilled negotiator must pick up on personality clues. The hostage taker may say one thing and mean another; i.e., he says he hates the world, but secretly he craves attention which may be fulfilled with media attention. The hostage taker may vacillate from calm to emotional madness within minutes. He may be emotional and responsive to sympathy, or he may be a cold-blooded individual who wishes only to establish his dominance over others. The negotiator must be prepared to deal with all personalities and to establish meaningful communication.

Negotiating does not mean giving in. In fact, the most successful negotiations are conducted with ground rules. The hostage takers must be made aware that they are not going to be given everything they ask for. In spite of what they may say, most hostage takers wish to live and they realize that, if they kill their hostages, their chances for continuing to live become very small. It should be noted that, in international terrorist/hostage situations, the hostage takers have demonstrated greater negotiating expertise than the law enforcement teams.

In an impromptu hostage incident, where hostages and hostage taker(s) are barricaded in a building, the hostage taker and his hostages are contained in a confined space. As time goes by, the hostage taker may be induced to release some of his hostages, particularly women and children, since he will realize the difficulties of keeping them prisoner. The larger the number of hostages the more noise, illness, dirt, garbage, stench, and other unpleasant circumstances. Many things begin to be negotiable-- food, drinks, blankets, and other creature comforts. Negotiations sometimes make possible the release of hostages who are sworn to carry the hostage taker's message to the media. There should always be some trade-offs when demands are made to make it clear to the hostage taker that, while he may control the hostages, the authorities control him and the overall situation.

There are concessions which should not be made. Weapons should not be provided the hostage takers; nor should additional hostages be provided. Drugs and alcohol should not be provided, as these will surely escalate the situation. When demands are met, such as providing cigarettes or food, these should be provided sparingly, so that the hostage taker is continually dependent upon the negotiators.

Deadlines are difficult. If at all possible, the negotiators should try to avoid having deadlines imposed. If there is a deadline, an effort should be made to provide some token response that avoids the consequences of a missed deadline. Maintaining constant communication and not allowing the hostage taker to retreat into silence is helpful in easing through deadlines.

Generally speaking, time is on the side of the negotiators. As time goes by, and it becomes apparent that the hostage taker(s) cannot simply walk away or escape, and if the negotiator has succeeded in convincing the hostage taker that he will be dealt with fairly, the end may be in sight. Weariness and boredom make it desirable to simply end the affair.

If the hostage situation is in another country, the negotiators should be extremely conversant with the local language or the language of the hostage takers if they are from another country. Interpreters, alone, simply can't perform the job of negotiating.

In kidnap or overseas hostage situations, the hostage's family should be sequestered, if possible, in another location. If the hostage takers are able to contact the family, they may make separate, or higher, demands upon the family, which could derail the negotiator's position.

Violent Employees

One of the more prominent contingencies which should be covered is that of violent employees in the workplace. There have been numerous incidents in which disaffected employees have shot and killed fellow workers and supervisors. There have been fewer incidents of these workers holding fellow employees as hostages. Because of the importance of this subject, a chapter has been devoted to it.

BOMBS AND BOMB THREATS

Bomb threats have become something of a way of life for many businesses, and while it is calculated that between 90% and 99% of all bomb threats are hoaxes, even a one percent success rate is potentially devastating to those individuals and businesses who are attacked. The United States has been fortunate in that it has not sustained the number of indiscriminate bombings which occur on a regular basis in other countries. England has been targeted for these attacks by the IRA, with death and destruction to those unfortunate individuals who just happened to be in a place at the wrong time. In this country, the preponderance of bomb attacks are planned, targeted, and often warned of in advance, making it easier to prevent the kind of terrible injuries suffered by indiscriminate attacks.

Exceptions, of course, are the bombings of the World Trade Center and the Oklahoma City federal building. The February 1993 bombing of the New York City World Trade Center contained no warning, and it was a *big* bomb. While the damage was extremely severe to the building, a relatively few number of people were killed, although over 1,000 were injured. The Oklahoma City bombing also was conducted with no warning, and the death toll was horrible. In the aftermath of these incidents, corporate Crisis Management Teams became very busy structuring Crisis Management Plans to deal with the devastating effects of a major bomb incident. The estimates of damages and costs to the businesses lodged in the World Trade Center alone are in the multi-millions of dollars, possibly a *billion* dollars.

The World Trade Center is a nightmare (but textbook) example of the need for a Crisis Management Plan. It is not known what procedures were in place within the World Trade Center to evacuate the tenants and visitors, since the power, lights, back-up power, and water were knocked out by the blast. But, approximately 60,000 people (including 200 school children) were in the building, some trapped in elevators, and others on the roof of one of the two 110-story buildings waiting for helicopter rescue. The majority of the occupants walked down as many as 100 floors gasping for air. It is a testament to the toughness, tenacity, and courage of those people that a panic did not ensue. It could have been much, much worse.

The perpetrators of the World Trade Center bombing also planned to bomb two heavily trafficked routes into New York City plus other major sites. The possibility of an increased domestic terrorism effort is too evident to ignore.

A corporate CMP must include all aspects of, and procedures for, handling a bomb incident from prevention to aftermath.

Who's In Charge?

The composition of the Crisis Management Team (CMT) remains much the same in a bomb incident situation as it does for other crises. That is, it should be composed of decision makers from the ranks of senior management. Some very significant decisions will need to be made quickly, particularly if the bomb goes off. Management, legal, financial, security, communications, public relations/media relations, personnel and human resources, safety, and medical are the basic areas which will be involved. The CMT Coordinator is the key person on the team. Every team member must have a deputy.

A secondary support group of expert individuals may be needed. If it is a bomb extortion attempt, trained negotiators will be needed. The Chief Engineer must be included, since he will be required to deal with decisions regarding power and utilities. If the power is affected, as it was in the World Trade Center, the Chief Engineer becomes a very important team member. Someone(s) will be required to provide information about the critical and expensive equipment within the building. If the

computer system is complex and critical to the company, this may provide some prioritizing in terms of searching for a bomb, and for providing damage control measures. If there are hazardous materials within the building, who will provide information and assistance? The executive protection agent will probably provide the risk assessment and intelligence gathering.

The CMT must designate the individuals who will be in charge, assign responsibilities, and provide guidelines for their authority. Who will have overall authority, for example, to order an evacuation and under what conditions? Will this same individual have the responsibility of recruiting evacuation teams and providing training for them? Who will be given the responsibility for recruiting and providing training for search teams? Will that individual lead and supervise the search teams during an incident? CMT members must assign these functions.

Communications

During a bomb incident, communications must flow between the crisis team, command post, management, security, evacuation teams, search teams, employees and occupants, key individuals on site (Chief Engineer, hazardous materials engineer, computer manager, etc.), public safety officials, emergency medical services, and the various federal and local disaster agencies. Communications are critical and extremely complex in a bomb incident. While always important, the complexity of the communications in other crises (kidnapping) may not be as great, since fewer people are involved.

A communications coordinator, his or her deputy, and a network of people will be required to ensure that all communications flow smoothly, even if power is shut off or limited.

Communications equipment, including radios, cellular telephones, and short wave radios must be assembled to be ready and available on short notice. A public announcement (PA) system, with back-up, should be in place for large organizations.

Prior to and during an evacuation, a PA system will carry pre-designated messages to employees and occupants, giving directions and instructions, and exerting a calming influence. This procedure helps greatly to avoid panic conditions. The PA system must have back-up power.

Regular communications must be relayed to employees and occupants. Almost all adult individuals can deal with very difficult, even frightening, situations if they are told the facts and are kept informed. The reverse is also true; lacking factual information, wild rumors will circulate like wildfire, which will only make matters worse. Regular, truthful communications are a priority.

There is, of course, a problem. If the bomb is vulnerable to radio transmission activation, or it is directly wired into the power system, there is a chance that the bomb could be detonated. As in so many situations, this is a judgement call. The use of radios within an area being actively searched should be restricted.

Command Center

Information about CMT command centers has been covered in the preceding chapter. There is one difference with a bomb incident. If there is a bomb and it detonates without warning, the command center may necessarily have to be evacuated or it may be damaged. Therefore, an auxiliary command center should be located, probably off-premises. The location of this command center must be identified in the Crisis Management Plan. It should, at least, be minimally stocked with furniture, supplies, floor plans, and communications equipment as will be needed.

The command center should be capable of operating on a 24-hour basis, if necessary, during the bomb incident. As with other crisis incidents, this will become the "war room." Blueprints and floor plans must be available.

Public Agency Assistance

In constructing a Crisis Management Plan for

a bomb incident, assistance should be requested of the various public agencies, many of whom have very helpful printed information. Because of the concern about bombing incidents, the following agencies have printed pamphlets which are available:

- FEMA (Federal Emergency Management Agency).

- FBI (Federal Bureau of Investigation).

- Bureau of Alcohol, Tobacco and Firearms.

- County Emergency Services Coordinator.

- Metropolitan police bomb squads.

The American Society for Industrial Security (ASIS) has an extensive library, with many pamphlets and materials on the subject of bombing incident management.

The International Association of Chiefs of Police (IACP), located in Alexandria, VA, telephone # 1-800-843-4227, researches and writes perhaps the best training material on bomb management incidents available to civilians.

One member of the CMT should be designated as the liaison person for the public safety agencies. This person should meet in advance and establish a good working relationship with the local FBI, police officials, fire officials, emergency medical support agencies, local utility firms, any emergency bomb disposal support organizations, and civil defense officials. Procedures should be discussed and verified, as they will need to be included in the CMP.

Risk Analysis

A CMT member should be given the responsibility of conducting a specific bomb incident risk analysis of the facility. This person should also be responsible for collecting intelligence on an ongoing basis.

Intelligence to be gathered will include

information specific to the company and building, to the local area, and to the industry of which the company is a member. These are some of the questions which must be answered.

. Has the company or building ever received a bomb threat? Was the threat real or a hoax?

. Have there been several, or many, incidents?

. Have other companies or individuals in the area been targeted for a bomb incident? What is the history of bomb incidents in the area?

. Have other companies in the same or similar industry/business been targeted for bomb incidents?

. In each incident, was a bomb detonated and was there prior warning? What were the details of the warning (did the caller give time and location)?

. What kind of bomb was used, and what was its destructive power? Did the bomb appear to be constructed by a knowledgeable person or was it strictly the work of amateurs?

. What reasons were given by the bomber for the incident?

. What were the conditions regarding how the bomb was delivered or inserted, and how did the bomber gain access to the building?

. Is there any pattern to the incidents that could be used in formulating the CMP?

. Are the police aware of any theft of explosive materials in the community?

. Are there any known terrorist or criminal groups operating in the vicinity?

A site survey should be conducted from the standpoint of any vulnerabilities of the facility to a bomb incident. The survey should include a thorough inspection of the grounds, building(s), parking, access routes, power system(s), public areas,

employee and visitor access control, and mail room procedures. The report should include a review of the hiring, training, and supervisory policies regarding employees. Are they adequate to screen out potentially harmful employees? Are there currently any incident reports concerning employees who have made threats against the company or any of its employees?

The site survey should keep its focus specifically on the vulnerability of the facility externally and internally to a bomb incident--not a shooting or kidnapping. For example, if the physical security is adequate, are access control procedures sufficient to keep out the bad guys from accessing the public restrooms? Is the facility vulnerable to a bomb placed from within by an employee? Are the areas adjacent to and attached to the outside of the building cleared of extraneous objects and crevices that could conceal a bomb? How often and how well are these outside areas patrolled and examined?

Are the public areas designed so as to minimize the access for hidden placement of a bomb? For example, public restrooms are favorite spots for the placement of bombs and, for that reason, should be kept locked. Whenever possible, all containers such as towel dispensers and toilet tops should be locked or bolted. Trash containers should be of the mesh, or open, variety to facilitate viewing of any suspect items. Furniture in the public areas should be of the non-upholstered type, with crisp open lines, to deny bomb placement. Public areas should be kept spotlessly clean and rigidly maintained, so that foreign objects stand out clearly. Recommendations might be made to install video monitoring equipment of public areas.

The site survey should include a thorough review of the power, air conditioning, and heating systems to determine if they are vulnerable.

The parking should be controlled so that a car bomb would not be capable of creating more than localized destruction.

The survey should make note of all critical

equipment and its location, as well as hazardous materials. How well is the critical material protected? Should the walls be reinforced? Is any critical equipment located close to the public areas which might more easily be accessed by a bomber?

When all information regarding the history of bomb incidents in the area has been accumulated, it should be combined with the results of the site survey in a risk assessment report to include probability conclusions and recommendations.

The risk assessment report and its recommendations should be considered by the Crisis Management Team. All acceptable changes should be implemented without delay. Policies and procedures should be written and disseminated to the proper people. For example, if the report finds that mail room procedures are not adequate, written procedures must be written, and those procedures would serve as the basis for a training program for the mail room employees. If the report finds that all employees should be provided with safety awareness training, the training program must be written and implemented.

Prevention

Without question, the best solution for bombing incidents is to prevent their happening. As part of the CMP, a prevention program should be implemented. The elements of a prevention program are:

.	Good physical security.

.	Access control that denies the bomber access to the building.

.	Building design, traffic flow, and equipment placement that lowers vulnerability.

.	Design of public areas in such a way that it minimizes the ability of the bomber to hide a bomb.

.	Strict mail and package screening.

.	Scrutiny and control of all vehicles and parking.

.	Knowledgeable employee screening that reduces the potential for hiring potentially violent employees.

.	Employee awareness training that equips them to identify suspicious behavior on the part of strangers and fellow employees.

.	Concerned supervisors who feel that they are part of the security team, and who can monitor employee activities and behavior.

Search Teams and Procedures

The CMT must develop policies and procedures for the recruitment of search teams, their training, and incident procedures. One team member must be assigned the responsibility for the search teams. What will be the company policy on searching--will this be done covertly or overtly? Who will perform the searches? Who will provide the training for the teams? Who will be responsible for procuring search equipment? Will the company buy electronic stethoscopes? All search procedures should be captured in writing. Room cards must be designed. A reporting process should be established.

Written procedures and training should cover the actions to be taken subsequent to finding a bomb. These might include: evacuations, notifying the public safety agencies, isolating the area, taking measures to minimize damage, posting security, and working with the police bomb division.

It would be difficult to overemphasize the importance of search team training. Bomb searches can be dangerous, and the potential liability is very high. At the same time, the company is caught in a quandary. It has a responsibility to protect its employees, and that responsibility could include either a blanket decision to evacuate at the hint of a bomb threat or a decision to search. It is not likely that the police will assist with or lead a search; they do not have the manpower and tend to view searching as a company responsibility. Outside search teams can be brought in, but this is expensive and not always efficient. While outside professional teams know how to search, they do not know the building. Their search, therefore, is going to be very lengthy, as they will have to search every single item.

Training of in-house search teams can be provided from various sources. Information about this can be obtained from the public and private sources listed in this chapter.

Evacuation Teams and Procedures

The example of the bombing of the World Trade Center points out the need for rigorously controlled evacuation procedures to be followed in the event of an actual bombing. The Crisis Management Team must let its imagination go into overdrive in planning for the evacuation of its employees and/or occupants during, or subsequent to, a major bomb incident.

Employees and visitors must be evacuated from the building to a safe haven. In a high-rise building, this could include Evacuation Wardens and their alternates on each floor, trained to search for all occupants of the floor, and capable of calmly directing the evacuation procedures. Procedures could include the shutting down of computers and rescue of the most vital information. Evacuation as a result of a bombing (as opposed to an evacuation caused by a bomb threat) may mean that the occupants cannot come back into the building for days or weeks. Should they take personal possessions with them? Is there time? What if the stairwells are blocked by smoke? Is there a flat space on the building roof for a helicopter to land and evacuate people? Is there back-up power? (In the World Trade Center the lights went out!) Has the bombing caused fire to break out on any floors?

The old-fashioned fire drills served a very useful purpose, and are recommended for inclusion in the CMP.

If there are any medical problems, these must be dealt with. Smoke inhalation, heart attacks, physical injuries, and pregnant workers must be attended to. Who has been designated the responsibility of coordinating with the medical emergency services to deal with these problems?

The evacuated employees must be taken to a safe haven. If the bombing incident occurs in a major metropolitan city, this can be a problem. Traffic, vehicles, and pedestrians all will impede an orderly retreat. Do the employees know that, in the event of an emergency, they can assemble at a designated location? Relatives will be anxiously waiting for news. Help may be needed in providing transportation for workers to their homes; if they left without purses or wallets, they may not have money to take public transportation.

Hopefully, a major disaster will not happen with your corporation, but a doomsday scenario should be devised and implemented.

The Crisis Management Plan must address all of these issues, beginning with the designation of a team member to coordinate and supervise all evacuation procedures and issues. The team must include primary and alternate evacuation routes in the Crisis Management Plan. A clear corporate policy must be written to cover evacuations--who decides to evacuate and what considerations govern conclusions to call for partial versus total evacuations. The CMP must delineate the responsibilities and authority of the Evacuation Wardens.

The CMP must establish procedures for identifying and recruiting Evacuation Wardens from among the employees and building occupants. Each Warden must be given clear areas of responsibility. A training program must be written. Will it include First Respondent Medicine training so that, if someone is injured, the Wardens can assist? In a large building, what will be the order of evacuation (one floor at a time or other means)? Who will establish priorities to decide where the evacuation begins?

Communication and reporting procedures for the Evacuation Wardens must be designated and written. Equipment (radios, arm bands) may need to be purchased. Where will be they kept? How quickly will they be made available to the Wardens?

The CMT member designated as responsible for evacuation should also take responsibility for the identification of a safe relocation area or areas. In a large building, there may be a need for several areas. All areas must be adequately comfortable and accessible to communications from the Wardens and from the CMT.

An identification system must be established which ensures that all personnel have been evacuated from the building in a total evacuation. This involves a roll call procedure plus designation of one or more Wardens to check the public areas, restrooms, employee locker rooms, etc. The policy may dictate that a final clearance check of the building should be made.

A policy should be established regarding the length of time that employees and occupants can be held in the safe area. Will they be allowed to go home after one hour (or other designated time period), or will they be released for some period of time and then obligated to return? If the evacuation has been total, and is an emergency on a par with the bombing of the World Trade Center, will the company provide food? Emergency shelter? Money for transportation to go home?

If the evacuation is extended, and several weeks will pass before the employees can return to work, provisions must be made to maintain communications between management and the furloughed employees. Perhaps a communication network should be established that designates supervisors as having the responsibility of calling all employees in his or her department on a regular basis to provide information and to answer questions.

Handling of Bomb Threats

The CMT must establish written policies and procedures regarding the handling of called-in and written bomb threats.

A Bomb Call Checklist should be designed and placed at all appropriate telephone stations. All telephone operators taking incoming calls should be given periodic training in the procedures. Training scenarios that are realistic are an excellent idea.

Procedures should be written for analysis and response to the bomb threat. To whom will the Operator relay the threat? Who will debrief the Operator? Was a taping made of the call? The nature and specificity of the threat must be analyzed, using input of the intelligence gathered for the risk assessment. Who will do this? As a result of the analysis, who is the decision-maker who will be empowered to order a search and/or evacuation?

If the threat is a form of extortion, the entire issue of "ransom" money must be considered. A clear corporate policy must be written to cover this eventuality.

Detonation

Since not all bombs are delivered with warnings, and for that reason can be much more devastating, the Crisis Management Plan must cover this eventuality in detail. Also, even with a warning and subsequent searches, bombs sometimes blow up. Procedures and policies must be written to cover all aspects of an explosion. This is when the CMT, using the command center, goes into high gear. Every member of the Crisis Management Team will have a job to do.

With an unexpected explosion, the evacuation plan must be implemented. Notification to the police, fire, emergency medical services, and FBI must be made.

A damage assessment must be made and by that is not meant a dollars and cents loss. Rather, it means assessing the criticality of the damage. Are hazardous materials leaking? Who will monitor the power systems? Is there critical equipment and/or information which must receive priority protection? Unless a total evacuation has been ordered, or there is a serious fire, can records be retrieved--records that will greatly assist the company in its subsequent recovery? The CMP should identify and prioritize the equipment, records, and information which would be removed first from an endangered building? If you knew that you only had thirty minutes, what would be the most valuable items that you could remove? It should be obvious that all corporations and individuals should keep back-up records and information off-premises as well.

Back-up power and water for the fire-fighting crews must be available. In the event of an emergency shutdown of utilities, who will perform the shutdown? Who will authorize it?

The communications network must quickly ascertain if people have been either stranded in the building, unable to get out, or/and if there are injured people in the building who require assistance. A roll call procedure must be in place for supervisors to determine if any employees are missing. What about visitors? Who will have knowledge of this and is there a visitors log? A policy must be established as to whether employee search and rescue teams will be utilized to locate and evacuate stranded and injured occupants. Will teams be trained for this task? If so, a training program must be developed and implemented.

The CMT member responsible for public relations and dealing with the media must prepare a briefing. The success and speed of recovery may well rest on the positive or negative slant of the media stories which will report the incident.

The legal aspects will be daunting.

The Aftermath

The immediate problems of a bombing incident, horrible as they are, may be overshadowed by the aftermath problems. A company that is under-insured and that has not prepared, by way of a contingency plan, for a major disaster may face bankruptcy.

Customer confidence may be shaken. If the company is out of business for 30 days or longer, it may find that customers, all of whom were sympathetic in the beginning, have migrated to other resources.

Employees must be supported physically, emotionally, and financially, or they, too, will gravitate to other jobs, being unable to wait out the disaster.

OVERSEAS EVACUATIONS & OTHER DISASTERS

On the overseas front, disasters tend to fall into two categories--man-made and natural. The man-made incidents can be terrorist-inspired (bombs, kidnappings), or they are caused by insurrections and coups d'etat. The natural disasters are floods, chemical spills, earthquakes, typhoons, and the like.

If it is a natural disaster, there is little (or no) need for the protection agent (unless, of course, he just happens to be on the scene with his protectee). However, if the crisis is man-made, the agent may be called upon to play a key role. The executive protection agent may already be on the scene or may be a member of a corporate Crisis Management Team sent to coordinate with the local CMT on the scene. In this chapter we will deal only with the man-made emergencies which might involve the protection agent.

A local Corporate Management Plan (CMP) should be developed--written both in English and in the local language. CMP's will differ from country to country.

A local Crisis Management Team (CMT) must be formed which will operate within the guidelines of general authority set forth by the corporation Board of Directors or Executive Committee. Composition of the CMT will, depending upon company resources, closely resemble the headquarters Team, as will the duties and functions assigned to Team members. A Crisis Management Coordinator (CMC) must be appointed, and a Crisis Management Center should be established within the facility. A liaison should be established with the responsible regional security officer or the most appropriate official at the U.S. Embassy or Consulate.

Acts of Terrorism

The following are suggested contacts at the U.S. Embassy or Consulate who might respond to acts such as bombings, seizures of owned facilities, assassinations or attempted assassinations, assaults on personnel and/or dependents, kidnappings or attempted kidnappings, and hostage takings.

.   Ambassador or Principal Officer.
.   Deputy Chief of Mission.
.   Economic Officer.
.   Administrative Officer.
.   Commercial Officer.
.   Regional Security Officer or Post Security Officer.
.   Consular Officer.

Suggested contacts with the host government, depending on circumstances, might include:

.   Head of State.
.   Minister of Interior.
.   Government intelligence agency.
.   Chief of Police.
.   Senior police official responsible for company area.
.   Senior official responsible for airport.
.   Senior official responsible for investigations.
.   Senior official responsible for responding to acts of terrorism.

Upon receipt of a terrorist threat, the local CMC should notify the corporate headquarters security department and activate the local CMP. As much information as possible regarding the threat/incident should be quickly collected and relayed to headquarters. Information should include:

.   Date, time, and location of the threat or incident.

.   Nature of threat or attack and injuries and damages sustained.

.   Full data concerning affected employees, including names and addresses of next of kin.

.   Number and identity of terrorists, organization, weapons used, and other information, if known.

.   Terrorism demands or claims.

.   Local assessment of the situation.

.   Initial actions taken by host government and police to respond to terrorist action re arranging enhanced security, medical assistance, etc.

.   Precautionary measures taken for other employees at the location of the incident and elsewhere in the host country.

Intelligence to be collected:

.   What is known about the terrorists? What are their goals, philosophies, and tactics?

.   What are pressure points on terrorists? Local political parties, state supporters, religious groups, the logical sympathizers, or international organizations.

.   What are host government capabilities to negotiate with the terrorists?

.   What is host government policy regarding terrorist demands?

.   What are host country laws regarding negotiating and paying ransom to terrorists?

Regarding the hostages and/or victims, the following questions must be answered.

.   What is the significance of the hostages to the terrorists?

. Do hostages have any capability to assist in achieving their own release?

. If victims, what arrangements should be made for treatment of the injured or disposition of remains and personal property?

It must be established whether senior U.S. government officials or corporate senior executives should attempt to intervene with the host government. Some critical negotiating issues include the following:

. The potential crucial threat to the life of the hostage(s).

. The extent to which the corporation has the authority to negotiate release.

. The extent to which the company will cooperate with law enforcement officials.

Additionally, the company must decide:

. What company resources should be deployed to the scene of the incident? Will a negotiating team be deployed?

. Are aircraft available for negotiators, psychiatrists, medical staff, security, etc.?

. What immediate assistance should the company provide to victims' families?

. What security measures need to be taken to protect other senior employees of the company or its assets?

Additional information on hostage taking and kidnappings is found earlier in this chapter. More information on designing and implementing crisis management plans is found in the preceding chapter.

Evacuations

There are circumstances in which it is obvious that a U.S. corporation operating abroad must consider sending employees and dependents out, such as times of terrorist threat, insurrection, or other civil disorder or when a natural disaster or other event poses serious hazard to their safety or so overburdens the country's ability to protect, feed, and house its citizens that departure is the best course of action.

If the U.S. government were to sponsor an evacuation of Americans from a given country, it would be coordinated and controlled by the U.S. Department of State. The Chief of Mission of the U.S. Embassy cannot order private American citizens to depart, but must inform them of impending danger and may offer evacuation assistance from the U.S. government when necessary. However, it is prudent for overseas companies to develop individual evacuation plans.

A model evacuation plan can be found in the Appendix of this book.

Resources

The U.S. Department of State Operations Center (202/647-1512) is a 24-hour communications facility which monitors worldwide developments that may affect the protection of U.S. interests abroad. In the event of a crisis overseas affecting U.S. citizens, the Center will become the site for a Washington task force staffed by representatives from various government agencies that will support the U.S. response to the incident.

The Center also works with the Washington Task Force or Working Group, an ad hoc working group activated only when necessary to work closely with the U.S. Embassy in the country where the incident or problem exists.

U.S. Government International Disaster Response coordination is provided by the Office of U.S. Foreign Disaster Assistance of the Agency for International Development (202/647-8924).

Every U.S. Embassy and consulate is required to have an Embassy Emergency Action Committee to function in the event of a crisis or emergency.

And, Finally

Someone is going to be nasty enough to, yes, sue, claiming that they were not properly dealt with by the corporation, or that the corporation did not properly prepare all necessary safety and security procedures.

The Crisis Management Plan with its written policies and procedures, and the subsequent training programs, will provide the company's best hope that it acted responsibly and to the best of its ability to prevent and mitigate the disaster.

The media will be hounding the company for any tidbit of news, good or bad.

A good CMP should take all of these factors into consideration with an aggressive plan to counteract them. A "heads-up" ad campaign saved Tylenol after product tampering almost torpedoed the company. A prominent Denver, Colorado restaurant chain combatted and survived a food poisoning incident with widely publicized news briefings of their efforts in coordinating with health authorities to locate and support victims.

A post-incident critique is a necessity. The Crisis Management Team must collect as much information as possible from reports and debriefings. This critique will aid in assembling the information which the legal department and the insurance people will need to decide if the company has any liability and to start the insurance recompense process. The Crisis Management Plan should be reviewed and updated to introduce any changes which might improve its performance. Any weaknesses should be corrected.

Any disaster can be minimized with careful planning. A bombing incident can be a nuisance or a disaster, but it can be made more tolerable by careful preliminary planning.

EXTORTION CALL

Call taken at:_____ Call ended at:_____ Date:_____ Call taken by:_____

Caller statement (Ask him to repeat it and ask for details -- Who, What, Where, When, Why it happened)

_____

_____

_____

_____

_____

_____

_____

What is it that you want? (Get specifics on currency, where and how to be delivered) _____

_____

_____

_____

_____

_____

Who is making this call? (A terrorist group may give its name)_____

May I speak with (victim)?_____ Is he/she harmed? (If injured try to ascertain nature and extent of injuries)

_____

_____

What is he/she wearing?_____

I must relay your demands to my superior, and I will do this as quickly as possible. When will you call back?

_____

So that we know you are the right person, let me give you a code word to use whenever you call, so that we can give you immediate attention. The code word is _____

Caller Details

Sex of caller_____ Approximate age_____ Accent_____ Did caller sound familiar?_____

Anything unusual about the voice or speech?_____

Caller's attitude (excited, calm, angry, etc.)_____

Background noises_____

Did caller seem familiar with the company or its employees? (explain)_____

_____

_____

Since all of the preventive measures in the world won't avoid all kidnapings, hijackings, and hostage takings, it is only prudent to include in the Crisis Management Plan a segment on crisis survival. Just as an executive is given a pre-departure briefing on the situation which he will find in the country to which he is traveling, every executive who might be considered a target for abduction should be briefed on how to react and survive if he is taken. And while, unfortunately, bodyguards are usually killed immediately in a kidnapping incident, there are some hijack and hostage situations which might include the protection agents as part of the crowd. For example, if the protectee and his agent are traveling together overseas and the plane is hijacked, both will need survival knowledge. If the agent and his protectee are rounded up along with other innocent bystanders in a bank stand-off, both must preserve their health and lives.

HIJACKING

In many ways, a hijacking is the preferred hostage incident of choice. Most passengers survive, do not pay ransom, and spend a relatively short time in discomforting circumstances. It isn't guaranteed since, occasionally, one or more passengers are killed to demonstrate the hijackers' demands. But, if the protectee and agent have followed the advice given in this book for keeping a low profile and sanitizing identification documents, they will probably not be chosen for demonstrative execution; and, if they don't do anything dumb like trying to overpower the hijackers, they may survive the hijacking with the minimum of discomfiture and the loss of watch and rings.

Once an incident begins, your job is to remain calm and to help keep your fellow hostages quiet and under control. However, do not do anything that could set you apart from the other

hostages in the eyes of the hostage takers. This is especially important for the security agent since being identified as such by the hostage takers would provide a great reason to be sacrificed first.

The first 15 to 45 minutes are the most dangerous. Most criminals and terrorists will be excitable, nervous, and determined. They are also very well trained. The passengers should do as they are told, without argument. Trying to be a hero or to intimidate the hostage-takers with vows of vengeance can lead to disaster. Adopting a calm, polite, quiet demeanor will set a good example for the other passengers. You should listen to commands and do as told without protest or complaint. You may be told to put your head in your lap, to put your hands behind your head, etc. It doesn't matter--just do as you are told.

The hijackers may feel that they have to prove that they mean business, and that proof may take the form of violence with the beating, or even killing, of a passenger. You may not be able to prevent this, and you certainly do not want to be picked as the sacrificial victim. Try to become as low profile as possible. Some of the experts advise that you avoid eye contact, while other experienced hostage negotiators tell us that you should look your hostage taker in the eye, calmly but not fixedly, maintaining a certain inner neutrality. By doing so, you appear "human" and take on an identity which will make it less likely that you will be harmed. There is general agreement that, at the beginning of a hostage taking, you will wish to keep your eyes down and present no threat to the hostage takers.

You will probably be asked to give up your passport, jewelry, money, and possessions. The flight crew will be forced to participate in collecting these items. The crew will be as protective of you as they can, and you should take your lead from their instructions and behavior. Flight crews receive special training in dealing with incidents of this nature and generally have good success in defusing violent incidents. If you are carrying your tourist passport, cleansed of any incriminating visas, and your identification has been sanitized of anything that identifies you as a corporate bigwig, a Security Agent, a Personal Protection Specialist, CIA, or member of the Jewish Defense League, you will probably not have a problem. Since you may be interrogated, you should mentally rehearse your stories to be sure that you and the protectee are together in anything that is said.

The hijackers have, in the past, devised some strategies for maintaining control of the passengers. They may require that seat belts be kept fastened and that all movement be restricted. Passengers may be asked to change seats. Window shades may be pulled. Until the situation can be stabilized, it is prudent to follow instructions without argument. This is where mental discipline comes in handy. Once the initial adrenalin shock is gone, it is going to be mostly boring. Playing mental games (writing a book, composing poetry, inventing a new computer software) will help to pass the time.

Avoid conversation, even whispered conversation, with other passengers. It is dangerous to confide in anyone. Sometimes one terrorist remains anonymous for a time among the passengers. Under stress, other hostages have traded information for favors from the terrorists. And, finally, you may fall under suspicion of conspiracy. If there is the slightest suspicion that an executive and bodyguard are among the passengers, the bodyguard will most likely meet an untimely end, and the executive will be targeted for special handling.

Think twice before volunteering to become a spokesperson or leader among the passengers. You may be asked to produce results which cannot be granted, and the failure could well be laid at your feet. There are a fair number of don'ts--don't argue, volunteer, ask any other than necessary questions, debate political philosophies, try to ingratiate yourself, ask for favors, or complain. Listen calmly and politely

and avoid sneering or showing any visible signs of disapproval.

No one should volunteer a conversation with a terrorist; however, if you are plucked out of the crowd for an interrogation or discussion, you should be polite and noncommittal. You may be required to listen, but you are not required either to argue or present your own views. Volunteering opinions will only lead to complications. Maintaining a calm, controlled demeanor is far better than exhibiting belligerence or obsequiousness. Terrorists often hold in contempt those prisoners whom they consider to be fawning or cowardly.

If you or your client has a medical problem which requires medicine or a doctor, wait until the situation has calmed down and relay a request to the hijackers for medical assistance. The terrorists would prefer to keep you alive and may include your request along with demands for food and supplies. Providing medical assistance gives them a chance to show concern for humanitarian requests and may assist in getting your protectee an early release, especially if they believe keeping him would only continue to complicate their plans.

Your preparations should come to your aid at this point. Be ready for an unpleasant, and perhaps long, experience. Before the incident is over, the air conditioning will go out, the toilets will overflow, the food and water will be sparse, and anxiety will go hand-and-hand with boredom. Unless you feel that the food will actually make you ill, you should accept all food that is offered, no matter whether you like it or not. You will need sustenance and strength.

Mental exercises, meditation, and isometric exercises will help to keep you alert and relieve the boredom. In an unobtrusive way, you should memorize details about the terrorists--names they may have used with each other, facial features and distinguishing characteristics, types of arms, etc. You may be released early, and all information will be of immense importance to the authorities in deciding how to terminate the incident. It is very likely that a low profile female protection agent, mistakenly identified as the protectee's sister or assistant, may be released early, before the male hostages. Her information will be of great value to the authorities.

In a cautious way, look around and memorize the location of the exits. If a rescue attempt is made, the lights may go out. If this happens, you will probably first be hit with concussion grenades. Stunning noise and light will then sweep the area. Smoke, noise, yells, and gunfire may erupt. Hit the floor, even if the hijackers demand that you stand up! The rescue team will not immediately be able to distinguish passengers from terrorists and anyone standing is likely to be hit. Also, unless you possess information of immediate importance (such as, a hijacker is wired with a bomb and has the pull in his hand) do not yell instructions to the rescuers. *They* will also be yelling instructions to you and you need to hear and react. Be prepared for the fact that your rescuers will treat everyone, including the passengers, with suspicion until they have sorted out the good guys from the bad guys. Be prepared to evacuate yourself and your protectee immediately, with or without possessions. If anything goes wrong, the airplane may be blown up.

KIDNAPPING AND HOSTAGE TAKING

Actual kidnappings and hostage takings take only moments to complete and can be totally disorienting. The speed with which the incident progresses, together with the noise, shock, and disbelief, produce a highly traumatic experience. One moment you are driving or riding in your vehicle or walking the protectee down the street, and the next there may be gunfire, shouts, screams, a sack over your head, even a blow that renders you nearly unconscious. Victims react in various ways. Some freeze, others panic, some fight. The protectee will probably react differently from you, his protector, being less conditioned to the possibility of a kidnapping or hostage taking.

If your captors do not kill you immediately, it is vital that you gain self control as quickly as possible, and this at a time when the captors will try

to establish *their* control. You may be handled roughly, tightly confined or bound, perhaps blindfolded, possibly locked in the trunk of a car. If your captors are terrorists, they are probably well armed and trained. Faced with too much resistance, the kind that could delay their escape, they may decide that assassination suits their purposes as well as taking hostages. Having selected you and your protectee as targets, they may feel only dislike and contempt for you. For these reasons, most of the experts advise against any attempts to escape. Others argue that this may be the *only* opportunity to escape, while there is confusion and relatively open avenues of escape. Later, under lock and key, blindfolded, naked, and chained, escape will be almost completely impossible.

There are some factors which should guide your decision as to whether to attempt to escape. If you have reason to believe that you will almost certainly be executed at a later time, you may choose to make your fight while there is even the smallest chance of success. There have been cases (the California McDonalds and the Texas restaurant where hostages were shot almost at leisure) when it would seem to all involved that death was inevitable if no resistance were made. If resistance is your choice, you must be in good physical shape, trained, alert, and prepared to act decisively and ruthlessly. Even then, it is a small chance. It is each person's judgement call.

Most people go through a range of psychological reactions immediately after being taken hostage, but the most common experiences are fear, denial, and withdrawal. At some point, everyone questions his or her ability to cope. Denial is common . . "this isn't happening to me."

In the case of a kidnapping, terrorist groups move the victim as quickly as possible from the site where the victim was taken. The rough treatment may, and probably will, continue, and drugs may be used to render the victims unconscious. If not unconscious, the victims will probably be blindfolded and confined out of sight, either in the car trunk or under a blanket. The feeling of disorientation can be overcome if the victims make a concerted effort for alertness. Although it may do no good in the long run, you should make every effort to notice such things as odors, sounds, left and right turns, and distances traveled. It may be of help in a future escape attempt or in directing authorities to the abductors after release.

In a hostage barricade situation, of course, the scenario changes. Hostages may be locked away or they may be used as human deterrents, placed by windows or doors to discourage rescue attempts. It is especially important to make mental notes of anything that could help the authorities if you are released prior to the other hostages. Sometimes women and children and/or sick or injured hostages are released in return for food or other favors. The authorities will want to know how many captors and hostages are involved in the takeover, numbers and types of weapons, description of the captors physically and emotionally, any names used, and the layout of the barricade.

In a foreign kidnapping, once the kidnapping is complete and you are safely (for them) in your prison, your captors will probably move quickly to establish their dominance. You may be stripped of all clothing, treated roughly, accused of being a spy, and threatened with imminent execution. All of this treatment is intended to reduce your resistance and establish your captor's control. You may be drugged and, worse, you may be isolated from other hostages. Solitary confinement can be horribly debilitating and disorienting. It helps to remember that courageous victims have been held in solitary confinement for years and survived to live meaningful lives.

To counteract the feelings of disorientation and isolation, it is important to establish a personal schedule and adhere to those personal rules of cleanliness and orderliness which civilized people need to hang on to their self-worth. Ask politely for soap, water, and a broom. Ask if they will allow you to shower. Feeling *clean* is a boon to morale.

Determine from the outset that you could be held for a very long time and that you *will* survive.

If you can accept the fact that you may be held for a year, you can devise a calendar for yourself and set about keeping your life and your health. If you have made the right preparations, you can be assured that your family is taken care of and that your business will continue to operate. You should reassure yourself, daily, that "out there" people are working for your release. You should also be prepared for the fact that your captors will probably take some pleasure in providing you with false information and in telling you that you have been abandoned. They may try to involve you in the negotiations to gain ransom money or other concessions. They may also require you to cooperate in making recorded statements, statements which may be embarrassing to you, your protectee, or your supporters.

Poor conditions may be compounded by a total lack of privacy and feelings of utter helplessness and dependency upon the terrorists for every necessity of life. The result is a tendency to lose dignity and self-respect. You must condition yourself to maintain these qualities as best you can. Your self-respect and dignity may be the key to retaining your status as a human being in the eyes of the terrorists. Insofar as you can, you should try to maintain your health, appearance, and personal cleanliness. Make your cell your home and take care of it by maintaining a kind of orderliness. Establish routines for the way in which you use your makeshift home.

If you are incarcerated with other hostages, try to establish some ground rules. Divide the space. Encourage each other to stay clean and healthy. Have respect for the other person's belongings, and take care of your own.

Fear in such a situation is very real. It is used as a tool by the terrorists against both you and the authorities. They will often use tactics to reinstill fear into hostages after the initial fear of the seizure has subsided. They have been known to load and unload weapons in the hostages' presence, show dramatic displays of temper, employ physical abuse, or even stage mock executions with unloaded weapons. They will try to intimidate you by criticizing your personal life.

If you can hang onto your dignity, your self confidence, and your optimism, you will survive and you will probably gain some respect from your captors. While the passage of time without rescue or release can be depressing for you, this lapse is actually to your advantage. Past experience has shown that the greater the time elapsed, the better the hostages' chances are of staying alive.

Boredom is a serious problem for hostages. If not combatted, it can make captivity intolerable and can, over an extended period of time, adversely affect one's physical and mental health. Experts stress the need for hostages to develop and maintain a daily physical fitness program and to engage in some creative mental activity such as reading, writing, memory exercises, problem solving, or simple daydreaming. Hostages have written novels in their heads, designed their dream home in their imagination, and mentally walked across the United States. Mental games with goals work well . . "I will survive and I will make that walk from New York to California." Many victims, upon release, have acted out the dreams that kept them alive over months and years.

A side effect of captivity for some hostages is weight loss, and although this may be considerable, it generally does not cause severe health problems. Weight loss may occur even with adequate food supply since hostages can suffer a loss of appetite. In some cases, hostages may experience gastrointestinal upset including nausea, vomiting, diarrhea, and constipation. Although these symptoms can be debilitating, they are usually not life-threatening. Since hostages are more valuable alive than dead, you should ask for medication. It is important to eat, even if the food is unfamiliar and disgusting. Maintaining one's strength is an absolute necessity.

If your captors attempt to engage you in political debate, listen and remain neutral. If they try to discuss with you the terms they propose for your release, listen but do not give them any information (such as your company's policy toward ransom). Trained negotiators will be devising strategies, and your input will get in their way. Remain firm in your

confidence that your release will be arranged, as this will motivate your captors to continue the negotiations.

As time goes on, you may be able, slowly, to build a friendly or at least mutually respectful relationship with your captors. The more human you become to them, as a person with family, hopes, and dreams, the better your chances of surviving. Discuss your family, show pictures of your family, and talk about how much you miss them. Talk to them about their families. Try to maintain a neutral attitude to their philosophies, neither arguing nor agreeing. It is okay to concede that they have a point of view, even if it is not your point of view.

You will probably be interrogated, if only to obtain information that helps the captors to obtain the highest possible ransom money. Interrogations will vary from simple and brutal to very sophisticated. Terrorists are trained in many areas, including interrogation. They will use the old "white hat, black hat" routine, balancing a friendly, compassionate interrogator against a cold, brutal one. Although you may be threatened with torture, it is more probable that other methods will be utilized to extract information such as deprivation of food, water, light, or the companionship of other hostages. A quiet, measured response that does not volunteer or collaborate is the best approach. As heartless as it may sound, if you are tortured you should resist as long as you can. Captors almost universally admire courage and despise weakness. If they feel that you give in too rapidly to torture, they may employ it more often.

Should you attempt to escape? There are two sides to a hostage-taking. While the first 15 minutes are the most dangerous, they also provide the best chance for escape--maybe. Once the captors have established their control and perhaps moved to a secret place, chances for escape go down to a very low possibility. Escape is a personal choice and may depend on your physical condition, your successful appraisal of escape opportunities, and luck. Escape attempts can result in your death or serious injury, and at best will enrage your captors and result in a much tighter incarceration. You should consider escape only if the chances for success are virtually assured.

Finally, at long last, release! Is it over? The incarceration, humiliation, filth, and confined space may be over. The experience is not. As with all traumatic experiences, there will be emotional and psychological problems. There may be feelings that the family does not understand, that the corporation did not make enough effort to gain release, or that they haggled with the captors over the amount of the ransom and thus extended the captivity. There may be continuing feelings of low self-esteem.

If the corporation has done its job in correctly writing the Crisis Management Plan, there will be provisions for dealing with these post-incident problems. If you and your protectee were worth ransoming, you and he are certainly worth the continuing support of his corporation. With professional counseling and the compassionate care of peers, both can be brought back to a position of corporate asset. If the victim's family has felt well treated by the corporation throughout the victim's captivity, they will assist in the rehabilitation process. It should be a team effort.

Since terrorism is an ongoing concern, it is well to put some definition to this act and to the people who perpetrate the violence. There may be some misconceptions about terrorists which should be cleared up. Not all terrorists are poor and oppressed, nor do they all wear beards and khaki. Many terrorists are middle or upper class idealists and come from families of doctors, lawyers, and engineers. They are generally young, since the surviving terrorists from the 1960's and 1970's, if still active, are aging. It's a stressful life, and even the master terrorist, Abu Nidal, is in poor health. Some of the old gangs are still around with names like the Shining Path, Red Brigade, and certainly the irrepressible IRA of Northern Ireland, though they no longer represent the numbers and force they once were. While there have been, and are, numerous groups of terrorists, their individual numbers are few. In spite of the relatively few numbers, terrorism has had some remarkable successes.

A short history of terrorism may be needed to set the stage for a discussion of modern terrorism and terrorist behavior.

In its purest sense, terrorism has been around almost since the dawn of history. Dreadful, destructive acts of terror were perpetrated by Ivan the Terrible, Genghis Khan, and other leaders. While enormously destructive, these acts were simplistically motivated: to gain territory; to destroy an enemy; to terrorize an enemy into submission; to acquire slave labor; and to eliminate competition and future problems. These were acts of terror on a grandiose scale, often eliminating and/or uprooting hundreds of thousands of people.

It is generally conceded that modern political terrorism has it roots in Hassan Ben Sabbah, the Old Man of the Mountain (1007-1091). Ben Sabbah was a fanatical member of a dissident Shia Moslem sect who initially attempted to sway all Moslems to join his sect and, when his more reasonable attempts failed, turned to terrorism. Legend has it that Ben Sabbah constructed a heavenly garden filled with riches and rewards as described in the Holy Koran (Muslim equivalent to the Christian Bible). He chose his potential assassins, drugged them with hashish and transported them to his heavenly garden where they awoke to its delights. After spending a few days in the garden, the potential assassins were again drugged and returned home, where they awoke believing they had dreamed their experiences. Ben Sabbah would then send for these individuals and recount their "dreams," convincing them that he was the personal emissary of the god Allah. Ben Sabbah was able to rather easily recruit these people to his army of assassins. Ben Sabbah's assassins were so sworn and dedicated to him that they undertook suicidal missions, because they believed that in dying "for the cause" they were ensuring their place in heaven. It also helped that they were given hashish prior to a mission.

The Cult of the Assassins, always with an "Old Man of the Mountain" to guide it, was extremely successful, killing hundreds of political and religious leaders and dominating much of the politics of the entire Middle East until the middle of the 13th century.

The modern day Shiite terrorists are not unlike the older Assassins. Hard core Shiite Muslim extremists do not hesitate to recruit young men, give them honorable funerals in advance of a mission, and send them to glory and Allah.

While modern terrorism may have had its roots in the Cult of the Assassins composed of Ishmaili muslims, many modern terrorist groups owe a debt to the Jewish terrorists of the 1930's and 1940's, primarily the Irgun and the Stern Gang.

These two groups committed assassinations and murders, blew up strategic sites, and are credited with having created so much trouble that the British decided to withdraw from the Palestine territories. The Irgun was eventually outlawed by the Israeli government. It has been said that the strategies and tactical operations of the Irgun and Stern Gang have been copied and adapted by PLO extremists, as well as other terrorist organizations--a true irony.

Within the United States, terrorism is a relatively new phenomenon. This is not surprising-- this is a relatively new country. Prior to the 1960's, there were only sporadic acts of terrorism, although it could be argued that acts of terrorism were perpetrated during the American Revolution. It was not a clean Revolution. There were many Loyalists who wished to remain under British Crown rule, and numerous violent acts were perpetrated against them by extremist revolutionaries. The same, of course, is true in regard to the American Civil War. The firing by Confederates on Fort Sumter can be labeled a terrorist act. And, it is certain that Native Americans believe that America systematically practiced terrorism in its efforts to remove the Indian from his traditional lands and to open the country to colonization by the "white man."

The term "terrorism" is always open to debate. When Native Americans attacked emigrant wagon trains and killed women and children, were these acts of terrorism or strategic moves in defense of traditional hunting grounds? And when "white" Americans attacked undefended Indian camps and slaughtered women, children, and old men, were these acts of terrorism or "ethnic cleansing" as we have witnessed in Bosnia and Kosovo? Is there a difference?

One of the oldest organizations born and bred in the United States and dedicated to achieving results if necessary through terrorist acts, is the Ku Klux Klan. At the height of its power in its original incarnation, there were over 500,000 Klan members. The original Klan was disbanded in 1869, and in 1871, Congress declared the Klan to be a group of criminals. In 1915, the Klan was resurrected and rose

to new heights of influence with over one million members. The Klan was disbanded in 1944 but was reinstated for the third time in 1946. The Klan, preaching its hatred of Jews, Catholics, blacks, and unions may well have served as a model for some of the modern right-wing white supremacist organizations which came into being in the 1980's. The Klan refuses to die. In one Presidential election, an avowed leader of the "new" (gentler?) Klan, complete with blow-dried hair, declared himself a Presidential candidate.

In the 1960's and 1970's, a number of revolutionary parties came into existence, and for the first time, the United States faced a challenge to overthrow the government, accompanied with calculated acts of violence. The heated controversies of this period resulted in the deaths of President John Kennedy, Robert Kennedy, Martin Luther King, Malcolm X, and the attempt on the life of George Wallace. The Weathermen, a radical left-wing group, is believed responsible for a number of bombings on college campuses and against businesses. "Civil disobedience" became a byword of those times. Civil disobedience is a concept which has been adopted by many of the radical groups of the 1980's and 1990's, with good reason. It worked before--and it can work again.

In the 1980's, we witnessed a rise in the numbers of right-wing extremist organizations, many of them dedicated to racial and/or religious concepts. We are now seeing a resurgence of the white supremacist Aryan movement both in the United States and in Western Europe. In Germany, "skinheads" and those who espouse the Aryan philosophy have committed violent acts of terror against expatriates in that country, primarily those of Turkish origin. In Austria, a right-wing populist who once praised the integrity of the Nazi SS officers and who opposes all immigration heads a party supported by half the Austrian population.

Domestic terrorism, or terrorism within the United States, can be somewhat loosely divided into two major groups, plus a small newly emerging group. Left-wing terrorist groups, as in most countries, advocate either the overthrow or significant reform of the government. Right-wing terrorist groups are deeply conservative, are sometimes anti-government or, conversely, may be deeply patriotic, are sometimes religiously based, may espouse white supremacy, and often target particular groups such as Jews, blacks, gays, Hispanics, Asians, and pro-abortionists as objects of hate.

The third, and emerging, group is composed of refugees to this country who hold nationalist or separatist views. The FALN is an example of this group, holding that Puerto Rico (an American colony) should be separated from the United States. A rising number of Palestinian and Middle Eastern refugees are residing in the United States, and their anger against what they perceive as America's bias in favor of Israel may have prompted the attack on the World Trade Center.

As a part of this expatriate group, one must also include transients who enter the United States either legally or illegally and who are linked to terrorist individuals and groups. In late 1999, the arrest and investigation of an Algerian attempting to cross the border with bombmaking equipment linked him to Osama bin Laden, accused of instigating the bombing of two U.S. embassies in Africa.

If terrorism is again becoming a major concern for the protective agent, it deserves further examination. Let us look now at the motivations of terrorists to determine if we can assign degrees of dangerousness to them.

One person has divided terrorists into three groups: criminals, crusaders, and crazies (Frederick J. Hacker, 1976). It may be simplistic but it is roughly correct. Criminal terrorists want money, power, and the good life just as we all do, and they have no compunction about taking it. Crusading terrorists are idealistic and perform their terrorist acts in the name of a "cause," though often committing criminal acts for money to finance their operations. Those labeled crazies are the emotionally and mentally disturbed who perform their terrorist acts for reasons that are clear to them but obscure to the rest of us. These

three groupings sometimes cross over the line. The idealistically inspired terrorist may, given time and success, find that a craving for power has blunted his/her ideals. Motivations are rarely one-dimensional; they can be very complex.

One prevailing, very strong motivation is the politically and racially inspired terrorist. This is the person who is intensely dedicated to a political ideology and a political goal. The white supremacist views white supremacy as a political goal, and often rails against the in-power government as being dominated by "impure" (usually Jewish, Catholic, and Black) influences and, hence, may advocate the overthrow of the legitimate government. The terrorist inspired by a political ideology can be incredibly insensitive to the results of terrorist acts perpetrated by himself and his/her group. The "ethnic cleansing" carried out in the Bosnian Republic (formerly part of Yugoslavia) and Kosovo is repugnant and horrible in the eyes of the world but has been staunchly defended by the Serbs.

Politically inspired terrorists seemingly have a very high need for control and power and may endure great economic hardships with smug satisfaction in order to retain control. Political terrorism is often an outlet for old enmities, unleashed with a viciousness that is stunning.

Closely akin to the political terrorist is the religiously inspired terrorist. If anything, the religiously inspired terrorist can be even more dedicated to an ideal and goal with a commitment and passion that exceeds the political terrorist. Often, the two motivations are joined. The Muslim fundamentalists, for example, are not satisfied to merely accomplish religious freedom and power; they are determined to topple the "godless" non-fundamentalist governments of the Middle East. It has become a holy crusade which has claimed hundreds of thousands of lives and plunged Iran and Afghanistan back into the dark ages.

The leaders of the religiously motivated terrorist movements are apparently able to justify any form of atrocity in order to accomplish their goals. It has been reported that, in Iran, small children were sent ahead of military troops in order to trigger any land mines. Make no mistake, the religiously inspired terrorist recruit is formidable. Shiite Muslim recruits to the "cause" have undertaken suicidal missions for their leaders, comparing themselves to the Assassins of the Old Man of the Mountain of former times.

It seems clear to the observer that the leaders of the religious terrorist groups, contrary to their avowed religious goals, actually lust for absolute power and control. What is incredible is that these leaders are able to recruit, in the name of religion, huge numbers of fanatically dedicated followers.

A variety of terrorist acts are committed as a part of the political or religious strategy to acquire power. Terrorist acts may be committed to demonstrate the powerlessness of the government to protect the people or to force the government into taking repressive measures which frustrate the people. Assassinations are commonly conducted against "enemies of the people," usually leaders seen as effective and strong. Terrorist acts may be conducted at a level calculated to discourage the in-power government. Prior to declaring a cease-fire, the Irish Republican Army (IRA) for many years conducted a campaign of terror, much of it indiscriminate in nature, in an attempt to force the British into abandoning Northern Ireland.

Terrorist acts may be committed in order to force concessions from the government, such as freeing political prisoners. The multitude of aircraft hijackings of the 1980's often were perpetrated both to publicize the "cause" of the terrorists and to free comrades from prisons.

The good cause extremists, both in the United States and abroad, have sometimes used violent tactics. Anti-abortionist organizations have picketed abortion clinics, harassed pregnant women entering these clinics, published "WANTED" posters with the pictures of abortion doctors, and killed practitioners. Animal rights activists in Louisiana forced the termination of a highly regarded U.S. Army-funded program which used cats in experiments of head

wounds.

The good cause extremists closely resemble the religiously inspired terrorists in their intense zeal, and in their seeming ability to condone acts of violence (including murder) with perfect aplomb. In the United States, these people present a very real threat to clients who may have any association with those activities targeted by the extremists.

Whatever their avowed motivations (white supremacy, political, religious), terrorists are very dangerous adversaries. Terrorist groups, like cults, offer social acceptance and goals to people who may have felt, prior to joining the group, as outsiders. Some have suffered personal failures and humiliations; others with giant-sized egos feel "unappreciated," and many have an inner rage that finds an outlet in terrorist acts that are praised by their comrades. Terrible things can be done, and *it's okay* (in their eyes), justified because of the goals. Success brings empowerment.

They may feel that they are victims of injustice perpetrated by an uncaring society which can only be eradicated by terrorist acts. For the individual who is suspicious, even paranoid, it is a perfect environment.

One characteristic of the religiously and politically inspired terrorist is an inability to see the world in other than black and white terms. Compromises, negotiations, and the ability to see both sides of an argument are not in his/her nature. Absolute obedience to an ideal is required. This one-sided view of the world is reinforced by the literature, teachings, and "gospel" of the organization and its leader(s).

On the other hand, the criminal terrorist who kidnaps, robs banks, and extorts corporations has a firmer grip on reality. With this individual, deals can be struck. For the protective agent, this is the preferred terrorist adversary. Being on a more realistic level, this terrorist will be more likely to pursue the "soft" target and can be dissuaded from attacking the well protected client. Heightened opportunities for criminal terrorists may now exist with the excess of nuclear weapons and unemployed technical experts in unstable areas of the world. Many novels have been written around the theme of a nuclear extortion threat, and it would now seem that at long last these themes may have a chance at reality.

Non-criminal terrorists who are idealistically inspired tend to have a warped view of the world and are often unrealistic in their perceptions of the world. Good cause organizations tend to draw converts who are naive in their beliefs, much like the "flower children" of the 1960's who believed that "if we only love each other, the world will have peace."

Interestingly, the terrorist leader may have a secret agenda of his/her own. While preaching a political or religious ideal, he/she may at heart have a desire for nothing so much as total power and control. Terrorist leaders are often well educated, extremely bright, charismatic, may have a high degree of paranoia, and are often pitiless. In order to command complete obedience, the leader may invent a new religion or doctrine, may write copiously, and is generally an eloquent speaker. It is important both for discipline and for ego satisfaction that the leader be regarded as omnipotent.

Where does this information lead us--to what conclusions? The terrorist is a formidable adversary, particularly the idealist terrorist. Complete devotion to a cause can remove the natural inhibitors to violence and to self-preservation. Terrorism as we knew it in the 1970's and 1980's, and which had begun to wane in the early 1990's, may be returning in new forms and with fresh impetus. Within the United States, terrorism may once again be on the rise, wearing new labels.

Kidnappers

For practical purposes, kidnappers do not differ greatly from terrorists. Their actions, how they go about doing what they do, and how they pick their targets, are very similar. Kidnappers and terrorists, at least the good ones, are well organized and meticulous in their research of the target. They are

avid collectors of information, most of which is readily available to them. Corporations publish annual reports listing key executives and, often, their salaries, along with the net worth of the corporation. News stories relate personal information about individuals who receive awards, information that lists number of children, ages, and other personal data. Servants can be met casually and used to obtain gossipy details. Surveillance can reveal travel habits, routes driven routinely, social activities, work schedules, and defensive measures. Kidnappers and terrorists are skilled intelligence gatherers. Raids of terrorist hide-outs have produced voluminous files documenting the personal lives of different individuals, thus giving the attackers a choice of targets. In gathering their intelligence, terrorists and kidnappers sometimes conclude that the original target is too well protected to undertake the risk. A much-quoted example of this is the case of Aldo Moro, a highly placed Italian politician, who was kidnapped and subsequently killed by the Red Brigade. Moro was not the Brigade's first choice. The Brigade originally intended to kidnap two other men, but decided that both men were too heavily guarded, so they chose the easier target of Aldo Moro. No matter--they still accomplished their political purpose.

Hate Groups

The Anti-Defamation League of B'nai B'rith, a New York-based Jewish organization, states in its *Hate Groups in America* that it has identified 67 hate groups in America that are violently inclined. Not surprisingly, the hate groups include a high percentage of white supremacist groups. Listed in B'nai B'rith's document are the Ku Klux Klan, several Neo-Nazi groups, and a number of pseudo-religious hate groups.

The hate groups are close kin to and include many of the goals and ideals described in this chapter to the domestic terrorists. At the heart of the doctrine of these hate groups is the concept of white supremacy over Blacks, Jews, Hispanics, Asians, and others. The more radical of these hate groups advocate a separatist doctrine, creating a "whites-only" territory. Many of the members of these hate groups are capable of violence. There have been some notable incidents, some targeting specific individual victims, and others merely spraying bullets into a targeted group.

Members of these groups, well labeled as hate groups, are motivated by a raging need to establish the white man and woman as supreme among the races and a hatred that is obsessive for other races, primarily Blacks and Jews. Often, religion and race are mixed in the same doctrine. Leaders of these groups tend to be highly charismatic and unscrupulous in their manipulation of their converts. The more virulent and active groups maintain their own training camps and enforcers.

The members of these groups tend to be undereducated, conservative, often from rural communities, and living in low economic circumstances. While the Ku Klux Klan had a history of political influence in its heyday, none of the other hate groups have established a popular political power base. The philosophy is too unsophisticated to legitimize a coherent political message. Still, the Neo-Nazis in Western Europe have managed to attract a fair number of followers, using as their political message the influx of foreigners who have displaced Germans from jobs. At a time of economic decline and/or high unemployment, this political message can find sympathetic ears. Recently, groups in Austria and Switzerland have begun to campaign to bar new immigrants and/or to deny them citizenship in their adopted country.

Although it had its beginnings in 1978, the "skinhead" movement in America made little headway until recent times. "Skinheads" are the foot soldiers for the white supremacist organizations and are generally believed to be the most violent segment of what authorities call the hate movement.

According to a report by the Anti-Defamation League of B'nai B'rith, it is estimated that there are several thousand active skinheads in 40 states, more than double the number reported in 1988.

In 1993, Federal and local authorities in Southern California arrested eight people on charges of conspiring to kill Rev. Al Sharpton, a controversial New York minister; Rodney King, a black motorist beaten by white Los Angeles policemen; and other well-known Blacks.

The eight, who are members of groups called "The Fourth Reich Skins," the "White Youth Alliance," and "White Aryan Resistance," allegedly also were plotting to blow up the First African Methodist Episcopal Church in Los Angeles and to gun down its parishioners.

The acknowledged founder of the U.S. skinhead movement, Greg Withrow, said he was brought up to be a racist. While he was growing up in Sacramento, his father made him study the life of Hitler and read hate literature. He formed a racist group that went around mugging Japanese tourists and homosexuals.

Members of hate groups are inflexible in their hatred and see the world in extreme black and white terms. They view themselves as the true inheritors of the earth and are enraged that others (Jews, Blacks, Hispanics, Asians) enjoy the good life while they are living at the bottom of the economic heap. Many farmers and ranchers who lost their lands and homes in the 1980's blamed the "Jewish bankers" for their losses.

Members of hate groups see themselves as righteous and justified in their hatred. It is only a small step to justifying violence. These are not all "crazies," although they may be suffering from delusionary notions and some are sociopaths. They are deeply suspicious and see conspiracies to deprive them of their God-given "rights" around every corner. Because hate feeds on hate, it is a self-reinforcing doctrine. And there is plenty of literature available to feed the flames. According to the Simon Wiesenthal Center, there are at least 2,100 Internet "hate sites" which have been identified.

How much of a threat do these groups represent to a client? It depends on several factors, including the client's ethnic and religious persuasion, and upon his/her possible exposure. If the client is the black president of the bank in a southern rural area which has been forced to foreclose on a number of farms belonging to white farmers, the exposure is high. In fact, bank presidents as a group have traditionally been at risk. If the agent's job is protecting Rodney King, the exposure is high. The danger from hate groups to a client is situational. Because of the insular nature of these groups, their secrecy, and suspicious outlook, the members are not outgoing. These are not well-funded terrorist groups who conduct sophisticated surveillance on targets. They are, for the most part, semi-content to fester in dark places and to prey on undefended targets. However, they are capable of causing great harm, and should never be underestimated.

On July 20, 1993, the Tacoma, Washington office of the National Association for the Advancement of Colored People was bombed. This was apparently only one incident in a planned string of attacks by a white supremacist group calling itself the American Front. This group had planned a campaign of bombings and murders aimed at Jewish temples, U.S. military facilities, radio and television stations, and rap stars Ice-T and Ice Cube, an admitted member told the FBI. The group had accumulated a cache of assault weapons, rifles, homemade bombs, and false identification. They also planned additional indiscriminate, racially directed sniper actions to be taken along their general route through the United States.

Lone Wolves

Top-level law enforcement officials and terrorism experts believe that what has emerged is a new style of "leaderless resistance," of very small cells, pairs, or individuals, called lone wolves, acting independently. Hate groups, often using the Internet, provide the philosophical framework. Individuals with few or no tangible connections to these groups do the killing. The notion being preached in pamphlets and on web sites is a romantic vision of the heroic loner who fights his own private war, committing violent acts against the government, Jews,

and racial minorities.

Unlike the pyramid type of traditional terrorist groups, the lone wolf operates from a "phantom cell" mode of organization, described as "leaderless resistance." These independent cells operate independently of each other and never report to a central headquarters or single leader for direction or instruction. The reasoning is that these cells cannot be betrayed or infiltrated by the FBI.

Timothy McVeigh and his alleged two co-conspirators are the most visible examples. McVeigh apparently had no real connections with any organized group, but he took inspiration from the right-wing milieu. Buford O. Furrow, Jr., the loner who shot five people in a Los Angeles Jewish community center, may be another example.

Three white supremacists who had bombed a bank, a newspaper, and an abortion clinic in Spokane, Washington in 1996 called themselves Phineas Priests. (Phineas was an Old Testament priest who slew an interreligious couple.)

Another loner, Eric Robert Rudolph, a fugitive who disappeared into the Carolina woods, is charged with four bombings that left two people dead, including a police officer, and 124 injured. These attacks included the bombing at Centennial Olympic Park in Atlanta in 1996, the bombings of an Atlanta abortion clinic and of a nightclub with a gay clientele in 1997, and the bombing of an abortion clinic in Birmingham, Alabama in 1998.

Those who participate in leaderless resistance, either through phantom cells or individual action, must know exactly what they are doing, and how to do it. It becomes the responsibility of the individual to acquire the necessary skills and information as to what is to be done. Rudolph has demonstrated these skills very efficiently.

Anarchists

They call themselves anarchists, anti-authoritarians, or humanists, and their basic belief is that all governments and corporations are bad and should be drastically curtailed if not abolished. They came to national attention for their aggressive participation in the street demonstrations in Seattle, Washington during the World Trade Organization (WTO) meeting in December 1999. Another group showed up at a Northwest anarchist conference in Eugene, Oregon in June 1999, and shortly thereafter eight police officers were injured when a march called by the anarchist Action Collective turned into a riot. Anarchists' protests in Eugene have often focused on environmental issues.

The protests in Seattle were so vehement and intrusive that meetings were disrupted, and WTO members could not reach their destinations. These protests severely rattled government officials.

No one, at this point, knows whether the anarchists pose a terrorist problem or merely a nuisance. It is clear that they should be monitored.

Good Cause Extremists

So as to clear the air, let us take a moment to distinguish between activists and extremists, in the context of this book. Political activism has a long and highly respectable history. Political activism preceded the American and French revolutions. The political activism of the 1960's and the 1970's resulted in positive cultural, economic, and sociological changes worldwide. In the United States, the Civil Rights Act, as well as other significant legislation, benefitted a great many of us women, Blacks, Hispanics, disabled, seniors, Catholics, gays and lesbians, among others.

Civil disobedience was an effective strategy of political activism during the 60's and 70's. While demonstrations, peaceful marches, non-destructive sit-ins, and pickets were initially met with police resistance, these active but essentially non-violent techniques were later accepted as legitimate forms of political protest. They are the strategies of today's protests as well.

In the 1980's, we witnessed the politicizing of good cause issues, prominent among them

religious, environmental, and animal rights issues. These issues, initially (and sneeringly) referred to as representing "bleeding hearts," "tree-huggers," "little old ladies in tennis shoes," and just plain crazies have burgeoned into some of the hottest, most powerful, most divisive issues of modern times. Organizations representing these issues and the people who support them have become increasingly powerful and competitive.

Unfortunately, powerful issues and emotion-charged messages tend to attract those individuals who are looking for a "home" for their own private agendas; i.e. the extremists who either attach themselves to an organization or who splinter an organization from within. Every activist organization has at least one or more individuals who believe that the organization is not sufficiently effective and that only extreme behavior (almost always violence or coercive behavior) will achieve results. These, then, are the extremists.

Good cause extremists are often described as individuals who start with good intentions and who then "go bad." This is certainly true of a portion of these individuals. There is ample opportunity for this behavior. The individuals who are active in fighting for their cause are impassioned, dedicated, and often one-dimensional in their outlook. However, without question, activist causes also attract a certain number of individuals who join, not so much because of a vested belief in the cause, but because of their need to be a part of a highly visible, ego-building activity. Some seek out causes as an avenue for their passion for violence.

Good cause extremists see themselves as soldiers fighting for God, country, the planet, innocent animals, etc., and against greed, cruelty, sin, and other unlovely virtues. "Baby killers" is the epithet flung at abortion doctors. As soldiers fighting the good fight, extremists find it perfectly acceptable to inflict casualties. After all, they reason, any conflict has unavoidable casualties. And, besides, didn't that abortion doctor (baby killer) get what he deserved when an inflamed anti-abortionist hanger-on shot him in the back and killed him?

Activists and, hence, extremists tend to fall into several broad categories, with many sub-divisions: environmental, religious, and animal rights.

Good cause activism now touches or has the potential to touch every politician at all levels--city, county, and national; every government worker; every corporate CEO; every research facility and its workers; every medical and health care worker; and some surprising others, such as archaeologists and National Park Service workers. Therefore, the potential danger of a violent confrontation to a client from good cause extremists is very high.

Environmental

There are dozens of environmental issues, some of which deal with: pollution, holes in the ozone layer, rain forests, preservation of hundreds of wildlife inhabitants, save the whales, save the dolphins, nuclear plants, effect of electrical power lines on health, polluted waterways, the inundation of the wilderness by dams, preservation of forests and wilderness areas, chemical waste, and chemical dumping. New to the list is the sudden emergence of those opposing genetically altered products. Apologies for those important issues which have been left out.

Logging and mining companies have been stopped dead in their tracks from performing their activities in public lands. In most cases, the successes have been achieved by the more conservative and credible Sierra Club, Audoban Society, National Wildlife Federation, and other organizations with long histories of activism tempered with discretion and a firm grip on reality. However, definite successes have been chalked up to the smaller, more impassioned environmental organizations.

There have been numerous ecotage incidents, many of them in the lush, heavily wooded northwestern portion of the United States. The total cost of these incidents is not reported, but individual incidents tend to be in the $60,000 to $100,000 range. And, they have been very effective in stopping

the logging and mineral development of public lands. In addition to the costs of ecotage, the environmentalists have managed to capture the public attention and have been quite successful in projecting their image as brave defenders doing battle against corporate and governmental greed.

The environmental protection movement is worldwide. In save the whale efforts, fishing vessels have been rammed, shots have been exchanged, and at least one vessel bombed. In other ecotage efforts, the British Columbia Hydro Substation on Vancouver Island was blown up, as was the Alta Dam in northern Norway.

The extremists believe that they serve a useful purpose in assuming the role of aggressive firebrands, thus making more conservative organizations such as Sierra Club appear as moderates.

Up until now, most of the ecotage has been directed toward property damage, although there have been more or less accidental human casualties resulting from acts of vandalism/ecotage. There has not been a concerted effort to directly cause human casualties. The property damage took a quantum leap in the fall of 1998 when Earth Liberation Front (ELF) admitted setting fires that caused more than $12 million in damage. The stated goal was to halt another expansion of Colorado's Vail Ski Resort because of fears it could harm a potential habitat for the lynx, a threatened species of mountain cat. One other theory is that ELF, which advocates nonviolence, meant to scare skiers away and hurt the resort economically.

There are some factors which could move the radicalism from its focus on property damage to attacks on people. There is a rising feeling of urgency to the environmental movement; disappearance of the rain forests, acid rain, and ozone breakdowns have produced some doomsday prophecies if action is not taken now to remedy the problems. If the economic condition in some parts of the world does not improve and, in fact, continues to deteriorate, resistance to environmental concerns may increase. If jobs are lost because of the shutdown of a nuclear plant, or the prevention of logging, or the ban on strip mining, heretofore neutral people who have not been touched by the environmental battles may find themselves on opposite sides. If the logger's job is gone and cannot be replaced, and his family is facing tough times, that logger may line up on the anti-environmental side. If the environmentalists believe that their position is being reversed, frustration could lead to violence. As it is, many radical environmentalists believe that a return to nature, and a de-emphasis of technology is the only way to save the planet. Wasn't this the message of the Unabomber?

Thus far, the environmentalists have been sufficiently successful in achieving progress so that targeted personal violence has not been a significant problem. Indeed, having achieved a credible reputation of respectability, even with the extremists indulging in ecotage, the environmentalists in general are anxious to preserve their legitimate state, and would not welcome the kind of violence associated with some of the other extremist groups. Given a status quo, this attitude will probably not change. On the other hand, circumstances that show a rapidly worsening ecological condition could give strength to the extremist factions.

What is the exposure to a client? At the current time, if the client has been lucky enough not to become involved in an environmental issue, the exposure is not likely to be significant. If the client has been targeted as a polluter or destroyer of the environment, he/she has a higher exposure to some sort of confrontation, possibly of a violent nature, but more likely concentrated on property damage.

There is a cautionary note. Every "cause" attracts a fringe element of deeply disturbed individuals, even when active participation on their part is discouraged. The rhetoric, alone, is attractive to those individuals who feel disenfranchised and victimized, and who have inner rages which are searching for an outlet. Events are now so well publicized in newspapers and on television that the "message" is certain to be received by anyone who is listening. Because much of the ecotage activity has

been reported in a brave and attractive light and as portraying the perpetrators as heros and defenders, the subliminal message might be interpreted as, "It is okay to cause harm if it is done for a good cause." Those individuals sitting on the fringes of the movement might be able to easily distort the message, moving the extra step to personal violence.

Abortion and the Right to Life Movement

It is not an exaggeration to say that the issue of abortion versus the right to life is one of the most emotional, invective-filled, hate-charged issues in America today. Perhaps because of the visceral emotions attached to abortion and the strategies employed by many of the followers of the right to life movement, there is a history of violence attached that poses real threats to doctors, nurses, health care workers, politicians, and corporate owners of abortion clinics.

Here is a highly simplified rendition of the two opposing sides' arguments and goals in the abortion issue.

The right to life advocates wish to put an end to all legal abortions now performed in clinics, doctors' offices, and hospitals. Further, the most idealistic goal for them is an amendment to the U.S. Constitution which would declare that the right to life is vested in each human being from the moment of fertilization without regard to age, health, or condition of dependency. The true believers in right to life extend the right to life to zygotes, a zygote being an egg at the moment of fertilization. Thus, true believers also object to those birth control methods which allow fertilization to take place but prevent implantation of the zygote on the uterine wall (intrauterine devices and low-estrogen pills).

The pro-choice advocates believe the opposite, that each woman has a right to privacy and the right to decide whether she will or will not practice birth control and will or will not have an abortion. *Roe vs. Wade* decision gave them these rights legally and they defend them vigorously.

The right to life movement is heavily oriented toward religion, and many anti-abortionists are fundamentalist in their beliefs.

This highly charged issue is, interestingly, a fairly recent phenomenon. Throughout history, abortion and even infanticide has taken place, usually to avoid the economic burden of extra children. Abortion was prevalent in primitive societies and was considered normal in ancient Greek and Roman cultures. In various cultures and at different times, there were various perceptions as to the question of when the fetus was considered as "human" or possessing a soul.

Even within the Catholic church there has been a history of dissention on the question of abortion and birth control. Adding to the confusion is the fact that there is no direct reference within the Bible to abortion or contraception. St. Augustine of Hippo, who lived in the late fourth and early fifth centuries, was influential in the formation of early church philosophy. As often happens, Augustine thoroughly enjoyed his early sexual exploits, only to turn later to spiritual purity. His writings and those of other Christian intellectuals, emphasized woman as the temptress and preached chastity as the road to God and heaven. Thus began a history of church teachings that sex should never be practiced for pleasure--only for procreation. Thomas Aquinas, the 13th century scholar who was so influential in forming the body of accepted Catholic thought, viewed women as appendages to men. Aquinas wrote that the soul entered the male fetus 40 days after conception and the female fetus 80 days after conception. Thus, early abortions were acceptable to the church at that time.

Regardless of religious thinking, abortion remained legal in the United States until the mid-1800's. Once abortions were outlawed, it drove pregnant women to illegal abortions, many of them dangerous and terminal. By the second half of the 19th century the medical community, the church, and the government had united in a campaign against abortion. This campaign was vested both in the moral issue of the right to life and in the practical

issue of female emancipation. As women began to emerge from the centuries-old role of subservience and to seek more freedoms, more laws were enacted. The Comstock Law made it a crime to import, mail, or transport any article or medicine for the prevention of conception or for causing an abortion.

Margaret Sanger, a nurse in New York City ghettos during the early years of the 20th century, realized that much human suffering could be alleviated if contraceptive education could be made available to women. Sanger was a fighter for women's rights and in 1921 formed the American Birth Control League which eventually became the Planned Parenthood Federation.

It was not until 1965 that the Supreme Court declared that states could not forbid the sale of contraceptives to married couples. This ruling was extended in 1972 to include unmarried individuals. The sexual revolution moved with breathtaking speed, and by 1966, it was estimated that six million American women (about one fifth of those of childbearing age) were using the birth control pill. The Catholic church has staunchly resisted not only abortion but contraception in any form except for use of the "rhythm method," although the church hierarchy has been widely split on this issue.

Abortion was legalized in 1973. The landmark case, first tried in Texas, then appealed to and won in the U.S. Supreme Court, was *Roe vs. Wade*. *Roe vs. Wade* rested on the right to privacy and the concept of personal liberty set forth in the Fourteenth Amendment, which forbids the State to "deprive any person of life, liberty, or property without due process of law . . ." Since then, there have been many challenges to *Roe vs. Wade*. It was particularly galling to anti-abortionists that several hundred thousands of poor Medicaid recipients were able to obtain publicly funded abortions. This publicly funded access to abortions by poor people was ended with the Hyde Amendment which was affirmed in the U.S. Supreme Court.

From 1973 to 1976, the Catholic church was the most outspoken and the most effective opponent of abortion. Then, in the late 1970's, the fundamentalist Protestants emerged as an active political force to be reckoned with, with an agenda of morality. The "moral majority" was angered by many issues: immorality, abortion, pornography, homosexuality, the breakdown of the family unit, bussing, and others.

The "moral majority" emerged as a cohesive, powerful force during the Presidential campaigns of Ronald Reagan. President Reagan was championed by the moral majority, and he gave great legitimacy to the fundamentalist movement. One leader of this movement, Pat Robertson, seriously considered running for the presidency of the United States.

This issue has struck a deep inner chord. The right to life movement is a complex one. Its avowed purpose is both religious and moral--to protect human life and to protect the sanctity of the family. "Family values," which is terminology closely associated with right to life, sees the family as the stabilizing unit and the woman as mother and helpmate. Many right to life proponents see today's society as lacking in moral virtues, rampant and evil in its sexuality, and yearn for the return of women to a more traditional role.

The women who favor abortion rights, on the other hand, see abortion as their guarantee of independence and freedom.

The abortion issue has, from the start, been an activist issue. The two sides drew up battle lines. Initial victories went to the pro-choice side and they were accomplished without undue violence. Women did not bomb clinics which refused to perform abortions. Quite simply, it was the right time for the issue. The pro-choice victories, however, served as a rallying point for the right to life proponents, and the elections of Ronald Reagan and George Bush gave them political clout to rejoin the battle.

When the right to life movement came into full flower, it did so with enormous force. The anti-abortionist movement has learned from others' experiences, particularly those freedom fighters of recent years. While the anti-abortionist movement espouses non-violent behavior, there are guerrilla arms to the movement. Operation Rescue, with close to 100,000 members, is extremely well organized. Its members block entrances to abortion clinics, wave pictures of aborted fetuses, and scream "Don't Kill Your Baby" at women entering the clinics.

Abortion clinics have been bombed and burned. Anti-abortionist organizations publish manuals on harassment techniques. Abortion doctors and nurses have their pictures published on "WANTED" posters. Abortion doctors' homes have been picketed. Children of abortion doctors are targeted at school with whisper campaigns.

There is no question that the anti-abortion issue has attracted a fringe element of hangers-on and admirers who are easily inflamed by the rhetoric engendered by the movement. The murder of a Florida abortion doctor by a demonstrator who coldly shot the doctor in the back is proof of this.

In Kansas an abortion doctor was shot (not fatally) as he sat in his car near his clinic. It is reported that his attacker, a woman, wrote at least 25 admiring letters and sent money to the man accused of killing the Florida abortion doctor. She is reported as writing, "I know you did the right thing. It was not murder. You shot a murderer. It was more like anti-murder. I believe in you and what you did, and really want to help if possible. I wish I could trade places with you." She wrote further, "I think it would be a good time to picket with a sign that says 'Execute Murderers/Abortionists.'"

It is probably fair to state that every doctor practicing in abortion clinics has received death threats, and many have endured endless vituperative telephone calls directed to their families. It is not so much the right to life proponents who pose the direct threat; it is the fringe element who inflame and encourage violent action.

The threat to the client? If he/she is not involved in this issue, the direct threat is low. If he/she is active on the pro-choice front, the threat is extremely high. And, if the client is on the hit list targeted by anti-abortionist foes, the threat is not only high, it is not to be taken lightly. The emotional level is sufficiently high to remove some of the inhibitors to violence.

Animal Rights Activists

Among the more violence-prone of the good cause extremists are the animal rights followers. The emotions of these believers are equal to those of the anti-abortionists. Advocates of animal rights are so certain of the justice of their cause that they break laws, destroy property, and have threatened those executives and doctors who lead the research units using animals for experiments.

If emotions run high on abortion issues, it is incredible that the emotions which are expended on animals of all kinds are sky-high. We are a nation devoted to our pets. We lavish the attention upon our domestic animals which we are often prevented from expending upon our children. At the very least, our pets do not judge us nor leave us. As a reward, pets are given food, medical attention and lavish accoutrements which generate many millions, even billions, of dollars each years.

Animal research has been performed upon a number of animals including monkeys, dogs, cats, rats, rabbits, and guinea pigs, among others. If all animal research were done upon rats and roaches, it is highly suspect that there would be so much commotion about animal rights. True, there have been a number of purists who have eloquently defended the rights of all living matter, but it is difficult to imagine that the current dissatisfaction would have occurred if research experiments were conducted only against slugs, beetles, and spiders.

This does not take away from the absolute purity and intensity of the goals of the animal rights proponents. These individuals are passionately dedicated to their cause. As with abortion, it is an issue that has visceral appeal. As also with the abortion issue, violence in defense of animal rights is viewed by many as a forgivable trait if it accomplishes a "greater good."

Animal rights is an issue which goes back some 200 years, but is newly popular. The term "speciesism" was first heard in 1973, but a book written by Peter Singer, *Animal Liberation*, pushed animal rights on to the international stage in 1975. Singer did not argue for equal rights for animals; he argued for equal consideration. Singer recognized that animals are not our equals in terms of voting and decision-making but he conceded to them equal rights to attention and care.

True animal rights activists believe that we should not kill animals for food, clothing, or research. *Really* pure animal rights activists extend their concerns to vegetables and give credence to the "death scream" of the carrot as it is wrenched from the ground. (This is a very low minority group.)

The more moderate animal rights advocates argue against the inhumane conditions of "factory farming" of chickens, calves, and beef cattle, while the more dedicated activists argue against the killing of any animals for food.

Animal research, or specifically research using animals, is a multi-billion dollar business. There are approximately 1,200 research institutions using animals in the United States. This research entails using animals for research in medicine, for refining surgical techniques, diagnosing diseases, defining pregnancies, determining whether products (chemicals, cosmetics) are safe, and for biological education in schools. Moderates would like to abolish the "frivolous" use of animals (such as testing for safety of cosmetics) in research, while allowing continued but humane treatment for research in drug and surgical testing. Activists wish to put a stop to all use of animals in research. Radical advocates have freed laboratory animals and damaged some research facilities, and in some extreme cases have threatened researchers and families with death and injury.

To their credit, the animal rights activists have been able to create better, more humane conditions for many animals used in research and in school science programs. A number of laws have been passed at the state level to protect animals. And, in truth, these laws were long overdue, since the environment in which many of the laboratory research animals were kept has been inhumane and insensitive.

As with the abortion issue and the use of pictures of aborted fetuses, the descriptions and pictures of research animals with severed limbs and pitiable living conditions has aroused intense emotions. In 1985, animal rights activists stole documents and carried off several hundred research animals from the biology and psychology labs at the University of California at Riverside. In 1987, activists set fire to a building under construction at the University of California's Davis campus. It was to have been used for research on diseases of farm animals. The Federal Bureau of Investigation labeled the Animal Liberation Front a terrorist group.

The issue of using dogs and cats from pounds in research is very controversial. Forced removal of animals from pounds has almost been stopped (although it has not prevented the euthanizing of the millions of unwanted pets held by the nation's animal pounds).

To the animal rights true believers *all* uses of animals are wrong, including zoos, circuses, rodeos, and racetracks. Some animal rights advocates even give up keeping pets. At the same time, all attempts to stop the use of animals has, not surprisingly, met with strong opposition from research scientists, farmers, ranchers, pet shop owners, fur stores, hunters, and trappers.

Predictions are that this is a movement that is not going to go away. It will probably continue to grow, somewhat dependent upon the national economy. If the economy should take a dramatically downward turn and unemployment becomes an issue, animal rights will undoubtedly lose some of its impetus. When people are worried about their security, they have little time left over to worry about the condition of animals. This could have two effects. Animal rights as a hot issue could simply cool down

and become semi-toothless, or the extremists, seeing a diminution of activity, could increase the violence as a way of keeping the pressure on.

The danger to a client? As we have already stated, the danger lies in direct proportion to the client's involvement or non-involvement with the use of animals. Thus far, the violence has been more or less confined to research institutes and those corporations funding research using animals. There was, however, one well reported incident involving the bombing of a vehicle belonging to the feisty CEO of a surgical manufacturing company which included research carried out on animals.

Refugees

America has long had a reputation for accepting the "poor and huddled masses," the refugees from politically chaotic countries. Ironically, while there are strict quotas on immigrants entering this country under normal circumstances, political refugees who claim that if they return to their homes overseas their lives will be in danger can find refuge within the United States. This has engendered some very troubling problems.

Hundreds of radical operatives now live in the United States, making up a loose network with possibly terrorist objectives. These potential terrorists often have a love-hate relationship with this country. They have communal and family roots in the United States, and many have started businesses. So, on the one hand, they have found a supportive refuge. On the other hand, they have brought with them the "baggage" of old enmities from other countries, notably Middle Eastern countries.

It is believed that there are now in this country members of Egyptian Jihad, Hamas, Hezbollah, Islamic Jihad, and others who use the U.S. as a base to coordinate attacks in their home countries.

The World Trade Center bombing has been claimed as the work of a group calling itself the Liberation Army Fifth Battalion. In a letter to the New

York Times, they stated that the bombing was in response to "American political, economic, and military support for Israel, the state of terrorism, and to the rest of the dictator countries."

The World Trade Center bombing was not only devastating, it was significant. This was the first major terrorist act by transplanted activists.

Also living in the United States, Britain, France, and Germany are hundreds of demobilized Islamic resistance fighters who were recruited and fought in the Afghan conflict. Many thousands of Islamic fighters were recruited and trained in guerrilla warfare. When the fighting ended in Afghanistan, it is believed that Iran and other fundamentalist countries redirected the residual rage toward the West. The United States and other Western countries have, in the past, recruited, trained, and funded activists to fight in conflicts which represented a vested interest for the U.S. and the West. Once the conflicts are ended, either as a win or loss for the West, the trained fighters often cannot go home, and their only trained skills are in guerrilla fighting.

The activist refugees closely resemble violent employees in the workplace in many ways. Like the violent employee, the refugee may undergo a metamorphosis in his feelings toward his "provider" (the corporation/boss for the employee and the government for the refugee). The government may have been perceived as the benevolent provider of money, guns, food, employment, and eventually a refuge, or home. However, as time goes on, the refugee wishes to return home. Many refugees lost family members, ancestral homes, and money. The refugees are enraged by these losses and wish both to recover their lost lives and possessions and to punish the offenders. The refugee may expect the government to aid him in his endeavors, either as a reward for his prior service or because his cause is "just." When this does not occur, when in fact the government appears to favor the offenders, the activist refugee and his fellow refugees, already ghettoized by language and cultural differences, may feel betrayed and turn on the government.

While it is to be hoped that the World Trade Center bombing may have been an isolated incident, it may also have been the first blow of a terrorist campaign within this country of a nature not heretofore experienced.

If the latter is true, the potential dangers to a client would sharply increase. While the World Trade Center bombing was an indiscriminate act, not targeted toward any particular individual, it makes no difference if your client just happened to be parking his car on that day or had his suite of offices on a collapsed floor. If this new terrorism were to take root, clearly the need to target particular clients would rise, both to obtain needed campaign money and to use as "object lessons."

International Terrorism

Worldwide, terrorism may once again be on the rise. The disintegration of the U.S.S.R. has left a greatly troubled legacy. The former Communist-dominated countries now squabble over the ownership of nuclear weapons. At the same time, there are bloody battles over the control of territory. And last, almost all of the former communist "States" are in dire economic straits. It must surely pose a tempting opportunity to trade nuclear weapons for money, support, and power. Nuclear weapons in the wrong hands would raise the stakes in the terrorism game to a new high.

By one account, from January 1968 to the end of December 1975, almost 1,000 transnational international terrorist incidents occurred. These incidents included aircraft hijackings, kidnappings, assassinations, murders, arson, bombings, and assaults. Well over 100 terrorist organizations from 50 or more countries were involved. New groups formed and networked, trained together in camps in Libya and Cuba, exchanged information, and copied successful incidents. During this period, Americans and American business in particular became targets of choice for many. American business came to be viewed as imperialist and neocolonial in nature, exploiting the poor, glutted with riches, and traitors to the cause of human rights.

Much of the terrorism of the 1960's and 1970's can be attributed to the left-wing, primarily Marxist and Marxist-Leninist groups.

The 1980's saw the emergence of the right-wing and fundamentalist groups, as well as a growing number of ethnic conflicts and national insurgencies. The 1990's witnessed the end of the Cold War, the splintering of the Russian Empire, a continuation of right-wing terrorism, and an expansion of ethnic conflicts. The 90's also witnessed several new terrorist expressions--narcoterrorism, biochemical terrorism, a marked increase in the numbers of kidnappings for ransom, and cyber-terrorism.

These, then, are some of the potential threats to clients.

If the client does business in Colombia, the danger of kidnapping is extremely high--not without reason has Colombia been dubbed the "kidnap capital of the world." 1998 saw an average of four to five kidnappings every day. Most were carried out by leftist rebels to finance their insurgency or to use as bargaining chips in negotiations with the government. But, right-wing paramilitaries and purely criminal gangs also regularly carry out abductions. Colombian rebel groups have tripled their numbers over the past ten years, funding much of their growing military strength with the proceeds of kidnappings. In April, members of the National Liberation Army (ELN) hijacked an internal flight, then on May 30 abducted more than 100 worshippers, including two diplomats, from a Roman Catholic mass in an upper-class urban neighborhood. The larger guerrilla group, Revolutionary Armed Forces of Colombia (FARC), dubs their kidnappings as "collecting taxes." Guerrillas set up roadblocks along a main highway and take away all passengers who appear affluent enough to warrant a ransom.

Mexico and Chechnya rate second-place in the kidnapping sweepstakes. Kidnappings in Mexico have become a cottage industry, with gunmen abducting people from cars, cabs, and off the street. Chechnya, now embroiled in a conflict with Russia, is located in a key area in the oil-rich Caucasus.

Chechens have become infamous, not only for kidnappings but for their criminal activities on the streets of Moscow. Criminal gangs elsewhere in the Caucasus also took part, often selling their hostages to people in Chechnya. Chechen rebels are blamed for two apartment house bombings in Moscow, incidents which infuriated the Russians and fixed their determination to wipe out the rebels.

Narcoterrorism poses a threat in that it is so widespread and involves so much money and corruption, that the danger of violence spilling over into other areas is evident. In February 2000, the police chief of Tijuana, Mexico was killed. Gunmen in cars ambushed Chief Marquez as he drove on a highway. He was hit by dozens of bullets. The state governor said that drug traffickers (blamed for the killing) were out of control at least partly because many federal authorities were in their pay. Tijuana, located on the border just a few miles south of San Diego, is also home for a number of American and foreign-owned factories. A few years ago, a Japanese businessman was killed there, as was a leading Mexican Presidential contender. The violence in Tijuana is scary.

Insurgencies have the unfortunate habit of occurring, often, in undeveloped, resource-rich areas-- oil, natural gas, diamonds, and gold being some of more desirable items. Insurgencies also occur in areas such as Indonesia and the Philippines, which have until recently been hotbeds of financial and economic growth, but are now somewhat unstable. Clients tend to be drawn to these areas because of the potential wealth of their resources.

.   A long-running rebellion in Algeria has threatened the stability of other North African countries. Over 100,000 people have perished in Algeria.

.   The Balkans are still in turmoil with new strife in Kosovo. U.S. and Nato air strikes in Yugoslavia were an unpopular issue in neighboring Greece, where protesters bombed two U.S. banks.

.   In Yemen, tourists and business people have

been frequent kidnap targets of disgruntled tribesmen, who have also regularly bombed and damaged a main pipeline from the east of the country to the Red Sea coast. The U.S. State Department issued a travel warning for Yemen on October 21, 1999, saying the level of risk for overseas nationals in Yemen is very high.

.   In Sudan, a new oil pipeline was bombed 20 days after it opened. The civil war in oil-rich Sudan is estimated to have cost as many as two million lives. The pipeline project is owned in part by Talisman Energy Inc. of Canada and is also financed by the state oil companies of China, Malaysia and Sudan. In the 1970's, Chevron spent tens of millions of dollars to develop two oil fields in Sudan, but in 1983, the civil war heated up. In 1984, rebels attacked a Chevron base near the town of Bentiu, killing three oil workers. Not long afterward, Chevron pulled out of Sudan.

.   In Kyrgyzstan, 13 people, including four Japanese geologists who were prospecting for gold, were captured by Tajikistan militants. The militants are thought to have as their goal an Islamic state on territories now belonging to three Central Asian nations, Kyrgyzstan, Tajikistan, and Uzbekistan. The main Islamic movement is the Islamic Renaissance Party. The militants are believed to be financed by Osama bin Laden, who is wanted in connection with the bombings of two U.S. embassies.

Following is a mere sampling of terrorist incidents in 1998 from the U.S. State Department's publication, *Patterns of Global Terrorism, 1998*.

.   January 5--Yemeni tribesmen kidnapped three South Korean citizens, including the wife and daughter of the First Secretary of the Korean Embassy.

.   February 3--Bombs detonated at two McDonald's restaurants in Greece.

.   March 23--Angola--Rebels from the Front for the Liberation of the Cabinda Enclave-Cabinda Armed Forces abducted two Portuguese citizens employed by a Portuguese construction company. Another

Portuguese construction representative was abducted april 22.

.   June 7--Pakistan--A bomb ripped through an 18-car passenger train en route from Karachi to Peshawar, killing 23 persons and wounding 32 others.

.   August 1--A 500-pound car bomb exploded outside a shoe store in Banbridge, Northern Ireland, injuring 35 persons and damaging 200 homes. The Real IRA claimed responsibility.

.   August 7--Bombs exploded almost simultaneously outside the U.S. embassies in Kenya and Tanzania.

.   August 12--Democratic Republic of the Congo--Suspected former Rwandan soldiers abducted six tourists from Canada, Sweden, and New Zealand) after the tourists crossed into the Congo from Uganda.

.   August 25--South Africa--A bomb exploded in the Planet Hollywood restaurant in Capetown, killing one person and injuring at least 24 others. The Muslims Against Global Oppression claimed responsibility.

.   August 29--Belgium--Arsonists firebombed a McDonald's restaurant. The Animal Liberation Front (ALF) claimed responsibility.

.   September 9--Philippines--Three Hong Kong businessmen were kidnapped in Mindanao.

.   November 8--Angola--50 armed assailants attacked a Canadian-owned diamond mine, killing one Portuguese national, two Britons, three Angolans, and wounding 18 others. The secretary general of UNITA claimed responsibility.

.   December 7--Italy--During the week of December 7, the Animal Liberation Front sent panettone cakes laced with rat poison to two branches of the Italian news agency ANSA. Two Italian subsidiaries of Swiss Nestle were forced to halt production, costing the company $30 million. According to Italy's ALF founder, the poisoned cakes were sent to protest Nestle's genetic manipulation food.

.   December 26--Angola--A transport plane carrying United Nations officials and crew members was shot down.   It is believed that UNITA was responsible.

As if this were not enough, on October 8, 1999, U.S. Secretary of State Madeleine K. Albright designated 28 organizations as Foreign Terrorist Organizations. In the following list, note how many are fundamentalist, religious, and/or insurgent in nature.

.   **Abu Nidal Organization (ANO).** Split from the PLO in 1974. Has carried out terrorist attacks in 20 countries, killing or injuring almost 900 persons. Major attacks included the Rome and Vienna airports in December 1985, the Neve Shalom synagogue in Istanbul and the Pan Am Flight 73 hijacking in Karachi in September 1986, and the City of Poros day-excursion ship attack in July 1988 in Greece.

Abu Sayyaf Group (ASG). Smallest and most radical of the Islamic separatist groups operating in the southern Philippines.   Some members have studied or worked in the Middle East and developed ties to Arab mujahidin while fighting and training in Afghanistan. Uses bombs, assassinations, kidnappings, and extortion payments to promote an independent Islamic state in western Mindanao and the Sulu Archipelago, areas in the southern Philippines heavily populated by Muslims.

Armed Islamic Group (GIA).   An Islamic extremist group, the GIA aims to overthrow the secular Algerian regime and replace it with an Islamic state.   Attacks civilians, journalists, and foreign residents.   Uses assassinations and bombings, including car bombs, and it is known to favor kidnapping victims and slitting their throats.

Aum Shinrikyo. A cult established in 1987 by Shoko Asahara, Aum aims to take over Japan and then the world.   Its organizational structure mimics that of a nation-state, with "finance," "construction," and "science and technology" ministries. On March 20, 1995, Aum members simultaneously released sarin nerve gas on several Tokyo subway trains, killing 12 persons and injuring up to 6,000. Operates in Japan, but previously had a presence in Australia, Russia, Ukraine, Germany, Taiwan, Sri Lanka, the former Yugoslavia, and the United States.

Basque Fatherland and Liberty (ETA). Founded in 1959 with the aim of establishing an independent homeland based on Marxist principles in Spain's Basque region and certain southwestern French provinces.   Primarily bombings and assassinations of Spanish government officials and French interest.   Finances its activities through kidnappings, robberies, and extortion.

Gama'a al-Islamiyya (the Islamic Group, IG). Egypt's largest militant group, active since the late 1970's.   Signed Osama bin Laden's fatwa (edict) calling for attacks against U.S. civilians but publicly has denied it supports bin Laden.   Armed attacks against Egyptian security and other government officials, Coptic Christians, and Egyptian opponents of Islamic extremism. Al-Gama'at has launched attacks on tourists in Egypt since 1992, most notably the attack in November 1997 at Luxor that killed 58 foreign tourists. Also claimed responsibility for the attempt in June 1995 to assassinate Egyptian President Hosni Mubarak.

HAMAS.   Formed in late 1987 as an outgrowth of the Palestinian branch of the Muslim Brotherhood, with a goal of establishing an Islamic Palestinian state in place of Israel. HAMAS activists have conducted many attacks, including large scale suicide bombings, against Israeli civilian and military targets, suspected Palestinian collaborators, and Fatah rivals.

Harakat ul-Mujahideen (HUM).   An Islamic militant group based in Pakistan that operates primarily in Kashmir.   Operates terrorist training camps in eastern Afghanistan and suffered casualties in the U.S. missile strikes on bin Laden-associated training camps in August 1998. Has stated that HUM would take revenge on the United States.

Hizballah (Party of God) a.k.a. Islamic Jihad.
Radical Shia (Muslim) group formed in Lebanon; dedicated to creation of Iranian-style Islamic republic in Lebanon and removal of all non-Islamic influences from the area. Strongly anti-West and anti-Israel. Closely allied with, and often directed by, Iran but may have conducted operations that were not approved by Tehran. Known or suspected to have been involved in numerous anti-U.S. terrorist attacks, including the suicide truck bombing of the U.S. Embassy in Beirut in September 1984. Elements of the group were responsible for the kidnapping and detention of U.S. and other Western hostages in Lebanon.

Japanese Red Army (JRA).
An international terrorist group formed around 1970. Led by Fusako Shigenobu, believed to be in Syrian-garrisoned area of Lebanon's Bekaa Valley. Stated goals are to overthrow Japanese government and monarchy and help foment world revolution. Has had close and longstanding relations with Palestinian terrorist groups. During the 1970's, JRA conducted a series of attacks around the world, including the massacre in 1972 at Israel's Lod Airport, two Japanese airliner hijackings, and an attempted takeover of the U.S. Embassy in Kuala Lumpur. In April 1988, JRA operative Yu Kikumura was arrested with explosives on the New Jersey Turnpike, apparently planning an attack to coincide with the bombing of a USO club in Naples and a suspected JRA operation that killed five.

al-Jihad a.k.a. Egyptian Islamic Jihad.
Egyptian Islamic extremist group active since the late 1970's. Appears to be divided into two factions: one led by Ayman al-Zawahiri--who currently is in Afghanistan and is a key leader in terrorist financier Osama bin Laden's new World Islamic Front--and the other led by Ahmad Husayn Agiza, now in jail. Primary goal is to overthrow the Egyptian government and replace it with an Islamic state. Increasingly willing to target U.S. interests in Egypt. The original Jihad was responsible for the assassination in 1981 of

Egyptian President Anwar Sadat. Has not conducted an attack inside Egypt since 1993 and never has targeted foreign tourists there. Has threatened to retaliate against the U.S., however, for its incarceration of Shaykh Umar Abd al-Rahman and, more recently, for the arrests of its members in Albania, Azerbaijan, and the United Kingdom.

Kach (many a.k.a.) and Kahane (many a.k.a.).
Stated goal is to restore the biblical state of Israel. Organize protests against the Israeli government. Harass and threaten Palestinians in Hebron and the West Bank. Have threatened to attack Arabs, Palestinians, and Israeli government officials.

Kurdistan Workers' Party (PKK).
Established in 1974 as a Marxist-Leninist insurgent group primarily composed of Turkish Kurds. Seeks to establish an independent Kurdish state in southeastern Turkey, where the population is predominantly Kurdish. Primary targets are Turkish government security forces in Turkey but also has been active in Western Europe against Turkish targets. Conducted attacks on Turkish diplomatic and commercial facilities in dozens of West European cities in 1993 and again in spring 1995. In an attempt to damage Turkey's tourist industry, the PKK has bombed tourist sites and hotels and kidnapped foreign tourist.

Liberation Tigers of Tamil Eelam (LTTE) a.k.a. Tamil Tigers.
The most powerful Tamil group in Sri Lanka, founded in 1976. Has integrated a battlefield insurgent strategy with a terrorist program that targets not only key government personnel in the countryside but also senior Sri Lankan political and military leaders in Colombo. LTTE political assassinations and bombings have become commonplace, including suicide attacks against the Sri Lankan President in 1993 and Indian Prime Minister Rajiv Gandhi in 1991. Has refrained from targeting Western tourists.

Mujahedin-e Khalq Organization (MEK or MKO) (many a.k.a.).
Formed in the 1960's by the college-educated children of Iranian merchants, the MEK sought to counter what it perceived as excessive Western influence in the Shah's regime. Following a

philosophy that mixes Marxism and islam, has developed into the largest and most active armed Iranian dissident group. Its history is studded with anti-Western activity, and, most recently, attacks on the interests of the clerical regime in Iran and abroad. Supported the 1979 takeover of the U.S. Embassy in Tehran.

National Liberation Army (ELN). Pro-Cuban, anti-U.S. guerrilla group formed in January 1965. Primarily rural-based in Colombia. Conducted assaults on oil infrastructure; extortion and bombings against U.S. and other foreign businesses; annually conducts several hundred kidnappings for profit. Forces coca and opium poppy cultivators to pay protection money and attacks government efforts to eradicate these crops.

Palestine Islamic Jihad-Shaqaqi Faction. Originated among militant Palestinians in the Gaza Strip during the 1970's; a series of loosely affiliated factions rather than a cohesive group. Committed to the creation of an Islamic Palestinian state and the destruction of Israel through holy war. Because of its strong support for Israel, the U.S. has been identified as an enemy of the PIJ. Also opposes moderate Arab governments that it believes have been tainted by Western secularism. Conducted suicide bombings against Israeli targets in the West Bank, Gaza Strip, and Israel.

Palestine Liberation Front-Abu Abbas Faction a.k.a. the Palestine Liberation Front (PLF). Broke away from the PFLP-GC in the mid-1970's. Later split again. The Abu Abbas-led faction has conducted attacks against Israel. Responsible for the attack in 1985 on the cruise ship *Achille Lauro* and the murder of U.S. citizen Leon Klinghoffer.

Popular Front for the Liberation of Palestine (PFLP). Marxist-Leninist group founded in 1967 by George Habash as a member of the PLO. Subsequently suspended participation in the PLO. Committed numerous international terrorist attacks during the 1970's. Since 1978 has conducted numerous attacks against Israeli or moderate Arab targets.

Popular Front for the Liberation of Palestine-General Command (PFLP-GC). Violently opposed to Arafat's PLO. Closely tied to both Syria and Iran. Has conducted numerous cross-border terrorist attacks into Israel using unusual means, such as hot-air balloons and motorized hang gliders.

al-Qa'ida (many other names). Established by Osama bin Laden about 1990 to bring together Arabs who fought in Afghanistan against the Soviet invasion. Helped finance, recruit, transport, and train Sunni Islamic extremists for the Afghan resistance. Current goal is to "reestablish the Muslim State" throughout the world. Works with allied Islamic extremist groups to overthrow regimes it deems "non-Islamic" and remove Westerners from Muslim countries. Issued statement under banner of "The World Islamic Front for Jihad Against The Jews and Crusaders" in February 1998, saying it was the duty of all Muslims to kill U.S. citizens, civilian or military, and their allies everywhere. Conducted the bombings of the U.S. embassies in Kenya and Tanzania that killed at least 301 persons and injured more than 5,000 others. Claims to have shot down U.S. helicopters and killed U.S. servicemen in Somalia in 1993 and to have conducted three bombings targeted against the U.S. troop presence in Yemen in December 1992. Linked to plans for attempted terrorist operations, including the assassination of the Pope during his visit to Manila in late 1994; simultaneous bombings of the U.S. and Israeli Embassies in Manila and other Asian capitals in late 1994; and a plan to kill President Clinton during a visit to the Philippines in early 1995. Bin Laden is sheltered in Afghanistan.

Revolutionary Armed Forces of Colombia (FARC). The largest, best-trained, and best-equipped insurgent organization in Colombia. Has been anti-United States since its inception in 1964. Armed attacks against Colombian political, economic, military, and police targets. Many members pursue criminal activities, carrying out hundreds of kidnappings for profit annually. Foreign citizens often are targets of FARC kidnappings. Group has ties to narcotics traffickers. Began in 1998 a bombing campaign against oil pipelines.

Revolutionary Organization 17 November. Radical leftist group established in 1975. Anti-Greek establishment, anti-U.S., anti-Turkey, anti-NATO, and committed to the ouster of U.S. bases, removal of Turkish military presence from Cyprus, and severing of Greece's ties to NATO and the European Union (EU). Initial attacks were assassinations of senior U.S. officials and Greek public figures. Added bombings in 1980's. Since 1990, has expanded targets to include EU facilities and foreign firms investing in Greece.

Revolutionary People's Liberation Party/Front a.k.a. Devrimci Sol. A splinter faction of the Turkish People's Liberation Party/Front. Espouses a Marxist ideology and is virulently anti-U.S. and anti-NATO. Finances its activities chiefly through armed robberies and extortion. Assassinated two U.S. military contractors and wounded a U.S. Air Force officer to protest the Gulf War. Launched rockets at U.S. Consulate in Istanbul in 1992.

Revolutionary People's Struggle (ELA). Extreme leftist group is a self-described revolutionary, anti-capitalist, and anti-imperialist group that has declared its opposition to "imperialist domination, exploitation, and oppression"; strongly anti-U.S. and seeks the removal of U.S. military forces from Greece. Since 1974, has conducted bombings against Greek government and economic targets as well as U.S. military and business facilities.

Shining Path (Sendero Luminoso). Larger of Peru's two insurgencies, SL is among the world's most ruthless guerrilla organizations. Stated goal is to destroy existing Peruvian institutions and replace them with peasant revolutionary regime. Also wants to rid Peru of foreign influences. Has engaged in particularly brutal forms of terrorism. Has bombed diplomatic missions of several countries in Peru, including the U.S. Embassy. Involved in cocaine trade.

Tupac Amaru Revolutionary Movement (MRTA). Marxist-Leninist revolutionary movement formed in 1983. Aims to rid Peru of imperialism and establish Marxist regime. Bombings, kidnappings, ambushes, assassination. Previously responsible for large number of anti-U.S. attacks; recent activity has dropped off dramatically. In December 1996, MRTA members overtook the Japanese Ambassador's residence in Lima during a diplomatic reception, capturing hundreds. Government forces stormed the residence in April 1997, rescuing all but one of the remaining hostages and killing the attackers. Has not conducted a significant terrorist operation since then.

Information Warfare

The United States government and terrorism experts are taking very seriously the threat of information and infrastructure warfare. Tactics would involve computer viruses and invasions; High Energy Radio Frequency (HERF) guns which focus a high power radio signal on target equipment, putting it out of action; and Electromagnetic Pulse (EMP) devices which can be detonated in the vicinity of a target system. Such devices can destroy electronics and communications equipment over a wide area.

It is primarily the civilian sectors that are most vulnerable, with consequences in both the military and the political sphere. Nearly every aspect of the military industry depends on civilian information networks; over 95 percent of military communications use the civilian network.

The increasing flow of information, the evolution of the global economy, and the creation of the Internet are all factors in creating the modern global village. It is clear that the changes in human society will entail changes in the way we wage war. Among other trends, warfare is shifting more and more toward civilian targets. This is because it is in our civilian lives that we are most vulnerable to the techniques of information warfare. We have become almost totally dependent on the digitized flow of information to control our electric power supplies, run the national water system, control the air traffic into and out of the country, manage our bank accounts, and keep track of every aspect of our personal lives. All of these information systems are vulnerable.

In the past, there was no compelling reason for terrorists to be computer literate. This is changing fast. Today, the majority of university degrees in Computer Science are given to students from developing countries, the vast majority from Islamic countries.

It is rumored that, during the Gulf War, a group of Dutch hackers offered to disrupt the U.S. military's deployment to the Middle East for one million dollars. The offer was, fortunately, turned down.

Closer to home and our immediate personal lives is the fact that we are currently engaged in an economic warfare. Battles are being fought in the race to acquire information that will give a country or entity or individual an "edge," particularly in the technological field. We're all listening in on each other and, yes, engaging in spying. Corporations still only vaguely understand what is going on--how much of their proprietary information (estimated in the billions of dollars) is being lost. Crisis Management Plans are detailed in those sections dealing with natural disasters such as floods and chemical leaks, but are woefully deficient in dealing with information warfare. The Global Network (cyberspace) is redefining the way we do business--and cyberspace is not a safe place to be; it is riddled with real and potential security leaks.

Information warfare has been described as low risk/high reward endeavor. The chances of being caught are low and the potential rewards are very high.

Furthermore, adversaries do not depend solely upon computers and the Internet to gain information and create mischief. A proliferation of satellites are even now collecting images and sounds from around the world, feeding them into databases, and spitting out summaries.

Narcoterrorists and other criminals have not ignored the advantages of going high-tech. From the rebel gangs using cell phones and fax machines to the very sophisticated information centers of the mafia, these people are part of the information warfare. It is said that Osama bin Laden runs his terrorist network through modern communications equipment.

The executive protection agent who is not computer literate is way, way behind the curve.

More to Come

There are at least three issues which will undoubtedly become involved in the terrorism arena: genetic alteration of food and drink products; worldwide globalization of just about everything; and the "haves" vs. the "have-nots."

One can already see the first indications. There is a growing resentment of the genetic alteration of food products. Note the incident of the Animal Liberation Front sending panettone cakes laced with rat poison to the Italian news agency ANSA, protesting Nestle's genetic manipulation of food.

The Seattle street riots protesting the World Trade Union are significant. There is a strongly felt feeling that we are losing our identity as individuals and as ethnic groups sharing a common language and culture. There has been, for years, a deeply felt suspicion of the United Nations and NATO. This has been exacerbated by the blinding speed with which globalization is taking over our world. If the European Union has produced a common currency and no trade barriers, will the result be a mongrelized "European" common culture? Previously noted was the August 25, 1998 bombing of a Planet Hollywood restaurant in Capetown, South Africa; responsibility was claimed by the Muslims Against Global Oppression. This issue is also tied to immigration. Open borders and access to economic benefits is attracting millions of immigrants, legal and illegal, to each and every prosperous country. Within these countries, there is a visible rift, with many resentful of this, feeling that their hard work is providing welfare, medical care, and economic benefits to "foreigners."

The technologies developed in the 1990's have far outstripped the understanding of them by the ordinary individual. It will surely heighten the fears of the right-wing elements who have long feared the "black helicopters" and mind-altering genetic tinkering of our food and water.

The high-tech times we live in, and the booming economies of some (primarily Western) countries have greatly exacerbated the divide between the haves and the have-nots. Most third-world countries lag far behind in the technological and information field, which--in addition to the fact that they are governed by some of the most corrupt people on the planet--dooms them to poverty and hard times. The gap between the rich and the poor is growing, and millions of people are left in the hopeless position of seeing no way to narrow that gap. And, even within those countries with booming economies, America among them, there are those who have not shared in the prosperity, and who bitterly resent that fact.

When you combine these three trends, the result is--loss of control, loss of pride, loss of empowerment, and deep resentment. It is inevitable that some will lash out in the only way they know--by smashing the infrastructure, bringing down the arrogant governments and corporations which have emasculated them--or perhaps, simply carving out their own places in the sun where they, too, can be rich.

This chapter has given only the slightest overview of the subject of terrorism. There are a number of very good books which deal with the subject, and the protection agent is urged to acquire several, read them, and keep them on the bookshelf for easy reference and research.

VIOLENT EMPLOYEES IN THE WORKPLACE

In one dramatic headline, a newspaper writer asked, "Have the killing fields moved from the streets to the workplace?" This is not exactly the case; there are, in fact, conflicting reports. One report states that workplace violence *incidents* have slightly decreased, whereas the numbers of *victims* have increased with each incident claiming more victims. There are some criminologists who, noting the overall decrease in violent crimes from all causes, refer to murder in the workplace as the fastest-growing form of murder in America.

Women are particularly at risk of accidental death and homicide on the job. A report from the National Institute for Occupational Safety and Health stated that murder is the leading cause of death of American women in the workplace and the third leading cause of occupational death for both sexes. One source states that more than 500,000 rapes, robberies, and aggravated assaults take place each year at U.S. workplaces. Other estimates of the total number of violent incidents on the job are close to one million a year. The U.S. Department of Justice, in a Special Report of Workplace Violence for the years 1992-96, concluded that each year between 1992 and 1996 more than 2 million U.S. residents were victims of a violent crime while they were at work or on duty.

While some of the homicides which occur in the workplace are attributable to outside factors (armed robbery which escalates into murder), some of the most violent crimes have been caused by fired and disgruntled workers, or husbands of workers. Murder is not the only crime committed by unhappy workers; other costly damages have occurred. Hostile workers and ex-employees have taken hostages, destroyed equipment, inserted false data into computer systems, and stolen company secrets. While these non-murderous acts cost businesses millions of dollars, it is the homicidal acts which are on the rise. Here is but a sampling of workplace mayhem.

In Louisville a man entered the plant where he used to work, armed with five guns and "looking for bosses." For half an hour, he methodically shot his way through the building, wounding 13 and killing seven. In Escondido, California, a letter carrier killed his wife, then drove to the post office and murdered two co-workers. A disgruntled ex-employee opened fire on his former supervisors in Georgia. In San Diego a man shot and wounded his supervisor, then chased and killed another manager.

Ex-US Air employee David Burke boarded a PSA plane (parent company US Air) with the express purpose of killing PSA executive Raymond Thompson, whom he believed was responsible for his firing from US Air. Burke went a giant step further; he killed Thompson and the plane's pilot and co-pilot, causing the plane to crash, killing all 44 passengers.

Investigators in New Jersey believe the man who pleaded guilty to Federal charges in connection with the kidnapping of Exxon Corporation executive Sidney J. Reso may have wanted revenge against Exxon for his 1987 firing.

In two of the most recent incidents Byran Uyesugi allegedly opened fire on his Xerox co-workers in Hawaii, killing seven people, and a man showed up at a Seattle shipyard and shot four people, killing two.

Even so, homicide totals do not tell the full story of workplace violence. There were hundreds of nonfatal shootings and stabbings of workers on the job in 1998.

Part of the problem, analysts say, may be rooted in the growing diversity of the American workplace. At no point in our nation's history have so many men and women of different racial and cultural backgrounds worked alongside each other. While all acknowledge that diversity is a good thing, it can also bring resentment and conflict.

The threat can come from at least three sources: a disgruntled employee; an outsider who is related to or otherwise knows an employee; or a stranger with no ties to the organization but who infiltrates through poor access control and security.

Steven Smith was arrested for the rape and strangulation murder of a pathologist in New York City. Smith was able to gain access to Bellevue Hospital Center where the pathologist worked by wearing a hospital uniform and stethoscope and by acquiring stolen identification. At the time, Steven Smith was homeless and living on the streets of New York City, until he surreptitiously found a way to shelter within the hospital.

Hospitals and schools with traditionally open environments have become quickly vulnerable to outside intrusion and violence. Within schools and universities, shootings and other assaults have horrified us all. Students shoot students and instructors and, of late, outsiders have infiltrated schools containing young children.

Street gangs have been able to infiltrate the workplace, to establish or take over a drug business, or to steal goods, often with the help of an employee or employees.

And it does not end there. It is estimated that business loses several billion dollars annually from family violence-related absenteeism and $100 billion in abuse-related medical costs. One organization has estimated that 25 percent of all problems in the workplace stem from violence at home, and an equal number of medical claims stem from family violence.

Family violence costs business more than the lost work hours and increased use of health care benefits. A worker with a troubled family life may reflect his/her problems in ways ranging from conflicts with co-workers, poor performance and poor morale among co-workers, to violence toward co-workers and supervisors. Ultimately, employees with records of poor performance and disruptive behavior must be replaced, costing the company even more money. Some estimates peg the cost of acquiring and training a new employee at an average $15,000, while replacing a top executive may run as high as $50,000.

The workplace has traditionally been considered a haven of security for its workers. Safety from occupational accidents has been an issue for many years, but the personal security of the workers within the workplace was taken for granted. One could be killed on the streets or at home, but the workplace was relatively free of violence. This is no longer the case. The type of aggression and violence which takes place in families and the types of emotions which cause family violence are spilling over into the workplace. Indeed, for the violent employee, the workplace may be his last bastion. He may have failed in marriage and in other work situations, and an additional failure in his current job may send him over the line.

There is a pattern to workplace violence. The violent employee is typically male, white and under the age of 35, although the "berserkers" (those who kill several people in a sudden incident) tend to be in their early to middle forties. There is a history of job-related problems and frequent job changes, indicating difficulty in getting along. The violent employee blames other people for his problems and feels unjustly treated.

The late 20th century male has particularly defined himself as a worker more than a family man or active member of a church community. Or, if first priority is with family, a high second priority relates to his work environment. Therefore, when he strikes out, he strikes out against the most significant part of his life.

Not only is work becoming a high priority with males, a high sense of "entitlement" and a low sense of reality may be present in his attitude. Beginning with the establishment of unions and the subsequent acquisition of civil rights in the 1960's and 1970's, many young people also acquired a different attitude towards their jobs. Traditionally, throughout history, jobs as means of employment were totally dependent upon the worker measuring up to the standards (and often whims) of the employer. Emphasis was on dependability, loyalty, and good performance. It was a mainly patriarchal approach to management, with the (male) boss making decisions and the workers responding to those decisions.

Unions made the first inroads, by organizing workers and acquiring legal entitlements for them. If a worker performed to a certain stated standard, he/she could not be fired. Gradually, these entitlements increased until they encroached upon standards of performance, as union leaders struggled to gain power. The automobile industry, among others, woke up to a world in which American auto workers were deemed substandard by the Japanese and Germans.

The civil liberties acquisitions of the 1960's and 1970's enlarged the area of entitlements by opening up the workplace to antidiscrimination suits brought against employers who discriminated against workers based on race, gender, age, and other standards. These civil liberty acquisitions, like the unions, benefitted a good many of us. But, as time went on, fuzzy interpretations and increasing litigation forced many employers to sacrifice standards of performance. Disciplining and/or terminating a worker became more difficult, with the burden of proof on the employer. "Entitlement" often became interpreted as, "I am entitled to keep this job as long as I want it." The Japanese introduced "Theory Z," which was based on guaranteed lifetime employment.

The low sense of reality which may be perceived by today's worker is that the world is changing once again. The pendulum swing is now moving in the opposite direction. In the late 1980's and very early 1990's, plant closings and consolidations, coupled with job downsizing, resulted in the loss of many jobs. This proved frustrating for the affected workers, many of whom had worked a good part of their lives in one spot. At the same time an increasing focus was placed on quality production, as a means of competing on the world market.

By the mid-1990's, the American economy had changed, and, for the past several years, the United States has been in a period of sustained growth and prosperity. The key word is "productivity." Inevitably, as this country works to maintain and increase a wider foothold in the world for American-made goods, emphasis on the worker will be more on quality, loyalty, good workplace qualities, and conformity. The phantom "entitlements" will be eroded. Some futurists believe that an erosion of the civil liberties gains acquired during the 60's and 70's will also be eroded. For marginal workers, this means the potential loss of a job. For those workers who measure up, fat paychecks are the reward.

The more sensitive employers who are alert to potential problems have begun to look at the areas of identifying, assessing, and managing workplace violence. They are also adding to their corporate Crisis Management Plans, which has spawned a new industry--violence counseling services. Employers must have some way of determining who is potentially violent--an imprecise skill at best.

The employee who kills typically has a high interest in guns and owns a variety of weapons. In the documented cases of workplace homicide, the violent employee carried one or more handguns and either a shotgun or an assault weapon. The violent employee is prone to watching violence on the television or in the movies, as he relates to the emotions expressed there. He may also have read a number of the "get even" books published by Paladin Books, Loompanics, or other publishers. There is almost a cult which has grown up to consume books with titles like *Get Even, Make 'Em Pay, Mad as Hell,* and *Revenge Book.*

The violent employee tends to have a migratory job history. Checking his job references may disclose that he has had previous job problems, including an inability to get along with others. He may have trouble in accepting authority. He (or she) may also be going through extreme private stress such as a divorce. Past encounters with violence are commonplace with the violent employee, who may well have come from an abusive family background.

Psychologists say the most actively disgruntled share common histories of depression, paranoia, and violence. An individual suffering from paranoia may regard the world as being involved in a conspiracy against him/her. One violence consultant has stated that the prototypical person at high risk often suffers from paranoid disorders which account both for his troubles on the job and his exaggerated fascination with weapons. He is seen as permanently disgruntled and quick to perceive unfairness, injustice, or malice in others which is not warranted.

Personality disorders, sometimes called narcissistic personality disorders, are characteristic of individuals who are manipulative, charismatic, and determined to be in control. When denied this control, they are capable of showing narcissistic rage. This is typical behavior for some domestic stalkers, and can also be applicable to violent employees and "significant others" to employees. This narcissistic rage can take the form of suicide or homicide.

Some violent individuals are subject to impulse control disorders. Impulse control disorders reduce some individuals' ability for impulse control. Persons who were hyperactive as children or who have brain injuries or other neurological disorders are more prone to aggressive behavior and are less able to inhibit themselves than the average person. These are the individuals who, given what seems to be minor provocation, can fly into rages. Their built-in inhibitors disappear.

Other contributors to or triggers for aggression and violence can include depression, panic attacks, repressed feelings of anger or resentment, and alcohol and drug abuse. All of these conditions tend to remove the natural inhibiting factors to violence and self-destruction. Some distort already existing conditions. Someone who is depressed, and who has

repressed feelings of early childhood abuse, may be a candidate for either suicide or homicide. Any combination can be lethal.

Often, violent employees are loners. They tend to be suspicious of others and may intimidate co-workers, thus validating their feelings of being outcasts. If and when they do try to relate to someone else, it is to release a string of gripes and perceived injustices which extend backward to cover months and years during which time they have nursed feelings of rage and resentment. They are not likely to take responsibility for their mistakes and problems, but instead blame others. Even when someone attempts to help by suggesting that they get rid of their gripes, they perceive this attempted help as another rejection. If the other person does not agree to share their rage, that person becomes just another enemy.

Conversely, there is a second type of potentially violent employee who may be much harder to spot. He may be a quiet, steady, long-time employee who, because of personal and family failures, considers his job to be his life. Thus, if he loses that job, he may snap. Without his job he has, literally, no life. And, he feels that, in spite of the fact that he has dedicated years of his life to his employers, they have unfairly deprived him of his entitlements, his livelihood and his very existence. Although he may never have exhibited any violent characteristics in the past, he may change that in one lethal incident.

A third type of potentially violent employee has stalker traits. In particular, this employee may be subject to *erotomania*, a condition wherein a person believes not only that he/she is in love with another person, but that the other person returns that love. It becomes obsessive and may lead to stalking. There have been a number of workplace incidents involving an employee (usually a male) who fastens his attention upon another employee. When that person does not return his affection and spurns his advances, he turns to stalking his victim and either kills or attempts to kill the victim. Typical of this type of stalker/co-worker is Richard Wade Farley, who shot

Laura Black, leaving her permanently disfigured and disabled, and killed seven of her co-workers at ESL, a Silicon Valley high-tech defense firm.

Traits and Clues

While alcohol and drug abuse have not been present in every violent incident taking place in the workplace, this is one factor which, together with others, may help to indicate the potentially violent employee. Traits to look for, besides substance abuse, most significantly include a history of violence, paranoia, emotional imbalances, wide mood swings, lack of impulse control, migratory work history, and (for a long-time employee) any significant and protracted behavioral and personality changes.

Depression, if it is intense and prolonged, may indicate that the individual is losing the ability to cope with reality or the problems of everyday life. Carried to an extreme, a severely depressed person can conclude that death is the only solution. Sometimes that death may include other persons beside himself, particularly if he believes that someone else has caused or contributed to his depression and lack of ability to cope. As with any prolonged behavioral changes, severe and lasting depression in a person who would normally be positive and cheerful is an indicator of deep and powerful emotions.

Delusions are fairly competent indicators of abnormal behavior. Delusions include hearing non-existent voices and loud music. The voices may issue instructions or whisper (imagined) secrets about other people or, conversely, may be unintelligible. The voices may be an echo of the person's own thoughts or a stratagem which allows him to act out a fantasy, usually of violence. If not voices, the person may smell odors that do not exist or see visions. These odors and visions are almost always unpleasant to the person, and, to rid himself of them, he may take violent action, particularly if he thinks the odors and visions are caused by another entity or person.

Talking to oneself is not necessarily a sign of mental illness, but if the person talks loudly, with

great emotion and is not aware that other people are present, it is at the very least an indicator of deep emotion. People who talk to themselves loudly, with gestures, are usually engaged in a hostile conversation. There is usually a person or situation who/which is the subject of the emotional dialogue.

At the heart of the delusions is generally the feeling that he, the "victim," has been wronged, that other people are causing his problems or have wronged him or are plotting against him. He may believe that others are talking about him or whispering untruths. He imagines slights. The delusions are generally not happy, cheerful delusions; indeed, they are seemingly rationales to explain why the individual feels so bad. He feels bad, lonely, angry, and unhappy because *others are at fault*. He may wish to strike back at these unfair people, to get even, to be in control--and the voices help him.

The most important clue to an act of imminent violence may be any references by the worker to other incidents of violence. For example, in the case of John Taylor, the postal worker who killed his wife at home, two co-workers and then took his own life, Taylor made vague references to a shooting incident three years earlier in which letter carrier Patrick Sherrill killed 14 people before taking his own life. Likewise, Larry Hansel, who killed two executives at the Elgar Corp. electronics plant, referred to the Taylor killing just before his rampage.

In the case of Robert Earl Mack, it was a case of a termination meeting that had unexpectedly violent repercussions. A hearing had been called to contest Mack's firing from General Dynamics, Convair Division plant. Immediately following the hearing, Mack shot and wounded his supervisor, then chased and killed a labor negotiator. At his trial, there was no dispute that Mack fired the shots that killed labor negotiator Michael Konz, but Mack's counsel convinced jurors that mitigating circumstances lessened the degree of his guilt, portraying his client as a loyal blue-collar worker who had been victimized by company managers more concerned with the bottom line than with the human costs of a layoff.

Almost all companies of any size now understand that they will, at some point, be saddled with the problem of the violent employee and many have incorporated strategies for managing the violent employee and dealing with the aftermath of an incident in their Crisis Management Plans. The company has a responsibility to take reasonable and prudent actions to provide a safe workplace for its employees. Wounded employees and slain workers' families have brought suit against the employer company, based on their perceptions that the company did not provide adequate security. Worker trauma, business disruption, and the adverse publicity associated with any disaster can cost millions of dollars.

Clearly, corporations must take action to stem the rising tide of workplace incidents of violence. AMTRAK lost a multi-million dollar claim in a case in which a disgruntled employee, angry about being reprimanded, shot and seriously injured his supervisor. The case involved negligence, asserting that AMTRAK did not sufficiently discipline the employee for previous acts which indicated violent tendencies. In another case, the husband of an insurance company employee who worked on the 18th floor of a building came to see his wife with the pieces of a 12-gauge shotgun in a flower box. He accused his wife of infidelity with her supervisor, opened the flower box and assembled the shotgun. He shot his wife, her supervisor, and eventually killed two people and injured nine others before being killed by the police. His wife and seven of her co-workers or families sued her employer and the building owners as having failed to provide proper security.

Workplace crimes are increasingly being viewed by the legal system, the government, and employers themselves as occupational health threats that are potentially preventable, rather than as random acts. Companies or people other than the killers are being held accountable for the murders and being made to take responsibility for protecting their workers. Survivors of murdered employees have won sizable sums in civil suits against employers or others with responsibilities in workplaces.

The experts agree that there are definite steps which can be taken to prevent or at least mitigate the number of violent incidents taking place in the workplace, and in diminishing the costs incurred by abusive family relationships which cause absenteeism and poor job performance.

HIRING PROCEDURES

The first step in controlling violence in the workplace seems simple. It is to ***not hire the violent employee in the first place***. This is yet another argument for checking references and past work histories. The selection process is the first step toward building a competent and trustworthy staff, and the background investigation is an integral element in this process.

In today's litigious climate, preventing problem incidents before they occur is only sensible. There is a body of case law that holds an employer liable for injuries to third parties when injuries occur because the employer's negligent hiring practices resulted in hiring an unfit or dangerous person. An increasing number of legal actions have alleged that the employer was negligent in placing an employee in a position in which the employer knew or should have known that the employee might cause injury. Other cases have raised the issue of employer negligence in retaining an employee known to be unfit or dangerous to others.

There are several steps in the hiring process.

.   Thoroughly checking application forms and resumes. These forms of documentation can provide a great deal of information even before an expensive and time-consuming background check is undertaken.

.   Written (pencil-and-paper) tests are now widely used to assess applicants' attitudes toward personal behavior and the work environment. These tests are by no means infallible, but, coupled with interviews and background checks, they can uncover a certain percentage of problem applicants.

. Interviews are invaluable--provided they are conducted in an imaginative and creative manner. Interviews are NOT very helpful if all they accomplish is to read the application form and ask a few perfunctory questions. In addition to checking and obtaining additional information from the applicant, interviews provide an invaluable opportunity to set forth company policy--for example, zero tolerance for harassment, violence, drug/alcohol abuse, and theft.

. Reference, credit, criminal, and other background checks are essential. Period! And, yes, they are time-consuming and often expensive. Failure to perform these checks can open the employer to negligence suits.

Application Forms & Resumes

Application Forms. These forms are important in providing initial information and in protecting the employer from legal entanglements. A well-designed application form can also send a subtle message to the applicant that the company views its hiring practices seriously. Malefactors and unstable individuals have been known to opt out after reading the application form, choosing not to continue with their quest for employment with a particular company.

First, a warning. State and Federal laws restrict certain topics which, years ago, were routinely included in application forms. Questions which should not be asked refer to:

. Date of birth (possible age discrimination).

. Arrests -- although convictions are a different matter.

. Height or weight.

. Home or vehicle ownership.

. Gender.

. Marital status.

. Number and ages of children.

. Race, national origin, political or religious affiliation.

Questions regarding these subject areas should not be asked in interviews (unless the applicant volunteers the information). There are, however, two additional forms which can be used, and which will provide the essential information. These are: a release form and an I-9 form.

Waiver. Many former employers will not release any information on a current or past employee without a signed release from that employee. The waiver allows the company to check references and employment history of the applicant. It also contains an important element, namely, that the applicant understands and agrees that omission, falsification, and/or misrepresentation of information on the application form is cause for immediate termination. For best results, the waiver should be notarized--this makes it more official and is impressive to those references contacted.

In essence, the waiver, which must be signed by the applicant, states that he/she agrees and understands that all information entered on the application form by the applicant is correct and that no attempt has been made to conceal or withhold relevant information. That any omission, falsification or misrepresentation of information on the application form is cause for denial of employment and/or immediate dismissal from employment. In addition, it states that the applicant authorizes all corporations, companies, credit agencies, educational institutions, persons, law enforcement agencies, and former employers to release information they may have regarding the applicant. It should also include a statement that information obtained is regarded as private and will be treated as such by the requesting company. The waiver should be signed by the applicant and by a company representative.

Employment Eligibility Verification (I-9). The Immigration Reform and Control Act of 1986 obligates every employer to verify, within three days of hire, the identity and employment authorization of every employee hired. Although it is not necessary to obtain a signed I-9 form until the applicant has been hired, there is no reason to delay, and very good reasons for obtaining this up front. If the applicant is reluctant to sign, a red flag should go up. The I-9 form contains information useful for the background check. For example, it includes date of birth, and requires the employer to check identification such as driver's license, passport, social security card, etc. (Forms can be obtained from government offices.)

Criminal Release Form. This is a simple form which contains applicant's name, address, telephone number, aliases (if any), driver's license, and social security number, and, when signed by the applicant, authorizes the company to conduct a criminal background check through a law enforcement agency.

Resume. Resume fraud is common; one report finds that 30% of resumes contain false information. Some of the more common resume misrepresentations include:

. Falsification of education credits.

. Omitting a period of employment or stretching dates of employment.

. Exaggerated or misleading claims of expertise and experience.

. Claims of self-employment when actually the applicant was unemployed.

. Same for claims of working as a "consultant."

Information contained on a resume can only be verified by a probing interview and a background check.

NOTE: From the beginning of the hiring process it is important to open a file and maintain documentation of the evaluation of the applicant. This includes evaluation of the application form, resume, interviews, and background checks. Numerous legal suits have been filed against companies, claiming discrimination. A well-documented file will go a long way to prevent problems and avoid judgments.

The Employment Interview

The employment interview is a key element in the screening and hiring process. If properly structured, it can reveal potential problems. The way in which job interviews are conducted now differs widely from job interviews of the past. In the old days, the interview was based largely around the application form which the candidate filled out, using questions that were unimaginative and superficial. Today's interviewers, while verifying the information on the employment application, conduct a more in-depth interview. Questions could include:

. What did you like best about your former job?

. What did you like least?

. Did you feel that your former job gave you an opportunity for promotion?

. Which of your supervisors did you like the best? Why?

. Were there problems at work that you think should have been changed? How?

. Were your co-workers cooperative and pleasant to be around? Will you miss them?

. What were the reasons for your leaving your last job(s)?

. What are your reasons for applying for this job?

. What would you expect to gain from employment with our company?

. As best you can, describe yourself -- your attributes, your goals, your social and team skills, etc.

. What do you look for in other people?

If answers tend to be overly emotional, or to indicate that the candidate feels wronged, or unjustly treated by his former bosses, or at odds with his former co-workers, a red flag should go up.

Interview questions should be as open-ended as possible, avoiding those questions which can be answered with a simple "yes" or "no." The applicant should be given time for answers -- firing questions in staccato fashion is a terrible modus operandi.

All information listed on the application blank and resume should be double-checked, particularly noting any omissions and any information that has been scratched out and rewritten. Questions should be fully answered. The application **must** be signed.

Paper and Pencil Tests

As an aid in screening job applicants, many employers now make use of the psychological, honesty, and skills tests on the market. Employers are increasingly using the honesty tests in an effort to cut down on internal theft. The psychological tests could be instituted as a means of spotting the potentially violent worker.

Generally speaking, there are three types of pencil and paper integrity tests: single purpose tests, personality tests, and multidimensional tests. Single purpose tests are aimed primarily at establishing the applicant's attitudes toward honesty. Answers are keyed against a base of information collected on numbers of individuals.

Personality tests can be described as being of at least two different types. One type is designed to obtain information about the applicant in terms of his/her ability to work with others and to determine whether the applicant is extroverted or introverted, etc. (This is a *very* simplistic explanation!) In other

words, is this applicant who is applying for a job as manager a dynamic, forceful personality with organizational skills and personal charisma who can lead his employees in a highly competitive business -- or is he a retiring, do-it-by-the-book hard worker with underdeveloped social interrelationship skills who prefers to work alone without input from others?

A second type of personality, or psychological test is designed more to establish the applicant's propensity for interaction with his/her fellow workers, his/her feelings about authority, his/her feelings about violence, etc.

Multidimensional tests, which are looked upon as the wave of the future for pre-employment screening, combine the overt and personality tests and look at the individual from several aspects. These tests typically contain an honesty scale but are beginning to include test scales to help companies control illicit drug use, reduce accidents, control damage and waste, and lower turnover rates. Specific multidimensional tests designed for specific job settings are also on the drawing boards.

The Minnesota Multiphasic Personality Inventory (MMPI) is an instrument which has been used with very good success in predicting violent behaviors, and in identifying other dysfunctional behavior. The MMPI is complicated and requires professional interpretation, but has proven over the years to be successful in determining and predicting certain behavioral patterns. It is used, for example, in screening some law enforcement and private security personnel. The results of the MMPI are interpreted on readings of scales. One scale, for example, with very high readings might indicate an individual who exhibits psychotic behavior, who has delusions of persecution or grandeur, feels mistreated and picked on, is angry and resentful, and harbors grudges.

While the MMPI is not for everyone, the London House Personnel Selection Inventory (PSI) is another widely respected test. It is designed to determine those persons likely to engage in counterproductive work activities. The items measure perceptions of the prevalence and acceptance of deviant actions and the likelihood the individual will engage in such behaviors in the future. Various versions of the PSI measure an individual's propensity for physical, assaultive violence; for non-violent aggression with co-workers and supervisors (verbal, argumentative, threatening, intimidating); and for relations with customers.

Caveats

There are some caveats to the interviewing and screening processes. Be aware that "workplace privacy" is an important issue. Some of the questions which must not be asked of an applicant are whether he is homosexual, or whether he smokes marijuana at home, or anything pertaining to other personal matters that are not job related. All interviews should be conducted equally, and all interview and job requirements should be equal for all job applicants. For example, paper and pencil testing should not be randomly administered -- if one interviewee is required to take the test, all interviewees should take the same test. Applicants should be asked to sign a waiver attesting to the fact that they understand the purpose of the test, that test results will be kept confidentially, and that the test represents only one component in the job hiring criteria.

At least two states regulate the use of paper and pencil pre-employment tests.

In the screening process, the paper and pencil test(s) should never be used as the sole criteria for hiring. While these tests have proven their worth, they are not considered 100% correct in their predictive value. Using them exclusively without additional criteria could leave the employer open to charges of discrimination and negligent hiring practices. When combined with good interviewing practices and background investigations, these tests have been extremely helpful.

Staff must be thoroughly trained in the use of, and scoring of, these tests, or some arrangements must be made with the test publisher for scoring and interpretive support. In the past, insufficiently trained personnel reached erroneous conclusions and often

"read into" the results the characteristics which they wanted to find. The trend, increasingly, when using paper and pencil tests, is to work out an arrangement with the producer for help.

Background Investigations

Access to records, the position being applied for, and the rules regarding invasion of privacy vary from one jurisdiction to another. The company's job application form should include an authorization to be signed by the applicant which allows the company to check references, credit, and criminal, educational and other information listed by the applicant. It should also include a statement to the fact that the company has the right to disqualify any applicant or fire an employee who falsifies information on his/her application.

All hiring procedures and background investigations must meet certain regulated guidelines and comply with a specific number of laws, acts and regulations.

The background investigation is intended to compare the information filled in on the application form by the applicant and to expand this information to include any pertinent facts not recorded there by the applicant. The key elements to a background investigation are employment history and performance, credit, criminal record, education, military record, and references (both personal and work related). Whenever possible, background investigations should be conducted in person rather than by telephone and, if this is not possible, should be conducted by telephone rather than letter.

Social Security Number. The application form should provide space for the social security number. Once obtained, a check can be made through a commercial service such as Trans Union, Equifax and Experian. Results should show any additional names and addresses, as well as additional social security numbers if used by the applicant.

Employment. Properly phrased questions can

elicit information that may indicate a workplace problem. First, facts must be checked, by asking the following questions. "Was the applicant employed as claimed?" "Was he/she employed for the time period claimed and in the capacity claimed?" "Did he/she leave for the reason(s) stated?" "Were earnings as claimed?" The question, "Would you rehire this person?," is usually answered honestly since it does not require any further explanation. Co-workers may be more willing to relate information about any disciplinary incidents and to give a more honest evaluation of the applicant than are supervisors. If there are any indicators of problems, a more thorough background check should be made and the applicant re-interviewed. Any gaps in the candidate's work history should be questioned and checked.

Credit. Credit reports are important in that they may indicate financial problems. Heavy debt to more than one creditor, that is not being repaid, should be investigated with the applicant to see if this is a one-time event or indicates a more serious problem. However, as with all segments of the background investigation, each element must be taken in context with the other elements. All credit investigations must be done in accordance with the Fair Credit Reporting Act. There are some firms which legitimately do a very good job of investigating not only credit records, but also education, military and other details.

Criminal. Criminal history checks are difficult. There is no national database available to employers (or the general public). Almost all states have a central state agency that collects criminal record information; however some states deny access and others are very restrictive in releasing information. Normally, state agencies require name, date of birth, social security number, and the range of years to be checked for a search. If additional names (aliases) are known, that information should be provided for the search. This is a situation where the use of a professional search agency might be highly advisable. These people know where to search and, more importantly, can do so much more quickly than an employer may manage. There have been numerous

cases where a person was hired, and the criminal records were not made available for such a long time that the new employee had already committed a crime.

Where there is not cooperation at the state level, one can check at the local (county, town) level.

Arrest records are generally *not* available for inquiry, but criminal convictions should be a matter of public record. Failure to check on criminal convictions is a primary fact which will weigh against an employer in any suit brought for negligence should a violent incident occur with the employee. To put it another way, if an applicant is hired without a check of his criminal record, and if the applicant does have a record of criminal conviction, and if the subsequently hired employee shoots a fellow worker, the corporation will be liable for *big* dollars.

Note: a conviction for a misdemeanor would not necessarily be grounds for employment rejection or post-hire discharge unless the applicant falsified his application, or the crime was directly related to the scope and nature of employment.

Also, under the Federal Civil Rights Act, no question may be asked about prior *arrests*; questions may be asked as to prior *convictions*. Applicants may not be categorically rejected because of one or more convictions. Consideration must be given to the nature of the conviction, the elapsed time since the last occurrence, relevance of conviction to the job applied for, and the social ambience at the place of the last occurrence. Example: a 30-year-old male who was arrested and convicted of possession of a small amount of cocaine when he was 18 years old and living with foster parents and who has been "clean" ever since, who passes all other portions of a background check, and who answers honestly about his criminal record would have a very good case against any employer who rejected him for employment based on the one conviction.

Education. Verification of an applicant's educational record is easily done by contacting the

Registrar or Director of Admissions for any school listed by the applicant. An applicant who lies about his/her educational record may have lied about other background data. If available, any disciplinary measures taken by a school against an applicant should be explored. Hard data, such as social security number, address, and age should be compared.

Military. A check of an applicant's military background (if any) provides another indication of the applicant's honesty. In one case, an applicant claiming to be a Navy Seal applied for the job of Director of Security for a small security firm. In checking his military record, it was revealed that he had never served in the Seals, but instead was a Marine deserter. The Marines were delighted to be informed of his whereabouts. Had he been hired, and subsequently a crime committed, the security firm could well have been put out of business.

Form 180 can be obtained from the National Personnel Records Center in St. Louis, Missouri.

Motor Vehicle and Driving Records. An applicant's driving record check is essential if the individual is being hired for a job that requires his/her driving for the company. It is also potentially helpful in assessing the person. An unduly large number of traffic offenses may be indicative of undesirable traits such as lack of inhibitions, reckless disregard for safety, and possibly ungovernable rage. Records can be checked at the state level using the individual's driver license number.

References. Many employers either do not check references or do so in a desultory manner, because they believe that no applicant will list a reference that is not supportive of him and will tender a good recommendation. This is not, however, the case. Incredibly, applicants will often list references who either do not know him/her, or who give negative reports. The applicant (unless this is his first job) should furnish work references as well as personal references. If he/she does not do so, the interviewer should ask for them. The interviewer

should always ask the applicant if he/she has permission to call the references. This is done for two reasons. If the applicant is still working, he will probably not wish to have his current employer contacted. If he is not currently working, a refusal to having his references contacted should be a warning signal that all is not right.

Drug Testing

For some years, pre-employment and random drug testing has been legal. However, all drug testing procedures should be established in writing. Policies stated should include which substances are prohibited, the conditions under which testing will be required and what will happen if an employee tests positive or refuses to submit to testing.

MANAGEMENT INTERVENTIONS

What about the potentially violent employee who slips through the interview process or the old-time steady employee who, because of a violent home life or job layoff, goes berserk? There are a number of steps which should be taken to minimize the risk of violence in the workplace. They include: proper orientation, training and supervision; employee awareness programs (EAP's); early disciplinary and counseling interviews; well-managed terminations; and reasonable security measures.

The Workplace Environment

In 1982, a book entitled *In Search of Excellence* was copyrighted, and in 1983 it hit its mark as one of the most successful books of the year. Its success has continued with over 5,000,000 books sold to date. This is an astounding record for a non-fiction book, particularly one whose subject is about how to achieve excellence within the corporation.

What, you ask, does this have to do with controlling workplace violence? Answer--a great deal, since the control of workplace violence is a valuable by-product for those corporations who know how to achieve excellence. Because, they cannot achieve excellence without excellent employees, and excellent employees (who are often made, not born) are developed, nurtured and instilled with pride. The techniques described in this wonderful book for achieving excellence could be a blueprint for removing some of the root causes of violence in the workplace.

For many years, Americans took pride in their work. Standards of quality were high, from the CEO of the company down to the least paid worker. Corporations were often family owned and privately held, with the result that long-term objectives were the goals. Employees were considered part of the corporate family and, as such, their personal problems were of concern to the company. There were not many total strangers within the company. Families were stationary, for the most part living and dying within the same communities. It was not unusual for the male head of the household to enter the company in his early twenties and continue to work for that company until retirement. Customer service and satisfaction were of primary concern, since customers tended to be largely localized. Reputation, integrity, permanence, and interpersonal concerns were the rule. The corporate environment was patriarchal, in keeping with its family orientation. Workplace violence was almost unknown. To the contrary, the workplace was a sanctuary of permanence and orderliness.

During the 1960's and 1970's, this corporate structure and environment began to change. America was hitting its stride as a world leader in politics and economics. World markets were opening, and in this heady atmosphere, competition and "the bottom line" began to gain ascendance over quality and reputation. New technologies were arriving with such breathtaking speed that successful corporations found it necessary to restructure themselves. Subsidiaries were formed. Employment was at an all-time high. Women went to work en masse, finding a higher receptivity within the workplace. The two-paycheck family had arrived. Markets became national rather than local, and multi-national in many cases. Corporate profits were huge and many corporate leaders believed that the growth would be permanent.

Who cared if the customer was happy, so long as he/she/it bought the product? Corporate objectives began to shift from an emphasis on long-term goals to short-term profitability which could lead to mergers and acquisitions. If it was bigger, it was better. If you didn't grow you were dead. If employees did not turn out a quality product, fire them and replace them. Time became a critical issue. No more did the CEO "walk the floor" to interact with his/her employees; he/she was too busy in the daily exercise of reading financial statements, looking for mergers and acquisitions.

Meanwhile, young people began the process of self-actualization, saying, "Is this all there is to life - - marrying the girl/boy next door, working for the company store, and never seeing the rest of the world?" Many began to question the motivations and actions of their "elders" while Vietnam destroyed their innocence. More young people than ever in history went to college, thanks to student loans and the advent of affordable community colleges. More career opportunities became available, often necessitating a move from the home community to other areas. Now there were many strangers among the work force. As the need for workers increased, the performance standards began to weaken. The personal accountability was gone.

By the 1980's, corporate America was beginning to realize that something was wrong. The trade deficit was growing by leaps and bounds, as other countries out-sold the United States. Crime, including employee theft and substance abuse in the workplace, had grown substantially. Dysfunctional job performance had increased, as had absenteeism. And, a new occurrence, violence in the workplace, had begun to capture national notice. Clearly, the workplace as a safe sanctuary was no longer the case. Just as families had fragmented, leaving damaged survivors, so had many corporations. With the Wall Street scandals, corporate leaders as role models looked badly tarnished.

By the early 1980's, many corporations had begun to reexamine themselves and, looking at Japan's economic success, began to take a new look at their employees. A number of strategies were inaugurated. "Quality circles" became very popular -- a new name for an old custom of involving the employees in team building and problem solving. Automakers, long tired of being pictured as shoddy performers, instituted new line procedures to re-build American pride and know-how.

Increasingly aware of the tremendous toll taken by internal employee-related problems of family abuse, drugs, alcohol, and high employee turnover, corporations instituted Employee Awareness Programs (EAP's), corporate counseling programs. These counseling programs were aimed at retrieving employees, many of whom cost $15,000 to $50,000 to replace. The EAP's today are alive and well and have begun to show some success in improving the welfare of employees and in improving workplace performance.

In 1983's *In Search of Excellence*, authors Peters and Waterman essentially told corporate America that it had better get back to essentials-- among them to rebuild inner pride among its employees, to reinstitute standards of integrity, honesty, quality standards, permanence, long-term goals, customer service, and the personal and career development of its employees. Further, it made the point that this rebuilding must begin at the very top levels of management. No more "doublespeak" with employees being exhorted to work harder and at the same time rewarding unapproachable CEO's with obscene salaries and bonuses.

To be successful in the 1990's, corporations had to restructure themselves in more wholistic and socially conscious ways. They were made to realize, once again, that their employees are potentially their greatest assets--and that, to achieve results, the corporation must set clear corporate policy and provide corporate role models. Management at all levels must be committed to demonstrating and practicing the behavior which is expected of all employees, and motivating all employees to conform to company policy.

If honesty is a quality expected in all employees, management must demonstrate integrity and honesty in all its dealings. It must be a stated goal. It must be clearly articulated in orientation, training and ongoing goal expectations. It must be rewarded. Conversely, a lack of honesty must have consequences--at all levels.

The same should apply to the area of harassment, aggression, intimidation, and violence. The company must have a clearly articulated policy that states it will not tolerate anti-social behavior, and that breaching this policy will have immediate consequences. Just as the company will not tolerate petty theft, it will not tolerate small aggressions. The company must clearly demonstrate its commitment to providing a safe workplace, to setting safety standards, and to providing an environment free of harassment.

The key word is "commitment." The company must dedicate its resources to building a strong employee work force, to treating its employees with respect and dignity, to helping every employee to achieve success, to lending support to those in need of counseling, and to taking immediate steps to rid itself of employees who are hostile, intimidating, harassing, and/or violent. The employer/employee relationship must be built carefully and strongly on mutual trust.

In order for violence to flourish, it must find a receptive environment. If the corporation is perceived as one which is detached, uncaring of its employees, and interested only in the "bottom line," the work force feels disenfranchised and resentful. Resentment leads to frustration which, in turn, can lead to violence. If there is a tolerance for harassment, female or otherwise, it is an open invitation to aggressive behavior, intimidation, and violence. Sexual harassment of a female employee can lead to stalking.

If, on the other hand, the corporation is perceived as caring and trustworthy, and at the same time as tough on theft, harassment, and malingering, those who are violently inclined and the regular bullies will find that their behavior is not accepted either by their co-workers or their bosses. All of us respond--for better or worse--to our environment and our peers. Even the most dysfunctional look to peers for approval. In really good, well-run organizations, the bullies and malingerers tend to feel uncomfortable and will often disqualify themselves by quitting to seek a more conducive workplace for their behavior.

Of key importance is the behavior of managers and supervisors. These people must serve as role models, abiding by the company's policies and setting clear examples of wanted behavior. If this does not happen, the company program will be compromised. If the company policy states "no sexual harassment" and Joe X, the line supervisor, says to his male employees, "Look at the boobs on that Nancy," it sends a clear signal that company policy doesn't mean anything down on the production line. For the program to work, that supervisor must either be removed or treated to a lobotomy to correct his attitudes.

Company policy must be stated in writing with guidelines developed and included in all policy manuals. It must be made a part of the screening and hiring process. It must be incorporated as an intrinsic part of the orientation and training of each new employee. It must be supported on a continuing basis with good supervision and management. It must be sensitive to worker needs, supplying goals and incentives which are attainable. It must incorporate Employee Awareness Programs (EAP's) in its structure--programs which help to identify the troubled employee and supply help before it is too late. It must be firm in its commitment to root out the bad apples among employees.

Orientation, Training and Supervision

Orientation. Orientation is the process whereby new employees are introduced to the corporation. It is said that first impressions are the most lasting; therefore, it is critical that an orientation program should leave the correct perceptions about the company and its policies. Orientations which consist only of giving the new employee information about working hours, the location of the restrooms and cafeteria, job specifications, and a quick introduction to his/her supervisor fall far short and miss a golden opportunity to set the right attitudinal tone. Good orientation programs stress the pride which the company feels in its products and its employees and emphasizes the things which the company does to make the workplace a more comfortable, more productive environment. Effective corporations spend serious money in developing top quality motivational video tapes for orientation, thus clearly demonstrating the importance which the company gives to its employees. With formalized orientation classes, top management personnel often address the new employees, reemphasizing company policies and goals.

Training. Training which is developed from standardized procedures and fitted to job descriptions and company policy is one of the finest management tools available. Good training is not a "nice-to-have;" it is an absolute necessity and an employee entitlement. Every employee deserves to know the company policies and procedures, including rules of conduct. The company policy manual should describe that conduct which is acceptable and that conduct which is not acceptable, with appropriate disciplinary action. This approach has worked extremely well in cutting down on employee theft. A majority of companies now state up front that they will not tolerate theft of company property, and that the result of proven theft will be immediate dismissal and prosecution, no matter how small the theft. It has worked very well to deter theft when the policy has been implemented and administered fairly across the board.

The same approach should be taken with the issue of intimidation, harassment' and violence. The company policy should be clearly stated and the disciplinary action implemented. Disciplinary action might include counseling for the first offence and dismissal after the second. If would-be violent offenders do not find an allowable breeding ground for their bullying tactics, they may be deterred or they may leave the company for more fertile fields. It is during the period of indoctrination and training that early indicators of future employee problems may be noted. He (or she) may attempt to argue the merits of the conduct rules or the performance standards. Clear rules and good training can help to take away the potential offender's alibis and rationale for violence.

Good training procedures are a valuable help to legal defense if an incident should occur and legal action is brought against the company.

Supervision. Good, fair, even-handed supervision is another employee entitlement. Lack of supervision is a clear lack of company responsibility. Supervisors are (or should be) there to guide employee performance and conduct on the job, and to make note of jobs well done and jobs inadequately done. Good supervision prevents problems whenever possible, and when not possible, takes action to solve problems. Supervisors should provide an "early warning system" for the company. These are the line people who should have a daily awareness of developing problems. At the same time, supervisors are often the target of violence; thus, it behooves them to sharpen their people skills.

Supervisory training should include specific training in the recognition of workplace personnel problems. Few supervisors are provided with this special training.

Sexual Harassment

Sexual harassment in the workplace represents a very real threat, primarily to women, and can serve as a precursor to violence if allowed to continue unchecked. Unfortunately, many employers still do not recognize sexual harassment for the serious problem that it is and have even less understanding of the problems created. In companies where sexual harassment is allowed as a relatively benign or harmless endeavor, the message which is telegraphed is clearly that management is hypocritical and insensitive, even *permissive*. If sexual harassment is allowed, how about bullying and intimidation of co-workers? How about just a little illegal drug abuse or some "harmless" gambling in the employees' locker room?

The employer's responsibilities in this area are serious and real. There are legal consequences to appearing to allow or foster sexual harassment. Sexual harassment claims brought to the Equal Employment Opportunity Commission numbered 4,400 in 1986 and jumped to 5,600 in 1990. Informally, the commission reported a 25% increase for 1991 over 1990.

While both sexes have complained about harassment, a significant majority of women are the victims of sexual harassment. Women who have complained of sexual harassment stated that in slightly over half the cases the harasser was a supervisor or person in power in the corporation, and that somewhat less than half of the harassers were co-workers and peers.

The problem has significant proportions, since more than half of all American women now work outside the home, and all reliable projections show that an ever-increasing number of women (and minorities) will enter the workplace, often filling non-traditional jobs formerly held almost exclusively by (white) males. Men have had a lot of adjusting to do in the workplace as well as at home, as women have invented new roles to meet new needs.

As part of this new working demographic revolution, both men and women are often working more hours, placing work priorities before other social outlets. Work, therefore, has become for many the primary social environment for the sexes to intermingle and relate to each other. Not surprisingly, men and women have difficulty keeping their working and nonworking lives separate.

At another level, many traditional males have viewed the onslaught of women in the workplace as threatening the dominant male role and as displacing male workers. This tends to build resentments which can result in a retaliatory behavior. Other males still view all women outside the home as potential (and available) prey for sexual pursuit. Male workers who experience abusive relationships at home often view female workers as extensions of the abusive home relationship and may direct a great deal of hostility toward these female workers.

Yet other male workers, perhaps unused to being in close contact with females who are educated, attractive and independent, may feel romantically drawn to these women, forming delusions about relationships that will never be. Worse, they may become obsessed with the notion that the women of their dreams return their romantic feelings. Clearly, female workers may experience the same emotions toward male co-workers. With both sexes, these attitudes can lead to harassing behavior, frustration, and violence. In a number of violent and fatal incidents in the workplace, a male worker formed an attachment for a female co-worker and, when rejected, stalked the female and killed or injured her.

An appalling form of sexual harassment involves supervisors or other persons in power in the workplace trading sexual favors for promotions, pay raises, or simply retaining a job. This is referred to as "quid pro quo" harassment. Historically, the Equal Employment Opportunity Commission has ruled that the employer is held in strict liability for quid pro quo harassment, regardless of whether the employer knew the harassment was taking place. This liability is known as "respondeat superior." A simplified meaning is--the master is responsible for the acts of his servant, and the principal for the acts of his agent.

Unlike quid pro quo harassment, hostile environment harassment can involve anyone in the workplace as well as off-premises at work-related functions, such as business trips, office parties, dinners, etc. This form of harassment can include off-color sexual jokes, lewd comments, displays, or visual materials of lewd or sexually off-color material, and/or repeated requests for a sexual or dating relationship. With hostile environment harassment the offensive conduct is repetitive, frequent, or continuous.

Sexual harassment can occur between members of the same sex, although this is not as prevalent as harassment between sexes.

Defining sexual harassment is often difficult and may appear differently to the harasser and the harassee. Many males, in particular, are genuinely confused as to what constitutes a joke, or a compliment, or harassment. Some accepted definitions of sexual harassment include:

.   Sexually suggestive or vulgar language, pictures, posters, magazines, or other materials.

.   Denigrating or vulgar comments about someone's gender or gender characteristics.

.   Touching someone in a sexually suggestive way or touching of another's breasts, genital areas, or derrieres.

.   Repeated and unwanted requests or demands for dates, off-work social contact, or sexual relationships.

Employers have a responsibility to promptly and thoroughly investigate charges of sexual harassment. In addition to the fact that employers have this as a legal responsibility, it sends a clear signal that abusive behavior in the workplace will not be tolerated at any level, and that management takes its responsibilities seriously in providing a safe work environment. And, last, it provides an opportunity for the accused individual to clear his/her name and defend his/her actions.

A designated investigator must have the trust and respect of both accuser and accused, as well as co-workers and management. The job will not be easy. The investigator must understand the legal aspects of sexual harassment, must be familiar with the company's written policies as well as company structure, hierarchy, and work environment, and must be totally fair and sensitive to the issue. Confidentiality is an essential element, and the rights of all parties must be protected. While the charges of sexual harassment must be given very serious consideration, there is always the possibility of innocence for the accused. If a qualified in-house investigator cannot be found, an outside consultant, someone specifically trained in the subject area, should be brought in.

A thorough investigation will involve interviewing the accuser and accused; in the case of group harassment, members of the group must be individually interviewed. Some determinations must be made as to whether the offensive behavior was invited, either intentionally or unintentionally. Corroborating witnesses must be interviewed and corroborating evidence (letters, offensive posters, etc.) examined. All evidence must be thoroughly documented. Since sexual harassment is usually not an isolated occurrence, an exploration of a pattern of behavior should be made. Have either the accuser or accused a history of related incidents? A background investigation of both should be conducted to determine if any similar behavior or complaints have occurred in the past.

Whoever handles the case should be a competent interviewer with an understanding of such concepts as commitment to denial, deceptive behavior, withholding of information, behavior provoking questions and confrontation.

Denial. Once an individual presents a denial, he/she is apt to become locked in that denial, even if it is untrue. For that reason, it is best not to ask the individual immediately if the accusation is true or untrue. Good interviewing technique consists of gradually leading up to the crucial question and by introducing some questions which will elicit affirmative responses.

The first portion of the interview should be spent asking nonthreatening questions--questions which can easily be answered in the affirmative. This could include questions about dates of employment, general attitudes towards co-workers, etc. Once having elicited some affirmative answers, an open question concerning the incident can be inserted. This might be, "Danny, some allegations have been made concerning a recent incident which involved you. Can you think of what that incident might be and who might have reported it?" The person might

then shrug and say, "Oh, Nancy is pissed with me about something I said, but it was just a joke." The interviewer might answer, "Can you tell me exactly what you said and why you think this might have upset Nancy?" This opens the incident to discussion, and further questions can narrow the field to precise statements and actions.

One of the concepts of good interviewing is that it is easier for an employee to make an admission if he or she is offered a face-saving reason for the incident. This does not mean letting the offender escape with a slap on the wrist; it does mean showing the person some respect and acknowledgment of his/her humanness. It can also open the discussion to company policy and to the company's strict interpretation of harassment.

Nitpicking. A good interviewer carefully phrases questions and statements. Some employees are skilled at nitpicking statements and pouncing on one word, or feeling justified in denying the incident simply because of one wrongly placed word.

Overload. In interviewing all parties, the interviewer should never let the incident get buried in an avalanche of accusations and counter-accusations. If the complainant says, "This isn't the first time something like this has happened," etc. etc., the interviewer must carefully structure the interview so as to obtain information first on the reported incident, and then separately obtain information on any other incidents. If there have been prior incidents, the investigation will necessarily have to be expanded.

Specifics. Once the incident has been brought into the open, specific details must be procured. This is not the time to gloss over details and obtain a provisional or nonspecific admission. Questions such as, "How close were you standing to . . . when this happened?" and "Did she touch you at any point? Where?" "Would you be willing to sign a statement as to exactly what you said?"

Attitudes Toward Punishment. One interviewing technique is to ask the accused what punishment should be handed out to someone guilty of harassment. "What do you think should happen to someone who locks the office door and attempts to kiss his secretary?" Usually, a truthful person will not hesitate to suggest a harsh punishment, while an untruthful person may waffle and recommend leniency for a "first offence."

Going Straight to the Point. If the interviewer is reasonably convinced that the person is guilty, he has two options for getting a confession from the employee. He can state that he does not believe the person is telling the truth, or he can attempt to offer some face-saving solution.

If the interviewer chooses the first option, the statement should not be confrontational. It should center around the facts and list any inconsistencies. This may then lead to the second option--the face-saving solution. For example, "I suppose all of us at some point have been tempted to step over the line and Nancy is very pretty." Then, the interviewer allows the person to respond affirmatively. The objective is to obtain the guilty statement. Once the admission is obtained and documented, company policy must dictate the actions to be taken.

This is an appropriate point at which to emphasize that not all complaints are true. Careers have been damaged, even ruined, by false accusations. Sexual harassment investigations must be conducted fairly, and every effort made to ensure justice on both sides.

If a sexual harassment investigation concludes that harassment has taken place, it can have several outcomes and subsequent courses of action. Some situations can be resolved fairly easily by determining what the complainant wishes to have done.

If the accusation is obviously true, but is of a minor nature, the accused may quickly agree to desist. Transfer of the offender to another department may be possible. Some complainants prefer less harsh resolutions of this nature than terminations, legal suits, and the like. When this happens, both parties must

agree to the reasonable settlement, thus preventing future problems. The complainant must be made to feel that she(he) has been fairly heard, and that there is no loss of position or prestige. All too often, victims of sexual harassment are victimized twice by being shabbily treated, even when their claims are proven correct.

The offender may be recommended for counseling and, depending upon the seriousness of the offense, may find that counseling is mandatory as a condition of job retention. If necessary, both parties may require counseling. This is particularly helpful in those cases which are borderline and which may have involved misperceptions on the part of both accuser and accused.

In more severe situations, options include written warnings of termination should another incident of inappropriate conduct occur; suspension; and termination.

If the incident(s) uncover(s) the fact that sexual harassment is a serious problem within the company, reeducation seminars may be needed for workers and supervisors, as well as a restatement of the company's policy regarding harassment.

Many organizations prefer to include sexual harassment issues as part of a general policy statement on all forms of harassment. However, many feel the issue is so important that it must be addressed separately to make certain the message is loud and unmistakable. A policy should specifically include a definition of sexual harassment, a description of procedures undertaken in response to harassment charges, mediation procedures, and consequences.

Preventing sexual harassment from occurring in the first place is infinitely preferable to the disruptive, expensive, and time-consuming course of investigating and/or litigating incidents. One of the most effective prevention tools is a well written, well communicated policy statement. Other prevention strategies include training, employee awareness programs, and exit interviews.

Exit interviews are one of corporate management's most valuable tools. Exiting employees are often willing and able to describe workplace conditions and to touch upon situations which are normally considered too touchy to discuss while one is on the company payroll. It behooves the company to take advantage of this unparalleled opportunity to ask questions about many situations, including the question of sexual harassment in the workplace.

Employee Awareness Programs

The shame and guilt attached to drug abuse, alcoholism, domestic abuse, sexual harassment, violent behavior, and other personal problems often cause workers to avoid seeking help because they feel they could lose their jobs or face criminal charges if the problem becomes public knowledge. It is this reluctance to seek help that makes it necessary for business to be proactive rather than reactive in addressing the problem.

A high percentage of companies now have drug and alcohol abuse counseling programs. Many companies have additional counseling programs to provide workers with education and support on how to prevent family violence, identify troubled employees, and get help for those who are involved in family violence. Managers, personnel staff, shop stewards, and company nurses require training in identifying signs of family violence and the propensity for violence within the workplace.

A valuable step is the development of an employee sensitivity program designed to alert employees to indicators within the workplace of emotional problems evidenced in fellow workers. There are several reasons for such a program. It might save a valuable employee who is undergoing emotional problems and who, lacking the ability and courage to solve them, might resign, thus depriving the company of a real asset. Sensitivity training could spot behavioral changes which precede violence. And, finally, sensitivity training might help the potentially (but not yet) violent employee to realize that he or she has problems which require counseling. To succeed, sensitivity programs must not only teach

employees how to note and recognize problems, but must encourage those employees to refer these problems in the strictest confidence to a trustworthy company representative. A good supervisor who is trusted by his or her employees is more likely to be given valuable information about fellow employees who might pose problems.

Employees and supervisors should be taught to look for and recognize some of the indicators of emotional problems. Certainly, any indicators of intimidation, bullying, harassment, or violence should be related in confidence to a supervisor or other company representative. Here are the indicators which might point to potential problems with an employee. These are listed in an ascending order, from early warning signals to indicators of imminent violence. Note: these signals are particularly meaningful if the employee has a history of drug or alcohol abuse, dysfunctional family relationships, prior or current emotional problems, or a work-related history of problems--reprimands, demotions, denial of promotions, poor evaluation reports, fighting, displays of violence, etc.

Early Warning Signals

. Does not cooperate with supervisors--accepts authority and criticism with difficulty--holds grudges against others, particularly supervisors.

. Is argumentative with co-workers, supervisors and customers--attitude is belligerent.

. Has a strong sense of entitlement and is unbudging in defending his/her position.

. Displays anti-social behavior--shows an increasing "loner" tendency and a social isolation--is withdrawn. May have a history of interpersonal conflicts.

. Has severe mood swings.

. Holds and expresses extremist opinions and attitudes and is angered when his/her opinions are not accepted by others.

. Uses coarse language, swears at others, and uses denigrative terms when referring to others. Spreads harmful (false) gossip and rumors about others.

. Makes sexual comments to and about others.

Escalating Trouble Signals

. Argues more with co-workers, supervisors, vendors, and customers. Engages in verbal abuse.

. Has increasing difficulties in controlling his/her temper. Is more demonstrative in showing anger--agitated pacing, slamming or throwing objects, punching the wall, yelling, clenching fists, breaking objects.

. Sabotages company equipment, steals property, damages co-worker property.

. Increasingly sees himself/herself as being "picked on" and victimized by management and co-workers.

. Writes sexual or violent notes to co-workers and/or supervisors--may begin stalking behavior.

. States desire to harm co-workers and/or management--may verbalize as provisional threats ("If . . . doesn't stop picking on me, he'll be sorry and I'm not kidding.") Or, may couch threats as jokes. ("I'm going to introduce him to my friends, Mr. Smith and Mr. Wesson.")

. Shows intense interest in previous acts of workplace violence and demonstrates in-depth knowledge of such acts--weapons used, circumstances, etc.

. Shows a fascination with weapons--may bring a weapon to work to display it.

Volatile Stage

. Makes and repeats suicidal threats.

. Assaults others.

. Uses weapons to harm others.

. Commits or attempts to commit arson, rape, and murder.

Trigger Points

The build-up to the violence stage may culminate with a trigger point.

. Involved in a current disciplinary, grievance, or arbitration action--an action which does not seem to be going in his/her favor.

. Facing lay-off or firing.

. Death of a spouse, divorce, or marital separation.

. Death of a parent, loved one, or close friend, someone who has provided an anchor and a stabilizing influence.

. Break-up of relationship with girl- boyfriend.

. Financial problems--foreclosure of home, unpaid bills, repossession of automobile, denial of a loan, etc.

. Owes back child support payments and is being hounded for them.

. May have been served with a restraining order.

. Arrest or run-in with law enforcement.

. Views problems as unsolvable and places responsibility upon the workplace. Sees a violent act as the only way out, or as justification and revenge.

If the company has done its job well by making clear its policy and written guidelines on the handling of violent incidents, and has developed a trustworthy, humane relationship with its employees, those employees will feel confident in reporting the incidence of or potential for a threatening or violent incident. The company policy should clearly relate that any threatening statement which is made by an employee concerning another employee, the company, a family member, or the person him/herself should be reported to the proper company authorities. This might be designated as a supervisor or manager, the security department, or the personnel/human resources department.

The company policy should be very specific as to the reporting procedures to be followed. These could include: the statement made, as verbatim as possible, or an exact accounting of any violent incident; names of any witnesses to the incident; the circumstances surrounding the incident or statement; and any additional information which might have a bearing. If the report is deemed sufficiently accurate and requires further action, the company designate should discreetly conduct verifying interviews.

Threat Incident Report

All threatening incidents should be documented with a Threat Incident Report. The report serves as information for the Threat Management Team, and provides an important piece of evidence should legal action be taken or instituted. At least the following facts should be included in the Report.

- Name of the threat-maker (subject), his position within the company, and his relationship to the victim or victims.

- Name(s) of the victim(s) and their position(s) within or outside the company (employee, vendor, customer, etc.)

- Date, time, and location where the incident occurred.

- Actions, facts, and circumstances occurring immediately before the incident.

- The specific language of the threat and any physical conduct which would indicate an intention to follow through on the threat.

- The demeanor of the subject--physical, emotional.

- Names and company positions of any others who were involved.

- Specific actions which transpired, including words and statements.

- Names and company positions of witnesses.

- What occurred after the incident.

- Names and positions of any supervisory staff involved and how they responded.

- Event(s) which may have triggered the incident.

- Any history leading up to the incident.

- Recommendations and immediate action to be undertaken by management.

Clearly, all such information must be handled with total trust and discretion. The employee who is experiencing problems deserves fair, confidential treatment and, if possible, counseling. Those employees who are encouraged to report abnormal behavior must themselves be protected by giving them as much anonymity as possible.

Accurate and careful documentation at every stage of the investigation and subsequent handling of the incident are important, both in fairness to the offending employee and to avoid litigation. All employees must perceive that the company handles such incidents in good faith and with concern for all parties.

If no one on staff is considered sufficiently trained to assess employees deemed to be potentially violent or threatening, the company may wish to contact a specialist, someone who is specifically trained in the assessment of violence. Depending upon the outcome of the assessment, the violent or potentially violent employee might be recommended for disciplinary action and/or counseling or might be recommended for termination.

As part of the assessment, the industrial psychology specialist or company designate handling the incident should review the offender's personnel file. If information prior to his/her employment with the company is inadequate, a thorough background check should be made, to include prior employment. Special focus should be placed on locating any information which would indicate previous violent or threatening incidents and on any personal pressures which might cause or contribute to the offender's problems. These pressures might be financial, marital, drug-related, or sexual. If the offender has a record of military service, a careful review of his military background should be made and, if possible, it should be determined if he has an undue interest in (and possession of) weapons.

One of the best predictors of current behavior is past behavior. This is a recognized and accepted theory by almost all experts--though it is not necessarily a palatable theory. It is an aspect of the American personality that we like to "forgive and forget" and to give second chances to people. We want to believe that all human beings have the ability to correct their deficiencies, and that everyone deserves the chance to "clean the slate." We believe it so strongly that our legal system requires that an individual's right to privacy includes the right to have arrest records withheld, and criminal (conviction) records are often difficult to obtain. Litigation potential for defamatory charges have caused many employers to be extremely reluctant to discuss a former employee's record of abusive or violent behavior. We are all aware, as well, that many individuals have managed to "go straight" after years of misbehavior, while others have received counseling which turned their lives around.

Nonetheless, as an element of prediction, past behavior provides a significant clue. If an individual has a record of abusive behavior, his chances for current and future abusive behavior are high. In assessing an employee in terms of predicting violence, some of the following questions should be considered.

.   Is there a record or evidence of abusive, assaultive, or violent behavior in the past?

.   What was the nature and severity of the past assaultive behavior? Was it a shouting match, a slap, or an attack with a weapon?

.   Has the aggression escalated over the years/months? Have the assaults increased or decreased? Have the attacks progressed from slapping a wife to brutally beating a companion while drunk?

.   What type of person was the victim of the assaultive behavior--is there a pattern or similarity? For example, were the victims all young, pretty women with long brown hair who might resemble someone for whom the offender carries an obsessive rage? (It is said that all of the victims of serial killer Ted Bundy bore a striking resemblance to the ex-fiancee who jilted him.)

.   If there is a record of only one or two past violent incidents, were there extenuating circumstances? What were the circumstances and are they likely to occur in the future, thus provoking more incidents?

.   What, if anything, was effective in the past to help stop the offender from becoming increasingly assaultive?

Information of this sort might be gathered in a background check of an employee who is being assessed to determine whether he/she will be retained or fired after an assaultive incident. It would be particularly useful in those cases in which an employee is to be terminated, to help determine his/her reaction in advance.

Depending upon the nature and extent of the threat or violent incident, it may be advisable to check with the police, who might be willing to review the offender's record for possible prior arrests and criminal record. This would also put the company on record as having filed information with the police, thus providing prudent documentation.

Depending upon the seriousness of the incident, prior to an interview with the offender, it might be prudent to alert the security department to monitor the interview. This is particularly true if the interview is scheduled in such a manner that the offender has advance time to brood over the affair and to come to the interview prepared for further violence. This does not necessarily mean that security people should be placed within the interview room, as this might escalate the level of tension and could easily disrupt a meaningful exchange between the offender and the interviewer. Security might be adjacent. This is a judgement call, since the offender might suddenly attack the interviewer, causing harm before security could intervene. Another option would be to have one security person in plain clothes (not in uniform) in the room, but sitting off to one side and close enough to provide protection.

Early Disciplinary and Counseling Interviews

Once a problem has surfaced and an incident reviewed and documented, the worker should be brought in for an interview. The interview should not be confrontational; it should be conducted calmly but firmly. The employee should be presented with facts relating to the incident and given a chance to present an explanation. The employee may react by attempting to bully his (or her) way through the interview--trying to intimidate the interviewer. While it is not pleasant to confront the workplace aggressor, it would be disastrous to allow oneself to be intimidated. It only pushes back the problem to a later time for resolution, and it allows the problem to escalate in nature. The aggressive employee has now won through intimidation and the number of aggressive incidents are certain to grow in nature and potential violence. Winning through intimidation validates his behavior and gives him another reason

to behave badly. If the interviewer is calm, refuses to be intimidated, and sticks to company policy, the aggressive employee may back down and agree to cooperate.

Interviews of this nature are likely to be highly charged. It is extremely important that the interviewer remain calm and project an attitude of confidence, patience, and empathy. The interviewer's posture should be relaxed but attentive and positioned at a right angle rather than directly in front of the other person, and placed so that access to an exit is not blocked. All interviews should be conducted in a quiet, private place, away from other employees.

Some specific tips are:

. Acknowledge the person's feelings; indicate that you can see he/she is upset and encourage him/her to explain this.

. Show genuine concern. Tell the employee that you are concerned he may lose control and hurt himself or someone else.

. Give the person time to calm down. Offer a drink of water. Allow him/her to smoke.

. Establish ground rules. Calmly point out the consequences of any violent behavior.

. Offer alternatives to abuse and violence. Tell the employee that if she doesn't stop yelling and making threatening gestures, you will have to terminate the interview. Assure the employee that you are ready to listen if he/she will calm down.

. Listen for what is really being said, and, just as importantly, what is the true meaning behind what is being said. The initial concern is rarely the whole story.

. Once the troubled person starts talking, don't interrupt, no matter how much you may want to jump in and start asking questions or giving commands.

. Use restatement and reflective questions to clarify and communicate what has been said.

. Be reassuring and point out choices. Problems can often be broken down into smaller, more manageable parts.

. Accept any deserved criticism. The company may be at least partially wrong. Ask questions.

. Ask for his/her recommendations. Repeat back to him/her what you believe he/she is requesting.

There are some real inhibitors to counseling interviews. Here are some negative attitudes and actions which should be avoided.

. Abrupt, hostile, authoritarian communication does not induce good results and is guaranteed either to raise the level of rhetoric or cause the individual to retreat into a cold shell.

. Gestures which challenge the individual should be avoided. These include standing over him/her with arms crossed or hands on hips, pointing a finger, staring with fixed eye contact for overlong periods, or making any physical contact with the person. That person's personal space should not be invaded; three to six feet is considered good spacing.

. Criticizing, demeaning, threatening, or attempting to bully the individual is disastrous.

. Showing impatience and cutting off the individual's explanations is nonproductive and demonstrates to him/her that management really doesn't care.

. The interviewer should listen carefully but

should never bargain with a threatening individual.

. The interviewer should never take sides or jump to conclusions even if the individual has a history of interpersonal conflict.

. It is usually unproductive for the interviewer to attempt to maintain control by using too much technical and legalistic terminology.

. The interviewer should never make promises which cannot be kept.

. The interviewer should never put an employee in a position where he or she has nothing to lose.

In the absence of a valid explanation, and if the facts are well established, the employee should be advised of his options. Depending upon the specifics of the incident(s), the person may be advised to seek counseling and warned that, should an incident again occur, disciplinary measures as outlined in the company's policy manual will be implemented. If the incident warrants it, a second interview may be scheduled, or the individual may be told that management will advise him of any actions to be taken.

If the employee shows any signs of carrying a grudge, continuing his unacceptable behavior, or actually makes threats, a warning flag should go up. This is an employee who should be kept under close supervision, and security measures should be taken to deter an incident.

Following the interview, a final assessment and determination must be made of the employee beginning, of course, with the decision of whether to attempt to retain the employee or to terminate him/her. If a trained psychologist has not been involved in the interview, the information gathered to date should be shared with him/her for his/her assessment. If a second counseling interview is to be scheduled, the psychologist may request that he/she be involved. Since a second interview may be alarming to the employee, it would be wise to consider what security considerations should be taken to protect the interviewers.

Strategic placement of security personnel is essential. They should be close enough to intervene with and forestall any violent actions, but not so close as to inhibit good communication.

Following the conclusion of the interview, the subject should be furloughed for the rest of the day and advised not to return until contacted by a company representative.

At this point, a meeting of the Threat Management Team should be held to determine further actions. If the employee is to be retained, further considerations would include whether to merely recommend counseling or to make counseling mandatory as a condition of employment, and whether to place the employee on probation pending the outcome of counseling. A recommendation might be made to transfer the employee to another department, thus affording him a chance for a "fresh start." Other courses of action include firing the employee or allowing him to resign.

All actions and recommendations taken from beginning to end **must** be documented, beginning with the Threat Incident Report. Recommendations include recommended actions to be taken in regard to the threat-maker, recommendations for improving the safety of the workplace, and the removal of any situations or circumstances which may have triggered or contributed to the incident under examination.

Well-Managed Terminations

Once it is determined that an employee is a troublemaker, is overly aggressive, is potentially violent, or makes threats, and this can be documented, he or she should be terminated. Not later, not given another chance (or warning), not forgiven with a hope for the best--*now*. Prolonging the inevitable termination does no good and can create a lot of bad. The longer the employee remains on the job, the harder it will be to dislodge him or

her without repercussions. If the aggressive employee feels that he is winning through intimidation and becomes locked into an attitude, he is likely to resent bitterly any attempt to dislodge him. After all, if he wasn't doing his job, they would have fired him a long time ago, right? Allowing him to continue his behavior without repercussions and then terminating him will "prove" to him, once again (and perhaps for the last time), that all employers, and this one in particular, are unfair and pick on him for no reason.

Because of the increasing number of violent incidents in the workplace, an imprecise but still recommended "management of terminations" style has been developed. That style does not include harsh confrontation, angry rebuttals, counterthreats, or even, necessarily, the cold, hard truth. Therefore, one objective of the termination interview will be to rid the company of the employee without prejudice; that is, to let the employee go without skewering him with his own misbehavior.

Increasingly, companies are making use of industrial psychologists who specialize in the management of violent individuals, both in assessing violent employees and in terminating aggressive employees or employees who have made threats against the company. The psychologist can offer two advantages; he (or she) can sit in on the termination interview and help to defuse the atmosphere, and he/she can advise the company as to his/her perception of the terminated employee's predilection for violent revenge.

With or without the help of an industrial psychologist, the termination interview should be carefully managed. The first decision should determine who will be present at the meeting and who will conduct it. This is dependent, to a large extent, upon the assessment of the individual about to be terminated and his conduct which has led to the termination. If the employee has been recently hired, but has already demonstrated indicators which management believes tag the employee as a troublemaker or potentially violent person, the meeting may be fairly straightforward. The employee is not as yet entrenched. The person conducting the termination interview should be at an authoritative management level, not merely an everyday supervisor. The employee must feel that he is not the victim of an immediate boss, but is being fairly dealt with at a corporate level.

If, however, the employee has been on the job for some time and has either demonstrated strong evidence of potential violence or has actually made threats, the termination interview takes on a much more serious nature. This is the time when consideration should be given to bringing in a psychologist experienced in dealing with violent employees. At least two people should be present at the meeting to show a solid corporate front. If threats have been made, the Security Director should be present but should take a non-aggressive, quiet role. The goal is to show that the company is not intimidated but, at the same time, is not showing a confrontational front.

The timing of the meeting is important. Generally, it is agreed that the best time for a termination interview is late in the day on Friday or the last day of the employee's weekly shift. The theory is that the employee will have time to go home and cool off. It delays the shock of not going to work. The timing and nature of the interview should not be revealed to the employee or his co-workers in advance. This is a security measure which will hopefully deter him from bringing a weapon to the meeting. And, it does not allow him time to build up a head of steam. The meeting should, of course, be conducted away from co-workers and held in strict confidence. The results of the meeting should also be confidential, and any gossip should be discouraged among fellow workers.

The meeting should be conducted with calm courtesy and kept at a professional level. Many people make the mistake of using the termination meeting to recite a litany of the mistakes and wrongdoings of the about-to-be-terminated employee. They probably do so because they are uncomfortable with firing another person, and listing that person's transgressions gives them a feeling of comfort that they are doing the right thing. However, it is a mistake. Firing someone, and at the same time telling him he is a failure, can provide the flash point for a violent individual. This may be the last straw for someone who has failed at other jobs or with family, and who needs to blame other people for his failures.

There are other, more tactful ways to terminate the employee (although the reasons must be legally correct). Sometimes it is a matter of how the information is worded. Instead of saying, "We are firing you because you broke the rules and we can't allow a bully to work for us," something like the following might work. "We have given careful consideration to your contribution to the company, and while we believe you have a future in the ____ _____ (electronics, manufacturing?) field, we believe that this company is not the proper setting for you. We are pretty set in our ways, and while we appreciate your suggestions, we think your future lies outside this company." Or, another tactful approach might be to suggest that the company is reorganizing the jobs within the department and is looking for someone who can bring a new and different approach to the job. Will this fool the employee? No. But, does it leave him with some dignity? Yes. It does not accuse him; it allows him to take a graceful exit if he chooses.

Be prepared for the interview to go one of three ways. The employee will accept the graceful exit; or he will attempt to argue to save his job; or he will make threats. If he goes more or less gracefully, well and good. If he attempts to argue, it is important to listen courteously, but remain adamant. If he makes threats, the response should not be with counterthreats. The calm response should be, "I am sure you don't mean that--we all say things under stress that we don't mean--we have great respect for you here at the ABC Company and would like to see you settled in a job that is more to your liking--we are sure that you can put your talents to good use--etc. etc." Responding to a threat with counterthreats or signaling for security guards to throw the bum off the premises could be a total disaster.

Even with the most skillful handling of the termination interview, there are no guarantees that the employee will not go home, brood over the perceived injustice, and come back bent on revenge, fortified with an arsenal of guns. It is only prudent to heighten the security measures within the company.

Prudent Security Measures

If the termination is "for cause," the terminated employee should not be given notice or permission to return to his or her job for any period or reason. He should be asked for any company keys and identification, and he should be given a final paycheck. It helps if the final paycheck contains a two-week pay addition. If the meeting has been held at the end of the day (or shift), the employee should be able to leave the premises without having to face any co-workers who know him.

If needed, locks and passwords to which the employee had access should be changed. If threats have been made or the assessment is that the employee is definitely prone to violence, it may be necessary to increase the physical security with additional guards and electronic enhancements. If specific threats have been made about company executives or co-workers, these individuals should be warned to be especially vigilant. Personal protection may be provided to company executives or others. If the threat, for example, is from the terminated employee to another co-worker, that co-worker may need protection.

If it is appropriate and possible, post-employment counseling for the terminated employee may be suggested and paid for by the company, although this counseling should take place off-premises. Every effort should be made to defuse the ex-employee's anger or feelings of mistreatment.

In extreme circumstances, the police should be informed and a follow-up investigation done to track the terminated employee. If threats were made, it will be desirable to accumulate quickly as much background information on the employee as possible. Will an injunction or restraining order be needed to keep the person away from the company or from company individuals?

The Threat Management Team should be alerted. The TMT will need to develop possible scenarios, such as an attack on the company or/and company personnel. The TMT should determine and authorize the extent of the security measures to be employed and the length of time expected to be needed. Should the police be alerted? Should a restraining order be secured? Should an executive protection team be placed with an employee or manager, and how many teams will be needed? If the company is located in a building with other tenants, those tenants should be alerted, as well as the building security personnel. Must protection be extended beyond the workplace to an employee's or executive's home? These and many questions must be considered and acted upon.

A complete post mortem end report should be made as to how the employee was hired, supervised, and handled on the job. What could be done in the future to avoid hiring dangerous employees? Was an old-time loyal employee allowed to develop emotional problems that drove him over the brink without anyone in the company noticing? Should training be enhanced? Does the company need expanded employee counseling services? Learning from the past helps to avoid the same mistakes. The problem of the violent employee will not go away, but it may be contained and managed.

Decisions must be made as to how and when to communicate actions which have been taken to company employees. This should be accomplished as soon as possible. If the incident is of sufficient scope and importance, it may leave lasting impressions. It may be advisable to provide counseling for some or all employees. Most importantly, the company must assure all employees that the highest priority is given to providing a safe, secure workplace and, where appropriate, company actions to strengthen security should be described.

If arrests are made and court action scheduled, the company should provide support for those employees who may be called upon to testify.

In some jurisdictions, an employer,

employment counselor, or therapist may have a duty to warn an identified employee, spouse, or third party of a threat made by another to do bodily harm to that person.

In the event that an employer warns employees of an individual's threat of violence, the employer could be liable for defamation if the employer is subsequently proved to be mistaken.

Also, an employee terminated for having violent tendencies could file a wrongful discharge suit against the employer if the employee disputes his employer's characterization. (All of these considerations indicate clearly why legal counsel should be included in the Threat Management Team.)

Stalkers are a relatively new phenomenon, particularly in their growing numbers and in the degree of their obsession. While the majority of stalkers are a nuisance at worst, many stalkers are potentially very dangerous. An obsessed stalker can be as dedicated in his quest as a suicide bomber. Many stalking cases have lurid twists: the man hiding in the attic with a gun; the murder of a pet; the defacing of old pictures, gardens, clothes, or automobiles. Domestic stalkers have killed ex-wives and members of her family, as if to wipe out her entire existence on earth.

A stalker can be of any age from lonely teenager to fixated middle age. Harassment can take the form of endless streams of telephone calls, letters, personal visitations, and trackings. While there are some female stalkers, the dangerous stalkers, those who kill, are primarily male.

Unprecedented interest in stalking over the past decade has produced media accounts of stalking victims, numerous television programs, and a spate of movies such as *Cape Fear, The Fan, Fatal Attraction,* and *Sleeping With the Enemy.* Captain L. Snow in his excellent book, *Stopping A Stalker*, states,

> "Stalking will likely become the crime of the twenty-first century.

> "Many people in law enforcement believe stalking will become the next 'in-vogue' crime in America because we are a nation of copycat criminals."

In addition to the copycat aspect, there are other reasons for the escalation of stalking incidents. There are several reasons but right at the head of the pack is the fact that, even now with antistalking laws in force in all 50 states, stalking has a high success rate. Unless and until the stalker commits a violent act, his/her chances of spending more than a few days or weeks at the most in jail are quite small. This is somewhat like white collar crime, in that the rewards (to the stalker) are high and the downside risks fairly negligible.

The stalker is not, normally, him/herself in any danger. Victims are usually well chosen, with few 250-pound linebackers elected. An interesting story from Associated Press, however, did relate an unusual incident. An individual who stalked a woman for months was shot and killed by the woman after he entered her home with a handgun and rope. Unfortunately, there are no statistics relating to victims fighting back; thus, it is not known whether this would be an effective deterrent.

National Violence Against Women (NVAW) Survey

What is most surprising are the numbers of stalkers. A study by the NVAW, jointly co-sponsored by the National Institute of Justice and the Centers for Disease Control and Prevention indicates that stalking is far more prevalent than had previously been thought. Using a definition of stalking that requires victims to feel a high level of fear, the survey found that 8% of women and 2% of men in the United States have been stalked at some time in their life. Based on U.S. Census estimates of the number of women and men in the country, one out of every 12 U.S. women (8.2 million) has been stalked at some time in her life, and one out of every 45 U.S. men (2 million) has been stalked at some time in his life. The survey also found that 1% of all women surveyed and 0.4% of all men surveyed were stalked during the 12 months preceding the survey. These findings equate to an estimated 1,006,970 women and an estimated 370,990 men who are stalked annually in the United States. While there are "serial stalkers" who pursue more than one victim at a time, this is relatively rare. Thus, if we combine 1,006,970 women and 370,990 men who are stalked annually, we have well over one million pathetic, obsessed individuals who need to "get a life," and, instead, are making life hell for their victims each year by spending their own lives in a 24-hour a day crazed, never-ending chase.

Though stalking is a gender-neutral crime, women are the primary victims of stalking, and men are the primary perpetrators (though not always). Four out of five stalking victims are women. Overall, 87% of the stalkers identified by victims were male.

Young adults are the primary targets of stalkers. 52% of the stalking victims were 18-29 years old and 22% were 30-39 years old when the stalking started.

The survey confirms previous reports that most victims know their stalker. Only 23% of female victims and 36% of male victims were stalked by strangers. The survey also indicates that women tend to be stalked by intimate partners, defined as current or former spouses, current or former cohabitants, or current or former boyfriends or girlfriends. It has been reported previously that, when women are stalked by intimate partners, the stalking typically occurs after the woman attempts to leave the relationship. Somewhat surprisingly, just over half of the victims reported that the stalking occurred either before the relationship ended or both before and after the relationship ended. Thus, contrary to popular opinion, women are often stalked by intimate partners while the relationship is still intact.

The survey found that men tend to be stalked by strangers and acquaintances, 90% of whom are male. It is unclear from the survey data why men are stalked by male strangers and male acquaintances. There is some evidence that homosexual men are at greater risk of being stalked than heterosexual men. Stalking prevalence was significantly greater among men who had ever lived with a man as a couple compared with men who had never lived with a man as a couple. Thus, in some stalking cases involving male victims and stranger or acquaintance perpetrators, the perpetrator may be motivated by hatred toward homosexuals, while in others the

perpetrator may be motivated by sexual attraction. It is also possible that some men are stalked by male strangers and male acquaintances in the context of inter- or intragroup gang rivalries.

Although men tend to be stalked by strangers and acquaintances, women are at significantly greater risk of being stalked by strangers and acquaintances than men.

When asked to describe specific activities their stalkers engaged in to harass and terrorize them, women were significantly more likely than men to report that their stalkers followed them, spied on them, or stood outside their home or place of work or recreation. Women were also significantly more likely to report that their stalkers made unsolicited phone calls. About equal percentages of female and male victims reported that their stalkers sent them unwanted letters or items, vandalized their property, or killed or threatened to kill a family pet.

Many state antistalking laws include in their definition of stalking a requirement that stalkers make an overt threat of violence against their victim. Survey findings suggest that this requirement may be ill-advised. By definition, stalking victims in this survey were either very frightened of their assailant's behavior or feared their assailant would seriously harm or kill them or someone close to them. Despite the high level of fear required, the survey found that less than half the victims -- both male and female -- were directly threatened by their stalker. This finding shows that stalkers do not always threaten their victim verbally or in writing; more often they engage in a course of conduct that, taken in context, causes a reasonable person to feel fearful. The Model Antistalking Code reflects this reality by not including in its definition of stalking a requirement that the stalker make a credible threat of violence against the victim.

The survey provides compelling evidence of the link between stalking and controlling and emotionally abusive behavior in intimate relationships. The survey found that ex-husbands who stalked were significantly more likely than ex-husbands who did not stalk to engage in emotionally abusive and controlling behavior toward their wife.

Persistence Pays

One of the elements of stalking--persistence--should be addressed. There is no question that, in our society, we reward persistence. Indeed, it is considered an admirable virtue, whether in sales or love. As a society, we are goal-oriented, driven toward success. "Quitters" are held in contempt, as is less than one's best effort. It is embodied in the American Dream and underscored in poetry, movies and song. "Her lips said 'no' but her eyes said 'yes'" or highly similar lyrics are to be found in any number of love songs. Somehow, courtship rituals have evolved into stalking behavior. This is the reason so many stalkers, when confronted, are either outraged or stunned that their behavior is regarded as wrong. In their eyes, they are only showing admirable persistence.

Stalking behavior is sometimes "encouraged" by the victim's initial reluctance to hurt the persistent suitor's feelings. In the beginning, many victims find their suitor's attentions to be flattering, perhaps romantic, something to talk about. And, what's the harm in letting the guy/woman show such devoted attention? It bestows bragging rights--until the time the stalking becomes, first annoying, then more serious and frightening. Real stalkers don't easily move on. And where the majority of us would be humiliated by a series of rejections, the stalker is not daunted. He is neither discouraged nor shamed; he is energized and driven to more serious exploits.

As a society we should know better. We have only recently accorded women the right to say "no" to sex. The same should apply to stalking--"no" should mean "no," delivered in unequivocal terms. We must stop rewarding the stalker.

Control

One should not be simplistic in attributing sanctioned persistence as the only reason for stalking.

It is generally accorded by the experts that the dedicated stalker is (in modern language) a control freak, driven by an obsessional, raging need to dominate. This is certainly the major impulse of the domestic stalker. However, more of this follows.

Who are the Stalkers?

There are two accepted methods of categorizing stalkers. In the first category, stalkers are divided as: intimate partner stalkers, delusional stalkers, and vengeful stalkers.

Intimate partner stalkers are among the most persistent. These are the individuals, almost all male, who "just can't let go." Well over half of stalkers are in this category. These people are not stalking out of love. Their entire self-worth is caught up in the process. These are often the same individuals who have shown abusive behavior in the relationship on an escalating scale.

Delusional stalkers generally have had no or very little contact with their victims. The typical profile shows an unmarried, socially immature or misfitted loner who is unable to establish or sustain close relationships with others. He rarely dates and has had few sexual encounters. He/she may have had a disastrous experience in attempting to attract a partner--disastrous in terms of humiliation and failure. Since he is unable to establish normal relationships and yet yearns for closeness, he often pick victims who are unattainable in some way. Victims may be in the helping professions--mental health, clergy, doctor, or teacher. These are the people who have shown warmth, kindness, and support, all of which may have been transformed in the stalker's mind to love. Or the victims may be in the star category, having appeared in the stalker's living room via the television set and is now firmly ensconced in his fantasy world.

A delusional stalker's fantasy may tell him that his victim is destined to be with him, that they are intertwined by fate. Severely delusional stalkers may believe themselves to be married to their victims.

Erotomania is a delusional condition in which the individual sincerely believes his victim to be in love with him (or her). It may start with an imaginary love which gradually robs the dreamer of any sense of reality. (One of the best and most graphic books on erotomania is Dr. Doreen Orion's *I Know You Really Love Me*.)

Delusional stalkers come primarily from a background which was either emotionally barren or severely abusive. They may have major mental illnesses such as schizophrenia or manic depression. Some studies show that delusional stalkers are the most tenacious of all, although it would be difficult to challenge the tenacity of the intimate partner stalker. Both categories of stalkers have their lives and self-esteem invested in the pursuit of their victims.

The third category of stalker is the vengeful stalker, though perhaps vengeful is an overly strong description. These stalkers become angry with their victims over some real or imagined matter. Politicians and activists attract many of these stalkers who become angry over some piece of legislation of program.

An often much more dangerous, vengeful stalker is the angry ex-employee who targets either his former employers or co-workers. Former intimate partner stalkers and delusional stalkers can become vengeful when they find that their efforts are being thwarted. Restraining orders can push a stalker to a new and vengeful level. In Sunnyvale, California, Richard W. Farley, 39 years old, a computer programmer, was dismissed two years previously from his job for harassing a female colleague. He returned to the workplace, killed seven people and wounded Laura Black, who had spurned him. There have been a number of cases of employees fantasizing about co-workers, casting them in the role of fantasy lovers, and stalking them. Other employees, co-workers, and supervisors have been stalked and killed by husbands and ex-lovers who convince themselves that the victim is having an affair with a fellow employee or boss.

The second method of categorizing stalkers is one upon which all mental health professionals agree. This includes four categories.

Simple Obsessional. These stalkers, being the most common, are also the most well studied. They are to be found in the intimate partner relationships. They are generally immature, socially incompetent, and unable to maintain normal relationships. They are characterized as jealous, insecure, paranoid, feel helpless and powerless, and have very low self-esteem.

These stalkers fear and detest nothing so much as seeing the end of a relationship; they often view the relationship as their entire life, the only thing that gives them worth and power. They are often batterers as well as stalkers and attempt to exercise as much control as possible, often isolating partners from friends and family.

When this stalker realizes that the partner is, yes, finally ending the relationship, he feels total panic and fear. He simply canNOT lose the object of his control--and this makes him very dangerous. The simple obsessional stalker may stop at nothing to prevent the loss of control. This can include murder or murder/suicide. To the obsessional stalker this is a small price to pay, since life without the victim is not bearable.

Love Obsessional. One of the more famous examples of this kind of stalker is John Hinckley, who not only stalked movie star Jodie Foster, but attempted to kill President Ronald Reagan "to prove his love." Love obsessional stalkers entertain fantasy images of somehow linking up with the objects of their love. At the very least, they wish to have some connection--to be noticed by their "love."

Hinckley is a classic example of the love obsessional stalker. He fell in love with Jodie Foster after seeing her in the movie *Taxi Driver*. He wrote to her a number of times but received no response and no recognition. This was not entirely surprising to him since he knew from his high school days that he was not socially adept with or attractive to the opposite sex. Hinckley felt his exploit in shooting

Reagan was well worth his loss of freedom. He declared proudly that forevermore his and Jodie Foster's names would be linked, that she would never again be able to ignore him. Typically, Hinckley had persisted in his pursuit of Jodie Foster. He had fantasized about her being his romantic partner, but when that fantasy clashed with reality, he escalated his behavior to a violent level to obtain her notice and make her a recognized part of his life.

Hinckley represented yet another trait common to some (but not all) stalkers -- the desire to "rescue" his beloved from some unsavory fate. Hinckley's fascination with Jodie Foster originated with his seeing her in her *Taxi Driver* role of a young prostitute, and his identification with Robert De Niro in his attempt to "save" her from a sordid life. This delusionary "rescuer" role is more often to be found in celebrity stalkers who have problems in differentiating between the celebrity's role playing character and his/her real character. Madonna's stalker was inflamed by her sexually suggestive and provocative public image and wanted to rescue her from "defilement."

Failed, and the subsequent absence of, social and sexual relationships are the rule among these stalkers. The National Victim Center suggests that the vast majority of love obsessional stalkers suffer from a mental disorder.

While love obsessional stalkers are persistent, even relentless, in their pursuit of their victims, they are reported to be only about one-fourth as common as simple obsessional cases.

Erotomania. Related to love obsessional stalkers is a condition known as erotomania. These are truly delusional individuals, as they believe their fantasies to be true. That is, the stalker may believe him/herself to be married to the object of his/her love, may believe that they have had a child together, and may show incredible efficiency in invading the victim's home and life. Television star David Letterman was stalked for years by a woman who claimed to be his wife and who broke into his home

and stole his car. (She subsequently committed suicide.) Erotomanics believe that the lack of response on the part of their love object is due to fantastic conditions such as aliens are preventing their meeting or other nonsense. The point must be made that the erotomanic ***absolutely, genuinely believes that the victim returns his/her love***.

Erotomanics constitute a high percentage of those individuals who stalk celebrities. Any number of movie stars and performers--Madonna, Whitney Houston, Vanna White, Kathie Lee Gifford, Janet Jackson, Michael J. Fox, Suzanne Sommers, Anne Murray, and Barbara Mandrell being just a few--have been pursued by these people.

False Victimization Syndrome. With these individuals the stalker may believe that he/she is the victim--may even report to the police that he/she is being stalked by the very person he/she is stalking. It is quite odd behavior. The stalker may so admire his victim that he imitates his victim's life style, clothes, job, home, and vehicle, even making career switches to gain closer contact.

Some Common Characteristics

Stalkers share a certain number of common characteristics which often seem to be social isolation, loneliness, perhaps a series of failures, and lack of normal social and bonding skills.

Stalking typically begins with unwanted communications--telephone calls or letters, e-mail, fax messages, etc.--which at first may seem only inappropriate or somehow sad, pathetic. The stalker may then escalate to physical approaches and, as time goes on, to physical intrusion. Stalking victims report that the most unsettling and debilitating effects on their lives result from the fact that the stalker seems to know everything about them, where they live, where they work, their friends, their social environment, where their children go to school--everything. The message is clear. "No matter where you go, I'll be there. You can't ever get away from me."

Some studies show that most stalkers are not necessarily violent, though the likelihood of physical attack is always there. When physical attacks do occur, the stalker may grab, choke, hit, slap, kick, or punch the victim. When a gun or knife is shown it is not usually used. Victims killed by their stalkers grab the headlines, but one figure places the homicide rate at less than 2%. Still, if one uses the figures contained in the NVAW survey of 1.4 million stalking victims yearly, the 2% figure could result in 28,000 deaths annually. The percentage may be higher in domestic stalker cases.

Stalker Traits

Irrespective of which category a stalker may fit into, all stalkers share some common traits. And, to the victim, categorization is of no importance. What is important is to recognize whether persistent, inappropriate behavior indicate a stalker or merely a pest who can be discouraged.

Persistence pays. Remember, this is the mantra of the stalker. This person will not take "no" for an answer, or at least for a final answer. Add to this the fact that the stalker does not believe that the victim really means "no." Stalkers possess a high degree of self-rationalization which enables them to believe that the victim does not mean "no," but really means "maybe," or "ask me enough times and I'll change my mind." This is winning at all costs. This is the person who revels in expressions such as, "Keep your eye on the ball," and "eyes on the prize." All will be well once the prize (stalkee) is acquired.

Intelligence. Most studies indicate that stalkers are not stupid--deluded, perhaps worse--but not stupid. Indications are that stalkers are somewhat above average in intelligence. They are extraordinarily cunning, persuasive, and manipulative. They are very inventive in acquiring information about their victims. Many are versed in the new technologies and have shown a disturbingly effective talent at hacking into computers, tapping phone lines, surveiling their victims, and using pretexts to gain entry to their victims' workplace and apartment buildings. John

Hinckley was able to penetrate the defensive security measures around Jodie Foster to slip notes under her door and, on one or possibly two occasions, to speak with her (briefly) by telephone. Many have also been quite successful in duping their mental health caretakers with their ability to anticipate questions and profess rehabilitation.

Absence of Normal Feelings of Embarrassment or Humiliation. The stalker does not totally lack these feelings. He or she may be embarrassed, as anyone would, at some clumsy accident or social faux pas. But he/she completely sublimates these feelings when engaged in stalking behavior. He is not at all embarrassed at being caught hanging around his victim's home, or peeping in her windows, or writing overwrought letters, or being screamed at to "leave me alone . . I hate you." He feels entitled to express his love/attachment through his stalking behavior. He is convinced that "no" doesn't really mean "no," and therefore it behooves him to press his case. Of course, rejection may ultimately kindle and fuel rage.

Obsessive Single-Mindedness. The stalker is totally focused in his/her pursuit of his/her victim. He is prepared to give up all else to continue the pursuit. The stalking has become his/her life, the reason for living. No cost is too much to pay. The dedicated stalker will quit or change jobs and travel thousands of miles to be close to his/her victim. The violent stalker bent on killing will pursue his victim knowing that, in the end, he will himself die or lose his freedom.

Loners. Many, though not all, stalkers are loners, socially inept, and unable of sustaining normal relationships. Many stalkers have a history of either childhood abuse or childhood deprivation, having an indifferent, uncaring parent or no parent at all. This is a "hit me" person, seeking out yet another example of rejection, or at the other extreme, seeking salvation. These stalkers are unable to identify with others or form meaningful and enduring relationships. They have no true friendships.

The Non-Loners--Domestic Stalkers.

The domestic stalker may differ from this profile, may even exhibit a considerable amount of charm among his friends. He may initially appear, even to his victim, to be rational, logical, and normal. However, he is apt to be unreliable and irresponsible. He will disregard the truth and lie comfortably and confidently. He will lie recklessly, but with great conviction to extricate himself from accusations.

Once the stalking begins, then escalates and finally consumes more time, even those stalkers with some friends will retreat from them, having no time to waste outside the single-minded pursuit of the victim. The increased loss of reality-based perceptions may persuade them that others are threatening to them, or are actively thwarting them in their attempts to be close to their victim.

Low Self-Esteem. Most stalkers suffer from low self-esteem. This is why so many stalkers choose as their victims individuals who are above them in terms of education and/or success, or who may have strong professional skills, or who are rich, famous, and high-profile. If the stalker can only succeed in capturing the attention and romantic interest of the stalkee, his/her self-esteem will receive salvation. Mr. Nobody will become Mr. Somebody.

Lack of Empathy. The stalker does not see, nor care about, the harm which is being caused to the victim and to the people and loved ones around the victim. Most stalkers do not consider their actions to be wrong or, when caught, criminal. So convinced are they of the virtue and rightness of their endeavor, that they simply cannot imagine that their actions are misplaced. In this respect, they show a sociopathic attitude. Bottom line is that they don't care if their actions hurt others, and they do not believe that their behavior warrants consequences. They may claim some responsibility for the trouble they have created, but do so with the intent to continue their manipulations. They deny culpability and blame everyone but themselves for their actions and the consequences for their actions.

Other Aspects. Some stalkers are psychotic. Many are paranoid. Some are schizophrenic. Some few are paranoid schizophrenic. And, 2% homicide figures not withstanding, all are potentially violent. One must never forget this. Thus, it becomes a matter of violence assessment and management, subjects which will be addressed later in this book.

The protection of stalking victims now, increasingly, involves the use of protective agents. Celebrities and dignitaries have long used bodyguards to protect them from cranks and stalkers. The problem for the domestic stalking victims in hiring protection is that the majority of these ex-wives and ex-lovers cannot afford to pay for protection. However, there is some encouraging news for these female victims. There are several organizations providing some help either at no, or minimal, cost. Victim protection services at the state level are increasingly savvy in their support of stalking victims.

CELEBRITY STALKERS

Celebrity stalkers, while similar to, differ to some extent from their counterparts who stalk dignitaries, Congressmen, Senators, U.S. Presidents, and high profile executives--and diverge rather sharply from domestic stalkers. Celebrity stalkers tend to romanticize their feelings about their targets, often expressing feelings of love. They may identify with their targets to such a degree that they form delusions of unrealistic bonding. They may believe that they are actually related to, or married to, the target. Stalkers who prey on high profile victims may also indulge in grandiose sexual fantasies involving themselves and their quarry. It is the stalker's fervent hope that the object of his obsession is reciprocal in his or her feelings.

The celebrity stalker often believes that he or she shares a common destiny of profound and privileged magnitude with the target. Such a stalker may determine to kill his victim, feeling that death will provide a perpetual bonding, a "marriage" of sorts. This was the motivation for Theresa Saldana's attacker, Arthur Jackson, who wished to be united with her forever in death and who attempted to facilitate that fantasy by stabbing her ten times. Saldana survived and later starred in a television production about her ordeal; it was excellent.

As their obsession grows, and if there is not a friendly response, the stalkers' feelings of love may turn to hopelessness, resentment, and anger. They have, after all, devoted considerable time and effort to their obsession. A clear and resounding rejection may incite the stalker to escalate to violent retaliation.

Stalkers, even those with romantic, benign feelings about their quarry, should *never* be underestimated nor automatically regarded as harmless pests. John Hinckley, Jr. (the man who shot President Reagan), while professing his love for Jodie Foster, nonetheless devised scenarios in which he killed her, then killed himself. No one who is obsessive in his/her passion for a celebrity can be regarded as harmless, although most are, relatively speaking.

For celebrities, the stalker is particularly worrisome. Celebrities--movie stars, rock stars, television performers, talk show hosts, artists, and writers--build careers based upon their desirability, popularity, and seeming access and yet, the last thing any one of them wants is some fan obsessing to the point that he/she breaks into the celebrity's home or claims to be sent from God to "take her to heaven."

Celebrities and the Illusions of Intimacy

The celebrity stalker is relatively new to the scene. But then, celebrity status is also relatively new to the sociological scene. To understand the celebrity stalker it is first necessary to understand the evolution and impact of modern-day celebrities.

Prior to the twentieth century there were no celebrities as we know them today. There were kings and queens, presidents, politicians, and the rich and famous but, while a few names were known and reported in the newspapers, the majority enjoyed a huge amount of anonymity. Without television and the movies, there were few stars and these stars were known primarily as "serious artists," being dramatic, operatic, musical, and sometimes comic and circus performers. They performed either in world capitals or on road circuits. Buffalo Bill, for example, was a star performer, and probably came as close to a modern celebrity as we might find; yet, he did not enter that area of intimacy with his fans which we see today.

While these stars enjoyed celebrity status, little was known of them. Stars and celebrities had the advantage of distance, both physical and emotional, from their fans. They made no pretense of being friendly to, or accessible to, their fans.

Physically, these stars were remote, being seen almost exclusively on stages or in arenas (wild west shows, circuses, sports). If one were persistent and willing to linger around a stage door, one might catch a glimpse of a star as he or she walked a few steps to a carriage. Or, if one were wealthy and able to afford the first-class passage, one might see a star aboard a cruise ship. Otherwise, travel was very private--private railroad cars and private carriages. Details of the stars' lives were not available to aid the stalker in pursuing his quarry. Communications were too slow to permit effective advance knowledge of the stalkee's whereabouts other than specific performances on tour.

Thus, it was difficult, if not impossible, for a celebrity stalker to make sufficient headway in developing a dangerous obsession. While many fans carried worshipful dreams about their favorite stars to their graves, these were unfulfilled for the most part.

The emergence of the cult of celebrities follows closely the evolution and progress of modern transportation and communications, particularly communications. Without modern communications it would, of course, be a very different world--no movies, television, radio, or mass circulation newspapers to create and package new stars.

By the late nineteenth century, newspapers were enjoying their greatest popularity, as these were the primary instruments of communication. A major metropolitan city might have a dozen popular newspapers, all competing for news. Savvy newspaper owners and editors began to realize that their readers were more interested in reading about some people than others. That is to say, it is more fun to read about someone who is beautiful or eccentric or despicable or rich than our next-door neighbor. For that reason, politicians became some of the first media celebrities. Politicians, even more so at the turn of the century, gave speeches, held hell-raising rallies, granted interviews, and loved the publicity generated by the newspaper stories.

From time to time, politicians attacked each other with fist fights on the floor of the Senate and House of Representatives, and occasionally a disenchanted voter might attempt to thrash his senator, but stalkers were almost unknown.

The politicians were followed by the rich and social as media personalities. Henry Ford, Andrew Carnegie, the Vanderbilts, and Rockefellers, among others, became increasingly prominent in the newspapers. In those more innocent years, the rich and social were more admired than hated. Hard work and devotion to duty were patriotic and religious icons. Surely, if a person were rich it meant that he had labored diligently for his wealth and thus had attained his just rewards. It was the American Dream.

Then came Hollywood, the granddaddy of all starmakers. Hollywood occurred at the same time that transportation and communications were speedily making it possible for people to move freely and to disseminate news within hours. Without question, Hollywood and the movie industry played one of the most significant roles of the twentieth century in changing and shaping the cultural mores.

As film making progressed technically, the close-up was invented. The importance of the close-up in creating a feeling of intimacy between actor and audience cannot be overemphasized. Think of it. Most of us never see the faces of our friends in as close proximity as we now see the faces of actors and actresses--and, for that matter, the faces of politicians

in news broadcasts. It was the close-up which enabled the camera to move as close to a star's face as to the face of a loved one in the most intimate setting. Therein began the love affair with stars.

Not only does the close-up permit us to truly see the star's face, we are permitted to do so intimately, for as long as we wish, without restraint or apology. For many years, the price of a movie ticket permitted the ticket holder to sit in a darkened movie house for as long as it was open, for hours on end, seeing the same scenes over and over. Now, of course, a movie can be rented, played on a VCR and, if we are truly in love, we can freeze-frame a close-up and stare at it for as long as we wish. It is almost as if we have control over the star. When the gorgeous actress stares straight into the camera and whispers "I love you," she may be speaking directly to you.

Once the star system was established, the stars' salaries escalated. Whereas before, actors and actresses lived more or less like anyone else in rented digs, *stars* now could afford to buy glamorous homes, wear suave and slinky clothes, ride in limousines, and kick up their heels at places like the Brown Derby and the Coconut Grove.

Enter the publicity agents, the fan magazines and the gossip columnists to feed the frenzy for news of the stars. Gossip columnists were, in their heyday, all-powerful. They literally made and broke stars, often with the connivance of the film studios. They wrote glowingly of their favorites and chastised the stars whose behavior they felt was not correct. The gossip columnists became our surrogates to ask questions and discipline our stars. Stars could be *punished* if they did not behave in ways acceptable to their fans and the studio. They could have their contracts canceled, be barred from the studio, placed on suspension, or denied privileges.

One could buy pictures of favorite stars and pin them on the wall where they could be endlessly dreamed about or stared at while writing fan letters. And, of course, the studios encouraged the writing of fan letters. Fan clubs were organized to further build the popularity and mystique of the stars, and they were highly successful.

But, almost nothing can compare with the advent of television. Television, with its growing technology, has placed our celebrities squarely within our living rooms and bedrooms in the most intimate settings. By bringing television into our homes we have come within inches, it would seem, of bringing our celebrities into our homes. These stars are like our best friends, and are as real to us.

Whether they come from movies, plays, music, sports, politics, business, or crime, our celebrities will, absolutely, appear on our television screens. Many will appear on the television talk shows, and their most private secrets will be laid bare in front of us. Some of these secrets may shock us, even turn our love to another less worthy emotion. Or, our affection (love?) for our celebrities may deepen. Or some strange mixture of both emotions.

Nathan Trupp killed two security guards at Universal Studios because they stopped him from entering to see Michael Landon of television fame. Trupp had decided that Michael Landon was a Nazi and needed to be killed.

Michael Perry, an escaped mental patient, saw singer/actress Olivia Newton-John in a movie and was immediately smitten. He moved from Louisiana to Los Angeles, where he stalked Newton-John, several times trying to break into her home. After being sent home to Louisiana, Perry drew up a list of ten people whom he intended to kill. These were a disparate group, including Newton-John, her husband, Supreme Court Justice Sandra Day O'Connor, and several members of his own family. And, in fact, within weeks, Perry had killed his parents, two cousins and a baby nephew, deliberately shooting out the eyes of his victims. Which points to another characteristic of some stalkers--not content merely to pursue their obsessions, some shoot members of their family.

Olivia Newton-John was simultaneously stalked by Michael Perry and by Ralph Nau. Prior to his Newton-John obsession, Nau had attempted to find a young lady in Arizona who (for a fee) wrote steamy, sex-laden letters. Nau tried without success to find her, after which he switched his obsession to Olivia Newton-John. He moved to Los Angeles, where he wrote numerous letters to her. He also flew to Australia to be near her. When all of his efforts failed, Nau returned home, moving in with his mother and new stepfather. Not long after, a stepbrother was killed with an axe, and Nau was committed to a mental hospital.

Helpfully, there are magazines, brochures, and other sources of information which tell us how to find our celebrities. There are maps for sale of Hollywood homes. Information about public appearances and tours is published. And while our celebrities are now well screened from the public, a clever person can get close.

And so, the stage is set for the celebrity stalker, the fan who has "gone over the line" and now poses a threat, either nuisance or physical, to a celebrity client. To the obsessive fan in search of an identity, the fantasy goal seems so close, so obtainable.

Television also offers another attraction for the celebrity stalker--it has the capability of turning the stalker himself into a celebrity.

Celebrity Stalking Incidents

The following provide only a small glimpse of the celebrity stalking incidents which have been documented.

. **John Lennon** was shot and killed by Mark David Chapman on the sidewalk in front of his apartment building, the Dakota, in New York City on December 8, 1980. It was an event that shocked the world. John Lennon, an ex-Beatle rock star, was a living legend, both for his music and for having crusaded for world peace, and denouncing political repression, hypocrisy and bigotry. Chapman stalked Lennon relentlessly and had become so closely identified with Lennon that he felt he "was" Lennon.

. **Rebecca Schaeffer**, a young television actress, was shot and killed by Robert Bardo. Bardo, a loner whom school officials once described as needing psychiatric help, at age 16 discovered Schaeffer, watching her on a television program. Bardo began writing to her. She sent him a postcard, signing it "Love, Rebecca." After receiving the card, he wrote in his diary, "When I think about her I feel that I want to become famous and impress her."

He traveled in June 1987 to the Burbank studios where the series was filmed, carrying a large teddy bear and a letter for Schaeffer. He was turned back by the security guards. He returned a month later, carrying a knife "because I thought she was turning arrogant." He again was turned back. After reading in *People* magazine about Arthur Jackson, a stalker who stabbed actress Theresa Saldana numerous times, Bardo paid a private detective to find Schaeffer's address (from California motor vehicle records.) He procured a gun and hollow-point cartridges. He wrote a letter to Schaeffer, then left for Los Angeles. Arriving at her apartment building, he pressed the buzzer, and, when she answered the door, he handed her the letter.

He then went to a diner and called his sister who told him to come home immediately. He returned for a second time to Schaeffer's apartment building and, as she opened the door, he shot and killed her.

. **Madonna** seems to have been a popular target. In 1994, in yet another stalking incident, a fan crashed his truck through the gates of her home. (It was reported that he was actually looking for Olivia Newton-John who had previously owned the property.) And still another individual, claiming to be her husband, scaled her eight-foot fence.

. **Sonny Bono** obtained a restraining order against a stalker who had harassed and followed him for eight years.

. **Bob Conrad** was stalked by a woman who eventually began a trek to his mountain home. When stopped, she was found to have a shotgun in her truck.

. **George Harrison,** a former Beatle, received a series of threatening letters.

. **Johnny Carson**, famed nighttime talk show host, was the recipient of numerous letters containing death threats. His stalker was finally arrested when he showed up at the studio.

. **Paula Abdul**, the popular singer, was the target of a wildly deluded stalker, Scott Isley. Isley believed that Abdul was his lover and that mobster John Gotti and President George Bush had cared for him when he was a youngster.

. **Sharon Gless**, of *Cagney & Lacey* fame, was stalked by a fan, Joni Leigh Penn, who tried unsuccessfully to visit her on the set, sent numerous letters, and broke into Gless's office with the intent of raping and killing her.

Stalker Profile Characteristics

It would be unfair to term each and every stalker as being mentally deranged or dangerous; however, it is fair to assume that almost all truly obsessed stalkers and all of the dangerous ones show evidence of some mental disorders. Dr. Park Dietz, an expert in the field of forensic psychiatry, has stated that 95% of stalkers have some form of mental disorders (although he was referring specifically to celebrity stalkers). Gavin DeBecker, an expert in the field of celebrity stalking, believes studies point out that more than 90% of people who might deliberately cause harm to public figures are mentally ill.

It seems obvious, and is confirmed by experts in the field, that people stalk celebrities because they have not been able to establish or maintain real-world emotional relationships and thus attempt to do so through their delusions and fantasies about celebrities. Many keep diaries and files of clippings to feed their need for knowledge about "their" celebrities. However, it is the stalker who attempts to *approach* his/her celebrity who is the problem.

There are many personality disorders, but the ones which would typify a stalker might include an exaggerated sense of entitlement, an inflated sense of self-importance, and a tendency to manipulation and exploitativeness. These characteristics are particularly typical of domestic stalkers. Other characteristics include a preoccupation with idealistic fantasies such as perfect love, and an unrealistic self-perception. Some stalkers suffer from erotomania, convinced beyond a shadow of a doubt that their target loves them in return and belongs to them.

Indications of personality disorders may be evidenced by overly dramatic behavior or ideas, intense expressions of excitement or anger, a history of unstable or abusive relationships, inappropriate or uncontrolled anger which may result in abuse or attack or self-damaging acts.

Stalkers are driven by a variety of emotions: love, adoration, hate, despair, jealousy, vengefulness, envy, and sometimes, happiness and devotion.

It is safe to say that stalkers, more often than not, have already established a history of aberrant behavior and/or anti-social acts. These may include abusive relationships, poor work history, unsatisfactory or non-existent family relationships, poor or non-existent social relationships, abusiveness or violence in the workplace, fighting, excessive use of alcohol and/or drugs, and record of crimes (both misdemeanors and felonies).

Celebrity stalkers most likely to approach a client, insofar as research has shown, are primarily white and male, ranging in age from teenagers to much older individuals, with the largest number in their late twenties to late thirties. Dedicated stalkers tend to be loners, unmarried or divorced, while the overall population of celebrity stalkers includes many who are married and reasonably well adjusted in their social relationships. While some are either unemployed or minimally employed, a surprising number hold down jobs in the mid-echelon business world.

It is well to repeat that the majority of celebrity stalkers are not dangerous -- merely fixated. They come in all sizes and shapes, ages, religions, ethnic backgrounds, and educational history. What is important is to recognize those stalkers who have the capability and intention of approaching and harming a client.

Evaluating the Stalkers

Not all stalkers are dangerous or pose a threat of more than nuisance value to a client. What is needed, therefore, is some method of detecting and evaluating stalkers to determine which of them is potentially dangerous to a client.

The prediction of dangerousness is an extremely imprecise science, as any psychiatrist is quick to tell you. However, some headway has been made in studies about stalkers, and this information is very helpful to protection agents.

We start with the fact that stalkers, unlike terrorists, do not set bombs or throw grenades or missiles at automobiles. Of the known cases of stalkers attacking, injuring, or killing a celebrity or other public figure, a physical encounter took place. That is, the stalker approached the victim at close range and used either a gun, knife, or similar instrument carried in the hands. The greatest distance between attacker and victim is the distance between Lee Harvey Oswald and President John F. Kennedy, and in this incident Oswald somewhat untypically used a rifle rather than a handgun.

This narrows the field considerably. Stalkers who merely send letters or make telephone calls, while a pain in the derriere, pose no danger to a client unless they actually attempt to approach the client. Let us be clear. Not every dangerous stalker attempts to approach a client, but if they do not approach, their dangerousness is not an issue. By the same token, not every stalker who approaches or attempts to physically approach a client is dangerous-- but each must be *considered* as being potentially dangerous and treated accordingly. A protection agent cannot afford to do otherwise as the consequences are too severe.

As a further aid to the agent, it has been shown that in many, if not most, of the attacks upon celebrities and dignitaries there were pre-attack signals. These signals, which could include written communications, telephone calls, conversations with third parties, visits, and surveillance, have been too often ignored and not reported to the proper people.

Example: Mark David Chapman called his wife during his first visit to New York City and told her that he had intended to kill John Lennon but that her love had saved him. Clearly, he was sending a signal but either she did not have the ability to recognize it, or she chose to disbelieve it. John Hinckley, Jr. wrote numerous letters to Jodie Foster and, while he did not talk about killing the President until his last letter, the sheer volume and intensity of his correspondence and personal visits should have sent a signal of his potential dangerousness to *someone*. Many obsessed and dangerous stalkers have histories of mental health problems and have related their fantasies to mental health workers, or to the police.

In fairness, pre-attack signals are not always clear to the recipient. The volume and intensity of Hinckley's correspondence to Jodie Foster and his subsequent visits were clear signals of his dangerousness, but, because he endlessly declared his love for her, his letters could easily be misinterpreted as evidence only of a hopelessly lovesick young man. Hinckley spoke of his obsession for Jodie Foster to his psychiatrist, but this condition was apparently not probed nor evaluated by the psychiatrist. Had he done so, there is a good possibility that the signal could have been properly interpreted.

There are celebrities and public figures who were killed by persons not termed stalkers. Some were killed by persons known to them and some (such as Malcolm X) by groups, cults or others. Sharon Tate was killed by followers of the Manson group/cult. Alan Berg (a Denver talk show host) was killed by Aryan Nation followers. Berg was not so much stalked as surveilled. Whether these groups or

known intimates signalled their attacks is not known. The methods of targeting and killing these public figures are more typical of terrorist or assassination attacks rather than stalker tactics.

Stalkers are diverse in their approach techniques. Many are clever at devising pretexts to allow them to get close to their person/obsession. Others behave in such a bizarre fashion that they are immediately spotted. Their delusions may be so severe that they are utterly convinced that the celebrity will be happy to see them. Some make repeated visits to the celebrity's home, are turned back and even arrested by security personnel, yet return again and again.

One man illegally entered a star's unoccupied home, firm in his belief that God had ordered him to take the star to Heaven. He persisted by breaking into a second home belonging to the star. On yet another trespass he was caught, at which time he stated that he was there "to serenade you and me to Kingdom Come."

A relatively popular delusion is that God is directing the stalker to either join with the celebrity or kill the celebrity (take him/her to Heaven). Others are more direct in their intentions. In one case, a man with an arrest history and known to possess weapons had also drawn diagrams of a celebrity's home for use in a sniper attack.

An overwhelming number of approaches are relatively benign and naive. A surprising number ask for money.

While many stalkers retain their obsessions for one particular celebrity for many months and years, some are relatively fickle and, if the object of their obsession rebuffs them and no progress is made, they may turn their attention to another star. Some waffle between celebrities and other public figures, notably Members of Congress. One man who was convinced that he was the son of a television star was known to the Federal authorities, as he had created a disturbance in the office of a member of Congress, and he also stalked several entertainment figures.

One mentally disturbed man, having previously written to an entertainment celebrity, escaped from a mental hospital and traveled over 1,500 miles to the celebrity's home. His attempts to enter the home and approach the celebrity were deterred by the celebrity's security. He then drew up a hit list of people to be killed, including his family, a U.S. Supreme Court Justice and the celebrity. Subsequently, he murdered his mother, father and three other relatives. Previously, he had told relatives that the celebrity was evil and should die.

Communications

If we accept the premise that only those stalkers who approach or attempt to approach a client represent a danger, and that many approaches are pre-signaled, it is very important to both limit the possibilities of approach and to detect the approach indicators (signals).

Let us start with the ways in which fans and stalkers communicate with their targets. Without a doubt, letters are the primary form of communication. Fans write to their stars, request pictures, stand on the sidewalk to view their stars at events, request autographs, and pay an admission price for movies, concerts, and sports events featuring their celebrities. Normal fans do not overstep the boundaries in attempting to approach their stars.

A stalker, however, in addition to the above activities, may attempt to call the celebrity on the telephone, may surveil the star's home, may use a pretext to try to gain entrance to the celebrity's home, may commit the crime of breaking and entering to gain access to the celebrity's home, or may simply attack the celebrity. The bigger the star, the more difficult it is for the stalker to get close, since the star will usually travel even short distances with someone or several persons and, in addition, may have close-in security. However, as always, a gun is an effective equalizer and a determined stalker might rather easily get close enough for a shot unless the client star and his/her security have pre-warning.

Like fans, stalkers rely primarily upon letters to communicate with their stars. Not all stalker letters are abnormal. They tend to send many letters, and it is both the tenor or content of the letters and the quantity of letters which may send up a "red flag."

Abnormal, Improper Communications

Following are examples of letters which have been changed and edited but which are reasonably close to the originals that were sent to celebrities and which should be considered not normal, or inappropriate.

1.   "Help. I have written to you before and I do not want to be a problem but you are the only one I can turn to. They are trying to get me and no one believes that I am really two people and the other one is the bad guy. He makes me do terrible things and I am afraid that they will put me away. If I do not hear from you I will come to your house. . . . . ."

2.   "You have not heard from me because the police put me in jail. They put me in jail because I was kinda crazy and first they put me in the hospital and I couldn't eat the food. I don't trust those people. Anyhow I'm getting out soon and I just want to see you and be with you and hold your hand. No one loves you the way I do and will take care of you. We can watch pornographic movies if you want to but I will not wear condoms because I don't want anything between me and you. Do you have orgasms? With me you will, my darling . . . "

3.   "I can't understand why you have not answered my letters and why you do not want to see your new son. He is a beautiful boy and looks just like you. It is no good denying that I am your wife or that we had that beautiful night together. That other woman living with you all these years and claiming to be your wife is really your sister. Why are you so cold? If you don't want me just say so, but I will call that other woman who claims to be your wife and has your

name, and I will tell her to leave you and maybe I will kill myself . . . "

4.   "I'm saving my money so that I can buy a plane ticket or maybe a car so that I can come to Los Angeles and be with you. It will be perfect. You don't know me in person yet but YOU WILL. We will make love day and night and you will beg for more. I can come sooner if you will send me the money. I called your agent and asked for $1,000 but it hasn't come . . ."

5.   "When you were in New York I went to every appearance you made and I sent flowers to your dressing room. I found out you were staying at the Plaza Hotel and I waited inside the lobby every night just to see you. I tried to follow you in the elevator but the bellman looked suspicious. If I could have found out which room was yours I was going to pick the lock and wait for you inside. I have loved you for years and I can't wait any longer. If you can't love me the same way, it will be sad but I will have to do something . . . "

Many letters are more graphic, or explicit. Some are more directly threatening. It is not unusual, as well, for fans and stalkers to enclose objects in their letters or to send gifts. Some of these enclosures are harmless and may include religious objects, poems, pictures (usually of the sender), and even valuable objects such as a ring. Many are simply strange, such as a shampoo coupon, candy wrappers, playing cards, a sample box of cigarettes, and a child's thermometer.

Many of these objects, however, are strange, even bizarre, some are threatening, and some are revolting. Blood, semen, feces, and sexual fetishes have been sent to celebrities, as well as drawings intended to frighten the star. For example, a rendition of a heart with a knife impaled in it, or the star's picture torn into pieces and smeared with blood, or a corpse with the star's picture superimposed have all been used.

Letters sent by stalkers and those not classified as normal fans vary a great deal in length, content and volume. In one study which was made of abnormal letters sent to celebrities, it was found that the subjects sent from one to several ***thousand*** letters to the celebrity of their choice, with an average number of eight. Over half of the writers in the survey had sent two or more letters. Letters included a diverse number of pages, ranging from one to two thousand pages. The mean number was surprisingly high at 35 pages, and a median of six and one-half pages. An astonishing ten percent of letters contained more than 80 pages. The average duration of the correspondence from first to last letter was 11 months.

The same study indicated that, for the most part, the letter writers gave information within the letter which identified their name and address, with only five percent maintaining full anonymity. While most sent their letters from one state or locale, a smaller number sent letters from two or more states or countries, some from several locations. The highest percentage of letters were hand written or hand printed, followed by typed letters. A few sent greeting cards. A very surprising finding was that only one letter writer had composed a letter of cut-and-paste materials--the typical suspicious missive depicted in movies.

In the study it was found that at least 12 percent of the letter writers also attempted to reach the celebrity by telephone or used other means of communication to do so.

One of the most interesting findings of the survey is that less than half of the subjects who approached the celebrity were known to have previously communicated with the celebrity. This figure may be open to some error since letters received by agents of celebrities may not be kept on file unless they are positively recognized as being abnormal.

Letters sent by stalkers and obsessed fans, and which can be classified as abnormal or inappropriate, tend to cast the sender (fan) and receiver (celebrity) in certain roles and relationships. In many cases, the fan implies a personal relationship which does not exist and is sheer fantasy. He/she may cast him/herself in the role of lover, spouse, friend, or adviser. A very few take on more bizarre imaginary roles as religious advisor, business associate, rescuer, enemy, or family member.

With multiple communications, the writer may change roles. However, a strong characteristic of abnormal communications is the presence of a persistent and repetitive theme or obsession. The theme may be love or persecution or sex, but it will almost certainly be present. Along with the thematic content of the letters can be found an intensity of feeling and expression. In the unsuitable letters the writers tend to express feelings of urgency or graveness, or implore the recipients to respond with some recognition, or demand certain actions. The intensity of feelings expressed is, in itself, abnormal. Writers of abnormal letters almost always ask for something. They crave recognition of the imaginary relationship which they have created. Sometimes the recognition sought may be as simple as a telephone call or granting a visit to the writer. Others ask for marriage, love, sex, or money.

In addition to asking for something, typically the writer may attempt to ensnare the celebrity by provoking some emotional response appropriate to the role in which he/she has been cast by the writer. The writer most frequently may attempt to evoke feelings of love on the part of the celebrity, but may also try to instill feelings of sexual excitement, remorse, guilt, shame, anxiety, or fear.

The writers of abnormal letters to celebrities (as opposed to other public figures) seem to have a preoccupation with sexual activity. Many describe sexual activities, either with the celebrity or as having been engaged in by the writer, or as approved or disapproved by the writer on an almost clinical basis. Some letters are overly explicit, using detailed descriptions of vaginal intercourse, fellatio, cunnilingus, or other sexual acts, and/or referring to sexual organs in fearful detail. Some also refer to masturbation, sex with children, sexual fetishes, rape, and sexual humiliation.

Because of the high number of loving, adoring and/or sexual themes of inappropriate letters sent to celebrities, it is not surprising to find that most do not threaten the celebrity. The letters have more of an insistent or imploring nature. However, some of these letters do contain threats, either direct, veiled or implied. Some threats are preceded by expressions of love, then followed with "if you do not respond, I will be forced to . . . ." Some threats have a religious undertone, implying that God is going to punish the celebrity if he/she does not repent or correct some behavior. Some threats appear to be non-lethal and directed to the writer, ". . . and if you do not consent to marry me, I will never marry and I may kill myself." Some threats are made against members of the celebrity's intimate circle, such as his/her agent or business manager, family, or friends and associates. Some threats are vague and involve God and God's justice to sinners. Some threats are against the writer, and a surprising number of threats are made against other public figures.

In the bulk of communications with celebrities, there is a low level of specific threats of violence; the implied threats are primarily of nuisance and embarrassment value. The worrisome threats, which are in the low minority, are those which seem specific and logical, which imply a *plan* and *an ability to carry out the plan*. These are the letters which should be immediately referred for investigative and preventive action. All unsuitable or abnormal letters should be evaluated as part of an ongoing threat assessment, but letters written with specific information about the celebrity and implying a threat to the celebrity should flag a higher "red alert" for investigation.

This may be an appropriate place to pause and examine the logistics of attempted communications with celebrities.

Celebrities closely guard private information about their geographic address and telephone numbers. A dedicated and clever stalker can, by examining property and tax records, determine where a star lives, but even then the star, if famous and sufficiently wealthy, will have a secretary and/or staff who opens mail and responds to appropriate requests. The bulk of all fan mail, therefore, is sent to an agent, agency office, manager, or studio, where it is opened, screened, and appropriate requests (for pictures, etc.) fulfilled. Some stars are more assiduous than others in answering mail. In any case, any inappropriate or abnormal letters and enclosures will normally be received and read by office personnel.

Therefore, it is logical that staff and office personnel should be trained or given guidelines as to which mail is not only abnormal, but specifically which correspondence indicates a potential or probability of dangerousness. In this way, the "red flag" letters could be diverted to security personnel for evaluation and follow-up. It is particularly important that abnormal correspondence not be thrown away. Any mail flagged as abnormal should be kept for a period of time and filed in such a way as to be easily retrievable. Thus, if a second and subsequent correspondence is received, the entire correspondence can be evaluated to determine if the sender is escalating his/her determination. It may signal that an approach to the celebrity is imminent. Whenever correspondence is flagged, the envelope or packaging material should be kept together with the correspondence itself so that it can be analyzed.

Some of the red flag issues which should be integrated into guidelines for mail screeners have been discussed within this chapter. Guidelines might include flagging all correspondence which mention:

- An obsession of any nature. If the sender seems fixated upon a theme or idea or passion, it should be noted. Certainly, if the obsession concerns love or sexual activity either with the celebrity or another public figure, this would be a red flag.

- Any threats, direct or implied, either against the celebrity or any other person, including staff, children, other public figures, or the writer's family and friends.

- Any indications of intense anger and/or persecution, particularly when coupled with

requests for help from the celebrity.

- Indications of highly intense and/or erratic emotions.

- Indications that the writer may be suffering from delusions, such as stating that he is someone or something other than himself, or that unusual agencies are attacking the writer (CIA beaming thoughts into his head, etc.).

- Overwrought religious themes, particularly when they involve the celebrity, such as directions from God to meet the celebrity or to share a destiny with the celebrity (take her to heaven, etc.), or to warn the celebrity to change his/her lifestyle, etc.

- Pretensions to a common history or a shared relationship or destiny which might include the illusion that the writer is married to, or loved by, or is related to the celebrity. References to a shared destiny may indicate that the writer will approach in order to fulfill the destiny.

- Requests based on the belief that the celebrity owes something--money, love, gratitude, recognition--to the writer.

- Any references to death, suicide, guns, knives, or violent events. This could include a preoccupation with violent movies and television, or serial killers, cults, gangs, etc.

- Any references to violence and abusive relationships in connection with family, friends and/or workplace.

- References to persons and events which included attacks against public figures, either the persons attacked or the attackers. (Hinckley, Lennon, etc.)

- Any references to criminal or mental health problems on the part of the writer.

- Indications that the writer intends to contact the celebrity or that the writer is abnormally preoccupied with the need/desire to do so.

- Any indications that the writer may be stalking the celebrity--for example, references to traveling in order to see the celebrity, or attempted approaches, or information indicating that the writer has secured the celebrity's home address and other personal information.

- References to an abnormal flow of correspondence and/or gifts to the celebrity-- indications that the writer has written previously and insistently.

- Letters with obscene, lewd, or pornographic references or enclosures.

- Letters with bizarre or gruesome enclosures.

Celebrities have not thus far suffered the potential for letter bombs and packages which has plagued politicians, public figures and executives. However, there is no reason to believe that this possibility does not exist. Therefore, training of mail screeners should include letter and parcel bomb recognition points.

The training of letter screeners is not difficult and can be easily and quickly accomplished. Key points can be reproduced on posters which can be placed on the wall for easy reference. It would be highly desirable to specify certain individuals as responsible for opening all mail. These individuals would, through practice, develop a fairly accurate perception of abnormal mail to be referred to security. Further, they might more readily become familiar with those fans/stalkers who should be red flagged.

Approaches

Screening and analyzing celebrity correspondence is important as a tool in predicting the likelihood of the writer's **approaching** the celebrity or someone else, such as a family member

or staff person. The writer can be dangerous, but unless he/she approaches the celebrity and succeeds in inserting him/herself in the physical proximity of the celebrity, the dangerousness is of minimal consequence to the celebrity. This is not to say that there does not exist a responsibility to notify the authorities of a dangerous suspect, since that suspect might attempt to attack someone else. The emphasis, however, for the protection agent is to attempt to determine in advance (predict) which abnormal fans and stalkers will attempt to approach the celebrity, since this could provide an attack situation.

What are the signals found in communications which might predict an approach attempt on the part of the fan/stalker? Any of the signals listed in the screening guidelines should "red flag" the screener(s), who would then refer the correspondence to the protective agent for evaluation and investigation.

It is the subsequent investigation which will add the information needed to predict the approach potential. In order to investigate an individual, certain personal information is needed. Letters must be analyzed to ascertain, if possible, name, address, telephone, and physical description. A high percentage of inappropriate letters contain some personal information, enough to enable an investigator to find out more about them.

There are computer databank services which are remarkably efficient in obtaining information about individuals if a name and address can be provided. With sufficient personal information, these service companies can investigate criminal, driving, employment, education, and credit records. These services are reasonably priced and worth every penny. There are some caveats. The protection agent should check the laws of the state in which he is working to assure compliance, and the computer databank investigative service must be reputable and conform to any restrictions and laws governing the use of information.

Mobility and travel are elements to be examined. Does the writer indicate in the correspondence that he/she has moved to be close to the celebrity? Has he/she traveled to see or be close to the celebrity? If so, how far did he travel? Has she moved or traveled more than once for this purpose? Does he indicate that he knows where the celebrity actually lives? Does the writer indicate that he has stalked the celebrity or has attempted to approach the celebrity? Subjects who write abnormal letters to celebrities are quite likely to indicate information in their letters which would provide answers to these questions, as evidence of their passion and commitment to the celebrity, and their belief in a pre-ordained destiny. That is, if the writer has moved to be near the celebrity, he is very likely to volunteer this information in the letter. Or, if he has stalked the celebrity, he may well boast of it, or use this information as a form of intimidation.

Whether or not the suspect writer possesses a car is not particularly indicative of approach mobility, since suspects have traveled by automobile, hitchhiking, bus, train, airplane, and walking. However, possession of a car enables the investigator to check Division of Motor Vehicles (DMV) records to obtain information about the suspect.

In the study previously mentioned in this chapter of abnormal and inappropriate correspondence to celebrities, the following factors were found to be approach signals. It should be noted that these are the results of a very specific study, and the figures may not apply in other studies. However, some very interesting results were tabulated.

. A greater number of communications. It was estimated that subjects who sent between 10 and 14 communications were most likely to approach.

. Long time span or duration of correspondence period. Subjects who corresponded for longer than one year were more likely to approach.

. Multiple communications, including telephone contact. Subjects who both telephoned and wrote to the celebrity were more likely to approach.

. Multiple letters from different geographic locations. Subjects who wrote from different states and countries were more likely to approach.

. Expressed desire for face-to-face meeting. Subjects who expressed an intense desire for a face-to-face meeting were more likely to approach.

. No return addresses. Subjects who did not supply an address of any kind were more likely to approach.

. Specific times, locations, and events. Subjects who described specific locations and events to take place were more likely to approach.

. Subjects who made repetitive mention of entertainment products were more likely to approach.

. Subjects who mentioned any stressful life event or, conversely, expressed happiness, contentment, and peace of mind were more likely to approach.

. Mention of a vehicle was associated with approach status.

Some interesting and unexpected results were tabulated. Again, it should be emphasized that these results are of one study only. There is still much research to be done.

. Subjects who made repetitive mention of public figures were less likely to approach.

. Subjects who made mention of sex, sexual activities, or marriage were less likely to approach.

Subjects who sent hate mail and obscene

mail were less likely to approach.

. Subjects who provided full addresses were less likely to approach.

. Subjects who attempted to instill shame in the celebrity, or who expressed intense or uncontrolled anger, were less likely to approach.

. Subjects who reported any mental health treatment were less likely to approach.

. The inclusion of threats in the correspondence did not significantly increase the likelihood of an approach. However, a significant number of subjects who mentioned a weapon approached.

It should be noted once again that not all approaches are preceded by communications. A significant number of approaches to celebrities are made without prior communication by letter or telephone. It was stated earlier in this chapter that most attacks are pre-signaled, although these signals may be made to third parties who do not understand them or who do not communicate them to the intended victims. These third parties include family, friends, mental health workers, and the police.

Good advice is to keep personal information safe and to avoid, whenever possible, allowing one's residential address to become public. It is best not to give interviews or permit photo shoots at home; these are best held elsewhere. Fan mail should be handled by a professional service and should be stripped of any messages which could be construed as "personal" or meaningful to a delusionary fan.

DIGNITARY AND PUBLIC FIGURE STALKERS

Public figures, and by that is meant politicians, dignitaries, members of government, and high-profile executives and professionals, have long been regarded as targets for attack. These are the people who have the power to enhance or restrict our lives, to grant favors, to pass laws, to remove part of our money through taxation, to punish us, and to reward us. These people have real power and they are highly visible. It is not surprising, therefore, that public figures should be targeted for praise, envy, anger, revenge, persistent demands, and requests. They function almost as lightning rods, attracting the (usually unwanted) attentions of those with a complaint, a cause, or a victim of real or imaginary persecution.

Every lawmaker must inevitably make decisions and vote on such issues as gay rights, abortion, acid rain, logging in the national forests, taxation, aid to the handicapped, gun registration, and women's rights. Each legislator has the capability of fighting to obtain military bases and build dams within his state, thus bringing millions of dollars in benefits but uprooting some worthy citizens to make room for the project.

Public figures such as George Wallace (Presidential candidate when shot by Arthur Bremer) and Martin Luther King (civil rights leader shot and killed by James Earl Ray) are so imminently controversial that it seems inevitable they will attract the attention of stalkers and would-be assassins.

There is another aspect which makes public figures such attractive targets. Their power and identity beckon to those mentally disordered individuals who yearn for recognition and who believe that by killing a powerful public figure they will themselves acquire a powerful identity.

Increasingly, corporate executives are becoming regarded as public figures. With the exception of a dozen or so public figure executives such as Henry Ford, the Rockefellers, and the Vanderbilts, corporate executives have, until recently, managed to remain relatively invisible. The "man in the gray flannel suit" who ran the company may have made decisions which affected our lives but we never knew his name. This has changed in the past 20 years. Corporate executives are highly visible and are often reported in the newspapers. Many corporate executives and CEO's have become involved in support of charities, the arts, and "good causes." Too, many corporate executives have become increasingly vulnerable because of adverse publicity. Plant closings, failed savings and loan banks, inflated CEO salaries, and bankruptcies have tarnished the image of corporate America. In the past two decades, corporate CEOs involved with companies which are considered bad ecological neighbors or which are engaged in animal research have become targets of stalkers, just as have abortion doctors and support staff.

Lynette Fromme, who was arrested after a failed assassination attempt on the life of President Gerald Ford, previously plotted to kill corporate executives, urging a friend to kill William Roesch, President of Kaiser Company.

Labor strikes--the really down-and-dirty ones-- almost always contain some elements of stalking. One of the first security measures taken by the corporation involved is to provide protection for its top executives.

One might also include other professionals in the group vulnerable to public figure stalking--judges, lawyers, mental health workers, college professors, police officials, and others. Because these professionals are so visible and are perceived as figures of power, they are often irresistible to stalkers, some of whom hold a grudge against the victim.

There is little hard data available on the volume of abnormal, threatening, or inappropriate correspondence to corporate executives and many other public figures. However, there have been some records kept on the abnormal and unsuitable correspondence sent to Members of Congress (protected by the Capitol Police) and to the President and Vice President (protected by the U.S. Secret Service). Records have also been kept on some of the more bizarre or threatening telephone calls, but, unfortunately, these records are very incomplete.

The illusions of intimacy so prevalent with celebrities are not as noticeable with public figures. That is, we are not so apt to believe that our Senator

or Vice President is our best friend; nor are we as likely to call him/her by a first name. We may think of Johnny Carson as "Johnny" but one almost never hears someone refer to Vice President Al Gore as "Al," unless it is his wife or the President. It is hard to imagine considering the CEO of Chrysler Corporation as a best friend or intimate.

There is, however, a strong feeling of "ownership" and entitlement. We feel that, by voting for our lawmakers they "owe" us. We made them, gave them their power. Are they not referred to as "public servants?" The president of the failed savings and loan bank who enticed us into investing millions of dollars in one of his schemes is directly accountable to us. These public figures must listen to us--or else!

There is a surprising amount of harassment in the form of love and/or sexual identification with public figures from individuals convinced that they are lovers and spouses. It is perhaps the aura of power of public figures which makes them seem romantically attractive.

Members of Congress are particularly susceptible to a constant barrage of correspondence, telephone calls, and visitors, much of which is unsuitable and some of which is bizarre and threatening. These politicians try to build the illusion of being accessible to their constituents and, of course, they attend many public events. Their whereabouts are not secret. They are good targets for harassment and for stalkers. It should be noted, however, that public figure stalkers are more likely to kill someone close to home than the individual being stalked.

CORRESPONDENCE

Clearly, not all attacks on public figures are preceded by illuminating correspondence. It is not known whether Arthur Bremer ever corresponded with President Nixon (whom he stalked) or George Wallace (whom he shot) but it is highly doubtful that he did so. James Earl Ray apparently simply fulfilled a contract in killing Dr. Martin Luther King. Do would-be attackers, then, ever write to their public figures? Indeed they do, just as they write to celebrities. Again, as with celebrities, not all attackers write in advance, nor do all individuals who write threatening or bizarre letters later attack.

There is a constant stream of correspondence to public figures and a certain proportion of that correspondence is abnormal or improper. The following examples have been changed from the original, but are indicative of the tenor of some correspondence.

1. "I am demanding the arrest and impeachment of the President of the United States. It is his fault that I have been harassed and followed by the CIA and the Justice Department. They have bugged my house and taken my wife who left me after the house was bugged. I am very angry and very anxious to recover my wife. This is not an idle threat! You must help me."

2. "I have heard that you want to marry me. It was on the television. I am coming to Washington and want you to meet me at the airport. If you cannot come to the airport I will come to your office so that we can be married right away."

3. "It has been twelve months since my son left home with that wife of his. Now, I don't usually get angry but I am so mad now that I slam things and I broke my alarm clock. They took my money and are living the life of Riley and I want them to pay for it. SLAM! I will call your office so that you can get the CIA to investigate."

4. "I am tired of being a nobody. I want to be a CIA agent or lead a battalion of raiders in any war. I am a weapons expert."

5. "I'm mad as hell and I'm coming to Washington and I'm going to stand in front of your office for as long as it takes. Your

bunch of crooks stole my property. I gave up my life for three years in the Army and now you took my property."

In a study made of bizarre and inappropriate letters sent and telephone calls made to Members of Congress, it was found that there were some similarities and some differences as compared with bizarre and unsuitable correspondence to celebrities.

The volume of correspondence compares similarly with an average number of two and one-half communications per sender sent to a public figure. For senders of multiple letters, the span of time during which the letters were written averaged about four months while the more persistent and prolific writers averaged about 12 months time during which they maintained their correspondence. It should be noted that some persistent and obsessive writers have sent hundreds of letters over a span of many years to a public figure.

Subjects also attempted to communicate with Members of Congress in other ways, primarily by telephone or by hand-delivering letters. Hand-delivered letters are often forwarded to the Capitol Police for review, particularly if the letters seem unusual in any respect. As with celebrities, subjects who telephoned in addition to writing were much more likely to approach the public figure than those who were satisfied merely to correspond.

As with celebrities, a certain percentage (approximately one-third) of letters contained enclosures, primarily media clippings and photographs. The enclosures tended to be much less bizarre than those sent to celebrities (blood, semen, feces). In addition to clippings, enclosures included copies of papers, documents, business and religious papers. The presence or absence of enclosures was not linked to approach behavior, and could not be used as an indicator of an approach.

The writers tended to give full information about themselves. A major proportion gave full names and addresses, with many giving other descriptive personal information.

The most significant desire expressed by the writers was for a face-to-face meeting, thus indicating approach behavior. As with celebrities, those subjects who wrote obscenely about love and sexual activities were not likely to approach. Perhaps it has something to do with preserving a fantasy and not having the fantasy punctured.

The writers of improper letters often perceived a (non-existent) personal relationship with the public figure, although these perceived relationships differed from those with celebrities. Correspondents to public figures most often cast themselves in the role of enemy, persecutor, or judge. The second most popular role was of constituent or fan. A lesser number saw themselves in the role of friend, adviser, associate, or someone with special powers (religious, rescuer, etc.) A very small percentage cast themselves in the role of lover or spouse. Interestingly, those who portrayed themselves as enemies were much less likely to approach than those who cast themselves in the role of special constituent. By the same token, those subjects who placed the member of Congress in the role of benefactor or rescuer were much more likely to approach.

Not surprisingly, the letters were heavily laden with references to political issues, other government figures, and political parties.

A significant number of letters mentioned or dwelled on a theme or idea. The highest number (almost half) of the letters mentioned injustices to themselves. The next most popular focus was on politics and government. This was followed by these themes: law enforcement, security, intelligence, military, the specific Member of Congress, the President, other public figures, violence or aggression, religious issues, racial issues, love, marriage, and sexual activity. Fully one-quarter of the letters mentioned violence or aggression either to the writer or others, or religion and/or mysticism.

The study showed that the writers almost all evidenced a high degree of intensity, ranging from indicating that their concerns were of extreme importance to begging and beseeching. At least one-third demanded or ordered the member of Congress to take some action. Interestingly, the degree of insistence indicated in the letters did not match approach behavior. That is, it could not be demonstrated that either a high or low degree of intensity predicted an approach.

Not only was there a high level of intensity in the letters, the writers almost unanimously attempted to elicit some sort of emotional response from the member of Congress. Fully half tried to instill a sense of anxiety or worry. One-third attempted to cause a feeling of fear. Others tried to create feelings of upset, shame, guilt, and anger. At the bottom of the list was any attempt to invoke a response of love or sexual excitement.

The study found that in almost all cases, the writer wanted something. Those writers who wanted a face-to-face contact and those who wanted rescue or assistance were more likely to attempt to approach. Those who sought marriage, sex, or merely a written response were found not likely to approach.

Slightly more than half of the letters contained some kind of threat, either to the specific member of Congress or to another (usually) public figure or to significant others. Some threats were direct; others were conditional ("If you do not do such and such, I will . . ."); and others were veiled. Some were too vague or unrealistic to be taken seriously. The high number of threats was not matched by approach behavior.

A further conclusion to the study showed that there was a significant association between writers who approached and their mentioning any mental health treatment. Approach status was strongly associated with subjects who suffered from delusional disorders and paranoid feelings of persecution.

The study concluded that certain factors were associated with approach behavior. Subjects more likely to approach were those who:

. Were constant letter-writers. Subjects who

wrote six or more letters were most likely to approach.

. Provided any identifying information, such as name and address.

. Telephoned in addition to sending letters.

. Wrote polite letters.

. Assumed the role of constituent.

. Assigned the role of benefactor or rescuer to the member of Congress.

. Expressed a desire for assistance, valuables of some sort, recognition, or rescue.

. Expressed a desire for face-to-face contact.

. Mentioned traveling to see the member of Congress.

. Repeatedly expressed love, marriage, or romance.

. Reported having received mental health treatment, particularly in association with a paranoid delusion. Also, all subjects who believed themselves to be married to or lovers of the member of Congress pursued face-to-face encounters.

. Expressed feelings of social isolation.

. Thought others were talking about them.

Those who were less likely to approach included subjects who:

. Sent only one letter.

. Sent no personal information as to name and address.

. Assumed the role of enemy or judge.

. Assigned the role of enemy, persecutor or conspirator to the member of Congress.

. Attempted to instill feelings of fear, upset, or worry.

. Sent hate mail.

. Sent obscene communications.

. Made threats of any kind.

The findings regarding threats is both surprising and worrisome. The conclusions reached were that subjects who threaten are less likely to approach. However, it is known that attacks are often preceded by signals, including threats. Thus, the pre-attack signals (threats) are more likely to be communicated to third parties rather than to the person attacked. The second disturbing conclusion is that we cannot afford to focus our attention only on those individuals who make threats, since studies show that individuals who do not make direct threats are equally or even more likely to approach.

Some of the differences in the abnormal and inappropriate letters sent to celebrities and to Members of Congress are readily apparent in the study.

Letters to celebrities tended to be more intimate and personal with a high focus on love, romance, and sexual activity, whereas correspondence to public figures tended to be more formal and had its highest focus on perceived injustices. Correspondents to celebrities more often requested face-to-face meetings than correspondents to public figures; they preferred instead to request something (rescue, information, valuables). There were a greater percentage of threats made in letters to Members of Congress, but the threats were less precise than those made to celebrities. There were more instances of a plan and opportunity to carry out the threats made in letters to celebrities than were apparent in those threats made to Members of Congress.

Further Conclusions

The studies made of abnormal and inappropriate correspondence to celebrities and Members of Congress showed some further characteristics.

The correspondents are primarily male--80 percent for writers to celebrities and 85 percent to Members of Congress.

High rates of mental disorders were apparent in both groups with paranoid delusions representing the most commonly perceived disorder. It was estimated that more than half of the subjects had thought disorders, with about ten percent reporting hallucinations. The most common diagnosis was schizophrenia (believed to be evident in one-half to two-thirds of the writers). Narcissistic, histrionic, schizotypal, and borderline personality disorders were identified in subjects, as was substance abuse. About ten to twenty percent mentioned suicide.

Correspondents to celebrities and Members of Congress often mentioned other public figures, sometimes referring to multiple public figures. These public figures included other celebrities, corporate executives, sports figures, and political assassins.

Correspondence indicated that some writers had previously stalked another celebrity or public figure.

Twelve percent of those writing to celebrities attempted to physically approach the celebrity. The 12 percent figure may be too low, as correspondence is not always preserved; therefore, an approach may have been made and perceived as having been accomplished without prior correspondence when, in fact, a letter may have been sent but tossed away. A comparable figure was not available for the correspondents writing to Members of Congress, as mail may have been routed to Capitol Police and subsequently discarded.

While 12 percent seems a high number of approaches, it should be remembered that an "approach" may include simply hand-delivering a letter or gift, or harmlessly attempting to talk with a celebrity. An approach should not be equated with an attack. *However*, approaches should always be viewed with concern since an approach is required for an attack. From the study which was conducted and has been described in this book, no figures are available as to which (if any) of the approaches resulted in an attack or attempted attack.

Subjects who approached celebrities did so primarily at the celebrity's home, whereas subjects approached Members of Congress almost exclusively at their offices or the Capitol Building. A second proportion of subjects approached their public figures at public appearances. When doing so, subjects approaching celebrities tended to be more law-abiding than the subjects who approached Members of Congress; these individuals were more likely to be charged with crimes of illegally carrying a weapon, trespass and/or disorderly conduct. This may be due, in part, to the fact that the Capitol Police and other law enforcement agencies attending the Members of Congress are more likely to press charges than the private sector. For example, private security personnel may not be empowered to search an individual for a weapon.

Subjects writing abnormal or inappropriate letters to celebrities were three times more likely to have actually stalked their celebrities than those correspondents to Members of Congress, who were apparently more content simply to bombard the public figure with multiple communications.

The study reached some additional conclusions which could not be scientifically proven but for which there is strong belief. The following are almost certainly strong predictors of impending attack:

. Excessive interest in famous assassins and killers of celebrities, and copying of behavior. For example, both Chapman and Hinckley carried a copy of the book, *Catcher in the Rye*. This copy behavior may be an attempt to emulate a "role model" in the hopes that the results will be as dramatic in creating recognition for the subject.

. The making of a "hit list" of persons targeted for attack (almost always public figures). Certainly, with terrorists, putting together such a hit list is very common in signaling a serious intent to attack. This may be equally true with stalkers.

. Keeping a diary of the stalk. Stalkers who keep intimate thoughts and intentions about their target and the logistics of their stalking appear to be more seriously involved in an attempted attack. Perhaps the diary helps to keep them on track toward their intended goal. (Bremer, Chapman.)

. Random travel, not necessarily travel spent stalking a target, may be a predictor of attack. Chapman and Hinckley both engaged in what appeared to be aimless travel, taking trips that bore no direct relation to the whereabouts of the target. It may be that the apparently aimless travel is a form of play-acting and preparation for the "real thing." Since many of the stalkers are relatively unsophisticated individuals, the travel may serve to "educate" them as to the logistics of getting from one place to another. Or, it may simply be indicative of a very confused and disordered thinking.

. Acquiring a weapon for the express purpose of attacking a target seems an obvious predictor of attack. Acquiring the weapon not only provides the means of attack, the mere possession of the weapon would appear to form some kind of commitment on the part of the subject. Or, perhaps it provides a sense of empowerment and seriousness that persuades the stalker to take the next step.

APPROACHES

Approaches, while not necessarily dangerous, are viewed very seriously by those assigned to protect public figures and by the public figures themselves. In order for the public figure to be endangered he/she must be approached. Thus, physical approaches are prerequisites to attacks, though not all approaches result in attacks.

Following are some of the more bizarre examples of approaches to public figures.

. A man who had been arrested at least twice for sending threatening letters to the President visited a U.S. Senator's office, loudly demanding to see him because "he had proof that he was being surveiled by the C.I.A. and that the President was selling out the country to the Communists."

. An individual attempted to enter the office of a Member of Congress to enter a complaint about a worker in the building whom he claimed had sexually assaulted him. He claimed that he knew the Congressman, having met him while the two of them were sleeping in a public park.

It is not at all unusual for public figure stalkers to pursue more than one person, sometimes serially and sometimes simultaneously. This can include both dignitaries and celebrities. For example:

An individual who caused a loud disruption outside the office of a Member of Congress was later picked up and questioned by police when he attempted to "crash" the set of an actress. His goal was to make her his "First Lady." He later pursued a male actor.

There is, still, a paucity of information about stalkers, particularly stalkers of public figures. It is to be hoped that, with greater recognition of the stalking problem, efforts will be made to retain, analyze, and continue the study of abnormal and inappropriate correspondence to determine whether other attack predictive factors can be identified.

CAUSE STALKERS

Among the movements which actively use

stalking as a weapon are the highly activist anti-abortionist groups. These people have perfected a method of identifying and stalking abortion clinic doctors and workers and have shown little restraint in ruthlessly using their methods to halt what they believe is murder.

Abortion doctors and their families have been relentlessly stalked and harassed. Activities have included placing signs emblazoned with "BABY KILLER" in doctors' front yards, passing out similar flyers in neighborhoods, sending threatening letters, following doctors and their families, vandalizing cars, and harassing doctors' children at their schools. In one Florida case, "wanted" posters against a doctor were posted offering a reward for information leading to his arrest or revocation of his medical license.

One assumes that members of these organizations sincerely believe in their goals--to stop abortions, to stop the "murder" of babies, and to use any legal or near-legal methods to do so. One also assumes that their sanctioned methods stop short of one of their own members committing murder, though sentiments may come down on the rationale that it is "for the greater good."

What is also true is that every red-blooded, high rhetoric, emotion-ridden cause is absolutely guaranteed to attract some less desirable individuals looking for acceptance, love, respect, and support. If those individuals are suffering from some form of anti-social behavior or mental disorder(s), he/she may step over the line. This is the danger for "good cause" organizations, that their zeal and rhetoric will attract the "loose cannon."

In March 1993, a protester identified as Michael Griffin shot Dr. David Gunn, a physician who performed abortions at a Pensacola, Florida clinic. Dr. Gunn had attempted to avoid the anti-abortion picketers outside the clinic by using the back door. Griffin is reported to have raced up shouting, "Don't kill any more babies," and then he shot Dr. Gunn three times in the back. Gunn later died at the hospital.

In August 1993, an antiabortion activist, Rachelle Shannon, shot a doctor outside the Wichita Kansas Family Planning clinic. She shot Dr. George Teller as he sat in his car outside the clinic. Shannon was also involved in attacks on abortion clinics in California, Oregon, Nevada, and Idaho. It was later discovered that Shannon had been in communication with a man being held by police in Florida for murdering a doctor at an abortion clinic there.

In 1994, again in Pensacola, Florida, right-to-life advocate Paul Hill used a shotgun to kill Dr. John Britton and Britton's escort/"bodyguard" James Barrett outside an abortion clinic. Because of the violent atmosphere and prior killing in Pensacola, abortion doctors there had been provided with volunteer escorts. This was unfortunate for Mr. Barrett, as well as the doctor. It was reported that Hill had been seen previously carrying a sign that said, "Execute Abortionists." At his trial, Hill claimed "justifiable homicide" to protect unborn children. It was also reported that a "justifiable homicide" statement signed by some 30 anti-abortion activists stated, "We, the undersigned, declare the justice of taking all godly action necessary to defend innocent human life including the use of force. We proclaim that what ever force is legitimate to defend the life of a born child is legitimate to defend the life of an unborn child." (An interesting application of the Use of Force doctrine.)

In December 1994, in Massachusetts, John Salvi entered the Planned Parenthood clinic and opened fire with a semiautomatic rifle. He then drove to a nearby clinic where he murdered two receptionists and wounded five other people. Not quite satisfied, he then drove to Virginia, where he fired shots at another clinic. This shooting spree might have been avoided. Salvi had previously argued with the leader of Operation Rescue (a pro-life organization) when she stated that Michael Griffin (Dr. David Gunn's killer) could not really be pro-life if he committed murder. Salvi, however, declared angrily that Griffin was a hero. The director was sufficiently concerned that she reported her feelings and Salvi's identity to the police. It is not known what use was or was not made of the information.

Anti-abortionist extremists do not believe they are stalkers (although a number of anti-abortion activists have been convicted of stalking); indeed, they feel completely, unshakably righteous in their behavior. Attitudes not markedly different from other stalking behavior, one might contend.

In February 1994, Cathy Rider was convicted of stalking the director, Lorraine Maguire, of the Charleston Women's Medical Center. Her stalking took a violent tone when she told Maguire to wear a bulletproof vest and hinted that the director might come to a violent end.

In 1995, a Dallas jury awarded a doctor and his wife over $8,000,000 in damages, money which the court ordered three anti-abortion organizations and seven individuals to pay.

Not all anti-abortion organizations support the extremists' hard-core activities. However, do not look for a reduction in the protests. In 1997, the U.S. Supreme Court held that activities such as confronting women and doctors en route into abortion clinics and attempting to dissuade them from having an abortion are protected speech under the First Amendment--so long as the activities take place on public (not private) property. Protesters are *not* allowed to push, shove, or prevent entry into the clinic.

REVENGE STALKERS

Minnesota District Judge Joanne Smith has been the victim of a stalker since 1985. The stalker, John Patrick Murphy, was sentenced to jail for 90 days by the judge for assault on a woman. Judge Smith has endured slashed tires on her car, obscenities spray-painted on her house, and other assaults. And that's not all. Apparently, Murphy is a serial stalker, having stalked at least three judges, three prosecutors, two probation officers, two halfway house workers, and two correctional workers.

Financial firms and Wall Street brokers have been stalked by individuals who lost money in their stock trading or by discharged employees. Kidder,

Peabody Group is just one such firm. College and university professors have been stalked, usually for awarding less than satisfactory grades to a student.

Included in the arena of revenge stalking is a related form of stalking -- hate stalking. There are numerous recorded incidents of individuals being harassed and stalked simply because they are of a different race, religion, or sexual persuasion.

DOMESTIC STALKERS

Domestic violence related stalking is significantly more prevalent but less publicized than stalking of high profile victims. It is primarily, but not entirely, a crime of men stalking women.

Domestic violence victims are primarily women who have experienced domestic violence at the hands of their spouse, former spouse or "significant other." There is an established cycle of violence and, therefore, a very real threat and probability that the perpetrator will attempt to attack, injure, or kill the victim. The most dangerous period of time for domestic violence stalking victims is when they leave the relationship with their stalker. In the great majority of reported spouse assaults, the victim was divorced or separated at the time of the incident.

Domestic stalkers are very direct in their stalking. Any correspondence is likely to be specific and threatening, and, unlike inappropriate correspondence sent to celebrities and public figures, these are threats to be taken very seriously. Domestic stalkers are extremely obsessive and violence-prone. They seek face-to-face confrontations above all else. Stalking can, and often does, precede assault and injury, abduction and kidnapping, vandalism, and homicide.

Domestic violence victims are contained in a prison of fear perpetrated and perpetuated by the stalker. Prior to being stalked the victim was comfortable conducting her daily routine unhampered as a private citizen. Now nothing can be taken for granted. Daily routines are hampered and influenced by fear of the stalker. The victim is unable to maintain or resume a normal lifestyle. Her life has become based on avoiding the stalker's wrath, terrorism, and retaliation.

Unlike the high profile victim who may view the stalker as merely a nuisance, the domestic violence victim views the threat extremely seriously. The victim has been stalked and/or attacked at home, at work, in her car, grocery shopping, the movie theater, in courtrooms, and in her family's and friends' homes. The level of menacing, domination, invasion, and violation inflicted by the stalker can be acute. The victim justifiably views herself as prey and the stalker as a hunter. The victim has probably experienced violence at the hands of the stalker before and therefore knows that he is capable of carrying out his threats.

Whereas the high profile victim usually does not know the stalker personally, the domestic violence victim knows the stalker intimately. She knows her stalker's habits, cycle of violence, pattern of stalking, and what incidents will provoke or escalate the stalker's behavior. The fact that the stalker knows the victim intimately contributes to the victim's terror.

With high profile victims, the threat to the victim is usually taken seriously by authorities, media, and the public. Because the victim is well-known, he or she is usually considered to be unequivocally credible, and, therefore, the threat to the victim is regarded as being credible and valid.

With the domestic violence victim, the victim's credibility is often criticized by the authorities, media, and public, because the victim is a previously unknown person. There is often a "blame the victim" mentality because the victim and stalker know each other. The victim is often prejudged and accused of being vindictive and making false accusations about the stalker. An ignorant but prevalent attitude is that somehow the victim must have provoked the stalking and deserves it. Another inappropriate banality is, "How could the victim be stupid enough to be involved with anyone

like the stalker in the first place?" Authorities have a tendency to focus on what they perceive to be the dynamics of a relationship, rather than to acknowledge that crimes have been committed and to respond in the same manner they would if the victim did not know the stalker. Attitudes are changing, both in the general public and within the law enforcement communities, but it is still an uphill battle.

Why Do Domestic Perpetrators Stalk Their Victims?

Domestic violence stalkers strive to repossess and maintain the complete control that they previously held over their victims. Stalkers believe they have the irrefutable right to control whomever they select to prey on. Stalkers also seek retaliation for offenses they perceive their victims have perpetrated against them (leaving the relationship, filing for divorce, asserting independence, improving their lives, dating someone else). Domestic violence stalkers are obsessed with their relentless attempts to subjugate, dominate, and control their victims' lives. Their profound need to control consumes the stalker's own life and dominates his thoughts, actions, and behavior.

Domestic violence stalkers will not reconcile themselves to the obvious--the relationship with their victim is over. The victim can no longer endure the cycle of violence and has chosen to end the relationship. Stalkers refuse to acknowledge that the dissolution of the relationship was a direct consequence of their abusive and violent behavior. Stalkers will go to any measure to hang onto a relationship that is no longer consensual. Stalkers have a raging need to control and punish the victim for not adhering to control. Their control has terminated, leading to feelings of extreme impotence. In an attempt to expunge their intolerable feelings of impotence and loss of power, they strive to regain that control. The stalking begins after attempts to cajole and manipulate their former partner into reconciliation fail.

Stalking accomplishes many purposes. Isolating the victim deprives her of social support and diminishes the impact of outside encouragement and assistance. When the stalker continually makes his presence known, it impairs mental and physical ability to resist. Threats effectively foster anxiety and despair. Flaunting omnipotence and ability to avoid police intervention conveys the futility of resistance. All of these tactics strive to coerce the victim into returning to the stalker, who thus regains the complete control which he craves.

Stalkers want their former partners to comply with their demand that they return to the relationship. Stalkers strive to show that resistance can be more dangerous than surrendering into submission. The average battered woman escapes and returns to her batterer seven times before she leaves permanently.

An estimation of an aspect of the stalker's rationale is, "I will never love anyone like that again. I will never find anyone for whom I will have those feelings again. Therefore, if I can't have her, then no one else will."

If the stalker's attempts at coercion fail, his actions can escalate to murder. Murder is the final act of control. Murder is the deliberate act of the stalker to get the final say.

Occasionally stalkers tire of their victim and redirect their attention and fixation to new prey that is more vulnerable because they are not yet intimately familiar with their dangerous patterns. It is sometimes less of a challenge and more entertaining to seduce someone new than to try to recapture someone who is alert to their treachery.

Domestic stalkers can be almost demonic in their single-minded obsessions. Unlike their counterparts in celebrity and public figure stalkers, domestic stalkers will pay any personal price to reach their victims. Note the fanatic quality in the following cases.

CASE STUDY--JUDGE SOL WACHTLER

Sol Wachtler was a top judge in New York

with a distinguished career and a brilliant future. He had a wife and four grown children. Wachtler, well regarded in the Republican Party, was chief judge of New York's Court of Appeals from 1985 until he resigned, three days after his arrest for harassing and stalking a female Republican fundraiser, Joy Silverman, with whom he had an affair.

Wachtler conducted a 13-month campaign of harassment which included threatening letters, calls, and a threat to kidnap the victim's daughter. He also mailed the teenager a condom along with a sexually explicit letter. Wachtler then attempted extortion, demanding $20,000 in exchange for photos of Joy.

Wachtler claimed that he suffered from bipolar depressions (manic depression) and that he should have killed himself.

Wachtler could have been sentenced to five years in prison and fined $250,000; instead, he was sentenced to 15 months in prison, fined $30,000, and must make restitution of $31,000 to the victim, as well as undergo two years probation.

Surely, someone of Wachtler's intelligence and criminal justice background knew the dreadful consequences to himself of pursuing the destructive behavior in which he engaged. His career is over, his future gone. This case shocked his associates and friends.

CASE STUDY--STEPHANIE SUND

Stephanie Sund was shot by her ex-boyfriend, Jeff Thomas, in February of 1992 in front of the Fort Collins, Colorado police station. As she reached the front door, a bullet grazed her head. A second bullet struck her arm and the third hit her in the middle of the back. At the time, she was clutching a restraining order against him in her hand. She survived, but she spent months recuperating--learning to sit up, turn over, walk, doing those things that come naturally to the rest of us.

Thomas was unrepentant and maintains his

"innocence" while pursuing an appeal from a life term in prison, where he is currently serving out his sentence. Thomas was not a stupid man--he was a man possessed, to throw away all caution as he did, shooting Stephanie Sund in front of a police station.

. **Connie's Story.** When Connie filed for divorce from her husband, he said, "If you go through with this, I'll kill you. Marriage is for life and the only way out is death." Connie filed for and received a protective order which her tormentor violated over a dozen times. Connie quit her job and went into hiding to escape. Actually, she did all of the right things--almost. She protected her new address from friends and family. But, her husband caught up with her when, several months later, she stopped by a friend's house to pick up mail. Her husband, who had maintained a relentless vigil, shot her and then killed himself.

. **Sonja's Story.** Sonja and Al were married only after several years of courtship, during which time she found him to be considerate and caring. Once married, all changed. Sonja, after abuse and threats against her life, obtained a restraining order against her estranged husband, Al. As often happens, the restraining order served only to send Al into a more violent, vengeful mode. His stalking behavior include vandalizing Sonja's car, slashing her tires, surveiling her constantly, invading her property, cutting her electricity, sending threatening messages, and, finally, physically threatening her with a gun. Sonja moved, but to no avail. Al leaves little messages in unexpected places, just to prove that he can get to her anytime he chooses to do so. Al was Sonja's second husband (and she his second wife). Sonja now carries a gun with her, always.

. There are hundreds, thousands of stories just like these. The striking parallel is that, in almost every single case, in the beginning the abuser is charming and caring. And, then, it's like a game of "Gotcha!" The charming courtier turns into the creature from Hell, first establishing control and then active abuse. The woman attempts to leave or does leave, and the really frightening stalking begins.

Battering

In cases of domestic violence, battering often precedes the stalking. It's a vicious circle. The victim is battered. Then, when the battering becomes unbearable, the victim takes action to leave the relationship. The batterer may already have begun stalking his victim, but now the stalking activities increase in intensity. The final result usually falls into one of three categories: the stalker continues to harass his victim for years; the stalker grows tired of the situation and seeks out a new victim; the stalker takes the ultimate last step and kills the victim.

There are women who are not certain if they are battering victims. The battering may be more psychological than physical. Or, the woman may become convinced that she (not the batterer) is at fault. In all too many cases, family and friends actively work to convince the victim that she is the one at fault. And the batterer may take a break when he senses that his victim is about to leave, by promising better times and undying love.

In these cases, a reality check may be in order. The following guidelines offer some clues as to whether an individual is in a battering situation.

Does the person the victim loves/is married to/is in a relationship with:

. Discourage/hinder contact with family and friends?

. Forced isolation may occur, with victim locked in the house or a room or tied up.

. Isolation may be achieved by frequent moves and/or by living in a secluded location.

. Mail and telephone calls may be monitored.

. Believe that others are "out to get him?"

- Abusers blame the victim's friends and family for problems and believe that others are unfair in their judgement of him.

Demand to know where she is all the time?

- Victim may be required to report where and when she is gone and with whom.

- Frequent daily telephone calls are made to check up on the victim.

- The abuser may surveil the victim.

Demand that she stop working or attending school?

- Abuser may harass her at work by telephone or in person.

Constantly criticize her and use disparaging remarks, often in public?

- Name-calling ("stupid," "worthless," "lazy," "bitch") can be used deliberately to destroy the victim's sense of competency and self worth.

- A deliberate effort may be made to convince the victim that she is mentally ill or so worthless that no one else would put up with her.

- Manipulation and lies may actually convince the victim that she is crazy or, at best, incompetent and lazy.

Make constant use of coarse, abusive language when talking to the victim or about the victim's friends and family?

Insist upon control of the money and all expenditures, making the victim account for all expenses? or . .

- Refuse to keep a job and force the victim to pay all the bills?

- The victim may be forced to spend excessively long hours on housework and cleaning to unreasonably scrupulous standards.

Have a "hair trigger" and an uncontrollable temper? Does he break things when he is angry?

Use drinking or drugs to excuse anger and abusive behavior?

- The abuser may force his victim to drink and/or take drugs.

Destroy the victim's personal property and items of sentimental value?

- The destruction may be eerily symbolic, such as marring a face or cutting it out of a photograph.

Threaten to harm physically, to further restrict the victim's freedom, to abandon, to commit suicide?

- Abusers use threats to control the victim and are clever at twisting the punishment to convince the victim that she "deserves" it. ("I swear I'll kill myself and, if I do, it will be your fault.")

- Threateners do so to maintain control and to perpetuate the relationship, factors which are of preeminent importance to the abuser.

- Abusers couch the relationship as "forever" and use phrases such as "no matter what," "You'll never get away," and the worst, "If I can't have you no one else will."

- Hit, slap, punch, pull hair, twist the victim's arm(s), shake, or otherwise physically abuse the victim? Or the children?

- Refuse to acknowledge the abuse, take responsibility for it, or, at the least, attempt to minimize it?

- Accuse the victim of being unfaithful?

- Force the victim to participate in sex when the victim does not wish to, or to perform unwanted sex acts? Indulge in pornography?

  - Conversely, the abuser may totally withhold all affection, love and sex, leaving the victim in a cold, isolated position.

- Threaten with or brandish a weapon? Like to play with gun(s)? Collect weapons?

  - Abusers who possess weapons are particularly scary. They are often infatuated with stories of individuals who have committed violent crimes. They view weapons as empowering.

If several (not necessarily all) of these behaviors are present in a relationship, it's a good bet that it is a battering situation.

Domestic Violence Stalkers: Traits and Patterns

Domestic violence stalkers are more overt in the nature of the contact with the victim. The extent of the contact may include attempts to confront or threaten the victim in person; breaking into the victim's residence or car; vandalism of property; or assaulting relatives, friends, children, and pets. Stalkers make terrifying threats to kill the victim and the victim's loved ones and acquaintances, and to sabotage or bomb the victim's car.

Domestic violence stalkers often utilize child visitation or/and child support as opportunities to manipulate and terrorize the victim.

Domestic violence stalkers invariably have a prior criminal record and/or a history of domestic violence.

Domestic violence stalkers frequently kill their victim in public and in full view of witnesses, the most probable locations being the victim's residence or job, family and friends' homes, restaurants, supermarkets, shopping malls, traffic intersections, and even courtrooms. Friends, family, and bystanders are often killed or seriously injured. Approximately one-half of the stalkers who kill subsequently commit suicide.

Occasionally stalkers murder their victim's loved ones or friends; the message they're sending the victim is, "The person I killed could have been you, so you better give in to my demands or you're next."

Other traits are:

- Dr. Jekyll/Mr. Hyde personalities--alternating between abuse and "hearts and flowers."

- Reconciliatory behavior after abuse or stalking. ("Hearts and flowers.")

- Profound need to control, assume a dominant and dictatorial role, and isolate their victim from outside influences.

- Inability to handle rejection, criticism, or responsibility. Resolve conflicts with intimidation, bullying, and violence.

- Erratic driving habits that endanger others such as excessive speeding, dangerous maneuvers, anger expressed at other drivers, cutting off other drivers.

- Recidivist domestic violence offender. Abusers have probably battered in prior relationships.

- Blatant disregard for the law; have strong feelings of entitlement and find nothing wrong with their behavior.

- Misogynistic -- basically do not like women.

- Possessive and punitive.

- Irrational. Capricious. Unpredictable.

- Jealous and insecure.

- Poor self-esteem.

- Narcissistic and emotionally immature.

- Masochistically dependent; they are convinced that their psychological sustenance can only be fulfilled by their victim. (This is not to be confused with love, which has nothing to do with it.)

- Pathological liar.

- Erratic work history and poor work habits.

- Experienced lax, unreasonably violent, or inconsistent discipline by parents as a child.

- Experienced an early onset of delinquency, misconduct and antisocial behavior as a juvenile.

- Experienced or witnessed violence in their formative years. Of the children who witness domestic violence, 60 percent of the boys eventually become batterers. Seventy-three percent of male abusers were abused as children.

Additional Stalker Traits

Both celebrity stalkers and domestic violence stalkers display elements of pathological and sociopathic behavior. They:

- Don't believe their behavior warrants consequences.

- Are extraordinarily cunning, persuasive, and manipulative.

- Lack social conscience, empathy, or concern for the welfare of others.

- Exude charm that is not easily discernable as superficial. They initially appear to be normal to the untrained eye; i.e., intelligent, rational, logical, and competent.

- Fail to display anxiety and nervousness in situations that would normally produce these feelings.

- Are unreliable and irresponsible; they make no effort to attain long-range personal goals.

- Are insincere and untruthful; they disregard the truth and lie comfortably and confidently. They will lie recklessly, but with great conviction, to extricate themselves from accusations.

- Lack remorse. They may claim some responsibility for the trouble they've created, but do so with the intent to continue their manipulations. They deny culpability and blame everyone but themselves for their actions and the consequences for their actions.

- Display poor judgement about how to obtain what they want. They consciously refuse to learn from experience and repeat antisocial and other self-defeating behavior. They are chronically maladjusted.

- Display an inability to identify with others or form meaningful and enduring relationships. They do not nurture true friendships. They display surface indications of love, sacrifice, generosity, and compassion but are incapable of experiencing these emotions deeply and truly.

- Consciously decide not to conform to social mores or obey the law. Violate the law with impunity.

. Display a chronic refusal to defer gratification, tolerate frustration, or control impulses.

. Can become very irrational and destructive, regardless of whether or not they are under the influence of alcohol or drugs. Alcohol or drugs only serve to remove inhibitions that modify behavior.

The Cycle of Stalking

The cycle of stalking is very similar to the cycle of domestic violence, in which there are three phases.

The **Tension Building Phase** consists of telephone calls, hang-up calls, unsolicited letters, cryptic "gifts," trespassing and hiding on property, threats, surveillance of the victim by the perpetrator, following the victim, minor acts of vandalism, increased attempts to control the victim, and psychological terrorism.

The **Explosive or Acutely Violent Phase** may include assault, burglary, kidnapping, rape, violence against the victim's family and friends, acute acts of vandalism, murder of pets and display of carcasses, and murder/suicide.

The **"Hearts and Flowers" Phase** is simply a new tactic and sometimes is signified by a temporary lapse in stalking during which the victim can become complacent about safety.

The cycle of phases is repeated, escalating in frequency and severity and can continue for years. The stalker may escalate to murder/suicide after the cycle has been repeated several times and it becomes apparent to the stalker that all attempts at coercion have failed.

Scale of Lethality -- Domestic Violence Stalking

1. Unsolicited letters.

2. Second-party threats.

3. Threatening phone calls.

4. Pattern of violence.

5. Indications of intensive search to locate victim such as calls made to employers, friends, family, ex-boyfriends, school, post office, veterinarian, etc.

6. Indications of presence in or near victim's home; i.e., cigarette butts, condoms, wine glasses.

7. Disregard of restraining orders.

8. Vandalism to victim's property.

9. Following victim.

10. Escalation of violence.

11. In-person threats against the victim and/or others.

12. Suicide threats.

13. Death threats (direct or indirect).

NOTE: It is imperative that anyone using this scale to determine a threat level must include the victim's opinion about the dangerousness. If a victim informs you that her situation is more dangerous than the scale indicates, believe her!

The lethality scale is also affected by several factors:

. The stalker possesses weapons.

. The stalker is psychiatrically impaired or exhibits evidence of mental disorder(s).

. Current life stresses in the stalker's life.

. Stalker's previous criminal history.

. Victim has a new personal relationship.

With some stalkers, there are times of specific and greater danger to the victim. When spouses go to court for divorce hearings, or decide to date another man, or appear to be happily working at a new job, the danger level goes up. Any of these circumstances threaten the stalker with loss of control over the victim. These are times for greater security awareness.

Police Intervention

Law enforcement officers are not always adequately educated about the applicable laws pertaining to stalking, harassment, domestic violence, and restraining order violations. Inadequate education about domestic violence and applicable laws contributes to an exhibited tendency to arrest both the victim and perpetrator rather than ascertaining the facts or attempting to interpret the law. Consequently, when the case is heard before a judge, the violent incident becomes a matter of the victim's word against the perpetrator's word. This consequence also contributes to society's skepticism of the victim's credibility.

Current laws do not adequately address the severity of the crimes, primarily because the fundamental consideration remains that the victim and perpetrator know each other.

Domestic violence-related crimes are not regarded as seriously as commensurate crimes committed by strangers against strangers. The domestic violence stalker knows how to "walk a thin line" and get away with his behavior. Stalkers choose to believe they aren't doing anything wrong and that they won't be apprehended. They don't believe their behavior warrants consequences. If arrested, stalkers rationalize that easily manipulated loopholes exist in the criminal justice system that will enable them to avoid harsh consequences.

Unfortunately, due to erroneous myths and the excessive offer of plea-bargains, the stalker often receives a slap on the wrist. Judges, attorneys, jurors, and psychiatrists are inconsistent and imperfect. Existing sentencing practices are erratic and weakened by erroneously exercised judicial discretion. Glaring irregularities and a lack of uniformity contribute to the difficulty of dealing with stalking.

Many law enforcement agencies could not take action against stalkers until now because they had not committed a crime. In 1990, California became the first state to pass antistalking legislation. That law was passed in response to several high-profile cases in which the perpetrator stalked and eventually killed the victim. In some cases, the victim had notified the police of her stalker's threatening behavior. Yet, the police said that unless the stalker acted on those threats, there was nothing they could do legally.

Since the enactment of the 1990 California law, all states and the District of Columbia have enacted laws making stalking a crime. In 1996, a Federal law was enacted to prohibit stalkers from traveling across a state line in pursuit of their victims. This legislation enabled Federal prosecution in instances where the interstate feature of a stalking case created additional challenges to effective state investigation and prosecution of such crimes.

State antistalking statutes vary widely. For instance, at least four states and one territory--Alaska, Michigan, Oklahoma, Wyoming, and Guam--specifically prohibit stalking through electronic means, such as e-mail. Nine states--Alaska, Connecticut, Florida, Iowa, Louisiana, Michigan, Minnesota, New Mexico, and Vermont--permit enhanced penalties in stalking cases involving victims who are minors. As of March 1998, legislation to enact new laws and strengthen existing ones addressing stalking of children is pending in 12 states.

Most of the laws require harassing, a credible threat, and repetition of the harassment on more than one occasion.

Antistalking laws will undoubtedly provide some deterrence to less dedicated stalkers and, very importantly, will provide the law enforcement authorities with a means to arrest a stalker, thus removing him or her at least temporarily.

But what about those deadly stalkers who cleverly do not make a "credible threat" and who are obsessed with reaching a victim? Since the antistalking laws provide little relief in this situation, victims may either hire a protection agent to be responsible for providing the needed security, or the victim, him- or herself, must manage his or her own safety.

Providing Protection to Domestic Stalking Victims

For a professional protection agent, the job of providing protection to a domestic stalking victim can be challenging on several points.

The primary distinction when providing protective services to a domestic violence stalking victim is education on and sensitivity to domestic violence and victim issues. It is imperative that the agent learn these subjects thoroughly if he or she intends to provide protection to victims of domestic violence or domestic violence-related stalking. Genuine sensitivity and compassion are essential qualities when protecting domestic violence stalking clients. It is vitally important that the agent be sensitive to the client's emotional equilibrium. The agent should *not* contribute to the revictimization of the client. Braggarts, wanna-be's, and womanizers need not apply! Information on this issue can be obtained by contacting the National Coalition Against Domestic Violence.

The domestic violence client, more often than not, has limited financial resources and may have the additional responsibility of being a single parent. The client has had no choice but to be responsible for her own safety prior to contact with protective agents. Because the client has had to be solely responsible for her safety and physical security prior to contact with protective agents, she will usually insist on remaining actively involved with the planning and execution of any protection provided her. She may be grateful for, but not completely trust, the agent's ability to protect her. The client has often learned some principles of

protection by experience, trial, and error. Some of the survival skills a client may have cultivated prior to contact with an agent include:

.   Intelligence gathering on the stalker.

.   Documentation of stalking.

.   Dealing with law enforcement and other authorities.

.   Evasive driving.

.   Protecting herself and her children to the best of her ability.

.   Developing an escape plan and executing it if necessary.

.   "Disappearing" through paperwork; i.e., changing name, appearance, habits, location, etc.

.   Instructing children on what to do if a violent incident occurs.

.   Keeping an emergency escape kit prepared, including:

    .   Weapons, if any.

    .   Money.

    .   Copies of car, house and work keys.

    .   Clothing for self and/or children.

    .   Copies of important documents.

    .   Phone numbers of police, shelters, service providers, friends, and relatives.

Another distinction of providing protection to domestic violence stalking clients is that, unlike their high profile counterparts, they will be financially unable to retain a protection agent for the remainder of their lives. Therefore, an agent should instruct the client on how to take responsibility for her own safety and physical security. The agent should not assume that, if the client has learned some principles of protection on her own, she knows everything she needs to know.

Additionally, it is vitally important that everything be thoroughly and competently documented in the protective detail log book. Doing so could make a critical difference for the client if her situation ever progresses to the courtroom.

Remember that there is an established cycle of violence and therefore a very real probability that the perpetrator will attempt to attack, injure, or kill the client.

A typical domestic violence stalking protection detail is comprised of escorts to and from:

. Work.

. Court.

. Child visitation exchanges.

. Recreational activities.

. Visits to friends and family.

. Running errands.

Occasionally a detail will require 24-hour protection in the client's home. Discretion is often a necessity; it is important not to alienate or aggravate the client's relationship with neighbors and friends. Domestic violence stalking clients do not ordinarily lead a high-visibility lifestyle and want to maintain a discreet existence.

Agent Specifics: DO'S AND DON'TS

DO

. Encourage the client to actively participate in the planning of a protective detail.

. Encourage the client to reclaim her normal lifestyle.

. Assure the client that she does not have to apologize for being a victim or for needing protection.

. Assure the client that her victimization is not a reflection on her character, on her worth as a human being, or her ability to make decisions.

. Acknowledge the high level of stress and fear in the client's life.

. Be sensitive as to how the client is feeling.

. Assure the client that you are there to protect her, not to judge her.

. Encourage the client to take active steps to empower herself and reclaim her life.

. Assure the client that she is a valued human being.

. Understand that the client may display passive behavior and that the passivity is her response to a crisis situation. Encourage her to set up a list of tasks and activities which she wants or needs to do.

. Recognize that the client has probably been socially isolated for a long time. As a result, she may be starved for company; she may be lonely; she may no longer have confidence in her social skills.

. Understand that the client may be suffering from low self-esteem.

. Understand that many clients may be suffering from Post Traumatic Stress Disorder or a variety of levels of depression. Recognize that these are normal responses to what the client has endured. Be sensitive and compassionate in recognizing that something you may consider to be insignificant or irrelevant could trigger a PTSD flashback or depressive episode.

. Try to be empathic and pay attention to underlying messages and clues.

. Be more sensitive to the *impact* of your actions and conversations with a client, rather than your *intent*. You may have great intentions but be inaccurate in your assessment of how you will affect the client.

DON'T

. Ask the client why he/she dated/married the perpetrator.

. Ask the client why he/she stayed with/lived with the perpetrator for so long.

. Ask the client why she didn't "see through" the perpetrator's con earlier.

. Offer to screen or interview future dates, boyfriends/girlfriends, or spouses.

. Infer that the client is dumb for pursuing further legal action against the perpetrator; i.e., lawsuits, child support, alimony.

. Minimize the client's feelings or the violence she has experienced.

. Assume a professional counselor or medical role.

. Assume control of a client's home or assume control of a client's decisions in the home.

Most particularly, the agent should not do everything for the client; instead, she should be encouraged to take responsibility for herself. The client's situation may go on for years! That being the case, the following advice should be imparted.

Self-Protection Survival Tips for the Client

If you find that you are on your own and must now be responsible for your own safety, there are some safety tips which have been developed by others in your predicament. At first, it will seem daunting, but, if you are on your own, your survival is the most important goal. Once you have begun to take responsibility for your own safety, you will feel stronger and more empowered. Taking control of your personal safety is akin to taking control of your health. It is a positive move in the right direction.

Remember, if you are being stalked, your stalker has time, leisure and motivation to watch you. But you can outwit and outlast him. All but the most dedicated stalkers will eventually tire of the game and seek out an easier target.

Personal

. Keep your gas tank full and have cash and credit cards on hand.

. Keep a small bag packed and ready with clothes, toiletries and medication in case you need to get away fast.

. Keep copies of all legal documents, telephone numbers, and other important data with you or close at hand.

. Get a dog. Dogs are very efficient alarm systems. But, keep an eye on the dog and do not let it run loose, even in a yard, without keeping a sharp watch. Stalkers often kill pets as a warning.

. Take a self-defense class, particularly one that addresses the issues of awareness and prevention.

. Carry an air horn with you.

. Document everything. Even if you have decided not to take the legal route of obtaining a restraining order or filing charges, you may change your mind. Keep answering machine tapes, letters, gifts, etc. Keep a log of all stalking incidents and suspicious occurrences.

. Don't accept any packages unless you personally ordered them or can verify the sender. Simply refuse them if they arrive at your residence. If they arrive at your mail box, throw them away.

. Destroy all discarded mail. If you don't have a shredder, bag the discards and drop them in a garbage container away from your home.

. Try to find and join a support group. Because of the growing menace of stalking, many stalking support groups have come into being. But, be extremely careful about trying to do this via the Internet. Stalkers love those web sites. Find out what your state and local community have to offer for victim assistance.

At Work

. Inform your employer, co-workers, and building security personnel of the situation. Give them a recent photograph or a good description of the stalker. Provide the license number(s) and description(s) of the vehicle(s) driven by the stalker. Provide copies of restraining orders.

. Ask co-workers to screen your incoming telephone calls at work. Instruct them to take messages and inform callers that you will return the calls. Instruct co-workers not to reveal your whereabouts or personal information.

. Ask co-workers to restrict visitor access to your work station or office.

. If you leave the building to smoke or during lunch, take someone with you. Vary the times that you take a break or leave for lunch.

. Vary the times you enter and exit the building. Vary the routes you take to your office once inside the building. Alternate between riding the elevator and taking the stairs.

. Avoid working alone after hours or early in the morning. Inform friends if you have to work during non-peak hours and maintain telephone contact with them. If possible, arrange for an escort to your car.

. Avoid listing your residential address and telephone number in the company directory.

. Establish a safe room at work. Determine escape routes.

. If you are self-employed and you have business visitors, rent an outside office. Your business stationary should reflect this outside address and telephone number.

Mail

. Rent a post office box through an independent carrier. Make sure that you have 24-hour access to the box. Do not rent a post office box from the U.S. Postal Service. Do not obtain a post office box located near your residence or employment. Never establish a routine or pattern of when you pick up your mail. Always take non-direct routes home after picking up your mail.

. For those places that will not accept a post office box, change "PO Box" to "Apt." and enter the number. Put this address on your bank checks.

. Do *not* file a change of address form with the post office for your new address. Your new address can be easily obtained.

. If you enter in sweepstakes or fill out information forms on coupons and rebates, provide your post office box address, not your home address. It is wise simply not to use these forms. The information is sold and traded in numerous ways.

. Never answer any mail addressed to "Occupant." A pursuer can send the same mailing to every mail box in the post office or private mail drop. Responding could provide him with a "hit."

. Have your name, home address, and home telephone number removed from your checks, stationary, and business cards.

Vehicle and Driving Tips

. Always have spare keys to your vehicle readily accessible in the event that you need to leave quickly.

. Check up and down the street before leaving a building or vehicle.

. Check for signs of entry or sabotage as you approach your vehicle. Straighten out a clothes hanger and use it to make sweeping motions to check for nails under the tires. Look for fluid leakage, such as power steering fluid, brake fluid, or antifreeze. Check your hood, trunk, and doors for visible signs of tampering.

. Equip your gas tank with a locking device that can only be activated from within the vehicle.

. Keep car doors locked and windows rolled up at all times, in or out of the car.

. Avoid traveling along the same routes every day--alternate your times and routes of travel. Shop at different grocery stores. Be aware of your location and surroundings. Heighten your peripheral awareness of surroundings when you are within three blocks of your destination.

. Drive in the center lane--this provides more options for evasive maneuvers and thwarts attempts to run you off the road.

. Constantly check the rear view mirror and look for cars that appear often or follow you for a long period of time. Always observe who is beside you in traffic and at traffic stops. Be alert to the actions of pedestrians.

. If you think you are being followed:

    . Drive around the block or drive into and out of a parking lot. Make quick, unsignaled turns into side streets. This will help to determine if you are being followed.

    . Attempt to place a slow moving vehicle between yourself and your follower.

    . Drive to the nearest police station, fire station, bank, or hospital--armed personnel are almost always present. If you were followed, repeatedly honk your horn and flash your lights to draw attention to yourself and your follower.

    . Do not try to drive faster than your follower. Try not to be stopped in traffic by the perpetrator or by traffic lights. Occupants in a moving vehicle are more difficult to attack than the occupants of a stationary vehicle. Drive at a normal speed and watch for a police car.

. If you are stopped at a red light and the perpetrator attempts to approach your car, make a right turn (if it can be safely done) while the perpetrator is away from his car. It may be better to pay a traffic ticket than to confront a perpetrator.

. If you can travel with companions, do so.

Maintain frequent contact with family, friends, and others (such as baby sitters, etc.)

. Block your address at DMV (Department of Motor Vehicles) and Voter Registration. In almost every state, this information is easily obtainable by anyone. You should also list your DMV address as your mail box address, not your home address. Ask for a new driver's license to reflect this. You can file for private voter registration.

. Keep your gas tank more than half-full, and get a locking gas cap that can only be operated from within the vehicle.

. If your name appears on a parking space either at work or at home, have it removed.

At Home

. Make sure that your doors, windows, door screens, and window screens have good locks, and keep them locked.

. Install protective grills on windows, preferably on the inside.

. Always lock your door after you enter your residence. Always lock your door after you exit your residence, even if you leave momentarily. Close and lock your windows when you leave in the summer.

. Window shades or drapes should be drawn after dark. Indicate the presence of other people by leaving lights on in two or more rooms.

. Do not stand or sit in front of windows when blinds are open. If you work at a table or desk, make certain it is against a wall, and away from windows.

. Rearrange furniture often. Do not reveal the design or layout of your home.

. Keep the entrance to your residence and yard free from overgrown shrubbery and trees. Provide clear visibility at night by utilizing outside security lighting.

. Always utilize the peep hole viewer in your doors at all times. If your doors do not have peep hole viewers, install them.

. Do not leave ladders in the yard.

. Lock your exterior fuse and switch boxes.

. Keep an inventory and serial numbers of your valuables. Have your social security number engraved on your valuables.

. Never allow a stranger to enter your home. If someone requests help, offer to call for help while he/she waits outside.

. When answering the telephone, do not identify yourself until you are sure who is calling. Do not reveal unnecessary information, even if it seems trivial. Never say that a family member is not home, only that he/she cannot come to the telephone.

. Never tell anyone you are alone in your residence, whether that person calls or is at your door.

. Try to obtain two telephones: one standard telephone and one portable telephone or, better, a cell phone. Do not use your portable or cell telephone for calls that you do not want to be rather easily monitored by someone. Keep your cell phone with you at all times.

. Get an answering machine and have someone else (a male voice is usually preferable) leave a message that does not identify you. Get Caller I.D. so that you can determine who is placing those hang-up calls. If the caller has placed a "block" on his/her line to prevent identification, contact the telephone company and ask that they work with you to identify and stop the harassing telephone calls. (The company can un-block the Caller I.D.) Another valuable tip is this: if you receive a hang-up call, hang up, then dial *69, and the caller's number will be given you.

. Get a new (second) unlisted and unpublished telephone number. Be very discriminating as to whom you give the new number. Always let the answering machine pick up on the old unlisted number. Gradually, only your stalker will be using your old number. If it is upsetting to hear the calls, put the answering machine in a closet where you can't hear it.

. If you have business contacts who must be in touch with you, consider getting an answering service--a good one--which will call you instantly or, better yet, patch through any business calls to you.

. Be extremely careful about giving out your name, address, telephone number, social security number, or other personal information. If possible, try to live without credit cards. (There is no privacy in the credit card world.) The same applies to magazine subscriptions. Subscription lists are frequently sold.

. Do not display your name on the exterior of your residence or apartment (welcome mat; mail box).

. Demand identification from individuals at your door. Confirm credentials with the agency they claim to represent before opening your door to them. Don't be fooled by uniforms; these can be stolen or purchased. Independently verify identities-- that is, do not simply call a number given you by the person at your door (it may be answered by an accomplice)--look it up in the telephone directory or call Information.

. Be cautious about entering an elevator or laundry room with an unknown person present. Better to wait for another time.

. After moving into a new residence, change the door locks. Previous tenants or former employees may still have keys.

. Some condominium and apartment buildings require that all tenants furnish management with duplicate keys (for use in an emergency such as a fire). Be very cautious about this. Request that management share with you their security arrangements for key lock-up. You may decide it prudent to tell them that you have been harassed by a stalker, so that they are doubly careful. Management should NEVER give out the extra key to ANYONE other than you.

. Use good quality, pin-tumbler locks (deadfall or deadbolt variety with pick-resistent cylinders) and bolts of at least 1-1/4" to 1-1/2" in length on your doors. Install a lock of equal strength on the bedroom door and LOCK it every night. Install industrial strength, heavy duty sliding chain bolts on the front and back doors. If either the front or back doors have a window, install a stout grill over the window.

. Use an internal door jam device on all entrances to your residence. This will make it more difficult for the doors to be kicked in.

. If a door or window has been forced or broken while you were absent, do not enter or call out. Someone may still be inside. Use your cell phone or a neighbor's phone immediately to call the police and wait outside or in a safe place until they arrive.

. Learn ways of marking the entries to your residence so that you can ascertain if entry has been gained during your absence. One example is to place some scotch tape bridging across your door and the door frame. Place the scotch tape anywhere but at eye level.

. When you go on a trip, do not advertise your absence. Stop all deliveries. Your lights, television, and radio should be set on timing devices which alternate turning on and off. (If the lights go off and on every day at the same time, it's a clear signal that no one is home.)

. Participate in a neighborhood crime watch program.

. If you relocate to a new residence, move late at night or very early in the morning. Use a variety of evasive travel routes while transporting belongings.

. Establish a simple code word or effective signal (such as rapid opening and closing of drapes) you can use to indicate danger covertly and notify your neighbors, children, family members, friends, and business associates.

. If you trust your neighbor(s), inform them of your situation. Give them a recent photograph or a good description of the perpetrator. Provide the license number(s) and description(s) of the vehicle(s) the perpetrator drives. Provide copies of restraining orders. Ask them to call the authorities if you signal for help or if they observe unusual activity.

. Be aware of seemingly innocent activity in your neighborhood. For example, phony repair crews and solicitors may be conducting surveillance for your perpetrator. Be alert to unusual activity and lack of activity.

. Stroll around the immediate neighborhood. Try to familiarize yourself with neighbors' vehicles. If you spot an unknown parked vehicle, investigate--cautiously.

. Alarm systems can be a great comfort, but they can also be difficult to live with. And they can give a feeling of false security. If you do decide to install an alarm system:

. Only deal with a reputable dealer-- one you think you can trust.

. USE IT! That means turning it on and off religiously.

. Continue to practice all of your safety tips. An alarm system will not protect you--it can only alert you.

Establishing a Safe Room at Home

. Designate a safe room in your home. This is a place that you can get to quickly and can remain within for several hours. If at all possible, it should have an alternate entrance/exit.

. The room should have a solid door, preferably metal-sheathed. The door frame should be anchored securely to the adjoining walls. In addition to top quality locks, it should have an industrial strength sliding bar to reinforce the door.

. A portable or cell phone is a must to call 911. (Program the phone to speed-dial 911.) The perpetrator may cut phone lines. Keep a list of emergency telephone numbers.

. The room should have good ventilation.

. The room should be stocked with a flashlight, first aid kit, fire extinguisher, food and water, and a weapon if desired and allowed.

Protecting Information

. Be discriminating as to whom you release information. Do not reveal details regarding:

. The location of your residence or

employment.

. The location of friends or family.

. Your social security number or date of birth.

. Your vehicle description, license plate number, or driver's license number.

. Your routes, destinations, or times of travel (unless you wish to give this information to a trusted friend).

. Social activities, favorite hang-outs, club memberships (including health clubs), or hobbies.

. Plans for vacations, or visiting friends and family.

. Patterns of shopping (these should be varied and alternating--don't be predictable).

. Information regarding your children, schools attended, routes taken to school, babysitters, day-care providers, playmates, etc. Instructions should be given to all that NO ONE except yourself is authorized to pick up your child, even when given a written and signed note.

. Your security precautions and plans.

. Do not participate in census surveys or opinion polls. Never, NEVER respond to a "prize" or "free gift" offer. These offers sometimes seem irresistible, but they may be simply a trick.

. Instruct family members, children, neighbors, friends, and business associates not to provide people with information concerning

you. This cannot be over-emphasized. Wily pursuers and experienced investigators have a repertoire of stories almost guaranteed to pry loose information. These stories may include, among others:

. (bogus) unclaimed property.
. a dying friend.
. money--a paycheck, lottery, etc.
. blood test results--HIV!

Safety on the Internet--Avoiding Cyberstalking

. Guard your address and telephone number and other personal information when you are online and avoid giving your true name. Do not sign up with various "clubs," or respond to banner ads and survey offers, or provide information for Internet "guest books."

. Avoid chat rooms. These are nurturing areas for lonely, angry, disaffected, non-social individuals who have their own agenda. Do not enter them even if you do not actively participate. If you have a stalker on your trail and he/she knows of your interest in growing exotic orchids, do not join the exotic orchids chat room. Your stalker will be lurking in the background, just waiting to pounce on your e-mail address.

. If you receive an e-mail message and do not know who is contacting you, ASK. If you do not get a satisfactory, straight-forward answer, don't hesitate to tell them not to contact you again.

. Do not engage with the on-line dating services.

The author is not aware of any letter or package bombs sent by stalkers to their targets, provided one does not regard the Unabomber as a stalker. Stalkers tend to focus their harassment on up-close-and-personal tactics. However, just to be on the safe side, the information given in the chapter on Bombs should be related to the client.

Documentation

There is some dispute as to the wisdom of obtaining restraining orders. To put it plainly, obtaining a restraining order is sometimes the trigger that sends a stalker into a killing rage. On the other hand, without a restraining order, the police are unable to provide help.

If a restraining order is obtained, it should be properly and legally served on the stalker. The victim should carry a notarized copy of the restraining order and proof of service on her/his person at all times, and a copy should also be kept at work, as well as with an attorney, a friend or relative, and the children's school administrators.

ALL incidents, no matter how trivial, should be documented with the date, time, and location of incidents, names of witnesses, and specific details (statements, threats, vehicle description and license plates, etc.)

Hang-up telephone calls as well as all messages left on the telephone answering machine or on the computer should be carefully documented.

Any communication and encounters with the police should be recorded, just as if a report were being written. This should include:

.   The date, time, location, and details as to incidents and reasons for calling the police.

.   Date and time the police were called.

.   The name of the dispatcher or/and officer spoken with.

.   The date and time when an officer arrives in response to the call.

    The badge number and name of the responding officer.

.   Details of what is said between the police officer and the victim.

.   The case number assigned to the police report filed.

.   Details regarding any subsequent contact with officers, detectives, victim advocates, etc.

This information will prove to be invaluable if the case progresses to an arrest and arraignment. The stalker's attorney will undoubtedly attempt to deny that any harassment has taken place. A well-documented case will aid the prosecuting attorney.

Much of the material on domestic stalkings was provided by Victim Protection Services, formerly of Denver, Colorado. Victim Protection Services was one of several private agencies which were established in the past few years specifically to help stalking victims in protecting themselves from their pursuers. Services provided included self-defense classes, educational seminars on domestic violence and stalking, escorts to and from court appearances and for various outings, and 24-hour protection when warranted. VPS and other private agencies generally provided services either free or charged according to the victim's ability to pay. It is a marvelous idea, but these agencies have experienced severe difficulties in obtaining funding.

In providing protection, the agent's primary job is planning ahead so that security problems do not occur. If the agent has done his/her job properly, the client is happy and comfortable, and is not badgered, embarrassed, or attacked by an adversary, including overly enthusiastic fans or obsessed cranks. This is much more desirable than being constantly embroiled in aggressive and dangerous confrontations, which tend to be "Lose-Lose" situations.

To provide this protection, the agent must:

. Have some understanding of how people behave, particularly when they behave aberrantly or badly.

. Recognize the signs of dangerousness and have some skill in predicting dangerousness.

. Know when and how to intervene when it appears that an individual poses a threat or seems determined to approach the client.

. Possess some skill in determining when an individual is lying or practicing some form of deceit.

. Provide ongoing management of some individuals who pose a threat or high nuisance to a client.

Successful agents, like successful cops and investigators, are lifetime observers of human behavior, constantly honing their observational and intervention skills.

It is well to keep in mind that protecting the client may be the first priority, but a second priority is in dealing humanely and fairly with those individuals who may be disturbed and in deep inner pain. Understanding them can provide some clues to helping them.

Threat management is a process of steps which manage (or attempt to manage) a threat and which may or may not include direct intervention(s). For our purposes, let us define interventions as some form of interacting with and/or direct contact with the pursuer. Next, we should state that there are several ways to manage a threat. There is no one best way, no guarantees of success, and a fair amount of controversy regarding the use of interventions.

While it requires a certain amount of generalizing, it can be said that the controversy breaks down into two schools of thought. One group, primarily those from the law enforcement field such as the Los Angeles Police Department Threat Management Unit (TMU), tend to recommend and employ the "hard line" proactive policing approach which relies on interventions. The private security experts view interventions more as a last resort in the face of imminent danger to a client.

That there is a strongly felt difference in tactics is not surprising. Police have, traditionally, taken the offensive, going after bad guys, arresting them, and bringing them in for prosecution and punishment. This is even more apparent in these days of "zero tolerance" in criminal matters. It is the classic police response.

Private security practitioners, having never had police powers, have been more open to other approaches and more dependent on creative techniques in managing a threat. The classic approach, even among the U.S. Secret Service, has been to avoid problems, deflect the threat, retreat, remove the client, and harden the target. Private protective agents do not attempt to chase bad guys and do not necessarily seek justice--only safety.

Clearly, these are two different philosophies and mind-sets. And, they often call for different case management tactics.

The mental health community, while split in their thinking, have come down more forcefully on the side of the private security philosophy. The feeling is that the traditional police approach, with its use of restraining orders and court-ordered injunctions, relies on the fact that the majority of people are rational beings who, when presented with a restraining order, will obey it and will understand the consequences of further harassment. What that thinking fails to take into account is that stalkers and violent, explosive workers are not behaving rationally and often have zero concern for consequences to themselves. Their obsessions and delusions have rendered them impervious to threats, arraignments, and jail. As we have seen in our case studies, many are prepared to die to satisfy their relentless pursuit of fulfillment.

There is a huge amount of data which shows that restraining orders and injunctions simply provide "triggers" for an obsessed pursuer, sending him/her into a killing rage.

In fairness, it should be pointed out that the L.A.TMU has had great success with their antistalking program. The problem is that their database is much smaller than that of the private sector, so it is difficult to provide comparisons of success and failure rates.

One of the greatest success areas of police Threat Management Units is that it indicates a change in the attitude of the police to the crimes of domestic abuse and stalking. Before the formation of these special units, the typical police reaction to stalking cases was at best "ho, hum" and at worst contemptuous, derisive, and sometimes abusive in itself. Just as domestic abuse was considered a private (not criminal) matter, stalking was such an aberration there was no understanding of the dimensions and violent nature of the problem. They simply could not understand how letter writing and gift-giving might seem distressing or harmful.

Several highly publicized events altered these attitudes (at least on the part of some police units). One event was the killing of television star Rebecca Schaeffer by her stalker, Robert Bardo. Another incident was the multiple stabbing of Theresa Saldana by her stalker. And a third series of events involved singer/actress Madonna, in which her pursuer, Robert Hoskins, threatened to "cut her throat from ear to ear"; he was later shot by a bodyguard when he attempted to enter Madonna's home. These and other events highlighted the problem of the stalker.

Because these events (and others) occurred in the Los Angeles area, the impetus for the formation of a special police unit to deal with stalking was there. It was aided by the efforts of Gavin deBecker, arguably the best-known private security individual with a specialty in celebrity stalking. DeBecker's firm has handled thousands of cases and he has developed both a formidable database and threat management strategies with proven success records.

DeBecker was active in the creation of the L.A.TMU, headed by Detective Robert Martin. It was believed at first that the work would be largely taken up with celebrity stalkers, but it soon became apparent that the problem was much, much bigger and that domestic stalkers composed the bulk of pursuers.

The TMU was soon turned over to Lt. John Lane. It soon became very proactive. A more or less standard procedure was developed for dealing with a stalker. It begins with obtaining a restraining order that denies the stalker the right to approach the victim. It may also include visits to the stalker's home and/or office for an up-front talk, plus background checks and surveillance. The TMU liking for restraining orders is not based on the belief that they will always prevent further stalking incidents but, rather, that they allow the police to arrest the stalker if he violates the order. Arrest can lead to incarceration though, unfortunately--not always, and not for very long.

Thus began the controversy dividing proponents of two styles of management techniques.

DeBecker was, and one assumes still is, opposed to the TMU hard tactics.

The mental health community is also divided. Agreeing with deBecker is Dr. Park Dietz, an old hand at researching stalking incidents. Dietz believes that active interventions as used by the LAPD TMU can be extremely harmful, particularly in domestic stalking cases, where they can provide the trigger for a killing rage.

One of the advantages of special police Threat Management Units (there are now a number of them within the United States) is their ability to tap into the law enforcement databanks on an interagency basis. In Los Angeles, for example, the TMU is able to interface with other agencies to determine if the suspect has a history of mental health problems or a criminal record, if there were prior police incidents and interventions, and the results.

TMU's and private security agents have a valuable avenue in that they can contact the suspect's family members to determine if the suspect has undergone in the past or is currently undergoing psychiatric treatment. While mental health people are prohibited from divulging information about clients, even to the police, simply relating current information to them can be very helpful. Patients undergoing therapy and counseling are not always honest with their mental health practitioners. They may claim that they are no longer engaging in stalking when, in fact, they have intensified their activities.

An improvement in police handling when a victim has access to a TMU is the fact that a case file is opened and the same detective handles each incident relating to the victim. In the past, a victim might find him- herself telling his/her story a number of times, each time to a different detective. Having to deal with only one detective, one who is familiar with the circumstances and who is sympathetic, is an enormous relief.

Restraining Orders

This may be an appropriate point to briefly discuss restraining orders.

Generally, these orders require offenders to stay away from and not interfere with the complainant. If violated, they may be punishable by incarceration, a fine or both. These orders are typically obtained through a magistrate's office or local court. Information can be obtained from the local clerk of court's office about where to obtain orders.

Restraining orders are not foolproof. They often do not extend beyond certain lines of jurisdiction and can only be enforced if they are broken. In addition, some states only provide protective (restraining) orders to former spouses or intimates. Finally, restraining orders are not a slam-dunk; they are issued at the court's discretion.

Many stalking victims are routinely told to get restraining orders. When they do, they often assume that the stalking will finally end, either because the stalker will stop on his own or because the police will stop him. Neither of these outcomes happens with any frequency. About 25% of stalking victims obtain restraining orders; in two-thirds of these cases, the restraining order is violated. About half of all stalking cases are reported to the police; a quarter of these result in an arrest.

As we have indicated in this chapter, there are two points of view on the value and risk of obtaining restraining orders. The police viewpoint is to obtain these orders as a necessary first step to stopping the stalker.

The opposite point of view is that, in many instances, restraining orders only make a bad situation worse. The stalker may feel humiliated that "outsiders" have been brought into a private situation. Worse, he may feel doubly rejected by his target; she has announced to the world that she wants nothing to do with him, that he is unworthy. It can be a killing blow to an already fragile self-esteem. There have been many, many cases of stalking victims found murdered after they had obtained restraining orders, some with copies of the order in their possession or even on the body (pinned to the chest in one case).

Restraining orders probably have the least success with domestic stalkers. Spouses and ex-lovers already have an intense investment in the relationship and have probably already succeeded in controlling the victim in the past. The domestic stalker often visualizes himself as being involved in a "war" which is being waged for control. A restraining order raises the stakes and calls for a counterattack.

By the same token, delusional stalkers cannot be reasoned with. These stalkers are convinced beyond all arguments that their quest is right and proper, may even believe (as in erotomania) that the restraining order has been issued by enemies bent on preventing him from being united with his true and yearning lover. A piece of paper has no significance to the delusional stalker.

The conundrum becomes: Should a restraining order be obtained, and, if so, when and under what circumstances? On the private security side of the argument, the answer is that a restraining order should not routinely be obtained. Each case may be different. Good advice is for the victim to research how these orders are enforced in her jurisdiction in similar cases. If, in the victim's jurisdiction, violation of a restraining order is a misdemeanor, it is much less likely to be enforced. Joining a support group and talking to other victims may provide a clue. The police will almost always declare that they will arrest the offender for violation of the order, but does this mean jail or merely a warning and citation. When a restraining order violation occurs and the police just go out and talk to the stalker or give him a citation, they may have just made the situation worse. What the police have done in this instance is to give the stalker further proof that nothing will happen to him, that he can act more or less with impunity and he will not be punished. The victim is seen as even more powerless.

Threat Management from the Private Security Viewpoint

One noted private security threat management expert stated that, out of several thousands of stalking cases handled by his organization, direct interventions had been applied in only about 10-15% of the cases. The U.S. Secret Service and the U.S. Marshals Office have received, between them, tens of thousands of threats, reports of threats, inappropriate letters, and attempted encounters, but have applied direct interventions in only a fraction of the cases. There are simply too many cases for this action; thus, alternative threat management approaches have been developed.

By contrast, the L.A.P.D. reported early in their history that, out of 74 cases, they had applied direct interventions in roughly 49% of the cases.

Determining whether to intervene, and when, in a threat management situation remains one of the most puzzling questions. There are no hard-and-fast rules. Threat management is a relatively new phenomenon in the private sector.

Remembering the figures presented in the National Violence Against Women Survey--10 million individuals have been stalked at some point in their lives--one fact is evident. The sheer enormity of the problem does not allow the luxury of actively managing and providing interventions in each and every case. Thus, the prediction of violence and the pre-incident indicators of those individuals most likely to approach and possibly harm an individual are the areas of concentration.

As was noted in the chapter on celebrity stalking, in communications with celebrities there is a low level of specific threats of violence. The implied threats are primarily of nuisance and embarrassment value. The worrisome threats, *which are in the low minority*, are those which seem specific and logical, which imply a plan and an ability to carry out the plan. These are the letters which should be immediately referred for investigative and preventive action. All unsuitable or abnormal letters are evaluated as part of an ongoing threat assessment, but letters written with specific information about the celebrity and implying a threat should be "red flagged" for investigation.

Each case is unique, but may contain similarities to other prior cases. Thus, some general data may be available upon which to base a decision as to whether to institute an intervention. At this juncture, it behooves us to repeat some facts. No matter what the circumstances, the victim **must** be made aware that she/he is ultimately responsible for her/his own safety. The victim **must** be a part of the team and must be made aware of the possible results, good and bad, of decisions made regarding interventions and non-interventions.

As we have previously discussed, there are several different types of stalkers. The domestic stalkers who are desperate to retain or regain control and who may be experiencing extreme feelings of rejection are probably the most likely to react badly to interventions. They may already be in an enraged stage and an intervention is likely to send them "over the wall." These are the stalkers who believe they are involved in a "war." There are attacks and counter-attacks, wins and losses, and, as with all wars, escalation and casualties. As also happens with wars, often the attacker forgets precisely why he/she went to war.

The delusional stalkers who pursue celebrities and others may also be inappropriate candidates for active interventions. They are like bombs, feeling okay about themselves as long as they are left alone, but if moved may explode. Celebrity stalkers can often be managed without overt intervention and, of course, celebrities have the resources to afford protection. Non-celebrity delusional stalkers are more difficult. They can make life hell for their victims but, like domestic stalkers, may escalate to a dangerous level if they feel they have been rejected and humiliated.

Those stalkers who pursue dignitaries, professionals, and executives may present better opportunities for interventions. These pursuers may be seeking redress of some sort or simply recognition. They are also more likely to be rational. Thus, the opportunity to pour out their hearts to someone may help to persuade them to desist in their stalking campaign. They have been provided with recognition, been treated with respect, and this may provide satisfaction. They have, after all, been validated. Having said this, much depends upon the issues which have propelled the stalker. If the issue is relatively non-inflammatory, it may be easily satisfied. On the other hand, if the issue is emotion-charged (abortion, animal rights, environmental), the individual will not be so easily deterred.

The situation of the violent employee is different, unless the employee is also a stalker. As discussed in the chapter on Violent Employees in the Workplace, emphasis is placed on good hiring, training, and supervisory practices. When these techniques fail, or the employee is a long-time employee gone bad, intervention is swift and straightforward.

The facts are that, of the extraordinary number of stalkers, most are non-violent--incredibly worrisome, efficient at making life hell for the victim, but not violent. Note: once again, the domestic stalker is a different story, being more likely to escalate to violence.

Do all interventions end in bloodshed? No, of course not. The LAPD TMU is a good case in point. They have had success pursuing active interventions in a high number of their cases. But for the private sector, and for individuals who decide to or are forced to take active management of their own threat, the question remains--whether and when to intervene. Perhaps a rule of thumb should be, to initiate interventions when less overt threat management tactics have failed and/or when it becomes apparent that the pursuer is showing signs of escalating to a dangerous level, to an extent that all other action is inadequate.

As difficult as it sounds, non-direct interventions may be the best course. The harassing letters and telephone calls may provide a way for the pursuer to "vent." So long as he/she can wage a campaign, it may provide some relief and satisfaction which keeps him/her relatively satisfied. In this regard, the victim must be aware that this is not perfect justice, and that a great deal of patience and fortitude will be called for. One way of addressing the problem is to have someone else (trained employee, answering service, private mail box service) accept the messages and mail, thus eliminating the incredible strain of being harassed at home. The objective is to wear down and bore the pursuer to the point that he will turn his attention to an easier target or a healthier goal.

Another argument against intervention is that the messages, both telephone and mail, provide potentially valuable information. Has the tone of the missive changed--for better or worse? Have the return addresses and/or postmarks changed? Is the stalker showing signs of approaching? Remember, in the final analysis, the victim can only be harmed if the stalker successfully approaches.

Interventions can send the pursuer "underground." This may be the most dangerous situation of all. With the disappearance of the pursuer goes all hope of keeping a close watch on him/her. Now it becomes impossible to monitor his/her whereabouts.

One intervention which seems attractive is the involuntary confinement of a person to a mental health facility. On the face of it, this seems to be a good solution and it may well be. There are, however, some potential risks. The suspect may not be helped by the treatment--may, in fact, be made worse. Much depends upon the quality of the treatment and the realistic assessment of the mental health practitioner. Is real progress made, or is the suspect merely dosed with soothing drugs for a period, then declared stabilized and sent home with the admonition to continue taking the drugs. What happens when the suspect decides to stop taking the drugs and the realization sets in that the victim *caused him/her to be incarcerated.* Those who are institutionalized are much like those sent to jail--they NEVER want to go back, and to prevent that, they may go into hiding, thus escalating their feelings of detachment and loneliness and reinforcing their delusionary feelings, not to mention their feelings of rage for having been sent there in the first place.

If non-intervention seems to be (for the moment) the safer course, what can and should be done?

To begin, the victim must be accurately and realistically apprised of the situation and the fact that a great deal of discomfort is going to be present, possibly for a long time. Is this just, fair? No. But, the victim must be persuaded that it is the safer course.

An overall assessment should be made of the victim's attitude, resourcefulness, and sense of reality. The victim must, as previously noted, be made aware of his/her responsibility for his/her ultimate safety. If the victim refuses to accept this responsibility, the situation becomes much, much more difficult. This becomes similar to the case of the abused spouse who complains but then waffles and refuses to bring charges or to leave the abusive situation. There is little which can be done for this person. The police have long been plagued with this problem, which probably contributed to the "ho, hum" attitude accorded stalking victims in the beginning.

The victim must be interviewed with the purpose of getting all of the facts: the circumstances surrounding the harassment; the length/duration of the incidents; any signals/signs that the harassment may be escalating and why; and the victim's actions and responses. Of particular importance is obtaining information about any previous attacks or indications that attacks may be imminent. Threats should be thoroughly analyzed to determine violence predictors.

.   What is the history and relationship, if any, of the victim to the suspect? If a relationship existed, did the suspect's behavior change during this period? Did a pattern emerge, indicating a propensity to rage and violence and/or to unrealistic delusions?

.   If an attack has already occurred, exactly what happened and to whom?

.   If it is a current threat, how specific is the threat, how detailed?

. Does the suspect have the means/ability to carry out an attack?

. Does the tone of the messages/threats appear to be escalating?

. What seem to be the motivations behind the attack(s) and/or threat(s)? What does the suspect hope to accomplish? What are his/her goals? Can these goals at least partially be satisfied in a non-violent way?

. Has something happened in the victim's life which might have triggered a threat (new boyfriend, etc.)?

. Does the victim know of any stress factors in the suspect's life, stress factors which might be addressed and alleviated?

. Does the victim know of any inhibitors which might be applied? (Family, friends, etc.)

. Does the victim know if the suspect has, or has had, any mental health problems. Was he treated for such problems?

The victim must disengage, must break all contact, and, if possible, must make it difficult or impossible for the harasser to find her. This is easier said than done. In extreme cases, the victim will have to leave, change locations, certainly change telephone numbers, and employ all of the safety tips given in the chapter on domestic stalkers.

The victim must be convinced to keep meticulous documentation of all messages, telephone calls, letters, gifts, surveillance, chases, and all other incidents. This is absolutely necessary in terms of eventually arresting and incarcerating the harasser.

The police should be notified and a case file opened even if a restraining order is not sought. The police are noticeably less sympathetic and supportive when the victim belatedly informs them that she has been stalked for a year or more and is now seeking help. They have much more respect for those victims who come to them early in the process and ask their help. If a restraining order is sought, the victim must determine--what next? Will she/he be provided any protection? Is there a safe location to which she can go for a time when the restraining order is served, thus removing her temporarily from the reach of a now enraged stalker? If the stalker ignores the order, what decisive action will the police take?

Can the victim's surroundings be made more safe? An assessment of the security in place should be made, both at home and work, to determine what should be done to "harden the target."

The victim's employer should be made aware of the threat to the victim and, possibly, to other employees. In many cases, the employer may provide some form of counseling and support for the victim.

Background information should be obtained on the suspect. This could include, where available:

. Any criminal records.

. History of treatment for mental illness.

. Military service.

. Drug and/or alcohol abuse.

. Current financial status--divorce, job loss, failure to pay alimony and/or child support, civil judgements, loss of residence, loan default(s), automobile repossessions.

. Suspect's access to, or possession of weapons.

. Suspect's access to, or possession of a vehicle.

This information should be examined to determine intent, the seriousness of the threat, and the apparent resources of the suspect to carry out a threat (means, ability).

In some circumstances, discreet surveiling of the suspect may be helpful. This, of course, depends upon whether the subject is in the area and whether the victim can afford to pay for it.

After careful consideration, a "soft" intervention, interviewing the suspect, might be accomplished. Considerations might include:

.   A determination regarding the rationality of the suspect. Is this someone who might be reasoned with, persuaded to desist or gently guided toward other goals.

.   The goals of the suspect. If the suspect seeks redress for a real or imagined wrong, an interview and possibly other action might satisfy him/her. Those suspects merely seeking identity and ego-stroking might be at least defused.

.   Possible accessible inhibitors: family, job, community standing.

It is vital to keep in mind that an interview could simply escalate the suspect's delusions or feelings of rage. Much would depend upon the tenor of the interview. It should NOT be threatening, should not demean the suspect, and should be held within a calm, rational, empathetic atmosphere.

Ongoing monitoring might be called for. Messages and communications would continue to be examined. If the suspect is incarcerated or institutionalized, requests would be made to be notified if and when the suspect is released, preferably prior to release.

If the victim lives in a state which provides victim assistance in stalking and harassment cases, the victim should be advised to seek help. This might include financial assistance for non-reimbursed medical and income losses and job retraining expenses. Generally not covered are personal property losses. (Caution: this helpful assistance is not provided by every state.)

Eligible recipients might include:

.   Persons who suffered physical injury, or the threat of injury, and/or emotional injury.

.   Anyone legally dependent upon the victim for support.

.   A member of a victim's family or someone who has a close relationship to the victim and is medically required for the successful treatment of the victim.

.   A member of the victim's immediate family who incurs emotional injury as a result of the crime (usually limited to medical and/or mental health counseling expenses).

When assistance of this sort is available, there are usually conditions. For example, most require that the victim must report the crime and must cooperate in the investigation and prosecution of any known suspects.

Imminent Danger

It is important to remember that danger is not necessarily accompanied by a threat. A fairly large number of attacks have occurred without the benefit of a threat. Violence predictors should be based on approach indicators. The victim may be made miserable by a campaign of harassment, but can only be harmed through contact with the pursuer. *Are there indicators that predict the suspect intends to physically contact the victim? Does the suspect have the means and ability to carry out an attack?*

Does non-direct intervention work when the victim is determined to be in imminent danger? Probably not. At this point, aggressive intervention may be the best course: restraining order, injunction, arrest, vigorous prosecution, and incarceration for the maximum period.

The victim may be advised to move, even disappear, for a period of time.

Security should immediately be increased at the victim's home and workplace.

Bodyguards, when affordable, might be employed, at least for the times of trigger points--the serving of restraining orders; court appearances; etc.

In the case of a celebrity or dignitary stalking, consideration should be given to canceling any publicized engagements. If not cancelled, increased security and access control should be provided.

It is imperative to know the stalking laws within the victim's state. It may be possible to have the suspect arrested or remanded for involuntary treatment without having first issued a restraining order and provided that documentation of harassment and/or threats is complete.

Prediction of Dangerousness

The prediction of violence is an area of expertise that has been debated by psychiatrists and clinical psychologists throughout the past few decades. Only recently has there been a special impetus given to reaching some determinations on potential violence, as there are now legal aspects specifically directed toward the duty of psychotherapists to warn and protect potential victims.

The ability to correctly predict violence is imprecise, but progress has been made.

Along with other intervention measures, the one which would be most useful to protective agents is the ability to predict dangerousness and imminent violence. Because, while there are an enormous number of violent incidents, there are many more threats of violence which are never consummated. We cannot simply lock up everyone who looks dangerous or who makes a threat. There are not enough hospitals and prisons to contain them. Therefore, we must concentrate our protective efforts upon those who are definitely dangerous, mean what they say (threaten and have ability to carry out the threat), and need restraint. It follows, therefore, that an ability to predict dangerousness is needed.

From the psychiatric standpoint, the process of predicting violence is a methodical, often timid, one. To the psychiatrist, the consequences of violence prediction may be daunting. There can be legal ramifications, for example, if a patient is deemed to be non-violent, then released and he/she kills or injures someone. Often, the prediction of violence means involuntarily hospitalizing a patient. If the patient's family is not supportive of the treatment, they may demand the release of the patient. The psychiatrist may feel that hospitalizing the patient will only contribute to his/her propensity for violence, and that the most effective therapy lies in keeping the patient in outpatient therapy.

The more thoughtful and concerned psychiatrists have developed some criteria which has adaptive uses for the protective agent.

First, from the psychiatric standpoint, violence in the future can only be predicted by basing it on past violence. That is, from their point of view, an accurate prediction of violence starts with the fact that the patient has already committed one or more violent acts. The protective agent does not have the luxury of predicting violence only with those individuals who have behaved violently in the past, since he cannot afford to take the chance that the first violent incident will happen to his client.

However, it is a point well taken. Individuals who have committed violent acts in the past are likely to commit violent acts in the future, and should be considered as potentially more dangerous.

Second, in order to accurately predict violence, one must have as much applicable information as possible on the individual being assessed. This should include all relevant background information on the subject.

.   Criminal record. Juvenile record.

.   Drugs and/or alcohol abuse.

.   Mental health problems, anti-social and/or obsessive behavior, delusions, hallucinations.

. History of child abuse. Subjects who have themselves been victims of abuse may have a tendency to exhibit the same behavior as adults.

. Violent role models (father, sibling).

. Permission or encouragement to engage in aggressive behavior as a child.

. School problems. Aggressive or assaultive behavior toward school and playmates.

. Feelings of hostility toward parents, siblings, or others.

. History of firesetting or cruelty to animals.

. History of repetitive abnormal correspondence and/or telephone calls made to an individual or individuals.

Preference for violent films and television.

. History of violence. If one or more violent incidents have occurred, information should be procured and analyzed to determine the:

   . Circumstances which precipitated the violence.

   . Degree of violence.

   . Number of incidents.

   . Time period between violent incidents.

   . Time elapsed since last violent incident.

   . Indications of an escalation of violence within incidents.

   . Type of violence.

   . Use of weapons.

The pertinent considerations are: frequency of incidents; severity; type; recentness; escalation of degree of violence; and whether weapons were used. Individuals with a history of repetitive, severe, and recent violent incidents are considered the most likely to commit imminent or future violent acts.

Third, with a violent act there may be a possible linkage or interrelationship between the subject and the intended victim--spouse, lover, celebrity, public figure, co-worker, boss, etc., possibly linked through correspondence, telephone calls, etc.

Fourth, every violent act requires a trigger, which may be only the short fuse attached to accumulated stress caused by problems related to money, job security, love, sex, self-esteem, inadequacy, or frustration. Drugs and alcohol can provide the trigger or break down the barriers.

Fifth, to commit the violence the perpetrator must have opportunity and ability. If the subject cannot approach or be in close proximity to the victim, he cannot carry out his violent act. And, if he does not have the weapon or mechanism, plus the ability to use them, he cannot consummate his violent act.

These are the broad factors that lead to a violent act. There may be some offsetting, built-in inhibitory factors which will deter the subject from committing a violent act against his victim. He may be an adoring fan who would not dream of injuring his star, but may shoot his mother. Or, he may have discovered God in a genuine Christian conversion and will never be violent again. (But don't bet on it!)

These broad factors can be translated or broken down into some specifics.

The following background considerations seem to indicate the highest potential for violence and can function as predictors when combined with other factors such as triggers, opportunity and ability:

   . Past violent incidents are multiple (more than one); are severe (murder, rape, assault, and/or fatal); and recent (no more than a year ago).

. A gun or other weapon was used in the incident(s).

. The violent incidents escalated in severity, particularly when stimulated by victim's pain and suffering.

. Arrests and convictions for violent crimes, particularly when first occurring during teenage years.

. History of family violence, particularly when the violent individual was a role model.

Less important but still significant as background predictors, particularly when combined with other factors, are such incidents as: history of property destruction and firesetting; school problems involving assaults on teachers and/or fellow students; juvenile record for non-violent crimes; alcohol and/or drug abusing parents and/or siblings; history of physical or sexual abuse; and preference for violent movies and television.

Some of the incidental considerations which may stimulate or reinforce violent behavior are:

. Lack of, or migratory, employment and lack of skills to procure steady employment

. Low economic status and sub-standard living environment.

. Poor language skills.

. Fantasies, delusions, and nightmares, particularly when of a violent nature.

. Self-destructive behavior, threats of suicide, self-mutilation.

. Feelings of impotence, low self-esteem, powerlessness, inability to reach goals.

. Low frustration tolerance; tends to act out

stress; blows up.

. Feelings of suspiciousness, persecution, revenge, and/or hostility.

. Obsessional behavior.

. Low need for affection.

. Feelings of loneliness, and of denial from normal social relationships; is considered a loner.

. Belief that violence is an acceptable, or the only, way to solve otherwise unsolvable problems.

. Strong feelings of entitlement and/or justification for violence.

The triggers, which are intense and recent, and are most often associated with violence include the following:

. Alcohol and/or drug intoxication taken singly or in combination.

. Loss of job.

. Loss of status on the job, loss of promotion, or demotion.

. Prolonged conflict with or loss of love/sex relationship.

. Financial problems.

. Loss of status in peer group.

. Severe or continued threats to self-esteem.

. Severe threats to basic needs group, primarily sex, territory dominance.

. Peer pressure (gang rape, wilding, gang fights, gang initiation).

.   Sudden pain.

Opportunity and ability are needed to carry through the violent act. Factors associated with these might include:

.   Proximity and availability of victim.

.   Possession of weapons and/or recent purchase of weapon.

.   Mobility, such as possession of a vehicle.

.   Release from confinement in prison or hospital, particularly when combined with a denial or cessation of stabilizing medicine.

All of these factors--background, personality, environment, triggers, opportunity, and ability are interrelated. While each has a predictor element, it is when they are combined that one is able to more closely predict the potential for and imminence of violence.

Of the studies made in the past on violence and dangerousness, it has been found that the best predictors of imminent violence, in combination, include:

.   Multiple (more than one) triggers which are severe in nature and of short duration.

.   A background of violent incidents.

.   Opportunity and ability.

Most severe triggers include break-up or denial of love/sexual relationship, deteriorating work environment, and peer pressure, aided or stimulated by substance intoxication, command hallucinations, paranoia, and obsessive thoughts of violence or revenge.

The second group of predictors, indicating slightly less potential for violence or a less severe degree of violence include:

.   One trigger.

.   History of violence.

.   Conditions associated with or known to lead to violence.

.   Young males of some races and minority groups, from a lower socioeconomic base.

.   Substance abuse.

.   Acceptance of or belief in violence as a problem-solver, or association with violent peers.

.   Lack of verbal skills.

The third group of predictors is less strong, less imminent, but still worthy of consideration, and include:

.   History of violence.

.   High hostility and low frustration level.

.   Distrust of others.

.   Feelings of persecution.

The fourth group of predictors indicate the lowest probability of violence and/or the lowest degree of severity of violence and include:

.   History and nature of past violence.

.   History of child abuse

.   School problems, firesetting, fights, vandalism.

INTERFACING WITH THE LAW ENFORCEMENT AND MENTAL HEALTH COMMUNITIES

Everyone agrees that the best and safest results would be achieved if the law enforcement, private security, and mental health areas could be persuaded to interact with each other to the highest degree possible and permissible by law. This has not worked very well in the past, but there are signs that improvements have been made. The *Tarasoff* decisions have compelled the mental health community to interface more significantly and openly with both law enforcement and private individuals. (*Tarasoff I* and *II* established the strictures that a doctor or psychotherapist has a duty to warn intended victims of threats made by a patient and, further, to use reasonable care to protect the intended victim against such danger.)

The formation of police threat management teams has increased and results have been encouraging.

Both the National Institute of Mental Health and the American Psychiatric Association estimate that, during any year, a startling percentage of all Americans--perhaps as many as 25%--suffer some sort of mental disorder. Yet, few of them get proper treatment and, of those who do receive treatment, many are recidivist. Those diagnosed as dangerous and committed for treatment are not guaranteed as cured when released. The same individuals turn up again and again for observation. Considering that a majority of stalkers suffer some form of mental disorder, it is disquieting news.

The move to deinstitutionalize the mentally ill began some 40 years ago. The reasoning was that the best path for all but the most dangerous and the hopelessly deranged would be to refer them to community mental health centers where they could be treated and medicated, preferably in their home communities. Even those considered as potentially dangerous or perhaps violently inclined could not then and cannot now be involuntarily committed for more than a few days unless they have actually committed a violent act or pose an immediate threat to themselves or others.

This leaves victims and potential victims in a very bad situation. Their pursuers may not be considered as posing an *immediate* danger, and, after

being held for a few days for observation, may be released. Treatment may consist of periodic counseling and medication which may show good results but which is useless if the patient stops taking the medication and terminates counseling.

Even when patients are institutionalized and treatment seems to produce good results, there is little communication between the mental health practitioners and either the law enforcement authorities involved or private individuals at risk. That is, if a stalker is committed and treated, there is seldom any notification when that person is released from treatment.

Patient confidentiality is carried to some notable extremes. It is very difficult, if not impossible, to obtain helpful information about patients. This is exacerbated when the patient is transferred from one institution to another. Some institutions are unwilling to accept dangerous individuals and so may transfer him/her one or more times. This makes effective treatment difficult and tracking of the patient almost impossible. Some of these individuals end up back on the streets or returned to the same situation and environment which they left. And all without benefit of notification to those most concerned.

The mental health practitioners have at best a 50-50% record of being able to predict dangerousness. Thus, many release patients or recommend that they be placed in out-patient care because they do not believe the patient is dangerous. They may also believe that treatment will be jeopardized if the patient is exposed to outside influence (law enforcement, private security, etc.) But, most of all, it is the adherence to patient confidentiality that is the stumbling block. Violating patient confidentiality may expose the mental health practitioner to ethics violation charges and lawsuits. In the past, refusal to share information about a patient provided a safety net for the counselor.

The situation has, of course, changed to some extent, driven by the 1974 and 1976 *Tarasoff* decisions. However, many psychotherapists were left confused in the interpretation of *Tarasoff*. Many still are, and are still inclined to shelter behind the cloak of patient confidentiality.

If the mental health community and the courts could be convinced of one simple fact, the protection of intended victims could be greatly strengthened--that fact being the notification to all involved of an impending release of a patient considered to be potentially dangerous. This should be mandated.

In addition, every effort should be made for the law enforcement and mental health communities to interact positively with each other. When possible, information should be shared and compared. All too often in the past, these two vital communities have not only not cooperated, they have viewed each other with hostility. This makes it extremely difficult to predict dangerousness and to monitor dangerous individuals.

It is not known how many police departments have their own psychiatric division. The Los Angeles Police Department does, the LAPD Mental Evaluation Unit. This is surely a great step forward. The Mental Evaluation Unit operates on a 24-hour basis. Specially trained police officers track and profile mentally disordered people who come in contact with the police. They advise and warn police officers of probable danger. They are involved in the recommendation to refer suspects determined to be in need of psychological assistance to a psychiatric facility. Officers have access to a Department of Mental Health hot line, and there are systemwide mental assessment response (SMART) teams to provide hands-on assistance. These teams are composed of unit officers and specially trained psychiatric nurses, and, importantly, the teams can compare and share mental health and criminal justice information about a suspect. These teams assist in emergency handling and also do regular follow-ups of suspects. The SMART teams are linked to the Threat Management Unit. This is an excellent arrangement. It is to be hoped that more police departments have, or will have in the future, similar assets.

Passage of antistalking laws has greatly

improved the situation. The police now have more options in dealing with stalkers. Notoriety has brought the seriousness of the situation to the forefront and placed pressure on the law enforcement community to view stalkers as criminals to be prosecuted and/or mentally disordered individuals to be institutionalized.

INTERVIEWS

One of the intervention strategies discussed is that of interviewing the subject. To what purpose? To attempt to determine why he/she wishes to approach the client, and whether he/she is dangerous. If dangerous, how dangerous? Does he/she have a plan, and would the plan work? What is the stress level of the individual--does he/she appear to be dangerously stressed?

To successfully conduct an interview, the interviewer must possess good conversational and communication skills. Effective interviewers know how to phrase questions which will elicit information and, very importantly, *know how to listen.* "Active listening" is a phrase which has been used to describe the process of listening intently as opposed to merely hearing. Active listening involves a process of listening for real meaning, of picking up key words and phrases, and of probing for hidden messages, instead of merely hearing the other person's words.

All aspects of the interview are important and include much more than merely what the subject says. Gestures, tone of voice, facial expressions, attitudes, emotions, level of agitation--all play an important role.

Whenever possible, interviews should be held privately, in a quiet setting. Ideally, the interviewer and interviewee should be sitting within easy distance of each other without an intervening barrier, such as a desk. *However,* these conditions are not always available or even desirable. With an intruder, there is always the possibility of violence; thus, a safe distance should be maintained. On the other hand, if one is interviewing, say, a neighbor as part of a background investigation, the setting should be comfortable, informal, non-threatening, and friendly, with as few distractions as possible. Turn off your cell phone and all other beepers and signals; it is distracting and rude to ask for an interview, then interrupt it to take calls. Get rid of any clutter between you, if possible.

The best interviewers are polite, empathetic, friendly, and adept at establishing a form of personal rapport with the interviewee. A good interviewer establishes a form of bonding between him/herself and the interviewee. In order to establish that bonding, the interviewer must be perceived as fair-minded and trustworthy. This means approaching the interview without fixed prejudices and without preconceived judgements. The interviewee must feel that he is getting a fair hearing.

The interviewee may display any of a number of attitudes and emotions, ranging from distraught, obsessed, resentful, angry, and aggressive to calm, helpful, apprehensive, frightened, devious, and secretive. The first chore, therefore, is to put the subject at ease and deflate any excess emotions. It does little good to interview someone who is upset, frightened, or angry. All elements of confrontation must be removed. The goals are to determine whether the subject poses a danger to the client and, if possible, to discourage any further attempts to reach the client. Ideally, it means sending the subject away feeling that he or she had a fair hearing, but that any further attempts will come to nothing.

Begin by introducing yourself and establishing your credentials. You are a professional, and you have the right to ask a few questions, although this should never appear to be an intimidating position. If the subject is upset, angry, or frightened, try to deflate the emotions by adopting a low, soothing tone of voice. Never let your own emotions escalate. The great majority of individuals who attempt to reach the client are misguided but harmless and, because of an intense frustration in achieving their goals, may appear overly emotional.

You should appear interested, concerned, and

non-judgmental. Maintain a conversational approach and, if appropriate, talk for a few minutes about other topics of interest--anything that establishes a friendly atmosphere. Refrain from jumping straight into the problem, and try not to hurry the subject. He or she may, given time, get to the point without urging. The interview will be more productive if the interviewee is set at ease. There is a pacing to every interview, with the normal progression of communication moving from the general to the specific, the casual to the meaningful, and the impersonal to the personal.

You should show a sincere interest in the subject (even if you do not feel it), but do not do so in a phoney or condescending manner. People are quick to spot insincerity, and, if they do so, it may spoil any chances to regain the subjects's trust. If you cannot fake an interest, at least be cordial and dispassionate.

The trick is to get the interviewee to talk and then to encourage him to continue talking. By talking, he may reveal all of the information which you need to know to make a determination about him. Therefore, ***do not interrupt the flow of his discourse unless necessary***. Let the subject tell his story naturally and save your questions until his free narrative has wound down. Make mental notes and, if possible, written notes so that you can follow up with questions later. With a receptive audience, an interviewee often finds satisfaction and even pleasure in revealing information. It may make him feel successful and powerful in revealing his "achievements." If he is frustrated, having a sympathetic listener will often be sufficiently satisfying to get rid of, or at least minimize, the cause of the frustration.

When you interrupt someone, you run the danger of throwing him off-track. He may forget exactly what he was saying. Or, he may resent the interruption and "clam up." Keep in mind, there are ways in which we interrupt other than verbally--looking bored or distracted, fiddling with a pencil, checking our watch. A good interviewer keeps all such motions to zero level, looks directly at the interviewee, and ***listens***. A caveat, however--listening intently does not mean staring with a fixed, unblinking look; this can be intimidating. The interviewer must appear as empathetic, not a "cold fish."

Another conversation-stopper is to argue with or patronize the interviewee. If the person mispronounces a word or mis-states a common fact, resist the urge to correct him/her. And, *never* indulge yourself by stating, "Well, of course, we all know that," or "Everyone knows that . . ." With an employee, for example, don't lecture--"Well, with your past history, what did you expect?" or "I can't understand why you're so upset--after all, you've been warned lots of times that calling in sick would get you fired." Or with an intruder who has announced that he is Madonna's husband, resist the temptation to respond, "Yeah, sure, and I'm Little Miss Muppet." These rejoinders may boost the interviewer's ego but do nothing to further a meaningful interview.

You must try to maintain an open mind. Do not feel that you must either disagree or agree with the interviewee. You may not approve of his actions, but at least try to be understanding of what motivates him. It is, in fact, alright to say from time to time, "I understand" or "I can understand how you might feel that way." And, no matter what the subject says, do not visibly react with disgust, disapproval, contempt, anger, or sarcasm.

Asking Questions

Once the subject has told his story, you will undoubtedly need to ask questions. Questions are intended to obtain and clarify information--often information that the subject does not wish to reveal. There is an art to asking questions and, if the stage has been properly set by preparing the interviewee and placing him at his ease, the right questions can motivate the right answers.

Questions should be simple, plainly worded and uncomplicated. Try to find the communication comprehension level of the subject and then stick to that level. It is useless to ask questions that contain words or jargon unknown to the subject. Keep it

simple and keep it short! Long, convoluted sentences will only confuse the subject. For some ego reason, many (unsuccessful) interviewers cannot resist the temptation to show off their superior intellect by asking impossibly long and contorted questions. Short questions are best by far.

Each question should cover only one point, rather than a number of points. There is less confusion and the answer can be more direct and concise. This is a very good interviewing rule--one point, one question. If a question is asked and the answer brings out several relevant points, subsequent questions should deal with these points--one by one. Questions should be stated in clear language to avoid being misunderstood. If the subject appears to be confused, restate the question, perhaps giving an example for clarification. Confusing questions not only provoke confusing answers, they provide a smoke screen behind which the subject may choose to hide. Short, simple, uncomplicated questions demonstrate the interviewer's control of the interview.

All questions should be asked in a neutral manner and should avoid the use of emotional language. There are words which are inflammatory, which carry an emotional impact, or which seem to impute guilt or threat. These words should be avoided.

The easier, less vital questions should be asked first. The strategy is to place the subject at ease, feeling good about the interview, and then in a logical, sequential manner lead him/her through the more complicated, important issues. Avoid the interrogator's way of throwing in unrelated trick questions designed to throw the subject off the track. This will only dry up the flow of information. The interviewee should feel confident and relaxed, with an impulse to reveal his innermost thoughts to his new friend, the interviewer. Questions should flow in a natural, logical sequence. There is always the possibility that the subject is at least momentarily suffering from a mental disorder and unable to cope with complicated conversational switching. If necessary, repeat the question slowly and wait for the answer.

It is often helpful to repeat or summarize the subject's answers. For example, if the subject has given a long, rambling response to a question, it is useful to quietly summarize the key points of the answer by saying, "As I understand it, you are saying that . . . . . Is that correct?" Conversely, if the subject's answer is short and complete, it often helps to repeat his answer, ending with a questioning tone, then pausing to see if the subject will add details to his response. For example, let us say that your question is, "And after you had written to Ms. Movie Star for a year without getting a response, what then?" And his answer is, "And then I decided to visit her." Your strategy may be to restate as a question, "And then you decided to visit her?" Pause -- wait for details.

Yet another strategy is to ask a probe or add-on question such as, "And then?" or "What happened next?" or "What else?" or "Tell me more about how you did that." Sometimes this technique can be most effectively used by pretending some confusion, such as saying, "I'm not certain that I understand that-- could you explain a bit more?"

Questions should be asked is such a way that the answer provides more information than "yes" or "no." Asking, "Were you attempting to break in Ms. Movie Star's house?" is likely to get a simple "No" answer. Instead, you may choose to ask either an open-ended or close-ended (leading) question.

Open-ended questions do not require specific answers; rather, they invite narrative-style answers. Open-ended questions might include something like, "Tell me a little bit about how you became interested in Ms. Movie Star." This invites a longer, more richly detailed, sometimes rambling answer. The advantages are that the free flow of information can reveal important details that could be missed by asking narrowly specific questions, and they give the interviewee his/her "day in court" by providing an opportunity to "vent" emotions and feelings. The disadvantages include rambling, often confusing answers which can effectively disguise or hide important information, or which meander off in irrelevant areas. Open-ended questions are often

difficult to handle for mentally disordered individuals who find it hard to stay on track.

Even if you need very specific information, a good strategy is to start with a few open-ended questions and become more focused as you go.

Close-ended questions are sometimes referred to as leading questions. Questions of this nature are based on assumptions and tend to lead the interviewee to a pre-designed conclusion. Example: "When did you decide to attack Ms. Movie Star?" (when no attack has in fact taken place). Or, when interviewing a witness about a subject, "Isn't it true that you observed the subject loitering near Ms. Movie Star's residence on a number of occasions?" as opposed to the more straightforward question, "Have you ever noticed the subject in the vicinity of Ms. Movie Star's residence?"

Close-ended questions are also used to gain precise, specific answers. These are the "Who," "What," "When," "Where," "Why," and "How" questions. Close-ended questions are used when asking for an address, telephone number, etc. They are also used when vital information is needed quickly. "Will you tell me if you are carrying a weapon?"

Close-ended questions allow the interviewer to maintain close control of the interview and they save time in gaining specific information. They are very useful in cross-checking information. The disadvantages are obvious, primarily in limiting the free flow of information which could be lost by not asking the right questions or by asking questions that are so limited in scope that the answers reveal only partial information. Too many close-ended questions, particularly when asked too abruptly, can make the interviewee feel as if he or she is being interrogated or cross-examined, which could have the unhappy result of turning a friendly interviewee into a hostile one who deliberately withholds information.

In probing for information it is a good rule to ask for all information even if it is known. In fact, known information should be asked for as if it were not known. This is a strategy for testing the interviewee's veracity or knowledge of details. By the same token, in asking for information which is *not* known it often works well to ask questions as if the information were known by the interviewer.

Hidden Meanings

Almost every interview contains some confusion and hidden meanings; total honesty is rare. Listening for hidden meanings and nuances is critical.

Unresponsive. If an interviewee does not respond or appears to avoid answering a question, there may be more than one reason. Start with the fact that the interviewee may not understand the question, and may not wish to admit it. Try this first--repeat the question but rephrase it, perhaps cutting down on the verbiage and using simpler words.

However, if several questions are not answered, you will have to try another tack. You might wish to leave the subject momentarily and then return to it. Or you may wish to take a more direct approach, saying something like, "I sense that my question may have made you uncomfortable--is there some way I can make it easier for you to answer?" or "Is there some reason for not answering, something that we can talk about and get it out of the way?"

Not Denying or Explaining When It Would be Logical to Do So. Common wisdom is that innocent, honest people are quick to deny any wrongdoing, and that those individuals who do not deny wrongdoing are more probably guilty. The author believes it is a bit more complicated than that.

It is true that honest people are usually quick to establish their innocence, but be aware that some people are made so nervous by interviews that they may protest too much, all the while sweating freely. One cannot go by these signals alone.

On the other hand, the guilty party may too quickly and too vigorously deny wrongdoing, using expressions such as, "I swear to God that I didn't do

anything wrong." Swearing "by God" or "on my mother's grave" is often a dead giveaway of a guilty person.

To get to the truth, the interviewer must have patience, must somehow make it comfortable and non-threatening for the interviewee to answer. When all else fails, a direct close-ended question may have to do, perhaps accompanied by something like, "Well, John, you realize that if you are not willing to answer the question, I must assume that you were involved in . . . Is this your choice? I would really rather hear your version to see if there is some common ground we can work on."

Short Answers. These are truly maddening. Short answers leave us with little to go on and looking foolish in the bargain. Once again, patience is called for with careful probing and follow-up questions such as, "Can you elaborate on your comment about . . .?"

Long Answers. Some people are prone to giving long answers to everything; it is a natural part of their personality. Lonely people may feel it is a great opportunity to have human dialogue. Nervous people sometimes act out their nervousness by giving rambling, semi-incoherent answers.

Dishonest people, especially the con artists, as well as honest people who have something to hide, often use long answers to bury the facts. Long answers can contain the truth, but the facts are so intertwined with extraneous material that the truth gets lost. The dishonest person hopes he has diverted you. The honest person has reached an accommodation with himself by giving the interviewer the facts but in such a disjointed manner, that the truth is obscured (I didn't really lie).

Answering A Question With A Question. This is another maddening tactic, one that has traditionally been employed by mental health professionals.

Example: "Were you trying to gain entry to

Ms. Movie Star's residence?" Answer: "What makes you think I'm trying to see Ms. Movie Star?"

Or, "Were you involved in the incident with Joe in the employee cafeteria?" Answer: "Does Joe claim that I was there?"

A common reason for employing this tactic is to gain time, time to find out what the interviewer knows before answering. Another reason may be that the interviewee wants to redirect the interview, perhaps to safer ground. In any case, when the interviewee consistently attempts to use this tactic, the interviewer should be alert. Something is wrong.

Signals of Withheld Information and/or Guilt. Interviews consist of more than questions and answers. A good interviewer must be alert to indications of intensely felt emotions, body language, contradictory signals, and withheld information.

An individual who is emotionally distraught will be difficult to successfully interview. It is even possible to misdiagnose emotions, mistaking them for signs of guilt. An emotionally distraught individual may be experiencing fear, anxiety, over-excitement, and, yes, guilt--or this may indicate that the individual is withholding information.

Some signals of an emotional manifestation include:

.   Excessive swallowing, sometimes followed by a "catch" in the throat and/or a momentary loss of voice.

.   Dryness of mouth perhaps accompanied by a licking of the lips.

.   Sweating--forehead, hands, armpits.

.   Fidgeting and restless motions--frequent changes of sitting or standing position--picking at hands or fingernails--plucking at hair--gripping chair arms--foot waving or tapping--tapping of fingers or pencil.

.   Either very pale or very florid (red) complexion.

.   Trembling or twitching of mouth or one side of mouth.

.   Pulsing artery in temple or neck.

.   Direct gaze avoidance -- inability to meet the interviewer's eyes.

These signals indicate intense emotions though not necessarily of guilt. Many people who indicate these symptoms are guilty of nothing more than a latent guilt complex which is a carryover from childhood. What is important is to calm the interviewee so that he/she can remember and describe important, accurate information. An interviewee who is under emotional stress may think only of providing *any* information which will allow him/her to escape. This can lead to false information and errors.

Withheld information is another problem. Even honest interviewees may withhold information. They do so out of fear of consequences, fear of reprisal, fear of falsely condemning another person, fear of becoming involved in a situation not of their choosing, fear of being inconvenienced, or merely resentment directed toward the interviewer. Or, they may withhold information which they consider to be irrelevant or of no significance. The skilled interviewer must learn to recognize the signals of withheld information.

Contradictions of words, or of words and behavior, may be a signal of withheld information. This may take the form of contradictory revelations or an inconsistency of reporting certain facts. Sometimes the contradiction occurs between what is being said and what is being shown in facial expressions and body gestures.

Another fairly reliable signal is vagueness on the part of the interviewee when, previously, he/she was clear and precise. If a certain area of information is approached and the interviewee suddenly begins to make statements such as, "I don't understand your question" or "I don't know why you are asking me that question," he/she is probably signalling that he/she does not want to reveal that information.

Any efforts to avoid answering questions, particularly when the interviewee has been forthcoming previously, is probably indicating an area of discomfiture and withheld information. Vague and incomplete answers or sudden attempts to appear ignorant of details are signals. Or, the interviewee may attempt to evade answering by deliberately changing the question and veering in another direction. A good interviewer looks for gaps in information, for the breaks in sequence which indicate that information is missing or being withheld. If the interviewer knows that the interviewee was in a position to know certain facts, and yet denies knowing them, he/she is undoubtedly withholding information.

The emotional signals of distress previously discussed may also indicate that the interviewee is withholding information.

And then? If the interviewer is relatively certain of this, he may want to ask a direct question such as, "Is there something that you feel uneasy about telling me?" or "I have this feeling that you are reluctant to discuss this with me--is there something I can do to reassure you?" Sometimes a direct appeal can be made, such as, "I need your help in order to resolve this situation satisfactorily for everyone." Most people do feel an obligation to be helpful, and if given the proper reassurances, they will be forthcoming. It is their hesitancy to "become involved" that is the primary problem.

False and Misleading Information. Yet another interviewing problem is that of securing false, misleading or inaccurate information. If you are conducting background interviews to obtain information on a possible suspect, you must avoid the pitfall of collecting only the information which "fits" your preconceptions. Information which is gathered should be tested against other known facts, and should represent only one aspect of an investigation.

Information collected about a suspect from other sources should be double-checked for veracity. However, having stated this, all information is potentially valuable and should be carefully examined.

AVOIDING CONFRONTATIONS

In any encounters with individuals who attempt to approach a client it is important to keep these as non-confrontational as possible. In this context, of course, we are not considering the violent encounters with assorted bad guys who are shooting at or otherwise attempting to harm their targets. The encounters most found by protective agents in their careers will be non-violent and non-threatening in a physical sense. Nonetheless, since clients do not want encounters of any kind with strangers, protective agents have two goals: to intervene and prevent contact with the client; and to keep the encounter as non-confrontational as possible. The worst handling of an encounter is to allow it to become violent or to result in anger that escalates to a future threat.

Dealing with someone who is deranged and violent at the outset or is under the influence of drugs is very difficult. Controlling that individual may require force, and a call to the police.

But, what about encounters with individuals who are determined but not crazy? Much has been written in the past 25 years about defusing anger and avoiding confrontation. Out of this body of knowledge the protective agent can extract some very effective points.

One approach which is interesting refers to "verbal judo." Martial artists know that using force against force may not be as effective as using the opponent's force against him. That is, going with the opponent's force to your advantage can be very useful. The same tactic can apply to verbal encounters. If a person attempts to approach a client and in so doing is yelling and cursing, it is very *in*effective to retaliate by yelling and cursing in return. This "force against force" is certain to prompt an unpleasant, if not violent, confrontation. Even if the individual is not yelling or behaving obstreperously but is attempting to approach, or is some place where he should not be and will not leave, the agent yelling "What the hell do you think you're doing? Get out of here or I'll throw you out." is very likely to cause a *big* problem. Instead, a calm, reasonable and *empathetic* approach can defuse the situation.

Another non-confrontational technique which became very popular in the 1970's was Transactional Analysis (TA), known best as "I'm OK, You're OK." The term "Win-Win" is a legacy of TA. While TA had several aspects to it, including the Parent-Child-Adult roles which all of us alternately play at given times, one of its best maxims dealt with how we approach and treat other people. Using our script in the preceding paragraph, it is easy to see how this approach could arouse a similar response, something like, "Oh, yeah? Well, buddy, I've got a right to be here and if you think you can throw me out, go ahead and try it, because I'm going to whip your ass!"

TA advocates a different approach, one which is softer yet remains firm, and which treats the other person as adult-to-adult. Let us examine the following script which presupposes that someone is attempting to gain entry to a client's property.

You, as the agent, state, "Is there any reason or justification for your being here?"

The intruder either does not answer or replies rudely, "Get lost, buddy, I've got a right to be here."

You then say, "Are you aware there is a law being broken here?"

He/she does not leave and says, "F... your law."

You continue in a firm but reasonable manner to say, "If you do not choose to cooperate, this is what will happen (we will be forced to call the police, etc.). Do you understand?"

He/she still does not leave.

You continue, "Look, is there anything I can say or do to get your cooperation at this time?"

During the encounter, the person may state a reason for the attempted approach, such as the need to broach a complaint or to leave a "gift" in person. A good response is for you to say, "I appreciate that, but . . . ." or "I understand, but . . . . ."

This approach to solving a problem has several elements. It treats the other person as an adult. It does not demean him/her. It does not contain any emotional or emotion-arousing words. It remains firm. It suggests options and courses of action. It extends a certain empathy. It exudes calm and reasonableness.

In any encounter we can attempt to persuade (not force) the other person by an appeal to his reason, or his emotions, or to character or personality. In talking with the other person you may find yourself using all three approaches or shifting from one to another when the first does not work. It is well to remember that when another person is caught up in his emotions and is behaving irrationally, he, himself, may believe that he is behaving completely rationally. An appeal to his reason may persuade him that he is over-reacting to some real or imagined complaint.

In all encounters, it is important that the agent has control of his emotions, prejudices and preconceptions. If the agent has had a bad day, been criticized by his client for a slight infraction, and is overly tired, he may have trouble controlling his emotions--but it is essential. If the other person in the encounter is someone whom it would be easy to despise and for whom the agent bears some kind of prejudice, the encounter will not go well unless the agent is able to sublimate his bias and go in with a clean attitude. Preconceptions can lead to trouble, since they may have little meaning in the current encounter.

With a clear mind and attitude, the agent can be free to truly listen to the individual. This goes beyond merely hearing words; it requires close attention both to what the individual is saying and what he is implying. Often, people who are caught up in their emotions do not say what is truly in their hearts but, instead, go off on vocal tangents. It is important to listen for the hidden message(s).

For example, an aggressive person, John Doe, attempts to approach Senator Brown, angrily denouncing the Senator as having "cheated him and caused his marriage to break up." Agent Smith, in probing empathetically, finds that John Doe has been laid off from his job with reasons given as lack of business and cutbacks. This layoff has caused John so much anxiety that he has begun drinking heavily and arguing with his wife, who leaves him. John has been reading the negative comments on NAFTA (North American Free Trade Agreement) and believes that his job has "gone South." Senator Brown is one of the strongest and most visible supporters of NAFTA.

If Agent Smith is a good listener and can empathetically "put himself in John's shoes," he stands a good chance of reasoning with John and giving him some solid advice about sobering up and re-training for another job. John is going to feel a lot better. He found a sympathetic audience and had a chance to vent his frustrations. He may even vote for Brown in the upcoming election.

There are some very good suggestions for effective listening which include:

.   Be quiet--stop talking and listen.

.   Look at the other person and concentrate on what that person is saying and what he may *not* be saying.

.   Be a responsive listener--smile, nod, and acknowledge with an occasional "I understand" or "Of course."

.   Control your own emotions and biases, and get rid of distractions. Focus your entire attention upon the speaker.

.   Ask clarifying questions and try to gain the main points; don't be distracted with side issues that have no importance.

.   Avoid jumping to conclusions; make certain that you have all the facts.

.   Avoid making moral or emotional judgements or showing these judgements by making derogatory comments.

The word "empathy" has been used several times as being the most effective element of communication. It means identifying with the other person--"standing in his shoes." Even if you do not agree with the other person, you must try to see his point of view. You may even give a quasi-agreement to the basis of his viewpoint.

For example, John X has attempted to gain entrance to Ms. Movie Star's residence and Agent Smith has foiled his attempt. John is angry, frustrated, and determined to try again. Agent Smith wants him to give up his attempts to approach the client. In his conversation, John X rails against women and celebrities in general as being "stuck-up" and uncaring and states that Ms. Movie Star "ought to be taught a lesson."

Agent Smith listens carefully, asks a few questions, and finds out that John's wife left him last year and that, in his loneliness, he has been sending weekly fan letters to Ms. Movie Star.

Agent Smith shows his empathy by saying, "I can understand how you feel. Loneliness is a terrible thing. And, it's true that celebrities can give the appearance of being stuck-up and unreachable. But, I can assure you that they are real people. It's just that they are so stressed by their schedules and constant demands on their time. Ms. Movie Star is constantly torn between her responsibilities as a good wife and mother to her two children and her career. She honestly works very hard to be kind to everyone, but there simply is not enough time. I know that she appreciates your support and the support of all her fans. Have you given your best effort to finding out whether you can put your marriage back together again, or finding someone else with whom you can feel comfortable? Marriage is such a great thing when both people try to make it work. Why not go home and put your energies into working out a good relationship that has a chance of success instead of spinning your wheels?"

Agent Smith is attempting to re-focus John into a more rational path by saying, "I understand, but . . ." He is attempting to use John's energy (force) by deflecting it into another area. If he succeeds he has practiced good TA, and the results will be "Win-Win." Ms. Movie Star and Agent Smith have one less crank to worry about, and John may actually try for a more productive and positive goal.

Does it always work? No, but it works in a majority of encounters or at least defuses some of the dangerousness.

Personal Space

Any encounter carries with it the potential for danger. This calls for constant awareness on the part of the agent.

There has been a fair amount of research which examines personal space, a phenomenon which affects all of us. Personal space is the area around an individual within which others are not expected to intrude. Understanding personal space is one of the most important aspects of non-verbal communication. Although an individual's ideas of personal space vary according to upbringing, age, sex, and ethnic background, an acceptable yardstick is a distance of four feet. In locations such as cars, bedrooms, or offices, the entire area may be considered a personal zone. When you enter a person's personal space, it either makes that person angry or it makes him afraid. It raises his anxiety

level, his blood pressure goes up, adrenalin starts to flow, pulse rate goes up, and so on.

Cornering is a concept related to personal space. When people are cornered, like animals they have the option of resisting, submitting, or fleeing. If we do not give them the means to flee, then they will either submit or resist, and in too many cases they will resist. Physical contact such as placing a hand on the person's elbow is another form of cornering, and can cause a violent reaction.

Cornering can be physical or psychological. That is, cornering can mean placing an individual in a space that does not allow him/her an escape route. Psychological cornering is giving someone a direct order without offering options--for example, saying, "Get out NOW!"

The eyes offer another clue to potential violence. Many individuals give signals with their eyes. People's eyes start looking around when someone corners them. Eyes that jerk, dart, or look around may indicate high anxiety that could result in aggressive action. If an individual's eyes alternately look at your eyes, chest, hands, or weapon he may be sizing you up and may be signaling an imminent attack. If the eyes focus upon a particular body area, that may be the area which is intended for the attack.

It makes good sense, therefore, to maintain at least four feet of distance from an individual, to respect his/her personal space, to watch the eyes carefully, and to avoid striking an aggressive posture. The agent should always present himself as calm and in control of the situation. Stance should be slightly sideways to the other person, with arms at the side of the body. Speech should be reasonable, calming in content and moderate in volume.

SPECIAL EVENT SECURITY

As an executive protection agent, you will find that, at some point, you will be asked to organize the security for a special event, or contacted as a consultant for a special event, or your client will be an integral part of the planning of a special event. This is not an easy task; very large special events can be enormously complex, and the potential for injuries and even death is great. This means that the potential for litigation brought against the sponsors and organizers is equally great. If the client's corporation throws a giant shindig for its 1,000 regional customers and their families, and someone is seriously injured by a fall in an unmarked hole, a lawsuit for negligence will be served forthwith. The fact that the corporation hired an outside event organizer who was supposed to take care of insuring safe and secure conditions will, in all probability, not excuse the sponsoring corporation.

Many special event organizers, promoters, and contractors tend to concentrate on aspects such as lighting, sound, ticket sales, entertainment, etc., and give too little attention to security. Even worse, some organizers and promoters of special events are neophytes in this area and know nothing of security. The purpose of this chapter is to explore the many factors which will influence the security needs for a given event. It is not intended to instruct the reader in every aspect of organizing and staging a special event; hence, there is no information included on such event components as booking entertainment, marketing, public relations, catering, etc.

There is a wide variation in the type of special events which are held each year throughout the world. A special event may be an award dinner with 200 people, the Academy Awards Ceremony, an international soccer match with 100,000 spectators, the Ride the Rockies Bicycle Race, the Winter Olympics utilizing five different locations, a Trade Show with 50,000 in attendance, or the Pope's outdoor sunrise mass for 500,000. Obviously, preparations will differ for each. There are a number of factors that impact a special event. These factors are something of a mix-and-match affair. The reason for the event, combined with its location, size, and timing can change the outcome. A Ku Klux Klan conference held in the winter in Colorado is going to be greatly different from a Klan rally held outdoors in the middle of summer in Washington, DC. The event components--the who, what, where, when, and why-- plus a number of other considerations will dictate certain security measures.

In every respect, planning a special event is akin to putting together a threat model. One must identify the threat, the vulnerabilities, and the recommended countermeasures, resulting in the security plan.

EVENT SECURITY FACTORS

There are some inherent, inescapable security risks associated with special events. Special events tend to attract large numbers of people in attendance, and the attendees may not be a cohesive group. That is, while many events--religious, professional and other--are designed for groups of people who are more or less alike in their goals and behavior, many events draw from diverse markets. Sporting events are a good example of this. A sports event may draw people of all ages, backgrounds, cultures, and ethnic makeup. Non-cohesive crowds in large numbers can be an increased security concern.

Budgets may skimp on security needs. If there is not an understanding and concern on the part of management for safety and security, there may not be money budgeted for enough guards, training, or equipment. This is often the case with events which are held for the first time, or, even worse, they are one-time-only events. The organizers may be inexperienced "do-it-yourselfers." Or, as a one-time-only event, the organizers may care less about security and more about gate receipts. Corporate events sometimes concentrate more on "fluff" (the public relations aspect) than security, not because corporate sponsors are unfeeling, but because they are often naive about security. Although, in today's litigious society, corporations are becoming much more liability-conscious. The nature, or sponsorship, of the event itself can be controversial.

These and other factors can turn special event security into an art form.

The Type or Nature of the Event

There is a big difference in providing security for a one-day meeting of the regional Girl Scouts and one for the Jewish Defense League. The profile of the attendees will be very different. Are the security problems likely to be generated from within or without? Sporting events, for example, tend to generate internal security problems which emanate from the fans. Soccer events are notorious for riots. International soccer matches have involved as many as several hundred deaths and injuries. On the other hand, if there is a Klan conference, the security problems will probably stem from outsiders.

What is the purpose of the event? It may be to enhance the corporate image or promote new products. It may be religious, political, or charitable. Sporting events differ. Whereas soccer games are apt to be riotous, bicycle races held either as fundraisers or corporate events tend to be totally without violence.

What kinds of security problems can occur in and around the event? Have there been any previous incidents associated with the same or similar events? If it is a rock star event, have there been instances of violence or drugs? Are there any current threats? Interviews should be held with the event promoter or sponsor and, if possible, with the manager of the star headliner group. For example, at a meeting of the prestigious American Society of Travel Agents in the Philippines, a bomb blast injured a number of attendees. Be assured that at the next year's conference security was greatly increased and enhanced. Any threats or previous incidents should automatically dictate greater security concerns.

Does the event have the backing and cooperation of the local community? If not, there can be serious problems not only from outsiders within the community but perhaps from the police and fire departments as well. It has been said that President Kennedy was warned not to campaign in the Dallas area because of the hostile feelings within the Dallas community. Whether or not this contributed to his assassination in a motorcade in Dallas will never be known.

Size and Type of Attendees

It is obvious that the size of the attendance will influence the security. The attendees, themselves, will have an influence on security. If there is a ticket cost for attendance, this may signal the kind of person who will be attending. If the event has been held previously, it may be possible to get a profile of sorts. Is the attendance predominantly male or female? What is the average age? If the conference is for the American Association of Retired Persons and the average age is 68, there will be other security concerns than for the Madonna National Fan Club, average age 23.

Is it an international event bringing individuals from countries that may be hostile towards each other? If it is a local event, will there be a mix of ethnic backgrounds that could spell trouble? In 1986, in Long Beach, California, gang members beat and stabbed at least 42 people at a concert by a popular "rap" group.

Location and Size

There are a number of concerns regarding location of the event. In some cities, conference centers have been built in downtown locales that have suspect surroundings. Some events take place in areas that border on crime zones or gang-related areas. Can parking, and access to parking, be secured? Does the facility have a history of accidents or crime-related problems?

Is the event to be held indoors or outdoors? Is it a "moving event" that changes locales? For example, the Olympics are now structured so that several events are held simultaneously in different locations, sometimes many miles apart. Bicycle races and marathons are moving events, sometimes stretching over several days, and include constantly changing locales. Are there problems to any one of the locales in the moving event? First aid and emergency equipment must be stationed at intervals to deal with injuries, exhaustion, or heat/cold problems for race participants and spectators. Bicycle races and marathons can be logistical nightmares, as many take place on public highways with traffic only barely controlled and routed. The potential for accidents is very high. If the event takes place within a city, the streets and intersections must be cordoned off, clearly marked, and manned.

What is the size of the location or building? Can the perimeter(s) be secured? At the State Fair, you will find indoor and outdoor events, many being held simultaneously, with evening events that headline such country music stars as Willie Nelson. The fair grounds cover many acres. If indoors, a floor plan and diagrams must be obtained; if outdoors, a sketched map of the area must be obtained or drawn.

The location may have some weather-related problems. If it is outdoors, are there covered facilities nearby or located on the property to which the event can be moved? Will the speakers or stars of the event be provided cover?

Is the location a public or private one? If it is a public location, there may be some help from the public law enforcement agencies. If it is a purely private location, is there some support from the owners? For example, if it is a hotel ballroom, the event sponsors can rightfully expect security reinforcement from the hotel security staff.

If outdoors, are there bleachers which must be checked for safety and sturdiness? Is there adequate fencing to separate the people on the field from the spectators in the bleachers? If it is a parade, what security measures must be implemented to separate the crowds lining the street from the parade participants and floats? In one famous southwestern river parade, one year, hooligans on a bridge spanning the river threw bottles and rocks at river floats, injuring several people.

Is the site one regularly used for special events, or has a public park been converted for the event? Temporary facilities can present special problems, particularly with access control, traffic, and parking.

If the event is being held overseas, is the locale reasonably safe and free from threat, or have there been a number of protest bombings against the host country? At the ASTA Conference held in the Philippines there was a bombing incident. It is believed that the attackers wanted to make a political statement and felt that by killing or injuring some travel agents it would discourage tourism to the Philippines and cause the government to lose the confidence of the people. It is not known whether there had been any prior bombing incidents leveled against tourists, but the Philippines has a history of political upheavals.

Season, Date, Time and Length of Event

The season may influence the security factors of an event. Is the event a celebration of some national holiday or event? If this is a Martin Luther King event held outdoors in 100-degree heat, this could have some security repercussions. Events held during school spring break periods may suddenly experience an influx of hordes of college students, bent on rowdy entertainment. Is it a weekday or weekend event? If it is a weekday event, this diminishes the number of school youngsters attending. Events held during a long holiday weekend (Labor Day, Memorial Day) will be impacted.

The time of day during which the events are held will influence security. If events are primarily nighttime, extra lighting and guards will be needed.

Access to parking lots will have an increased security risk.

The duration of the event will influence the extent of security. If it is a three-day or five-day event, the numbers of security personnel will increase--and increase. It will require more guards, working in shifts. If the event is one day, lasting one to 12 hours, it may be possible to work with one shift. If the event is one long day and one short day, well, now there are shifts, relief periods, etc. to contend with.

Weather Conditions

At the time the original edition of this book was being written, the author listened to a news report of a storm flood in Tempe, Arizona which unexpectedly washed out a building in which an event was being held--no further details available. Did everyone escape? Was anyone injured or killed? It is a troublesome example of what can go wrong with special events trapped in weather conditions that exceed simple rain. Part of the security survey that should be written for an upcoming special event is a survey of the location to determine if it could withstand a dramatic weather upturn. Would flooding occur? A less dramatic aspect is the consideration of cover in the event of rain. Weather also sometimes determines whether alcoholic beverages will be served. If it is an outdoor event, held in the winter, will there be alcohol smuggled in to ward off the cold? If it is hot summer, will there be beer flowing to excess? In fact, will alcoholic beverages be provided or sold? If so, this affects security.

Would adverse weather conditions dictate additional emergency equipment? In hot summer, should there be a doubling of ambulances available for those felled by heat prostration? In winter, is hypothermia likely to become a problem?

Security Personnel

Decisions must be made as to the number of security personnel needed, whether any of them should be armed, and whether the security should be visible or low profile. There is also the issue of equipment for the security people. Will they be provided radios? Will there be a command post? Where will the command post be located? Access control and surveillance posts must be designated. In terms of access control, if it is an outdoor event, how will the perimeters be controlled? How will access be handled?

Are sufficient numbers of trained guards available in the immediate vicinity or will it be necessary to hire untrained personnel and provide training? At the 1984 Olympics, a huge number of neophyte security personnel were hired and then trained for specific security duties during the events. The 1984 Olympics in Los Angeles produced a very nervous event. 1984 was a year marked by overseas terrorism, and there was great fear that a terrorist incident might be in the making for the Olympics. Background checks were made on countless security personnel. Hotels in the Los Angeles area, especially those housing competing Olympic teams, provided security and anti-terrorism training to their staffs. Access control was a major issue. And, the various interagency bomb squads were everywhere to be seen.

For many special events, there will be volunteer (non-professional) security people. This is particularly true with sporting events such as ski races, bicycle races, and marathons which require enormous numbers of control people to man the streets and intersections. These volunteers must not only be trained, they must be carefully screened to make certain that they are there to work, not merely get into the event free. They should also not be underestimated nor ignored; these people can be very valuable adjuncts to the professional security staff. They should be stationed at very low-risk posts, or they may be intermingled with the regular (professional) security staff, for example, at access control points where their diplomatic skills may be invaluable.

Where are volunteers used in the security context? They can profitably be employed at street checkpoints and intersections at outdoor street events, at access control points, ticket sales (they will zealously protect receipts), interpreting, medical, parking, and transportation, among others. It is important that these volunteers be made to feel that they are important, that they are doing a useful job, and that they are as highly regarded as other components to the staff. Never forget--volunteers are free--they can help to stretch a security budget to meet the goals.

Along with volunteers there may be law enforcement personnel assigned to an event and these people will have to be integrated into the overall security plan. In an event such as the Olympics, there will be a mingling of public law enforcement officials, volunteers, and professional security personnel. A real consideration is how to schedule and assign these three diverse groups of people to the security objectives. Law enforcement personnel are most usefully employed in those situations that might require either an armed response or powers of arrest. This is why they can be very well used in access control checkpoints.

Special Considerations

The event may include some surprising features which, if not known about and planned for in advance, could present problems. Will there be fireworks? Skydiving? Will all the lights be turned out for "a moment of silence to commemorate the . . . . ."? a cannon salute? Never to be forgotten was an event held in San Antonio, Texas honoring the heroes of the Alamo. As part of the tableau, there was a surprise cannon salute. Two cannons located only about 50 yards in the rear, which had been covered with cloths, suddenly roared into life. People leaped over chairs, old ladies fainted, and a concerted rush was made for the exits before the loudspeakers could calm the crowd. As noted earlier in this book, it is essential to have a detailed itinerary of events in advance. If special security must be added to cover the "added attraction," this can be planned for. In any case, there should be no surprises.

Are there event-related activities? Do any of these activities take place outside the event site? Will

there be special luncheons, dinners, barbecues, fiestas? Is there a separate stream of activities for spouses? This is often the case with conferences and trade shows. Spouses are often offered outside entertainment consisting of tours, picnics, and meals. Are there any security problems attached to these event related activities? What about the children? Will there be animal rides? carnival rides?

Will there be a large number of foreign attendees? Will it be desirable to use international codes on directional signs--the little stick figures which indicate traffic directions, "Don't walk," etc.?

If the event is being held outside the United States, are there any environmental concerns? Is the water safe to drink and the food safe to eat? How reliable is the power supply and is there back-up power? Is the building fire-safe? Are there environmental hazards? Who is expected to provide security?

CONTINGENCY PLANNING

Special events pose an excellent opportunity for contingency planning as well as risk management. There are endless numbers of "what if" questions which should be considered. The matter of event insurance coverage should be addressed in this context. "What if a child falls off the carnival ride or the ride itself malfunctions? How would we respond to an accident? Who is liable? What kind of insurance should be obtained? How can we make sure that the rides don't malfunction and the kids are all strapped in or accompanied by an adult?"

Let us say that Agent Brown has been retained to provide security for a special event held by a charitable organization. Before Brown can put together his security plan, he needs to find out some important facts, starting with who-what-where-when-why-how. Brown is going to approach this assignment as he would any protection assignment by gathering intelligence, pinpointing vulnerabilities, devising "what-if" scenarios, and organizing his conclusions into a security plan, much as he would put together a threat model or a security component to the Crisis Management Plan for a corporation. Fortunately, there are sources of information which Brown can access.

Background Information

Brown knows who is sponsoring the event, who (and how many) are expected, what the event is, whether it is a regular or first-time or one-time-only event, where and when it will be held, and the reasons for holding the event. Brown also needs to know if the event will be organized by the sponsors themselves, or whether they are bringing in an outside professional event organizer. Another important question is whether the event organizers have designated, or intend to designate, a Safety Director. This is a key point, because safety is of as much concern as security and the two functions are mutually dependent upon each other. If there is no Safety Director, will each event department manager be responsible for the safety of equipment, buildings, and activities directly related to his department? If there is no Security Director and no one to coordinate the safety functions, will Brown be expected to take over this area?

Brown can ask to review any documents which have been prepared.

Budgets. How much money has been allocated to security, and is this amount fixed or is it flexible? Brown will have to come back to the budget later, but, for the moment he has an indication of whether the sponsors are low-balling it or will allow a realistic amount of money.

Contracts. Any agreements and contracts let with event organizers, caterers, facility/site managers, concessions operators, maintenance and clean-up, parking, entertainers, etc. should be reviewed, and copies requested. Brown will need to interview the various people or their representatives.

Licenses, permits, and insurance. Brown wants to know that any event he is associated with is legal and has the proper permits. Insurance is very important. Brown will need to review the insurance policies to determine what they include and the limitations of coverage. Will the insurance be negated if certain safety and security conditions are not met? For example, if a security guard assaults a young girl and it is discovered that no background checks were performed on security personnel, will the insurance company refuse to cover any damages awarded as a result of the assault?

Event plans, itineraries, and schedules. Well organized events have very minutely orchestrated flow charts to indicate what is happening, when, and where. Production schedules may deal only with staging and entertainment but will necessarily have to dovetail into overall planning. The plans may be further broken down into departmental plans. These will indicate the overall length of the event, the complexities of multi-activities, and indicate any potentially hazardous attractions or activities.

Marketing and promotion plans. How and to whom is this event being marketed? What is the message? Is it a private, closed-to-the-public affair, with high confidentiality? Is the marketing designed to pull in the maximum crowd, including all income levels and ethnic backgrounds? Is the hype misleading and thereby likely to cause problems? Is it inflammatory?

Files from previous events (if this is a regular event). How does this event differ from events held by the sponsors in the past? Are there old security plans? Are there incident reports, complaints, citations, press clippings, video tapes, post-event wrap-ups?

List of special guests, speakers, and entertainers. These people must be individually considered as to their security and the impact which they may have on the overall security of the event. Will they have their own security with them? Must special security be provided them by the event sponsors?

Volunteer structure. Will there be volunteers who can be brought into the security function? How many are there? Will they need training? Have assignments been made for them?

Facility/site diagrams and maps.

Library. If the event has been held in the same city previously, there is sure to be newspaper coverage of the event kept in the library's backdated files. Brown will want to research this to see if he can acquire any additional information which perhaps has not been revealed to him by the event organizers. Brown will also want to research the backgrounds on any contract parties (caterers, facility operators, etc.) to determine if they have had any security-related problems in the past.

Meetings

Agent Brown has reviewed all of the documents and concluded his initial research. He has put together a hit list of questions, and now needs to meet with various individuals and entities.

Event Department Managers. Brown has some questions about events, staging, etc. He particularly wants to know if the event activities have a past history or if they are new to this event. Will Brown be permitted to work with the managers during the planning stages to build in safety and security measures? Is there to be paid admission, and, if so, who will be responsible for handling the cash receipts? Brown may need to arrange for special security. Should this security be armed? Will there be a safe on the premises, or will an armored car service be needed to pick up cash receipts on a regular basis? Do any of the managers foresee safety or security problems? What is the overall security awareness level of the staff?

Safety Director. Brown will need to work closely with the Safety Director, whose responsibilities will include a thorough inspection of the buildings and equipment to determine if they meet safety codes. Are the buildings equipped with sprinklers and alarms? Are they properly equipped with emergency signs and directions of what to do in case of fire? Are the hallways cleared of rubbish and obstructions? Where are hazardous and inflammable materials stored? Who is supervising the construction of new or temporary bleachers to make certain they are safe? Are all exits clear and either unlocked or equipped with panic bars? Are there a sufficient number of fire extinguishers placed at strategic locations, properly charged, and with instructions on how to use them given to all employees?

Have repairs been made or will they be made to all rips, cracks, and other potentially harmful items such as carpets, furniture, etc.? Do lights work? Is there back-up power? Are engineers and maintenance people available in sufficient numbers to handle breakdowns? If fireworks are to be included in the event, will there be safety officers stationed to keep all nonauthorized personnel away from the staging area? Will the fireworks handlers be properly trained so as to avoid injury? If it is a Fourth of July event, what measures can be taken to prevent attendees smuggling in firecrackers?

Unfortunately, if there is no Safety Director, Brown may have to take over these duties. If so, this should be made clear to the event organizers, and a sufficient budget allowance made to handle this sector. Brown may need to bring in a Safety Engineer on a temporary basis to provide support.

Legal. Brown should meet with the sponsoring organization's legal counsel to determine specific areas of liability and negligence. Brown wants to be crystal clear as to his security functions and their interrelationship with insurance coverage. Brown is aware that *negligence* is "the failure of omission or commission, or both." In other words, Brown knows that if certain security measures are taken which, in fact, result in injuries, or if security measures are not undertaken and injuries result, the event sponsors and organizers and he (Brown) may be liable.

Service Contractors. Brown wishes to review

the details of the contracts insofar as security is concerned. (Brown has no business quibbling over menus, appearance, or any other non-security matters.) Will the caterers provide background checks on their employees and, if not, have they at least checked employee references? If a caterer's employee assaults an event attendee, and it is later proven that the caterer did not check references, does this pose a liability for the event sponsors? Will the contractor allow his employees to be badged, so as to provide tight access control? What insurance does the caterer, and facility manager, and maintenance crew carry? Have there been any problems in the past? What has the contractor done to correct the problems? Will alcoholic beverages be served? What provisions have been made for checking I.D's and carding young people?

Insurance. Brown has some questions about certain limiting conditions written into the insurance policy and wishes to have clarification, particularly as concerns the service contractors. Who does the insurance cover? attendees? employees? volunteers? Does the insurance cover damage to property, including borrowed equipment? Brown may wish to ask the insurance officials about incidents which have occurred with other events they have insured and the results.

Entertainment and Attractions. Brown wants to know if the entertainment group has its own security. Can Brown coordinate and work with them? Will their security need to be augmented? What do they consider to be their security concerns? Have there been problems in the past? Brown knows that the risks are higher with some groups than others. Some musical groups, for example, have invited their audience on stage with resulting injuries. Brown has reviewed the entertainment contract to determine how much control the event organizers have over the entertainers' actions. Are there any current threats against the entertainment group? What is the entertainer's history in allowing hangers-on and underage admirers backstage? Is there a history of drugs used by the group?

Guard Companies and Volunteers. Have guard companies been contracted with? If not, are there reliable guard companies in the immediate area who can be used? What arrangements have been made for armed guards? Are they needed? Do the guard companies carry their own insurance? Are their employees drug tested? Are background checks made by the guard company?

Law Enforcement, Fire, and Emergency Services. Will the police provide traffic control? Is there a history of incidents attributed either to the event sponsors or to events in the area generally? What was the nature and the outcome of the incidents? How do the local officials feel about the event in general? This may have an influence on their response to an incident.

Can ambulances be provided at strategic points during the event? Will the ambulances be staffed with EMT's or paramedics? First aid stations will need to be located at strategic points to handle minor medical problems. The medical services should be prepared to work with the police in drug-related cases. Depending on the type and locale of an event, medical problems run the gamut of: heat exhaustion, broken limbs, cuts and abrasions, heart attacks, drug overdoses, electric shock, burns, breathing problems, and many others. If a fight has broken out, there can be serious knife or gunshot wounds. In a worst-case scenario with multiple injuries and/or deaths, are the local emergency services adequate to handle the crisis? Is there a Crisis Management Plan to cover low, medium, and high medical emergencies?

With very large events such as the Olympics or political national conventions, the active cooperation and integration of the local law enforcement, fire, and emergency services will be needed. These officials become active players in the security plan. Brown wants to know about the jurisdictional prerogatives. Who's in charge, and of what? What security services are being provided by each jurisdiction? Will the state police be involved? (They will if the Governor is to give the Opening

Address.) This tricky ground is where some important security measures can fall in the cracks unless it is very clear who is doing what, where, and when. For this situation, Brown will be in constant touch with the law enforcement, fire, and emergency officials, and his timetable will be integrated with that of the public officials. Security for major international events will involve SWAT teams, helicopter surveillance, bomb sniffing dogs, and lots of high tech equipment.

Is it an event that takes place along the coast and in the water? Is it an Air Show? Here are some (not all) of the governmental agencies that might be involved in a security stance with a special event: U.S. Secret Service (protection of the President and Vice President, and presidential candidates); Federal Aviation Administration (airport security); State Police and Department of Highways (dignitary protection and interstate highway traffic control; U.S. Coast Guard and coastal commissions (beach, water, boats); Federal Emergency Management Agency (disaster planning and response); Department of State (overseas activities); Bureau of Alcohol, Tobacco and Firearms (alcoholic beverage licenses and firearms); Drug Enforcement Agency (drugs); Federal Bureau of Investigation (crime, possible background checks); U.S. Immigration (possible hiring infringements if event is held close to the border of another country); local police, sheriff's department, fire department, and emergency medical services. For very unique special events, other government agencies may be involved with security planning and the implementation of security measures.

If the event is being held overseas, are there special laws and regulations which Brown must factor into his plan? Will they be more, or less, supportive than their American counterparts? Are the medical facilities adequate to handle injuries? What is the quality level of the medical facilities? Is the blood supply clean and tested for AIDS?

Special Guests, V.I.P.'s, Speakers. Brown will need to meet with the advance people and administrative assistants for these people. Will the V.I.P.'s have their own security people? Will they be armed? Will a command post be commonly shared? What particular security concerns do the V.I.P.'s have? Are there any threats? Have there been past incidents?

Site Surveys

Thorough walk-throughs and site surveys must be performed for the site, parking, and indoor facilities, including an inspection of storage rooms, catering facilities, dressing rooms, electrical outlets, power input, exits, and seating. Is there back-up power? How will perimeters be secured? How many security personnel will be required to secure the perimeters, provide access control, and guard the gate receipts? Where will the command post be located? What equipment is available and on hand for the command post? Will there be a necessity for in-depth bomb searches? How far in advance should the site/facility be searched? After the bomb search, will the area be sealed off? What provisions have been made for background or reference checks on facility and site personnel? Do the facility/site owners or managers have security personnel of their own who can be integrated into the overall security plan? Where is parking? Will it be lighted? patrolled?

Will there be media coverage? If so, Brown will need to determine if arrangements have been made for the media to set up their equipment in a controlled area. If media interviews are to be conducted, arrangements must be made for a separate room or rooms which can be lighted by the media and which can be used by the media for work. They will need telephones and work space. Are there licensing agreements with the media which allow only certain media to be present? For example, for sports events, one or more stations may have agreements which give them exclusive rights to coverage; all other media must be excluded.

Can private rooms be set aside for the VIP's, rooms which have a telephone, a separate entrance, and, ideally, a restroom away from the public sector? Is there a private entrance? Will there be special VIP parking?

Will any special use permits or inspections be required for the facility because of the special event activities?

Meeting with the Event Organizers

Brown now has completed his background research and has met with the key people involved with the event. Brown has pinpointed some vulnerabilities. Brown has put together a preliminary schedule with numbers needed of security guards and volunteers. Brown has also concluded that, in order to provide good security coverage, he must have volunteers to augment his security, as well as security communications equipment. Brown believes that, because of the nature of the event, some equipment might be donated or loaned. Included with Brown's report is a timetable for security, detailing when he will need to bring in his security equipment and when he will need his security guards and volunteers to meet for training and specific instructions. Brown will include in his report any recommendations for safety improvement and special considerations. Brown will have a plan for controlling access and perimeter security. Brown's plan must include provisions for loss prevention (protection of property against theft). Brown believes that he can work reasonably well within the budget, but he needs a lot of cooperation from the event organizers and service contractors.

Or, a second scenario is that Brown believes that the initial budget is not adequate to provide necessary security coverage, even with the help of volunteers, and that the event organizers must be made aware of this. Brown has put together his security plan with hard figures and his reasons for requesting the additional money. If Brown has documented his report, he should be able to present a good case. Brown has been careful not to request "fluff" items; he has budgeted his needs as minimally necessary to do the job.

The Plan

Having secured the agreement of the event organizers, Brown must now refine and implement his

written security plan. Brown's timetable must be minutely constructed with a countdown to the event. In planning the security for an event such as the Olympics, security planning will begin in earnest at least one year in advance, with some elements of security being integrated four years in advance during the construction phase of the Olympic Village.

Brown will need to include in his security plan procedures for handling crises: bomb threat and search procedures, evacuations, and terrorist incidents.

His plan will also include provisions for, and the equipping of, a command post. He will need to develop written post assignments, which will eventually be lodged together with the work schedules in the command post.

Ideally, Brown should be provided with an office close to the management team. Brown will need to continually coordinate with the department managers, legal counsel, financial, and support people. This gives Brown a base to keep records, receive calls, and be in touch with any changes as they develop. If Brown does his job properly, he will work well with the organizers and they will keep him informed. And, it provides Brown with the opportunity to extend confidentiality and security to the administrative offices. Leaving the marketing and promotion aside, the planning details for the event should be kept confidential and protected from leakage of information to outsiders. This is particularly important if the event is controversial or has had actual threats. In fact, one of Brown's first jobs will be to implement security procedures for the planning and administrative staff.

Brown must implement security procedures from the outset to protect materials, equipment, and buildings earmarked for the event. Depending upon the size and extent of the special event, valuable equipment may be acquired which will need to be warehoused and protected. If special construction is required, security must be provided for the construction materials and the construction site. If donated equipment or materials are acquired, they must be documented and kept secure.

As with all protective assignments, Brown will need to establish up front the procedures for handling expenses and reimbursements incurred in the course of his work for the event. All contracts let by Brown must be reviewed by legal counsel, reviewed, and signed by management. Brown will not sign these contracts since, by so doing, he may become financially liable for them.

Equipment. Brown's plan must include each and every security item which he recommends for purchase, lease, or rental and a date entered as to when it is initiated and completed. Brown may need to secure bids on security equipment. Is it available? Can it be reserved for use on event days and picked up (or delivered) sufficiently in advance to make certain that the security team knows how to use the equipment and make certain that the equipment works? Last minute decisions to purchase equipment can be very costly, as it may be too late to shop for the best prices; or, worse, the equipment may not be available in time for use with the event.

Security Employees. Brown will need to put together a hiring schedule which includes any time needed for training. Brown may need to bring in some employees early in order to provide security for property and equipment and for maintaining the security of the administrative offices. Brown may contract with a guard company to provide security guards or, if not available, Brown may have to hire his own people, do the background checks, and train them. He will certainly need to have his volunteers brought in well in advance of the event for instructions and training. Will security personnel be drug tested?

Volunteers. Brown will need a schedule for volunteers showing how many are needed, where they will be assigned, duties, and when they will be brought in for training and subsequent work. Will Brown have any input in the selection of volunteers, and can he set some standards for their inclusion? For example, will he be allowed to obtain references

and/or background checks on volunteers? Or, is the event so small that everyone knows each other and can vouch for the volunteers?

Policies, Rules, and Job Descriptions. Brown will need to put together some working policies, and to write up job descriptions and job procedures for his security guards and volunteers.

Rules and policies are common sense but, nonetheless, should be put in writing and signed off on by paid employees and volunteers. Rules should include such items as: no drinking of alcoholic beverages on the job; refusal to accept bribes; and agreement to report any crimes or suspicious behavior to management. Other rules should relate to: reporting for duty on time; proper attire; uniform requirements; parking; use of time clocks; turning in lost and found items; relief breaks; meal provisions; and all other behavioral requirements for the job. These rules can be typed up on a single sheet or, for large events and complicated hiring procedures, a simple Policy Manual can be written.

Job descriptions are basic instruments that define a certain job and list the duties assigned to that job. For example, one job might be termed "Ticket Seller," and a simple job description for the job of Ticket Seller should include shifts, hours, locale, and duties. Duties should be written in a how-to style.

Simple job descriptions are better than overly elaborate ones. Job descriptions are wonderfully useful instruments. They make sure that all parties understand what is to be done, and they form the basis for a training program. Job descriptions are essential in labor disputes, job complaints, and disciplinary action.

Training. Training sessions should include an orientation to the event project, a review of rules and policies, a description of job duties, and, in addition, special instruction in safety and security awareness and security procedures which should be followed by all employees and volunteers. For example, all employees and volunteers should either have proof of, or receive, CPR training. All employees and volunteers should be aware of how to fill out an accident report and an incident report. Making all staff part of the safety and security awareness team is essential.

Security guards and volunteers should be trained to look for and report any unsafe conditions such as broken glass, slippery floors, broken equipment, or fences. They should also be instructed to report any persons who appear to be unwell, intoxicated, argumentative, destructive of property, or exhibiting any other behavior which might cause a safety or security problem. Instructions must be very clear as to how to handle situations which might lead to an arrest: dealing or taking drugs; pickpocketing; sneaking into restricted areas; fighting; or attempting to gain entrance without purchasing a ticket. Will security guards have arrest powers or will they only be allowed to report criminal behavior? Will they be permitted to break up fights? If so, what is the liability if someone is hurt, including the security guard?

Security guards and volunteers should be given instruction in conflict avoidance (how to defuse situations) and crowd control. As noted before, sporting events tend to attract violent behavior. A fight can break out at some point that involves hundreds of people, with many hundreds of other people simply trying to escape. Will the security guards be prepared to take measures and what are these measures? The legal aspects of the security guard's job should be thoroughly explained, particularly those aspects which deal with searches, arrests, use of force, and ejection of anyone for good reason.

Volunteers should be carefully instructed in what they are *not* permitted to do. Volunteers should never be placed in positions of potential harm. If volunteers are to be used in searches of ladies' purses or briefcases or are expected to participate in "patdowns," they must be trained to recognize any contraband items.

Security personnel and volunteers should be briefed on emergency procedures for riots, demonstrations, fires, evacuations, bomb threats and searches, armed confrontations, etc.

Security personnel assigned equipment should be trained in the use of the equipment. If electronic equipment or computers are to be used, personnel should be assigned who already know how to use the equipment or can be most easily trained.

Legal Issues. A significant legal issue is that of negligence. One area particularly vulnerable to negligence problems is that of the security guard. This is covered in the chapter on Legal Aspects of the Agent's Job.

Fighting is another potential problem for special events. Every effort must be made to avoid fights and, when unavoidable, to contain the fights. The issue must be addressed in training and reinforced in daily supervision. Security guards should never allow themselves to become a party to a fight, except in circumstances of self defense. If one or both of the fighters initiates an attack, an arrest may be necessary, which is best done by a law enforcement officer. In any case, the fight must be kept at the lowest level possible, both to mitigate injuries and to prevent the fight from spreading.

Ejections fall into categories--immediate ejections and ejections as a last resort after warnings have failed to produce desired results. Reasons for immediate ejections can include: a criminal or lewd act, entering without a ticket, fighting, use of illegal drugs, and excessive intoxication. Lesser reasons tend to fall into the category of public nuisance and/or endangerment and include: continued failure to take an assigned seat, impeding traffic or blocking exits, badgering others, refusal to cooperate with safety and security requests, etc. Ejections are never desirable and, when possible, warnings should be given before taking this action. If a criminal act is involved, a law enforcement officer should be given the task, since an arrest may be necessary.

Arrests by a security guard are classified as

citizens arrests and must be based on a specific incident witnessed by the guard. In some states, detainment can constitute arrest. (If a person is ordered to remain in a specific place, and a reasonable person concludes that he/she cannot leave, this could be interpreted as arrest). The entire matter of arrest is fraught with problems, and arrests should only be performed by a security guard if a law enforcement officer is not available, and the evidence is irrefutable, or failure to arrest could result in endangerment either to the person or another.

Bribes. Brown is aware that, with huge special events, bribes are a special problem, though not such a problem with small, internally controlled events. The corporate picnic is not likely to be vulnerable to bribes. An international event, in the planning stages for two to four years, may be ripe for bribes. Providing security may also mean internal investigations, mostly undercover, of illegal bribes and contract-letting.

Local, State and National Government Officials. Brown will spend a fair amount of his time coordinating with, and building good relationships with, the local establishment. Brown knows that, if agreeable, the city establishment can provide licenses, parking permits, signage, friendly inspections for fire and safety, and cooperation regarding emergency services. Brown may agree to take on a certain number of off-duty policemen to augment the security personnel for the event. Off-duty police personnel offer some real advantages, not the least of which is the "license to carry." If there is a government connection to the event, in terms of security, Brown will need to make connection with the proper authorities. Is the Governor going to make the commencement address? Be assured that his security will be present. Is the Vice President going to be a featured speaker? The Secret Service will have special requirements. Brown will want to coordinate with these people as early on as possible.

If it is a major international event, Brown will spend even more time with local, state, and national government officials, coordinating with them on safety

and security issues. Brown will put together a minutely detailed graph of who is doing what, when, where, who (is in charge), and the reporting structure. For very large events, Brown must be prepared for any safety and security contingencies.

Unions. Union problems are not usually the province of the security people unless the security companies are union-organized. This would be very unusual. However, it is useful to be conversant with union regulations if only to know where there may be some problems in terms of security scheduling and assignment of duties. Union regulations often dictate relief breaks and other aspects of the job.

Access Control. A plan must be developed that will handle access control. This has been covered in some detail in previous chapters. For any events which have received a threat or for which there is the potential for an incident, the site/building may be sealed off several days in advance of the event. Thereafter, access will be tightly controlled for staff, employees, construction people, contractors, and service personnel. A system of identification badges must be developed. Once the area is sealed off, parking should also be restricted. Employees may be requested to leave their cars in outside locations. In very high threat situations, incoming vehicles (delivery trucks, etc.) should be searched.

Crowds, Riots and Demonstrations. For these situations it is to be hoped that the police will be on hand to handle the problems. However, during the planning stages of an event, some consideration must be given to these potential problems. Preventive measures are always preferable to reactive measures.

There are certain factors which can contribute to a riot or an unruly crowd. Alcohol is a contributor, whether it is sold on the premises or sneaked inside. The nature or content of the event may attract a rowdy crowd or can turn a normally quiescent crowd into a swirling mass. This can consist of an entertainer who either deliberately stirs up the crowd by inviting them on the stage or who taunts the audience with obscene language, insults, and/or sexual language and gestures. The advertising for an event, if it promises or hints at overheated attractions, can pull in a crowd just waiting for something to happen. If the music is extremely loud with sound effects or hysterical lighting, and the lyrics contain violence, it can stir up the crowd to assaultive behavior. If any or all of these factors are known in advance, preventive measures can be taken, and extra security provided for the event.

There are some basic rules for handling crowds. The event should not be oversold, if at all possible, and should never exceed the legal allowable limit of people. The Fire Department inspectors can be helpful in determining crowd capacity, and notices are usually posted in buildings which list the maximum number of people allowed legally within an area. The crowd should be channeled properly, with clear signage, wide access aisles, and clearly marked exits. There should be an adequate number of exits, unlocked or equipped with panic bars, and unobstructed. Exits should flow either outdoors or into hallways which allow easy egress to the outside. If at all possible, entrances and exits should be separated so that, in the event of a mass exodus, the crowd does not trample on people coming inside.

Crowds should never be allowed to bunch up. There should be tickets for sections which are clearly marked and separated, so that the crowd is broken into smaller segments. If there is a problem in one section, it can be contained there. It is much harder to do this outdoors. Security personnel and volunteer ushers should be uniformed or attired in a clearly defined manner, trained to detect trouble in

advance and to maintain a calm posture in the face of trouble. A good loudspeaker system is essential to give instructions and to calm the crowd. Troublemakers should be spotted and pointed out to security who should *quietly* remove them. Uniformed police may be a deterrent. It is very helpful to have additional security personnel (not in uniform) mingling with the crowd, looking for potential problems.

Controlling the crowds to make certain they don't turn into mobs is essential. It is wise to understand that a crowd, even a friendly crowd, can turn into a hostile mob with the wrong treatment. There is a delicate line which should be drawn in dealing with crowds. If there is one or more troublemakers, the line is drawn at when to deal with the troublemaker, and how. Too much force in ejecting this problem may turn a friendly crowd into a hostile mob. On the other hand, failing to take action when a bully intimidates others can unleash other troublemakers in the crowd. Adequate staffing and training are essential.

Other. There are, obviously, many aspects of event security to be considered. It is an area of expertise which is closely akin to the protection agent's job. There is a similarity between event planning and threat modeling, contingency planning, and crisis management. Special event security, therefore, is an opportunity and a challenge to the protection agent. A number of experienced executive protection agents have gravitated to special event security as a specialty.

SPECIAL EVENT CORPORATION
JOB DESCRIPTION

Job Title: Ticket Seller   **Location:** Front gate ticket cage
Shift: Day   **Hours:** 8:00 a.m. - 5:00 p.m.
Reports to: Ticket Seller Supervisor

DUTIES FOR DAY SHIFT

- Reports for work at the central ticket office at 8:00 a.m.

- Picks up and signs for assigned number of tickets, listed by numbers.

- Picks up, counts, and signs for cash bank of $500.00. Bank is broken down as $300.00 in one-dollar bills, $100.00 in five-dollar bills, and $50.00 each in ten-dollar and twenty-dollar bills.

- Reports to ticket cage at 8:15, sets up counter, and is ready to greet customers at 8:30 a.m.

- Sells tickets and makes correct change. Leaves customer's currency on top of the cash drawer until change has been handed to customer and transaction is completed.

- Lunch break is provided from 12:00 noon to 1:15 p.m., allowing fifteen minutes for work-related activities. Signs tickets over to relief person, noting beginning and ending ticket numbers. (Relief person will provide his/her own bank.) Takes bank to central office and turns it in together with numbers of tickets sold. Bank is counted and countersigned.

- Picks up bank after recounting and countersigning and reports for work in the ticket cage by 1:15 p.m. Accepts tickets from relief person and notes ticket numbers.

- Closes ticket office at 4:30 p.m. Turns in bank after counting and countersigning. Turns in tickets, noting beginning and ending numbers.

- Over-and-under numbers in the bank should not exceed $20.00; losses and excesses which occur more than twice will be subject to disciplinary action.

- Any complaints which cannot be handled and completed quickly should be turned over to the Ticket Seller Supervisor on duty. All personnel will deal courteously and helpfully with customers at all times, even if complaint seems unreasonable.

- If ticket seller detects any suspicious behavior such as anyone trying to sneak inside without paying, or intoxicated, or hostile and threatening, he/she should immediately notify a supervisor or a security guard.

Every book on the market dealing with executive protection (insofar as we have found) refers to protection agents as males. It is true that, traditionally, men have filled the ranks of bodyguards. However, in today's world, women are making inroads into this male-dominated field and doing so very capably. We asked three successful female agents to give us their comments and advice about this field. We asked them to tell it "the way it is" for female protection agents. We are indebted to these women for this chapter, which they wrote.

WOMEN AS PROTECTORS
By Sharon Frink and Shanti Khalsa

Only since the early 1980's have women had career opportunities in executive protection. Although, traditionally, a man's profession--a *BIG* man with forearms the size of my thighs and knuckles that drag the ground when he walks--the need for women protection professionals has resulted in the integration of women into this vocation. This is a career with many rewards and many hardships.

The role that women play in executive protection is varied. While it is true that opportunities do exist, the facts are that these types of jobs are not plentiful. You will need to seek out any opportunity as an entrance into the business, even if the pay is not what you expect, then build your reputation and your contacts so that you will be offered a broader range of employment over time. It is hard but not impossible, and is certainly a career worth the effort.

The Advantages of the Female Protector

Today, there are many more women business executives and public figures who require protection, especially when traveling. Since the single most important goal of bodyguarding is security, the luxury of privacy and modesty must sometimes be sacrificed

when men are assigned to protect women. This is not a problem when the bodyguard is a woman. Many women executives feel it is less of an invasion of privacy to have a female protector who can accompany them to the gym, the restroom, and other gender-specific activities.

It is lower profile and less expensive to hire a female bodyguard who can share the hotel room. It is socially safer for a female political person to share a close proximity to a female rather than a male bodyguard, as it reduces the risk of gossip and scandal.

When a male bodyguard has close-quarter contact with a woman protectee for an extended period of time, several problems can develop. Some women are so independent and stubborn that they ignore a male bodyguard's directives for their security and try to evade him. Others will sexually taunt and tease the bodyguard, setting him up for an infraction of security policy or sexual assault charges. Still others may have so little self-esteem as to be uncooperative in threatening situations and jeopardize their own and their bodyguard's security. Assigning a woman to protect a woman can create a more productive and professional bond between the protector and protectee.

Clients who are of an orthodox religious orientation may require female protectors by protocol for the women in the principal detail. In this situation, you become part of a larger team, and your area of responsibility will be hands-off to the male members of the detail.

Security details that include children will often need female protectors. Women more often have certain skills with children that many men lack. Don't confuse this with babysitting or child care. It is not. Children are prime targets for kidnapping, and your role as protector is a serious one. This is an excellent opportunity to display your professionalism and, as a result, to be considered for further work.

Also, as in my case, a male principal may require a protector that doesn't *look* like a bodyguard. I started out as a secretary and my boss told me that, if I got security training, he would use me as a bodyguard. I did, and he did, and now that is my main career focus.

The characteristics that make a good bodyguard are often the traits expected of the female gender. Generally speaking, women are very organized people. It is part of our early childhood training. We have good attention to detail and the ability to conceive a plan in a comprehensive manner. Women are also very intuitive. I have used my intuition on numerous occasions to identify perpetrators and avoid confrontation. It is not that men are incapable of the skills of organization and intuition; in fact, those men who excel in these two areas are the leaders of our industry. But, it is my opinion that these are natural gifts of women that can easily be put to professional use.

Disadvantages to Overcome

Executive protection is traditionally a man's field of work, and there is a social stigma to overcome for a woman to be a success. It requires a great deal of professionalism and self confidence to combat the existing prejudice. Recognize the problem and embrace it. Be hungry for work, work hard when you get it, and never rest on your achievements. Don't let anyone discredit or demean you, but avoid reacting defensively when you encounter this. Respond with dignity and professionalism.

Only in North America and Western Europe have women risen in social status to even be considered for protection work. Be sensitive to this when working outside of these geographic areas. Play the male game of domination because, if you fight it head-on, you risk losing. You are smart or you wouldn't have qualified for this job, so work around the social limitations placed on female protectors in

foreign countries. It doesn't matter if a man thinks he is bigger/badder/meaner/stronger as long as you get your mission accomplished, which is the safety and comfort of the principal. This may mean using a male intermediary when dealing with police, military, or government officials instead of doing it yourself.

You may be posing in the role of nanny, mother, sister, or confidant, but don't allow your "cover" to become a detriment to security. Your demeanor need not be gruff and uncompromising; you can honestly say, "I'd really like to talk with you, but right now it's very important that I pay attention to the road (or the window, or the crowd)." If you have developed a proper professional rapport with your principal, she will understand and cooperate.

Another cover for your presence may be that of secretary and, to the extent that you must play the role convincingly, you will have to engage in secretarial duties. Don't, however, let those duties compromise your security function.

Gender Differences--Physical

Generally speaking, I am smaller, lighter, and not as strong as my male counterparts, but I do not allow this to become a significant factor in my safety and that of my client. By dealing with the reality of this, you find ways to overcome it. Your first responsibility is to avoid confrontations and maintain the comfort and safety of your client. But when it cannot be avoided, then develop the confidence, aggression, and proper timing to compensate for being shorter and lighter than your adversary. Know your physical limitations and work around them. Regularly practice martial arts with men bigger than you are so that you can learn to accurately judge a developing situation of physical violence. Use your equipment (gun, baton, etc.) at the appropriate time in the confrontation to ensure your success. Be very skilled with your equipment, because this may serve as your equalizer.

Because of my body shape, carrying a concealed weapon is a challenge. When wearing a shoulder holster or a concealed belt holster, the outline of the weapon may be visible to the watchful eye. When you are carrying a legal, concealed weapon, this is not a big problem. However, the reality of protection in the private sector is that most of the time, you are not in a situation where a concealed weapon is legal. I am not advising you to illegally carry a concealed weapon, nor am I endorsing this activity. However, in those times when I have made the decision to do so, I carry my gun in a custom-made handbag or hipsack, depending on the situation.

Working 12 or more hours on a protection detail can be a real problem during your menstrual period. If it is convenient for you to arrange your days off for the heavy days of your period, do so. However, it will be to your disadvantage to have the reputation of being unavailable for work during your period. And if you are on an extended out-of-town job, you will likely have no choice in the matter. Stay in good shape physically so that your periods are short and manageable. For days that you cannot get to a bathroom regularly, figure out a solution that works for you. If possible, pack high protein food with you and eat small amounts at regular intervals to keep your temperament even. Work with it, and don't involve others in your drama because you will be quickly criticized.

In countries outside the United States, Canada and Western Europe, public bathrooms for women are rare or nonexistent. If you are working for a female principal, then you have a joint problem which you can solve together. But if you are working for a male principal, you have a singular and serious problem. You can expect to go 12 to 14 hours without having the chance to relieve yourself. On these types of trips you have to reduce your liquid intake to accommodate the situation. In other words, drink almost nothing from the time you wake up until the end of your shift. This is not healthy for extended periods of time, so make a point of rehydrating at the end of your shift each day. Pack natural laxatives because constipation is an unwelcome side effect of restricting your fluid intake. In extreme situations, wear adult diapers. It sounds ridiculous, but it is not. What is really ridiculous is wetting your pants when

all the guys on your team get to pee into a bottle. And again, keep this drama to yourself. You will not be given sympathy, only ridicule.

Sexual Harassment

Sexual harassment, discrimination, and stereotyping are facts that you will live with from the first day on duty to the last. You must develop a thick skin and a personal professionalism that will carry you through these experiences and, hopefully, will make it easier for the next generation of women protection specialists. You will hear from secretaries, staff members, and spouses of the principal that a man, or worse, a "professional," would be better suited for the job than you. If you can make light of it, tell them you are a "200-pound Marine in camouflage," and if you can't, tell them you will "look into it." But never, never react to these comments. They are spoken from ignorance. If the principal felt that way, you would not have been hired in the first place. Your actions and your contribution to the mission will prove them right or wrong.

Because you are female, you may be asked to perform domestic or secretarial tasks which are outside of your protective duties. Like male bodyguards who are asked to carry luggage, you are obliged to politely refrain from these activities and keep security first. If these duties are directly for the principal and in no way interfere with your protective duties, then the choice is yours. But if these tasks compromise your ability to protect, then politely but firmly turn them down. Don't take it personally or allow it to make you insecure. This will happen throughout your career, so maintain a professional demeanor.

Sexual harassment from peers or employees of the principal which is intended to embarrass or intimidate you should do neither. Filing a complaint is your right, and you may choose to do so. But that could result in drying up your work opportunities, because you become unfairly known as a liability instead of an asset. Here again, a thick skin comes in handy. If possible, ignore it. Avoid making a joke of the situation unless you truly find it funny. If it is too serious to ignore or if it interferes with your ability to perform, take the "high road" and turn the humiliation back on the perpetrator by exposing the aggression for what it is. Above all, be on guard and keep yourself safe.

If the harassment is from your client, draw a very firm line. You cannot protect your client and simultaneously have any kind of a sexual relationship with him. It is a no-win situation, and to succumb to sexual pressure will never save your job, it will only ruin your professional reputation. If you are firm in this, you have a good chance of cooling off your client. If he won't take "no" for an answer, then find another client.

Sexual assault is another reality of this business. You are out there on the other side of the safety line, and rape is an ugly possibility to be faced. If you are a rape survivor, then you know what I am talking about. If you've avoided this topic in the past, face it now. Head on. Read about it, talk to rape victims, contact your local rape crisis center, and expose yourself mentally and emotionally to this topic. Be an expert. You become a danger to yourself and your mission if you either deny the possibility of rape or give in to hysteria out of fear of rape. Instead, be aware, alert, and listen to your keen intuition. That will go a long way in keeping you safe. You may be discriminated against by well-meaning males who try to keep you out of the action because of the possibility of rape. If you have faced this topic in your own soul, you will be able to stand your ground.

Dress for Duress

Professional dress for a female protection specialist is a combination of practical and appropriate. You must look consistent with your purported role, but clothing that inhibits your ability to move, such as straight skirts and high heels, will prevent you from doing your job. Choose clothes such as jackets, medium-length skirts full enough for wide strides, or dress pants, and low or flat shoes with good soles. If you can't run and fight in your clothes, then you are wearing the wrong style.

Keep jewelry to a minimum, although wearing a wedding band is advised (even if there is not a husband attached to it). Necklaces and earrings that dangle can be used as tools against you in a physical confrontation. Avoid bracelets that jingle, but wrist jewelry that aids in preventing wrist locks are appropriate and recommended.

Cosmetics should be kept at a minimum and perfume should be eliminated. You are seeking a low profile and should not draw attention to your physical appearance. Realize that your hair can be grabbed in a physical confrontation. It should be a simple style that allows you to wake up and be out the door in a minimum amount of time, will not obstruct your vision in high wind, and cannot be used against you in a fight.

Night clothes, such as tee-shirt and sweat pants, should allow you to deal with any situation in the event of an emergency. Also, plans may change mid-trip and you may find yourself sleeping in a foyer, on a couch, or in a hotel hall.

Communication and Relations

With your peers, your communication should be confident, reserved, and professional. With your subordinates, learn to give orders with an even tone, clear enunciation, and simple syntax. With your superiors, receive orders and report information with a manner that inspires respect and transmits your inner confidence. Make an effort to stay informed in all aspects of the detail so that your communication can be accurate and informed. But do not indulge in gossip about non-essential or personal details. Arrange to conduct briefings and other business with male associates in the command post or other public places. To avoid problems, keep this activity out of your hotel room.

For your own benefit and the success of the team, refrain from personal or sexual relationships with anyone connected to the protection detail. This includes team members, the client, or the client's employees and associates. Sometimes a job might last for months and, in the stress of the situation, it is natural for relationships to occur. But these will inevitably result in disappointment for you or worse. Complications arising from sexual relations on duty can abruptly end your future in executive protection. If you feel driven to pursue a relationship, wait until you are no longer professionally connected to that person.

Executive Protection as a Career

There are some realities to be considered before investing time and effort into an executive protection career. Not the least of which is your expectations for marriage and children. One is not exclusive of the other but, like most demanding careers, it is difficult to sustain both simultaneously. Because you are under a great deal of stress and away from home for long periods of time, it is a challenge to maintain a stable relationship and home life. This requires a very giving and supportive spouse.

You must maintain a reasonable level of fitness and training. This is critical to your stamina and to your ability to keep yourself and your client safe. Between the ages of 35 and 40, the long hours and physical demands force many people, men and women, out of the profession unless they have rigorously maintained their physical fitness and stamina. Bodyguards over 40 are those who have been able to keep themselves at physical and mental excellence.

Certainly, security work is rewarding and exciting. The sacrifices made are more than compensated for by the benefits received. As a woman, you gain a rare confidence and self respect that will serve you throughout life. Through your travel and business contacts, you expose yourself to a variety of opportunities and advantages. And friendships forged under situations of hardship are very enduring. I certainly wish you the best of luck and success in your career.

Sharon Frink provided protection for high-ranking corporate, government, and diplomatic clients for nearly a decade. She was a paramedic and a bodyguard, and carried with her both a stethoscope and a gun. She currently runs an investigation firm in the southwestern United States and is active in professional security associations and public safety.

Shanti Khalsa has worked in executive protection since 1982. Her clients have been male, female, and children both in this country, Europe, and the Far East.

FEMALE AGENTS
by Judith M. Robinson

Perhaps the place to start in talking about female agents is to make some comparisons with male agents. Generally, women's minds are grid-like, men's linear. Women tend to see the entire situation with its ramifications and leads. Men tend to take care of the immediate situation without regard to the consequences. Neither is right nor wrong. Women do well at interrogations because of their mind-set, the tendency to listen to a story and wonder what if-- how come--yes, but. They are also disarming when interviewing men when they can make use of MPS, the Male Power Syndrome, which makes men believe they are smarter, trickier, and able to fool others-- women especially. This female mind-set also produces good advance work. Women naturally want to fill in all the squares in the grid. They will more easily think of all contingencies before the event, leaving fewer surprises.

Women generally have better small muscle coordination. Their smaller physical size can be useful in performing chokeholds, and they are often better shooters than men, once they have conquered the initial shooting trauma. Women are usually more flexible than men, allowing greater ease of evasive movement; the smaller female size is easier to fit into tight spaces.

Females are often easier to train than males; not having MPS, they come to training with a more open mind. The social conditioning that trains women to please and to be dependent upon others prepares them to be more aware of their surroundings, including the intentions of the people around them. This skill is useful in an executive protection proactive environment.

Women have two speeds--off, and kill. They will go into a mother bear mode to protect their client. In terrorist groups, women are frequently the assassins. Still, females are not perceived to be as threatening as males and are easier to disguise in a low profile detail. They are able to defuse situations that arise without resorting to intimidation and force, an important asset to protection work.

Problems

The problems female agents encounter are those that women in a male dominated society encounter generally. They need to be more qualified than a male to be taken seriously by a client or a detail leader. They need to know that there is a double standard for women. Men communicate differently than women, and women are misunderstood by the males they work with. Most men in protection work do not believe women can do the job, that they don't have the stamina. So, women must work longer hours, volunteer more, and not show any sign of stress of fatigue.

Usually, it is impossible to be one of the guys. The men on most details will keep women out of the information loop. They will sometimes gossip about the women and watch for any mistake. They will not cover for the woman and will try to blame her for things that go wrong. In the male hierarchy, females are at the bottom of the ladder and will be treated that way. The answer is for women to be always super-professional in actions, words, and dress. Do not appear to threaten in any way; don't talk about your martial arts training, your shooting scores, your weapons collection, and don't know too much about sports. Women need to keep their guard up at all times, learn as much as possible about how men operate, and never take anything personally. The predominate male attitude is, "No matter how much training, you can't make a donkey into a racehorse."

Dress

As a woman, you can never dress too well. Constantly upgrade your wardrobe. Buy your shoes one size larger than usual because you will be on your feet for long hours. Wear flat heels whenever possible. Buy clothes you can run in. Have jackets for every outfit. When working for clients from other cultures, respect their customs. With Middle Easterners, start out with longer skirts and wear blouses with sleeves until you determine how westernized they may be. Be conservative in your dress, blend in with your client, get clothes with pockets, and have your dress belts handmade so they are heavy enough to carry a gun without looking like a gun belt.

Carrying Concealed

Women and Guns magazine has invaluable information about holsters, guns that are easy to conceal, manufacturers of purse-holsters, and general information that is very useful for females in protection work. Women are usually more comfortable with shoulder holsters, but you need to try different things on your particular body shape to determine what is most comfortable for you. Belly-band holsters also work well for most women. Belts on skirts help distribute the weight of a gun. The current loose jacket styles are great for concealing, and just being a woman keeps people from giving you the same scrutiny (for a gun) which a man would receive.

Relating to the Client

There is only one thing to say on this subject--be professional! Completely and at all times. Clients tend to be erratic. A wise old executive protection agent once said, "In this business you get ahead not by how fast you can shoot but how much s--- you can take."

Job Opportunities

There are fewer job opportunities than for men. Having a concealed weapons permit is a great help in securing jobs. You must network constantly. Still, if you are prepared to work hard, market yourself, and do the job, it can be a very satisfying career. Breaking into the executive protection field is akin to breaking into law enforcement, fire fighting, and many of the other traditionally male dominated career fields. As time goes by, inevitably more and more women will enter the field and prove their worth. Good luck!

Judith Robinson is a graduate of Executive Security International (ESI), and is a credit both to her gender and her profession. Judith raised five children on her own before trading in her mother career for one in executive protection. She lives in the southwestern United States and has served on a number of executive protection details.

The subjects of protocol, etiquette, and the social and working interrelationships between client and protection agent are very important. The protection agent is expected to provide top level protection and, at the same time, allow the client to enjoy his or her life style with as little interruption as possible.

Good manners are part of working smart. Anyone who doesn't understand this issue would be more successful seeking employment elsewhere. How the agent looks, appears, speaks, conducts himself and herself, and interrelates with others will, in large measure, determine his and her success in the field of executive protection. The executive or dignitary may not want protection and has accepted it only from necessity. In order to get the job done, the agent must win the respect of the client, which means looking and acting like someone the client is used to being with. The client does not want to be embarrassed among his friends and associates by having someone following him around who looks dreadful and acts worse.

If manners, etiquette, and protocol do not come easily to you, there are a number of excellent books on the market which cover the subjects in detail. Most of the books on the market today deal with modern manners, the manners and etiquette practiced in the business, social, and personal environments of today's world. Modern manners also include the special etiquette required in dealing at an international scope. James Bond would fit right in!

In the turbulent 60's and early 70's, manners, along with other "establishment" customs, were largely rejected by young people who later entered the executive world and found themselves at a clear disadvantage. In the past few years, a new emphasis on manners and protocol has arisen in the business world. Women have entered the executive chambers in increasing numbers, and U.S. business is now heavily invested with foreign entities. Thus, some of the rules have changed, and etiquette has adapted to these new situations. Manners are no longer as rigid as they were 20 years ago, but they are as important. In major corporations across the country, executives are going back to school to learn business and social etiquette. To be lacking in this area is to limit your potential.

Many executives and private individuals feel they cannot afford to employ an agent strictly for protection. The same holds true for corporations. A protection agent who is equipped to function in other areas (executive assistant, personal assistant, etc.) and who has the appearance and manners to blend in with the workplace, has an excellent advantage.

Manners and good behavior are an integral part of interpersonal relationships. The way in which we deal with each other spells the difference, and often determines the outcome, between success and failure. Protection agents often encounter resentment on the part of co-workers who may perceive the agent as a barrier between them and the boss. This problem can be greatly reduced by a conscious effort on the part of the agent to deal in a sensitive and mannerly fashion with co-workers. The agent must never be the cause of problems; rather, he should be a problem solver.

There are instances when the protection agent may have to bend the rules of etiquette to provide the best security for the protectee. For example, a gentleman normally allows a woman, the boss, or a senior executive to enter a door or room first; however, a good security agent will almost always precede the protectee into a "strange" room, to be certain that there are no problems. You will undoubtedly learn much of this on your own. Whenever you find that you must breach the rules of etiquette, it helps to quietly explain your action to the protectee in advance, if possible. There will be other instances when you will have to sacrifice maximum security for the sake of the protectee's comfort. For example, if the protectee is the guest speaker at a banquet, you may not be allowed to stand or sit close to him or her. You will simply have to cope with a less than perfect situation, weighing the potential risks and striking a balance between security and comfort.

APPEARANCE

The agent must fit into the client's world and, therefore, should take his cue as to clothing style from the client. Since the preponderance of clients are older and successful, their clothing will undoubtedly be of a conservative nature and expensive. Of course, if the client is a rock star who spends half his time on the road, the correct clothing will be more casual. For the most part, however, the agent's clothing will be business wear. For the men, this means suits and ties; for female agents, suits, conservative dresses, skirts, blouses, and jackets.

Investing in a Wardrobe--Men

Clothing is an investment, always, and this certainly holds true for the executive protection agent. You are going to have to spend enough money to buy clothing of very good quality. If you intend to make top dollar, you have to look like top dollar.

If you feel that you need help in spending your hard-earned dollars for the right clothes, you may choose to put yourself in the hands of the experts, the top salesmen and saleswomen in a top quality store. These people are the reality experts. They know quality and style--not the sometimes far-out styles you see in fashion magazines. The clothes you see in the magazines are apt to be overly trendy and chosen for their dramatic characteristics. It is in the stores that you will see the real clothes. This is particularly true with men's stores, where the average salesman has worked there for ten years or longer, has seen styles come and go, and can steer you in the right direction. The salesman will oversee the fitting and alterations and help you pick the right shirt and

tie. Men's stores and their salesmen take the long view. They build customer loyalty by giving the right advice.

Women have a tougher time. Women's stores tend to be more trendy. The fashions change dramatically with bewildering speed. Still, with diligence, one can find a good store with a sensible, long-time salesperson who will be invaluable in steering the female client beyond fashion to the right selections, the dresses and suits that are timeless in look and quality.

Business suits for men are available in three ways. Off-the-rack suits are often excellent choices if you have a good physical build and you insist on alterations to make the fit perfect. If off-the-rack won't work, there are semi-custom and custom-made suits which are more expensive, but which can be cut and fitted to any shape or form. Custom suits are, naturally, more expensive. To be avoided are the so-called designer suits, the ones with the little nipped-in waists that look like they belong on an Italian movie star.

Single-breasted suits are the only way to go for the male protection agent. Double-breasted suit jackets must be kept buttoned at all times or, with the extra material hanging in front, they look dreadful. If the agent is carrying a gun, he needs a single-breasted suit. Besides, single-breasted jackets are slimming.

There is nothing quite like a fine all-wool suit; however, there are now available some excellent wool and synthetic blends which make a good appearance and are easy to maintain. A fabric should have a fine appearance, be resistant to wrinkling, have the inherent strength to hold its shape, and be easy to maintain through brushing, spot cleaning, and pressing.

To be on the safe side, stick to dark blue and grey as suit and jacket colors, either plain or pin-striped; these colors are acceptable in almost any business circumstances and, in a pinch, will be acceptable at a black tie affair. In the south, or in a more relaxed environment, beige is acceptable.

Alterations are usually needed to make the fit of a suit perfect. The jacket should fit smoothly across the back and not stand away from the shirt collar. When you are standing still, the jacket should not pull or wrinkle. Wrinkles are a sign that something is not fitted properly. The vent, or vents, should hang smoothly, not gaping open. One mark of a good suit is the way in which the sleeves are fitted. It is the most difficult part of fitting a suit. When you move your arms in a jacket the sleeves should not hike up or pull. Sleeve length is at the wrist bone. If the suit has a vest, the vest must be fitted as well as the pants and jacket. The most noticeable flaws in a poorly fitted vest are wrinkles across the tummy and gaposis at the armhole; the vest should fit smoothly under the arms. Pants should hang smoothly and not gap. The length of the inseam (crotch seam) and the length of the pant must be correct. Pants should be long enough to "break" slightly across the top of the shoe in front, and to hang slightly longer in back. If in doubt, it is better for pants to hang one-quarter to one-half inch longer all around than to be too short. An important tip for getting the best fit in your alterations is to wear the shoes and shirt (or at least the same weight and fabric of shirt) which you intend to wear with the suit. Also, if you will be carrying a gun, it is very important to have the suit fitted while you are wearing the gun. It may necessitate a slightly larger jacket to conceal the weapon and still appear presentable.

Shirts are simple; choose good quality white or pastel, long-sleeved, and well fitted shirts. Custom-made shirts are not as expensive as you might think, and because they are well fitted and lie smoothly under a suit, they are worth every penny. A shirt may have button cuffs or more formal french cuffs (which require cuff links). Sleeves should be long enough to extend about one-half inch to one inch beyond the jacket sleeve. Cotton is the fabric of choice, winter and summer. Silk and other shiny soft fabrics simply do not have the crisp look needed for business. Shirts with or without tab collars are acceptable.

Buy the best ties you can afford. Silk ties are wonderful; they look beautiful and they are easy to tie, although there are some combination silk and synthetic ties on the market which are quite good. Be certain that the material is thin enough to tie without bulk. Consult with a good salesman as to the current fashion in ties--wide vs. narrow, etc. While bow ties are a matter of personal preference, they tend to make the wearer look either young or professorial. Because they are unusual, they attract attention and are not as low profile and conservative as is most desirable for an agent. Very tall men need extra-long ties, which can generally be bought off the counter but may have to be custom-made. Plain and printed ties are acceptable, and paisleys of muted colors are always correct.

Shoes are of great importance for looks and comfort. An agent spends many hours on his feet, so shoes that can be polished and have a soft, thick sole for solid footing are most desirable. Laced shoes are more conservative, but slip-on shoes are perfectly acceptable. Black is the color of choice since it will go with any other color except brown. Investing in good shoes is as important as investing in good clothes, since shoes are always in view. Good shoes will last for years if maintained properly with new heels and soles, polish, waterproofing, and a pair of shoe trees lodged inside them at night to hold the shape. Some manufacturers of sports shoes are now designing good-looking, comfortable walking shoes which are acceptable for daytime wear with suits. Socks should match the color of the suit and should be long enough to cover the calf of the leg; this avoids the possibility of showing bare leg when sitting, a definite breach of etiquette.

Jewelry for men and women should be less rather than more. A good watch, a class ring, a wedding band, cuff links, studs for a dress shirt; that's about all that is recommended for a man in business. Belts should match shoes in color and should be strong and of good quality. If the agent carries a gun, his belt and holster must be compatible in fit and appearance.

There are other articles of clothing needed to round out the minimum wardrobe of the male agent. A good rain-resistant trench coat, plus a winter overcoat, are needed items. Sports coats for casual occasions are acceptable attire with a plain shirt, tie, and pants. For winter, a pullover v-neck sweater is another acceptable piece of casual clothing. For special circumstances (client on vacation), appropriate sports clothes may be needed, which could include anything from snorkeling gear to skiwear, blue jeans, and black tie.

Black tie occasions require a special form of dress. If the occasions upon which you will be required to appear in formal dress are few, and because good tuxedos are expensive, you may choose to rent rather than buy. However, if a tuxedo is to be part of your life, invest in the purchase of a good one. Black-tie evening wear means a black jacket with matching pants in good (lightweight wool) fabric. The suit is usually trimmed with a stripe of satin or grosgrain. The jacket can be single or double breasted. The shirt is white, front-pleated (no ruffles!) with small fold down collar. The bow tie and cummerbund can be black (traditional) or red. A vest can be worn in place of the cummerbund. A double breasted suit does not require a vest or cummerbund. Shirt studs and cuff links are an elegant touch although white dress shirts have quite acceptable pearl buttons. Many agents wear suspenders (called "braces") with their tuxedos to keep the trousers in place and support the weight of a hand gun. Black dress shoes and black socks complete the ensemble.

Investing in a Wardrobe--Women

The basic rules of dress are the same for male and female agents. Dress conservatively for a low profile, invest in the best quality you can afford, and choose non-trendy, timeless fashions. Female agents have one disadvantage, in that it is harder to carry a concealed weapon than it is for men. Women's suits are generally too form fitted and jackets are too short to provide concealed cover; and, of course, a dress allows no room for a concealed weapon. Pants on women in business have been out of fashion for several years, but the latest fashion magazines indicate that they may be back "in." Suits, dresses, dresses with jackets, skirts with blouses, and jackets all are good choices.

It is not necessary to appear overly mannish. Suits and dresses should have a professional appearance, but it is a mistake to try to look like a female version of a man. It should be obvious that frilly clothes, sequins, plunging necklines, and brilliant colors are poor choices since they call attention to the wearer (often unflatteringly).

It is important to have clothes that fit well and are properly maintained. Whatever the fashion in hemlines, mini-skirt to ankle-length, you are better off selecting a length that is attractive for you and is midway between extremes. Mini-skirts should be a definite "no" for work, and ankle-length skirts are cumbersome (try to run in one!). Accessories can be very useful in changing the appearance of a plain suit or dress; however, loose, dangling scarves and accessories are a problem. Clothes should be anchored so that no fussing or tugging is needed to keep them smoothly in line. Jewelry should be kept to a minimum. A good pair of earrings, watch, small ring, pearl necklace, small pin; these are elegant items and are always in good taste. Dangling earrings and bright costume jewelry are distractions best left for leisure hours.

Shoes should be attractive but conservative, and *comfortable*. You will be on your feet for many hours at a stretch, and you never know when you may have to jog trot or run with your client firmly in tow. This precludes high, spikey heels and thin soles. Fortunately, in this health conscious society, sensible shoes can be found that are attractive and can be polished. While expensive, real leather is great. It looks good for years, can be polished to a lovely sheen, and bespeaks quality. If you are going to invest in good shoes, you must keep them in good repair. Heels and soles should be replaced at the first obvious signs of wear. Shoe trees are great for maintaining the shape of shoes overnite.

For black-tie occasions, women have a choice of wearing a short cocktail dress or full length dress. A female agent should take her cue from the client as to which is preferable. As always, the dress and shoes should be comfortable and allow for movement. Accessories, make-up, and jewelry should be low key.

Casual wear while accompanying the client on a vacation or week-end can run the gamut from shorts, ski wear, hiking clothes, and bathing suits to skirts, blouses, and lightweight jackets.

Grooming and Personal Appearance

Surely everyone agrees that personal hygiene is absolutely essential in business, but just to be on the safe side, let's cover the issue. Daily baths, a deodorant, clean hair smoothly styled, teeth well maintained to prevent mouth odor, and clean clothes are a necessity 100% of the time. Clothing must be fresh, clean, with no rips and tears, well fitted, and comfortable. Shoes must be polished and well heeled and soled. If the agent's job includes frequent travel, clothes should be selected with their maintenance in mind. Adequate dry cleaning may not be always available within the time frame of the agent's schedule. Clothes which are wrinkle-resistant are a godsend. Every agent should have in his and her personal bag a small portable steam iron, a small cleaning kit, and a compact sewing kit to reattach buttons and mend small rips. If you do not know how to perform small sewing chores--learn!

Hair should be styled so that it does not require tugging, combing, and preening. Styling should be conservative. Although some men like to wear their hair long, or pulled back in a ponytail, they should reconsider. Very, very few clients wear *their* hair in a ponytail (unless they work in the entertainment industry), and they do not work with people who wear ponytails; hence, they prefer their security agents to wear their hair in a style that looks more like the people they associate with every day. Women with long blowing hair may look attractive, but they may also appear frivolous or self-preoccupied. Hair should be as close as possible to "wash-and-wear," since long shifts and short nights leave little time for elaborate hair styling. Facial hair is another matter. Neat beards are, sort of, acceptable, better if they are on an older man and enhance his appearance. Some clients have no-beard rules in their workplace, and the agent should

comply.

Many people do not realize how distracting and downright annoying some personal "grooming" habits can be. Here is a short list of things to avoid:

.   Touching one's hair (comb it in the morning before leaving, or in the bathroom-- otherwise, keep your hands away from your hair).

.   Stroking one's mustache or beard (maddening--a preening gesture that seems overly ego-centered).

.   Rubbing one's bald head (even worse than preening one's mustache--looks like a baboon).

.   Rubbing one's face or body for any reason (keep your hands away from your body--no scratching, thoughtful nose rubs, thoughtful tummy rubs, picking at ears, noses, or complexions).

.   Slouching (stand up straight--it looks more professional and it's better for your health--you will tire more easily if you slouch).

.   Nail biting and picking at one's cuticle (looks like a child).

.   Chewing gum (ugly).

.   Loud honking and blowing of one's nose (disgusting).

.   Sneezing without the use of a handkerchief (equally disgusting).

.   Squirming and constantly moving while seated (childish).

.   Drumming fingers on a surface, and waving one's foot like St. Vitus Dance (very distracting--sit *still*).

.   Constantly using one's hands to "talk"--jabbing, pointing, and waving them (keep quiet, be smooth and professional).

Demeanor and Conduct

Demeanor is "the manner in which one behaves or bears oneself," according to the dictionary. The old style demeanor of the agent was tough-guy, heavy-handed, and mean-talking. The demeanor that the professional agent wants to portray is very different. The new demeanor is that of the U.S. Secret Service--polite, professional, efficient, capable, mannerly, and able to blend in with the client's world. Demeanor is our perception of another individual, how that individual appears to us. Demeanor is the sum total of his appearance and bearing.

Conduct, on the other hand, is more precisely how a person behaves, acts, and relates to others. The agent's conduct will tell others whether he is trustworthy, competent, and professional. Does he treat corporate and family matters confidentially? Is he pleasant to be around? Does he have good work habits? Is he a facilitator and problem-solver or a pain in the neck? Are her manners such that she is an embarrassment?

Here are some of the more glaring conduct flaws which can sink the agent's career:

. Pretends to know it all, and has an answer-- no, a *suggestion*--for everything.

. Isn't around when you need him.

. Is around and underfoot all the time, making life difficult for other staff.

. Tries to get special perks, such as personal parking space, all touted as necessary for the protection of the client.

. Talks really tough, and doesn't bother to clean the obscenities and vulgarities from his language. This is supposed to be "telling it the way it is."

. Gossips about the client and family, or about co-workers, or about prior clients.

. Displays racial, gender, and sexual insensitivities; loves telling jokes about women, blacks, "New York Jews," and others.

. Uses his position and job to flirt with female workers and brags of his sexual prowess.

. Dresses and speaks so inappropriately everyone is embarrassed.

. Reacts inappropriately to personal provocations; is quick to take offense.

There are other conduct flaws which can cause career setbacks for the agent, but this list is an important one.

A few words here on the subject of male/female relationships. There will be those temptations throughout the agent's career to respond to, or initiate, a sexual liaison with a client, or a member of the client's family, or a close working associate. It's a very bad idea and has blighted some promising careers. Don't do it.

Another point: male agents should be courteous and show respect to their female agent team members. More and more women are entering the executive protection field and are doing an outstanding job. They are equal team members and should be treated as such. There is no excuse for male agents to harass female agents, embarrass them in front of the client, or treat them unfairly. That is very unprofessional behavior.

Last, it is only realistic to state that executive protection can be difficult on marriages, particularly if the agent is required to travel often. Enforced separation is tough enough on the stay-at-home spouse--don't make it more difficult by engaging in sexual games.

COMMUNICATING WITH OTHERS

If how you look is important, how you speak and write is equally important. If you want to be taken seriously, you must look and sound like a professional.

Somewhere along the line our schools have failed to educate a majority of young people in the rudiments of good grammar and vocabulary. It is a flaw that is embarrassing, like bad breath or body odor. People are reluctant to tell you that you sound like a yokel and your writing is even worse. If you suspect that this is a problem, seek help immediately. There are numerous opportunities to correct speech and writing flaws. Community colleges, libraries, and books are readily available. Purchase a dictionary if you do not already own one and use it. Have it at hand while you are reading your daily newspapers and news magazines or listening to the newscasts. Work crossword puzzles. Learn five new words and their correct pronunciation every day to build your vocabulary. If your vocabulary is limited, you will not be able to express your thoughts. If you improve and expand your vocabulary, your horizons broaden and new opportunities open up.

Business communication means speaking and writing correctly, and it also means speaking and writing in a clear, organized manner. We have all had the painful experience of listening to people who can't get to the point; they lack the ability to organize information and present it in a clear, logical sequence. Good language skills are so important that they can affect how you feel and think. People who lack the ability to communicate are prone to incoherent anger and fits of rage. They have thoughts but they can't translate those thoughts into speech. Learning to organize thoughts and ideas is not difficult. A good speech class is helpful. A report writing class is another good exercise, since it concentrates on concise writing.

The quality of the speaking voice is another important element. It is a composite of tone, pitch, inflection, delivery, and speech mannerisms. If you are curious to know how you sound, tape record yourself. It is usually something of a shock to listen to oneself.

Tone and pitch are usually regarded as much

the same. Is the voice pitched high or low? Is it nasal or deep? Does the tone grate or is it soothing? Is the voice pitch squeaky, so that the person sounds like a mouse, or is it deep and impressive?

Inflection and delivery are those qualities which can make a voice interesting or hopelessly boring. If the speaker delivers his speech in a monotonous, mumbling fashion, the listener loses interest. Dynamic speakers are able to place an inflection on key words and deliver them in a clear tone that holds the listener's interest. Speech that is paced too slow or too fast is irritating.

Speech mannerisms are those annoying little speech habits which many people use to their disadvantage. Conversations heavily sprinkled with "Y'know?" are particularly annoying. Speakers who constantly use "uh" can drive the listener to distraction. "I, uh, just wanted to know, uh, if you will want to, uh, leave for work, uh, at 8:00?" is not an exaggeration for those people addicted to the use of "uh." These are terrible speech mannerisms and should be drilled out of one's speech. Listening to a taped conversation, not the reading of a set piece, will disclose whether you are one of the offenders. If you are, sign up for a speech class tomorrow!

Other speech mannerisms which are undesirable include those tiresome cliches and jargon which either exclude the listener or bore him to death. Cliches are expressions such as, "You can't make an omelet without breaking some eggs." Cliches are often used as excuses for unpleasant action. "You can't make an omelet without breaking some eggs" has been used as an excuse for everything from mass lay-offs to killing thousands of people in resettlement plans. Jargon makes heavy use of initials and funny expressions. Police jargon includes "perpetrator" shortened to "perp." Jargon, if used, belongs strictly among those people who share it, preferably relegated to the locker room. Using jargon around a client is akin to a death wish. Clients do not wish to hear the manly jargon of the executive protection trade. They are comfortable only with the language they understand and that they are used to hearing in their own world. Jargon-spouting agents are usually classified just to the left of contract guards.

Strong regional accents are generally not a good thing to have, unless you intend to spend the rest of your life living in that region. A soft or faint accent is perfectly acceptable, but strong accents will always place the speaker at a disadvantage. A strong southern accent sounds to many people as ignorant or redneck. A New York accent straight out of the Bronx has been portrayed in too many movies as uneducated or gangster style. Again, a good speech class can help to soften a strong accent.

Making Conversation

No one expects, or wants, the protection agent to be a chatterbox. An agent is not expected to be "Mr. or Ms. Charm." He, or she, however, is expected to be able to conduct a conversation with a certain amount of ease and confidence. Just as the agent is no longer portrayed as a thug, he is no longer perceived as a person of no words and all action. An agent who fits into the client's environment, and maintains his low profile by doing so, is an asset. Besides, it's fun.

Good conversationalists are those people who look others straight in the eye when they are talking and appear to be genuinely interested in what the other person is saying. Being well informed and well read can provide the means for good conversations. Knowing something about business, art, music, theater, and sports provides the opening gambit for an interesting and lively conversation. Conversely, the person who knows only one subject and can only talk about that subject quickly bores all listeners. While being well read and possessing some knowledge on a subject is useful, it is a mistake to appear as an expert. Reading about the budget deficit does not equip a person to become a self-proclaimed economics expert with all the answers for correcting the problem.

A good conversationalist makes an effort to direct the conversation to the interests of the listener, asking questions that draw out the listener. It helps to pay attention to the listener's reactions. Is the conversation making the listener bored? nervous? angry? upset? Conversations are not arguments to be won; they are civilized social exchanges which can be lively and interesting without being confrontational. It is not useful to skewer the other person when he or she makes a conversational blooper or to make the other person feel stupid. "Winning" the conversational point can be a social disaster. Real conversation-stoppers are when you correct someone else's grammar, or correct their statistics, or say bluntly, "Well, you're wrong about that; I happen to know that the real truth is . . . . . ." The other person now feels like a fool and hates you.

Showing a genuine interest in the other person does not mean probing in a gossipy fashion or asking personal questions. It is perfectly alright to ask another person what he or she does for a living but not alright to ask how much the person makes in salary and benefits. It is alright to ask where the other person lives but not appropriate to say, "Oh, *that* part of town--aren't you afraid to live in that high-crime district?" Prying into another's affairs is not socially acceptable unless the other person happens to be a close friend, and your interest is based on genuine concern.

There is a fine line between business conversations and social encounters. Refusing to talk about anything but business is boring; on the other hand, interrupting a conversation about business with some inane comment about sports is poor timing. Being sensitive to the others in a social group can provide clues to the direction the conversation should take.

While there are no black-and-white rules for polite conversation, there are some points of etiquette which should be observed. Everyone in a social group should be included in the conversation. If you see four people standing in a group, one of whom is a friend or someone whom you wish to talk with, it is alright to join the group but not alright to monopolize the friend and ignore the others. Everyone in the group, including strangers, should be included in the conversation.

It is not polite to interrupt another speaker. You should wait until he or she pauses to draw breath before jumping in. Attempting to dominate a conversation is bad form, something like being the bully in the playground. Sadly, many bright, knowledgeable people can't resist showing off by taking charge of the conversation and refusing to let anyone else participate.

There are some subjects which should be avoided in conversations, particularly when you do not know the opinions of the others. Politics and religion are riddled with controversial subjects. Saying to a total stranger, "Isn't it ridiculous that in this modern age the Catholic church still opposes abortion?" is likely to set off a conversational powder keg if the listener is a staunch Catholic or Family Values charter member. You should not launch these conversational bullets and should dodge them if they are hurled in your direction. So, what do you do if someone else asks you the same question? Try to avoid answering it and, if you can't avoid it, try something nondescript such as, "Not being a family man, I'm afraid I don't know much about the subject," or, "Not being a Catholic, I guess I am not familiar with their views."

Health and personal misfortunes are other conversation depressors. No one except your immediate family is really interested in your health, good or bad. Nor are they interested in your recent hard times, loss of a job or contract, divorce, or the fact that the treasurer of the company hates you and has tried to convince the client that he doesn't need you. And, it is a conversational death wish to ask others about their misfortunes. If you are close to and genuinely concerned about another person, ask him or her privately about his/her poor health or family tragedy, but don't surface it among strangers.

The worst possible conversation bloopers are those that are racist, gender, or sexual in nature. Telling dirty jokes, Italian jokes, Jewish jokes, or any other form of stupid jokes should and probably will cast you into a conversational Siberia. Nor will it help to tell a Jewish joke and follow up by saying, "Hey, some of my best friends are Jews."

Other conversational subjects which should be taboo are those embarrassing personal questions which none of us like to answer. "Is that a wig you're wearing? It looks great." "How old are you?" These and other personal questions are forbidden, even among friends. Other personal remarks can be backhanded slaps, such as, "You look great; you must have lost a lot of weight." (Oh--does that mean I was a disgusting fatso before?) Or even, "You look better than I've ever seen you!" (What, I looked terrible before and my friends all knew it?) Instead, if you want to give a compliment try saying something like, "You look great, as always, maybe even better!"

Everyone appreciates a compliment, particularly at work. Saying something complimentary about another person's report or presentation or any work-related project is greatly appreciated if the compliment is genuine. Trying to win points by flattering someone with false compliments usually backfires as it becomes apparent that it is not true. Many people in business feel so competitive, or are so insecure, that they never compliment a colleague's work. In fact, they may rarely compliment the performance of an employee working for them. A pity, since the right word for a job well done is worth more than money to the recipient. Graceful compliments and "thank-you's" are not forgotten.

Gossip is not conversation. It's a bad habit, somewhat like smoking. In the end it will probably kill you professionally, and your smoke will undoubtedly injure innocent bystanders.

Listening

Listening is a form of communication, but most of us do it poorly. There is a communication style, called "Effective Listening," which is taught in all communications classes. The premise is that *hearing* is not *listening*. Most of us have radios and television sets which we turn on and then we promptly turn to other pursuits. We hear the program, but mostly as compatible noise, and we don't listen to what is being said. Most studies show that we listen with very poor efficiency, one reason being that we can hear and process information twice as fast as the average person can speak. Therefore, we tend to listen inefficiently, paying only partial attention to what is being said, and at the same time are thinking of other matters. We "tune out" the other person, and often lose valuable information.

Effective listening is based on several points, most of which are common sense. Listening is an active process, not a passive one. To listen effectively you must concentrate, pay attention, and refuse to let yourself become distracted. You must listen for the message as opposed to merely hearing the words. Many people have a problem in coming to the point and often will cloak the message with word distractions. If you are receiving and processing information you must constantly ask, "What is this person really saying or trying to say?" Often, the word distractions are emotional words which can mask the real message.

Listen not only for the message but for central ideas and refuse to be sidetracked with statistics or secondary arguments. All too often, two people participate in a conversation, at the conclusion of which each thinks he knows what he heard and agreed to, only to find later that each heard a different message. Effective listening requires asking questions that expand ideas and pinpoint facts. And, it requires a summation at the end of the conversation. A good, effective listener might say, "Let me see if I understand the facts of what we have been discussing, and what we agree needs to happen. You have a problem in . . . . is that correct? And you are asking that we . . . . I believe that it would be possible to do this within 30 days. Is this your understanding of what we have agreed to?" This summation restates, concisely, the facts, and asks for the other person's agreement both as to facts and conclusions.

There are some barriers to effective verbal communication. If the listener has a "private agenda," he may hear only part of the message, or may distort the message. If a team member attempts to tell the Detail Leader that certain conditions are not working well within the command post, and the Detail Leader is privately worried about his job, he may interpret

the team member's comments as criticisms and receive the wrong message. If one person dislikes another or has no respect for him, he may listen to that person with resistance or inattention, thus missing valuable information.

Effective listening is an excellent technique to use in business, and with some modifications, is a good conversational tool for social occasions. In a strictly social setting, it is not necessary to use a summation. The active element of listening with attention is immensely flattering to the speaker. It can also save the listener from the embarrassment of having to ask the speaker to repeat something that he did not listen to but realizes he needs to know.

An agent must guard all information which he receives, either directly or indirectly, with total confidentiality. Oddly enough, there is a tendency to remember information which is overheard as a bystander with greater efficiency than information heard as a participant. All information is confidential unless directed otherwise.

Grammar

There is not enough room within this book to examine the rules of grammar. However, because correctly written and spoken grammar is so important, every agent should take pains to learn, or re-learn, this subject. The most widely read, interesting, and amusing person will conversationally fall on his face if he murders the English language. It is painful to be part of a group in which one person tries hard to be a good conversationalist and whose every sentence makes the listeners wince. It may be unfair but it is reality, that someone who sounds grammatically ignorant will usually be taken as incapable of doing his job. What, you ask, does correct grammar have to do with straight shooting? Actually, nothing. But the client does not wish to listen to advice from someone whom he considers to be ignorant and unschooled. There are many, many remedial classes in basic English language and grammar. If you have any doubts about your spoken or written grammatical style, ask someone.

A speech class is excellent training and is highly recommended. It teaches the student how to organize material and present it in a clear and interesting manner. Instructor and class critiques help to point out grammatical, dialogue, and vocabulary flaws. Classes are composed of strangers who are in no position to help or hinder a participant's career, and for that reason, their critiques can be accepted without loss of face.

Public Speaking

Good public speaking skills are important for an agent. Giving a report before a group of people, either strangers or co-workers, is a form of public speaking. Making a presentation, instructing a class, leading a seminar, and giving a speech at the monthly meeting of the agent's professional association are other forms of public speaking. The first few times that you have to get up in front of other people and engage in some form of public speaking can be terrifying, but the terror can be overcome by using good speaking skills.

Doing one's homework, organizing the material, and knowing it very well all help to overcome public speaking fear. Practice smooths out the rough edges. When practicing, it is a good idea to time yourself and to speak out loud just as if it were the real thing. Taping yourself will tell you how you sound, the quality of your delivery, and the tonal qualities. Are you speaking too quickly? too loudly? hesitantly? Do you sound confident? Are there too many pauses while you desperately try to find your place in the presentation? Timing yourself will help to avoid the problem of running overtime or out of time, before you are finished. If you still feel uncertain, practice your presentation before a "live" audience of family, friends, or co-workers and ask for their comments.

Some people like to speak from notes or key words; others write out a complete script and read from it. Both are perfectly acceptable although each has drawbacks. Speaking from notes can lend a more spontaneous quality, but also allows the speaker to wander off the track and lose his place. Reading from

a script helps to stay on track, but can sound wooden and "canned." Everyone has to find his and her best style of speaking. Probably the worst approach is to try to memorize a speech and then give it word for word. The probability of getting a memory blackout midway through the presentation is very high.

In writing notes, key words, or a script for a speech, remember that the lighting may not be good, and, if the writing is too small or cramped, it will be very easy to get lost in your presentation. Use type that is very large, black, and bold with double spacing and wide white margins. Keep separate subjects and thoughts on one page or card, so that you do not have to shuffle pages just to complete a sentence.

Any body language will be exaggerated. Tapping one's fingers, or jingling the change in pockets, or rubbing one's head will become massively annoying to the audience. A good public speaker remains still, doesn't stride around, and is all but motionless in every aspect except face and voice. Face and voice should be animated. A voice that drones on monotonously puts the audience to sleep. An interesting speaker is one who knows how to vary the pitch and cadence of his voice, and can add a slightly dramatic air to his presentation. Some movement of the hands is acceptable, so long as it does not become a distraction. Some occasions, such as political rallies, call for more animated gestures. An experienced speaker has the ability to vary his or her presentation according to the nature of the gathering.

If you are using a podium or lectern, use it properly. It is meant to provide a surface for speeches and notes. It is not intended as a prop for the human body, nor a shield for shaking knees. Some speakers drape themselves across a podium as if they were too weary (or bored) to stand erect.

There are two problems with podiums and lecterns--lighting and the microphone. Sometimes the light causes a glare that, in a dark room, makes it impossible to see the audience clearly. If you can do so, try to adjust the light so that it is not a barrier between you and the audience.

Whenever possible, you should adjust the height of the microphone and the volume *in advance*. It is embarrassing to step up to the "mike" and find that it is six inches too high or low, and you cannot find the screw that allows you to adjust it. All of us, I am sure, have cringed when a speaker stepped up to the microphone, spoke two words and it screeched with a most horrible feedback noise. If you are scheduled to make a presentation, it is appropriate for you to arrive early and ask the host/sponsor if you can test the mike volume. This will also give you the opportunity to play with the screws and adjustments, and to determine if you will need your glasses in order to see.

As with social conversation, you should include everyone in the audience in your presentation. Establish eye contact with people throughout the audience and believe that you are speaking straight to each of them. Allow your eyes to move to all sections of the room, so that everyone in the audience feels included in the presentation.

In a way, good public speaking closely parallels good conversation, except that conversational bloopers are intensified and spotlighted in public speaking. Mispronunciations, and unending "uhs" and "y'know?s," will be glaring.

A touch of humor is always welcome if you can carry it off and if you do not overdo it. Less is always better than more when referring to jokes. And do not, under any circumstances, include any offensive jokes. After-dinner speakers, in particular, sometimes feel that the rules do not apply to that situation and relate embarrassing, foolish jokes. Don't be tempted. A meal and a glass of wine are not sufficient to change the rules of good behavior.

In the long run, you will be a real success if you know your subject, organize your material, start and finish on time, and speak with some enthusiasm about your subject. You will be doing yourself a favor if you ask a friend or associate to critique your presentation; then, listen carefully to the feedback. This is where speech classes are so helpful. Like it or not, this is where you and your presentation will be made better.

Telephone Manners

The executive protection agent spends a certain amount of time on the telephone, either screening calls or in seeking information for an advance or threat assessment. Whereas in face to face conversations you can see the reactions to what you are saying, this is not always so apparent over the telephone. Many otherwise courteous and intelligent people do not know how to communicate over the telephone.

Good telephone manners are simply good manners. The voice should be courteous and warm. Nothing is so offputting as making a telephone call to someone who growls into the phone and who is curt and impatient, and yet this is the telephone style of a great many people.

As with public speaking, you should organize your thoughts before you make a call. Know what you want, and be prepared to ask for it or describe it in a short, succinct, organized way. Making a telephone call for information and then sounding hopelessly addled will not bring success. In addition, it helps greatly to say, "I would really appreciate," and "Thank you," and "Please," even if the other person hasn't been particularly helpful or friendly. You may have to be patient and work your way through their bad manners. Demanding information, losing one's temper, or being curt simply won't work.

An excellent thing to do when calling someone is to ask, "Is this a good time for us to talk?," or "Do you have a few moments so that we can discuss . . . . ?" Sometimes the timing of the call is not good, and the recipient of the call will be distracted and unable to pay attention. Much better to give him or her the chance to say, "This really isn't the best time; can I call you back after lunch?" The other person will appreciate your thoughtfulness, and you will get a better listener.

Another excellent suggestion is--avoid using the speakerphone! Many people are so intensely annoyed by having to listen to calls on a speakerphone, they simply hang up.

Answering the telephone requires a certain style which should be thoughtfully decided upon. If the agent is screening calls for the client, he should get some guidance as to how the client wants his or her calls handled, and whether his name will be identified. In screening calls, one should always be courteous and not too abrupt in extracting information about the call. It is not courteous, for example, to say, "What is this call about?" (too abrupt). Better to take a softer approach; "Will Mr. X know what this call is concerning?," or "Mr. X is not here; may I be of assistance?"

All calls should be handled meticulously, with a written record kept of each call, containing full information as to name, telephone number, and any message to the recipient. Messages should be given promptly to the client. In a command post, calls should be logged in some fashion, and a record kept.

If you are the recipient of the "screen," and a secretary or assistant asks you "the nature of your call," don't react with hostility or bad manners. Be prepared to state your business and do so immediately. Trying to take an end run around the secretary usually backfires. Indeed, the secretary can become your best ally. After all, she (or he) has the unpleasant chore of screening calls all day and will appreciate your saying something like, "Yes, indeed, and perhaps you could help me as well. I am looking for information about . . . . . I would greatly appreciate your help." Very often, the secretary will become a real ally instead of an obstacle.

Calls, even nuisance calls, made to the agent should be returned promptly. A real gentleman and lady is one who takes the time to return all calls, and does so as soon as possible. Besides, you never know, today's nuisance could be tomorrow's hero.

Other good telephone manners include answering the telephone, if possible, within the first three rings, and never putting anyone on "hold" for one second longer than is needed. If information

must be acquired for the caller, it is much better to offer to call back rather than keeping them on hold. Try not to constantly interrupt a call by taking other calls or by talking to someone in your office at the same time. When you are talking to someone, try to give them your full attention. It is rude to eat, play loud music, or allow other background distractions to interfere with the conversation. Don't dominate the conversation, and try not to interrupt.

Terminating a long-winded conversation is actually a simple affair. There are several acceptable excuses, which are business related. One can say, "I'm sorry to have to cut this short, but I've just been told that a call from Moscow which I was expecting is holding for me," or "I've just been handed a note that says they are waiting on me in the meeting," or "I appreciate your calling and will pass along your message to Mr. Client, but a call which he was expecting is holding for me."

When you are leaving a message with someone, stick to the essentials, and do not leave long-winded, overly detailed messages. This applies both when talking to a real person or leaving a message on an answering machine. If you are talking to a real person, he/she has no time or interest in chatting with you or recording lengthy passages of information. A long message on the answer machine is not only tedious to listen to, it eats up the time on the machine tape. At the same time, do not leave mysterious messages ("he'll know what this is about")--the call will probably never be returned.

Resist with all your might the temptation to leave "funny," loud, stupid messages on your own answer machine--it is totally unprofessional. Write out your message, practice, and then record it. It should be simple but complete, perhaps something like the following:

"John Brown's office. At the signal please leave your name, number, a short message, and the date and time of your call. Your call will be returned as quickly as possible. Thank you."

Practice good voice modulation, which means

not shouting or whispering. Practice good voice cadence--avoid the rapid, staccato delivery used by people who wish to appear busy and oh-so-important. If you are disconnected during a call, immediately ring the other person, regardless of who or what caused the disconnection.

WRITTEN COMMUNICATIONS

Letters, reports, business plans, recommendations, proposals, and memorandums are a part of everyday business life for the agent. These written documents highlight the agent's efficiency and knowledge to clients, potential clients, and employers. An agent must not only write, he must write well. The people who read these documents are almost always well educated and are used to reading documents that are factual, correct, concise, complete, and well organized. In submitting written documents, the agent is competing with executives who have long experience in writing reports and plans.

Letters

In writing a letter your goal is to convey your message across space to someone else. People who are able to write in a personal, human manner are more successful as letter writers than those who write in a stilted, cold fashion. This is not to say that letters should be informal, breezy, or chatty. There is a middle ground that allows the writer to sound like a human being without being an old pal.

If it is a business letter, you need to organize your thoughts. Why are you writing? What are the facts? What is the decision or conclusion that you want? And, you need to get to the point without a lot of dancing around the subject. A rule of thumb is, whenever possible confine the letter to one page, two at the most. One of the common mistakes is to try to cram what really amounts to a report into a letter format. If there is too much to say in one or two pages, consider formatting it as a one page letter with an enclosure.

Avoid repetitions. Say it once; that's enough. Many letters are stuffed with redundancies and unnecessary words. For example, in this sentence the unnecessary words are italicized . . "*Past* experience has shown that to bring an incident to its *final* conclusion, it is necessary to . . . " The words *past* and *final* are redundancies and unnecessary. Another example: "At this point *in time*." *In time* is a redundancy. While few people enjoy reading a letter that is overly bare and terse, most of us err on the side of saying too much.

Most importantly, you should resist using a lot of words that you don't understand but that you like the sound of. If these are words that you do not normally use in everyday conversation, don't try to sound like a different person in a letter; there is always the danger that you may misuse an unfamiliar word. Long sentences are another mistake made by novice writers. Sentences should contain one thought only, not a mishmash of different ideas or subjects. The same applies to paragraphs. A paragraph deals with one subject, not a long string of different ideas and subjects.

As is true with conversations, business letters should be courteous, grammatically correct, and careful not to be offensive. Jokes, slang, jargon, and emotional words should not be included.

The appearance of a business letter is as important as the contents, and there are some fairly rigid rules which, if you follow them, will tell the reader that you are a professional.

.   Letters should be either single-spaced or, if the letter is very short, can be one-and-a-half spaces, but never double-spaced.

.   A letter should be balanced so that it is neither top-heavy nor too close to the bottom. Depending upon the length of the letter, the date line should be three to six spaces below the letterhead or top margin. The date line can be flush with the left margin or flush right.

.   Left and right margins should be one to one-and-a-high inches. Overly wide margins look peculiar.

. The inside address (name and address of the person to whom you are writing) should be positioned at least three spaces, and preferably four to six spaces, below the date line. Check the spelling of all names and addresses. Nothing is as irritating as receiving a letter with one's name misspelled. Include the middle initial of a person's name if it is known.

. If there is a reference or code number, it should appear two spaces below the inside address, and two spaces above the salutation. A reference might be, for example, "Reference Case #29433."

. If there is no reference, double-space--repeat, that is two spaces down, no more and no less from the inside address--and type the salutation, "Dear . . . ." followed by a full colon (:) at the end. It is not permissible to use other than two spaces between the inside address and the salutation.

. The salutation should be either formal, "Dear Mr. Brown:" or, if the person is a friend or peer, "Dear Joe:" is acceptable. You should never address someone whom you barely know, or an older person (unless related to you), or an executive who outranks you, with the informal salutation. It is not proper to address someone using first and last names, for example, as "Dear Joe Brown:". There are standard formal salutations and titles for heads of state, legislators, clergymen, and other individuals of rank and title. The correct forms can be found in any good book on writing business letters and reports.

. Double-space down--again, two spaces, no more and no less--and begin the letter. Paragraphs can be indented five spaces, or not indented and flush against the left margin. Indented paragraphs are considered less formal. The right margin can be "justified" (straight against the right margin) or "ragged" (uneven right margin). Justified margins are more formal.

. After the last paragraph of the letter, double-space--two spaces, no more or less--to the closing phrase (called the complimentary closing). The closings, "Sincerely," "Yours truly," and "Sincerely

yours," capitalize only the first word, and the phrase is finished with a comma at the end.

. Go down four spaces exactly for the name and title of the sender of the letter.

. The complimentary closing, name, and title can be flush against the left margin or centered on the page.

. If the sender has a secretary who has typed the letter, this is indicated by double spacing (two spaces) down from the sender's name, and typing in the initials of the sender in all caps followed by a colon or slash mark, and the initials of the typist in small case letters or full caps. Like this: MB:ab, or MB/ab, or MB:AB.

. If there are enclosures to the letter, double space (two spaces) down below the name and title of the sender and type "Enclosure(s)" followed by a colon, two to five spaces, and a description of the enclosures.

. If a copy of the letter is being sent to someone else, this is indicated by double spacing (two spaces) down below the sender's name and title, or if there are enclosures, below the enclosures notation.

These are the bare essentials of writing proper business letters. There are numerous subtleties and differences which can only be learned by reading one of the numerous books about business letters and business writing on the market.

The following is an example of the "open" style with indented paragraphs, complimentary closing, and signature. It is a more informal, friendly appearance. Note it is balanced left, right, top, and bottom. The dateline appears on the left to counter-balance the ESI logo. Because it is a long letter, the left and right margins are one inch. The notations at the bottom are aligned for a symmetrical look.

June 31, 1993

Ms. Martha J. Braunig
400 West Main Street
Aspen, Colorado 81611

Dear Ms. Braunig:

I would like to personally congratulate you on your decision to enroll in the ESI Advanced Executive Protection Program. You have just made an investment in one of the most important career decisions of your life. In fact, like many of our ESI students, this experience will undoubtedly change your life. The opportunities for trained, professional protection agents are growing rapidly. ESI graduates are working in private security jobs around the world.

And now we would like to help you get started in the right way. It is going to be an exciting challenge for you. Home study is one of the most convenient forms of education. But, you need to set a schedule and stick to it! Try to spend an hour or two every day working on your lessons, and before you know it, I will have the pleasure of seeing you in Aspen for Resident Training.

In fact, we would like to schedule your Resident Training class but, before we can do so, you need to complete your first Home Study course. I would like to see you complete this course within four weeks, and it's easy! As an incentive to you we are enclosing the ESI Home Study Record Form with personalized pen. If we receive your first test results within four weeks, we will send you our official ESI cap, along with the scheduled date for your Resident Training in Aspen.

In 1992 almost 200 students graduated from our AEP Program. We were tired but happy when the last program was over, having spent long, action-filled days (and some nights) with shooting, defensive tactics, executive protection driving, and protection scenarios. Our graduates were unanimous in their opinions--"absolutely fantastic," and "just great." We take pride in our graduates. They are unique, one of a kind, and very important to us.

It gives me great pride to welcome you to ESI and our powerful network of ESI students and graduates. I am sending a copy of this letter to the Home Study Director, and I will be checking on your progress, so don't let me down. I am counting on you to be one of our 1993 graduates!

Sincerely,

Bob Duggan
President

BD:mb

Enclosure: ESI Home Study Record Form
Personalized pen

cc: Home Study Director

Executive Security International, Ltd., 605 West Main Street, Aspen, Colorado 81611 • 303/920-2323 • 1 800-874-0888

The following sample letter is short and needs to be positioned on the page so that it is not top heavy. It is an example of the blocked, or flush left letter.

This style is the faster method of letter writing, as no thought has to be given to indentations.

January 31, 1993

Mr. Alfred R. Jones
The ABC Corporation
225 Teal Place
Williamsburg, New York 10014

Dear Mr. Jones:

I would like to take this opportunity to forward our new 1993 ESI Catalog. We at ESI were so pleased to include Doug Jones and Ray Sharkey of your company in our Resident Training last year. We are hoping that, as we discussed last year, you will send the other members of your executive protection driving team to ESI for one of our 1993 classes.

Have you given any thought to visiting with us during one of our classes? You will be most welcome. I look forward to hearing from you.

Sincerely,

Bob Duggan
President

BD:mb

Enclosure: Catalog

Executive Security International, Ltd., 605 West Main Street, Aspen, Colorado 81611 • 303/920-2323 • 1 800-874-0888

Memorandums

Memorandums can be informal notes, short reports, or requests sent primarily within an office or company from one individual to another or several other individuals. Memorandums used in small offices are usually informal with no formalized structure; however, in larger organizations there is a formalized style used for sending interoffice memorandums. You should always ask for the correct format. Generally, a memorandum looks something like the following example.

ABC MANUFACTURING COMPANY

September 12, 1992

From: Robert Benson, Engineering Department

To: Ralph Jones, Design Department
        Mary Holmes, Purchasing Department

Re: Completion of prototype of new widget

The engineering department has completed the prototype of the new widget, in accordance with the design specifications given us by the Design Department. We encountered a potential problem in the final assembly of the racket arms. Originally planned for robotic assembly of the racket arms, we found it necessary to hand-assemble them. This will undoubtedly mean a repricing, unless we can alter the design.

I would like to meet with you at 4:00 p.m. tomorrow in Engineering, Room 12, if this is convenient, so that we can decide how we are going to handle this. Please confirm to me by noon tomorrow. Notwithstanding the racket arms, the finished product looks great! I look forward to your comments.

                                Robert Benson

Memorandums, as you see, are short, concise, and to the point. While the format of the memorandum is structured to a certain style, a memo is considered to be a form of informal or semi-formal communication. There are no expressions of "Sincerely yours" or other formal courtesies of that nature used in memorandums. It is understood that the memorandum is a business communication.

Many companies use pre-printed memorandum forms which ensure that the essentials are included. The important points to remember about memorandums are: they should be well organized, easy to read, and get to the point. They are essentially information pieces. If any action is required as a consequence of the memorandum, this should be included together with a date and time for conclusion of the action.

Reports

There are many different kinds of reports. Report writing for investigations and police reports have a style of their own, with a very structured format which concentrates on legal facts. The Target Study in the Appendix is an excellent example of a different kind of report, written in precise outline form. Other reports are presented in narrative (or prose) style.

Whatever the format, the business report has identifiable parts: the Title Page, Table of Contents, Introduction or Methodology, Executive Summary, Contents, and Conclusions.

The Title Page is simple and clean: *who* prepared the report, *what* is the report (title), *when* (date), and for *whom*. The Table of Contents is self-explanatory; it lists the contents of the report by page number.

After the Table of Contents is the Introduction or Background or Methodology, whatever is appropriate. In brief, it should state why the report was compiled, the goals or objectives of the report, and the methods used in compiling the report. It may include background information such as, "This report was compiled in response to the numerous terrorist incidents which have occurred in the area, leading the ABC Corporation to commission a Threat Survey . . ." It establishes the justification for the report (why this report is being written?). The scope is important and might be referred to as . . ."In compiling this report a study was made of terrorist incidents in the immediate area of Pakistan, but not of adjoining countries or the region in general." This tells the reader that the scope is limited or broad. This is also the appropriate place to define terminology used in the report.

The Executive Summary is a short (usually one page) version of the contents and conclusions of the report. A busy executive can read the Executive Summary and know the "bottom line" of the report. For more information, of course, he or she must refer to the body of the report which shows the report findings in detail. Mr. Executive might read something in the Executive Summary which he finds surprising or disagrees with, and can quickly turn to the body of the report for details. But, busy executive that he is, by reading the Executive Summary he can find in one or two minutes the answers he is seeking: what the problem is, how it can be corrected, and what it will cost.

The contents of the report represent the major part of the report. This section should be presented in a logical, sequential form--not a fuzzy, wandering narrative. Referring to the Target Study in the Appendix, you will see that this report moves in a straightforward manner, examines each potential situation, and presents recommendations to solve each problem encountered.

In the memorandum above, a problem is targeted as the attachment of the racket arms to the widget. A subsequent report would be constructed which examines the problems and makes recommendations for solutions. This would be an example of a highly focused report. An example of a report closer to the protection agent would be a survey of the physical and electronic vulnerabilities of the client's residence or office.

The last section of the report lists the conclusions and recommendations of the report. Recommendations are just that, recommended suggestions, and should not be worded as commands. "In order to secure the building properly we *must* install CCTV in the . . . " is worded too strongly. Again, look at the Target Study in the Appendix. The facts, conclusions, and recommendations are written in a straightforward manner and presume that the reader has the right to agree or disagree.

COMMUNICATING WITH FOREIGNERS

An agent working with a client who either travels overseas, lives overseas, or hosts foreign dignitaries and businessmen will inevitably need to interact with agencies and individuals who have different languages and customs. Each nationality and grouping of nationalities has customs which are not only different, they may create problems if you do not understand them. Here are a few examples of customs which could be troublesome if you are not aware and sensitive to them.

.   For Muslims the normal work week is Saturday through Thursday. Friday is the holy day, and a day of rest.

.   Devout Muslims do not drink alcohol, do not eat pork products, and eat only with the right hand because the left hand is used for bodily hygiene and is considered unclean.

.   In Muslim countries it is impolite to sit in any position which shows the soles of the feet.

.   In Japan it is considered impolite to hold or maintain eye contact.

.   The Japanese are too polite to say "no" as brusquely as Americans. They may, instead, give a nondescript "maybe" which really means "no."

.   In the Middle East and North Africa, men greet each other by hand clasping and kissing both cheeks. Men frequently hold hands as they walk together.

.   People in many countries do not bother to be punctual; it simply is not important to them. Time has a different meaning, and "tomorrow" may become next week. Westerners attempting to do business in the Middle East and Saudi Arabia are frequently frustrated by this point.

.   In Spain the main meal is between 1:00 and 4:00 p.m., and the evening meal is rarely taken before 10:00 p.m. or later.

There are, of course, numerous other cultural differences which an astute agent would be wise to learn. Fortunately, there is help. Many business schools now offer programs in fields of intercultural development. Kennedy Center for International Studies at Brigham Young University in Provo, Utah, (801) 378-3377. The Center publishes a series called

Culturgrams, one for each of 104 countries, at $1.00 each. These *Culturgrams* offer information on the lifestyle and culture of each country. These are highly recommended for anyone doing business with foreigners either in their own country or within the United States.

There are other books which deal with international business. Two of the best are *Do's and Taboos Around the World*, and *Do's and Taboos of Hosting International Visitors*, author Roger E. Axtell, publisher John Wiley and Sons. They are crammed with useful information, short, easy, and fun to read. Good books such as these are usually available in a library of any size.

RELATIONSHIPS

Perhaps the best time to structure the working relationship with the client is at the initial interview. This is the time to ask the client any questions about his expectations, his reasons for employing a professional protection agent, and his life style. Often the client does not fully comprehend the role of the protection agent and expects services that are not specifically within the area of protection. If the interview results in a job offer, a contract should be drawn. This sets a professional tone.

It is important to gain the respect and trust of the client. You will need his active cooperation to properly protect him. Do not confuse this with overeager efforts to impress him. Start off by reviewing the information about your client, his family, and business. Get a medical history. Do a site survey. Meet the staff. And do all this with a minimum of interference or irritation to those involved.

It is well to remember that you are on the job to provide security, and to direct some of the logistics of movement for the client. You are not there to give advice on business, investments, health, food, entertainment, or personal relationships. The client is seldom interested in the protection agent's opinion on those subjects. A polite, but respectful, distance between the client and the agent generally provides a healthy working relationship.

On the other hand, a protection agent in a family situation is often regarded by his client as a friend or companion. This feeling should not tempt the agent to take advantage of the situation by becoming overly familiar with the client. The client is the boss and deserves the respect given a boss. It is particularly important to maintain a professional demeanor with the client's family and to have the respect of the family. Confusing the roles of protector and friend can be extremely dangerous. On the other hand, fitting into the household with ease can diminish the irritation which is almost inherent in the agent's job.

An agent should be considerate of the client's need for privacy, and without compromising security, should allow as much private space as possible to the client, the client's family, and their relationships with their friends. Protecting the client's privacy includes not gossiping or discussing anything seen or heard with the other staff members or outsiders.

Courtesy, manners, and a sensitivity to others are good qualities for a professional agent.

MODUS OPERANDI

The agent should establish with the client some simple codes and procedures, particularly for emergencies. If an emergency should occur, there is no time to argue with, or explain to, the client. The client is more inclined to trust the agent if the agent has made the right judgement calls and not cried "wolf" too often.

Never lay hands on the client or his family except in an emergency, when you will need to get them away fast, covering their retreat with your body. Explain to the client and his family why you will precede them into public and unfamiliar buildings.

EXPENSES

An agreement should be reached as to how

expenses will be handled, who will pay the bills, and how the agent will be reimbursed for out-of-pocket job related expenses. It is very important for the agent to have a VISA/Mastercard and an American Express card. The AMEX card will generally permit a higher limit. Credit card bills should always be paid promptly to build up and keep the highest possible credit limit.

Keep all receipts as back-up to the credit card and cash purchases and use them to put together an expense report. Printed expense report forms can be purchased in any office supply store. List expenses, attach back-up, be certain that you have all receipts, and submit for payment. Reimbursement from the client should be made immediately upon receipt of the expense, as an accepted routine. It is not a good idea for the agent to "front" too many expenses, as this is the client's responsibility.

ASSOCIATIONS

It is an excellent idea to join one, two, or more law enforcement associations. This is particularly useful when doing advances in other cities and establishing a liaison with the police and sheriff's department. Before leaving on an advance, you can check the roster of your association to find the name and rank of the law enforcement office in your target city. You may wish to ask a local member of the association to call ahead and arrange for a meeting.

Volunteer to become a special deputy for the sheriff's department, or assist in some way with his political campaign. Being a member of the sheriff's department can ease the way to obtaining a carry permit for your gun.

LEAVING THE JOB

What about the other side of the relationship? What should the protection agent expect from the protectee? Certainly the agent should be treated with professional respect.

He has a right to expect that his client is not involved in illegal activities, and that the client does not involve the agent in illegal activities. Bribes, kickbacks, drugs, gambling, and alcohol can all constitute trouble. There may be a time when the agent feels that the situation is too compromising, and that the sensible decision is to resign. If this should occur, you must leave the job in a professional way, without acrimony--but leave! An agent's reputation is his stock in trade, and to jeopardize it because of a client's activities is a bad bargain. More normally, a working relationship ends for less dramatic reasons. The client may feel that he no longer needs protection. The agent may feel that he is not progressing in his job, or that the personal interrelationship isn't working comfortably, or that he has better opportunities elsewhere.

If the agent makes the choice to leave, he should give ample notice to effect a replacement for himself. He should always ask for a reference to add to his resume.

Note: An obvious omission in this chapter is that of table manners and restaurant conduct. The subject is too broad to be dealt with in this book; however, this is a HIGHLY important issue and the reader is urged to read two excellent books:

. *"Letitia Baldridrige's New Complete Guide to Executive Manners," published by Rawson Associates of New York.*

. *"The New Etiquette," by Marjabelle Young Stewart, published by St. Martin's Griffin, New York.*

If you are looking for something short and simple, try "The Idiot's Guide to Etiquette," published by Alpha Books.

The executive protection agent needs to have a basic understanding of the American legal system and how it affects his job. There are numerous laws which the agent will not necessarily need to know, but there are a few concepts which he should know very well. The agent's job carries inherent risks and the potential for liabilities.

A first matter, one which should be kept constantly in mind while reading the following discussion, is that there are at least 55 different sets of laws in the United States and its territories (i.e., one set for each of the 50 states, Puerto Rico, the Virgin Islands, Guam, military law, and U.S. law). Consequently, the following discussion is highly generalized and should be understood to be a cursory analysis at best. In confronting a specific legal problem, questions must be addressed to an attorney who is qualified to practice law in the jurisdiction and venue where the problem has arisen.

We start with the fact that the legal system is made up of two parts: *civil law* and *criminal law*. Criminal law concerns itself with the commission of crimes; civil law, on the other hand, deals with non-criminal disputes among individuals, businesses, and governments.

Another way to see this distinction is to look at the differences in possible outcomes of a legal action under each system. In civil law, the offender is subject to pay the injured party for injuries and/or losses; under criminal law the offender may be fined, imprisoned, put to death, and/or made to provide restitution or perform community work. In civil law, when a wrong (called "tort") has been committed, the wronged person brings a lawsuit to correct the wrong. In criminal law, the government (federal, state), acting in the name of the People, brings the alleged wrongdoer to court.

It is possible for a person to be subject both to criminal prosecution and tort liability; that is, a person may be tried for a crime and, even if found not guilty, he can be sued for the same act in a civil action and found culpable. The reason is that, in a criminal action, the standard for conviction in all jurisdictions is that the jury is convinced "beyond a reasonable doubt" that the defendant committed the crime; whereas, in a civil action, the jury merely has to find that it is "more probable than not" that the defendant committed the tort.

CIVIL LAW

Civil violations usually fall into two categories: breaches of contract, and commission of torts.

Contracts

There is an entire body of law known as contract law, but for the purposes of the protection agent, only relevant points have been included in this chapter.

A contract is an *enforceable* agreement (a set of mutual promises) between two or more parties. A contract is said to exist when the following elements are present: **an offer** ("I offer you a job as my executive protection specialist."); **acceptance** ("I accept."); **consideration** ("The pay is $1,500.00 a week."); **mutual assent to the same proposition** ("This is a security position; I don't do baby-sitting or shopping . . ."); **the subject matter of the contract is legal** ("This agreement does not include participating in drug transactions with you . . ."); **all parties have the legal capacity to enter into a contract** (i.e., non-adults, the mentally ill or persons of insufficient intelligence to know what they are doing are presumed, by law, to be incapable of exercising the intent to form an agreement); and **the absence of**

duress (i.e. no one is forced into the agreement by threat of physical force, etc.)

Disagreements and, therefore, lawsuits over allegations of breach of contract are almost invariably caused by ambiguity in the terms of the agreement; that is, what exactly was to be done, when was it to be done, and how much was to be paid. It is obvious that proving these things in court is immeasurably aided if the agreement is in writing; however, oral contracts are just as enforceable as written ones. They are simply more difficult to prove.

Express contracts are those contracts containing terms and conditions communicated orally or in writing at the time of making the contract. *Implied contracts* may be inferred by courts who look at the history of the conduct of the parties and conclude that a contract exists between them.

An important concept is that of *agency*. *Agency* is a relationship in which one person's acts have a binding legal effect on another. You will see agency relationships expressed as those of a Master/Servant, Employer/Employee, or Principal/Agent. Agency, too, may be created by express or implied contract, or inferred by law.

What all of this boils down to is that the employer, or client, *will* have legal responsibility for the wrongful acts of the employee or agent; whereas, the agent does not have legal responsibility for the wrongful acts of his or her principal. This principle is referred to as *vicarious liability*.

A principal is generally not responsible for the acts of an independent contractor, but a crucial question is simply whether or not someone is an "independent contractor." This is determined by asking such questions as: Who maintains control in the contract?; Who has actual control?; Who hires, fires, evaluates, disciplines, trains, assigns duties, supervises, sets hours of employment, pays, provides uniforms and equipment, prepares post orders, establishes and enforces policies and procedures?

Other elements which determine independent contractor status are: length of employment contract; method of payment, whether by time or by the total job; and whether the one employed is engaged in a distinct occupation or business.

Torts

Torts impact on security personnel, as they include such actions as assault, battery, false imprisonment, negligence, trespass, invasion of privacy, vicarious liability, and infliction of emotional distress. It is within the tort aspect of the law that security personnel are particularly vulnerable. There have been numerous cases, in particular of assault, battery, and unlawful imprisonment, brought against security personnel. There are three kinds of torts: *intentional torts, negligence,* and *strict liability torts.*

Intentional Torts

The basic elements of intentional torts are: a *wrongful act* (tortious act) by a person; with *intent* to do wrong; and which *"proximately" causes* an injury to another person.

There are three concepts of *intent* under tort law:

. *Specific*--an actor intends the consequences if his goal in acting is to bring about these consequences.

. *General*--an actor intends the consequences of his conduct if he knows with substantial certainty that these consequences will result.

. *Transferred*--the transferred intent doctrine applies when the actor intends to commit a tort against one person but instead commits a different tort against that person; commits the tort unintentionally against another person; or commits a different tort against another person unintentionally.

Assault. The definition, or elements, of assault are: an act; with intent to cause immediate harmful or offensive contact; or to cause the apprehension of immediate harmful or offensive contact coupled with the immediate apparent capacity to carry out that threat or harm. The plaintiff's (victim's) apprehension must be reasonable in light of the circumstances. It may be reasonable even though the defendant is not actually capable of causing the plaintiff injury; the defendant's apparent ability to cause the plaintiff injury is sufficient. Apprehension must be of imminent contact; threats of future harmful or offensive contact are insufficient.

What does this mean? Let us take an example. In manning a check post at the client's residence, a crank (known to you) attempts to gain entry peacefully. You decide that you are tired of this particular crank, and you want to get rid of him in such a way that he will not come back. You raise your voice and tell him that you are tired of his incursions, that he is to leave immediately, and if he doesn't leave immediately, you are going to "make him sorry he ever came back"--and you raise your arms so that your weapon is visible, or you plant your hands on your hips, glower at him menacingly, but don't touch him. You have just committed an assault, and the crank can bring suit against you.

Battery. Battery requires an unconsented-to touching of the plaintiff's person. It includes touching, poking, spitting, and other contacts. If a crazy looking female runs up to your client and says, "I must have your autograph," and tries to push a pencil and paper in the client's hands, and you shove her out of the way forcefully, you are liable for the charge of battery.

False Imprisonment. This charge is probably more applicable to security guards but can also apply to agents. False imprisonment is the unlawful confinement or restraint of a person to a bounded area. The confinement may be by physical barriers, by physical force, by direct threat of force, or by acts or words reasonably implying such force. The plaintiff need not resist an act of confinement. However, no confinement exists if the plaintiff has a reasonable means of escape, and of which the plaintiff is aware.

Many, many suits have been brought and won based on the premise of false imprisonment, particularly in retail stores where security guards apprehend individuals on false charges of shoplifting and restrain that person from leaving the store. A protection agent would be in danger of having caused false imprisonment if he stopped an individual attempting to sneak past his hotel hallway check post, and then forced that individual to go into the command post and held him there against his will while he summoned the police. The individual has broken no laws, nor made threats, but merely by appearing to be suspicious in his intent, he was held against his will and prevented from leaving. Big dollars for the settlement!

Defenses to Intentional Torts

There are some acceptable defenses to the committing of intentional torts which are of particular interest to the protection agent.

Consent. There are two types of consent; *express (actual) consent*, and *implied (apparent) consent.*

Actual consent occurred when the plaintiff actually told the defendant that the defendant could commit the intentional tort on the plaintiff. If, however, the plaintiff's consent was induced by fraud or duress, the consent will not be a valid defense to the intentional tort.

Apparent consent is present when a reasonable person would infer from the custom or usage of the plaintiff's conduct (such as the normal contacts inherent in body contact sports: football, hockey) that consent was granted. There is another apparent consent which is *consent implied by law, where the defendant's action is necessary to save a person's life or some other important interest in person or property.* If the defendant exceeds the implied consent and does something substantially different than that which the plaintiff consented to, then the defendant may be liable to the plaintiff for the intentional tort.

Self-Defense. A defendant has the defense of self-defense where the defendant has a reasonable belief that he is being or is about to be attacked. The defendant's reasonable mistake as to the existence of the danger does not invalidate the defense. Usually, a person using self-defense need not attempt to escape. The modern trend imposes upon the defendant a duty to retreat before using deadly force where retreat can be done safely, unless the attacked person is in his own home. The self-defense privilege does not exist after the commission of a tort (retaliation is not allowed).

One may only use the degree of force which reasonably appears to be necessary to prevent harm. If more force than is reasonably necessary is used, the defense is lost. Self-defense may extend to third party injuries (caused while the defendant was defending himself). The defendant may be liable to a third person if the defendant deliberately injured the third party while the defendant was trying to protect himself.

Defense of Others. A person may come to the aid of and defend another person. The aiding person may use as much force as the person defended could have used. More on this in the criminal law section.

Defense of Property. One may defend his property. However, before defending his property the defender must request the person harming the property to desist (unless it is clear that such would be futile or dangerous). The defense is limited to torts that are being committed upon plaintiff's property. Once the tort is complete, the defender may no longer use force to defend his property. The defender may use reasonable force to defend his property. Deadly force is *not* reasonable in defense of property.

Negligence

Negligence is usually defined as the failure to exercise a reasonable care in a situation where someone could foreseeably be injured, and where that failure causes harm to someone or something.

There are three elements of negligence: *duty, breach of duty,* and *causation.*

Duty of care. Since the law requires all persons to conduct themselves with due regard for the safety and rights of others, the failure to do so amounts to negligence. There is a standard referred to as the "reasonable person standard." Was the conduct which caused or constituted the negligence that of a "reasonable person?" The standard of care is higher for a professional, or a person who has a higher level of knowledge or skill, or for someone who is attempting to act as a professional or undertakes the job of a skilled worker.

Negligence has severe application and ramifications for liability for those who do not adequately screen, hire, train, appoint, entrust, supervise, discipline, and terminate its personnel, and for those companies that rely heavily on risk management insurance coverage to meet their obligation of providing adequate security.

The defendant can be deemed negligent for his own actions directly against the plaintiff (direct first party negligence). He can also be deemed negligent for damage to the plaintiff for damage caused by a third party (employee). Example: if a training officer negligently trains an officer in the use of a firearm, and the plaintiff is injured by the officer because of the negligent training.

Negligent Screening and Hiring. The employer has a duty to carefully screen prospective employees. Hiring an employee without checking references or performing some sort of background check, and subsequent placement of an unfit individual into a position, as a result of which the unfit employee injures someone, could leave the employer open to a charge of negligence. Negligent retention is another issue. If an employee is hired and subsequently found to be unfit for the job, but nonetheless is retained, and thereby causes an injury, the employer could be found negligent.

Negligent Training and Direction. The

employer has a duty to train employees. The difficulty within the security industry is a lack of national standards. For this reason, it is very important that the employer provide a written manual of policies and procedures, from which training programs can be designed and implemented.

Negligent Assignment, Supervision, Discipline, and Retention. If a subordinate is obviously unfit for an assignment, then the supervisor is under obligation to change that subordinate's assignment. If the supervisor "knew or should have known" is the key. If an injury were to occur, failure to supervise properly could result in a lawsuit for negligent supervision. Insufficient or negligent discipline of an employee, who subsequently causes an injury due to the action which occasioned the negligent discipline, could be grounds for a lawsuit based on negligent discipline. If an employee is obviously unfit to properly perform his duties in a sensitive area, then the employer has a duty to terminate his employment or move him to a position not likely to cause harm.

Breach of Duty. When a person's conduct falls short of that level required by the applicable standard of care (e.g. reasonable person) owed to the injured person, there has been a breach of duty. It must be shown that, in fact, a wrong took place, and it must be shown from the facts that the accused acted unreasonably.

Cause. It is well to note that an "act or omission" can be the cause of an injury. Serious problems with resultant lawsuits have stemmed from omission. For example, if the owner of a restaurant which is located in a high crime district fails to provide proper lighting for the parking area, and a customer is assaulted in that area, the owner may be liable for negligence in failing to provide proper lighting.

CRIMINAL LAW

Criminal law defines crimes and establishes the punishment for those crimes. Crimes are public wrongs--illegal acts or failure to act--violations of the governing body's penal code. Most crimes have two essential elements: "Mens Rea," a guilty mind; guilty or wrongful purpose; a criminal intent, guilty knowledge, and wilfulness--and "Actus Reus," which translates as a "wrongful deed." Thus, for most crimes, there must be a guilty mind and a guilty act. Some crimes, however, are "strict liability" crimes. That is, all that is necessary is the wrongful deed; intent is never an issue.

There are a few other simple concepts about criminal law which are useful to know.

Actus Rea Methods. The act must be done either by or through:

. The suspect's own hand;

. An innocent agency, such as a bomb on an air carrier;

. An innocent person, such as smuggling by means of another person's baggage;

. The use of other means, such as animals or machines; or

. The failure to act, as well as an affirmative act.

Mens Rea. The *general rule* is that the act of the accused and the intent to act must occur simultaneously (it is not a defense for the accused to repent after the act). *Motive* is not an essential element of the crime; the suspect's motive does not have to be proven. However, the motive may be proven by the prosecutor as a means of proving the suspect's guilt. *Transferred intent*: when the accused intends one criminal act but accomplishes another, the law holds that the Mens Rea is present in the resulting act by means of "transfer" from the original intent; or if the accused's actions injure the wrong person, the accused's intent shall be transferred to the person actually harmed.

Intent. There are two categories of intent, general and specific. Under *general intent* the law presumes that a person intends his acts and, therefore, a jury can infer the required general intent merely from the doing of the act. All that the prosecutor must show is that the accused had the mental capacity of knowing right from wrong. Some crimes require a higher level of proof of intent. In these cases, the existence of *specific intent* cannot be presumed from the doing of the act. Defenses such as involuntary intoxication and reasonable mistake of fact apply to specific intent crimes. Some specific intent crimes which an agent might be subject to are: assault, false pretenses, and first degree premeditated murder.

Recklessness. This is interpreted as a wrongful state of mind of a lesser degree than intent but may nevertheless be criminal, dependent upon the circumstances. It is a state of mind which implies one has acted in complete disregard for the rights and safety of others, resulting in harm. The accused must have taken an unjustifiable risk, and it must be shown that he had knowledge of the risk and consciously disregarded the risk.

Negligence. This is also interpreted as a wrongful state of mind of a lesser degree than criminal intent, but may nevertheless be criminal. A defendant must have taken a very unreasonable risk, and the defendant failed to recognize that his actions were a substantial deviation from the normal standard of care owed to the general public under similar circumstances. Four elements of criminal negligence are: a standard of care; a breach of the standard; proximate cause; and harm or injury. As in tort law, the standard of care and breach thereof is usually determined by the "reasonable person test" or standard. However, in criminal law it is not just the reasonable person test but also proof that the defendant took a very substantial risk at the expense of the victim.

An act or omission is "willfully" done if done voluntarily and intentionally and with the specific intent to do something the law forbids, or with the specific intent to fail to do something the law requires to be done.

Wanton. An act done in reckless disregard of the rights of others, indicating a reckless indifference to consequences to the life or limb, or health, or reputation, or property rights of another, and is more than negligence, more than gross negligence.

The Law of Causation. In order to amount to criminal conduct, there must be a causal connection between the "forbidden act" and the criminal intent. The law presumes that a person intends the natural and probable consequences of his/her acts. The accused takes his victim as he finds him. The accused might have only intended to scare his victim, but in fact the accused killed his victim. The charge may be changed from assault to homicide.

The prosecutor must prove that the defendant's act was the "proximate cause" of the end result. One method of determining "proximate cause" is to clearly show a direct cause and effect relationship. There is also the "But For" test: the act of the defendant set in motion a chain of events that caused the victim's damages. It is said that "but for" the acts of the defendant, the victim would not have been injured. A third method is to clearly show that the acts of the accused substantially increased the likelihood of injury to the victim by another cause.

For example, a man who is obviously drunk is badgering your client and suddenly shoves you. You, in turn, shove back, intending only to get rid of him, but he falls through a plate glass door and is badly cut. You caused him to be cut. Were it not "but for" your actions, the man would not have been grievously lacerated.

Defenses

Legal defenses to crimes include: diminished capacity; insanity; intoxication; infancy (a minor); and self-defense. Note that ignorance of the law is *not* a viable defense. Of these defenses, that of self-defense is the more important for an agent.

USE OF FORCE

All agents and security personnel should be trained in the methods of solving problems without using force whenever possible. Using force, either lethal or non-lethal, should be a last resort only.

Laws regarding the use of force are not necessarily the same in every state. A good model, however, is the Model Penal Code; a criminal code which was drafted by criminal law scholars originally in 1962 as a benchmark for use by legislatures. It has been used by a majority of the states to revise and codify their criminal laws. The applicable provisions of the Model Penal Code regarding Use of Force are as follows:

1.   *Use of force justifiable in the protection of the person.* Subject to the provision of this section and of section 3.09, the use of force upon or toward another person is justifiable when the actor believes that such force is immediately necessary for the purpose of protecting himself against the use of unlawful force by such other person on present occasion.

2.   *Limitations on justifying necessity for using of force.*

   a.   The use of force is not justifiable under this section:

      (i)   to resist an arrest which the actor knows is being made by a peace officer although the arrest is unlawful.

   b.   The use of deadly force is not justifiable under this section unless the actor believes that such force is necessary to protect himself against death, serious bodily harm, kidnaping, or sexual intercourse compelled by force or threat, nor is it justifiable if:

      (i)   the actor, with the purpose of causing death or serious bodily harm, provoked the use of force against himself in the same encounter; or

      (ii)   the actor knows that he can avoid the necessity of using force with complete safety by retreating or surrendering possession of a thing to a person asserting a claim of right thereto, or by complying with the demand that he abstain from any action which he has no duty to take, except that:

         (1)   the actor is not obliged to retreat from his dwelling or his place of work unless he was the initial aggressor.

         (2)   a public officer justified in using force in the performance of his duties, or a person justified in using force in his assistance, or a person justified in using force in making an arrest, or preventing an escape is not obliged to desist from efforts performed such duty, effect such arrest or prevent such escape...

In plain language, what does this mean? A person without fault may use such force as reasonably appears necessary to protect himself from the imminent use of unlawful force upon himself. A person may use deadly force if: he is without fault; he is confronted with "unlawful force"; and he is threatened with imminent death or great bodily harm. The response to the threat of force must be proportionate; that is, if an individual threatens you with a stick, you cannot shoot him. Your response would be excessive. If someone shoves you, you cannot smash him in the face and break his jaw.

Again, your response is unreasonable. This works in reverse as well. If someone is threatening to kill you, and has the means to do so (gun, knife), and you have not provoked the attack, you can match his lethal force.

This sounds simple and, of course, is not so. Unless there are witnesses lined up waiting to testify in your behalf, *proving* self defense after you have broken someone's jaw or killed him is often difficult. Ask any police officer who has been involved in an altercation or shootout. You must prove that you did not provoke the attack, that escape was not possible, and that your response to the other person's show of force was commensurate (equal) or less. There is, for example, the Deadly Weapon Doctrine, a rule which allows juries to assume that if a deadly weapon was used, the defendant intended to kill his victim (as opposed to merely wounding him).

Defense of Others. In some jurisdictions, the person acting in defense of another is only permitted to use that degree of force that the victim is entitled to use. If the victim was not entitled to use force in self defense, the party acting in the defense of the victim is likewise not able to use force ("stands in the shoes of the victim"). Modern interpretations, however, are slightly different, stating that defense of others is only valid if the defender reasonably believed that the person being rescued had the legal right to use force in his own right. All that is necessary is the reasonable appearance of the right to use force.

From the Model Penal Code:

(1)   Subject to the provisions of this section and of section 3.09, the use of force upon or towards the person of another is justifiable to protect a third person when:

(a)   the actor would be justified under 3.04 in using such force to protect himself against the injury he believes to be threatened to the person whom he seeks to protect; and

(b)   under the circumstances as the actor believes them to be, the person whom he seeks to protect would be justified in using such protective force; and

(c)   the actor believes that his intervention is necessary for the protection of the other person.

Under this interpretation, the defender "stands in the shoes of the victim" and can take those actions which the (client) would be entitled to take in order to protect him. By the same token, the agent cannot acquire or exercise any rights which do not belong to the client. If the client, for example, has provoked an attack, the self-defense premise evaporates.

Defense of a Dwelling. Non-deadly force may be used to prevent or terminate an attempt at unlawful entry into the dwelling or an attack upon defendant's dwelling. Deadly force can only be used to prevent violent entry made with intent to commit a personal attack upon an inhabitant, or to prevent an entry to commit a violent felony in the dwelling. The rule to follow is to only use deadly force in self-defense or defense of another who would be justified in the use of deadly force in self-defense.

Defense of Personal Property. Reasonable non-deadly force may be used at any time to prevent property in one's possession from being wrongfully taken. Deadly force may not be used to regain possession of property wrongfully taken. The courts have taken the stand that there are summary legal mechanisms available to recover property and that a human's life is worth far more than mere property. Force may not be used if a request to desist or refrain from the activity would suffice.

EXAMPLE

You are offered a two-year contract as a Security Specialist for a corporation which manufactures products for the Defense Department. Your contract spells out your rate of pay, ancillary benefits (i.e., medical and dental care, insurance, per diem, transportation, clothing allowance, etc.), and your duties.

One evening, while you are on duty, protestors climb the security fence, break into a high security building, and begin to smash valuable computer equipment which contains the fruits of years and billions of dollars of research. When they break in, a central alarm system alerts you to the intrusion and you take a squad of your subordinates to the site. There you witness the ongoing destruction noted above.

In confronting the problem you have priorities, those assigned to you by your employer and those assigned to you by law.

From your employer's point of view, your first effort must be to stop the destruction. This is permissible by law because the protestors are both trespassing and committing destruction of property not their own (which, in some jurisdictions may define the felony of burglary). You cannot use "undue" force to prevent the destruction; however, you may apprehend them (place them under arrest) for the commission of a felony and turn them over to the police upon their arrival. In doing so, you risk charges of assault (intent to commit bodily harm), battery (unconsented to touching), wrongful imprisonment (holding for the police), intentional infliction of emotional distress (lawyers always throw that in because it sounds good to juries and because there's no consistent definition of it), violation of civil rights (wrongful use of force, if you have general police power).

If, in preventing further destruction, one of

your subordinates uses his PR-24 to strike one of the protestors, you as well as your employer can be sued for negligence in screening and/or training that individual.

It is thin comfort to you that these protestors were committing crimes and, at the very least, serious torts at the time you subdued them. If, of course, you or one of your subordinates should shoot a protestor, or kill one, the level of potential damages rises seriously.

On the other hand, if you or any of your men are injured by the protestors, you may have legal recourse against them . . . good luck to you in collecting. You will, more than likely, have a workers compensation claim against your employer in the event you are injured, which claim you would be injudicious to exercise unless the employer's insurance doesn't cover your injury.

Other legal issues may arise from this event. If you or your subordinates sustain an injury, was that because your employer was negligent in failing to hire sufficient security personnel to cope with a foreseeable event? Did the employer provide training, proper liaison with the local police department, or adequate equipment for you to deal with protestors on a non-lethal basis, etc.? These aspects of the matter may all provide grounds for a legal recovery but, the question really is, are you wise to avail yourself of them? And that is one only you can answer.

A much better practice would be to foresee these potential problems and address them in your employment agreement.

The job and business opportunities for executive protection trained individuals are broader than might first be imagined. Executive protection agents have used their skills in an extended work environment to include personal protection, property protection, and asset protection. Agents work: for corporations, security companies, private families, and individuals; as couriers and limousine drivers; for airlines and cruise ship companies; and as the executive protection and property protection teams for strike protection companies. Many agents, either on their own or teamed up with one or more other agents, open their own businesses. Some use their experience to move into other areas of security, such as special event security or campus security. Others, with experience and specialized skills, provide consulting services.

For the fledgling agent, it is important to make some targeted decisions which are primarily-- "Do I want to work for a corporation or company, or a private family or individual, or do I want to open my own business?"

WORKING FOR A CORPORATION

There are pros and cons to every job situation, and if you are thinking that you would like to work for a corporation, here are some factors that you should consider.

Pros and Cons

On the "pro" side, if you are successful in getting a job with a corporation, you will (hopefully) have job stability, at least for a period of time. Companies and corporations who are able to afford the hiring of executive protection agents are probably in good financial condition. Regular payroll checks are issued, making income predictable. Corporate benefits can total at least one-third of the payroll

dollars and can include health and dental insurance, paid vacations, paid holidays, tuition assistance, child care, employee cafeteria with inexpensive meals, perhaps a car, and a sharing of the social security taxes, among other benefits.

Another advantage to working with a corporation is that you may be able to work your way up to an even better-paid job. For example, an agent might eventually achieve a Security Director's job. Because of the close proximity of the agent to the client (probably the CEO of the company), the agent can enjoy the good wishes of the client for career advancement.

An advantage of working with a corporation is the corporate support, the secretarial pool for typing letters and reports, the legal counsel, sophisticated communications, lots of office supplies and stationery, the Crisis Management Team, the transportation pool, possibly corporate aircraft, and more. These are wonderful advantages, although they have a tendency to spoil the individual who may, later, go off on his own.

An advantage for some is the caliber of people with whom the agent will interact. Corporate people tend to look good, smell good, and use good social manners. The client will be a sharp, intelligent business man or woman, easily able to understand protection concepts (whether he/she practices them or not). For the most part, these are not crazy, drugged-out clients who will make life hell for the agent(s). While the corporate client may or may not be fully cooperative, he is not dumb.

Working for a major corporation does wonders for a resume. If an agent can list that he or she worked for a Fortune 500 company and had a successful tour, it places him/her in the company of heavy-hitters.

So, what's to complain about? The very infrastructure which supplies the secretaries, communications, legal counsel, etc. will supply something else--office politics. Corporations are riddled with hungry, ambitious sharks, all striving to improve their individual careers at anyone else's expense. The agent will, because of his close proximity to the client, undoubtedly be viewed with suspicion and jealousy. Corporations harbor endless ways to torpedo a good idea or a good person. If the agent is perceived as a threat, the corporate sharks will meld together to get him. Corporate sabotage is ruthless and effective.

It can be boring. Because of the many layers of management and protocol, an agent will experience terrible feelings of helplessness. The agent cannot simply walk in and say, "This the way it's going to be." An agent may end up as a glorified flunkey, primarily driving the car.

There is a finite upper level of income which the agent can make within the corporation. For example, the agent might, under the most ideal circumstances, make $50,000-plus and benefits (often much less), working for a corporation. And, at the end of his or her tenure with the corporation, that's pretty much *"it."* He may or probably will not be a part of the pension plan, so that at the end of his job, he is out without ongoing income. This is as opposed to putting together one's own business with an equity that can be sold.

A clear disadvantage to getting a job with a corporation is the need to show a very high level of qualifications. If you are young and lacking in education and experience, you will probably not even be considered for a corporate position. Corporations tend to hire people who have college degrees and in-depth experience. They don't like the concept of on-the-job training for protection people. Therefore, if you are 21 and have never protected anyone, you will probably not be considered for employment.

Targeting the Corporation

Before you show up at the door of the corporate personnel office, there are a number of things to be done. This is akin to saying that, before you can conduct an advance, you must do your research and put together your threat assessment. So, before you even ask for an interview, you must put together a Target Model for each corporation with whom you will seek employment. You will want to know as much as possible about the corporation. There are some readily available sources for this information.

Most corporations, whether private or publicly traded on the stock exchange, publish an Annual Report. Annual Reports (intended for present stockholders and future investors) are marvelous repositories of information about the company. The Annual Report "tells the story" of the corporation, describing its history, activities, products and services, financial information, often the names and titles of top executives, as well as indicators of numbers of employees. An Annual Report for a corporation can usually be obtained simply by asking for it. Many public libraries contain the Annual Reports for major corporations in their area.

Other sources of corporate information contained in good libraries are:

. *Lexus/Nexus*--a sophisticated computer news database.

. *Standard and Poor's Register of Corporation Directors and Executives*--gives names, business addresses, and biographical data.

. *Standard and Poor's Corporation Records*--gives industries, geographic penetration, corporate structure, history, names of key managers, addresses, financial data.

. *Moody's*--covers similar topics as does *Standard and Poor's.*

. *New York Times Index*--indexes articles published in the *New York Times* newspapers by subject and name.

. *Wall Street Journal Index--Corporate*--gives brief summaries of all *Wall Street Journal* articles published.

. *Wall Street Journal Index--General*--gives brief summaries of *Wall Street Journal* articles by subject or an individual person's name.

. *Dunn's Million Dollar Directory*--different data.

. *Dunn's Career Guide*--hiring trends in corporations and work force needs.

. The business-oriented magazines, back issues kept by libraries--*Forbes, Business Week, Fortune*, and any local business magazines such as *Colorado Business Magazine*. The local business magazines list the top 100 to 300 corporations in the state with brief descriptions.

From these sources you should be able to find the answers to most of these questions.

. How long has the corporation been in business? (An indicator of stability.)

. Is it privately held or publicly traded on the stock exchange? (Stockholder meetings can be dangerous for a CEO's health.)

. What are its primary industries? (If it is animal research or abortion clinics, there is a high potential risk factor.)

. Is it an international company? Where are its subsidiaries and branch offices located? (Lebanon? Iran? or other high-risk countries?)

. Who are their primary customers and markets? (Are they selling nuclear initiators to Saddam Hussein?)

. Who are their major competitors? (Research them as well; have they had security problems?)

. What is the history of the stock prices traded

for the company, and what is the stock selling for now? (Financial stability.)

. Has the company announced lay-offs, downsizing, or other signs of retrenching? (This is a good-news, bad-news story--the company may be in severe financial straits--or, conversely, it may be taking bold, needed steps to achieve financial success, thus making some employees unhappy.)

. Does the company contribute money to any causes and, if so, what are they? (If the corporate gift-giving is focused on abortion, it can be a security problem.)

. Are they unionized? (Ugly union negotiations can heighten the risk to key executives.)

. Have they had problems in the past which were covered by the media, such as product tampering, sabotage, or suits brought against either the company or key executives? (There may be some unhappy, brooding, potential stalkers out there.)

. Is, or has, the company taken a controversial position on any issue? (More potentially unhappy, dissatisfied people with a grudge.)

. Does the company have a history of being associated with environmental crises, contaminations, or hazards? (There are some violent "anti" groups out there.)

. What is the corporate structure of the corporation? (It helps to know who are the decision-makers.)

. Are corporate officers (Chairman of the Board, President, etc.) widely covered by the media, listing hobbies, charities, addresses, etc.? (This makes the executives very vulnerable.)

If you have done your homework, you now know enough about the corporation to apply for a job. Instead of sitting in an interview as a non-informed nerd, you can intelligently discuss alternatives with your interviewer. Also, as a result of your research, you have targeted the companies you want to work for instead of blindly cold-calling on multiple corporations. Which are the handful of corporations which offer the challenge, and show the need, for you to demonstrate your skills?

How do you know which corporations are looking for executive protection agents? You don't, unless you have received a tip from someone. However, having done your research, you now know which corporations *might* have a need for protection and can afford it. If you have maintained your membership in the right associations, such as the American Society for Industrial Security (ASIS), and have participated actively in the local ASIS Chapter meetings, you will have met a number of Security Directors from major corporations. From them you may receive information about jobs. If there are no insider tips, you will need to make appointments and prepare to interview.

Getting the appointment for an interview will probably be the toughest hurdle. You should have some idea as to who would authorize the hiring and who will interview the potential agent. Is it the Security Director? Probably not, since his, or her, job is primarily to protect the company assets from being stolen either from outside or inside. Is it the CEO himself? Probably not. He is too busy to conduct initial interviews. Try one step down from the CEO and you may be on the right track. If you are on good terms with the Security Director, you might want to take him to lunch and ask his advice. Tell him what you are looking for, and emphasize the fact that you would greatly appreciate his help in contacting the right person. Try *hard* not to present a challenge to the Security Director; instead, leave the impression that executive protection and corporate security are two different but complementary fields. If the Security Director is reluctant to steer you to the right person within his own corporation, he may cheerfully give you valuable information about other corporations in the area.

Once you have determined who should be contacted for an interview, you can try one of four strategies. Best strategy is to find someone through

your professional network who can, and is willing to, request the interview for you. If this is not possible, you can send your resume with a cover letter to your target, stating that you will follow up with a phone call to set up an interview. Or, you can bite the bullet and, without preamble, make the telephone call, asking for the opportunity to meet with the individual. Or, fourth, you can try walking into the office and asking the secretary (known as the "gatekeeper") to assist in making an appointment with the individual.

With the three latter techniques you will probably be confronted by the "gatekeeper," the (usually) female person whose job it is to protect her boss's privacy and time. There is absolutely no advantage in trying to circumvent the gatekeeper. Instead, you must get this person on your side. Do not lie to the gatekeeper; do not be flippant with her; do not try to intimidate her. Be courteous and be brief. If you are met by a stony refusal, thank the gatekeeper and ask if she would recommend the person whom you should contact for an interview. Surprisingly, you may find that once she does not feel under pressure to arrange an interview with her boss, she may be very willing to help you find someone else, even going so far as to calling that person's office for you. If you are faced with a brick wall, and no one will grant the interview, thank each and all, and tell them that you will be in touch with them at a later date. You may have to try several times before you succeed in getting the interview. Even if you are turned down, send a thank-you letter, stating that you appreciate their courtesy in talking with you.

Assuming that you are successful in making an appointment for an interview, you will need several items to take along with you to the interview.

Business Cards

A business card of good design and high quality is absolutely indispensable. It is a tool of the trade. A business card is, in a sense, you! It gives the recipient as idea of how you regard yourself. It provides the necessary information for the other person to get in touch with you. Not to have a card, nor to have one on your person, is an indication that you are a nonentity, not worth remembering. On the other hand, worse than not having a card is having a dirty, crumpled, badly designed, or poor quality card.

Because of the important message which a business card sends to the receiver, you may wish to use a graphic artist to design and commission your cards for you (as well as your stationery, all of which should match in logo, design, paper, and color.) A good graphic artist can design a card that is in good taste and harmony, and that looks as handsome as the cards used by those executives whom you need to contact. A graphic artist can design a distinctive logo, which is often, in itself, worth the price of her services. If you feel that you cannot afford the services of a graphic artist, then go to a high quality printing firm, not one of the cheap, fast quick-print companies. The quickie companies provide no design assistance and little help; they are primarily order-takers. A good printing firm, on the other hand, will actively assist in suggesting appropriate paper quality and weight, colors, and a graphically balanced card.

There are several elements to a business card, beginning with the *paper stock* on which it is printed. Cards can be dull matte finish or shiny, but must be of sufficient weight not to tear or easily crumple. If in doubt, ask the graphic artist or the printer for advice. These people print thousands of business cards for companies and executives and have an excellent sense of what is appropriate.

Cards may be *printed* or *engraved*. Engraving is more expensive than printing but is a sure indicator of quality. Many people have their cards printed but pay a little additional to have either the name of the company or their own name engraved, thus giving a little touch of class. The *type* used for lettering may be simple and straightforward or more script-like. Many professions have adopted a particular type of lettering; for example, attorneys tend almost invariably to use elegant script lettering. As an executive protective specialist, you should use a type that is strong, clear, and straightforward without being overly bold. Remember, the card represents the real you; a

card that is too high profile might indicate that *you* are too high profile.

The *size* of the lettering can be controlled. It should be easily read without squinting, but not so large as to cover the face of the card. As with all documents, a business card should have a sufficient amount of what is called "white space"; that is, space that is not covered with print or graphics.

Which leads to the next design elements, the *logo* and the *text* printed (or engraved) on the card. A logo is where most people go wrong. Many logos are badly designed or are overly cute. This same flaw pertains to the choice of a company name. I have seen business cards with names like WORLD'S GREATEST BODYGUARDS and a logo that sports a grossly muscled guy with arms crossed and scowling. Is that supposed to be tough or what? It gives entirely the wrong impression. A logo should be discreet, in good taste, and can be quite simple. For example, some people opt to have as a logo their company name with a small but distinctive arrangement of lines or symbol. The logo must be in harmony with the company name, and the text printed on the card.

The *text* (or information) contained on the card should always include the company name, your name and title (if you have one), business address, telephone, fax number (if pertinent), and e-mail address. If you have more than one office, you may also include the address and telephone number of both offices. If your title is bonafide, use it, but avoid convoluted titles and initials that are added on because you think you need them. Many agents use Personal Protection Specialist, or Certified Protection Specialist (if they are, indeed, certified by a recognized body such as a school). The titles "Mr., Mrs., Ms., and Miss" are not used on business cards unless the first name is unclear as to whether it is male or female. For example, if a female is named Cameron White, she will probably need to add "Ms." in front of her name.

If the name of your company or your name and title do not easily indicate the nature of your business you may need to add a *descriptive line*. For example, if your company name is "Executive Protection International," it is clear what your business is engaged in; but, if your company name is "Excalibur" with no additional description, it is not at all clear what and who you are. In this case, you might wish to use EXCALIBUR and underneath add a smaller line that states, "Personal and Estate Protection."

Many people choose to design their cards so that it includes a description of their services. You can use a double card (see example) which on the outside has the usual company name, individual name and title, address, and telephone--and on the inside lists the services offered.

In deciding what to put on your card, remember, less is better. Do not cover your business card with print from side to side, and top to bottom. A business card is not a brochure. It is an "introduction," and as such, states only the necessary facts.

The color of the paper stock and the print should be the same as used on your stationery, envelopes, and presentation folders and brochures (if you have them). If in doubt, stick to the safe side. White and light grey with black lettering is always acceptable. Sometimes, for very little additional money, an additional color can be added; for example, a logo that is dark red or dark blue on a light grey card with black lettering is a handsome presentation.

Purchase a card case, one of good quality, (avoid using the tacky freebies which the printing companies hand out) to keep your cards clean and uncrumpled. For some dim reason, many men (in particular) carry their business cards in their wallet, along with credit cards, pictures of the kids, etc., etc. It is painful to see a person looking through bits and pieces of their lives to find the company business card. Card cases, even leather ones, cost very little.

You should refill your card case every day, so that you always have about 20 business cards with you. If you are going to a conference or other event

where there will be many people, you may need to carry another 20 or 30 cards with you in an easily accessible pocket. Don't be shy! When you find an appropriate opportunity, hand your business card to anyone whom you think will be a good networking partner or a potential client.

JUDITH M. ROBINSON

Personal Protection Specialist

855 E. River Road #111 • Tucson, AZ 85718 • 602 887 3986

Education • Services • Audio-Visual Productions

POLO INTERNATIONAL™
PROTECTING OUR LOVED ONES

Robert L. Bishop, Ph.D.
Director

P.O. Box 150058
San Rafael, CA 94915
(415) 453-9774

TELEPHONE SYSTEMS CONSULTANTS

BARRY A. CRYER
PRESIDENT

303-963-0545   FAX 303-963-9617

320 ARAPAHOE CARBONDALE, COLORADO 81623

Below is shown an example of a double card, with a listing of services on the inside of the card.

MARTHA J. BRAUNIG
DIRECTOR, PROGRAM DEVELOPMENT

200 PARK AVENUE • NEW YORK, N. Y. 10017 (212) 973-3210

TOURISM EDUCATION CORPORATION

- MULTI-MEDIA PERSONALIZED INSTRUCTIONAL PROGRAMS FOR HOTELS/MOTELS/RESTAURANTS.

- SUPERVISORY DEVELOPMENT COURSES FOR IN-HOUSE GROUP INSTRUCTION.

- DEVELOPMENT OF STANDARD TASK PROCEDURES FOR TOURISM/HOSPITALITY INDUSTRY.

- TASK UNIT JOB DESCRIPTION MANUAL.

- HOSPITALITY MANAGEMENT SKILLS PROGRAMS.

- TRAINING AND COACHING TECHNIQUES COURSES.

- CUSTOM-DESIGNED INDIVIDUAL TRAINING PROGRAMS.

TOURISM EDUCATION CORPORATION

Resume

A good resume is an absolute necessity! OK, why am I highlighting this fact? Because, even though everyone knows this, *an astonishing number of executive protection agents do not have ANY resumes, or have long, outdated resumes.* Writing good resumes is not easy and is not very much fun to put together, but if you accept that it is an absolute necessity, you can then move on to doing it.

Some common alibis for not having a resume are: I'm too busy; I don't know how; I don't need a resume; I'll get around to it later. Well, stow away all those tired alibis and let's get started. While not simple, it's not that hard.

The basic functions of a resume are to summarize your background by accenting your unique accomplishments, to "advertise" you to a prospective employer, and to obtain an interview. As much as a business card, a resume is a picture of you. Visually it represents you. If it is sloppy or poorly organized, the impression is that you are likewise. A resume is worth spending several hours writing it originally, and it should be constantly revised, added to, and refocused to target specific companies and job possibilities. A resume is not static. Your resume should be customized to fit specific job situations. It is well to remember that, generally, the resume will not get you the job, but it can get you the interview, and it can leave a memory pictorial of who you are and what qualities you have that are unique and desirable.

Resumes are so critical that many people pay goodly sums of money to professional resume writing services. If you feel that you simply cannot cope with writing your own resume, this is an option. However, the disadvantages are several. A top quality resume writer may charge as much as $100 or more to write your resume. Once you have the resume, you will still need to customize it from time to time, either adding to or reformatting it. And, the exercise that you will go through in writing your own resume will be helpful to you in your interviews, as you will spend a number of hours interviewing yourself in order to write the resume. If possible, you should write your own resume, then have someone else or several people read it for accuracy and content.

Whether you write your own resume or pay someone else to do so, there are some simple rules to be followed.

. If possible, keep your resume to one page, and never more than two pages. A resume should not be confused with a curriculum vitae, which can be multiple pages, containing letters of recommendation, copies of diplomas, etc. Guaranteed, a busy executive will not read more than two pages unless he has specifically requested a curriculum vitae. Curriculum vitaes are sometimes requested when one is bidding on a contract, and the reader may be making decisions long distance rather than in person, sitting in front of you. A one or two page resume will still allow space to list and describe your professional qualities and accomplishments.

. Keep sentences and paragraphs short, and avoid embellishing simple facts.

. Be honest. Although it is calculated that a high percentage of resumes contain false information, this is a trap that can be fatal. If you lie on your resume and are caught, your name will be muddied throughout the private security world.

. Don't "gild the lily" by embellishing the facts. State the facts in simple but action-oriented words. The interviewer does not need to think that you are the greatest protection agent since the invention of the U.S. Secret Service. The interviewer wants to know about you, what you have done and accomplished. Interviewers are too smart and have listened to too many braggarts to be fooled by a flowery resume. Eliminate overlong works, phrases, and sentences.

. Use action words, such as *planned, designed, created, negotiated, completed, evaluated, identified, implemented, changed, reduced (costs), produced, directed, handled, identified*, etc.

. If you have properly researched the company or individual with whom you will be interviewing, your resume should be targeted directly to that company or individual. Let us say, for example, that Company X is interviewing for an agent to be assigned to the CEO's wife, who spends half her time traveling in Europe. Your resume should highlight your experience in working with female clients, your language capabilities (if you speak another language), your experiences with foreign advances, your ability to work as a one-man (or woman) team, and other applicable qualities--rather than focusing on how you ran several four-man teams for the CEO of the abortion clinics.

. While the appearance of the resume is important, you should not attempt anything too fancy. One of the problems with professional resume writers is that they have fallen in love with desktop publishing and are apt to turn a resume into some sort of quasi-brochure with fancy headings, borders, and typographic add-ons. A resume should be simple, well organized, easy to read, and tell the story--period. Skip the bells and whistles.

. Use a simple format that is easy to read, that is free of all typographical and grammatical mistakes, is spotlessly clean, and is on good quality paper. If you have written your own resume, go to a secretarial service and have it printed out on a high quality laser printer. It is perfectly all right to photocopy (xerox) additional copies (since laser print copies can cost as much as $1.00 per page) so long as the paper is of better quality than the usual photocopy paper. Buy a good bond paper from the office supply place and use it in the copy machine.

The following information appears on all resumes:

. Name.

. Address.

. Telephone number at which you can be reached or receive messages.

. Experience.

. Education.

The experts recommend that you include a "Summary of Qualifications section which, in one paragraph of five to six sentences, strongly illustrates your top selling points--what you would bring to perform the job. This should appear close to the top.

Many resumes also contain the following:

. Job or career sought. While many resumes

begin with a statement of job or career objectives, this can be a trap. If I state that my career objective is "to make a career as a professional executive protection agent in the private security field," it is too general. If I say that my career objective is "to achieve employment with a Fortune 500 corporation, heading up their executive protection division of security," it is too specific. Remember, your objective in furnishing your resume is to obtain an interview, at which time you and the interviewer can discuss company goals and your abilities to fit those goals. (Some of the best assignments and jobs the author has experienced were so unique that had I listed some specific job being sought, I would probably not have been offered the exciting jobs about which I knew nothing.)

. References. You can save space by stating, "References furnished upon request." The only reason for listing references would be if the references are known to the interviewer and carry weight with him. An exception to this is the resume provided by a consultant or independent agent who might list "Clients" rather than "References." For example, a consultant might provide on a separate page something entitled, "Partial List of Clients for Whom Services Were Provided," followed by name, address, telephone number, and contact name of several clients. If you provide this, be certain that the clients do not mind having their names used, and that they will testify to your accomplishments for them.

. Special talents. Special talents may, or may not, be of interest to an interviewer depending upon whether those talents are uniquely fitted to the corporate goals and the specific job. Language skills are always useful, but your interest in medieval poetry is probably not. If you possess specialized computer skills or other business-related skills, this would be a good place to list them, as they may be of benefit to a corporation. A corporation reluctant to bring in a protection agent might be more willing to do so if that agent can bring other skills to the job.

. Military experience. This is a valuable addition for executive protection agents (as is law enforcement experience). Many employers prefer agents with military or law enforcement experience, so this should be included in a resume.

. Association memberships, awards, accreditations. This can be a valuable category if you are a member of ASIS (American Society for Industrial Security) or other industry associations. This marks you as a professional. On the other hand, if your only memberships are with the Kiwanis Club and the Senior Boy Scouts, that's nice but not of much use, so leave it off the resume.

. Boards of Director memberships. Some consultants who have been in the business a long time have served on the Board of Directors for notable corporations. This is then a valuable add-on, as it lends prestige. It is not usual for a protection agent new to the business to have this experience.

. Personal information--marital status, age, height, weight, sports. While personal data such as marital status and age may be important to the interviewer, you may not wish to limit your opportunity for an interview based on volunteering personal data. The interviewer may prefer someone over 35 for the job and you are 25, but if you can get as far as the interview, you may be able to impress the interviewer with your unique abilities to perform the job. It is illegal for an interviewer to ask some personal questions (age, religion) or to discriminate in job hiring based on age, sex, or ethnic values. Why then gratuitously provide this information?

The space you save by not listing unnecessary add-ons will give you full scope to list your accomplishments and the results which you have achieved, and which may make you uniquely desirable for the job being interviewed.

There are some "don'ts." Don't include your picture unless asked to do so. You do not know what they are looking for and your picture may torpedo you. Don't waste money on fancy binders; it looks like you are trying to dress a poor resume in a fancy cover. If your references are not top-drawer, don't list them; your relatives or church minister are not going to be impressive. Do not list salary expectations in your resume. It is *after* you have bowled them over with the interview that you get into the serious business of salary and benefits.

The organization of a resume is very important. Some resumes are never even read because at first glance they appear badly organized and unsightly. There are, in broad terms, two ways to organize a resume; chronological, and functional (sometimes called targeted).

In a chronological resume, work history is highlighted, shown by working backward with the most recent job listed first. This is the usual old-style resume format and is useful if you have a solid work history without gaps between jobs, if the jobs clearly show a steady progression and growth of career, and if the jobs and/or companies listed are impressive. Clearly, a chronological resume is not advantageous if you are just starting out and have little work experience to speak for you, or worse, you have a spotty work history with long gaps between employment.

With a chronological resume, do not feel that you have to list every piddly job you have ever held. List the important jobs of the past ten years and summarize the others in one descriptive paragraph. You do not have to list the exact day and month. If someone wants to check your work history, you can supply this later.

In the example of a chronological resume shown, note that the applicant has a strong, steady job history with no perceptible gaps between employment. He has improved his employment potential with each new job. His education follows his job history. This is a professional who is dedicated to self-improvement and has proven his value with his accomplishments. It is a straightforward resume with no embellishments or fancy wording.

With a functional, or targeted, resume, the information is organized differently and allows you to highlight your accomplishments and areas of strength rather than work history. This format works well for those individuals with short ("thin") work histories, or who are changing career areas, and for those people who are targeting a specific job. It is more future-directed than the chronological resume and allows you to list capabilities as well as accomplishments.

Many experienced consultants use the functional resume rather than the chronological, as they may have dealt with many clients but do not wish to list a long, long history of work in chronological order.

The functional resume provides an opportunity to highlight some valuable abilities which do not surface in a chronological resume. For example, if you possess those qualities which fit you for working very well with children, how do you say this in a chronological resume? It is easy with a functional resume.

The example shown of a functional resume is targeted for a specific job. The XYZ Corporation is preparing to hire an individual for a low-profile, low-risk, one-man or one-woman team to protect the wife of the CEO of the XYZ Corporation. The wife is interested in volunteerism and spends a good part of the year traveling to Europe on missions for the United Nations, specifically with issues concerning children. The wife is a very private person although she maintains a busy social schedule, and whoever works with her must fit in discreetly with her life style.

Yet another approach is to work with a combination resume--one that combines the best features of the chronological and the functional resume.

The important point is to individually target the resume toward the company and/or job wanted, and to do so in a way that emphasizes the applicants best qualities and experience. It is good practice to construct one each of the different styles of resumes; then, show them to friends and ask for their opinion. If you have written the resumes on your computer, you can make any necessary adjustments, as needed.

```
CHRONOLOGICAL RESUME
```

GEORGE J. BUTLER
1422 Seelig Street
Houston, Texas 76210
(713) 522-5313

WORK EXPERIENCE:

1989 - Present   JONES INTERNATIONAL, INC.   Houston, NY

Director of Security

Report directly to Vice President, Operations. Plan and submit yearly strategic plan for security, with budget. Provide all in-house security, supervising staff of 50 employees. Provide executive protection for CEO and Chairman of the Board, utilizing two teams of two protection agents each. Designed and implemented computer and information protection program to safeguard proprietary information. Reduced internal theft from $150,000 in 1988 to $70,000 in 1992. Designed and implemented security program for overseas subsidiary. Participate in corporate Crisis Management Team.

1986 - 1989   BROWN MANUFACTURING, LTD.   Chicago, IL

Assistant Director of Security
Team Leader, Executive Protection Team
Team Member, Executive Protection Team

Joined Brown Manufacturing in 1986 as member of four-man team, assigned to CEO and his family. During first month of assignment found and identified bomb attached to vehicle. Nine months later, appointed team leader and, as such, made out all work schedules, conducted or supervised all advances for team, and contracted for new security system for CEO's residence. In 1988, appointed Assistant Director of Security with specific responsibility for all executive protection provided company officials, total of four teams. Conducted and supervised all undercover operations to diminish internal theft and drug use.

1984 - 1986   SINGLEY HOTEL   Chicago, IL

Supervisor, Security

Joined the security staff in 1984 as member of the security staff. Within three months promoted to Supervisor, Security, reporting to the hotel Director of Security. Supervised staff of 12. Assigned for six months to Singley Hotel, Houston, Texas, as undercover operator. Broke case of internal theft involving theft of $120,000, identified culprits, and succeeded in obtaining indictments against three ringleaders.

EDUCATION:

1988   Executive Security International, Ltd.   Aspen, CO
A.A.S. in Criminal Justice

1986   Executive Security International, Ltd.   Aspen, CO
Certified Protection Specialist

1985   Houston Community College   Houston, TX
A.A.S. in Hotel Management

MEMBERSHIPS: American Society for Industrial Security
International Association of Chiefs of Police (Associate Member)
Reserve Deputy Sheriffs of Texas

FUNCTIONAL RESUME

MARY R. RINGOLD
1212 South Elm Street
Denver, Colorado
(303) 355-9788

JOB TARGET: Member executive protection team

ABILITIES:

- Excellent handgun shooting skills, NRA certified instructor, with license to carry. Excellent defensive driving skills; trained at convoy driving as well as escape and evasion maneuvers. Graduated with honors from Executive Security International's Executive Protection Driving program.

- Good language skills; speak/write, in addition to English, Spanish and French.

- Very good social skills, having attended private schools with wide experience in social events. Worked as social secretary to private club director.

- Very good communications skills, including report writing, letters, and proposals. Worked for two years as volunteer for non-profit organization.

- Very good typing and computer word processing skills. Am accurate and understand formatting of documents.

- Work exceptionally well with families and children. Am one of seven children, five of whom are younger. Volunteer work with needy families has honed my communication skills with children and youngsters.

ACHIEVEMENTS:

- Graduated from Executive Security International with honors, highest-scoring student in class of 1992. Courses included defensive driving, defensive shooting, principles of protection, observational psychology, first respondent medicine, profiles of terrorism, and bomb search and identification.

- Received commendations from ABC Volunteer Group for work with poor children.

- Worked three summers at the Cherry Creek Country Club as assistant to the Social Director of the club, arranging special events, luncheons, dinners, and sports activities. Served as secretary to the social director, learning valuable communications skills.

- Completed several computer classes, thus building skills with IBM and McIntosh computers, focusing primarily on word processing and desktop publishing.

- Volunteered for protection team and received commendations for work with presidential candidate Jerry Brown. Worked with campaign for six weeks. Identified several potentially dangerous individuals who were subsequently turned over to authorities.

WORK HISTORY:

1987 - 1989   Cherry Creek Country Club, Denver, CO. Assistant Social Director

1992   Executive protection team, presidential candidate Jerry Brown.

1990-92   Volunteer worker, Disadvantaged Children of Metro Denver.

1990-1992   Deputy Sheriff, Arapahoe County Sheriff's Department.

EDUCATION: Certified Protection Specialist, Executive Security International, Ltd.
               A.A.S. in Criminal Justice, Arapaho Community College, Denver, Co.

MEMBERSHIPS: American Society of Industrial Security (ASIS)

The young lady whose functional resume you will see is 25, a graduate of a private security school and, while she does not have an impressive work history, in many ways she is perfect for the job. She is low-profile, conversant in three languages, possesses to a high degree social interactive skills, and is experienced in child issues--all elements that are important to the CEO's wife, and which may be lacking in the resumes of older, more experienced executive protection men. Her resume must, somehow, catch the attention of the interviewer, compete with the more experienced people who are also interviewing for the job, and overcome her age and lack of on-the-job experience. She needs to highlight those features that will make her seem employable and comfortable with the CEO's wife, who may be very uncomfortable with the typical macho image.

Cover Letter

To secure your job interview, you may wish to send your resume with a cover letter to your targeted employer. It is important to send the letter to the right (decision-making) individual. If your research has failed to turn up a name, take a chance by calling the office of the executive you think is the person you should see and ask his secretary for his name and title. You do not have to say that you are trying to arrange for a hiring appointment; simply say that you have some information to send to the individual and would like the correct spelling of his name, plus his title.

A good cover letter is short and to the point. It is as personalized as you can make it, with some kind of reference to the company or the executive to whom you are writing, information which you should have obtained from your research. Stress your value to the company as opposed to how much you would like to work for the company (what the company can do for you.)

In the first paragraph, state why you are writing. Name the position, or field, or general occupational area about which you are asking. If you know of a specific job opening, mention it.

In the second paragraph, state why you are particularly interested in the company, location, or type of work. If you have had related experience or specialized training, point this out, mentioning one or two qualifications you think would be of greatest interest to the employer.

In the third paragraph, refer the reader to the enclosed resume, and close by making a specific request for an interview. Always ask for the interview by including a sentence something like this. "I would like to meet with you to discuss the possibilities of my working with you. I will call you in a week to arrange a meeting."

Follow through. Keep a copy of your letter and stay on schedule, so that within a week (or the time you state) call and ask when the interview can be scheduled. If the person whom you have contacted says, "I really see no point in our meeting, as we are not hiring at the present time," your response might be, "I can appreciate that; however, if you could spare 15 or 20 minutes I would still like to meet with you to get your opinion on some ideas which I have put together about your company which might be useful at some future time." While your primary objective may be to get a job, it never hurts to meet people and let them form a personal, and hopefully favorable, impression of you, thus leaving the door open to re-contact them at some point.

The Interview

A job interview is your showcase for merchandising your talents. During the interview, an employer judges your qualifications, appearance, and general fitness for the job opening. It is your opportunity to convince the employer that you can make a real contribution. Equally important, it gives you a chance to evaluate the job, the employer, and the firm. It enables you to decide if the job meets your career needs and interests.

In preparing for the interview, assemble in easily available order all the papers you need to take with you. The principal item is your resume. Even if you have sent or submitted one in advance of the interview, carry a spare as you may be asked for one. If you have submitted a resume but you also have a curriculum vitae, take along a copy of the c.v., as you may have an opportunity to present it to the prospective employer. Carry your business cards. If your resume does not list specific dates of employment, military service, etc., prepare a sheet of paper with all pertinent information so that you can refer to it if necessary.

Dress conservatively and with careful grooming. If possible, you should tailor your appearance to that of the company executives where you will be interviewing. You wish to appear as dependable, steady, professional, and entirely trustworthy. Whenever possible, wear something that is not brand-new, but rather a suit or dress that you know you look good in. New clothes, never worn before, can present surprise problems, pinching or twisting in unexpected ways.

You should be on time, actually two to three minutes early. Be prepared to present your business card to the gatekeeper, smile, and say something like, "Good morning, my name is George Brown; I have an appointment to meet with Mr. Sinclair at 10:00." If you are asked to wait, because Mr. Sinclair (the executive) is running late, smile again, saying, "Of course, no problem," sit down, and *don't fidget*. You are relaxed and cool. It helps if you have thoughtfully brought along a copy of *Business Week* or *Fortune*, which you can read while you are waiting. No matter how long it takes, be patient and remain calm. If the executive is running late, he probably has good reasons for doing so.

If the executive himself greets you and offers to escort you to his office, be quick to rise, shake hands firmly, and say, "Mr. Sinclair, thank you so much for agreeing to meet with me. I know that you are busy, and I will not take too much of your time."

During the interview, remain pleasant, friendly, and businesslike. The interviewer normally controls the interview. He/she may ask questions and may also say something like, "What can we at XYZ corporation do for you?" or, "Tell me a little more about your reasons for requesting this meeting." Be prepared to give a succinct, organized statement as to why you are specifically interested in the XYZ Corporation, and what you feel is your potential value to the company. Loose, rambling statements filled with your hopes, dreams, and ambitions will quickly bring a close to the interview. Stress your relevant qualifications without exaggeration. Make your statements and answers brief and to the point.

As you speak with the interviewer or answer questions, occasionally lean forward in your chair to show your interest. But, do not lean on his desk or touch items on his desk. Always maintain eye contact.

Following are a list of questions which are frequently asked by interviewers:

. Tell me something about yourself.

. Do you prefer a larger or smaller company?

. Why are you particularly interested in our company?

. Why do you think that you are qualified for the job?

. How did you hear about our company?

. What do you know about this job, or company?

. What would you like to tell me about your self?

. What are your major strengths? What are your major weaknesses?

. What type of work do you like to do best?

. What are your interests outside work?

. What did you like best and least about your last job?

. How does your education or experience relate to this job? this company?

. What are the advantages and disadvantages of the job you are seeking?

. Are you willing to relocate?

. What is your best quality?

. What aspect of your personality would you like to improve upon?

. What are your professional goals?

. Describe your personality.

. Why did you leave your last job?

An interview provides an opportunity for you to ask some questions, and once you have answered the interviewer's questions, it's your turn. You might want to ask these questions. Whom would I report to? May I meet this person? How important is this job to the company? What advancement opportunities are offered? Why did the last person leave this job? What is the greatest challenge of this position? Is the company growing?

While you are selling yourself, do this by letting your appearance, demeanor, and calm, precise statements sell for you, as opposed to trying to sell yourself by stampeding over the interviewer. Avoid negative statements or complaints. Keep the interview upbeat.

At the end of the interview, you should know what the next step will be: whether you should contact the interviewer again, whether you should provide more information, whether more interviews must be conducted, and when a final decision will be reached. You should end the interview on a positive note. Even if the interviewer tells you, regretfully, that the company cannot at the current time utilize your talents, thank him for taking the time to meet with you. And, *ask him for his suggestions as to where you might most successfully use your abilities.*

Surprisingly, many people do have suggestions, particularly if you have impressed them. If he has no suggestions, ask if he will keep your resume and perhaps allow you to contact him again in the future.

You should follow up every interview with a letter to the interviewer covering these points: thanking him for taking the time to meet with you; telling him that you enjoyed discussing with him the corporate environment of the XYZ Corporation; and suggesting that you will stay in touch with him in the future. Don't give up! Be persistent. Stay in touch. It may take months for the right corporate job to turn up. Meanwhile, if you have made the right impression, your interviewer may recommend you to someone else.

Listed below are some of the major reasons why individuals are rejected for jobs for which they have interviewed.

. Poor personal appearance.

. Overbearing; overaggressive; "knows it all."

. Unable to express oneself clearly; poor voice, diction, grammar.

. Lacks interest and enthusiasm; passive; indifferent.

. Lacks confidence and poise; nervous; ill-at-ease.

. Overemphasizes money; interested only in best dollar offer.

. Evasive; hedges; makes excuses.

. Lacks maturity.

. Lacks courtesy, tact, social understanding.

. Little sense of humor.

. Limp handshake; fails to look interviewer in the eye.

Two last tips. #1. If interviewing does not come easy for you, you should get a friend (or friends) who will agree to practice with you. Outline to the friend a job situation and supply him/her with some questions to ask you. When the practice interview is over, ask your friend for his *genuine*, no-holds-barred opinion of your performance.

#2. "Burn" some unimportant interviews, which is an old sales trick. It means that you make appointments for interviews that represent jobs you are not particularly interested in; then, go through the interview and when the interview is over, ask the interviewer politely for his candid impression of your interview (don't tell him you are practicing with him!) and your resume. He will probably tell you the truth. After you have six or eight interviews under your belt, you will become more comfortable with the interview process. You may go through 25 or 50 interviews before you find the "real thing."

WORKING FOR YOURSELF

Many agents, whether just starting out or widely experienced, like the concept of being independent contractors.

Pros and Cons

Working for yourself is not for everyone but, if you are full of energy, a self-starter, confident of your abilities and willing to take risks, having your own business can be great! No more complaining about the boss, since you are the boss. You can be as creative as you choose. You can set your own standards. You can be as successful as you determine you are going to be. And, finally, there are some individuals who simply are not cut out to work for other people; they are only happy when they are on their own.

As an independent contractor, you have the option of hiring other people to work with you, either regularly or (more often) on an as-needed basis. As the boss, you can set the rules, and establish the prices for the contracts. Typically, as an independent

contractor, you may bid and win a contract, then bring in the help you need to fulfill the job. If you have a good reputation and can command top dollar, you can make excellent money for short assignments; then, if you like, you can relax for a few weeks.

Many independent agents like the notion of working non-stop on an assignment, making good money, then relaxing and taking some time off. Taking different assignments can be interesting, and it always provides a variety of experiences. The top agents generally build up a reputation and a clientele that keeps them as busy as they care to be.

Perhaps the most significant advantage to owning one's own business is that of possibly selling it, profitably, at a future time. If you have been successful at starting and operating your own business, you may find that others are interested in buying your business, thus providing for your retiring years.

There are, clearly, some very serious disadvantages to working for yourself. Starting out, you are bound to find some lean times with *no* income and with bills to pay. Many independent contractors work for a year or two, or more, before they build up a sufficient clientele and reputation to be able to predict a stable income. Probably, the most severe disadvantage to being on your own is that you must handle everything, including the marketing, advertising, bookkeeping, telephone calls, and the protection work. There is no corporate infrastructure to provide the supplies, secretary, communications, legal advice, or insurance. You will need to commission stationary, write your own proposals, do your own advertising, and work up your own budgets.

There will be times when you think your telephone will never ring and other times when you are working alone, long hours, every day, until you think you will drop. The times when your telephone doesn't ring, you will wonder how you are going to pay your bills, and no matter how independent you are, you will sometimes be lonely.

Even with the disadvantages many, many agents work on their own, or start their own businesses. Some of the most successful executive protection companies in the country were started by agents who tired of working for "the company store" and struck off on their own. They wouldn't have it any other way.

Legal Forms of Doing Business

There are basically three ways of doing business: as a *sole proprietorship*; a *partnership*; or a *corporation*. There is also a handy business form called an *S Corporation*. While there is not enough room within this chapter to examine in detail the various business formats, there are a few points which may help you in the initial decision-making stage. For more information, go to the library where there are excellent books. One handy little paperback is a book called *The Law (in Plain English) for Small Businesses*, Second Edition, by Leonard D. DuBoff, publisher John Wiley & Sons.

Sole Proprietorship. A sole proprietorship is generally what we think of when we decide to go into business on our own. It is an unincorporated business owned by one person. It is simple and uncomplicated. You may be required to register the name of your company, and you might be required to obtain a license in your home city. The sole proprietor is taxed on all profits of the business and may deduct losses. There are some disadvantages to a sole proprietorship. You have no "corporate veil" to protect you against litigation, and your personal property and assets are at risk.

Partnership. Inevitably, many agents decide to partner up with one or two others and open their own business. There are obvious advantages to having a partner, someone to share the work and the worry. Two people may have somewhat different but complementary talents which, when combined, get good results. One partner may have better writing, communication, and marketing skills; the other may have better protection skills. It would seem, in many ways, to be an ideal situation, but there are definite

hazards to partnering that should be carefully examined.

Partnerships have destroyed more friendships than can be imagined. To begin, equal partnerships are really tough. Who can define "equal?" Almost inevitably, particularly as times get tough, the partners are each going to feel that the other is not pulling his or her weight. There are going to be disagreements about decisions that must be made about marketing, pricing, and just about everything else. Who will solve these disagreements? The income will almost certainly not be enough in the early stages to support one person, much less two or three people.

Partnerships are legally tricky. A partnership is a form of business wherein two or more persons associate together to conduct, as co-owners, a business. No formal agreements are needed; however, if the partners do not have a formal agreement, some very difficult problems exist. For example, without a formal agreement, all members have an equal vote in the partnership management of the business, and share equally in the profits and losses no matter how much capital they have contributed or work they have done. Without a formal agreement, any one partner can withdraw and force the dissolution of the partnership. It is essential in a partnership that the partners clearly understand and agree to a formal agreement regarding contributions of capital, voting rights, dissolution of the partnership, distribution of profits, management responsibilities, and duties of partners. The major advantages of a partnership are the pooling of talents, efforts, credit ratings, and mutual goals. The major disadvantage, in addition to those pointed out, is that each partner is *fully and personally liable for all the debts of the partnership*. There are no particular tax advantages to a partnership over a sole proprietorship, as they are handled similarly regarding income and deductions. Partnerships are difficult, and any good attorney will give many reasons why a partnership should not be attempted.

Limited Partnership. A limited partnership is sometimes a viable way to get investment dollars for a small business. This is a formalized agreement, registered with the state, much as you would register a corporation. The limited partner generally provides investment money in return for a (usually quite high) share of the profits of the business, but cannot be involved to any extent in the management or day-to-day operations of the company. The limited partner does not, therefore, share the risks of the company and is not liable for them or for debts incurred by the company. These responsibilities belong to the general partner. Needless to say, a limited partner must have a great deal of faith and trust in the abilities and prospects of the general partner to invest good money without any ability to supervise its use.

Corporation. If you believe that you and one or two others should get together, the best legal structure is a corporation. A corporation is a formal business structure which is composed of shareholders (also called stockholders), a Board of Directors, Articles of Incorporation, and Bylaws. There are some distinct differences between a corporation and a partnership or sole proprietorship.

The shareholders of the corporation are not personally liable for the corporation's debts; however, the "corporate shield" does not protect a shareholder or individual from his or her wrongful acts. So, if a shareholder agent negligently injures someone else while engaged in corporate business, he has exposed the corporation to liability, as well as himself personally.

A shareholder has full voting rights, in proportion to the number of shares which he holds, in electing the Board of Directors and appointing Officers. By controlling the Board of Directors, the shareholders control the management decisions of the corporation. Unlike a partnership, a shareholder cannot cause the dissolution of the corporation; he can only sell his shares.

One disadvantage of a corporation is the double taxation which occurs when profits of the corporation are taxed to the corporation before they are paid out as dividends, and then dividend income is again taxed to the shareholder.

In putting together the corporation, you must spend as much time as is needed to specify who is in charge, who will be the final decision-maker, what positions the principals will occupy, who is putting up the money to fund the expenses of stationery, telephone, office rent, etc., and the goals of the corporation. Are the goals to be the biggest executive protection corporation in the country or merely the best? (There may be a difference). What activities will the corporation engage in? strike protection? contract guard security? or, only executive protection? Who will be responsible for bringing in the contracts? Will each of the principals initially be responsible for bringing in enough contracts to pay his or her salary? Will the principals even take a salary, or will they plow the income back into the business?

These are only some of the questions which should be very seriously considered and answered before friends and professional associates put themselves together into a corporation or partnership.

The S Corporation. Many small businesses (and individuals) choose to incorporate as an S Corporation. The major advantage is that the owners can elect to be taxed as if they were a partnership, and they can absorb the losses of the corporation against their personal income, which cannot be done with a standard corporation.

Partnerships registered with the state and all corporations are required to file regular (usually annual) reports and tax returns. The annual reports are generally quite simple; the tax returns are somewhat more complicated than the tax returns for sole proprietorships.

Whatever you do, seek legal counsel. While it is possible to go to the library and check out a book on how to incorporate yourself, you will run the risk of making some serious mistakes. Find an affordable attorney and do it right.

Bookkeeping and Accounting

Whether in business as a sole proprietorship, partnership, or corporation, you will need to keep detailed records of your income and expenditures. Tax returns will be required for all individuals and businesses, and annual financial statements for the corporation will be required. At some point, you will be well advised to engage in some realistic financial planning for your business, with cost analyses and projected earnings. At the very least, you should become familiar with basic financial statements: the Balance Sheet and Statement of Income, and the Cash Flow Statement, as well as simple bookkeeping methods.

A very economical thing to do is to engage an accountant to set up your business with a set of very simple books which you, yourself, can keep. Then, at the end of the year, the accountant can prepare your tax return and financial statement.

Insurance

Liability insurance, if you can get it, is highly recommended. The agent's work is riddled with the potential for lawsuits. The agent can be sued, and his client can also be sued. If you are working for a corporation, you should check with the corporation's legal counsel to make certain that you and the corporation are covered in the event that something goes wrong. If you are working on your own, find a good insurance agent (one who specializes in or is at least very familiar with liability insurance) and determine what can be done. Liability insurance for bodyguards is hard to find and, unfortunately, very expensive. It is one of the hazards of the occupation. If it is a one-time gig, such as providing protection for a jewelry show, you may be able to buy an affordable short-term policy covering theft but probably not liability for injuries. If you are married, life insurance should be on your list as well.

If you accept a long-term assignment with an individual client, part of your contract might be the inclusion of both liability and life insurance. This should be one of the negotiating points. If the client

is a good businessman he will quickly understand the fact that, if someone is injured or even claims to be injured by the protection team, the client will be the "target of choice" for a lawsuit. It is, therefore, to his or her benefit to make certain that the protection team is covered with liability insurance.

Contracts

Contracts should be a regular part of the agent's working modus operandi. Contracts clearly tell the participants what services will be performed. They tend, therefore, to avoid later disagreements. Contracts help to keep the parties involved honest, for while contracts can always be litigated, the process of bringing suit can be costly and painful.

A "contract" is just a legal term for an enforceable agreement. The key terms of that sentence are *enforceable* and *agreement*.

Whether an agreement is enforceable, and by that I mean can any of the parties to the agreement be made to perform according to the terms of the agreement, or be made to pay money for damages resulting from their failure to perform, depends upon the laws of the state or country in which the contract is sought to be enforced or where it is made (signed). There are a number of reasons which a court might use to invalidate an agreement. Examples: the agreement was illegal; the agreement was an oral one where it was required to be in writing; one of the parties to the agreement was a minor; the critical terms of the agreement were not set out or were not sufficiently specific; etc. Consequently, it is advisable to have any agreement reviewed by an attorney.

Aside from pure enforceability, the real issue in a contract is whether, in fact, there was an agreement ("a meeting of the minds"). For example, suppose you hire on to do security work for $750 per week. If your contract just states ". . . the bodyguard will be paid $750 per week . . . ," does this mean a seven-day week? Twelve hours per day? Time off for meals? Recompense for damage to bodyguard's equipment? From the simple term, "$750 per week," a court could not necessarily know what other aspects are meant by the partners. A court could then enforce its own idea of what that phrase should imply. Or, it might very well declare the contract void (unenforceable).

There are two theories about contracts. The more traditional theory states that all the details (all possibilities) are discussed and put in writing. In other words, what you are obligated to do, when, where, how, and under what circumstances. The underlying rationale of this theory is that if you ever have to go into court over the contract, all the rights and obligations of each party will be clearly spelled out in great detail. In theory, it should be clear who breached the contract (broke the agreement). In practice, especially in unusual circumstances, this doesn't always work out so well.

The other theory states that contracts should be fully negotiated, not with a view towards enforcement in the courts, but for the purpose of increasing understanding among the parties so that there will be no unintentional breach of the contract.

In practice, you do about the same thing, discussing each party's obligations and duties in detail, but one perspective anticipates litigation and the other seeks to avoid it. Which brings us to the last concern; do you intend to sue the other person?

After all, he may live in a different state, or country, than you. It will probably cost you money to hire an attorney. It may cost you more to sue than you stand to recover. The cost of your time in preparation of the suit, travel, and time for testifying may exceed your recovery or interfere with other employment. There is always the significant chance that you could lose. Finally, do you want it known about you that you are a trouble-maker? All of these considerations, and more, should make you cautious about suing.

In the Appendix can be found a suggested form of contract which might be used by bodyguards and agents. It should be pointed out that sometimes the client will balk at signing such an ironclad contract. It then becomes a judgement call as to

whether you, as the agent, wish to have the assignment with no contract or with a less strict contract. Working without a contract leaves the agent open to many problems and vulnerable to legal action.

Working Tools

Business cards and resumes are an invaluable start, but there are other working tools which the independent agent or new business will need. An office, even an office at home, is needed, a place where work can be done and records kept, without distraction or outside noises. Some bare essentials include a computer, telephone, answering machine or answering service, a small typewriter (for typing envelopes and labels), a small printer, office supplies, and a filing system to contain research and client records.

If working at home is comfortable, and a small space can be dedicated to an office, well and good. However, if the agent is married with children, this can be difficult. Nothing is as depressing as calling someone (in this case the agent) on a business matter only to have a small voice wailing in the background or a tiny child answering the phone with unintelligible patter. Only slightly better is a harried wife trying to cope. The at-home business telephone should be on a separate line with a separate number, dedicated to business and hooked into an answering machine or linked to an answering (or secretarial) service which can take messages in a professional manner. A useful and inexpensive addition is "call holding," which permits you to receive two callers at the same time. Any modern answering machine permits you to call in from any point and receive messages from the machine.

Another option is to rent a small office called an executive suite. This is usually found in a complex of small offices which are all served by a common receptionist, and which include access to a copy machine, fax machine, mail drop, and answering service. Some suite arrangements provide secretarial services on an as-needed basis. These offices are often surprisingly inexpensive.

An active, busy agent will find a cell phone and/or beeper to be useful, since these communication devices enable him to stay readily available. However, these are relatively expensive services, and an answering service may be more cost-effective if the agent is just starting his or her own business.

Simple stationery, of good quality, with the agent's logo or company name imprinted, adds a definite professional tone. It is, of course, cost-effective to commission all printing at one time, to include business cards, letterhead stationery, envelopes, and presentation folders. Presentation folders are very effective for use with proposals and contracts. Presentation folders can also be used to contain promotional information about the agent or company.

Marketing Yourself and Your Business

Successful marketing is usually a blend of activities, most of which are either relatively free or very inexpensive and cost-effective.

Networking. It has been estimated that fewer than 25% of all jobs are filled through job advertisements, job recruiters, or referral services. Most people get jobs by networking, by knowing someone who knows someone. It's particularly true in the executive protection business. The most successful agents are the most accomplished at networking. The private protection business is essentially a small world, which makes it doubly important to maintain an impeccable professional reputation and to constantly network with friends, acquaintances, associates, and professionals. It also means positioning yourself in places where you will meet those people with whom you can network. Be prepared at all times to hand out your card and to collect business cards from others, even competitors. Networking means staying in touch, regularly, by telephone and by letter. If you meet someone at a seminar with whom you want to network, write to him after the seminar saying how much you enjoyed meeting him and perhaps enclose an article which

might be of interest to him. Find opportunities to contact your network people.

Associations. Join the associations which can produce business for you or can enhance your reputation and professional skills; and once having joined them, become active within the association. You should certainly join and become active with your local chapter of the American Society for Industrial Security (ASIS). Also, inquire with your local Chamber of Commerce as to their dues. If affordable, this is a good showcase for your business. In most metropolitan cities, the Chamber of Commerce regularly holds "hospitality get acquainted" social events, where you are encouraged to circulate, talk with members, and hand out your card. With all associations, you should attend meetings, meet fellow members, and inquire about business. With these people you do not necessarily have to be bashful. It is well understood by the members that one of the primary purposes of belonging is to either get business or get a job. Volunteer for committee work and as a speaker for meetings of the association. These are perfect opportunities to showcase your talents.

Seminars. Many associations and private professionals give seminars. If affordable, plan to attend those where you think you will meet people with whom you can network. One of the most valuable aspects of seminars is the networking and social time allowed in recesses and at the beginning and end of each day. Volunteer to give a seminar, thereby establishing yourself as an expert. Many successful consultants use this technique by giving affordable seminars to an audience that is likely to produce future clients.

Teaching. If you have the time, try to teach a course for a community college. If your schedule is busy or erratic, you may only be able to volunteer as a guest teacher, which means that you might teach only one day in a Private Security or Criminal Justice program. Again, teaching gives you credentials and establishes your expertise.

Speaking. If this is something you do very well, you may be able to promote yourself as a guest speaker with some prestigious associations. It is not easy to become accepted, which means you will have to market yourself. There are speakers' bureaus which book speakers at events and meetings. The best way to work with these bureaus is to develop and polish a "set" speech on a particular subject, let us say a 45-minute speech on "PERSONAL PROTECTION . . What is It and Who Needs It?" Then, put together a one-page promotional piece which lists your name, address, telephone, credentials (why are you an expert?), experience, and highlights or key topics of your speech. This gives the speaking bureau something in writing that can help to sell you.

Media Contacts. If you have been involved with something noteworthy, write out a simple news release and send it to the press, then follow up with a telephone call. Sometimes a significant event will provide an opportunity to contact the press. When Kevin Costner's very successful film, "The Bodyguard," appeared on movie screens around the country, some media-aware agents contacted the press who were only too happy to interview a "real" bodyguard. Newspaper stories of the right kind can provide a huge audience of readers, some of whom might be prospective clients. Unless you are determined to work very low profile, it would be useful to have a good, professional picture (head shot) taken which could be provided to the press. (Don't be tempted to do some sort of stupid "action" picture, such as crouching with guns cocked at an invisible enemy.) Your picture should be taken by a professional photographer, not your next-door neighbor; a bad picture is worse than no picture. The other "no-no" is to reveal confidential information to the media--NEVER use a client's name, even though this is precisely what the media wants to hear.

The kind of story you want is something like this:

"John Jones, a highly regarded private protection specialist based in Denver, Colorado, has recently returned from a most unusual assignment in Russia. Mr. Jones was employed by the ex-Director of the KGB to assist in overhauling the security programs for the three major tourist hotels in Moscow and St. Petersburg. Mr. Jones was also instrumental in setting up the first executive and dignitary protection teams employed by the State Police . . . (etc.) . . ."

John Jones is now known by some 500,000 readers of that newspaper as "the" expert in executive protection with an international reputation. That should be good for six or eight new clients! And the publicity was free.

John Jones can also have that article about himself reproduced, and he can mail it with a cover letter to the top 100 corporations in the Denver and Colorado area, requesting an opportunity to meet with Mr. . . (the executive), then follow up with telephone calls for interviews.

Peripheral Contacts. Make appointments with the major legal firms in your city, then spend 15 minutes or so telling them what you do and asking them to refer you to any of their clients who might need protection. The same applies to major accounting firms, major real estate and property management firms, and homeowner associations, all of whom come into daily, close contact with individuals and corporations who could use your skills, and will some day have a need for them.

Marketing is a creative activity. Some agents have volunteered to work free for presidential candidates on campaign swings. Others volunteer for civic events in providing free protection services. For example, if the Pope is visiting your city, volunteer to work with the civic and church authorities on one event so that you get a chance to provide a service, get a letter of commendation, and pass out at least 50 business cards to people along the way. In some cities and communities, agents have volunteered to provide protection in a highly publicized, volatile "stalking" case where the victim cannot afford to pay. Just be certain that your marketing is in good taste and does not violate any confidentiality.

More Marketing.

Advertisements. Should you or shouldn't you? Having learned that most clients are secured through word-of-mouth, referrals, and networking, you may have concluded that advertisements are not particularly effective. In the executive protection field, particularly if you are a lone contractor or small business, advertising can be extremely expensive and not as cost-effective as other means of marketing. You may, however, want to consider a small ad in the yellow pages of your telephone book. That's right, the telephone book is exactly where some private individuals will look for bodyguards; they do not know where else to look.

If you do decide to advertise, shop carefully for the best price, and be prepared to advertise not less than three times. A one-time ad (unless it is for a one-time event) is the poorest, least effective, most expensive form of advertising. Many, many people shopping for a serious product may notice your ad but not respond for weeks, months, even a year.

Ad design is almost an art form. Designing good, effective ads is difficult. Unless you have some talent for this, find a friend or professional acquaintance who can help you. "Homemade" ads can be as damaging to your image as bad pictures. If all else fails, use your business card as your ad; at least it will be clean and direct.

Brochures. A good brochure can be extremely effective and much less expensive than an ad. Brochures have many uses. They can be mailed to prospective clients, taken to seminars and association meetings, and left with prospective clients and referrals (such as legal firms) after interviews. The author is sold on brochures as effective marketing tools. *However* (and this is the catch), the brochure must be of good quality and appearance--quality and appearance equal to the brochures and reports which your prospective clients are used to looking at.

Basically, for our purposes, there are two kinds of brochures. There is the folded brochure which you see promoting hotels, resorts, schools, and businesses. These are relatively easy to produce and fairly inexpensive. A good graphic artist (the one who designed your logo) can often come up with very innovative ways to design brochures, with different ways of folding, use of color or half-tones, and other catchy devices. The drawback to this kind of brochure is that, in order to make it affordable, you must print a quantity at one time. This means spending a chunk of money on a brochure before you know whether it is going to be effective.

If you are going to use this kind of brochure, there are some tips which you should keep in mind.

.   The cover of the brochure is the key point. The cover is like the headline of a story. Whether or not the reader opens the brochure depends upon whether the cover is interesting. It must tell the story.

.   Brochures are much more effective with pictures or graphics, but the pictures must tell a story, must have meaning.

.   You should identify pictures by putting captions under the pictures.

.   Use enough copy to tell your story. Not everyone understands the phrase, or scope of, "executive protection." Often, the client must first be educated, then sold.

.   Avoid cute or stereotyped pictures and material. An action picture is very effective, but avoid the dumb pictures of bodyguards in dark glasses shoving bystanders away from the client. Brochures are not movie posters; they should be professional, dignified, trustworthy sales instruments.

.   Don't produce this brochure unless you can spend enough money to have a quality product. There is nothing as demeaning as a cheap, flimsy, tacky brochure turned out by the local quick-print store. Those brochures are best used for selling used cars, not personal protection.

The second kind of brochure is very different. It looks more like a corporate report. It will usually have a handsome cover with the company name and logo printed on it and a matching plain back cover. Inside, on good quality white paper, will be several sheets of paper which "tell the story" of the company. These sheets can be composed on your computer and printed on a laser printer. A simple binding holds it together. It is very effective with many advantages. It looks like the kind of documents that corporate executives are used to reading. It is dignified. It allows sufficient room to include all pertinent information. It is very inexpensive, even when using the best quality paper. You can produce one, 20, or 100 copies. You can tailor the material to target the audience. It is a good corporate sales tool.

Press Releases. For those who have never written a press (or information) release, there are some guidelines which should be followed, to make it easy for a newspaper or magazine to use your information.

Releases should be typed, double-spaced, on 8-1/2 x 11 white paper with wide margins on both sides. This gives an editor plenty of room to pencil in edits and changes. Use only one side of the paper. A sentence or paragraph should never be split between two pages. Keep each sentence and paragraph on one page. If the release if more than one page, at the bottom center or bottom right-hand side of all but the last page you should type, "more" and a page number as: "1 of 3," or the appropriate number of pages. On the last page, at the bottom, you should type "* * * * *," which indicates the end of the release. News releases should be kept as short as is possible to adequately tell the story.

At the upper left or upper right side of the first page of the release, you should type, "FOR IMMEDIATE RELEASE," or give a specific release date. Underneath, type, "FOR MORE INFORMATION CONTACT:" and then type in a person's (your) name and telephone number.

A headline should indicate the contents of the release. It is the headline which will, or will not, capture the attention of the editor.

The information which follows the headline should answer some basic questions--who, what, where, why, when, how. The release should be timely, of human or public interest, intriguing, sexy, exciting, meaningful, humorous, tragic, or have some quality of excitement.

A release is constructed something like a pyramid. The most important information is contained in the first paragraph. Succeeding paragraphs contain more detail. The theory is that an editor could, conceivably, chop off your last paragraph or last two paragraphs without ruining the story. The meat of the story is in the first paragraph, so don't save the punch line for the last.

An example of a press release can be found in the Appendix.

Continuing Education

As with all professional fields, it is important for executive protection agents to continue and further their education. While the basics remain the same, new technology (particularly in the use of enhanced electronics) has brought changes to the profession. As a goal-oriented career agent, you should stay on top of the technology within your chosen field, and you should acquire some auxiliary education as well.

College degrees always look good on a resume, and within the private security industry, they are very important if you wish to work with a corporation or as a consultant. In order to reach the top of your profession, you need credentials.

Specialized training is equally important. Within this book are recommendations for acquiring EMT (Emergency Medical Training) certification. A knowledge of, and basic proficiency with, computers is a must in order to prepare resumes, reports, proposals, and letters.

Highly recommended is the acquisition of

investigative skills. Not only do these skills help the agent to perform his and her job, if you plan to open your own business, you will acquire an enhanced opportunity to do business. For example, if you were to approach a legal firm with the hope of performing services for them, being able to offer your services as an investigator and a protection agent would double your value.

Above all, never think that you know everything there is to know about your trade. There is always more, and the knowledge is available through networking, seminars, trade shows, training, and schools.

Read the security magazines from cover to cover. When you find a useful article, clip it. Never stop learning, and never be embarrassed to use someone else's good ideas.

END RESULTS

We have reached the end of this book, and the exhaustion of advice for the professional protection agent. If you have faithfully studied the information, by now you have acquired a great deal of knowledge which should, God willing, assist you in pursuing your career to a successful conclusion. The author wishes you the best of luck, and success in your endeavors.

APPENDIX

TARGET STUDY

OVERSEAS EVACUATION PLAN

CONTRACT FOR PERSONAL SERVICES

PROTECTEE PROFILE

SAMPLE PRESS RELEASE

CHECKLISTS AND SURVEYS

PROFESSIONAL RESOURCES

TARGET STUDY

MJB AVIATION FACILITY

DELHI, INDIA

PREPARED BY

ROBERT E. AGENT

TABLE OF CONTENTS

*To protect the identity of the client, photographs have been eliminated in this reproduced report. Photographs are desirable additions as they graphically illustrate to the client what has been presented in the report.

INTRODUCTION

This report presents observations, conclusions, and recommendations resulting from our inspection of MJB aircraft, ground facilities, and flight operations. This study was specifically directed toward an evaluation of the following five topical areas:

. Current security procedures in effect at Delhi Airport.

. Security procedures followed within the MJB hangar complex.

. Vulnerability of MJB executives and aircraft during arrivals and departures at Delhi Airport.

. Vulnerability of MJB executives during helicopter flights in the Delhi area.

. Security of MJB aircraft while on the ground away from the MJB/Delhi hangar complex.

TARGET STUDY METHODOLOGY

Determining the viewpoint from which the potential attack scenarios are planned is the first order of business. This determination was based on our analysis of the size and skill levels of groups and individuals who have participated in operations against targets with related characteristics. Acquisition of target data was the next step. This included maps, photographs, newspaper clippings, and our observations notes. Reduction of the target data to operational scenarios and the comparison of these scenarios against the existing defenses comprised the third phase. The fourth phase was the pinpointing of those elements which can be modified or introduced to thwart the predicted operational scenarios.

EXECUTIVE SUMMARY

During the month of November, 1992, we surveyed the MJB aviation facilities located in Delhi, India. Our purpose was to evaluate the vulnerability of MJB executives using corporate aircraft. Threat models were formulated, operational scenarios considered, and conclusions derived. The following is a brief synopsis of our recommendations.

1. Passengers should board corporate jet aircraft on the runway rather than in the hangar area.

2. A uniformed observer/countersniper should be positioned on the roof of the MJB hangar during the arrivals and departures of MJB executives.

3. A response car with two uniformed men should be present on the flight line during arrivals and departures.

4. Minor variations should be incorporated into the routine flight path of MJB aircraft in the Delhi area.

5. Ballistic armor should be incorporated within the Dauphine 300 helicopter.

6. The proposed two-part microwave/physical security system should be evaluated for use with corporate aircraft.

THREAT MODEL

The operational scenarios necessary for an evaluation of the vulnerability of a specific target, in this case corporate aircraft, require the formation of threat models. The hypothetical threat used for the preparation of this report assumes that a small group (from six to twelve individuals) will carry out the kidnap or assassination attempt.

For our purposes we are presuming that the protagonists are well rehearsed in the planned operation and technically proficient in the required skills. Further, we can assume that adequate target analysis has been conducted and that they have access to modern military weapons and explosive devices.

I. **VULNERABILITY PRIOR TO TAKE-OFF**

A. <u>Jet Aircraft</u>

1. <u>Operational Scenario</u>

An attack is launched against one of the MJB Falcon aircraft after the executives have boarded and the aircraft is taxiing from the MJB hangar to the runway. The best place for this ambush is just outside the MJB compound on the road leading to the runway. (See photo #1, Item A) <*NOTE: all photos have been deleted from this report to protect the identity of the client*>. The attack would most likely be initiated by blocking the aircraft's route with a car, thereby effectively immobilizing the plane. The attackers would then direct small arms fire toward the plane and place a small explosive charge beneath it. The combination of small arms fire, explosives, and burning jet fuel would ensure the death of all passengers and crew. The attackers need not cluster in the area prior to the assault, but could converge on signal when the intended victim boarded the aircraft.

2. <u>Conclusion</u>

This type of assault would have a particularly high probability of success owing to the almost total lack of maneuverability of the aircraft in this situation, the absence of ballistic armor, and the presence of significant quantities of fuel.

3. <u>Recommended Countermeasures</u>

a. Passengers should board the aircraft on the runway just prior to take-off. This will accomplish two things:

(1.) Remaining in the relative security of the armored car increases the executive's ability to evade blocking maneuvers by potential kidnappers or assassins.

(2.) Increasing the distance between the auto and the assassin's shooting position would augment the relative effectiveness of the car's armor.

b. A uniformed observer should be posted on the roof of the MJB hangar (see photo #1, Item B) during arrivals and departures. This individual's responsibilities would include visual surveillance of the airport. Ideally, he should also be capable of acting as a countersniper, providing suppressing fire to cover the executive's escape. The observer/countersniper should be equipped with a radio that enables him to communicate with the executive car, the airplane, the tower, and the airport security force. Binoculars (10 x 50mm) for observation and a telescopically sighted rifle (cal. 7.62 x 51mm) of the type shown in photo #2 are the other equipment requirements. Adequate training in the use of this equipment is, of course, necessary.

B.   Helicopters

1.   <u>Operational Scenarios</u>

a.   A sniper armed with a suitable rifle shoots the executive as he walks from his armored vehicle to the waiting helicopter. The assailant would pick either the roof of building A (see photo #3, Item A) or a window in the building to the north of the MJB hangars as the best vantage point from which to fire his shot.

b.   From either of the buildings mentioned above, the assailant launches either a shoulder-fired anti-tank rocket or a rifle grenade. These weapons are powerful enough that pinpoint accuracy is not required.

2.   <u>Conclusions</u>

a.   The fences surrounding the MJB compound significantly obstruct the vision of the potential assassin attempting to fire his weapon from ground level. This obstruction forces the would-be assassin to seek higher elevation to insure a clear shot over the fence. Assuming a reasonable degree of marksmanship, this type of attack has a moderate probability of success. It should be noted that, although this particular scenario (long-range sniping) does not occur frequently, the significant probability of a fatal shot mandates some attention to appropriate countermeasures.

b.   The employment of shoulder-fired rockets or rifle grenades as described above constitutes a significant threat with a high probability of success. This assumes that the executive is in the immediate vicinity of the helicopter and not in his armored car. The armor in his car would protect him from anything except direct hit by either a rocket or a rifle grenade (HEAT type).

3.   <u>Recommended Countermeasures</u>

The observer/countersniper is the most viable countermeasure available. We assume that the helicopter is warmed up and takes off immediately when the executive boards. If not, a further suggestion would be to encourage him to remain in either his armored vehicle or in one of the buildings until the helicopter is completely ready for departure.

C.   <u>Jet Aircraft or Helicopter</u>

1.   <u>Operational Scenario</u>

A fuel contaminant or explosive incendiary device is introduced into the fuel tank by the fuel handling crew.

2.   **Conclusion**

This is a viable, proven technique, though it is not most commonly employed by the probable assailants.

3.   **Recommended Countermeasures**

a.   Refueling operations should be closely supervised by trusted crew members.

b.   Where possible, fuel suppliers should be selected at random.

II.   VULNERABILITY DURING TAKE-OFF AND LANDING

A.   **Jet Aircraft**

1.   **Operational Scenarios**

a.   As the aircraft lifts off, and as it lands, it passes over the open, uncontrolled areas at the ends of the runway. At this moment, our would-be assassins attempt to cause the aircraft to crash or explode by firing small arms rounds, shoulder-fired rockets, or a heat-seeking missile at the aircraft.

b.   The plane is on the ground preparing for take-off or slowing to a halt after landing. A pre-positioned vehicle near the flight line buildings (Photo #3, Item B) speeds out to intercept the helpless aircraft. As the car full of terrorists comes abreast of the plane or to a blocking position in front of it, the terrorists shoot the pilot, blow up the plane, or commit some combination of these actions.

2.   **Conclusions**

a.   Given the relatively high take-off and landing speeds of a jet aircraft, it is unlikely that a group armed with the typical mix of handguns and submachine guns would hit the aircraft a sufficient number of times to cause a crash due to mechanical failure. The greatest risk in this scenario is that of a random bullet striking either the executive or the pilot. Attackers positioned directly under the flight path pose the greatest threat due to the advantage of head-on fire.

b.   A significant variety of shoulder-fired, free flight (unguided) rockets have been used by terrorist groups (Photo #4). The majority of these are stolen or Soviet supplied anti-tank weapons, any of which will destroy an aircraft in flight. Since these weapons were intended for use against targets moving at less than 30 km/hr, their launch systems are not well adapted for use against jet aircraft. Additionally, the maximum range for these rockets is generally less than 1,000 meters. These facts combine to yield a low probability of success if used against a jet aircraft. The only launch position which affords any real possibility of success is directly beneath the aircraft's flight during a landing.

c.   Shoulder-fired heat-seeking missiles (see Photos #6-8) have been used on several occasions by terrorists and are believed to be available in India. These missiles have a maximum slant range of 3.5 km and will probably cause a small executive aircraft to crash or blow up in the air. Launch positions are not critical, and numerous locations in and around the airport offer the required clear, unobstructed view of the aircraft's flight path. The most likely launch positions would be just outside the perimeter fence on one of the small roads close to the north end of the runway or from one of the fields off the south end of the runway.

d.   The nearly complete absence of control over the movement of vehicles in the flight line area makes the use of a vehicle to intercept a taxiing aircraft a tempting proposition. The drivers of the intercepting vehicles would time their movements so that they would arrive at the point furthest from the flight line at approximately the same moment that the target aircraft does. This would maximize the time it would take for help to arrive once the attack began, and would put the kidnappers or assassins closer to one of the many unguarded perimeter gates, thus aiding their escape. The obvious ease in stopping the aircraft and the close proximity of the assailants armed with the weapons of their choice would virtually insure the success of this type of operation.

3.   **Recommended Countermeasures**

a.   An observer/countersniper be positioned on the roof of the MJB hangar building as described.

b.   A "sweep car" be utilized prior to arrivals and departures. This vehicle would be manned by two uniformed security men and equipped with appropriate radios to allow communication between the observer, the aircraft, and the tower. Additionally, an automatic rifle or submachine gun should be available in the passenger compartment. The sweep car should insure that no vehicle is allowed to approach the aircraft unchallenged. The sweep car would also work in conjunction with the observer to investigate suspicious activities and respond to specifically threatening situations.   A further benefit derived from the sweep vehicle/observer team is a psychological one. The presence of uniformed, visible professional security may persuade the potential attacker that the operation is just too difficult to attempt.

c.   (1)   An electronic countermeasures system exists that will reliably confuse the guidance system of a heat-seeking missile. This system is in use by at least one major airline and is potentially adaptable to the Falcon aircraft. While the effectiveness of such a system is reasonably assured, the cost, over $500,000 per plane, is high. Unless there is a marked increase in the use of these missiles, this system is probably not warranted at this time.

(2)   A more reasonable approach is to change the flight path of the aircraft such that the angle of approach and departure is steeper, thereby reducing the time period spent within the range of the missile. This tactic has been used with success by numerous airlines in Africa and the Mideast where the threat of heat-seeking missiles is currently greatest.

B.   Helicopters

1.   Operational Scenarios

Assailants in or around buildings adjacent to the hangar complex fire small arms rounds, shoulder-fired rockets, or heat-seeking missiles at the helicopter as it arrives or departs the MJB hangar complex.

2.   Conclusions

a.   American experience in Vietnam demonstrated the vulnerability of helicopters to small arms fire. The most vulnerable period for the helicopter occurs during vertical flight (lift-off and landing). At this moment the aircraft requires maximum stability and the pilot is preoccupied with flying considerations. Helicopters are relatively fragile and present a large cross section; this combines to make them a tempting target which is relatively easy to bring down. Additionally, to save weight, helicopters are constructed of the lightest materials available, thereby increasing the risk of projectiles penetrating the fuselage and killing or injuring a passenger or pilot. In sum, helicopters are very susceptible to ground fire, and assassination attempts which exploit this vulnerability would have a high probability of success.

b.   Given the large cross section mentioned in the preceding paragraph and their slow speed, helicopters are vulnerable to shoulder-fired rockets. Of the various rockets currently in use by radical groups, the Soviet designed RPG-7 and RPG-2 (Photo #4) present the most serious threat. Not only are these rockets compact, accurate, and powerful, but some versions have a self-detonating element incorporated in the fusing system that automatically causes the warhead to explode after a flight of approximately 1,000 meters. Since the warhead has a payload weight of slightly less than one kg, such an explosion would be of little practical significance if it were not for its lined cavity shaped charge design. When this warhead detonates, it produces an intensely concentrated jet of molten metal and explosive products. This jet will severely damage a helicopter in flight at distances of up to one hundred meters. There, the assassin need only predetermine the probable direction the helicopter will take away from the airport and position himself so that he will have a shot at the helicopter from directly in front or behind. This type of attack is very feasible but actually enjoys only a low-to-moderate probability of success due to the limited firing experience of most terrorists.

c.   The use of shoulder-fired, heat-seeking missiles against helicopters during take-off and landing almost guarantees success, due to the aforementioned vulnerability of helicopters in general and the close proximity of the helicopter's heat-producing components to the passenger area. The detonation of the one kg warhead virtually assures a crash or at least significant injuries among the passengers.

3. **Recommended Countermeasures**

a.   An observer/countersniper be employed as described. This would maximize the probability of detecting and preventing an attempted assassination.

b.   Ballistic armor be applied to the Dauphine helicopter to protect the passengers, crew, and critical components from small arms fire. A quick estimate indicates that an acceptable level of protection could be achieved with the addition of less than 100 kg. Incorporation of this armor would vastly reduce the aircraft's vulnerability to ground fire.

c.   No scheme has yet been devised that will protect a helicopter from a direct impact by a shaped charge warhead. The ballistic armor mentioned in the preceding paragraph will offer some protection from the effects of the "jet" previously described. The only viable defenses against unguided rockets are to avoid predictable flight paths and to minimize the time the helicopter spends near structures that offer concealment for potential assassins. A possible alternative flight path would entail descending to near ground level over the runway, then proceeding directly to the MJB hangar with the minimum of altitude necessary to safely clear buildings. This would tremendously increase the difficulty in making a clear shot from outside the airport perimeter.

d.   The available electronic means of defeating the guidance systems of heat-seeking missiles is not applicable to helicopters of the type in question due to the size and weight of the system's components. The countermeasures of an observer and modification of flight path would minimize the vulnerability to heat-seeking missiles.

III.   VULNERABILITY IN FLIGHT

A.   **Jet Aircraft and Helicopters**

1.   **Operational Scenarios**

A shoulder-fired heat-seeking missile is employed to cause the crash of an MJB aircraft.

2.   **Conclusions**

a.   Heat-seeking missiles are the only credible threat to a jet aircraft in flight. This threat is minimal at best, due to the limited range of these missiles (3.5 km slant range) and their relative scarcity.

b.   Due to their low altitude and relatively slow speed, the helicopters in question are constantly vulnerable to heat-seeking missiles. Almost any roof top in Delhi that is beneath the flight path is a suitable launch point.

3.   Recommended Countermeasures

a.   No specific countermeasure is necessary for a jet aircraft in flight once an altitude of 2.0 km above ground has been achieved.

b.   The helicopter should routinely vary its flight path slightly to decrease its predictability when flying over Delhi.

IV.   PHYSICAL SECURITY FOR AIRCRAFT

A.   Observation

MJB aircraft are, of necessity, frequently left in unsecured locations which offer the clever assassin ample opportunity for sabotage.

B.   Conclusions

Discussions with the MJB pilots and others indicate that an aircraft security system incorporating the following features is desirable.

The system should detect any actual penetration of the aircraft such as opening of inspection covers and access plates. It should also detect someone reaching into the internal recesses directly accessible from the exterior of the aircraft--for example, those recesses located inside the wheel wells. The system should not go into alarm if an individual approaches the aircraft out of mere curiosity, and should be lightweight and entirely covert.

C.   Recommendations

The requirements mentioned above are met by a two-part system designed especially for MJB. Part One is a series of miniature microwave sensors with associated radio transmitters. These sensors are located in the various parts of the aircraft that are routinely accessed during preflight or postflight operation. Wheel wells and the main access hatch are examples of such areas. When an intrusion is detected, the sensor relays this information to a master memory module located within the aircraft. As the pilot approaches the plane for preflight inspection he activates his small handheld unit, which interrogates the master memory module and then lights up an LED display indicating where penetration occurred. Armed with this information, the pilot can be certain to include these areas in his routine inspection. (See photos #9 and 10.)

Part Two involves the use of a quick drying glue and fluorescent powder to provide a seal visible only under ultraviolet light. This mixture is applied to a screw head on any access panel that is only infrequently opened. It is impossible to remove the panel without breaking the seal. During preflight inspection, the pilot would use a small ultraviolet light to inspect the integrity of the seals.

For those access panels that do not lend themselves to either of the aforementioned techniques, a paper seal provides the same protection for larger openings that the fluorescent seal does for smaller ones. Since the seal cannot be removed without being torn, it is an effective security device even though it is somewhat more visible than the fluorescent technique.

V.   DELHI AIRPORT

A.   Airport Security -- General

1.   Observations

Our inspection of the portions of Delhi Airport not under MJB control revealed several weaknesses. Employees of the various entities located at the airport come and go freely with no system of identification to pinpoint which persons are authorized in the various areas. Visitors are not subject to even the most rudimentary screening, nor are they required to display any visible identification even when on the flight line. The perimeter fence, where it actually exists, poses no deterrent to free access to the runway (Photo #11). Various houses and other buildings, some unoccupied, are immediately adjacent to the perimeter and provide excellent cover for surveillance of MJB activities (Photo #12). Finally, no patrols by airport or military security personnel were observed though it is reported that they are occasionally undertaken.

2.   Conclusions

The overall security at Delhi airport is incredibly lax. Penetration of the airport perimeter and subsequent free movement without challenge requires little or no advance preparation. The lack of adequate perimeter fencing and security patrols encourages this penetration. The situation is such that the initiation of offensive operations from within the airport is entirely feasible.

B.   MJB Hangar Complex

1.   Observations

As one nears the MJB hangar complex, it is impossible not to notice the recent installation of a taut wire fence completely encircling the complex. Also in evidence are two new strategically placed guard posts of sufficiently sound construction to provide protection from small arms fire. An inspection of the hangars revealed an array of CCTV cameras which provide effective video surveillance of any activities.

2.   Conclusions

Careful consideration was given to perimeter security and the surveillance of activities within the perimeter. These measures are all excellent and will deter clandestine penetration attempts. It is, however, possible to envision situations wherein additional measures might be necessary. These include situations that require a guard to leave his post to physically examine something, or the use of an otherwise authorized vehicle to transport unauthorized persons or things into the compound.

3.   **Recommendations**

a.   The large gate meant for passage of aircraft should open from the opposite direction. This would insure that someone attempting to slip through a partially open gate would be forced to do so directly in front of the guard post.

b.   Two guards should be posted in the booth at the entrance gate. This allows the post to remain manned if one guard must be absent from his post.

c.   A panic alarm should be mounted on the wall of the guard booth at the main gate. This should be in series with the gates so that if the gate is open, one guard must be physically depressing a button to prevent an alarm from sounding. This version of the traditional "dead man" switch insures that, in the event a guard is shot or otherwise forced away from his post, the gate cannot be opened without the alarm sounding. This, of course, presupposes that a second guard is available for checking identification.

d.   A visitor's log should be maintained by the guard. This will insure that the guards are aware of the number and approximate location of all visitors within the compound.

e.   Employees should be provided with and required to wear some form of identification badge. Ideally, this would be part of a badge exchange wherein the person authorized with routine access presents his employee identification card to the guard who then issues him or her the corresponding badge maintained by the guards. This special badge, which authorizes free movement within the hangar area never leaves the compound, thereby minimizing the opportunity for theft or duplication. This system is especially useful when new or relief guards are used, since it requires only a matching of employee ID card and the person presenting it with the corresponding badge maintained in the guard booth.

f.   If possible, employees should be prevented from bringing their private automobiles inside the perimeter gate. Presumably, the employees do not carefully inspect their cars nor maintain them in a secure area. Therefore, it would not be difficult to attach to the employee's car an explosive device which could be detonated upon an executive's approach. Enough vehicles should be maintained within the hangar complex to allow for efficient movement of people and material within the complex. Any other vehicle entering the hangar area which is not kept under appropriate security should be thoroughly inspected prior to being admitted.

SUMMARY

Within the context of this study MJB executive personnel are vulnerable to kidnap and assassination attempts, especially while aboard MJB aircraft awaiting take-off or landing. The countermeasures recommended would significantly reduce this vulnerability without appreciably restricting the individual executive's mobility or privacy.

Security in general at Delhi airport is virtually non-existent. The MJB hangar complex enjoys first-rate security coverage and a few minor adjustments would improve the security even further.

MJB aircraft are completely open to sabotage attempts when parked away from the MJB/Delhi hangar complex. The proposed security package will provide the necessary increase in security to further insure the safety of MJB executive personnel.

ABC CORPORATION

CRISIS MANAGEMENT PLAN

SECURITY EVACUATION

OVERSEAS COUNTRY

**ABC CORPORATION
CRISIS MANAGEMENT PLAN - SECURITY EVACUATION
OVERSEAS COUNTRY**

Table of Contents

EMBASSY TELEPHONE NUMBERS: North City   252-5555

South City   511-1111

1.   COORDINATE ALL ACTIONS WITH THE COUNTRY MANAGER

2.   ASK THE STATE DEPARTMENT:

____   Should Americans consider evacuation at this time?

____   To notify you if they issue warnings to Americans.

____   To include you in their evacuation plans, if possible.

____   For any additional help if needed.

3.   DO:

____   Prepare a family contingency plan, in case the family is apart in an emergency situation.

____   Coordinate with others who represent American or other companies, if possible.

____   Know how to get exit and other necessary visas.

____   Know how to get "open" airline tickets for employees and dependents.

____   Know how to get sufficient cash to make the trip.

____   Know best way to the airport and alternate routes.

____   Get together all travel, I.D., and other personal papers.

____   Pack one suitcase and/or backpack per person.

____   Prepare residence--inventory, pack, and store items.

____   Prepare office--identify documents to be removed and to be destroyed. Consider disposition of outstanding contracts, accounts, etc. Inventory, pack, and store all office equipment and supplies.

4.   KEEP CORPORATE CONTACTS INFORMED!

An evacuation plan is designed to cope with those situations that could require expatriate or foreign national employees and their dependents to be removed from a variety of sources of threats relative to their overseas location of assignment. The goal of this, and supporting documents, is to recommend procedures which will effect a safe, orderly, and expeditious evacuation.

Authorized subsidiary representatives should consider these recommendations and make certain decisions regarding aspects of that plan finally adopted.

An evacuation plan should complement other corporate programs, such as the headquarters' and foreign offices' Crisis Management Plans; each entity's plan should be implemented by a Crisis Management Team and coordinated by a Crisis Management Coordinator. Guidelines for Crisis Management Plans, Teams, and Coordinators are presented in the Appendix to this document.

The U.S. Department of State has said:

Past experience has shown that companies and employees in foreign locations show a reluctance to develop, maintain, or implement evacuation plans. This reluctance stems from a false sense of security developed through the absence of personal threats and the lack of access to uncensored news reports.

The fundamental factors in conducting a safe and efficient evacuation in a destabilized overseas environment are prior planning, continuous and comprehensive analysis of potential security threats, and timely decision-making concerning the evacuation itself. Effective management of these factors should facilitate the evacuation process . . in a timely and orderly fashion.

PLANNING

An objective of an evacuation plan is to secure as much time as possible to accomplish tasks necessary to effect an evacuation. Accurate planning can greatly assist in meeting this objective. Timetables used for planning an evacuation should provide generous estimates for executing tasks and allow for breakdowns in continuity. The alternative--racing against time--increases anxiety, and in the worst of cases, induces panic. Clearly, if an evacuation is necessary, it is far better to be a little ahead of schedule than behind.

Our government does not necessarily move faster in a crisis. To accommodate this, planners must allow time for obtaining clearances, exit permits, and the like. Generally, the timing requirements for making specific decisions and taking specific actions must be identified.

In planning, priority must be given to the safety and security of employees and their dependents over that of the company or personal property.

In an evacuation, the human element should be given constant sympathetic attention. An emergency evacuation is capable of generating strong emotions and resentments. Often overlooked are the psychological damages suffered, even by those who have safely made it out of the danger area. Counseling and other help may be needed and ought to be considered in the planning process.

The evacuation requires careful planning and close supervision to ensure the correct degree of urgency. Too much time can be as great a problem as too little. The best amount of time is that which will allow the job to be done thoroughly without undue tension being forced upon those concerned.

These are among the many reasons why an evacuation should be reviewed for accuracy and applicability, and practiced. Any time is appropriate for review and practice, but at least every six months is recommended. It is especially important when implementation of the evacuation plan appears increasingly likely.

No one can anticipate all factors which could potentially influence an evacuation. However, for the purpose of planning, hypothetical scenarios should be considered in which personnel would be forced to leave the country.

By way of example, a planner might consider a situation in which decreasing availability of goods and services results in an increasing frequency of civil disorder. It could be predicted that authorities might react to this situation by imposing a state of complete police control. Such a reaction could restrict our employees' ability to communicate or evacuate.

Scenario 1: This situation may be anticipated by planners and afford them the opportunity to react. If so, they could react by effecting either a complete or partial evacuation. Alternatively, if planners believe this situation to be short-lived and would not result in the targeting of foreigners, they may elect to manage it by staying in touch with the U.S. Embassy and recommending that personnel remain in their homes (or in a predetermined safe haven) until the threat of danger has passed. Planning for this scenario must, therefore, consider crime trends, past reactions by authorities to similar occurrences, the existence of recent anti-American sentiments, opinions of State Department officials, the length of time expected for waiting-it-out, and other variables.

Scenario 2: As an alternative to Scenario 1, the situation may develop precipitously and *not* allow time for implementing evacuation plans. Therefore, personnel would be required to wait-it-out (unless, for example, the State Department sponsored an evacuation).

A thoughtful response to either Scenario 1 or 2 requires anticipation and planning; to include preparations not only for an evacuation, but also for staying in place and waiting-it-out.

It is crucial that planners anticipate the need to move personnel *prior to* the development of an emergency situation.

There are circumstances in which a U.S. corporation operating abroad must consider sending employees and/or dependents out of the country. For example, evacuation should be considered during times of serious terrorist threat, conditions of insurrection or other serious civil disorder, or when the environment poses other serious hazards to safety, or overburdens the country's ability to protect, feed, or house its citizens.

3

Serious trouble may be preceded by signs which are less obvious such as a gradual, almost imperceptible, decline in services, a decline in attitudes of established contacts, a decline in internal security, an increase in travel restrictions, or capital flight. Country managers should be vigilant in their monitoring of such changes.

THE PLAN

NOTE: Individuals authorized to initiate the following phases should be designated in advance of need. These individuals should be located both within the U.S. and at the foreign office location. Hereinafter, these individuals will be referred to as coordinators.

Planners should also be reminded that neither the company nor any of its entities nor employees can promise or deliver protective security or any other measures not commercially available.

A. **THE ALERT PHASE**

This phase is characterized by: an intensification of data collection regarding local events; a recognition of host country instability; a communication of local conditions to other designated corporate employees; and a preparation of measures for possible use if conditions deteriorate.

1. The coordinator should intensify data collection by meeting with:

- Employees to review current trends and events, to develop a procedure to deal with rumors, and to communicate preliminary evacuation instructions.

- The Regional Security Officer (RSO) and/or other staff members of the U.S. Embassy.

- Other American or friendly companies.

- Company Risk Management, Security, and their independent consultants and analysts.

2. In this phase the local coordinator should notify specific individuals of the potential for evacuating our personnel. The local coordinator should inform:

- His or her superior.

- Corporate headquarters, to include the company Risk Management organization.

- Other resident company employees in the city (both expatriates and nationals) and any others visiting the area, if known.

- The RSO of the nearest U.S. Embassy or Consulate, or other appropriate embassy officials.

. *If* the evacuation plan has been prepared with their cooperation, other local American or friendly companies should also be consulted.

The coordinator's notification to corporate headquarters and his/her superior may include:

. A description of the current threat environment.

. An accounting of *all* resident employees and other individuals who are included in the coordinator's area of responsibility.

. A statement of criteria to be used for the decision to evacuate.

. Any other information about future communication times or mechanics, if necessary.

. Any questions which the coordinator requests to have researched; i.e., assistance with the decision to evacuate.

. Any requests for assistance with addressing specific needs; i.e., increased physical security of facilities or residences, increased security for those staying behind, or assistance with managing local contracts, investments, bank accounts, personnel, etc.

. Any requests for assistance with logistical needs; i.e., the arrangement of charter aircraft, medical examinations, reception, ground transportation, or accommodations at the destination.

. If known, a statement of anticipated evacuation date, time, means of transportation, and destination.

. *If designated*, the location and telephone number of the local Crisis Management Center and alternate.

3.   The coordinator should also assist his or her group with other measures during this phase, such as the following.

. Confirm registration of all group and family members with the nearest U.S. Embassy or Consulate. All telephone numbers and addresses of expatriate's homes, offices, and schools should be provided, as well as any other information which might be necessary for the emergency notification of an impending evacuation. Other travel documentation, such as passport and visa numbers, may also be needed by embassy personnel. (It may also be wise to determine the RSO's opinion regarding the appropriateness of seeking security assistance from the host government for the staging and embarkation areas and movement along convoy routes.)

. All contacts and procedures necessary for facilitating exit formalities, such as arranging for necessary visas (exit visas and those required for the country of destination), should be identified. In fact, it may be prudent to begin to arrange for the requisition of these documents during this phase.

. Investigate any other departure formalities for employees in connection with taxes, etc.

. The group's participation in embassy-sponsored Alert Call Procedures (also known as Warden Systems). If available, such a program would likely include other Americans. This would have the advantage of affording our personnel an opportunity to get acquainted with other Americans and to cooperate with them in preparing for evacuation. Regardless of whether or not the embassy sponsors an Alert Call Procedure, an emergency communication program for the group should be set in place. See Appendix 2 regarding guidelines for developing an Alert Call Procedure.

. Begin assessing travel options. See Appendix 5 for transportation recommendations.

. Choose the location of the Crisis Management Center, and communicate to all group members. Ideally, this should be located within a company facility. It should have equipment needed during an emergency, to include as a minimum: communications equipment; tape recorders; emergency plans and procedures; a log to record all actions taken during the crisis; necessary office equipment and supplies; and appropriate maps and building plans.

. Choose safe havens in the event personnel's homes or hotels are deemed unsafe or otherwise unacceptable--if they are forced to "wait-it-out."

. Choose the staging area(s) to be used for the collection of personnel prior to actual evacuation. A staging area should be selected with consideration for security and other logistical factors, such as size, parking availability, location, etc.

. Choose the embarkation point, the selection of which will be determined by the mode of evacuation transportation selected.

. Select the assembly point(s).

. Select routes to the assembly point(s) considering potential choke points, bridges, and areas that could be congested, and identify alternate routes if possible. Consider developing maps for each route.

. Select support personnel and assign responsibilities (see Appendix 1).

. Identify evacuees. It should be noted that if the decision to evacuate is made, it may *not* be necessary for all expatriate employees, dependents, and foreign nationals to leave at once. The coordinator must establish and individually assign evacuation priorities. For example: first priority--dependents; second priority--individuals other than key expatriate employees; third priority--key expatriate and foreign national employees. (The best contingency for foreign nationals may be to send them to safe areas within their countries.)

. Confirm communication alternatives. Besides using the above sources for identifying alternatives, see Appendix 3 for the communication plan recommended.

. Hand Appendix 4, "Personal Security Recommendations," to group members.

. Ready the mechanics of reassembly to include: arranging for housing relocated personnel; integrating them into the new business organization and environment; compensation; and other adjustments. If evacuation is effected with embassy sponsorship, the embassy will designate the reassembly location. From this point, plans for additional transportation, if required, will have to be made by the coordinator or the company.

. In managing the business, documents and computer software and other critical data should be identified and set aside for possible future destruction or transportation out with evacuees.

NOTE: **all aspects of security evacuation plans, including assembly locations, movement plans, transportation itineraries, and methods, etc., should be protected from unauthorized disclosure.**

B.   THE READINESS PHASE

This phase should be initiated when, in the judgement of the coordinator, the situation has reached a level of tension or instability that could lead to a partial or complete evacuation. (Again, the earlier an evacuation decision is made, the more likely it is that the evacuation will be effected in a calm, secure manner, and with the least political sensitivity and implications.)

During this phase, all mechanics of evacuation should be reviewed and placed in a ready state. All personnel should prepare to move on short notice. The Alert Call Procedure should be readied.

1.   In this phase the following general recommendations should be communicated to personnel:

. Reduce movements.

. Avoid incidents.

. Avoid attracting attention.

. Stay away from politically volatile areas, such as potential military or terrorist targets.

. Refuel personal vehicles frequently, keeping fuel tanks full. (If appropriate, additional gasoline reserves may also be stored at employee's home in safe plastic containers.)

2. The following recommendations should be communicated to personnel regarding their personal papers and affairs:

. Account for current passports of all family members.

. Collect all host country identification papers.

. Collect all essential personal papers such as birth certificates, marriage licenses, etc.

. Arrange for and collect transportation tickets, if applicable. (The coordinator should supervise transportation ticket acquisition and distribution.)

. Collect copies of U.S. federal income tax returns, if applicable.

. Bring a blank copy of an expense statement (to keep track of expenses).

. Provide for sufficient cash in U.S. dollars and travelers checks for at least three days of travel. Include sufficient currency in small denominations to take care of incidental expenses while en route.

. Review National Certificates of Vaccination, if applicable.

. Prepare an inventory of household goods. This may include photos of personal effects, particularly items of high value.

. Prepare a small first-aid kit, if space available, and bring along necessary medications.

. Package all possessions and place all other personal affairs in order.

. Do not expect to bring along more than 66 pounds of clothing and personal effects, per individual. (This weight is the absolute maximum permitted on a U.S. government sponsored evacuation aircraft.)

. Carry the most essential items in a small handbag or carry-on bag, in case it becomes necessary to restrict further baggage.

.   Do not bring firearms, other weapons, or liquor.

3.   Standing Fast.

As stated previously, in addition to being prepared to evacuate, it may also be necessary to be self-sufficient, without the support of the local service infrastructure.

The decision to prepare for standing fast (or waiting-it-out) should be made by the coordinator early on. Standing fast should be implemented in the event evacuation may not be prudent (as described in Scenario 2). This decision should be made considering such variables as the situation's rapidity of onset, its expected longevity and severity, and the reliability of transportation methods, in addition to other variables previously mentioned.

In standing fast, employees and dependents should remain in their quarters or other designated safe location until tensions abate.

Business operations may slow down or be suspended.

Employees and dependents should be reminded to use common sense and caution relative to their discussions and mechanics of preparation.

In addition to the above recommendations, the following should be communicated to personnel in preparation for standing fast:

.   Without hoarding, maintain a reasonable (five to seven days, at least) supply of food, water, and fuel.

.   Determine how cooking, etc. can be managed without power.

.   Consider trash disposal, especially in hot weather.

.   Make sure vehicles, if available, are ready for immediate use. For example, fuel tanks should be kept full, a reasonable supply of spare parts should be kept on hand as necessary, and the oil, water, fluid levels, and tires should be checked periodically.

.   Maintain a family-size first aid kit and an adequate supply of necessary prescription medicine(s).

.   Have a flashlight with fresh batteries and/or candles.

.   Keep a supply of matches, preferably waterproof and windproof.

. Keep a small battery operated short-wave, or other radio, with fresh batteries. This can be used to closely monitor the local news media, *Voice of America*, and the *British Broadcasting Company*, if available, for relevant announcements from the local government or U.S. Embassy. The embassies will be closely monitoring any situation and will provide further information to the coordinator or liaison contact person if this procedure has been established in advance.

. Have at least one blanket and/or sleeping bag for each family member.

. If available, two-way radios may be distributed to key individuals having critical duties in the evacuation process.

4. The coordinator should review all evacuation mechanics with embassy staff, to include primary and alternative transportation methods and proposed destination(s).

5. The coordinator should simultaneously complete an evacuation plan independent of that offered by embassy staff, if any. Any and all resources should be considered in the development of such a plan, including the coordinator's group, other Americans, and friendly nationals.

6. If not previously finalized, all mechanics of evacuation should now be ready, such as the securing of exit and other visas, other clearances, and the securing of open airline tickets (on possibly more than one airline).

7. Mechanics of reassembly should be confirmed.

8. Normal business and work routines should continue as best as possible. In doing so, the following should be considered:

. Individuals may need to be designated, and delegated authority, to handle company business during the absence of evacuated personnel.

. All valuable documents should be identified for protection, removal, or destruction. Company accounting records, contracts, pending proposals, and other important documentation should be carried out by trusted personnel, as should the inventory of high value office items left behind.

. Consideration should be given to requirements of timing related to the mechanics of office closure. For example, local nationals may need to be hired to watch the office (if it is going to be closed and no foreign national employees are going to be assigned to watch it); an inventory of all high-value office equipment may need to be made; the office equipment may need to be packaged and moved to the safest locations(s) possible, for storage under lock and key.

C.   THE STAGING PHASE

This phase should be initiated when, in the judgement of the coordinator, the local conditions have deteriorated to the point that the decision to evacuate is imminent.

1.   The decision to evacuate.

When the company employee authorized to make the decision to evacuate believes the safety and security of personnel or dependents may be in imminent danger if local conditions continue to deteriorate, the mechanics of the evacuation should be implemented.

Planners should be aware that the U.S. Department of State cannot order the departure of private American citizens from a strife-torn country. However, State Department officials may inform citizens of impending danger, may recommend evacuation, and may offer U.S. government assistance in evacuation. Clearly, any notices provided to planners by the State Department should be given strong consideration, if not followed to the letter.

Planners must use all available resources in planning and implementing an evacuation. Multinational companies caught up in international crises have learned that it is largely up to them to devise and execute plans to protect their employees. They have found embassies in crisis situations, straining to protect American tourists, students, and others who have no other point of contact. Flexible plans must be developed to react to events quickly, and on behalf of corporate interests.

If a country manager or coordinator delays evacuation until the U.S. Department of State closes its embassy and/or recommends all American citizens leave the country, obtaining transportation and evacuating under possibly adverse security circumstances will be difficult.

2.   Evacuation from a hostile environment.

Evacuation of personnel from a situation of hostility is usually not advisable. The risk of harm to personnel is usually greater when trying to move about the country than when maintaining a low profile and staying indoors. Again, waiting for a hostile situation to stabilize is generally far safer than traveling about.

If a hostile evacuation is necessary, it is hoped that all dependents and nonessential personnel will have already been withdrawn by commercial airline. The decision to evacuate personnel under hostile conditions should be made only when the risk of staying becomes greater than the risk of being exposed. Under no circumstances should an action be taken if that action places personnel and dependents in more jeopardy than they were already in.

The evacuation plan should also consider the prudent assistance of local nationals employed by the company, who may become threatened or endangered as a result of local conditions.

3.   Evacuating the sick.

In the event an employee or dependent is hospitalized in the country at the time of a required evacuation, he or she should also be evacuated, if possible. It is likely, however, that ill employees will have already been moved out of the country, due to the requirement that most illnesses be treated outside the country.

If evacuation cannot be effected for these individuals, alternative plans for their continued protection and care during the crisis should be developed as best as possible, to at least include attempts to develop evacuation procedures for use when the situation allows.

4.   Movement for staging.

Generally, during the staging phase, personnel and their dependents will be moved from homes and offices to a prearranged staging area or areas, in preparation for air, land, or seas exits.

As a general rule, it is preferable to utilize a phased departure procedure in which evacuees are assembled at a secure staging location, then moved to an embarkation point or points in groups. In deciding whether to use a staging area, security risks should be weighed for assemblage at a staging location versus remaining in individual homes until departure, and versus having individual employees independently make their way to embarkation points.

If a phased departure is to be used, evacuee groups should be sized according to the transportation capacities planned for movement to the embarkation point. The movement schedule should be calculated to minimize exposure and to coincide with the scheduling of transportation planned for departure. This phased movement is recommended because it is effective in securing and facilitating the evacuation operation; however, circumstances out of the control of planners may prevent a phased movement. An alternative plan must, therefore, be considered in advance.

Movement from the staging area to the embarkation point should not occur without approval by the coordinator, or designate.

5.   In managing the business, withdrawal or cessation of business will be imminent or underway; management plans, as mentioned previously, will need to have been implemented by this time.

6.   Inquiries received from the media regarding a planned evacuation, or one in progress, should be managed carefully. Speculative reasons for the evacuation could be harmful to the evacuation and the company's relationship with the host government. Communication with the media, and statements expected to be made to them, should be considered an essential component of the overall evacuation plan, and necessary responsibilities assigned for their management.

D.   THE EVACUATION PHASE

This phase involves the movement of evacuees from staging area(s) to the embarkation point, then on to planned transportation, continuing to the reassembly point(s).

As with the selection of the staging area, security of the embarkation point must be considered.

At the time of the evacuees' departure from the embarkation point, the coordinator, or other designated individual left in country, if any, should notify corporate headquarters or the reception team at the reassembly point(s), of the following:

> .   The flight or other transportation data; i.e., departure date and time, estimated time and location of arrival.

> .   The names of all evacuees to include: those needing additional assistance with transportation to other destinations; those staying at the reassembly point and needing arrangements for lodging, etc.; those who are victims of injuries, etc.; and those with other medical needs, such as medical examinations and psychological care.

> .   The identification of other needs requiring advanced planning or scheduling at the reassembly point, such as protecting personnel from the media, should also be communicated.

E.   THE REASSEMBLY PHASE

This phase may require complete repatriation of employees and dependents, of dependents only, or of any variation of these. Alternatively, evacuees may simply be moved to another foreign office location where business and residence may be safely and temporarily resumed.

A.   GENERAL CONSIDERATIONS

The purpose of a Crisis Management Plan (CMP) is to resolve fixed issues in advance, so that only the variable elements must be addressed during a crisis. A CMP provides the corporation direction in responding to various emergency situations, and helps ensure correct reactions by those involved.

Emergency situations with the potential for negatively impacting business operations can occur both within and outside the U.S. and can include civil unrest, demonstrations, extortion, bomb threats, kidnapping, hijacking, natural and environmental disasters, as well as other corporate emergencies such as expatriate evacuations.

Corporate headquarters and each principal business and foreign office should develop (or have developed) CMPs with necessary management approval.

CMPs should reflect thorough risk and business impact analyses and outside advice, if solicited. The company security department is available to assist in conducting risk analyses and developing CMPs.

CMPs should be developed to address possible "worst-case" disaster scenarios, as such plans often apply to less serious emergencies as well.

Plans should include such elements as providing for the presence of security and other services at the incident site, for accurate documentation of events and for media control.

In addition, business recovery strategies should address such considerations as inventory control, insurance coverages, and temporary work locations. The role of communications in managing a corporate calamity should be given special consideration, as history has shown its importance cannot be overstated.

Each CMP must coordinate with those in other corporate entities. For example, forms used throughout the corporation in key crisis management processes should be standardized. CMPs must also coordinate with those of other governments and their agencies, and comply with local laws.

Each entity should designate a Crisis Management Team to develop, evaluate, update, and implement their CMP. Each team should be supervised by a Crisis Management Coordinator and should develop a method for emergency notification of team members, in the event the CMP is activated.

All CMPs should be considered CONFIDENTIAL for disclosure and distribution solely to employees of the company, having a need to know.

B.   THE CORPORATE CRISIS MANAGEMENT TEAM

1.   Functions.

The corporate Crisis Management Team manages incidents directly affecting corporate headquarters, such as their management, employees, or assets. In some cases, the corporate team also manages incidents at subsidiary companies and acts as the decision-making authority for the local teams' management of incidents.

The corporate team is responsible for developing and communicating to other teams applicable procedures and practices to be used. This coordination creates consistency and offers senior management an opportunity to address entity-specific aspects of CMPs. For example, consistency can be enhanced by the corporate team dispatching a representative to the incident location.

2.   Organization.

The corporate team should be chaired by a senior company official who functions as the team's coordinator. This position is often filled by the corporate CEO. However, the CEO may elect to relinquish authority to an alternate in cases where the alternate possesses expertise in managing the specific crisis at hand.

Other team members should represent departments such as legal, risk management, finance, human resources, personnel, and public/governmental relations.

Other support functions may include an executive assistant, a liaison officer for the victims' families (possibly even one per family), rumor control, communications specialist, medical liaison, incident site liaison, and international liaison.

C.   THE LOCAL CRISIS MANAGEMENT TEAM

1.   Functions.

The local team must operate within the guidelines of authority set forth by the corporate team. From these guidelines, the local team formulates and develops detailed CMPs for handling local emergency situations.

In large corporations, local teams report to their corporate counterpart regarding any emergency situation or response.

Often the actual CMP, or portions thereof, should be both in English and the local language so all employees can contribute fully in implementing it in an emergency.

2.   Organization.

The organizational structure of the local team depends upon the availability of local corporate personnel and may represent the following specialties or functions:

.   Security Incident Coordinator.

.   Personnel/Medical Coordinator.

.   Legal Advisor.

.   Financial Coordinator.

.   Public Relations Coordinator.

.   Business Unit Manager.

.   Liaison(s) to Host Government.

As with the corporate team, a senior in-country executive should be appointed Local Crisis Management Team Coordinator. The local coordinator should speak English, receive proper training, possess the appropriate psychological makeup, and be known at the U.S. Embassy or Consulate.

He or she is responsible for directing, selecting, supervising, and assigning functions to members of the local team, and for preparing and implementing the local CMP.

        a.   The Local Crisis Management Team Coordinator:

                .   Implements the local CMP.

                .   Forwards the local CMP to the corporate team.

                .   Ensures that all corporate and local company employees are aware of the local CMP and its functions.

                .   Trains personnel having team responsibilities.

                .   Practices the local CMP and evaluates team responses.

.   Reviews the local CMP on a semi-annual basis to ensure its accuracy.

.   Coordinates the local CMP with responsible officials of other local corporate facilities or sites, where appropriate.

.   Establishes liaison with local law enforcement or other public emergency officials, and other corporate CMP teams; and, in foreign locations, interfaces with the U.S. Embassy or Consulate security officer.

b.   During a crisis the local coordinator:

.   Convenes the local team.

.   Verifies the threat.

.   Assesses the crisis, including possible outcomes. In civil unrest situations, for example, the crisis may threaten many corporate assets. As one asset is protected another may become vulnerable. A goal of crisis management is to develop and plan responses so that the asset threatened is protected, yet other assets are not placed in jeopardy.

.   Implements phases of the CMP.

.   Designates and communicates to appropriate personnel the name and location of the local crisis management center, and the alternative off-site location.

.   Advises the corporate team of the crisis and actions to be taken by the local team.

.   Determines company options and goals in responding to crises, for local application.

.   Delegates duties, not in the CMP, to be performed by team members.

.   Maintains liaison with the corporate security structure and others, and advises them of the problem and action(s) to be taken.

.   Advises the Regional Security Officer or other appropriate official at the U.S. Embassy of actions to be taken by the local team.

17

. Notifies host government and law enforcement agencies at the appropriate levels, where necessary.

. Establishes liaison locally, as deemed necessary (with other American or friendly company, chamber of commerce, etc.).

. In the event hostages are taken and released, prepares for evacuation, debriefing, and rehabilitation.

D. ADDITIONAL STATE DEPARTMENT CONTACTS

The names and responsibilities of various U.S. Department of State organizations which may offer additional assistance are listed below.

1. Operations Center.

This is a 24-hour communications facility which monitors worldwide developments that may affect the security of U.S. interests abroad. In the event a crisis overseas affects American citizens, the Operations Center normally becomes the site for a Washington Task Force, staffed by representatives from various government agencies who support the U.S. response to the incident.

2. Washington Task Force or Working Group.

This task force is an ad hoc working group, activated only when necessary, to work closely with the U.S. Embassy in the country where the incident or problem exists.

3. U.S. Government International Disaster Response.

Coordination of this service is provided by the OFDA of AID. This service can also assist ins exploring corporate involvement in disaster relief overseas.

4. Embassy Emergency Action Committee (EAC).

Every U.S. Embassy is required to have an EAC. The EAC includes representatives from the political, security, public affairs, defense, administration, consular, and economic sections as well as representatives of other government agencies represented at the embassy. The EAC is responsible for developing U.S. government CMPs and recommends appropriate actions to the ambassador in the event of a crisis or emergency.

A.   GENERAL CONSIDERATIONS

Experience has shown that an established network is an especially effective way to communicate with employees residing in a specific area during times of increased threat or actual emergency. Such a communication network is known as an Alert Call List and when activated is known as an Alert Call Procedure or Warden System. This procedure is an essential part of a corporation's foreign office Crisis Management Plan (CMP).

B.   ADMINISTRATION

It is the responsibility of the entity's Crisis Management Team Coordinator to organize the Alert Call Procedure in advance of need. In fact, it should be organized as soon as a foreign office is established having more than one expatriate or family.

The success of the procedure depends in part on the accuracy of the list(s) containing local employees' names, addresses, and telephone numbers; and, if elected to be part of the procedure, their children's schools' telephone numbers, addresses, and school contacts' names should also be included. To maintain accuracy, this list should be updated periodically. It should also be a permanent part of the local CMP, and considered **CONFIDENTIAL**.

The coordinator is responsible for testing the procedure periodically and activating it in a time of need. Besides testing and activating the procedure, the coordinator may also implement it (as may be the case if the employee population is small).

On the other hand, if the coordinator believes he or she would be unable to implement the procedure, due to the size of the employee population or the likelihood of having too many other responsibilities during a crisis, alternates should be selected to implement it.

Employees assigned to implement an alert call procedure are referred to as "wardens." These wardens should be selected for not having other, extensive responsibilities during a crisis; for having access to private telephones, radios, or similar means of communication; and for residing centrally in areas of concentrated employee populations. If wardens are to be used, a pyramid network of communication can be established with each warden responsible for communication to his or her constituency group.

1.   Functions of the Coordinator:

.   Prepares a contact list including the entire employee population (and possibly others) to be used in an emergency, including wardens.

.   Activates the Alert Call Procedure.

19

. Supervises information sent to, and received from, employee group.

. If wardens are used, coordinator prepares a pyramidal communication network. An example of how this can be accomplished is by having individuals with telephones contact each other, and those without telephones contacted in person by someone who has one and lives nearby.

. Selects and meets with wardens and alternates to review responsibilities and update requirements.

2.   Functions of the warden (if used):

. Prepares, updates, and maintains a contact list of employees residing in his or her area of responsibility.

. Appoints at least one alternate as a substitute in his or her absence and provides substitute with the list of employees within the area of responsibility.

. Contacts employees when instructed.

. Knows and, when instructed, communicates the location of the assembly areas, movement routes, and other necessary instructions.

C.   ACTIVATION

Activation of the Alert Call Procedure should occur whenever it is necessary to communicate with employees in an emergency, and the most efficient means of accomplishing this is the Alert Call Procedure.

1.   Functions of the Coordinator:

. Activates the procedure by contacting those who are on the list. If a warden system is used, the coordinator contacts the wardens who then contact others in their area(s) of responsibility.

. Instructs wardens or others to transmit messages verbatim, without interpreting or expanding on the content.

. In an emergency gives necessary instructions; for example, to remain at a location near a telephone or emergency radio network, if in place.

. In an emergency designates a Crisis Management Center. If designated, this center will be manned to receive instructions from the embassy and corporation, and to communicate that information to wardens or others.

2. Functions of warden if used, or additional functions of coordinator if wardens are not used:

. Forwards, receives, and distributes messages as instructed on the status of the emergency and suggested actions to be taken.

. Ensures that the information contained in the notice is communicated to all employees in their area of responsibility.

. Assumes responsibility for knowing the whereabouts of those within his/her area of responsibility and all necessary contact information.

. Ensures that an alternate individual is available to carry out assigned responsibilities.

D. **SPECIAL CIRCUMSTANCES**

1. School Children.

A provision should be considered for the collecting of children in the event it becomes necessary while they are in school. Such a provision may include an agreement with school officials and alternate officials, and should provide for children to be collected by the school and any two of specified parents. School officials should be required to check the parent's identification at the time they pick up the children and should have names and telephone numbers of other parents designated to be called if there are any questions at the time of collection. *Strict confidentiality of this procedure should be required of all involved.*

An alternative to this plan is for each parent to collect his/her own children himself/herself.

2. Employees who cannot be contacted.

In the event an emergency evacuation becomes necessary and some individuals cannot be contacted, every effort should be made to continue to contact them as long as possible. Attempts should also be made to furnish them with alternative contacts (possibly through the U.S. Embassy) and an alternative evacuation plan.

A.   GENERAL CONSIDERATIONS

A reliable communication system is essential in the successful management of a crisis. Considering the current atmosphere within the country, reliable communications may be necessary as a result of a variety of extraordinary situations.

B.   SCENARIO EXAMPLES

For planning purposes, it is useful to consider extraordinary situations in which expatriate personnel in the country would need to communicate outside the country.

A planner might consider a situation in which decreasing availability of goods and services results in increasing frequency of civil disorder. In this situation, it could be predicted that authorities may react by imposing a state of complete police control. Such a reaction could restrict our employees' ability to communicate or evacuate.

Scenario 1.

One consequence of this situation may be that planners anticipate the problem and are afforded the opportunity to react. They could react by either a complete or partial evacuation; they might otherwise elect to manage it by staying in touch with the U.S. Embassy and recommending personnel stay in their homes or in a predetermined safe haven until the threat of danger has passed.

In this scenario, local planners must attempt to communicate their observations and plans to corporate headquarters as soon as any critical situation has been identified and a strategy adopted.

Scenario 2.

As an alternative to Scenario 1, the above mentioned situation may develop precipitously and not allow time to implement plans. This would likely necessitate personnel to wait-it-out, unless the State Department sponsors an evacuation.

It is possible that this scenario could develop so precipitously that communication would not be possible in advance of the crisis, and may not even be possible during the crisis. However, it is important to emphasize that, if possible, local planners, as in the above scenario, should communicate observations and plans to corporate headquarters as soon as a critical situation is identified and a strategy adopted.

22

C. GENERAL RECOMMENDATIONS

To help ensure the availability of adequate communications in emergency circumstances, three general capabilities should be investigated by a designated corporate employee in-country. These are:

. A local communications network with employees and authorities, to include an employee emergency notification system (such as an Alert Call Procedures or Warden System).

. A national link to locations in the country where other facilities are located.

. An international link to the company's corporate headquarters or other designated location.

To investigate these for application in a Crisis Management Plan (CMP), it is recommended that planners contact representatives of the Emergency Action Committee of the nearest U.S. Embassy. This group creates updated CMPs for many potentialities which may affect American civilians and governmental personnel. For example, in past evacuation scenarios this group has sometimes made arrangements with local *Voice of America* radio relay stations to broadcast simple emergency and evacuation advice to Americans within the local broadcast area. While this example may not be appropriate in all situations, it illustrates the creative use of resources which may be offered our personnel.

Specifically, the following communication alternatives should be assessed for applicability by personnel on site:

. The ability of the local telex system to handle national and international calls.

. Possibility of linkage with the non-secure U.S. Embassy very high frequency (VHF) radio network for intracity communication.

. Development of our own radio network, VHF (intracity), high frequency (national), and/or short wave (national and international).

. Access to a satellite-based communication system other than those now in use.

. Communication capabilities via the U.S. Embassy or other friendly country embassies, for national or international communication.

D. SPECIFIC RECOMMENDATIONS

It is likely that an investigation into alternative communication capabilities, such as those mentioned above, would greatly increase our knowledge of alternatives for communication in a crisis setting. In the absence of such an investigation, however, the following are recommended:

1.   Managing Scenario 1

As stated earlier, as soon as planners anticipate a problem and determine which plans to implement, this information should be communicated to corporate headquarters.

The requirements for communication are availability and reliability.

a.   In communicating from the host country to the United States:

Telex is recommended to be used until the Sprint electronic mailbox service is available, if one-way communication and the time of message receipt in the U.S. are acceptable.

If two-way transmission is needed, and/or the time of message receipt in the U.S. is critical, communication should be relayed to corporate headquarters by enlisting the help of corporate personnel in Central Europe, as it may be easier to access Central Europe than the U.S. directly.

2.   Managing Scenario 2

This scenario would require in-country planners to communicate their situation, observations, and plans to corporate headquarters as soon as possible.

In addition to options mentioned above, communication alternatives which are not dependent on the local telecommunication infrastructure should also be investigated. If, for example, the imposition of martial law prevents communication via the local telecommunication system outside the country, or the situation does not provide for the maintenance of continued protection of that network, system dysfunction could result.

a.   In communication from the host country to the U.S.:

In the event the local telecommunication infrastructure is not available for necessary communication the Consular Section of the U.S. Embassy *may* make available alternative mechanisms otherwise available to American civilians in emergencies. If so, only those resources established in advance will likely be available. Therefore, such a potentiality should be reviewed with embassy staff in advance and should be adopted as part of that plan to be implemented.

The safety and security of those affected by security threats is of primary importance whether in a foreign country, in any environment characterized by political or civil unrest, or when evacuation of corporate personnel or dependents is being considered.

The following recommendations may be helpful in reducing risks in these and other risk scenarios.

IN ANY CIRCUMSTANCE

.	Never resist an armed robbery, as resisting usually leads to violence. In fact, it is helpful to consider in advance the possibility of being robbed so that one can think through reactions and thus be better prepared.

.	In any conflict with political implications, do not take sides. Plead ignorance of local politics and express only the desire to contact the U.S. Embassy or Consulate, for the purpose of being reunited with your family back home.

.	Do not attempt to gather intelligence. Any individual who attempts to gather information about a situation, particularly by an on-the-scene examination, is in jeopardy by both sides.

IF DISTURBANCES ERUPT AND PREVENT EVACUATION AND THE OUTSIDE ENVIRONMENT SEEMS DANGEROUS

.	Stay in your hotel or home.

.	Try to contact the U.S. Embassy or Consulate by telephone.

.	If unsuccessful, try to hire someone to take a note there for you.

.	If unsuccessful, try to contact other friendly embassies by telephone or note--Britain, Canada, West Germany, etc.

IF DISTURBANCES ERUPT AND PREVENT EVACUATION AND THE OUTSIDE ENVIRONMENT DOES NOT SEEM DANGEROUS

.	Go to, or telephone, the U.S. Embassy and request assistance.

.	If unsuccessful, consider seeking safety at the embassy of a friendly nation.

.	Do not attempt to circumvent roadblocks or document checkpoints, as you are likely to be shot.

- Stay away from the scene of disturbances. Consider it a life-threatening situation, not an attraction.

- If you hear gunfire or report of hostilities, take shelter inside a neutral building, meaning one that is not apt to be a military target. Government facilities of any sort are likely to be military targets, as are television and other communication centers.

- It may be inadvisable to leave that safe harbor, assuming it has sufficient food and water. This would not be prudent, however, if there is imminent danger of it becoming engulfed in hostilities or taken over by a military force. Otherwise, a safe harbor should only be left if evacuation is offered by an embassy or humanitarian organization, or authoritative communication indicates that hostilities have been suspended or terminated.

- If it is necessary to move out of a safe harbor, it is generally best to move in a direction away from hostilities--away from the troops, tanks, or circling helicopters.

- Under most circumstances it is inadvisable to make a run for the airport with hostilities still in progress. The airport probably will be closed. Moreover, it will likely be a magnet for fighting or military positioning, and in any case, your path to it will likely be impeded by military roadblocks.

IF STRANDED IN YOUR HOTEL OR HOME

- Seek out other guests and organize the group to take care of housekeeping chores and create an emotional support base.

- Do not watch activity from your window, particularly if sniper fire is being directed from your hotel, or area.

- Sleep in the area offering the greatest protection against gunfire from the outside.

- Move to a room that is not exposed to the area of gunfire.

- Know your escape routes in case of fire.

IF DETAINED BY HOSTILE INTELLIGENCE

- First, never do anything that would give a hostile intelligence service reason to pick you up.

- However, if you are arrested or detained, ask to contact the American Embassy. You are entitled to do so under international diplomatic and consular agreements, to which most countries are signatories.

. Phrase your request appropriately. Your request is more likely to succeed in a communist country if you present it as a demand. In third-world countries, however, making demands could lead to physical abuse.

. Do not admit to wrongdoing or sign anything. Part of the detention ritual in communist countries is a written report which you will be asked or told to sign. Decline to do so and continue demanding to contact the embassy or consulate.

. Do not agree to help the hostile service. They may offer you the opportunity to help them in return for releasing you or foregoing prosecution. Either refuse outright or delay a firm commitment by saying that you have to think it over. Either action often leads to release.

. Report to the embassy or consulate and the in-country manager or corporate headquarters as soon as possible after such an incident. You should then request assistance in departing the country. Departure is generally possible with embassy assistance. However, you will risk rearrest on future visits, or may be denied future visas.

. Report to your corporate supervisor and security manager officer and the FBI immediately upon return to the U.S. This is especially important if you were unable to report to the embassy, consulate, or in-country manager.

IF YOU ARE ARRESTED

Every year thousands of Americans are arrested abroad, many on drug charges. The experience of being arrested overseas is notably different from being arrested in America.

. Few countries provide a jury trial.

. Most countries do not accept bail.

. Pretrial detention may last months, often in solitary confinement.

. Prisons may lack even minimal comforts of bed, toilet, and wash basin.

. Diet is often inadequate, requiring supplements from relatives and friends.

. Officials do not speak English.

. Physical abuse, confiscation of physical property, degrading or inhumane treatment, and extortion are possible.

KNOW YOUR RIGHTS

If you are arrested, ask permission to notify the nearest U.S. Embassy or Consulate. This is particularly important in countries with which the U. S. has status of forces agreements. Under international agreements and practice, you have a right to get in touch with the American Consul. If you are turned down, keep asking, politely but persistently. If you are unsuccessful, try to have someone else get in touch for you.

WHAT THE U.S. CONSULATE CAN DO

Consular officers will do whatever they can to protect your legitimate interests and ensure that you are not discriminated against under local law. Consular officers can:

. Provide lists of local attorneys.

. Help to find adequate legal representation.

. Visit you in jail.

. Advise you of your rights according to local law.

. Contact your company, family or friends.

. Arrange for the transfer of money, food, and clothing from your family and friends to prison authorities.

. Try to get relief if you are held under inhumane or unhealthy conditions, or if you are treated less favorably than others in the same situation.

WHAT THE U.S. CONSULATE CANNOT DO

Unfortunately, what American officials can do for you overseas is limited by foreign laws, U.S. laws, and geography. The U.S. Consulate cannot:

. Get you out of jail by posting bail or bond.

. Pay your legal fees or related expenses, serve as attorneys, or give legal advice.

A.   GENERAL CONSIDERATIONS

Accurate planning most influences the availability and selection of transportation methods used in an evacuation.

The country manager or Crisis Management Team Coordinator should use any sources available in the planning process including other multinational companies in the area.

The U.S. government *may* offer assistance with evacuation. However, they usually do not provide funds for the movement of persons, other than U.S. government employees and dependents. Normally, non-government individuals, evacuated by U.S. government funded transportation, must execute a promissory note to cover the cost of transportation.

B.   ASSESSING TRAVEL OPTIONS

If the need for transportation is anticipated, scheduled flights on commercial air carriers are recommended over any other mode of travel. However, the time needed for preparation of such a provision must be considered. For example, airline tickets should be obtained in advance of need. "Open" airline tickets should be acquired as they may be beneficial in the event evacuation is imminent, yet not certain. In fact, it may be wise to secure "open" tickets on more than one air carrier.

Air travel is recommended over other transportation modes for several reasons. Air travel is usually easier for those involved and may be safer due to the decrease in time of actual exposure to travel. However, before the decision is made to use air travel, it is important to carefully consider the relative risks of other travel options; for example, when the proposed flight path traverses a war zone, or when air carriers have recently been targeted by hijackers, etc.

One criteria for comparing the feasibility of various transport modes is to determine the frequency of scheduled travel to destinations of interest, and the normal capacity. One should compare all sources including commercial flights, ships, trains, buses, and automobiles departing the location of potential trouble.

C.   ASSESSING DESTINATION OPTIONS

The selected destination should have a correlation with the amount of time expected to be away. For example, the longer one anticipates being away, the more important it is that the destination be able to provide long-term supportive resources and may even result in repatriation, in some cases.

D.   SCHEDULED AIRLINES

One should also determine the capabilities of scheduled airlines to respond to evacuation requirements.

This should include scheduled frequencies, routes, capacities, ticketing and payment requirements, and procedures for obtaining using "open" tickets.

While flight schedules may change, those carriers who have the most flights to a destination now will likely have the most flights in the future. However, the final selection of a carrier must remain that of in-country planners.

Alternate routes to the airport(s) should be established and checked for traversability under emergency conditions.

E.   UNSCHEDULED (CHARTERED) AIRLINES

It is recommended that in-country planners use all available resources, including U.S. Department of State contacts, to determine carriers that have the capability of engaging in evacuations during periods of civil emergency. Their ability to do so under varying degrees of danger should also be determined. Company contacts and other mechanics of managing such a service should be investigated.

A reliable carrier, either foreign or domestic, should be selected. Suitability of equipment should be confirmed. Response times, such as time required for obtaining required overflight and landing authority, fuel, etc., should be determined. This data should then be communicated to corporate headquarters in the event expatriates need the service but are unable to handle it.

F.   SEA TRANSPORTATION

Shipping companies or agents that serve the area should be identified. Shipping or charter agents should be selected. The ship, response time, capacity, and time required to reach the planned destination should be identified.

One should also consider chartering small oceangoing yachts or cabin cruisers as a possible method of evacuating small numbers of essential personnel who have remained in-country after the evacuation of others. This is particularly important if airport embarkation points may be closed, yet seaport or shoreline use may still be available.

G.   LAND TRANSPORTATION

Transportation by personal vehicle out of the country should be considered a last resort only, and is not recommended to be used in most cases. The use of trains is normally less risky.

If, however, personal vehicles are required to be used, assistance from a local guide will likely be required. In fact, such an evacuation should not be attempted without careful consideration of the likelihood of needing a local guide.

The name, location, and potential for accessing any sources of vehicles that could be used in an emergency should be identified, whether by rental, loan, or pooling with cooperating companies.

The following checklist for road convoys should be considered:

. Designate primary and alternate convoy leaders.

. Select routes (primary and alternates) that avoid choke points.

. Plan for rest stops.

. Determine availability of vehicles to meet convoy requirements.

. Ensure adequate supplies of personal medical or other special needs. Inventory and have available spare fuel, food, water, tools, first aid, comfort supplies, maps, and compasses with each convoy.

. If the convoy is expected to cross an international boundary, have appropriate documentation for each person and vehicle.

. Arrange security for the convoy from local authorities, if possible. If environment is expected to be hostile, contact the U.S. Embassy for security assistance.

. Reconnoiter route in advance by sending advance vehicle approximately thirty minutes or more ahead of convoy.

. Provide communication capabilities for advance, lead, and rear convoy vehicles.

. Make preliminary arrangements to have local nationals available to drive and translate at road blocks, checkpoints, etc.

. Where possible, overland evacuation by convoy should be coordinated with other entities, particularly U.N. agencies and diplomatic groups.

. If the overland route is long, consideration should be given to stashing gasoline supplies along the route, possibly hiring an over-the-road trucker to place a supply of gas at a designated, strategic location along the route.

1. Parties:

   This contract is between Joe Wealthy Target (hereinafter referred to as TARGET) of Filthyrich City, Stuck-up County, New York, and Bob Bodyguard (hereinafter referred to as BODYGUARD) of Pot Luck, New Jersey.

2. Purposes of this Agreement:

   TARGET has a well-founded belief that, due to his personal circumstances, he and his family are vulnerable to various forms of criminal activity. TARGET, by this agreement, agrees to hire BODYGUARD to provide security services for TARGET and his family for the period of this agreement.

3. Duration of the Contract:

   This Contract shall become operative when executed by both parties, and shall remain in force and effect for one year from that date, unless terminated pursuant to the provisions of paragraph 4, herein.

4. Termination of this Agreement:

   This agreement may be terminated as follows: (a) TARGET may terminate this agreement at any time; (b) BODYGUARD may terminate this agreement upon twenty-four (24) hours notice, or at any time upon TARGET's substantial violation of the terms of this agreement.

5. Start-Up Costs:

   Upon execution of this agreement TARGET agrees:

   a.   to provide BODYGUARD with certificates of insurance for:

      i.   term life insurance in the amount of One Million ($1,000,000) Dollars to a beneficiary to be named by BODYGUARD;

      ii.   major medical insurance in the amount of One Million ($1,000,000) Dollars;

      iii.   disability insurance in the amount of Two Hundred Fifty Thousand ($250,000) Dollars; and

      iv.   a bond, in the amount of One Million Five Hundred Thousand ($1,500,000) Dollars, covering TARGET's performance of the covenant for legal services and continuing salary in case of incarceration, as detailed in this agreement.

1

6.   Remuneration:

TARGET shall pay to BODYGUARD, as salary, the sum of Eight Hundred ($800.00) Dollars a week, each week in advance, the first week's salary to be paid upon the execution of this agreement.

TARGET shall also pay the sum of Two Hundred ($200.00) Dollars an hour for ultra-hazardous work (said work shall be deemed ultra-hazardous when TARGET is under attack or threatened with imminent attack).

TARGET shall allocate to BODYGUARD the sum of One Hundred ($100.00) Dollars a month for minor expenses, and TARGET shall reimburse BODYGUARD for all expenses not covered by that allocation.

TARGET shall pay all ordinary and necessary living expenses of BODYGUARD during the term of this agreement.

TARGET shall pay to BODYGUARD, or his representative, extraordinary expenses as follows:

a.   If BODYGUARD is charged with any civil or criminal offense, in any jurisdiction, for any action connected with his employment by TARGET, TARGET shall pay for all legal expenses in connection with BODYGUARD's defense and reimburse him for any judgement made against him.

b.   If BODYGUARD is incarcerated for any activity connected with his employment by TARGET, BODYGUARD's salary, as set forth in this sub-paragraph, shall continue unabated until he is at liberty.

c.   Performance of these obligations shall be guaranteed by a bond in the amount of One Million Five Hundred Thousand ($1,500,000) Dollars, in accordance with paragraph 5 (a)(iv), above.

7.   Duties:

a.   It shall be BODYGUARD's primary duty to use his best efforts to protect TARGET from personal injury due to criminal or terrorist activity; secondary duties shall involve protecting TARGET's family and property from criminal or terrorist attack;

b.   BODYGUARD shall be available for duty twenty-four (24) hours a day, though his actual hours shall conform to TARGET's convenience. TARGET acknowledges that efficiency is impaired when BODYGUARD is required to be "on duty" for more than twelve (12) hours and, therefore, agrees to pay BODYGUARD one and one-half (1-1/2) his normal hourly rate for any on-duty hours in excess of twelve during any 24-hour period.

c.   TARGET guarantees that BODYGUARD's duties shall be of a legal character in whatever jurisdiction they are to be performed;

d.   TARGET guarantees that he has disclosed all the relevant information in his possession to BODYGUARD so that BODYGUARD can perform his assigned duties--breach of this guarantee shall be cause for immediate termination of this agreement.

8.   Severability Clause:

If any part of this agreement is found to be illegal, both parties agree that the remainder of the agreement shall remain in force and effect and, further, that all the terms of this agreement shall be construed, where possible, to provide for full enforcement of the agreement.

9.   Jurisdiction and Enforcement:

Both parties agree that, in any action involving the terms of this agreement, BODYGUARD shall stipulate that he may be served by first class mail at his residence in Pot Luck, New Jersey, and TARGET similarly stipulates to service by mail at his residence in Filthyrich City, New York; and further, both parties agree that this contract shall be construed according to the laws of the State of New Jersey.

10.   Attorneys Fees:

Both parties agree that should any action be instituted to enforce the terms of this agreement, the party who prevails shall be paid, in addition to any other recovery, all reasonable attorneys fees and costs in prosecuting the action.

11.   Arbitration:

If any party to this agreement files an action to enforce its terms, either party may demand, and both parties do hereby agree, that said action shall be heard by an arbitrator selected by and under the rules of the American Arbitration Association at Trenton, New Jersey.

12.   Inclusionary Statement:

This agreement embodies the entire understanding of the parties hereto; it supersedes all negotiations and all prior agreements, written or oral, and it may not be modified except by a writing signed by the parties hereto.

_____   _____
Joe Wealthy Target   Date

_____   _____
Bob Bodyguard   Date

PROTECTEE PROFILE

1. Protectee's Name_____ Nickname_____

2. Permanent Residence Address_____

   _____

   Telephone_____ Fax#_____ Floor Plans Available?_____

3. Secondary (Vacation) Residence Address_____

   _____

   Telephone_____ Fax#_____ Floor Plans Available?_____

4. Office Address_____

   _____

   Telephone_____ Fax#_____ Floor Plans Available?_____

   Secretary Name_____ Home Phone #_____

   Other Telephone #s and Description (Skypage, etc.)_____

   _____

5. Physical: Age_____ Height_____ Weight_____ Hair Color_____ Eye Color_____

   Glasses?_____ Prescription_____

   Scars/Identifying Marks_____

   _____

6. Personal Data: Sex____Race_____ Date of Birth_____Birthplace_____

   Social Security #_____Passport#_____Passport Exp.Date_____

   Driver's Lic.#_____State/Country_____Int'l Driver's Lic.#_____

   Major Credit Cards & #s_____

   _____

   _____

7. Medical: Physician's Name_____ Telephone_____

   Address_____

   Physician's Name_____ Telephone_____

   Address_____

   Dentist's Name_____ Telephone_____

   Address_____

   Illnesses/Operations_____

   Medication Required_____ Blood Type_____

   Allergies/Drug Allergies_____

8. Vehicles: Make_____ Model_____ Year____Color_____Lic.# & State_____

   Make_____ Model_____ Year____Color_____Lic.# & State_____

   Make_____ Model_____ Year____Color_____Lic.# & State_____

9. Plane: Type/Description_____I.D.#_____

10. Boat: Type/Description_____I.D.#_____

11. Health Ins.Carrier_____ Policy#_____

    Auto Ins. Carrier_____ Policy#_____

    Other Ins. Carrier_____ Policy#_____

    _____

    Kidnap/ransom insurance? _____ Carrier_____Policy#_____

12. Attorney's Name_____ Telephone_____

    Address_____

    _____

13. Protectee's Chief of Security_____ Telephone_____

    Address_____

14. Bank: Name_____Telephone_____ Contact_____

15. History of threats against family:_____

    _____

    _____

16. Any known enemies?_____

    _____

17. Club Memberships_____

    _____

    _____

    _____

18. Spouse Name_____ Nickname_____

    Physical: Age_____ Height_____ Weight_____ Hair Color_____ Eye Color_____

    Glasses?_____ Prescription_____

    Scars/Identifying Marks_____

    _____

    Personal Data: Sex____Race_____Date of Birth_____Birthplace_____

    Social Security #_____Passport#_____Passport Exp.Date_____

    Driver's Lic.#_____State/Country_____Int'l Driver's Lic.#_____

PROTECTEE PROFILE

Medical: Physician's Name_____ Telephone_____

Address_____

Physician's Name_____ Telephone_____

Address_____

Dentist's Name_____ Telephone_____

Address_____

Illnesses/Operations_____

Medication Required_____ Blood Type_____

Allergies/Drug Allergies_____

Club Memberships_____

_____

_____

_____

19.   Ex-Spouse Name_____ Nickname_____

Physical: Age_____ Height_____ Weight_____ Hair Color_____ Eye Color_____

Glasses?_____ Prescription_____

Scars/Identifying Marks_____

_____

Personal Data: Sex____Race_____Date of Birth_____Birthplace_____

Social Security #_____Passport#_____Passport Exp.Date_____

Driver's Lic.#_____State/Country_____Int'l Driver's Lic.#_____

Parent of Children?_____ Terms of Custody_____

_____

20.   Children or Other Persons in Household:

Name (**Child #1**)_____ Nickname_____

Physical: Age_____ Height_____ Weight_____ Hair Color_____ Eye Color_____

Glasses?_____ Prescription_____

Scars/Identifying Marks_____

_____

Personal Data: Sex____Date of Birth_____Birthplace_____Passport#_____

Name of School_____ Telephone_____

School Address_____ Contact_____

If living away from home, telephone/address_____

PROTECTEE PROFILE

Medical: Physician's Name_____ Telephone_____

Address_____

Dentist's Name_____ Telephone_____

Address_____

Illnesses/Operations_____

Medication Required_____ Blood Type_____

Allergies/Drug Allergies_____

21. Name (**Child #2**)_____ Nickname_____

Physical: Age_____ Height_____ Weight_____ Hair Color_____ Eye Color_____

Glasses?_____ Prescription_____

Scars/Identifying Marks_____

_____

Personal Data: Sex____Date of Birth_____Birthplace_____Passport#_____

Name of School_____ Telephone_____

School Address_____ Contact_____

If living away from home, telephone/address_____

Medical: Physician's Name_____ Telephone_____

Address_____

Dentist's Name_____ Telephone_____

Address_____

Illnesses/Operations_____

Medication Required_____ Blood Type_____

Allergies/Drug Allergies_____

22. Name (**Child #3**)_____ Nickname_____

Physical: Age_____ Height_____ Weight_____ Hair Color_____ Eye Color_____

Glasses?_____ Prescription_____

Scars/Identifying Marks_____

_____

Personal Data: Sex____Date of Birth_____Birthplace_____Passport#_____

Name of School_____ Telephone_____

School Address_____ Contact_____

If living away from home, telephone/address_____

_____

PROTECTEE PROFILE

Medical: Physician's Name_____ Telephone_____

Address_____

Dentist's Name_____ Telephone_____

Address_____

Illnesses/Operations_____

Medication Required_____ Blood Type_____

Allergies/Drug Allergies_____

23.   Name (**Child #4**)_____ Nickname_____

Physical: Age_____ Height_____ Weight_____ Hair Color_____ Eye Color_____

Glasses?_____ Prescription_____

Scars/Identifying Marks_____

_____

Personal Data: Sex____Date of Birth_____Birthplace_____Passport#_____

Name of School_____ Telephone_____

School Address_____ Contact_____

If living away from home, telephone/address_____

_____

Medical: Physician's Name_____ Telephone_____

Address_____

Dentist's Name_____ Telephone_____

Address_____

Illnesses/Operations_____

Medication Required_____ Blood Type_____

Allergies/Drug Allergies_____

24.   Grandchildren? If yes, attach separate sheet(s) with same information as for children.

25.   Household employees: Name_____ Telephone_____

Address_____

Name_____ Telephone_____

Address_____

*Client should provide:

.   fingerprints, photographs, voice tapes, and handwriting samples of each family member

.   blueprints of all residences

FOR IMMEDIATE RELEASE

For More Information Contact:

> Mary K. Jones
> ESI Protection International
> 1212 Lincoln Street
> Denver, CO 80202
> (303) 988-0200

RUSSIANS SEEK AMERICAN SECURITY KNOW-HOW

John Jones, the highly regarded private protection specialist whose firm, ESI Protection International, is based in Denver, Colorado, has recently returned from a very unusual assignment in Russia. Mr. Jones was employed by the ex-Director of the KGB to assist in overhauling the security programs for the three major tourist hotels in Moscow and St. Petersburg. Mr. Jones was also instrumental in setting up the first executive and dignitary protection teams employed by the Russian State Police.

"Russian police authorities are baffled in their attempts to solve their growing street crime problems," states Jones. "For decades, there was no street crime in Moscow. It would have been unthinkable for anyone to attempt to mug, assault, rape, or murder a tourist on the streets of Moscow, but now it is an everyday occurrence. And, the crimes of theft and assault in the tourist hotels are very serious." A tour group of Americans staying in the Rostenskaya Hotel in Moscow lost two people to crime. They were attacked in a back hall, robbed, and killed. This incident sparked the Russian concerns for tourist safety.

Jones' firm, ESI Protection International, was contacted in late summer, with a real cry for help from the Russian authorities. EPI President John Jones agreed to work with the Russian Director of Tourist Security in developing an overall hotel security program, and to train the Russian security police within the hotels. The Director of Tourist Security is the ex-Chief of Security, Russian KGB. "I was shocked," said Jones, "when I found that the man in charge of tourist safety was ex-KGB--it seems like a wild difference in jobs. But, we worked very well together. The problems for the Russians, to put it delicately, is that they do not know how to handle security problems in a 'civilized' manner. In the old days, they would have simply knocked heads and dragged them off to jail without much of a fuss. But, now, they have to deal with crime in a more western fashion."

While there, Jones set up an executive/dignitary protection program for the Russian State Police, a program more in keeping with the U.S. Secret Service rather than the old heavy-handed guard programs of the past.

Jones was impressed with the sincerity of his Russian counterparts. He says he hopes to go back, soon.

* * * * *

There can never be a "perfect" checklist, as each should be custom-tailored for the client and assignment and, for that reason, it is with some trepidation that the following checklists have been included in this book. There is the danger that if one were to accomplish only the items included on the checklist(s) some very important items could be left undone. Some of the best agents in the business do not use checklists for this reason and, instead, rely on their in-depth experience to trigger all the right moves. However, if you are (like the author) reliant upon the written word, checklists are a necessary part of life. Therefore, the checklists included within the Appendix should be viewed only as a starting point, to be added to and revised for each assignment. In fact, the author would be very pleased to have any suggestions, additions, deletions, etc. for revision of these checklists.

Please note that these checklists are not as minutely detailed as some, but instead, look at "the big picture." For example, some excruciatingly detailed checklists include . . . "Did you remove the keys from the vehicle?" Well, if you cannot remember to remove the keys from the vehicle, all of the checklists in the world will not help you--you're hopeless. Along with your preparation checklists (particularly with advances) you should make notes, including names, of anything that will help you in the future.

RESIDENCE

1. What are the crime statistics for the neighborhood? _____

2. What is the response time for police? fire? ambulance? _____

3. What is the quality of the police, fire, and ambulance services? _____

4. Have you introduced yourself to the local authorities? _____

5. Have you walked/driven around the neighborhood? _____

6. Have you introduced yourself to the neighbors? Is there any neighborhood interaction on security matters? _____

7. Have you made a notation of neighbors' vehicle license #s and description of vehicles? _____

8. What is the layout of the grounds and surrounding terrain? Have you produced a map or sketch? _____

9. Are there security problems caused by the terrain, such as ditches, body of water, trees, high point overlooking the house and grounds? _____

10. What delay/deterrent protection is provided by the perimeter? Is there a fence? Is it in good repair and of sufficient height? Is there a hedge? _____

11. If there is a fence, is the gate stoutly built with a good lock? _____

12. Is the gate locked at night? Is it locked during the day? _____

13. Is the gate-mounting hardware secured so that it can not be unfastened to permit an intruder to enter? _____

14. Can the gate be unlocked with a remote control device from within the automobile? _____

15. Have shrubbery and trees close to the fence and/or house been cut back to deny hiding places? _____

16. Are there trees, poles, or structures near the fence which would enable an intruder to more easily climb the fence or avoid contact if there are electronic sensors? _____

17. Has debris been cleared from both sides of the fence? _____

18. Is there sufficient lighting for the grounds and the exterior of the house? _____

19. Are light (power) switches well protected? _____

20. Is there back-up power for all lighting on the grounds and in the house? _____

21. How many access points to the grounds and house are there? (alley, secondary access road, etc.) _____

22. Does someone regularly check the grounds and perimeter to make certain that fence, gates, locks, lights, etc. are in good repair and have not been tampered with? _____

23. Are light bulbs replaced on a regular schedule? _____

24. Is the ground sufficiently level around the perimeter to enable the installation of barrier-type intrusion detectors? _____

25. Are there trees, poles, or other obstacles which would hamper the use of invisible barrier-type sensors? _____

26. Are there animals on the grounds during the night which would preclude the use of motion detectors? _____

27. Are there guard dogs and, if so, who is responsible for handling and exercising them? _____

28. If not guard dogs, are there (pet) dogs which bark to warn of intruders? Are they secure from intruders? _____

29. Is the lighting sufficient to enable the use of CCTV? _____

30. Are there guards and, if so, who is responsible for supervising them, assigning schedules, etc.? _____

31. Do the guards vary their patrol schedules so as not to be predictable? _____

32. Are the guards armed and, if so, what is the firepower and condition of the weapons? _____

33. Do the guards supply their own weapons, or are these provided by the client? _____

34. Do the guards carry radios, and is there a strict code for their use? _____

35. Are the guards proprietary (hired and supervised by the client or agent) or provided by a contract service? _____

36. If guards are provided by a contract service, is the liability issue clearly defined, and does the company carry liability insurance? _____

37. Have the guards, in your opinion, been properly trained, particularly in the use of and maintenance of firearms? _____

38. Are firearms properly secured when not in active carry? _____

39. Are all firearms regularly checked, repaired, cleaned, and maintained? _____

40. Are weapons licensed and in compliance with local regulations? _____

41. Can entrances to the residence be seen from the street or any area off-premises? _____

42. Are entrances well lighted? Has shrubbery been cut back? _____

43. Are exterior doors of solid core and/or contain steel facing? _____

44. Do exterior doors fit and close snugly without gaps or "give"? _____

45. Are there steel/glass security storm doors? _____

46. Are door hinges well-secured and, if not located on the inside, protected against the removal of the hinge pins? _____

47. Are all locks on exterior doors either deadbolt (with at least a 1" throw) or double cylinder? _____

48. Are all exterior doors equipped with auxiliary locks? _____

49. Have strike plates been used and securely fastened with deep-set screws? _____

50. Is there glass in the door which could be broken and the lock reached from outside? If so, is the door fitted with a double cylinder lock and the key hung out of reach from the outside? _____

51. If there is no glass in the door, is there a peephole? _____

52. Is there a pet entrance which would permit entry by a small person, or can lock be accessed through the pet door? _____

53. Are all sliding glass doors hung so that the sliding door is mounted on the inside? Are doors secure from being lifted off the sliding track? _____

54. Is there a jimmy-proof lock or charley bar on all sliding glass doors? _____

55. Are all sliding glass doors of reinforced (bullet-proof) glass? _____

56. Is the garage door equipped with a good locking system which can be unlocked and opened electronically from inside the vehicle? _____

57. Does the garage door automatically lock itself when closed? _____

58. Is the garage kept closed and locked at all times? _____

59. Are vehicles inside the garage kept locked? _____

60. Is the door from the garage into the residence of solid core and does it have not only a good quality deadbolt lock, but an auxiliary lock operated from the inside? _____

61. Is the door from the basement into the upper floor of solid core and equipped with a deadbolt plus auxiliary lock? _____

62. If there is an outside entrance into the basement, has this entrance been equipped with the same security specifications as other exterior doors (solid core door, solid fit, solidly emplaced hinge pins, deadbolt lock)? _____

63. Do all outbuildings (storage sheds, pool house, etc.) have sturdy locks, hasps, and good security? _____

64. Have trellises and ladders which could be used to gain access to upper floors been removed? _____

65. Are external fuse boxes, control panels, and power sources well secured from environmental hazards and against intrusion? _____

66. Is there a swimming pool? If there are small children, is pool well secured with a fence, gate, locks, and a floating alarm? _____

67. Are unused doors and windows permanently closed and secured? _____

68. Have louvre windows been replaced with solid windows of tempered, shatter-proof glass? _____

69. Do all windows have locks? Are windows kept locked when closed? _____

70. If windows are opened, can they be locked in the open or half-open position? _____

71. Do all windows have screens or storm windows which can be locked from the inside? _____

72. Are all of the windows and doors protected either with iron bars or an alarm system? If so, are they (particularly bedroom windows) equipped with quick release fire escape devices? _____

73. Are window air conditioners bolted and secured against removal? _____

74. Are basement and garage windows fully secured? _____

75. Do any upper floor windows open onto a porch, balcony, or other structure? If so, have they been fully secured? _____

76. Do all windows have adequate window coverings (curtains, drapes, shutters) to prevent someone from seeing inside? _____

77. Are skylights fully secured against intrusion? _____

78. Is the roof fully secured against intrusion? _____

79. If it is a flat roof, has a pole or something been erected to deter a helicopter attack? _____

80. Can the roof be accessed by scaling with grappling hooks? _____

81. Does the master bedroom have a solid core door with deadbolt lock and hinge pins which cannot be removed from the outside? Is there either a separate secure telephone line or a cellular telephone? _____

82. Has a safe room been designated? _____

83. Is the safe room equipped with a separate secure telephone line or a cellular telephone? _____

84. Is the safe room rated fire safe for at least one hours? _____

85. Is the door to the safe room solid core, steel plated, and secured with a deadbolt, strike plate, reinforced door frame, and non-removable hinge pins? _____

86. Has the safe room been equipped and stocked with a battery-operated light, fire extinguisher, first aid kit, two-way radio, weapon(s), and water?   _____

87. Does the residence have an electronic alarm system?   _____

88. Is it an audible or silent alarm system?   _____

89. Is the alarm system connected to a central station, or is it connected to a residence command post?   _____

90. Has the system been recently (and is it regularly) tested?   _____

91. Who is responsible for servicing and maintaining the system?   _____

92. Is the system subject to a higher than normal rate of false alarms?   _____

93. Does the alarm system need updating and/or enhancement or is it adequate?   _____

94. What is the response to an alarm intrusion? What is response time?   _____

95. Is the residence equipped with panic switches to signal an emergency? What is the response?   _____

96. Is there a CCTV detection system? Is it adequate, with sufficient lighting?   _____

97. Who is available to monitor the CCTV? What is the planned response to a detection?   _____

98. Do you have layout and a set of blueprints for the residence and the electronic system? Where are they kept?   _____

99. Is there a fire detection system?   _____

100. Are batteries regularly checked for the system?   _____

101. Is there back-up power?   _____

102. Are fire extinguishers strategically placed around the residence?   _____

103. Who is responsible for charging and maintaining the extinguishers?   _____

104. Are all occupants of the residence trained in the use of the extinguishers?   _____

105. Is the residence equipped with interior fire sprinklers?   _____

106. Is there at least one (or more) folding ladder(s) on the upper floors to facilitate escape in the event of a fire? _____

107. Do the occupants regularly practice a fire drill? _____

108. Do the occupants regularly practice an intrusion drill, with retreat to the safe room? _____

109. Is there a command post on the grounds or within the residence? _____

110. Is the command post manned on a 24-hour basis? _____

111. Are schedules made and adhered to for the protection team? _____

112. Are weapons safely secured within the command post? _____

113. What form of communications system is available for the command post? Is it secure? _____

114. Is the command post off-limits to employees other than the protection team? _____

115. Is the command post stocked with:

    . radio(s)? _____
    . medical kit? _____
    . office supplies, table, chairs and bulletin board? _____
    . typewriter? _____
    . flashlight? _____
    . fire extinguisher? _____
    . extra keys (vehicles, residence)? _____
    . layout and plans of house and grounds? _____
    . updated client itinerary? _____
    . telephone numbers? _____
    . agent schedules and post assignments? _____
    . intelligence reports? _____
    . polaroid camera? _____

116. Are procedures in place for screening visitors? _____

117. Is there a locking mailbox or arrangements for delivery of mail to the command post? _____

118. How are deliveries to the residence handled? Are they taken to the command post? _____

119. Is garbage/trash in a secure area, or is it shredded? _____

120. Do you have names, addresses, and telephone numbers for all staff? _____

121.	Have the household employees been screened with background checks?

122.	Has a Personal Profile been obtained for the client and family members?

123.	Have family members and household staff been given "security awareness" training to alert them to excessive wrong numbers and indications of surveillance?

124.	Does family and staff understand the workings of the alarm system and use it?

125.	Are windows and doors kept locked?

12ι.	Does family and staff understand the use of (and any codes for) emergency communication procedures?

127.	Have serial numbers been recorded for possessions, and have possessions been marked with an ID number?

128.	Have family and staff been alerted to the signs of a possible mail or package bomb and been given procedures for handling?

129.	Is there a strict system for key control?

130.	Have the client and family been given a security briefing including how to keep a low profile, varying driving routines, defensive driving, and crime prevention measures?

131.	Have procedures been established with the children's school officials to prevent the children being picked up by strangers?

132.	Do the children have escorts and secure transportation to take them to and from school?

133.	Do you have make, model, and license numbers of all client and household staff vehicles?

134.	Has the residence been checked for eavesdropping devices?

135.	Are the telephone lines regularly checked against wiretaps?

APARTMENT/CONDOMINIUM

In addition to the above, the following apartment-specific security details should be checked. All items on the above checklist should be checked and, where necessary, security alterations made to the apartment--for example, with doors, locks, hinges, window locks, sliding glass doors, etc.

8

136. What is the history of crime within the building? _____

137. Have the neighbors in close proximity (either side, above, and below) been checked out? Do you believe them to be secure neighbors? _____

138. Have you introduced yourself to your (close) neighbors within the building? _____

139. Is there a tenant association, and is mutual security an issue which can be established? _____

140. How secure, overall, is the building? _____

141. Is someone on duty in the lobby 24 hours a day to screen visitors, deliverymen, and repair/maintenance people? _____

142. Does the apartment have a balcony (balconies) which could be accessed from the outside? _____

143. Are the apartment grounds patrolled? _____

144. Are the grounds well lighted? _____

145. Is there an inside parking garage? _____

146. How secure is the garage against intrusion? _____

147. Is the garage well lighted? _____

148. Is there a telephone and/or panic switch located at strategic points within the garage? _____

149. Is garage area patrolled? _____

150. Are you certain that no keys, or master keys to the client's apartment, are in other hands such as the building management? _____

151. Have background checks been made on building management staff and employees? _____

152. Is there back-up power for the building? _____

153. Is there an adequate number of elevators in the building? _____

154. Are the elevators well lighted and equipped with a mirror which reveals all occupants? _____

155. Is there an adequate intrusion detection system in the building? _____

156. What is the response time to the alarm? _____

9

157. Have you checked to be certain that the building alarm system is regularly inspected and maintained?

_____

158. Does the building have a fire detection system?

_____

159. Is it well maintained?

_____

160. Are there fire extinguishers in each hall of the building?

_____

161. Have you checked the tags to be certain that fire extinguishers have been charged and maintained?

_____

162. Is the building well sprinklered?

_____

163. Is the client's apartment located within reach of the fire trucks and ladders?

_____

164. Does the apartment have its own intrusion detection system?

_____

165. Has the system been maintained properly?

_____

166. What is the location of the closest emergency hospital?

_____

167. Have you located the primary and secondary routes to the hospital?

_____

168. Have you checked all hallways and exits to determine the best escape route(s) in the event of a fire?

_____

169. Are hallways, stairs, and exits free of obstructions, equipped with handrails, and well lighted?

_____

170. Can roof doors and skylights only be opened from the inside, and are they kept locked at all times?

_____

171. Are there bars covering roof doors and skylights?

_____

172. Are recreational areas (swimming pool, weight/exercise room, library) secure and not available to the public? Are there outside doors to these areas and are they kept locked from the inside?

_____

173. Have you acquired a set of plans or at least a detailed layout of the building?

_____

OFFICE

1. Is the building proprietary to the client; that is, is the client's company the only one occupying the building? _____

2. If not, have you introduced yourself to the other tenants? _____

3. Have you performed a background check on any of the other tenants? _____

4. Do any of the tenants present a security problem for your client-- either with their employees, their product/service, or their inattentiveness to security? _____

5. Are there building security programs which encourage interaction between the tenants? _____

6. Is there a building Director of Security? _____

7. What are the crime statistics for the neighborhood? _____

8. Is there anything about the building, grounds, or location that would make it an unusually attractive target for crime or terrorism? _____

9. Are there any environmental concerns within or about the facility which should be addressed (poor water, asbestos, flooding, etc.)? _____

10. What is the response time for police? fire? ambulance? _____

11. What is the quality of the police, fire, and ambulance services? _____

12. Have you established liaison with the police authorities? _____

13. Have you walked/driven around the neighborhood, noting anything unusual? _____

14. Have prior security surveys of the building and grounds been made and are they available? What were the results of those surveys? _____

15. What is the layout of the grounds and surrounding terrain? _____

16. Have you produced a map or sketch? _____

17. Are there security problems caused by the terrain, such as ditches, body of water, trees, high point overlooking the facility and grounds? _____

18. Is access to the facility open or restricted? _____

19. If open access, is there visitor parking on the grounds? _____

20. How is employee parking handled? _____

21. What delay/deterrent protection is provided by the perimeter? Is there a fence? Is it in good repair and of sufficient height and strength? Is the entry road/street straight or angular? _____

22. If there is a fence, how many access gates are there? _____

23. Is/are the gate(s) locked at night? Locked during the day? _____

24. Is the gate-mounting hardware secured so that it can not be unfastened to permit an intruder to enter? _____

25. Is the gate(s) equivalent in strength and security to the fencing? _____

26. Is the main gate manned by a guard? _____

27. Have shrubbery and trees close to the fence and/or facility been cut back to deny hiding places? _____

28. Are there trees, poles, or structures near the fence which would enable an intruder to more easily climb the fence or avoid contact if there are electronic sensors? _____

29. Has debris been cleared from both sides of the fence? _____

30. Is there sufficient lighting for the perimeter, fencing, gates, grounds, and the exterior of the facility? _____

31. Are light bulbs replaced on a regular schedule? _____

32. Is the lighting sufficient to enable the use of CCTV? _____

33. Are parking lots adequately lighted? _____

34. Is the lighting mounted so that it is beamed in the direction of the fencing (in the eyes of the intruders), leaving the guards in a non-highlighted area? _____

35. Are light (power) switches well protected? Is the lighting tamperproof? _____

36. Is there back-up power for all grounds and building lighting? _____

37. Who is responsible for controlling the lights? _____

38. Who is responsible for checking and maintaining the lights? _____

39. How many access points (alley, secondary access road, etc.) to the grounds and facility are there? _____

40. Is there an interior perimeter road for the use of the guards? _____

41. Does someone regularly check the grounds and perimeter to make certain that fence, gates, locks, lights, etc. are in good repair and have not been tampered with?

_____

42. Is the ground sufficiently level around the perimeter to enable the installation of barrier-type intrusion detectors?

_____

43. Are there trees, poles, or other obstacles which would hamper the use of invisible barrier-type sensors?

_____

44. Are there animals on the grounds during the night which would preclude the use of motion detectors?

_____

45. Are there guard dogs and, if so, who is responsible for handling and exercising them?

_____

46. Are there guards and, if so, who is responsible for supervising them, assigning schedules, etc.?

_____

47. Are background checks performed on guards at hiring?

_____

48. Do the guards vary their patrol schedules so as not to be predictable?

_____

49. Are the guards armed and, if so, what is the firepower and condition of their weapons?

_____

50. Do the guards supply their own weapons, or are these provided by the client?

_____

51. Do the guards carry radios, and is there a strict code for their use?

_____

52. Are the guards proprietary (hired and supervised by the client or agent), or provided by a contract service?

_____

53. If guards are provided by a contract service, is the liability issue clearly defined, and does the company carry liability insurance?

_____

54. Have the guards, in your opinion, been properly trained, particularly in the use of, and maintenance of, firearms?

_____

55. Are firearms properly secured when not in active carry?

_____

56. Are all firearms regularly checked, cleaned, and maintained?

_____

57. Are weapons licensed and in compliance with local regulations?

_____

58. Does the facility have an electronic alarm system?

_____

   .   perimeter intrusion detectors?

_____

   .   fence disturbance/motion sensors?

_____

13

.   exterior door alarm sensors?

.   interior motion detectors, microwave, or other sensors?

.   window sensors?

59.   Is it an audible or silent alarm system?

60.   Who will monitor the alarm sensors?

61.   Is the alarm system connected to a central station, or is it connected to a command post?

62.   If a central station is used, are there dedicated telephone lines to carry the signals?

63.   Who will respond to an alarm signal?

64.   What is the response time?

65.   Are there guidelines for a response to an alarm signal? Will the response team be armed? What are the limitations to the response?

66.   If the alarm signal is transmitted from within the facility, will the response team be able to enter? How? Will they have keys?

67.   In the event of an alarm signal, who on the company staff will be notified?

68.   Has the system been recently (and is it regularly) tested?

69.   Who is responsible for servicing and maintaining the system?

70.   Is the system subject to a higher than normal rate of false alarms?

71.   Does the alarm system need updating and/or enhancement, or is it adequate?

72.   If there are no proprietary guards, who will respond to an alarm signal? What is response time?

73.   Is the facility equipped with panic switches to signal an emergency? What is the response?

74.   Is there a CCTV detection system? Is it adequate, with sufficient lighting?

75.   Who is available to monitor the CCTV? What is the planned response to a detection?

76.   Are all outdoor switches located in weatherproof, tamper resistent areas?

77. Do you have a sketched layout and a set of blueprints for the grounds and the electronic system?   _____

78. Are all entrances to the building well lighted?   _____

79. Are secondary doors (fire exits) solidly constructed and equipped with panic bars--and otherwise kept locked?   _____

80. Are unused doors securely locked?   _____

81. Is the exterior of the building itself of sufficient strength and integrity to withstand intrusion?   _____

82. Is there an alarm system which controls access through the exterior door(s)?   _____

83. Are exterior doors of solid core and/or contain steel facing?   _____

84. Do exterior doors fit and close snugly without gaps or "give"?   _____

85. Have strike plates been securely fastened with deep-set screws?   _____

86. Are door hinges well-secured and, if not located on the inside, protected against the removal of the hinge pins?   _____

87. Are all locks on exterior doors either deadbolt (with at least a 1" throw) or double cylinder?   _____

88. Is there glass in the door which could be broken and the lock reached from outside? If so, is the door fitted with a double cylinder lock and the key hung out of reach from the outside?   _____

89. If there is no glass in the door, is there a peephole?   _____

90. Are all sliding glass doors hung so that the sliding door is mounted on the inside and/or secure from being lifted off the sliding track?   _____

91. Is there a jimmy-proof lock on all sliding glass doors?   _____

92. Are all sliding glass doors of reinforced (bullet-proof) glass?   _____

93. Are all windows within access from the ground connected to the alarm system?   _____

94. Are ground floor windows protected by shatterproof glass and iron bars?   _____

95. Is the roof accessible from the ground or from adjoining buildings?   _____

96. Have the roof, skylights, ducts, and other accessible entryways been secured? _____

97. If it is a flat roof, has a pole or something been erected to deter a helicopter attack? _____

98. Can the roof be accessed by scaling with grappling hooks? _____

99. Do you have a layout and/or blueprints of the building? _____

100. Is there an inside parking garage? _____

101. How secure is the garage against intrusion? _____

102. Is the garage well lighted? _____

103. Is there a telephone and/or panic switch located at strategic points within the garage? _____

104. Is the garage area patrolled? _____

105. Has a safe room/area been designated? _____

106. Is the safe room equipped with a separate secure telephone line or a cellular telephone? _____

107. Is the safe room rated fire safe for at least one hour? _____

108. Is the door to the safe room solid core, steel plated, and secured with a deadbolt, strike plate, reinforced door frame, and non-removable hinge pins? _____

109. Has the safe room been equipped and stocked with a battery-operated light, fire extinguisher, first aid kit, two-way radio, weapon(s), and water? _____

110. Is there a fire detection system? _____

111. Are batteries regularly checked for the system? _____

112. Is there back-up power? _____

113. Are fire extinguishers strategically placed around the facility? _____

114. Are fire extinguishers regularly charged and maintained? _____

115. Is the facility equipped with interior fire sprinklers? _____

116. Do the occupants regularly practice a fire drill? _____

117. Are there lighted exits which are well marked? _____

118. Are there signs by the elevators directing occupants to use the stairs in the event of a fire? _____

119. Are procedures in place to handle bomb threats and evacuation? _____

120. Are evacuation drills practiced on a regular basis? _____

121. Has a safe assembly area been designated for use in an evacuation? _____

122. Are there an adequate number of elevators in the building? _____

123. Are these elevators regularly inspected? _____

124. Are the elevators well lighted and equipped with a mirror which reveals all occupants? _____

125. Are all hallways, stairs, and exits free of obstructions, equipped with handrails, and well lighted? _____

126. Is there a Crisis Management Team which meets regularly? _____

127. Is there in place a Crisis Management Plan? _____

128. Are CMP scenarios and drills practiced? Does top management participate? _____

129. Does the company carry kidnap/ransom insurance on its top executive(s)? _____

130. Does the CMP include procedures for handling a kidnap or hostage taking of a top company executive? _____

131. Is there a command post on the grounds or within the facility? _____

132. Is the command post manned on a 24-hour basis? _____

133. What form of communications system is available for the command post? Is it secure? _____

134. Is the command post off-limits to employees other than the protection team and guards? _____

135. Is the command post stocked with:

    . radio(s)? _____
    . medical kit? _____
    . office supplies, table, chairs and bulletin board? _____
    . typewriter? _____

	flashlight?	_____
.	fire extinguisher?	_____
.	extra keys (vehicles, office)?	_____
.	layout and blueprints of building and grounds?	_____
.	telephone numbers?	_____
.	agent schedules and post assignments?	_____
.	intelligence reports?	_____
.	polaroid camera?	_____

136. Is strict key control maintained within the facility? How is this handled? _____

137. Is a record kept of all persons issued and holding company keys? _____

138. What procedures are in place for handling lost keys? Are locks changed? _____

139. Are mail handling procedures in place to alert mail handlers to possible mail and/ package bombs? _____

140. Are all deliveries to the building or company space received at a central place? _____

141. Do all new employees receive security awareness training as part of their orientation? _____

142. Are background checks made, and/or references checked, on all employees? _____

143. Are executive briefings prepared for all executives going overseas? _____

144. What access controls are in place to handle visitors and tradespeople:

   . at the gate? _____
   . in the lobby? _____
   . in the anteroom of the company offices? _____
   . in the executive offices? _____
   . in restricted areas? _____
   . at the loading dock? _____

145. Is it open access within the building for employees, or are they restricted to certain areas? _____

146. What access controls are in place to handle restricted employee access? _____

147. Are employees badged? _____

148. Are visitors issued badges, and are these badges collected upon the end of the visit? _____

149.   Is there a visitor escort service?   _____

150.   Are outside repair/maintenance people escorted and supervised
        during their entire visit?   _____

151.   Are packages and/or briefcases searched?   _____

152.   Are stairwells locked from the inside (self-locking) except at the
        ground floor and each five floors?   _____

153.   Do the receptionist/secretary and top executives have a silent distress
        (panic) signal?   _____

154.   What is the response to the distress signal?   _____

155.   Are restrooms kept locked?   _____

156.   Are closets and maintenance rooms kept locked?   _____

157.   Is an outside cleaning service used? Have they been checked?   _____

158.   Are meeting rooms and executive offices regularly checked for
        eavesdropping devices?   _____

159.   Are telephone lines secure? Are they regularly checked for wiretaps?   _____

160.   What procedures are in place to protect proprietary company
        information?   _____

161.   Is there good computer security?   _____

162.   Is the client's staff (assistants, secretary) willing to assist in providing
        information to the protection team about the client's itinerary and
        plans? Are they cooperative?   _____

163.   Is the client's staff aware of the need to protect the confidentiality of
        the client's itinerary and personal information?   _____

164.   Is the Security Director aware of the need to work with the protection
        team? Have good relations been established?   _____

OVERSEAS

165.   If overseas, have all the above security measures been followed and
        upgraded to provide even more in-depth security?   _____

166.   Is client and family fully aware of the need to keep a low profile and
        to be even more aware of the need for security in a foreign country?   _____

167. Have household employees and company staff, particularly foreign nationals, been fully background checked?   _____

168. Have you obtained the names, addresses, and telephone numbers for household employees and company staff?   _____

169. Are household employees trained in security awareness and in the handling of mail, deliveries, and strangers at the door and on the telephone?   _____

170. Have you established contact with local authorities and with the U.S. Department of State?   _____

171. Have you prepared an intelligence report and threat assessment for the host country and location?   _____

172. If you have employed a guard service, did you get recommendations from the U.S. Department of State, and did you check on the company?   _____

173. Have you communicated with the security personnel in other American companies in your location and discussed mutual security plans in the event of an evacuation?   _____

174. Have company logos and other identifying marks been removed from client vehicles and residence?   _____

175. Is client's vehicle of a low profile make and model common to the vehicles of the host country?   _____

176. Have you prepared an emergency evacuation plan in the event that the client and family must leave quickly?   _____

177. Have you prepared a stock of emergency rations to be kept at the residence in the event that an emergency prevents you from leaving the country?   _____

178. Are more stringent security measures taken to avoid having a bomb placed in or near the residence or offices, such as:

    .   removing any bicycle racks adjacent to the building?   _____

    .   not allowing unidentified bicycles or vehicles to be parked adjacent to the building?   _____

    .   placing covers or screens over all openings (ducts, vents, mail slots, etc.) on the building?   _____

    .   regularly inspecting the public areas of the building to note any unidentified or suspicious objects left there?   _____

. securing and/or locking paper towel dispensers, boxes, toilet tank tops, etc. in public restrooms?

. designing access road/street to the building so that it is not a straight shot, requiring the driver to drive slowly?

179. Have children's school(s) been thoroughly checked to be certain they are safe and reliable?

180. Have school administrators and teachers been given instructions regarding not allowing children to be picked up by anyone other than family, agents, and other identified individuals?

181. Have children been given a code to identify any unknown persons contacting them, or attempting to remove them from school?

182. Has a code been established with the client which would be used in the event of a kidnapping?

183. Has a safe been installed in the residence and in the office to hold sensitive personal documents?

184. Has client left a power of attorney, will, list of assets, and other personal information with a trusted associate or family member in the United States, to be used in the event of a kidnapping?

185. Does the corporate Crisis Management Plan cover the eventuality of a kidnapping, hijacking, or hostage-taking?

186. Are you aware of the host country's national holidays, and are you particularly vigilant during these times?

VEHICLE & TRANSPORTATION CHECKLIST

1. Is the client's vehicle of a size and weight that gives comfort and solid safety features?

2. Does the vehicle have an automatic transmission?

3. Have engine, transmission, radiator, alternator, battery, suspension, and tires been upgraded for the heaviest duty available?

4. Is the vehicle equipped with a high intensity spotlight mounted on a swivel?

5. Is the vehicle air conditioned?

6. Does the vehicle have automatic controls for the windows and door locks?

7. Is the vehicle equipped with an alarm system?

    _____

8. Can the alarm system be controlled electronically with a hand-held clicker from outside the car?

    _____

9. Are tires fully inflated, and are all four tires kept at exactly the same level of inflation?

    _____

10. Is the spare tire regularly inspected and kept fully inflated?

    _____

11. Is the vehicle in good condition overall?

    _____

12. Is it regularly maintained?

    _____

13. Who performs the maintenance? Is the vehicle taken to the same mechanic each time?

    _____

14. Do you carry in the trunk (in addition to the spare tire) flares, fire extinguisher, flashlight, tire sealers, tool kit, tow chain, jack, lug wrench, jumper cables, extra motor oil and engine coolant, and a fully maintained medical kit?

    _____

15. Does the trunk have an inside latch release to permit escape if locked in the trunk?

    _____

16. Do the hood and gas cap have locks controlled from the inside?

    _____

17. Is the car armored? Should it be?

    _____

18. Is the window glass bullet resistant?

    _____

19. Have the radiator and gas tank been reinforced?

    _____

20. Are the tires a "run flat" type which will continue to roll even if pierced by a bullet?

    _____

21. Is the vehicle equipped with a cellular phone, and is it programmed for speed dialing? Do you have a two-way radio?

    _____

22. Do you keep your gasoline tank at least half full?

    _____

23. Do you keep all doors and windows closed and locked at all times?

    _____

24. If the vehicle is not always under your direct control or well secured, do you always perform a quick inspection of the vehicle and its immediate surroundings before getting in?

    _____

25. If a driver is employed for the client's vehicle, has the driver been fully briefed as to logistics, safety, and security procedures?

    _____

26. If permanently employed, has the driver been fully trained in executive protection driving procedures and escape and evasion driving maneuvers? _____

27. Is the driver aware that travel routes and times should be varied to avoid predictable behavior? _____

28. Is driver aware that, in an emergency, he/she must drive away immediately, even at the cost of damaging the vehicle? _____

29. Is the driver armed? _____

30. Has driver been trained in defensive shooting? _____

31. Have all identifying marks (logos, vanity license plates, etc.) been removed from the vehicle? _____

32. Have all identifying marks been removed from the parking space habitually used for the vehicle? _____

33. When not in use is the vehicle kept locked and inside a locked garage whenever possible? _____

34. If there is an escort car, does it function as the lead vehicle? _____

35. If a rental limousine and driver have been hired, has the driver been informed that the agent (rather than the client) will issue instructions? Has the limo driver been given explicit instructions? _____

36. Are rental vehicles checked as to spare tire, fluid levels, trunk contents, cleanliness, and general condition? _____

ADVANCES

PRE-DEPARTURE

1. Have you put together a preliminary threat assessment? _____

2. Have you reviewed your files to find any prior reports and advance information which might be useful? _____

3. Do you have client's itinerary and all pertinent information about the proposed trip/visit? This includes:

    . Dates and locations to be visited. _____

    . Itinerary. _____

23

    .   Names, titles, and description of protectee(s) and other members of the client party.   _____

    .   Transportation arrangements. Have reservations been made?   _____

    .   Billing arrangements for transportation.   _____

    .   Name and address of hotel or residence protectee will use. Have reservations been made?   _____

    .   Billing arrangements with the hotel.   _____

    .   Transportation at host site. If rental vehicles will be used, have reservations been made?   _____

    .   Billing arrangements for local transportation.   _____

    .   Amount of luggage.   _____

    .   Has luggage been tagged and color coded?   _____

    .   Protectee's medical requirements.   _____

    .   Are extra quantities of prescription drugs being brought, in separate bags?   _____

    .   Are there any special requirements protectee may have regarding rooms, food, diet, etc.   _____

    .   Transportation, housing, and billing arrangements for advance agent and protective detail. Have reservations been made?   _____

    .   Budget authorization and inclusions (rental equipment, extra people, tips, etc.)   _____

    .   Special dress requirements.   _____

    .   If going out of country, will an interpreter be needed?   _____

    .   Transportation and customs requirements for protective equipment--weapons, radios, alarm kit).   _____

    .   List of individuals who may be of help, with telephone numbers.   _____

4.   Have you made the following pre-departure contacts:

    .   Local contact at the site to be visited?   _____

    .   Hotel, to check reservations?   _____

   . Auto/limousine rental agencies to check reservations?   _____

   . Federal, state, and local law enforcement or intelligence agencies, as appropriate?   _____

   . Airline and/or transportation agency being used by advance agent to location?   _____

5. If travel is by private aircraft, have captain and crew been alerted? Have you secured information about: _____

   . Type of aircraft, owner, call signs, and tail number?   _____

   . Anticipated departure and arrival times?   _____

   . General aviation facility or FBO at the departure and arrival sites with telephone numbers?   _____

   . Ramp stairs required?   _____

   . Storage location for the aircraft at the FBO?   _____

   . Alternate arrival site?   _____

   . Any special requirements?   _____

ON SITE AT SITE/CITY

6. Observe general layout of the airport. How good is security?   _____

7. How is luggage handled?   _____

8. Will unloading and processing of the client in a special place be required?   _____

9. Airline Service Representative contacted for any special handling requests?   _____

10. Obtain a good map of the area and orient yourself to important reference points and locales.   _____

11. Obtain rental car, reconfirm reservations, and discuss any special requirements.   _____

12. Proceed to hotel, observing traffic conditions, road conditions, and prominent landmarks.   _____

13. Check into hotel, noting parking areas, lobby configuration, elevator locations, restaurants, emergency exits, areas of congestion, etc.   _____

14. Telephone home office and inquire about any changes in plans. _____

15. Notify host, sponsor, or contact of arrival, and make appointments if appropriate. _____

16. Make appointment(s) to meet with local law enforcement officials. _____

Hotel

17. Meet with General Manager or Resident (Assistant) Manager. _____

18. Request meeting with Reservations (Front Desk) Manager, Security Director, Night Manager, Food and Beverage Manager, Chief Hotel Telephone Operator, Head Bellman, Concierge, and Head Housekeeper. _____

19. At the meeting, obtain telephone numbers for General Manager, Resident Manager, and key personnel, and explain any special requests for room arrangements, food, access control, screening visitors, handling of incoming calls, need for privacy and security, etc. _____

20. Obtain all information about hotel restaurants and room service.

    . Locations and hours restaurants are open. _____
    . Room service hours. _____
    . Name of Maitre d'hotel and/or Chief Host/Hostess. _____
    . Menu(s) for breakfast, lunch, dinner. _____
    . Request that all food service orders mail and packages be delivered to command post. _____

21. Determine if employees wear identification badges. _____

22. Determine what services (barber, beautician, drug store, health club, masseuse, clothing store, safety deposit boxes) are within the hotel. _____

23. Select rooms for protectee and his/her party, and determine who is in close proximity rooms (either side, above, below). _____

24. Examine rooms to be certain they are in good repair, safe, free of hazardous objects, comfortable, and contain any items of special request by the client. Check for electronic bugs and wire taps. _____

25. Obtain duplicate keys for all rooms to be used by client. _____

26. Locate emergency exits, fire extinguishers, fire hoses, and smoke alarms--establish primary and secondary exit routes for emergency. _____

27. Check fire extinguishers to see if they have been charged. _____

28.   Check hallways and stair wells for any obstructions, hand rails, and lighting.

_____

29.   Select location of command post. Check for bugs and wire taps.

_____

30.   Arrange with Head Housekeeper to rearrange furniture, and obtain chalk board, bulletin board, extra waste baskets, and bathroom towels.

_____

31.   Obtain long cord for telephone in command post.

_____

32.   Obtain supplies for command post: typewriter, local telephone books, pens, paper, legal pads, paper clips, stapler, expense vouchers, time sheets, tags for labeling keys, etc.

_____

33.   Other supplies and equipment recommended for command post:

.   Folding stock pump shotgun.   _____
.   Extra ammunition for shotgun and handguns.   _____
.   5-cell heavy duty flashlight with extra batteries.   _____
.   ABC type fire extinguisher.   _____
.   Handcuffs or flex cuffs.   _____
.   Electrical appliance extension cord(s).   _____
.   Telephone extension cord.   _____
.   Long telephone handset cord.   _____
.   Small screw driver set.   _____
.   Key block locks.   _____
.   Smoke mask for each protectee.   _____
.   Two-way radios, chargers and spare batteries.   _____

34.   Portable alarm equipment should include:

.   Smoke detector, door motion sensor, and panic alarm for room.   _____
.   Alarm annunciator for remote sensors.   _____
.   Paging system with sufficient pagers for off-duty personnel.   _____

35.   Medical kit for command post should include:

.   Oxygen cylinder, regulator and mask.   _____
.   Bulky trauma dressings.   _____
.   Bandage material.   _____
.   Splints.   _____
.   Comfort items.   _____
.   Aspirin and Tylenol.   _____
.   Di-Gel, Pepto Bismol.   _____
.   Antihistamine.   _____
.   Protectee and protective detail medications.   _____

36.   Meet with Security Director and ask for a walk-through of the hotel, checking entrances, exits, parking, emergency equipment, banquet and conference rooms, kitchens, maintenance, engineering, employee locker rooms, employee entrances, and storage areas.   _____

37.   Determine from Security Director if there have been in the past, or are currently, any particular security problems. What is history of crime within the hotel and in the surrounding area?   _____

38.   How many security personnel are on the hotel staff? Can they be utilized to assist in extending special security to client?   _____

39.   Determine from Security Director locations of nearest fire station, ambulance service, and emergency hospitals.   _____

40.   Ask Security Director for floor plans of hotel, or make sketches of hotel layout.   _____

41.   Make certain that there are sufficient baggage handlers, with carts.   _____

42.   Reaffirm all billing arrangements, and charges to master ledger.   _____

Residence (not belonging to client)

43.   See above checklist for Residence.   _____

44.   If alarm system is not in place, attach portable alarms.   _____

45.   Determine if a temporary command post can be set up.   _____

46.   Determine if a temporary safe room can be set up.   _____

47.   Determine if all mail, gifts, and packages delivered to the residence can be checked first by the agents.   _____

48.   Household staff should be briefed on procedures for handling telephone inquiries and visitors.   _____

49.   Obtain a list of service providers (garbage collection, gardeners, pool service, newspaper carrier, etc.) and approximate times when they are to be at the residence.   _____

50.   If appropriate, conduct an electronic sweep of the premises to determine if there are any eavesdropping devices or wire taps.   _____

Restaurants

51.   Obtain floor plan or make sketch of layout.   _____

52. Request most secure, private table(s) for client and party. _____

53. Request privacy and confidentiality for client. _____

54. Check exits, restrooms, and access to telephones. _____

55. Determine where to park the protectee's vehicle. _____

56. Make arrangements for feeding protective agents. _____

57. Make reservations and arrangements for billing or payment. _____

58. Determine primary and secondary routes to nearest emergency hospital with trauma unit. _____

59. Determine primary and secondary routes to restaurant from client's location. _____

Ballrooms, Banquets, and Auditoriums

60 . Meet with liaison person for Host Committee, Banquet Manager, Facility Management, and Program Manager. _____

61. Obtain telephone numbers for these people. _____

62. What is the purpose of the function? _____

63. What is the *detailed* program? _____

64. How many attendees? _____

65. What is the suggested dress for men and women? _____

66. Request that all awards and gifts be mailed or delivered to protectee. _____

67. Determine seating arrangements--ask to see Function Sheet. _____

68. Will client be seated at head table? _____

69. If so, what is above, below, and behind head table and how is access gained? _____

70. Is there a buffer in front of the front table? _____

71. Examine podium, raised platform, stage, steps, and chairs for loose carpet, wires, and general stability. _____

72. Are stairs to podium well lighted or should tape be affixed? _____

73. Obtain a floor plan of facility, showing entrance and exit routes under normal and emergency conditions, fire extinguishers, restrooms, telephones, holding room, and parking. _____

74. Select and indicate agent posts on floor plan. _____

75. Determine if protectee can be brought in through a special entrance. _____

76. Identify control boxes for heat, air, light, sound. Are they secure? _____

77. Is there back-up power? _____

78. Where will protectee's vehicle be parked? Will it be secure? Under constant supervision? _____

79. Who is handling security for the event? How large is the security staff? _____

80. Have there been any problems associated either with the event, the facility or the neighborhood? _____

81. Do a walk-through of the facility. _____

82. Make arrangements for agent meal tickets. _____

83. Determine what will be needed for access control. _____

84. Is entry free and open to the general public? _____

85. Were tickets sold? At what price? _____

86. Is the event by invitation only? _____

87. Are invitations numbered and cross-referenced by name on a master list? _____

88. May guest who chooses not to attend give his invitation to another? _____

89. How many people are expected? _____

90. Where is the main access control point? _____

91. Who will be there to check tickets or verify invitations? _____

92. Who will handle guests who have forgotten or lost their invitations? Where? _____

93. Are handbags and parcels to be searched? By whom? _____

94. Will metal detectors be required? _____

95. How will access via service or stage entrances be limited to authorized personnel?   _____

96. How will authorized personnel be identified?   _____

97. How will exits to restrooms and re-entry to ballroom be handled?   _____

98. Have arrangements been made and space/electricity been provided for the media? Is the space contained in some way?   _____

99. Has a press room been set up? Is it adequate?   _____

100. Will bystanders and hecklers standing outside be contained in a roped-off area?   _____

101. Establish primary and secondary travel routes to the event.   _____

102. Establish primary and secondary travel routes to the closest emergency hospital with trauma unit.   _____

Outside Events

103. Establish liaison with event sponsors, and obtain details as listed in above checklist.   _____

104. A diagram or sketch of the area should be made.   _____

105. A walk-through should be conducted of the entire area.   _____

106. Is the area fenced?   _____

107. Is there high ground overlooking the event area (stage)? Can it be secured?   _____

108. Who is handling security for the event? How large is the security staff? Is it sufficient?   _____

109. Is it a seated affair?   _____

110. Can attendees and spectators be confined behind ropes or barricades?   _____

111. Have "friendlies" been contacted to fill the front sections of the roped-off areas?   _____

112. Has space and arrangements been made for the media?   _____

113. Is there a "foul weather plan"?   _____

114. Do you have a large umbrella for the protectee?   _____

115. If it is a night time event, who is handling the lighting and will they be on hand for the event? _____

116. Is there back-up power? _____

117. Determine primary and secondary routes to the event. _____

118. Determine primary and secondary routes to the closest emergency hospital with trauma unit. _____

Ground Transportation

119. Are you dealing with a large, reputable rental car agency? _____

120. Have reservations and billing arrangements been made and reconfirmed? _____

121. Does the car/limousine have an automatic transmission? _____

122. Is it air conditioned? _____

123. Does it have an alarm system, and can the system be controlled electronically from outside? _____

124. Are tires fully inflated at exactly the same level? _____

125. Is there a spare tire in good condition and fully inflated? _____

126. If using a rental car, check the fluid levels and conduct a general examination of the under-the-hood mechanisms. _____

127. Test all controls--air conditioning, heat, power windows, power locks, automatic seat belts, and radio. _____

128. Rental car or limousine should have, in the trunk, jumper cables, jack, small tool kit, and lug wrench. _____

129. Trunk should be equipped with flares, flashlight, tire sealers, tow chain, fire extinguisher, jumper cables, extra motor oil and engine coolant, and a fully maintained medical kit. _____

130. If using a limousine, has driver been fully briefed and given a typed list of instructions? _____

    . Report with clean car and a full gas tank--refill at night. _____

    . Speak only when spoken to. _____

    . Stay with limo at all times unless relieved. _____

. Driver does not open and close the car doors. _____

. If trunk needs to be opened, use the interior release. _____

. Don't drink alcoholic beverages prior to or during work. _____

. Don't eat in the car. _____

. Don't smoke in the car. _____

. Obey all traffic laws. _____

. Do not turn on radio unless requested. _____

. In high profile motorcade, keep headlights on. _____

. Keep one car length between vehicles. _____

. Follow agent-recommended travel routes. _____

. Follow instructions of security agent rather than client. _____

. Establish duress code and emergency procedures. _____

131. Is the car/limousine equipped with a cellular telephone or two-way radio? _____

132. Obtain duplicate vehicle key(s). _____

133. Is an escort car to be rented? If so, all of the above should be checked. _____

134. Is a stash car to be rented? If so, all of the above should be checked. _____

135. Where will the vehicle(s) be parked? Is the parking secure? _____

136. Is there a contingency plan for what will be done if the limo or rental car breaks down? _____

137. Do you have name, home telephone number, and address for limo driver? _____

138. Have you picked a primary and secondary route to each destination to be visited by the protectee? _____

139. Have you tested the routes during rush hour, at night, and at times similar to when event will be held? _____

140. Have you produced maps and detailed instructions regarding the travel routes for the drivers and agents? _____

141.   Are the maps clearly marked and easily read?   _____

Charter or Corporate Aircraft

142.   Have captain and crew been alerted to departure and travel schedules? Filed flite plan and alternate foul weather plan?   _____

143.   Have arrangements been made for ramp steps, if needed?   _____

144.   Is de-icing equipment available?   _____

145.   What is length of runway and will it accommodate the aircraft?   _____

146.   Do you know the hours of airport operation?   _____

147.   Do you have the telephone numbers and names of airport operations people?   _____

148.   Is there a VIP holding area at the local and site FBO's?   _____

149.   Where are the restrooms and telephones?   _____

150.   Are there any customs regulations and clearances?   _____

151.   Are there any special requests for food, equipment, etc.?   _____

152.   Obtain a diagram or map of the airport and ramp areas. Be sure to brief all drivers on primary and secondary routes into and out of the airport.   _____

153.   Brief drivers on the primary and secondary routes to the hospital from the airport.   _____

154.   Will aircraft be guarded when unoccupied?   _____

155.   Are aircraft crew fully aware of security procedures?   _____

156.   Establish any security posts.   _____

157.   If additional security is needed, ask the operations supervisor for recommendations for an outside security company.   _____

158.   What is aircraft identifying information?   _____

159.   After a departure, wait several minutes and then notify advance agent at next stop that party is on the way.   _____

Commercial Air Travel

160. Have you established primary and secondary routes from the client's locale to the airport?

161. Is there a private airline club where the client can wait for his/her flight? Does he possess a membership card? Do you?

162. Have you produced a layout plan for restrooms, telephones, gift shop, barber, shoe shine, departure gates, etc.?

163. Have you reconfirmed reservations?

164. Has pre-boarding been arranged?

165. Are departure gates known and identified?

166. Have primary and secondary routes to the closest emergency hospital been identified?

167. Are on-site airport medical facilities identified?

168. Are on-site airport security facilities identified?

169. Has Airline Service Representative been contacted for any special requests (boarding, luggage, menu)?

Emergency Services

170. Where is the closest hospital with shock/trauma unit and a doctor on 24-hour duty to the hotel or site?

171. Have you established primary and secondary routes to the hospital from the hotel, event, etc.?

172. Do you know the locations of the emergency entrances?

173. Is there a suitable landing area for a helicopter?

174. Is there a VIP room?

175. Is there a room for security and staff?

176. What is the response time for the Fire Department to the various locations where the protectee will be?

177. What is the response time, and quality of service, of the ambulance emergency services?

FOREIGN ADVANCES

178. Do you have a valid passport which will not expire in less than six months? _____

179. Do you have the appropriate visas for the countries to be visited? _____

180. Have you received the appropriate medical and immunization shots for the countries to be visited? _____

181. Do you have a supply of medicines (for colds, allergies, diarrhea) which might be used in the countries to be visited? _____

182. Do you have an International Driver's License? _____

183. Do you have valid and current credit cards? _____

184. Do you have a small amount of local (foreign) currency for payment to taxicab drivers, etc.? _____

185. Do you have a current guidebook for the country (countries) to be visited? _____

186. Have you considered prepaying an amount to your credit card companies, so as to extend your charge potential? _____

187. Have you purchased travelers checks? _____

188. Have you given careful consideration to the choice of an air carrier? _____

189. Have you booked an "open" return flight? _____

190. Are you carrying a supply of prescribed medicines, and do you also have a copy of your prescription? _____

191. Are you carrying with you those items which might be difficult or expensive to replicate overseas? _____

192. Have you noted serial numbers of and declared any firearms, and packed them away, unarmed, in the stowed luggage? _____

193. Have you made copies of your passport and visa information, and your travelers checks and credit card numbers? _____

194. Have you committed to memory a few basic phrases of the local language? _____

195. Will you need an interpreter? _____

196. Upon arrival, did you check in with the U.S. Embassy and introduce yourself to the U.S. Embassy personnel?   _____

197. Have you asked the U.S. Embassy for recommendations for additional/supplemental security personnel?   _____

198. Did you conduct a briefing of, and are you aware of, any special security problems in the area(s) to be visited?   _____

199. Have you introduced yourself to other security personnel of American companies in the area?   _____

200. Have you written and implemented an emergency evacuation plan for the protectee and company?   _____

WRAP-UP

201. Have you collected all expense vouchers and submitted a final expense report?   _____

202. Have you written thank-you letters, and filed your notes?   _____

Listed herein are some of the key periodicals, publishers, associations, institutes, schools, and companies which might be of use to the executive protection professional. There are many, many additional competent providers of products and services who are much too numerous to list, as they number in the hundreds. The reader is directed to the American Society for Industrial Security's publications, in particular the *ASIS Directory and Buyer's Guide*, for names, addresses, and telephone numbers of product and service providers. The *Buyer's Guide* lists these providers by specific categories (executive protection, contingency and emergency planning, countersurveillance, etc.) and by location. *Security* magazine and *Police* magazine also publish buyers' guides annually. Any protection agent worth his and her salt should investigate and become familiar with the sources available for networking, consulting, co-venturing, and training.

Periodicals

The ASLET Journal
American Society of Law Enforcement Trainers
Box 361
Lewes, DE 19958-0361
(302) 645-4080

Black Belt
P.O. Box 918
Santa Clarita, CA 91380
(661) 257-4066

Combat Handguns
Harris Publications
1115 Broadway
New York, NY 10010
(212) 807-7100

Corporate Security Newsletter
1340 Braddock Place, #400
Alexandria, VA 22314
(703) 706-0207

Guns & Weapons
Harris Publications
1115 Broadway
New York, NY 10010
(212) 807-7100

IACP News
International Association of Chiefs of Police
515 North Washington Street
Alexandria, VA 22314
(703) 836-6767

Law Enforcement News
899 - 10th Avenue
New York, NY 10019
(212) 237-8442

National Directory of Law Administrators, Correctional Institutions and Related Government Agencies
National Police Chiefs & Sheriff's Information
        Bureau
Box 365
Stevens Point, WI 54481
(715) 345-2772

The National Sheriff
1450 Duke Street
Alexandria, VA 22314
(703) 836-7827

Police Chief
International Association of Chiefs of Police
515 North Washington Street
Alexandria, VA 22314
(703) 836-6767

Police Marksman
6000 E. Shirley Lane
Montgomery, AL 36117
(800) 223-7869

Private Security Case Law Reporter
Strafford Publications, Inc.
590 Dutch Valley Road
Atlanta, GA 30324
(404) 881-1141

Public Risk
Public Risk Management Association
1117 North 19th Street, Suite 900
Arlington, VA 22209
(703) 528-7701

Risk Management
Risk and Insurance Management Society
    Publishing Company
205 East 42nd Street
New York, NY 10017
(212) 286-9364

Rusting Publications
-     *Hotel/Motel Security And Safety Management Newsletter*
-     *Parking Security Report*
-     *Hospital Security and Safety Management Newsletter*
-     *College Security Report*

P.O. Box 190
Port Washington, NY 11050
(516) 883-1440

Security (Magazine)
P.O. Box 5080
Des Plaines, IL 60018
(847) 635-8800

Security Management
American Society for Industrial Security
1625 Prince Street
Alexandria, VA 22314
(703) 518-1471

Security Law Newsletter
Crime Control Research Corporation
2125 Bancorst Place NW
Washington DC 20008
(202) 337-2700

The Economist
111 West 57th Street
New York, NY 10019

Washington Crime News Services
-     *Training Aids Digest*
-     *Corporate Security Digest*
-     *Crime Control Digest*
-     *Organized Crime Digest*

3702 Pender Drive, #300
Fairfax, VA 22030
(703) 573-1600

Women and Guns
P.O. Box 488
Buffalo, NY 14209
(716) 885-6408

Associations and Institutes

American Red Cross
430 - 17th Street N.W.
Washington, DC 20006
(202) 737-8300

Association of Threat Assessment Professionals
11301 W. Olympic Blvd., #307
West Los Angeles, CA 90064
(310) 312-0212

Board of Certified Safety Professionals
208 Burnwash Avenue
Savoy, IL 61874
(217) 359-9263

Business Espionage Controls and Countermeasures
Association
Fort Washington, MD
(301) 292-6430

Centers for Disease Control
National Center for Prevention Services
Atlanta, GA 30333
1-888-232-3228

International Association of Chiefs of Police
515 North Washington Street
Alexandria, VA 22314
(703) 836-6767

Int'l Assn for Medical Assistance to Travelers
17 Center Street
Lewiston, NY 14092
(716) 754-4883

National Crime Prevention Institute
University of Louisville
School of Justice Administration, Shelby Campus
Louisville, KY 40292
(502) 852-6987

National Institute of Justice
NCJRS User Services
Box 6000
Rockville, MD 20850
(800) 851-3420

National Rifle Association
1600 Rhode Island Avenue, N.W.
Washington, DC 20036
(202) 267-1000

National Sheriff's Association
1450 Duke Street
Alexandria, VA 22314
(703) 836-7827

Public Risk Management Association
1815 No. Fort Meyer Drive, Ste. 1020
Arlington, VA 22209
(703) 528-7701

Risk and Insurance Management Society
205 East 42nd Street
New York, NY 10017
(212) 286-9364

United Nations Disaster Relief Coordinator
Palais des Nations
1211 Geneva 10
Switzerland

United Security Professionals Association
4934 Borchers Beach Road
Waunakee, WI 53597
(608) 231-3676

World Health Organization
525 23rd Street, N.W.
Washington, DC 20037
(202) 974-3000

Government Resources

Central Intelligence Agency
McLean, VA 22101
(703) 482-1100

Defense Department
The Pentagon
Washington, DC 20350
(703) 545-6700

Department of the Treasury
Bureau of Alcohol, Tobacco and Firearms
Washington, DC 20226
(202) 927-7777

Environmental Protection Agency
401 M Street, S.W.
Washington, DC 20460
(202) 260-2090

Federal Aviation Administration
800 Independence Avenue, S.W.
Washington, DC 20591
(202) 366-4000

Federal Bureau of Investigation
Pennsylvania Ave bet. 9th and 10th Sts, N.W.
Washington, DC 20535
(202) 324-3000
(for local field offices, check telephone directory)

Federal Emergency Management Agency
500 C Street, S. W.
Washington, DC 20472
(202) 646-2500

Office of Foreign Disaster Assistance
Agency for International Development
2201 C Street, N.W.
Washington, DC 20520
(202) 647-4000

Superintendent of Documents
U.S. Government Printing Office
Washington, DC 20402
(202) 512-0000

Superintendent of Documents
U.S. Government Printing Office
P.O. Box 37954
Pittsburgh, PA 15250

U.S. Public Health Service
Washington, DC 20201
(202) 690-7536

U.S. State Department
2201 C Street, N.W.
Washington, DC 20520
(202) 647-4000
(202) 647-5225 (Citizen's Emergency Center)

The White House
1600 Pennsylvania Avenue, N.W.
Washington, DC 20500
(202) 456-1414

Private Sources

Ackerman Group, Inc., The
1666 Kennedy Causeway
Miami Beach, FL 33141
(305) 865-0072
Consulting services for counterterrorism, crisis mgt., contingency planning, risk assessment

Frank A. Bolz Associates, Inc.
P.O. Box 2678
Huntington Station, NY 11746
(516) 462-9706
Hostage negotiations

Control Risks, LTD (North America)
1749 Old Meadow Road, #120
McLean, VA 22102
(703) 893-0083
Executive security, hostage negotiations, crisis mgt., counterterrorism

Gavin de Becker Inc.
11684 Ventura Blvd., Suite 440
Studio City, CA 91604
(818) 505-0177
Celebrity protection services

Dr. Robert Kupperman
Center for Strategic & Int'l Studies
1800 K Street N.W., Ste. 400
Washington, DC 20006
(202) 775-3229
Counterterrorism consulting services

International Association for Medical Assistance to Travelers
417 Center Street
Lewiston, NY 174092
(716) 754-4883
        and
57 Voirets
1212 Grand-Lancy
Geneva, Switzerland
International medical assistance

International Legal Defense Counsel
24th Floor, Packard Building
111 South 15th Street
Philadelphia, PA 19102
(215) 977-9982
International legal services

Public Safety Group
12608-B Lake Ridge Drive
Woodbridge, VA 22191
(703) 491-5236
Executive protection consulting and training, threat assessment, contingency planning

Vance International
10467 White Granite Drive, Suite 210
Oakton, VA 33234
(703) 385-6754
Executive, dignitary, and asset protection services, uniformed guards, training, investigative services

Schools, Training, and Training Materials

Bob Bondurant Driving School
Firebird International Raceway
Box 51980
Phoenix, AZ 85076
(800) 842-7223

Butterworth-Heinemann Publishers
225 Wildwood Avenue
Woburn, MA 01801
(800) 366-2665

Executive Security International, Ltd. (ESI)
Gun Barrel Square, #206
2128 Railroad Avenue
Rifle, CO 81650
(800) 874-0888

Executive Protection Institute
Richard W. Kobetz
Route 2, Box 3645
Berryville, VA 22611
(540) 955-1128

Lethal Force Institute
Massod Ayoob
Post Office Box 122
Concord, NH 03301
(603) 224-6814

Vance International
10467 White Granite Drive, Suite 210
Oakton, VA 22124
(703) 385-6754

Publishing Houses

Paladin Press
P.O. Box 1307
Boulder, CO 80306
(800) 392-2400

Charles C. Thomas Publishers
2600 South First Street
Springfield, IL 62794
(217) 789-8980

Useful Websites

State Department Overseas Security Advisory
Council
http://ds.state.gov/osac/

State Department Office of the Coordinator for
Counterterrorism
http://www.state.gov/www/global/terrorism/index

State Department
http://travel.state.gov/travel_warnings.html

State Department
http://travel.state.gov/yourtripabroad.html

State Department
http://travel.state.gov/foreignentryreqs.html

State Department
http://travel.state.gov/medical.html

Centers for Disease Control
http://www.cdc.gov

INDEX

ABOUT THE AUTHOR

M.J. Braunig is Vice President of Executive Security International, Ltd. (ESI), a private security training academy located in Aspen, Colorado. ESI is recognized worldwide as offering the most complete, in-depth executive protection program outside the U.S. Secret Service. During the 20 years of its existence, ESI has pioneered in the development and codification of much of the executive protection information now practiced in the field. Ms. Braunig has, as one of her responsibilities, the writing of much of the material used in ESI's programs. During the past 16 years, Ms. Braunig has actively participated in ESI's training programs.

Ms. Braunig's background in security includes the development of a series of security programs which were held nationwide during 1984, in conjunction with the Democratic and Republican national conventions, and the Olympics held in California of that same year. She has worked extensively with the hotel industry in developing in-house security programs.

Ms. Braunig's career experiences also include five years working as a Program Director for a major international hotel chain. During that time, she traveled extensively throughout the world, implementing training programs in the Philippines, Afghanistan, Lebanon, the Caribbean, and Europe.

Ms. Braunig has authored a number of safety and security articles, is a noted lecturer, and has consulted with a number of clients in the development of training programs and manuals.